# Poetry
# Criticism

# Guide to Gale Literary Criticism Series

| For criticism on | Consult these Gale series |
|---|---|
| Authors now living or who died after December 31, 1959 | *CONTEMPORARY LITERARY CRITICISM (CLC)* |
| Authors who died between 1900 and 1959 | *TWENTIETH-CENTURY LITERARY CRITICISM (TCLC)* |
| Authors who died between 1800 and 1899 | *NINETEENTH-CENTURY LITERATURE CRITICISM (NCLC)* |
| Authors who died between 1400 and 1799 | *LITERATURE CRITICISM FROM 1400 TO 1800 (LC)*<br><br>*SHAKESPEAREAN CRITICISM (SC)* |
| Authors who died before 1400 | *CLASSICAL AND MEDIEVAL LITERATURE CRITICISM (CMLC)* |
| Black writers of the past two hundred years | *BLACK LITERATURE CRITICISM (BLC)* |
| Authors of books for children and young adults | *CHILDREN'S LITERATURE REVIEW (CLR)* |
| Dramatists | *DRAMA CRITICISM (DC)* |
| Hispanic writers of the late nineteenth and twentieth centuries | *HISPANIC LITERATURE CRITICISM (HLC)* |
| Native North American writers and orators of the eighteenth, nineteenth, and twentieth centuries | *NATIVE NORTH AMERICAN LITERATURE (NNAL)* |
| Poets | *POETRY CRITICISM (PC)* |
| Short story writers | *SHORT STORY CRITICISM (SSC)* |
| Major authors from the Renaissance to the present | *WORLD LITERATURE CRITICISM, 1500 TO THE PRESENT (WLC)* |

ISSN 1052-4851

# Poetry Criticism

*Excerpts from Criticism of the Works
of the Most Significant and Widely
Studied Poets of World Literature*

## VOLUME 16

*Margaret Haerens*
*Christine Slovey*
Editors

## GALE

DETROIT · NEW YORK · TORONTO · LONDON

Library of Congress Catalog Card Number 91-118494
ISBN 0-7876-0475-5
ISSN 1052-4851

Printed in the United States of America

10  9  8  7  6  5  4  3  2  1

# Contents

# Preface

## A Comprehensive Information Source on World Poetry

*P*oetry Criticism (PC) provides substantial critical excerpts and biographical information on poets throughout the world who are most frequently studied in high school and undergraduate college courses. Each *PC* entry is supplemented by biographical and bibliographical material to help guide the user to a fuller understanding of the genre and its creators. Although major poets and literary movements are covered in such Gale Literary Criticism Series as *Contemporary Literary Criticism (CLC)*, *Twentieth-Century Literary Criticism (TCLC)*, *Nineteenth-Century Literature Criticism (NCLC)*, *Literature Criticism from 1400 to 1800 (LC)*, and *Classical and Medieval Literature Criticism (CMLC)*, *PC* offers more focused attention on poetry than is possible in the broader, survey-oriented entries on writers in these Gale series. Students, teachers, librarians, and researchers will find that the generous excerpts and supplementary material provided by *PC* supply them with vital information needed to write a term paper on poetic technique, examine a poet's most prominent themes, or lead a poetry discussion group.

## Coverage

In order to reflect the influence of tradition as well as innovation, poets of various nationalities, eras, and movements are represented in every volume of *PC*. Each author entry presents a historical survey of the critical response to that author's work; the length of an entry reflects the amount of critical attention that the author has received from critics writing in English and from foreign critics in translation. Since many poets have inspired a prodigious amount of critical explication, *PC* is necessarily selective, and the editors have chosen the most significant published criticism to aid readers and students in their research. In order to provide these important critical pieces, the editors will sometimes reprint essays that have appeared in previous volumes of Gale's Literary Criticism Series. Such duplication, however, never exceeds fifteen percent of a *PC* volume.

## Organization

Each *PC* author entry consists of the following components:

- **Author Heading:** the name under which the author wrote appears at the beginning of the entry, followed by birth and death dates. If the author wrote consistently under a pseudonym, the pseudonym will be listed in the author heading and his or her legal name given in parentheses in the lines immediately preceding the Introduction. Uncertainty as to birth or death dates is indicated by question marks.

- **Introduction:** a biographical and critical essay introduces readers to the author and the critical discussions surrounding his or her work.

- **Author Portrait:** a photograph or illustration of the author is included when available. Most entries also feature illustrations of people and places pertinent to an author's career, as well as holographs of manuscript pages and dust jackets.

- **Principal Works:** the author's most important works are identified in a list ordered chronologically by first publication dates. The first section comprises poetry collections and book-length poems. The second section gives information on other major works by the author. For foreign authors, original foreign-language publication information is provided, as well as the best and most complete English-language editions of their works.

- **Criticism:** critical excerpts chronologically arranged in each author entry provide perspective on changes in critical evaluation over the years. All individual titles of poems and poetry collections by the author featured in the entry are printed in boldface type to enable a reader to ascertain without difficulty the works under discussion. For purposes of easy identification, the critic's name and the publication date of the essay are given at the beginning of each piece of criticism. Unsigned criticism is preceded by the title of the journal in which it originally appeared. Publication information (such as publisher names and book prices) and parenthetical numerical references (such as footnotes or page and line references to specific editions of a work) have been deleted at the editor's discretion to enable smoother reading of the text.

- **Explanatory Notes:** introductory comments preface each critical excerpt, providing several types of useful information, including: the reputation of a critic, the importance of a work of criticism, and the specific type of criticism (biographical, psychoanalytic, historical, etc.).

- **Author Commentary:** insightful comments from the authors themselves and excerpts from author interviews are included when available.

- **Bibliographical Citations:** information preceding each piece of criticism guides the interested reader to the original essay or book.

- **Further Reading:** bibliographic references accompanied by descriptive notes at the end of each entry suggest additional materials for study of the author. Boxed material following the Further Reading provides references to other biographical and critical series published by Gale.

# Other Features

**Cumulative Author Index:** comprises all authors who have appeared in Gale's Literary Criticism Series, along with cross-references to such Gale biographical series as *Contemporary Authors* and *Dictionary of Literary Biography*. This cumulated index enables the user to locate an author within the various series.

**Cumulative Nationality Index:** includes all authors featured in *PC,* arranged alphabetically under their respective nationalities.

**Cumulative Title Index:** lists in alphabetical order all individual poems, book-length poems, and collection titles contained in the *PC* series. Titles of poetry collections and separately published poems are printed in italics, while titles of individual poems are printed in roman type with quotation marks. Each title is followed by the author's name and the volume and page number corresponding to the location of commentary on specific works. English-language translations of original foreign-language titles are cross-referenced to the foreign titles so that all references to discussion of a work are combined in one listing.

# Citing *Poetry Criticism*

When writing papers, students who quote directly from any volume in the Literary Criticism Series may use the following general formats to footnote reprinted criticism. The first example pertains to material drawn from periodicals, the second to material reprinted from books:

[1]David Daiches, "W. H. Auden: The Search for a Public," *Poetry* LIV (June 1939), 148-56; excerpted and reprinted in *Poetry Criticism*, Vol. 1, ed. Robyn V. Young (Detroit: Gale Research, 1990), pp. 7-9.

[2]Pamela J. Annas, *A Disturbance in Mirrors: The Poetry of Sylvia Plath* (Greenwood Press, 1988); excerpted and reprinted in *Poetry Criticism*, Vol. 1, ed. Robyn V. Young (Detroit: Gale Research, 1990), pp. 410-14.

# Comments Are Welcome

Readers who wish to suggest authors to appear in future volumes, or who have other suggestions, are cordially invited to contact the editors.

# Acknowledgments

The editors wish to thank the copyright holders of the excepted criticism included in this volume, the permissions managers of many book and magazine publishing companies for assisting us in securing reprint rights, and Jane Currier for assisting with copyright research. We are also grateful to the staffs of the Detroit Public Library, the Library of Congress, the University of Detroit Public Library, Wayne State University Purdy/Kresge Library Complex, and the University of Michigan Libraries for making their resources available to us. Following is a list of the copyright holders who have granted us permission to reprint material in this volume of PC. Every effort has been made to trace copyright, but if omissions have been made, please let us know.

**COPYRIGHTED EXCERPTS IN *PC*, VOLUME 16, WERE REPRINTED FROM THE FOLLOWING PERIODICALS:**

*American Literature,* v. 59, December, 1987. Copyright © 1987 Duke University Press, Durham, NC. Reproduced with permission of the publisher.—*Ariel: A Review of International English Literature,* v. 5, April, 1974 for "The Narrator of 'Don Juan'" by David Parker. Copyright © 1974 The Board of Governors, The University of Calgary. Reproduced by permission of the publisher and the author./ v. 9, January, 1978 for "The Byronic Heroine and Byron's 'The Corsair'" by Gloria T. Hull. Copyright © 1974 The Board of Governors, The University of Calgary. Reproduced by permission of the publisher and the author.—*Best Sellers*, v. 33, July 15, 1973. Copyright 1973, by the University of Scranton. Reproduced by permission. *boundary* 2, v. VIII, Spring, 1980. Copyright © boundary 2, 1980. Reproduced by permission. *Chicago Review*, v. 24, Winter, 1973. Copyright © 1973 by Chicago Review. Reproduced by permission./v. 32, Spring, 1981. Copyright © 1981 by Chicago Review. Reproduced by permission./ v. 33, Winter, 1983. Copyright © 1983 by Chicago Review. Reproduced by permission.—*CLA Journal*, v. XVIII, September, 1974. Copyright, 1974 by The College Language Association. Reproduced by permission of The College Language Association.—*Diacritics*, v. III, Winter, 1973. Copyright © Diacritics, Inc., 1973. Reproduced by permission. *Epoch*, v. XVIII, Fall, 1968. Copyright 1968 by Cornell University. Reproduced by permission./v. XXVI, Spring, 1977. Copyright 1977 by Cornell University. Reproduced by permission.—*Harper's*, v. 258, May, 1979. Copyright © 1979 by Harper's Magazine. All rights reserved. Reproduced by special permission.—*Michigan Quarterly Review,* v. XXIIX, Winter, 1989 for an interview with A. R. Ammons by William Walsh. Copyright © The University of Michigan, 1989. Reproduced by permission of A. R. Ammons and William Walsh.—*Modern Language Quarterly*, v. 33, December, 1972. © 1974 University of Washington. Reproduced by permission of Duke University Press./ v. 35, September, 1974. © 1976 University of Washington. Reproduced by permission of Duke University Press.—*Modern Poetry Studies*, v. 11, 1982. Copyright 1982, by Media Study, Inc. Reproduced by permission.—*New England Review and Bread Loaf Quarterly,* v. 14, Fall, 1991. Copyright © 1991 by Kenyon Hill Publications, Inc.— *Nineteenth-Century French Studies*, v. XIII, Summer, 1985. © 1985 by T. H. Goetz. Reproduced by permission.—*Parnassus: Poetry in Review*, v. 9, 1981. Copyright © 1981 Poetry in Review Foundation, NY. Reproduced by permission.—*Partisan Review*, v. LXI, Spring, 1994 for "Wild Plots" by Stephen Yenser. Copyright © 1994 by Partisan Review. Reproduced by permission of the author./ v. XXXVI, Spring, 1969 for "Mixed Bag" by Robert Boyers. Copyright © 1969 by Partisan Review. Reproduced by permission of the publisher and the author.—*Pembroke Magazine*, n. 18, 1986. Copyright © 1986 Pembroke Magazine. Reproduced by permission.—*Poetry*, v. CVII, January , 1966 for "Muse & Hearth" by Jim Harrison. © 1966 by the Modern Poetry Association. Reproduced by permission of the Editor of Poetry and the author./v. CXXXV, January, 1980 for "Summer Birds and Haunch of Winter" by Peter Stitt. © 1980 by the Modern Poetry Association. Reproduced by permission of the Editor of Poetry and the author.—*Raritan: A Quarterly Review,* v. X, Winter, 1991. Copyright © 1991 by Raritan: A Quarterly Review. Reproduced by permission.—*Salmagundi*, ns. 22-23, Spring-Summer, 1973. Copyright © 1973 by Skidmore College. Reproduced by permission./ns. 90-91, Spring-Summer, 1991. Copyright © 1991 by Skidmore College. Reproduced by permission.—*Southwest Review,* v. 60, Summer, 1975. © 1975 Southern Methodist University. Reproduced by permission.—*Studia Neophilologica*, v. 61, 1989. Reproduced by permission.—*Studies in Bibliography*, v. 30, 1977. Reproduced by permission.—*The American Poetry Review,* v. 4, July-August, 1975 for Louise Gluck's 'The House on Marshland'" by Anna Wooten. Copyright © 1975 by World Poetry, Inc. Reproduced by permission of the author.—*The Antioch Review,* v. XXIV, Winter,

**COPYRIGHTED EXCERPTS IN *PC*, VOLUME 16, WERE REPRINTED FROM THE FOLLOWING BOOKS:**

# A. R. Ammons
## 1926–

(Full name Archie Randolph Ammons) American poet.

## INTRODUCTION

A prolific writer, Ammons is widely considered among the most significant contemporary American poets. Sometimes referred to as an Emersonian Transcendentalist for his visionary view of the relationship between humankind and nature, Ammons is praised for his sensitive meditations on our capacity to comprehend the flux of the natural world. Furthermore, he frequently endows his verse with resonant images of detailed landscapes rendered in a conversational tone and flowing style similar to that of an interior monologue. Though features of traditional literary movements are evident in his work, Ammons's poetry is pervaded by a modern skepticism that stems from his refusal to attach universal significance to religious or artistic doctrines. Abstaining from offering any facile resolutions to the tensions in his verse, Ammons is concerned with broadening his readers' perceptions of their relationship to the world. Donald H. Reiman observed: "A. R. Ammons has engaged the fundamental metaphysical and psychological issues of twentieth-century man—concerns about the relationships of the individual with the Universe and with his own familial and social roots—and he has shown us a way to triumph without relying on dogmatisms or on mere palliatives."

## Biographical Information

Born in the rural community of Whiteville, North Carolina, Ammons was raised on a farm, where his appreciation for nature was fostered. A good student, he graduated near the top of his class in elementary school and high school. Upon completing high school in 1943, Ammons worked in the shipyards in Wilmington, North Carolina, and in 1944 joined the Navy for two years of service. He began writing poetry while in the Navy and, after World War II, enrolled at Wake Forest College, North Carolina, receiving a bachelor of science degree in 1949. For one year he was the principal of an elementary school in Hateras, North Carolina, then enrolled for a short while at the University of California, Berkeley. Ammons returned to the east coast, settling in south New Jersey, and there held several jobs, including that of a vice-president of a glass company. His poetry began to appear in magazines in 1953, and an inaugural collection, *Ommateum with Doxology*, was published in 1955. With the publication of a second volume, *Expressions of Sea Level*, nine years later, Ammons garnered widespread critical attention that established him as an important American poet. That same year, 1964, he began to teach in the English Department at Cornell Uni-

versity, Ithaca, New York, where he continues to work as a professor. Ammons has received many honors during his career, including the 1973 National Book Award for *Collected Poems: 1951-1971*, the 1982 National Book Critics Circle Award for *A Coast of Trees*, and the 1993 National Book Award for *Garbage*.

## Major Works

*Ommateum with Doxology*—the title refers to the compound eye of an insect—conveys a broad range of expression. In his attempt to present a multifaceted view of humanity's relationship with the universe, Ammons vacillates between a scientific and a transcendental perspective. In the collection *Expressions of Sea Level*, his conception of the interdependence between humanity and nature becomes more complex as he begins to focus on the educative and restorative aspects of the universe. Often using images of sea and wind to represent nature's perpetual motion, Ammons suggests that man is only partially cognizant of external forces. In "Unsaid," one of his most acclaimed pieces, Ammons acknowledges the limitations of human expression and apprehension as he asks his readers, "Have you listened for the things I have left out?" In *Corson's Inlet* and *Northfield Poems* Ammons continues to examine the complex association between man and nature.

During the period in which he produced the above-mentioned collections of short lyric verse, Ammons also published two book-length poems, *Tape for the Turn of the Year* and *Sphere: The Form of a Motion*. Noted for its innovative structure, *Tape for the Turn of the Year* takes the form of a daily poetic journal and chronicles Ammons's thoughts on the mundanity of everyday life. In *Sphere* Ammons focuses on humanity's futile attempts to impose structure on the environment and to halt natural forces. While this work is arranged in 155 numbered sections of four tercets each, Ammons's minimal use of punctuation endows *Sphere* with a fluid style that conveys nature's inexorable motion. In the much later volume *Garbage*, Ammons returned to the long format of *Tape for the Turn of the Year* and *Sphere*, composing a poem that comprises what appears to be a single extended sentence, divided into eighteen sections, arranged in couplets. Starting with the image of a trash dump beside a Florida highway, the poem develops into a series of meditations about different kinds of waste, decay, and debris, but eventually makes the point that what we term garbage is part of the cycles of nature, evolution, and renewal. In other volumes, Ammons has tended toward a less discursive style. In such collections as *A Coast of Trees*, *Worldly Hopes*, *Lake Effect Country*, and *Sumerian Vistas*, he employs short-lined forms to create increasingly philosophical explorations of the natural world. *A Coast of Trees* presents a spiritually oriented view of nature and aligns Ammons's work more closely with the Romantics in its adherence to the primacy of human instinct and emotion. In *Worldly Hopes* and *Lake Effect Country*, Ammons fuses his empirical perceptions with hymn-like tributes to nature.

### Critical Reception

Commentators have been almost uniformly complimentary of Ammons's work. Most commend his ability to provoke thought about the complexity of human nature through reflection upon our attitudes toward and understanding of the environment. Because of his iconoclastic views and association of nature and humankind, Ammons is customarily acknowledged to be a literary descendent of Ralph Waldo Emerson and Walt Whitman. Clearly critics perceive Ammons's poetry to be distinctly American, and other comparisons find him frequently linked to Wallace Stevens, William Carlos Williams, and Emily Dickinson. Though Ammons has received high praise for his Whitmanesque extended interior monologues, some reviewers object that his poems can be self-indulgent and wordy, problems exacerbated by the occasional impression of structural arbitrariness and by his preference for minimal punctuation. *Tape for the Turn of the Year*, for example, has been called gimmicky because it was composed on an adding machine tape, which artificially prescribed the shape of the poem. Nevertheless, Ammons's manipulation of language is also recognized as one of his strengths. Com-

mentators remark on the rhythm and phrasing of his poetry, finding them imitative of spoken language, and judge his vocabulary to be engaging and stimulating.

## PRINCIPAL WORKS

### Poetry

*Ommateum with Doxology*  1955
*Expressions of Sea Level*  1963
*Corson's Inlet*  1965
*Tape for the Turn of the Year*  1965
*Northfield Poems*  1966
*Selected Poems*  1968
*Uplands*  1970
*Briefings: Poems Small and Easy*  1971
*Collected Poems, 1951-1971*  1972
*Sphere: The Form of a Motion*  1974
*Diversifications: Poems*  1975
*For Doyle Fosso*  1977
*Highgate Road*  1977
*The Selected Poems: 1951-1977*  1977
*The Snow Poems*  1977
*Breaking Out*  1978
*Six-Piece Suite*  1978
*Selected Longer Poems*  1980
*Changing Things*  1981
*A Coast of Trees: Poems*  1981
*Worldly Hopes*  1982
*Lake Effect Country: Poems*  1983
*Sumerian Vistas: Poems, 1987*  1987
*The Really Short Poems of A. R. Ammons*  1990
*Garbage*  1993
*The North Carolina Poems*  1994
*Fear*  1995
*Brink Road*  1996

### Other Major Works

*Set in Motion: Essays and Interviews*  1996

## CRITICISM

**Laurence Lieberman  (essay date 1964-65)**

SOURCE: "Poetry Chronicle: Last Poems, Fragments, and Wholes," in *The Antioch Review*, Vol. XXIV, No. 4, Winter, 1964-65, pp. 537-43.

[*Lieberman is an American poet and critic whose verse combines the particular and the visionary in its celebration of the physical world. The long, flowing lines and eloquent language of his poems set them apart from the works of his contemporaries. Unassigned Frequencies:*

American Poetry in Review, 1964-1977 *(1977) collects Lieberman's reviews of the works of many important contemporary poets. His most recent book,* Beyond the Muse of Memory: Essays on Contemporary American Poets, *continues his exploration of modern American poetry. In the following excerpt from a review of Ammons's* Expressions of Sea Level *and several books by other poets, Lieberman calls attention to the talent of Ammons and James Dickey in the long poem genre.*]

James Dickey and A. R. Ammons are evolving a poetic line that works wonders in the extended lyric. In composing the longer poem, most poets rely on sectional subdivisions and distinct variations in form between sections to keep the poem from growing tedious. But in so doing they jeopardize the key advantage that Dickey and Ammons get from writing on a broad scale—the unbroken flow of language.

For Ammons, words on the page weave in and out like crosscurrents in a calm river:

> . . . shapeless, undependable
> powerless in the actual
> which I rule, I
>
> will not
> make deposits in your bank account
> or free you from bosses
>         in little factories,
> will not spare you insult, will not
> protect you from
> men who
>     have never heard of modes, who
> do not respect me
> or your knowledge of me in you;
>         men I let win,
> their thin tight lips
> humiliating my worshippers:
>
>     I betray
> him who gets me in his eyes . . .

There is a quality of hesitation and search in the variable movement of the line down the page. The center of gravity in the lines shifts from left to right to center. In most of Ammons's poems, a sort of variable but recognizable stanza pattern emerges from the movement. In others, there is a relatively unbroken thrust down the page, as in the passage quoted. . . .

Many a contemporary poet handles language like a mason laying a foundation for a house—the words are so many concrete blocks to be cemented into a wall. Dickey and Ammons treat language with special attention to tone, modulation, and breathing space; all are suavely managed. Particular words and phrases rarely call attention to themselves; they must swing with the abiding rhythm and movement. It is hard to conceive of this poetry being composed slowly, word by word. There is too much continuity and rhythmic sweep. . . .

Both Dickey and Ammons tend to write very long sweeping verse sentences that read quickly. There is more technical excitement for the reader of Ammons; I find myself moving down the page and weaving back and forth simultaneously, hunting the rhythmical center of each line. It's a poetry of crosscurrents, and a reader finds he is rowing *with* the current and *into* the current at once.

A quality that makes both of these poets better able to work on a larger scale than most of their contemporaries is the extraordinary power of mind they bring to bear on experience in their poems. In both, the depth and breadth of concentration is astonishing. Surprisingly, neither poet suffers from abstractness or obscurity, two hazards that poetry which thinks very hard is usually prone to. Their poetry seems to think its way *into* experience and things in life, not *around* them, and never loses a close touch with the contours of creature, landscape, and seascape:

>         . . . here on the
> bottom of an ocean of space
> we babble words recorded
>     in waves
> of sound that
> cannot fully disappear,
>     washing up
> like fossils on the shores of unknown worlds . . .

(from **"Risks and Possibilities"**—Ammons)

Ideas in the poems seem less important in themselves, more important as conveyors or conductors that lead the mind into the center of happening.

I think the extended lyric is one of the most fertile and inviting territories for the poet of today, and I hope we can look to Ammons and Dickey for more solid achievement in this genre. It will take some doing to offset the movement toward fragmentation of experience set in motion by the shorter lyrics of William Carlos Williams in the twenties, and to initiate a return to structures that are large enough to cope with our most important experiences.

**Jim Harrison  (essay date 1966)**

SOURCE: "Muse & Hearth," in *Poetry,* Vol. CVII, No. 4, January, 1966, pp. 330-31.

[*An acclaimed American novelist, short story writer, and poet, Harrison is best known for his fiction but has published nine collections of verse. In the following review, he perceives some flaws in* Tape for the Turn of the Year *and* Corsons Inlet *but states: "In both books, I sense a poet on the eve of a breakthrough."*]

A. R. Ammons' *Tape for the Turn of the Year* was composed on a roll of adding machine tape; it purports to be a long poem in the form of a journal covering some thirty-five days in the poet's life. There are a dozen or so things that make it fatally wrong as a long poem—the fact of its length alone was predicated by the size of the tape, its form determined by the width of the tape and the number of days. The whole idea is more than a bit fey; we have weather descriptions, nature walks, all manner of cracker barrel phenomenology; the poet pumping out large un-leavened portions of his brain, the day in shorthand, creak-ing dross, rather house-broken observations on poetics, jokes, much fallow ground that might better have been left that way. It is a disastrously ambitious piece of work; the marriage of the poem and journal a bad one.

Despite these crude reservations *Tape for the Turn of the Year* has much to recommend itself. There are many fine short lyrics hidden within it, sections of incredible fertil-ity, the texture rich, the poet in completely new territory. I think it is the poem's total intemperance that saves it. Ammons is a poet with an essentially sweet consciousness at home with the quality of strangeness that makes him a very individual poet. Ammons does not limit himself to colonizing like so many of his gifted contemporaries; he explores. When he invokes the muse he does not do so fatuously; rather than the small household god or mistress of the academy that we are accustomed to, she takes the form of the "perpetual other woman" whom poets have served for centuries. It is a tribute to the poet that he sometimes makes her whine in the same sense that John Skelton did in his *"Merry Margaret,"* makes her yield to him the volatile gift of the poem. Ammons writes, "the predator / husbands his prey". He might well take this as a cautionary note for himself, an admonition.

Much of *Corsons Inlet* is perhaps too typical of the better conservative poetry being written now; a poetry of things closely observed and gracefully described, of the imagina-tion at reasonable harmony with itself. There's a great deal of unpretentious technical solidity and little of the diffuseness and ambling that marred *Tape for the Turn of the Year*. I think, though, that the more successful poems in the collection are the least orthodox. Of the seven ex-ceptional poems in *Corsons Inlet* (I would draw attention to **"Moment," "Jungle Knot," "Dark Song," "Butter-flyweed," "Two Hymns," "The Strait," "Libation"**), **"Jungle Knot"** and **"Two Hymns"** are truly fine. Our senses rupture, are enlivened, awed; there are no false notes. I quote part of the first of the **"Two Hymns"**:

So when the year had come full round
I rose
and went out to the naked mountain
to see
the single peachflower on the sprout

blooming through a side of ribs
  possibly a colt's
and I endured each petal separately
and moved in orisons with the sepals . . .

In both books I sense a poet on the eve of a breakthrough, a poet who has far from exhausted his equipment. I think A. R. Ammons' success—it could have very large dimen-sions—will depend on his ability to harbor, to cage his gift with greater cunning while still taking those steps in the dark that make his best work so radically original and fresh.

**John Logan  (essay date 1967)**

SOURCE: "Interior and Exterior Worlds," in *The Nation*, New York, Vol. 204, No. 17, April 24, 1967, pp. 541-42.

[*Logan is an American poet and critic whose verse is gen-erally regarded as intense and personal as well as distinct-ly humanist in its central concern with humankind and its potential. He has served as the poetry editor of both the* Nation *and the* Critic *and is also the founder and coeditor of* Choice, *a magazine of poetry and graphics. In the fol-lowing review of* Northfield Poems, *Logan comments on the relationship between the external world and the poet's internal life, as they are depicted in Ammons's early poet-ry. Logan concludes by declaring Ammons "a major tal-ent."*]

A. R. Ammons is one of the most prolific and, at the same time, most intelligent gifted poets of recent years. *North-field Poems* is his third book to appear in two years—with *Corsons Inlet* and *Tape for the Turn of the Year*—and there were two others in the previous ten-year period; *Om-mateum* (which was privately printed) and *Expressions of Sea Level*.

*Tape for the Turn of the Year,* perhaps the most interest-ing single volume, is a continuing poem, mainly unrevised, which Ammons composed by inserting one end of an adding machine tape in a typewriter and proceeding to the other end. The imposed limitation of form apparently provided a pressure which helped to produce some very beautiful writing, all 200 pages of it in the mode of a journal extending over a period of about a month. The long, thin poem is occasionally ascetic in its effect (as an El Greco figure) and again it is snakelike. There is a passage where the poem shows a striking self-recognition of its phallic character:

> If I had a flute: wdn't
> it be fine
> to see this long thin
> poem  rise out of the waste-
> basket:
> the charmed erection,
> stiffening, uncoiling?

Another passage catches from inside the work, toward its end, the speaker's sense of his own utterance:

> I wrote about these
> days the way life gave them:
> I didn't know
> beforehand what I
> wd write, whether I'd meet
> anything new: I
> showed that I'm sometimes
> blank and abstract,
> sometimes blessed with song: sometimes
> silly, vapid, serious,
> angry, despairing.

The free form of the poem (despite its strict limitation on line length) and its willingness to risk "prose" and looser diction, has given it an utterly original tone, a curious blend of confession, lyricism and observation of two kinds—the strikingly concrete and the near abstract.

All three of these qualities recur in other books though there is less of the first—indeed less personal portraiture of any direct kind—in *Ommateum*. Confession begins with *Expressions of Sea Level* where, combined with childhood reminiscence as in **"Nelly Myers"** and **"Silver"** it has given us some of the most beautiful poems of our time:

> I will not end my grief, earth will
> not end my grief,
> I move on,
> we move on, some scraps of us together,
> my broken soul leaning toward her to be touched,
> listening to be healed.

A number of poems in *Expressions, Corsons Inlet* and *Northfield,* as the names of the latter two hint, are based on experiences of places in South Jersey—where Mr. Ammons was for many years an executive in a chemical glass factory before turning to teaching.

Ammons' voice is unique and would not fail to be recognized even in the first book:

> So I said I am Ezra
> and the wind whipped my throat
> gaming for the sounds of my voice
> I listened to the wind
> go over my head and up into the night.

There is a return to the oracular, Old Testament-like persona of "Ezra" in the poem **"The Wind Coming Down From"** in the present volume. The poems of this book reiterate several motifs we are familiar with from the others, and they range from the highly abstract game-stance of **"The Numbers"**:

> be confident;
> as you turn to the numbers
> veracity
> links segment to segment: a sausage bliss!

through the lecture-like sound of **"The Motions"** to the Biblical incantation of **"Joshua Tree"** on the one hand or the very direct, sure, imitative dialect of **"First Carolina Said Song"** on the other:

> We got there just in time to see her buried
> in an oak grove up
> back of the field:
> its growed over with soapbushes and huckleberries
>     now.

**"Joshua Tree"** is a moving piece in which the speaker relates to the wind, who instructs him to

> settle here
> by this Joshua Tree
> and make a well.

The speaker, after lamenting that he is

> consigned to
> form that will not
> let me loose
> except to death

so that he "must go on" until then, asks that later the wind—muse-like and yet like a man—

> enter angling through
> my cage
> and let my ribs
> sing me out.

The wind is a frequent persona in the poems, as breath itself becomes fleshed out. Considering wind as breath one begins to see the connection between the poems of external landscape and the elements (which fill the first book and reappear here) and the poems of internal geography.

> When I go back of my head
> down the cervical well, roots
> branch
> turning, figuring
> into flesh.

I don't like the line "mcat's indivisible stuff" because its texture jars with the rest of the *coulage* of diction, but otherwise this poem, **"Landscape with Figures,"** is one of the strongest in the collection.

There is a constant playing off of the interior world of mind and cells against the exterior world of things where self lies dispersed and in need of the gathering force of a poem. The rapport of interior and exterior is itself expressed in a perfect short poem entitled **"Reflective,"** which I give here entire:

> I found a
> weed
> that had a
>
> mirror in it
> and that
> mirror
>
> looked in at
> a mirror
> in
>
> me that
> had a
> weed in it.

The half-solipsistic character of this is projected beautifully to trees in a fuller sense in the poem **"Halfway"**:

> birches stand
> in
>
> pools of them-
> selves, the yellow
> fallen
>
> leaves reflecting
> those on
> the tree that
> mirror the ground

From the idea of external—reflected—in—internal, one can move rather easily to the notion of the cosmos reflected in small in one of its parts, as in the striking poem. **"The Constant,"** where the galaxy-like, moving film of sand in the water of a clam shell seems to reflect the scope of sky, so that:

> a gull's toe could spill the universe:
> two more hours of sun could dry it up;
> a higher wind could rock it out. . . .

There is a marvelous imaging of the tentativeness with which things "live and move and have their being" as the Old Fellow said. This mood is seconded in **"Contingency"** where, contemplating all the life and change started by a sprinkler, one reflects that:

> a turn of the faucet
> dries every motion up.

And it is brought into a new key in the poem, **"Zone,"** which suggests that a myth of creation is completed only by its parallel myth of uncreation. There is a constant need for recovery, whether for the shadows of trees (in **"Recovery"**) or for time future (in **"Passage"**)—

> tomorrow emerges and
> falls back shaped into today: endlessly

—or for the life of a man himself. For poets this latter kind of recovery is accomplished by the writing of poems, and when the poems are as good as these, it is sometimes accomplished for others by reading them.

Intellectuality is a prime trait of Ammons' work, as is suggested by the abstract character of several titles in the new book: **"Height," "Reflective," "Contingency," "Interference," "Saliences."** Sometimes, as in the latter poem and in **"One-Many"**—two of the most ambitious and strongest poems in the book—there is too much cerebration demanded of the reader, I believe, before the poem begins to burgeon. There are some other faults. Occasionally the poems seem to lack vigor. Occasionally influence obtrudes itself, as that of Marianne Moore in **"Uh, Philosophy"** or of Dylan Thomas in these punning, elegiac lines:

> If bleak through the black night
> we could outrun
> this knowledge into a different morning!

or of T. S. Eliot in this passage: "though the world ends and cannot end" and "To death, the diffuse one going beside me, I said. . . ." (Yet the most pervasive influences—those of William Carlos Williams and Ezra Pound—have been well assimilated to form a highly original body of work.) There are occasional bad lines: "O ablutions!" Yet, a careful look at the whole body of Ammons' work, particularly *Tape for the Turn of the Year* and the new book, will show that we are dealing with a major talent, one who has the courage and the heuristic power to discover new form, as well as the eye and the ear and the mind to hold us and to give us what Thomas called "the momentary peace of the poem."

### A. R. Ammons (essay date 1967)

SOURCE: "A Poem Is a Walk," in *Epoch,* Vol. XVIII, No. 1, Fall, 1968, pp. 114-19.

[*In the following essay, which was first presented as a lecture in 1967, Ammons considers the difficulty of defining poetry. He concludes by offering two observations: "poetry is a mode of discourse that differs from logical exposition. . . . [and] leads us to the unstructured sources of our beings, to the unknown, and returns us to our rational, structured selves refreshed."*]

> *Nothing that can be said*
> *in words is worth saying.*
> Laotse

I don't know whether I can sustain myself for thirty minutes of saying I know nothing—or that I need to try, since I might prove no more than you already suspect, or, even worse, persuade you of the fact. Nothingness contains no images to focus and brighten the mind, no contrarieties to build up muscular tension: it has no place for argumentation and persuasion, comparison and contrast, classification, analysis. As nothingness is more perfectly realized, there is increasingly less (if that isn't contradictory) to realize, less to say, less need to say. Only silence perfects silence. Only nothingness contributes to nothingness. The only perfect paper I could give you would be by standing silent before you for thirty minutes. But I am going to try this imperfect, wordy means to suggest why silence is finally the only perfect statement.

I have gone in for the large scope with no intention but to make it larger; so I have had to leave a lot of space "unworked," have had to leave out points the definition of any one of which could occupy a paper longer than this. For though we often need to be restored to the small, concrete, limited, and certain, we as often need to be reminded of the large, vague, unlimited, unknown.

I can't tell you where a poem comes from, what it is, or what it is for: nor can any other man. The reason I can't tell you is that the purpose of a poem is to go past telling, to be recognized by burning.

I don't, though, disparage efforts to say what poetry is and is for. I am grateful for—though I can't keep up with—the flood of articles, theses, and textbooks that mean to share insight concerning the nature of poetry. Probably all the attention to poetry results in some value, though the attention is more often directed to lesser than to greater values.

Once every five hundred years or so, a summary statement about poetry comes along that we can't imagine ourselves living without. The greatest statement in our language is Coleridge's in the *Biographia*. It serves my purpose to quote only a fragment from the central statement: that the imagination—and, I think, poetry—"reveals itself in the balance or reconciliation of opposite or discordant qualities." This suggests to me that description, logic, and hypothesis, reaching toward higher and higher levels of generality, come finally to an antithesis logic can't bridge. But poetry, the imagination, can create a vehicle, at once concrete and universal, one and many, similar and diverse, that is capable of bridging the duality and of bringing us the experience of a "real" world that is also a reconciled, a unified, real world. And this vehicle is the only expression of language, of words, that I know of that contradicts my quotation from Laotse, because a poem becomes, like reality, an existence about which nothing that can be said in words is worth saying.

Statement can also achieve unity, though without the internal suspension of variety. For example, All is One, seems to encompass or erase all contradiction. A statement, however, differs from a work of art. The statement, All is One, provides us no experience of manyness, of the concrete world from which the statement derived. But a work of art creates a world of both one and many, a world of definition and indefinition. Why should we be surprised that the work of art, which over-reaches and reconciles logical paradox, is inaccessible to the methods of logical exposition? A world comes into being about which any statement, however revelatory, is a lessening.

Knowledge of poetry, which is gained, as in science or other areas, by induction and deduction, is likely to remain provisional by falling short in one of two ways: either it is too specific, too narrow and definite, to be widely applicable—that is, the principles suggested by a single poem are not likely to apply in the same number or kind in another poem: or, the knowledge is too general, too abstract and speculative, to fit precisely the potentialities of any given poem. Each poem in becoming generates the laws by which it is generated: extensions of the laws to other poems never completely take. But a poem generated by its own laws may be unrealized and bad in terms of so-called objective principles of taste, judgment, deduction. We are obliged both to begin internally with a given poem and work toward generalization *and* to approach the poem externally to test it with a set—and never quite the same set—of *a priori* generalizations. Whatever we gain in terms of the existence of an individual poem, we lose in terms of a consistent generality, a tradition: and vice versa. It is Scylla and Charybdis again. It is the logically insoluble problem of one and many.

To avoid the uncertainty generated by this logical impasse—and to feel assured of something definite to teach—we are likely to prefer one side or the other—either the individual poem or the set of generalizations—and then to raise mere preference to eternal verity. But finally, nothing is to be gained by dividing the problem. A teacher once told me that every line of verse ought to begin with a capital letter. That is definite, teachable, mistaken knowledge. Only by accepting the uncertainty of the whole can we free ourselves to the reconciliation that is the poem, both at the subconscious level of feeling and the conscious level of art.

One step further before we get to the main business of the paper. Questions structure and, so, to some extent predetermine answers. If we ask a vague question, such as, What is poetry?, we expect a vague answer, such as, Poetry is the music of words, or Poetry is the linguistic correction of disorder. If we ask a narrower question, such as, What is a conceit?, we are likely to get a host of answers, but narrower answers. Proteus is a good figure for this. You remember that Proteus was a minor sea god, a god of *knowledge,* an attendant on Poseidon. Poseidon is the ocean, the total view, every structure in the ocean as well as the unstructured ocean itself. Proteus, the god of knowledge, though, is a minor god. Definite knowledge, knowledge specific and clear enough to be recognizable as knowledge, is, as we have seen, already limited into a minor view. Burke said that a clear idea is another name for a little idea. It was presumed that Proteus knew the answers—and more important The Answer—but he resisted questions by transforming himself from one creature or substance into another. The more specific, the more binding the question, the more vigorously he wrestled to be free of it. Specific questions about poetry merely turn into other specific questions about poetry. But the vague question is answered by the ocean which provides distinction and non-distinction, something intellect can grasp, compare, and structure, and something it can neither grasp, compare, nor structure.

My predisposition, which I hope shortly to justify, is to prefer confusion to over-simplified clarity, meaninglessness to neat, precise meaning, uselessness to over-directed usefulness. I do not believe that rationality can exhaust the poem, that any scheme of explanation can adequately reflect the poem, that any invented structure of symbology can exceed and thereby replace the poem.

I must stress here the point that I appreciate clarity, order, meaning, structure, rationality: they are necessary to whatever provisional stability we have, and they can be the agents of gradual and successful change. And the rational, critical mind is essential to making poems: it protects the real poem (which is non-rational) from blunders, misconceptions, incompetences; it weeds out the second rate. Definition, rationality, and structure are ways of seeing, but they become prisons when they blank out other ways of seeing. If we remain open-minded we will soon find for any easy clarity an equal and opposite, so that the sum of our clarities should return us where we belong, to confusion and, hopefully, to more complicated and better assessments.

Unlike the logical structure, the poem is an existence which can incorporate contradictions, inconsistencies, explanations and counter-explanations and still remain whole, unexhausted and inexhaustible; an existence that comes about by means other than those of description and exposition and, therefore, to be met by means other than, or in addition to, those of description and exposition.

With the hope of focusing some of these problems, I want now to establish a reasonably secure identity between a poem and a walk and to ask how a walk occurs, what it is, and what it is for. I say I want a reasonably secure identity because I expect to have space to explore only four resemblances between poems and walks and no space at all for the differences, taking it for granted that walks and poems are different things. I'm not, of course, interested in walks as such but in clarification or intensification by distraction, seeing one thing better by looking at something else. We want to see the poem.

What justification is there for comparing a poem with a walk rather than with something else? I take the walk to be the externalization of an interior seeking, so that the analogy is first of all between the external and the internal. Poets not only do a lot of walking but talk about it in their poems: "I wandered lonely as a cloud," "Now I out walking," and "Out walking in the frozen swamp one grey day." There are countless examples, and many of them suggest that both the real and the fictive walk are externalizations of an inward seeking. The walk magnified is the journey, and probably no figure has been used more often than the journey for both the structure and concern of an interior seeking.

How does a poem resemble a walk? First, each makes use of the whole body, involvement is total, both mind and body. You can't take a walk without feet and legs, without a circulatory system, a guidance and co-ordinating system, without eyes, ears, desire, will, need: the total person. This observation is important not only for what it includes but for what it rules out: as with a walk, a poem is not simply a mental activity; it has body, rhythm, feeling, sound, and mind, conscious and subconscious. The pace at which a poet walks (and thinks), his natural breath-length, the line he pursues, whether forthright and straight or weaving and meditative, his whole "air," whether of aimlessness or purpose—all these things and many more figure into the "physiology" of the poem he writes.

A second resemblance is that every walk is unreproducible, as is every poem. Even if you walk exactly the same route each time—as with a sonnet—the events along the route cannot be imagined to be the same from day to day, as the poet's health, sight, his anticipations, moods, fears, thoughts cannot be the same. There are no two identical sonnets or villanelles. If there were, we would not know how to keep the extra one: it would have no separate existence. If a poem is each time new, then it is necessarily an act of discovery, a chance taken, a chance that may lead to fulfillment or disaster. The poet exposes himself to the risk. All that has been said about poetry, all that he has learned about poetry, is only a partial assurance.

The third resemblance between a poem and a walk is that each turns, one or more times, and eventually *re*turns. It's conceivable that a poem could take out and go through incident after incident without ever returning, merely ending in the poet's return to dust. But most poems and most walks return. I have already quoted the first line from Frost's "The Wood-Pile." Now, here are the first three lines:

> Out walking in the frozen swamp one grey day,
> I paused and said, 'I will turn back from here.
> No, I will go on farther—and we shall see.'

The poet is moving outward seeking the point from which he will turn back. In "The Wood-Pile" there is no return: return is implied. The poet goes farther and farther into the swamp until he finds by accident the point of illumination with which he closes the poem.

But the turns and returns or implied returns give shape to the walk and to the poem. With the first step, the number of shapes the walk might take is infinite, but then the walk begins to "define" itself as it goes along, though freedom remains total with each step: any tempting side-road can be turned into on impulse, or any wild patch of woods can be explored. The pattern of the walk is to come true, is to be recognized, discovered. The pattern, when discovered, may be found to apply to the whole walk, or only a segment of the walk may prove to have contour and therefore suggestion and shape. From previous knowledge of the terrain, inner and outer, the poet may have before the walk an inkling of a possible contour. Taking the walk would then be searching out or confirming, giving actuality to, a previous intuition.

The fourth resemblance has to do with the motion common to poems and walks. The motion may be lumbering, clipped, wavering, tripping, mechanical, dance-like, awkward, staggering, slow, etc. But the motion occurs only in the body of the walker or in the body of the words. It can't be extracted and contemplated. It is non-reproducible and non-logical. It can't be translated into another body. There is only one way to know it and that is to enter into it.

To summarize, a walk involves the whole person; it is not reproducible; its shape occurs, unfolds; it has a motion characteristic of the walker.

If you were brought into a classroom and asked to teach walks, what would you teach? If you have any idea, I hope the following suggestions will deprive you of it.

The first thought that would occur to you is, What have other people said about walks? You could collect all historical references to walks and all descriptions of walks, find out the average length of walks, through what kind of terrain they have most often proceeded, what kind of people have enjoyed walks and why, and how walks have reflected the societies in which they occurred. In short, you could write a history of walks.

Or you could call in specialists. You might find a description of a particularly disturbing or interesting walk and then you might call in a botanist to retrace that walk with you and identify all the leaves and berries for you: or you might take along a sociologist to point out to you that the olive trees mentioned were at the root—forgive me—of feudal society: or you might take along a surveyor to give you a close reading in inches and degrees: or you might take a psychoanalyst along to ask good questions about what is the matter with people who take walks: or you might take a physiologist to provide you with astonishment that people can walk at all. Each specialist would no doubt come up with important facts and insights, but your attention, focused on the cell structure of the olive leaf, would miss the main event, the walk itself.

You could ask what walks are good for. Here you would find plenty: to settle the nerves, to improve the circulation, to break in a new pair of shoes, to exercise the muscles, to aid digestion, to prevent heart attacks, to focus the mind, to distract the mind, to get a loaf of bread, to watch birds, to kick stones, to spy on a neighbor's wife, to dream. My point is clear. You could go on indefinitely. Out of desperation and exasperation brought on by the failure to define the central use or to exhaust the list of uses of walks, you would surrender, only to recover into victory by saying, Walks are useless. So are poems.

Or you could find out what walks mean: do they mean a lot of men have unbearable wives, or that we must by outward and inward motions rehearse the expansion and contraction of the universe; do walks mean that we need structure—or, at an obsessive level, ritual in our lives? The answer is that a walk doesn't mean anything, which is a way of saying that to some extent it means anything you can make it mean—and always more than you can make it mean. Walks are meaningless. So are poems.

There is no ideal walk, then, though I haven't taken the time to prove it out completely, except the useless, meaningless walk. Only uselessness is empty enough for the presence of so many uses, and only through uselessness can the ideal walk come into the sum total of its uses. Only uselessness can allow the walk to be totally itself.

I hope you are now, if you were not before, ready to agree with me that the greatest wrong that can be done a poem is to substitute a known part for an unknown whole and that the choice to be made is the freedom of nothingness: that our experience of poetry is least injured when we accept it as useless, meaningless, and non-rational.

Besides the actual reading in class of many poems, I would suggest you do two things: first, while teaching everything you can and keeping free of it, teach that poetry is a mode of discourse that differs from logical exposition. It is the mode I spoke of earlier that can reconcile opposites into a "real" world both concrete and universal. Teach that. Teach the distinction.

Second, I would suggest you teach that poetry leads us to the unstructured sources of our beings, to the unknown, and returns us to our rational, structured selves refreshed. Having once experienced the mystery, plenitude, contradiction, and composure of a work of art, we afterwards have a built-in resistance to the slogans and propaganda of over-simplification that have often contributed to the destruction of human life. Poetry is a verbal means to a non-verbal source. It is a motion to no-motion, to the still point of contemplation and deep realization. Its knowledges are all negative and, therefore, more positive than any knowledge. Nothing that can be said about it in words is worth saying.

## Harold Bloom (essay date 1973)

SOURCE: "The New Transcendentalism: The Visionary Strain in Merwin, Ashbery, and Ammons," in *Chicago Review,* Vol. 24, No. 3, Winter, 1973, pp. 25-43.

*[Bloom is one of the most prominent contemporary American critics and literary theorists. In* The Anxiety of Influence *(1973), he formulated a controversial theory of literary creation called revisionism. Influenced strongly by Freudian theory, which states that "all men unconsciously wish to beget themselves, to be their own fathers," Bloom believes that all poets are subject to the influence of earlier poets and that, to develop their own voice, they attempt to overcome this influence through a process of misreading. By misreading, he means a deliberate, personal revision of what has been said by another so that it conforms to one's own vision. In this way the poet creates a singular voice, overcoming the fear of being inferior to poetic predecessors. In addition to his theoretical work, Bloom is one of the foremost authorities on*

*English Romantic poetry and has written widely on the influences of Romanticism in contemporary literature. Here, Bloom, who was a prominent early supporter of Ammons, calls upon his theory of the anxiety of influence to help explain the development of Ammons's poetic voice within the American poetic tradition established by the nineteenth-century literary figure Ralph Waldo Emerson.]*

In turning to A. R. Ammons, the wisest and I prophesy most enduring poet of his generation, we confront the most direct Emersonian in American poetry since Frost. For an account of Ammons' work from its origins to the lyrics of *Uplands* (1970) and *Briefings* (1971), I refer to my book, *The Ringers in the Tower* (1971). Here I wish to describe the great achievement of the latest Ammons, as gathered in the large *Collected Poems* (1972), particularly three long poems: **"Essay on Poetics," "Extremes and Moderations," "Hibernaculum,"** but also two crucial recent lyrics.

The **"Essay on Poetics"** begins by giving us Ammons' central signature, the process by which he has made a cosmos:

>     Take in a lyric information
>     totally processed, interpenetrated into
>     wholeness where
>
>     a bit is a bit, a string a string, a
>     cluster a cluster, everything beefing up
>     and verging out
>
>     for that point in the periphery where
>     salience bends into curve
>     and all saliences bend to the same angle of
>
>     curve and curve becomes curve, one curve, the
>        whole curve:
>     that is information actual
>     at every point
>
>     but taking on itself at every point
>     the emanation of curvature, of meaning, all
>     the way into the high
>
>     recognition of wholeness, that synthesis,
>     feeling, aroused, controlled, and released . . .

Ammons' "periphery" is at once the "circumference" of Emerson and Dickinson, and also the nerve-ending of the quester who goes out upon circumference. Ammons' "salience" is the further projecting or outleaping from the longest periphery that the seer has attained. That makes Ammons' "salience" his equivalent of the Pound-Williams "image" or the Stevensian "solar single,/ Man-sun, man-moon, man-earth, man-ocean." Far back, but indubitably the starting-place, Ammons' **"Essay on Poetics"** touches Whitman's 1855 "Preface" and Whitman's fecund ground, Emerson's "The Poet," a prose rhapsody mostly of 1842. Ammons expounds a "science" that now seems curious, but Emerson called it "true science." More than Whitman, or even Thoreau or Dickinson or Frost, Ammons is the Poet that Emerson prophesied as necessary for America:

. . . For through that better perception he stands one step nearer to things, and sees the flowing or metamorphosis; perceives that thought is multiform; that within the form of every creature is a force impelling it to ascend into a higher form; and following with his eyes the life, uses the forms which express that life, and so his speech flows with the flowing of nature. All the facts of the animal economy, sex, nutriment, gestation, birth, growth, are symbols of the passage of the world into the soul of man, to suffer there a change and reappear a new and higher fact. He uses forms according to the life, and not according to the form. This is true science. The poet alone knows astronomy, chemistry, vegetation and animation, for he does not stop at these facts, but employs them as signs. He knows why the plain or meadow of space was strown with these flowers we call suns and moons and stars; why the great deep is adorned with animals, with men, and gods; for in every word he speaks he rides on them as the horses of thought.

As in "Tintern Abbey," standing closer to things is to see into their life, to see process and not particulars. But it is not Wordsworthian nor even neo-Platonic to possess a speech that is magic, to speak words that are themselves the metamorphosis. This violent Idealism is Emerson's Transcendental science, a knowing too impatient for the disciplines of mysticism, let alone rational dialectic. To read Emerson's "The Poet" side-by-side with any British Romantic on poetry, except Blake, is to see how peculiar the Emersonian wildness is. Only a step away and Emerson will identify a true poet's words with Necessity, as though nature's absolute confounding of our faculties simultaneously could make us skeptics and scientists affirming an inevitable insight. Emerson, here as so often, seems to break down the humanly needful distinctions between incoherence and coherence, relying upon his tone to persuade us of an intelligibility not wholly present. Ammons, like any strong poet, handles influence by misprision. His Emersonianism is so striking and plausible a twisting askew of that heritage as to raise again the labyrinthine issue of what poetic influence is, and how it works.

To talk about a poem by Ammons in terms of Emerson or Whitman is to invoke what one might term the Human Analogue, as opposed to Coleridge's Organic Analogue. No poem rejoices in its own solitary inscape, any more than we can do so. We have to be talked about in terms of other people, for no more than a poem is, can we be "about" ourselves. To say that a poem is about itself is killing, but to say it is about another poem is to go out into the world where we live. We idealize about ourselves when we isolate ourselves, just as poets deceive themselves by idealizing what they assert to be their poems' true subjects. The actual subjects move towards the anxiety of influence, and now frequently are that anxiety. But a deeper apparent digression begins to loom here, even as I attempt to relate the peripheries and saliences of Ammons to the great circumference of his ancestors.

Reductively, the anxiety of influence *is* the fear of death, and a poet's vision of immortality includes seeing himself free of all influence. Perhaps sexual jealousy, a closely related anxiety, also reduces to the fear of death, or of the ultimate tyranny of space and time, since influence-anxiety is related to our horror of space and time as a dungeon, as the danger of domination by the Not-Me. Anxiety of influence is due then partly to fear of the natural body, yet poetry is written by the natural man who is one with the body. Blake insisted that there was also the Real Man the Imagination. Perhaps there is, but he cannot write poems, at least not yet.

The poem attempts to relieve the poet-as-poet from fears that *there is not enough for him,* whether of space (imaginative) or time (priority). A subject, a mode, a voice; all these lead to the question: "what, besides my death, is my own?" Poets of the Pound-Williams school, more than most contemporary poets, scoff at the notion of an anxiety of influence, believing as they think they do that a poem is a machine made out of words. Perhaps, but mostly in the sense that we, alas, appear to be machines made out of words, for poems actually are closer-to—as Stevens said—men made up out of worlds. Men make poems as Dr. Frankenstein made his *daemon,* and poems too acquire the disorders of the human. The people in poems do not have fathers, but the poems do.

Ammons . . . is aware of all this, for strong poets become strong by meeting the anxiety of influence, not by evading it. Poets adept at forgetting their ancestry write very forgettable poems. Ammons' **"Essay on Poetics"** swerves away from Emerson by the exercise of a variety of revisionary ratios, cunningly set against mere repetition:

> the very first actions of contact with an ocean say ocean over and over: read a few lines along the periphery of any of the truly great and the knowledge delineates an open shore:
>
> what is to be gained from the immortal person except the experience of ocean: take any line as skiff, break the breakers, and go out into the landless, orientationless, but perfectly contained, try
>
> the suasions, brief dips and rises, and the general circulations, the wind, the abundant reductions, stars, and the experience is obtained: but rivers, brooks, and trickles have their uses and
>
> special joys and achieve, in their identities, difficult absoluteness but will you say, what of the content— why they are all made of water but will you, because of the confusion, bring me front center as
>
> a mere mist or vapor . . .

This is the faith of Emersonian Self-Reliance, yet severely mitigated by the consciousness of latecoming. At the close of the poem, Ammons attains a majestic bleakness not wholly compatible with this apparent humility:

> . . . along the periphery of integrations, then, is an exposure to demons, thralls, witcheries, the maelstrom black of possibility, costly, chancy, lethal, open: so I am not so much

arguing with the organic school as shifting true organisms from the already organized to the bleak periphery of possibility, an area transcendental only by its bottomless entropy . . .

The later Ammons writes out of a vision "transcendental only by its bottomless entropy," yet still Emersonian, though this is the later Emerson of *The Conduct of Life,* precursor of Stevens in *The Rock* and Frost throughout *In The Clearing.* **"Extremes and Moderations"** is Ammons' major achievement in the long poem, written in "the flow-breaking four-liner", starting out in an audacious transcendentalism and modulating into the prophetic voice Ammons rarely seeks, yet always attains at the seeking:

>                      . . . O city. I cry at
> the gate, the glacier is your
> mother, the currents of the deep father you, you
>     sleep
>
> in the ministry of trees, the boulders are your
>     brother sustaining
> you: come out, I cry, into the lofty assimilations:
>     women, let
> down your hair under the dark leaves of the night
>     grove, enter
> the currents with a sage whining, rising into the
>     circular
>
> dance: men, come out and be with the wind, speedy
>     and lean,
> fall
> into the moon-cheered waters, plunge into the
>     ecstasy of rapids:
> children, come out and play in the toys of divinity:
>     glass, brick,
> stone, curb, rail are freezing you out of your
>     motions, the
>
> uncluttered circulations: I cry that, but perhaps I am
>     too secular
> or pagan: everything, they say, is artificial: nature's
>     the
> artwork of the Lord: but your work, city is aimed
>     unnaturally
> against time: your artifice confronts the Artifice:
>     beyond
> the scheduled consummation, nothing's to be
>     recalled: there is
> memory enough in the rock, unscriptured history in
> the wind, sufficient identity in the curve
> of the valley . . .

This is the extreme of which Ammons' earlier and masterly lyric, **"The City Limits,"** was the moderation. By "extremes" Ammons signifies what Emerson's circle called the Newness, onsets of transcendental influx. "Moderations" are the rescues of these evaded furies that Ammons attempts for the poetry of life, while carefully distinguishing even the extremes from mere phantasmagorias: . . . that there should have been possibilities enough to include all that has occurred is beyond belief, an extreme the strictures and disciplines of which prevent loose-flowing phantasmagoria . . .

Though the poem concludes in a moving ecological outrage, an outrage the poet appears to believe is his theme, its concerns hover where Ammons' obsessions always congregate, his resistance to his own transcendental experience. This resistance is made, as all constant readers of Ammons learn, in the name of a precarious naturalism, but the concealed undercurrent is always the sense of an earlier bafflement of vision, a failure to have attained a longed-for unity with an Absolute. The latest Ammons rarely makes reference to this spent seership, but the old longing beautifully haunts all of the difficult recent radiances. Here is a typical late lyric, **"Day,"** manifesting again the extraordinary and wholly deceptive ease that Ammons has won for himself, an ease of mode and not of spirit, which continues to carry an exemplary burden of torment:

> On a cold late
> September morning,
> wider than sky-wide
> discs of lit-shale clouds
>
> skim the hills,
> crescents, chords
> of sunlight
> now and then fracturing
>
> the long peripheries:
> the crow flies
> silent,
> on course but destinationless,
>
> floating:
> hurry, hurry,
> the running light says,
> while anything remains.

The mode goes back through Dickinson to Emerson, and is anything but the Pound-Williams "machine made out of words" that Hugh Kenner describes the praises in his crucially polemical *The Pound Era.* "The long peripheries," for Ammons, are identical with poems, or rather with what he would like his poems to be, outermost perceptions within precise boundaries, or literally "carryings-over" from the eye's tyranny to the relative freedom of a personally achieved idiom. What now distinguishes a lyric like **"Day"** from the characteristic earlier work in the Ammons canon is the urgency of what another late long poem, **"Hibernaculum,"** calls "a staying change," this seer's response to our current time-of-transition from our recent confusions to whatever is coming upon us: "I think we are here to give back our possessions before/ they are taken away." This is the motto preceding an immense intimation of another Newness:

>           . . . I
> accost the emptiness saying let all men turn their
> eyes to the emptiness that allows adoration's life:
> that is my whole saying, though I have no intention

> to
> stop talking: our immediate staying's the rock but
> the staying of the rock's motion: motion, that spirit!
> We could veer into, dimpling, the sun or into the
>   cold
>
> orbital lofts, but our motion, our weight, our speed
> are organized here like a rock, our spiritual stay:
> the blue spruce's become ponderous with snow:
>   brief
>
> melt re-froze and knitted ice to needles and ice
> to snow so the ridges eight inches high hold: the
> branches move back and forth, stiff wailers:
>
> the cloud-misty moonlight fills small fields, plots,
> woodnooks with high light, snow transluminant as
> fire. . . .

Contrast to this an equal superb Emersonian epiphany:

> Last night the moon rose behind four distinct pine-tree tops in the distant woods and the night at ten was so bright that I walked abroad. But the sublime light of night is unsatisfying, provoking; it astonishes but explains not. Its charm floats, dances, disappears, comes and goes, but palls in five minutes after you have left the house. Come out of your warm, angular house, resounding with few voices, into the chill, grand, instantaneous night, with such a Presence as a full moon in the clouds, and you are struck with poetic wonder. In the instant you leave far behind all human relations, wife, mother and child, and live only with savages— water, air, light, carbon, lime, and granite. . . . I become a moist, cold element. 'Nature grows over me.' Frogs pipe; waters far off tinkle; dry leaves hiss; grass bends and rustles, and I have died out of the human world and come to feel a strange, cold, aqueous, terraqueous, aerial, ethereal sympathy and existence. I sow the sun and moon for seeds.

Emerson and Ammons share a nature that on the level of experience or confrontation cannot be humanized. Yet they share also a Transcendental belief that one can come to unity, at least in the pure good of theory. Their common tone is a curious chill, a tang of other-than-human relationship to an Oversoul or Overall that is not nature, yet breaks through into nature. Like Emerson, its founder, Ammons is a poet of the American Sublime, and a residue of this primordial strength abides in all of his work.

*Collected Poems 1951-1971* closes with a magnificent poem that is Ammons overt *apologia,* and I will close this essay by giving the poem entire, and then attempting a defining observation upon its place in the tradition of American poetry. Here is **"The Arc Inside and Out"**:

> If, whittler and dumper, gross carver
> into the shadiest curvings, I took branch
> and meat from the stalk of life, threw
>
> away the monies of the treasured,
> treasurable mind, cleaved memory free
> of the instant, if I got right down

shucking off periphery after periphery
to the glassy vague gray parabolas
and swoops of unnailable perception,

would I begin to improve the purity,
would I essentialize out the distilled
form, the glitter-stone that whether

the world comes or goes clicks gleams
and chinks of truth self-making, never
to be shuttered, the face-brilliant core

stone: or if I, amasser, heap shoveler,
depth pumper, took in all springs and
oceans, paramoecia and moons, massive

buttes and summit slants, rooted trunks
and leafages, anthologies of wise words,
schemata, all grasses (including the

tidal *Spartinas,* marginal, salty
broadsweeps) would I finally come on a
suasion, large, fully-informed, restful

scape, turning back in on itself, its
periphery enclosing our system with
its bright dot and allowing in nonparlant

quantities at the edge void, void, and
void, would I then feel plenitude
brought to center and extent, a sweet

easing away of all edge, evil, and surprise:
these two ways to dream! dreaming them's
the bumfuzzlement—the impoverished

diamond, the heterogeneous abundance
starved into oneness: ultimately, either
way, which is our peace, the little

arc-line appears, inside which is nothing,
outside which is nothing—however big,
nothing beyond: however small, nothing

within: neither way to go's to stay, stay
here, the apple an apple with its own hue
or streak, the drink of water, the drink,

the falling into sleep, restfully ever the
falling into sleep, dream, dream, and
every morning the sun comes, the sun.

The "arc" here, like Dickinson's "Circumference", ultimately
derives from Emerson's subtle essay, *Circles*:

> Our life is an apprenticeship to the truth that around
> every circle another can be drawn; that there is no end
> in nature, but every end is a beginning. . . . The natural
> world may be conceived of as a system of concentric
> circles, and we now and then detect in nature slight
> dislocations which apprise us that this surface on which
> we now stand is not fixed but sliding . . . The one thing
> which we seek with insatiable desire is to forget

ourselves, to be surprised out of our propriety, to
lose our sempiternal memory and to do something
without knowing how or why; in short to draw a new
circle. . . .

Ammons' "little arc-line" is both his Blakean Minute Particular or vision that cannot be further reduced, and his
Emersonian "new circle" or vision that cannot be further
expanded. He begins his poem by a vehement reduction to
"the face-brilliant core stone" and proceeds by an equally
vehement expansion to a "suasion, large, fully-informed."
Both reduction and expansion are lovingly dismissed as
rival dreamings. This poet's reality, still transcendent, is the
arc-line, at once peripheral and salient, a particular apple or
a particular gulp of water, that itself is dream-inducing, but
this is a dream of Whitman's or Steven's colossal sun, of
a reality so immediate as to carry its own transcendence.
Ammons remains, somewhat despite himself, the least spent
of our seers.

## Ammons with D. I. Grossvogel (interview date 1973)

SOURCE: An interview in *Diacritics,* Vol. III, No. 4,
Winter, 1973, pp. 47-53.

[*In the following excerpt, Ammons discusses his ideas about
poetry.*]

[Grossvogel]: *You seem to be suspicious of mentalisms. In
your poem "Uh, Philosophy," isn't that "uh" a disclaimer?*

[Ammons]: Yes. At the first level of the critical I tend to
think of the discursive as assuming limits which then prevent it ever from encompassing the work that is before it.
So I always think of that mode as a lesser mode than the
imaginative. There is nothing new about that; most people
grant it, I believe. Along the same lines as when Laotse
says that nothing that can be said in words is worth saying.
He means, I think that by the time we have embodied into
limitation any sort of reality, it has limited itself out of the
total adumbration. It is true that I use the discursive in my
work a good deal, but always as a character in a play: I
don't particularly care what I say; I care only that the dramatic placing of the thought is accurate in the piece as if it
were a stage play. So and so enters from the left and says
his thing, and it either fits in and promotes the dramatic
action, or it doesn't. Whether or not it is literally true is of
little interest to me because I don't think that the truth can
be arrived at in that mode; but I do believe a character can
represent that truth.

*Let me quibble with you, nevertheless. My sense of your
chronology is that in the beginning you were more dependent on specific myths or stories; this may be inaccurate.*

No, I think it's accurate.

*If it is accurate, would you not agree that a myth is al-
ready, as opposed to the freedom of pure poetry, the encapsulation of an idea?*

No, I don't think so. I think that a narrative provides the configuration from which many ideas may derive. In some short poems, I tell a little story. The story is quite plain; it's the first level of apprehension of the poem, but it becomes mythic in what it might suggest. It can suggest any number of facets. Consequently, it is not formulable into a concept. In other words, I think the narrative is a body in motion and the concept is of a different order. I can give you a good example, a little poem called **"Mountain Talk."** You may know it.

*I was very much sensitized to your mountains by Harold Bloom who makes a big thing of them—mountains out of mountains.*

It tells a very simple story. Actually the poem investigates the feelings that might be said to surround certain objects. A person is walking along a dusty highroad. What does a dusty highroad mean? It's almost in a religious realm—you know, *dust, height, abstraction, separation* from the landscape, in a sense of perhaps being lost in it. And then, the moment of recognition when the person who is walking along becomes aware of a presence near him and he turns and it is not something that is wandering at all. It's a mountain that is always there. It occupies a single position and, as the poem says, it retains a single prospect. So the narrative then becomes the play of these two possibilities, of being stable and of occupying a massive view about things that is unalterable; or being tiny enough to go up and down pathways, to become lost. And the speaker finally prefers that mobility, that changeability, to occupying a single space. Now, it seems to me that the center of the poem is not a concept but a polarity; something like the two separate parts of a metaphor.

*When you write that poem, you're a poet, but when you talk about that poem you're a critic.*

Right.

*And what dissatisfies you, presumably, in any dialogue of this kind, is that you're being forced out of your true role.*

I just feel incomplete.

*You are being forced to do what you may legitimately not want to do. The poem stands as the totality of your statement.*

There is a lovely thing in, of all people, Carlyle, where he describes our present age beautifully—you know, bombed out—but, he says, we still have action left. Well that's exactly the mode I try to jump into; it's as if you were reading a newspaper—"I was walking along a dusty highroad. . . ." You get to that ordinary level of things and, in a normal, almost journalistic way, you go into action, things happen, and then they end. Meanwhile they describe a curvature of some sort that's either narrative, or myth or structure or whatever, but it *is*, it *exists* and is no longer susceptible to analysis, to destruction by analysis or to further creation by analysis. *It's there.* It was just something that happened and it was a series of actions and somehow those actions were

so interrelated that they described a synthesis, a curvature of sentences; and that is the myth, or whatever, lying at the center of the imagination. It's just there; it doesn't do anything.

*When you say "myth," what you mean seems to be the synthesis effected by the poem.*

Right. The essential configuration. That structure upon which all the meanings depend.

*But I was thinking of an evolution in your poetry that goes from a more specific fabulation to a much freer (if I may use the word) verse.*

I think you're right.

*In that case, if we subtract from the earlier verse the freer verse of your later period, there is a residual armature that I wanted to call "myth"—a more formal way of showing; not a simple statement, but a relatively learned structure drawing on oriental or Indian philosophies, or folktales. And it seems to me that all this raises a more fundamental question about the legitimacy of criticism. Your primary responsibility is that of the poet; but what about the rest of us, the teachers or those whose function is to provide a bridge to your poetry, for those who may not know it, or who may not know how to get to it? Is it a legitimate function? I understand to what extent your suspicion of the critical function determines that it is an illegitimate exercise. But what about the possibility of teaching poetry in the classroom? My first caution in a poetry class is that we are going to do the one thing we should not be doing with a poem. We are going to analyze it, that is to say we are going to destroy it. But then I go ahead and do it anyway. My rationale is that it is a necessary sort of destruction. I am hopeful that the student will be able to effect his own syntheses later on.*

My feeling is that the critical function, at least at the lower level about which we were speaking earlier, engages the intelligence primarily as a conceptual function and I take that to be a very small part of a possible human response—that is, the physiological, the emotional, the visceral, whatever, so that I distrust the conceptual in that it separates out and over-emphasizes one particular function of the human organism. I think that what is gained at the cost of that separation is clarity, and to the extent that criticism can offer clear opinions, opinions obviously superior to some other set of opinions, it does a great service to the poet and everybody else. But here again, as Edmund Burke says, the clear idea is another name for a little idea. Now this is not to say that there cannot be large critical ideas. It's just to say that the critical idea itself illuminates only a part of the work of art at a time. It may be that, seriatim, the critic would get around the whole periphery. But there would never be any one moment when the poem was apprehended in its entirety.

*I can't help feeling that you are describing a bad critic.*

Well, I don't know. All I'm saying is that criticism does not enable you to embrace the whole work of art at an instant—a moment of sudden coalescence—a tripping of the feeling when the whole being is suddenly imbued with a heightened energy and a feeling of understanding, though its an understanding of *seeing into,* or *through.* The mind can exist in all kinds of ways. It can be too rigid, it can be loose to the point of lunacy, it can be disoriented, disconcerted, and so on. This suggests that there may be some desirable state that the mind could be in, that might vary from culture to culture, but that might be substantially the same in any given culture. I think this would apply also to the whole body. The entire body is functioning, perhaps at a slightly stepped-up rate, and all the energy is available, and it is directed, as in coitus for example; but also in a focusing of the attention when the mind is fully awake, fully focused and penetrating (if I may get back to coitus) and realizes the experience that is to be shared. That might be what we would calla desirable state of being. It seems to me that in teaching, beginning with images, or rhythms, perhaps going through several motions, situations or strategies within the poem, one might gradually be lifting the student into the kind of comprehensive attention that would enable him to move into a desirable state of being, where there is a complicated, free (though directed) functioning of his energy. I think that the poem is an image of this complex activity. And not only the poem: I think this is true of any work of art.

*Any art form that enables its beholder or participant to rehearse an essential moment of the human condition?*

To rehearse, to alert, to freshen, to awaken the energies, not to lunacy and meaningless motion, but to concentration and focus. That is the desirable state to which art should bring you, and to the extent that the poem becomes an image of this, and a generator of it, it is a desirable thing. No computer, no bank of computers, can keep track of the physiological events that must occur for that state of being to be reached. So dozens of sciences have as their objective an analysis of one part of this complicated process. I think that the poem, or the work of art, has underneath it this entire physiology. I believe it is so complicated that you cannot say anything clear about it except about a small part of it. Through the concatenation of such clarifications one can heighten one's own attention so that by exposure to the thing itself, one comes into a sense of coordination with the work of art. Ultimately there is no value to this except the experience of having been there and felt the heightened focus and the heightened release of energy. Once again I think that the whole thing is very close to the experience of coitus. I think that's one reason why the University cannot get closer to the imaginative moment because it's a little bit embarrassing to be that close to coitus; it's safer to talk about it than to be in it. Take a boy and a girl, they see each other. It's like the first line of a poem. It either sets up an immediate attraction so you want to know more, or it doesn't. If the attraction is there, what happens? The two people manage somehow to get close to each other and what happens next?—not silence but an outbreak of dialogue whereby they try to sense where the other person is, with the anticipation, I believe, that whatever comes of this experience will be deepened, will be colored and made more

beautiful by whatever they do know, which apparently cannot be shared in any other way, except through dialogue, through conversation and through doing things together. A poem is just that way; it begins by talking; that's all it does—talk. Because as the two people come closer and closer together, and—say everything is going fine—and the thing is consummated, speech begins to fail and finally there's not much more than a grunt. The reaction to a poem that is especially effective is just that—a grunt. I think the parallel is just too close to be dismissed. Now when the poem starts to take on radial completion, that is to say that, whatever the structure might be, it is now complete, you are left in a state of silence. You now know where all the motions are—you know all the words, you know all the images, you are in it, and you are almost without words, but you're still able, through that focus, to meditate, to contemplate, to move deeper into the poem and sometimes far beyond the poem. But the most meaningful thing happens at the non-verbal level. The motions are all reconciled when motion ends.

*Does that mean that we are supposed to leave out of all conversation talk about poetry?*

No, not at all. Certain levels are discussable. That is what bothers me so much about some of the French critics, as I understand them. They have arrived at the point where there is no text. It's impossible that there should have been an author; it's inconceivable that there could be an audience. Now it just won't work, because human life and human organisms go right on. Maybe not precisely in the same way, but generally in the same way. And if you locate meaning there, then it's idle, it's sophistry to take things apart until nothing means anything at all.

*Since you have introduced French critics . . .*

. . . about whom I know little . . .

*. . . let me ask you about something that one of them has said. I am thinking of Mauron, who practiced what he termed "psychocriticism." In reading poetry (and we should think of critics like Mauron as people who enjoy reading poetry), he discovers what he calls obsessive images, something the poet may not have been aware of.*

Why not? I'm aware of obsessive images in my poems. I can see how the poet might not know at first because the images have not had a sufficient chance to recur, but surely after he has written for a few years I would think that it would start to be very plain to him.

*It is possible that the individual does not necessarily hear himself as accurately as an outsider hears him. His inner landscape may be more accurate as he perceives it . . .*

But he may not be able to translate it as well?

*No. I mean he might not be able to see it in exactly the same way, or from exactly the same perspective, as an outsider.*

He would see it in a different way.

*Right. He sees it by virtue of being in it. The critic, being outside, allows no more than another view of the forest. But isn't that important? Or is it irrelevant?*

It's important. It's finally not very interesting to me, but I can see how it might be to someone else.

*Tell me why it isn't very interesting to you.*

Well because here again, I think that a person and a poem are very close images of one another. I've never been psychoanalyzed but I understand that you can go along for eight or ten years and at a certain point you quit, but you never come to that very deep point where you can reach absolute formulation and say "this is I, and this is the reason I am I." What do the French critics ultimately hope to arrive at through psychoanalysis, structuralism, or whatever? What is the energy behind the effort?

*I have a feeling that their answer would be similar to yours when I asked you about poetry. Their interests are just postures of the mind. I don't think they claim that they are arriving at an ultimate truth or even an ultimate object. They are merely interested, as is the poet, in exploring the object of their respective attentions.*

That makes the critics' attention a little more provisional than that of the poet who, though he's involved in mortality and time—as everyone else—has in his imaginative work a stabilizing center. The work of art is complete, however unexhausted. Works of art are complete moments that stop. I don't think that the critic would be satisfied to say, "Here is another aspect of the systems which we already have going: now let's see how we can sort it out and move forward."

*Of course, the critic cannot live within a closure in the same way as the poet does within the completeness—I believe you use the image of the orb—of his poem. The critic lives in a speculative realm which, by definition, cannot be closed. But even though you know when the poem is finished, you also know that the poetic investigation continues, and there is a first similarity between the critic, any critic, and the poet. But the modern French critic in particular confronts a poetry that is, generally, less storying than is a good deal of English and American poetry. He is therefore less likely to formulate final truths or ideas about it. Rimbaud moves from storying poems to a free kind of discourse that tells only very dimly a discernible story. This kind of poem really defies intellective interpretation or analysis at the level of ideas. As for your detecting a diffidence when these critics talk about the text, or the text's author, you are perfectly right: you distrust the critic in what he might leave unsaid about the poem: many modern French critics distrust the very act of saying. But they are not really the critics I would like to talk about. I would like to know more specifically, about the critics who have written about your own work. As a critic, I would like to know how an author feels about the criticism he elicits. In his book* Alone with America*, Richard Howard quotes a line*

*of yours, "Teach me, father: behold one whose fears are the harnessed mares of his going!" That seems to confirm two of Harold Bloom's theories about you: one about your anxiety, and one about your anxiety of influence. And this runs counter to a sense that I have of you. I do not detect the quotient of anxiety which a line like that, taken in isolation, would seem to indicate.*

Well, Harold Bloom says somewhere that those who reject their poetic fathers write very forgettable poetry. I think that what he is suggesting is that there is a continuity of some kind, a continuity that moves on through the centuries and remains largely the same, but that is consequently very hungry for, and suspicious of, any novelty, or shift, or change, that it can incorporate into itself, to make itself a more adequate river of the mind. I think he means that if you do not acknowledge the river, the river can easily pass your contribution by. It seems altogether probable that anyone raised in a culture takes in, if unconsciously, much of the gesture and significance of that culture; even if he thinks he is writing counter-culture, he's writing out of the culture in order to be against it. But the culture, if you consider it as this stream, has no need greater than to step outside of itself, and see itself. In personal terms, that's what I'm talking about in that poem called "**Laser**" where an image or representation is seen, and the mind is then locked with it obsessively, and what the mind needs most is some other, disorganized energy that it can use to break free. And I believe cultural influence acts a little in the same way. Culture is always hungry, at the same time that it questions novelty or change.

*Isn't culture many things?—first of all a language, certain rhythms, certain life rhythms? One cannot be for or against these; one can only* be *that culture, so defined. But can't a culture be also a self-consciousness—a thing of conscious learnings and rehearsals? I feel more comfortable with, say, an analysis that tells me about the rhythms or cadences of a Southerner as opposed to those of a Northerner. In a poem of yours, I believe it is called* **"Mansion,"** *you write that when the time comes for you to cede yourself, you choose the wind, and the wind says that it is glad because it needs all the body it can get to show its motions with. That seems to be a good image for the way in which a non-self-conscious culture might inform the individual. When one speaks of culture, must one not speak of these more fundamental definers of the culture? Harold Bloom and Hyatt Waggoner see you writing in the lineage of Emerson. Such an influence would be more than your native culture speaking through you—it would be the cultural acquisition of a culture, what I was calling a self-consciousness. When Bloom analyzes your "anxiety of influence," I feel that he is placing you within such a more formal concept of culture in order to make you part of an historical, evolutionary process. And I wonder whether he is on safe ground, speaking of a specific cultural influence, like Emerson, or the "visionary" sense that is supposed to be yours, just as it is supposed to have been (or maybe because it is supposed to have been) that of a number of your cultural ancestors? The reason I ask this is that I* *feel this influence much less in your writing. But perhaps this is due to my ignorance.*

About the "anxiety of influence," you know that Emerson is supposed to have felt that very little. I have experienced very little anxiety of that kind that I could identify—a need to come, and a fear of coming, to terms with a literary father. It is nearly impossible for me to identify closely with Emerson because he comes from Concord, and I from a rural and defeated South. You know, there are just too many wave lengths that we don't share; it's impossible for me to imagine myself belonging to any culture because of that rural South, which, in growing up, I tended to discredit religiously and intellectually, though I could not emotionally—you know, I am there, that's who I am. But that culture contained no elements, either religious or intellectual—formulable elements—that I could maintain to this moment. And it may be because I have no culture that I have not experienced what Harold Bloom talks about when he speaks of culture in the formal sense. My feeling about the anxiety of influence is that it is so generalized a theory that it could be applied to corporations or to body politics, and that it is really an introductory topic into the larger subject of hierarchy. Hierarchy would include the pantheon of which we, in the universities, are the guardians: we very carefully sort our authors; you know, Donne goes up and Shelley goes down; and then after a while we say oh, no, Shelley has been down too long, Shelley must come back up; he has been up and down so many times, that now he doesn't have to go down anymore. And we have widened our scope so that we can tolerate both Donne and Shelley at a fairly high level in our pantheon. I am convinced that this kind of sorting goes on all the time and it may be valuable: what we are trying to do is give structure and definition to our minds. I don't see anything wrong with that. But a theory that enables us to do this, such as the theory of influence, is so general that it has to be explored in any number of other ways. But I have no feeling that it should be discounted. I believe it provides very strong insights into some figures, and one of its specific applications can be literary. As to my own anxiety, my *Angst,* that is a different matter. I tend to think of it in a much less apocalyptic way than Bloom does. I have been fascinated by social orders of animals, baboons in particular: there is this creature called the solitary; he's a very strong baboon, but he's not quite strong enough, he thinks, or he lacks the courage, to test the dominant male in the structure—he is afraid he would be defeated. So he can't stand to live in that structure, out of pure hatred, jealousy and envy of the dominant male. So he goes off into the woods as a solitary baboon, self-exiled from the group. His deepest longing is to be back with the group. He's less safe because he's alone, where before the group might have protected him; it is a very fearful situation to be in. And I identify myself as one who has not found the group in which I feel safe, or welcomed, or by which I feel realized and expressed. Consequently, I feel that my terrors, which in my life have been at times quite severe, though not so much lately perhaps because my work has been more accepted, have as their root a secular, social structure, deriving from something situated somewhere down all of our spines, and racial experience—a sense

that we do better within the compromises of the group than in the terrifying precision of being alone.

*And yet your poetry is so much a close attention to the natural world that, although you have spoken somewhere about all poetry being about impermanence, I feel that in this attention to nature there is a constancy of permanence and renewal.*

What would the solitary baboon amuse himself with? The people aren't there. Not the people: I mean the other baboons aren't there; nature is there, the day and the night, the things around him.

*But he has been forced out there.*

Forced out or self-willed.

*But there is no Western tradition for baboons and there is a tradition for humans, and in particular for poets. It tells us that it is not all bad to be forced out into nature, whether by your own choice as Democritus, or by the ill will of the group, as Rousseau believed. Perhaps the gregarious virtue is, I don't know, a part of the puritan ethic?*

Oh, I think it has a lot to do with it: you remember when Frost says it is not sex but grex—that we will make nearly any compromise in our sexual life in order to continue being with grex, with the group, with the society, with the body politic? We make these puritanical sacrifices all the time.

*So what you are describing then is an uneasiness born of a cultural need and a cultural rejection.*

I think so. Perhaps you can extend that directly into the anxiety of influence. At any rate it would be an analogy for such a theory. I myself have not experienced it in those terms. I have experienced it more in social and hierarchical terms. When Joyce exiles himself, he says that he will survive by cunning. That too reminds me of the solitary individual, who has a fury in him to go back to his own order and possess it somehow. But he cannot do that in an open way, so that he has to resort to exile, cunning, sulking, deviousness. Rather a bad set of characteristics.

*Is there no virtue at all then in solitude?*

Yes: one writes one's poems. And then one day, perhaps, one is astonished to find that people belonging to the order of which one does not feel a part identify with them.

*Perhaps we are too much with the world and our society enforces too much this gregariousness. When a critic like Bloom says that your poems enable him to live, maybe it is there that we should look for the meaning of his words: perhaps the poem enables us in a very necessary way to rehearse our own sense of solitude. This would be a less negative way of envisioning solitude.*

Yes. However negative the sources of the energy, may be, it is energy and, hopefully, imaginative energy, and can be multiplied reader by reader. It is always astonishing to me that while the relationship of author to reader is one to one, this sort of energy can be endlessly multiplied without necessarily compromising it.

*It must be wonderful to be at the source of such renewal.*

It is. I received a letter from a man who said that he was listless, ready to call it quits. A very lovely letter: he said he had read my book from beginning to end and he now felt that he had the energy to live and to die. That may have been a gross overstatement on his part, but I said to myself afterwards that I would never have to ask myself again why I write poems. If a man who wakes up with no energy in the morning finds himself in possession of energy, then I need no further justification.

*That's also a little frightening.*

Yes, it's terrifying.

*But then, that is the function of art, isn't it?—if art has any function . . . .*

That's what I would like it to do—to give people the energy to move through their lives. . . . I mean to contribute a small part—obviously it's a small part—of the energy needed to move through life. The source of this energy is, I believe, quite obviously a bad state of life, confusion and terror, with momentary releases and flashes, concentrations of energy and, in those moments, you get that energy onto the page and then the recipient of that energy doesn't have to share in its source, in the negative aspect of its source. He has the energy which he can put to his own use.

*Art most likely serves a number of purposes. It is clearing in our social and industrial wilderness. In that desert, it is one of the last remaining genuine plants. And then, there is also what you see as the awakening and mustering of energy in coming to terms with the work of art. Those are the sources of what I would like to call a natural function. But what about the other culture, the self-conscious or acquired culture? If you acknowledged literary fathers, who would they be?*

I think that Bloom is right. In American literature, it's Whitman and Emerson. But Emerson led me to the same sources that he discovered himself—to Indian and Chinese philosophy which, when I was younger, I read a good deal, finally coming to Laotse, whom I mentioned earlier. That's my philosophical source in its most complete version. So that when I look back at Emerson, Emerson looks derivative to me of certain of those oriental traditions in the same way as I am derivative of them. In an immediate sense, my forebears are Whitman and Emerson, but in a larger sense my source is the same as theirs.

*I have the feeling that as one moves into your later poems, this influence is progressively less important as the influence of nature is progressively more important.*

Yes, I think that is correct. I identify civilization (the city) with *definition*, as against the kind of center-and-periphery,

closed-openness that I identify with nature. That's why I'm not in the city; that's why I am not an urban person. The city represents to me the artificial, the limited, the defined, the stalled, though obviously the city changes. I often think the city represents the confrontation of the artificial in man with the natural process and I tend to think that the natural process produced everything—including the city.

*The problem is that, even though secreted by the human mind, the city has secreted in turn such a thick overlay that it now seems to determine all further secretions of the mind. Still, the human race appears to endure, somehow. Since I am in such a rashly optimistic mood, let me suggest another theory of history, one which might be opposed to the apocalyptic view. It's the laundry list theory, the view that everything is lustered by time. The belief that if you took a laundry list written in the days of Henry IV, something that was simply functional in the fourteenth or fifteenth century—a completely dismissible object— would now be informed with a density of time and the careful scrutiny that we would give it, since we are always looking back for our own traces in what has endured as long or longer than we have. If that is a possible interpretation of history, then everything is in the process of becoming better, if you will only give it time.*

I think I understand the idea: but I have another view of history that means more to me. I have written a little poem about it which I have never published, whose last line is "history is a blank." Whatever you see when you look out of the window at any particular moment is history—is the truest history surviving into the immediate moment. The whole history of the planet earth is in your body at this moment, and so on. So that I don't have to structure it into time periods. Perhaps this is another reason why I do not have problems with the anxiety of influence, because I believe that what is here now, at this moment, is the truest version of history that we will ever know. Consequently, I have as much right to enter into it with all the innocence of immediacy as anyone else possibly ever could.

*I understand that history can never exist for anyone except through the percipient's view of it. But history yields its own precipitations regardless of whether or not there is a percipient: when the perceiving consciousness becomes aware of those precipitations, is it not affected by them, is it not in some way altered? Is not an alteration due to the thing that was a working of the historical process?*

You may remember my rather long "**Extremes and Moderations**." At one point I'm addressing the city directly and the poem says that the cities' work and the cities' artifice confront the *artifice* in capital letters—that is, God's creation. And then it says

> beyond
> the scheduled consummation, nothing's to be
>   recalled: there is
> memory enough in the rock, unscriptured history in
> the wind, sufficient identity in the curve
> of the valley. . . .

And what I mean is that if you see the shape of the valley, it's there, immediate in this moment. But in that shape is the entire history of its coming there.

*You have cosmic sense of history—the thundering course of the planets and the molecules to which they gave birth . . .*

Some of that. But I also think of the human parallel. Take language: language is the same kind of history as survival. In the case of language, any discontinuity between its beginning and its present would interfere with our use of it now.

*We may not be so very far apart. It is just that you appear to focus on a presentness which you inform with the density of history. Your sense of the archeology of language is after all the sense of an object that was. Perhaps that's what a poetic sense of language is—an awe of its resonance in time as well as in space. What does a poet do? Does he pay more attention to the resonances of a language or to the people that give it rise? I ask you that question because I do not find many people in your poetry. In a review of your selected poems by Reed Whittemore—a review that did not particularly turn me on—I found, nevertheless, something that corresponds to a feeling that I too have about your writings. Whittemore says that although you are very good with objects, and sometimes even with people, he finds that you are "weaker on people." Would your baboon theory shed any light on this?*

I think it would, yes . . .

*Nature is really nature in your poems. One of the significant differences between you and the romantic poets is that you do not anthropomorphize nature.*

I use the pathetic fallacy quite a bit, but always quite deliberately, with full knowledge of what I'm doing. There is probably some psychological explanation that is better than the baboon theory, or the hierarchy thing. I have to insist though that I am a human being and that the feelings I experience, I am somewhat surprised to find, are shared by other human beings: so that though you say I write about nature, I might insist that I write about nothing at all except *human* nature. I may not be able to form characters or vessels of human nature in poems. But that doesn't eliminate human nature.

*Yours is a humane poetry. It is simply that its humanity is contained mainly in your reaction to the world of nature.*

It's much cooler to find the objective correlative in that which does not answer back—nature—rather than in the furies and anxieties, jealousies, envies and whatever else a human correlative would contain. I take this to be the rightful province of the novelist; although great poets are able to do it, too. I don't know anything about nature. I am not a dislocated part of anything you call nature. I am a human being who has entered into certain kinds of expres-

sive relationships with the external world. And while I may not have been able to manage those expressions as expressions by other human beings, they are the elements of human nature.

*In your first "Carolina Said Song," you take a character that may be indeed, as you say, a member of your family and you have her talk about an incident that occurred; but you seem to be interested in relating the incident mainly because the richness of the language contrives a mood, rather than in the interpersonal developments that one might have stressed.*

In the other **"Said Song,"** I think it was the same stimulus that awakened my attention to that particular experience in which a man calms a swarm of bees that could represent chaos, disorder or whatever, and reduces them to a perfectly manageable order so he could put them on a limb over his shoulder and take them home. Just that motion from the chaotic to the ordered is a complete motion to me.

*And yet I would be willing to bet anything that the source of this abstract notion was a real man you met, an actual event that occurred in your life.*

Oh yes, it's an actual fact. That's as nearly as I could reproduce the man's speech. It's not my poem. These are things that I remembered—tried to remember—as they were being said. If only we had someone to record the poems that are being said every day, it would be marvelous.

*I would like to get back for a moment to your way of masking the human in your poetry. In your poem "Nelly Myers," the heroine turns out not to be a girl, the mother turns out not to be a mother—these immediate sources of a possible tenderness are once again hidden, at least at the surface. But in a poem like "Coon Song," there is an outburst of real anger. What triggers that sort of thing?*

I think that wherever there is energy, it is as likely to be violent energy as anything else. Energy is violent. Under the proper controls and uses, it is beautiful; and only when it is mismanaged, is it destructive. So if you're saying, under my quiet exterior, is there a tiny little volcano, the answer is yes. Sure.

### Hyatt H. Waggoner (essay date 1973)

SOURCE: "The Poetry of A. R. Ammons: Some Notes and Reflections," in *Salmagundi*, Nos. 22-23, Spring-Summer, 1973, pp. 285-93.

[*An American educator and critic, Waggoner was known for his expertise in the works of Nathaniel Hawthorne. His writings also include* American Poets from the Puritans to the Present *(1968) and* American Visionary Poetry *(1982). In the following excerpt, Waggoner compares and contrasts Ammons's poetry to that of Ralph Waldo Emerson.*]

What follows is simply some of the thoughts, and a few reflections on those thoughts, that have come to me as I have read through seven volumes of [Ammons'] poetry, the product of something more than a decade of writing. I do not own, am not near a library that contains, and so have not seen Ammons' first volume, **Ommateum** (1955), an omission which must qualify anything I may say about Ammons' development.

I write these notes seated in a mountain meadow, facing north towards a spruce woods fringed with poplar and balsam fir, the short-lived forward units of the woods as it edges across an unused pasture beyond the meadow. I have been watching the woods take over the pasture for more than thirty years now but have seen no movement. All I know is that the woods are a hundred or so feet closer to engulfing the spot where I sit and the house behind me than they used to be, and from that I can deduce that they are coming toward us all the time, moving in stillness.

So much for the permanencies of nature. I find this helping me to understand and respond to a good deal of Ammons' poetry, in which nature is the subject, the exemplum, or the setting of a good many of the best passages and poems.

Ammons is a visionary poet in the Neoplatonic tradition introduced and best represented in our (American) poetry by Emerson. I would guess that he has read a good deal of Emerson and pondered much on what he has read. Maybe not. Maybe he has read only a little and gotten all his Emersonianism from that little, working out for himself, as Emerson did, the consequences of a few major ideas about the relations of the Many and the One. Or maybe it has come to him at second and third hand, through Pound and Williams, Whitman and Frost, all of whom make their appearance in his poetry. It is clear at least though that he has read "Brahma"—which could have been sufficient for the right kind of mind—for he alludes to it and paraphrases it in **"What This Mode of Motion Said"** in *Expressions of Sea Level*. Emerson: "When me they fly, I am the wings"; Ammons: "I am the wings when you me fly"; Emerson: "I am the doubter and the doubt"; Ammons:

> I am the way by
> which you prove me
>      wrong,
> the reason you
> reason against me.

Some other "Emersonianisms" in the poetry. (This could be a full-length article itself. It would have to treat important poems in each of the seven volumes I have read. [In a footnote, the critic adds: For such a study, **"Hibernaculum"** in the new *Collected Poems* would be particularly important. In it Emerson is mentioned by name and linked with Plotinus in a passage that seems to me to say in effect, This is the philosophic tradition that means the most to me. Some of the Emersonianisms are jocular, as when Ammons finds in Shakespeare the same virtues and same defect that Emerson had found, then adds that he is cheered by this because "I can't reconcile the one with the many either."]) **"Raft,"** the opening poem in *Expressions of Sea Level*, a

somewhat self-consciously Romantic poem in which the sought-for unity with nature—or with the undefinable Reason behind nature—is distanced by a tone of playful make-believe, is central Emerson: let go, yield, be blown by the winds of spirit. *Spiritus*: breath, wind. The Muse, the deeper self, the Holy Spirit. The boy on the circular raft is swept out to sea by the tides to where the winds control his motion toward the east, the rising sun. Neoplatonists: sun, source of light, life, and goodness; emanation. Christian Neoplatonists: sun = Son. . . . The Romantic sea-voyage; the "innocent eye" of the child. Several poems in the same volume make explicit what **"Raft"** implies by the story it tells. For instance, **"Guide"**: "the wind that is my guide said this"; and **"Mansion"**:

> So it came time
>      for me to cede myself
> and I chose
> the wind
>      to be delivered to.

The word *soul* can be used only in actual or implied quotation marks by contemporary poets. Since Ammons takes what the word refers to very seriously, he seldom uses it: there is nothing "so-called" about spirit in his work. Like Emerson, he is ambiguous about what he refuses to name. Emerson usually preferred to define the "Over-Soul," "World-Soul," "The Spirit," "The Real" in negative terms, as he does in the opening of the essay on the subject, following the long tradition of "negative theology." He was surer about Immanence than about Transcendence: "A light from within or from behind," with the ambiguity kept. Only in "Circles," in the early essays, does he drop the subjective-objective ambiguity and attribute unqualified Transcendence to the One: "the eternal generator of circles," that is, the Creator of the circles of physical and spiritual reality. Ammons' poetry keeps both Emerson's theoretic ambiguity and the intensity of Emerson's search for vision.

Ammons has a *mind*, too good a mind to be content with the kinds of superficial Romanticism that are becoming fashionable in contemporary poetry. I would like to call him a philosophical poet—except that description might turn away some of those who should read him, and except also that the phrase is in part intrinsically misleading in its suggestion that he deals principally in abstractions. He deals with the perfectly concrete felt motions and emotions of the particular self he is and, like Emerson again, looks for and often sees "Correspondences" between these motions and those of animate and inanimate nature, both nature-as-observed (winds, tides, seeds, birds) and nature-as-known-about (the chemistry of digestion, entropy).

The title poem of *Corsons Inlet* is such a philosophical poem, treating the relations and claims of logic and vision, order created and order discovered, being and becoming, art and nature. Rejecting any "finality of vision," it still prefers the risk of vision to any "easy victory" in "narrow orders, limited tightness." The poet's task is to try to "fasten into order enlarging grasps of disorder," the task Emerson set before the poet in "Merlin" and "Bacchus." I find significance in the fact that the poem was first entitled "A Nature Walk." If there is no order discoverable in nature, the order of art is a contrivance without noetic value. Ammons, like his Romantic and Transcendental poetic forebears, is not content to make pretty, or even interesting because intricately fashioned, poems. **"Corsons Inlet"** seems to me at once one of the finest and one of the most significant poems written by any of our poets in recent years. It is a credo, a manifesto, a cluster of felt perceptions, and a demonstration that, up to a point at least, vision *can* be both achieved and conveyed.

Though I am persuaded that my frequent mentions of Emerson up to this point do not distort but rather illuminate Ammons' work, still they might prove misleading if I failed to mention the ways in which the poet's vision is *unlike* Emerson's. (Emerson, I should explain, is very fresh in my mind these days, for I have just spent a year rereading and writing about him. But I am still not importing my own preoccupation into Ammons' poetry: Emerson is there, and I happen to be well prepared to notice his presence—in many more ways, and more poems, than I have mentioned or will mention.) Let me try to generalize the difference first. Ammons comes as close to rediscovering the Romantic Transcendental vision of Emerson as any thoughtful and well-informed man of the late twentieth century is likely to be able to, but as a man of our time he simply cannot be a "disciple," he can only learn from, be stimulated by, walk the paths of, and be honest about his differences with, the poet who more than any other foreshadows him, as I see it.

A few of the differences. Ammons allows to come into consciousness, and so into his poetry, much more freely than Emerson did, the existential *angst* that Emerson must have felt but usually repressed. (See "1 Jan." in *Tape for the Turn of the Year* for Ammons' statement on this. The point he makes there—"I know the/ violence, grief, guilt,/ despair, absurdity"—is clear in all the volumes without being stated.) Death, disorder, entropy (one of his few technical philosophical terms) are never far from the surface of any of Ammons' poems, and frequently they are central in them. Poetry, he says in *Tape,* has "one subject, impermanence." Never unaware of "a universe of horror," Ammons knows that "we must bear/ the dark edges of/ our awareness," but the goal of his search remains "a universe of light" (*Tape,* "1 Jan.*").

A different man in a different age, Emerson erected his defenses against fear and grief stronger and taller than Ammons', though I should say that in his best poetry—in prose as well as in verse—he was sufficiently open to all his feelings, even these, to allow his wonderful intelligence to work freely. Still, it is true, however one may take the fact, that Ammons does not transcend so easily or so far.

Related to this as a symptom is to a cause is the much greater concreteness of the way Ammons' imagination works, and so of his poetic language. As Emerson was more concrete, specific, even local (think of the first line of "Hamatreya") than the Pre-Romantics whose style his often resembles, so Ammons is more concrete, specific, local, and *personal* than Emerson. On this matter, as on style in general, Ammons' affinity seems to be with Pound and

Williams, but of course Pound and Williams were more Emersonian than they knew.

A difference that is more strikingly obvious but I think finally less important is that of verse-forms. Emerson's theory, at least the part of it we are most likely to remember, called for organic or open form, but only a few of his best poems put the theory successfully into practice, and then only partially. Ammons, like most of his best contemporaries, has moved all the way toward practicing the theory announced in "The Poet" and elaborated in "Poetry and Imagination." Still, there is not an immeasurable gap, formally speaking, between "Merlin" and **"Poetics"** in *Briefings*.

*Tape for the Turn of the Year,* Ammons' "long thin poem" typed on a roll of adding-machine paper, a poetic journal which keeps turning into a poetic meditation, is the most continuously interesting, the strongest, the finest long poem I have read in I don't know how many years. It is as concrete as *The Cantos,* but the facts in it are not exotic lore out of the library and they are not illustrations of theories. It is at once personal and historical, like *Paterson,* but I don't feel, as I do in that poem at times, any attempt to impose the larger meanings. The meanings rise from the facts of personal history, the life the poet led from December 6 to January 10, the meals, the weather, the news, the interruptions, the discrete perceptions, and are presented for just what they are, felt thoughts. *Tape* proves—for me, anyway—the point Ammons makes in it somewhere, that poetry is "a way of/ thinking about/ truth" even while, as an art form, its distinctiveness is its way of "playing" with language to create untranslatable meanings.

Stylistically, *Tape* is "good Emerson," not so much in resembling Emerson's poems (though it does resemble them in certain ways, at times) as in following-out Emerson's theory. Transcendental poetic theory puts enormous emphasis on the single word, the single image, the discrete perception that may become an intuition. The short lines of the poem would seem merely stylish if they could not be justified in terms of this aspect of Transcendental Poetics. "Stylish" they may be, but the reason for the style emerges from the lines surprisingly, astonishingly. Prosaic, lyric, meditative, philosophic by turns, *Tape* is a wonderful poem. Read it.

Ammons' latest poems strike me as showing two developments. Stylistically, they are somewhat less "open," more thought-out, "reasonable," logically disciplined. They have pulled back a little from the letting-go and letting-out of the earlier work. There is less abandon, more control. Stylistically firmer perhaps, they seem to me less daring. Their style might be described as more "mature," but maturity brings losses as well as gains. The transparent eyeball narrows slightly to shield itself against the too-dazzling light. Ammons said toward the end of *Tape* that after the long, in a sense "dictated," poem he wanted to write short, artful lyrics, and he's doing it. And of course art is artificial. But I hope he will continue to leave openings, cracks maybe, in his conceptual boxes.

In any poet as fine as Ammons, a stylistic change signals a change in sensibility and vision. **"Transaction"** in *Uplands* ("I attended the burial of all my rosy feelings") describes the new "resignation" (Is this the right word? I'm not sure.) explicitly, but a good many of the poems in the two latest volumes exhibit it.

In *Tape* he reminded us—warned us?—that "I care about the statement/ of fact" and suggested that "coming home" meant "a way of/ going along with this/ world as it is:/ nothing ideal," but he still invited us to the dance. Wisdom involves a kind of resignation, I suppose, as one of its elements, but I think of it as contrasting with rashness and inexperience rather than as first cousin to prudence. I should hate to see Ammons become too prudent. I don't think he will.

The most recent poems may be less ambitious philosophically and less openly Romantic-Transcendental in their imaginative questing, but the quest itself has not been abandoned and the conception of how the journey should be undertaken—how thinking, feeling, imagining, responding can find expression and thus be realized, recognized, identified, and shared in a particular verbal object we call "this poem"—has not essentially changed. In the inseparable union of physics and metaphysics in Ammons' imagination, the emphasis may have shifted a little from the *meta* to the *physics,* but the union has not been dissolved, as of course it must not be if poetry is to continue to have noetic value. (Heidegger's "What Are Poets For?" in his recent *Poetry, Language, Thought* is relevant here. What are poets for in a dark time?) **"Poetics"** in *Briefings* should send any readers of it who don't remember the essay back to Emerson's "Poetry and Imagination." "Ask the fact for the form." Imagination and circles, imagination and possibility, the expanding spheres of possibility—of apprehension, of recognition, of meaning—finding their forms in poems. Here's the poem:

I look for the way
things will turn
out spiralling from a center,
the shape
things will take to come forth in

so that the birch tree white
touched black at branches
will stand out
wind-glittering
totally its apparent self:

I look for the forms
things want to come as
from what black wells of possibility,
how a thing will
unfold:

not the shape on paper—though
that, too—but the
uninterfering means on paper:
not so much looking for the shape

as being available
to any shape that may be
summoning itself
through me
from the self not mine but ours.

Harold Bloom is quoted on the back cover of *Briefings* as saying that the lyrics in the book "maintain an utterly consistent purity of detached yet radiant vision." Right on target. But I'd like to shrink the ambiguities of this a bit if I can without putting us and Ammons into a mentalistic box. "Consistent": consistent with all the other lyrics in the volume, yes, but not entirely consistent, in tone or statement, with the best of the earlier lyrics or even with the prayer (**"14 Dec."**) and the several credos (*credo*: I believe) in *Tape*. A little more defensive, more guarded, more "intellectually prudent." There's a concern with defining differences: ". . . keep me from my enemies'/wafered concision and zeal" (**"Hymn IV,"** *Briefings*). A fear almost that vision may harden into doctrine.

"Purity": Yes, of style, of tone, of vision too. The wonderful thing is that the purity is at once a purity of style and a purity of vision, in both cases (or perspectives: two sides of the same coin) a unique balance maintained between conflicting perceptions of the One and the Many, the Real and the Actual, etc.—to borrow some Emersonian terms for what is not easily talked about in any terms.

"Detached": "Wafered concision" suggests that the detachment is from High Church zealots who localize "the eternal generator of circles" (Emerson's term in "Circles") in the manageable little round wafer of Communion. But the detachment is equally, I think, from the rationalistic formulations of the ineffable that betray an idolatrous attitude not toward a common substance, bread, but toward the results of a process, directed abstract thought. I say this not from the evidence of this poem, which, by its emphasis, might not seem to prompt it, but from the evidence of the whole corpus of the poetry as I have read it.

"Radiant": No need for clarification (if that's the word for what I'm trying to do) here. "Radiant" in the sense that applies to Blake, Emerson, Whitman, Cummings, Roethke.

"Vision": Right again, of course. But "vision" and "visionary" can be a way of throwing positivistic enemies off the scent. Vision of what? Assuming that God is not a "being" among other beings, and so, being unlimited spatially and temporally ("God is the circle whose center is everywhere and circumference nowhere"—the practitioners of the "negative theology," and Emerson, said), is undefinable, still I'd say a sense of God's reality, whether as immanent or as *deus absconditus,* is everywhere present in the poems and should be recognized, for it does more than anything else (of the many factors at work, some unknown, some unknowable,) to give the poems their special *kind* of "vision." Heidegger, "What Are Poets For?" again.

I'd like to make the word *religious* respectable once again among literary critics, rescue it from Freud ("the future of an illusion") and give it to Jung, who used the word not to clobber the naively pious but to point to something real and permanent in human experience. ("Permanent" until *now,* maybe.) Ammons is a poet of religious vision who is as wary of intellectualist abstractions as he is of pious dogmas. *That's* the peculiar feature of the "purity" of his "vision," it seems to me. Peculiar in our time, not peculiar if we think of the poetic visionaries who are his ancestors, whether he knows it or not—and he probably does, for he seems to know everything.

The "veracity" of Ammons' poetry (his word, and Emerson's before him, in "Poetry and Imagination"), the sense it creates in us that the radiance, when it comes, is real, discovered, not invented or faked, is causally related, I suspect, to the steadiness with which the poet has looked into the Abyss. The gains for the imagination from such looking are incalculable, but it must be hard on the nerves. One wants to survive as well as write "short rich hard lyrics," as Ammons is doing now. I want Ammons to do both—that is, survive and write. Perhaps the slight narrowing of the eyelids over the transparent eyeballs I seem to detect in the later work is necessary for the survival. But the transparency remains essential to his kind of vision. Dilemma. Poets age, like the rest of us.

I don't try very conscientiously to "keep up" with all the new poetry in the magazines and the slender volumes, but I can say that of the "new" poets I've read since Roethke's death, Ammons seems to me at or near the top. His poetry is, among other things more important, a "sign" granted for the strengthening of the faith, the faith that in a dark time light may still be seen, not invented (no **"Supreme Fiction,"** no fiction at all), by the unguarded eye.

At his best (I don't much like **"Summer Session 1968"**), Ammons is a highly distinguished poet of religious vision who grants the Transcendence but finds his occupation chiefly in searching out the traces of the Immanence. May he survive, save himself for this, and be visited often by the Muse, indulging as little as may be in the writing of merely fashionable poems.

**Jerald Bullis (essay date 1977)**

SOURCE: A review of *The Snow Poems,* in *Epoch,* Vol. XXVI, No. 3, Spring, 1977, pp. 304-11.

[*Bullis is an American poet and critic. In the following review of* The Snow Poems, *he finds that Ammons is one of the few poets to successfully undertake the challenge of the non-narrative long poem. Bullis claims that one of Ammons's greatest strengths, demonstrated in* The Snow Poems, *is his ability to express the interrelationship of all things, thereby overcoming artificial categories and divisions.*]

*The Snow Poems* are actually one poem. It is a diary of the 1975-76 year: a record of Ammons's own experiences, observations, attitudes that begins in the fall with the bird migrations heading south and ends in the spring, with welcoming (the last word of the poem is "we(l)come") "a

young/ birch frilly in early-girlish/ leaf." *The Snow Poems* is at the same time an almanac—a compendium of useful and interesting facts, proverbs, weather news. It is also an adventure story in which Ammons, in Ithaca, wanders far and the extravagance of the wandering becomes a reaffirmation of the poet's role as adventurer, as Odysseus (Odysseus's name, in Greek at least, meant trouble—it was his fate to Odysseus himself and others heroically). Ammons's own wandersong precisely distinguishes the heroic potentiality of now from the models of unreclaimable times: without coming on in a high-hatted, grandeurish way, *The Snow Poems* radiates nobility, that quality Wallace Stevens remarked as being most conspicuously absent from modern literature. *One* of the values of this poem is its bulk, the overweeningness of its cry: it approximates the plenitude of the novel without falling into the worn-out procedures of the novel. It is Ammons's richest exemplification to date of the resolution made in the concluding lines of **"Corsons Inlet"** to "try/ to fasten into order enlarging grasps of disorder, widening/ scope." The extempore explorations of this long poem affirm Emerson's assertion that "the vision of genius comes by renouncing the too officious activity of the understanding, and giving leave and amplest privilege to the spontaneous sentiment."

This book could have been done as four or five books, but done in that way it would have been a piecemeal offering of several kinds of more-or-less acceptable poetic styles. In his earlier work Ammons has already experimented with lyric and meditative modes, testing the limits of free verse, incorporating levels of diction—such as the scientific—that have enlarged the scope of poetry; he has made the fable appear like a new genre, as if Emerson's mountain and squirrel had never had a quarrel (in which Bun replies—Bun being the squirrel—that "all sorts of things and weather/ Must be taken in together,/ To make up a year/ And a sphere"—a wisdom about spheres that applies as well to *The Snow Poems* as it does to *Sphere: The Form of A Motion*). Ammons's successes with the medium-length conversational poem (after Coleridge's "Frost at Midnight"), the hymn, the metaphysical lyric, the "song," the pastoral-walk poem (after Frost's "The Wood Pile") are exemplary: in such poems as **"The City Limits," "Saliences,"** and **"Configurations,"** Ammons has extended the range of the short poem.

If Ammons were a *moderate* poet . . . (designation oxymoronic if not entirely moronic) then I suppose he would have kept plunking-out the kind of performance for which he has already received acclaim. But *The Snow Poems* is a more extravagant poem than any of the earlier poems, including the resuscitations of the *essai* in its original aleatory form: **"An Essay in Poetics," "Hiburnaculum," "Extremes and Moderations,"** and **"Summer Place"** (forthcoming in *The Hudson Review*); it is more openly autobiographical than any earlier poem: and it challenges our assumptions about what makes a statement "poetic" to an extent that even *Tape for the Turn of the Year* did not. Most of the "poems" of this poem have an entropic "organization"—the conclusions irrelevancies, seemingly—a kind of dribbling-off format, even to the shapes on the page. The sections are believably extra-vasational or, more like snow, precisely improvisational. Some of the sections seem to derive their forms from the spatial limitations and freedoms of the 9" x 11" page, written upon by a typewriter. In some of the sections one "poem" will proceed down the left side of the page, going right about half-way, and another—contrapuntal, complementary, dialectically?—will begin somewhere right-of-center. This technique seems a further development of Ammons's statement concerning nonlinear prosody published in *Poetry* (vol. cii, 3, June 1963): "What I think is illustrated by [the versification of a poem like Ammons's **'Close-Up'**] is that both ends are being played against a middle. The center of gravity is an imaginary point existing between the two points of beginning and end, so that a downward pull is created that gives a certain downward rush to the movement, something like a waterfall glancing in turn off opposite sides of the canyon, something like the right and left turns of a river."

Such typographical pyrotechnics aren't new. They get their freshness in **The Snow Poems** from Ammons's ability to amalgamate ranges of discourse—heretofore largely excluded from poetry—with such techniques. Though these poems may superficially resemble work by Charles Olson, look like some of Pound's *Cantos,* or portions of Williams's *Paterson,* Ammons's work actually exhibits a far different rhetorical stance. The discursive tendency of much of Carl Sandburg's and Robinson Jeffers's poetry—two unfashionable precursors with whom Ammons has not been allied—anticipates the openness of **The Snow Poems** more directly than the work of the above mentioned poets. Not even Wallace Stevens, whose improvisatory and essayistic ensembles are more apparent prior attempts at making nonnarrative long poems, could manage more than uneasy fusings of imagistic-symbolic and discursive writing, a problem Ben Belitt pointed out in a review of Stevens: "moved to formal discourse in the quest for order and certitude. [Stevens's] art has not up to the present permitted him to pursue such discourse or his temperament to accept it." To which Stevens replied in a letter to Belitt: "While you pointed out my difficulty in the second sentence of your review, it is a difficulty that I have long been conscious of and with which I am constantly struggling." Stevens struggled with this problem to the end, though late poems exhibit an Ammons-like acceptance of the antipoetic, as in "Reality Is an Activity of the Most August Imagination": "Last Friday, in the big light of last Friday night,/ We drove home from Cornwall to Hartford, late." Ammons is the only modern poet I've encountered who seems to have gotten beyond the bugbears of imagism and symbolic systematising: who doesn't seem to feel that the propositional, the baldly discursive, is innately antipoetic: who doesn't write as if abstractions were the Death of Poetry, as if proverbial announcement were something old-timey sayers could get to the sooth of, but that we cannot. At random:

> so much works flawed
> it makes you think
> perfection not one of
> nature's hangups
> how could you, walking in the mts,
> be big as the mts: only by

> wandering: aimlessness
> is as big as mts
> it is not for the poet to
> speak the speakable
> that which long known & said
> requires no energy
> of finding or forming but to
> murmur, stammer, swear, and
> sing on the edges of or around
> or deep into the unspeakable—

> the reason it makes
> no difference what people
> think
> is that they don't think
> enough to make any
> difference

> you can't imitate
> anybody really
> and the extent
> to which
> you can't is
> enough originality

> poets add
> obscurity
> to the
> inexplicable
> for critics
> who can't
> get their
> tools sharp on
> the obvious

The intelligence and smiling acerbity of this aspect of **The Snow Poems** reminds me of the poetry of the T'ang poet Han-Shan:

> A certain scholar named Mr. Wang
> Was laughing at my poems for being so clumsy.
> "Don't you know you can't have two accents here?
> And this line has too many beats.
> You don't seem to understand meter at all
> But toss in any word that comes to mind!"
> I laugh too, Mr. Wang, when *you* make a poem.
> Like a blind man trying to sing of the sun.
> *(translated by Burton Watson)*

But the strength of **The Snow Poems** can't be demonstrated by snippets of quotation. And, though the problem of judgment with respect to this long poem may seem difficult, I think it is actually not. For those who have read Ammons's work from **Ommateum** (1955) through **Diversifications** (1975), including this poem's important prelude, **Tape for the Turn of the Year** (1964). **The Snow Poems** will seem the necessary unfolding of Ammons's venture. As Warner Berthoff has remarked of Emerson, "Once we begin to get the sense of how [Ammons] operates as a writer, our experience of reading him is likely to be full of double takes, and our admiration, sluggish and reluctant at first, so little taste remains with us for the mode of pastoral exhortation he seems to employ, springs forward by a geometric progression." Ammons's mode of pastoral exhortation is to try to hold in interpenetrant relation the dualistic categories with which, in order to communicate easily though imprecisely, we have oversimplified our language: I mean such categories as imagination/reality, inner/outer, self/other, man/nature. This interpenetration of word and world, whereby abstract "themes" are divulged or adumbrated through hollyhocks, blue spruce, jays, brooks, mudpuddles, mountains and so on, is summarized ideogrammatically in **"The Word Crys Out"**: "wor(l)d." Ammons's insistence on seeing books in the running brooks, poetic theory in the ministrations of snow, enables a ghostly demarcating of rigid, highfalutin categories *within* a discursive context. For instance, in **"It's Half an Hour Later Before,"** the self is presented as a winter tree, probably about fifty years old, whose fine branches, as of imagination, snatch lyric flakes before they reach the ground they'll end up groundwater of, and whose big branches take on ridges-worth of saying, holding the evanescent in beads that light up nature, and man, for a spell:

> winter trees aren't good
> winnowers
>
>         nevertheless,
> fine branches snatch flakes
> and big branches take
> single ridges: the chaff
>   hits the ground
>   but the caught
>   turns to lit melt beads
>   that light up
>   trees in a different light:

If this poem is directed in any particular way, it is directed against destructive clarification. Ammons balks at harping on small ideas, neat schema, paradigmatic bliss. So the big idea that drifts through and settles on everything here like snow is that all is in all—the idea enunciated as fable in **"Ballad"** (*Diversifications*), in which the water oak and willow defend their respective territorial rights, with the poet as mediator. In this poem Ammons repeatedly asserts, exhorting by example, that

> I do not, can not, will not
> care for plain simple things
> with straightforward fences round them:
> I prefer lean, true
> integrations of ongoing
> with recurrences.
> resemblances, half-adventitious or fortuitous
> or as some would say accidental,
> half-accidental,
> not under a third

—the hedging on how much accidence is necessary typifies the complexity of statement in this poem, the major subject of which is poetry. Poems, like crows in the initial segment (**"Words of Comfort"**), "emphatically find dead/ trees to sit in,/ skinned branches, line up/ into the wind/ a black countercurrent/ drippy but cool." This venturing

begins "in a fallish time,/ the birds' gatherings and flights/ skim treetops, not/ much entering in now, no nests, pausing to consider/ or dwell, the wide/ storm winter coming." And while *The Snow Poems* is a venturing away from "the wide/ storm winter coming"—the winter of frozen possibility, personal extinction (always coming, but inevitably closer when one is "pushing fifty")—the book is at the same time a venturing into what can be found possible, established as abundance, *in* the venture of "pushing fifty" and heading into winter, unlike the birds.

One of the central ways in which this poem projects itself is to identify the poetic self with snow, an identification that is sometimes accentuated by the resemblance of snow to age, the winter of life, and discontent, a sense of lessening power, ("the sexual basis of all things rare is really apparent": *Sphere*); and so this poem prays for a snowing "of the/ right consistency,/ temperature, and/ velocity" that will enable the cold-bright diffuse but still consistent leeself to fall in a "building out over/ space a/ promontory of/ considerable/ reach in/ downward curvature." The poem wondrously demonstrates that "snow/ will do this/ not once/ but wherever possible,/ a similarity of effect/ extended/ to diversity's/ exact numeration."

I find this aspect of the generalized snow-metaphor beautiful as poetic defense—an offense not at all offensive. But I don't think Ammons is falling in downward curvature: the promontory of this poem speaks against that drift.

Actually, most of this poem, so far as I can tell, was written in that time when winter begins to fade into spring's necessary muckiness: from **"The Prescriptive Stalls As"** on, we're going from February toward and into April-May. The major gesture of the poem is away from, contrary to stasis, delimitation, ice—the easy victory of the professionally-wrought lyric—and toward enlarging possibility, spanglings of snowlight-meltings-and-meldings from the reservoirs of evergreens: "I stand for/ whatever will not come round/ or be whole/ or made out or reduced."

*The Snow Poems* is a great poem. It tries to make the mind—rather, *let* the mind—accord with "necessity's inner accuracy": necessity's inner accuracy is nature's accuracy. The poem is a habitat, ecosystem, world, galaxy, universe—in which there are events and creatures of little note and others on up (or down) the scale to events and creatures of great note, magnificent with their breakings-out of the brush of silence, in order to leave a greater silence after their going again. It shows how the great poem of earth, if this isn't it, may be written: it reveals how what has been taken for the great poetry of earth is only "the smooth walks, trimmed hedges, posys and nightingales" of insular tradition. *The Snow Poems* calls for a view of nature (to continue to quote Whitman) "in the prophetic literature of these States," that would place man in the light and dark of "the whole orb, with its geologic history, the cosmos, carrying fire and snow, that rolls through the illimitable areas, light as a feather, though weighing billions of tons"; it supports W. C. Williams's indictment of us by saying in its own way how the first settlers "saw birds with rusty breasts and called them robins," thought what they saw were not "robins" but thrushes "larger, stronger, and in the evening of a wilder, lovelier song."

This poem raises more questions about out aesthetic assumptions than a review can honestly deal with. If the segments of *The Snow Poems* were normal (Academico-American?) Western Adult Lyrics, then clearly some of the stuff would have to be left out. But to make that assertion seems more a criticism of our lyric-based poetics than a criticism of this particular poem, or any similar to it. The problem with aesthetic dicta is that they are of no use when one is confronted with work of major importance. Ammons's intention is obviously *not* to make a great pile of well-wrought urns. As Whitman asserted in the 1855 preface to *Leaves of Grass,* prophesying Ammons but speaking primarily of his own audacity. "Here is action untied from strings necessarily blind to particulars and details magnificently moving in vast masses. Here is the hospitality which forever indicates heroes." He was speaking of These States too: and said they await the gigantic and generous treatment worthy of them. And of the American poet: "he is greatest forever and forever who contributes the greatest original practical example. The cleanest expression is that which finds no sphere worthy of itself and makes one." And: "Great genius and the people of these states must never be demeaned to romances. As soon as histories are properly told there is no more need of romances." And: "The great poets are also to be known by the absence in them of tricks and by the justification of perfect personal candor." Here is one of my favorite properly told moments of history in *The Snow Poem:*

> what my father enjoyed
> most—in terms of pure,
> high pleasure—was
> scaring things: I remember
> one day he and
> I were coming up in Aunt
> Lottie's yard
> when there were these
> ducks ambling
> along in the morning sun,
> a few drakes, hens, and a string of
> ducklings,
> and my father took off his
> strawhat and
> shot it spinning out sailing in
> a fast curving glide over the
> ducks so they
> thought they were being
> swooped by a hawk,
> and they just, it looked
> like, hunkered down on their
> rearends and slid all the
> way like they were
> greased right under the house
>   (in those days houses
>     were built up off the ground)
> my father laughed the purest,
> highest laughter
> till he bent over

> thinking about those
> ducks sliding under
> there over nothing

---

**On the essence of Ammons's poetry:**

Ammons is the poet of perception, of vision as experience. Like Louis MacNeice, the "I" of Ammons's poetry feels "the drunkenness of things being several," but instead of fusing the separateness of creation in one mind, he holds it as it is, utterly particularized, in an orgy of precision. No matter how numerous the bricks, for him no building emerges; the whole of experience is always *less* than the sum of its parts: "Overall is beyond me: is the sum of these events/ I cannot draw, the ledger I cannot keep, the accounting/ beyond the account." Everything, in fact, is "magnificent with existence," and must be "interpenetrated" individually.

The nature of poetry and the place of art in this world are hazy. Certainly there must be no coalescing into significance, for this presupposes reduction. Similarly, the value of poetry cannot be located in the charting of a man's mind by its principles of ordering, for there *are* no such principles. . . .

The supreme principle is freedom. The freedom of "I," the experiencer, to chart his own course, his freedom to write what *he* wants ("you want to hear me describe it,/ to placate the hound's-mouth/ slobbering in your own heart:/ I will not tell you"). And ultimately, as he realizes, the freedom of the *reader* to choose within the choice presented: "I change shape, turn easily into the shapes you make."

> *Duncan Kenworthy, "Contemporary Poets: Six Touchstones," in* American Scholar, *Summer, 1973.*

---

**Alfred S. Reid   (essay date 1979)**

SOURCE: "The Poetry of A. R. Ammons," in *The South Carolina Review,* Vol. 12, No. 1, Fall, 1979, pp. 2-9.

[*Reid was an American educator and critic. In the following essay, he traces Ammons's emergence as a major postmodern writer who has rejected modernist sensibilities and seeks humankind's integration with the universe.*]

We can scarcely read a literary review or critical essay these days without finding the word *post-modern.* One critic has even described certain writers as *post-contemporary.* These usages of *post-,* paralleled by equally frequent occurrences of *neo-* in combination with *romanticism, realism,* or *experimentalism,* might be a mere passing semantic fad, but more likely they suggest a pervasive sense of cultural transition. As one reviewer has put it, the transition has progressed to the point that our literature is "no longer 'post-modernist' but 'pre-something.'" Perhaps other critics are saying the same thing when they recognize no literary orthodoxy. Nevertheless, some critics still insist that modernism is not over. Despite the deaths of all the great moderns and our lengthening distance from the peak of modernism, these critics say that modernist poetry continues in different ways. One critic speaks of early moderns and late moderns. Others use the term for its mystique. Still others use the label *modern* only as a term of convenience or habit, more in its popular sense of *now* than in its critical sense of a body of writing that flourished in the teens and twenties of this century and had certain definite characteristics, such as repudiation of rhetoric, a reliance on formalist techniques of myth, symbol, and subjective states, an ironical, analytic detachment, and a numbing sense of alienation and nihilism.

If we define modernism by two of these most essential features—first, its impersonality, its formal separation of art and reality, its attraction to personae and fictions to live by, as in Pound, Yeats, Eliot, and Stevens—and, second, by its hollow despair, its inability to accept absolutes, we cannot help being struck by the newer tendencies of certain representative contemporary poets to take the opposite attitude of demythologizing the poem, of personalizing it, of blurring the line between art and reality, and of making more than tentative attempts to re-attach man to his world within a context of faith. I refer mainly to the recent work of Robert Lowell and A. R. Ammons but also to such poets as Allen Ginsberg and Imamu Amiri Baraka (formerly LeRoi Jones). The latter two are special cases, and Lowell is already well recognized as probably our major contemporary or post-modernist poet. He abandoned the mythic approach for the semi-autobiographical, and in 1973 in *The Dolphin,* he surprised us all with his optimism, his "heaviness lifted."

To develop this controversial point of an emerging post-modernist sensibility, I shall therefore concentrate on A. R. Ammons, who is less well known than the others in spite of his recent winning of the National Book Award in 1972 for his **Collected Poems** and the Bollingen Prize in 1974 for his latest book **Sphere**. I realize the risks of oversimplification in arguing that a post-modernist sensibility can be demonstrated at this point and that it can be reduced to two features. I make the assertion less as dogma than as a hypothesis, something to be explored. But the truth is that some kind of break has definitely been taking place since the 1950s and that essentially it includes a blurring of the line between poetic art and reality and an urge to religious synthesis. Let us look at these phenomena in the poetry of A. R. Ammons.

Ammons began his poetic career in 1955 as a descendant of the wasteland poets in a little book called **Ommateum**. It is clearly modernist in technique and tone. The dominant image is that of a mythic wanderer, a sort of priestly poet or kingly exiled figure, often nameless, often named Ezra or Gilgamesh, one who seeks wisdom for himself and restoration for his people. He shuffles over the dry desert land, over "the bleached and broken fields," over the ravaged cities, hoping to hear the eternal word in the wind, but "there were no echoes from the waves." "The sap is gone out of the trees." There is only a "great vacuity." Death, disease, war, and destruction stalk the land

and leave it in ashes. Wells are polluted and yield only muddy water, beer cans, and innertubes; there is scant shade under the willow trees. The wanderer is as often dead as alive and yet finds some minimum insight in this dying state. Coming to a primitive shore, he is killed by an aborigine's arrow shot in his throat. Although taken off by the wind, he returns to find his own dry bones, draws pictures with one of his ribs in the sand, and sings Devonshire airs. He dies in a more "mirthful place" and hears the buzzards engaged over him in talk that sounds "excellent to my eternal ears" while they wait for a "savoring age to come."

The book shows the obvious influence of Eliot's *The Waste Land* but contains a few more hints of redemption, as in the desire to experience an eternal unity beyond the flux, the image of working in the barn by a sheaf of light torn from a sunbeam, a love affair with a lion at a waterhole, and especially the various miracles of moonlight, grass, and autumn harvest. In **"When I Set Fire to the Reed Patch,"** Ammons experiences not only pleasure and beauty but "mulch for next year's shoots/ the greenest hope/ autumn ever/ left this patch of reeds."

Eight years later, in 1963, in his second book, **Expressions of Sea Level,** Ammons abandoned the formalist imagery of the mythic wasteland and the hollow despair. He describes the familiar landscape of farms and inlets of his youth in Whiteville, North Carolina. Instead of the dramatic masque of the wandering Ezra-Gilgamesh figure, he adopts the more general speech of meditation. Instead of a forlorn search for faith, apocalyptic and surrealistic, he focuses on a belief in an orderly world in which finite and natural boundaries reflect an immense universal order. We live amid these forms, these "expressions of sea level," he writes, on the periphery of being, far from the center, yet not so far that we do not recognize the unity of creation in its multitudinous identities and motions, its mysterious comings and goings, its harmonious and wonderful operations. The book celebrates this sense of union and order in the universe: "an order of instinct prevails/ through all accidents of circumstances," he writes in **"Identity."** Along the edge, the crust, one can find "disorder ripe,/ entropy rich, high levels of random,/ numerous occasions of accident." But these multitudinous forms or modes are possible because the "underlying" essence is "all and/ beyond destruction/ because created fully in no/ particular form." We cannot know the essence, only "its forms, the motions . . ./ its/ permanence," but we know the essence is there because its manifestations work so well and appear so universally. Therefore the poet in **"Raft"** drifts out through the inlet to the sea, letting "the currents be/ whatever they would be,/ allowing possibility/ to chance/ where choice/ could not impose itself." In **"Hymn"** he says he will find this eternal essence both by leaving the earth and by staying:

> and if I find you I must go out deep into your far
> resolutions
> and if I find you I must stay here with the separate
> leaves.

The book represents a striking departure from the modernist sensibility in which the poem is artifice and man is cut off from his world. Ammons is both a neo romantic and a pragmatist, fusing certain modern scientific principles of indeterminacy and closed structures with an older Platonic metaphysics of matter and form and of the one and the many.

In his subsequent books of short lyrics—*Corson's Inlet, Northfield Poems, Uplands,* and *Briefings* in the 1960s and early 1970s—Ammons, for the most part, expands and illustrates his theories of peripheries and identities of nature. The bulk of his output consists of short nature poems about the familiar objects in his experience—inlets, dunes, rivers, animals, butterfly weeds, morning glories, pea vines, a favorite mule, and trees in the snow. He invites his friends to visit him and see the glories of nature, to be blessed as he by the destruction of self in the epiphanies of natural experience, be "released from forms" into the "eddies of meaning" and into the transcendental mysteries of the "over-all" presence. He has his dark moments, his struggles and losses; he knows violence and change; but he consistently holds to a world of open possibilities and the pervasive order of objects perceivable by the human mind and traceable to a vitality at the core. Ammons comes close to a Whitmanesque absorption into the One but strives to maintain a wholesome pragmatic balance between the oneness and the manyness of reality. Facts are facts, regardless of the freedom of philosophy, and he insists that we take the world as we sense it. With a similar stubbornness, he insists that we take the spiritual essence as we intuit it. In many of his poems, he professes to talk to mountains, rivers, and trees but wisely recognizes that his capacity for synthesis and flexibility of perspective makes man superior to, if slightly confused by, these other stable identities that he can take apart and re-order (**"Zone"**). As he says in **"Poetics"** (from *Briefings*), he looks for ways that things will turn out spiraling from a center.

In the midst of these personal nature lyrics spoken in his own voice, Ammons departed still further from the modernist sensibility of mythical analysis by writing a spontaneous autobiographical book-length poem, *Tape for the Turn of the Year*. With this work he explicitly joined the postmodernist movement begun ten years earlier by Ginsberg and Lowell. The Beats had aggressively challenged the modernist theory of the objective correlative of subliminal experience. They had advocated direct autobiographical treatment of reality and favored spontaneity over art. They argued too that the intellectual imposition of form on expression distorted reality. In *Life Studies* of 1960 Lowell had likewise departed from his earlier modernist works by demythologizing poetry in the confessional mode. Ammons' *Tape* similarly blurs the line between reality and art. Inserting an adding-machine tape into his typewriter, he proceeded to write a journal of his feelings, reminiscences, thoughts, and activities—a "long thin poem," he called it—between early December, 1963, and early January, 1964. "Anti-art and nonclassical," the book ridicules both the modernist and classical theories of poetry as artificial and obscure. Ammons accepts the "frazzling reality" of his daily life as more genuine, a "way of going along with the world as it is": "I care about the statement/ of fact:/ the true picture/ has a beauty higher/ than Beauty." He put the idea better

ten years later in *Sphere* when he scoffed at the tightly made modernist poem: "I don't know about you, but I'm sick of good poems, all those little rondures/ splendidly brought off, painted gourds on a shelf." In *Sphere* and in *Tape* he wanted to write something more personal, something massive, more synthesizing, something that touches "the universal anywhere you touch it everywhere." Yet he was not fully satisfied with the artlessness of *Tape* and concluded at that time that one cannot get too free: reality has to accept some form because form, as he is fond of saying, is part of reality; the identities of matter have their confinements though seemingly looser than the strict oneness of the center. *Tape* therefore is only a temporary launching, an experiment to see how far spontaneity will go without much imposed order, and it will not go very far. He returned to his short lyrics of natural insights until he finally devised a series of more controlled verse-essays or lectures to provide the "play-shapes" that satisfied him.

The first of these verse-essays, **"Essay on Poetics,"** defines poetry as a synthesizing principle. A poem, he says, draws out the multiple stimuli of reality, those essential designs and configurations that curve to the wholeness of meaning. Language is a level of abstraction that only appears to suppress reality while actually holding it in a stasis: "poems are arresting in two ways: they attract attention with/ glistery astonishment and they hold it: stasis: they gather and/ stay: the progression is from sound and motion to silence and rest." The poem must not violet the bits and pieces of reality but must tidy them up. There is a living organism in life's structures, and the poet's task is to locate that law at the centers of the various blobs and clusters so as to find their meanings and preserve the living core. Ammons' tone is slightly whimsical, and the view of poetry is not new: as others have noted, it is Whitmanesque. What is mainly interesting is the almost banal perspective of a lecturer trying out illustrations, deliberately avoiding the "locked clarity" of finished poem for a "linear"—perhaps he means rhetorical—mode that keeps open all options and possibilities of thought. To Ammons, poetry is "fun," a "superior amusement." He deplores the "Scoffers," the "party-poopers who are/ afraid they ought to believe in history or logical positivism and/ don't have any real desire to do so: they are scarcely worth a/ haircut: organisms, I can tell you, build up under the trust of joy and nothing else can lift them out of the miry circumstances: . . . poems are pure joy, however divisionally they sway with grief: the way to joy is integration's delivery of the complete lode. . . ." As did *Tape for the Turn of the Year,* this long poem repudiates the Pound-Eliot-Yeats-Stevens tradition of recondite myth and the cynical historical complicators of the very simple romantic truth of a harmonious creative center.

In a second lecture-poem called **"Extremes and Moderations"** Ammons delights in this great principle of harmonious balance that moderates nature's extremes of winds, floods, lightning, and body sickness, but he expresses fear that human beings have technologically tampered with nature so as to upset the balances. Such things as factories, automobiles, and chemical insecticides have jeopardized the balancing principle: "blue green globe, we have tipped your balance/ though we have scalded and oiled the seas and/

scabbed the land and smoked the mirror of heaven, we must try/ to stay and keep those who are alive alive." Like Blake and Hopkins and others before him, he believes that nature's balances are superior to our own and that we are headed for destruction unless we can align our psychic forces with nature's. Extreme calls to extreme, and moderation is losing its effect and quality. Yet all is not dreary; he has faith that we shall recognize our folly and save our world.

The third of these lectures, **"Hibernaculum,"** attempts more ambitiously than the earlier verse-essays to define the poet's own emerging mental and physical identity. It catalogues the welter and tangle of his sensations that are bursting into a recognizable personality. He sees himself coexisting with nature without conscious will. Compared, however, to Whitman's brilliant poems on the subject of the self's becoming—"Song of Myself" and "Crossing Brooklyn Ferry"—Ammons' poem is unsuccessful. It does exactly what he says he hopes he will not do: "I must not when I get up on/ the soapbox wash out." The bobs and bits never synthesize, and the tone is proudly clever rather than penetrating. A few isolated passages are splendid, but earlier shorter poems about nature—**"Identity," "Risks and Possibilities," "Expressions of Sea Level," "Gravelly Run," "Corson's Inlet"**—say much better what he seems to be trying to say here about his own identity as a consciously complex person in the process of organizing his various multiplicities.

Ammons' *Sphere* reaffirms the ideas of the one-many and center-periphery that have guided his thought for more than fifteen years. It brilliantly succeeds in showing the underlying unity of diversity that leads up to the Most High. It is the finest of his autobiographical verse-essays, a meditative philosophical lecture on the unifying forces in nature. It is also a work in the grand American tradition of Emerson-Thoreau-Whitman-Frost, the blend of the practical and the idealistic, the semi-cantankerous and garrulous amateur thinker eliciting universal meanings from commonplace details. It is a joyous book, a celebration of living, a humble awareness of the mysteries of cycles and changes.

Beginning with a statement of his usual theme of the mystery of an integrated universe, Ammons proceeds to illustrate its working in lively examples: sexual imagery, geometric imagery, the seasonal changes, nature's ways of renewals and balancings, the eternal springing of water in a well, numerous kinds of objects like chairs or fictions that imitate the ideas of these things, daily routines that identify him, history ever on the move toward newer meanings, biological formations, and so on—a constant flux of organization and divine recreation in which "fragments/ cease to be fragmentary and work together in a high flotation." It is one long ecstatic book-length sentence of 1,860 lines arranged into 155 numbered sections of four three-line stanzas. Like Whitman, Ammons addresses "vague hosannas: evaporation without arithmetic of loss." He feels so blessed that he invites others to join him: "send folks over: I have/ plenty to pass around . . ./ I go/ on the confidence that in this whole magnificence nothing is/ important, why should this be, yet everything is, even this/ as it testifies to the changing and staying." Abandon your scrambling for so-

cial status, he chides modern man: "let go and let your humanity rise to its natural/ height, said the star, and you will in that smallness be as/ great as I." The attitude extends to patriotism as well. He ecstatically praises his country and its citizens and attacks the radical, nay-saying, unpatriotic tradition:

> I can't understand my readers:
> they complain of my abstractions as if the United
>     States of
> America were a form of vanity: they ask why I'm so
>     big on the
>
> one-many problem, they never saw one: my readers:
>     what do
> they expect from a man born and raised in a country
>     whose
> motto is *E pluribus unum:* I'm just, like Whitman,
>     trying to keep things
>
> half straight about my country. . . .

And what he keeps straight is the unity, the federation, the comradeship, the continuing possibilities:

> I figure I'm the exact
> poet of the concrete *par excellence,* as Whitman
>     might say:
> they ask me, my readers, when I'm going to go
>     politicized or
> radicalized or public when I've sat here for years
>     singing
>
> unattended the off-songs of the territories and the
>     midland co-ordinates of Cleveland or Cincinnati:
>     when I've prized multeity
> and difference down to the mold under the leaf on
>     the one
> hand and swept up into the perfect composures of
>     nothingness
> on the other. . . .

But he has no intention of radicalizing or politicizing, only of asserting hope and reassurance, of singing "that tireless river system of streaming/ unity: my country: my country; can't cease from its/ sizzling rufflings to move into my 'motions' and 'stayings'":

> when I identify my self, my work, and my country,
>     you may
> think I've finally got the grandeurs. . . .

His hope is to achieve "a broad sanction that gives range/ to life," to achieve a "context in which the rose can keep its edges out of/ frost" and in which the "knots of misery, depression, and disease can/ unwind into abundant resurgence."

Often facetious and witty, often a bit tedious and overblown, *Sphere* is never merely clever or dull for long. It securely grounds its observations, unlike the other essay poems, on a progression of events, natural and human, that take place during one season: the melting snow of spring, the blast-off of Apollo 16, "April 23rd and still not a daffodil," returning from a trip to Baltimore on April 29 to find daffodils in bloom, the first mowing of the lawn, a cook-out at a friend's house on May 6, planting a garden, trimming a quince, being chased by a hornet while picking veronica from the lawn. In this respect the poem resembles *Walden* as well as *Leaves of Grass,* a kind of writing in which the assertions lead to concretes and the concretes rise again to universals.

Only in the most careless meaning of the term *modern* is Ammons a modernist poet in **Sphere**. He has rejected nearly everything that the modernists stood for. Like the other post-moderns he has extolled personality, blurred the line between art and reality, demythologized the poem. He is no confessionalist of a broken life, no advocate of poems-as-bullets, no extremist as A. Alvarez has called Plath, who tragically fulfilled the meaning of her poems in her suicidal death. He has rediscovered his own kind of personal expression, the lecture, the verse-essay, the Emersonian sermon. More than any of the others of his time he has attempted to re-integrate man into a whole person in a whole nation in a whole world, a part of a synthesis of man, nature, and God. He is the new poet of hope and faith, national and cosmic, who prophesies a "climb/ up the low belly of this sow century, through the seventies,/ eighties, right on upward to the attachments, the anterior/ or posterior fixation, anything better than the swung pregnancies of these evil years."

A movement as pervasive and successful as modernism will not succumb easily to change. It will continue to shape the work of contemporary poets for years to come. Yet Ammons is only one of several poets in the past fifteen years who has challenged the formalist theories and practice of modernism, not only by outright argument but by the more glacial emergence of a new sensibility. In the process he has lost some of the dramatic intensity that we associate with modernist poetry, but he has made up for the loss in urbane phrasing and the energy of a new affirmation.

## Helen Vendler  (essay date 1981)

SOURCE: "Reason, Shape, and Wisdom," in *The New Republic,* Vol. 184, No. 17, April 25, 1981, pp. 28-32.

[*Vendler is regarded by many as one of America's foremost critics of poetry. Since the mid-1960s she has contributed reviews and articles on poetry to prominent literary publications, in particular the* New York Times Book Review, *and since 1978 has served as poetry critic for the* New Yorker. *In addition to her reviews and articles, Vendler is the author of acclaimed book-length studies of poets W. B. Yeats, George Herbert, Wallace Stevens, and John Keats. Her most noted work, the award-winning collection of criticism* Part of Nature, Part of Us: Modern American Poets *(1980), is recognized as a thorough and informed view of contemporary American poetry. In the following review, Vendler offers an enthusiastic appraisal of Ammons's* A Coast of Trees *and states: "Ammons's own new-*

*ness . . . lies in his finely calibrated sense of the actual, non-transcendent motions of the natural world."*]

A classic poem, when it appears, comes not as a surprise but as a confirmation:

> I have a life that did not become,
> that turned aside and stopped,
> astonished:
> I hold it in me like a pregnancy or
> as on my lap a child
> not to grow or grow old but dwell on
> it is to his grave I most
> frequently return and return
> to ask what is wrong, what was
> wrong, to see it all by
> the light of a different necessity
> but the grave will not heal
> and the child,
> stirring, must share my grave
> with me, an old man having
> gotten by on what was left

This is the beginning of A. R. Ammons's revelatory poem, "**Easter Morning**." The central sentiment is not altogether unprecedented—Robert Lowell said, "Always inside me is the child who died"—but Lowell was speaking of a younger self continuous in some way with his adult self ("Always inside me is his wish to die"). Ammons is talking about a self that stopped, that never became, that is buried in a grave that does not heal. And yet that self is not dead; it is a "child, stirring." Robert Frost talked, more distantly, of a road not taken in the past; Ammons's metaphor of the child—buried, or in a womb, or on a lap—is alive with pain and quick with dismay. Ammons's lines rivet us where we stand and we find ourselves uttering them as though our own life had suddenly found its outlet-speech: "I have a life that did not become . . . the grave will not heal." Ammons's arrow strikes straight to the heart, and to the unhealed grave in it. "How did you know," we ask Ammons, "when we didn't know, ourselves, till you told us?" This is a poetry of eerie power, dependent not so much on the particular circumstances of Ammons's life as on his unsettling skill as an allegorist. Anything he tells us about his life ("I have a life that did not become") turns out to be true of everyone: he is a poet of the universal human condition, not of particular idiosyncrasy. This great poem, "**Easter Morning,**" turns out to be about the damage which every child undergoes as members of his family—a sibling, an aunt, a grandparent—die. It is an elegy in a family churchyard. When Ammons now goes back to North Carolina, the relatives he knew are dead:

> When I go back to my home country in these
> fresh far-away days, it's convenient to visit
> everybody, aunts and uncles, those who used to say,
> look how he's shooting up, and the
> trinket aunts who always had a little
> something in their pocketbooks. . . .

The catalog goes on to include uncles and teachers and Ammons's mother and father—all in the churchyard, dead, their world gone. And Ammons remembers himself as a child, shocked and blighted and deflected out of ordinary growth by these deaths:

> the child in me that could not become
> was not ready for others to go,
> to go on into change, blessings and
> horrors, but stands there by the road
> where the mishap occurred, crying out for
> help, come and fix this or we
> can't get by, but the great ones who
> were to return, they could not or did
> not hear and went on in a flurry and
> now, I say in the graveyard, here
> lies the flurry, now it can't come
> back with help or helpful asides, now
> we all bury the bitter incompletions.

In the desolate market of experience where none come to buy (as Blake said) Ammons stands, with his uncanny plainness of speech, the lines running on like an explanation and an apology atonce, heedless and pell-mell, every so often stopped by a pulling-up short, a bewilderment, an obstacle, an arrest in emotion:

> I stand on the stump
> of a child, whether myself
> or my little brother who died, and
> yell as far as I can, I cannot leave this place, for
> for me it is the dearest and the worst
> it is life nearest to life which is
> life lost: it is my place where
> I must stand and fail.

I am not sure whether the strange and complex resolution of the poem (in which Ammons watches the flight of eagles, and is grateful for perennial natural patterns and fresh insights alike) serves to resurrect the dead on this "picture-book, letter-perfect/ Easter morning." And I wonder whether the long anguish of the poem can be excerpted at all. But to review *A Coast of Trees* is first of all to give notice of the existence of **"Easter Morning"** as a new treasure in American poetry, combining the blankest of losses with the fullest of visions. It is a poem which should be published all alone, in a three-page book by itself; it is so complete it repels company.

Nevertheless, it has company, and distinguished company, in this new collection of short poems. Ammons always oscillates interestingly between the briefest of brief lyrics (**"Briefings," "Uplands,"** etc.) and the longest of long poems (**"Sphere," "Tape for the Turn of the Year"**). Ammons's bedrock is his conviction of the absolute interconnectedness of all phenomena. The atmosphere (so to speak) over his bedrock is formed by his quick, almost birdlike, noticing of all epiphenomena constantly occurring in the universe—a flight of moths here, a rill of snow-melt there. The short poems record the noticings; the long poems offer the metaphysics of multiple connection. Yet even this description is too divisive. Even in the short poems, Ammons's metaphysics of multiple connection is present in an abbreviated form, represented sometimes by syntax,

sometimes by rhetorical figure (notably repetition of a word or a word-root in syntactically significant positions). For instance, Ammons writes about the difficulty of putting a name, or names to reality—and about the attendant paradox that the closer the approximation of the name to the event the more acutely one feels the frustrating gap between what has been achieved and what absolute fidelity to reality would be. Using his favorite dense repetition, he grieves, ". . . the name nearest the name/ names least or names/ only a verge before the void takes naming in."

The sound of the writing verges on riddle, and hovers near theological paradox, but the sentiment is neither a riddle nor a mystification. It is a precise denomination in a series of self-joining words: "the name nearest the name names least or names only. . . ." This statement of a divergence takes on itself semantically the form of an obsessive connection. And though the creation of the formal barrier of art excludes "reality," it is surely a wonderful mutual relation that makes the terrain of the excluded ("cast out") equal exactly, as a two-piece verb, the terrain of the included ("shut in"): "when the fences foregather/ the reality they shut in is cast out." Almost every statement of fear or loss in Ammons occurs in a line that paradoxically consolidates a strict, practical linguistic gain—often as simple a gain as a word humming in resonance with another word, or a triumphant conclusion to a long syntactical suspension. The suspended syntax arises from Ammons's inexhaustible wish to explain; he is the poet *par excellence* of the bifurcating line of argument, a line that is interspersed with "I suspect" or "well, maybe" or "in fact" or "after all" or "that is" or "probably" or a sequence of "but's." To that extent his poetry is the utterance of that endless rhetoric he calls "reason":

> Reason can't end:
> it is discourse, motion
> to find motion, reason to
> find reason to abandon reason

But against the straight "thruway" of reason Ammons sets another formal motive, which he calls "shape": shape wants to wind discourse up, to give it a rondure, a closure. The shapeliness—almost spherical—of so many of Ammons's short lyrics asserts that a moment or a mood has its own being to proclaim in a determinate form. If that form is violated, something else is produced—even another poem perhaps, but not the original one, which, in being amended, is forever gone. The shape of a poem is inviolate:

> it is as
> it is: it can't be cast
> aside except to cast
> shape aside, no part in it
> free to cast free any part.

The rigidity of this verse defies us to shift a single word, to misplace a single "it" or "cast." The verse rejoices in its imperviousness to tinkering: it braces its "no" against its "any," its "free" against its "cast free," its "part" against "part," creating a wind-proof, storm-proof shelter against the inversions of chance. Ammons's loquacity of "reason" so plays against his geometry of "shape" that the exhilaration of the combat of the two motives equals in interest the plangent tales he tells of the life of the spirit.

These are twice-told tales; Ammons moves easily in the line of our poets. Like Traherne, he calls a poem **"Poverty"**; like Herbert, he sees a silk twist (in Ammons, "silk lines") coming down in radiance from heaven; like Keats, he stands (in the majestic poem called **"Swells"**) on the shore of the wide world till love and fame sink to nothingness. Like Yeats, he feels the pull of the balloon of the mind (Yeats tried to tether it; Ammons says, "I have let all my balloons aloose"); like Emily Dickinson, he feels an affinity for that "neglected son of genius," the spider, working like the poet "airy with radiality"; like Oliver Wendell Holmes, he writes **"An Improvisation for the Stately Dwelling"**; like Williams and Hopkins, he offers perpetual praise of the world of sight. In Ammons these earlier poets have found the ideal reader—the reader who himself writes a new poem as a variation on the older one.

Ammons's own newness—it bears repeating—lies in his finely calibrated sense of the actual, non-transcendent motions of the natural world. He is not in a hurry, as most of his predecessors (Emerson, Whitman, Dickinson, Hopkins) have been, to move from natural fact to patriotic or religious or philosophical enthusiasm. Ammons is true to himself in ending **"Easter Morning"** with the natural fact of bird-instinct, seen in a new configuration, rather than with the transcendent resurrection of the body in spirit. The natural universe is so real to Ammons's imagination that his poem about the earth rolling in space is spoken with an ease foreign to most efforts to "imagine" a cosmic perspective. Only Wordsworth had a comparable iron sense of fact:

> We go around, distanced,
> yearly in a star's
> atmosphere, turning
> daily into and out of
> direct light and
> slanting through the
> quadrant seasons: deep
> space begins at our
> heels, nearly rousing
> us loose: we look up
> or out so high, sight's
>
> silk almost draws us away.

(Frost, who yearned for vision, said we can look "Neither out far nor in deep"; Ammons, in his love of sight, is silently corrective.) Ammons is tugged between sentiment and stoicism, and the play between those two motives is as entrancing as the play between the flow of discourse and the shape of poetry. He is as tender as Keats and as harsh as Keats, reaping some of the same benefits. He does not rise to Wordsworth's full bleakness, but he has more humor and more waywardness than Wordsworth.

**"Swells"** gives full range to Ammons's sentiment and stoicism alike, to his precise sense of physical motion (in this case, wave-motion), and to his firm momentum-rounding-

into-shape. When hundreds of conflicting motions are assimilated into one wave, a paradoxical calm results:

> The very longest swell in the ocean, I suspect,
> carries the deepest memory, the information of
>    actions summarized . . .
>    so that the longest swell swells least.

Ocean floor or mountain are alike places where gigantic motions have been summarized into a near stillness:

>    I like to go
> to old places where the effect dwells, summits or
>    seas
> so hard to summon into mind, even with the natural
> ones hard to climb or weigh; I go there in my mind
> (which is, after all, where these things negotiably
>    are)
> and tune in to the wave nearly beyond rise or fall
>    in its
> staying and hum the constant, universal,
>    assimilation.

To climb the summit or find that summary so hard to summon to mind, and there to hear the hum (as Stevens called it) of the universal pantomime, might be in another poet a forgetful sublimity. But Ammons, like Keats, cannot forget the world where men sit and hear each other groan; he ends his poem by saying he has sought out the summit for "rest from the ragged and rapid pulse, the immediate threat/ shot up in a disintegrating spray, the many thoughts and/ sights unmanageable, the deaths of so many, hungry or mad." Mortality swells so agitatingly into presence at the end of the poem that the hoped-for contemplative calm is shaken and bruised. The ills of the body and of the spirit are all there are; we die hungry or mad, our pulse ragged or rapid. In nature, of course, there is nothing "unmanageable"; the word is meaningless in the cosmos, and takes on meaning only through human will, afflicted by thoughts and sights too painful to be borne. If only, like the geologic strata or the ocean floor, we could manage "the constant, universal assimilation: the/ information, so packed, nearly silenced with majesty." But we do not, and cannot, for long. The possibility, and the impossibility, of psychic assimilation are held in equilibrium in the long oceanic swell of this Stevensian poem—which should be read with Stevens's "Somnabulisma" and "Chocorua" as its predecessors.

It is a mark of Ammons's variety that it is very hard to generalize about his practice in this volume. Almost every poem has a distinctive shape and a set of new strategies, imitating the variety of nature:

>    a dance sacred as the sap in
> the trees, permanent in its descriptions
> as the ripples round the brook's
> ripplestone: fresh as this particular
> flood of burn breaking across us now
> from the sun.

Ammons matches his loneliness and his freshness to the solitary, permanent, and renewed acts of nature; and in his

*Ammons and the novelist E. Annie Proulx on the evening of the 1993 National Book Awards ceremony.  Ammons, a previous winner, took honors in poetry for his collection* Garbage.

"central attention" he keeps the universe alone. The poems enable us to watch this poet going about the business of the universe, both its "lost idyllic" and its present broken radiance. He has been about this business for years now, but I notice in reading this new collection how much more secure his language has become. Once, he was likely to err both in amassing scientific words too lavishly and in affecting too folksy a tone. Now the scientific world in Ammons is beautifully in balance with the perceptual one, and the tone is believably, and almost perfectly, colloquial. The lines are as near as we could wish to the ripples round the ripplestone.


**Thomas A. Fink  (essay date 1982)**

SOURCE: "The Problem of Freedom and Restriction in the Poetry of A. R. Ammons," in *Modern Poetry Studies,* Vol. 11, Nos. 1-2, 1982, pp. 138-48.

[*In the following essay, Fink explores the tensions between the concepts of individuality and unity as presented in Ammons's poetry, claiming that this polarity gives rise to a political dimension in the poet's work.*]

A number of highly regarded contemporary poets, among them Robert Creeley, John Ashbery, and A. R. Ammons, have been accused of evading the responsibility of bringing political concerns into their writing. In his long poem, *Sphere: The Form of a Motion,* Ammons summarily dismisses this charge, suggesting that his readers are simply blind to the political aspect of his poetry:

> they ask me, my readers, when I'm going to go
>   politicized or
> radicalized or public when I've sat here for years
>   singing
> unattended the off-songs of the territories and the
>   midland
> coordinates of Cleveland or Cincinnati: when I've
>   prized
> multeity and difference down to the mold under the
>   leaf
> on the one hand and swept up into the perfect
>   composures of
> nothingness on the other: my readers are baffling
>   and
> uncommunicative (if actual) and I don't know what
>   to make of
> or for them. . . .

In referring to his concern with "multeity and difference" and "nothingness," Ammons is reaffirming his long-time obsession with what he has termed the "one:many problem," the desire to maintain a sense of unity and diversity in poetry, perception, and other forms of experience. Coleridge in his *Biographia Literaria* had insisted that great poetry has a felicitous balance of unity and multeity, and Ammons implicitly indicates that the United States of America (with its motto, *E pluribus unum*) is in many respects exemplary of this aesthetic principle:

> I'm just, like Whitman, trying to keep things
> half straight about my country, my readers say,
>   what's all
> this change and continuity: when we have a two-
>   party system,
> one party devoted to reform and the other to
>   consolidation:
>
> and both trying to grab a chunk out of the middle. . . .

In his poetry Ammons never subjects the "one:many" structures of American politics to any rigorous analysis; in fact, he rarely speaks of any overtly political matters for more than a few lines. Nevertheless, he wants the impatient reader to understand that the salient features of the "endless" speculation on unity and diversity, abstract as they may sometimes seem, can be seen to have fundamental political ramifications. In order to demonstrate the validity of this statement, I will consider Ammons' treatment of the "one:many problem" in several poems as a reflection of the dynamics of a particularly political concern: the interplay of restriction (one) and freedom (many) in various aspects of human experience.

According to those who quest for unified, eternal, and totalized vision, the possibility that the spatial and temporal limitations of ordinary reality can be transcended constitutes the greatest imaginable freedom. In the relatively early lyric, **"Guide,"** however, Ammons declares that the attainment of this supposed freedom turns out to be an *absolute* restriction of individual possibility; it is the "unity" of nothingness or death:

>     You cannot come to unity and remain
>   material:
> in that perception is no perceiver:
>     when you arrive
> you have gone too far:
>     at the Source you are in the mouth of Death:
> you cannot
>     turn around in
> the Absolute: there are no entrances or exits
>         no precipitations of forms
> to use like tongs against the formless:
>     no freedom to choose:

Like Yeats in "A Dialogue of Self and Soul," Ammons warns that the diverse, uncontrollable flux of life is incompatible with the fixity of absolute unity. The "material" forms of life—both their physicality and their relevance to the living—must be sacrificed when an individual embraces a static, metaphysical paradigm of totality. If the "perception" of this absolute is supposed to be the highest kind of vision, Ammons claims on the contrary that no seeing is actually involved; the unified view of all phenomena is an *absence* in the world of the living.

Of course, those who desperately desire the unity that can be "found" only in death have already ceased to perceive their immediate environment as it is, and they have experienced a death-in-life of "material" concerns. Ammons' warning may apply to anyone with a fixed idea of reality or an inflexible ideology in which it is possible to "turn around." The stasis of an idealized paradigm precludes the possibility of movement or development, and so the "freedom to choose" is obliterated. What had at first seemed a liberation from uncertainty is now a seemingly irrevocable imprisonment in a tyrannical sameness.

Ammons' later poem, **"He Held Radical Light,"** describes the conflicts of a man who feels torn between the delight of the influx of transcendental power and the desire to remain within the security of a human community. In the opening stanza, the "radical light" of transcendence is figured as a version of the "music of the spheres" which came to "the furrows" of the man's "brain/ into the dark, shuddered,/ shot out again/ in long swaying swirls of sound. . . ." This remarkable energy, evoked grandly by the alliteration, seems an almost sexual release from "the dark" of limited perception and the constraints of ordinary experience. As indicated by the use of the word "radical" in the title and first line, the visionary/ musician thinks that he has been allowed to return to the "root" or origin of his being, the source of unlimited power.

But the second stanza immediately discloses that he is afraid this liberating energy will uproot him from the context he has known all his life, a world full of other people. Understanding that "reality had little weight in his transcendence," the man has been terrified of losing contact with the ground (in a literal and figurative sense) "and liked himself, and others, mostly/ under roofs. . . ." Comically, he can appreciate the commonplace restriction or "government" of a roof, because he has the paradoxical awareness that this agent of limitation is actually a source of *liberation* from a seemingly external force that would (in the name of freedom) *coerce* the individual to abandon the people and things he values so highly.

If the man finds at times that he desires to experience the powerful influx of "radical light," he knows that to adopt some version of transcendence as a permanent, unchanging attitude would prove an insupportable restriction of possibility, and so he must be satisfied with temporary flashes of transcendence. Furthermore, as much as the visionary/musician may hope to discover the "radical" truth of his self-identity (whatever distinguishes him from all other entities), he desires even more strongly to gain psychological strength from his identification with—or sense of being rooted in—his community:

> released, hidden from stars, he ate,
> burped, said he was like any one
> of us: demanded he
>
> was like any one of us.

As in Whitman's "Song of Myself," the reference to burping is a sign of liberation from the tyrannical allurement of the Sublime, the immaculate starlight, which would reduce the diversity of human behavior into the unity of inhuman perfection.

Although much of Ammons' poetry shows he believes, as he asserts in the long *Tape for the Turn of the Year,* that "we can approach/ unity only by the loss/ of things—/ a loss we're unwilling/ to take," he clearly perceives the dangers of diversity without any sense of provisional order. As evidenced by a lengthy criticism of industrial polluters in **"Extremes and Moderations,"** Ammons is extremely concerned with the survival of man and nature, and he recognizes that unlimited freedom would result in the ultimate imprisonment of global destruction. "Rampaging industrialists" are "filling vats of smoky horrors because" they desire "to live in long white houses on the summits/ of lengthy slopes," but they forget that "common air moves over the slopes, and common rain's/ losing its heavenly clarity: if we move beyond/ the natural cautions, we must pay the natural costs. . . ." How, then, does Ammons arrive at a satisfactory midpoint between the disastrous poles of anarchy and totalitarianism? In a handful of poems, Ammons presents either a partial or provisional conclusion to this monumental problem. The world of nature often provides examples of the balance-in-movement that mankind must learn in order to ensure its own and the earth's survival. After announcing, "*ecology* is my word: tag/ me with that," in *Tape for the Turn of the Year,* the poet celebrates a natural symbol of positive growth:

        the circular lichen
        spotting the tree
    trunk
    is
    like a moral order: there
    is a center
    where with threads the
    lichen knits in, the
            "holding-on" point
        that gathers stability
        from bark: and there
        is
    the outward multiplication
    of forms (cells & patterns)
    to an unprescribed
    periphery
    that marks the
    moment-to-moment edge of growth:

On the one hand, the lichen is not a static pattern governed by a center that prescribes the periphery, and on the other hand, the growth of the periphery does not destroy all sense of pattern or stability. The center is both the beginning-point of growth and the reassuring foundation or base of support for the periphery. But, like an ideal form of government for citizens who are all trustworthy and responsible, this center does not interfere with the freedom of the periphery to expand in whatever way it finds necessary and desirable. While the center is providing a sense of unity or coherence, the periphery's "unprescribed"

growth from "moment-to-moment" is providing a sense of spontaneity and diversity. In simple abstract terms, survival can be viewed as the center, and adaptability to change as the expansion of the periphery. As Ammons notes a few pages later in *Tape,* his "other word" (besides "ecology") "is *provisional,*" and "the center-arising/ form" he admires continually "finds a new factor,/ utilizes a new method,/ gains a new foothold,/ responds to inner & outer/ changes."

It is one thing to find an ideal "model" for development and maintenance of continuity in the environment; it is quite another to apply it, however beautiful or efficient it seems, to the extremely complex functioning and interactions of human beings. In **"Corsons Inlet,"** perhaps his best known poem, Ammons directly addresses the problem of how the individual perceiver can both regulate and yet open up possibilities for understanding and growth in his encounter with the natural world.

As the speaker of the poem is walking "over the dunes again this morning/ to the sea", he finds himself liberated from rigid geometrical forms and exposed to more changeable, uncertain, and—to use the poet's own word—provisional shapes:

    the walk liberating, I was released from forms,
    from the perpendiculars,
        straight lines, blocks, boxes, binds
    of thought
    into the hues, shadings, rises, flowing bends and
      blends
          of sight:

Static formulations give way to an awareness of process; the confinement of "blocks" and "boxes" gives way to "rises" and "flowing." As the aural imagination moves from "binds" to the off-rhymes of "bends and blends," the speaker is released from the reductive impulse of abstract categorization and experiences the "unprescribed" and ever-expanding "periphery" of phenomenal perception. He goes on to emphasize the beauty of vigorous movement: in the "geography" of the poet's work are to be found "eddies," "a stream" and "swerves of action." None of these phenomena can be captured in a snapshot, and the experience of an Ammons poem cannot be squeezed into an aphorism or paradigm.

The poet refuses to give a name to the "Overall," the totalization of the experience from a retrospective position, although he celebrates the diversity of "the overall wandering of mirroring mind." The value of the experience of nature is the transition or "wandering" from perception to perception; there are continual surprises. Since every artificial boundary or limitation proves unable to contain what the speaker sees, as "manifold events of sand/ change the dune's shape that will not be the same shape/ tomorrow," he can have the confidence that embracing the *temporality* of experience is the only "logical" choice he can make: "so I am willing to go along, to accept/ the becoming/ thought . . .". Once "thought" is considered a process and not a final, static formulation, it can be valued along with the "bends and blends/ of sight."

Realizing that "the demand" among nature's denizens "is life, to keep life," the perceiver can admire to some degree even the savagery of predatory birds satisfying their hunger, as opposed to the lifelessness of placing the world's elements in metaphysical "boxes." Without any trace of revulsion, the speaker reports that one gull "ate/ to vomiting," while another "squawking possession, cracked a crab,/ picked out the entrails, swallowed the soft-shelled legs. . . ." Is the poet implying here that all survival is based on the necessity of depriving others of life? This is only one small aspect of the workings of nature; Ammons is careful to differentiate his view of natural process from the notion of anarchy. "Thousands of tree swallows/ gathering for flight" toward a warm climate are "a congregation/ rich with entropy: nevertheless separable, noticeable/ as one event,/ not chaos . . ." .

At this point, Ammons' *persona* feels sufficiently liberated from the tyranny of falsely uniforming or unifying forces, and now he is concerned that his exercise of this freedom will be misconstrued as total disorder—without the possibility of provisional understanding. The balance-in-movement is achieved when he describes a continual process of the "many" springing out of the "one" in his field of vision and experience:

> in the smaller view, order tight with shape:
> blue tiny flowers on a leafless weed: carapace of
>   crab:
> snail shell:
>     pulsations of order
>     in the bellies of minnows: orders swallowed,
> broken down, transferred through membranes
> to strengthen larger orders: but in the larger view,
>   no
> lines of changeless shapes: the working in and out,
>   together
>     and against, of millions of events. . . .

In metaphysics and theology, disorder is generally conceived as existing within a comprehensive order, diversity within unity, words within the Word (*Logos*). The Ammons of **"Corsons Inlet"** articulates the exact opposite of this position: although small orders may be "broken down" and their fragments later used in the composition of larger orders, every larger order at some point is destined to prove inadequate or be dismantled. Furthermore, given the multiplicity of possible factors involved in any transformation, one cannot predict the pattern of a future synthesis from a present one. With every expansion of the individual's perspective comes an "unassimilable fact" that "leads [him] on"—to account for the diversity that bursts out of a limited unity.

The poet, then, considers the small instances of order that he sees, such as the pattern of "blue tiny flowers on a leafless weed," provisionally valuable, but no more valuable than the loss of order. The most important thing is that movement continues, because movement is a sign of *survival,* which has to be the greatest solace for the poet who tosses aside metaphysical consolations: "all possibilities/ of escape open: no route shut, except in/ the sudden

loss of all routes . . . ." No one can find guaranteed protection against death, but the poet's common-sense approach can help to avert the horror of death-in-life. He strives for maximum freedom within severe external limitations, and this aim is accomplished through the interplay of small freedoms and restrictions: "I will try/ to fasten into order enlarging grasps of disorder, widening/ scope, but enjoying the freedom that/ Scope eludes my grasp, that there is no finality of vision. . . ." The poet's desire to confine the swarming elements of his perceptions for a time within a unified "scope" can be viewed as a way of liberating himself from the undifferentiated mess of chaos. The breaking of order cannot be appreciated without the prior existence of order. Likewise, the individual is set free from a futile quest for "Scope"—freed from the universal in order to experience the power and pleasure of the particular—only because he has agreed to restrict the scope of his ambition, to acknowledge his human limitations.

In **"Uh, Philosophy"** Ammons suggests that the kind of freedoms assumed in poems such as **"Corsons Inlet"** must be used with a strong sense of political responsibility, lest one individual or group mistakenly believe that the highest form of personal liberty is domination of others. In an age such as ours in which, according to the poem's speaker, philosophers say "that truth is so much a method" and therefore one should be permitted to believe anything he chooses or nothing, the proliferation of ideologies makes it extremely difficult for people to live peaceably with one another:

> philosophy is
> a pry-pole, materialization,
> useful as a snowshovel when it snows:
> something solid to knock people down with
>   or back people up with:
> I do not know that I care to be backed up in just
>   that way:
>     the philosophy gives clubs to
> everyone, and I prefer disarmament:
>   that is, I would rather relate
> to the imperturbable objective
>   than be the agent of
> "possibly unsatisfactory eventualities":
>   isn't anything plain true:
> if I had something
>   to conform to (without responsibility)
>
> I wouldn't feel so hot and sticky:

The word "rhetoric" can usefully be substituted for "philosophy" in this poem, since philosophizing here is an exercise of the individual will. If a rhetorical pattern is like a "snowshovel" that clears away the vast accumulation of data that cannot be satisfactorily assimilated ("possibly a hundred sensations per second, conscious/ and unconscious . . ."), it can certainly help someone make his way through various experiences. But when the snowshovel is turned into a club, when defense is converted into offense, Ammons' speaker does not want his arguments to be "backed up" or supported by such rhetoric, because he knows that he could just as easily be "backed up" or caused to retreat by someone else's. The more people who are vying to club one another, the less chance that any particular one of them will succeed in subjegating the others, and, in any case, it is hard to imagine the genial speaker of **"Uh, Philosophy"** wanting to impose an ironclad will on everyone he meets.

Most crucially, the speaker prefers "disarmament" because he is convinced that "the imperturbable objective" of collective survival must always be cherished more than an individual's personal gain or that of his country. He longs for peaceful coexistence to be established as the truth beyond all mere questioning, but feels "hot and sticky" because he knows that no authority, no central force, has been able to check the escalation of the ideological and military arms buildup.

There is irony, though, in the speaker's desire for "something/ to conform to (without responsibility)." The voluntary shouldering of responsibility—on *everyone's* part—is precisely what is needed to ensure global survival. If we are free to choose our ideologies, we should be happy to honor others' right to enjoy this freedom. But the "overall" "message" of poems like **"Corsons Inlet"** has already taught us that it is a grave mistake to impose *any* fixed version of "Being"—much less one of our own total mastery or control over anyone else—on ourselves or those we encounter. If we accept the continual becoming (be-*ing*) of our individual and collective experience, as Ammons and several other influential modern American poets (among them Williams, Olson, Creeley, and Ashbery) have in their various ways urged us to do, we will not need the threats of external authority to keep us in line; we will exercise *restraint* on our will to power, with the confidence that it is the most *liberating* and best possible course of action. Unfortunately, few world leaders at the present time seem to cherish this way of thinking.

In presenting various acts of individual liberation (and its attendant restrictions) in many of his poems, A. R. Ammons sets implicit examples for others to liberate themselves and to help protect individual freedom in general through their actions. Although some readers are put off by what they consider a plethora of "inhuman" abstract philosophizing in the work, Ammons' poetry is filled with inherent generosity, much like the light that the poet praises in **"The City Limits"**:

> When you consider the radiance, that it does not
>     withhold
> itself but pours its abundance without selection into
>     every
> nook and cranny not overhung or hidden . . . .
>     when you consider
> that air or vacuum, snow or shale, squid or wolf,
>     rose or lichen,
> each is accepted into as much light as it will take,
>     then
> the heart moves roomier, the man stands and looks
>     about, the
> leaf does not increase itself above the grass, and the
>     dark

> work of the deepest cells is of a tune with May
>     bushes
> and fear lit by the breadth of such calmly turns to
>     praise.

---

**Ammons on his constant interest in poetry:**

. . . In 10th grade, I wrote a poem on Pocahontas, and in the Navy at the age of 18, whisked away to the South Pacific, I began to write poems in a log I kept. After the war in 1946, I enrolled on the G.I. Bill at Wake Forest College, where the following year I met Phyllis Plumbo, whom I later married. Phyllis moved away for a couple of years but our correspondence included poems to each other, an exchange that deepened the life in words for me. I could I think show a retrospective track of incidents that might have produced me as an artist, preacher, singer, doctor, mycologist, etc., but the string of events I've listed brought me in 1955 to publish through a vanity press my first book of poems, *Ommateum,* and led nine years later to the appearance of my first accepted book, ***Expressions of Sea Level,*** which was published by Ohio State University Press. Nineteen years elapsed between the time I began to write continually in the South Pacific and the appearance of the Ohio book. They were years of working alone, while working at something else for a living, years in which I received little acceptance or encouragement. But I take no credit for the persistence. Writing poetry is what I did. I had no place else to turn.

*A. R. Ammons, "'I couldn't wait to say the word,'" in* The New York Times Book Review, *January 17, 1982.*

---

**Gilbert Allen  (essay date 1986)**

SOURCE: "The Arc of a New Covenant: The Idea of the Reader in A. R. Ammons' Poems," in *Pembroke Magazine,* No. 18, 1986, pp. 86-103.

*[Allen is an American educator, poet, and critic. In the following essay, he asserts that Ammons's poetry constantly challenges the traditional conception of poetry, as well as the standard roles of the poet and reader.]*

Most writers cultivate their ability to satisfy expectations. A. R. Ammons is a notable exception. Through his defiance, he hopes to make us question the assumptions behind—our ideal of Good Poetry and to join with him in creating new, provisionally more satisfying standards. Then, in the next poem, or in the next book of poems, the process of denial and revision begins afresh: or, as Ammons succinctly puts the matter at the end of **"Corsons Inlet,"** "tomorrow a new walk is a new walk."

Not all readers are comfortable with this responsibility. David Young, for example, complains that Ammons does not always provide us with the verbal *richesse* traditionally

Perhaps the verse essay is a respectable and legitimate genre, but I wish it wouldn't be confused with lyric poetry; if you order bourbon and get ginger-ale because someone thinks they are roughly the same thing, you have a right to protest. ["Language: The Poet as Master and Servant," in *A Field Guide to Contemporary Poetry and Poetics,* edited by Stuart Friebert and David Young, 1980]

The central metaphor in this passage is revealing. It implies that the relationship between audience and author is a fundamentally commercial one. Readers like Mr. Young know what they want from poems; the writer should be smart enough either to want the same things, or at least to pretend that he does; the writer then hands over the bourbon to his patrons and hopes for his critical gratuity.

This strikes me as precisely the relationship between writer and reader that Ammons has been questioning for thirty-five years. In a 1973 interview with David Grossvogel [in *Diacritics* 3 (Winter 1973)], Ammons' profession of interest in John Ashbery's poems underscores his own aesthetic principles:

I respect [Ashbery] very much as a courageous man who has not thought to himself "What is most likely to succeed?" Which is what most of the poets that I don't respect ask first.

Ammons does, of course, ultimately wish to please his readers. Like Roland Barthes, he perceives the relationship between text and reader as an erotic one:

Take a boy and a girl, they see each other. It's like the first line of a poem. It either sets up an immediate attraction so you want to know more, or it doesn't. If the attraction is there, what happens? The two people manage somehow to get close to each other and what happens next?—not silence but an outbreak of dialogue whereby they try to sense where the other person is. . . . [Interview, *Diacritics*]

But lovers often please us most by telling us things that we initially did not want to hear, and that we come to see as beautiful only through their efforts. That is, poets don't *sell* us anything but manage to *engender* it in our deepest, best selves. And just as we change, they change, and we must all try to rekindle that love in ever-various ways.

Young shows an unwillingness to entertain Ammons' notion of the shifting, recriprocal relationship between poet and reader; he assumes that Ammons, especially in his longer poems, is either too stupid or too untalented to provide verbal flourishes for our edification. Denis Donoghue has a different problem with Ammons' work, but it also hinges upon a reluctance to question the customary relationship between author and audience. Donoghue chastises Ammons for being insufficiently concerned with other human beings in his poems:

He protests that he is concerned with Nature, including human nature, but he rarely makes me feel that he cares much about any human nature but his own. His

poetry is rural in the sense that you can walk for miles in it without meeting anyone; so the dramatic sense of life never appears. Ammons could write his poetry if there were nothing in the world but mountains, winds, weather, birds, fish, sand dunes, beaches, and a poet accustomed to living in his art alone. ["Ammons and the Lesser Celandine," *Parnassus* 3 (Spring-Summer 1975)]

Donoghue is wrong as well as uncharitable here, for such a world would also be devoid of readers. For Ammons, the essential humanity of poems lies not within them but between them and their audience. That is, his poems rarely dramatize relationships between persons, but rather present speakers who are surrogates or adversaries for the reader. The resulting tension between the voice in the poem and the reader's response to it becomes the poem's social being—which often incorporates the isolation of the speaker within it. Thus, the typical Ammons poem is at once alienated and in quest of the social completion that is available only through the reading process.

Critics like Harold Bloom, despite their maddening jargon, posit an active, creative reader: a concept that helps them to realize and to enjoy the many tasks that Ammons sets before them. My chief reservation about Bloom's commentaries, apart from their prolixity, is their tendency to pursue theoretical points at the expense of the poems themselves. (Bloom would call my position a canonization of "weak misreading," but that is another matter.) Because Bloom's theory is, in general, much closer to the spirit of Ammons' work than more traditional theories of interpretation are, it produces some rich, persuasive readings. Yet it also produces excesses like the following:

As I read the most recent Ammons [Bloom is writing in 1973] I keep remembering fragments out of Emerson's *Journals* (not because Ammons browses in them, but because his Lurianic misprision of Emerson operates most fiercely when he has not read the ancestral sage). ["Emerson and Ammons: A Coda," *Diacritics* 3 (Winter 1973)]

If one practices this sort of intertextuality-run-wild—an influence is strongest when it isn't there—then there is no longer the dialog that Ammons envisions between poet and reader. Instead, the reader has taken over the whole show.

Although Ammons' manners are too good to call Bloom specifically to task for this critical imperialism, he has commented upon the excesses of contemporary criticism in general:

Certain levels [of poems] are discussable. That is what bothers me so much about some of the French critics, as I understand them. They have arrived at the point where there is no text. It's impossible that there should be an author; it's inconceivable that there could be an audience. Now it just won't work, because human life and human organisms go right on. [Interview, *Diacritics*]

In his helpful study of Ammons' work [*A. R. Ammons*, 1978], Alan Holder sets up groups of "polar clusters" to indicate the extremes "between which Ammons' sensibility oscillates":

| One (Unity) | Many (Multiplicity) |
|---|---|
| formlessness | form |
| order | disorder (entropy) |
| stasis | motion |
| height | ground level |
| center | periphery |

The list suggests that Ammons habitually concerns himself with provisional, informing tensions rather than with gem-like lyrics or narratives. To Holder's clusters I would add "author: readers" or "assertion: syntheses." Perhaps we should remember the littoral landscape of so many of Ammons' poems in the late 50's and early 60's. In metapoetic terms, the ocean becomes the author, shaping the land of the reader that both receives and deflects. The text of each poem is a point upon the vital, ever-changing periphery whose broadest outlines I shall now attempt to chart.

The world of A. R. Ammons' first poems is forbidding: often desert, usually hostile, always disorienting. Many readers who enjoy the more conversational later poems are baffled by the hermetic incantations of *Ommateum*:

> [T]he poetry is personal but abstract, intense but distanced. Taken as a whole, the volume is attenuated and unduly strange, coming to us from too far away. [Holder, *A. R. Ammons*]

Robert Morgan sums up the spirit of the early work more sympathetically:

> The *Ommateum* poems occur in remote points of desert and mind, which is their difficulty and purity. The later poems create a sense of space more accessible and easier to recognize. Their landscape is often the more life-promoting sea shore and marshes. ["The Compound Vision of A. R. Ammons' Early Poems," *Epoch* 22 (Spring 1973)]

The paradox of Ammons' earliest work is that it insistently asks the reader to identify with the poet's radical isolation, thereby qualifying that isolation in the reader's mind as it is qualified nowhere on the page. The world *ommateum* refers to the compound eye of an insect; if we extend the metaphor implied by the title of the book, Ammons himself becomes the insect, and the speaker of each poem is a fragment of the eye which is the I. The typical speaker in *Ommateum* is alienated from other human beings, from the landscape, and often from his own body:

> Leaving myself on the shore
> I went away

> and when a heavy wind caught me I said
> My body lies south
> given over to vultures and flies
> and wrung my hands
>                              (**"The Whaleboat Struck"**)

Even the refuge of language itself is flimsy:

> The pieces of my voice have been thrown
> away I said turning to the hedgerows
> and hidden ditches
> Where do the pieces of
> my voice lie scattered
>                              (**"Rack"**)

In his first book Ammons shows us, but rarely tells us, that the poem is the last, unassailable point of contact between human beings. Gestures of farewell dominate in *Ommateum*, yet the book goes on: the speaker dissolves into the night wind (**"So I Said I Am Ezra"**); he "Walk[s] out of the world" after seeing Jews burned alive (**"In Strasbourg in 1349"**); he disappears into the well of the inexpressible (**"Turning a Moment to Say So Long"**); he perishes while waiting for the resolving chord of divine unity (**"I Struck a Diminished Seventh"**); he disappears into the mushroom clouds above a leveled city (**"Dropping Eyelids Among the Aerial Ash"**). Yet he is magically resurrected, if not rescued, again and again in ways that are possible only in the transforming imaginations of writer and reader.

Ammons begins *Ommateum* with an assertion of unity: he adopts the voice of the prophet Ezra. But the world around him denies his gesture:

> So I said I am Ezra
> and the wind whipped my throat
> gaming for the sounds of my voice

And ultimately the speaker himself follows suit:

> As a word too much repeated
> falls out of being
> so I Ezra went out into the night
> like a drift of sand

Ammons goes on to become the Ancient Mariner of his own book, appearing and dissolving in different scenes, compulsively counting the many grains of his being that have been winnowed by the wind of life-in-death.

The wind games for the sounds of the speaker in **"So I Said I Am Ezra,"** suggesting the bewildering multiplicity of voice and vision throughtout *Ommateum*. Patterns of imagery are begun in one poem and transmuted in the next; the sea oats of the Ezra poem become the rye and oatgrains of **"The Sap Is Gone Out of the Trees"** while the "unremembered seas" of the first poem become the memories of the land of the speaker's birth in the next. Such patterns occur over and over again in *Ommateum*, the most thoroughly Heraclitean book of this Heraclitean poet.

Death is both the dissolution and the unity of *Ommateum*. Mortality eventually becomes **"This Black Rich Country"** at the end of the 1951-1955 section of the *Collected Poems*. The shifting perspectives, ambiguous line-divisions, and broken images of *Ommateum*, however disorienting, do not preclude the poet's resurrection on the next page. To enjoy Ammons' early work, a reader must be willing to embrace this rapid, paradoxical shifting, to become its flux, to see, at least provisionally, through the compound eye of *Ommateum* to the I beyond.

Although *Ommateum* is a book of dislocations—in time, place, syntax, and patterns of imagery—in tone it is all of a very dark piece. But in the rest of the 1971 *Collected Poems* a new Ammons emerges. His tone is often playful, and as various as his many voices. His language becomes more conversational and more accessible. Frederick Buell summarizes these new tendencies:

> Most immediately striking in the poetry dated in the *Collected Poems* between 1956 and 1966 is the great variety of voices and lyric selves that Ammons has created. Sly or serious inquirer, chanter, celebrant, country skeptic, diarist, observer, reasoner: the speakers range in utterance from the formal, hortatory, or celebrative Whitmanian chanter of songs to the wry, ironic doubter of prophecy.

> ["'To Be Quiet in the Hands of the Marvelous': The Poetry of A. R. Ammons," *Iowa Review*, Winter, 1977]

Ammons largely abandons his desert landscapes and becomes more interested in field, forest, river and seashore. The inner and outer weather in his poems appropriately becomes more temperate and more changeable. Ammons now implies that all emotions, somber and glorious, joyful and humble, deserve equal consideration as psychic forces, and that the mind must celebrate its changes. Richard Howard notes astutely that "it is only in Ammons that I find all three moments—the changing from, the changing, and the changing to—exalted equally" [*Alone with America,* enlarged edition, 1980].

Ammons' relationship with the reader undergoes an equally dramatic change in this period. No longer is the speaker an isolated seer, hoping for the empathy that he seems unable to extend to anyone else. Now he frequently addresses the reader in the second person; this rhetoric gives the poems of the late 50's and early 60's an explicitly social dimension absent from *Ommateum*. For example, Ammons begins **"Risks and Possibilities"** with a garland for the reader:

> Here are some pretty things picked for you:
>     1) dry thunder
>         rustling like water
>         down the sky's eaves
>
>     is summer locust
>     is dogfennel weed

The *Ommateum* poems renounce the everyday world and its rhetorical gestures, but Ammons' impulse five or ten years later is to "honor a going thing" (**"Mechanism"**). The farewells of the early poems have become arrivals and returns. **"Hymn"** begins with a perception similar to the one that dominates *Ommateum*:

> I know if I find you I will have to leave the earth
>     and go out
>             over the sea marshes and the brant in bays

But in its second stanza, the poem makes an assertion more characteristic of the newer Ammons:

> And I know if I find you I will have to stay with
>     the earth inspecting with thin
> tools and ground eyes
> trusting the microvilli sporangia and simplest
>     coelenterates

This acceptance of what Richard Wilbur calls "the things of this world" is the most substantial difference between the first book and the half-dozen that follow it. Ammons' "things" are characteristically smaller or larger than Wilbur's, however, and Ammons never has the certainty of vision that is the center of Wilbur's art. Indeed, in a 1968 essay, "A Poem Is a Walk," Ammons suggests that the perception of poetry should be a battle against such certainty:

> Having once experienced the mystery, plenitude, contradiction, and composure of a work of art, we afterwards have a built-in resistance to the slogans and propaganda of over-simplification that have often contributed to the destruction of human life.

But uncertainty does not preclude education, and Ammons frequently employs a lecturing tone in the middle of his *Collected Poems*. **"Bridge,"** for example, begins with the enigmatic advice that "A tea garden shows you how." As we adopt the identity of the "you" in the poem and become Ammons' pupil, we enjoy the midafternoon sun and watch "lovers and single people" walk over a steep, small bridge arcing above a pond's narrowest point. As the people ascend the bridge, their reflections seem to go deeper into the pond, "where bridge and mirrorbridge merge at the bank." Then they descend on the other side, "returning their images to themselves" as they disappear into a grove of trees that "screens them into isolations of love or loneliness." At this point, the speaker invites us to imagine the spirit making a similar ascent and descent on the "bridge of consciousness." As in Frost's "Birches," this mental journey is good both going and coming back, but especially coming back:

>     paradise was when
> Dante
> regathered from height and depth
>     came out onto the soft, green, level earth
>
> into the natural light, come, sweat, bloodblessings,
>     and thinning sheaf of days.

The reintegration into the world that took place silently *between* poems in **Ommateum** now is occuring *within* the poems themselves. Poet and reader have become fellow observers, fellow walkers—even if, like the objects and reflections in **"Bridge,"** they never wholly meet in the water of the text.

This new convenant is most playfully clear in "**Coon Song**." The poem begins as the speaker watches a raccoon fall from a tree and lands in front of some hounds. Just as we're ready for the bloody dismemberment to occur, the speaker interrupts the story with some "uh, philosophy":

> Dostoevsky would think
> it important if the coon
>   could choose to
>       be back up the tree:
> or if he could choose to be
>   wagging by a swamp pond,
>       dabbling at scuttling
> crawdads: the coon may have
>   dreamed in fact of curling
>       into the holed-out gall
> of a fallen oak some squirrel
>   had once brought
>       high into the air
> clean leaves to: but
>
>       reality can go to hell
> is what the coon's eyes said to me

Then the speaker both whets our curiosity and delays its satisfaction by presenting the coon's death in graphic but hypothetical terms;

> . . . I thought the raccoon
>       felt no anger,
> saw none; cared nothing for cowardice,
>   bravery; was in fact
>       bored at
> knowing what would ensue:
>   the unwinding, the whirling growls,
>       exposed tenders,
> the wet teeth—

At this point, Ammons incorporates the reader into the poem directly, and raises the fundamental issue in the relationship between author and audience, the issue of power:

> you want to know what happened,
> you want to hear me describe it,
>   to placate the hound's-mouth
>       slobbering in your own heart:
> I will not tell you: actually the coon
>   possessing secret knowledge
>       pawed dust on the dogs
> and they disappeared, yapping into
>   nothingness, and the coon went
>       down to the pond
> and washed his face and hands and beheld
>   the world: maybe he didn't:
>       I am no slave that I

should entertain you, say what you want
>   to hear, let you wallow in
>       your silt: one two three four five:
> one two three four five six seven eight nine ten:
>   (all this time I've been
>       counting spaces
> while you were thinking of something else)

In this remarkable passage, Ammons suggests that in conventional narrative the writer is the slave of the reader's expectations. He must, like Samuel Johnson's playwright, please to live. But Ammons is trying to give poetry its thirteenth amendment. With the phrase "I am no slave that I/ should entertain you," Ammons deftly turns the poem's title into a racial pun. The poet who renounces his slavery is singing **"Coon Song"**; we should also remember that "coon songs" were a staple of the record industry at the turn of the century.

Of course, readers are ultimately the slaves of their expectations as well. Once Ammons forces us to admit that our hunger for narrative closure makes us long for the poet-coon's death—once we recognize the "sloppy silt" of our conventional expectations—then the wily beast paws more dust into our eyes and reverses the reversal:

> the hounds disappeared
> yelping (the way you would at extinction)
>   into—the order
>       breaks up here—immortality:
> I know that's where you think the brave
>   little victims should go:
>       I do not care what
> you think: I do not care what you think:
>   I do not care what you
>       think: one two three four five

When we've barely finished acknowledging our lust for blood and certainly, Ammons makes us acknowledge our guilt for rejoicing in the disappearance of the hounds. We may have switched from sadism to sentimentality, but Ammons wants us to see that both are conventional poses that he wishes to avoid. To acknowledge the shattering of the order that he himself has helped to create, the poet violates his customary pattern of line indentations.

If Ammons has not purged us of our preconceptions, he at least has encouraged us to recognize them for what they are. We never find out what "really happens" to that raccoon; but if we don't like leaving the possibilities open, we can provide our own closure while the poet takes time off to count. Thus, the poem is a collaborative enterprise in which the reader has the responsibility to listen to the poet, but not the duty to obey him. Similarly, the pet takes into account the reader's expectations but feels free to subvert them. We have, in short, an interpretive game whose rules lie somewhere between the ones posited by David Young and Harold Bloom in the passages quoted at the beginning of this essay.

The "two philosophies" at the end of the poem are not "spheres roll, cubes stay put," because both statements imply a similar fatalism. Rather, thc second philosophy is to be provided by the reader while Ammons counts:

> spheres roll, cubes stay put: now there
> one two three four five
> are two philosophies:
> here we go round the mouth-wet of hounds:
>
>> what I choose
>> is youse:
>> baby

At first glance, the last stanza might seem a non sequitur as well as a solecism. Once again, Ammons violates the pattern of indentation that hc has established, just as the streetwise colloquialism violates the rural setting of the poem. Yet these lines remind us of the digression in the second stanza ("Dostoevsky would think/ it important if the coon/ could choose"), and in doing so underscore an important difference between poetry and experience. There need be no practical constraints upon our choices as writers or readers: we are free to make our own chains. Ammons chooses to address us, just as we choose to read his poem, so the adversarial relationship between the *I* and the *you* is only one part of a deeper community of concerns. After upbraiding us for our imagined shortcomings throughout the poem, Ammons playfully embraces us in the last three lines: the slave who refused to entertain us has become the friend who does entertain us. This new relationship is mysterious, subversive, erotic, and just plain fun.

In more stately poems such as **"Expressions of Sea Level,"** the text can become the interface between writer and reader as it explores the interaction between ocean and land. In Richard Howard's fortuitous phrase, Ammons is "a littoralist of the imagination" [*Alone with America*], for he believes that both world and mind are most vital at their outer edges, where they are at the point of becoming something or someone else. Here, the possibilities and the dangers of change are greatest:

> The sea speaks far from its core,
> far from its center relinquishes the
> long-held roar:
>
> of any mid-sea
> speech, the yielding resistances
> of wind and water, spray,
> swells, whitecaps, moans,
>     it is a dream the sea makes,
>
> an inner problem, a self-deep
> dark and private anquish
>     revealed in small,
> by hints, to
> keen watchers on the shore:
>
> only with the staid land
> is the level conversation really held:
> only in the meeting of rock and
>     sea is
> hard relevance shattered into light

The poet, like the sea, finds expression and completion only on the periphery, only in contact with the other. Such contact can be observed but not explained or even entirely understood. The ocean-as-poet "erodes and/ builds" the land-as-reader in a never-ending meeting that can be both destructive ("shattered") and illuminating ("light").

The Ammons of the 1960's usually seems comfortable with the social dimension of his art. Yet on occasion he feels nostalgia for his earlier, more difficult work:

> I've come down into the
>     odor and warmth
>     of others: so much so that I
>         sometimes hit the ground and go
> off a ways looking, trying out:
>
> if startled, I break for the tree,
>     shinny up to safety, the eyes and
>     mouths large and hands working to my
> concern:
>     my risks and escapes are occasionally
> spoken of, approved: I've come down a lot.

> ("The Fall")

The fall from the isolation of the **Ommateum** poems "into the/ odor and warmth/ of others" seems problematic here. At the end of the 1970's, Ammons will shinny up that lonely tree once more in writing one of the most baffling works of his career, **The Snow Poems**.

**The Snow Poems** is easily the most controversial of Ammons' many books. Hayden Carruth's assesment of it is typical:

> In spite of a bright, attractive technique, which could be used perfectly well in real poems, and in spite of lyric parts that remind us of earlier work, **The Snow Poems** is a dull, dull book.
>
> ["Reader Participation Invited," *The New York Times Book Review,* September 25, 1977]

[In "Book Reviews: *The Snow Poems* and *The Selected Poems 1951-1977*," *The Georgia Review* 32 (Winter 1978)] Peter Stitt bluntly refers to "the disaster of **The Snow Poems**" while praising the earlier lyrics.

There's no denying that it is a strange and often maddening book—292 pages of whistling in the slush. When I first read it, my response was similar to another critic's reaction to **Tape for the Turn of the Year,** Ammons' most idiosyncratic work of the 1960's: "not so much a poem as the ground of a poem, the dark backing of a mirror out of which all brightness may, as a condition, come" [Howard, *Alone with America*].

But after rereading **The Snow Poems** (twice!), I have come to regard it not as a notebook in verse but as a measured, finished work which, oddly enough, encourages us to wonder whether the "finish" of poetry is a kind of death-worship.

The book begins with the aging poet's guilt and resentment:

by the time
a poem is the world
the author is
out of town
pushing fifty—

("**Words of Comfort**")

As the poems accumulate, the melting and reappearance of their snow is reminiscent of the dissolution and reappearance of the self in **Ommateum**. The desert has been replaced by a seemingly endless Ithaca winter dragging on into spring, and the atmosphere of the new book is less rarefied than what we find in the early poems. Yet the obsession with death, alienation, and discontinuity is remarkably similar.

The individual poems often end with abrupt shifts in voice, tone, and subject. In the critical lingo of our time, *The Snow Poems* contains a strong deconstructive impulse that Ammons has expressed more directly in other forums. He states in a 1978 interview with Cynthia Haythe that "All I mean to do [in my poems] is to overturn the Western mind!" [*Contemporary Literature* 21 (1980)]. He goes onto explain his preference for appreciation over analysis:

. . . I have a very strong attachment to readers. Now on the other hand, if you live in a university community, you constantly hear things being explained. It gets to the point where it looks as if the explanation is going to replace the reality.

*The Snow Poems* could be subtitled "A Diatribe Against Explanations." It contains spoofs of the spirit behind academic literary criticism:

I do not care what anybody
thinks of anything, really:
that is to say, I have not
found the flavor of orange
juice diminished or increased
by this or that approach to
Heidegger or Harmonium: I
believe the constituency of
water has remained constant
since the Pleides:
I don't think that any
attitude I take to spider webs
will faze flies: have you seen
Stanley Fish in the flesh:

("**You Think of the Sun That It**")

Things and feelings are ultimately stronger than ideas. All the poems in *The Snow Poems* have their first lines as their titles; Ammons tries to avoid even the appearance of the overarching orders that his commentators so inordinately prize.

The entire book is aggressively fragmentary, and therein (perhaps) lies its purpose. X. J. Kennedy's appraisal of the earlier *Tape* is relevant here:

It is as if [Ammons] were trying to prove how much dull junk his barge can triumphantly float.

["Translations from the American," *The Atlantic Monthly,* March, 1973]

But in *The Snow Poems,* Ammons is out to sink the barge, not just to test it. He seems to be asking the following question: Whatlies before or beyond or after the lyric experience that both poets and readers worship? "**Hard Lard,**" for example, contains the following reminiscence:

here's little poem I jotted down this
morning: it's about a complete action,
ah, except for the purple do: the starlings,
having hung sideways on the music building's
ivyvine collection while picking the berries,
sit meditatively high in the branches of the
oak to rest and then the berries
that had not fallen from the vines fall
from the lofts of oak, empurpling do's
sparse rain:
        [-]
the starlings barely
got the berries
off the vines
before snow
lineations loaded
them up again

As the poet listens to snow fall on the windowpanes, he willingly supplies the "do" that is absent from his earlier work. Do also deserves its due, he implies. Although the urge to purify in lyric poetry may please our nostrils, it can also impoverish the mind's soil.

In the next stanza of "**Hard Lard,**" Ammons recalls pulling up a small maple tree that was growing too close to his garage. For purely practical reasons, the tree had to go. But there is no practical imperative in poetry. We can have the purple do and the tree next to the garage if we wish. And if we lose something in the process, we gain something also.

In *The Snow Poems,* Ammons often subverts the lyric impulse behind his earlier, shorter poems by showing how random thoughts (especially sexual and scatological ones) occur at the most inopportune moments—even, great heavens, while we're writing poems. "**Poetry Is the Smallest**" has the strangest ending of any work celebrating poetry's ability to number the streaks of the tulip:

poet friend of mine's          still his fat wife's
dick's so short                radiant every morning:
he can't pull it long enough   he humps well, probably,
to pee straight with:          stringing her out far and
not to pee on                  loose on the frail hook:
anybody by surprise            and, too, I notice she
sideways, he hunkers           follows his words
into the urinal so far         closely like one who
he looks like, to achieve,     knows what a tongue can do
relief:

Throughout *The Snow Poems,* Ammons is making jokes: juxtaposing philosophy with flatulence, NFL games with High Culture, the sublime with the absurd, in order to make us question our very classification. He is establishing a new periphery here—the one that lies between sense and surprise—to replace the beaches of his earlier lyrics as the locus of imaginative activity. Ammons writes like a man who is afraid of selling out to the glorified version of himself created by the literary establishment. By 1977, he is determined to flaunt his warts.

The contrapuntal technique of *The Snow Poems* echoes this whimsically aggressive nose-thumbing. Two stanzas develop side by side, irreconcilable yet (somehow, we want to trust) part of the same whole. "[A]rrange these words so that they make/ sense," Ammons tells us in **"Hard Fist"**; this is the battle cry to the reader throughout the book.

As long as we take this challenge in the right spirit, and don't insist upon our "sense" of the poem being unique and determinate, then there's no problem. We can let the ideas, images, and emotions of *The Snow Poems* accumulate and dissolve, just as the snow does in the many passages involving the weather. It's only when we wish to freeze *The Snow Poems* permanently in our minds—when we become pedants eager to make "the explanation replace the reality"—that we feel uneasy:

> if you could,
> for example, set poetry off
> into 10 orders of this and
> that, subsidiary systems spelled out, lifted into
> interpenetrative connection
> with what is perceived to be,
> you could call it preserved
> territory, a public or private
> garden, identity certain:
> but poetry resists this, yielding to erosion,
> horse manure, bird droppings,
> pine needles, the wind, moss,
> bracket, bract, stone of change,
> a troublesome, marvelous garden:
> fertility inexhaustible, a milling:
>                     **("The Prescriptive Stalls As")**

So the poet becomes a befuddled befuddler, one of whose most important tasks is to reveal our blind confidence in the too-easy orders of the lyric impulse, just as **"Coon Song"** revealed our blind confidence in narrative momentum. The poet seeks not closure, but an openness that can sometimes include closure:

> poetry operates, not to deny
> the abstraction or the
> particular and not to diminish
> the distance between them but
> to hold in relation the
> widest play between them
>                     **("A Seventeen Morning")**

*The Snow Poems* contains a mixture of insults and apologies, neither to be taken entirely seriously, for seriousness

is one of the most insidious of the lyric closures that we must resist:

> may a fart pule brow billows
> about your earlobes
>
>         . . . . .
>
> I am not wise
> please forgive for writing
>                     **("Quilted Spreads")**

But just as the author of **Ommateum** finally comes to question his own questioning, so does the author of *The Snow Poems* occasionally wonder whether he's gone too far:

> I suppose I've
> worried too much
> abut the outbreak
> of destructive
> clarification
>                     **("As for Fame I've Had It")**

The dominant tendency of *The Snow Poems,* however, is to eschew this single vision and to concentrate instead upon trying "to/ murmur, stammer, swear, and/ sing on the edges of or around/ or deep into the unspeakable . . ." (**"I'm Unwilling"**). The final poem of the book gives us perhaps the best advice for considering it as a whole. **"They Say It Snowed"** is a lyric encapsulation of this often anti-lyrical work. Here, the snow that covers the rest of the book gives way to its memory, as the book itself recedes into the reader's own past. Ammons is outside his home, cleaning up after the profligate "lord of volition," the cruising teenagers who pass by on Hanshaw Road:

> I pick up after them and find
> the slug has made a home under
> the gumwrapper or grass is
> holding and hiding a
> Schaefer can
> filled with the plump, pulp
> bellies of mosquito larvae:
>     the lords of volition
>     caring for their own
>     natures care for nature
>     around them; they expend,
> satisfy, create . . .

Ammons, assuming the role of homeowner and lyric poet, is busy tidying up the excesses of others. If we have been tempted to become impatient with the author of *The Snow Poems,* just as he is tempted to become impatient with those teenagers, we should also remember the value of raw vitality—something that doesn't get through the gate at garden parties or in lyric poems.

The reader and writer walk off into the future at poem's end. Ammons tells us that he will catch up on his correspondence; then, after he has already given us nearly 300 pages of poems, he offers to send us not one letter, but several:

> how many

should I
put you
down for

The poem's final word, "we(l)come," contains a greeting within its insistence upon sexuality and the future. Writer and reader are never finished; the world is never exhausted.

I am intrigued by **The Snow Poems,** but in the end, I must say that my reaction to it is much like my reaction to John Ashbery's work: I find it more enjoyable to talk about than to read. I am glad Ammons has written the book, but I hope that he doesn't write it again; a little deconstruction (as any reader of recent literary theory will attest) can go a long way. Ammons may be right in saying that the lyric impulse is incomplete, but it is the kind of incompleteness that I think poetry ultimately needs.

Ammons has renewed his alliance with change in the early 1980's. His new journey seems to be toward silence, as Helen Vendler notes in her review of the 1982 volume, **Worldly Hopes**:

> The short poems here are more of Ammons' experiments in the minimal. The question is how few words can make a poem, and how densely can a few words be made to resonate. ["Spheres and Ragged Edges," *Poetry*, October, 1982]

If **The Snow Poems** is insistently garrulous, insistently more inclusive and therefore more diffuse that the poetry to which we are accustomed, **Worldly Hopes** (like the earlier **Briefings**) is just as insistently exlusive, inviting extensions rather than consolidations from the reader. Once again, Ammons has changed the focal length and the field of vision in his work.

His 1981 volume, **A Coast of Trees,** is the lyrical midpoint between his macrocosmic and his microcosmic extremes. The book begins with the "thesis" of **The Snow Poems:** all orders, however tentative, are ultimately false, and we must embrace the particular, the absence (hole) of order if we are to find the wholeness and holiness of the world:

> how are we to find holiness,
> our engines of declaration put aside,
> helplessness our first offer and sacrifice,
> except that having given up all mechanisms of
> approach, having accepted a shambles of
> non-enterprise, we know a unity
> approach divided, a composure past
> sight: then, with nothing, we turn
> to the cleared particular . . .
>
> ("**Coast of Trees**")

But this poem is within the realm of lyric assertion as it qualifies assertions of unity. In "**Continuing,**" one of the most moving poems in the new book, the fiftyish poet tries to discover "the accumulation/ of fifty seasons" of leaves beneath a tree, but he can discern only two:

. . . under that

sand or rocksoil already mixed
with the meal or grist:
is this, I said to the mountain,
what becomes of things:
well, the mountain said,
one mourns the dead but who
can mourn those the dead mourned

Here, the elegiac tone of **The Snow Poems** is reunited with the lyric impulse. "**White Dwarf**" presents us with an image of the poet that will become the aesthetic center of his next book:

> As I grow older
> arcs swollen inside
> now and then fall
> back, collapsing, into
> forming walls:
> the temperature shoots
> up with what I am not
> and am: from
> multiplicities, dark
> knots, twanging twists,
> structures come into sight,
> chief of these
> a blade of fire only now
> so late, so sharp and standing,
> burning confusion up.

This vision of the aging poet seems close to the "old man's eagle mind" that we find in Yeats' last poems. But Ammons' rag and bone shop of the heart is less rhetorically heightened. He sees his earlier works not as a collection of circus animals but as the balloons of "**Breaking Out**":

> . . . they are all let loose
> yellow, red, blue, thin-skinned, tough
> and let go they have put me down
> I was an earth thing all along
> my feet are catching in the brush

**Worldly Hopes** is a book of small motions: squirrels in trees, a leaf in the wind, a shrub rising when the ice is kicked from it, a hermit lark singing. Ammons gives us his new aesthetic in "**Progress Report**":

> Now I'm
> into things
> so small
> when I
> say boo
> I disappear

Assertions of Ammons' kinship with Emerson have become commonplace; many critics note, usually with praise, his tendency to become on occasion the "transparent eyeball" of *Nature*: "I am nothing," Emerson tells us; "I see all." This is clearly the spirit behind poems such as "**Spruce Woods**":

> It's so still
> today that a

dipping bough means
a squirrel has gone through.

Ammons' long poems tend to operate in a Heideggerean universe: *Die sprache spricht;* language itself is the foreground. That is how *The Snow Poems* achieves many of its disquieting effects. But the Ammons of *Worldly Hopes* tries to shake us up in a different way: here, *das ding spricht,* as Husserl and Williams say that it should, and Ammons eagerly follows his own line of sight, phenomenological pencil in hand. Ammons' new short poems encourage the reader to say boo and disappear along with him, to abandon momentarily the ego's labyrinth of language.

Ammons seems to draw strength from the extremes of his art. I am not entirely comfortable with either his smallest poems or his largest ones. Yet I see that without these poles, the marvelous, informing tension between concentration and expansiveness might not exist in poems such as **"Expressions of Sea Level," "Coon Song" "Corsons Inlet," "The City Limits,"** and **"Easter Morning."**

And my experience with the long works has expanded my notion of what poetry can be. Donald Davie has had a similar response:

> Whatever the opposite of an ideal reader is, I ought to have been that thing as far as [*Sphere*] is concerned. How could I be anything but exasperated by it, profoundly distrustful, sure I was being bamboozled, sure I was being threatened? And how is it, then, that I was on the contrary *enraptured?* Have I gone soft in the head? . . . No. I am as suspicious as ever I was of Ammons' initial assumptions and governing preoccupations . . . And yet I can't refuse the evidence of my senses and my feelings. . . . [*The New York Review of Books* March 6, 1975]

Like Davie, I am a formalist at heart, and I share some of his skepticism along with much of his enchantment. After reading Ammons' work, I still feel that a form of my own choosing liberates me from a confusion that is not of my own choosing. But Ammons has given me the black rich country of another point of view; I have chosen to walk with him in it, and I am grateful for his company.

---

**Contrasting impulses in Ammons's poetry:**

A. R. Ammons means to be a meditative poet, but he keeps getting distracted. He would, like Wallace Stevens, write the poem of the mind in the act of finding, but what he finds, as often as not, is natural appearance or natural fact. He is thus led around to a conflicting tradition, that of Frost, in which ideas are presented not directly but through the medium of natural imagery. His poems shuttle back and forth between image and abstraction, description and discursion, even seeming, on occasion, to blur those distinctions. Confusing those opposites, Ammons at times successfully accommodates both; when he attempts to compromise, he more often falls down between them.

*Vernon Shetley, "Nature and Self," in* The New York Times Book Review, *May 10, 1981.*

---

**Stephen B. Cushman  (essay date 1987)**

SOURCE: "Stanzas, Organic Myth, and the Metaformalism of A. R. Ammons," in *American Literature,* Vol. 59, No. 4, December, 1987, pp. 513-27.

[*Cushman is an American educator and critic. In the following essay, he attempts to define the structural principle of Ammons's verse, focusing on such features as stanza shape and length, typography, and linguistic patterns.*]

In his long poem **"The Ridge Farm"** (1983), A. R. Ammons continues his persistent meditation on poetic form:

> don't think we don't
> know one breaks
> form open because he fears
> its bearing in on him . . .
> and one hugs form because
> he fears dissolution, openness,
> we know, we know:
> one needs stanzas to take
> sharp interest in and
> one interest the stanza
> down the road to the wilderness:

This passage uses the word "form" in suggestive ways. Unlike the "completed, external form" Ammons renounces in the "Foreword" to *Ommateum* (1955), where "external" suggests nonorganic rigidity and "completed" implies the kind of autotelic closure Charles Olson, among others, was lobbying against when Ammons wrote his first poems, "form" in the later poem both repels and attracts. In a characteristic gesture, the passage opens with Ammons' version of epanalepsis, an enjambed line which begins and ends with the same word: "don't think we don't." Here this self-enclosing pattern, one Ammons uses in different ways throughout his work, is revealed by the conventions of Ammons' lineation rather than by the unaided contours of his syntax. In this opening line, Ammons breaks his syntax against a line in order to discover a buried repetition, one to which the syntactic pattern alone would not normally call attention. If "one breaks/ form open because he fears" it, one also breaks form, such as the form of a syntactic pattern, in order to reveal other hidden structures.

The humor implicit in this passage arises from its deliberate self-betrayal. While the passage extols the stanza, it builds no stanzas, although other parts of **"The Ridge Farm"** do. In fact, the passage neither breaks nor hugs form in any remarkable way. Ammons casts this passage in the familiar shape of a left-justified stichic column, the lines of which fall mostly between the lengths of traditional trimeters and tetrameters. In his *Collected Poems* (1972), this shape appears only twice among poems written between 1951 and 1955 (**"Chaos Staggered"** and **"Bees Stopped"**), but with the poems written between 1966 and 1971, grouped mostly in *Uplands* (1970) and *Briefings* (1971), it becomes, along with the tercet, one of his dominant visual patterns. At least once in the passage, the faint trace of an iambic sequence becomes audible:

```
     /        /        /        /        /
  because he fears/ its bearing in on him
```

Because Ammons is a self-proclaimed "free-versite" [*The Snow Poems*], an occasional iambic string may seem like a simple accident of language, inhering in the structure of English. But to argue this is a bit naive, since iambic forms can be broken, and usually are by Ammons, as easily as they can be constructed. Furthermore, this particular iambic eddy corresponds neatly to an expression of formal claustrophobia.

At its best, the breaking of form establishes a principle of "uneasy pleasures" [**"The Ridge Farm"**]. The poet breaks in order to remake in order to break again. The flight from form is constant and the refuge in form temporary. Behind the ironic humor of Ammons' know-it-all voice and his stanza-less advertisement for the stanza lies a deep confusion, confusion that vexes not only this passage but also the entire poem **"The Ridge Farm"** and much of the thirty-year work which precedes it. The confusion is about the relationship of polarities, specifically the polarity of form and formlessness.

The blending, or "confusion" in its radical sense, of form and formlessness is especially evident in Ammons' use of stanzas. More often than not, his stanzas do not satisfy Paul Fussell's requirement that "in poems written in fixed or nonce stanzas separate and different shapes should embody separate and different things" ["Poetic Meter and Poetic Form," revised edition, 1979]. In other words, Ammons' stanzas have little or no logical integrity, an integrity Fussell includes among his "principles of excellence in stanzaic forms." Furthermore, since they have no such integrity, they do not satisfy another of Fussell's requirements that they, like a particular meter, "should give the illusion of having arisen intrinsically and subtly from within the uniqueness of the poetic occasion." Since Ammons' stanzas make no attempt to give this illusion, but in fact often seek to dismantle it, Fussell would say they are not organically part of his poems.

Ammons' stanzas appear to challenge the Romantic myth of organicism, particularly its boldly hyperbolic American versions initiated by Whitman. As John Hollander comments on the fulfillment of Emersonian prophecy in "The Poet" by *Leaves of Grass,* "Organic form is to be the emblem, then, of the authenticity of the text, although the precise nature of the form is not made clear" [*Vision and Resonance: Two Senses of Poetic Form,* 2nd edition, 1985]. In fact, the vexingly imprecise nature of what poetic form has to do to be considered "organic" harasses many discussions. Is organicism a condition the poem aspires to in its imaginative movement but not necessarily in its prosody? in its prosody only? in both? Donald Wesling's definition of organic form, which echoes Fussell's emphasis on "illusion," is helpfully clear and usefully concise: "This, or the illusion of it, is what the successful poem has when it justifies the arbitrariness of its technique; and what the failed poem lacks, when its technique seems obtrusively imposed. . . . I would define organic form as convention in its innovative guise" [*The Chances of Rhyme:*

*Device and Modernity,* 1980]. Although Wesling singles out rhyme to stand for technique and convention, one would assume that other techniques and conventions, of genre (lyric, dramatic, narrative), type (song, monologue, dream), and prosody, would also work with this definition.

In Ammons' poetry, the myth of organicism, which his seemingly arbitrary stanzas appear to reject, in fact embodies itself in subtle and complex ways, although Hyatt Waggoner is not alone in taking Ammons' organicism at face-value: "Ammons, like most of his best contemporaries, has moved all the way toward practicing the theory announced in 'The Poet' and elaborated in 'Poetry and Imagination'" ["On A. R. Ammons," in *Contemporary Poetry in America,* edited by Robert Boyers, 1974]. But for someone who "has moved all the way" toward practicing Emersonian theory, Ammons has much to say on the subject of artifice and artificiality in poetry, and in his poetry in particular. In *Tape for the Turn of the Year* (1965), for example, he states baldly: "poetry is art & is/ artificial: but it/ realizes reality's/ potentials." In **"Extremes and Moderations,"** he adds:

> everything, they say, is artificial: nature's
>    the
> artwork of the Lord: but your work, city, is aimed
>    unnaturally
> against time: your artifice confronts the Artifice:

And in **"Hibernaculum,"** he ponders artifice in the context of the promotion of art over nature which Oscar Wilde preaches, for example, in his essay "The Decay of Lying."

Predictably, Ammons' only explicit commentary on organicism comes in the course of a poem, the long **"Essay on Poetics,"** originally published in 1970. The earliest of the longer poems which use the long-line tercet (**"Hibernaculum," Sphere,** and **"Summer Place"** are the others), **"Essay on Poetics"** maintains a relentless loyalty to its own stanzaic regularity, even as it interpolates into various stanzas three shorter poems, three long quotations from scientific texts, and one column of words. After each of these interruptions, the respective stanzas pick up where they left off, often in the middle of lines. Apparently a meditation on the nature of the lyric versus its own longer "linear mode," Ammons' **"Essay"** at one point reads Williams' dictum "no ideas but in things" into various alternatives: "'no things but in ideas,'/ 'no ideas but in ideas,' and 'no things but in things.'" This revision of the famous refrain of *Paterson* leads to an extended figuring of different poetic modes in terms of the stages of water flowing, as it goes from snow-melt to brook-rapids, to slow river, and finally to sea:

> genius, and
> the greatest poetry, is the sea, settled, contained
>    before the first
> current stirs but implying in its every motion
>    adjustments
> throughout the measure:

Both the word "measure" and the image of a river running to the sea suggest that the dialogue with Williams and

*Paterson* continues throughout this section. [In *A. R. Ammons,* 1978] Alan Holder contends that here Ammons is pointing up "the inadequacy of William Carlos Williams' famous prescription for the poet." Certainly, Ammons is examining that prescription critically ("one thing/ always to keep in mind is that there are a number of possibilities"); yet in the adoption of Williams' image of the river running to the sea, an image which despite his own brooks and falls he does not use often, Ammons may also be making his pact with Williams, who in his own way challenges the organicist label too often applied to him.

As Henry Sayre has argued convincingly, Williams' "notoriously inadequate explanations of the so-called variable foot are most usefully seen as efforts to defend as organic what through the 1940s and 1950s is more and more evidently a formally mechanical and arbitrary practice" [*The Visual Text of William Carlos Williams,* 1983]. Like Williams, Ammons invents a three-line stanza that is mechanical (in Schlegel's sense of the word), arbitrary, and artificial. But unlike Williams, Ammons does not try to defend that artificiality with a rhetoric of traditional organicism. Instead, the exact opposite is true. He challenges the rhetoric of traditional organicism and flaunts the artificiality of his form. The challenge to organicism, or more precisely, literary organicism, comes near the end of **"Essay on Poetics"** in a long passage which begins

> the point of
> change, though,
> brings me to a consideration of the adequacy of the transcendental
> vegetative analogy: the analogy is so appealing, so swept with
> conviction, that I hardly ever have the strength to question it:

In his "consideration of the adequacy of the transcendental/ vegetative analogy," Ammons demystifies the literary rhetoric of organicism by confronting it with scientific literalism. As this passage argues, it is naive to think that a particular tree realizes itself according to innate individual laws. In fact, what is innate in a particular tree is not its own uniqueness, but quite the opposite, its pre-ordained genetic code, which nature protects against "haphazard change." The uniqueness of a given tree, then, results when its genetic "print-out" is modified from outside by "the bleak periphery of possibility," which includes "variables of weather,/ soil, etc."

Ammons' revised organicism has important implications for his poetics. If a tree develops according to a code that is genetically pre-ordained, and a given tree varies only according to local external modifications, then a truly organic poem is one that figuratively does the same. A truly organic poem reflects both the predetermination of structures it cannot change and the local variation of those structures where other conditions modify them. In Wesling's terms, Ammons' poem justifies the arbitrariness of its stanzaic regularity by letting that arbitrariness stand for predetermination, the poetic analogue of a locked-in genetic code. Each stanza is a print-out of the predetermined pattern; and

yet, like a given tree, a given stanza varies according to local effects, effects, in its case, of syntax, diction, rhythm, enjambment, and typography. Subsequently, Ammons multiplies organic analogies by quoting passages of prose, as Williams does in *Paterson.* One passage celebrates "a good worm," which has "developed segmentation or reduplication of parts, permitting increase in size with completely coordinated function," an apt self-description of **"Essay on Poetics."** Another passage describes "the molecular bricks out of which living matter is made," adding that "a mere random pile of such bricks does not make a living structure, any more than a mere pile of real bricks makes a house." By analogy, this statement also describes Ammons' own poem, as its stanzas are the brickshaped blocks that attempt to build a living structure instead of a mere pile.

**"Essay on Poetics"** provides a key to Ammons's formal intentions, especially in those poems which seem at first to organize themselves arbitrarily around regular typographic patterns, such as stanzas or indentations. In those poems, short and long, arbitrary regularity is the artifice by means of which Ammons, as he explains in *Tape,* "realizes reality's/ potentials." Although what nature predetermines for a white oak evolves through a series of favorable mutations, and so is not arbitrary in the way the selection of a stanza shape may be arbitrary, the stanza shape nevertheless represents the given, whether it be the organic given of a genetic pattern, the mental given of binary concepts, the linguistic given of modern American English, or the literary given of poetic tradition. One does not invent these; one inherits them. When Ammons closes **"Hibernaculum"** with the outrageously flippant stanza

> I'm reading Xenophon's *Oeconomicus*
> "with
> considerable pleasure and enlightenment" and with
> appreciation that saying so fills this stanza nicely.

he tweaks the noses of both the traditional formalist for whom the stanza is necessarily a metrical and auditory reality, never merely a typographic one, and the naive organicist who believes that a poem should never compromise content in order to fulfill the demands of a predetermined form. But beneath the humor lies more serious meaning. Disciple of Socrates, military leader, and historian, Xenophon presides over the close of **"Hibernaculum"** as a representative of the accumulated weight of a philosophical, historical, and literary past. His *Oeconomicus,* undoubtedly a model for the chapter "Economy" in Thoreau's *Walden,* casts Socrates in a dialogue on household management and married life, two subjects the domestically hibernating Ammons contemplates in **"Hibernaculum"** and elsewhere. In its casual way, Ammons' final stanza is about demands and expectations generated by the past, demands and expectations he did not create but still must meet. These exert a pressure on him which, no matter how much he may wish to believe otherwise, shapes his utterances.

**"Extremes and Moderations,"** which falls between **"Essay on Poetics"** and **"Hibernaculum"** in the 1966-1971 section of *Collected Poems,* opens and closes with remarks on its own four line stanza, unique among Ammons' longer poems. The introduction of the stanza again recalls Wesling's formulation that successful organicism involves the justification of arbitrary technique:

> constructing the stanza is not in my case
>   exceedingly
> difficult, variably invariable, permitting maximum
>   change
> within maximum stability, the flow-breaking four-
>   liner, lattice
>
> of the satisfactory fall, grid seepage, currents
>   distracted
> to side flow, multiple laterals that at some extreme
>   spill
> a shelf, ease back, hit the jolt of the central
>   impulse:

The admission that the construction of stanzas "is not in my case exceedingly difficult" anticipates the end of **"Hibernaculum"** in its unabashed acknowledgment of an artificiality which neither the traditional formalist nor the conventional organicist could justify. Meanwhile, the description of the stanza as "variably invariable" continues the argument from **"Essay on Poetics,"** abstracting it from the realm of white oaks and genetic printouts, yet preserving the conjunction of general predetermination with specific modification. Although "variably invariable" takes the rhetorical shape of oxymoron, Ammons' version of organicism demonstrates the necessary congruity of the variable and invariable. Images of water flowing through the stanza, "the flow-breaking four-liner, lattice/ of the satisfactory fall, grid seepage, currents distracted/ to side flow," prefigure images of form in *Sphere* (1974). In both poems, Ammons' images of flowing water recall the etymological meaning of "rhythm" (Greek *rein:* to flow), while his images of the stanza as "lattice," "grid," "log the stream flows against," and "mesh" describe the phenomenology of verse structure in new terms.

Etymologically, a "stanza" is a stopping-place, a place to stand. The word suggests a phenomenology of writing and reading that involves a series of stops between which one crosses white space or silence to get to the next stop. More recently in poetic tradition, occasional enjambment between stanzas may vary the stop-and-go pattern; yet such enjambment remains exceptional in most verse and should remain exceptional, according to those, such as Paul Fussell, who place high value on stanzaic integrity. The stanzaic repetition of stops and starts reflects the origin of stanzas in the strophic divisions of song, divisions which allow a singer to sing new verses to a recycled tune. As verse becomes more removed from its historical origins in song, structures that originated asauditory modes become increasingly visual. In Ammons' stanzas the removal from auditory origins is complete, his various images of the stanza implying a different model for writing and reading. Instead of a phenomenology of stopping and going, his stanzas generate one of speeding and slowing. If going ever stops, it stops only partially with a colon, and even then it stops much less than it continues.

The speeding and slowing of perpetual going, the presentation of some resistance or channel that flow must overcome or follow, revises another Romantic metaphor, that of the Aeolian harp. Although that image runs on wind and Ammons' on water, they share the fiction of an essential passivity. For Shelley in "Ode to the West Wind," the desire for inspiration leads to the petition "Make me thy lyre," while for Coleridge in "The Eolian Harp," the image prompts him to ask whether "all of animated nature," himself included, "Be but organic Harps diversely framed" over which "sweeps/ Plastic and vast, one intellectual breeze,/ At once the Soul of each, and God of all?"

At the close of **"Extremes and Moderations,"** written about the time that, as Harold Bloom points out [in "A. R. Ammons: 'When You Consider the Radiance,'" *The Ringers in the Tower,* 1971] "the motions of water . . . replaced the earlier guiding movements of wind" in Ammons' poetry, the Romantic metaphor surfaces in final remarks on the stanza:

>       the cumulative vent of our primal
> energies is now and
> always has been sufficient to blow us up: I have my
>   ventilator
> here, my interminable stanza, my lattice work that
>   lets the world
> breeze unobstructed through: we could use more
>   such harmless
> devices:

Punning on the Latin for wind (*ventus*), Ammons describes his ventilating stanza as both a device for passively letting the world breeze through and for venting his prophetic anger over our use and abuses of nature. Whether he describes the stanza in terms of wind or water, it remains his typographic version of the Romantic harp. In each case, the image of sweeping over, or breezing through, functions to naturalize poetic artifice. If the poetic imagination simply presents itself in the form of a harp or stanza to be acted upon by a wind or a stream, then that imagination cannot be held responsible for what results. The burden of structuring the poem shifts away from the poet, so that, at least in Ammons' case, he escapes having to account fully for his form. Whereas Ammons' revision of organicism allows him to justify arbitrariness by redefining "organic" in terms of scientific literalism, his version of the Aeolian harp allows him to do so by trivializing his own role as maker of "harmless/ devices."

Nowhere in Ammons's work have issues of form and formlessness, arbitrariness and organicism, poet as artificer and poet as innocent bystander, caused more disagreement and more misunderstanding than in *The Snow Poems* (1977) [in *American Poets: From the Puritans to the Present,* revised edition, 1984]. Waggoner pronounces the volume "a thick book of dull, tired poems that prompt us to wonder, does Ammons write too much?" *The Snow Poems* appeared too late for consideration by Holder, which is unfortunate, since the ways in which his judgments differ from Waggoner's represent a larger critical disagreement over Ammons' work. (Waggoner applauds *Tape for the*

*Turn of the Year,* calling it "good Emerson," but doesn't "much like" **"Summer Session."** Holder ranks **"Summer Session"** "among Ammons' most interesting poems," while in *Tape* he finds "egregious examples of the imitative fallacy," "verbal doodling," and tastelessness.) Amidst a swirl of negative reviews, such as Hayden Carruth's ("a dull, dull book") [*The New York Times Book Review,* [September 25, 1977]), Bloom has remained determinedly silent, while Helen Vendler has given the book limited but sympathetic attention: "Ammons has delineated that landscape and that climate [of Ithaca, New York] for good and all, with an Emersonian wintriness of voice diluting the ebullience he inherited from Williams" [*Part of Nature, Part of US,* 1980].

But most interesting is the reappraisal of *The Snow Poems* made by Michael McFee after the appearance of *A Coast of Trees* (1981) signaled Ammons' return to the short lyric. Although McFee blusters a bit too much against what he calls the "popular critical pacifier, as manufactured by Bloom and others, . . . that Ammons had come into the world to fulfill the Romantic Transcendental heritage, to realize the promise of Organic Form" ["A. R. Ammons and *The Snow Poems* Reconsidered," *Chicago Review,* 33, No. 1 (1981)], he does settle down to make two significant points. The first is that "as Ammons became more prominent, the form of his poetry became more conservative, taking on a more orderly and regular appearance." The second is that "the heart of *The Snow Poems*" is "Ammons' deep anti-formalism." Both of these assertions need re-examination, but they do serve to focus attention and lead toward conclusion.

When McFee argues that Ammons' form becomes more conservative as it takes on the orderly and regular appearance of uniform stanzas, he makes two mistakes. The first is that he reduces poetic form to mere format, or the typographic shape of a poem on the page. Williams often veered dangerously close to the same error, sometimes even committing it, but Ammons never does. For him, "form" is far too large and suggestive a term to let itself be contained within the boundaries of a stanza shape. Any account of his poetic forms must also reckon with rich phonetic configurations, syntactic patterns, rhetorical figures, and occasional metricality, as well as with the larger contours of his characteristic meditative habits. The second mistake is that McFee uses the unhelpful term "conservative" to describe what he apparently believes to be Ammons' devoted guardianship of the traditional stanza. If indeed he does believe that Ammons' stanzas imply an uncritical acceptance of at least one aspect of prosodic tradition, he is badly mistaken. In Ammons' hands, the stanza format is an instrument of humor, parody, playfulness, figuration, self-description, and poetic revision. The irreverent liberties he takes with his stanzas should disabuse us of any notion that his growing fame has caused him to think twice about formal experimentalism. As Ammons' more recent work has shown, especially **"The Ridge Farm,"** he can take or leave the stanza with no trouble at all.

But McFee's second statement, that the heart of *The Snow Poems* is a deep anti-formalism, reveals a crucial misunderstanding of Ammons' poetic program. To support his con-

tention, McFee quotes part of the poem **"One at One with his Desire"**:

> this stanza compels
> its way along: a
> break will humble it:
>
> form consumes:
> form eliminates:
> form forms the form
> that extracts of the elixir from
> the passages of change:

A full reading of this passage requires placement in its immediate context, but even without that context, McFee's reading is hard to justify: "He endorses the 'hellish paradise' susceptible to shit and wind change, not the artificial order of a stanza." Yes, a break will humble the stanzaic compulsion to repeat and rescue Ammons from the fear of overbearing form he expresses in **"The Ridge Farm."** But the subsequent lines about form consuming, eliminating, and extracting must not be misread to mean only that form constructs "inflexible structures which drain the elixir vitae of motion." The sequence of consumption, elimination, and extraction also suggests the digestive processes of an organism. In other words, although form may threaten to assume a Frankenstein-like autonomy, and so must be humbled if creator is to retain control over creation, still that form does have a life of its own. In fact, "the form/ that extracts of the elixir from/ the passages of change" performs a kind of alchemy, as it rescues from the rush of impermanence and dissolution a precious essence which remains. When this passage joins with a long one preceding it, the full complexity and pathos of Ammons' ambivalence toward his stanza, and toward abstractions of form it represents, emerges. This important passage, too long to quote in full, begins

> art's
> nonbeing's
> dark consolation:
> what a nice stanza! imagine just going
> on:

and ends

> what a numb pale
> paradise! how constant
> the music
> dwelling among the constant
> bushes, the deathlessness only
> lifelessness can know
> one not at one with his
> desire still has to desire
> so much more than nothing

This is not the voice of one who hates form. Instead, it is the deep, moving confession of a man who realizes that he has been shut out from rooms where life goes on immediately and unconsciously, shut out from the places where his desire can be fulfilled. As a result, the rooms that stanzas build, and the poems for which they stand as synecdoches, provide the only places for him to dwell. He is fully, radically disillusioned about the "numb pale/ paradise!" form encloses, its drug-like power that makes erasure bliss, or the misery "the uneasy" use it to cover. This last phrase recalls the "uneasy pleasures" Ammons identifies in **"The Ridge Farm."** But he sees no alternative. Life may be preferable to form, but form is the dark consolation of lifelessness. Against the background of these stark choices, the familiar figure of epanalepsis, "desire still has to desire," looms with uncanny power. Like the line McFee quotes, "form forms the form," in which repetition threatens to hollow "form" of its substance and meaning, this self-enclosed, self-mirroring line figures both the entrapment of desire and the poetic self-consciousness that gives desire form, if not fulfillment. Ammons gives the repetition of "desire" a twist, as he uses the word first as a noun and second as an infinitive, binding a state or condition to the process which generates it. These nuances may not be much, but they are "so much more than nothing."

This hugging of form for preservation, consolation, and in a displaced, deflected, uneasy way, pleasure, makes for its own peculiar formalism. Admittedly, Ammons cannot be considered a formalist in the same strictly limited sense in which his contemporaries Richard Wilbur, Anthony Hecht, John Hollander, James Merrill, and Howard Nemerov can. As he says in "A Note on Prosody" [*Poetry*, 102 (1963)], "the box-like structure of rhymed, measured verse is pretty well shot" in his verse, and so are his credentials as a traditional prosodist. But what McFee identifies as "antiformalism" in *The Snow Poems* is in reality something else. It is the "strong antivisionary current flowing in Ammons' poetry," to which Waggoner calls our attention [in *American Visionary Poetry*, 1982]. Similarly, McFee's suggestion that some have rejected *The Snow Poems* for its lack of stanzaic regularity is questionable. The end of the twentieth century is far too late in the history of American poetry to squabble about whether or not traditional prosody should rule, but it is never too late to question whether the proper business of the poet is simple notation or transforming vision. Those who reject *The Snow Poems*—and I am not one—object to its antivisionary overinclusiveness, not its alleged antiformalism.

Ammons, then, cannot be considered a formalist, in the usual sense of the term, but neither can he be dismissed as an antiformalist. His need of some form of form remains too acute, his explicit considerations of form too insistent. Instead, Ammons' work embodies a kind of metaformalism. In the same way that Stevens produced a metapoetry about poetry, Ammons has produced and continues to produce poetic forms about themselves, their own phenomenological power, and their own ontological significance. In this way, he resembles Williams, especially the Williams of the often self-descriptive *Paterson*. But unlike Williams, whose poems also struggle to engage the world of people and history, in its many social, political, and economic phases, a struggle which sometimes burdens his fictions of form, Ammons has meditated on form to the exclusion of these other concerns. Such exclusion betokens aloofness, but for him aloofness is not so much a conscious choice as a condition he wakes to find himself in. Through poetic

form, and the poetic fictions it generates, he struggles to reattach himself, first to the larger capabilities of the human mind, second to the natural world which preceded and remains separate from him, and third to whatever else, beyond these, is available.

## A. R. Ammons with William Walsh (interview date 1988)

SOURCE: An interview in *Michigan Quarterly Review,* Vol. XXVIII, No. 1, Winter, 1989, pp. 105-17.

[*In the following interview, which was conducted in March 1988, Ammons speaks about his literary career and his poetry.*]

[Walsh]: *I read an interview the other day where the guest was asked if there was a question he had always wanted to answer, but had never been asked.*

[Ammons]: Most of the questions I have been asked have had to do with literary reputations rather than what I considered the nature of poetry, that is, what is poetry and how does it work? In what way is it an action or a symbolic action? In what way does poetry recommend certain kinds of behavior? Questions like that are of absorbing interest to me. What Robert Bly or somebody else is doing is of no interest to me whatsoever. I've written my poetry more or less in isolation without any day-to-day contact with other writers. Though I have read tidbits in anthologies of other people, I've made no study of anybody else's work, except in school where I read Shelley, Keats, Chaucer, and so on. I like questions that address, if they can, the central dynamics of this medium we work with, not that any answer is possible, but that we meditate the many ways in which it represents not only our verbal behavior but other representative forms of behavior—how poetry resembles other actions such as ice skating or football. That is to say, I think poetry is extremely important because it's central to other actions, and it should not be pushed far to the side as a strictly academic study or a technical investigation.

*Do you think poetry is threatened by becoming an academic subject?*

To the extent that it is a mere object of study, yes. I worry about that, because it means that the action of the poem and the mind, the action of the body of the poem itself, is going to be paraphrased into discursiveness—something is going to be said about it which will be different from the original action. And while I don't know how classes can be conducted any other way, that's not why poems are written. They are not written in order to be studied or discussed, but to be encountered, and to become standing points that we can come to and try to feel out, impressionistically, what this poem is recommending. Is it recommending in a loud voice, extreme action, or is its action small, does it think we should look closely at things, should we forget the little things and look at some big inner problem, should we understate our stances toward the world, or does hyperbole work better, is this a shallow poem, or is there some profound way that it achieves something it didn't even mean to achieve? In other words, we're trying to live our lives and we go to these representative, symbolic actions to test out what values seem to have precedence over others. If human beings in this country or wherever could approach poetry more in that way rather than as an historical or strictly theoretical form of study, then they might feel the ball of strength in poetry and come to it because it would inform and excite them the way Madonna does or punk rock does. Of course, I'm not insisting that poetry become a popular medium. It requires the attention that few people are willing to give it. I kind of wish that weren't so.

*Many of the people I've come in contact with who don't read poetry say it's because they don't understand it.*

"Understanding something" has been defined for them as a certain system of statements made about something. If they don't get a very good statement about the poems, it means they haven't opened themselves to the rhythm, pacing, sounds of words, colors, and images that they are supposed to move into. Who understands his own body? I mean the gorillas have been walking around for two hundred and fifty thousand years with extremely complicated enzymic and other operations going on in their blood streams that they know nothing about, which prevented them not at all from being gorillas. We're the same case. What are we supposed to understand about poetry? I've studied and worked with poetry since I was eighteen. Poetry astonishes me day after day. I see something else that is somehow implicated in that. I never expect to understand it. You see, there's where the problem is. The kind of understanding that was defined for these people, most people, has been trivial and largely misses the poem.

*You spent the first seventeen years of your life in the South, in Whiteville, North Carolina. Could you discuss your background leading up to your first interest in writing?*

It covers the period people like to cover in ten years of psychotherapy and don't give up and walk away until they have an answer. [*Laughing*] I was born in 1926, just toward the end of the good times—the Twenties into the Depression. Our family had a pretty rough time on the farm. We had a small subsistence farm of fifty acres on which my grandfather had raised thirteen children, and which in my father's hands became a cash crop farm that was not large enough to raise enough cash. Yet, we didn't do the dozens of things that would have continued it as a subsistence farm. Apparently, my grandfather had done very well. So we were caught in that kind of bind, aggravated by the Depression, about which you've heard endless rumors—all true. [*Laughing*] It was a rather desperate time until the beginning of the war provided jobs for people, and changes—radical changes. Do you realize that when I was born in 1926 something like 85 percent of the people in the country were rural, lived on a farm, and now it's about 3 percent? So the most incredible silent revolution has taken place just in my lifetime.

After I graduated from high school in 1943 I worked for a shipbuilding company in Wilmington, then entered the Navy when I was eighteen. I was in the South Pacific for nineteen months, came back and entered Wake Forest College in the summer of 1946 on the G. I. Bill. Nobody in my family had gone to college before. It was a truly daunting experience for me. My major was pre-med and I minored in English, and then everything collapsed into a kind of general science degree.

*You started in a pre-med program with hopes of becoming a doctor?*

Yes, I did. I think it came out of a general interest in things and people and feelings. To be a doctor would have been to get completely out of the mess I was in as a farmer. It was a different social and economic level. I didn't pursue it beyond my undergraduate degree. I had wanted to stay a farmer, but my father sold the farm. So, that option was eliminated. I love the land and the terrible dependency on the weather and the rain and the wind. It betrays many a farmer, but makes the interests of the farmer's life tie in very immediately with everything that's going wrong meteorologically. I miss that. That's where I got my closeness and attention to the soil, weeds, plants, insects, and trees.

*Prior to studying English in college had you written very much?*

The first poem I wrote was in the tenth grade, where you have to write a poem in class. It was on Pocahontas. Then I didn't write anymore until I was in the South Pacific and discovered a poetry anthology when I was on the ship. Then I began to write experimentally and imitatively. There was a man on ship who had a Master's degree in languages and I began to study Spanish with him. We didn't have a text; he just made it up as he went along. It somehow gave me a smattering of grammar—you know how helpful it is with your own grammar to study another language. Pretty soon I was writing regularly. Then I came to Wake Forest where there were no creative writing classes, but I continued to write for four years. About a month before I left Wake Forest I finally got up the nerve to show some of my poems to the professors and they were very encouraging. From then on, my mind, my energies, were focused on poetry even though I had to do what everyone else does—try to figure out some way to make a living.

*You didn't begin by sending your poems to small magazines, did you?*

I didn't even know they existed. I was just totally ignorant of the literary scene. What a load that is on the mind not to know what the configuration, the landscape of the literary world is. I got married the year I was the principal of the elementary school in Cape Hatteras. From there we went to Berkeley, where I did further study in English, working toward a Master's degree. I took my poems to Josephine Miles, a fine poet and critic who died a couple of years ago. She consented to read my poems and said I should send them out. That's where I first heard about literary magazines.

*Your first book of poetry, **Ommateum,** failed terribly.*

I believe the publisher knew it wouldn't sell and so they only bound one hundred copies of the three hundred sheets pressed. It sold sixteen copies the first five years. Five libraries bought it—Princeton, Harvard, Yale, Berkeley, and Chapel Hill, only because they bought everything. My father-in-law sent forty copies to people he knew in South America. I bought back thirty copies for thirty cents each. So I guess you could say it failed miserably. One review in *Poetry* magazine, my first review, was favorable. But now **Ommateum** goes for about thirteen hundred dollars a copy.

*The reason I brought this up is because you did not publish another collection of poetry for nine years. What transpired in those nine years, between the time you wrote* **Ommateum** *and* **Expressions of Sea Level,** *that produced a resounding critical change in your work?*

We cannot imagine, sitting here, how long nine years is. I just kept writing, resubmitting manuscripts, tearing them apart, putting them back together, getting rejected, trying again, and so on until I was finally rejected by everybody. I took my work to a vanity publisher in New York City and I was turned down by them, too. I went to Bread Loaf in 1961 and met Milton Kessler, who at that time was teaching at Ohio State University. He said their press was starting a poetry series and I should send my poems early on before the hundreds of manuscripts began to arrive. I did and they took it. It was favorably reviewed, but it took ten years for them to sell eight hundred copies. I used to get monthly statements from them saying this month we've sold three copies, this month we sold four. For ten years this happened, and I'm not sure they ever sold all one thousand copies. It is amazing how favorably it was reviewed. I just saw *The Oxford Companion to American Literature* which has an article on me saying from the day *Expressions of Sea Level* was published, A. R. Ammons was a major poet. . . . Nobody told me then that I was a major poet.

Now, as to what happened to the poetry itself, that's a story so long I wouldn't know how to tell you. I'd have to go back over the stages, the failures, the rebeginnings, and so on. It isn't easy to be a poet. I think if the young poets could realize *that* they would be off doing something else. It takes a long time. It took me a long time. I do believe there are poets who begin right at the top of their form, and usually are exhausted in five years. In a way I wasn't bad either early on. **Ommateum** remains a very powerful influence with me.

*Who do you see as starting at the top of their form?*

I just happen to think of James Tate, who won a national prize when he was twenty-two. I don't mean to say he burned out. There are poets who seem to be at their best right away. I'm a slow person to develop and change. The good side of that is that it leaves me so much more to do.

*When you look back at the poems in* **Ommateum** *as a whole what is your reaction? Do you still feel the same way?*

It's a very strong book. It may be my best book. *Expres-*

*sions of Sea Level,* though more widely welcomed, more obviously ingratiates itself to an easier kind of excellence. The **Ommateum** poems are sometimes very rigid and ritualistic, formal and off-putting, but very strong. The review I got said, these poems don't care whether they are listened to or not. Which is exactly true. I had no idea there was such a thing as an audience; didn't care if there was. I was involved in the poem that was taking place in my head and on the page and that was all I cared about. If I had known there were millions of people out there wanting to buy my book, which of course is not the case, it would have been nice. But an audience meant nothing to me. Someone else said that I was a poet who had not yet renounced his early poems. I never intend to renounce those poems. [*Laughing*] I have published some inferior poems in each volume— that's inevitable. But as Jarrell said, if you are lucky enough to write a half a dozen good poems in your life, you would be lucky indeed.

*Critics have traced your creative genealogy to several influences: Whitman, Thoreau, Emerson, Pound, Stevens, Frost. One critic stated, "Ammons's poetry is founded on the implied Emersonian division of experience into Nature and the Soul." Would you agree with their findings?*

First of all, one has been influenced by everything in one's life, poetic and otherwise. There have been predominant influences, such as Robert Browning, whom I imitated at great length as an undergraduate, writing soliloquies and dramatic monologues, trying to get anywhere near the marvelous poems he wrote. I failed miserably. Whitman was a tremendous liberation for me. Emerson was there in the background; though I am said to be strongly Emersonian I sort of learned that myself. I haven't read him that much. When I read Emerson I see a man far wiser and more intelligent, and a better writer than myself, saying exactly what I would say if I could. That's scary in a way. We're still different in so many ways. But then I do believe I hear, at times, in my poems, distant echoes from every poet, not in terms of his own words, but as a presence. Frost is there, also Stevens. I have read very little Stevens, and basically he's not one of my favorite poets, though I think he's a good poet. They do say of me, even though the influences are there, that my voice remains my own, which is a mystery to me, but apparently it's true. I believe I assimilate from any number of others and other areas. I'm that kind of person—one who is looking for the integrated narrative. That's where my voice finds its capability of movement. It is my voice, but it is an integrated one. Does that sound right?

*Oh, yes.*

I just made it up. [*Laughing*]

*How, then, would you describe your poetry?*

It's a variable poetry that tries to test out to the limit the situation of unity and diversity—how variable and diverse a landscape of poetry can be and at the same time hold a growing center. I have written some very skinny poems you might call minimalist and I've written some very long-lined poems, such as "**Sphere**." In my early poems I was contemplating the philosophical issue of the One and the Many.

*Your poetry deals principally with man in nature, the phenomena of the landscape-earth's nature. I've wondered, because of your scientific background, if you have ever thought about taking man off the earth into space? I don't mean to say science fiction poetry, but into the nature of space.*

I don't believe I have, though I've thought a great deal about it—billions and billions of galaxies and billions and billions of stars in each one. Who was it said that if you stick out your arm at the end of space what does it stick into? If space is limited, what happens?

*In about 90 percent of your poetry the reader is brought into the poem to witness the solitude of the speaker. Is this solitude your poetic vision of loneliness?*

Yes.

*Is it your loneliness you're writing about?*

Yes it is. I really don't write to an audience. I never imagined an audience. I imagine other lonely people, such as myself. I don't know who they are or where they are, and I don't care, but they're the people whom I want to reach. It seems to me that the people who are capable of forming themselves into groups and audiences have something else to go on besides poetry. So let them go ahead. It could be political, sociological, mystical, or whatever. They're welcome to it and I hope they do a good job, but I am not part of that. I'm really an isolationist. And I know there are others like me. There is some element of ultimate loneliness in each person. In some people it's a crisis. Those are the pieces of loneliness I would like to share at this distance.

*You published three major collections in a row:* **Collected Poems 1951-71, Sphere: The Form of a Motion,** *and* **The Snow Poems**. *How does this affect a writer's sense that since what you're doing is working, you might as well keep doing the same thing?*

I can't get stuck in a pattern, because I don't believe in patterns. I believe in process and progression. I believe in centralizing, integration, that kind of ongoing narrative, more than I believe in the boxes of identification and completion. That's just the way I am structured as a human being. *The Collected Poems* contains two or three other previously unpublished books. I just dumped them in there. I had them, but didn't want to bother sending them out to magazines.

But *Sphere,* finally, was the place where I was able to deal with the problem of the One and the Many to my own satisfaction. It was a time when we were first beginning to see an image of the earth from outer space on the television screen, at a time when it was inevitable to think about that as the central image of our lives—that sphere. With *Sphere,* I had particularized and unified what I knew about things as well as I could. It didn't take long for me to fall apart or for that to fall apart, too. Thinking of the anger and

disappointment that comes from such things . . . I wrote *The Snow Poems,* where I had meant to write a book of a thousand pages. I don't know why I didn't go ahead and do it, because I wanted to say here is a thousand pages of trash that nevertheless indicates that every image and every event on the planet and everywhere else is significant and could be great poetry, sometimes is in passages and lines. But I stopped at three hundred pages. I had worn myself and everybody else out. But I went on long enough to give the idea that we really are in a poetically inexhaustible world, inside and out.

*Your work has been anthologized in many publications over the years. They usually publish* **"Corsons Inlet," "This Is," "Bridge,"** *and* **"Visit."** *Of all your poems which do you think is your best work and will most likely survive?*

I have always liked two poems of mine that are twins, **"Conserving the Magnitude of Uselessness"** and **"If Anything Will Level with You Water Will"** from the *Collected Poems*. I think those are fine poems, but other people don't reprint them. I think anthologists tend to imitate each other. If they find a poem anthologized, they put it in their anthology. I have a great many poems, to tell you the truth, that could just as well have been chosen for an anthology as the others.

*Donald Justice said at one time that the United States has not produced a major poet in the last thirty years. Do you agree with this?*

I agree with that. The possibility is that Ashbery is a major writer, but other than that I don't know any major writers, except possibly myself. The great poets of the first half of the century are not as great as we thought they were, but they are greater than anything since. I think Eliot was a great poet. I like Ransom a lot. I don't believe Lowell and Berryman are going to prove to be as strong as was thought. I hope I'm wrong about that. It seems to me that there are a million poets that write interesting verse, but I can't think of a single one that I would think of getting up in the morning and going to to find my life profoundly changed and enlightened and deepened by. Not a single one. Isn't that amazing? Or do I just not know about them? I don't mean an answer to life, I mean an encounter of intelligence, sensibility, feeling, vision. Where do I go for a verbal encounter that will be sufficient to cause me to feel that I should come back the next day and the next day to drink from that fountain again?

*Do you think we will see a major poet evolve out of the last eleven or twelve years of the century or has the well dried up?*

I think not. This century has had it. Like others, I believe that we've been replaying the seventeenth century in which a great deal of poetic energy in the first part of the century dried up into Dryden and Pope. Dryden at the end of the seventeenth and Pope at the beginning of the eighteenth. And we have started to take on a formalist cast now. Maybe we're going to need a century or two before we get back on line.

*You've taught at Cornell since 1964.*

Yes, that's right. Denise Levertov was poetry editor of *The Nation* and she wanted to take off for six months and she asked me to fill in for her. During that period I accepted a poem by David Ray. I didn't know who he was, but I published his poem. Some months later I was asked to read at Cornell, and it turned out that David Ray was a teacher there. I guess he was glad I published his poem and wanted to meet me. I went to read and they asked me why I wasn't teaching and I said because no one had ever asked me. They proceeded to ask me. I became a full professor in seven years. Some years later Yale made me an offer, so Cornell countered their offer and gave me an endowed chair. They have just honored me beyond all dreams. I teach part-time . . . one course that meets once a week. It's like having your life free. I go over every day and talk to students and go to meetings, but I don't have to.

*Is it stimulating for your work to meet with the students everyday?*

Not much any more. I need human contact, but it needn't be profound. To see someone and have a cup of coffee really restores me. See, I don't like to live alone. I don't think that I'm much of a teacher, but that's not what the students tell me. I never feel very competent. I don't think anyone who teaches poetry can feel very competent, because the subject is so overwhelming and it's easy to miss the center of it. Can you imagine in a creative writing class the interplay between the teacher and the student—how complex that is on both sides? Superficial, no matter how profound. It's so superficial and so mixed, "Help me, don't help me. Criticize this poem but only say good things. Don't tell me what my next move is. Tell me, but don't let me know that you told me what my next move is, so it will seem that I discovered it for myself. When I owe you something please be the first one to say I owe nothing." That is to say, the relationship is extremely complex and draining on that account. You would have to be superhuman to know what to do in that situation. I am, as it turns out, not superhuman. But they say I'm a good teacher, nevertheless. I do the best I can. I must say that I have a pretty quick eye on a poem. I can tell what it is likely to amount to or not amount to rather quickly. It's just a wonderful job, but I'm tired of it, only because of something they call "burnout." After having done something for twenty-five years I don't know what happens. I guess you begin hearing yourself say the same thing, repeating yourself.

When I first began to teach, I would go into the classroom and see eighteen or twenty individuals and I believed they were individuals. After about five years of teaching six courses per year, I would come into a writing class knowing full well that there were three or four basic problems. Diction—there is always too much poetic diction. There's the problem of shape, or the lack of it—some contact with an ideal form. There's the problem of consistency. It's not sufficient to have a good line and a good image, you need to write a whole poem. Then, as a teacher, you have to begin to nudge yourself and say, "This person sitting in front of you is not an example of one of these problems,

he's a person." After awhile, if you have to nudge yourself too much, then it's time to quit.

*If the burnout begins to weigh too heavily upon you, is there something that you would prefer doing instead of teaching?*

I would like to, now, be designated, as anything in this world, POET. Not teacher, not professor, not farmer, but one who writes poems. What I would like to do now, since I have not allowed myself to do it in twenty years, is to go out and meet the people who read my poems. I have been giving poetry readings lately which I did not do for a long, long time. I would like to stay home when I go back to Ithaca and write my poems, send them to magazines, go see people, because I don't know how to tell somebody else how to write.

*You don't categorize yourself as particularly Southern, a Southern writer.*

I feel my verbal and spiritual home is still the South. When I sit down and play hymns on the piano my belly tells me I'm home no matter where I am. So, yes, I am Southern, but I have been away from the immediate concerns of the South a long time. I guess we should define Southerner. Who are Southerners? Are they white, black? Does a black Southerner want to be separated from a Northerner? Does he feel the same boundary in the North as the Southerner often does? Also, the South has changed so much demographically that it's difficult to know. I was just in the bank the day before yesterday and I told a young lady I was going back home to Ithaca. She had just moved down from Kingston, New York. She said she liked it, but missed the snow. At the next teller's window was a woman who said she was from New York. So there we were, the three of us, adjacent to each other from New York. The very same thing happened in the post office one morning.

*How does a poet deal with this change?*

I wonder. I don't think it has very much effect on me. The sources of poetry, by the time you are as old as I am, sixty-two, have taken all kinds of perspectives, and while the work may be changed in tone and mood by recent events, it's changed only slightly. Curvature of the narrative, by that time, becomes fairly well established, and while it can change, it won't change much.

*You never dreamed of becoming a poet in the sense of receiving recognition for your work. You thought of yourself as being an amateur poet and not a "Poet." Once you began publishing, when did you begin to think of yourself as a "Poet?"*

When I said "amateur poet," I meant that I didn't want to professionalize it. It seems to have more spontaneity, immediacy and meaning to me when I think of it as just something I do. I worry when poetry is professionalized. I think maybe I am a poet. I keep getting letters from all over the world from people who say they are moved by this and that. Whatever it was that they were moved by is in the past for me. I just wrote a poem this morning. That's where I'm at. I try to live each day as I can. If I write a poem, fine. If I don't, that's fine. I think life ought to come first. Don't you? One is alive in the world with other people. I write poetry. Other people collect insects or rocks. I don't think I have answered this question very well, but you know how at some point in your life you have meditated deeply on a subject—you remember that you have meditated on it, you file it, and the next time you try to remember it you can't access it. You have to take thirty minutes to work your way there, then you might have something to say, or you might not. That's what just happened. [*Laughing*]

*Do you think there are writers, poets, who take poetry too seriously, that they feel poetry is almost more important than life?*

The solemn, the pompous, the terribly earnest are all boring.

*We touched upon your childhood earlier and I'd like to ask if you have a favorite childhood memory?*

I remember one Christmas when I got a little tin wagon with milk cans drawn by a mule or a horse. I must have been five or six. I remember getting back into bed and playing with that on top of the quilt, thinking it was absolutely marvelous.

*Turning this around, do you have a least favorite childhood memory?*

The most powerful image of my emotional life is something I had repressed and one of my sisters lately reminded me of. It was when my little brother, who was two and a half years younger than I, died at eighteen months. My mother some days later found his footprint in the yard and tried to build something over it to keep the wind from blowing it away. That's the most powerful image I've ever known.

*Throughout your career you've professed formlessness and boundlessness. Have you found either?*

I guess the other side of that question is, is there anything, in fact, in our world and perception that isn't formal in one way or the other? I guess not. The air between me and that oak tree is invisible and formless. I can't see the air. So I see nothing but form out the window. I know the air is there because I see it work on the trees, and so I begin to think there is an invisible behind the visible, and a formlessness, an ongoing energy that moves in and out of a discrete formation. It remains constant and comes and goes and operates from a world of residual formlessness. That space, at some point, develops what we perceive. In a way I have experienced the idea of formlessness and boundlessness, but these are imperceptible thanks to our senses.

For the last three or four months I have been profoundly occupied with the conceptual aspect of poetry—poetry that has some thought behind it. But also, the poem is a verbal construct that we encounter, learn from, make value judgments with, and go to to sort out possibilities in relation to our own lives in order to try to learn how to live. I'm sick and tired of reading poets who have beautiful images that don't have a damn thing to say. I want somebody who can think and tell me something. You reintegrate that into a larger thing where you realize that thought and loss are certainly not the beginning and end to things, but are just one element in the larger effort we are making, which is to try to learn how to live our lives.

**Frank J. Lepkowski  (essay date 1994)**

SOURCE: "'How Are We to Find Holiness?': The Religious Vision of A. R. Ammons," in *Twentieth Century Literature*, Vol. 40, No. 4, Winter, 1994, pp. 477-98.

[*In the following essay, Lepkowski perceives religious sentiment and motifs in Ammons's poetry.*]

Critical attention to the religious element in the poetry of A. R. Ammons has generally subsumed it in an overall argument placing him as a modern Romantic visionary poet. Locating Ammons in this way has obscured somewhat the extent of his spirituality and its unique emotional tonality. A reading of Ammons sensitive to these may find in his development a spiritual pilgrimage with distinct phases. His idea of God, clearly present in the early poetry, undergoes a period of doubt, reconstruction, and denial in the middle of his career, and after a strong negation becomes a renewed theme in his later poetry. Meditation on the nature of God and interrogation of the visible world for revelation of the Divine occasion some of his most powerful writing.

Marius Bewley in an early review first pointed out that "Ammons *is* a mystical poet in the same sense that Whitman was" ["Modes of Poetry," *Hudson Review*, 1968-69]. Somewhat later, Hyatt Waggoner discerned that "a sense of God's reality, whether as immanent or as *deus absconditus,* is everywhere present in the poems and should be recognized . . . . Ammons is a poet of religious vision" ["Notes and Reflections," *A. R. Ammons: Modern Critical Views,* edited by Harold Bloom, 1986], a view to which he has held true in subsequent assessments of Ammons's career, although he stresses a skeptical Ammons as well for whom religious beliefs "are like mirages, existing somewhere between fact and delusion" [*American Poets,* revised edition, 1984]. Helen Vendler has identified one of his greatest poems as a "a colloquy with God" [*The Music of What Happens: Poems, Poets, Critics,* 1988], yet elsewhere she qualifies Ammons as manifesting no more than a belief in a Quakerish "inner light," and certifies his work as being happily free of "disabling religious or ideological nostalgia" ["Veracity Unshaken," *The New Yorker,* February 15, 1988]. Vendler's uneasiness with Ammons's religiosity, even as her critical acuity registers its existence, indicates the difficulty others have had acknowledging it.

The age wants to celebrate the poet, but is uncomfortable with the spiritual commitments that animate his work.

Ammons's belief in God's presence in the universe does not arise from allegiance to a particular institutional mode of revelation; in fact, while his early work can be quite overtly Christian, his later work includes elements of eastern religion. Furthermore, as both mystic and inheritor of the Williams branch of modernist tradition, he operates under Pound's injunction to "make it new," to perceive God and to articulate that knowledge without reference to institutions and sacred texts. Yet however syncretic or idiosyncratic his synthesis, there seems little doubt that Ammons, rather than showing "characteristic concepts and patterns of Romantic philosophy and literature" of "displaced and reconstituted theology or . . . a secularized form of devotional experience" [M. H. Abrams, *Natural Supernaturalism,* 1971], instead shows a return to mystical devotion and meditation on the works and mind of God.

In the criticism of Ammons's work the religious has often been elided into the philosophical or psychological. Favoring the latter was Harold Bloom, who during the period of his own greatest influence was one of the first to champion Ammons. He applied a reading which relentlessly psychologizes the poet's work. Ammons is a Romantic seer whose achievement is the result of a creative will to power, continuously threatened by the universe's recalcitrance, and by the poet's awareness of the limits of his own mind. Bloom, like Waggoner, places Ammons in a visionary company of Strong Romantic Sensibilities, an avatar of his American predecessor Emerson. While philosophical similarities between Ammons and Emerson have been often noted, Bloom makes it an issue of filiation and treats the tensions in that relationship as the actual matter of the poetry.

Bloom invites us to admire the heroic struggle of a doomed subjectivity to establish its vision for a time, a struggle with the very fact of vision itself, a project in which "a poem is . . . as much an act of breaking as of making, as much a blinding as a seeing" ["A. R. Ammons: The Breaking of Vessels," *A. R. Ammons: Modern Critical Views,* edited by Bloom, 1986]. When he traces the development of a poem he does so in primarily psychological terms, as when he sees the language of Ammons's **"Guide"** enacting "the psychic defenses of undoing and isolation, but only in order to recoil from this limitation so as to mount up into a daemonic Sublime, itself based upon a repression of this poet's deepest longings." To see Ammons's concern as the Sublime in isolation from what he tells us about the Divine is the "strong misreading" which has skewed the critical debate over Ammons. The primary question of interest for such critics becomes that of how successful a belated Romantic can be when transcendence has been rendered by the Zeitgeist an untenable alternative.

Portraying Ammons as a Romantic obscures the way his poetry reenacts spiritual inquiry and devotion, with a piety quite unlike anyone else in the American tradition, linking him more to the humility of George Herbert than to the vatic optimism of Ralph Waldo Emerson. In the present reading our goal is to show through a thorough examination of his *ouevre* the importance of the Divine in Ammons, who in his poetry offers a vision in which science tells of the works of God, whose presence is revealed to the patient and faithful inquirer.

Ammons's earliest strong expression of the Divine we find in the much-commented upon **"Hymn,"** in which the poet addresses God directly, uniting the question of His nature with Ammons's abiding philosophical preoccupation with the one:many problem. The first stanza begins with the line "I know if I find you I will have to leave the earth," and the second with the line "And I know if I find you I will have to stay with the earth," and between the poles of transcendence and immanence we may track Ammons's project.

To know God at His most universal, the poet will have to ascend past sea marshes, hills, crater lakes, and canyons, through the atmosphere and out into space: "way past all the light diffusions and bombardments/ up further than the loss of sight/ into the unseasonal undifferentiated empty stark." The poet's unpurgeable humanity and affiance to the things of this world make him pause when going out "past the blackset noctilucent clouds/ where one wants to stop and look." God at His most absolute is infinite and eternal, hence "undifferentiated" and "unseasonal," and radically unembellished with anthropomorphic presence beyond the intimacy of address implied in the second person pronoun. To cross over into a transcendence so radical is incomprehensible and involves leaving the human completely behind.

Instead of pursuing God beyond this world, then, the poet seeks to find how God's presence may be revealed in the world of nature as perceived by the poet, moving from the macrocosm to the microcosm, "inspecting with thin tools and ground eyes" of science. In this direction faith ("trust") reposes in minute details of cell structure visible only through electron microscopy ("microvilli") or the tiny spore sacs of fungi ("sporangia") or animals so basic and rudimentary that they lack vascular systems ("coelenterates"). The Naturalist ultimately finds himself reduced to another point of human reluctance in this direction as he finds himself praying "for a nerve cell/ with all the soul of my chemical reactions," which is to say that the scientific mode of perception, which helps the poet to understand creation at one level, when carried too far begins to radically diminish his humanity. Threatened in transcendence by expansion to a universal starkness, in the microcosm he is threatened by diminution through subdivision into the tiniest part of the whole.

These two motions are unified by the statement, "You are everywhere partial and entire/ You are on the inside of everything and on the outside." The presence of the Godhead is everywhere in the universe; there is no place into which it does not reach, yet the poet's recognition of this still leaves him with an unavoidable human predicament. He is drawn both ways himself, for "if I find you I must go out into your far resolutions/ and if I find you I must stay here with the separate leaves." He reiterates the two poles of spirit, essence and articulation, transcendence and immanence, one and many, with the final sense obtaining of the poet's remaining caught between them.

That the universal spirit we commonly call God is the object of address in this poem seems a not illogical supposition. The title of the poem, after all, is **"Hymn,"** referring to a genre in which "you" almost always means "God." All the aspects of the presence Ammons attributes to what he is addressing are easily comprehended within what has commonly been thought of as the Deity. Of the poem's many commentators, however, only Bewley unambiguously observes that Ammons is "addressing a cosmic God who is diffused throughout nature, yet presumably transcends it." Waggoner refers to the object of "you" as "One" (as in One:many) and circumspectly notes that "In traditional religious terms, which he normally avoids, these lines would imply the simultaneous Immanence and Transcendence of deity" (*American Poets*). Alan Holder states that "The *you* appears to be a principle of absolute being, existing outside the realm of seeing" [*A. R. Ammons,* 1978]; Nathan Scott holds that "it is Being itself, the aboriginal reality from which everything else springs. . . . Ammons choice of an anthropomorphic idiom for his salute to this aboriginal reality is merely a conceit" ["The Poetry of Ammons," *Southern Review,* Autumn, 1988]; Bloom sees "you" as "Emerson's 'Nature,' all that is separate from 'the Soul' . . . the found 'you' is: 'the NOT ME, that is, both nature and art, all other men and my own body'" [in the introduction to *A. R. Ammons,* edited by Bloom]. These last are strategies for eliding the religious into the philosophical or psychological, as the Divine is replaced with a principle or abstraction embodying some aspect of it. We can see in this one example the critical resistance that Ammons's religious sensibility faces.

Early in his career Ammons explicitly embraces Christianity. One poignant expression of it may be found in **"The Foot-Washing"** as the poet, summoning man and woman alike, enacts the same service that Christ performed for the Apostles (John 13:5-14). The ablution he has to offer is a healing one, which will cleanse the dust-humbled feet of his "brother," will heal with "serenity" the woman's "flat feet/ yellow, gray with dust,/ [her] orphaned udders flat." Of both brother and sister he asks forgiveness for himself, as if in apology to the broken and human for his visionary ambitions: "if I have failed to know/ the grief in your gone time,/ forgive me wakened now." The Christian pilgrimage here stands in rebuke, in its reminder of earthly suffering and requirement of charity, to the temptations of the egotistical sublime.

Another striking example of the Christian theme is **"Christmas Eve,"** in which he juxtaposes an account of the nativity with that of a contemporary American husband, trying to sneak a nap and decorate the tree before his wife comes home. The poem begins, however, with an evangelical excursus, seeming to preach the totalizing gospel of science:

> When cold, I huddle up, foetal, cross
> arms:
> but in summer, sprawl:
>
>    secret is plain old
> surface area,
> decreased in winter, retaining: in summer no
>    limbs touching—
> radiating:
> everything is physical:
>
>    chemistry is physical:
>    electrical noumenal mind
> is:
> (I declare!)

But the sleepy poet finds his "electrical noumenal mind" picturing Mary's experience by his own lights, the muse for the moment more morphic than orphic:

> Christmas Eve tonight: Joseph
> is looking for a place:
> Mary smiles but
>    her blood is singing:
>
>    she will have to lie down:
>    hay is warm:
> some inns keep only
> the public room warm: Mary
>
> in thinking, Nice time
>    to lie down,
> good time to be brought down by this necessity:

His reverie is repeatedly interrupted by such travelers from Porlock as a telephone call and the need to find an extension cord for the lights, so that the poem plays back and forth between the mundane and the spiritual. This oscillation, with its gently comic tone, reaches a sudden, wrenchingly personal fusion of the two realms:

> I better get busy
> and put the lights on—can't find
>    extension cord:
> Phyllis will be home, will say, The
> tree doesn't have any lights!
> I have tiny winking lights, too:
>    she will like
> them: she went to see her mother:
>
>
> my mother is dead: she is
> deep in the ground, changed: if she
> rises, dust will blow all over the place and
>    she will stand there shining,
> smiling: she will feel good:
> she will want
> to go home and fix supper: first she
>    will hug me:

an actual womb bore Christ,
divinity into the world:
　　I hope there are births to lie down to
back
to divinity,
since we all must die away from here:

I better look for the cord:

The figure of Ammons's dead mother being resurrected, embracing him, all told in a guilelessly childlike tone, quite movingly bridges the personal and religious levels of the poem. That divinity ultimately receives the poem's assent over physics we see in the conclusion's treatment of Christ's mission:

　　　Christ was born
in a hay barn among the warm cows and the
donkeys kneeling down: with Him divinity
swept into the flesh
　　and made it real.

This final affirmation that the ultimate meaning of human life is a spiritual reality clarifies the irony involved in Ammons's initial invocation of physics to explain "everything." Scientific knowledge, while having its profound uses, does not begin to address human reality at the level Christ does.

We find a Christmas scene as well in Ammons's first long poem, the book-length poetic journal ***Tape for the Turn of the Year*** (1965), which contains the following description of a church service, notable for the his sincere, unironic, unalienated participation in it:

　　I held a lighted candle
　　in my hand—as all the
　　　others did—and helped
　　sing "Silent Night": the
　　church lights were doused:
　　　　the preacher lit his
　　　　candle & from his the
　　　　deacons lit theirs &
　　then the deacons went down
　　the aisles & gave light to
　　each row
　　& the light poured
　　down the rows &
　　the singing started:

The song and light create a setting for Ammons to testify to the nature of his religious faith. The communal celebration of the very origin of Christian belief contextualizes his more individualist credo regarding fundamental spiritual realities, given the scientific, objectifying name of "forces":

　　　though the forces
　　　　have different names
　　in different places &
　　times, they are
　　real forces which we

don't understand:
　　I can either believe
　　in them or doubt them &
　　I believe:
I believe that man is
small
& of short duration in the
great, incomprehensible,
& eternal: I believe
it's necessary to do
good
as we can best define it:
I believe we must
discover & accept the
　　terms
　　that best testify:
I'm on the side of
whatever the reasons are
　　we are here:

　　　we do the best we can
& it's not enough:

What is most interesting about this passage is the humility with which Ammons treats the divine mysteries; in fact, as Frederick Buell has observed, "his acceptance of uncertainty is Judeo-Christian in overtone." He accepts the limits of his knowledge yet accepts the knowledge as well. The relentless clarifications and revisions of the reasoning, scientific mind in Ammons pause at the threshold of revealed belief. Such intellectual humility and acceptance of the insufficiency of the human will is not what we think of as a trait of the dauntless Romantic seer.

This poem not only includes a credo specifying the articles of faith, but also manifests faith's action in the form of a prayer for strength and guidance:

　　　God, help us: help us:

we praise Your light:
give us light to do what
we can with darkness:

　　　courage
　　　to celebrate Your
　　　light
　　　even while the
　　　bitterdrink
　　　is being drunk:

　　　give us the will
　　　to love
　　　those
　　　who cannot love:
　　　a touch of the dark
　　　so we can know how one,
　　　hungry for the light,
　　　can
　　　turn away:

Ammons concludes with a plea for "a song/ sanctified/ by Your divinity/ to make us new/ & certain of the right," lines which, in their naming the Lord as his muse emphasize what Vendler observes elsewhere in his work as the "utter congruence between Christian grace and *poiesis*" (*The Music of What Happens*). What is more audacious tonally than this public testimony of faith and prayer is the way he goes on to tell us that he "had/ lunch after/ 'who cannot love'—/ soup, sandwich, milk" (*Tape*), much as he used the mundane details of **"Christmas Eve"** to contextualize that poem's vision of divinity. The diary-like accumulation of the quotidian in this lengthy work makes the outbursts of religious vision all the more remarkable.

None more extraordinary, perhaps, than this act of surrendering himself to God's purposes, and in effect dedicating his poetic work to be part of His work:

> Lord, I'm in your
> hands: I surrender:
>     it's your will
>     & not mine:
>     you give me
>     singing shape
> & you turn me into dust:
>
> undefined &
> undefinable, you're
>     beyond reach:
>
> what form should my
> praise take?

The fruit of submission to God's will is poetic inspiration. Its result, seen in this key word of "praise," will appear often in Ammons, including poems during his middle period most commonly seen as purely Romantic. Clearly its object is divine, the Creator of all and His creation; the praise is the poet's just prayer. In *Tape* we encounter both spiritual longing and deep faith expressed so unaffectedly as to seem as natural as the meals, weather patterns, and other incidents that make up this extraordinary poetic journal. The absolute dependency of the human upon God for solace, for meaning, and for healing has not been more convincingly portrayed since Eliot. Ammons at this point in his career seems to view his own poetic vocation as a ministry in Christian terms, that of spreading testimony to God's grace and works.

The Divine continues as an abiding concern of Ammons in the work from the late 1960s through the early 1970s, but the perspective he takes on it changes. The poet comes to view God as a construct of the human imagination rather than as an independent, noumenal entity, the creator of the universe; he seems to agree with Blake that "all Deities reside in the human breast," and to begin to embrace a Religion of Man more Emersonian in tone. The reading of Ammons as latter-day Romantic may most convincingly be applied to works from this period.

In **"Hibernaculum,"** when Ammons addresses God there is uneasy qualification alien to the earlier poems: "dear

God (or whatever, if anything, is/ merciful) give us our lives, then, the full possession,/ before we give them back." Diffidence about knowing *what* God is is a sign of piety; diffidence about knowing *whether* God is at all is a sign of profound religious doubt. A tone of resentment has entered into the prayer as well, understandable since God seems to exist only as an endlessly fillable blank, a sort of floating signifier, rather than a powerful being who would care to hear and answer prayers:

> I address the empty place where the god
> that has been deposed lived: it is the godhead: the
> yearnings that have been addressed to it bear
>     antiquity's
>
>                    18
>
> sanction: for the god is ever re-created as
> emptiness, till force and ritual fill up and strangle
> his life, and then he must be born empty again: I
> accost the emptiness saying let all men turn their
> eyes to the emptiness that allows adoration's life:

The focus has changed from the originary, constitutive presence of God in creation, which animates the spiritual seeking of the early poems from **"Hymn"** through *Tape,* to the promptings of the human imagination that needs to create an object of veneration. Rather than witness to God's presence in creation, Ammons offers only "antiquity's sanction" to validate faith. Making the Divine the creation of the human, though much more easily assimilable to the rationalist and secularizing thrust of intellectual history since the eighteenth century, is a significant reversal of the stance we have seen in his earlier work.

The long poem *Sphere: The Form of a Motion* marks a certain climax of this humanistic version of the Divine. Here the will to believe poses grave dangers, because people invest the objects of their belief with considerable power over themselves, conceptions to which they become captive:

>                make a mighty
> force, that of a god: endow it with will, personality,
>     whim:
> then, please it, it can lend power to you: but then
>     you
> have created the possibility of its displeasure: what
>     you
> made to be greater than you is and enslaves you

From being the transcendent and immanent creator of all toward whom the spirit yearns, the Divine here has become a treacherous projection of the mind which usurps our freedom.

In keeping with the circularity of *Sphere*'s motion, Ammons returns to this theme in a tone more seemingly reverential, referring to God in the second person rather than the third:

spirit-being, great one in the world
beyond sense, how do you fare and how may we
    fare to Thee:

               69

           . . . . .

what is to be done, what is saving: is it so to come
    to know
the works of the Most High as to assent to them
    and be
      reconciled
by them, so to hold those works in our imaginations
    as to
      think

them our correspondent invention, our best design
    within the
governing possibilities: so to take on the Reason of
    the
      Most
High as to in some part celebrate Him and offer
    Him not our

flight but our cordiality and gratitude: so to look to
    the
moment of consciousness as to find there, beyond
    all the
individual costs and horrors, perplexing pains and
    seizures,
joy's surviving radiance:

The initial voice of prayer recalls *Tape,* but the view Ammons takes toward the Most High here is considerably more qualified. He seems to be uneasily fusing two contradictory propositions, that God is a creation of the human imagination, and that God has the omnipotent existence of the creator of all. He argues that the same power of mind by which we repeatedly imagine and destroy our gods is itself the acting power of God's imagination re-making itself. By looking inside ourselves to our own consciousness, we find the Most High's way at work, and in so doing our imagination serves as an essential vehicle of God's self-creation. This is Ammons's closest approach to the Emerson who declared "that man has access to the entire mind of the Creator, is himself the creator in the finite."

The overall movement of *Sphere* is toward affirming the world the way it is, in secular terms, as the place in which we have our happiness or not at all. In it alone may we find sufficient beauty to sustain us. We find "joy's surviving radiance" in the "moment of consciousness," that is through enjoying the motion of our minds in the here and now rather than in anticipation of a future transcendent state beyond our mortal life. This argument animates some of the great poems of his middle period, as for example **"The Arc Inside and Out,"** which, after luxuriating in both poles of thought, ends with an injunction to inhabit a state between both of these motions of the mind, to accept this life as it is as a resting point and enjoy it as such:

               stay
here, the apple an apple with its own hue
or streak, the drink of water, the drink,

the falling into sleep, restfully ever the
falling into sleep, dream, dream, and
every morning the sun comes, the sun.

The poet articulates so remarkably an edenic equipoise of mind and feeling that it seems churlish to question its durability as a position for living, or its suitability as an answer to the spiritual searching that drives so much of Ammons's earlier (and, as we shall see, later) verse. But it is hard, after reviewing the whole corpus of his poetry to date, not to assent to Waggoner's criticism of the poems of this middle period as being "not entirely consistent, in tone or statement, with the best of the earlier lyrics or even with the prayer . . . and the several credos . . . in *Tape*. A little more defensive, more guarded, more 'intellectually prudent'" ("Notes and Reflections"). The poems of the period, roughly speaking, from *Uplands* (1970) through *Diversifications* (1975), "have pulled back a little from the letting-go and letting-out of the earlier work. There is less abandon, more control. . . . Their style might be described as more 'mature,' but maturity brings losses as well as gains." Ultimately this position would not satisfy the poet, and in fact it inspired a thorough demolition of the optimistic humanism on which it is based.

After the climax of critical reception attendant upon the publication of *Collected Poems* (1972) and *Sphere* (1974), which received the National Book Award and Bollingen Award respectively, Ammons shocked many of his readers with *The Snow Poems* (1977), a book Waggoner found "trivial and dull" (*American Visionary Poetry*), which moved him to wonder aloud, "Does Ammons write too much?" (*American Poets.*) In context of our argument here, *The Snow Poems* is a descent to the underworld, an exploration of the abyss of mind and will wrestling with the most intractable material of the human condition in isolation from God and His grace. In this book (at almost three hundred pages his longest single work) the poet seems awash in ennui and depression alternating with terror, confined by quotidian life, taking tranquilizers to get by, haunted by memories of his dead father. Precious little of the buoyancy of his previous work is to be found, and even the qualified, constructed God of *Sphere* has vanished. Earlier in his career he pictures God's universal, beneficent consciousness as

    someone [who] has a clear vision of it all,
    exact to complete existence;
    loves me when I swear and praise
    and smiles, probably, to see me
    wrestle with sight

In *The Snow Poems* comes the bleak negation:

    is no one watching, of
    course not,

not even a gentle, universal
principle with a calming circularity

The poet has a sense of utter cosmic abandonment so
intense it pushes aside the effect of the tranquilizer he
uses to blunt it:

        one is helpless: one weeps:          e
        terror raves beyond the tear:        q
        one is without help:                 u
        and then one sees or recalls         a
    that on the balance line between         n
    purchases and payoffs                    i
    indifference looks neither this          l
    way nor that:
    our help is the call of
    indifference that says
    come where there is no
    need of help
    and have all the help you need.

Over the course of this book the poet enacts the drama of
a resourceful mind isolated and unable to find a way to
live with his human brokenness, most tellingly in the way
in which he is haunted by the memory of his father, but
really including all the other people and things in his life.
In this record of spiritual isolation and alienation the vehicle of his "redemption" proves to be, oddly enough, a
spring encounter with a neighbor's dog, whose kindly recognition endorses his existence from outside:

    . . . old fellow,
    friend, frizzled schnauzer
    runs out of the driveway
    and whines grievous
    pleasure
    stretching up toward my face:
    he knows me: we were
    friends last fall:
    I am myself:
    I am so scared and sad I can
    hardly bear to speak
    and yet delight breaks
    falls through me
    and drives me off laughing
    down a dozen brooks:

From this point the book's mood begins to rise from the
Slough of Despond in which the poet has been caught, and
move toward an acceptance of the world and his life in it,
seen inessentially natural, secular terms.

In tracing the spiritual theme in Ammons's work, *The Snow
Poems* stands as an oddly compelling record of a long, dark
night of the soul, when the seeker feels himself abandoned
by God, by the grace he had previously been able to find
in the world of things, by what his understanding of the
universe and his life has been. It is Ammons at his most
reduced, least transcendental, least religious, least visionary; it is his fullest exploration of the estranged self in an
abandoned universe. Its example points out as by relief the
importance of the Divine in his work overall.

*The Snow Poems* contrasts dramatically with the book
that follows it, *A Coast of Trees* (1981), as Ammons takes
up again his spiritual searching. The first poem, **"Coast of
Trees,"** invokes the Taoist Way to describe the origin of
observed creation and its ongoing course for the pilgrim,
one who is asking a question absent throughout the preceding book, "How are we to find holiness?" Only by accepting our fallenness, our "helplessness" of which we make
"first offer and sacrifice," by accepting "a shambles of/
non-enterprise" which represents our conscious, calculat-
ing, making-sense-of-the-world's failure to control reality
the way we want it to, may we come to "know a unity
approach divided, a composure past/ approach." It is after
thus emptying ourselves of the pretensions and intrusions
of willful consciousness that "with nothing, we turn/ to the
cleared particular, not more/ nor less than itself," seeing
things for what they are and neither exaggerating nor deprecating their significance, their proper place in creation.
Which is to say that we see things in their place in the
Divine Nature and the Divine Nature's place in them: "and
we realize/ that whatever it is it is in the Way and/ the Way
in it, as in us, emptied full."

Seeing things in themselves and in their place in the Way
reminds us of our nature, and of our place in the Way. The
poet's acceptance of the "shambles" in this poem denotes
a chastened return to the spiritual humility seen in his earlier work; a taste of earth now leavens his religious sensibility, and the optimistic humanism of his middle period
has been replaced by an acknowledgment that this life is a
Vale of Sorrow to be endured before our emergence after
death into a better life.

In the elegy **"In Memoriam Mae Noblitt"** this world,
instead of being our sufficiency, is rather a temporary abode
before the eternal one: "this is just a place," whereas

    our home which defines
    us is elsewhere but not
    so far away we have
    forgotten it:

Rejecting with Flannery O'Connor the notion that we are
our own light, he questions:

    is love a reality we
    made here ourselves—
    and grief—did we design


    that—or do these,
    like currents, whine
    in and out among us merely
    as we arrive and go:

Our ultimate consolation turns out to be our destination
after death, a return to our true home:

    the reality we agree with,

    that agrees with us,
    outbounding this, arrives

to touch, joining with

us from far away:

The consolation of this eternal frame of reference in no way eliminates the death and suffering that blight our earthly life. Looking forward to the next hundred million years in **"Rapids,"** Ammons predicts that "the universe will probably not find/ a way to vanish nor I/ in all that time reappear." **"Sweetened Change," "Parting," "Givings,"** and **"An Improvisation for the Stately Dwelling"** are all in some sense meditations on death, the last marked particularly by spiritual compensation for earthly travail:

> I know a man whose cancer has
>  got him just to the point
>  he looks changed by a flight of stairs
> people pass him and speak
> extra-brightly
> he asks nothing else
> he is like a rock
> reversed, that is, the rock has a solid
> body and shakes only
> reflected in the water but he shakes
> in body only,
> his spirit a boulder of light

The problem of mortal suffering constitutes a counterpoint to spiritual reward which checks whatever temptation to the egotistical sublime the poet may still feel. In **"Swells,"** a symbolic meditation on the magnitude and amplitude of the waves of the ocean, the climax comes not in lofty cresting but rather in a shattering collapse back into the rag-and-bone-shop base of human life from which this meditation has sought to ascend but will not be permitted to escape: "the immediate threat/ shot up in a disintegrating spray, the many thoughts and/ sights unmanageable, the deaths of so many, hungry or mad." Ammons recognizes, in **"Breaking Out,"** that he has been "an earth thing all along," whose "feet are catching in the brush" now that the "balloons" of a self-deceiving afflatus have been released.

This dialectic of human sorrow and divine grace which consoles may be seen no more clearly than in the much-commented-on **"Easter Morning."** In fact, the poem could have been titled **"Good Friday and Easter Morning"** for it is a two-stage construction in which suffering and death in the first meets its complement of saving grace and resurrected spirit in the second. The *via dolorosa* is represented in a child's desperation, loneliness, and abandonment by his elders in which the poet sees that

> the child in me that could not become
> was not ready for others to go,
> to go on into change, blessings and
> horrors, but stands there by the road
> where the mishap occurred, crying out for
> help.

The aborted life of this child within him the mature poet holds onto, suffers with over the course of his life. Ammons speaks from the center of his brokenness and sorrow:

> I stand on the stump
> of a child, whether myself
> or my little brother who died, and
> yell as far as I can, I cannot leave this place, for
> for me it is the dearest and the worst,
> it is life nearest to life which is
> life lost:

He finally embraces this locale, and the suffering it represents, as his own:

> it is my place where
> I must stand and fail,
> calling attention with tears
> to the branches not lofting
> boughs into space.

Finally he clings to that failure and the pain it holds with a certain tenacity, almost pride, since it defines him more truly than any exultation in his power as a seer.

The reclamation of the poet's spirit arises in the final section from finding holiness in the purpose and beauty of the natural world, or, as Vendler puts it [in *The Music of What Happens*], "grace—not offered by Ammons as an 'equivalent' to Bunyan's grace, but as *the same thing*, a saving gift from an external source," an observation as true of **"Easter Morning"** as it is of **"Grace Abounding,"** the poem she has in mind. The contemplation of the flight of a pair of eagles allows Ammons his "assuaging human clarification":

> it was a sight of bountiful
> majesty and integrity: the having
> patterns and routes, breaking
> from them to explore other patterns or
> better ways to routes, and then the
> return: a dance sacred as the sap in
> the trees, permanent in its descriptions
> as the ripples round the brook's
> ripplestone: fresh as this particular
> flood of burn breaking across us now
> from the sun.

The divinity revealed by nature, as announced by the poem's title, makes **"Easter Morning"** a capstone of the rest of the book's preoccupation with the human and the Divine.

The poem in which Ammons addresses God at the highest and most reverent level of expression of which he is capable comes from a later collection, *Lake Effect Country* (1983). **"Singling & Doubling Together"** is like **"Hymn"** in that the poet refers to God in these cond person, achieving here something of the tender familiarity we see in the poetry of George Herbert. Unlike **"Hymn,"** in which God is sought by moving outward into an unimaginable transcendence, or downward into the minute particulars of the physical universe, the later poem finds Ammons recognizing God's grace as a personal gift in his own human identity: "My nature singing in me is your nature singing." The poem elaborates the felt intimate presence of the Lord from His articulation as well in the world of appearances:

> you have means to veer down, filter through,
> and, coming in,
> harden into vines that break back with leaves,
> so that when the wind stirs
> I know you are there and I hear you in leafspeech

The poem does replicate the motion of the earlier **"Hymn"** in tracing out a polar relationship between the most remote and unknowable manifestation of the Godhead and its particular expressions in local nature, both the "far resolutions" and the "separate leaves":

> though of course back into your heightenings I
> can never follow: you are there beyond
> tracings flesh can take,
> and farther away surrounding and informing the
>   systems,
> you are as if nothing, and
> where you are least knowable I celebrate you most
>
> or here most when near dusk the pheasant squawks
>   and
> lofts at a sharp angle to the roost cedar,
> I catch in the angle of that ascent,
> in the justness of that event your pheasant nature

God at His most infinite and eternal is remote and inconceivable to the poet's mind, but in the natural world of creation reveals Himself in a variety of forms and ways of being, including a "creaking/ and snapping nature" in the motion of bushes. In human form God shows a failing nature. Here as in **"Easter Morning"** failure summarizes what it is to be human, a state of brokenness and pain, in which God participates completely and sacrificially:

> and you will fail me only as from the still
> of your great high otherness you fail all things,
> somewhere to lift things up, if not those things
>   again:
>
> even you risked all the way into the taking on of
>   shape
> and time fail and fail with me, as me,
> and going hence with me know the going hence
> and in the cries of that pain it is you crying and
> you know of it and it is my pain, my tears, my loss

The final motion is that of testifying to God's forgiving grace, as the poet rededicates his art to His service, as he had done in *Tape for the Turn of the Year*. Ammons can see the desired end of his life's pilgrimage, the annihilation of his self in death, to be reunited with his Creator. Finally the poet looks forward to being liberated from his own particular voice to be blended with God's pure expression:

> what but grace
> have I to bear in every motion,

> embracing or turning away, staggering or standing
>   still,
> while your settled kingdom sways in the
>   distillations of light
> and plunders down into the darkness with me
> and comes nowhere up again but changed into
>   your singing
> nature when I need sing my nature nevermore.

At this point in his poetic career Ammons is, like the George Herbert of "Love (III)," in communion with his creator. We sense a familiarity with God wrought of concentration, persistence, suffering, prayer, the reward of which is a trust foretelling eternal salvation.

Among Ammons's critics it has been easier to speak of the Sublime rather than the Divine, perhaps because the former is an ultimately subjective mode of expression, and can be tailored to the needs of the occasion as a one-size-fits-all spirituality replacement. Harold Bloom makes of it the centerpiece of an elaborate psychodrama in the poet's mind, the various discharges from which are the heart of his reading of Ammons. A critic like Nathan Scott can make it just consoling enough so that it becomes almost divine, without setting off the reflex of disbelief endemic to the modern mind. Given the ardor of Ammons's spiritual expression in these late poems, the lengths to which an otherwise sympathetic and acute commentator like Scott will go to elide the presence of God in **"Singling & Doubling Together"** indicates the operation of a powerful taboo:

> In short, the "you" being addressed in **"Singling & Doubling Together"** is simply the Wholly Other, the Incomparable, the "dearest freshness deep down things": it is none other than Being itself. . . . And this aboriginal reality is addressed as "you," not because Ammons conceives it to be *a* being with personal attributes but rather, presumably, because he feels it to present itself with the same sort of graciousness that one encounters in the love of another person. He chooses not, in other words, to talk about "God" but, rather, to speak of that which approximates what Teilhard de Chardin called *le milieu divin*. Or, we might say that Ammons is a poet of what Stevens in a late poem, "Of Mere Being," in *Opus Posthumous*, called "mere Being": we might say that he is a poet of that which, though not coextensive with all things, yet interpenetrates all things with the radiance of its diaphanous presence.

This fails to be a satisfying account of the poem because as we have just seen, Ammons addresses an omniscient creator who feels his pain, who participates in his fallen human life even though having high and eternal origin, which is to say it is exactly "a being with personal attributes" and not merely some abstraction of "Being itself," which would indeed be "mere Being." The poem is addressed to a sympathetic consciousness who shares the poet's sufferings and who, moreover, will ultimately save the poet from them. In short, the address is not to some abstraction of Being but rather to the God in whom "we live and move and have our being," not the milieu but the Presence itself, such convincing witness to which is quite rare in contemporary poetry.

The later poems in their working toward a state of communion represent a culmination of Ammons's engagement with the Divine as a poetic subject, which has taken several phases. In the earliest, he combines an examination of nature for signs of the Creator with a faith basically Christian in origin as seen in **"Hymn," "Christmas Eve,"** and *Tape for the Turn of the Year*. In his middle period, seduced by the egotistical sublime, he revises God into being a necessary construct of the human imagination, which needs to create a space to venerate. With the scorched-earth demolition in *The Snow Poems* of Romantic optimism Ammons shows the extremity of life without God in his most willful, isolated, and harrowing work, which clears the field for renewed spiritual pilgrimage in the later books. In these Ammons is strengthened to endure the trials of earthly life which threatened to undo him in *The Snow Poems,* and fixes his hope on eternal reward after death, nourished in his faith by signs of grace that he encounters in the natural world,and by God's speaking directly to his heart.

In its most affective lineaments, the idea of God that Ammons articulates is not dogmatic but partakes, rather, of the emotional context of personal spiritual encounter, and is revealed in an examination of nature as probing and scientific as one can imagine any poet performing. In the rigors of this unsparing intimacy we may see Ammons more fruitfully not as our Emerson, but rather our Herbert, not Romantic so much as truly Metaphysical. Such attention to nuance of thought and depth of feeling in spiritual experience grounds the rest of his concerns and makes Ammons's enterprise a singular achievement in modern American poetry.

---

## FURTHER READING

### Criticism

Baker, David. "The Push of Reading." *The Kenyon Review* 16, No. 4 (Fall 1994): 161-76.
> A review of four books, including Ammons's long poem *Garbage*. Baker observes that the poem illustrates the interconnectedness of all things: "We become witness to something of a generative and evolutionary process— the turning of garbage into utility, decay into new life, an idea into further ideas."

Bloom, Harold. "A. R. Ammons: When You Consider the Radiance." In his *The Ringers in the Tower: Studies in Romantic Tradition*, pp. 256-89. Chicago: The University of Chicago Press, 1971.
> Examines Ammons's handling of ideas treated previously by American poets in the Romantic tradition, especially Ralph Waldo Emerson, Walt Whitman, and Wallace Stevens. This essay was originally published in 1970.

————. "A. R. Ammons: The Breaking of the Vessels." In his *Figures of Capable Imagination*, pp. 209-33. New York: The Seabury Press, 1976.
> Explores Ammons's poetry apropos of Bloom's theories of poetic influence and creative misreading. This essay was originally published in *Salmagundi*, Fall-Winter, 1975-76.

Bullis, Gerald. "In the Open: A. R. Ammons' Longer Poems." *Pembroke Magazine*, No. 18 (1986): 28-53.
> Identifies characteristics of Ammons's long poems while attempting "to offer explanations for the specific form and content" of these works.

Costello, Bonnie. "The Soil and Man's Intelligence: Three Contemporary Landscape Poets." *Contemporary Literature* 30, No. 3 (Fall 1989): 412-33.
> Discusses varying stances of American poets with regard to the landscape. Labelling Ammons an analogist poet— defined here as the individual who "pursues the parallels between landscape and mind, allowing each its autonomy and authority"—Costello contrasts him with the immanentist poet Gary Snyder and the transcendentalist poet Charles Wright.

Cushman, Stephen. "A. R. Ammons, or the Rigid Lines of the Free and Easy." In his *Fictions of Form in American Poetry*, pp. 149-86. Princeton, N.J.: Princeton University Press, 1993.
> Studies line, meter, and form in Ammons's poetry, focusing on the tenion between rigor and freedom in his verse.

*Diacritics* III, No. 4 (Winter 1973).
> Special issue devoted to Ammons. Among the essays included here are "The Cosmic Backyard of A. R. Ammons" by Linda Orr, "Ammons' Radiant Toys" by David Kalstone, and "Light, Wind, Motion" by Josephine Miles.

Doreski, William. "Sublimity and Order in the *Snow Poems*." *Pembroke Magazine*, No. 21 (1989): 68-76.
> Presents Ammons's *The Snow Poems* as an exemplar of the neo-Romantic lyric because it achieves its effects without reliance on epiphany, mystical language, or pathetic fallacy. Doreski maintains that the success of *The Snow Poems* is closely linked to the diction and structure of the poem.

Hans, James S. "The Aesthetics of Worldly Hopes in A. R. Ammons's Poetry." *Essays in Literature* XVII, No. 1 (Spring 1990): 76-93.
> Asserts that Ammons's poetry evinces the ideas of a poet "who sees life as an essentially playful activity that affords one a perspective on the tragic joy that life embodies when it is seen aesthetically."

Holder, Alan. *A. R. Ammons*. Boston: Twayne Publishers, 1978, 179 p.
> Biographical and critical overview of Ammons's career.

Howard, Richard. "'The Spent Seer Consigns Order to the Vehicle of Change.'" In his *Alone with America: The Art of*

*Poetry in the United States since 1950*, pp. 1-17. London: Thames and Hudson, 1970.

> Identifies transcendentalism as the primary impulse of Ammons's poetry. Howard defines Ammons's artistic aim as "putting off the flesh and taking on the universe."

Morgan, Robert. "The Compound Vision of A. R. Ammons' Early Poems." In his *Good Measure: Essays, Interviews, and Notes on Poetry*, pp. 45-74. Baton Rouge: Louisiana State University Press, 1993.

> Explicates Ammons's poems that originally appeared in *Ommateum* or soon thereafter. Morgan contends that the major emphases of Ammons's poetry—namely the discovery of unity in contradiction, an interest in language that mirrors the diversity of life, and a sense of the provisional nature of insight—are apparent even at this early stage in his career. This essay originally appeared in the journal *Epoch*, Spring, 1973.

*Pembroke Magazine*, No. 18 (1986).

> Special issue devoted to Ammons. Among the items included here are the essays "Poetic Metaphysic in A. R. Ammons" by D. R. Fosso and "Scholar of Wind and Tree: The Early Lyrics of A. R. Ammons" by Sister Bernetta Quinn, and an interview conducted by Shelby Stephenson.

Scott, Nathan A., Jr. "The Poetry of Ammons." *Southern Review* 24, No. 4 (Autumn 1988): 717-43.

> Declares Ammons "a poet of the Sublime," meaning that "the most fundamental premise of all his principal meditations is that the sheer ontological weight and depth of the world are such as to invest all the finite things of earth with an incalculable complexity and inexhaustibility, so much so indeed that really to savor the full-fledged otherness of the immediate givens of experience is to find them testifying to their own finitude by their silent allusions to a transfinite dimension within themselves."

Spiegelman, Willard. "Myths of Concretion, Myths of Abstraction: The Case of A. R. Ammons." In his *The Didactic Muse: Scenes of Instruction in Contemporary American Poetry,* pp. 110-46. Princeton, N.J.: Princeton University Press, 1989.

> Examines the manner in which Ammons merges science and poetry to create successful philosophical verse.

Wolfe, Cary. "Symbol Plural: The Later Long Poems of A. R. Ammons." *Contemporary Literature* 30, No. 1 (Spring 1989): 78-94.

> Contends that Ammons's verse aspires to be true organicist poetry, aiming "to engage a poetics of the centrifugal, to consciously resituate poetry—and, by extension, culture—in a network of relations both biological and social."

---

**Additional coverage of Ammons's life and career is contained in the following sources published by Gale Research:** *Authors in the News*, Vol. 1; *Contemporary Authors*, Vols. 9-12 (rev. ed.); *Contemporary Authors New Revision Series*, Vols. 6, 36; *Contemporary Literary Criticism*, Vols. 2, 3, 5, 8, 9, 25, 57; *Dictionary of Literary Biography*, Vol. 5, 165; and *Major 20th-Century Writers*.

# George Gordon (Noel) Byron, Lord Byron
## 1788-1824

English poet, dramatist, and satirist.

## INTRODUCTION

Both celebrated and vilified during his lifetime, Byron was one of the most flamboyant of the English Romantic poets. He is now perhaps best known as the creator of the figure of the "Byronic hero," a melancholy man, often with a dark past, who rejects social and religious strictures to search for truth and happiness in an apparently meaningless universe.

## Biographical Information

Byron was born in London to John "Mad Jack" Byron and Catherine Gordon, a descendent of a Scottish noble family. He was born with a clubbed foot, with which he suffered throughout his life. Byron's father had married his wife for her money, which he soon squandered and fled to France where he died in 1791. When Byron was a year old, he and his mother moved to Aberdeen, Scotland, and Byron spent his childhood there. Upon the death of his great-uncle in 1798, Byron became the sixth Baron Byron of Rochdale and inherited the ancestral home, Newstead Abbey in Nottingham. He attended Harrow School from 1801 to 1805 and then Trinity College at Cambridge University until 1808, when he received a master's degree. Byron's first publication was a collection of poems, *Fugitive Pieces,* which he himself paid to have printed in 1807, and which he revised and expanded twice within a year. When he turned twenty-one in 1809, Byron was entitled to a seat in the House of Lords, and he attended several sessions of Parliament that year. In July, however, he left England on a journey through Greece and Turkey. He recorded his experiences in poetic form in several works, most importantly in *Childe Harold's Pilgrimage.* He returned to England in 1811 and once again took his seat in Parliament. The publication of the first two cantos of Childe Harold in 1812 met with great acclaim, and Byron was hailed in literary circles. Around this time he engaged in a tempestuous affair with Lady Caroline Lamb, who characterized Byron as "mad—bad—and dangerous to know." Throughout his life Byron conducted numerous affairs and fathered several illegitimate children. One of his most notorious liaisons was with his half-sister Augusta. Byron married Annabella Millbank in 1815, with whom he had a daughter, Augusta Ada. He was periodically abusive toward Annabella, and she left him in 1816. He never saw his wife and daughter again. Following his separation, which had caused something of a scandal, Byron left England for Europe. In Geneva, Switzerland, he met Percy Bysshe Shelley and his wife Mary Godwin Shelley,

with whom he became close friends. The three stayed in a villa rented by Byron. During this time Mary Shelley wrote her famous novel *Frankenstein,* and Byron worked on Canto III of *Childe Harold,* which was published in 1816. In 1817 Byron moved on to Italy, where he worked on Canto IV, which was published the next year. For several years Byron lived in a variety of Italian cities, engaging in a series of affairs and composing large portions of his masterpiece *Don Juan* as well as other poems. In 1823 he left Italy for Greece to join a group of insurgents fighting for independence from the Turks. On April 9, 1824, after being soaked in the rain, Byron contracted a fever from which he died ten days later.

## Major Works

Byron is difficult to place within the Romantic movement. He spurned poetic theory and ridiculed the critical work of William Wordsworth and Samuel Taylor Coleridge. Although he was a friend of Shelley, Byron was not, as his friend was, part of the mystic tradition of Romanticism. Byron's first successful work, *English Bards and Scotch Reviewers,* is a satire in the neoclassical tradition of Alexander Pope. His Eastern verse tales—including *The Bride of Abydos. A Turkish Tale* and *The Giaour, A Fragment of a Turkish Tale*—and, especially, such poems as *Childe Harold's Pilgrimage* and *Manfred* are more typically Romantic, with their portraits of outlaws and brooding heroes. *Beppo, A Venetian Story* dispenses with the Byronic hero and turns again to satire, as does *Don Juan*, a mock epic which casts a critical eye on society, presenting its title character not as the notorious womanizer of legend but as a naive victim. This complex, digressive satire, influenced by Italian burlesque poetry, was condemned on its publication as obscene and has been described by some as careless and meandering; however, most critics now regard *Don Juan* as Byron's masterpiece, citing its skillful rendering of a variety of narrative perspectives and its treatment of an array of topics, including politics, society, and metaphysics.

## Critical Reception

Byron's poetry was extremely popular during his lifetime, although some reviewers regarded both his personal life and his writing as immoral. He was nearly forgotten by critics in the second half of the nineteenth century, and during the first half of the twentieth century, he was often ranked as a minor Romantic poet. Since then, however, his poetry has met with increasing critical interest—in particular for its employment of satire and verbal digression, for its presentation of the individual versus society, and for its treatment of guilt and innocence. Finally, Byron's place within the Romantic movement and his debt to the eighteenth-century neoclassical writers before him are a source of ongoing interpretation and reassessment.

## PRINCIPAL WORKS

### Poetry

*\*Fugitive Pieces*  1807
*English Bards and Scotch Reviewers*  1809
*Childe Harold's Pilgrimage: A Romaunt*  [Cantos I and II]  1812
*The Bride of Abydos. A Turkish Tale*  1813
*The Giaour, A Fragment of a Turkish Tale*  1813
*Waltz: An Apostrophic Hymn*  1813
*The Corsair, A Tale*  1814
*Lara. A Tale*  1814
*Ode to Napoléon Buonaparte*  1814
*A Selection of Hebrew Melodies Ancient and Modern*  1815
*Childe Harold's Pilgrimage. Canto the Third*  1816
*The Prisoner of Chillon, and Other Poems*  1816
*The Siege of Corinth. A Poem. Parisina. A Poem*  1816
*The Lament of Tasso*  1817
*Manfred, A Dramatic Poem*  (verse drama)  1817
*Beppo, A Venetian Story*  1818
*Childe Harold's Pilgrimage. Canto the Fourth*  1818
*Don Juan*  [Cantos I and II]  1819
*Mazeppa, A Poem*  1819

*Don Juan, Cantos III, IV, and V*  1821
*Marino Faliero, Doge of Venice. An Historical Tragedy, in Five Acts. With Notes. The Prophecy of Dante, A Poem*  (verse drama and poetry)  1821
*Sardanapalus, A Tragedy. The Two Foscari, A Tragedy. Cain, A Mystery*  (verse dramas)  1821
*The Vision of Judgment*  1822
*Don Juan. Cantos VI.–VII.–and VIII*  1823
*Don Juan. Cantos IX.–X.–and XI*  1823
*Don Juan. Cantos XII.–XIII.–and XIV*  1823
*Heaven and Earth*  1823
*The Island; or, Christian and His Comrades*  1823
*Werner, A Tragedy*  (verse drama)  1823
*Don Juan. Cantos XVI. and XVI*  1824
*The Deformed Transformed; A Drama*  (verse drama)  1824

## Other Major Works

*The Parliamentary Speeches of Lord Byron*  (speeches)  1824
*Letters and Journals of Lord Byron, with Notices of His Life.* 2 vols.  (correspondence and journals)  1830
*Byron's Letters & Journals.* 12 vols.  (correspondence and journals)  1975-1982

\* This work was revised and reprinted in 1807 as *Hours of Idleness, A Series of Poems, Original and Translated.*

## CRITICISM

### M. G. Cooke  (essay date 1969)

SOURCE: "The Fatal Bounds of the Will," in *The Blind Man Traces the Circle: On the Patterns and Philosophy of Byron's Poetry,* Princeton University Press, 1969, pp. 61-90.

[*In the excerpt below, Cooke analyzes the nature of the self and the strength of individual will as they are presented in Byron's dramatic poem* Manfred.]

Critical theorists celebrate as one of the outstanding marks of romanticism the realization that the seat of value is in the self, and the obligation of the self the apprehension of its home beyond brute circumstances of time and place; its "heart and home," as Wordsworth declares, "is with infinitude." A decisive shift in orientation takes place here. For where traditional Christianity had promised redemption of the individual from eternal wretchedness by a briefly incarnate Christ, Agent of Infinitude, romanticism is seen propounding a redemption of infinitude from entrenched materialism by the self, Bearer of Infinitude—so that Christ, as used by Blake for example, comes to represent man-as-God more truly than God-as-man. It would appear quite fitting, then, for Byron to have been brought home to himself in 1816, just as it would appear standard for him, in the name of that self, to have laid claim to infinitude. But Byron's situation and his response admit of features that have no exact parallel within the romantic complex.

The cardinal quality that sets Byron's presentation of the self apart in its time I would describe as starkness. The frustrating interaction of circumstances and personality which almost systematically in **Childe Harold** III strips the self of armor, integument, and salve leads to a minor metaphysical insight in Byron's work, in the implicit recognition that self-assertion counts more than self-regulation in a difficult universe. Of course one cannot be blind to moments of starkness undergone by the other great romantics: as when Keats finds himself tolled back from the nightingale, the blessed world of vision, to his *"sole self"*; or when Wordsworth experiences "a sense, / Deathlike, of treacherous desertion . . . / In the last place of refuge—[his] own soul"; or in Coleridge's "Dejection: An Ode" or in certain of Blake's *Songs of Experience* or *Europe: A Prophecy*. But these instances only remind one that the romantic poet's affirmation of the Self Infinite is rarely divorced from the context, if not the formal process, of argument. It bears emphasizing that the inevitable recoil of romantic self-concern is the recognition of the way others will stand as strangers to one's own presuppositions and predilections, and the recoil of romantic vision the awareness of profane, even antagonistic views. An undernote of philosophical differing, of necessary, if muted argument continually impinges on the reader's consciousness in the most affirmative romantic poetry; but not as a distraction. Rather it leads attention unresisting back to the main theme with little further need for a suspension of disbelief. There has been a barely audible clashing and getting done with the adversary mind, such as we may perceive when Wordsworth writes: "And I must think, do all I can, / That there was pleasure there." The interpolated phrase "do all I can," acknowledges opposition which is obviously made futile (I *must* think). Wordsworth's claim to vision, and by the same token, the claims *of* his vision have to be made good against the possibility of error. "If this be but a vain belief . . ." he worries in "Tintern Abbey," and goes on to purge himself and his reader alike of such misgivings, the force of his renewed conviction breaking the grammatical pattern with an anacoluthon:

> . . . yet oh! how oft—
> In darkness and amidst the many shapes
> Of joyless daylight; when the fretful stir
> Unprofitable, and the fever of the world,
> Have hung upon the beatings of my heart—
> How oft, in spirit, have I turned to thee,
> O sylvan Wye! thou wanderer thro' the woods,
> How often has my spirit turned to thee!

His doubt, played out on a rationalistic, argumentative speculation, shows itself to be unsupportable in the real order of fact and faith. The moment of argument becomes a foil to the moment of affirmation as the verse paragraph swells with exclamations and nearly ritual repetition ("often" works in diction *and* in experience) to annihilate the potentially crippling doubt with which it commences. The doubt, not the belief, is vain. Yet the element of doubt, the

possibility of negation appears in a way necessary to the visionary affirmations of romantic poetry. To recognize the immortality of the bird's voice in "Ode to a Nightingale" or "To a Skylark" or "To the Cuckoo" is also inevitably to recall mortality. And to express immortality is impossible except through denial, or suspension, or actual time and transitoriness. These latter must keep a half-life in the mind for the very sake of one's belief in immortality. The visionary poet thus with equal validity enjoys, or has hopes of, or only continues to believe in, vision. His poetry may be a matter of pursuit as well as of possession, and need do no more than set itself positively on the spiral of aspiration.

This dualistic idea of aspiration and relationship, the concept of ex-stasis that is bound up with the romantic portrayal of the Self, Byron brings to its lowest pitch. The possibility of negation gets in him the kind of substance that represses aspiration into unbending defiance, replacing identification in, and with, the Universe with general self-assertion. It is a rhetorical emblem of a metaphysical orientation that Byron has no nightingale or urn, no cuckoo or solitary reaper, no skylark or west wind, no mountain and no light with which he can collaborate in the discovery and perpetuation of value. At least, not in 1816. He has his special passages of passion, of symbolism, of action, but these eliminate more than they create, building up, as it were, to nakedness. As in **Childe Harold** III they create the image of a man unaccommodated though unlamenting, undefended and yet not reduced to defeat. In **Manfred** that figure is again presented, and for the first time substantially characterized.

The profile of unaccommodated man, as critics have perennially remarked, has another and doubtless more spectacular side from which Manfred appears as unaccommodating man—defiant, seemingly solipsistic, and in less danger of being possessed than self-possessed. But Manfred develops into something more than an all-repudiating hero. He crackles with an aggrieved superiority, but actually by this enables us to observe that the fierceness of his rejection of whatever he has or is offered corresponds to the depth of his fixation on what is, more than coincidentally, unattainable. He typifies the perfectionist and iconoclast in collision with reality, and ordained to recover strength and sanity through acceptance rather than action and aggression.

Notwithstanding Manfred's apparent energy and self-involvement, the play is moving toward an ideal of acceptance from the start. Thus Manfred early implies a repudiation of his past deeds, or misdeeds; "I have ceased / To justify my deeds unto myself—/ The last infirmity of evil" (I.ii.27-29). It is worth stressing that Manfred becomes a hero less for what he can do than for what he can do without. A major rhythm is established in the play with his rejection of an assortment of orthodox forces and relationships. His opening speech—and the first words of the drama—straightway engages us in the mystique of doing without. It recapitulates the things ("Philosophy and science," etc.) which have "avail'd not" for him, presenting him as the disengaged man:

> I have no dread,
> And feel the curse to have no natural fear,
> Nor fluttering throb, that beats with hope or wishes,
> Or lurking love of something on the earth.

What he does have is a purpose ("Now to my task") or, to put it more abstractly, a will. That will must seem curiously thwarted if compared with the will of a Tamburlaine [in Christopher Marlowe's *Tamburlaine*]: Manfred fails to achieve anything, and even puts aside such particular goals as knowledge, benevolence, conquest, and happiness. His will goes practically unsatisfied. But Byron's play, concerned with a different order of will than Marlowe's, plants its standard on a different peak. Tamburlaine triumphs over all obstacles and opposition, only succumbing to death; Manfred defies all dangers and powers, including death. The emphasis in *Tamburlaine* falls primarily on material operations, in Manfred on a spiritual condition, so that the creature's death experienced in common by the two heroes becomes for one a reversal, for the other a culmination of his career. Manfred, as a hero who excels by doing without, proves in his most perfect moment capable of the ultimate excellence of doing without life.

It is crucial to see that Manfred rises above the things he rejects, and at the same time to see that in this he only achieves a negative victory, indicating what he is too strong to submit to, not what he is strong enough to realize. And the latter does not depend on an exercise of will. Manfred's ultimate state takes him clearly beyond mere strength of denial, or of assertion, beyond what Shelley calls "the anarchy / Of hopes and fears." The drama itself seems so far from centering around the manifestations of a substantive will that no other character evinces even Manfred's passing and partial reliance on will, whereas the will of Tamburlaine for example gets its basic definition by outtowering the stilted will of others.

The early spectacle of Manfred's emphatically self-conscious and self-confessing determination too easily seduces attention from the fact that he is met in a pattern of self-discovery and self-acceptance, just as his outbursts of pride tend to drown out a steady note of eagerness for reconciliation and calm. This needs to be remembered in judging his relationship with the rest of the characters; his haughty rejection of them, seemingly progressive in its sequence from Chamois Hunter to Abbot to otherworld Spirits, actually serves to show him arrested at a point of psychological and spiritual crisis; he is living in the trap which the Stranger so dispassionately sets for Arnold in *The Deformed Transformed,* with "no bond / But [his] own will, no contract save [his] own deeds" (Pt. I, i.150-151). These widely differing figures, however, are not the ciphers they are often taken for; they show us a sort of abortive excellence in Manfred, and help to define the impasse of Manfred's situation.

On the cliffs of the Jungfrau and in the mountain cottage, at the outset of the drama, Manfred is seen in a natural and human context. He is divorcing himself from both, finding nature's beauty and man's compassion alike irrel-

evant and impotent for himself. But he leaves his impress behind. The Chamois Hunter defers to him as a superior man, and he signalizes Manfred's spirit rather than his agility in saying that the latter,

> Who seems not of my trade, . . . yet hath reach'd
> A height which none even of our mountaineers,
> Save our best hunters, may attain.
>
>                                     (I.ii.60-62)

Untouched by the world he is leaving, Manfred is also untouched by the underworld he dares to enter. He disdains the shock and indignation of the attendant Spirits in the Hall of Arimanes (III.iv), and indeed extracts from them the same simultaneously personal and professional praise the Chamois Hunter has accorded him, as one of the Spirits breathlessly recognizes in him a "Magian of great power, and fearful skill." There is, finally, the world that comes to Manfred, in the person of the Abbot of St. Maurice who, working in the human sphere in the interest of a spiritual, divine order, in himself comprehends features of two worlds. The indefatigable Abbot shares the experience of the Chamois Hunter and the chthonian Spirits; he can do nothing with Manfred, but finds something admirable and attractive in him, sensing qualities that normally enable one to take a fair place among the brotherhood of man and, ultimately, the communion of saints (II.i). The degree of Manfred's excellence, as well as the degree of his separateness can be discerned in the subjunctive with which Hunter, Abbott, and Spirit all express their responses to him: "You should have been a hunter," "This should have been a noble creature," "He would have made / An awful spirit." The range of his influence can be gauged by the way he moves representatives of the secular, the religious, and the chthonian orders.

Yet it is all too evident that his impregnable loftiness hinges on a secret defect. Certainly there are points at which the "noble" and "awful" uniqueness of Manfred presents itself in a dubious light. In the guilty action with Astarte which Manuel speaks of to the Abbot *offstage,* and which Byron coyly drags in without unwrapping, Manfred has without doubt been the aggressive, the demanding, the reckless party. He is thus liable to the charge of selfishness, and his conduct after realizing that he has in effect victimized Astarte by inducing her into a passing act of passion contrary to her profoundest principles turns his supposed individualism into something more like peevishness. He repudiates philosophy, altruism and so on (I.i) because he has failed to maintain "a kind of transcendental state outside ordinary human experience, . . . an ineffable absolute irreconcilable with the world, . . . [and] *more real than the world*" [Denis de Rougemont, *Love in the Western World,* trans. Montgomery, 1956]. He does it impressively, philosophically even, with *sententiae* like "Sorrow is knowledge," and "The Tree of Knowledge is not that of Life," but it remains tantamount to striking out at others to beguile personal pain.

The emphasis in the early scenes of the play on Manfred's will and what it can make others do tends to corroborate this judgment. Manfred, with the Seven Spirits, and on the

Mountain of the Jungfrau, seeks to prescribe terms to the Universe, seeks to act and be immune to consequences. Even his implied yearning toward "serenity of soul," which he recognizes as a form of "immortality" (II.ii), betrays a known imperfection in his individualism. The root conflict of the drama occurs inside Manfred's mind, and is but intimated in the more conspicuous confrontations with Chamois Hunter or Abbot or otherworld agents. Its root issue has finally two distinguishable terms to be resolved: can Manfred keep from losing himself to various outside forces, can he withstand the "temptation" to "the abandonment of his will"? And if so, can he further find for himself, instead of deadened detachment, a more than mortal "serenity"?

In a sense, the play drives Manfred toward the fullest experience of his somewhat irritable boast that he is, like the lion, "alone"; his metaphor expresses life's literal truth, and life's uncompromising challenge. His difficulties with truth and challenge alike arise chiefly out of his relation to Astarte, whose universe he has not expanded but shattered in pressing her toward some uncanonized transaction. Manfred must learn to *accept,* albeit without sacrificing his essential self; and he must learn not to *expect,* and this is a lesson that he takes longest to learn where Astarte is concerned. His intensest expectation, and gravest weakness, appears as he presses her, or her Phantom, for an expression of forgiveness, then of love, at the end of Act 11. He is denied, and as one of the Spirits present vindictively observes, "He is convulsed—This is to be a mortal / And seek the things beyond mortality." But what looks like the final humbling for Manfred is only the sign of a crisis, in dramatic as well as spiritual terms. Manfred responds superbly. Another Spirit reports on the scene:

> Yet, see, he mastereth himself, and makes
> His torture tributary to his will.

These lines, perhaps, tend to revive the idea of Manfred's predominance of will. In fact, what gets "mastered" here is the curl of the interested self; the will works as a rectified will, not aiming toward (or away from) objects, but purely sustaining the integrity of the existential self. The present "tributary" does not swell the hero's store, or consciousness of will. If anything it destroys it. Manfred emerges from the scene purged of the defects which had led him into it. He remains alert and involved, but he is no longer harshly purposive; in his brief exchange with Nemesis as the scene and act come to a close he shows himself above all ready for whatever may arise. Significantly Astarte now virtually disappears from the play, and Manfred enjoys a new state:

> There is a calm upon me—
> Inexplicable stillness! which till now
> Did not belong to what I knew of life.
>
> (III.i)

Here Manfred attains a dignity beyond what merely "lies in his conscious awareness of, and defiance of, the fates which are his antagonists" [Peter L. Thorslev, "Freedom and Destiny: Romantic Contraries," *Bucknell Review* XIV,

May, 1966]. The serenity for which he has yearned has in effect befallen him, and that in the unlikeliest of places, where he has been thrust through the final gate of agitation.

Clearly this experience of serenity on the part of the "mortal" affords the immortality which he had expected of it, inasmuch as it frees him from the sense of incompleteness and instability inherent in mortality; it is the Emersonian idea of immortality as being "not length of life, but depth of life, . . . not duration, but a taking of the soul out of time." We may note, too, that the singular experience of immortality is given a universal moral bearing in Manfred's identification of it as "the golden secret, the sought 'Kalon'." He has discovered mankind's "good," not just his own; and he has discovered it neither in enormous energy nor in vacant self-forgetfulness, but in the strength of vital peace. And where before he has been bent on rejecting or destroying all terms of existence, his new state proves harmonious and inclusive. It brings back the scholar in him, for one thing, and we may find in his recollection of his "tablets" a noteworthy echo of Hamlet, in an affirmative chord befitting one to whom has been revealed not evil but unprophesied grace:

> It hath enlarged my thoughts with a new sense,
> And I within my tablets would note down
> That there is such a feeling.

Manfred's feeling, his knowledge of spiritual goodness and self-accord opposes as it also redeems his earlier condition of desperate stagnancy, which even he recognized as a "curse." If his "pride and defiance" have any "moral-philosophic value," it must be the negative one of constituting symptoms of a soul dis-eased, of representing the problem rather than the foundation of the play. Manfred's "Promethean" ability to withstand various orthodox and systematic attacks on his self-possession should finally be taken as ambiguous, being but a half-way stage between the ultimate degradation of surrender and his ultimate attainment of a more than personal "calm of mind, all passion spent." For while it could seem that Manfred ceases "to struggle toward resolution," in actuality resolution has befallen him. He knows what it means "wenn ein Glückliches fällt."

Two other problematical points are resolved less successfully as regards Manfred's character. The first is the relation of Manfred to the Abbot, who, unlike the Chamois Hunter and the assorted servants and Spirits parading through the play, ends up in the final version of the play as much more than a foil to the hero. He is a considerable character in his own right, and his position carries substantial weight; because of him *Manfred* escapes being "a one-character drama." Manfred, rejecting his aid, is far from negating his values. Ultimately he fails to break out of the orbit of his priestly function, as he does out of the orbit of the Chamois Hunter and Astarte. The Abbot is present and active to the end, and his persistence, without arrogance or prurience as it is, adds at once to his credit as a priest and to his stature as a character. This is not to gloss over the fact that he is practically stymied. He has, and can have, no proper answer to the serene and simple finality of Manfred's expiring words: "Old man! 't is not so difficult to die." But the play allows him the concluding statement:

> He's gone, his soul hath ta'en its earthless flight;
> Whither? I dread to think; but he is gone.

In this way Byron himself has partially "destroyed the whole effect and moral" of the drama. Manfred avoids the merely conventional piety of Maturin's Bertram: "Lift up your holy hands in charity"; but a problem remains. Has Manfred transcended, or only ignored the possibility intimated in the Abbot's summary? Hasn't the "noble" and "awful" resolution of his last words—the "serenity" which we have been invited to take as a form of "immortality"—been impugned by the fact that the Abbot has the last word? Or do we interpret it that the Abbot retains enough of the intellectual obtuseness and institutional rigidity of the original version to prevent him from appreciating a new existential sanctity in the hero?

*Manfred* ends on an ambiguous note of affirmation and uncertainty. That uncertainty, however, does not concern the power of the will, which is at best irascible and negative. It concerns the possibility and efficacy of purging the will, and constitutes the final problem to be recognized in the play. Is the hero's philosophy ultimately viable? Is his conscience respectable, his character plausible? Even with the affirmative force of "earthless flight" to temper the Abbot's misgivings, the play offers nothing like an answer to such questions, which indeed it raises at the eleventh hour. But as the figure of the self-subsistent hero, most powerfully limned in Manfred, reappears in Byron's work, so does the element of doubt as to his ultimate status. More than this, doubt seems to get amplified into disapprobation as Byron gets closer to the terms of actuality and, in particular, to the contemporary European scene.

## Michael V. DePorte (essay date 1972)

SOURCE: "Byron's Strange Perversity of Thought," in *Modern Language Quarterly,* Vol. 33, December, 1972, pp. 405-19.

[*In this essay, DePorte analyzes Byron's depiction of the struggle for individual freedom in* Childe Harold's Pilgrimage, *claiming that for Byron the desire for freedom can ultimately result in a form of madness.*]

Byron's affection for Augustan satire is well known, but *Childe Harold* is hardly the poem one would turn to for echoes of Swift. Nevertheless, canto 3 contains lines strikingly reminiscent of the "Digression on Madness" [in Swift's *Tale of a Tub*], where the lunatic is pictured as a man unwilling to "pass his Life in the common Forms" and intent on "subduing Multitudes to his own *Power,* his *Reasons* or his *Visions,*" and where it is argued that all conquerors, contrivers of philosophical systems, and founders of new religious sects are thus mad.

> there is a fire
> And motion of the Soul which will not dwell
> In its own narrow being, but aspire
> Beyond the fitting medium of desire. . . .

> This makes the madmen who have made men mad
> By their contagion; Conquerors and Kings,
> Founders of sects and systems, to whom add
> Sophists, Bards, Statesmen, all unquiet things
> Which stir too strongly the soul's secret springs,
> And are themselves the fools to those they fool;
> Envied, yet how unenviable! what stings
> Are theirs!
>
> (3.42-43)

Byron has been reflecting on the fate of the latest conqueror, praising him really. The assessment of Napoleon seems balanced because of the careful antitheses—"An Empire thou couldst crush, command, rebuild, / But govern not thy pettiest passion" (3.38)—yet the balance turns out to be mainly grammatical. That Napoleon can sway empires and at the same time be unable to control himself is not the paradox for Byron it might be for others. He expects irrationality and imprudence of his heroes. After all, what is control to Napoleon? His reforms, his wars, his crimes are alike inspired by a consuming impulse to throw off controls. Such a man hungers after a freedom that is total, a freedom that is above all unchecked from within. Byron understood these aspirations; to a great extent he shared them and tried to act them out. Washington, the responsible revolutionary, he admired; Napoleon, the grasping, extravagant adventurer, bewitched and implicated him. How startling, then, yet how typical of Byron, that he should deflate the portrait of Napoleon with a moral from Swift, reveal the source of the magic charisma as lunacy.

The effects of this shift are interesting. Most immediately we see Byron trying to have things both ways. He has given us Napoleon the demigod; now, to temper awe with pity, he gives us Napoleon the victim. The greatest man of the age, he shows, was inwardly sick and suffering. True, he tricked and betrayed others, but he also betrayed himself. He could not even relish power because he kept hungering for more. There is, we learn, no lasting joy for the mighty: "tempted Fate will leave the loftiest Star" (3.38). Byron has a way of bringing all topics to bear on himself, and in this case he adds "Bards" to Swift's list of archetypal madmen lest we forget that he too is one of the unhappy great, and mistakenly envy the rich and famous poet when we should be shedding a tear for the tormented, misunderstood genius. This is the familiar, self-indulgent mood of *Childe Harold,* a mood established in the first canto by the description of Harold as a scornful, "pleasure drugged" youth who can find nothing worth loving . . . yet whom, alas, "none did love!" (1.6, 9). It is a kind of self-indulgence far removed from Swift.

But tone aside, the passage on madmen is a remarkably close para-phrase of Swift's theory that madness is born of the impulse to spurn tradition and common sense. For Byron is not only out to elicit every emotional response he can; he is after a kind of perspective as well. Why else, in casting about for a means to understand Napoleon, should he evoke the perceptions of a writer less apt to sympathize with his hero than almost anyone he could have thought of? Such is Byron's honesty, an honesty which promises not so much to speak the truth as to admit the worst. Unlike many of his contemporaries in the romantic movement, Blake in particular, Byron seldom inverts traditional values by arguing, say, that excess is wisdom, or that hell is bliss, or that imagination leads to truth while reason deludes. Thus his observation on the madness of conquerors, poets, and philosophers is not a rhetorical ploy introduced to show that what seems mad to the common mind must in fact be sanity of a rare order. That he can allow his heroes to be judged by Augustan criteria without feeling a need to revise definitions does not mean his sympathies are Augustan; it means simply that he feels no compunction to accept the conclusions implied by those definitions. On the contrary, Byron tends to affirm his independence by reacting against the implications of the very definitions he accepts. He will admit that Napoleon is a madman and a fool, and like him the more for it. His view of Rousseau is similar. Rousseau is both a genius *and* mad. His genius lay in the single-mindedness of his love:

> not the love of living dame,
> Nor of the dead who rise upon our dreams,
> But of ideal Beauty, which became
> In him existence, and o'erflowing teems
> Along his burning page, distempered though it seems.
>
> (3.78)

His passions, wild and ignoble as they often were, suffused everything. He could make a casual kiss or glance seem a thing of piercing beauty and significance. His urgent visions of a new, just society were "oracles which set the world in flame, / Nor ceased to burn till kingdoms were no more" (3.81). But he was also single-minded in his hate; he made his life "one long war with self-sought foes" (3.80); he injured those who loved him most. Rousseau's madness is not his genius, yet neither is it separable from it. While madness is no virtue for Byron, it is the mark of an uncommon soul, of a mind resolved to impose rather than accept conditions.

Blake's theories, though radical, are ultimately normalizing; that is, they aim at exploding one set of norms for the sake of another. He meets the old standards head on. He rejects utterly the Augustan's distrust of private inspiration as bordering on madness: "Who shall dare to say . . . that all elevation is of self & is Enthusiasm & Madness, & is it not plain that self-derived intelligence is worldly demonstration?" To Reynolds's insistence that the ability to formulate general truths is "the great glory of the human mind," Blake replies: "To Generalize is to be an Idiot." The abnormal per se could have no appeal for Blake; in his terms it is conventional wisdom and morality that are abnormal. Byron, however, is fascinated with madness *as* madness, not as disguised good sense, in the same way that he is obsessed with incest not as a possibly natural relationship, but as an irresistibly criminal one.

The lure that madness has for Byron cannot be understood without understanding his vision of the Fall. In his mythology, the Fall is less a fall from righteousness into sin, or from reason into passion, than it is a fall from ignorance into awareness. "The Tree of Knowledge is not that of Life," Manfred laments (1.12); the Tree of Knowledge deprived man of Eden, and in the world outside Eden the Fall is relived again and again. Each new thing we learn qualifies our hopes and diminishes the possibilities for happiness. Cain is at first eager for the knowledge Lucifer offers him, since knowledge is the only compensation for the loss of Paradise. But he becomes increasingly despairing as Lucifer's harsh truths unfold. He does not really want to know that the beauty of his beloved Adah is a thing of the moment and will soon fade, or that man will continue to degenerate until human life is more unbearable than he could ever have imagined. After Lucifer has left Cain with these thoughts, he finds himself looking with envy on his sleeping infant son, looking with half a mind to dash the child against a rock and so spare him the agonies of consciousness. Like Wordsworth, Byron has many poems regretting the loss of childhood. But whereas Wordsworth longingly recalls childhood as a time of vision and intuitive wisdom, Byron cherishes it as a time of ignorance, as in these lines from **"I Would I Were a Careless Child"**:

> I would I were a careless child,
>   Still dwelling in my Highland cave,
> Or roaming through the dusky wild,
>   Or bounding o'er the dark blue wave. . . .
>
> Once I beheld a splendid dream,
>   A visionary scene of bliss:
> Truth!—wherefore did thy hated beam
>   Awake me to a world like this?
>
> (1-4, 21-24)

Childhood is a dream: there are no laws of probability that will not bend to desire; horizons are without limit; the child is in a kind of psychic womb where no sally of imagination is stopped cold by reality and the self seems all.

When one awakens from this dream, he awakens to the misery of Cain. Ordinary men may accept the awakening and resign themselves, but for others the awakening is often too violent, or the misery too intense, and they go mad. In Byron madness always results from some sort of confrontation of the self with external realities intolerable to it. When Don Juan is cut down before Haidée's eyes, and her dream of happiness suddenly violated, she falls into a swoon. When, days later, she regains consciousness, she is hopelessly mad: "Thought came too quick, / And whirled her brain to madness" (4.67). The tales are rife with such grief-maddened heroines: Parisina, Medora, Zuleika, Lara's faithful Kaled, who refuses to leave the spot where he was killed in battle but sits cradling an imaginary figure in her arms. Nor need the shattering of expectation be so violent for it to induce madness; the suggestion in **"The Dream"** is that the everyday suffocations of adult life are alone enough to derange a sensitive soul. Once Mary Chaworth has attained the conventional goals of a husband and children, a shadow settles over her. "What could her grief be?—she had all she loved" (136). The implied answer is that though she had all she loved she had nothing left to hope for; her horizons had begun closing in; only in madness could she break out and regain the sense of freedom and possibility she had known earlier:

> Oh! she was changed
> As by the sickness of the soul; her mind
> Had wandered from its dwelling, and her eyes
> They had not their own lustre, but the look
> Which is not of the earth; she was become
> The Queen of a fantastic realm; her thoughts
> Were combinations of disjointed things;
> And forms, impalpable and unperceived
> Of others' sight, familiar were to hers.
>
> (168-76)

Byron's fragile, suffering heroines typically retreat from reality into delusion or death; his outlaw heroes, on the other hand, declare war: they seem consumed by a need to punish the world for its crimes against their sensibilities. At the death of his beloved Leila, the Giaour is overwhelmed by a maniacal passion for revenge which becomes for him a despairing affirmation of the self's right to fulfillment. He would not forget Leila if he could; to do so would not only compromise her memory, but call in doubt the power and validity of personal vision:

> Earth holds no other like to thee,
> Or, if it doth, in vain for me:
> For worlds I dare not view the dame
> Resembling thee, yet not the same.
> The very crimes that mar my youth.
> This bed of death—attest my truth!
> 'Tis all to late—thou wert, thou art
> The cherished madness of my heart!
>
> (1184-91)

Byron's heroes are always afflicted by a "madness of the heart," that is, by a madness of response rather than of perception, a madness like that which the bishop predicted would befall Marino Faliero in his old age when he becomes unbearably sensitive to anything which opposes his will, or like that of Jacopo Foscari, whose passion for Venice is so intense that it blinds him to every consideration of prudence and family responsibility, or like that of Lara, which does not manifest itself in obvious ways:

> 'Tis true, with other men their path he walked,
> And like the rest in seeming did and talked,
> Nor outraged Reason's rules by flaw nor start,
> His Madness was not of the head, but heart;
> And rarely wandered in his speech, or drew
> His thoughts so forth as to offend the view.
>
> (1.355-60)

Lara, Conrad, the Giaour are not self-deceived; they do not retreat into illusion. Indeed, as M. G. Cooke has said [in *The Blind Man Traces the Circle: On the Patterns and Philosophy of Byron's Poetry,* 1969]: "They are heroes who bear the primary stap of consciousness." They see the reality others see, but they refuse to accept or be guided by that reality. They see the distinction between inner and outer worlds only too clearly and know that whatever dreams of happiness or fulfillment they once had are only dreams and can never be actualized. But if they cannot be happy they can yet be free. In Byron, madness is a supreme expression of the desire for freedom because for him freedom demands an uncompromising assertion of the self. Barriers to experience, whether physical, societal, or psychological, must be overcome if the self is to get the measure of that assertion.

The obvious difficulty with such a notion of freedom is that it borders on the psychopathic; it requires a commitment to self so great as to reduce other people to instruments. Ruinous collisions are bound to occur. Of this Byron was painfully conscious. In *Childe Harold* he writes of Cromwell: "What crimes it costs to be a moment free" (4.85). His thoughts on Napoleon in *Childe Harold* no doubt lead him to echo the "Digression on Madness" in part because of its savage attack on the aspiring self. To Swift, total freedom for the individual means slavery for everyone around him; one cannot impose his will without others resigning theirs. Swift thus loathes conquerors, innovating philosophers, and enthusiasts, as tyrants or would-be tyrants, as men who would "reduce the Notions of all Mankind, exactly to the same Length, and Breadth, and Height of [their] own." Byron's view of freedom and self-fulfillment is close to Swift's except that the priorities are reversed:

> He who ascends to mountain-tops, shall find
> The loftiest peaks most wrapt in clouds and snow;
> He who surpasses or subdues mankind,
> Must look down on the hate of those below.
>
> (3.45)

Swift worries about the harm ambitious men do their fellows; Byron laments that their yearnings should be frustrated, that those who brave the free life should be so ill-fated. Byron is not blind to the suffering a man like Napoleon might inflict. Nor does his idea of heroism *require* psychopathic indifference to others. He often railed at the butcheries of Napoleon's wars and was always sensitive to abuses of power by leaders he disliked. But Byron's imagination was more engaged by the plight of the hero pitted against the many than by that of the many at the mercy of the one. His wish would be for a natural coincidence of interests. This is why Napoleon originally so captivated him. During Napoleon's years of glory he seemed to have come close to achieving the ideal: he did just what he pleased, yet in working out a personal destiny received the adulation of the masses and gave Europe hope of a new order.

Byron's fantasy, then, is of a situation in which the hero achieves the fullest self-expression without injury to others. It is, though, a fantasy he seldom indulges for long; he sees that like all fantasies it can never be realized. A life given up to single-minded assertions of will is inevitably destructive of friends, enemies, and followers alike.

The heroes of the tales, not to mention Napoleon, leave a legacy of devastation. And finally such madness of the heart destroys the self; it marks a man out for violent, untimely death or for lacerating despair. Indeed, Byron's sympathies are so often with the conqueror or the outlaw because, despite a genuine abhorrence for their crimes, he identifies with their doomed passion for freedom, with their unreasoning determination either to transcend the limitations imposed by the Fall or to wreak their vengeance on the created order of things. The problem of freedom takes on a special urgency in canto 3, which Byron wrote the year after Napoleon's final defeat in 1815, and only months after his own humiliations in London. Here Byron seems to resign once and for all the possibility of being free in society, any society. From the beginning Harold was an outsider and a renegade, but in the first canto his motives for leaving home are uncomplicated. He is simply tired of his life of ease and pleasure—"the fulness of Satiety" (1.4) has left him melancholy—and he is eager for adventure. By the third canto his disillusionment with society is far more serious and irresolvable:

> But soon he knew himself the most unfit
>   Of men to herd with Man, with whom he held
>   Little in common: untaught to submit
>   His thoughts to others, though his soul was quelled
>   In youth by his own thoughts; still uncompelled,
>   He would not yield dominion of his mind
>   To Spirits against whom his own rebelled,
>   Proud though in desolation—which could find
> A life within itself, to breathe without mankind.
>
>                                             (3.12)

"A life within itself"—Byron, always preoccupied with the priorities of the self, considers now the possibility of voluntary withdrawal from the world in order to enjoy the unchallenged freedom of contemplation. His reflections on Napoleon and heroism force him to conclude that solitude alone offers the self a chance for fulfillment:

>               true Wisdom's world will be
> Within its own creation, or in thine,
> Maternal Nature!
>
>                                             (3.46)

In isolation man can do and think as he wishes without danger of contradiction. He need make no compromises with the world; he need fear no intrusions. One who has suffered and been disillusioned like Byron or Harold is best able to understand what it is the hermit seeks in the wilderness:

>             he can tell
>   Why Thought seeks refuge in lone caves, yet rife
>   With airy images, and shapes which dwell
> Still unimpaired, though old, in the Soul's haunted
>     cell.
>
>                                             (3.5)

The solitary man has the best hope of preserving his ideals because he is unexposed to abrasive contacts with other men. Nature, as opposed to society, lays no claims upon

the freedom of the mind. Indeed, what most impresses Byron about "Maternal Nature" is that her beauties are malleable. He likes the passivity of nature, the way she responds to the suggestions of imagination. "Like the Chaldean," Harold

>             could watch the stars,
>   Till he had peopled them with beings bright
>   As their own beams; and earth, and earth-born jars,
>   And human frailties, were forgotten quite.
>
>                                             (3.14)

He appreciates the way nature can become almost an extension of the self—"Are not the mountains, waves, and skies, a part / Of me and of my Soul, as I of them?" (3.75)—and give us a new sense of ourselves by drawing out of us feelings hitherto unknown:

>   I love not Man the less, but Nature more.
>   From these our interviews, in which I steal
>   From all I may be, or have been before,
>   To mingle with the Universe, and feel
> What I can ne'er express—yet can not all conceal.
>
>                                             (4.178)

Significantly, Byron is moved less by what is revealed *to* him than by what is revealed *in* him. Though there are Wordsworthian moments in ***Childe Harold*** when Byron believes he senses a divine presence animating the forms of nature, his deepest experience of nature is not one of communion. Nature most inspirits Byron by calling forth in him the fullest expression of self, by exciting the discovery of new emotions and sensitivities, and thus enriching and intensifying his experience of himself. She permits him a feeling of participation in the life around him without curtailing his freedom because he encounters nothing there but the various manifestations of his own being.

In his life of Byron, Moore remarks on this all-encompassing preoccupation with the creations of self [Thomas Moore, *Life, Letters, and Journals of Lord Byron,* 1892]. Byron, he observes, cultivated his imagination to the point where he could not accurately perceive the external world and saw only "the reflection of his own bright conceptions." A state of mind which for the Augustans would have been a symptom of madness is for Moore "the very nature and essence of genius." Moore, in fact, maintains that precisely those qualities of mind which unfitted Byron for life assured his greatness as a poet. He suspects, for example, that despite Byron's reputation as a lover, he much preferred dreaming of women to sleeping with them. In the company of a mistress he was soon bored; alone in his study, however, he could adore his mind's image of her:

> It was there that, unchecked by reality, and without any fear of the disenchantments of truth, he could view her through the medium of his own fervid fancy, enamour himself of an idol of his own creating, and, out of a brief delirium of a few days or weeks, send forth a dream of beauty and passion through all ages.

There is much in Byron to bear out Moore's insistence that he gave highest priority to the world of imagination. For Byron the freedom of solitude, or of poetry, is the freedom to regain the child's world of projected realities by asserting the primacy of mental experience. He was fascinated by dreams as pure creations of mind; dreams, he wrote, "divide our being." They are proof of the mind's ability to make

> Substance, and people planets of its own
> With beings brighter than have been, and give
> A breath to forms which can outlive all flesh.
> ("The Dream," 20-22)

The poet he sees as the man who can dream waking, whose imagination, like Tasso's, is such that he is able to behold "The visions which arise without a sleep" (*The Lament of Tasso,* 165). His own *Childe Harold* Byron calls a "protracted dream," which ends only when his power to reify images begins to fail:

> I am not now
> That which I have been—and my visions flit
> Less palpably before me. . . .
> (4.185)

And earlier, at the opening of the third canto, he had described the writing of the poem as a process of giving body to imagination:

> 'Tis is to create, and in creating live
> A being more intense that we endow
> With form our fancy, gaining as we give
> The life we image, even as I do now.
> (3.6)

But Byron's attitude toward the imaginative process is more complicated and self-conscious than Moore would make it seem. Having said in one stanza that he writes as a way of extending the provinces of the self, he reproaches himself in the next:

> Yet must I think less wildly:—I *have* thought
> Too long and darkly, till my brain became,
> In its own eddy boiling and o'erwrought,
> A whirling gulf of phantasy and flame:
> And thus, untaught in youth my heart to tame,
> My springs of life were poisoned.
> (3.7)

It is as if he has suddenly seen what he has written through the eyes of a Swift or a Johnson and realized that to have poetry born of the impulse to impose fancy on actuality is to make poetry a kind of madness. Clearly, Byron does not share Moore's view, or for that matter the views of Coleridge and Wordsworth, that to write from such impulse is simply to be a genius. Though he may echo Coleridge's "Dejection" and exclaim that neither "Worth nor Beauty dwells from out the mind's / Ideal shape of such" (4.123), his meaning is different from Coleridge's. For both Coleridge and Wordsworth the mind's impositions on the external world were evidence that one could not

---

**Francis Jeffrey on *Childe Harold's Pilgrimage*:**

[*Childe Harold's Pilgrimage*'s] chief excellence is a singular freedom and boldness, both of thought and expression, and a great occasional force and felicity of diction, which is the more pleasing that it does not appear to be the result either of long labour or humble imitation. There is, indeed, a tone of self-willed independence and originality about the whole composition—a certain plain manliness and strength of manner, which is infinitely refreshing after the sickly affectations of so many modern writers; and reconciles us not only to the asperity into which it sometimes degenerates, but even in some degree to the unamiableness upon which it constantly borders. We do not know, indeed, whether there is not something *piquant* in the very novelty and singularity of that cast of misanthropy and universal scorn, which [are] . . . among the repulsive features of the composition. It excites a kind of curiosity, at least, to see how objects, which have been usually presented under so different an aspect, appear through so dark a medium; and undoubtedly gives great effect to the flashes of emotion and suppressed sensibility that occasionally burst through the gloom. The best parts of the poem, accordingly, are those which embody those stern and disdainful reflexions, to which the author seems to recur with unfeigned cordiality and eagerness—and through which we think we can sometimes discern the strugglings of a gentler feeling, to which he is afraid to abandon himself. There is much strength, in short, and some impetuous feeling in this poem—but very little softness; some pity for mankind—but very little affection; and no enthusiasm in the cause of any living men, or admiration of their talents or virtues. The author's inspiration does not appear to have brought him any beatific visions, nor to have peopled his fancy with any forms of loveliness; and though his lays are often both loud and lofty, they neither 'lap us in Elysium,' nor give us any idea that it was in Elysium that they were framed.

> *Francis Jeffrey, in an unsigned review of*
> Childe Harold's Pilgrimage. A Romaunt,
> *in* The Edinburgh Review, *Vol. XVIII,*
> *May-August, 1811, pp. 466-77.*

---

talk about "reality" apart from the way it is perceived. "Reality" is a construct of external stimuli and internal response; each mind in some measure creates the world it perceives by transforming raw sensory data into a uniquely personal vision. Since the object becomes in the instant of perception what it is perceived to be, the richer a man's imagination, the richer his experience of reality. There is none of this affirmation of fancy in Byron. He rates highly the textures imagination gives to life, but for him the textures remain imaginary. His sense of frustration is too keen for him not to insist on an irrevocable division between inner and outer; he desperately wants "Worth" and "Beauty" to have objective existence.

Thus for most of the last canto of *Childe Harold,* Byron's pose is that of the heroic victim, the man done dirt both by the world and by his own perceptions. In the famous opening stanzas Byron relates how he conquered his disappointment over the shabbiness of modern Venice by recreating the glories of her past in imagination and filling her streets with characters from Shakespeare and *Venice Preserv'd.* As in his appreciation of nature, he is drawn once more to the life of subjective experience in which pattern, tone, and significance are projected on external reality. He sees that by turning inward the self retains absolute integrity: "The Beings of the Mind are not of clay" (4.5); they cannot be touched or compromised. Yet he no sooner affirms the attraction of imagination than reason intervenes and he pulls back:

> I saw or dreamed of such,—but let them go,—
> They came like Truth—and disappeared like dreams;
> And whatsoe'er they were—are now but so:
> I could replace them if I would; still teems
> My mind with many a form which aptly seems
> Such as I sought for, and at moments found;
> Let these too go—for waking Reason deems
> Such over-weening phantasies unsound,
> And other voices speak, and other sights surround.
>
> (4.7)

Another unexpected turn on imagination: dreams, he decides, bear only semblances of truth, the power of fancy is madness akin to that of poor Mary Chaworth who ruled as "Queen of a fantastic realm," and he perhaps rejects it in part because he sees it as a response essentially feminine and unheroic. This rejection can be taken as evidence of Byron's realism, of a hardheaded refusal to accept the "transcendental ideal." Or, as in the case of his curious epitaph to the portrait of Napoleon, it can be seen as one more attempt to elicit from his readers the double response of admiration and pity. He cannot present the isolated self as a completely happy sanctuary from reality without sacrificing the pathos of the poem. Yet at the same time the sharpness of the reversal suggests a certain intellectual perversity. Given the way he has set up the dilemma of the individual in society, a life of inward meanings is the logical solution. But Byron's instinct is always to recoil from such logic, to resent as an imposition on his freedom conclusions which seem "necessary." He characteristically reacts "in spite of," not "because." He is, as he pictures himself in *English Bards and Scotch Reviewers,* a man "skilled to know the right and choose the wrong."

As has often been said, it is the outlaw's scorn for common morality which compels Byron's imagination. For him, freedom is experienced as an act of definance: the more radical and dangerous the defiance, the stronger the sense of freedom. Thus Byron's outlaws are never merely outlaws. The ordinary criminal may oppose the laws of his society, all the while adhering to some other carefully rationalized system of values—a personal code, the code of the underworld. Byron's outlaws, however, resist all systems of thought, all logic, whether externally imposed or internally conceived. If, like Lara, they have come to scorn the life of virtue, yet they will not become totally criminal. For at times Lara can

> resign his own for others' good,
> But not in pity—not because he ought,
> But in some strange perversity of thought,

> That swayed him onward with a secret pride
> To do what few or none would do beside.
>
> (1.338-42)

In Byron, as in his heroes, contradictions are intensified rather than resolved. He too is possessed by "some strange perversity of thought." When he sees the decaying palaces of Venice, he longs for the city of his imagination. When he raises up that vision, it immediately begins to fade: "other voices speak, and other sights surround." Canto 4 comes back repeatedly to the point that objects take on a richness in contemplation which they never have outside the mind:

> Of its own beauty is the mind diseased,
> And fevers into false creation:—where,
> Where are the forms the sculptor's soul hath seized?
> In him alone. Can Nature show so fair?
>
> (4.122)

But Byron refuses the obvious inferences: that one should either commit oneself to the inner life or be resigned to reality. He refuses because he is unwilling to limit himself by denying any feeling or thought. Throughout **Childe Harold** he laments the passing of youth as a time when self and surroundings might easily merge. But he sees that to return more than momentarily to the illusions of childhood would curtail radically the experience of self which is had through confrontation with a reality alien to it. Harold's journey itself is a metaphor for the kind of freedom to be had by constant change. The discontent with his homeland, the subsequent traveling, the refusal to settle any place reflect Byron's own restlessness of mind. He knows that the man of action's bid for freedom is doomed, yet he finds it impossible to withdraw entirely into the freedom of reverie or solitude. What remains is the exhilarating freedom of change. Here, as in the tales and plays, the uncompromised self emerges as a tangle of conflicting thoughts and desires; the celebration of freedom becomes finally a celebration of ambivalence. In this ambivalence we perhaps see most clearly Byron's own madness of heart. Byron does not altogether share Cain's malignant resentment of creation, nor is his rejection of conventional society, much though he liked to dramatize it, ever so explosive as that of Conrad or Lara. But his outcry against those conditions of mortality which prevent a man's being both happy and fully conscious is every bit as deeply felt, and his willful assertions of self every bit as startling and intense.

**David Parker (essay date 1974)**

SOURCE: "The Narrator of *Don Juan*," in *Ariel: A Review of International English Literature,* Vol. 5, No. 2, April, 1974, pp. 49-58.

[*In the following essay, Parker contends that the narrator of* Don Juan *is intentionally inconsistent and that Byron patterned him after the literary figure of the rogue.*]

As a poet and as a man, Byron was a poseur, everyone agrees, but some of Byron's posturing is more interesting than most poets' sincerity, and by no means everyone disapproves of it. Nevertheless, for those like myself who feel that what there is of value in Byron is not to be dissociated from this posturing, there is a problem; not one that immediately affects our enjoyment of the poetry, but one that can ultimately do so, once we start puzzling about meaning: it is often difficult to know who is saying what is said, how seriously, and with what shade of irony, if any. The problem has been complicated by current intellectual fashions. Problems of identity are all the go, and it is tempting to see Byron as a Regency Borges with a passion for masks, as a precursor of existentialism, or as a devotee of the absurd. I think he probably does have some importance in the history of these phenomena, but simply to say that Byron was doing what lots of writers today are trying to do seems to me neither accurate, nor a good way of seeing where he stands in literary history, nor indeed a reason why we should admire what he wrote.

One critic who has managed to state the problem, without falling into the pedantry encouraged by intellectual fashion, is John Wain [in "Byron: The Search for Identity," in *Essays on Literature and Ideas,* 1963]. Byron's failure to establish his own true identity, he argues, prevented him from having "a fully successful relationship with his poetic imagination." Byron's method, he suggests, was to project an image of himself, "and then let the image do the writing." Because he lacked the confidence to look deeply into his own mind, he fell into the trap of projecting oversimplified images, who wrote oversimplified poetry for him.

I agree that Byron failed to establish his own true identity, that his life and his poetry may be seen as a series of experimental postures, and, like John Wain, I cannot see how he would have developed had he lived, but it seems to me that in one poem at least this failure was no handicap. In **Don Juan,** I believe, Byron exploited his lack of firm identity, his posturing habit, to create a work of enduring value, in which the oversimplification is transmuted into something richer and more satisfying.

The oversimplification is found in each of the multiple narrative voices that all wakeful readers of **Don Juan** notice. Some critics have been offended by these multiple voices, but most readers enjoy them, and it seems to me that the critic should be wary of finding blemishes where the common reader finds only things to enjoy. I am thinking of the narrator's trick of appearing in alternative and contradictory guises. At one point he tells us he is past his "days of love"; at another, that he is "fond of a little love," fond of the "old pleasures," "so they but hold." Almost as soon as the prevailing worldly and tolerant attitude towards sexual irregularity has been established, we come across stanzas such as the following, expressing a prudish distaste for amatory verse:

> Ovid's a rake, as half his verses show him,
>   Anacreon's morals are a still worse sample,
> Catullus scarcely has a decent poem,

> I don't think Sappho's Ode a good example,
> Although Longinus tells us there is no hymn
>   Where the sublime soars forth on wings more ample;
> But Virgil's songs are pure, except that horrid one
> Beginning with 'Formosum Pastor Corydon.'

(1.42)

One could go on listing examples for a long time.

Objections of the sort John Wain makes are set aside by critics who favour the interpretations endorsed by intellectual fashion. They explain the multiple voices of **Don Juan** by making Byron out to be a modern, with a taste for the absurd, in the modern sense. The meaning of the poem, they suggest, is to be found in the ironic dissonance of the many voices. "Its irony," says William H. Marshall [in *The Structure of Byron's Major Poems,* 1962], "is terminal rather than instrumental." This is not an explanation likely to satisfy an enquiring mind; its anti-historical tendency has obvious disadvantages. Indeed, it has been opposed, and fairly successfully I feel, but it seems to me that the way the different narrative voices are united has yet to be fully explained.

The notion that the irony is "terminal" is no longer tenable, once we recognize the pervasive mocking tone, which suggests a judging mind, the narrator's or Byron's, assessing each of the multiple voices. It is only at one level, a fairly low and immediate one, that we find ourselves thinking of, and responding to, the sort of mind that prefers "decent" to "chaste," that speaks with relief of Virgil's "pure" songs, and that dare not refer to the second eclogue, except as "that horrid one / Beginning with 'Formosum Pastor Corydon.'" Most of today's readers, I suppose, see that there is a joke in such passages, first of all because they know Byron. A reader new to Byron might recognize the mockery in this passage, because it is out of tune with what's gone before. But you don't need to know Byron, or to have read any but this single stanza, in order to see that there is a joke. By itself, the stanza makes us aware of the judging mocking mind, a mind that delights in human absurdity (I'm not now using the word as a modernist slogan), but delights also in rising above it, in fixing or placing it, by giving it a crazy elegance of a sort the mind mocked could never devise and would never approve. In this stanza, the rhymes alone make us aware of the judging mind. And whenever the dissonant narrative voices chime in, the comic rhymes, the seemingly casual versification (in truth cunning)—all the things that give the unmistakable air of pretence—clearly indicate that there is something behind the diversity, that the irony is not terminal. The oversimplified images suggest a hidden complexity.

By itself, of course, a tone is not enough to provide a poem with unity. We don't recognize a tone as such, unless it suggests something deeper. My contention is that the multiple voices are united in our recognition, partly induced by the tone, that the narrator is a version of the rogue, who traditionally discovers identity in diversity. Byron's admiration for eighteenth-century literature is well-known, and some critics have demonstrated, specifically, his debt to picaresque fiction. I should say, however, that

I feel the narrator's roguishness is not to be explained simply by the identification of a specific "influence." He has qualities fundamental to rogues found throughout the long tradition of rogue literature.

Juan himself is a version of the rogue, but the narrator, in his mode of thought rather than in his actions, is the one who evokes more often the sentiments that belong to rogue literature. It is his commentary that gives the work its distinctive flavour. It is he who focuses the hatred of cant and hypocrisy, such as we find in *The Alchemist;* he who glorifies faith in impulse and truth to nature, such as we find in *Tom Jones.* And it is he who, through being protean, attains to a higher, freer identity. From Mak the sheep-stealer in the Towneley Mysteries, to Felix Krull, rogues have always been lovers of disguise, mimicry and imposture. The narrator of **Don Juan** takes his place in this tradition. Like the character in *The Importance of Being Earnest* (Wilde is surely one of Byron's literary progeny), he discovers that one is more alive, more alert to the possibilities of life, the more one stretches oneself to embrace alternatives and contradictions. He discovers that, when it is difficult to approach truth at all, it is better to approach it obliquely, from many points, than to pretend it is easy from one.

Recognizing that the narrator is a version of the rogue helps solve not merely the puzzle of the multiple narrative voices; it helps solve the puzzle of how far we should allow ourselves to hear Byron's own voice in the poem. It doesn't matter whether we tell ourselves we are listening to Byron, or to an image projected by Byron, or to a dramatically conceived narrator. The important thing is, we are listening to someone discovering identity through diversity, someone getting at the truth with the help of a variety of alternative disguises. This someone stands behind, concealed, knowable only through deduction and intuition. Perhaps the most sensible thing to say would be that Byron himself is the figure we ultimately sense or detect, and that the narrator is a projected image, the last layer of disguise. That, however, is by no means the only profitable way of imagining the latent structure of the poem. The point is, there is something complex behind the surface simplicities, but it is definable only in terms of those simplicities.

It might be objected that considering **Don Juan** as a piece of rogue literature is no more helpful than considering it as a piece of absurd literature. Both traditions suggest that there is something wrong with conventional attitudes towards truth and identity, and that imposture is a significant activity. Yet there are differences, and **Don Juan,** I feel, has some of the qualities that distinguish rogue literature from absurd literature. The latter usually suggests that there are no certainties: that what we think of as truth is convenient fiction, what we think of as personal identity is role-playing. Sometimes this postulate produces a grim or freakish comedy, but almost always, in the background, there is despair, or at best glum stoicism. Rogue literature, too, questions what is normally accepted as truth, and casts doubt on the fixity of human identity, but it usually does this on the understanding that it is primarily the certainties

endorsed by society it is criticizing; rarely does it strive towards the metaphysical nihilism of absurd literature. If it is in any way nihilistic, it is not so glumly; rather, in the dissolution of certainties it finds freedom and scope for the imagination; not a pretext for *angst.* Even while we criticize them morally, we admire the imagination and appetite for life of Lazarillo de Tormes, of Falstaff, of Roderick Random. We find their scepticism about rules and theories exhilarating, not dismaying. **Don Juan** provokes the same exhilaration. In it, the feeling of moral liberation and the gusto, that belong to rogue literature, blend imperceptibly with the love of freedom and of truth to nature, characteristic of romantic literature. The narrator of **Don Juan** is the rogue as romantic sensibility.

It is not just that looking at **Don Juan** as rogue literature makes us see it better than looking at it as absurd literature. It seems to me that this way we are more likely to do justice to the intelligence and sanity of the poem. Rogue sentiment and the romantic love of freedom both easily turn into superficial gesturing, but not so easily as the existentialist *angst* that seems to be at the heart of absurd literature. The trouble with this *angst* is that it is well-founded only if you believe the universe has let you down, if you feel it has neglected its clearly defined duty to provide you with certainties. Absurd literature is the literature of an age of transition; its value lies more in the way it records characteristic experiences of the age, than in its insight into enduring truths. Too often, it amounts to little more than the formalized self-pity of the generation. **Don Juan** is altogether more robust than most absurd literature. There is a continuous energy behind it that stops it from ever degenerating into superficial gesturing (however much it makes superficial gesturing its subject matter). Its clarity of vision demands that the poem be put in a different category from absurd literature.

Some readers might resist thinking of the narrator of **Don Juan** as a rogue, because he is aristocratic in temperament and style. He is familiar with members of the Spanish gentry, and he writes in a lordly fashion, with the manner of a man who finds it easy to laugh at modish ideas, persons and institutions, because his breeding sets him above them. It would be wrong to see this as something disqualifying him from being a rogue. Rogues are drawn to gentlemanly and aristocratic styles, and there seems to be an obscure link between rogues on the one hand, gentlemen and aristocrats on the other. Some rogues, like Mak the sheep-stealer and the hero of Quevedo's *La Vida del Buscón,* are enthusiastic mimics of upper-class styles. Some, it is suggested (ironically or otherwise), are good at upper-class styles because of a natural affinity with gentlemen and aristocrats: Robin Hood in the ballads, for example, Macheath, and Fielding's Jonathan Wild. And some rogues have an easy command of upper-class styles because, like the heroes of Restoration comedy and Roderick Random, they really are gentlemen or aristocrats.

During the Restoration era, in fact, it became fashionable to assume that all true gentlemen had something in common with rogues (it helped distinguish them from the hypocritical bourgeoisie). The old equation, "rogues are like gentlemen," was reversed. But the way had been well-prepared by the rogue tradition in literature. In the ballads, Robin Hood is a yeoman with a courtly style. At the end of the sixteenth century, Anthony Munday made him a real aristocrat, the wronged Earl of Huntingdon. Within a few years, it became natural to think of rogues as possessing a certain elegance. In *Volpone,* Mosca speaks admiringly of

> . . . your fine, elegant rascall, that can rise,
> And stoope (almost together) like an arrowe;
> Shoot through the aire, as nimbly as a starre;
> Turne short, as doth a swallow; and be here,
> And there, and here, and yonder, all at once;
> Present to any humour, all occasion;
> And change a visor, swifter, than a thought:

The rogue's very protean nature is thought of as elegant. By the time of *A New Way to Pay Old Debts* (1625), we find an old-fashioned low-class rogue, Sir Giles Overreach, being defeated by one of the new upper-class gentleman-rogues, Welborne, whom Massinger evidently thought naturally superior in wit and resourcefulness. In the Restoration era, as I say, both in comedy and, it seems, in life, gentlemen and aristocrats thought of themselves as rogues. The tradition was carried forward by *The Beggar's Opera* and by eighteenth-century fiction. During the Regency period, the Restoration feeling about rogues and gentlemen was evidently revived in social life and, by Byron among others, in literature.

The style, or rather styles, of *Don Juan* is one of the things that points to a link with the rogue tradition. "Carelessly I sing," the narrator tells us, "But Phoebus lends me now and then a string" (VIII.138). This is a fair description—of the effect at any rate. We admire the ramshackle gracefulness of the verse, and the way it moves imperturbably from one contradictory note to another. Rogues are always masters of style, and of quick changes between styles. It is part of their delight in disguise, mimicry and imposture. This is another area, too, in which the rogue and the gentleman meet. We can think of the narrator of *Don Juan* as one of the mob of gentlemen who write with ease, or we can think of him as a rogue with a love of brilliant surface. For a complete response, we have to think of him as both.

As many critics have pointed out, there is an exactness of control lying behind the seeming carelessness of the verse of *Don Juan*. Byron had a good ear, and a sure taste for effect. The effect of carelessness is carefully contrived. It is largely a matter of courting poetic disaster, striking a pose, or moving from one pose to another, in such a way that the reader is convinced the precarious balance will be lost, and is disproportionately pleased when it's not. The narrator behaves, verbally, like one of those circus performers who are both clowns and acrobats. Doing a trick, he always manages to give an impression of clumsiness, of impending failure, but always at the last moment he converts clumsiness into grace, and succeeds. And like the acrobatic clown, the narrator makes those he mockingly pretends to imitate seem silly and dull; what he does is

a sort of demonstration of his contempt for such actions, such postures.

It shouldn't, then, be too difficult for us, when we are reading *Don Juan,* to identify with sufficient precision who is saying what is said. It is a rogue, a prankster, whom we perceive precisely because we are addressed by so many contradictory voices. It makes little difference whether we assume this rogue to be Byron or a dramatically conceived narrator. It is a little difficult to tell how seriously any particular utterance is made, and what shade of irony, if any, we are supposed to detect, but not much more difficult than it usually is in ironic literature, or, speaking more specifically, in rogue literature. Reading the poem, we get to know the rogue behind the various disguises; our sense of character, our natural discernment, teaches us how to assess each utterance, for its degree of seriousness and degree of irony. Most sensible critics have realized this, and I don't propose to demonstrate what they already have. The judicious reader will agree with Helen Gardner's reply to the charge that *Don Juan* is amoral (a charge implicit in the notion that it is a piece of absurd literature). "It is preposterous to call *Don Juan* an amoral work," she says [in *"Don Juan," The London Magazine* 5, July, 1958]. "Apart from the obvious moral passion in many passages, we are in no doubt as we read that Byron admires courage, generosity, compassion and honesty, and that he dislikes brutality, meanness, and above all self-importance, hypocrisy and priggery." We are in no doubt, that is, that Byron's values, formally presented through the medium of the narrator, are ultimately the values that lie behind most rogue literature worth reading. They are the values of Ben Jonson and Henry Fielding.

Supporters of John Wain's thesis might object that the rogue tradition is not something a poet can devote his creative life to exploiting. He may try it once, or a few times even, but he has to go on. At best it offers only a provisional adjustment to social and psychological fact. It doesn't offer a mode for discovering the deepest truths. I would agree; but I would also point out that such an objection, severely adhered to, puts out of court a great deal of literature most qualified readers admire. It implies that we should admire only the very greatest. What I am trying to suggest is this: I don't think it is true to say that Byron's failure to establish his own true identity prevented him from having "a fully successful relationship with his poetic imagination," if by that it is meant that Byron never wrote anything of significance in which this failure is not manifest, and which is not in some way spoiled by it (I think that's what John Wain does mean). *Don Juan* might not tell us whether Byron ever discovered himself, but it doesn't matter. In *Don Juan* we have a poem, unique in its way of course, but at the same time very nearly perfect of its type. And paradoxically, in the very diversity of voices heard within the poem, we perceive a man who, if he has not actually discovered himself, has got very near to it (close enough, indeed, for the purposes of the poem), through a process of exclusion: through identifying a multitude of inadequate and despicable moral postures, and thus disowning them. Negative though this process may be, it shows us a complex and volatile personality achieving at least a provisional stability, and that's no mean feat for a poem to perform.


**Howard H. Hinkel   (essay date 1974)**

SOURCE: "The Byronic Pilgrimage to the Absurd," in *The Midwest Quarterly,* Vol. XV, No. 4, Summer, 1974, pp. 325-65.

[*In the following essay, Hinkel contends that Byron's poetry reflects his continuing attempts to come to terms with a world he considered chaotic and meaningless.*]

In 1821, only three years before his death, Byron wrote in his diary: "It is all a Mystery. I feel most things, but I know nothing except—." He then covered the page with a series of blanks. The best of Byron's poetry is variation on that theme. The theme assumes nearly as many different emphases as the poet assumed poses, but the recurring motif, from *Childe Harold's Pilgrimage* through the fragmented Canto XVII of *Don Juan,* asserts an essentially absurdist view of the world. In one sense, Byron was born out of phase with time. While Coleridge and Wordsworth affirmed the organic unity of life and the blessedness afforded one who participates in an ultimately benevolent process, Byron traced the shrineless pilgrimage of Childe Harold who searches relentlessly for he is not sure what. While Shelley—even in Byron's presence—found "flowering isles" in the "sea of life and Agony" (imaginatively, if not actually), Byron allowed Manfred to die out of an unbearable, guilt-ridden existence. While Keats was steeling himself against misery with his doctrines of disinterestedness and "soul-making," Byron prepared Don Juan to play cleverly and sometimes heartlessly with a world which shifted constantly beneath his feet. Unlike his contemporaries, who were capable of affirmation in the face of misery, Byron affirmed, then doubted his own affirmations. Unable to realize, intellectually or emotionally, the stability and sanctity of Wordsworth's and Coleridge's organically unified world, Byron faced a world in which there was yet no adequate defense against chaos.

Like T. S. Eliot one hundred years later, Byron felt the need to shore some fragments against his ruin. In his poetry he first explores a fragmented world, then builds a refuge against it. Byron spent the balance of his poetic career haunted by what Harold Bloom has called the "specter of meaninglessness" (*The Visionary Company,* 1961). He used the force of his poetic genius to deal with this specter, first by shouting defiance of the world, then by mocking it, laughing that he might not weep. Ironically, the power of Byron's opposition made the specter materialize; the poetry from *Childe Harold's Pilgrimage* through *Don Juan* progressively reveals an incoherent, essentially meaningless world.

Although there are moments in *Childe Harold's Pilgrimage* when the pilgrim seems to have found what he seeks, something of extraordinary beauty and value, most of the pilgrimage wanders from one disillusioning experience to another. From the beginning there is a poignant sense of burned-out life, of energy so purposelessly spent that only a void remains. In the very first stanza the poet sets the tone by denying himself a muse: "Nor mote my shell awake the weary Nine / To grace so plain a tale—this lowly lay of mine." This initial humility is the poet's, but the pilgrim will eventually realize it as well. No muse could elevate and inspire the poem, for the subject itself is base. From "Childe Harold's Good Night" till the end of Canto IV, the pilgrim wanders; less heroically than Tennyson's Ulysses, he defines his existence in terms of quest and new experience. Each new experience, though, disappoints. The shining, enchanting beauty of Lisbon seen from afar becomes the wretchedness and poverty of the city seen in close-up. Heroic and legendary Greece has a modern sculptor; an Englishman, Lord Elgin, hacks away at Grecian monuments, forcing Byron to write "The Curse of Minerva." Countless experiences and themes from the poem might be cited to support the claim that the poet is beginning to develop a nihilistic view of things: the lasting disparity between ideal and real, aspiration and achievement, imagination and reason; the *sic transit gloria mundi* theme which informs Cantos III and IV; the lonely soul theme which the alien Harold reiterates so boldly but sadly. But ultimately there is hope in *Childe Harold's Pilgrimage.* The poet found at least one way of dealing with a disappointing world: the creation of art. The fear of nothingness leads nowhere, so Byron seized, almost in desperation, the idea of living through imaginative structuring of experience:

> 'Tis to create, and in creating live
> A being more intense, that we endow
> With form our fancy, gaining as we give
> The life we image, even as I do now. . . .
>
> (III, vi)

This concept, reinforced by the Shelleyan-Wordsworthian optimism that appears in the middle of the canto, suggests that Byron had reached despair but passed beyond it. Shelley's optimism, though, is unnatural to Byron, and there is a regression to bleakness in Canto IV. But the notion of living by creating gave Byron one defense against chaos; he finds another in Canto IV, a tremendous faith in the power of the human mind and will.

As Childe Harold enters Venice in Canto IV, Byron is still sustained by his newly achieved conviction that the creative imagination gives structure and meaning to the poet's existence. In an echo of the passage from Canto III, vi, Harold identifies "The Beings of the mind" as being of more than clay. They are "essentially immortal," and they afford us eventually a more "beloved existence" (IV, v). Eventually, though, the creations, the "Beings," yield importance to the mind itself. In stanza xxi Byron affirms an even greater strength in the mind:

> Existence may be borne, and the deep root
> Of life and sufferance make its firm abode
> In bare and desolated bosoms: mute
> The Camel labours with the heaviest, load,
> And the wolf dies in silence—not bestowed

In vain should such example be; if they,
Things of ignoble or of savage mood,
Endure and shrink not, we of nobler clay
May temper it to bear,—it is but for a day.

The poet's eye is turning yet more inward, scanning the
creations of the mind for their beauty and life, but praising the mind even more because it can will endurance for
our mortal clay. No longer seeking to transcend bodily
life by momentary engagement with the higher world of
art, Childe Harold gradually adopts a quite acceptance of
his unrewarding quest. In stanza cxxvii he says that it is
"a base / Abandonment of reason to resign / Our right of
thought—our last and only place / Of refuge. . . ." This
last proclamation reaffirms his suspicion, first voiced in
stanza xxv, that perhaps the best he can do on his pilgrimage is "To meditate amongst decay." The very power of
art to revitalize life depends upon the mind's receptivity;
the mind itself is our last refuge.

Byron's belief in the shaping power of poetry undoubtedly influenced his notion of the indomitable force of the
mind; poetry, which gives life to the poet, is of course a
creation of the mind. But the Prometheus myth added
another dimension to Byron's developing conviction that
the mind itself is man's greatest resource. Prometheus had
long fascinated Byron, enough so that he wrote an entire
poem about the rebellious Titan. His defiance of Zeus,
his opposition to a force supposedly greater than himself, made Prometheus attractive to Byron at this point in
his development. The Titan epitomizes heroic volition,
terrifying assertion of one's own will. Zeus stood as a
judge who enforced illogical and indefensible laws. Through
an act of will, Prometheus became the soul judge of
himself by refusing to accept any external standard or
law. He became a law unto himself, and it is to this same
position that the poet himself came. Having failed to
find coherence and stability in a world of orthodox standards and conduct, Byron concluded that coherence could
at least be achieved within the individual mind. With this
pervasive sense of individual order, *Manfred* was composed.

Simply stated, *Manfred* dramatizes the refusal of the mind
to yield to anything outside itself. Manfred, then, at least
in part, develops from Childe Harold whose last refuge is
the mind itself. As did Childe Harold, Manfred sought for
something more than the "humble virtues," "hospitable
home," and "spirit patient" represented by the Chamois
Hunter. But like Childe Harold, Manfred was destined to
be an alien: "though I wore the form, I had no sympathy
with breathing flesh" (II, ii, 56-57). Tormented by his
sense of guilt for having loved "as we should not love"
(II, i, 27), Manfred seeks forgetfulness. He is offered what
he needs by the Witch of the Alps if he will only yield his
will to her. Manfred's reply to the Witch of the Alps might
be the poet's to the world:

> I will not swear—Obey! and whom? the Spirits
> Whose presence I command, and be the slave
> Of those who served me—Never!
>
> (II, ii, 157-159)

Even at the moment of death when the spirits come to
claim him, Manfred asserts the supremacy of his own will:

> I do not combat against Death, but thee
> And thy surrounding angels; my past power
> Was purchased by no compact with thy crew,
> But by superior science—penance, daring,
> And length of watching, strength of mind, . . .
>
> (III, iv, 112-116)

Strength of mind, the impassioned assertion that the individual will is the most powerful of forces. Manfred's
anguish came not from any external imposition, but from
within—and so does his death. The common mind (the
abbot), shaped by orthodoxy, is at a loss to understand
Manfred's willful death. It is this same common mind,
nourished by traditional values, which both Byron and
Manfred repudiate. Childe Harold tentatively asserted the
supremacy of the individual will; Manfred glorifies it.

Heroic defiance cannot last indefinitely. Either it must
consume its possessor, as it does Manfred, or be consumed, leaving a void behind. The tone of the poetry after
*Manfred* suggests that the latter may have happened to
Byron, that at least in his art the will to command experience absolutely slowly diminished. In the best poems,
especially in *Don Juan,* there is a resignation which accepts incoherent meaninglessness and deals with it. In his
epic, Byron's outright defiance fades, and he doubts the
sanctity of most things, the individual will and poetry
included. Having lowered his two earlier defenses against
ruin in the face of chaos, Byron adopted new ways of
dealing with an essentially absurd world. Sentimental visions of innocence, shrineless pilgrimages, aesthetic imposition of order, heroic self-assertion, and Shelleyan transcendence all failed to uncover the coherent, ordered world
he sought. By 1818, then, Byron concluded that no order
was to be found. His consequent acceptance of chaos is
even reflected in the form of his greatest works. The earlier poetry usually had been written in rhymed forms dignified by the weight of tradition. Pope and the heroic
couplet stood behind *English Bards, and Scotch Reviewers,* supporting an interesting but lame satire. Spenser and
all his imitators gave aged authority to the stanza form of
*Childe Harold's Pilgrimage.* Even the plays, although
unique in many ways, show obvious indebtedness to the
rich English and Greek dramatic traditions. But in English
there was no *ottava rima* tradition, no precedent for the
unlikely rhymes, the diversified metrics, sometimes Mil-
tonic in grandeur, sometimes deliberately doggerel. Byron
was on his own, free from serious concerns for propriety
and structure. The rejection of most literary standards
complemented his rejection of the idea of an ordered
universe. With the freedom afforded by the *ottava rima,*
Byron developed his last defense against incoherence.
Childe Harold's quest and Manfred's peculiar knowledge
had turned up relatively little to be celebrated in the world.
The world, though, could be neither transcended nor ignored, but had to be faced. Laughter, even when it tended
toward the hysterical, offered a way of coping without
going mad.

A cursory look at *Beppo* confirms that Byron had begun to laugh. The material for an explosive melodrama is here. After years away, Beppo returns home to find his wife, Laura, keeping the company of a "Cavalier Servente." If Beppo had had Childe Harold's idealism and Manfred's grand passions, he could have turned his unexpected home-coming into an Italian domestic tragedy. The poem, though, gives nothing of the sort. The hero accepts his plight calmly, makes necessary adjustments. Laura occasionally enrages Beppo by henpecking him, but his fury is soon spent. Indeed, the Count, the "Cavalier Servente," and Beppo "were always friends." No heroic vengeance; no epic destruction of Penelope's suitors. Beppo simply accepts things as they are, and his acceptance resembles Byron's own; things may occasionally enrage him, but he is now amiable on the whole.

*Mazeppa* reaffirms the notion that nothing now is very important. Much of the poem approximates the emotional depths Byron had examined in *Childe Harold's Pilgrimage* and *Manfred*. The tale relates events of passion, violence, and revenge, and Byron seems to have exposed his pulse in public once again. But finally *Mazeppa* is an elaborate joke, a shaggy-dog story constructed in 868 lines leading to a punch line which deflates the serious tone of the narrative. The fact that the King, the intended audience, slept through the balance of the narrative implies that the poet's art is really a soporific. The poet may have participated in a greater world created by the imagination in *Childe Harold's Pilgrimage* (III, vi), but in *Mazeppa* poetry has become dull entertainment which may or may not reach the intended audience; it really does not matter, though, because the joke is for the poet's sake.

With the peculiar calm which resulted from his realization of nothingness in the world, and with the relaxed freedom afforded by the *ottava rima*, Byron wrote *Don Juan*. To demonstrate in this poem the despair at a meaningless world is easy. Indeed, the unlimited scope of the poem makes it likely that nearly anything can be proved by reference to the text. But the idea of nothingness permeates the poem because it appears at so many strategic and dramatic moments. For example, the following stanza might be cited as evidence of Byron's vision of nothingness:

> Ecclesiastes said, "that all is vanity"—
>   Most modern preachers say the same, or show it
> By their examples of true Christianity:
>   In short, all know, or very soon may know it;
> And in this scene of all-confessed inanity,
>   By Saint, by Sage, by Preacher, and by Poet,
> Must I restrain me, through the fear of strife,
> From holding up the nothingness of Life?
>
>                                         (VII, vi)

Canto VII is of course one of the war cantos; consequently its dominant tone is seriously satirical. War is shown to be violent, and Don Juan, at least for a while, fights violently beside the best of the Russian troops. Yet the high seriousness of the tone and the subject matter is regularly undermined. While monstrous war goes on in Canto VII, in the next canto, after the Russians have besieged the city, the serious tone is interrupted by levity. In the best Roman-Sabine tradition, the raping begins:

> Some odd mistakes, too, happened in the dark,
>   Which showed a want of lanterns, or of taste—
> Indeed the smoke was such they scarce could mark
>   Their friends from foes,—besides such things from haste
> Occur, though rarely, when there is a spark
>   Of light to save the venerably chaste:
> But six old damsels, each of seventy years,
> Were all deflowered by different grenadiers!
>
>                                         (VIII, cxxx)

The flippant couplet alone turns a sad situation into a comic episode. In the next stanza, though, the narrator points out "that some disappointment there ensued," and the following stanza tells why:

> Some voices of the buxom middle-aged
>   Were also heard to wonder in the din
> (Widows of forty were these birds long caged)
>   "Wherefore the ravishing did not begin!"
>
>                                         (VIII, cxxxii)

The nothingness which Byron holds up here is not the fact of war, but the inane responses to it. Against the cruelty of war and the subsequent inanity which informs man's response to war, Byron protects himself with laughter. On the whole, the war cantos reveal a depth of compassion and sense of the sanctity of human life. But to be only serious about such matters is again to invite despair. Byron chooses to laugh, and then to move on to the Court of Catherine the Great. Rapid movement and laughter becomes his defense against senseless cruelty and inane human behavior.

That laughter and acceptance of nothingness have replaced the earlier defense against ruin which Byron found in the creative act is reflected in his expressed attitude toward poetry in *Don Juan*. At the beginning of Canto VII the poet identifies his tale as a "versified Aurora Borealis / Which flashes o'er a waste and icy clime" (VII, ii). The light of his verse, though, is not to redeem or to elevate, but to lay bare a wasteland of a civilization that we may know it for what it is. The following passage tells what the Aurora Borealis elucidates:

> When we know what all are, we must bewail us,
>   But ne'erthless I hope it is no crime
> To laugh at all things—for I wish to know
> What, after all, are all things—but a show?
>
>                                         (VII, ii)

Poetry now induces laughter; no longer does it allow its creator to participate in a better world of art, rather to live with his lesser world of factual nothingness—a "show." Among myriad possibilities, several stanzas from Canto XIV reflect the persistency of Byron's now casual attitude toward poetry. In stanza viii "Poesy" is "a straw, borne on my human breath." Whimsical by intent, it acts "according as the Mind glows." Like straw, poetry is essentially hollow, lacking the passionate emotion which surfaced so regularly in *Childe Harold's Pilgrimage* and *Manfred*. The couplet of stanza viii comments further on poetry:

> And mine's a bubble, not blown up for praise,
> But just to play with, as an infant plays.

After admitting in stanza x that "I can't help scribbling once a week," Byron expresses a defense of poesy that must have shocked his friend, Shelley:

> But "why then publish?"—There are no rewards
>   Of fame or profit when the World grows weary.
> I ask in turn,—Why do you play at cards?
>   Why drink? Why read?—To make some hours less
>     dreary.
> It occupies me to turn back regards
>   On what I've seen or pondered, sad or cheery;
> And what I write I cast upon the stream,
> To swim or sink—I have had at least my dream.

Writing is like a pointless game of cards or is a soporific, like reading and drinking. It pacifies. All these passages, and countless other, suggest that Byron had become obsessed with emptiness and futility. Art became a game, played only as earnestly as suburban housewives might play bridge, to keep blankness away.

This affable but calloused appraisal of the world finally leads Byron to train his hero quickly for the insubstantial, hypocritical society he will find in the English Cantos. After several stanzas of cataloguing ignominious historical events and figures in England's past and present, the poet instructs Juan in how to survive in the inanity of the English society Juan has entered:

> But *"carpe diem,"* Juan, *"carpe, carpe!"*
>   To-morrow sees another race as gay
> And transient, and devoured by the same harpy.
>   "Life's a poor player,"—then "play out the play,
> Ye villains!" and above all keep a sharp eye
>   Much less on what you do than what you say:
> Be hypocritical, be cautious, be
> Not what you seem, but always what you see.
>
>                         (XI, lxxxvi)

All races and days in this society are transient, and Juan must learn self-annihilation and shape-shifting if he is to play in a frivolous world. This is self-annihilation, though, which is manifested in convenient refusal to be a person; Juan must always be whatever the situation demands. This capacity to disguise one's essential self while playing various roles is identified in Canto XVI as "mobility." While Lady Adeline entertains her husband's political supporters, she assumes her role so elegantly that Juan "began to feel / Some doubt how much of Adeline was real" (xlvi). Furthermore:

> So well she acted all and every part
>   By turns—with that vivacious versatility,
> Which many people take for want of heart.
>   They err—'t is merely what is called mobility,

> A thing of temperament and not of art,
>   Though seeming so, from its supposed facility;
> And false—though true; for, surely, they're sincerest
> Who are strongly acted on by what is nearest.
>
>                         (xcvii)

"Want of heart" is precisely what is wrong in the world Juan inhabits. Strong will and heart moved Childe Harold and Manfred through anguished existences, though, and Byron, like Juan and Lady Adeline, has learned that an emotional commitment to an essentially meaningless existence can only bring anguish. Don Juan will prosper in England; like Lady Adeline he learns to adjust to the moment at hand. Persistent and flippant inconsistency is the only way to deal with an insubstantial, incoherent world.

*Don Juan* is something of a labyrinth, though, and around each corner and at each dead-end is more evidence that the poet has determined existence itself to be an incoherent maze. Rather than proceed with more particular illustrations, perhaps it is better to look at three general points about the poem to show that it is finally about nothingness. First, the very fact that the poem concerns everything suggests that it is ultimately about nothing. Byron admitted in a letter to his publisher (April 23, 1818) that the poem "is meant to be a little quietly facetious upon every thing." A central theme is impossible to locate. At times the theme seems to be the old discrepancy between illusion and reality. Or perhaps it is, as several critics recently have argued, the theme of the Fall with elaborate variations. Or perhaps a desire to expose gross hypocrisy motivated the poem. Or perhaps. The possibilities are countless. The focus is finally nowhere. By being everywhere, *Don Juan* is not anywhere—it is constantly in the process of becoming, but it never simply is, nor could have been until it ended, and it could end only with Byron's death. To look too closely at any single subject, or to narrate in a single tone of voice, would be to edge toward consistency, and consistency is more than the hobgoblin of small minds; it is madness. Byron's "mobility," though, allows him to keep playing opposites off against one another in a desperate defense against despair. If love becomes painful, it must be mocked. If war is violent and cruel, there must be women wondering when the raping will begin. If there is an Aurora Raby, there must be a Lady Adeline. Rapid movement with a shifting world is the only means of survival.

Secondly, the character of Juan himself demonstrates the emptiness of the world Byron inhabited. Mobility becomes the habit of Juan's soul. A reader spends an immense amount of time with Juan, but finally knows very little about his character. Even more important, Juan almost completely lacks the will which sustained Childe Harold and Manfred. As numerous critics have pointed out, the world acts upon him. Even his few willed acts, like the saving of Leila, are vague gestures that go nowhere. Like Auden's unknown citizen, "When there was peace, he was for peace; when there was war, he went." When there is an empress to pamper him, he lets her. But that is Juan's victory; the moment determines both his actions and his essence.

Finally, the essential formlessness of the poem reflects Byron's conviction that life is ultimatley incoherent and chaotic. The poem literally sprawls from Spain to Greece, from Greece to Turkey, from Turkey to Russia, and from Russia to England. Byron was too much an artist to try to impose strict, traditional artistry on Juan's meandering. He simply terminates episodes when they no longer interest him, and numerous digressions interrupt and defy a strictly coherent narrative. This formlessness, though, comes not from incompetence, but from Byron's understanding of how he had to operate within his world in order to stay sane. From one canto to the next he wrote what pleased him, how it pleased him. If he decided that the reader did not need to know how Juan escaped from the Seraglio, Byron did not bother to tell. If Leila, who was the occasion for Juan's one really heroic and compassionate act, virtually disappears from the poem though she remains with Juan, the poet does not care. What did it matter? The poem meant more to Byron as process than as achievement. With urbane laughter and the emotional detachment afforded thereby, Byron survived in his poetic world which earlier had nearly devoured him. Byron's own comment that parts of **Childe Harold's Pilgrimage** were written by a man much older than he would ever be is appropriate. Childe Harold's idealism-to-anguish journey tired the poet; the endless growth and process of **Don Juan** not only kept him young, but sustained him in a world which he intellectually knew and experimentally proved to be imperfect.

### Edward E. Bostetter   (essay date 1974)

SOURCE: "Masses and Solids: Byron's View of the External World," in *Modern Language Quarterly*, Vol. 35, No. 3, September, 1974, pp. 257-71.

[*In the essay below, Bostetter examines Byron's ideas regarding the relationship of the human mind and the physical world as expressed in his poems.*]

John Locke's theories affected all the major Romantics, even those like Coleridge who repudiated them with such scorn. In particular, they were influenced by his separation of senses into primary and secondary sensations, the external world versus the inner world. The distinctions Locke drew were simple and dramatic: the "primary" qualities of objects—solidity, extension, figure, motion or rest, and number—are those that really exist in the objects, whether anyone's senses perceive them or not; and secondary qualities—colors, sound, tastes, etc.—"in truth are nothing in the objects themselves but powers to produce various sensations in us by their primary qualities, i.e., by the bulk, figure, texture, and motion of their insensible parts" [*An Essay Concerning Human Understanding*].

> Take away the sensation of them, let not the eyes see light or colours, nor the ears hear sounds; let the palate not taste, nor the nose smell; and all colours, tastes, odours and sounds, as they are such particular ideas,

---

**Walter Scott on the characteristics of the Byronic hero:**

It is a remarkable property of the poetry of Lord Byron, that although his manner is frequently varied—although he appears to have assumed for an occasion the characteristic stanza and style of several contemporaries, yet not only is his poetry marked in every instance by the strongest cast of originality, but in some leading particulars, and especially in the character of his heroes, each story so closely resembled the other, that managed by a writer of less power, the effect would have been an unpleasing monotony. All, or almost all, his heroes, have somewhat the attributes of Childe Harold:—all, or almost all, have minds which seem at variance with their fortunes, and exhibit high and poignant feelings of pain and pleasure; a keen sense of what is noble and honourable, and an equally keen susceptibility of injustice or injury, under the garb of stoicism or contempt of mankind. The strength of early passion, and the glow of youthful feeling, are uniformly painted as chilled or subdued by a train of early imprudences or of darker guilt, and the sense of enjoyment tarnished, by too intimate and experienced an acquaintance with the vanity of human wishes. These general attributes mark the stern features of all Lord Byron's heroes, from those which are shaded by the scalloped hat of the illustrious Pilgrim, to those which lurk under the turban of Alp, the Renegade. The public, ever anxious in curiosity or malignity to attach to fictious characters real prototypes, were obstinate in declaring that in these leading traits of character Lord Byron copied from the individual features reflected in his own mirror. On this subject the noble author entered, on one occasion, a formal protest, though, it will be observed, without entirely disavowing the ground on which the conjecture was formed.

*Walter Scott, in an unsigned review of* Childe Harold's Pilgrimage, Canto III *and* The Prisoner of Chillon, a Dream; and Other Poems, *in* The Quarterly Review, *Vol. XVI, October, 1816– January, 1817, pp. 172-208.*

---

vanish and cease, and are reduced to their causes, i.e., bulk, figure, and motion of parts.

Most of the Romantics, except Byron, were enthralled by the secondary sensations. They dismissed Locke's conception of them as illusory and decided, contrary to Locke, that they were actually as real as the external world of primary sensations. Wordsworth and Coleridge sought to dramatize the interaction of internal and external worlds; Keats and Shelley sought through the visionary experience to find evidence for a world of beauty and truth to which the present external world is inferior and which is indeed molded and shaped by the imagination; Blake boldly reversed Locke's position and saw imagination as the only reality, and the external world as illusory. Indeed, most of the Romantics sooner or later developed such a conception of the imagination and clung to it, even though the younger Romantics like Keats and Shelley became increasingly disillusioned and skeptical about its powers to discern the ultimate truth.

Byron, in contrast, was the only major Romantic poet who wrote within the empirical tradition. The external world is the ultimate reality for him. His poetry abounds with the mountains, seas, and infinite spaces of the physical universe. But he was skeptical of the visionary experience and had little or nothing to do with it. There are surprisingly few images of color, and perhaps a few more of sound; but on the whole Byron uses the secondary sensations sparingly as subsidiary to the primary, except when he is dealing wholly with the human world, as in the third canto of *Don Juan* (Haidée's feast) or in the last cantos (e.g., the Epicurean feast).

This is not to say that Byron does not explore an interrelationship between man and the physical world (or more often a relationship between himself and that world). But he confronts the external world not so much through imaginative vision as through the naked ego, defying, supplicating, probing, always seeking some answer, as from an oracle or an allegorical painting, to the mystery of his own identity. For Byron believes that beyond yet immanent in Nature is a power of Mind (though he vacillates on this in his view of nature, which ultimately perhaps he sees as indifferent or hostile, activated by a power or energy similar to mind, but subordinate in the short run at least to the power of mind in the human being). This power manifests itself in reason, which can control both human society and the natural world. One notices that these terms are well-grounded in the eighteenth-century empirical tradition.

Byron's reaction to his world is ambiguous, often contradictory, oscillating back and forth according to his moods and experiences until *Don Juan,* when his attitude tends to stabilize. There are at least four possible ways in which he views the external world:

(1) as the deteriorating world of a lost pastoral paradise, of which remnants still remain (the first act of *Cain,* Haidée's island, *The Island*). The prehistorical earth may have contained superior beings, or there may have been other worlds with such beings before our own, with its inferior beings, was created. At any rate, past nature was the Ideal by which to measure the present.

(2) as a benign universe in which man finds comfort and solace, into which he can project himself, and with which he can identify (the Alps in the third canto of *Childe Harold's Pilgrimage,* the end of the fourth canto, Haidée's island, and other portions of *Don Juan*).

(3) as an active, often malevolent universe, both creative and destructive, a world of titanic power which man, to survive, must defy with the power of his mind—or one which Byron can admire and identify himself with as superior to other men—a power of nature himself (*Childe Harold, Manfred,* the second canto of *Don Juan*).

(4) as an indifferent world of bleak masses and solids, of an infinity of worlds, unfathomable, other than which there is emptiness, nothingness, meaninglessness; a world that will ultimately sweep away man and his works and

leave nothing except a wasteland; beyond this world no God, no purpose, no prime mover (**"Darkness,"** the third canto of *Childe Harold, Manfred, Cain, Don Juan* throughout).

At the same time, Byron was in conflict; the opposite side of the coin was his conviction that mind was superior to matter and could well prevail. If so, there was a great design beyond nature, an omniscient Mind. Here again Byron comes close to the eighteenth-century tradition, Deism.

Let me now examine episodes in representative poems in illustration of these generalizations.

I

The "lost" earthly paradise of Byron was the world of his childhood: the Scottish Highlands, Newstead Abbey, Harrow. In his earliest poems—most of them in *Hours of Idleness*—he writes about these places frequently with nostalgia and yearning. The poems on the Scottish Highlands indicate the origin of his love of mountains and oceans and point toward *Childe Harold's Pilgrimage, Manfred,* and other later poems. In **"Lachin Y Gair"** he writes:

> England! thy beauties are tame and domestic,
> To one who has rov'd on the mountains afar;
> Oh! for the crags that are wild and majestic,
> The steep, frowning glories of dark Loch na Garr.

And in **"When I Roved a Young Highlander"** he writes of how he would climb snow-covered Mt. Morven:

> To gaze on the torrent that thunder'd beneath,
> Or the mist of the tempest that gather'd below;
> Untutor'd by science, a stranger to fear,
> And rude as the rocks, where my infancy grew . . .

and later on, "I lov'd my bleak regions, nor panted for new." Here are the elemental forms which loom so large in Byron's later poems; and here is one of the first expressions of identifying with them—mountains, torrents, crags, rocks, ocean ("Place me among the rocks I love, / Which sound to Ocean's wildest roar," in **"I Would I Were a Careless Child"**). One other feature goes into these memories of childhood: there is always some human being whom he loves and who loves him. This becomes one of the most poignant and powerful elements in the childhood paradises he so wistfully recalls—giving them the warmth of human love to make the landscape meaningful.

Newstead Abbey and Harrow are pastoral landscapes described in the traditional language of the English pastoral. As Byron matured as a poet, Newstead became increasingly important to him, and he individualized it more and more. The old Gothic ruins of the Abbey in the center of the lovely landscape gave an additional charm to his memories. In the **"Epistle to Augusta"** Lake Leman and its environs take on special meaning because they recall

Newstead Lake and its environs. But it is in canto 13 of
*Don Juan,* where he describes Norman Abbey, the seat of
the Amundevilles, in terms of Newstead Abbey (stanzas
56-58), that he gives his most intense reconstruction of
the childhood paradise:

> It stood embosomed in a happy valley,
>    Crowned by high woodlands, where the Druid oak
> Stood like Caractacus, in act to rally. . . .
> Before the mansion lay a lucid Lake,
>    Broad as transparent, deep, and freshly fed
> By a river. . . .
>
> Its outlet dashed into a deep cascade,
>    Sparkling with foam. . . .

And he describes the stag, the wild fowl nestling in the
brake and sedges, the woods sloping downward to the
lake.

Byron's paradise is in many respects like Rasselas's happy valley. He seems always to view his paradise through
a frame, as if it were a picture, or through a camera ob-
scura. Newstead Abbey is always framed by its woods;
the Scottish Highland valleys, by their mountains. An
important result is the aesthetic distancing that Byron attains. In numerous poems, he provides a glimpse of an
Earthly Paradise (similar to but with no reference to his
childhood paradise). In *The Prisoner of Chillon,* the prisoner climbs to the window where he glimpses the wondrous world surrounding Lake Geneva framed by his prison window. In *Manfred,* the protagonist has a glimpse
through the Chamois Hunter of a pastoral paradise no
longer accessible to him. Cain has his parents' memories
of Eden. In canto 3 of *Childe Harold,* Rousseau's Clarens
becomes the center of an idyllic landscape. But the two
major constructions of dream paradises, wistfully built upon
memories and (as Byron knew) impossible hopes for the
future, are Haidée's island in canto 3 of *Don Juan* and
*The Island.* Haidée's paradise, isolated by rugged cliffs,
almost impenetrable and ringed by the raging sea from
which Juan had been tossed, has all the pastoral beauty of
the English landscape that Byron recalls. But it is ultimately marred by the corruption of the human beings who
live there, and Byron makes clear how ephemeral it is,
acknowledges that Haidée and Juan cannot long enjoy it,
and wishes that they could die in the high ecstasy of their
love. *The Island,* ironically perhaps the last work of Byron, except the final cantos of *Don Juan* (13-17), contains his most unabashed dream picture of paradise. Drawing upon accounts of the South Seas and his own wistful
memories and hopes, he describes the ultimate paradise
framed by wild cliffs and a dangerous sea. Neuha is truly
the innocent savage, more pure and simple than Haidée,
enamored of the barbaric splendor of feast and clothing
and furnishings. Torquil is the dashing young Highlander,
who still recalls the glories of his Highland youth. The
astonishing thing is that Byron allows them to escape from
their pursuers through the hidden cave and return to the
island, there presumably to live happily ever after. Here
just before setting off for Greece, he allows himself the
indulgence of a dream picture of an enduring paradise.

## II

Childhood memories and the influence of Wordsworth by
way of Shelley were mainly responsible for Byron's recurrent belief in the benignity of the natural world. A
strong pull toward Deism also contributed. In an early
poem, **"The Prayer of Nature"** (1806), Byron writes in
echo of the Newtonian-Lockean creed:

> Father! no prophet's laws I seek,—
>    *Thy* laws in Nature's work appear; . . .
>
> Thou, who canst guide the wandering star,
>    Through trackless realms of æther's space;
> Who calm'st the elemental war,
>    Whose hand from pole to pole I trace. . . .

In the later poems it is the Wordsworthian creed of the
immanence of a living and benign power in natural objects that dominates. This power is most evident in the
massive primary forms—mountains, ocean, the physical
universe of stars and planets. The most famous passage
demonstrating these points is the apostrophe to the Alps
in canto 3 of *Childe Harold,* but similar passages occur in
most of the poems. In fact, throughout the four cantos of
*Childe Harold's Pilgrimage,* with the exception of the
ambiguous apostrophe to the ocean at the end, the beauty
and goodness of nature are contrasted with the corruption of man. Even in the most somber poems this motif
recurs. In *Manfred,* though in most of the poem the elements are indifferent or destructive, there is the passionate cry in I.ii:

> Beautiful!
> How beautiful is all this visible world!
> How glorious in its action and itself!
> But we, who name ourselves its sovereigns, we,
> Half dust, half deity, alike unfit
> To sink or soar, with our mixed essence make
> A conflict of its elements. . . .

And there are the splendid apostrophes to the Witch of the
Alps (II.ii), the sun (III.ii), and the moon (III.iv). In *Cain,*
the physical universe, if left alone by God, is serene and
beautiful. When Cain is carried up into outer space, he
exclaims:

> Oh thou beautiful
> And unimaginable ether! and
> Ye multiplying masses of increased
> And still-increasing lights! what are ye? what
> Is this blue wilderness of interminable
> Air, where ye roll along, as I have seen
> The leaves along the limpid streams of Eden?
> Is your course measured for ye? Or do ye
> Sweep on in your unbounded revelry
> Through an aërial universe of endless
> Expansion—at which my soul aches to think—
> Intoxicated with Eternity? . . .
>     Let me die, as atoms die,
> (If that they die), or know ye in your might
> And knowledge!

The star had special symbolic significance for Byron; it was a sign of purpose in the universe. He called his destiny or fate a star and saw Augusta as a star guiding him on. The eye of a beautiful woman was like a star. The stars are "the poetry of heaven." Only in *Manfred* is the star destructive and malign. In *Cain,* as the quotation indicates, stars are the symbols of eternity and the ultimate mystery, the key to knowledge which Cain thirsts for so desperately. Cain—after his apostrophe—identifies them with good: "Within those glorious orbs . . . / Ill cannot come: they are too beautiful."

Even in *Don Juan* in the midst of the most flippant or realistic passages (as in the shipwreck), a nostalgic glimpse of benign Nature intrudes suddenly: in the description of Haidée's island, in the Ave Maria stanzas in canto 4, and in the description of Norman Abbey, for example. In *The Island,* Nature not only is benign, but actively aids and abets the lovers in their escape—though beyond the islands lie dangerous reefs and turbulent seas.

### III

The most recurrent motif is perhaps that of the ambivalence of the beautiful and powerful forces of the physical universe. They are at the same time creative and destructive, indifferent, even hostile, to man, capriciously capable of doing him—according to man's ethical standards—good or ill. With his view of man as part of the physical world, Byron contemptuously called him "clay"—molded from the clay of the earth and doomed to crumple like clay, struggling constantly to transcend his physical limitations through his reason—fighting a continuing battle of the spirit to dominate the flesh—but doomed in the end to destruction by the elemental forces of nature. The most striking example of the ambivalence in nature is given in the apostrophe to the ocean in stanzas 177-84 of canto 4 of *Childe Harold*. The passage begins with a return to the motif of benign nature in the section on the Alps in canto 3: "Oh! that the Desert were my dwelling-place, / With one fair Spirit for my minister," and he asks the elements "in whose ennobling stir / I feel myself exalted" if they can find him such a being. "I love not Man the less, but Nature more"—because his experiences in Nature have led him to mingle with the universe. But with the apostrophe to the ocean a shift in mood takes place. The ocean is an indifferent destructive power to man, sweeping away his ships and petty empires, despising "the vile strength he wields / For Earth's destruction." Byron seems to revel in this ruthless description of the meanness and insignificance of man before the titanic powers of the ocean—and the passage suggests that beneath the words "I love not Man the less" there is a partly unconscious Freudian delight in the annihilation of corrupt human beings—who had been responsible for his own exile—by the cleansing power of the ocean. The ocean is also a creative force, as Byron apostrophizes in one of his finest stanzas:

> —boundless, endless, and sublime—
> The image of Eternity—the throne
> Of the Invisible; even from out thy slime

> The monsters of the deep are made—each Zone
> Obeys thee—thou goest forth, dread, fathomless,
> alone.

It is with the ocean Byron identifies, superior himself to the rest of mankind. For him the ocean is benign: "For I was as it were a Child of thee, / And trusted to thy billows far and near."

Here, then, the ocean is presented as indifferent and destructive, creative and benign. For Byron the ocean remains a symbol of the awesome power of natural elements. There is the deluge in *Heaven and Earth,* in which the threat of man's annihilation in canto 4 of *Childe Harold* is realized, and there is the storm in canto 3 of *Don Juan,* followed by the description of the protective reef which insures the safety of Don Juan and Haidée; a similar alternation between menace and protection is found in *The Island*.

In *Cain* Byron subscribes to the deteriorationism of Cuvier. Once there were other worlds more magnificent than earth; there were mighty beings, "Intelligent, good, great, and glorious things," far superior to man; and there were the great mammoths of the land and leviathans of the sea. Cain views them as phantasms in the dark Hades to which Lucifer has led him. When Cain asks how they were destroyed (II.ii), Lucifer replies, "By a most crushing and inexorable / Destruction and disorder of the elements, / Which struck a world to chaos," and he implies that Cain's earth will be similarly destroyed, as it decays into "dull damp degeneracy."

But the most vivid use of destructive elements is in *Manfred*. When Manfred conjures up the spirits of earth and air (I.i), each declares his power of unleashing destructive forces. And the seventh spirit, no longer the benign star of other poems, is now malevolent. It tells Manfred that his star was once a world as fresh and fair as ever revolved around the sun. But now it is "A wandering mass of shapeless flame, / A pathless Comet, and a curse, / The menace of the Universe," rolling on with innate force, a bright deformity on high.

The destinies who do the bidding of Arimanes are akin to, perhaps are, the elements of the first act. But here they are openly destructive (II.iii) of the good—they restore tyrants to their thrones, sink ships, rescuing only the traitor, spread the black plague. And in II.iv they hail Arimanes as

> —Prince of Earth and Air!
> Who walks the clouds and waters—in his hand
> The sceptre of the Elements, which tear
> Themselves to chaos at his high command!

At his will, tempests shake the sea, clouds reply in thunder, sunbeams flee, earthquakes rend the world, volcanoes rise; his shadow is pestilence, and planets turn to ashes at his wrath. The Manicheism indicated here between the evil "God of this World" and what Manfred calls the "overruling Infinite" is developed on a fuller scale in *Cain*. There the God of Adam is responsible for human suffering, as Lucifer says in I.i:

Goodness would not make
Evil; and what else hath he made? But let him
Sit on his vast and solitary throne—
Creating worlds, to make eternity
Less burthensome to his immense existence
And unparticipated solitude;
Let him crowd orb on orb: he is alone
Indefinite, Indissoluble Tyrant. . . .

Lucifer, the tables turned as in Blake's *Marriage of Heaven and Hell,* presents himself as the good, and in Byronic eyes *is* the good.

### IV

Under these varying views of Nature lay a fundamentally bleak view of the natural world as made up of masses and solids, of infinite planets living and dead, and as inexorably moving toward the destruction of earth and its inhabitants. This view, which Byron had held at least from early manhood, lay not far beneath his surface consciousness and erupted at frequent intervals in his later poetry. We find a glimpse of it in the Hebrew Melody **"When Coldness Wraps This Suffering Clay"** (1815) and a more explicit statement in a letter to Annabella, March 3, 1814, in which he states, "Why I came here, I know not. Where I shall go to, it is useless to inquire. In the midst of myriads of the living and the dead worlds—stars—systems—infinity—why should I be anxious about an atom?" *Childe Harold's Pilgrimage,* particularly cantos 3 and 4, and *Manfred* have references to the earth as "wasteland," "desert," "With blasted pines . . . barkless, branchless," but these epithets are perhaps mainly the reflection of Byron's own moods. It is in **"Darkness"** (1816) that he presents a terrifying picture of the earth becoming a dead planet, returning to chaos:

The World was void,
The populous and the powerful was a lump,
Seasonless, herbless, treeless, manless, lifeless—
A lump of death—a chaos of hard clay.
The rivers, lakes, and ocean all stood still,
And nothing stirred within their silent depths. . . .
The waves were dead; the tides were in their grave,
The Moon, their mistress, had expired before;
The winds were withered in the stagnant air,
And the clouds perished; Darkness had no need
Of aid from them—She was the Universe.

In *Manfred,* the description of Manfred's star as "The burning wreck of a demolished world" gives us another glimpse into chaos, this time inextricably bound up with Manfred's sense of his own deterioration and doom.

*Cain* is a vivid illustration of Cuvier's theory of deterioration, which, as the preface indicates, fascinated Byron. Key features are the description of Hades with the dead worlds floating there, along with the titanic beings that once existed and the implication—spelled out by Lucifer—that tiny earth and its inhabitants will be destroyed in the same way, returning the Universe to chaos.

*Heaven and Earth* is perhaps the most spectacular presentation of the earth being overwhelmed by the surging waters of the ocean. The deluge fulfills Byron's implicit prophecy in canto 4 of *Childe Harold*. As one of the fiendish spirits says, "Earth shall be Ocean!" Japhet on Mt. Ararat exclaims:

Ye wilds, that look eternal; and thou cave,
Which seem'st unfathomable; and ye mountains,
So varied and so terrible in beauty;
Here, in your rugged majesty of rocks
And toppling trees that twine their roots with
    stone. . . .

                        Yet, in a few days,
Perhaps even hours, ye will be changed, rent, hurled
Before the mass of waters. . . .

And he muses on the thought that, all other living things dead, serpents shall escape

To hiss and sting through some emerging world,
Reeking and dank from out the slime, whose ooze
Shall slumber o'er the wreck of this. . . .

The fiends tell him that he will survive, but that his race will be inferior to what had gone before, as will other living things. He denies this and dreams of a new Eden.

When the deluge does come, the clouds "fixed as rocks" wait to pour out their "wrathful vials," the stars are no longer glorious, and in the sun's place, "a pale and ghastly glare / Hath wound itself around the dying air." And here, as in **"Darkness,"** the sun is at last obliterated. Mountains collapse, torrents rush down, and rocks crash into the deep. A chorus of mortals rushing by describes the chaos descending upon the world. The final touching note is the cry of a fleeing woman recalling the paradisical world that is being destroyed:

The pleasant trees that o'er our noonday bent,
And sent forth evening songs from sweetest birds,
The little rivulet which freshened all
    Our pastures green,
    No more are to be seen.

Here is a good time to digress for a moment and write of Byron's influence. In his emphasis on the massive effects of nature, he had little appeal for the poets who followed him—who were mesmerized by the preoccupation of the other Romantics with vision. Browning's *Childe Roland* and some later poems came closest. But painters and composers were greatly stimulated. In particular, John Martin, the English painter who has only recently come into his own, was spurred to some of his most impressive paintings. One of them, *The Deluge,* first displayed in 1826, was accompanied by a pamphlet in which he quoted from *Heaven and Earth,* "that sublime poem." Later, when he did a group of three paintings on the Deluge, exhibited in 1841-42, he again quoted from *Heaven and Earth.* He was also fascinated by *Manfred* and **"Darkness"** and did paintings inspired by them. Indeed, the massive mountains, rocks, and overpowering oceans in his nature pictures become a transformation of Byron's descriptions into painting.

The music of composers like Berlioz was also molded and shaped by the massive forms of Byron and Martin. To both Berlioz acknowledges his debt. The monumental orchestration in works like *Harold in Italy, Requiem, Damnation of Faust,* and *Te Deum,* often with several choirs and orchestras, plainly shows the transformation into music of the massive grouping of Byron and Martin. Heine, commenting on the influence of Martin, writes of the "orchestration placed tier upon tier, vistas, in music, disappearing into infinity." Berlioz's influence was not great during his lifetime, but he led the way toward the huge orchestras used by Schumann, Wagner, Brahms, and Tchaikovsky, all of whom were influenced also by Byron.

Now what are we to say about *Don Juan*? In this long "medley" of a poem, as John Jump calls it [in his *Byron,* 1972], Byron is mainly concerned with the relation of his characters to each other and to society, and with their physical vulnerability—the mutability of themselves and their civilization. He is less concerned with the physical universe outside him, except for the raging storm and implacable sea in canto 3. He touches upon every aspect of nature as his mood or the particular context prompts. But implicit in the poem, and increasingly pervasive as it proceeds, is a view of the natural world as, if not meaningless, at least capricious and indifferent to man, without purpose of its own, and ultimately absurd, a "glorious blunder." So he finally anticipates existential and absurdist literature of the present: man is on his own to make what he can of life. In reality, the universe has become unimportant to Byron, as he becomes involved in castigation of the "cant" of civilization, in efforts to promote a moral toughening therein by relentless exposure of the "facts" of human behavior, and therefore in working toward the improvement of civilization. The malevolent or indifferent deteriorating universe, its destruction millennia away, no longer disturbs him in his preoccupation with what man can do with his experience here and now. His new point of view is also affected by his shift from the serious to the comic perspective, always present in the *Letters,* but now through the ottava rima poems surging up to release Byron as poet in all his potentialities. The perspective of *Don Juan,* like Pulci's, is essentially comic, and increasingly skeptical as the poem proceeds into the English cantos. Byron questions the reality or truth of everything, except what he feels upon his pulses, as Keats said—in other words, the experience of his senses. But this is enough. The poem reveals throughout Byron's exuberant love of life on its own terms. He writes with gusto and evident enjoyment. He laughs at himself and his characters with genuine humor, and often with boisterous explosions. This is what gives the positive note which dominates the often nihilistic and pessimistic implications of the poem.

*The Island,* as we have seen, represents a startling change of pace and mood from the satiric realism of the English cantos into which it is sandwiched. Though an uneven

poem, it takes on a strange poignancy in the love affair between Torquil and Neuha. This is Byron's most nostalgic dream of the Earthly Paradise, with its innocent lovers (Neuha is Haidée stripped of her barbaric trimmings), secure in the protection of the ocean, rocks, cliffs, and caves.

Byron's death was a sad and miserable anticlimax, the opposite of the glorious death in battle of which he had dreamed. The wretched climate of Missolonghi, plus his own imprudence, killed him. But there was final spectacular moment. On the evening that he died, an approaching storm could be heard, with terrific claps of thunder and blinding lightning. For one who so wanted to identify with the elements, it was a fitting finale to his life.

From the beginning Byron was the spectator standing like Lucifer on his promontory, observing the world as it goes. To him the real world was the Lockean world of massive forms. He was irresistibly drawn to the titanic—the ocean, mountains, cliffs, lakes, storms, thunder and lightning. With these he identified, and felt himself superior to the rest of mankind. And yet he remained restless and dissatisfied. The mind, that "fiery particle," was surely superior to nature and linked to a power transcending both nature and man. In the mind and the reason he found his ultimate source of hope and affirmation. Though them man can control his destiny. He can control his environment, initiate the necessary social and political revolutions, and make a better world for himself. Thus he can triumph over the forces threatening to destroy him, with the exception of mutability and the ultimate deterioration of the universe. But that deterioration was a long way off (and now he was not quite sure that the universe was not eternal).

Byron's confidence in the triumph of mind over matter, if man will only follow his reason (and there is a doubt that he will), occurs as a recurrent theme through the major poems—the fourth canto of *Childe Harold, Manfred, Cain, Don Juan*. It becomes a more firm and constant conviction as Byron grows older.

Byron's most succinct statement is given in the *Detached Thoughts* No. 97:

> Matter is eternal, always changing, but reproduced, and, as far as we can comprehend Eternity, Eternal; and why not *Mind?* Why should not the Mind act with and upon the Universe? as portions of it act upon and with the congregated dust called Mankind? See, how one man acts upon himself and others, or upon multitudes? The same Agency, in a higher and purer degree, may act upon the Stars, etc., ad infinitum.

John Martin has painted a memorable water color of Manfred and the Chamois Hunter on the Jungfrau. The mountains are enormous and the figures tiny, insignificant creatures standing at the top of the picture, but placed as they are, they surprisingly dominate the scene. The picture captures Byron's conception of the relation of man to nature, and seems an admirable place at which to leave him for the time being.

## Gloria T. Hull  (essay date 1978)

SOURCE: "The Byronic Heroine and Byron's *The Corsair*," in *Ariel: A Review of International English Literature,* Vol. 9, No. 1, January, 1978, pp. 71-83.

*[In the following essay, Hull—focusing particularly on Gulnare in* The Corsair—*analyzes the general characteristics of Byron's heroines.]*

The phrase, "the Byronic heroine," usually evokes an image which is epitomized by a sketch executed for Byron's *Corsair* by Richard Westall, a contemporary painter famous for his mannered book illustrations. Westall's watercolor shows a tall, tragic-stricken young woman in Oriental dress—including billowy pants, a long camisole tunic, and a trailing, embroidered train—leaning forlornly against the outer wall of a vine-covered, Mediterranean cottage which is perched high on a rocky promontory overlooking the sea. Her hair straggles untended down her face, shoulder, and back; her figure is stooped; and her hands hang listlessly. She has turned from a departing ship which is disappearing into the distance, while the vast lonely horizon further accentuates her grief.

This character represents Haidée and the women of the narrative tales which Byron produced in 1813-14, and is usually considered to be "the Byronic heroine." More importantly, she is the figure so designated by Byron himself. Despite the excellence of some of his other female characters (for example, Aurora Raby in *Don Juan* and Myrrha in *Sardanapalus*), whenever he mentioned his "heroines," Byron catalogued only Leila from *The Giaour,* Zuleika from *The Bride of Abydos,* Gulnare and Medora from *The Corsair,* and Haidée (who will not be considered here). Unlike the Byronic hero, who has been the subject of much deliberation, the Byronic heroine has not received the primary attention which she deserves. Generally, she is not as compelling a figure as the hero (though this is not always true in individual cases) nor is she as central in English and European literary history. Nevertheless, these Byronic heroines are important and should be more carefully studied for the following reasons: they are fascinating and worthwhile in themselves, especially since they were drawn by the author who created the most notorious and influential English hero type; they are important for the additional insights which they give into the nature and use of the Byronic hero; they show some of the larger trends of Romanticism—for instance, the romantic dichotomy of light-dark characterizations seen in Radcliffe's and Scott's novels; and they document a stage in Byron's growth as a poet and reveal a facet of his personal character.

In 1823, the last year of his life, Byron explained these female characters to his friend, Lady Blessington:

> I flatter myself that my Leila Zuleika, Gulnare, Medora, and Haidée will always vouch for my taste in beauty: these are the bright creations of my fancy, with rounded forms, and delicacy of limbs, nearly so incompatible as to be rarely, if, ever, united; . . . so that I am obliged to have recourse to imagination for my beauties, and there I always find them. . . . I should leave [my mistress] . . . to dress her up in the habiliments of my ideal beauty, investing her with all the charms of the latter, and then adoring the idol I had formed [*Lady Blessington's Conversations of Lord Byron,* ed. Ernest J. Lovell, Jr., 1969].

And in a conversation that same year with Thomas Medwin, he added:

> My writings, indeed, tend to exalt the sex; and my imagination has always delighted in giving them a *beau idéal* likeness, but I only drew them as a painter or statuary would do,—as they should be. Perhaps my prejudices, and keeping them at a distance, contributed to prevent the illusion from altogether being worn out and destroyed as to their celestialities [*Medwin's Conversations of Lord Byron,* ed. Ernest J. Lovell, Jr. 1966].

In both of these statements, Byron outlines a method of characterization which is essentially non-realistic. He stresses the distinction between life and art and emphasizes the role of the idealizing imagination. Therefore what he says here shows his bias toward ideally-depicted women and further suggests that, in his art, this was the conscious level from which he worked. While this definition of his creative process falsifies some of Byron's other female characters and fails to tell the whole story about these five women, it does indicate the attitude which dominated the creation of "the Byronic heroine." No doubt, his poetic medium (which sanctioned romantic characterizations) and the fact that all of the women are non-English (and therefore exempt from the low opinion which he held of his countrywomen) helped him in projecting his beautiful ideals.

Though these heroines have traits which distinguish them as individuals, they share many common characteristics. They are all Eastern, young, and beautiful. They are fond of music, poetry, and romantic tales, and are often skilled in singing and playing. Refined and noble, these heroines seem to be highborn even when they have become harem slaves (as two of them are). In a sense, they are all orphans, alone with no close family or friends. Consequently, they are sequestered and are wont to live in spiritual and emotional solitude, their only meaningful contact being with the hero.

This hero is the object of their attention, passion, and eternal devotion, and they love him above all else. Even though they are usually quiet, mild, obedient and retiring, they can become vocal in expressing their love and exhibit strength and courage in its pursuit and defence. The Byronic heroines are essentially pure in soul and spirit despite their worldly crimes (like murder) and moral transgressions (like perfidy to their tyrant lords)—presumably because these "sins" are committed for the sake of a supra-human passion. All of these qualities make them eminently worthy of the hero's love, and they, in turn, provide his sole inspiration toward all that is good and human. Yet the heroines lead melancholy, troubled lives and end tragically. All of them die, three of broken hearts and one by being drowned for her infidelity.

This woman character is of the utmost importance to the purpose and effect of Byron's Oriental tales, and is one of the elements which justify T. S. Eliot's judgment of these *contes* as "readable . . . well-told . . . interesting" ["Byron," in *English Romantic Poets: Modern Essays in Criticism,* ed. M. H. Abrams, 1960]. Though these heroines are conceived within certain limits, if one does not misconstrue the limits as automatic artistic flaws and ignore the variety and excellence of their depiction within them, then they can be rightly appreciated as one broad type functioning in many ways. They provide the central plot motivation, and much of the narrative interest, thematic meaning, and poetic symbolism.

Of all the tales, *The Corsair* (written in 1814) is the one which best illustrates the complex role of the Byronic heroine. Leila does not actually appear in *The Giaour* and therefore remains a shadowy figure. Zuleika, Byron's first deliberate attempt at a heroine, is a full representation of her type—but what Byron does with her he achieves also with Medora. And Kaled in *Lara* principally derives her significance from her earlier characterization as Gulnare. Thus the two women of *The Corsair,* Medora and Gulnare, show what Byron is able to accomplish with the Byronic heroine during this phase of his career. The poem also boasts an exciting romantic plot and a towering Byronic hero.

Conrad, the Corsair, is the leader of a pirate band that returns to his island hideaway and immediately prepares for a raid on Seyd Pasha, his enemy. He takes a tearful farewell of Medora, the woman he loves, despite her beguiling attempts to dissuade him. The foray is all but successful until Conrad is moved by the frightened cries of Seyd's women and pauses in the fight to rescue them from the burning castle. Seyd's forces rally, and Conrad is beaten and thrown into the tower prison. Falling in love with him, the harem queen, Gulnare, frees Conrad, and escapes with him to sea where they are joined by the happy remnant of his followers. Back to the island, Conrad discovers that Medora has died, and disappears mysteriously with Gulnare.

Medora and Gulnare share certain functions in the tale. They contribute to the action, convey the symbolic meaning of the poem, and help to characterize the hero by allowing him to reveal aspects of himself which would otherwise remain hidden. Peter L. Thorslev [in *The Byronic Hero: Types and Prototypes,* 1962] points out an important instance of this last function in his discussion of women and their relationship with the Gothic villain, who was a prototype of the Noble Outlaw, Conrad. All of the villains were crass misogynists who delighted in feminine persecution. But,

> according to the sentiments of the age, of course, any act of cruelty or even of unkindness and disrespect for women was unforgivable; . . . and Byron and Scott take advantage of this fact when portraying their Noble Outlaws. Make your protagonist a Hero of Sensibility in his regard for women, and this characteristic alone will mitigate all of his other crimes, no matter how

**Percy Bysshe Shelley on *Don Juan:***

Many thanks for [Cantos III-IV] of *Don Juan*—It is a poem totally of its own species, & my wonder and delight at the grace of the composition no less than the free & grand vigour of the conception of it perpetually increase. . . . This poem carries with it at once the stamp of originality and a defiance of imitation. Nothing has ever been written like it in English—nor if I may venture to prophesy, will there be; without carrying upon it the mark of a secondary and borrowed light.—You unveil & present in its true deformity what is worst in human nature, & this is what the witlings of the age murmur at, conscious of their want of power to endure the scrutiny of such a light. . . . You are building up a drama, such as England has not yet seen, and the task is sufficiently noble & worthy of you.

*Percy Bysshe Shelley, in a letter to Lord Byron dated October 21, 1821, in* The Letters of Percy Bysshe Shelley, Vol. II: Shelley in Italy, *edited by Frederick L. Jones, Oxford at the Clarendon Press, 1964, pp. 357-59.*

Gothic. . . . a Romantic love for his mistress and a courteous attitude toward women in general is the "one virtue" amidst a "thousand crimes" which makes Conrad . . . a character over whose death readers could weep.

Further than this, it is a mistake to generalize about Medora and Gulnare together, for they are quite different. Their physical appearance provides the first and most obvious clue to their individualities. In making Medora blue-eyed and fair-tressed (468, 470) and Gulnare dark-eyed and auburn-haired (1008-09), Byron is drawing on the romance tradition of contrasting fair and dark heroines which was begun by Mrs. Radcliffe (whom he numbered among his favorite authors) and extensively used by later writers—Scott, for example. Eino Railo [in *The Haunted Castle: A Study of the Elements of English Romanticism,* 1927] describes these two romantic heroines:

> The first named type [the fair woman] breathes a fine femininity, a tender and sacrificial maternal spirit, fighting the battles of life with the weapons of resignation and tears, and bringing to love everything that is divine, passion excluded. The second type, [the dark woman] more spiritedly poetical, is represented in the independent and oppositional beauty, who feels deeply, demands freedom of movement and choice, and is not impervious to passion.

Railo's distinction, which conveniently categorizes the two basic types of women in Byron's poetry, is first clearly manifested in Medora and Gulnare.

Medora's character is not difficult to determine. She is Conrad's beautiful young mistress functioning as a positive love figure who softly expresses her adoration and concern for her roaming Corsair. She first appears in the metaphorical guise of a "Bird of Beauty" caged and singing a melancholy song high in the tower which suggests a prison atop Conrad's hill. She implores Conrad to end her agony by learning to share "the joys of peace"—if not for her, then for his own "far dearer life, / Which [now] flies from love and languishes for strife" (394-95).

Her gayer side emerges when she invites her lover to eat the fruit which she has carefully culled and dressed for him, to taste the sparkling sherbet, to watch her dance or sing, or to read Ariosto's tales. When he begins to leave, she becomes passionate, kissing and caressing him "in all the wildness of dishevelled charms" (471). He walks away, calling her "the dim and melancholy Star / Whose ray of Beauty reached him from afar" (511-12). In this way, Medora is identified with the beacon-fire which blazes in the tower to direct him home. By leaving her, the Corsair rejects what she represents; he goes off to war with his enemy—repudiating Love and Beauty for Hate and Death. Symbolically, then, Medora is probably the physical embodiment of Conrad's tender features and one of Byron's many counterpart figures.

But Gulnare is decidedly richer, more complex, and more engaging. Because she exhibits the typical characteristics of the Byronic heroine, she is representative of them and shows how these traits are incorporated into the tales. At the same time, she is given a more expanded and active role in the poem and made a more human and realistic character. Thus, she points toward fuller feminine characterizations in Byron's later poetry, and can therefore be viewed as a transitional figure in his artistic development. Furthermore, the way Byron handles her illuminates him as a man and simultaneously raises some worthwhile questions about the construction of the tales.

Within the symbolic framework of *The Corsair,* Gulnare's meaning is rather easily arrived at if one uses the suggestions given by earlier tales and by Medora's role. In an important sense, she belongs to the world of strife for which Conrad abandoned Medora and represents that part of his being and experience. Thus she is, as Jerome J. McGann aptly puts it [in *Fiery Dust: Byron's Poetic Development,* 1968], "the proper image of Conrad's divided spiritual aims." The ambiguity of his situation is reflected in her, for not only is she a part of what separates him from Medora, but she in turn comes to embody love and salvation from even greater violence by Seyd— yet primarily through the kind of violence which was, in the first place, and continues to be, the undoing of love. Furthermore, as William Marshall suggests [in *The Structures of Byron's Major Poems,* 1962], she intensifies the Corsair's psychological and emotional problems since she "(a Woman, therefore a Love symbol) has brought Death to the Seyd." And in any reading of the poem which stresses the bisexuality of human spiritual nature, she is certainly crucial, uniting as she does elements from both sides and suggesting the *Doppelgänger* theme which plays throughout these tales.

In further describing Gulnare, one must employ concepts and qualities which do not even arise with the other woman. The contradictory aspects of her character emerge with her initial appearance in the poem. Conveyed to safety in Conrad's arms during the fighting, she is "the Harem queen—but still the slave of Seyd"; and these opposites, queen and slave, first define her. Accustomed to the haughty wooing of the Pacha, she marvels at the courtesy shown her by her rescuer and becomes aware of what is due her, a female slave, as a person. She becomes even more human and appealing by musing sarcastically about her rescue:

> The wish is wrong—nay, worse for female—vain:
> Yet much I long to view that Chief again;
> If but to thank for, what my fear forgot,
> The life—my loving Lord remembered not!
>
> (875-78)

Gulnare's physical loveliness is emphasized as she appears late that same night in Conrad's cell, drawn there from sleeplessness at Seyd's side. This action gives the first hint of her intrepidity. Gazing in wonder at Conrad as he calmly sleeps, she voices a dawning of romantic love: "What sudden spell hath made this man so dear?" (1030). She immediately begins to rationalize it in terms of gratitude, then attempts to dismiss it with "'Tis late to think," and finally confesses to Conrad when he awakes: "I came through darkness—and I scarce know why— / Yet not to hurt—I would not see thee die" (1045-46).

In their ensuing conversation, Gulnare reveals her intelligence, initiative, pride, and strength. She promises to use her beguiling power with the Pacha to delay Conrad's impalement so that they can save him. When the Corsair despondently reflects on his situation and recalls Medora in a panegyric to their love, he yet shows his susceptibility to Gulnare's beauty: Until her form appeared, his "eyes ne'er asked if others were as fair [as Medora]" (1096). Gulnare, apparently affected by his declaration of love for another woman, gives a psychologically revealing response: "Thou lov'st another then?—but what to me / Is this?— 'tis nothing—nothing n'er can be" (1097-98). And then she tells him how she envies those who love without the sighing after visions which besets her. She cannot, despite her striving, love "stern" Seyd, for, as she hesitatingly puts it, "I felt—I feel—Love dwells with—with the free" (1008).

After Gulnare leaves the Corsair, she employs her charm and cunning with the Pacha to try to save him. When these fail, she becomes increasingly resourceful and active. The escape scene enacted when she tremulously returns to Conrad at midnight is masterful. After hearing her affirm his sentence of death, he persists in a strange lassitude. Gulnare exhorts him: "If thou hast courage still, and would'st be free, / Receive this poinard—rise and follow me!" (1474-75). Still he hesitates, worrying about the clanking of his chains and the unsuitability of his garments for flight. She assures him that she has safely engineered the escape, and explains the motivation for her actions in a forty-five-line speech (1480-1525). In it Gulnare decrees the Pacha's death because he prematurely accused her of infidelity. Though a slave, she refuses to be threatened and then spared simply to be "a toy for dotard's play / To wear but till the gilding frets away" (1510-11). The fire in her "Eastern heart" has only now been kindled, for her love of Conrad and hatred of Seyd are the first strong emotions she has felt.

After the Corsair refuses to knife a sleeping man and advises her to be peaceful, Gulnare decides herself to kill Seyd and springs to do so as the fettered Conrad trails behind. With wild eyes and streaming hair, she returns, and a spot of blood on her brow proclaims the murder. If he had shuddered at her passion before, Conrad is now thoroughly revulsed. Still in command while Conrad "following, at her beck, obeyed," she leads them aboard ship and they embark. Lost in contemplation, Conrad reviews the past and dreams of "his lonely bride" until the reality of "Gulnare, the Homicide," kneeling beside him and watching his "freezing aspect and averted air," compels his attention. The "strange fierceness foreign to her eye" has now disappeared in tears:

> "Thou may'st forgive though Allah's self detest;
> But for that deed of darkness what wert thou?
> Reproach me—but not yet—Oh! spare me now!
> I am not what I seem—this fearful night
> My brain bewildered—do not madden quite!
> If I had never loved—though less my guilt—
> Thou hadst not lived to—hate me—if thou wilt."
>
> (1637-43)

The change in her becomes even more pronounced when they join Conrad's men who so perplex her by their stares that she turns to him her—"faint imploring eye," "drops her veil," and stands silently. If she or Conrad had revealed how they escaped, the pirates would certainly have made her their queen. But they both scruple to have it known that he was rescued by a woman. Moved by her meekness and the knowledge of all she has done for him, Conrad embraces and kisses her. Had it not been for the "bodings of his breast" about Medora, "his latest virtue then had joined the rest" (1715-16). But he remains faithful, and Gulnare fades out of the conclusion of the poem.

Throughout, Gulnare manipulates the action in such a way that she becomes the one person with whom the Corsair *must* reckon. She compels him to respond—in admiration for her beauty, in horror at her violent love and "desecration of feminine gentleness," and in unbidden affection for her devotion. That self-containment on which he prided himself is shattered by the force of her individuality. In the escape scene, Conrad's inaction and revulsion are inconsistent with his expressed atheism (1083-84) and his reputation as a fearless outlaw. This lapse in his characterization is Byron's way of dramatizing the complete metamorphosis of Gulnare's personality and the horrible perversion of the "natural" scheme of things which has resulted in their both being "unsexed," Byron's symbol in these tales for a world which is out of joint.

Gulnare's change of character deserves even further comment. At the point where she confesses her love to Conrad, she launches into an accurate comparison of herself and Medora:

> Though fond as mine her bosom, form more fair
> I rush through peril which she would not dare.
> If that thy heart to hers were truly dear,
> Where I thine own—thou wert not lonely here:
> An outlaw's spouse—and leave her Lord to roam!
> What hath such gentle dame to do with home?
>
> (1466-71)

Interesting first for its characterization of Gulnare, this speech is doubly valuable because it raises some artistic questions about the Byronic hero and heroine. In the tradition which produced them, there were a dark and a light hero as well as the contrasting heroines mentioned earlier. The fair young types were generally linked together in a happy fate while their dark counterparts suffered tragedy. Byron merged the two kinds of heroes by taking over most of the characteristics of the dark one and some gentler elements of the light. The women, too, he merged, but in opposite proportions, appropriating more features from the fair heroine. Ordinarily, he used the resulting figure by herself in each poem. But here in *The Corsair,* the two feminine representations appear, and Byron tentatively feels his way (one might even say he stumbles) among this new material.

He first pairs his towering hero with a woman unlike him in command and power, and then with a parallel heroine drawn on a scale equal to his own. After having painted this bold portrait of a dark heroine, he tones down the colors and makes her, at the end, a light type in all but her appearance; and he even creates the impression that her looks, too, have faded: She "now seemed changed and humbled, *faint* and meek, / But varying oft the colour of her cheek / To deeper shades of *paleness*" (1701-03; my italics). Thus, he recaptures the contrast between the hero and heroine which was present in the first instance. His retreat from his headier creation back to the safer delineation of the one-dimensional woman and simpler Byronic heroine represents a capitulation to the orthodoxy of his genre and society, and also to his own ambiguous feelings about bold, strongly individualistic women. Considered from the point of view of his artistry, Byron's treatment of Conrad and Gulnare suggests that he did not wish to wrestle with two heroic figures in the same story, especially since handling them would not have greatly changed the outlines of his poem. He apparently felt that there was room enough for only one such character and made certain that nothing would detract from his male hero.

All of the female characters in Byron's Oriental tales are not as striking as Gulnare. Yet, as a group, they deserve recognition—especially when their socio-literary contexts are considered. These larger frameworks provide extensive avenues for further investigation which can only be suggested here.

Obviously, one fruitful approach is to compare them with the other women characters in Byron's poetry. When this is done, they emerge as deliberately balanced counterparts to his Byronic heroes who, together with these heroes, represent Byron's achievement in the romantic verse narrative on which he focused during this period of his artistic life. Furthermore, Byron's experimentation with these heroines was apprentice work for his more fully-developed women. Haidée, for instance, is the culmination of the artistic impulse which produced her sisters in these earlier tales, while anticipations of Myrrha can be seen in Gulnare.

When the Byronic heroine is placed against the background of Regency England, she stands out as a reflection of the prescribed—and primarily emotional—roles which that society accorded to its women. Ironically, Byron's depiction helped to perpetuate the stereotyped prevailing image which had first influenced him. He was also probably thinking of the numerous women in his audience when he laced his verse with chivalrous romanticism.

From the viewpoint of the literary historian, the Byronic heroine can be compared with other romantic female figures (Shakespeare's, for example, or the heroines of Gothic romances and verse narratives). She could be placed within the tradition of the *femme fatale* (where she does not strictly fit, even though some ambiguity attaches to her as a love figure since she is sometimes the indirect cause of the hero's death). And finally, she might fruitfully be related to the symbolic use of women by other Romantic authors (Shelley, for instance). Certainly, the Byronic heroine is a rich figure, and she becomes even richer when one fully realizes her intrinsic value and larger significance.

## Candace Tate  (essay date 1980)

SOURCE: "Byron's *Don Juan*: Myth as Psychodrama," in *The Keats-Shelley Journal*, Vol. XXIX, 1980, pp. 131-50.

[*In the essay below, Tate reads* Don Juan *as a "psychodrama," in which "the poem served the poet as a kind of therapeutic theater in which he could reenact certain of his own problematic amorous adventures."*]

In his "uncommon want" of a hero, Byron deliberately chose Don Juan as one whose myth satisfied his own needs both as poet and as private man. Examining Byron's poetic reworking of the Don Juan myth in relation to his own psychology yields a reading that lends continuity to a poem still being termed a "hold-all." The myth is descended from Tirso de Molina's *El burlador de Sevilla y convidado de piedra* (ca. 1616), which combines an account of the amorous adventures of a fictive character whom Tirso named Don Juan, with the Spanish folktale of a stone statue that comes to life and delivers the village rouge to hell. Both the amorous adventures of the Don and the avenging stone statue are central to Byron's presentation of the myth.

The classical, or pre-Romantic, Don Juan is renowned more for his ceaseless efforts than for his actual triumphs. He resorts to all sorts of chicanery: even his successes tend to be comically colored by the overintensity of his assaults. The Byronic Don Juan, on the other hand, is *l'homme fatal,* universally irresistible. The humor in Byron's **Don Juan** is provided only by the narrative voice. The narrator's skillful, satiric assaults upon humanity's sacrosanct foibles are counterpoised against the inadvertent quality of Juan's successes. The narrator jokes about Juan's innocence, but his tone remains light and playful when he speaks of him. The egoistic exuberance of the young Don's adventures contrasts with the diabolical character of the traditional Don, whose famed selfish, blustering cynicism Byron makes an attribute of the knowing narrator, rather than of his naive hero. In a sense, the cynical wisdom of the narrator is what the naive Juan is evolving toward throughout the poem. In fact, Byron seems to have created an entirely new version of the myth: he has given Juan the characteristic erotic prowess, but he leaves him uncharacteristically vulnerable to women. Juan's virility is not only subject to the taming influence of love, it is also coveted, manipulated, and subjugated by every female he encounters.

Similarly, in the traditional versions of the legend, Don Juan's insult to the spirit of the dead *commandante* animates the stone statue, and his defiance becomes the final offense for which all his lechery is punished; the last scene of fiery annihilation is appropriately heroic. Yet, the personality of Byron's Don Juan, by contrast, seems to fade, and the narrator becomes dominant just as the poem comes to a fragmented conclusion.

Juan's encounter with the lady ghost, and the disastrous effects of their night together—their mutual fatigue, the implications that sex as the ultimate sensation leaves Juan depleted and dissatisfied—completes Byron's irascible interpretation of the myth: the libertine who holds out his hand to specters or avenging spirits is inviting consummation, especially if his bedchamber is on hallowed ground. While the traditional Don Juan is visited by a stone statue from a monastery, and is consumed by flames, Byron's Don Juan is visited by a live woman simply disguised as the ghost of a friar and is annihilated by sexual consummation. Combining the memories of his own childhood terror of Newstead Abbey with the pattern of the original myth, Byron thus makes Juan the unfortunate prey of the restless ghost who haunts Norman Abbey in retribution of offenses the Amundevilles are still committing against the "glorious remnant of the Gothic pile," and the statues of the "Twelve saints [which] had once stood sanctified in stone." The offense against the statues is integral to the animation of the Byronic specter, and, in conformity to the traditional version of the myth, it is the crime for which the Don receives his ultimate punishment. His sexual energy is totally enveloped by female aggression. The legend of the Black Friar of Norman Abbey is a hoax, but so, in Byron's poem, is the myth of Don Juan's inexhaustible, indomitable sexuality. In fact, in Byron's version of the legend women are fatal to Juan; sex is anathema, and he is too enchanted with his own image to see the joke.

The neat reversals of the traditional elements of the legend indicate that Byron's poem does more than recast the *burlador* as Romantic hero. The narrator of the poem is ostensibly concerned with judging society in terms of Romantic idealism, but the poet is ultimately concerned with the etiology and evolution of Juan's delusions. The poem scrutinizes the pathology of being human. Everyone, including Juan, capitalizes on his charismatic sexuality. Juan is the key to the poem, yet he is only significant in relation to the other characters. The pattern of his relationships with other characters is essentially one of relationships with women and their men, established in Canto I and repeated throughout the poem. While traditional criticism says Byron makes small use of the Don Juan myth, the pattern of Don Juan's relationship with women and their men does, in fact, conform throughout the poem to the patterns of the original myth, but turned about for purposes that a psychoanalytic examination of the poem will clarify. The hero seems deliberately depicted as the personification of the Don Juan complex, as described by Otto Fenichel more than a century later [in *The Psychoanalytic Theory of Neuroses,* 1945]:

> Don Juan's behavior is no doubt due to his Oedipus complex. He seeks his mother in all women and cannot find her. But the analysis of Don Juan types shows that their Oedipus complex is of a particular kind. It is dominated by the pregenital aim of incorporation, prevaded by narcissistic needs and tinged with sadistic impulses. . . . The striving for sexual satisfcation is still condensed with the striving for getting narcissistic supplies in order to maintain self-esteem. . . . His narcissistic need requires proof of his ability to excite women; after he knows that he is able to excite a specific woman, his doubts arise concerning other women whom he has not yet tried.

Incorporation, or the infantile desire to engulf external objects, is the Don Juan personality's habitual response toward women: he sees sexual conquest as a means of reunion with the omnipotent external force that mother represents; yet, he also fears this reunion because of a concomitant fantasy of being engulfed by it—hence the oedipal relationship carries "a frequent and intense unconscious connection between the ideas of sexuality and death," between sexuality and an anticipation of retribution. As a result of his conformity to the Don Juan complex, Juan emerges as the least mobile character in the drama. Byron employs him in a particular role, with a severely limited repertoire of responses.

Given that Byron invented neither the Don Juan myth, nor the Don Juan complex, he does devote considerable effort to dramatizing the phenomenon. Byron himself was a man with a compulsion for self-dramatization, and the term "psychodrama," the reenactment of problematic past experiences, real or imagined, in an effort to resolve them, may well express what the poem was for Byron. By concentrating on Juan and the ladies, we can see how the poem served the poet as a kind of therapeutic theater in which he could reenact certain of his own problematic amorous adventures—such as incest both real and fancied—in an attempt to achieve relief from the anxiety that memory must perpetuate. The creation of *Don Juan* was Byron's attempt to fuse conflicting elements of his own personality, as well as those of the myth he had become:

> They made me, without my search, a species of popular Idol; they, without reason or judgement, beyond the caprice of their good pleasure, threw down the Image from its pedestal; it was not broken with the fall, and they would, it seems, again replace it—but they shall not.

He wrote this letter, as he wrote *Don Juan,* in exile, and both are public statements of hubris that refute the powers of social retribution. Byron was concerned with the reader's reaction to *Don Juan* only insofar as it related to his own need to be accepted as a Don Juan: Byron reserves judgment for himself, and the poem as psychodrama will reveal that his Nemesis, like Juan's, is a form of degraded eroticism which he may describe or reenact, but which he will not, cannot deny.

Freud's statement [in *On Creativity and the Unconscious,* 1958] about the poet's relation to his work is fundamental to our understanding of Byron's undertaking:

> Some actual experience which made a strong impression on the writer had stirred up a memory of an earlier experience, generally belonging to childhood, which then arouses a wish that finds a fulfillment in the work in question, and in which elements of the recent event and the old memory should be discernible.

Throughout the poem, we can see elements of Byron's childhood, his marriage and divorce, and the trauma of his relationship with Augusta Leigh interwoven into Juan's adventures. If we expand upon Freud, using [Jacob L.] Moreno's principles of psychodrama [in his *Psychodrama,* 1964] however, according to which the actor (who is also the author) in this genre is the protagonist, and all the other characters in the poem represent "auxiliary egos," actors who "play the roles of absent people involved in his problems or fears" [Ira A. Greenberg, *Psychodrama and Audience Attitude Change,* 1968], Canto I, as a deliberate innovation to the traditional Don Juan myth, is doubly significant then: we can see the poet's overt attempt to create a plausible source of Juan's eventual disorder, and Byron's own oedipal problems emerge as the ultimate conflict in his psychodrama, with Juan as the protagonist of myth and psychodrama both.

The evolution of Juan as a character spans the wealth of the poem, linking Byron's playful treatment of the sensuous innocent to his portrait of the weary *cavalier servente* of English drawing-room society. Byron devotes most attention to Juan's psychological development in Canto I, through the detailed description of Juan's childhood behavior and adolescent sensibility. While the Russian cantos make some reference to Juan's dissipation and a mysterious illness, it is only within the confines of Norman Abbey (Cantos XII-XVII) that Byron returns to an indepth scrutiny of the hero and once again explores the psychology of his malaise. Though the entire poem, particularly such episodes as those of Haidée, Juan, and Lambro, bears examination in terms of Byron's psychodrama, these cantos will serve to illustrate the ways in which Byron's own psychology informs his reinterpretation of the myth.

The poet points out that seeds of Juan's discontent were started in Seville. His mother, like Byron's, is repression personified: "Some women use their tongues—she *looked* a lecture." His father is a henpecked cavalier, "a mortal of the careless kind" (I.xix.1), whose indiscreet love affairs prove his undoing. According to the narrator, Donna Incz becomes incensed by the gossip and begins to torment her husband:

> But then she had a devil of a spirit
> And sometimes mixed up fancies with realities,
> And let few opportunities escape
> Of getting her liege lord into a scrape.
>
> (I.xx.5-8)

Juan is doted upon, yet undisciplined, because his parents are distracted by maintaining conduct that is "exceedingly well-bred," while "Wishing each other, not divorced, but dead" (I.xxvi.3). Inez attempts to dispose of Jóse by proving him insane, but, lacking enough evidence, she settles for divorce, gathering the forces of public opinion to do battle against her husband:

> The hearers of her case became repeaters,
> Then advocates, inquisitors, and judges,
> Some for amusement, others for old grudges.
>
> (I.xxviii.6-8)

With the added enforcement of social institutions, Inez's actual wish is fulfilled:

> The lawyers did their utmost for divorce,
> But scarce a fee was paid on either side
> Before, unluckily, Don Jóse died.
>
> (I.xxxii.6-8)

Don Jóse, like Byron, is doomed because his own "malus animus" prevents him from understanding his wife's pernicious hypocrisy; Jóse is too busy pursuing his pleasures to realize that under her cultivated air of stoic magnanimity, she has never ceased plotting revenge. In the contest of wills, Donna Inez's triumphs; Jóse's physical and spiritual strength are destroyed:

> Standing alone beside his desolate hearth,
> Where all his household gods lay shivered round him.
> No choice was left his feeling or his pride,
> Save death or Doctors' Commons—so he died.
>
> (I.xxxvi.5-8)

His power, his life force as symbolized by the household gods, is broken. The shattered gods, the desolate hearth, are touching images of depleted forms that once held life but now are cold, empty, and powerless. His death wish toward Inez, his magic, was no match for hers.

The chronicle of Don Jóse and Donna Inez's divorce parallels Byron's own, but the actual death of Jóse relates to the death of Byron's father, Captain John Byron:

> George was three and one-half years old when his father died, and less than three when he saw him for the last time, but he later told Thomas Medwin: "I was not so young when my father died, but that I perfectly remember him; and had very early a horror of matrimony, from the sight of domestic broils. . . . He seemed born for his own ruin, and that of the other sex" [Leslie A. Marchand, *Byron: A Biography,* 1957].

Mrs. Byron "assuaged her passionate grief by a mingled hatred and love of the son who reminded her of . . . [her husband]." Unfortunately for Byron, he was too early the man of the house, like Juan "An only son left with an only mother" (I.xxxvii.7).

Juan is left to Inez's care. She proceeds to discipline and shape his education, "Resolved that Juan should be quite a paragon, / And worthy of the noblest pedigree" (I.xxxviii.2-3). The futility of her excessive effort is intimated even in this early description of Juan's education: Juan's pedigree naturally includes Jóse's legacy, what Inez's lawyers call a propensity for cvil, and "paragon" implies excellence, but it is morally vague. Because of these earliest accounts of Juan's curriculum, his virtue is made something to joke about; one realizes from the narrator's sly remarks that Donna Inez cannot quite maintain control, and tension builds as Juan matures.

Byron shows Juan approaching manhood, amid the screaming protests of Donna Inez, and the docile machinations of Donna Julia. The "almost man" is thrilled and confused with Donna Julia, ignorant of the cause of these new feelings. The narrator vacillates between hinting that something "From sire to son to augur good or ill" is a scandalous possibility, and claiming that Juan is aware of something, but cannot imagine that it could be a "Thing quite in course, and not at all alarming, / Which with a little patience might grow charming" (I.lxxxvi.7-8). Juan as "Poor little fellow!" is incredibly dumb. He wanders, "silent and pensive," through the woods—in fact, he wanders through the entire canto without ever uttering a word. He is purportedly only aware of Julia's eyes, and even this conscious longing occurs in the midst of metaphysical ponderings. He is lost for hours to his scrutiny of leaves and flowers, hearing "a voice in all the winds," filled with imaginings of wood nymphs and "how the goddesses came down to men." These gentle, pensive imaginings of Juan's are sublimated erotic longings. The imagery couches his sexuality in such a manner as to make it palatable to the reader. By thus engaging the reader's approval of Juan's budding sexual appetite, Byron appears to be reshaping the symbol of Don Juan as the comically overassertive lecher, to that of a wandering innocent whose passion is linked to wood nymphs and goddesses. Juan's somnambulant sexuality is given a preternatural quality, which is essentially the characteristic that explains his appeal for women throughout the poem.

In contrast to Juan's passionate ignorance, Julia's knowing attempts at self-control appear contrived and ludicrous:

> Yet Julia's very coldness still was kind,
> And tremulously gentle her small hand
> Withdrew itself from his, but left behind . . .
>
> (I.lxxi.1-3)

She vow'd she never would see Juan more
And next day paid a visit to his mother.

(I.lxxvi.1-2)

She has prayed to the Virgin Mary as "the best judge of
a lady's case," but, when she misses seeing Juan, the Virgin
is "no further prayed." Her turmoil is declared in terms of
a Christian's inner struggle, that of the virtuous wife tempted by the devil "so very sly," amidst "love divine," angels, and "reveries celestial." Her serenity, however, has
a certain concupiscent smugness to it: deciding that her
honor is "a rock or a mole," she dispenses "with any kind
of troublesome control." She envisions a plan that makes
provision for her husband's death, while it ingeniously
allows her to begin immediate instruction of Juan in "the
rudiments of love."

Julia's fantasy about Alfonso's death exactly resembles
Inez's death wish toward Jóse:

And if in the meantime her husband died,
But heaven forbid that such a thought should cross
Her brain, though in a dream, and then she sighed.

(I.lxxxiv.1-3)

As Inez's social and psychological peer, Julia becomes a
parental substitute for Juan; as another character in Byron's
psychodrama, she embodies again his own mother's violent
hatred toward her husband and the emotional excesses that
her stern Presbyterian principles neither disciplined, nor
relieved, but as with Julia, and Inez, hatred is nicely submerged beneath a veneer of respectability, and the hated
husband is replaced by the more easily dominated son.

Byron has been pointing at similarities between Inez and
Julia since he first introduced Julia into Inez's domain.
The narrator imputes scandal to be the basis of their friendship. If "Inez had, ere Don Alfonso's marriage, / Forgot
with him her very prudent carriage" (I.lxvi.7-8), and in
"still keeping up the old connexion . . . / She took his
lady also in affection" (I.lxvii.1,3), then Julia's fifty-year-
old husband, as Inez's lover, doubles as a father figure to
both Julia and Juan, and the implication is, of course, that
the young pair could be sister and brother. Alfonso's relationship with Inez and the chance of his being Juan's
actual father, or at least old enough to substitute as the
father symbol in the exclusive "only mother," "only son"
affiliation, sets up an oedipal configuration between these
three characters, which is further complicated by the possibility that Julia is "sister-mother" to Juan. When she is
depicted as the young wife of a "jealous lord," innocently
caressing Juan, this passes as a kind of youthful familiarity. The psychic consanguinity becomes more complex,
however, as she assumes the role of older woman, guiding
him into a forbidden affair: then, her role as knowing
voluptuary and Juan's as the sexually precocious child set
the stage for the inevitable confrontation between father-
Alfonso and Juan.

Whereas in his own childhood Byron never actually confronted his father, he would have shared his mother's guilt,
that is, he would have been aware that his exclusive at-

tachment to her psychologically demanded his complicity
in the death wish she expressed toward his father. His
relationship with Augusta Leigh was similar to Juan's
relationship with Julia and Inez: the sister displaces the
mother in an incestuous relationship that could be actualized, and the guilt and anxiety that his father's death had
left with him would be resolved by the punishment the
incest would inevitably incur.

The confrontation scene is the only aspect of Juan's and
Julia's affair that Byron concerns himself with. After so
long and carefully preparing the seduction, he devotes only
a few lines to their enjoyment; the conflict and upheaval
are far more dramatically significant. Their passion is
mentioned only briefly, amid the comings and goings of
the chagrined Alfonso, and with the maid standing around
to chastise their foolishness. The lovers together are never
allowed to achieve the grandeur with which they are comically endowed as individual characters. Juan is still the
*enfant terrible,* the naughty man-child, while Julia has
developed into a fabliau harpy, the nasty mother-figure
capable of holding her own in their struggle with the cuckolded Alfonso. The incestuous implications of stanzas ix
through cxvii are no longer strained and snide. The maid,
Antonia, gives an indirect praise of Juan that makes the
contrast between Julia, the knowing dowager, and Juan,
the precocious child, humorous:

"Had it but been for a stout cavalier
Of twenty-five or thirty (Come, make haste)
But for a child, what piece of work is here!
I really, madam, wonder at your taste."

(I.clxxii.1-4)

"Stout" has some nice phallic qualities, and the phrase
"piece of work" quite explains Julia's "taste." Compared
to poor old Alfonso, whose "sword had dropp'd ere he
could draw it," and who comes off the impotent buffoon
of the scene, Juan is the virile figure who is all the less
culpable because he cannot quite pull off the escapade.
All he inflicts on Alfonso is a bloody nose, as he runs off
naked into the night. Whatever damage Juan has done to
Alfonso's sexual nose is innocuous, and the potentially
dangerous scene is farcically resolved. For Byron, Canto
I allows him to recreate through fantasy, and memory, the
bizarre relationships with his own overprotective mother,
and wife, and to joke about his own oedipal, or sister-
mother, relationship with Augusta Leigh. His treatment of
these ladies, within the context of the poem is also integral to the turnabout he makes upon the traditional Don
Juan myth: the Don cannot alter his fate: it is conceived
and delivered by women.

Byron's method of handling Julia's sexuality merits some
further explication, because it prefigures his pattern of
developing females as paradoxically predictable and mysterious. While Julia's soft sighs are actually expressions
of a powerful erotic appetite, Byron's laughing exaggeration of her feigned restraint, in terms of the Christian
metaphor, makes her seem only silly. Yet, as the source of
Juan's sexual initiation and the cause of his exile, her
sexuality becomes threatening. She claims little of the

reader's sympathy; stanzas of her farewell letter to Juan are touching, but the sentiment is immediately undercut by the narrator's description of the care with which the adieu is prepared—even her sorrow seems contrived; her tragedy is mere melodrama. Julia is important as Juan's first lover because she embodies all the puzzling aspects with which Byron endows women throughout Juan's adventures:

> Oh thou *teterrima causa* of all *belli*—
>   Thou gate of life and death—thou nondescript!
> Whence is our exit and our entrance. Well I
>   May pause in pondering how all souls are dipt
> In thy perennial fountain. How man fell, I
>   Know not, since knowledge saw her branches stript
> Of her first fruit; but how he falls and rises
> Since, thou hast settled beyond all surmises.
>
> (IX.lv.1-8)

> Some call thee 'the worst cause of war,' but I
>   Maintain thou art the best, for after all
> From thee we come, to thee we go . . .
>
> (IX.lvi.1-3)

Because they are a mystery, all women represent an external threat to Juan's sexuality, and Byron needs Juan to enact an escape from their motherly manipulations. Juan's role as the "innocent" in Canto I differentiates him from the traditional Don Juan character: he is the conquered, not the conqueror, and the parallel between the two heroes' adventures does not clearly emerge until the English cantos. Here, Byron fulfills the prophecy that he is writing about the same hero of the pantomimes, plays, and operas. The English episodes illustrate that Byron has kept the legend of Don Juan and the stone guest within his overall poetic design. With "new mythological machinery, / And very handsome supernatural scenery" (I.cci.7-8) he will manage "in canto twelfth . . . to show / The very place where wicked people go" (I.ccvii.7-8).

The Don Juan of the English episodes impresses us with the dispassionate savoir-faire he has learned in Russia. In contrast to the fabulous description within which Byron couched Juan's adolescent fantasies in Canto I, with its apotheosis of Juan's innocent eroticism, the itinerary of Juan's advance into the aristocratic circles of London appears merely matter-of-fact. He is the "young diplomatic sinner" who has come to England to regain his health after the dissipation that he was enjoying in Russia mysteriously made him sick. The narrator suggests the cause was "the Empress's *maternal* [my italics] love" (X.xxxii.8), because even as Juan did "his duty, / In royalty's vast arms he sighed for beauty" (X.xxxvii.7-8). Like the youth of Canto I, Juan barely escapes the dowager's engulfing embrace, but in the Russian canto Byron seems to be suggesting that Juan is becoming somewhat of a predator himself, because the "imperious passion," which Juan dedicates to Catherine in Canto IX, is the "self-love" that makes Juan believe himself "as good as any" (IX.lxviii.8).

We see him approaching the throne with a predetermined intent to serve the queen in a particular fashion. Like Byron, Juan has become a *cavalier servente;* these cantos were written while the poet was "settled into regular *serventismo*" to Teresa Guiccioli, and Byron's own ambivalence about his servitude is reflected in his delineation of Juan's Russian post:

> What were the actual and official duties
> Of the strange thing some women set a value on,
> Which hovers oft about some married beauties,
> Called *cavalier servente*—a Pygmalion
> Whose statues warm . . .
> Beneath his art.
>
> (IX.li.2-7)

Whatever his official duties were in Russia, this equation of women to statues who animate under his art has foreboding implications, both in relation to Juan's oedipal relationship to Catherine, and as a *figura* of the stone statue that comes to life and punishes Don Juan's lechery in the traditional myth: we would expect Byron to demand punishment from an aroused female statue, because of his own oedipal problems, and Juan's strange malady in Russia is yet another way in which the poet expresses his neurosis.

Since Byron's own displaced oedipal problem, his relationship with Augusta Leigh, is integral to his memories of England, by calling England hell in his version of the legend, and by demonstrating the omnivorous immorality of the aristocracy, the government, and the business magnates, he is attempting to invalidate the social condemnation that had forced his exile. Byron's idea of "the place where wicked people go," hell as expressed in Canto XII, is simultaneously different from and identical to the traditional Don Juan's destination. In a letter to Murray, written after the completion of Canto v, he claims that he has "not quite fixed whether to make . . . Juan end in Hell, or in an unhappy marriage, not knowing which would be the severest." His next remark about the tradition seems good evidence that he is still keeping the traditional legend well in mind: "The Spanish tradition says Hell: but it is probably only an Allegory of the other state." Hence, Juan's "last elopement with the devil" should conform to Byron's conscious interpretation of the traditional legend, as well as being part of the poet's psychodrama and reflective of his unconscious interpolations of the elements of the myth: the word "elopement" in connection with the "devil" points again toward Byron's connection of punishment with the wife-mother figure. Marriage is inherently bound to his transgression of the incest taboo. For the traditional libertine, marriage is an "Allegory" of hell because it represents external restrictions upon his own desire to engulf the objective world. The traditional Don is the aggressor; in London, Byron's Juan is still the obliging son-lover, whose hell is a continuum of falls, with sister-mother.

The epic similes of Canto x prepare the reader for a more spectacular hell than Juan encounters in Canto XII, yet the true map of Juan's descent does underlie Byron's description of his first view of London:

> The sun went down, the smoke rose up, as from
> A half-unquenched volcano, o'er a space

Which well beseemed the 'devil's drawing-room,'
As some have qualified that wondrous place.

                                                    (X.lxxxi.14)

Byron's metaphor of London refers to "the popular tradition that craters of volcanoes lead directly to the pit of hell, hence to the devil's drawing-room" [W. W. Pratt, in *Lord Byron: Don Juan*, ed. T. G. Steffan, E. Steffan, and W. W. Pratt, 1973]. The "pit of hell" in Canto XII is London, and the "Smithfield Show" a flesh market where all the members of drawing-room society survey each other in an endless parade of possible marriage bargains. Juan enters London, the "devil's drawing-room," with little hesitation; he hovers "undecided / Amongst the paths of being 'taken in,'" pausing only long enough to be received into the "best" society. Whereas the belching infernos of Canto XI and the repeated references within that canto to London as "damned" would seem to be setting the scene for our hero to enter a fiery hell—to meet death in submission or defiance, according to the heroic *burlador* tradition—perdition becomes only a metaphor of the change in Juan's psychology. In Canto XII, hell is an experience that polishes the skills he had begun to acquire in Russia, and Juan's resemblance to the traditional libertine becomes apparent: he has learned to see women as objects whom he may desire and engulf. He learns to maneuver within the social marketplace, only hesitating "at *first* because he did not think the women pretty." Like a mercantile Narcissus, he sees his own worth as a reflection of others' desires, and he proceeds to shop for a lady worthy of his charms. In Canto XII, our hero has wandered into an existential hell, where reality is the bartering experience endlessly perpetuated, and universally perpetrated. The narrator lambasts society; Byron refuses to differentiate between Juan and mankind. While the narrator delivers scathing descriptions of genial hypocrisy, Byron shows Juan indulging in the same peccadilloes. Juan is doomed to the ordinary, and in London he seems shallow and insignificant without his mythical trappings.

At the close of Canto XII, Juan has been left "exposed to temptation," but then Byron has done this to him so often that one does not take the narrator seriously when he insists on repeating it. The reader can see that Juan has developed a social cunning that makes the most of any occasion, and the defenseless man-child of the first canto has developed at last into the libertine after whom he is named: he no longer stands "in the predicament / Of a mere novice." His experience, his past servitude, seems to have equipped him to handle even "The loveliest oligarchs of our gynocracy." For Byron, the "English setting makes the last cantos, stanza for stanza, more personal than the preceding ten" [Truman Guy Steffan, *The Making of a Masterpiece: Byron's* Don Juan, Vol. 1 of *Byron's* Don Juan: *A Variorum Edition*], and he uses Juan to reenact the dynamics of his own social triumphs in England. The atmosphere is melancholic, however, and Juan seems to have settled into a "dreary void," an abyss of the "polished, smooth, and cold." The women are lewdly voracious, "marble," and "ice," another collection of cool statues, with an assortment of cuckolded husbands.

The Don Juan of the last English cantos is only a bored aristocrat whose sense of malaise seems part of the social disease he contracted in Canto XII. He is a sophisticated strategist, managing to keep one step ahead of Adeline and her matriarchal machinations. In fact, up until Canto XVI, it appears that Byron is going to ignore the traditional confrontation between Don Juan and the devil that he promised the reader in Canto I. Juan's offenses hardly seem to merit an avenging specter. Instead, Byron has shown that the betrayals are done by the women upon their husbands, and any shame they incur, they bear as emblems of the pleasure they knew with Juan. They never curse Juan or call upon their husbands or heaven to avenge their honor—the image of the ladies' being usually too busy plotting revenge upon their husbands is one of Byron's favorite and most autobiographical motifs. Byron's *cavalier servente* does receive a few curses from the husbands, or even from a father or two, but since immorality is ubiquitous in his version of the libertine's life and loves, their curses are a comic bluster, part of the overall social satire. Juan lacks the braggadocio that would force the comparison between his own fame as it is discussed in England and the renowned lechery of the legendary Don. The ordinary quality of Juan's dissipation and his sharing this doom daily with his peers leave the reader unprepared for any hell but a continuation of the ennui that has plagued our hero for six cantos.

Thus, when Byron creates a ghost at Norman Abbey, and refers to the curse of the Amundevilles, the family's offense to the stone statues, there would appear to be no connection to Juan or the ghost who leads Don Juan to hell in the stone guest legend. Juan's anxieties appear to be focused on Aurora's "self-possession"; even as he is sighing in his Gothic chamber, listening to the "rippling sound of the lake's billow, / With all the mystery by midnight caused," he is only "restless, and perplexed, and compromised." Byron has dropped the incest innuendoes, and Juan comes off so perfectly blameless in regard to his amorous adventures that one can only attribute our hero's nervous condition to his self-immersion in the powerful aura of superstition that surrounds the desecrated ruins. Juan's encounter with the monk, "The thing of air, / Or earth beneath, or heaven or t'other place," is given such comic-horror treatment that it seems a hoax, although Juan goes "Back to his chamber, shorn of half his strength." The narrator informs us that Juan's taper is "Burnt, and not blue," and, according to the rules of haunting-superstition, no malevolent spirit could possibly be present. Juan, however, does not seem to accept this evidence as any indication of the visitant's benignity, and he appears at breakfast distraught and imperfectly groomed for the first time in his career as a dandy.

The breakfast conversation, about the "Black Friar," is initiated by Lord Henry, but Adeline's perusal of Juan's reactions to her husband's ghostly tale would lead us to suspect that she could very well be the ghostly culprit:

She looked and saw him pale and turned as pale
Herself, then hastily looked down and muttered

Something, but what's not stated in my tale.

(XVI.xxxi.1-3)

She could be playing with him, distracting him from his quest of Aurora; or, in psychological terms, since Juan refused to allow Adeline to settle his marriage match for him, she would be the destructive mother figure, as voracious and repressive as Donna Inez, attempting to control Juan's virility to her own ends. She becomes the prime suspect in the ruse as the narrator questions her motives in singing of the Black Friar:

'Twere difficult to say what was the object
Of Adeline in bringing this same lay
To bear on what appeared to her the subject
Of Juan's nervous feelings on that day.
Perhaps she merely had the simple project
To laugh him out of his supposed dismay;
Perhaps she might wish to confirm him in it,
Though why I cannot say, at least this minute.

(XVI.li.1-8)

Byron returns to the metaphor of hell in Canto XVI, and, when he does, Juan, as a result of the previous visitation, is involved and expecting the spectral encounter. He sits in his chamber, as he did the night before, save this time "Expectant of the ghost's fresh operations" (XVI.cxi.8). The door opens with "a most infernal creak / Like that of hell" (XVI.cxvi.1-2). Juan seems about to be engulfed by something dark and dreadful: "A single shade's sufficient to entrance a / Hero, for what is substance to a spirit?" (XVI.cxvi.6-7). Like the legendary libertine from whom he sprang, who puts forth his hand to touch the stone statue of the commandant, Juan puts forth his hand, determined to touch the "stony death," resolved to pierce the mystery, brave and defiant with a wrath fed by fear. He puts forth an arm, but it touches "no soul, nor body, but the wall." He cowers. Suddenly, the ghost has "a remarkably sweet breath," fair hair, red lips, and "a hard but glowing bust"—it is "The phantom of her frolic Grace—Fitz-Fulke!" (XVI.cxxiii.7-8).

Within the dramatic context of the poem itself, this comic revelation is particularly effective in contrast to all the tension and terror that the legend of the Black Friar and the scenery of the Gothic ruins has evoked. Considering the format of the Don Juan genre, a female ghost seeking Juan in pleasure, as contrasted to the traditional figure of the avenging patriarch, is the final explosion of the myth that *malus animus* is unique to the *burlador*. The neatest reversal lies in Byron's setting up Adeline as the female figure most likely to be subverting Juan's strength: instead of the usual hypocritical, aristocratic, cold character, Juan meets damnation from the warm Fitz-Fulke. She is the one person in the English cantos whose "mind was all upon her face," who openly enjoys the "Tracasserie and agacerie." In linking Juan's last fall to such an apparently uncontrived appetite, Byron is intimating that any female, no matter how voluptuous, or openly flirtatious, is as destructive to Juan as the repressive, manipulative Donna Inez and Donna Julia, because women in general are the statues that warm, or become erotically animated, under his

art, and their aroused sexuality then threatens to engulf Juan. These fears and fantasies seem particularly meaningful to Byron, because he can employ Juan to play the role of *cavalier servente,* create continuous escapes for his hero, as he remains bound to Teresa Guiccioli; perhaps, even more significant than the vicarious pleasure that Byron derives from Juan's escapes is the satisfaction and relief he would derive in seeing Juan punished.

The fragment of Canto XVII is the end of **Don Juan**—Byron leaves his hero with nothing; the curse of the dissipated is only an absence of something:

Which best is to encounter, ghost or none,
'Twere difficult to say, but Juan looked
As if he had combated with more than one,
Being wan and worn, with eyes that hardly brooked
The light that through the Gothic windows shone.
Her Grace too had a sort of air rebuked,
Seemed pale and shivered, as if she had kept
A vigil or dreamt rather more than slept.

(XVII.xiv.1-8)

The ultimate irony is that even when sexuality escapes the moral confines, and appears spontaneous, it is deadly.

This final stanza and the one below, which immediately precedes it in the original manuscript, form an absolutely coherent conclusion to the poem:

But Oh! that I were dead—for while alive—
Would that I neer had loved—Oh Woman—
Woman—
All that I write or wrote can neer revive
To paint a sole sensation—though quite common—
Of those in which the Body seemed to drive
My Soul from out me at thy single summon
Expiring in the hope of sensation.

In terms of dramatic unity, the stanzas represent the only possible resolution to the poem's overwhelming variety of verifiable paradoxes and playful juxtapositions: together, they illustrate the fusion of the naively innocent Juan persona and the cynically experienced narrative voice. The description of Juan's dissolution echoes the narrator's desperate apostrophe to Woman. Juan's malaise is more than an elegant social disease. His psychic depletion corresponds to the narrator's "Soul . . . expiring in the hope of sensation." The narrator's howls about Woman's "single summon" belong to Juan's mute encounters with female sexuality. The speaking voice metaphorically articulates an awareness of the oedipal neurosis, which Juan has only been capable of acting out. The conflicting fantasies and fears of engulfment are expressed in both stanzas through Romantic expletives of guilt and anxiety. Fear and impotency are Byron's concessions to his own psychic reality, and about as close as he ever comes to a public statement of morality.

If one compares the merging of the narrator's emotion and Juan's physical state in the last two stanzas with Byron's feelings about his role as *cavalier servente* to Teresa

---

**Virginia Woolfe on the style of *Don Juan*:**

Having indicated that I am ready, after a century, to fall in love with [Byron], I suppose my judgment of ***Don Juan*** may be partial. It is the most readable poem of its length ever written, I suppose; a quality which it owes in part to the springy random haphazard galloping nature of its method. This method is a discovery by itself. It's what one has looked for in vain—a[n] elastic shape which will hold whatever you choose to put into it. Thus he could write out his mood as it came to him; he could say whatever came into his head. He wasn't committed to be poetical; & thus escaped his evil genius of the false romantic & imaginative. When he is serious he is sincere; & he can impinge upon any subject he likes. He writes 16 canto's without once flogging his flanks. He had, evidently, the able witty mind of what my father Sir Leslie would have called a thoroughly masculine nature. I maintain that these illicit kind of books are far more interesting than the proper books which respect illusions devoutly all the time. Still, it doesn't seem an easy example to follow; & indeed like all free & easy things, only the skilled & mature really bring them off successfully. But Byron was full of ideas— a quality that gives his verse a toughness, & drives me to little excursions over the surrounding landscape or room in the middle of my reading.

*Virginia Woolfe, in a diary entry dated August 8, 1918, in* The Diary of Virginia Woolfe, Vol. I: 1915–1919, *edited by Anne Oliver Bell, The Hogarth Press, 1977, pp. 180-81.*

---

Guiccioli, the oedipal conflicts of the poem and the poet appear contiguous. In August 1819, distracted from continuing Canto III, Byron sent the following letter to his friend John Hobhouse:

> I have been excited and agitated, and exhausted mentally and bodily all this summer, till I sometimes begin to think not only "that I shall die at top first," but that the moment is not very remote. I have had no particular cause of griefs, except the usual accompaniments of all unlawful passions. . . .

> I feel—and I feel it bitterly—that a man should not consume his life at the side and on the bosom of a woman, and a stranger; that this *Cicisbean* existence is to be condemned. But I have neither the strength of mind to break my chain, nor the insensibility which would deaden its weight. I cannot tell what will become of me—to leave, or to be left would at present drive me quite out of my senses; and yet to what have I conducted myself?

If adultery were the "unlawful passion" that tortured him, then the legal negotiations between Byron and Count Guiccioli, in 1820, should have eased the conscience of so infamous a libertine as he. Instead, the legal agreement seemed to irritate. Like the legendary Don Juan, Byron hated the rules and regularity of a contracted affair: "A man actually becomes a piece of female property." Like his pantomiming hero and melancholy narrator, Byron's engulfment anxieties, as expressed in this letter, outweight-

ed "the recompense" of his relationship with the Countess. As Teresa, herself, so aptly described the continuum of Byron's incestuous delusion:

> How often has he not spoken of [Augusta] to me! and, much as I loved him, how often I was irritated by his tender affection for his sister! Augusta. C'était un refrain perpétuel.

No matter what shape the relationship with Teresa assumed, legal or otherwise, or if the husband-father figure of the Count challenged or sanctioned the affair, it was still, for Byron, "unlawful" or threatening, and related to his sister-mother confusion.

Byron's separation from Teresa and the trip to Greece seem but another sequel to Juan's adventures. For Byron, ***Don Juan*** was his psychodrama: using the Don Juan legend throughout, but making significant alterations, he reshaped the myth in an attempt to confront his past within the present of the poem. In Moreno's terms, all the characters in the poem are the "auxiliary egos" in Byron's own oedipal drama. Byron's Juan is not, nor was he intended to be, a hero: he is only the protagonist of the drama, the man in a frenzy.

**Daniel P. Watkins**   **(essay date 1983)**

SOURCE: "Politics and Religion in Byron's *Heaven and Earth*," in *The Byron Journal*, No. 11, 1983, pp. 30-9.

[*In this essay, Watkins argues that in* Heaven and Earth *Byron demonstrates how religious beliefs can be manipulated to support authoritarian political views.*]

Byron's faith in the ability of readers to understand and appreciate his poetry seems to have disappeared completely in his later years. His famous response to the strong moral criticisms of ***Don Juan*** reflects his sense of how far the public missed his literary aims: "it may be bawdy—but is it not good English?—it may be profligate—but is it not *life,* is it not *the thing?*" Criticism of the history plays, too, derived from ignorance; the plays, he claimed, would be appreciated only when properly "understood." His impatience perhaps reached its peak in his sardonic comment that ***Cain*** was subtitled "A Mystery" "in honour of what it probably will remain to the reader."

That he had good cause to be touchy about the way his poetry was read is nowhere better exemplified than in ***Heaven and Earth,*** a serious work that (since its publication in 1821) has been consistently misinterpreted. It has always been assumed that Byron's objective in this play was to show "that the upper and the lower worlds in some way need each other, and that each constantly gravitates toward the other despite Jehovah's decree" [Jerome J. McGann, *Fiery Dust: Byron's Poetic Development*, 1968]. Or, as Bernard Blackstone puts it [in *Byron III: Social Satire, Drama and Epic,* 1971], "What is at issue here is the question of intercourse, or communication. How is the heaven-earth nexus to be achieved?" To exemplify this point, critics cite the sexual union between the daughters of Cain and the angels of God. But there is another, less metaphysical Heaven and Earth in the play that had occupied a central position in Byron's thought at least since the writing of *Cain,* and that, as far as I know, has never been recognized, certainly never explored. His immediate concern, I believe, was to define as far as was possible the connection between politics and religion; he wished to suggest that the religious values accepted unquestioningly by a society as being true, universal, and absolute can be used to sanction and justify political authoritarianism. The much noted angel-man union is subordinate to this larger interest, serving mainly to clarify and emphasize the play's political message.

Byron had become increasingly convinced in the history plays—*Marino Faliero, Sardanapalus,* and *The Two Foscari*—that politics could not be understood simply in terms of exterior political events. To say that the Doge Faliero committed treason only to avenge his wife's injured honour ignores the more far-reaching question of why a substantial portion of the Venetian population was willing to commit treason with him. Or to suggest that Nineveh succumbed to a rebellious uprising only because a pacifist king sat on the throne places blame on a single individual while ignoring the long-standing social problems that gradually had weakened the city. To understand politics properly, these plays suggest, one must look beneath surface events to the primary relationship between the governing values at society's core and the practical needs and drives that motivate people at any given moment in history.

This social perspective on politics is developed further in the two "mystery" plays, in which Byron turned his attention fully to underlying social values and tried to explain how they often create strife and unrest. Like *Heaven and Earth, Cain* is not so much about theology as about what religion means in terms of political and social reality. The play depicts a society built on a religious foundation, allowing Byron to stress the way religion can dictate society's conduct and outlook on life; every major character except Cain submits readily to the sacred order that man must toil, pray, sacrifice, and, generally, ignore independent human dignity. Cain's unhappiness and restless opposition to prevailing beliefs offer a way of examining the justice of a religious code that demands self-denial and of measuring religious values against the material situation in which they find expression. Each act of the play treats an aspect of the social implications of religion. Act I presents "the accepted social order" [Edward E. Bostetter, *The Romantic Ventriloquists: Wordsworth, Coleridge, Keats, Shelley, Byron,* 1963], the combination of fundamental religious and political ingredients that makes society what it is. Cain is not yet consciously rebellious because he is as yet unsure about the source of his distress; but he is alienated, torn by his inchoate sense that something is wrong with God's scheme, and driven to question the values that require his submission. The cosmic journey of Act II provides him with a perspective that is larger than the narrowly ideological one of his own culture, enabling

him to assess the way religion and society work together to control man's thinking and behaviour. The voyage shows Cain both the insignificance of the world when measured against the vastness of the universe, and—by revealing previous, greater races than man—undercuts man's central role in God's scheme. Act III then returns Cain to the world, where his frustration with the oppressive and evidently unjust "politics of Paradise" causes him to murder Abel. At every point Byron makes the religious story bear on conventional assumptions about man and society; he takes a hard and honest look at the practical significance of a subject most people prefer to leave sacrosanct and unconsidered, and he suggests that social unrest often traces back to the system of values that motivates human action. The play, in short, indicates the social context in which Byron had come to consider religion, and provides a firm foundation for the questions he raises later in *Heaven and Earth*.

*Heaven and Earth* pursues many of the interests established in *Cain.* The play describes both a ruling order and individual discontent with that order; it offers a perspective on social life that is not dictated by society itself; and it presents an openly defiant reaction against the way society is set up. But *Heaven and Earth* is finally more complex than *Cain* because it confuses even further the matter of "right and wrong" Rather than having Lucifer lure man into defiance of God's proclamations, Byron has God's own unfallen angels perform the deed; instead of having a traditional villain such as Cain question the laws of God and man, Byron has one of the Elect—Japhet—serve in this capacity; and rather than having the defiant rebels punished by the Deluge, Byron allows them to escape with God's legions—who become rebels to save them. These points emphasize Byron's refusal to label values abstractly as sacred or profane, and more importantly illustrate his belief that a value system—an ideology—is logically subordinate to social circumstance: no pre-determined system of values exists above and beyond man and society.

As the patriach of antediluvian society, Noah represents the controlling orthodox attitude in the play; he embodies a set of idealistic principles against which the other characters measure their individual needs and desires. Noah believes that society is built on laws, codes, and morals handed down by God, not created by the people who live in society; in fact, he believes that humanity has no real control over the world in which it lives, nor, indeed, any *right* to govern itself. A person gains social power only when he is pre-ordained (as Noah himself has been) by God to voice His wishes. This outlook generates at least two unfortunate practical consequences.

First, it promotes a rigidly authoritarian power structure that justifies tyranny by religious sanctioning. By attributing his power to God, Noah relieves himself of the responsibility attendant upon his position as ruler. As God's mouthpiece, he uses religion to control every facet of social conduct, not only sexual and domestic habits, but even geographical mobility. If individuals deviate from the accepted social norms Noah recalls them not by a threat of physical punishment but by the stronger threat of God's vengeance. To illustrate, Noah claims that his son, Japhet, has no business wandering the Caucasus because "It is an evil spot" (II. 91), nor any right to seek Anah's love because she is "of a fated race" (II. 94); Japhet's errant conduct in both cases is considered to be an affront to God, and punishable by "doom" (III. 466). The sanctions are vague, but effectively intimidating, and they systematically "over-awe" the sensual through their reference to the ideal. A second, even more disturbing consequence of Noah's calvinist understanding of social power is that it deadens human sympathy for mankind and endorses a vicious drive for self-preservation at the expense of others. Noah shows no compassion for the daughters of Cain; he is willing, even eager, to see them destroyed by the Flood. And he warns Japhet to dismiss them also. If Japhet hopes to survive the impending Flood, Noah says, he must "forget / That [the daughters of Cain] exist" (III. 495-96). The selfishness inherent in Noah's power is displayed even more forcefully when it becomes evident that he is willing not only to let the daughters of Cain die, but also to let his son Japhet die for continuing to love Anah despite his commands:

> Then die
> With them!
> How darest thou look on that prophetic sky,
> And seek to save what all things now condemn,
> In overwhelming unison
> With just Jehovah's wrath!
>
> (III. 756-61)

Noah's power rests not only on his ability to convince society that he is administering God's wishes, but also on his ability to keep individuals fixed in their assigned class positions. The importance of stratification to Noah's rule is presented most clearly in the Caucasus scene, which brings together those characters Byron has chosen to represent antediluvian society: Japhet, the tempted son who must be recalled to the moral norms of society so that eventually he can inherit his father's power; Anah and Aholibamah, the temptresses who challenged Noah's power, both by luring Japhet and by consorting with beings beyond Noah's control; the angels, overt representatives of the religious justification for Noah's rule; and, later, Noah himself, the exemplar of proper social conduct. Noah's frantic response to these characters collected together exchanging ideas openly, without any apparent regard for their appointed social positions, suggests the important role hierarchy plays in maintaining the social order he rules. He angrily reminds the others of their proper stations, threatening them with God's vengeance if they continue to violate the decreed order. He classifies Anah and Aholibamah as "children of the wicked" (III. 465) who deserve no human sympathy; he insists that the angels belong in heaven, out of man's sight—not in the daily routines of society: "Has not God made a barrier between Earth / And Heaven, and limited each, kind to kind?" (III. 475-76). He reminds Japhet that he is better than his associates, and that if he is to be assured of continued social and sacred favours he must forego such unseemly company (III. 494-98).

Plainly Noah's heated, politically shrewd commands—which go so far as to call God's angels themselves into question for intruding uninvited into the world—illuminate the requisites of the power he wields: the regimentation of individuals, the snuffing of any possible opposition before it can solidify, a single authoritarian ruling voice. Further, his comments reveal once more the way religion can be used for political ends: Noah justifies the division of society into classes not in terms of his personal rule but in terms of *God's* orders. These points not only show the close connection between Noah's religion and politics, but suggest as well the inhumanity and injustice at the heart of his religious beliefs.

One of the ways Byron makes the play's social theme more credible than in **Cain** is by having Japhet—traditionally associated with unquestioning conformity to God's commands—express many of the same social and religious doubts that Cain had expressed in the earlier mystery play. Japhet is alienated from the blind movements of society, he is expressly unhappy, and he questions many of society's accepted values. Although his immediate cause for distress is Anah's lack of interest in him, he is disturbed also because his emotional needs cannot be satisfied within the scope of Noah's power. He is told bluntly (III. 464-66) that Anah is off-limits to him because she is wicked and thus unacceptable to both Noah and to God. Compared with the ringing finality of this pronouncement, it actually matters little whether Anah loves him or not. Furthermore, he is bothered not only by his private difficulties with Noah and God, but also by the impending Flood, which he doubts is justifiable even in religious terms. If his initial prayer to God to preserve Anah (II. 74-75) suggests his desire for a single exception to God's will, rather than his discontent with the decree that everyone shall die, his later sympathy with doomed humanity as well as his questioning of the logic and virtue of God's plans show a more general concern for mankind and a dissatisfaction with God's law:

> My kinsmen,
> Alas! what am I better than ye are,
> That I must live beyond ye?
>
> (III. 16-18)

> Can we in Desolation's peace have rest?
> Oh God! be thou a God, and spare
> Yet while 'tis time
>
> (III. 703-05)

Japhet's position here recalls the defiant Cain boldly defending what he instinctively knows to be right; he tells Noah that he would have his lot with mankind: "Let me die with *this,* and *them*" (III. 498).

Unlike Cain, however, Japhet's gnawing sense of injustice in the world is outweighed by the heavy hand of religious and social pressure, and thus he never openly breaks with society. He is a potential son of Cain in his unrest and doubt that wilful harm to humanity can be good, but he does not have the courage to side with Anah (though he loves her) in opposition to Noah and God. Traditional attitudes eventually control his thinking and weaken his independence until finally he succumbs to his father's obviously unsatisfactory explanation that the tightening hold on the human race is necessary because "The Earth's grown wicked" (II. 65), and denies his own power to alleviate injustice (III. 51). He expresses his return to conformism when he learns that Anah is consorting with Angels:

> . . . unions like to these,
> Between a mortal and an immortal, cannot
> Be happy or be hallowed. We are sent
> Upon the earth to toil and die; and they
> Are made to minister on high unto
> The Highest.
>
> (III. 369-74)

This passage echoes Noah's law that man's role is to "die when he [God] ordains / A righteous death" (III. 687-88), and indicates Japhet's inability to stand against the controlling codes of social and religious conduct. Pressed to choose between open defiance and reluctant submission. Japhet cannot sustain the Cain-like posture because underneath his outward discontent he is afraid not to believe Noah's maxim that to "Be a man" (III. 694) means to submit to the dictates of God and society. Still, though he submits, he does point up in his final question the chilling irony of this great system of cosmic and worldly order that divides individuals from their fellow beings: "Why, when all perish, why must I remain?" (III. 929).

Anah and Aholibamah reveal more explicitly the problems embedded in antediluvian society by openly testing and challenging the combined religious and political forces that control their world. Although they display opposite personalities—Anah is introspective, sensitive, submissive, while her sister is proud, defiant, caustic—still they both embody the orthodox idea of human evil, and both are equally condemned by Noah and God. Aholibamah claims that her spirit, "though forbidden yet to shine" (I. 104), demands freer movement than orthodox attitudes permit; in fact, her confidence in her independent strength not only generates contempt for Noah's power, but even prompts her to exhort angels to "Descend and share my lot" (I. 96). The gentle Anah expresses with less assurance and vigour essentially the same radical sentiments as her sister; while lamenting on the one hand that in the world's present condition "Delight [is] / An Eden kept afar from sight" (I. 72-73), she also implies at the same time in her impatient longing for the angel Azaziel that she intends to find what pleasures she can despite Noah and God. Her timidity and her natural trepidation notwithstanding (see, for instance, I. 139), Anah shares with her sister a substantial opposition to the existing social order.

Their nonconformity is revealed clearly in their relationship with the angels. This relationship not only exemplifies their decided refusal to accept without question Noah's commands: it furnishes them with a larger perspective of reality than Noah wants to allow individuals, and thus challenges the absolutism of his political power; and, moreover, it implies their denial of God's cosmic scheme.

Anah and Aholibamah believe in a reality beyond the authoritarian rule that now controls the world; they believe in a human spirit that (they feel) has been smothered unjustly by existing laws and structures. Their union with angels manifests these beliefs, and actualizes their hatred of the unnecessary and unjust restrictions which govern antediluvian society.

The social relevance of their affair with the angels crystallizes in Aholibamah's exchange with Japhet, who, though frustrated with Noah and God, finds himself making a clumsy effort to defend the way the world is against what Aholibamah says it can be. The awkwardness of his position highlights the inconsistencies rooted in orthodoxy. For example, he defends his father's willing participation in the impending destruction of humanity as both "well-doing" and "Righteous" (III, 381-82). This statement alone perhaps would not show Japhet in such bad light, but he follows it with a desperate pronouncement of his love for the clearly wicked Anah, which pathetically demonstrates his dissatisfaction with Noah's "well-doing" and "righteous" ways by betraying his longing for things expressly forbidden by Noah. Worse, like Byron's heroes in the Turkish Tales, he rationalizes his love for Anah by deluding himself as to her real standing in the world: "My Anah / Thou who dost rather make me dream that Abel / Had left a daughter" (III. 402-04). Aholibamah recognizes the inconsistencies in Japhet's speech and condemns his spoutings as unhealthy and destructive hypocrisy: "Get thee hence, son of Noah; thou makest strife" (III. 411). His attitude, she knows—less polished but essentially the same as his father's—allows religious fear to fasten unjust authoritarianism and hierarchy on mankind. The clearest material example of the fear that governs his thinking is the Ark, which Aholibamah holds up to him as "The bugbear . . . built to scare the world" (III. 443) into doing what Noah says. Japhet's bumbling exchange with Aholibamah points up the social injustice at the heart of Noah's political and religious system and, more significantly, explains the importance of the angel-mortal union as a means of combating Noah's authoritarian politics.

Taken together, the characterizations in the play suggest Byron's twofold interest in *Heaven and Earth*. First, he tries to show the way society's religious foundation dictates man's outlook on life. The dominant social order of the play echoes that which Byron had presented in *Cain*: it is a paternalistic, restrictive, and authoritarian order that Noan commands as God's regent; it focuses on submission as the central virtue and thus at least seems to work against the best interests of humanity. Noah's pact with Heaven, in short, creates tyranny. This is shown in the Flood, which in the context of the play does not so much represent God's cleansing of the earth as the extreme practical consequence of Noah's philosophy. As the Flood gains momentum, doomed humanity repeats Aholibamah's bitter claim that "heaven and earth unite / For the annihilation of all life" (III. 770-71; see also III. 795-96, and 840-43). The Flood is the culminating illustration of the oppressive and destructive tendency of Noah's powers; it is the practical manifestation of how religion can be used to justify even mass murder.

The other *Heaven and Earth* union—Anah and Aholi-bamah linked with Angels—is more frequently comment-ed on, but just as frequently misunderstood. I have tried to suggest that this union not only demonstrates Jerome McGann's argument that Heaven and Earth naturally grav-itate towards one another, but also that it provides the rebellious characters with a means of rising above the system of values that controls the world, and of evaluating life from a perspective other than Noah's. Anah and Aholi-bamah represent the search for a freer reality principle by which to measure their potential in life. Their escape from the Flood with angels who desert God's tyranny to save them suggests both the nobility of their resistance, and the continuing physical and spiritual opposition to the clearly unjust system administered by God and Noah.

*Heaven and Earth* examines the source of many social attitudes and assumptions treated in Byron's earlier writ-ings, showing the profound impact of religion on soci-ety, and supplying thereby an explanation of how sys-tems of values can be used to manipulate people. Social control, even authoritarian social control, is not neces-sarily maintained by physical sanctions, but very often by ideological ones that derive their strength from reli-gion. Byron emphasizes the role religion can play in causing social injustice by clouding the distinctions be-tween characters traditionally assumed to be good or evil, illustrating more clearly than he had in *Cain* that the worth of one's values must be determined by material circumstances. That what Noah calls God's values are not automatically good is made evident both through Japhet's frustration and through the angels' evasion of God's command. The play concludes that "The politics of Paradise" and the politics of society in general, be-come dangerously oppressive when they are built upon so-called religious ideas that in reality deny man his free-dom to achieve full potential in the world.

**Edward Proffitt**  (essay date 1983)

SOURCE: "Byron's Laughter: *Don Juan* and the Hegelian Dialectic," in *The Byron Journal,* No. 11, 1983, pp. 40-3, 46.

[*In the essay below, Proffitt examines the function of the comic aspects of* Don Juan.]

In his preface to *Man and Superman,* Shaw ridicules Byron's Don Juan as being a mere "vagabond libertine." Shaw was wrong. Byron's "hero" is, by force of circum-stance, a vagabond; but he is no libertine. He is as essen-tially chaste and as passive as Shaw's own Tanner—never the seducer, always the seduced. Shaw, of course, dispar-aged Shakespeare, too—his disparagement being a sure sign of his debt. But my point is not that Shaw was influ-enced by Byron. Given Shaw's own chastity and contrar-iness, he would probably have come up with a chaste, passive Juan in any event. But Byron! What was he doing with such a hero?

Before I attempt an answer to this question, let me quickly establish the passivity—that is, with respect to matters sexual—of Byron's protagonist. The keynote of that pas-sivity is struck in Canto V, when Juan, in female disguise and known as Juanna, is to be taken from the seraglio to the Sultan. Bidden by his friend Johnson to "Keep your good name; though Eve herself once fell," Juan, as "maid," modestly replies:

. . . the Sultan's self shan't carry me,
Unless his Highness promises to marry me.

(st. 84)

Throughout, indeed, Juan seems more like a modest maid than the rake of legend. With Julia he is the victim of the plot of Donna Inez; with Haidée and Dudù he is the pawn of circumstance; and with Catherine the Great he could hardly be his own man. Byron's women, like Shaw's, are the active agents, not Juan. He might have "learned the arts of riding, fencing, gunnery, / And how to scale a fortress—or a nunnery," as we are told in Canto I (st. 38). But had he accomplished the latter, he would have to have found a particularly aggressive nun.

And even had such been waiting, nothing would necessar-ily have happened. For Juan is essentially chaste (as well as being chased). Thus, he heroically resists the advances of the tearful Gulbeyaz; and his affairs with both Julia and Haidée are innocent and pure—young love in full bloom. Byron was a bit disingenuous, then, when he described the poem as follows:

As to "Don Juan"—confess—you dog—and be candid—that it is the sublime of that there sort of writing—it may be bawdy—but is it not good English?—it may be profligate—but is it not life, is it not the thing?—Could any man have written it—who has not lived in the world?—and tooled in a post-chaise? in a hackney coach? in a Gondola? against a wall? in a court car-riage? in a vis a vis?—on a table?—and under it? [*Byron's Letters and Journals,* Vol. IV, ed. L. A. Marchand].

But here is the crux of the problem. Like da Ponte's Gio-vanni, Byron did those things; Juan does not. Why not?—especially given that the poem is in so many other re-spects autobiographical and that in terms of mundane particulars, at least, Byron certainly identified with his Juan. As Byron wrote to Murray: "Almost all Don Juan is *real* life—either my own—or from people I knew."

We are back to our original question: why did Byron choose to make Juan a passive agent, given the tradition he was derived from? Leslie Marchand [in *Byron's Poet-ry,* 1965] suggests one answer:

In general this follows Byron's own concept of his relations with women. Reputed to be a rake and a seducer, he felt himself the most pursued of men. Replying to a distorted story of his abduction of the Countess Guiccioli, he wrote: "I should like to know who has been carried off—except for poor me. I have been more ravished myself than anybody since the Trojan War . . ." And to Murray he wrote in 1819:

"Your Blackwood accuses me of treating women harshly: it may be so, but I have been their martyr. My whole life has been sacrificed to them and by them."

In the passivity of his protagonist, Byron reflects, no doubt, half wish and half fact. Especially once his reputation was established, Byron was in fact as often seduced as he seduced.

But a more penetrating answer, perhaps, involves the very reputation that led Byron to take Don Juan as protagonist in the first place. In many ways *Don Juan* is a parody of, specifically, *Childe Harold,* or more generally, of the pretensions, posings, and ego-mania of the Byronic hero. *Don Juan,* that is, marks a healthy comic rejection on Byron's part of the expectations of his audience, or Byron's refusal to become, as did Hemingway, for example, a living parody of his own hero or a writer of inadvertent parody (as Hemingway also became). Via his treatment of the Don, Byron escaped the traps that wait for any writer of his fame.

There is yet a third answer. In Canto IV Byron says in his own voice:

And if I laugh at any mortal thing,
  'T is that I may not weep; and if I weep,
'T is that our nature cannot always bring
  Itself to apathy, for we must steep
Our hearts first in the depths of Lethe's spring,
  Ere what we least wish to behold will sleep:
Thetis baptized her mortal son in Styx;
  A mortal mother would on Lethe fix.

(st. 4)

His treatment of the Don was not only Byron's artistic salvation but also his spiritual. Unable to move beyond an adolescent mentality, the Byronic hero falls into a posture of alienation; but that alienation became real and intolerable for Byron himself. What then? Werther shoots himself; Byron laughs. Laughter, then, became the final defence of a mind that could not move beyond youthful idealism and narcissism. Of poems composed while *Don Juan* was in progress, William Marshall [in *The Structure of Byron's Major Poems,* 1962] states: "Byron dramatized the ironic situations of those who were essentially unable to reconcile themselves to imperfection." Byron himself was no doubt one of those. In a late canto—Canto XI—Byron says:

What a sublime discovery 't was to make the
  Universe universal egotism,
That all's ideal—all ourselves!

(st. 2)

It is that that Byron laughs at. But his laughter, finally, has a defensive tone to it. Byron seems not to have been able to attain the wisdom of A. R. Ammons:

By the time I got the world cut down
  small enough that
I could be the centre of it, it wasn't
  worth having.

However much Byron laughs at our "universal egotism," or his own, he still hankers after the narcissistic ideal. His laughter, thus, is a defence against the pain of that hankering.

But that laughter can also be viewed as a way toward a more mature vision of things. That is, we might take *Don Juan* in an Hegelian context. Speaking of the advancement of "spirit" and consciousness, Hegel writes in the *Phenomenology* that spirit must become

conscious of its own distraught and torn condition and to express itself accordingly,—this is to pour scornful laughter on existence, on the confusion pervading the whole and on itself as well: it is at the same time this whole confusion dying away and yet apprehending itself to be doing so.

Laughter, thus, can move us to a higher state of self-integration, or, as Hegel says, "self-alienation . . . moulds itself into its opposite, and in this way reverses the nature of that opposite." In pouring laughter on himself, Byron—a most modern man in this regard—is pointing, perhaps, toward wholeness, the kind of wholeness postulated by Hegel or envisioned by Yeats when he wrote:

For nothing can be sole or whole
That has not been rent.

Of course, to see that rending, we must take *Don Juan* within the tradition of the Don as rake and seducer as well as within its Byronic context. A passive Juan? Yes, that is to rend and to pour laughter on. As to the Byronic context, we must, as I have suggested, read *Don Juan* against *Childe Harold*. So read, *Don Juan* becomes an antithesis and rings thereby with Hegel's laughter. Compare, for example, the ways in which Harold and Juan go into exile. Harold, wrapped in a cape and standing on the prow of the ship, takes up a handy harp and sings an heroic elegy to the waves as the sun sets. Trying his best to be a Childe Harold—in Juan's case, to maintain the posture of the heroic lover—our hero turned anti-hero gets seasick; and as he does, he gives rise to some of Byron's most scornfully comic lines:

He felt the chilling heaviness of heart,
  Or rather stomach, which, alas! attends,
Beyond the best apothecary's art,
  The loss of Love, the treachery of friends,
Or death of those we dote on, when a part
  Of us dies with them as each fond hope ends:
No doubt he would have been much more pathetic,
But the sea acted as a strong emetic.

Love's a capricious power: I've known it hold
  Out through a fever caused by its own heat,
But be much puzzled by a cough or cold,
  And find a quinsy very hard to treat;
Against all noble maladies he's bold,
  But vulgar illnesses don't like to meet,
Nor that a sneeze should interrupt his sigh,
Nor inflammation redden his blind eye.

But worst of all is nausea, or a pain
  About the lower region of the bowels:
Love, who heroically breathes a vein,
  Shrinks from the application of hot towels,
And purgatives are dangerous to his reign,
  Sea-sickness death! . . .

                        (II, 21-23)

To be sure, to laugh at Juan for being less than super-human is to deride our common mortality; Byron is not reconciled to our clay, but would have us made of more heroic stuff. Nevertheless, his vision of Juan vomiting, like his creation of a passive Juan in the first place, is a healthy counter to his and our infantile aspirations. In sum, though defensive in motive force, Byron's laughter is also liberating in potentiality; his treatment of the Don is a strategy of self-protection in part, but also a strategy of personal growth, that prime romantic value. So seen, the passivity of Byron's Juan is fully comic: funny, yet also instructive with respect to our arrested longings.

### Camille Paglia  (essay date 1990)

SOURCE: "Speed and Space: Byron," in *Sexual Personae: Art and Decadence from Nefertiti to Emily Dickinson*, Vintage Books, 1991, pp. 347-64.

[*In the following essay, which was first published in 1990, Paglia regards Byron as instrumental in the development of the phenomenon of the male sex symbol.*]

The second generation of English Romantic poets inherited the achievement of the first. Byron, Shelley, and Keats read and absorbed Wordsworth and Coleridge's poems and gave them new form. The younger men created the myth of the doomed Romantic artist. All three went into exile and died young, in pagan Italy and Greece. Publicity and fashion made them sex-heroes of European high society: they were real-life sexual personae, as Blake, Wordsworth, and Coleridge were not. The poems of Byron, Shelley, and Keats are theatrical gestures of self-definition. The first Romantic generation released the psychic energy in which the second swam and sometimes drowned. Achieving freedom is one problem, surviving freedom another. The early deaths of Byron, Shelley, and Keats demonstrate the intolerable pressures in the Romantic and liberal world-view. Blake and Wordsworth wanted identity without personality: but personality is ultimate western reality. Byron, Shelley, and Keats had a love-hate relationship with personality, their own and others'.

Lord Byron makes Romantic incest stunningly explicit. I see *Manfred* (1817) as a cross-fertilization of Goethe's *Faust* with Wordsworth's *Tintern Abbey*. Byron's passionate hero is tormented by guilt for some mysterious crime. He is obsessed with his dead sister Astarte, his twin in eyes, face, and voice. Byron relishes sexual criminality. Forbidden love makes his characters superhuman. Rejecting all social relationships, Manfred seeks only himself in sexually transmuted form. Wordsworth's sister allows him

to remain alone, sex-free, but Astarte (Phoenician Venus) lures Manfred into the vertigo of sex.

The sister-spirit appears in *Manfred* at exactly the point where she materializes in *Tintern Abbey*. Astarte died in Manfred's tower when her heart "wither'd" while gazing on his. She has no tomb. What happened? Where is she? Manfred's western lust for knowledge annihilates his sister, like Faust with Gretchen. Oscar Wilde reimagines the scene in the climax of *The Picture of Dorian Gray*, where two doubles, a man and his portrait, confront each other in a locked attic room. The man is found dead, hideously "withered"—Byron's word. Astarte, gazing at her brother's heart as if into a mirror, dies of daemonic narcissim. Brother and sister trespass the borderlines of western identity and exchange personality. Manfred merges too fiercely with his sister. He assimilates her. How else explain the disappearance of her body?

Manfred's union with his sister is a solipsistic sex-experiment that fails. His restlessness and remorse are symptoms of his engorgement by her. Like Thyestes, Manfred has eaten his own flesh; like Kronos, he must vomit it out. Because real sexual relations have occurred between Manfred and his double, the physical world becomes intolerable to him. Byron's poem is surrealistically expanded in Poe's *The Fall of the House of Usher*, where the sister, entombed in the skull-like house, returns as a bloody apparition to stalk her hysterical brother. In Byron, the sister-spirit's materialization promises psychic relief. Manfred appeals to her to speak, so she can regain her autonomy and *stay* externalized. But she only prophesies her brother's death and disappears. I say sister collapses back into brother, renewing his sufferings.

In *Tintern Abbey*, Wordsworth's sister does not need to speak. She is the *anima* in correct relation to the poet. The intercourse of brother and sister is spiritual, not physical. In *Manfred*, fraternal intercourse is violent and voracious. Blood is shed, which Manfred hallucinates on a wine cup. He has ruptured his sister's virginity. The blood-rimmed cup from which he cannot drink is a nightmare vision of the locus of violation. It is also his bloody mind and bloody tongue, thinking and speaking against nature.

Like Coleridge's *Christabel*, *Manfred* centers on a ritual sex act defying social and moral law. In the poem's pagan cult of self-worship, matrimony, communion, and last rites are simultaneous. The ritual victim is torn by the phallic knife and her flesh consumed. Astarte is tombless because she has been perversely absorbed, body and soul, by her brother. As in Poe's *The Tell-Tale Heart*, Manfred is tormented by the internal presence of another being, illegitimately enwombed like a daemonic fetus. Manfred is the Romantic solipsist who has devoured the universe, but it sickens within him. Amputation or self-gorging? Kleist's Achilles makes one choice, Byron's Manfred another. The self is out of sync with the object-world, which floods in or cruelly withdraws, marooning Wordsworth's puckered solitaries. In *Manfred* Byron makes illicit sex the lists of combat. Romantic sexual personae scratch and claw in attraction and repulsion.

Rumor said Byron committed incest with his half-sister, Augusta Leigh. True or false, the story added to his fame. Incest obsessively recurs in Byron's poems. *Cain* turns the issue into legal conundrum. God allows incest for mankind's second generation, who must marry their siblings. The poem dwells on the mutual love of Cain and his twin sister, incredulous at the prohibition of fraternal sexuality to their own children. In *Parisina,* the Phaedra-like incest is between wife and stepson, an exception to Byron's favorite brother-sister pattern. Originally, Byron's central characters in *The Bride of Abydos* were brother and sister in love. In the final version, they are first cousins. But their infatuation dates from childhood, and the girl still believes the boy her brother when, feverishly kissing him, she rejects an arranged marriage. Byron says, "Great is their love who love in sin and fear" (*Heaven and Earth*). Incest is sexual dissent. Its value is in impurity. Byron would spurn Blakean innocence. He takes the Sadean approach to sex and psyche: make a line, so I can cross it. Unlike Blake or Wordsworth, Byron wants to reinforce the boundaries of self. In incest, libido moves out and back, making a uroboros-circle of regression and dynastic exclusiveness.

Romanticism's feminization of the male persona becomes effeminacy in Byron. The unmanly hero of *The Bride of Abydos* is stranded among women. Incestuous feeling is incubated in an Oriental haze. *The Corsair* introduces seductive Gulnare, to appear transvestite in a sequel. Gulnare's relations with the corsair are like Kleist's Penthesilea with Achilles, a dancelike exchange of strength and weakness. There are heroic rescues, then capture, humiliation, and recovery. Byron ritualistically elaborates each stage of assertion and passivity, making the narrative a slow masque of sexual personae.

Until the end of *Lara,* Byron teasingly implies that the effeminate pageboy, Kaled, is homosexually attached to the chieftain Lara. The truth outs when Lara is killed and the boy faints. Bystanders reviving him loosen his garments and discover Kaled is the woman Gulnare, in love with the corsair Lara. Byron's rippling poetry makes sexual metamorphosis happen before our eyes. First we are admiring "the glossy tendrils" of a beautiful boy's "raven hair." Suddenly, he swoons into sensuous passivity. Now we join the voyeuristic marvelling at public exposure of a woman's breasts, as she lies unconscious. Homosexual and heterosexual responses have been successively induced or extorted from the reader. The blink-of-an-eye sex change recalls Spenser's switch of sexual perspective, but Byron retains his woman's male name to prolong her sexual ambiguity. Surely Gautier imitates this scene in *Mademoiselle de Maupin,* when a page is knocked unconscious from his horse and his shirt parted to reveal a girl's "very white bosom." I think it all ends up in *National Velvet* (1944, from Enid Bagnold's novel), where a fallen jockey, played by the young Elizabeth Taylor, is carried unconscious from the race course. The motif is now safely sanitized: a doctor, not titillated passersby, undrapes the succulent bosom.

*Lara*'s sex games echo Byron's own. After leaving Cambridge, Byron had an affair with a girl whom he dressed as a boy and called his brother. G. Wilson Knight [in *Lord Byron's Marriage,* 1957] suggests Lady Caroline Lamb masqueraded as a pageboy to rekindle the poet's fading passion. Byron probably models Kaled's service to Lord Lara on that of transvestite Viola to Duke Orsino in *Twelfth Night.* Byron's responses are as bisexual as Shakespeare's. He is equally and even simultaneously aroused by an effeminate boy and a bold cross-dressing woman. Byron's last poems are addressed to a handsome Greek youth with whom he was unhappily infatuated. His early poems to "Thyrza" were inspired by a Cambridge choirboy, probably John Edleston. The boy has a female name partly because the poems could not have been published otherwise. But this is also an example of my principle of sexual metathesis, a shift in gender producing a special eroticism. We feel it in Byron's lascivious delight in *Lara*'s open-air spectacle of sexual unmasking—the topos of deblousing, recreating the mood of the naughty Italian romances purified by Shakespeare.

In *Sardanapalus* (1821), Byron vies directly with Shakespeare. The poem recasts *Antony and Cleopatra*—with the hero as Antony *and* Cleopatra. In a prefatory note, Byron claims he got the story from Diodorus Siculus. The Greek Sardanapalus bore little resemblance to the Assyrian king and general, Assurbanipal. Delacroix's crimson tableau shows Byron's Sardanapalus amid the decadent conflagration of empire. Byron begins his poem as Shakespeare begins his play: a hostile bystander scorns the sexual degeneracy of the protagonist, who enters for our inspection. In Shakespeare, the cynical commentary is contradicted by Antony and Cleopatra's love. Byron's Sardanapalus, however, is just as unmanly as foretold. He sweeps onstage crowned with flowers and "effeminately dressed," followed by a train of women and young slaves. Sardanapalus is Euripides' Dionysus with his Maenads—but now Dionysus is king. We are in Shakespeare's Egypt, a liquid realm of woman, music, and perfume. Maleness dissolves. The king's companions include eunuchs, "beings less than women." Sardanapalus' brother-in-law calls him "the grandson of Semiramis, the man-queen." Who's the queen, Semiramis or Sardanapalus? Calling his hero a "she-king," a "*she* Sardanapalus," Byron develops an entire character out of Antony's transvestite game. Sardanapalus denies he is a soldier and denounces the word and all who identify with it. Byron tries to argue that Sardanapalus' manhood is more comprehensive than the ordinary. But morality is not the Romantic strong suit. Byron quickly flits off into sexual caprice, his best manner. Sardanapalus' feminized masculinity is far from efficacious. His kingdom is destroyed, and he with it.

*Sardanapalus* is an experiment in personae: how far can a male protagonist be shifted toward the female extreme without total loss of masculinity? The enervation in *Sardanapalus* is more extreme than anything in *Antony and Cleopatra,* which bursts with Renaissance energy. In his journal Byron speaks of the delightful "calm nothingness of languuour" and elsewhere describes a "voluptuous state, / At once Elysian and effeminate" (*The Island*). This floating condition sabotages *Sardanapalus*. The king laments the heaviness of objects, as if his muscles have atrophied. Sardanapalus is western personality submerged in Dionysian flux. When military crisis forces him into the social world, reality seems stubbornly dense.

Sardanapalus' most masculine moment is his arming for battle, prefigured in Shakespeare when Cleopatra acts as Antony's arms-bearer. Sardanapalus calls for his cuirass, baldric, helmet, spear—and mirror. He flings away his helmet because it doesn't look good. The king of Assyria, who should be psyching himself up for battle, seems more like a lady trying on hats. Shakespeare's hero is attended by his lover. In Byron, the lover becomes a mirror. Sardanapalus is the complete Romantic hero, in love with his mirror-image. He is his own audience and critic, a projected eye. Byron nullifies Sardanapalus' manhood with feminine narcissism. We saw this pattern in Lewis' *The Monk*, where each sexual movement immediately swings in the opposite direction. Sardanapalus risks his life by fighting bare-headed, apparently because he wants to show off "his flowing hair." This hair belongs to the poet of Coleridge's "Kubla Khan," whose sexual ambiguity Byron divines. Byron attaches Coleridge's whole line to the king's Amazon slave, Myrrha (Dante's incestuous sinner), who strides into battle with "her floating hair and flashing eyes." Poets, unlike critics, sense the sex and decadence in art.

As a program for androgyny, *Sardanapalus* is unconvincing. I find the poem more ominous than does Knight [in *Poets of Action*, 1967], who praises the "poet-like" hero for "joining man's reason to woman's emotional depth." Sardanapalus seems too vain and whimsical to lead a nation, or even produce art. The brawling Cleopatra gets more done. The effeminacy of Byron's hero is perverse, not ideal. *Sardanapalus'* richness of Shakespearean reference raises an interesting question. Byron always spoke negatively of Shakespeare. Lady Blessington concluded Byron must be feigning animosity, since he knew so much Shakespeare by heart. Bloom's anxiety of influence would suggest that Byron owed Shakespeare too much and was determined to deny it, even to himself.

In *Don Juan* (1819-24), his longest and greatest poem, Byron invents another sexually unconventional hero. The seducer Don Juan, a Renaissance Spaniard, is one of the west's unique sexual personae. In contrast to Mozart's Don Giovanni, Byron's Don Juan is smaller, shyer, more "feminine." He is "a most beauteous boy," "slight and slim, / Blushing and beardless," perfect as "one of the seraphim" (VIII.52; IX.53, 47). Juan is partly Byron and partly what Byron likes in boys. Knight, Frye, and Bloom comment on the hero's sexual passivity toward dominant women [G. Wilson Knight, *Poets of Action*, Northrop Frye, *Fables of Identity*, 1963; Harold Bloom, *The Visionary Company*, 1961]. When Juan is sold as a slave in Constantinople, a eunuch forces him into female clothing, supplemented by makeup and judicious tweezing. Juan has caught the sultana's eye. By transvestism he can be smuggled into the harem for her pleasure. Byron's sensual, self-enclosed harem world is like Blake's rose, femaleness multiplied and condensed in a small humid circle.

The sultana Gulbeyaz is one of Romanticism's most potent women. *Don Juan* continues *Sardanapalus'* maneuvering of an effeminate male along the sexual spectrum. Juan's tenuous manhood is near-obliterated by female drag. Now Byron shoves him next to an Amazon dominatrix. Juan in petticoats is a trembling pawn upon whom the raging queen bears down. Gulbeyaz is the Cleopatra missing from *Sardanapalus*. She is the androgyne as virago, luxuriously female in body but harshly male in spirit. Gulbeyaz has Cleopatra's vigorous duality: her "large eyes" show "half-voluptuousness and half-command." She is "imperial, or imperious," with a haughty smile of "self-will." Her eyes "flash'd always fire," blending "passion and power" (V.108, 110-11, 134, 116). Gulbeyaz wears a male poniard at her waist. Byron's sultana will end up as a smouldering Spanish marquise in Balzac's *The Girl with the Golden Eyes,* where that poniard is drawn and dreadfully used.

Gulbeyaz's entrance into the poem overwhelms Don Juan's residual masculinity. Introduced as a girl to sultan and harem, he blushes and shakes. Byron chooses not to defend his hero's virility and mischievously absents himself to take the sexually external point of view. Poor Juan is now simply "she" and "her." Even Spenser, after briefing the reader, allows his transvestites their proper pronoun. In the next canto, Byron allows "he" intermittent return. But it is rudely jostled by the harem's unflagging attention to the newcomer: "Her shape, her hair, her air, her everything" (VI.35). Gossip, admiration, envy: Juan's female alter ego is fixed by and projected to a captive audience. Asked his name, Juan replies "Juanna." And Juanna he is called for the rest of the Turkish episode, even by Byron himself. This sex transformation of his own name is a sign of Juan's developing sexual complicity, like Coleridge's Christabel lifting the vampire over the threshold. Apologizing for calling his hero Juanna, Byron wantonly stresses the sexual equivocal: "I say *her* because, / The gender still was epicene" (58). Even at his most perverse, Spenser is never this coy. Byron is flirting with the reader, something new in literature.

Logically, a young man spirited into a harem, like a fox in a hen-house, should soon profit from his access to, as Byron puts it, "a thousand bosoms there / Beating for love" (26). But this is a Romantic and not a Renaissance poem, and in a Romantic poem, as should now be clear, virility is granted no privileges. Juan becomes the object of desire not because he is male but because he is thought female. The harem women fight over who is to sleep with Juanna, and more than sleep is on their minds: "Lolah's eyes sparkled at the proposition" (82). Gulbeyaz is included in this steamy stuff. The sultan is "always so polite" as to announce his conjugal visits in advance, "especially at night." Since the harem is marked by "the absence of all men," the sultan would presumably not be surprised to find Gulbeyaz in bed with her own women (V.146; VI.32) *Don Juan*'s lesbian innuendos frustrate conventional sexual expectation. How does one defeat the virility of a man at happy liberty in a harem? The Romantic poem, with cross-sexual virtuosity, blithely replies: why, by turning him into a transvestite and making him the object of lesbian lust!

The rest of **Don Juan** is a series of sexcapades across Asia and Europe. The unfinished poem ends in female transvestism, a scene probably inspired by *The Monk:* Juan's bedchamber is invaded by a ghostly, hooded friar, whom the closing words reveal to be a "voluptuous" woman. The best things in **Don Juan** take place in the Near East, which Napoleon's expedition to Egypt in 1798 had made a subject of European interest. Knight says, [in *The Starlit Dome,* 1970] "Byron is saturated in oriental sympathies." Byron's Orient, like Shakespeare's, is an emotionally expansive realm liquefying European sexual personae. Genders proliferate: Byron calls eunuchs and castrati "the third sex." We cannot comprehend the mysteries of love, he says, until we imitate "wise Tiresias" and sample "the several sexes." Don Juan's teeming eunuchs—the sultan's eunuch train is "a quarter of a mile" long—are extreme versions of its androgynous hero. Transvestite Juan subject to Gulbeyaz is like a castrate priest of Cybele. The Byronic Orient is matriarchal. Don Juan's seraglio, a "labyrinth of females," is a drowsy Spenserian bower, the womb-tomb of the male will. As in *Antony and Cleopatra,* the Orient also stands for liberated imagination. It is the anarchic unconscious, a dream-world of unstable sex and identity where objects cannot hold their Apollonian shape.

**Don Juan**'s free and easy style is difficult to analyze. Style reflects poet. Spengler [in *The Decline of the West,* trans. charles Francis Atkinson, 1929] says western history demands "contrapuntally strong accents—wars or big personalities—at the decisive points." The huge influence of Byron's personality on the nineteenth century is still incompletely assessed. His early poems of brooding defiance, like **Cain** and **Manfred,** conform to the popular image of Byronism, but **Don Juan** actually captures the poet's essential spirit. **Don Juan** is emotionally various and comprehensive. Bloom says, "The last word in a discussion of **Don Juan** ought not to be 'irony' but 'mobility', one of Byron's favorite terms." Byron defined mobility as "an excessive susceptibility of immediate impressions." The mobile male is receptive and half-feminine. I myself hit upon "mobility" to describe the psychic volatility of Shakespeare's boys and women, whom his plays class with lovers, lunatics, and poets. The many moods of **Don Juan**'s omniscient narrator make him a Mercurius of multiple personae. The poem explores the emotional tonalities available to a poetic voice speaking for itself and not through projected characters. It is analogous to Chopin's development of the lyric potential of the piano. In **Don Juan** Byron takes himself for subject nearly as forthrightly as Wordsworth does in *The Prelude.*

Byron's dedication to **Don Juan** attacks Wordsworth, Coleridge, and Southey for "a narrowness . . . which makes me wish you'd change your lakes for ocean." A lake is enclosed and trapped by the conventional and known. No one point of view can do justice to ocean, vast and metamorphic. Byronic energy overflows Wordsworthian decorum. Impatiently, Byron overlooks the sexual ambivalences in Wordsworth and daemonic Coleridge. He charges them with parochialism, with damming up the waters of emotion in stagnant spiritual ponds. The English are traditionally a seafaring people. Their location on an island amidst a turbulent northern ocean contributed to the outpouring poetic vitality of the English Renaissance. By the early nineteenth century, the psychic fluidity of Shakespeare's England was long gone. Like Shelley, Byron, the most mobile of poets, fled the resentments of a closed society. The English had become emotionally and sexually landlocked. Frazer [in *The Golden Bough,* 1935] links ancient Egypt's stability and conservatism to its desert geography. Agriculture's "monotonous routine" gives the farmer "a settled phlegmatic habit of mind very different from the mobility, the alertness, the pliability of character which the hazards and uncertainties of commerce and the sea foster in the merchant and the sailor," with their "mercurial spirit." In **Don Juan,** Byron takes English imagination back to sea. As Juan is tossed and turned by adventure, the narrator's shifting voice recreates the ceaseless sea change of sex and emotion.

Like **Childe Harold's Pilgrimage,** which made Byron famous, **Don Juan** is structured by the archetypal journey theme. But **Don Juan**'s journeying has *speed.* Alvin Kernan [in *The Plot of Satire,* 1965] speaks of an "onward rush" in the poem, "a vital forceful onward movement." From locomotive to jet plane, speed has transformed modern life. The Renaissance reeled from its sudden expansion of space, as the known world doubled and tripled. Speed is western domination of space, a linear track of the aggressive will. Modern speed alters perception. As late as 1910, E. M. Forster's heroine in *Howards End* resists the new speed of the motorcar, which makes her lose "all sense of space." Mr. Wilcox sings out, "There's a pretty church—oh, you aren't sharp enough." Margaret's premodern eye moves sluggishly: "She looked at the scenery. It heaved and merged like porridge. Presently it congealed. They had arrived." Speed melts the object-world without remaking it. Revolutionary Byron senses an imminent change in the nature of space, which he did not live to see. **Don Juan** marks the first appearance in art of modern speed.

Critics sometimes speak of the "swiftness" of Shelley's poetry. But Shelley's movement is upward. He seeks rhapsodic exaltation (*exaltare* means "to lift up"). Byron is never exalted. His movement is secular and vehicular. Byron's space was created by the Renaissance Age of Discovery and measured by the Enlightenment. Speaking of Milton [in "Milton and the Descent to Light," in *Milton: Modern Essays in Criticism,* ed. Arthur E. Barker, 1965], Don Cameron Allen says Judeo-Christianity urges man "to abandon the horizontal movement of human history for the vertical motion of the spiritual life." Shelley is spiritual verticality, Byron earthly horizontality. Shelley is always subverting horizontals: the Witch of Atlas' boat defies gravity and sails upstream, or the procession of "The Triumph of Time" shows life as a leaden line of slaves. Shelley's objects . . . are weightless and porous, penetrated by vision. Byron's concrete objects are firmly fixed in space and time. Shelley's imagination moves, but what moves in Byron is the body. Byron is a Greek athlete, challenging and surpassing. Objects are his counters and stepping stones.

Shelley's and Byron's speed are energized by different principles of sex-transcendence. ***Don Juan***'s speed is a skimming, like Raphael's Galatea flying in her chariot across the sea. But Galatea is drawn by porpoises. Byron's speed is *self-motivating*. All self-motivating speed is hermaphroditic—in angels, Vergil's Camilla, or Giambologna's Mercury. Pope's Camilla "skims along the Main" (*An Essay on Criticism*, 373). Byron actually compares the dancing Don Juan to Vergil's Amazon: "Like swift Camilla, he scarce skimm'd the ground" (XIV. 39). Don Juan the character and ***Don Juan*** the poem are world-skimmers. The skimming is in both style and content. Byron's poetry is not "finished," that is, finely crafted and polished. Sir Walter Scott saw in Byron "the careless and negligent ease of a man of quality." Calling him "slovenly, slipshod," Matthew Arnold [in his preface to *Poetry of Lord Byron*, 1881] rebuked Byron for "negligence" and "want of art, in his workmanship as a poet." But this slapdash freedom gives Byron his relentless forward propulsion. Since the lines are not crisply formed, each tips into the next with breathless haste. Shakespeare's spilling lines are weightier, his diction craggier. I said vision in Coleridge and Poe often overpowers language, leaving it rude or weak: words run hot and cold, gorgeous splotches followed by shabby scrabble. But Byron's poetry has evenness of texture, a liquid fluency. Byron greatly admired the Augustan poets, but though his aristocratic satire is Augustan, his style is not. There is no braking midline caesura, nor is there Pope's massy orotundity. Byron cultivates a sensation of linearity. His verse is like a clear, rapid stream. Byron's objects have a friendly exactitude. His moods and objects are tumbled like smooth pebbles in the stream of his poetry. Love and hate, male and female, lobster salad and champagne: this is Byron's object-world in genial rolling flux. All come together in his poetry to make us feel we are skimming a surface.

Poetry began as music, and music began as dance. Shelley's movements are like those of classical ballet, which takes place in abstract space. Ballet ideologically defies gravity. Great male dancers are applauded for their ability to hover at the crest of their leaps, as if momentarily breaking their tie to earth. Female dancers mutilate their feet to remain inhumanly on point, keeping their contact with earth to the absolute minimum. The arms extended from the body, a gesture originating in the Baroque court, suggest wings, contempt for the earth's surface. Ballet is the body rising. Ballet is ceremonial and hieratic. Its disdain for the commonplace material world is the source of its authority and glamour. Ballet is Apollonian. Martha Graham invented or rather reinvented chthonian dance. Modern dance is primitivistic and pelvic. It slaps bare feet on mother earth and contracts with her spasms. The dance of Byron's poetry is neither Apollonian nor chthonian. Byron is attuned neither to sky nor to earth's bowels. He skims earth's surface, midway between realms. ***Don Juan***'s Byronic style is found in only one dancer: Fred Astaire. Astaire's supple dancing is a silvery gliding along hard polished surfaces. There is no balletic aspiration in Astaire. He is the here and now, a sophisticate moving in cosmopolitan space. Even when springing up on chairs or climbing the walls, Astaire is exploring the dimensions of

our common life. Rudolf Nureyev is a haughty Lucifer shut out from heaven, which he tries to reach in angry leaps. Nureyev is early Byron, tense and defiant. Astaire (and his admirer, Mikhail Baryshnikov) is late Byron. Astaire is a suave reed bending to the wind. He has Byron's "ease," the well-bred manners and gentle smiling irony. Astaire is as elegantly elongated as Giambologna's Mercury. With his smooth head and slim body, he is ageless and androgynous. He is a gracious host or guide, like Milton's Raphael, "the sociable Spirit" or "affable Archangel." Astaire's fluid grace is Byron's mobility, skimming across the world.

Byron knew both his speed and his space. His dedication to ***Don Juan*** proclaims to rival poets that, "wandering with pedestrian Muses," he will not contend with them "on the wingèd steed." He is not Nureyev, making Pegasus-like skyward leaps, but Astaire, spiralling across the earth's dance floor with merry carnal Muses (Ginger Rogers, Rita Hayworth). An eternal "wandering" or surface-skimming: like all picaresque works, Byron's travel poems have no necessary ending and could go on and on. I call ***Don Juan***'s lightness and quickness *breeziness*. A connection to Camilla: Jackson Knight [in *Roman Vergil*, 1944] says the idea of a fleet figure running atop the grain stalks may have originated in Volscian belief in "the presence of some spirit of the corn." So the meadows' wave-like motion is the wind's invisible steps. The breeziness of ***Don Juan*** is the freshness of a spring breeze, a new spirit entering and aerating history. The breeze emanating from Byron—literally, his emanation—is the spirit of youth, which was to have enormous impact upon European and American culture. Rousseau invented the modern cult of childhood; Goethe popularized Rousseau's moody adolescent. But Byron created the glamourous sexy youth of brash, defiant energy, *the new* embodied in a charismatic sexual persona. Hence Byron senses the dawn of the age of speed. Youth is swiftness in emotionally *transient* form. Transience, from the Latin *transeo*, contains the ideas both of travel and of the short-lived. Byron, portrayed by Goethe as the androgynous, self-thwarted Euphorion, died in 1824. The first passenger locomotive appeared in 1825. Byron's spirit seems to have transmigrated into the engine of speed.

Surveys show that two advertising words rivet our attention: "free" and "new." We still live in the age of Romanticism. When novelty is worshipped, nothing can last. Byronic youth-culture flourishes in rock music, the ubiquitous American art form. ***Don Juan***'s emotional and poetic style is replicated in a classic American experience: driving flat-out on a highway, radio blaring. Driving is the American sublime, for which there is no perfect parallel in Europe. Ten miles outside any American city, the frontier is wide open. Our long, straight superhighways crisscross vast space. Mercury and Camilla's self-motivating speed: the modern automobile, plentifully panelled with glass, is so quick, smooth, and discreet, it seems an extension of the body. To traverse or *skim* the American landscape in such a vehicle is to feel the speed and aerated space of ***Don Juan***. Rock music pulsing on the radio is the car's heartbeat. European radio stations are few and mostly state-controlled. But American radio-bands teem with music and voices, like the many moods of Byron's poem. Driving through upstate New York, horizontally slashed by six hours of straight-as-the-crow-flies Thruway, one hears music from Illinois, Kentucky, North Carolina, as distant as Italy is from England. Twirling the radio dial while travelling the open road, the American driver flies along on a continuous surface of music, with a sublime sense of huge space surveyed and subsumed.

Rock music is normally a darkly daemonic mode. The Rolling Stones, the greatest rock band, are heirs of stormy Coleridge. But rock has an Apollonian daylight style as well, a combination of sun and speed: the Beach Boys. *Don Juan* and the Beach Boys combine youth, androgyny, aeration, and speed. Lillian Roxon [in the *Rock Encyclopedia*, 1969] calls the Beach Boys' first album "a celebration of airiness and speed, speed on the water or the road." The romance of motion survives in the Beach Boys' soaring harmonies and chugging sound, like the chuff-chuff-chuff of a locomotive or steamboat. The Beach Boys made the California surfer a new American archetype, like the cowboy. Surfing, of course, is *skimming* in its purest form.

The Beach Boys use a falsetto lead voice set against a boyish chorale; their sound is effeminate and yet enthusiastically heterosexual, as in the immortal "California Girls." We find the same odd combination in Byron. Byron may have been partly or even primarily homosexual, but his poetry affects a distinctive eroticism of effeminate heterosexuality. The Beach Boys' seraphic boy voice gives an unexpected beauty and religiosity to their trivial high-school themes. The tone is Byronic: sympathy and satire, without cynicism. In their exuberance, hedonism, and mannered irrelevance, the Beach Boys epitomize the self-sustaining and annoyingly self-congratulatory modern youth culture that Byron began. The American teenager in a souped-up car bursts the confines of adult space.

Why did Byron's poetry turn to skimming? Bernard Blackstone remarks [in *Byron: A Survey*, 1975], "We know how much Byron objected to seeing his wife eating, and while this may have something to do with his own horror of obesity and recollections of his mother's gormandising, there were probably moments at which Byron saw himself as an homunculus between the steady munch, munch of Annabella's upper and lower jaws." Byron had a weight problem and struggled to keep thin, even by starving himself. Fat is femaleness, nature's abundance, symbolized in the bulging Venus of Willendorf. Femaleness, I argued, is primitive and archaic, while femininity is social and aesthetic. Byron courts femininity but flees femaleness. His fear of fat is his fear of engorgement by mother and wife. Woman gets under his skin. Skimming is keeping the fat off, in soup or milk. *Don Juan*'s skimming is a defense mechanism, a compromise between earth's primitive chthonianism and sky's repressive Apollonianism. Byron keeps moving, reclaiming space from mother nature. Byron's Sardanapalus eliminates and supplants Cleopatra because Byron fears the femme fatale and female stasis. Even fierce Gulbeyaz is trapped in a male world, the sultan's prisoner.

---

**Northrop Frye on the biographical content of Byron's poetry:**

The main appeal of Byron's poetry is in the fact that it is Byron's. To read Byron's poetry is to hear all about Byron's marital difficulties, flirtations, love for Augusta, friendships, travels, and political and social views. And Byron is a consistently interesting person to hear about, this being why Byron, even at his worst of self-pity and egotism and blither and doggerel, is still so incredibly readable. He proves what many critics declare to be impossible, that a poem can make its primary impact as a historical and biographical document. The critical problem involved here is crucial to our understanding of not only Byron but literature as a whole. Even when Byron's poetry is not objectively very good, it is still important, because it is Byron's. But who was Byron to be so important? certainly not an exceptionally good or wise man. Byron is, strictly, neither a great poet nor a great man who wrote poetry, but something in between: a tremendous cultural force that was life and literature at once.

*Northrop Frye, "Lord Byron," in his* Fables of Identity: Studies in Poetic Mythology, *Harcourt Brace Jovanovich, 1963, pp. 168-89*

---

Byron loved water and was so expert a swimmer that he wondered if he had been a merman in a previous life. He chose a mermaid for his carriage crest. Is the mermaid androgynous Byron—or archetypal woman closed to penetration? Swimming was club-footed Byron's freest motion. One of his feats was swimming the Hellespont: Byron honored liquidity but sought to dominate it, athletically. As much as Wordsworth, he wanted nature without chthonian danger. The clarity of Byron's late style is a denial of the murk of woman and water. Female fluids are opaque, resistant; fat, the wateriest part of our body, is mother nature's grip on the human will. Like Blake, Byron refuses to yield to Jehovah *or* Cybele. "Run, run, run," say a dozen classic rock songs. To grow, a plant must put down roots. So keep young and die. Byron's restless animal motion defeats his female vegetable flesh. *Don Juan* does not stop because Byron cannot stop.

A contemporary spoke of Byron's "magical influence" on people [quoted in E. M. Butler, *Byron and Goethe*, 1956]. Mary Shelley said of him, "There was something enchanting in his manner, his voice, his smile—a fascination in them" [quoted in Newman Ivey White, *Shelley*, 1940]. Byron had pure charisma, a power of personality divorced from the conceptual or moral. Charisma is electromagnetism, a scintillating fusion of masculine and feminine. Lady Blessington said Byron's "voice and accent are peculiarly agreeable, but effeminate." His friend Moore saw "a feminine cast of character" in "his caprices, fits of weeping, sudden affections and dislikes" [*Lady Blessington's Conversations of Lord Byron*, ed. Ernest J. Lovell, Jr., 1969]. Byron belongs to the category of androgyne I invented for Michelangelo's *Giuliano de' Medici*: Epicoene, or the man of beauty, an athlete of alabaster skin. Jane Porter found Byron's complexion "softly brilliant," with a "moonlight paleness." Lady Blessington called his face "peculiarly pale," set off by curling hair of "very dark brown": "He uses a good deal of oil in it, which makes it look still darker." White skin, dark oiled hair: Elvis Presley. In homage to singer Roy Orbison, Presley dyed his brown-blonde hair black and continued to do so to the end, despite friends' urging to let the natural color return. Presley, a myth-maker, understood the essence of his archetypal beauty.

Byron and Elvis Presley look alike, especially in strong-nosed Greek profile. In *Glenarvon,* a roman à clef about her affair with Byron, Caroline Lamb says of her heroine's first glimpse of him, "The proud curl of the upper lip expressed haughtiness and bitter contempt." Presley's sneer was so emblematic that he joked about it. In a 1968 television special, he twitched his mouth and murmured, to audience laughter, "I've got something on my lip." The Romantic curling lip is aristocratic disdain: Presley is still called "the King," testimony to the ritual needs of a democratic populace. As revolutionary sexual personae, Byron and Presley had early and late styles: brooding menace, then urbane magnanimity. Their everyday manners were manly and gentle. Presley had a captivating soft-spoken charm. The Byronic hero, says Peter Thorslev [in *The Byronic Hero,* 1962], is "invariably courteous toward women." Byron and Presley were world-shapers, conduits of titanic force, yet they were deeply emotional and sentimental in a feminine sense.

Both had late Orientalizing periods. Byron, drawn to oriental themes, went off to fight the Turks in the Greek war of independence and died of a mysterious illness at Missolonghi. A portrait shows him in silk turban and embroidered Albanian dress. The costume style of Presley's last decade was nearly Mithraic: jewel-encrusted silk jump-suits, huge studded belts, rings, chains, sashes, scarves. This resembles Napoleon's late phase, as in Ingres' portrait of the emperor enthroned in Byzantine splendor, weighed down in velvet, ermine, and jewels. Napoleon, Byron, and Presley began in simplicity as flaming assertions of youthful male will, and all three ended as ornate *objets de culte*. British legend envisions a "westering" of culture: Troy to Rome to London. But there is also an eastering of culture. We are far from our historical roots in Mesopotamia and Asia Minor; yet again and again, collective emotion swelling about a charismatic European personality instinctively returns him or her to the east. Elizabeth I also ended as a glittering Byzantine icon.

Another parallel: Byron and Presley were renowned for athletic vigor, yet both suffered chronic ailments that somehow never marred their glossy complexions or robust beauty. Both constantly fought off corpulence, Presley losing toward the end. Both died prematurely, Byron at thirty-six, Presley at forty-two. Byron's autopsy revealed an enlarged heart, degenerated liver and gall bladder, cerebral inflammation, and obliteration of the skull sutures. Presley suffered an enlarged heart and degenerated colon and liver. In both cases, tremendous physical ener-

gy was oddly fused with internal disorder, a revolt of the organism. Presley's drugs were symptom, not cause. Psychogenetically, Byron and Presley practiced the secret art of feminine self-impairment.

Discussing Michelangelo's *Giuliano,* I noted the statue's swanlike neck, strangely contrasting with the massive knees and calves. Countess Albrizzi said of Byron, "His neck, which he was in the habit of keeping uncovered as much as the usages of society permitted, seemed to have been formed in a mould, and was very white." (Shelley also appeared with "his white throat unfettered.") Most of Byron's portraits emphasize the neck. Narcissistically turning his feminine neck, the man of beauty offers his profile for our admiration. The feminine meaning of an exposed neck is plain in Flaubert's *Madame Bovary* when Emma flirts with her future husband by tossing off a liqueur and, head back, licking the bottom of the glass. I find similar provocative body language in Lucretius' Mars, Ingres' Thetis, Girodet's Endymion, Kleist's Achilles, George Eliot's Rosamond, and Tilly Losch as the vain Chinese dancer in *The Good Earth* (1937). One of the hallmarks of Elvis Presley's late Orientalizing period was his architectural stiff standing collar, elongating the neck and revealing the throat in a plunging V to the chest. In his Las Vegas shows, Presley ritualistically draped scarves about his neck and cast them into the audience—self-distribution as formulaic neck-remembrance. Do this in memory of me.

Where does charisma belong? Where should it stay? Byron was full of political ideas, which led him to sacrifice his life in the cause of liberty. But he was an Alcibiades whose glamour was too intense for his own society. England could not tolerate Byron's presence and convulsively expelled him. Perfect narcissism is fascinating and therefore demoralizing. Byron's narcissism released the archaic and asocial phenomenon of incest. What if Lord Byron had entered English politics? We have the precedent of another man of beauty, George Villiers, first Duke of Buckingham, favorite of James I and Charles I. Wandering through the Palazzo Pitti twenty years ago, I was electrified by an ill-lit, unmarked portrait of stunning androgynous beauty. It turned out to be Rubens' painting of Buckingham. Playing Buckingham in Richard Lester's *The Three Musketeers* (1974), Simon Gray is wonderfully made up to resemble Rubens' portrait. David Harris Willson says [in *King James VI and I,* 1956]:

> Buckingham was a seductive young man, with something of the allurements of both sexes. He was esteemed one of the handsomest men in the whole world. Tall, comely, and beautifully proportioned, he had great physical vigour and skill in bodily sports . . . The antiquarian and diarist, D'Ewes, recorded: "I saw everything in him full of delicacy and handsome features, yea, his hands and face seemed to me especially effeminate and curious."

As the man of beauty, Buckingham combined athleticism with feminine charm. Once again we find the contrast of dark hair and fine complexion. The political consequences of Buckingham's extraordinary beauty were severe and longlasting. Perez Zagorin states [in *The Court and the Country: The Beginning of the English Revolution,* 1970]:

> He rose to the meridian of power, there to shine in blazing splendour until the knife of an assassin extinguished his light. . . . A golden shower of wealth and offices descended on him. . . . Buckingham's domination formed an epoch of critical importance in the pre-history of the revolution. It deformed the workings of the King's government and the patronage system. It sowed disaffection in the Court and was a prime cause of enmity on the political scene. It brought the royal regime into hatred and contempt. To the favourite's ascendancy must be ascribed in no small measure the decline of the crown's moral authority—an authority indispensable to government which, once lost, can hardly ever be recovered.

> With all his sway over affairs, Buckingham had no real policy or extended aims. Unlike his contemporary ministers, Richelieu and Olivares, his predominant purpose in the use of power was to aggrandize himself and his dependents.

Alcibiades helped bring down the Athenian empire. Buckingham hastened England's regicidal revolution. Excess charisma is dangerous, to self and others.

Byron, the Romantic exile, did England a favor. Energy and beauty together are burning, godlike, destructive. Byron created the youth-cult that would sweep Elvis Presley to uncomfortable fame. In our affluent commercial culture, this man of beauty was able to ignore politics and build his empire elsewhere. A ritual function of contemporary popular culture: to parallel and purify government. The modern charismatic personality has access to movies, television, and music, with their enormous reach. Mass media act as a barrier protecting politics, which would otherwise be unbalanced by the entrance of men of epochal narcissistic glamour. Today's Byronic man of beauty is a Presley who dominates the imagination, not a Buckingham who disorders a state.

## Paul M. Curtis (essay date 1993)

SOURCE: "Byron's *Beppo*: Digression and Contingency," in *The Dalhousie Review,* Vol. 73, Spring, 1993, pp. 18-33.

[*In the following examination of* Beppo, *Curtis concludes that Byron used digressions from the main plot or theme of his poems as a metaphor for life experience.*]

> You ask me for the plan of Donny Johnny—I *have* no plan—I *had* no plan—but I had or have materials. . . . —Why Man the Soul of such writing is it's licence?— at least the *liberty* of that *licence* if one likes—*not that* one should abuse it.
>
> [Byron, letter to John Murray, 12 August 1819]

The Romantics valued narrative uncertainty, and Byron certainly was the rule rather than the exception. His brand of uncertainty was of a different order, however. Whereas the Ancient Mariner had "strange power of speech" or Wordsworth's *Prelude* prophesied "Something evermore about to be," Byron understood narrative uncertainty more as rhetorical liberty than the groping of one's consciousness in the effort to create one's self. Keats pointed out that Byron cut a figure and was one too; but, as his correspondence reveals, consciousness for Byron was often claustrophobic. The narrative uncertainty Byron preferred was boundless or encyclopedic like that of Sterne's *Tristram* or Burton's *Anatomy.* The use Byron made of digression—a relatively minor technique according to the classical rhetoricians—is essential to the mode of uncertainty Byron cultivated. Apart from great good fun, digression provided Byron with an alternative to the Romantic "monotony and mannerism" of which he had been guilty but later came to despise. In the pages following. I will examine as briefly as possible the history of digression as set forth by classical rhetoricians and then apply these findings to Byron's *Beppo,* the narrative experiment to be elaborated in *Don Juan.* As we shall see, Byronic digression departs from the narrative, of course, but in such a way that affirms the variability of living by means of the contingencies of language.

The genesis of *Beppo* is an interesting story, but it has been ably described elsewhere and need not be rehearsed here. Suffice it to say that the poem subscribes to a comic pattern. A disguised Beppo returns to Venice after an absence of more than six years, tracks down his wife whom he finds with her *Cavalieri Servente,* and then reveals himself in, of all places, a gondola. Unlike the practice in the "moral North" of Byron's forsaken England, marriage Italian style appreciates infidelity; and Beppo's return disturbs the delicate equilibrium of Venetian mores. The subscription to the comic pattern ends here, however. The poem's "plot" is more of a dodge than a design which is inherently meaningful. *Beppo* concludes with a *ménage à trois* rather than a wedding or even a reconciliation.

The extent of digression in the poem is unusual and much energy has been spent arguing what constitutes a digressive line, a digressive stanza or stanzas, or the manifold transitions between the modes of narration. The effort of fussing over the less evidently digressive segments outweighs the interpretative benefit. I believe that the poem's contingency has a lot to tell us about Byron's theory of language. For one, the poem is deliberately un-plotted as if to say that no story can account for the variability of life. Digression, in fact, has more fidelity to experience because life itself is a digression between birth and death.

> Between two worlds life hovers like a star,
> Twixt night and morn, upon the horizon's verge:
> How little do we know that which we are!
> How less what we may be! The eternal surge
> Of time and tide rolls on, and bears afar
> Our bubbles; as the old burst, new emerge,

Lash'd from the foam of ages; while the graves
Of Empires heave but like some passing waves.
                                        (**Don Juan**, XV, 99)

Digression, as the important second point, shows up the contingency inherent in language. A word's representational value might trigger a deviation into symbol, allegory, myth, or the *Morning Chronicle* for that matter, at any time. Byron does not subscribe to a notion of truth in the phenomenal world. That a sentence describes a fact may be true, but it is still a sentence first and exists apart from an inherent truth. Digression holds up (and delights in) this discontinuity between world, where we perform, and words, where that performance is verbalized. Before we apply this perspective to **Beppo,** let us fill in the background and turn to digression as it was understood by the classical rhetoricians.

## I

Digressions, incontestably, are the sunshine;—they are the life, the soul of reading;—take them out of this book for instance,—you might as well take the book along with them (Laurence Sterne, *The Life and Opinions of Tristram Shandy, Gentleman*).

Digression is usually a minor segment, a "dropped stitch" as Sir Walter Scott writes [in *The Heart of Mid-Lothian*], of a far greater design be it an oration or a text. While reading **Beppo,** the reader often forgets the premise that digressions must step away *from* some basis of plot. Etymologically, digression is a "stepping aside" from the narrative at hand. The Greek and Latin rhetoricians regard digression as part of a rigid oratorical method: however improvised a digression may seem to the auditor, it is a carefully conceived and artfully wrought element of a discourse. Our first landmark in the critical theory of digression, then, is oxymoronic: we may characterize digression as anticipated disorder, a momentary fracturing of narrative linearity that ultimately aids the intellectual direction of the whole.

Digression first appears in the performance art of classical theatre. *Parekbasis* is the technique in Greek Tragedy, whereas in the Greek Old Comedy of Aristophanes it goes by the name of *parabasis*. The older form of digression is ethical in import because *parekbasis,* within the context of tragedy, implies the moral transgression of some divine code. Such an infringement is in turn absorbed into literary theory, as Joel Black points out [in an unpublished dissertation], "where it comes to refer to a fault of style, or style which is carried to excess." Comic *parabasis,* however, is an interruption used by the author to insert his opinion by means of the chorus. The author speaks his mind on matters of a personal, a public, and often satirical nature. Two general types of indirection, therefore, make up the theory of digression: the idea of a fault or excess of style, which in the context of Greek Tragedy connotes an ethical fall from society; and the stylistic excursion or the stepping aside from a linear narrative progress. Byron employs both types: the one when he describes digression as a "sin," or the second when the narrator speaks of

himself as a "broken Dandy." In the history of western literature, digression is coeval with drama. As a mode of narrative indirection, its origin is found in performance art.

Of the classical rhetoricians it is Quintilian who singles out digression for separate analysis. He discusses digression within the context of forensic rhetoric and the five part division of a speech into the exordium, the statement of facts, the proof, the refutation, and the peroration. Foremost in Quintilian's discussion is its effect of pleasing the auditor, especially when pleading a case which concerns some horrible crime. Digression offers the "pleasures of a more expansive eloquence"; and within the natural order of the speech it usually occurs between the statement of facts and the proof. "Pleasures" and "expansive" are the words to note here. The first suggests that the impact of digression is psychological; the second that the affective pleasure of digression is a function of comprehensiveness.

Using the Greek word, Quintilian defines the device as follows: "[*Parekbasis*] may, I think, be defined as the handling of some theme, which must however have some bearing on the case, in a passage that involves digression from the logical order of our speech" [*The Institutio Oratoria of Quintilian,* trans. H. E. Butler, 1921]. The "bearing on the case" of apparently unrelated matter is perhaps the most important function of digression: to bring a point to bear upon the auditor's mind by virtue of the pleasure of indirection. And so digression is not simply performative in essence, it is an eminently psychological technique that imparts additional information but under the guise of a pause, a rest, or a delay in the text.

Examples of digression in eighteenth and nineteenth-century English literature conform less and less to classical theory as we might expect, in part because of the figure's proliferation from genre to genre. Hugh Blair regarded it as an essential feature of primitive lyric poetry, as in the odes of Pindar which are "perpetually digressive" [*Lectures on Rhetoric and Belles Letters,* 1965]. The psychological impact of the figure suited well the Romantic obsession with self and served to image the workings of the anti-rational imagination. Digression also became a figure of the heuristic activity of the creating mind. Coleridge, who was fascinated by theories of association, has his *Biographia* wander into surprising narrative modes such as the counterfeit epistle. What does the classical understanding of digression teach us about Byron's **Beppo**?

## II

But to my tale of Laura,—for I find
  Digression is a sin, that by degrees
Becomes exceeding tedious to my mind,
  And, therefore, may the reader too displease—
The gentle reader, who may wax unkind,
  And caring little for the author's ease,
Insist on knowing what he means, a hard
And hapless situation for a bard.

                                        (Stanza 50)

Byron often questions what a poem is supposed to be and to what canonical standard the reader might expect it to conform. Beginning at the beginning, we have the poem's title, for example. ***Beppo: a Venetian Story*** advertises and dissembles. It advertises a story—a sequence of events, in other words, presumably associated with or caused by Beppo. The colon in the title arranges a semiotic equivalence between Beppo and the story: man as a function of place. According to this line of thinking, our hero's name labels him as an individual, of course, with the nuance that this individual is the sum of a sequence of events. Beppo is synonymous with the story; moreover, he is a man who becomes a name thanks to his story. At issue here is more than lighthearted satire. Byron was suspicious of easy correspondences between language and reality; a synonymy between man and story presumes that language can represent the "facts" of a life or "truths" of human living. He uses ***Beppo*** to debunk such thinking. "I leave the thing a problem, like all things," runs the penultimate stanza of the fragment ***Don Juan***. All that language and reality share, Byron seems to say, is contingency. By not buying into the teleological promises of plot, process, or progress, the marginality of digression represents better the stew of living.

According to such a view, the title of the poem dissembles rather than advertises. It holds out a paradigm for telic narration that is subsequently dashed. Instead of equivalence, the title hinges upon the grammatical discontinuity between a proper noun and a noun phrase. The title puts us on a first-name basis with the "hero" and appears ingenuous thanks to this informality. Imagine a title like "Joe: a Soho Story" for a similar effect. The informality, however, goes one step further. "Beppo," as Byron notes, is a nickname, a familiar form of the Christian Guiseppe. That Beppo's name has been nicked suggests a higher degree of linguistic play; indeed, the titular hero is largely absent from the poem that goes by his name. If the individual is synonymous with his story, both have been nicked by a rhetorical technique, digression.

Tales are told, narratives are narrated, and digressions are . . . performed. The resistance of the noun "digression" to a passive formulation is a morphological indication of its essentially active significance. Byron's biggest debt to the classical tradition of digression is its history as performative discourse. A Sophoclean chorus was not simply a lyrical or ethical device but a character in itself whose discourse expanded the fictive limits of the theatrical experience. Digressions in ***Beppo*** read as "impromptu" monologues sound. The affective success of either depends upon making the reader aware of the extent of the departure. We can treat the departure's magnitude in at least two ways. In the first case, we can treat the poem in a formalist fashion. Assuming the poem is centred upon its plot, the narrative jeopardy incurred by each departure is in proportion to the degree of that departure. And what departs the most radically from the narration should be the most valuable since its potential effect on the reader outweighs the "risk" of its communication. More pertinent to Byron's poetry is a second case, that of contingency: the magnitude of departure has no relation to the worth of

what is imparted in the digression, the reason being that systemic thinking should not be the yardstick with which we measure the particular and discontinuous. Life has no unity, Byron implies, and the affect of digression is its claim to the particular—the bubbles of living—within a narrative context that might be general but remains unpatterned.

***Beppo*** relies upon drama intertextually as in the case of Shakespeare whose *As You Like it* provides the poem's epigraph. Shakespeare's play, like ***Beppo,*** is replete with disguise: Rosalind disguises herself and goes by the mythological name Ganymede as she pursues and courts her lover Orlando. Rosalind is in disguise when she utters the lines Byron takes for ***Beppo's*** epigraph and so the poem subscribes to an allusive degree of dissembling before the poem actually begins. Rosalind addresses Jaques whose melancholia she denounces: "And your experience makes you sad. I had rather have a fool to make me merry than experience to make me sad; and to travel for it too!" (IV.1.25). The nobleman Jaques—the "Monsieur Traveller" of the epigraph—is sentimental, cynical, a melancholy sensualist who echoes Byron and his self-imposed exile from a hostile society.

Byron's intertextuality goes beyond references to the dramatic tradition and yet remains performative. A case in point is allusion. In the poetry of Pope (much admired by Byron), allusion is the rhetorical mode of memory. Mnemosyne, and serves to approve tacitly artistic values of the past. Allusion, opposite to Pope's practice, is often the trigger for digression in ***Beppo***. Byron's allusions fracture the progress of the verse in two ways. Firstly, the moral or allegorical expectation conjured by the allusion is negated by its treatment. The allusion is, in effect, a miniature digression. Take for example Ariadne who, for Pope, might imply labyrithine terrors and a progress to the light of day directed by the power of love. Myth in ***Beppo*** is not a structure of knowing for Byron and so he reduces the allusion by means of sonic excess:

> 'Tis said that their last parting was pathetic,
> As partings often are, or ought to be,
> And their presentiment was quite prophetic
> That they should never more each other see,
> (A sort of morbid feeling, half poetic,
> Which I have known occur in two or three)
> When *knee*ling on the shore upon her sad *knee,*
> He left his Adriatic Ariad*ne*.
>                                   (***Beppo,*** Stanza 28, my emphasis)

The digression upsets the reader's expectations because Laura's apparent reverence for her husband Beppo finds no correlative in the concluding couplet. The redundancy of the pun is a grotesque of the human anatomy. Laura kneels on one knee only, and it is personified as being "sad." The effect is bathetic, of course, because Laura's body parts are mixed-up—her knee appears to have more feeling than her heart. Sonic excess such as this almost always implies the opposite of its literal statement: Laura's concept of marital fidelity exists only so far as it can satisfy her extra-marital appetite. The alliteration and ironic semioties of Laura's body language are clues to Byron's rhetoric throughout the poem. The "allusive digression" calls attention to itself in contradistinction to what it describes. As is the case with the "lost Pleiad" in Stanza 14, "Ariadne" is more a rhetorical jab at Romantic poetics than it is a description of Laura.

The second function of allusion in **Beppo** is to divide memory against itself. As we noted above, allusion is the mode of memory that presumes the knowledge of an entire culture's literary tradition as well as the wit to manipulate this tradition. The narrator's memory is unusually rich in material of a digressive nature such as Ariadne or the minute particulars of Venetian and English society. That part of his memory responsible for the narrative in progress, however, resorts to aleatoric accounting in Stanza 56. Or, the narrator forgets Beppo's response to Laura's questions which are recorded in detail (ll. 745-6), but remembers the *Morning Chronicle*'s particulars of Mrs. Boehm's London masquerade. In this dilatory fashion, **Beppo** contains more than a linear plot could accommodate.

To this point we have examined the digressions of **Beppo** as a performative device within an allusive context. A second performative aspect of **Beppo** is linguistically based but still augments the affect of digression. The frequency in **Beppo** of what J. L. Austin [in *How to Do Things with Words,* 1962] calls "performative" words is high. Austin describes non-philosophical language as being either constative or performative. Constative language states a fact and refers outward to some thing or idea. Performative language is significantly different. When one uses such language, ". . . the issuing of the utterance is the performing of an action—it is not normally thought of as just saying something." Austin gives the example of a wager; the clause "I bet you" signifies and performs the engagement between contestants. The narrator's utterances in **Beppo** are often performative—the words actually do what they state. The narrator and (willing?) reader, *call* Laura into poetic existence by making rhyme take priority over sense: "And so *we'*ll call her Laura, if you please. / Because it slips into my verse with ease" (ll. 167-8 my emphasis). Performatives such as "I charge ye" (l. 24), "Dine, and be d—d!" (l. 71), the verbalization of prayers or bribes (l. 173) are ironic, and therefore truthful, examples of the "name and thing aggreeing." Byron's reliance upon per-formative language within digression, a performative rhetoric, augments the poem's affective impact.

### III

What are the effects of digression as it is described above? For one, it affects time to a considerable degree in **Beppo**. Digression fractures the chronology of a linear sequence to the extent that it strains at a dimension of time that is beyond verbal representation.

> Of all the places where the Carnival
> Was most facetious in the days of yore,
> For dance, and song, and serenade, and ball,
> And masque, and mime, and mystery, and *more*
> *Than I have time to tell now, or at all,*

> Venice the bell from every city bore,
> And *at the moment when I fix my story,*
> That sea-born city was in all her glory.
>
> (Stanza 10, my emphasis)

Time is understood as a random collection of discrete bits of memory rather than as an absolute of experience. By putting forward an image of time that is at odds with duration. Byron exaggerates the moment of each event described. The exaggeration of the *moment* of action gives the poem tremendous rhetorical *momentum* forward. The present tense of the narrator is overwhelming to the point that each digression suggests an experience of time far beyond the actual elapsed time of reading the digression or beyond the experience of time the digression entails. As readers we are taken hostage since we have little or no way of knowing what will come next. This experience of reading is exciting in that it strains our desire to know and challenges us to make connections between the digressions themselves, or between the poem's digressive and narrative modes.

Such associative attempts are hazardous in "nested" digressions. Take for example the fiftieth stanza. Numerically, it is very near the poem's centre—the forty-third stanza of eighty-four in the first edition, and fiftieth of ninety-nine in the final. (It is the "centre" if one counts Byron's appended stanza at l. 368). Punningly heavy-handed, it addresses the issue central to **Beppo,** digression.

> But to my tale of Laura,—for I find
>     Digression is a sin, that by degrees
> Becomes exceeding tedious to my mind . . .

The stanza begins with a return to the primary narrative (abandoned fourteen stanzas previously) only to digress yet again. The second concurrent digression lists the detrimental effects of digression for the narrator and reader; it is a digression upon the nature of digression. Whereas a series of digressions might appear pleasingly haphazard, a digression that attempts to define digression as "sin" is very much to Byron's ironic purpose. We are presented with a digression that argues in favor of narrative continuity or, with respect to ironic contingency, simply continuation.

The more nested the digressions are, the closer we seem to get to the poem's "core."

> To turn,—and to return:—the devil take it!
> This story slips forever through my fingers,
> Because, just as the stanza likes to make it,
> It needs must be—and so it rather lingers;
> This form of verse began, I can't well break it,
> But must keep time and tune like public singers;
> But if I once get through my present measure,
> I'll take another when I'm next at leisure.
>
> (Stanza 63)

The stanza is unusual for the reason that it is triply nested. It is the third digression in a series that begins at 58 and ceases at 64. The narrator's insistence upon the priority of narrative is delivered in the midst of conflicting signals, the chief of which is the stanza's pronominal ambiguity. The performative "the devil take it!" is a mild oath and refers to the previous part of this line: "To turn,—and to return. . . ." Turning such as this epitomizes the poem as language folded atop itself; and since the "turn" is twinned within infinitive phrases, the impression of language as being contingent rather than representative is heightened. An infinitive phrase is neither verb nor noun, neither action nor thing, and yet the beginning of the stanza both describes and exemplifies digression. This coiling overlap of syntax and sense enacts the essential (and humorous) jeopardy of *Beppo*. The verbalization of what goes on in a poem creates more problems than it attempts to solve.

Exactly what is "it" by the time we get to the stanza's end? Of the five usages of the word, the first two *take it / make it* are direct objects. The next two *It needs must be—and so it rather lingers* are both subjects. The last example *break it* repeats the objective case. The duplication of "it" as object and subject is another example of the poem's rhetorical puzzle. Despite strongly transitive verbs, a meaningful carry-over from subject to object is lacking much as if the stanza occurs at a rhetorical still point. The ambiguity does not stop here. The intention to "keep time and tune" is heavily qualified by prosodic lapses. Each line surpasses the pentameter measure by one syllable, and the sylabic disharmony of feminine end rhymes diminishes the narrator's stated understanding of his chosen medium. "It" constitutes a list of a single word, not one of many discrete particulars, but a very full list nevertheless. In a digression on digression, subjects and objects tend to intrude upon each other's grammatical and conceptual territory. Byron's language gets us coming and going, as it were. If the object of the poem is to digress—to turn and return—its subject also digression.

*Beppo* concludes, or rather terminates itself, with:

> My pen is at the bottom of a page,
>  Which being finished, here the story ends;
>  'Tis to be wished it had been sooner done,
> But stories somehow lengthen when begun.

Byron's deferral of closure is not surprising. His poem insists gleefully upon a self-reference that recognizes that it has gotten out of hand. A "poem" that consistently shifts between rhetorical abstractions and concrete particulars is terminated by a trivial economy of paper. The inevitable ordering principle of storytelling which Byron resists compels him to specify grammatically, at least, *the* story at its conclusion. Such a specificity is qualified, however, by an ambiguity regarding the story's physical composition—*a* page. The indefinite article. "My pen is at the bottom of *a* page," instead of the definite article *the*, is the final grammatical loophole through which *Beppo* concludes the story of digressive storytelling: ". . . here *the* story ends."

One *can* write a story by digressing on what that story will not contain or how it shouldn't be written, but it still requires some container for what is contained. Byron situates his poem within a frame-tale of sorts. Shrovetide provides the narrative frame for Beppo's story: and as the last blow-out before Lent, the excesses of *Carnival* are part of a cycle of redemption completed at Easter.

> This feast is named the Carnival, which being
> Interpreted, implies "farewell to flesh":
> So call'd, because the name and thing agreeing.
> Through Lent they live on fish both salt and fresh.
> But why they usher Lent with so much glee in.
> Is more than I can tell, although I guess
> 'Tis as we take a glass with friends at parting,
> In the stage-coach or packet, just at starting.
>         (Stanza 6)

Linguistically, the word *Carnival* is a happy congruence of reference. One can bid "farewell to flesh" only after having partaken of its pleasures. The Carnival in effect compensates for the rigors of the liturgical season it introduces. Name and thing agree, in this case. But the ironic point Byron makes here is that word and thing agree especially when we digress from the normal arbitrary standard of social behavior, hence the fidelity of the digressive mode to the (contingent) representation of life. Byron's frame-tale serves obviously as an ironic counterpoint. The poem's rhetorical insistence upon digression is Carnivalesque because it is sinning narratively.

Whereas Shrovetide is made sense of by Easter, *Beppo* concludes inconclusively. The text adroitly avoids a centre or a narrative telos. Once "inside" *Beppo,* therefore, the reader doesn't necessarily come to the middle of a poem from its beginning and then proceed to its end. A narrative construed in such sequential terms misses the point because such thinking reduces the story to its aboutness ("Oh that I had the art of easy writing / What should be easy reading!" ll. 401-2) rather than engaging the vitality of its language ("I love the language, that soft bastard Latin, . . . [Un]like our harsh northern whistling, grunting guttural. / Which we're oblig'd to hiss, and spit, and sputter all" ll. 345, 351-2). If one accepts that the subject of the poem is not the titular hero, then his "return" home is superfluous. Subjects, be they grammatical ("I am but a nameless sort of person" l. 409) or thematic ("This feast is named the *Carnival,* which being / Interpreted, implies 'farewell to flesh'" ll. 41-42) lose their usual discriminations. The I of the persona and the eye of the historical Byron merge; the Carnival exists not so much in time and space, in Venice or in London, as it does in the poem's rhetorical gamesmanship. Objectives, be they satiric ("*England!* with all thy faults I love thee still" l. 369) or narrative (". . . stories somehow lengthen when begun," l. 792) are achieved by indirection. Adultery is adultery whether in London or Venice; English hypocrisy, however, is damned by the frankness of Venetian carnality. The fact that narratives don't arrive at their conclusions matters less than the drive through their ideas. Byron's usage of digression transforms the cliché that narrative art as fiction must mislead us to truth into the proposition that art must mislead to be "real."

At the risk of appearing contradictory for the moment, one pleasure of *Beppo* resides in the reader's liminal awareness that the apparent chaos of the poem is nevertheless a product of a mind—the narrator's or Byron's, it doesn't matter which—that contains a multiplicity of orders. Only by perceiving digressively, at a rhetorical distance, can the nature of plot as con(ned) text be understood. The distance between digression and plot seen in this way accounts, perhaps, for the many mentions of the unsaid, the unremembered, or the unknown. Instead of resolving the knot of plot, uncertainty mounts at the poem's conclusion. The knowledge of such unarticulated particulars on the part of the reader is not necessary since they belong to a moral order of storytelling that dwells on how the story turns out and who gets the girl. One senses that particulars such as these are known at a remove more comprehensive than the already encyclopedic experience of the poem.

In his early favorable review. Francis Jeffrey defines *Beppo* as "absolutely a thing of nothing—without story, characters, sentiments, or intelligible object." If we take a moment and conclude by examining the comment more closely, it *makes* sense both as a paradox and as a pun. The original meaning of paradox still lurks behind our modern usage: that which goes against heterodox opinion. We might take the comment to mean that *Beppo* exists without antecedence, that it comes out of nothing in the Latin sense, that it is, perhaps, an anti-poem. In the second case, a pun is the product of sophisticated linguistic play and exhibits, simultaneously, a residual unease with that play as a form of persuasion. *Beppo*'s *thingness* ("words are things, and a small drop of ink, / Falling like dew, upon a thought" *Don Juan* III, ll. 793-4) might exist as something distilled from the order of abstract poetics where ideas or *no*-things rule as opposed to events. Jeffrey's indefinite definition reveals the inadequacy of his (and my) vocabulary in coming to terms with *Beppo* as a narrative turned inside-out. Nevertheless, such readings reveal Jeffrey as trying to teach the "mere English reader" about *Beppo*'s unprecedented originality.

If we look elsewhere for help regarding a poem as thing. Byron praised *Don Juan* because it was a *thing* of life. In a famous letter to Kinnaird from Venice. 26 October 1818, Byron cajoled,

> confess—confess—you dog—and be candid—that it is the sublime of *that* there sort of writing—it may be bawdy—but is it not good English?—it may be profligate—but is it not *life,* is it not *the thing?*—Could any man have written it—who has not lived in the world. . . .

Experience is the key to poetic success especially if the experience lived is random, disjointed, even amoral. In most of Byron's later work, digression is the trope of lived experience. The arbitrary paths of life, Byron implies archly, are surveilled by the very people or institutions who stand most in need of their own counsel. Only by straying away from the arbitrary do we finally arrive at an understanding (however marginal) of life. A verbal act can only partially describe the variability of experience in that life (and can only come to terms partially with its own variability through time). But only through verbalization do we begin to approach an understanding of experience.

The efficiency of digression lies in its variability. Through several editions and additions. Byron worked hard to make *Beppo* exist more as a function of its attenuated form and specific manner than as a function of its setting, characterization or satire. The discrepancy between the plot of the story and the gamesmanship of its rhetoric is to such a degree that the discrepancy, and not Beppo's story, consumes our attention, leaving the poem a thing of no formal thing.

---

## FURTHER READING

### Biography

Quennell, Peter. "Lord Byron: Man and Legend." *The Critic* XXXIII, No. 2 (January-February 1975): 36-43.
　　Reassesses Byron's life and reputation 150 years after his death.

### Criticism

Beatty, Bernard and Newey, Vincent, eds. *Byron and the Limits of Fiction.* Liverpool: Liverpool University Press, 1988, 291 p.
　　Essays by various critics examining the narrative patterns in Byron's works.

Boker, Pamela A. "Byron's Psychic Prometheus: Narcissism and Self-Transformation in the Dramatic Poem *Manfred.*" *Literature and Psychology* XXXVIII, Nos. 1-2 (1992): 1-37.
　　Applies theories of psychology to the Byronic hero Manfred, judging him a projection of the author.

Bold, Alan, ed. *Byron: Wrath and Rhyme.* London: Vision Press, 1983, 216 p.
　　Essays by various critics examining Byron's works and ideas.

Brisman, Leslie. "Byron: Troubled Stream from a Pure Source." *English Literary History* 42 (Winter 1975): 623-50.
　　Examines Byron's ideas about humanity's origin as they are presented in his poems.

Chew, Samuel C. *Byron in England: His Fame and After-Fame.* New York: Russell and Russell, 1965, 415 p.
　　Discusses Byron's critical and popular reception in England before and after his death. Includes a bibliography of Byroniana.

Cooke, M.G. *The Blind Man Traces the Circle: On the Patterns and Philosophy of Byron's Poetry.* Princeton, N. J.: Princeton University Press, 1969, 227 p.
　　Critical study that treats Byron's poetry as a coherent unit rather than simply as a collection of individual works.

Elton, Oliver. "The Present Value of Byron." *The Review of English Studies* I (January 1925): 24-39.
Written for the centenary of Byron's death, this essay positively assesses Byron's poetry.

Fischer, Hermann. "Metre and Narrative Rhetoric in Byron." *The Byron Journal* 10 (1982): 38-53.
Defines Romantic verse narrative and discusses Byron's use of it.

Fisher, James R. "'Here the Story Ends': Byron's *Beppo,* A a Broken Dante." *The Byron Journal* 21 (1993): 61-70.
Evaluates the extent to which *Beppo* imitates Dante's *Divine Comedy.*

Hall, Jean. "The Evolution of the Surface Self: Byron's Poetic Career." *Keats-Shelley Journal* XXXVI (1987): 134-57.
Demonstrates that Byron's works belong to the Romantic movement of English poetry.

Manning, Peter J. "Childe Harold in the Marketplace: From Romaunt to Handbook." *Modern Language Quarterly* 52, No. 2 (June 1991): 170-90.
Surveys the early reception of *Childe Harold's Pilgrimage.*

McGann, Jerome J. *Fiery Dust: Byron's Poetic Development.* Chicago: University of Chicago Press, 1968, 338 p.
Collection of essays illustrating a variety of critical approaches and focusing on *Childe Harold* as well as on previously neglected texts by Byron.

———. "The Significance of Biographical Context: Two Poems by Lord Byron." In *The Author in His Work: Essays on a Problem in Criticism,* edited by Louis L. Martz and Aubrey Williams, pp. 347-64. New Haven, Conn: Yale University Press, 1978.
Argues that an adequate interpretation of two of Byron's short poems depends upon knowledge about the poet's life.

———. "Byron and the Lyric of Sensibility." *European Romantic Review* 4, No. 1 (Summer 1993): 71-83.
Looks at eighteenth-century sentimental poetry for the origins of Byron's style of lyric verse.

Michasiw, Kim Ian. "The Social Other: *Don Juan* and the Genesis of the Self." *Mosaic* 22, No. 2 (Spring 1989): 29-48.

Uses deconstructive theory to examine the concept of self in Byron's *Don Juan.*

O'Neill, Michael. "'A Being More Intense': Byron and Romantic Self-Consciousness." *The Wordsworth Circle* XXII, No. 3 (Summer 1991): 165-72.
Examines self-consciousness in Byron's poetry and how it compares to that of other Romantic poets.

Salvesen, Christopher. "Byron's 'Poetical System'—Revolutionary or Augustan?" *Dutch Quarterly Review of Anglo-American Letters* 20 (1990-91): 51-65.
Analyzes Byron's interest in both revolutionary causes and Augustan writers and assesses whether either influenced his ideas about poetry.

Shilstone, Frederick W. "The Dissipated Muse: Wine, Women, and Byronic Song." *Colby Library Quarterly* XX, No. 1 (March 1984): 36-46.
Asserts that Byron used aspects of his own life as metaphors in his poetry.

Stürzl, Erwin A. and Hogg, James, eds. *Byron: Poetry and Politics.* Salzburg, Austria: Institut für Anglistik und Amerikanistik, 1981.
Collection of essays from a symposium on the poet.

Thomson, Alastair W. "Method and Decorum in *Don Juan.*" In *Literature and the Art of Creation,* edited by Robert Welch and Suheil Badi Bushrui, pp. 186-203. Totowa, N.J.: Barnes and Noble Books, 1988.
Examines Byron's poetic language in *Don Juan* and compares it to that of other Romantic poets.

Van Doren, Mark. "*Don Juan.*" In his *The Noble Voice: A Study of Ten Great Poems,* pp. 283-302. New York: Henry Holt and Company, 1946.
Surveys the comic elements of the poem.

Watkins, Daniel P. "Byron and the Poetics of Revolution." *Keats-Shelley Journal* XXXIV (1985): 95-130.
Discusses Byron's poetry after 1820, when he focused upon revolutionary politics and abandoned the figure of the Byronic hero.

Webb, Timothy. "Byron and the Heroic Syllables." *The Keats-Shelley Review* 5 (Autumn 1990): 41-74.
Examines Byron's conflicting attitudes to warfare.

Additional coverage of Byron's life and career is contained in the following sources published by Gale Research: *Nineteenth-Century Literature Criticism*, Vols. 2, 12; and *Dictionary of Literary Biography*, Vol. 96.

# Louise Glück
## 1943–

American poet and essayist.

## INTRODUCTION

Initially associated with the confessional school of poetry, Glück (pronounced "Glick") has managed in each successive volume after her initial collection, *Firstborn,* to develop her handling of the lyric form. Consequently, her work has become representative of a contemporary "pure poetry" that is marked by precisely used common language, austere imagery, and a disengaged emotional tone. In this, Glück's work is more characteristic of the earlier poets H.D. and Emily Dickinson than confessional writers such as Sylvia Plath. Though Glück's poems are still grounded in a highly individualized personal response to everyday life, she is recognized for her unerring ability to place her individual experience in a larger human context through correlations with Greek mythology and the Bible. She composes clear, sharp, spare, rhythmic poetry that is noted for its ongoing experimentation with a formal structure and syntax.

## Biographical Information

Glück was born in New York City on April 22, 1943, to a Wellesley-educated mother and a father who was a first-generation American businessman of Hungarian descent. The firstborn daughter of this family, who died before Glück's birth, is the acknowledged source of the poet's preoccupation with the phenomenon of death, grieving, and loss that is a resonant theme in her work. As a teenager, Glück struggled with anorexia, another experience that was later reflected in her poetry. This condition had immediate practical consequences; Glück's formal education was interrupted in her last year of high school when she began a seven-year course of psychoanalysis. Glück has said that this process taught her to think, to analyze her own speech. Though she had from her early teenage years wanted to be a poet, the experience of psychoanalysis developed the requisite discipline for the task, so that a year later she enrolled in Dr. Leonie Adams's poetry workshop at Columbia University. After two years she went on to work with poet Stanley Kunitz, initiating a relationship that would be a major influence on her life as a poet. Four years later, in 1967, she received the Academy of American Poets Prize, and the next year *Firstborn* was published. Glück has received various awards and prizes throughout her career, including the Book Critics Circle Award and the Melville Cane Award for her 1985 volume, *The Triumph of Achilles*; the Pulitzer Prize in 1993 for her sixth book of poems, *The Wild Iris*; and the 1995 PEN/Martha Albrand Award for First Nonfiction for *Proofs & Theories,*

a collection of her essays. Since 1970 she has taught at numerous colleges and universities. Although Glück has indicated that she was at first hesitant about teaching, she ultimately embraced it as a means of surviving the extended silences she endures when it seems impossible to write poetry. She currently teaches at Williams College and lives in Vermont.

## Major Works

Even though *Firstborn* reflects the influence of the confessional tradition that was popular in the late 1960s, Glück's ability to manipulate the "I" to transcend strictly autobiographical topics led many critics to recognize her as a unique talent in contemporary poetry. *The House on Marshland,* published in 1975, saw Glück distancing herself from the confessional mode and developing a more distinct poetic voice. This voice achieves a wider range in *Descending Figure,* published in 1980. This collection continues to feature the examination of common human themes through a deceptively simple language, but the poet's use of extended poem sequences rather than individual lyrics allows her to sustain more complex emotional and intellectual engagement with her topics. For example, in *Descending Figure*'s poem sequence "The Garden," Glück painstakingly locates her own individual experience within the Garden of Eden story from the Book of Genesis so that the poem becomes a lesson in human history, an exercise in how to be human. In her fourth major publication, *The Triumph of Achilles,* Glück further explored the need for love in a limited human world. In doing so, she again employed classical myths and the Bible, using them to provide the metaphorical basis of the poems rather than relying heavily on imagery to convey meaning. This book also demonstrates an expansion of Glück's poetic line; the resulting language is similar to common speech, but also reflects meticulous attention to such poetic concerns as rhythm, alliteration, repetition, off-rhyme, and lineation. In *Ararat,* her first attempt at a book-length sequence, she addressed the death of her father and the implications that death held for the other members of the family, including her mother and sister. *The Wild Iris,* Glück's sixth volume of poetry, is another book-length poem sequence. Here, the poet establishes a range of individual voices for flowers, which alternate with the poet-gardener's voice and with the voice of a gardener-god. All combine to address the landscape of the poet-gardner's marriage and other issues related to her existence. *Meadowlands,* which appeared in 1996, deals with the failure of a marriage, exhibiting an ironic humor that has only been hinted at in Glück's earlier work. The book continues to feature elements characteristic of her poetry, including a concise style and the use of rewritten classical and biblical mythologies. Its primary design makes use of the epic Greek poem the *Odyssey* as an analogy for a marriage that is disintegrating.

## Critical Reception

From the publication of *Firstborn,* Glück was recognized as a significant poetic voice, though these earlier poems have also been criticized for being derivative of the confessional poets Robert Lowell, Sylvia Plath, and Anne Sexton. It was not until the publication of *The House on Marshland* and subsequent volumes that her unique abilities with the lyric form were more widely acknowledged and praised. Frequently, commentators have lauded Glück's use of mythic material, especially the unique way in which she retraces the patterns of these archetypal stories through an individual consciousness. Likewise, her sparse writing style and emotionally removed tone have received considerable attention, with critic Helen Vendler describing Glück's poetic voice as "disembodied ... transparently removed in space or time." Many, like Vendler, have found this voice to be striking and effective, but other observers have found her stark compositions to be less successful. In extreme cases, Glück's poetry has been dismissed as a type of stylistic affectation while others complain about the difficulty in comprehending the poems because, as Peter Stitt puts it, "the maker has excluded too much." Glück is sometimes faulted on technical grounds for favoring abstract metaphor over concrete image, explanation over suggestion. However, works such as *The Wild*

*Iris* have been judged successful by some critics because of Glück's very rejection of the poetic convention of image.

Glück has drawn the attention of many feminist critics who are interested in her treatment of gender roles and the identities and actions of the women in her poems. Some criticize her negative portrayals of female experience while others argue that Glück's work considers artistic expression and female sexuality to be opposing forces. Others, in contrast, view her work as a direct and necessary feminist response to male-dominated culture. The poet's evolving style is also the subject of much critical commentary. While some observers have disapproved of Glück's trend toward longer and more involved poem sequences, most reviewers have praised her efforts in this direction, especially the book-length works *Ararat, The Wild Iris,* and *Meadowlands.* The latter two, especially, have been viewed as significant, not only for their interrelated poems, but for their departures from the poet's perceived style—*The Wild Iris* employing the conceit of speaking flowers and *Meadowlands* displaying ironic humor in place of the grim tone Glück has been known for. Though her work has been greeted with a variety of responses throughout her career, these views are perhaps testament to the innovation and variety that are manifested in her poetry. As her list of publications has grown, so too has the consensus among many critics that Glück is an important author in contemporary American poetry and one who continues to produce a wide range of quality work.

## PRINCIPAL WORKS

### Poetry

*Firstborn*   1968
*The House on Marshland*   1975
*\*The Garden* (chapbook)   1976
*Teh*   1976
*Descending Figure*   1980
*The Triumph of Achilles*   1985
*Ararat*   1990
*The Wild Iris*   1992
*Meadowlands*   1996

### Essays

*Proofs & Theories: Essays on Poetry*   1994

\*This poem sequence was later published in *Descending Figure.*

## CRITICISM

### Robert Boyers  (essay date 1969)

SOURCE: "Mixed Bag," in *Partisan Review,* Vol. XXXVI, No. 2, Spring, 1969, pp. 306-15.

[*Boyers is an American educator and critic whose books include* Selected Literary Essays of Robert Boyers *(1977). In this review of* Firstborn, *he praises the craftsmanship of Glück's poetry while also voicing concerns about the melodrama and the lack of coherence that he detects in the volume.*]

Louise Gluck is an extraordinarily meticulous craftsman whose poems give promise of a really remarkable career. Working with materials associated with the confessional tradition, but speaking in a variety of voices, she has created a body of work that is painful and shocking, but without sufficient coherence to justify the relentless evocations of violence that reverberate in so many of her pages. In a poem like **"Thanksgiving,"** images of corruption and decay are marshaled, but we do not know why they must have anything to do with the people in the poem. . . . [All] we can really explain is the poet's desire that her images and observations fit together. Here is the poem:

> In every room, encircled by a name-
> less Southern boy from Yale,
> There was my younger sister singing a Fellini theme
> And making phone calls
> While the rest of us kept moving her discarded
>    boots
> Or sat and drank. Outside, in twenty-
> nine degrees, a stray cat
> Grazed in our driveway,
> Seeking waste. It scratched the pail.
> There were no other sounds.
> Yet on and on the preparation of that vast consoling
>    meal
> Edged toward the stove. My mother
> Had the skewers in her hands.
> I watched her tucking skin
> As though she missed her young, while bits of
>    onion
> Misted snow over the pronged death.

The echoes abound in this poetry. But echoes in the work of a young poet need not always be wholly assimilated if the poet is to achieve a voice of his own. A poem like **"Grandmother In The Garden"** is no less lovely and moving for the fact that it calls to mind a number of Jarrell's better poems, including one like "Next Day" from his final volume. Here is Miss Gluck's poem:

> The grass below the willow
> Of my daughter's wash is curled
> With earthworms, and the world
> Is measured into row on row
> Of unspiced houses, painted to seem real.
> The drugged Long Island summer sun drains
> Pattern from those empty sleeves, beyond my
>    grandson
> Squealing in his pen. I have survived my life.
> The yellow daylight lines the oak leaf
> And the wire vines melt with the unchanged
>    changes
> Of the baby. My children have their husband's
>    hands.

> My husband's framed, propped bald as a baby on
>    their pianos,
> My tremendous man. I close my eyes. And all the
>    clothes
> I have thrown out come back to me, the hollows
> Of my daughter's slips . . . they drift; I see the
>    sheer
> Summer cottons drift, equivalent to air.

The poise and serenity of this poem constitute a remarkable tribute to a poet so young, and the dense aural patterns are woven so casually that one cannot but wonder at this poet's mastery of her craft.

Miss Gluck is a poet of few themes, but these she develops with a ferocity that borders on obsession. She appears to write best when she is least herself, when she writes out of contexts which are relatively unfamiliar to her own experience, and which she need not invest with the accouterments of melodrama or terror in order to make them striking. The poems are often extremely lean, several cultivating a stenographic bluntness which owes more to Alan Dugan than to any of the woman poets I can think of. In fact, the more one thinks about the resemblance, the more one can identify Dugan as a presence behind these poems, especially in the many combinations of slang words and elaborate Latinisms, as in "Saturnalia": "Now northward some two-bit / vercingetorix sharpens his will. A star / Is born. Caesar snores on his perch above the Senate."

What informs Dugan's verse, though, is a moral passion, an earnestness which is largely lacking in Miss Gluck's volume. Instead of moral passion we too often get melodrama, the forcing of images to yield more than they can or ought to yield. Situations are unambiguously awful; mothers become prototypical predators, husbands monomaniacal in their obsessions, lovers indistinguishable from pimps. Details accumulate inexorably, as if by an energy of their own, an energy in no way responsible to the shaping intelligence that presumably controls the poem. A pregnant woman, miserable about the imminent birth of her child, surveys her room as follows (in the poem **"The Wound"**): "The air stiffens to a crust. / From bed I watch / Clots of flies, crickets / Frisk and titter. Now / The weather is such grease. / All day I smell the roasts / Like presences." The evocations are so patently horrible that one is inclined to dismiss them as the meanderings of a morbidly diseased psyche, and it is virtually inconceivable that any serious reader will sympathize with such a vision, for we are given no opportunity to understand why the speaker should see her world from the perspective that is developed in the poem. In a sense it is possible to say that neurosis is here exploited for itself, because its manifestations are bizarre and exotic. Miss Gluck would do well to cultivate the unusual capacity for compassion she demonstrates in her successful poems, among them **"Returning a Lost Child," "The Game"** and **"Letter From Our Man in Blossomtime."** On the basis of these we can safely predict a distinguished career. For those who have lamented the laxness and mediocrity of most recent work by younger practitioners, *Firstborn* ought to constitute a most encouraging sign.

**Anna Wooten  (essay date 1975)**

SOURCE: "Louise Glück's *The House on Marshland*," in *The American Poetry Review*, Vol. 4, No. 3, July-August 1975, pp. 5-6.

[*In the following review, Wooten compares Glück's first two books of poetry, asserting that in the second,* The House on Marshland, *the poet has achieved a wider control in her lyric treatment of the personal and mythical without sacrificing her unique poetic voice.*]

For the admirers of Louise Glück's first book of poems (*Firstborn*, 1968), the second may initially seem less a treat. *The House on Marshland* lacks some of the verve of the first volume—the characteristic muscularity of language, the skillful use of ellipsis, the yoking of some hard and unlikely images—but it gains in other ways. Part of the charisma of the new volume is its calm sure-handedness. Glück's ear never fails her; she manages to be conversational and lyrical at the same time, a considerable achievement when so much contemporary poetry is lamentably prosaic. Her range is personal and mythical, and the particular genius of the volume rests in its fusion of both approaches, rescuing the poems from either narrow self-glorification or pedantic myopia. Glück has a gift for getting the reader to imagine with her, drawing on the power of her audience to be amazed. She engages a "spectator" in a way that few other poets can.

The first lines of **"Nativity Poem,"** for example, catapult the reader back thousands of years: "It is the evening /of the birth of god." Glück makes you feel witness to a current miracle, as if you are a fly on the wall of the stable, where Mary and Joseph and Jesus and the animals huddle: "the beasts likewise gathering, / the lambs & all the startled silken chickens . . . And Joseph, / off to one side, has touched / his cheek." **"The Magi,"** too, has a touchable immediacy: "Toward world's end, through the bare / beginnings of winter, they are traveling again." Wonderful! Suddenly the sojourn of the Wise Men becomes an event that is still happening, that is always happening, as if a curtain has parted and we are allowed to see them rounding a corner of the globe, in their usual way.

Or a poem like **"Gretel in Darkness"** where the poet draws out a childhood myth and suffuses it with the indignant fear children feel from that grisly German tale. Gretel's account (the story is told from her point of view) is remarkably astute; she remembers the trees in the forest as "armed firs," and the event as happening yesterday, yet the witch is dead and she and Hansel have been firmly reestablished in their father's hut for years. "This is the world we wanted," Gretel says. "All who would have seen us dead / are dead." But the memory haunts her, "the witch's cry," "the spires of that gleaming kiln." Her self-interrogation—"Why do I not forget?"—illustrates the living and hallucinatory quality of a child's fear, and the tendency of children to color a past horror with all the vividness of a present one. She addresses Hansel:

Nights I turn to you to hold me
but you are not there.
am I alone? Spies
hiss in the stillness, Hansel
we are there still and it is real, real,
that black forest and the fire in earnest.

Her earlier reminder to Hansel, "But I killed for you," is a stark realization of her lost innocence. The words, from a child robbed of her childhood, are bone-chilling.

**"Gretel in Darkness"** has much in common with the poems of Glück's first volume because of its dramatic rigor. In a memorable poem from *Firstborn* titled **"The Egg,"** the female persona has gruesome, recurring visions of abortion and abortionist as she watches the ocean thrust up fishbones and waste on the shore:

The thing is
hatching. Look. The bones
are bending to give way.
It's dark. It's dark.
He's brought a bowl to catch
The pieces of the baby.

Again, as in **"Gretel,"** the effect is hallucinatory.

The *Firstborn* poems are outstanding for startling effects achieved thorugh the use of 'reversals': "Time and again, time and again I tie/ My heart to that headboard/ while my quilted cries/ Harden again his hand." (**"The Edge"**) In this poem Glück's mastery of the language goes beyond cleverness; the inverted image gives way to the inverted reality that suffering, too, has weapons. Other reversals are paradoxical. "I have survived my life" says the grandmother in the garden, regarding three generations of family laundry on the clothesline. And the images are brilliant, fresh: in its pot "a lone onion/ Floating like Ophelia"; the ceiling "a convention of leaks"; snow that fastens "like fur to the river"; a sister sunning by "the chiming kinks of the Atlantic Ocean".

Despite the brilliance, metaphors in a few of the *Firstborn* poems are too rich and sometimes distracting, similes too conscious. Even the force of a poem like **"The Inlet"** cannot very well sustain "the sunset leaked like steak blood."

*The House on Marshland* is the mature achievement of a rare poet who has found since her first volume—not a distinctive voice, since Glück is always unique—but a wider control. The poems of this second collection (excepting a few) are less vigorous, but more uniform, and they are written with a majesty of ease that belies craft. There is a mellow acceptance of some rankling ironies put forth in *Firstborn* (the topical matter of the two volumes is similar; the treatment is not). There is a panoptic sadness that mourns things lost (childhood, innocence), allowing the poet a greater range of vision than would have been possible in *Firstborn* because we can guess, Glück years later knows the meaning of taking chances. No poem better illustrates the reality of loss and

the meaning of adult fear, in this second collection, than
**"The Undertaking."**

> The darkness lifts, imagine,
>     in your lifetime.
> There you are—cased in clean bark you
>     drift
> through weaving rushes, fields flooded
>     with cotton.
> You are free. The river films with lilies,
> shrubs appear, shoots thicken into
>     palm. And now
> all fear gives way: the light
> looks after you, you feel the wave's
>     goodwill
> as arms widen over the water; Love,
>
> the key is turned. Extend yourself—
> it is the Nile, the sun is shining,
> everywhere you turn is luck.

The juxtaposition of the implied Moses narrative and the
ancient, seductive Nile, haunted by Cleopatra, represents
the tension between innocence and experience felt through
most of the poems. Both landscapes are auspicious, but
"the key is turned," and the darkness we are asked to
imagine being lifted is the dominant landscape of the book.

A subtle darkness pervades. So does loss. So do the ringing parables of the Old Testament as in, for instance, the
poem **"Abishag,"** where Abishag as a young girl is fetched
by David's kinsmen to bed down with the old and dying
king and restore him to life. The story is not explicit in the
poem; instead, Glück achieves a successful pathos by
having Abishag's father turn to her and say: *"How much
have I ever asked of you."* Abishag answers *"Nothing."*
The fate to which her dutiful and brave reply condemns
her is the source of her recurring dream in the second half
of the poem; in the dream she *has* a choice. She has a
choice of suitors, and she imagines that she chooses the
old king of her own volition. "I hear my father saying /
*Choose, choose.* But they were not alike / and to select
death, O yes I can / believe that of my body."

In a larger sense, the poem, powerfully wrought, illustrates the human need to believe that choice is possible,
and when it is not, to transfigure reality making it *seem*
possible. For this reason Abishag confuses her own will
with her father's in the dream, and assumes culpability for
choosing the wrong suitor:

> I tell you if it is my own will
> binding me I cannot be saved.
> And yet in the dream, in the half-light
> of the stone house, they looked
> so much alike. Sometimes I think
> the voices were themselves
> identical, and that I raised my hand
> chiefly in weariness.

**"Northwood Path,"** a less fine poem than **"Abishag,"**
also deals with choice, this time in a contemporary set-

ting. Two people, presumably lovers, walk through the
woods "where the pokeweed had branched into its purplish
berry." The female persona is reflecting on an earlier meeting ("For my part / we are as we were / on the path / that
afternoon"), and can still see "the sun sink / drawing out
/ our parallel shadows." As in so many other poems in this
collection, there is an under-riding sense of *taint,* coupled
with innocence, the symbols for which are trees bearing
white flowers and darkish-red or purple fruit—the plum,
the shad-blow; or trees and bushes producing red and white
flowers—japonica, azalea, rose; or just dark red fruit or
berries, such as pomegranate in the poem **"Pomegranate."** In this poem, pokeweed, with poisonous purple berries that leave a dark red stain, is the symbol for desire
that "called love into being." At first glance the choice the
lovers make seems voluntary, conscious, but the choice is
"characteristic," consigning to both people the path they
must take, given their respective natures. The last line,
then is ironic:

> But always the choice
> was on both sides
> characteristic,
> as you said,
> in the dark you came
> to need,
> you would do it again.

It is hardly an accident that so much of the imagery in *The
House on Marshland* is Eden-like, or that the titles of the
first and last poem in the volume are **"All Hallows"** and
**"The Apple Trees."** "All Hallows" is a harvest poem, but
it remains for the rest of the book to disclose what price
must be paid for "harvest," for experience. Glück is too
good to theorize, but in the last poem the father stands, a
resplendent Adam, "among trees hung / with bitten apples."
Choices have been made; a child has been born. The woman holds her son to the window for his father to see: "I
raised him to the window saying / *See what you have made*
/ and counted out the whittled ribs, / the heart on its blue
stalk / as from among the trees / the darkness issued . . ."
Already the son's future, by some deep dark inheritance, is
being written on his hand. "I wait to see how he will leave
me," the mother says without surprise. "Already on his hand
the map appears / as though you carved it there."

Other poems reflect Glück's concern with the myth of
Adam and the garden of Eden, such as **"The Fire," "The
Shad-blow Tree," "Pomegranate,"** and **"The Murderess."** None is overtly about Adam, Eve, and serpent; in
fact, the Biblical and classical allusions often overlap. But
there are tracings, parallels. The mother in **"The Murderess"** slays her daughter because "she would pare / her
skirt until her thighs grew / longer, till the split tongue slid
into her brain," the way the serpent's forked tongue be-
guiles Eve, seducing her imagination. Finally "the stain /
dissolved, and God presided at her body," absolving for
the murderess, not only the murder, but the soul of the
daughter who "had no fear."

**"Pomegranate"** is based on the myth of Persephone, but
it works equally well as a poem based on Old Testament

myth. Without any mythological context, it works as a poem based on a young woman's relationship with a man: "First he gave me / his heart. It was / red fruit containing / many seeds, the skin / leathery, unlikely." Obviously it is a temptation poem that operates against the backdrop of the situation of the daughter the man seduces, and her mother, who figures in the poem but does not appear. The final appeal the man/lover makes is the one Satan makes to Eve: he offers her knowledge:

> When he looked up at last
> It was to say My dear
> you are your own
> woman, finally, but examine
> this grief your mother
> parades over our heads
> remembering
> that she is one to whom
> these depths were not offered.

"These depths" are the domain of the underworld, the chambers of the pomegranate fruit, the dark gift of experience, or all three, and the poem is sufficiently complex to sustain all these interpretations.

Similarly, **"The Shad-blow Tree"** presents a backdrop of experience against innocence in the young man who takes a photograph of the Shad-blow "through sunlight pure as never afterward." And the lovers in **"The Fire,"** who cannot ward off the night in which they "see one another so clearly" are still able in the daytime to intuit their former Eden:

> And in the days we are contented
> as formerly
> in the long grass,
> in the wood's green doors and shadows.

The young bride in a poem called **"Bridal Piece"** from *Firstborn* says, "I want / My innocence. I see / My family frozen in the doorway / Now, unchanged, unchanged." The longing for innocence in *The House on Marshland* is more qualified. The necessity of being "likewise / introduced to darkness" has become Glück's reality; it has given her poems texture and tension almost unequaled by any other contemporary poet.

## Helen Vendler  (essay date 1978)

SOURCE: "The Poetry of Louise Glück," in *The New Republic*, Vol. 178, No. 24, June 17, 1978, pp. 34-37.

*[Vendler is an American educator and critic specializing in modern poets. Her books include studies of Wallace Stevens, John Keats, and William Butler Yeats, as well as* Part of Nature, Part of Us: Modern American Poets *(1981). Here, she focuses on Glück's second book,* The House on Marshland, *analyzing the poet's voice and lyric form. She contends that the separate lyrics in linked structures, as well as Glück's "transparently removed"*

*narrative voice, provide a highly personal and exciting alternative to confessional poetry.]*

**"All Hallows"** appeared on the first page of Louise Glück's *The House on Marshland* (1975). If there were echoes of Stevens and perhaps of Sexton, they were assimilated into a new voice. **"All Hallows"** is about bearing a child—or so it seems to me—but it is saturated by the poet's sense of her own birth. A mother has paid some unspeakable price into an invisible hand, has enabled the gold seeds, and the child victim is sold into bondage, enticed into the world. When a human couple takes on the unknown in the form of a baby, it is a time of "harvest or pestilence": their spring flowering is over, and, after the fashion of an archetypal Nativity, the baby is born in the cold. The "toothed moon," a savage Jack O'Lantern, rises in a sinister ascendancy, a parody of the Christmas Star. The deceptive title and peaceful beginning lead to the frightened child-soul leaving its tree nest, beckoned by the evil fairy-tale voice—*"Come here/ Come here, little one."* The helplessness of the child, the complicity of its mother, the cannibal jaws of the moon, make the title in one sense a blasphemy; but the pity for the child, the uncertainty whether this is harvest or pestilence, the sense of a waiting landscape, all make the title, in another sense, the most reserved of benedictions. The whole poem trembles on a verge: "And the soul creeps out of the tree." Nativity, said Shakespeare, crawls to maturity: where Shakespeare saw the crooked eclipses, Glück sees the toothed moon.

A powerful re-seeing of family life animates many of the poems in *The House on Marshland,* down to its last poem, **"The Apple Trees,"** spoken by a woman to a man who is leaving her; he is the father of her child. In a dream, she holds up the child to him, saying "See what you have made"—

> and counted out the whittled ribs,
> the heart on its blue stalk.

As a mother's view of her child, this is unnerving: she sees him as artifact and X-ray plate, with the dispassionate eye of a woodcarver or a radiologist. In that dispassionate eye so stiffened against the distortions of love, Glück exerts a clear sovereignty that attracts our assent rather than inquiry. One scarcely wants to ask the secret of certain impeccable lines:

> And the deer—
> how beautiful they are,
> as though their bodies did not impede them.
> Slowly they drift into the open
> through bronze panels of sunlight.
>
> **("Messengers")**

Glück's rhythm yearns toward the deer: we think of the isolate Mariner pained by "the many men, so beautiful," as we see that this speaker, "impeded" by her body, envies the natural paradise of the deer, drifting through sun as through some etherealized version of the Ghiberti doors. And yet, at the end, these natural messengers, if I read the poem aright, are superseded by the wounded, disembodied consciousness:

> . . . they come before you
> like dead things, saddled with flesh,
> and you above them, wounded and dominant.

The perverse dramatist of the poem has perhaps learned something from Sylvia Plath. But Glück's tone owes nothing to Plath; it is not Lawrentian or clinical (Plath's two extremes), but rather, as one auditor said after Glück's Harvard reading last year, "unearthly."

In fact there is something "disembodied, triumphant, dead"—Whitman's words—about Glück's usual voice (barring some uncollected songs, in a more demotic manner, which are I think not successful). She sees experience from very far off, almost through the wrong end of a telescope, transparently removed in space or time. It is this removal which gives such mythological power, in *The House on Marshland,* to the account of her parents lives and of her own childhood, and makes their family constellation into a universal one. In the brilliant **"Still Life"** she reconstitutes the overexposed Kodak shot in every reader's photograph album, revealing the impossibility of family relations, the aversion and separation in the poses family life makes us strike when, if we were animals, we would curl up out of the sun, out of postures, and be spared these stiff and unnatural configurations.

Glück's poems of family life tend to avoid the biographical, as a way of avoiding the inevitably helpless "I." Lyric has, historically, voiced a prayer or a complaint, both presupposing a listener, the "thou" of remedy. But if there is no "thou," the voice can make no leap to another ear, can scarcely conceive of itself as subject. An inflexible statement of what is must replace protest, plea, confiding, intercession, and defense. Glück resolutely gives the blank title **"Poem"** to her *ur*-poem of family life, with its inescapable images of man, wife, spring, a house, and an unborn child. The only unexpected component in the complex is the man's writing. He is a poet, and doubles for Glück herself in this archetypal tale. The woman's face in the mirror takes on the contours of an icon or a mandala, as she becomes a Muse and her mirrored reflection causes that writing which takes on the function of life, as ink replaces blood. The conundrum of marriage is set for the unborn child, a conundrum she can never solve; the house is immobile in the constricting universe; and once again, nature, unbidden, sends forth those weak blooms vulnerable to the first frost, the first too-rough airs of heaven. Such a poem appears to exhaust one form of life, and thereby earns its title: there is a house, a couple, suffering, "what binds them together," reproduction, a child, an utterance in ink: what else could there be? And the tale of life unrolls unstoppably on: the child who enters the parents' lives must go to school and propitiate the mysterious teachers, intent on silencing the children into the classroom order.

The first day of school is not an unattempted topic (though school itself appears less in poetry than one might ex-

pect): but Glück's **"The School Children"** takes it more seriously than any previous description I can recall. Glück's is post-Freudian poetry; its wide-eyed and appalled gaze takes seriously the gulfs and abysses of the child's experience, an experience shared by the mother frightened for her departing child. Glück's mothers find themselves in the last phase of fertility; the orchards—which are the mothers themselves—are yielding only a few late apples of maternity and love, "so little ammunition" to fortify the children with, before the mothers themselves turn into barren gray limbs. The children make the first great crossing—from the shore of the mothers to the shore of the teachers—and it is a sacrificial rite, the yearly tribute to the Minotaur. The nails are waiting for the children, the mothers are trapped in the orchards. There is no prayer, no protest, no outcry, even: only the primal simplicity of the narrator.

This narrator, who holds us with her tale of deadly ill so quietly told, is Glück's great resource. The telling is oblique but not self-mocking; divinatory, like that of a Fate, who can see the apples "like words from another language," mute signs to the teacher that the child is used to an Eden of nourishment, not a world of desks and nails and silence. The Fate impersonally pities both mothers and children, seeing the uneven battle, the pathetic armor of the children's "little satchels," the timid insufficiency of their ammunition.

Here and there, Glück's tone of doom modulates into something less deathly, as in **"Flowering Plum"** and **"Brennende Liebe"**; it lifts for a moment in the discovery of love, punning, in her Moses-fable, **"The Undertaking"** on her own name—"Everywhere you turn is luck." A benevolent euphony, in such happy moments, tunes her lines: *sh*rubs and *sh*oots appear, the *w*ill of *w*aves *w*idens, the river *f*ilms with *lil*ies, the N*i*le is *sh*ining. But this flooding light supervenes on some unimaginable incarceration in the dark: "The darkness lifts, imagine, in your lifetime." It is like the opening of the camps after the war: captives resigned to a lifetime of imprisonment hear the unhoped-for creak of widening gates. It is not surprising that even this expansive freedom, of spring and love, is soon incorporated into Glück's fateful sense of meaningless life-rhythms. Glück has some of Stevens's bitterness about the childish onslaughts of the spring, and some of Williams's naive power in encompassing birth and death in one breath. This, from the poem **"For Jane Myers,"** is one quick sequence of love, reproduction, and execution:

> Look how the bluet falls apart, mud
> pockets the seed.
> Months, years, then the dull blade of the
>   wind.
> It is spring! We are going to die!

Insight is of no use in spring; the bluet's power makes us follow the bluet's cycle:

> And now April raises up her plaque of flowers
> and the heart
> expands to admit its adversary.

By a single word—"plaque"—Glück confers on April all the monumentality of an allegorical goddess, stationed irresistibly on the heart's pathway.

Since *The House on Marshland,* Glück has published a memorable sequence, *The Garden,* prolonging her fixed glance and conclusive style into a linked series of poems. Sections of *The Garden* could stand alone, but each gains by juxtaposition. From its beginning in a rebirth of love to its diminished ending in death, *The Garden* combines Glück's almost posthumous tone with moments of quick proximate sympathy. From the one immobile focus she can say that "the past, as always, stretched before us / still, complex, impenetrable"; from the other, fluid point of view she can still feel tempted by the garden's "ecstatic reds" and feel certain that to be like the stone animals, beyond harm, is "terrible." *The Garden* speaks from the abstract knowledge of past losses ("one after the other, all supportable") but its present losses are made so exact that they are felt as if for the first time. Glück's eclectic mythology, combining Eden, feather-cloaked gods, classical stone animals and a helmeted sun, ends with a Christian, ghost, a spirit sitting on its own headstone, "a small rock." "The tomb in Palestine," said Stevens, "is not the porch of spirits lingering"; but Glück's ghost, like the gospel angels, lingers in the cemetery. The body is forgotten by the relentless village, its faint searchlights scanning the rows of gravestones. The earlier garden has become Keats's stubble plains—here, Glück's "sheared field"; the "poor body" has only its buckled shadow, having lost its spirit. The body waits to be claimed, like Jesus's by the Marys.

The remoteness of what was once common is Glück's central subject: the irreality of life in the orchard once one has passed through the doors of what Ginsberg once called in horror "the vast high school" but what Glück names elementary school; the incomprehensibility of the parents' marriage in the eyes of the child; the ungraspable elements of daily life, "the bread and milk . . . on the table" once one has left the land of the living. The very table at the end of *The Garden* would evanesce were it not for the weight of the daily bread; the house would disappear without its wooden doors; Glück poses "weight" and "wooden" against the shadowy otherness of the dead body and formless spirit alike.

*Lamentations,* Glück's most recent sequence, retells in four parts of what *The Garden* had told in five, but it fatally separates the woman into two: the woman she had been with the man, and the body that will bear a child. It is the child, with no one to turn to but its parents, who makes them into the only authority. And from this premise, everything else follows: these primal parents become human; their white flesh becomes the *tabula rasa* for those wounds which will give rise to the hieroglyphs of language; and God leaves Eden for Heaven, enabling his creatures for the first time to conceive, through their imagining of him, earth seen from the air. This parable, beginning with copulation and an indigenous God, passing on through splitting and panic to birth and authority, and ending with language and estrangement (though with

an uneasy joy in wide-ranging consciousness) will be read differently by different readers, who may recall, while reading Glück, Blake's ambiguous Genesis-parable stationing the angels, in the form of stars, as our surrogates.

The three recent lyrics included here—**"Portland, 1968," "Thanksgiving,"** and **"The Drowned Children"**—are all allusive in Glück's enigmatic manner, all hopeless, all staving off tears with finish and surface. In the first, male and female come to a standstill, conjoining like rocks and sea: the rocks are marred by the ocean, the sea triumphs "like all that is false / all that is fluent and womanly." The poem would be uninteresting if it did not attribute suffering to the fixed man who refuses to turn to be photographed, and transparent longing to the woman who mars him. The circular form of the poem—from the immobile man to the immobile man—itself makes a transparent wave of longing, curbed by the self-censure of the speaker and witness.

In Glück's bitter **"Thanksgiving"** the "summoned prey" come to eat, knowing that they will be eaten, tracked down and located by their hoofprints in the snow. In the ritual, eater and eaten have their role: the part of the eater is not to relent, the part of the eaten is not to forgive; all is order, all is a dying order. It may be an allegory of the generations. Nature is as meticulous as the feasters: before it destroys, it sorts. The summoned prey; the sorted leaves; the lethal wind; the treacherous snow; the waiting predators; the dying order: all this is prefaced by the name of America's most genial family feast.

I have put last Glück's chilling explanation of the event always considered the most unnatural of all—the death of children. "You see," she says ingenuously, "they have no judgment / So it is natural that they should drown," should resume their fetal condition—blind, weightless, suspended in water. Weightless again, but now in the pond, they wait in the water hearing their parents' fruitless calls, "lost / in the waters, blue and permanent." Glück's last line evades analysis: is it an accident that I link *blue* and *permanent* with ink? It is hard to fix the speaker's relation to the children: she wants death to have been easy for them, she wants them to think of their brief earthly life as a dream; but yet she wants them still to hear the beckoning earthly voices, passing above them like lures over fish suspended just below the surface. It is as though Glück were a mother excusing their fault, hoping they were not hurt and do not miss her, and yet unwilling that they should forget her utterly or be deaf to her voice. We are made to remember, with her, the last moment, the floating scarf, surrealistically prolonged; and we bequeath them, with her, to the pond's colder maternity. But the last act, against all reason, is the call, "come home, come home."

Glück's cryptic narratives invite our participation: we must, according to the case, fill out the story, substitute ourselves for the fictive personages, invent a scenario from which the speaker can utter her lines, decode the import, "solve" the allegory. Or such is our first impulse. Later, I think, we no longer care, in **"Thanksgiving"** for instance, who are the prey and who the predators: we read the poem, instead, as a truth complete within its own terms, reflecting some one of the innumerable configurations into which experience falls. Glück's independent structures, populated by nameless and often ghostly forms engaged in archaic or timeless motions, satisfy without referent. They are far removed from the more circumstantial poetry written by women poets in the last 10 years, but they remain poems chiefly about childhood, family life, love, and motherhood. In their obliquity and reserve, they offer an alternative to first-person "confession," while remaining indisputably personal.

The leap in style from Glück's relatively unformed first book (*Firstborn,* 1968) to *The House on Marshland* suggests that Glück is her own best critic. For myself, I would hope she might follow the advice Keats and Stevens gave themselves, and write a long poem: "All kinds of favors," said Stevens, "drop from it."

## Peter Stitt (essay date 1981)

SOURCE: "Purity and Impurity in Poetry," in *The Georgia Review,* Vol. XXXV, No. 1, Spring, 1981, pp. 182-89.

[*Stitt is an American educator and critic. This excerpt from a review of* Descending Figure *classifies Glück's work as "pure poetry," which Stitt defines as verse that is more concerned with superficial qualities of structure and technique than with the intellectual or emotional core of poetic experience.*]

Among many other things, there is pure poetry, there is impure poetry, and there is everything in between. The pure poem is exclusive, attends tea parties, breathes rarified air; the impure poem is democratic, tends to drink too much, revels in ribald stories. The impure poem is anxious to get everything in; the pure poem is concerned to leave most things out. The poetic age, the one in which we live, seems especially concerned to get everything in—every possible kind of poet and poetry, that is. Among the most maddening problems facing the critic of contemporary literature is the absence of reliable categories and definitions—where do all the poets belong, in what schools and classes? What order is to be found within the incredible mass of material that confronts us? Of course we aren't completely without touchstones—we can at least tell some of the pure poets from some of the impure poets, and both of these from some of those in between—at least some of the time. . . . Louise Glück would seem the epitome of purity. . . .

[In] Louise Glück's newest book, *Descending Figure,* we find ourselves ascending with great speed from the dirt and shine of ordinary lives and everyday passions to the pristine ethereality of an almost completely pure poetry. One of the most important points made by Warren about pure poetry concerns its tendency to avoid or underplay meaning. So it is with Glück, whose short book presents relatively little to engage the intellect. Its most serious theme concerns death—the "descending figure" of the ti-

tle, illustrated so beautifully on the dust jacket, is the angel of death. Throughout the volume, death is associated with childhood—Glück's preoccupation is not future-oriented (her own death, directly or indirectly regarded) but past-oriented. Much mention is made of a sister who apparently died in childhood or infancy. This is the dark presence that broods over these somber poems, from **"The Drowned Children,"** through **"The Garden"** and the title poem, into the concluding section, subtitled "Lamentations."

There is an unreal quality about such poems, which prevents them from engaging our feelings, our empathic passions. The poems seem to exist at a considerable distance from us, as though in a world or on a stage all their own. Perhaps a better figure would be a sound stage or the set for a film. Reading this book is a bit like sitting through "Last Year at Marienbad"—all is style and gesture; action and meaning come in brief scenes or passages, perhaps suggestive in themselves but adding up to no overall, coherent statement. Consider the opening stanza of **"The Drowned Children"**:

You see, they have no judgment.
So it is natural that they should drown,
first the ice taking them in
and then, all winter, their wool scarves
floating behind them as they sink
until at last they are quiet.
And the pond lifts them in its manifold dark arms.

The first two or three lines are controlled by the language of logical discourse but of course make no sense on that basis. The third line shows a transition to domination by imagery—Glück is here captivated by the visual beauty of the children drowning in wintertime. Of course, truth, logical disourse, is left far behind, for the fact of real drowning children makes neither sense nor beauty. In the final line, image is in the process of yielding to the power of language, its "manifold dark arms." This one little stanza is dominated successively by three powerful stylistic elements; what is of least substance is the truth, the actual meaning, of the poem.

Another poem here is entitled **"Palais des Arts"**—which would actually be an appropriate title for the book as a whole. The poems on these pages are like porcelains and vases in a museum; as we wander from one to another, we are aware of a decorous silence, a rarified tint to the air, an atmosphere not to be violated by grunts or expostulations. The objects of our interest, meanwhile, pose still before us, scarcely betraying the passion that *may* (we can only guess) have gone into their making. The poem itself—**"Palais des Arts"**—is (improbably, given its title, but appropriately, given Glück's method) about love, its warm birth after a protracted gestation. The poem is nicely illustrative of Glück's way of writing, but another poem—**"Pietà"**—may be even more revealing:

Under the strained
fabric of her skin, his heart
stirred. She listened,
because he had no father.

So she knew
he wanted to stay
in her body, apart
from the world
with its cries, its
roughhousing,
but already the men
gather to see him
born: they crowd in
or kneel at worshipful
distance, like
figures in a painting
whom the star lights, shining
steadily in its dark context.

The mother and her incipient child embody the ethereal desire of this kind of poetry to stay away from the real world and its "roughhousing." When the Magi enter, we have some hope or expectation that they at least will retain their shagginess, their earthbound reality. But no; so strong is the method of the poem that they are absorbed too, turned into paint, or porcelain, or marble. As the reader can tell from my quotations, Glück is a very skillful writer within her mode. But a poetry this pure makes inordinate demands upon our interest in style and style alone, unsullied by the complications of too great an engagement with reality. The water was poured delicately and well, and at the proper temperature; the teapot itself is rare and beautiful, of china seldom seen; but the liquid that one wishes amber tends toward a pale yellow—the maker has excluded too much tea.

---

**Glück's dispassionate violence:**

This is a poetry fascinated by violence, but equally fascinated by cool dispassionate renderings of it. There is a void at the center of much American poetry, an inability to love or to forgive. And there is arrogance too, a kind of competition among poets writing now to see who can write the most horrifying thing with the least discomfort. . . . Louise Glück makes no attempt, . . . to bring language and meaning together. Instead she talks of drowned children in a voice formerly reserved for things like root canal surgery or the birds and the bees.

*Greg Kuzma, "Rock Bottom: Louise Glück and the Poetry of Dispassion," in* The Midwestern Quarterly, *Vol. XXXIV, No. 4, Summer, 1983, pp. 468-81.*

---

**Calvin Bedient   (essay date 1981)**

SOURCE: "Birth, Not Death, Is the Hard Loss," in *Parnassus: Poetry in Review*, Vol. 9, No. 1, Spring-Summer, 1981, pp. 168-86.

[*In the following review of* Descending Figure, *Bedient discusses themes and techniques that appear in all of Glück's work. The critic finds that Glück's emphasis on the sensuality of the form of the poem raises it to the level of high art, at the same time as her subjects stand as testament to the poet's inherent humanity.*]

1.

Louise Glück once ended a poem, "Open my room, trees. Child's come." This nostalgia for flourishing apart from others, this nature-huddling, the little head-pat of "Child's come"—yes, charming; but it composes the only charming moment in her volumes—of which now, as of the Fates, there are three.

Glück's importance lies more and more in her stringency, which is an earnest of her truthfulness and courage. Her poetry is rock-bottom hard and final yet marked by a sentience next to clairvoyance, and subtle surprise, and strong beauty. Into the midst of the usual fumbling well-meant "delightful" efforts of the poetry of any age, poems like hers must come as a liberating rout of everything would-be, tepid, maundering, arbitrary.

What has grown upon her, insidiously and strengtheningly, is an "infamous calm." Any more of it, you think, and she will turn to stone; any less and hell will break loose. In **"Phenomenal Survivals of Death in Nantucket,"** an early poem, this calm is the spiritual aftermath of epileptic seizures: "Past what you hear in a shell, the roar,/ Is the true bottom: infamous calm." This is however the last we hear of it: the rest is incorporation. This calm is a being beside oneself even after the storm of ecstasy clears; survival on the other shore. Because it expects nothing, there is no undermining it; it is what Beckett's characters would die to have. Measuring the treacherous variability and, worse, radical insufficiency of life, it recognizes (unforgivingly) the relativity of life to something else, of which mortality is the mere sign. Just to be alive, normally conscious, is to violate the absolute and to love is to be ransacked by whatever wants to return to it—it feels like death. Glück's poems are full of a fated denial, timberline bleak, as if nothing were ever intended to root in the ramshackle shale of this world.

In certain poets the sense of deprivation runs so deep it has abducted them; there is no calling them back. Some seem to have been nabbed by the Father's "No." Evidence of male violence dots Glück's poems like scraps of clothing dropped behind to leave a trail. In *Firstborn* (1968), her first and most acid book, men are vicious, carnivorous; their hands swarm. A typical husband drives "into the gored / Roasts, deal[s] slivers in his mercy." Another's erotic murmurings *lurch* across his wife's brain. And still in *Descending Figure* men are wound-givers ("And then it didn't matter / which one of you I called, / The wound was that deep"). Yet here, at least once, a man is corroborative and that is **"Happiness"**:

*Look at your face,* you say
holding your own close to me

to make a mirror.
How calm you are. And the burning wheel [the sun]
passes gently over us.

In her mercy she here deals only a sliver of Lear's pro-Manichaean "You do me wrong to take me out o'the grave: . . . I am bound / Upon a wheel of fire." There are détentes.

Each of her volumes ends with a Father's "No." **"Lamentations,"** the shaky mythological sequence at the close of **Descending Figure,** concludes with a callously *ascending* figure:

> And from the meaningless browns and greens
> at last God arose, His great shadow
> darkening the sleeping bodies of His children,
> and leapt into heaven.
>
> How beautiful it must have been,
> the earth, that first time
> seen from the air.

At the end of **The House on Marshland** (1975) the male has evidently left the speaker behind with their son, of whom this exquisite palm reader says,

> I wait to see how he will leave me.
> Already on his hand the map appears
> as though you carved it there,
> the dead fields, women rooted to the river.

The name of the poem: **"The Apple Trees."** After the mundane Fall of birth, the Fall for this poet is sexual: men branching into women, women rooted and bearing, men taking off and getting the view. Or simply being out of it: at the end of the first book, Caesar, Father of his empire, "Snores on his perch above the Senate." "The wolf," notes the terrific opening, "takes back her tit. . . ." *Mater natura* abandons men to their own devices.

Another grudge: the phallic male can thumb a ride back to the absolute; the woman (the true Manichean) must wait it out. ". . . always to go to women / and be taken back into the pierced flesh: / I suppose memory is stirred." (Molly Bloom: ". . . theyre all mad to get in there where they come out of.") The vicious ones *nail* themselves in. As for the Father, he has already gone on. What is a Father? Freud asked. Dead, he answered. Perhaps the Father merely disappears behind what he represents: rule, space, Law, all delimitations, including language—for the Father, so Jacques Lacan argues, founds the relation of signifier and signified. In verse the poet may wish to follow his route but her lines switch back and down and back and down again and only leave her on the same side of language, out of breath.

Women of her generation expect one another to write polemically of men. They are less free than a Marianne Moore, an Elizabeth Bishop, a Stevie Smith to speak of anything they please, freer to say what they think about being women. There has been a narrowing as well as the application of a burning glass. Yet the glass burns women,

too. In Glück the moody criticism of the Father is a minor third above the tonic struggle against the Mother.

Where the Father, marking off, minces himself into the lines of a ruler, the Mother—that "inescapable body"—is oceanic. She tries to keep one here. "Come . . . Come to Mother"—she is lure and lair. *"Come here"* calls the wife with her gold seeds in **"All Hallows,"** in what Helen Vendler admirably pinpoints as an "evil fairy-tale voice," *"Come here, little one"*; "And the soul creeps out of the tree." Our true mother is nature, which is too kind to require us to be born. But, surrendered to the other mother, we gradually learn "Distance at [her] knee," and better so: in **Firstborn** "My mother / Had the skewers in her hands," notes a young woman home for Thanksgiving. "I watched her tucking skin / as though she missed her young." What is a fussy yes yes yes when *No* has been heard? It is the absent Father that one needs—"O pitiful," Glück says of the female primeval forest, "so needing / god's furious love."

Better, in his absence, to be "masculine" than "feminine," for the masculine is already a withdrawal, a partial absence. Nothing is more saving than a mind set like a house of crystal amidst the vegetable jungle of the instincts. True, **"For My Mother,"** in **The House on Marshland,** looks back with regret on "the absolute / knowledge of the unborn." It pictures the world as the wrong womb: "A marsh / grows up around the house. / Schools of spores circulate / behind the shades, drift through / gauze flutterings of vegetation." The cloying vegetable random seminal voluptuousness, the decadent fleshly flutterings, convey a horror of the sexual and organic; even the womb, then, may not be far enough back. But it is too late not to be conceived at all. Only intelligence can set one free.

"The woman who fights against her father," writes Jung in "Psychological Aspects of the Mother Archetype," "still has the possibility of leading an instinctive, feminine existence, because she rejects only what is alien to her. But when she fights against the mother she may, at the risk of injury to her instincts, attain to greater consciousness, because in repudiating the mother she repudiates all that is obscure, instinctive, ambiguous, and unconscious in her own nature." (We will find this repudiation brilliantly restaged in **"The Sick Child."**) Beginning with **The House on Marshland** Glück has shown both the "lucidity, objectivity, and masculinity" of "a woman of this type" and her "tardily discovered maternal quality" (a quality entirely lacking in **Firstborn**). So we find her siding compassionately with the mothers of **"The School Children,"** in whom the maternal is wide-awake, drying up, a prison. The mothers have dutifully and protectively sent their children off to the first day of school with "late apples, red and gold"; and now they "shall" (it is almost a command) "scour the orchards for a way out, / drawing to themselves the gray limbs of the fruit trees / bearing so little ammunition." The maternal has left them aging as if to match the gray limbs and, since they have given so much of themselves to their children, with fewer, not more abundant, resources. The apple not of propitiation but of discord and disobedience must be their ammunition. Yes, it is "late" and how desperate they are to escape motherhood. If they are less essentially remote from the children than the teachers who "shall instruct them in silence," it is not entirely by choice.

On balance, the Mother who lies mysteriously near the origin of life—too near—is more terrifying than the Father who perhaps mysteriously transcends it. The Father wounds, but the Mother represents the woundable.

In turning toward the Father, however, Glück hardly knows what she finds. What to make of an unilluminated Absence? Projecting denial into psychology, history, the physical, and the metaphysical or following the light of what extinct star? she sometimes glosses the absence as a withholding, as if he were merely snoring on his perch above the garden. God? "Who knew what he wanted? / He was god and a monster." "Who knew . . .": often her imagination seems to have forgotten everything it may once have known about otherness except that it exists, like a bright vacancy in the corporate air.

The absence is at once a gap and a limit. There is no way around it, no way out from woe, neither in life, which is confronted by it, nor in death, which represents it. Pity the dead, for they miss life; pity the living, for being unborn is the supreme good. Of drowned children Glück says in the lead poem of *Descending Figure*:

> . . . death must come to them differently
> so close to the beginning.
> As though they had always been
> blind and weightless. Therefore
> the rest is dreamed, the lamp,
> the good white cloth that covered the table,
> their bodies.

In an earlier stanza and even this one the soothing tone and rhythm form almost an argument for drowning. But "blind and weightless"? It is denial, refuse it:

> And yet they hear the names they used
> like lures slipping over the pond:
> *What are you waiting for*
> *Come home, come home, lost*
> *in the waters, blue and permanent.*

"*Blue and permanent*"—the hesitations!

Similarly, what should one desire, life in the body or life above it? In **"Messengers,"** in *The House on Marshland,* the deer, however magically they may "drift into the open / through bronze panels of sunlight," grow older, autumn comes and, standing still, they wait in their rusting cages of shrub for messengers—messengers like the geese flying over the black marsh water at the beginning of the poem; for above this stalled world is a mobile one. Because the deer are earth-bound they too, though so "beautiful," are eventual victims of a metaphysical impatience with what is "saddled with flesh"; and as human consciousness finally finds release from the flesh through contemplation, "like the moon / wrenched out of

earth and rising / full in its circle of arrows," it slays the deer, "until they come before you / like dead things . . . / and you above them, wounded and dominant." Feminine regret for the murder of flesh, masculine triumph over flesh—again, hesitation. Glück writes as one who loves the earth, where gravity (as in the young) approaches grace and where mobility (if only through art, the bronze panels) may coincide with permanence—but longs even more for something unspecifiable and preternatural. A marvel that her pen should hold so steady—in strength, beauty, poise—even as she writes on the tortured line between gnosticism and agnosticism, idealism and sensory enchantment.

Her vision is a poet's vision—groping, contradictory, excessive, obstinate, arresting, revealing. Hunger and more hunger is her burden. In *Descending Figure* she hears it in a girl's stark laugh:

> They cross the yard
> and at the back door
> the mother sees with pleasure
> how alike they are, father and daughter—
>
> I know something of that time.
> The little girl purposefully
> swinging her arms, laughing
> her stark laugh:
>
> It should be kept secret, that sound.
> It means she's realized
> that he never touches her.
> She is a child; he could touch her
> if he wanted to.

It should be kept secret but pain will out, anger too. Or a precocious descending figure fetches her dead sister part way back from Hades:

> I was playing
> in the dark street with my other sister,
> whom death had made so lonely.
> Night after night, we watched the screened porch
> filling with a gold, magnetic light.
> Why was she never called?
> Often I would let my own name glide past me
> though I craved its protection.

The "gold, magnetic light" of this life, its mothers' calls, do not prevent it from being *the place where we defer to the gods*:

> And the past, as always, stretched before us,
> still, complex, impenetrable.
>
> How long did we lie there
> as, arm in arm in their cloaks of feathers,
> the gods walked down
> from the mountain we built for them?

As for the body, its very "language" is "hunger." Of a gull's call Glück says in **"Aubade,"**

I feel its hunger
as your hand inside me,

a cry
so common, unmusical—

Ours were not
different. They rose
from the unexhausted
need of the body

fixing a wish to return:
the ashen dawn, our clothes
not sorted for departure.

". . . fixing a wish to return"—can she not say to what? Again she seems to suffer from a metaphysical amnesia, as if birth had deprived her of her native *gnosis* and left a bewildering nostalgia.

Excessive ("unexhausted") and deficient, always outside Origin, this for her is life at the sub-gnostic "bottom," life that cannot find its way up in the darkness, laughs its stark laugh, is never called to the gold magnetic light nor being of little faith has sorted its clothes for departure.

2.

Descending figure—moving sculpture. "There is a sort of poetry where painting or sculpture seems as if it were 'just coming over into speech'" (Pound). If a statue could think: infamous calm.

Even *The House on Marshland* was serenely moulded, the poems moving as if in a spell. Here, through her enchanted cast of speakers, Glück affected to be one of the slow to learn and the slow to leave the earth, one of the slow, the hypnotically slow, to speak. Honey of generation, honey on the lip had betrayed her honey-heavy heroines; honey like dream-bait poured from her vials. She caught us:

And always on the tray
a rose, and always the sun branded on the river
and the men in summer suits, in linen, and the
  girls,
their skirts circled in shadow . . . Last night
I dreamed that you did not return.
Today is fair. The little maid filled a silver bowl
shaped like a swan with roses for my bedside,
with the dark red they call *Brennende Liebe,*
which I find so beautiful.

Such writing is a charm, a serious encroachment.

The beauty of these poems was instant, helpless. But it was not cheap and even forebears, influences, dissolved in it. Absolute, it subdued everything to itself. The perfect cleanliness of the phrasing, the graceful syntax, the sorrowing subdued tone exposed the ordinary stammering world as a deception. Seriously slow and weighted, seductively turned, equitable, freestanding, the poems yet seemed

profoundly absorbed with their own impenetrable interior. Like Sirens some of them made you want to follow them inward, down. . . . You had to strap yourself to your chair.

By contrast *Firstborn* had been like quick deft daubings on a canvas. It altogether lacked the cool mystery of the undisclosed; it was hot dramatic surface. Yet after Lowell and after Plath as it was, it proved studied where all had been at risk. An obnoxious adolescent's sharp eye lit on things remorselessly: ". . . outside, dozing / In its sty, the neighbor's offspring / Sucks its stuffed monster, given / Time." "The crocus spreads like cancer"—spoken with a defector's malice. Out came the Plath stop: "You / Root into your books," "You do your stuff." Out came the Lowell: "They're both on Nembutal, / The killer pill." Out the Berryman: "Love, you ever want me, don't." But it was virtuosity on an electric organ, the floor did not shake and pour (as in Lowell and Plath) toward the Falls ahead.

Yet a few lines heralded the essential plainness of *Descending Figure,* above all "Birth, not death, is the hard loss," which also broached her inchoate gnosticism. The interruptive *House on Marshland* was but little digressive. Its ornament proved chastely limited; besides, the figurative—as with the mothers scouring the orchards for a way out—simply and hallucinatingly asserted itself as the real. You did not pause to distinguish; all was dream; it had to be some other world that was true. "What do you think of, lying so quietly by the water?" asked the speaker in **"The Pond"** as she gazed down. "When you look that way I want / to touch you, but do not, seeing / as in another life we were of the same blood." She thus spoke to herself as the other that all know themselves to be—as when one catches oneself looking back from a mirror before comprehending who it is. Otherness swamps the paper boats of the poems, much of it erotic. The treacherous otherness that love reveals, a new awareness that has all distance in it, in which intimacy too is mythified, had crept up on her imagination, overcoming it like a sweet gas. The erotic is so like a birth—or is it a death? It takes one fearfully and sweetly beyond known, safe, tired limits. *Firstborn* had been an outsider's study of insiders (parents, lovers) or of other outsiders (the cripple in the subway, the lady in the single, etc.) but now the speaker is inside more than she can understand: ". . . death / also has its flower, it is called / contagion, it is / red or white, the color / of japonica— / You stood there, your hands full of flowers. / How could I not take them / since they were a gift?" Love, you ever want me . . . death, you ever want me . . . paralyzing, this dilemma, if not for the somnambulism.

Toward all this one finds in *Descending Figure* a ferocious hardening. Now she treats death rudely: simply, don't. Gone is the miasma of eroticism. The love poems (still her staple) contain no preternatural nipple, no violable flesh. Some things can be said against them (for one she seems stuck on the genre: is she still looking for salvation in love?) but not that they are soft:

And pain, the free hand, changes almost nothing.
Like the winter wind, it leaves

settled forms in the snow. Known, identifiable—
except there are no uses for them.

The new style is an attack of purity. A severe wind has
cleared out every patch and drop of dreaminess. "Hard
light, clear edges"—the verse is Poundian. There is no
ground, all is figure, stark. In **"Phenomenal Survivals of
Death in Nantucket"** Glück had said: "My first house
shall be built on these sands, / My second in the sea" but
after choosing marshland she chose rock. Just as her
Aphrodite is what men desire against desire,

> On a hill, the armless figure
> welcomes the delinquent boat,
> her thighs cemented shut, barring
> the fault in the rock,

so an armless welcome is what she now wants from poetry—and what her poems give.

Few manifestoes could be so profoundly sympathetic yet
so intrinsically perverse, yet again so disarmingly poised,
so indifferent to what anyone thinks of it, at the same time
so modest, as **"The Deviation"**:

> It begins quietly
> in certain female children:
> the fear of death, taking as its form
> dedication to hunger,
> because a woman's body
> *is* a grave; it will accept
> anything. I remember
> lying in bed at night
> touching the soft, digressive breasts,
> touching, at fifteen,
> the interfering flesh
> that I would sacrifice
> until the limbs were free
> of blossom and subterfuge: I felt
> what I feel now, aligning these words—
> it is the same need to perfect,
> of which death is the mere byproduct.

Thus she directs us to the blood spot in the egg, the mark
of violence that is also the mark of creation.

Routing the terror implicit in its inception the new style
here examines itself as both "case" and triumph; the explanation carries no apology. One does what one has to
do; no "nerves," no grimaces. Infamously calm the word
"form" gradually takes over and where else does it know
better what needs to be done? "Diet on the denominative,"
it advises. "Little difference as there may be between *diet*
and *die*, there is one." It is accomplished: the poem contains so little blossom that when a metaphor appears one
lights on it hungrily—though "a woman's body / *is* a grave;
it will accept / anything" is both too shocking and too like
form (autopsy) to gratify except as insight. So apart from
"blossom" itself it is left to the six learned words—"dedication," "digressive," "interfering," "subterfuge," "aligning," and "byproduct"—to serve as subtle points of interest: *fleshless figures*.

Free of meter's "contract" (John Hollander), its physiological and emotional "herd commonness" (Christopher
Caudwell), the verse stands off from us, from the body,
from death, from life. "We know nothing and can know
nothing but the dance," Williams says in *Paterson V*, "to
dance to a measure / contrapuntally, / Satyrically, the tragic foot." But Glück sidesteps the tragedy implicit in pleasure—what Oscar Wilde meant when he said, "Pleasure.
One must always set one's heart upon the most tragic."
No foolish tapping, nodding; none of the innocence and
vulnerability of life heading toward its own destruction
such as makes death (as Susan Sontag says) haunt photo-
graphs of people.

What is behind all this? Pleasure, which in the first place
created the reality-principle to protect it. "Form," Glück
says solemnly and Death is to turn away from the austere
word in disappointment. But the form of the poem itself
is precisely an erotic body. A poem lives only so long as
it likes the way it feels and moves, narcissistically refers
to itself at every point. **"The Deviation"** wants, and gets,
some of the same things a human body demands—rhythm,
repetition, change, self-enlargement, climax. And resolved
"to die only in its own way," as Freud said of the organic
body, it too moves pleasurably toward the "reinstatement
of an earlier condition."

Above all it exacts for itself repetition-plus-variation—the
repetition without which, as Kierkegaard said, the universe itself would cease to exist. With the "death of God,"
Foucault notes in "Language to Infinity," language finds
itself headed toward death "and to stop this death which
would stop it, it possesses but a single power: that of
giving birth to its own image in a play of mirrors that has
no limits." God or no, poetry has always yearned for its
own mirror-infinity and the self-imaging of language here
takes, to begin with, familiar forms. With its lines the
poem claims over and over a certain space, as an animal
repeatedly marks a territory as its own. (The lineation is
at the same time a kind of self-stroking.) Then certain
phonemes iterate one another fondly, attentively, like birds
answering calls from other parts of the wood. The musing
almost elegiac long *i* in "quietly," "lying," "night," "digressive," "I," "sacrifice," and "aligning" is a notable instance, as is the *f* that (as the saving link between *flesh*
and *form?*) begins or ends so many syllables, forming a
net so flexible and fine the ear hardly knows it's caught.
The long *a*'s add ripeness (but are discretely few). Then
too "touching," loving to hear itself, recurs and "feel"
brings "felt" back to life. And in each of the pairs "blossom and subterfuge" and "soft, digressive," an ascetic
Latinate word beds down with a soft and blossomy Anglo-
Saxon word.

None of this redoubling is flaunted, for what is flaunted
will be snatched away. Where its own pleasure is concerned, the poem is poker-faced. Subtle too is the way it
offers itself as both written and spoken, composed and
spontaneous. Glück is a wizard at poising informality.
When she says, "What I feel now, aligning these words,"
is she speaking or writing? She is speaking of writing
while writing her speaking. The writing throughout opens

into speech, the speech stabilizes itself as writing, and the words in question bring this to the surface momentarily. We see that speech and writing escape their respective limits in one another, look to one another for energy or support, relate to one another in infinite circularity.

Further, with "aligning these words" the poem proves established enough to gaze on itself and in a mirror that is nothing but itself. Hoisting itself up deftly by its own bootstraps, it discovers itself on its own ground, safely removed from death.

Hence the justified assurance of the close. Where in "Edge" Plath had sickeningly rhymed "perfected" with "dead," here "death" is shoved to the side as a byproduct and "byproduct" is misaligned with "perfect" so as to seem all the more what it is. The need to perfect leads to death (doing anything leads to death) but on a road facing away from it. Perfection, which is chosen and which chooses to be choice, is the antithesis of death, which "will accept / anything." **"The Deviation"** is perfect and knows it.

3.

Glück's two earlier manifestoes (one per volume and each oblique) looked emulatively toward photography. Take **"Still Life"** in *The House on Marshland*. Here the photographer ("Across the lawn, in full sun, my mother / stands behind her camera") is privileged over the people being photographed: "Not one of us," Glück says with apt awkwardness, "does not avert his eyes." Only the photographer is spared the embarrassment of "face." She is brought outside herself by her medium (her medium becomes her insides). Photographing the photographer with her poem Glück in turn stands in "full sun." The place of plenitude is paradoxically the hidden position. Being seen displaces one from being; being is seeing.

Nonetheless, the photograph takes the picture of the photographer. Her decisions—of will, solicitude, taste, reticence—are in it. In her first two volumes Glück may resort to masks, but still the photograph goes off with her soul. Now she shows herself without fear but herself as a god, impersonal with the "power to expose the underlying body." She shows us herself *looking,* considering, as if she were an X-ray technician in her own poem. But she is not nearly so clinical as it may at first seem. Her way of seeing is, precisely, like a photographer's, "both intense and cool, solicitous and detached" (Sontag); it is informed by spirit, and impelled by heart. The photographer conceals a good Samaritan crossing the road to bring humanity where it seems needed. The hard and proficient manner is creative; it profoundly attends.

Despite its defences against innocence, her rhythm is where her poetry is most sensitive. No less supple than firm, it delineates in a plastic way without failing to space words out gravely, giving most of them a fitting emphasis and distinction. Though it keeps to a dependency-inducing even keel, the rhythm takes the impression of things, responds to them warmly, stirs us because it has itself been stirred by what it contemplates. It becomes the calm soul of what

is said. This is equally true of the syntax, which feels as intently inward as it is classically dispassionate. And within its usual elegant serenity it is well varied, beautifully balancing as it goes.

In the movement the passing is elevated into beauty:

> Public sorrow, the acquired
> gold of the leaf, the falling off,
> the prefigured burning of the yield:
> which is accomplished. At the lake's edge,
> the metal pails are full vats of fire.
> So waste is elevated
> into beauty . . .

Typical here are the bowing heads of what might as well be called the trochees ("Public sorrow"), the balanced pairing of falling and rising duple rhythms ("gold of the leaf"), the musing spondees ("So waste"), the not infrequent slack line-endings. These imposingly blend with the formal words—"Public," "sorrow," "acquired," "prefigured," "accomplished," "elevated"—and with the solemn syntax. Set on the frail column of "which is accomplished," the large capital of noun phrases in particular makes us feel a weight as of sorrow. And in the indecisive transactions of art even this weight, although free of dream, lies on us as a beautiful burden, a luminous resignation.

Yet the poetry simultaneously resists resignation. Glück's poems arise from protest; the only thing they are at peace with is themselves. Even infamous calm is a rebuke to the violence of its own birth—an unforgiving rejection. Yet on rare, wonderful occasions the calm buckles. Indignation stirs in the tone, ruffles the syntax. An instance of the first: the poem ending "She is a child; he could touch her / if he wanted to." The language piques with the hurting realization, uniting author and child. Something deep and beyond pacification has been roused.

The incomparable example is the little masterpiece **"The Sick Child,"** subtitled "Rijksmuseum":

> A small child
> is ill, has wakened.
> It is winter, past midnight
> in Antwerp. Above a wooden chest,
> the stars shine.
> And the child
> relaxes in her mother's arms.
> The mother does not sleep;
> she stares
> fixedly into the bright museum.
> By spring the child will die.
> Then it is wrong, wrong
> to hold her—
> Let her be alone,
> without memory, as the others wake
> terrified, scraping the dark
> paint from their faces.

Terrific the shift of tone with "then it is wrong, wrong," beyond praise the judgment that here was the place to employ once again the intensifying *epizeuxis* (Gr. "fastening upon") mechanically used in *Firstborn*. Out of cool description flares realization and out of narrative, urgent homily. One who had seemed but a tourist in the museum is transfigured on the spot into an intimate of the world of a particular painting, flushed and partisan in her humanity. Or should one praise first the way the placid rhythm— eternally tranquil—is shattered by the word "die," or the perfect limpidity of each word in its place, up to the end, or the frightening darkness and oil-like density of *scraping the dark / paint from their faces?*—an image beyond calculation, an instance of the purest finding.

The poem is—in Pound's phrase—of the "first intensity," meaning it does so well some of the things poetry is best suited to do that not a hundred other works in other mediums could usurp it. Besides, it unfolds and yet again unfolds to meditation, proving exquisitely complex. Of especial interest are two intermeshed conflicts: the subtextual one between language and paint and the dramatic one between the two strong women.

Language here protests the peace of pigment. Instinct with time and motion as it is, what choice does it have? All but few syllables squirm with phonemes active as maggots. Language is vital, it germinates, it proliferates. It rushes into the future like faith, like a compulsion. Here, with its too-active nature, it naively enters the painting to animate it with its own animation, its own assumption of the identity of the signifier and the signified. At the first gentle touch of the words the scene wakes from its long sleep in time and pigment; it is brought flush with the hour painted on it. With "is ill," the present tense erupts, immediately introducing mortality. Then "By spring the child will die"— as an inference from the mother's fixed stare—opens the future even as it fatally closes it. In its spatial mercy the painting had kept the child alive in perpetuity, then language with its running toward death cruelly makes her begin to die.

Language attacks the fixity, the aesthetic fatedness of the scene as if it were not too late to change it. The child will die, but movingly the poet acts to minimize the anguish she must feel at parting, by seeking to deprive her of any deeper attachment to the life she must so soon relinquish: the sweeter the comfort now, the bitterer the parting later. The exhortation "Let her be alone" is borne on the buoyant element of language-in-time beyond any sense of its own futility and falls on the painted scene with a force meant to alter its moral composition. The poem credits language absolutely. What it says, is. It has claimed the mother is conscious, it has even overheard her thoughts. Let her listen, then. Let her learn.

The painting is a noun, the poem a verb. The first is not a process but totally intransitive; it lullabies its own content. Passive, satisfied with itself, it hangs there, *through.* Where is the painter in the painting? Translating the scene into words the poet knows where *she* is, she is in the words and she cannot bear to keep silent as if she were not. Why should she? Language puts her at the helm of what it pirates. By comparison to her words the painting

sacrifices energy, activism, acumen, rectitude, the greatest kindness and the severest renunciation. The painting is surrender; the poem, combat. Pigment is foreclosure; language, opportunity. The painter exercises a permissive negative capability; the poet, moral passion.

Could any action be at once more tender and more harsh than the speaker's attempted intervention? Her logic is shocking only in being extreme, carrying compassion (that good thing) so far beyond its sweet accustomed bounds as to make it terrible as passion. What we hear is the free, decisive voice of an outsider. The speaker, luckily for her, is not the mother. But neither is she a moral philosopher: she is, rather, a character in a work: and struck by the costs of pleasure, knowing something of them, she raises a resonant cry of objection. The moment is dramatic.

The costs of pleasure: the healthy children will of course suffer these too. Their night-breathing might as well have betrayed them from beyond the lit area of the painting, so unexpected is their inclusion; they are brought into being by the poet's desire to insist on the costs. True, they could not be more skillfully linked to the painting than they are by the metaphor "scraping the dark / paint from their faces." It is as if here the painting had taken advantage of their sleep, which is as recessed from time as it is, to re-implant itself as a canvas. But to no good; in the same figure the poet rouses the children from an eternal rest and in a long, unprotective sentence exposes them to the harsh light of growing up. The tense of "as the others wake" sidles toward presentness, as if they were waking even now in blind terror fantasies fearful as the night-gum that glues children's eyelids together. 'They must struggle for truth, which is strength, light.' As she looks at the painting, the strongest and clearest of seers knows this last with a passion. And the mother staring fixedly into the bright museum—perhaps she knows it too.

But what keeps the children in the dark if not her kind of mothering? As one given to overcoming fear, the speaker is riled by one who hushes it. She seems to square up to the mother, to return her stare. Do you not see, she challenges, that what you protect you weaken? Comfort deludes—the stark lines themselves proclaim it. The child in the poet protests not only having been thrown upon the world and so deprived of "absolute / knowledge" but then being held back by a fierce compassion from regaining knowledge, however bleak and relative. It is the mother the children must scrape from their faces, her smothering and blinding love.

Everything in the poem is disputed, or disputes itself. The museum is a maternal chamber, sheltering the painting— but also the well-lit arena from which the poet looks at it with a god's power to expose its underlying body, and the space back into which the mother (as if nobly suffering the knowledge of death) stares no less fixedly. Then the stars, all but Bethlehem-sweet in the frigid peace of the hour—at the same time, cold and untouchable above the wooden chest with its warm earthliness and its *intimate* space (as Bachelard would say after Rilke). Subliming the domestic into the cosmic, the line-up of chest and stars is exhilarating. But this perspective is an illusion. Yes, pleasure deceives. The only trustworthy light is a severe one.

The basic dispute, the source of all the others, is over the value of pleasure, hence of life itself. On the one hand life attaches us to it so strongly that death rises as a horror. How subtly precious life is, and not least its family romance. Yet because pleasure necessarily entails its opposite, pain, how one must stand up to one's weakness for it. The ambivalence is unrelenting, wracking.

The total situation, as I see it, is this: into the space left empty in the painting by the father (there are no male symbols, even), a powerful caring voice, full of both truth and love, enters and puts to rights an appalling imbalance, countering softness with severity. The voice, to recur to Jung, is lucid, objective, and masculine, and at the same time maternal.

In **"The Sick Child"** a vehement tone develops like something untoward, something not expected to be in the photograph. The analogy between poetry and photography (never secure) breaks down and the poem enters, as was said, into drama. Another instance of dramatic tone, this time acerb from the start, is **"Rosy,"** deploring a friend's or relative's abandonment of a dog "on three legs: now that she is again no one's, / she pursues her more durable relationships / with traffic and cold nature, as though at pains / to wound herself so that she will not heal . . . what death claims / it does not abandon. / You understand, the animal means nothing to me." Linger too long by the poem and it bites tears from your eyes. A few other moral (mortal) swats. But always intensity, and often solicitude. ". . . it is wrong, wrong": all her most memorable poems bear this inscription. However gentle they may be, they impugn. Objection to being placed in the site of wounds is their inspiriting element.

Apart from her determined and wholly realized perfection and her clear-eyed terrible strength (which both detects pain and makes it back off) Glück is notable for her "furious love," given in the absence of God's. The glamour of being a visionary, if only a negative one, means less to her than befriending a sick child, or a girl whose laugh is give-away stark, or a dead sister without other playmates, or a three-legged dog back in the streets. "Thirty," she tolled in **"For My Mother"**; thirty-eight . . . her years may tally up to a minus but they have led to more than compensatory creation. They have made her tender toward the senselessly deprived, they have given her humanity.

**Robert Miklitsch   (essay date 1982)**

SOURCE: "Assembling a Landscape: The Poetry of Louise Glück," in *The Hollins Critic,* Vol. XIX, No. 4, October, 1982, pp. 1-13.

[*In this essay, Miklitsch charts the course of Glück's work over her first three volumes of poetry. By analyzing rep-* *resentative poems from each volume, the critic discusses the strengths and weaknesses he perceives in the poet's work. Miklitsch also declares that* Descending Figure *transcends the despair of the earlier two books by means of its technical sensibility.*]

Louise Glück is familiar to readers of contemporary American poetry. As early as her debut appearance in Paul Carroll's *Young American Poets* (1968), her work intimated a poet of consequence. There was something about the obvious technical facility and self-lacerating tone that was immediately engaging, not to say arresting. Her first book, *Firstborn*, initially published in the United States by the New American Library in 1968, substantiated that impression. In a review of the book, Robert Hass wrote that the poems were "hard, artful, and full of pain," characteristics of the poetic *épistémé* in which they were written.

True to its "confessional" sources, the poetry of *Firstborn* is, as Hass hints, formally strict, musically dense, and thematically elliptical, even obscure. But two poems, **"The Egg"** and **"The Wound,"** set forth Glück's obsessive subject, abortion, and form a kind of thematic matrix for the book as a whole, focusing its somewhat blurred emphases. And those emphases, the recurring themes of emptiness, sterility and death, are powerfully reinforced by their juxtaposition with the plenitude, fertility, and vitality of the natural world or, one might say, the natural fertility of the physical world. Hence, in the presence of nature ("Ripe things sway in the light / Parts of plants, leaf / Fragments"), not the "gored roasts" or "plot / Of embryos," abortion seems unnatural, *contra natura*. Furthermore, what the poems insist in their oblique way is that one can never be done with something like abortion. What is seemingly dead, past, returns—as Freud knew— to haunt the present and future, obsessively alive. Such, at least, is the poetic premise of *Firstborn*.

It is a commonplace that every poet has his or her subject and, as readers, we grant them this. Yet in an art that has been dominated by male obsessions (what Foucault calls the discourse of power), Glück's subject is an uncommonly female one, even as the style and models of *Firstborn* are not. Herein lies the contradictory nature and ambiguous achievement of the book. This is not to say that Glück polemicizes her subject as, I think, Adrienne Rich has in recent books. Although **"The Egg"** and **"The Wound"** are not wholly successful artistically speaking because of the unresolved disjunction between verse and voice, they are still too rich and complex for the reductionism of "right-to-life" or "radical feminist" slogans. Glück is not intent to teach, but to present. And what is presented—sometimes coolly, sometimes fiercely, always forcefully—is not easily dismissed. Which is simply to say that Glück is not a proselytizer but a poet, and an accomplished one at that.

Glück has, as they say, learned her craft. In fact, much of the abiding interest of *Firstborn* resides in the tension between her subject and her means, her particular voice and the vigorous pull of tradition. One can detect the influence of Berryman and Sexton, though her primary models are Lowell and Plath: specifically, the Lowell of *Life Studies* (1959) and *For the Union Dead* (1964) and the Plath of *The Colossus* (1960) and *Ariel* (1961). For instance, the beginning of **"The Lady in the Shingle,"** with its querulous tone and mixed diction, slant-rhymes and involuted syntax, sounds remarkably like Lowell's "Water," the first poem of *For the Union Dead:*

> Cloistered as the snail and conch
> In Edgartown where the Atlantic
> Rises to deposit junk
> On plush, extensive sand and the pedantic
>
> Meet for tea, amid brouhaha
> I have managed this peripheral still,
> Wading just steps below
> The piles of overkill:
>
> Jellyfish. But I have seen
> The slick return of one that oozed back
> On a breaker. Marketable sheen.
> The stuffed hotel . . .

On the other hand, Plath's influence, unlike Lowell's, is less explicit. Outside of tone and some imagery (e.g., the ubiquitous skulls and bald babies), it is most obvious in Glück's recourse throughout the book to epizeuxis, a favorite, almost signature device of Plath's.

However, and this is crucial, the dominant rhetorical figures of *Firstborn* (epizeuxis, catachresis, meiosis) are central to Glück's enterprise: respectively, in her "fastening upon" her subject again and again; her feeling that something has been "wrenched" out of the natural order; and her resolve to "understate" her subject because it is so emotionally charged. And yet, despite her preoccupation with abortion in all its literal and metaphorical senses, Glück is at her best when she weaves her poems out of a dim memory of life before the deluge, as in **"Cottonmouth Country,"** or when she finds her voice and subject by displacing it, as in **"The Racer's Widow."**

The latter poem, a fully realized lyric act that reveals a mastery of loose couplet form beyond mere apprenticeship, begins with a simple sentence, a characteristic gesture in her second book, *The House on Marshland*:

> The elements have merged into solicitude.
> Spasms of violets rise above the mud
> And weed and soon the birds and ancients
> Will be starting to arrive, bereaving points
> South. But never mind. It is not painful to discuss
> His death.

After a rationalization which "explains" why the speaker is able to discuss her husband's, the racer's, death ("I have been primed for this, / For separation, for so long"), the poem abruptly begins to re-enact it:

> But still his face assaults
> Me, I can hear that car career again, the crowd
> coagulate on asphalt

> In my sleep. And watching him, I feel my legs
> like snow
> That let him finally let him go
> As he lies draining there. And see
> How even he did not get to keep that lovely body.

The loose, run-on sentences and sometimes violent enjambments (especially "his face assaults / Me," which has an almost tactile quality) mimic the speaker's involuntary recollection, and cathartic recreation, of the "scene of pathos." The poem in turn seduces the reader, as Kierkegaard said art should, into *seeing* the truth, beautifully captured in the concluding couplet: no one gets to keep his or her body, lovely or not.

Yet what is perhaps more intriguing for the reader familiar with *Firstborn* is how Glück manages at the same time to evade and confront her obsessive subject. In light of **"The Egg"** and **"The Wound," "The Racer's Widow"** elicits quite a different scene and reading. It is not too hard to see, cued by the presence of repetition— diacope this time ("*let him* finally *let him* go")—and remembering Freud's notion of "negation," that despite how long the speaker has been "primed" for her racer-husband's death, it *is* painful to speak; that the "separation" which an unnatural death produces does not mend as easily as she would wish. With a little imagination, it is possible to imagine Glück's true "scene of pathos" in *Firstborn*: "And see / How even [she] did not get to keep that lovely [baby]." This re-vision accounts for the hint of prophecy in the poem, the emphasis on "seeing," as if the speaker (mother) were somehow secretly liable for her husband's (child's) death. Truly, abortion widows a woman.

Finally, though family romance is a poetic matrix for Glück in *Firstborn,* as it is in *The House on Marshland* (see, for comparison, **"Still Life"**), the most moving moments in the book, outside of those in the second, "persona" section, occur when she is not voicing or confronting the other but her own self, deeply wounded but obstinately alive. In what is arguably the best poem in the book, **"Cottonmouth Country,"** she is writing out of a place beyond pain and rage and despair, a place earned because built out of the slow, painful process of surviving:

> Fish bones walked the waves off Hatteras.
> And there were other signs
> That Death wooed us, by water, wooed us
> By land: among the pines
> An uncurled cottonmouth that rolled on moss
> Reared in the polluted air.
> Birth, not death, is the hard loss.
> I know. I also left a skin there.

If poems such as **"The Racer's Widow," "Cottonmouth Country,"** and a formal *tour de force,* **"Phenomenal Survival of Death in Nantucket,"** mark a poet of considerable talent at work in *Firstborn,* one not wholly subject to her poetic models, nonetheless the tone that pervades the book is so high-pitched that, finally, there is little of the quiet control that is often a sign of the mature poet. In a review of *The House on Marshland,* Calvin Bedient wrote in the *Sewanee Review* (Spring 1976):

> Her earlier poems are tense performances, the light a little too strong, with Robert Lowell, Sylvia Plath, and Robert Browning [evident in her frequent use of the dramatic monologue] noticeably coaxing from the wings. The poems are brilliant but lack resonance. . . . They suffer from a too-conscious subject and skill.

*The House on Marshland* however, is a major advance on its predecessor—brilliant and self-conscious as that book was—and evidence of an achieved poetic maturity. In poem after poem the subtle interweaving of myth and music produces an effect that can only be termed spellbinding. On its publication Stanley Kunitz wrote: "Those of us who have waited impatiently for Louise Glück's second book can rejoice that it confirms and augments the impression of a rare and high imagination." Yet that imagination, burdened by a difficult subject which seemed to necessitate a difficult style (or perhaps it was, as a Russian formalist or Glück herself might argue, vice versa), was occulted in *Firstborn*.

Reading *The House on Marshland* though, one senses that Glück could not have written the latter without the poetic travail of the former. The effect, evident from the very first poem of the book, **"All Hallows,"** is a poetry liberated of its creator's designs (and, as Keats knew, of the reader's as well). It also makes possible a situation in which, to paraphrase Heidegger, *poetry speaks us,* author and reader alike. While implicitly criticizing the clipped style of her first book, Glück in a recent, illuminating interview (*Columbia* [Spring/Summer 1981]) credits the transformation to a change in technique.

> *Firstborn* is full of those bullet-like phrases, the nonsentences. When I finished the poems in that book, it was clear to me that the thing I could not continue to do was make sentences like that. The earliest poems in *The House on Marshland* were responses to a dictum I made myself, to write poems that were, whenever possible, single sentences. . . . What it turned out to do was open up all kinds of subject matter that I had not had access to. . . . technical impositions precede change. I had become habituated to a mode of expression that was itself communicative of a certain state of mind and attitude. If you take that. . . . technique away, then by definition you are going to have something else. . . . The atmosphere of spontaneous deadedness will go. That was what I thought I was doing from Book 1 to Book 2.

Thus, as Glück notes, the terse voice and clotted verse of *Firstborn* give way to the off-hand tone and matter-of-fact rhythms of, say, **"Pomegranate,"** a representative poem from *The House on Marshland*:

> First he gave me
> his heart. It was
> red fruit containing
> many seeds, the skin
> leathery, unlikely.

The pomegranate or "grained apple," a persistent emblem in Glück's poetry (see, for example, **"The Apple Trees,"** the last poem in the book from which the second section takes its title), alludes to the myth of Demeter and Persephone. The "he" in the above stanza is Hades. In the Homeric Hymn, he steals Persephone from the upper world; however, when Demeter forces him to return her, he in turn forces Persephone to eat a pomegranate which will make her return to the underworld every year.

A smart poet, Glück twists the original:

> I preferred
> to starve, bearing
> out my training.
> Then he said Behold
> how the world looks, minding
> your mother. I
> peered under his arm:
> what had she done
> with color and odor?

Because no one, mortal or immortal, will tell Demeter what has happened to Persephone, she "hides the seed" so that nothing on earth will grow until she sees her daughter again:

> Whereupon he said Now *there*
> is a woman who loves
> with a vengeance, adding
> Consider she is in her element:
> the trees turning to her, whole
> villages going under
> although in hell
> the bushes are still
> burning with pomegranates.

Glück then twists the myth again, giving it a distinctly contemporary cast:

> At which
> he cut one open & began
> to suck. When he looked up at last
> it was to say My dear
> you are your own
> woman, finally, but examine
> this grief your mother
> parades over our heads
> remembering
> that she is one to whom
> these depths were not offered.

A startling re-vision of the Homeric Hymn, this conclusion yields the fruit of both classical myth and contemporary moment, though the measure of compassion it conducts is more remarkable yet. The syntactical emphasis on the word "finally" has I think both a specific reference (the female personae of *Firstborn*) and a generic one ("women") which highlight the lacuna between mother and daughter, between two generations of women, one bound to tradition, one liberated. Persephone, who is *finally* "her own woman," represents the "new woman" while Demeter, every daughter's mother, represents the old.

All this sounds rather pedestrian, not to say pedantic, compared to the measured pace and shifting nuances of **"Pomegranate"** (though it should hint at the historical context and implication of such a poem). In fact, all the explicitly "mythical" poems of *The House on Marshland* (**"Gretel in Darkness," "Jeanne d'Arc," "Abishag"** and **"Pomegranate"**) wear their learning lightly and this is what accounts, at least in part, for their grace and wit. This equipoise of talent and tradition in Glück's poetry reminds one of Marvell, that poet of consummate taste whose verse so effortlessly blends the classical and topical, the formal and colloquial (as, for example, in "The Nymph complaining for the death of her Fawn"); verse which betrays, according to Eliot's definition of wit, "a tough reasonableness beneath the slight lyric grace." Reading for instance the first few lines of **"Pomegranate,"** one almost forgets the other grand poet and tradition they recollect. In the *Vita Nuova,* Love makes Beatrice eat Dante's heart; glossing this dream, Frank Kermode in his introduction to Eliot's *Selected Prose* observes that it "leaves the poet sad" and "represents an unrepeatable, irreversible experience of a kind that may be associated with love and poetry." And isn't this, finally, what Glück's **"Pomegranate"**—what, in fact, all her poetry—is about: the power of love and poetry, forces which can move the sun and all the stars?

If *The House on Marshland* is rooted in "the intimacies of the heart," its variable language and weather, it is also frequently "about" poetry, about how myth comes into being, as in the poised opening of **"All Hallows,"** the *première* poem of the book:

> Even now this landscape is assembling.
> The hills darken. The oxen
> sleep in their blue yoke,
> the fields having been
> picked clean, the sheaves
> bound evenly and piled at the roadside
> among cinquefoil, as the toothed moon rises.

Reading these lines one somehow feels that there is more going on than meets the eye. Certainly, the poem acknowledges its "staging," the scene of production. Hence, the seemingly incidental presence of "cinquefoil" (a purple flower that grows on inland marshes), actually reflects the book in miniature, *en abyme,* like the infinitely-reflected image of the little girl with the umbrella on certain salt canisters. At the same time the first stanza of **"All Hallows"** is a set scene, a moment frozen for eternity as in a conventional landscape painting or stained-glass window. It is not surprising, then, that there is, as Helen Vendler suggests in a review-essay of *The House on Marshland* (*New Republic* [June 17, 1978]), a hint of the Nativity in the poem, a subject dear to Glück (cf. **"Nativity Poem"** and Eliotic **"Magi"**).

I do not, however, think the Nativity is the dominant topic or trope of **"All Hallows"** since the title and the beginning of the second stanza precisely mark the time:

> This is the barrenness
> of harvest or pestilence.
> And the wife leaning out the window
> with her hand extended, as in payment,
> and the seeds
> distinct, gold, calling
> *Come here*
> *Come here, little one*
> And the soul creeps out of the tree.

The feeling of seasonal ritual and ceremony is conveyed here through a subtle manipulation of antithesis and syntactical parallelism. In fact, the entire poem is constructed out of balance and repetition which, together with assonance and epizeuxis (preferred figures of *Firstborn*), makes reading **"All Hallows"** such an unsettling experience. The effect is most evident in the enigmatic—I won't say "creepy"—conclusion where the tamped meter and vocalic play of long *e*'s in the body of the poem are consummated in the final line, with its assonantal doubling ("cr*ee*ps" / "tr*ee*") and reversed accent in the second foot. We *feel* the first tentative steps of the anima as, answering the numinous appeal of the speaker, it emerges out of its abode. The last line also in effect reproduces the emergence of the poem itself, its "assembling." In this sense, **"All Hallows"** is as much "about" *poièsis* as anything else.

I have already limned how one might construe the self-reflexive character of the poem; no interpretation of it, though, can ignore its mythical aspect and still do adequate justice to its thematic complexity. "The Hallowe'en Fires" from Sir James Frazer's *Golden Bough* provides, I think, a necessary gloss; it even suggests itself as a possible source. Allhallow Even or Hallowe'en, Frazer reminds us, is on the thirty-first of October, the day preceding All Saints' or Allhallows Day:

> . . . when November opens, the harvest has long been reaped and garnered, the fields lie bare, the fruit trees are stripped, and even the yellow leaves are fast fluttering to the ground. Yet the first of May and the first of November mark turning points of the year in Europe; the one ushers in the genial heat and the rich vegetation of summer, the other heralds, if it does not share, the cold and barrenness of winter . . . [they] deeply concern the European herdsman, for it is on the approach of summer that he drives his cattle into the open to crop the fresh grass and it is on the approach of winter that he leads them back to the safety and shelter of the stall.

This provocatively "poetic" excerpt offers a context or "frame" (among others) for the mythical impulses of **"All Hallows."** In other words, it sheds light on the presence in the poem of the sleeping oxen and sheaf-harvested fields, the barren atmosphere and imminent approach of winter. It is even more useful to know that, according to Frazer, Hallowe'en conceals an "ancient pagan festival of the dead":

> Hallowe'en, the night which marks the transition from autumn to winter, seems to have been of old the time

of year when souls of the departed were supposed to
revisit their old homes in order to warm themselves by
the fire and to comfort themselves with the good cheer
provided for them in the kitchen or the parlour of their
affectionate folk.

Widening the focus of our reading, we see that **"All Hallows"** is not so much about an imminent birth (which is the
subject of another poem from *The House on Marshland*
titled, simply, **"Poem"**) as it is about a lamentable death, a
dead child. Accordingly, the implicit nostalgia of the above
passage from *The Golden Bough* underscores the tone of
the speaker's address at the end of the second stanza: *"Come
here / Come here, little one."* As in **"The Undertaking"**
where the speaker tells herself to "extend herself," the speaker of **"All Hallows"** extends her hand, offering the harvest
seeds like gold coins to lure the hungry anima out of its
heaven-tree, as if to repay it for its unfortunate death, for
coming back into this world of birth and death and desire.

**"All Hallows,"** finally, is not only about its own genesis
but about poetic production in general, about the fears and
anxiety that plague every poet; fear of sterility and the
periods of barrenness, anxiety that no more poems will be
forthcoming, that in the future there will be nothing to
harvest. **"To Autumn,"** Glück's unswerving address to
Keats, makes this abundantly clear:

> . . . and it is spring again.
> The willow waits its turn, the coast
> is coated with a faint green fuzz, anticipating
> mold. Only I
> do not collaborate, having
> flowered earlier. I am no longer young. What
> of it? Summer approaches, and the long
> decaying days of autumn when I shall begin
> the great poems of my middle period.

Fear and anxiety, this poem? Yet it seems to me that **"To
Autumn,"** despite or perhaps because of its light-hearted
irony, is as much wish as prognosis, as much petition as
prediction. Glück here *envisions* a future when a season not
of "barrenness" or "pestilence" but of Keatsian cornucopia,
a plentiful "harvest" of poems, will prevail.

However, in order to reap that harvest, she will in the future
have to successfully manage two sometimes demonic impulses in her work: stasis and decoration. In their negative
or perjorative aspects, they signify lack of dramatic tension
and stylization respectively. Positively speaking, stasis can
produce an aura about an object or scene so that it is as if
its "blaze of being" had suddenly been disclosed. Thus some
poems, and parts of poems, resemble stained-glass windows, highly-wrought, brightly-figured, emblazoned. And
when Glück is aware of her decorative impulse, that is,
turns it to her own purpose by bringing it into the full play
of the poem, it can be an asset, as in the first stanza of **"All
Hallows"** or the following stanza, or *frieze,* from **"The
Messengers"**:

> And the deer—
> how beautiful they are,

as though their bodies did not impede them.
Slowly they drift into the open
through bronze panels of sunlight.

Here the de-naturalized images are appropriate because
the poem is about disembodiment, about a "wounded and
dominant" being before whom the messengers come "like
dead things, saddled with flesh." Similarly, the arrested
presentation in **"Still Life"** is absolutely necessary for the
poem's effect:

> Father has his arm around Tereze.
> She squints. My thumb
> is in my mouth: my fifth autumn.
> Near the copper beech
> the spaniel dozes in the shadows.
> No one of us does not avert his eyes.
>
> Across the lawn, in full sun, my mother
> stands behind her camera.

Stasis can also allow one to speak in a voice that, since it
seems to come from the womb or the grave, the distant
past or the realm of dreams, is sovereign, illustrative or,
in Rilke's terms, angelic. It allows, finally, for a peculiar
and powerful kind of poetic transcendence.

Decoration too can work as long as it does not pretend to
substitute for what it is not. However, when it becomes
*mere* decoration, too painterly, and when stasis becomes
a form of petrifaction—when, that is, they are not integral
to a particular poem's action, then they betray a lack of
engagement on the part of the poet, feigned emotion or
impoverishment of genuine feeling that can stop a reader
cold. They can ruin an otherwise great poem. Bedient, for
instance, notes that the "'panes of color' [are] too decorative for a poem nearly so great as **'The Apple Tress.'**"
And sometimes, even when stasis or decoration would seem
to be appropriate, they work against a poem. Thus, in
**"The Shad-blow Tree,"** despite some fine writing, not
enough of the poet's sensibility has been brought to bear
for the poem to be successful. And there is ultimately
something unsatisfying about **"Departure,"** to cite another example:

> My father is standing on a railroad platform.
> Tears pool in his eyes, as though the face
> glimmering in the window were the face of someone
> he was once. But the other has forgotten;
> as my father watches, he turns away,
> drawing the shade over his face,
> goes back to his reading.
>
> And already in its deep groove
> the train is waiting with its breath of ashes.

The concluding couplet verges on being facile and, therefore, unconvincing not simply because of the less than
animated language ("breath of ashes") and commonplace
trope (we know from Freud that trains, especially departing ones, represent death) but because it functions more as
decoration than as a summation or amplification of the

first stanza. Yet when *cultivated,* used with a certain amount of restraint, stasis and decoration can produce magnificent and magisterial verse, "music and legend," an image or instant of time seemingly caught once and for all.

Which is not to imply that **The House on Marshland** does not have its grand successes. An unqualified success, **"Gretel in Darkness"** beautifully illustrates how Glück transmutes her *prima materia,* in this instance the famous Grimm brothers' fairy-tale, "Hansel and Gretel." Their ordeal over (or seemingly so), Gretel is speaking:

> This is the world we wanted.
> All who would have seen us dead
> are dead. I hear the witch's cry
> break in the moonlight through a sheet
> of sugar: God rewards.
> Her tongue shrivels into gas.

The beginning of this poem is familiar, rhetorically speaking; as in **"All Hallows,"** a simple declarative sentence sets the tone and scene. And at least in this first stanza, the poem is not incompatible with the original: the children, as at the end of "Hansel and Gretel," have completely vanquished their enemies, including their step-mother who persuaded their father to lose them in the woods. Good children who were not guilty of any wrong-doing, they have been properly rewarded: "All who would have seen [them] dead / Are dead." It would appear that there is a benevolent providence at work in the world, watching over the children, meting out justice.

But the dead, as Glück knows so well, do not die so easily. The past, "armed" with its terrible arsenal of memories, intrudes into and impinges on the present. The second stanza immediately announces a temporal shift:

> Now, far from women's arms
> and memory of women, in our father's hut
> we sleep, are never hungry.
> Why do I not forget?
> My father bars the door, bars harm
> from this house, and it is years.

Even though Gretel is safe at home and what she has had to do to survive is past, she is still haunted by memories of burning witches, bewitched women. Another common device of **Firstborn,** the rhetorical question ("Why do I not forget?") stresses the speaker's inability to forget what has happened. From the Grimm original—pun intended— we know Gretel had to kill, literally incinerate, a witch and figuratively "kill off" her step-mother before she was safe. Hence, she is a woman-killer and, since the witch and step-mother are surrogate mother-figures, she is guilty of matricide. Unfortunately:

> No one remembers. Even you, my brother,
> summer afternoons you look at me as though
> you meant to leave,
> as though it never happened.
> But I killed for you. I see armed firs,
> the spires of that gleaming kiln—

Like so many of Glück's anti-heroines, Gretel is alienated from her family, those who normally would, or should, comfort and protect her.

But what is her status in the poem? Is she a reliable narrator? Or obsessed, paranoid? Like numerous female personae in Glück's poetry, the speaker seems to be afraid that the man (or men) she lives with and depends on will leave her, alone and vulnerable to those who would do her harm. Perhaps, however, everything *is* okay "now," the children *are* safe and sound, and only Gretel is "mad" and, therefore, not to be trusted as a narrator? But setting aside this question for a moment, let me quote the third and final stanza:

> Nights I turn to you to hold me
> but you are not there.
> Am I alone? Spies
> hiss in the stillness, Hansel,
> we are there still and it is real, real,
> the black forest and the fire in earnest.

So powerful and spell-binding is this conclusion that it arrests any questions about the speaker's reliability just as it suspends distinctions between "dream" and "reality," "truth" and "obsession." A "tale of deadly ill so quietly told," as Vendler notes of another poem, **"Gretel in Darkness"** forces our "assent rather than inquiry"; in other words, it convinces us of its reality, makes us believers. And it accomplishes this, as in **"All Hallows,"** by its tone, a function of its consummate and compelling rhetoric. Hence, after the aposiopesis at the end of the second stanza where Gretel breaks off her discourse, her hallucinatory vision ("I see armed firs / the spires of that gleaming kiln—"), a rhetorical question follows ("Am I alone?") which reinforces the speaker's painful realization that her brother is absent ("you are not there"). The concluding three lines, dense with Glück's repertoire of rhetorical figures (apostrophe, consonance—sibilants especially, epizeuxis, etc.) accentuates Gretel's aloneness. Finally, the shift from the first-person singular that dominates the beginning of the poem to the first-person plural at the very end, together with the demonstratives and spondaic feel of the lines, all confirm the speaker's and our worst fears: the "black forest and the fire in earnest" are *real,* are *out there* still.

The final stanza, pervaded by an ominous atmosphere of impending doom, problematizes everything that has preceded: nothing is as simple as it seems (or as things would have us believe). Everything, for Gretel, is questionable now: her father (who, barring harm, also bars her escape), her brother (who might leave and therefore not be there to protect her), even her home, "this house" (which, I think we can safely say, is haunted). In "The Uncanny" Freud observed that many "people experience the feeling [of uncanniness] in the highest degree in relation to death and dead people, to the return of the dead. . . . Some languages in use today can only render the German expression 'an *unheimlich* house' by 'a haunted house.'" All of which accounts for the "unhomely" (*unheimlich*) effect of the poem, the uncanny feelings it evokes in us.

As in so much of Glück's poetry, we experience in **"Gretel in Darkness"** with terrible clarity the commonplace (which is not to say it is not true) that "we can never go home again." In this sense, the poem is one of experience, about irreversible loss (of innocence) and the costly wages of knowledge. Glück's achievement here is to take a story about children, a children's story, and expose its darker significance, its "adult" dimension, the terror and pity which make the originals the unforgettable stories they are and which later editors have glossed over, edited out, expurgated. **"Gretel in Darkness,"** like the original Grimm stories, does not spare its readers: in Auden's terms, it creates a world of illusion that simultaneously disenchants us of those same illusions.

If, as Helen Vendler claims, Glück's poems "are far removed from the circumstantial poetry written by women poets in the last ten years," they also suffer occasionally from a lack of immediacy, a sense of humor or wit (where there is no lessening of intensity, as Eliot defined it) which would leave her sometimes too deadly serious tone. Certainly Glück possesses, and is possessed by, a magisterial voice that has made for some astonishing poems. The danger is that it will produce mere magic, rhetoric devoid of the felt experiences of everyday life. This caveat, I suppose, accounts for some of the ambivalence I experienced after reading Glück's third and most recent book of poems, *Descending Figure*. At first glance, it merely seems to repeat the successes of *The House on Marshland*.

However, if Glück's tone and language have not changed appreciably (which readers familiar with her work might find vexing), *Descending Figure* does extend the emotional range of the first two books to accommodate events, one surmises, in the evolution of her personal life. Although still haunted by pain and loss and death, the poems are less obsessed with these topics and so less marked by a rather nostalgic desire for extinct states of being and non-being in general: the world of childhood innocence, the "absolute knowledge" of the womb and tomb. True, there are poems about dead children and deadlier male-female relationships, staples of the first two books, but there are also poems about the poet's husband and son, the domesticities of daily life and its small, though not insignificant, pains and pleasures.

**"Happiness,"** a representative poem from *Descending Figure*, recognizes figures of feeling that Glück's earlier work did, and perhaps could, not admit of:

> A man and woman lie on a white bed.
> It is morning. I think
> *Soon they will waken.*
> On the bedside table is a vase
> of lilies; sunlight
> pools in their throats.
>
> I watch him turn to her
> as though to speak her name
> but silently, deep in her mouth—
> At the window ledge,

> once, twice,
> a bird calls.
> And then she stirs; her body
> fills with his breath.
>
> I open my eyes; you are watching me.
> Almost over this room
> the sun is gliding.
> *Look at your face,* you say,
> holding your own close to me
> to make a mirror.
> How calm you are. And the burning wheel
> passes gently over us.

Here the intricate dream-like movement of the first stanza and the abrupt shift of gears that initiates the second are consummated in the beautiful but vaguely terrifying image of the last two lines. Though this poem has none of the regret or sorrow traditionally associated with the genre it echoes, the aubade, its relation to Glück's earlier poems, and their concern with the pain of separation, make **"Happiness"** the quietly powerful and complex poem it is.

Paradoxically, despite or because of its downward movement toward the things of this world, *Descending Figure* represents a slight upbeat impulse in Glück's poetry, one not perceptible perhaps to the general reader though one, more importantly, which two poets of pain and loss and death, Sylvia Plath and Anne Sexton, never lived to see and write about. "I have survived my life," a speaker in *Firstborn* says. Louise Glück has survived, and *Descending Figure* is a small testament to her canny craft and courage. In the future, no doubt, her poems will not only continue to move and amaze us but reflect more and more those moments when, just as we are waiting on what Rilke calls a "rising happiness" (steigendes *Glück*), "a happy thing *falls*" (*ein Glückliches* fällt). Descending figures such as these are also the stuff of poetry.

### Louise Glück  (1985)

SOURCE: "The Dreamer and the Watcher," in *Proofs & Theories: Essays on Poetry,* The Ecco Press, 1994, pp. 99-106.

[*In this essay, originally published in 1985, Glück elucidates the process through which a poem takes shape out of her ordinary experience. She also discusses particular tasks she has set herself concerning matters of form, structure, rhythm, and syntax.*]

I have to say at once that I am uneasy with commentary. My insights on what I perceive to be the themes of this poem are already expressed: the poem embodies them. I can't add anything; what I can do is make the implicit explicit, which exactly reverses the poet's ambition. Perhaps the best alternative is to begin in circumstance.

In April of 1980, my house was destroyed by fire. A burned house: a reprimand to the collector. Gradually certain benefits became apparent. I felt grateful; the vivid sense of escape conferred on daily life an aura of blessedness. I felt lucky to wake up, lucky to make the beds, lucky to grind the coffee. There was also, after a period of devastating grief, a strange exhilaration. Having nothing, I was no longer hostage to possessions. For six weeks, my husband and son and I lived with friends; in May we moved into Plainfield Village, which seemed, after the isolation of the country road, miraculously varied, alive.

At that time, I hadn't written anything for about six months. The natural silence after a book. Then the natural silence imposed by crisis. I was oddly at peace with it. What word did I use? Necessary, appropriate—whatever I said, the fact is that for once I relinquished the anxiety which, in my mind, ensured the return of vision. That first summer after the fire was a period of rare happiness—not ecstasy but another state, one more balanced, serene, attentive.

Toward the end of June, I began writing again, working on a poem called **"Mock Orange."** Then that poem was finished; in rapid succession, over a period of about two weeks, I wrote twelve more. Such experiences are, in many lives, a commonplace. But for me this was unprecedented and unexpectedly frightening. I kept feeling the poems weren't mine but collages of remembered lines. When I thought otherwise, I thought such fluency meant I was going to die, not sometime, but very soon. At such moments, for the first time in my life, I wished not to write; for the first time, I wanted survival above all else. That wish had no influence on behavior. Other factors—twenty years of discipline and obsession—were more powerful. When, of itself, the seizure ended, I was left with a sense of direction, a sense of how I wanted to sound. I wanted to locate poems in a *now* that would never recur, in a present that seemed to me utterly different from my previous uses of that tense. I had tried, always, to get at the unchanging. But, beginning at this time, my definitions of *essential* were themselves altering. I wanted, as well, poems not so much developed as undulant, more fire than marble. The work I'd just done suggested these possibilities. Meaning, it suggested a method, a tone. The chief attribute of that tone, as I heard it, was urgency, even recklessness. . . .

In practical terms, in the period before the fire I had set myself certain assignments. In the gloomy, unproductive winter of 1980, I was sorting, analyzing, trying to identify in my poems those habitual gestures—signature rhythms, tricks of syntax, and so on—that had to be discarded, trying, at the same time, to see what constructions I had tended to avoid. I had made a style of avoiding contractions and questions; it seemed to me I should learn to use them. Both forms felt completely alien, which was encouraging. That is, I allowed myself to believe something profound had been addressed. My work has always been strongly marked by a disregard for the circumstantial, except insofar as it could be transformed into paradigm. The poems in *Descending Figure* aim at a kind of terminal authority: they will not be distracted by the transitory, the partial; they reserve their love for what doesn't exist.

I expect that, to some degree, this disposition not to acquiesce will always inform my work: an aspect of character. An aspect, also, of the passion for form. But if writing is to be a discovery, it must explore the unknown, and the unknown, to me, was informality—contractions and questions specify the human, not the oracular, voice.

**"Night Song"** was written in the early part of 1981, about six months after the period I've described. It's not clear to me to what extent the poem reflects either these concerns or these events. I find traces of both in the lines. And yet, the poem could not have been predicted. All this is something like looking at an old photograph of a friend: you can see readily how that child came to be this adult. But it doesn't work the other way; you can't find in the blurred, soft face of an infant the inevitable adult structure.

The process of writing doesn't, in my experience, vary much. What varies is the time required. For me, all poems begin in some fragment of motivating language—the task of writing a poem is the search for context. Other imaginations begin, I believe, in the actual, in the world, in some concrete thing which examination endows with significance. That process is generative: its proliferating associations produce a broad, lush, inclusive and, at times, playful poetry; its failures seem simply diffuse, without focus. My own work begins at the opposite end, at the end, literally, at illumination, which has then to be traced back to some source in the world. This method, when it succeeds, makes a thing that seems irrefutable. Its failure is felt as portentousness.

**"Night Song"** began with its first stanza, heard whole. And a working title: "Siren Song." A seduction. Are all seductions riddled with the imperative? As I remember, I had been thinking, on and off, of Psyche and Eros, thinking specifically of the illustration which had introduced these figures to me in childhood: the mortal woman bending over the ravishing god. This image remained with me, an independent fact, so divested of narrative that for years I didn't remember that Psyche had to be pressured into this betrayal. In my mind, Psyche leaning over Eros stood for the human compulsion to see, to know, for the rejection of whatever comfort results from deception. The figures suggested, as well, the dilemma of sexuality: the single body split apart again, an old subject; the exhausting obligation to recognize the other as other, as not part of the self.

For some months, I had no idea what to do with this beginning. The lines did seem a beginning: they were a summons, after all. In some sense, the "you" at this point was myself. "The calm of darkness is the horror of heaven"—the lesson was the lesson I keep trying to learn. But the poem had, I thought, to be dramatic.

When work resumed (how, why, I don't know), it went quickly. The dramatic situation remains sketchy—perhaps there is not enough background, in both senses of the word. But the truth is I didn't care about how these people got to this beach, or where the beach was. I could imagine no answers to such questions that were not conventional.

What compelled me were the figures juxtaposed by this reunion: Eros and Psyche; the dreamer and the watcher.

What's essential is the idea of reunion; there has been provided, in reality, an exact replica of dream. Which event presumably erases the need for compensation or escape. And yet two primary responses suggest themselves: one can repudiate the translation or, in a kind of exorcism, one may permit the actual to supplant the dreamed. But immersion in time is a shock, involving real forfeits—of perfection, of the fantasy of eternity. That shock could be predicted. The surprise is that there are benefits to this perspective. To someone who feels, however briefly, without longing or regret, life on the shore, the life of dream, of waiting, seems suddenly tragic in its implications.

"Mild expectancy": what can be wrong with that? The lover hardly seems to be suffering. In his fatigue, he relaxes easily into the natural cycle, whereas the speaker's conscious determination places her outside these rhythms. This determination to stay awake is fueled by terror; it is, throughout the poem, a continuous, an active, choice. Expectancy, the sign of a heart set on the future—suddenly this seems a grave misuse of time. To dream, to yearn, or, in the realm of consciousness, to plan, to calculate— all a waste, a delusion. To live this way is to slight the earth. Not that the future isn't *real*. The delusion lies in projecting oneself into it indefinitely. One cannot live both there and here.

What the future holds is clear enough: the beach, the night world are dense with presentiments. Everywhere is stillness, the stillness of sleep which cannot help but resemble the stillness of death. What life there is regresses, the gulls, by example, transformed into clusters of cells. This is a warning, the message being: time is short. I hope a reader senses, in the poem's slow unreeling, interrupted with recurring commands, the degree to which this speaker is subject to the lure of the regressive. Her urgency reflects her own desire to capitulate and, in this sense, she sings to herself to keep awake, like someone on a vigil, a firewatch. There is, to put it plainly, an aspect of this which is pure pep talk.

The worst this poem can imagine is "what happens to the dreamers." The worst is to sleep through a life. By definition, it doesn't matter what the lover dreams; if he dreams, he isn't watching. Nor has the speaker's "weakness" been cured forever. Forever is, in itself, the dreamer's word. As for the peace passion gives: it could be called courage. Among the residual gifts of love is a composure, an openness to all experience, so profound it amounts to an acceptance of death. Or, more accurately, the future is no longer necessary. One is not rash, neither is one paralyzed by conservatism or hope. Simply, the sense of having lived, of having known one's fate, is very strong. And that sensation tells us what it is to live without the restrictions of fear. Such moments, in a way, have nothing to teach; they can be neither contrived nor prolonged by will. What they establish is a standard. Not forever, but for once it was possible to refuse consolation, to refuse the blindfold.

"Night Song" issues from, is made possible by, a sudden confidence. Whether finally or briefly, the soul can expose itself to "the revolutions," the massive cycles and upheavals of time. This is the greatest freedom we can know; its source, in the poem, is love, but the experience itself, the sense of being no longer "compelled," is an experience of autonomy. The lover's alert presence is necessary to confirm these sensations, since such experiences must be tested, witnessed.

What the speaker wants is *presence,* not union, dissolution, but the condition which preceded it. The choice is not between dreaming and lovemaking (another escape of self) but between dreaming and watching. Simultaneous consciousness, in other words—the exultant recognition of one soul by another. The ideal of balance has replaced the fantasy of incorporation. Contact of this sort seems to exist outside of time, beyond the laws of earth: all motion, whether toward fusion or separation, ends it. Motion is the first law. And as surely as the speaker's state dramatizes one of the soul's primary aims—to exist distinctly, to know where it ends and the blur of the world begins—so will the conflicting aim be asserted as the wish to dissolve, to be allied with, absorbed into another. The drive toward oblivion seems to me (as to many others) not a symptom of sickness but a true goal, and this wish of the self to do away with the very boundaries it has struggled to discover and maintain seems to me an endless subject, however we may try to subvert its grandeur.

I don't think of "Night Song" as a love poem. Love is a stimulus, and the advantage of writing out of situations of this kind seems to me an advantage of subject and attitude: one can write as lovers speak, of what is crucial in simple language.

The underlying subject seems to me to be individuality, without which no love can exist—groups do not love other groups. Love connects one irreplaceable being to another: the payment is terror of death, since if each person is unique, each death is singular, an eternal isolation. That we have common drives is consoling, but to dwell on them is to evade the issue of ultimate solitude. The relationships, in this poem, of the various forms of oblivion, of dream to orgasm to death, are less important than the perception of oblivion, in any form, as noncollective. If the pronouns in the last line are changed to "we" and "our," the line is instantly cloying, conventional; the sentiment thus expressed is paraphrased many times in the archives of Hallmark. Even if the second person is retained and only the possessive deleted, the thought turns vague—that in the second instance the line is also destroyed as a rhythmic unit is another problem. "You'll get oblivion"; "We'll get our oblivion": despite extreme discrepancies of tone, both sentences express the idea that oblivion is an alternative to self. Total eradication or complete union. "Night Song" suggests that the oblivion we ultimately achieve is an outpost of solitude from which the other is exiled—your oblivion is not mine; as your dream is not. This last line makes a mockery of placation; it damns the wish it grants. Against the relentless pronoun, the verbs are drumbeats, infantile, primitive. If what we want is oblivion, we are all lucky.

A last point. We are given to assume that morality depends on a regard for consequences. To some extent, this
is surely true. But the regard is felt as fear—in this light,
morality appears a product of intimidation. If **"Night
Song"** connects the idea of freedom to rejection of the
future, what is diminished, emotionally, is greed. Not
avidity, but compulsive acquisition, need projected into
time, the self straining to predict and provide for all foreseeable deficiency. I think the word *free* has no meaning
if it does not suggest freedom from greed. To live in the
present must mean being unerringly decisive, but choice,
there, is easier, not harder. I do not claim to live on this
plane, but I can imagine it.

It was clear to me long ago that any hope I had of writing real poetry depended on my living through common
experiences. The privileged, the too-protected, the man-
darin in my nature would have to be checked. At the
same time, I was wary of drama, of disaster too deliberately courted: I have always been too at ease with
extremes. What had to be cultivated, beyond a necessary
neutrality, was the willingness to be identified with others. Not with the single other, the elect, but with a human community. My wish was to be special. But the
representative life I wanted to record had somehow to be
lived.

Major experiences vary in form—what reader and writer
learn to do is recognize analogies. I watched my house
burn—in the category of major losses, this made only
the most modest start. Nor was it unexpected: I had spent
twenty years waiting to undergo the losses I knew to be
inevitable. I was obsessed with loss; not surprisingly, I
was also acquisitive, possessive. The two tendencies fed
each other; every impulse to extend my holdings increased
the fundamental anxiety. Actual loss, loss of mere property, was a release, an abrupt transition from anticipation
to expertise. In passing, I learned something about fire,
about its appetite. I watched the destruction of all that
had been, all that would not be again, and all that remained took on a radiance.

These are, in the deepest sense, ordinary experiences.
On the subject of change, of loss, we all attain to authority. In my case, the timing was efficient. I was in my late
thirties; perhaps I'd learned all I could about preparation, about gathering. The next lesson is abandon, letting
go.

Perhaps, too, in all this there were other massages to be
heard. And perhaps **"Night Song"** sounds much more of
a piece with my other work than this suggests. It wouldn't
surprise me. It seems these are the messages I'm equipped
to receive.

**Burton Raffel (essay date 1988)**

SOURCE: "The Poetry of Louise Glück," in *The Literary
Review*, Fairleigh Dickinson University, Vol. 31, No. 3,
Spring, 1988, pp. 261-73.

[*Raffel is an American poet, educator, critic, and translator. In this essay, he critiques Glück's poetry up to and
including* The Triumph of Achilles, *which Raffel judges
as not fulfilling the promise of the earlier work, and which
he assesses as sometimes disconcertingly bad.*]

Born in 1943, Louise Glück has published four volumes
of poetry: *Firstborn* (1968), *The House on Marshland*
(1975), *Descending Figure* (1980), and *The Triumph of
Achilles* (1985). She has won prizes and awards; she is
reasonably well-known. But the kind of acclaim I believe
she deserves has not come to her. She is not yet quite the
poet she is capable of being. In particular, her last book
represents a severe falling off (though the Poetry Society
of America gave it the 1985 Melville Cane Award and
The National Book Critics Circle gave it its 1986 poetry
prize: I do not pretend to infallibility). But the toughness,
complexity and, at its best, quite incredible insight and
hard, tested truth of her poetry, as well as its masterfully
lyric sweep, make her, at the least, one of the most interesting poets working today. Her work needs to be much
more fully and widely read, and thought about, and discussed.

*Firstborn,* obliquely dedicated to Stanley Kunitz, with
whom Glück had been studying ("to my teacher"), is rich
in promise. The poems are strong, well put-together, and,
as might be expected from a poet in her early twenties,
both faintly derivative and not yet fully individual. "South-
ward floated over / The vicious little houses, down / The
land." One thinks immediately, and properly, of early
Robert Lowell. But there is a clarity, and a complex lyricism, even in these early poems, which mark the young
Louise Glück as a poet of more than casual promise. "We
had codes / In our house. Like / Locks; they said / We
never lock / Our door to you. / And never did." Like her
early mentor, Kunitz, Glück is not prepared to sell out a
poem for the sake of an effect (as Lowell alas often did).
In poems like this she exhibits a conscientiousness, a
concern for her craft, and a determined non-pretentious-
ness; stout bulwarks upon which to build.

And there are poems in *Firstborn* that, for all their indebt-
ednesses, for all their youthful excesses, also transcend
both influences and juvenilities and flow clear and strong
to a wonderfully inexorable end:

**Memo from the Cave**

O love, you airtight bird,
My mouse-brown
Alibis hang upside-down
Above the pegboard
With its tangled pots
I don't have chickens for;
My lies are crawling on the floor
Like families but their larvae will not
Leave this nest. I've let
Despair bed
Down in your stead
And wet
Our quilted cover

So the rot-
scent of its pussy-foot-
ing fingers lingers, when it's over.

There is Lowell, here, and Anne Sexton. There is a super-abundance of the tricks that all poets, but especially young poets, dearly love. The last eight lines fairly explode with their own cleverness. And yet that cleverness does not obstruct or mask what is being said, which is both substantive and totally in key with what has come before. Let us not forget, either, that neither Anne Sexton nor Robert Lowell could do better than this at the same age. Indeed, the poems in Lowell's first book, *Land of Unlikeness,* have strength but far too much straining, featuring large gobs of clotted imagery, whole passages heavy with clumping, stumping over-passion, and in general frequently so over wrought (and overwrought) that one cannot give them credence—a point that Lowell himself proved by later re-writing or abandoning virtually everything in that first book. Glück at her early best is plainly far beyond that sort of thing.

Nor is **"Memo from the Cave"** the only fully achieved poem in *Firstborn*.

### Nurse's Song

As though I'm fooled. That lacy body managed to
    forget
That I have eyes, ears; dares to spring her
    boyfriends on the child.
This afternoon she told me, "Dress the baby in his
    crochet
Dress," and smiled. Just that. Just smiled,
Going. She is never here. O innocence, your
    bathinet
Is clogged with gossip, she's a sinking ship,
Your mother. Wouldn't spoil her breasts.
I hear your deaf-numb papa fussing for his tea.
    Sleep, sleep,
My angel, nestled with your orange bear.
Scream when her lover pats your hair.

Glück has commented, in a long and very helpful private letter: "I have little to say about *Firstborn*. For a long time I was ashamed of it (when I was writing the poems, of course, I felt quite otherwise). Then, as more years divided me from it, I came to feel toward it a sporadic tenderness. I didn't think it was good. I thought it was good for someone so young."

But **"Nurse's Song"** is not only very good, it also announces many of the subjects and attitudes of Glück's later and stronger poetry. The poet as social outsider; the strong but hopelessly ambivalent pull between child and surrounding, presumably nurturing adults; deft and deeply felt irony in the face of pretended rather than genuine truth ("I have known no happiness so based in truth," ends another poem in this first book); and a powerful longing for the peace and fulfillment that should have accompanied and embellished childhood but somehow, straitly and miserably, did not.

In the same private letter, Glück lays out a personal history that fully supports and to that extent helps to explain each and all of these themes. "From the first," she writes, "I belonged to my mother: I craved her absolute approval." And: "For about five years (at about age 18) I lived a strange, isolated life at home. In some ways, it was a quite wonderful time: a recreation of infancy. It went better the second time." She indicates, too, severe illness, both physical (epilepsy) and psychological. And not too long after *Firstborn* appeared, she notes, "in my late twenties, (I) went through a very long silence. Long, and agonizing. I wrote nothing for something more than a year."

Not surprisingly, the technique of *Firstborn* is distinctly more conventional than any of her later poetry. There are metrical poems, and a good deal of rhyming. Glück's letter is explicit about her reasons for dropping this more traditional approach in the poems that were to follow those of *Firstborn*: "I think I turned away from rhyme because I stopped wanting to write a harmonious whole. Also, I disliked the sense of virtuosity rhymed poems tended to produce. I didn't want, as a reader, to come away impressed with the writer's bravura. I didn't want skill to be so obvious."

*The House on Marshland* (1975), a full seven years after her first book, announces from its very first lines a vastly more mature, more individual, and more powerful poet. But it is not the subject matter that has changed, or the thematic pathways. The Glück who appears in this second book is not a different poet, but simply a very much better one. Here is the first poem:

### All Hallows

Even now this landscape is assembling.
The hills darken. The oxen
sleep in their blue yoke,
the fields having been
picked clean, the sheaves
bound evenly and piled at the roadside
among cinquefoil, as the toothed moon rises:

This is the barrenness
of harvest or pestilence.
And the wife leaning out the window
with her hand extended, as in payment,
and the seeds
distinct, gold, calling
*Come here*
*Come here, little one*

And the soul creeps out of the tree

The delicate ease with which Glück associates "harvest" and "pestilence" is typical both of her newfound authority and the stability in her attitudes and stances. Only the perpetual outsider could so casually link that which grows and nurtures to that which destroys. But only a truly mature poet could prepare the way for such a linkage with the patient portraiture of the first seven lines. Indeed, nothing in this poem is in any way labored. Nothing is obvious or calls attention to itself as lines and scenes in the earlier poems sometimes do. Glück wanted a non-virtuosic poetic, and—by age thirty-two—achieved it.

The intensely visualized scene of the first strophe is deeply realized: Glück is a poet who *sees* piercingly. But each item on which the poem's visual scan turns is given its plain, fair exposition. There is no scamping for effect, no subordination other than the natural, inevitable movement of the eye. And yet the poem's eye is kept focused, apparently effortlessly, on the scene as a whole, on the organic rather than the isolated effect. The control, the mastery, is quite simply dazzling.

Glück has learned, too, how to make leaping transitions, transitions she fashions so expertly that they do not seem to be hurdling the huge chasms that in truth they cross. Note, in the second half of the following poem, how time is crossed and re-crossed. We are first given the fact of pregnancy, then are taken back to the moment of conception ("waiting for my father"), then forward to the moment of birth ("spring . . . withdrew from me the absolute knowledge of the unborn"), then sharply forward to the mother, perhaps in a photograph, as seen by the child thirty years later ("the brick stoop where you stand, shading your eyes"), and then finally to an indefinite timelessness that is also the source of the book's title ("A marsh grows up around the house . . .").

**For My Mother**

It was better when we were
together in one body.
Thirty years. Screened
through the green glass
of your eye, moonlight
filtered into my bones
as we lay
in the big bed, in the dark,
waiting for my father.
Thirty years. He closed
your eyelids with
two kisses. And then spring
came and withdrew from me
the absolute
knowledge of the unborn,
leaving the brick stoop
where you stand, shading
your eyes, but it is
night, the moon
is stationed in the beech tree,
round and white among
the small tin markers of the stars:
Thirty years. A marsh
grows up around the house.
Schools of spores circulate
behind the shades, drift through
gauze flutterings of vegetation.

When Glück uses the chiming of internal rhyme, now, it is as unobtrusive as it possibly can be: "the small tin *markers* of the *stars*." Even the poem's powerful refrain,

"thirty years," is not signalled to us as a refrain. And not only is the refrain not set off by formal spacing, but each iteration is significantly separated, and by variable distances, in order not to call undue attention to what is a large part of the glue that holds the poem together. The visualization is vivid and intense: "moonlight / filtered into my bones," the then-fetus tells us, "as we lay / in the big bed, in the dark . . ."

Nor is the visualization simply aimless, merely what an eye happens to see. It is, like everything in this powerful book, tightly controlled. There is no notable amount of darkness in the poems of *Firstborn*. But *The House on Marshland* employs a pretty consistently nocturnal landscape. In **"All Hallows,"** the book's first poem, "the hills darken." The second poem opens with the word "night." The third poem, and one of my own favorites (I have anthologized it, as well as others of Glück's), **"Gretel in Darkness,"** opens with "moonlight" and ends with "nights" and a "black forest." The fourth poem is **"For My Mother,"** just reproduced, in which "we lay . . . in the dark." The fifth poem gives us "immense sunlight," but immediately frames it as "a relief." The sixth poem, **"The Magi,"** another favorite, ends with a "barn blazing in darkness." Shadows and mists, darkness and dusk, predominate in *The House on Marshland*—not oppressively, not pretentiously, but almost always there.

The sometimes savage stance of the first book, too (**"The Chicago Train,"** for example, ends: "I saw her pulsing crotch . . . the lice rooted in the baby's hair"), has now become a much more relaxed, even genial humor. The mordancy remains, and is indeed more effective. But it is not so far removed from us. "Summer approaches," ends **"To Autumn,"** "and the long / decaying days of autumn when I shall begin / the great poems of my middle period." "Do not think I am not grateful for your small / kindness to me," begins **"Gratitude."** "I like small kindnesses." There is a cutting edge to this apparent gentleness that the first book (and most young poets) cannot achieve. In **"The School Children"** we are shown how "all morning" the childrens' "mothers have labored / to gather the late apples, red and gold / like words of another language," and then we are immediately shown "those who wait behind great desks / to receive these offerings." One thinks of Sir Walter Scott facing up, manfully and accurately, to the superiorities of Jane Austen's work: "The Big Bow-wow strain I can do myself . . . but the exquisite touch which renders ordinary commonplace things and characters interesting *from the truth of the description and sentiment* is denied to me" (emphasis added). I think Glück would welcome exactly that praise, and clearly she deserves it.

Glück has also learned to look both inward and out, with equal facility and insight. Nor does she need vast quantities of words in order to encapsulate full, complete poetic statements.

**Departure**

My father is standing on a railroad platform.
Tears pool in his eyes, as though the face

149

glimmering in the window were the face of someone
he was once. But the other has forgotten;
as my father watches, he turns away,
drawing the shade over his face,
goes back to his reading.

And already in its deep groove
the train is waiting with its breath of ashes.

**Love Poem**

There is always something to be made of pain.
Your mother knits.
She turns out scarves in every shade of red.
They were for Christmas, and they kept you warm
while she married over and over, taking you
along. How could it work,
when all those years she stored her widowed heart
as though the dead come back.
No wonder you are the way you are,
afraid of blood, your women
like one brick wall after another.

The rhythmic progression in these two poems also requires some notice. **"Departure"** opens with an end-stopped first line, then swings easily into the kind of loping smoothness that is typical of this entire book, and typical too of Glück at her best. But **"Love Poem"** has a different theme, a different subject, and so has a different rhythm as well. The first three lines are rigidly end-stopped. Even when enjambement begins, in line 4, the poem does not take on a deep, sweeping movement until the next two sentences, each three heavily enjambed lines long, the second sentence ending the poem. Again, these are the furthest thing from obvious, underlined uses of poetic craft. But they are the mark of a master craftsman.

The wryly powerful lyricism of *Descending Figure* (1980), Glück's third book, is once more announced in the opening lines of the first poem, **"The Drowned Children"**: "You see, they have no judgment. / So it is natural that they should drown / first the ice taking them in / and then, all winter, their wool scarves / floating behind them as they sink / until at last they are quiet." It is hard to forget those "wool scarves," though the poet is scrupulous about not fussing over or sentimentalizing or even dramatizing them. The intrinsic truth of the lines takes care of all that for her. Glück is open about her debt to both T. S. Eliot and William Carlos Williams. They "are hugely important to me," she says in the letter already referred to. But at the end of **"The Drowned Children,"** when the lamentations rise and float over the frozen water, the sparse drama is entirely her own: *"What are you waiting for / come home, come home, lost / in the waters, blue and permanent."* Not many poets know how to use echoic repetitions like "come home, come home." The unfortunate tendency usually is to simply echo away all through a poem, as if the fact of echoing was itself significant. Not only does Glück prepare the way for such quasi-refrains, but she has absorbed and made her own Williams's large tact, his determinedly non-melodramatic discretion.

The influence of Eliot, which begins to manifest itself quite openly in *Descending Figure* (and becomes too obvious in her most recent book), is not so beneficent. Nor is it unconnected to a tendency to over elaborate descriptions, to landscapes in which some of the pigmentation suddenly strikes the reader as applied, laid on, rather than instrinsic. The second poem in a five-poem sequence, **"The Garden"**—and I shall say something more of Glück's growing fondness for such sequences in a moment—opens with a passage that is all too like many passages in *Four Quartets,* especially *Burnt Norton.* "The garden admires you. / For your sake it smears itself with green pigment, / the ecstatic red of the roses, / so that you will come to it with your lovers." Glück notes, in the same letter already referred to, that "'Four Quartets' I've liked least and read least." But the echoes seem both unmistakable and unfortunate—doubly so, because what is being said begins to become less important than the manner of saying it. "Admit that it is terrible to be like them," the second part of **"The Garden"** concludes, "beyond harm." That says, frankly, a great deal less than the poet appears to think it does. If it says anything, to be perfectly blunt, what it says is slight, even sentimental, and not worth saying—certainly not worth the skill and attention of a poet like Louise Glück.

The unevennesses of *Descending Figure,* though disturbing and quite marked, do not deeply disfigure the book. In the first part of **"The Garden,"** for example, Glück manages in three short, end-stopped lines to create a lyrical flow, as well as to analyze a profoundly true insight in utterly masterful style: "And then the losses, / one after another, / all supportable." This is brave as well as useful, cogent as well as quietly packed with strength. There are still further explorations of the "other," notably the male other—an exploration begun in the second book. In **"Palais des Arts"** a woman watches a small boy throwing "bits of bread into the water." The boy is apparently her son. The poem ends: "She can't touch his arm in innocence again. / They have to give that up and begin / as male and female, thrust and ache." In **"Aphrodite"** we are told that "A woman exposed as rock / has this advantage: / she controls the harbor . . . / her thighs cemented shut, barring / the fault in the rock." (The poem seems to me unrelievedly bitter, but Glück has assured me that it "was intended to be funny," adding that "some women find it so. Though not all. Some women take it for an earnest, fierce political statement. No men find it funny.") Glück's stance is not always sympathetic to women, by the way. In **"Portland, 1968"** she writes: "And the sea triumphs, / like all that is false / all that is fluent and womanly."

There is also a fine set of poems that begin to explore the endless cycles of human existence—a natural development in a maturing poet. As before, Glück can distill into a single line an entire philosophy, beautifully expressed. "What doesn't move, the snow will cover," she writes in **"Thanksgiving."** It is a poem quite as comfortable with the subtle, shifting interrelationships of external physical world and internalized human idea and emotion as anything in Wallace Stevens. So too **"Porcelain Bowl,"** where the references to (but not echoes of) Stevens are more pronounced still. "In a lawn chair, the analogous / body of a woman is arranged, / and in this light / I cannot see what time has done to her." The governing phrase, "in this light," seems peculiarly, uniquely her own. In **"Happiness,"** which opens with a "man and a woman" lying "on a white bed," the ending is a triumphant, transcendent embodiment of the title's assertion. They are asleep, it is morning. "Almost over this room / the sun is gliding. / *Look at your face,* you say, / holding your own close to me / to make a mirror. / How calm you are. And the burning wheel / passes gently over us." Perhaps the most powerful poem in the book is **"The Gift,"** again a favorite and one I have anthologized.

### The Gift

Lord, You may not recognize me
speaking for someone else.
I have a son. He is
so little, so ignorant.
He likes to stand
at the screen door, calling
*oggie, oggie,* entering
language, and sometimes
a dog will stop and come up
the walk, perhaps
accidentally. May he believe
this is not an accident?
At the screen
welcoming each beast
in love's name, Your emissary.

I know of no other poet now writing who could have written this poem. To use a pianistic metaphor, the "touch" is both utterly sure and absolutely individual.

But there are the strained, straining poems. And there are the poem sequences, six of them. In a book of only forty-eight pages that constitutes a significant presence. There are only two poem sequences in *Firstborn,* which is both a longer and more closely printed book. There is one two-part poem, and no true poem sequence at all, in *The House on Marshland,* which seems to me the most fully consistent of her collections to date. And since I find only two of *Descending Figure'*s poem sequences entirely convincing, and since *The Triumph of Achilles* (it has sixty pages), about which I have serious doubts, features no fewer than eight poem sequences, some of them quite long, I think some emphasis needs to be placed on these facts. And some explanation, no matter how tentative (and quite possibly how wrong), needs to be ventured for so errant and probably misguided a direction.

It should be said unequivocally that there is nothing intrinsically flawed about a desire to write longer poems, including longer poems composed out of shorter poems, some of those smaller poems having been initially published separately. Many superb poets, T.S. Eliot among them, have followed this practice with obvious success. The problem is not in the idea but in the fact that "Between the idea / And the reality . . . Falls the Shadow." I

have alluded to the straining in the sequence, **"The Garden."** If there is a unifying theme, it is overly intellectualized, insufficiently embodied. The next sequence, **"Descending Figure,"** is shorter (only three component poems) and structurally more fully, more tightly realized: it is one of the two sequences that seem really to work, in her third book. Built around the stark fact that Glück's parents lost their first child, also a daughter, seven days after the child's birth, **"Descending Figure"** moves carefully across a limited and sharply controlled poetic terrain. The same should be said of **"Illuminations,"** again composed of only three parts and again built around the growth of the poet's son. (Oddly, the poet says that she no longer likes this sequence. It seems to me finely done, ending with the child at "the kitchen window / with his cup of apple juice. / Each tree forms where he left it, / leafless, trapped in his breath.")

But **"Tango,"** in four parts, tries, I suspect, to do too much with the relationship between sisters—tries, that is, to find and assert truths that are only doubtfully true. Or, to put it differently, the sequence attempts to do more than the material will allow. Why are some sisters chosen by "the light"? "How they tremble," we are told, "as soon as the moon mounts them, brutal and sisterly . . ." If this is no more than a reference to physical maturation (i.e., menstruation), it is vastly overblown. If it is a reference to something else, the poem does not reveal what that something else might be. Nor do the succeeding lines help much: "I used to watch them, / all night absorbed in the moon's neutral silver / until they were finally blurred, disfigured . . ." So too the relationship between the sisters seems over-dramatized: "You were the gold sun on the horizon. / I was the judgement, my shadow / preceded me, not wavering . . ." This is not convincing, nor is it illuminating. The poem continues: "Your bare feet / became a woman's feet, always / saying two things at once." This is either obvious or pretentious; in either case, it does not make for good poetry.

**"Dedication to Hunger,"** which has five parts, seems to strike poses rather than directly deal with its subject, the relationship between daughters (and mothers) and their fathers. The grandfather's "kiss would have been / clearly tender," the second poem ends. "Of course, of course. Except / it might as well have been / his hand over her mouth." Not only is there nothing in the poem, or the sequence, to justify this final line, there is about it a strong sense of overstatement, an unpleasant flavor of far too easily achieved drama—that is, melodrama. **"Lamentations,"** the final sequence in *Descending Figure,* similarly mythologizes—but abstractly, unconvincingly—a basic human context, namely Adam and Eve in the Garden of Eden. The very language glitters too artificially. "But god was watching. / They felt his gold eye / projecting flowers on the landscape." This is ingenious, it is felicitously phrased. But it is also terribly intellectualized; it works far too hard at saying something that does not require anything like so much effort—and which, once said, does not have anything like the import, the weight, that the poet seems to think it has. "Against the black sky," we read in the third of the sequence's four poems, "they saw the massive argument of light." This too is strained and straining, trying to be and to say more than it either is or can possibly be.

With only two or three exceptions, *The Triumph of Achilles* seems to me to suffer from the same deficiencies, not only in its many and very long sequences, but in most of its shorter poems as well. Glück is too fine a poet, and I have much too much respect for her work, to belabor the point—or the book. Here is **"The Reproach."** Let me say in advance that I find it an embarrassingly bad performance, full of tritenesses, unfortunate echoes of H.D., and about as totally unconvincing as might be.

### The Reproach

You have betrayed me, Eros.
You have sent me
my true love.

On a high hill you made
his clear gaze;
my heart was not
so hard as your arrow.

What is a poet
without dreams?
I lie awake; I feel
actual flesh upon me,
meaning to silence me—
Outside, in the blackness,
over the olive trees,
a few stars.

I think this is a bitter insult:
that I prefer to walk
the coiled paths of the garden,
to walk beside the river
glittering with drops
of mercury. I like to lie
in the wet grass beside the river,
running away, Eros,
not openly, with other men,
but discreetly, coldly—

All my life
I have worshipped the wrong gods.
When I watch the trees
on the other side,
the arrow in my heart
is like one of them,
swaying and quivering.

This is perhaps the single worst poem in the book, and easily the worst by Louise Glück that I have ever seen. But the eight sequences in the book are almost as slack. **"Marathon,"** a nine-part sequence that occupies eleven printed pages, is a curious mixture of occasionally brilliant lines, flooded and ultimately drowned in a veritable sea of words—and many of them derivative words. "Finally, this is what we craved, / this lying in the bright light without distinction—/ we who would leave behind / exact

records." The echoes of T.S. Eliot, at such moments, are deafeningly loud. There are others. Even when she creates a viable image, Glück seems unable to leave it alone. "In the river, things were going by—/ a few leaves, a child's boat painted red and white." This would be a lovely pair of lines—if they were all Glück had written. But she goes on, the period after "white" being in fact a comma: "its sail stained by the water." This may seem a small matter; to a nonpoet it may seem even niggling. But it is neither small nor niggling—and there is much more of the same sort, sometimes a flickering alternation of bad and good passages, all jumbled hard upon each other. "And, where there are cities, these dissolve too, *the sighing gardens* [BAD: trite], all the young girls / eating chocolates in the courtyard [GOOD], *slowly / scattering the colored foil* [BAD: going on far too long]" (emphasis added). There is a great deal of what strikes me as pure verbiage, essentially empty of content. "I see / that ice is more powerful than rock, than mere resistance." "The calm of darkness / is the horror of Heaven." "Why did we worship clarity, / to speak, in the end, only each other's names, / to speak, as now, not even whole words, / only vowels?" "What began as love for you / became a hunger for structure." And so on. There is even a bit of secondhand Ernest Hemingway, of all things. "When my lover touches me, what I feel in my body / is like the first movement of a glacier over the earth, / as the ice shifts, dislodging great boulders, hills / of solemn rock."

**"The End of the World,"** a three-part sequence, seems like thinned-out talk, going nowhere—until the final, brilliant line: "There is no god / who will save one man." But nothing builds toward this line; it rises, solitary, out of the limp three pages that precede it—and no matter how brilliant, a final line must stand on something in order to reach any sort of proper height.

What has happened? "I ask you," says the fourth and last part of **"Baskets,"** "how much beauty / can a person bear?" Is it that the poet has at least for the moment become The Poet, and also the Prophet? There are prophetic poems in *The Triumph of Achilles,* and they are not good poems. In **"Morning,"** for example, we are told that "mothers weep at their daughters' weddings, / everyone knows that, though / for whose youth one cannot say." This is clearly not Glück's proper strength; she does this sort of thing drably. In **"Elms,"** which reads like an exercise poem, written to keep the machine running, the parts oiled, we begin with a sad Eliot echo: "All day I tried to distinguish / need from desire." This too is not Glück's forte, any more than is the last part of the poem: "I have been looking / steadily at these elms / and seen the process that creates / the writhing, stationary tree / is torment, and have understood / it will make no forms but twisted forms." But there is nothing to this, either in the poem or out of it. *Why?* we are obliged to demand. Why is it "torment" that creates the tree, or elm trees in particular? What is this about? The final line has all the force, and also all the credibility, of a famous television commercial, in which the late Orson Welles proclaims that the vintner for whom he speaks "will sell no wine before its time."

I do not mean to mock Louise Glück. She is an immensely fine poet. But for the moment, inexplicably, she strikes me as a poet who has lost her way. I cannot believe that she will not emerge, again triumphant, as the poet of *The House on Marshland* and *Descending Figure*. As she herself writes, in one of two beautifully realized poems in this most recent book, **"Seated Figure"**: "You could no more heal yourself / than I could accept what I saw."

---

**Glück's achievement in *The House on Marshland*:**

Just as the most depressing thing about ordinary well-meaning verse is its predictability—in logic, emotional "curve," and choice of language, so the most profound source of elation in reading a new species of poet is the surprise in every line as a new voice and a new sensibility declares itself. Glück no longer sounds at all like Hart Crane, Lowell, or Lawrence; she sounds only like herself.

*Helen Vendler, "A Quarter of Poetry," in* The New York Times Book Review, *April 6, 1975, pp. 4-5; 29-35; 37-38.*

---

**Lynn Keller  (essay date 1990)**

SOURCE: "'Free / of Blossom and Subterfuge': Louise Glück and the Language of Renunciation," in *World, Self, Poem: Essays on Contemporary Poetry from the "Jubilation of Poets,"* edited by Leonard M. Trawick, Kent State University Press, 1990, pp. 120-29.

[*Keller is an educator, a critic and the author of* Re-Making It New: Contemporary American Poetry and the Modernist Tradition. *In the following essay, she adopts a feminist critical perspective on the negative treatment of the female in Glück's first four books. The critic analyzes the relationship of the role of woman and that of poet and finds that, for the most part, Glück views the two as mutually exclusive.*]

It is a commonplace of American feminist criticism that, historically, linkage of the words *woman* and *poet* has yielded a powerful contradiction in terms, inevitably confronted by women attempting verse. Because those aspiring to the male status of poet have been caught in a conflict with their own female identity, as Gilbert and Gubar observe, "at its most painful the history of women's poetry is a story of struggle against . . . self-loathing" (xxiii). The poetry of Louise Glück testifies that being a woman continues to some contemporaries to seem an impediment to being a poet, and that women writers today may still struggle against consequent self-loathing. At the same time, Glück's achievement suggests that these pressures may, by providing major themes, compel or even enable women

to write. Her often extremely negative sense of womanhood—as both a biologically and socially determined experience—has been crucial in shaping the language, tone, and style, as well as the thematic content of her poetry. Her four collections of poems develop toward increasingly complex thought and flexible style, reflecting her changing responses to the dilemma of being at once poet and woman.

The shock-value of the opening poem in Glück's first volume, *Firstborn* (1968), asserts her desire to be different—perhaps especially her desire to stand apart from other women poets, just as earlier women struggled not to be taken for stereotypical "female songbirds" [as poet Louise Bogan put it in a 1935 letter]. Here is the complete poem, entitled **"The Chicago Train"**:

> Across from me the whole ride
> Hardly stirred: just Mister with his barren
> Skull across the arm-rest while the kid
> Got his head between his mama's legs and slept. The
>     poison
> That replaces air took over.
> And they sat—as though paralysis preceding death
> Had nailed them there. The track bent south.
> I saw her pulsing crotch . . . the lice rooted in that
>     baby's hair.

To begin one's book with such flaunted offensiveness—both in the speaker's implied politics (her attitudes toward the lower classes) and in her ghastly perspective—is a gesture of defiant individualism. Glück's mature work is neither so histrionic nor so technically awkward as this, but the poem provides a preview of her obsessions. It is immediately clear that Glück feels revolted by her bondage to the human body and the physical world. In her work, physical being is always a *memento mori;* the child always desires to press back toward the womb and prenatal weightless unconsciousness; and the woman's body, particularly the genitals that are the locus of her sexual desire, is the horrifying center of the death-that-infests-life. The pulsing of the crotch in this poem suggests sexual arousal, as if the woman were stimulated—willingly or not—by the pressure of the child's head. Here we have an indication of Glück's early preoccupation with woman's horrifying lack of control over her sexual desires—something that her poetry attempts to compensate for and counter.

That first poem is only one of many portraits and dramatic monologues in *Firstborn* through which the young poet examines the situations of women in her society, finding nearly all of them revolting. **"The Edge"** typifies the volume's sensationalized view of the wife's misery in marriage. The husband is bored, hardened, and associated with predatory violence; the wife is angry, wounded, yet subservient. Her role: bitterly to bear his children, tolerate his sexual demands, and sustain herself on his leavings: "Mornings, crippled with this house, / I see him toast his toast and test / His coffee, hedgingly. The waste's my breakfast."

A poet's vision, some early poems condescendingly assert, is far superior to that of the ordinary woman who accepts the roles of wife and mother—roles determined not only by society but by the woman's biological urges. Thus the speaker sets herself above her fertile, giggling relative in **"My Cousin in April."** The cousin, absorbed in playing with her first child and pregnant with her second, is seen as having given into the "stir" "in her body" despite anger at her husband. The cost of such accommodation is insensitivity, obliviousness: "she passes what I paused / To catch, the early bud phases, on the springing grass." In **"The Wound"** the paisley pattern of the speaker's bedroom walls is "like a plot / Of embryos," and "ripe things" are the walls of a prison. The association of woman with childbearing and physical life is for young Glück a deathly trap the female artist must struggle to avoid.

In view of Glück's aversion to the women's roles that conventionally accompany adult sexuality, it is not surprising that her work is filled with nostalgia for the presexual innocence of childhood. In the emblematic piece, **"Flowering Plum,"** from her second collection, *The House on Marshland* (1975), the adult woman looks with worldly cynicism and some longing at her neighbor's adolescent daughter who gives herself with wholehearted joy to spring and the thrush's "routine / message of survival." The innocent girl sits under the plum tree

> as the mild wind
> floods her immaculate lap with blossoms, greenish
> white
> and white, leaving no mark, unlike
> the fruit that will inscribe
> unraveling dark stains in heavier winds, in
> summer.

The poet who would inscribe meaning upon the world, if she is a woman, inevitably finds herself stained, battered, and written upon by the world. She remains the object rather than the writing subject, and that is the way of nature, not just patriarchy. Once again, the locus of vulnerability is her lap—the girl's not yet pulsing but vulnerable crotch.

Attempting to thwart this natural cycle of ripening and unraveling from childhood's spring to womanhood's summer, Glück's response in her personal history would seem to have been anorexia. Anorexia is both a retreat from adult sexuality to a childlike state safe from sexual drives, and an assertion of control—two desirable things for those who share Glück's sense of woman's powerlessness. The urges behind anorexia, and the relation between those urges and the drives behind poetic creation, are the subjects of **"Dedication to Hunger,"** an important sequence from Glück's third volume *Descending Figure* (1980).

The early sections of the poem suggest that coming into womanly sexuality is a loss and a deprivation, that even in the most loving instances, a man's kiss, "might as well [be] a hand over [the woman's] mouth." Gendered roles and heterosexuality itself silence and suffocate, perhaps even impose starvation on a woman. The fourth section depicts the anorexic's consciously chosen dedication to hunger as a way of defying death and renouncing female sexuality:

> because a woman's body
> *is* a grave; it will accept
> anything. I remember
> lying in bed at night
> touching the soft, digressive breasts,
> touching, at fifteen,
> the interfering flesh
> that I would sacrifice
> until the limbs were free
> of blossom and subterfuge

Eradicating one's blossom means sacrificing the body that invites male domination and silencing. Glück's rejection of female sexuality, then, does not simply reflect self-hatred. Paradoxically, it enacts positive self-assertion, since she believes that a woman may escape man's control only outside of the gendered roles of wife or lover. Only without her sexuality and the fleshy curves in which it is embodied can she be sure of having or creating an identity as subject rather than object. The anorexic's starvation, as clinicians put it, "is a statement about autonomy, not an attempt at self-destruction" [Garfinkel and Garner, *Anorexia Nervosa: A Multidemensional Perspective*, 1982]. Glück in an interview confirms this point when she identifies "the anorexic nightmare" as "the being taken over by sensation, and obliterated by it, obscured by it, your individual outline . . . dissolved in some larger shape." For Glück, denial of her body does not entail suppression of her essential womanhood, for, as she explains in **"Lamentations,"** God at the creation divided humankind not into two but into three: "the man, the woman, and the woman's body" (*Descending*). As she sees it, the woman's fulfillment may depend on her subduing the woman's body.

In starving away not just blossom but also "subterfuge," Glück attempts to purge herself of the deceptions and evasions patriarchy has long associated with women. Just as man and woman are, for Glück, opposed as "thrust and ache," men in her work have a rigidly phallic singleness, while women tend toward the bending, fluent, multiple or, in negative terms, the duplicitous. This duplicity is closely associated with the female body and also with female language. In **"Tango"** she addresses her younger sister: "Your bare feet / became a woman's feet, always / saying two things at once" (*Descending*). Rather than being a dancer like her sister, she has become a "watcher," as if by remaining on the sidelines she could keep from female double-talk. In **"Portland, 1968,"** female subterfuge, contrasted with upright singularity, is again tied to language. A stiff figure, presumably male, is likened to fixed rock that is being eroded by the sea's "transparent waves of longing":

> everything fixed is marred.
> And the sea triumphs,
> like all that is false,
> all that is fluent and womanly.

> (*Descending*)

Glück's words suggest her ambivalence toward what is womanly: the triumph of the womanly sea (and, implicitly, of the female speaker) is at once a tragic prevailing of the morally inferior ("false") and a valuable victory of what is live over what is static and death-like. One might expect a woman poet to value the association of women and fluency—linguistic fluency being the ability to control words effortlessly, smoothly—but it seems that for Glück fluency is too closely associated with stereotypically female gushing, with the absence of control over one's falsifying tongue.

The closing sections of **"Dedication to Hunger"** make it clear that the kind of poet who may be likened metaphorically to the anorexic does not aspire to write with fluency. Glück explains that as an adolescent dedicating herself to the sacrifice of her "soft, digressive" flesh,

> I felt
> what I feel now, aligning these words—
> it is the same need to perfect,
> of which death is the mere byproduct.
>
> (*Descending*)

The anorexic distinguishing herself through self-denial becomes "like a god" in her "power" to expose her own frame and to reverse the natural progress of temporal development. The poet, too, wants to remove young life from the progress of time, making it invulnerable to decay:

> I saw
> the hard, active buds of the dogwood
> and wanted, as we say, to capture them,
> to make them eternal.
>
> (*Deending*)

Since the natural world is infused with time, such a poetic achievement is as god-like, as supernatural, as the anorexic's.

In the fleshless rigor of her style, Glück establishes a language of almost super-human renunciation, the poetic equivalent of the anorexic's "expos[ure of] the underlying body." The driving principle is reduction. Her collections are of minimal length. She pares away at her lyrics to keep them short, restricts her lines to three or four stresses, and so concentrates on monosyllabic words that she often generates entirely monosyllabic lines. When not limiting herself to simple short declarations, Glück tends to chop sentences into small units, often rearranging them so the effect will not be fluid.

Glück's characteristic tone, which some reviewers (Greg Kuzma, for instance) have mistakenly heard as unfeeling, is one of enforced restraint. Pressured by nearly overwhelming fears and longings, the poet as metaphorical anorexic triumphs by controlling the urge to cry out, by forcing herself to speak calmly: "You see, they have no judgment. / So it is natural that they should drown" (*Descending*). Although employing conversational elements ("you see"), her manner avoids the relaxed talk or confessional outpouring common among contemporary women poets. Such apparent naturalness would be suspect; as she says in one poem, "nakedness in women is always a pose" (*Triumph*). Not surprisingly, some aspects of Glück's style involve adopting conventionally masculine modes such as a reasoned explanatory manner and frequently abstract diction. When not abstract, her diction tends to be simple, providing the reader with the bare minimum of contextual information. Glück's figures often employ jarring linkages. Near incompatibility of their contributing elements—their derivation from disparate realms or their contrasting connotations—forces recognition of their separateness, as if each were a separate bone exposed in the poem's skeleton. Even her frequent use of the definite article reinforces the distinct outlines of semantic and syntactic units. As Glück put it in an interview: "My poems are vertical poems. They aspire and they delve. They don't expand. They don't elaborate, or amplify."

In that interview, conducted while Glück was working on her 1985 collection, *The Triumph of Achilles,* she immediately added that she was presently trying to write poems that *would* elaborate and amplify, precisely because she had "so clearly seen the absence of this strategy" in her earlier work. Her efforts to put some flesh on the bones of her poetry have, I think, meant true aesthetic growth, evident in much of *Descending Figure,* as well as *The Triumph of Achilles*.

Ironically, the female "duplicity" that in some contexts so troubles her has been crucial to her poetic success. Her best works capitalize on the rich "subterfuge" of paradox, oxymoron, homophone, and pun, as well as the suggestive power available in even the most pared-down phrases. These strengths are particularly evident in her most recent collection, in which she imposes less rigorous divisions than before between language and life, between spoken language and body language, between man and woman, even between woman and her body. Rather than taking the fanatical either or stance of the anorexic, she now tries, in her own words, to present something "in its full complication—the yes and no being said at the same time."

Formally, this means she allows herself greater syntactical flexibility and more variation in descriptive manner. She even provides luxurious lists of blossoms and fruits: "camellia, periwinkle, rosemary in crushing profusion" (*Triumph*); "Crates of eggs, papaya, sacks of yellow lemons" (*Triumph*). Where her early collections contained only one or two poems of more than one section, her recent works are often sequences of lyrics; in *The Triumph of Achilles,* nearly a third of the poems are sequences, some with as many as nine sections. This expansion permits greater emotional range and fuller consideration of a subject.

Thematically, Glück has not relinquished her yearnings for an unchanging absolute, but at least in parts of *The Triumph of Achilles* she now admits her need for others and her need to give in to need itself. Significantly, in this collection anorexia and hunger are no longer dominating images, though the problem of desire and the need to restrict its satisfaction remains. This volume's preoccupation is with a solitude necessary for the artist, one thwarted by the body's erotic fulfillment, just as the anorexic's urge to expose underlying structure would be countered by satisfying her hunger. But where *Descending Figure* stressed the god-like triumph of the anorexic perfector, *The Triumph of Achilles* regards human imperfection and yearning with more compassionate ambivalence. Thus, in a poem tellingly titled **"Liberation,"** Glück's speaker relinquishes her (anorexic) need to be in the position of control. She lays down the phallic gun of the hunter to take up the role of fleeing rabbit. This reversal is prompted by her recognition that resistance to life's processes condemns one to a condition of death-in-life, while willing participation in life's motion-toward-death is at least a temporary freedom:

Only victims have a destiny.

And the hunter, who believed
whatever struggles
begs to be torn apart:

that part is paralyzed.

(*Triumph*)

Like Achilles in the title poem, she lets the mortal part free of her god-like ambitions and is rewarded with love as well as loss.

In *The Triumph of Achilles,* the body, its hungers and attachments, the "part that loved / the part that was mortal," are more genuinely appreciated than before. In **"The Embrace"** Glück's lover enables her to relearn the "original need" to be touched, leading her back to "a kind of splendor / as all that is wild comes to the surface" (*Triumph*). The volume overflows with passion, and that passion is welcomed more often than before. Glück seems now to believe that while one cannot simultaneously be a poet and a lover, one can appreciate being each in sequence. She emphasizes the joy of sensually satisfied lovers, even when they have been changed "to a mute couple." Their desires for language and a permanent verbal record are incompatible with their desires for a transitory physical union that dissolves ego boundaries and transcends language, but the situation seems merely ironic, not desperate or threatening:

Then why did we worship clarity,
to speak, in the end, only each other's names,
to speak, as now, not even whole words,
only vowels?
Finally, this is what we craved,
this lying in the bright light without distinction—
we who would leave behind
exact records.

(*Triumph*)

**"The Reproach"** also presents this conflict humorously; the poet reproaches Eros because he has given her what every woman supposedly dreams of finding—her "true love." In so doing, he has nearly deprived her of her art:

What is a poet
without dreams?
I lie awake; I feel
actual flesh upon me,
meaning to silence me—

(*Triumph*)

Art depends on desire; the artist, Glück still insists, must remain dedicated to hunger.

Yet there has been a shift in emphasis. She no longer sees this renunciation as a distinctly female necessity or as something to counter particularly female weakness. Nor is her abstinence governed by the terror of growth and development, by the anorexic's fanatical devotion to starvation, or, for the most part, by the disturbing abhorrence of female sexuality that characterized her preceding volumes. Thus, in the poem **"Summer,"** both she and her artist husband relinquish without regret the sating passions of summer for the creative isolation of autumn. As desiring, separate individuals, "We were artists again, my husband. / We could resume the journey" (*Triumph*).

A happy ending to one poet's "struggle against self-loathing"? No, nothing so reassuringly simple. Certainly from a feminist perspective, Glück's increasing acceptance of herself as a woman, and her higher valuation of female sexuality and of female linguistic powers mark definite progress. Yet any individual's ability to change is inevitably limited. Glück's poetics were founded on the anorexic's renunciative orientation, and though flexed and stretched somewhat, they remain largely unchanged. The attitudes expressed in her recent work also remain strongly linked to those in her earlier collections. That Glück's model in her latest volume is the male hero Achilles indicates the continuation of a male-centered perspective. Some of her recent poems still present her own sexual desire and orgasmic experience as imprisoning forces before which she is despicably and terrifyingly out of control. Glück has not passed beyond self-loathing, and this makes reading her work still a profoundly uncomfortable experience. Yet it would be false to suggest that in Glück's case the ongoing nature of her struggle has greatly restricted the power of her art; on the contrary, one could argue that this inner battle is precisely what electrifies her poetry. Nor should feminist readers and critics turn away from her and others like her, devoting attention solely to artists who themselves bring feminist analyses to bear upon their experience or whose more inspiring personal histories better point us toward positive change. Feminist scholarship will be enriched by remaining in touch with the varied perspectives of the many women writing today, including those like Louise Glück, whose poetry raises crucial, disturbing issues about women's complicity in their own oppression.

**Calvin Bedient (essay date 1991)**

SOURCE: "'Man Is Altogether Desire'?," in *Salmagundi*, Nos. 90-91, Spring-Summer, 1991, pp. 212-30.

*[In this review excerpt, Bedient discusses Glück's* Ararat, *finding the direct tone to be different than her previous volumes. Nonetheless, the critic finds the collection to be successful due to the precision and concentration of poems.]*

Desire has become the most commonplace of topics, and not only because, like the weather, it is always with us, but because it doesn't know what to make of itself now that its own gaudy theological and philosophical trappings have been emptied of gas, like giant passenger balloons, and cut into rectangles and put on the wall as abstract art.

What poets (the house experts on the subject) may now regret is that walking naked is all that's left to them. The Plotinian *There,* the Fall, millions of flaming swords drawn from the things of mighty Cherubim, the light that never was on sea or land, progress, usury, supreme fictions—the whole panoply of grand and cranky themes has rusted.

Stripped-down desire—desire without transcendental dignities—is the burden of new books of poems by Louise Glück, Robert Hass, and Robert Pinsky. All three poets are in what looks like mid-career and all three are among the finest now writing in English. And partly because their new books are so marvellously accomplished, one wants to say that this is a rich time for American poetry. And I believe it is. But if the big themes are dead? If the ladder has been lifted from the rag and bone shop of the heart? Or is desire, for all its present sorriness, even yet a great subject?

With some ambivalent exceptions, the three poets treat it as merely inescapable and necessary: you will dress your bones in rags, won't you, rather than walk naked?. . . .

In *Ararat,* Glück's few allusions to Greek tragedy may essay a heroic resonance, as if she thought desire could still be construed as tragic; but is she not, all the same, an A+ analysand who's been sealed in the almost airless bubble of her own lucidity? (Her commitment to this last *is* her heroism.). . . .

Still, a certain passionate toughness in Louise Glück makes you feel that this poet *could* have been a Greek heroine—Electra, perhaps. That is why she's scary when she steps into the delicate, habitually evasive sphere of family grievances (though Sylvia Plath and Sharon Olds have so opened the way that it's now posted: *Anything goes*). She enters and the walls tremble; the sphere is so small, in its way, so unarmed, in its way, and she—she is equipped with a child's accusations of betrayal and deprivation, with her adult, fearful intelligence, and with the sharpest verbal instrument around.

Not that she raises her voice; she doesn't need to—she makes every word say, *I am only going to tell you this once*; she is all deliberation, and then some. But her topics scathe: indeed, they telescope into the one topic, desire as the scathed and the scathing, not least the self-

scathing ("in childhood," she says in the final poem, **"First Memory,"** "I thought / that pain meant / I was not loved. / It meant I loved"). Her burden is less the legendary loss of a fusional bliss than the heart's reasonable/unreasonable fixation on it. The heart! The instant it gains consciousness it is kicked out the door and it reacts as if something had injured it! And you don't comfort *Louise.* She isn't having any of it. No, you respect her instead:

> It's very sad, really: all my life, I've been praised
> for my intelligence, my powers of language, of
>   insight.
> In the end, they're wasted—
>
> I never see myself,
> standing on the front steps, holding my sister's
>   hand.
> That's why I can't account
> for the bruises on her arm, where the sleeve ends.
>
> In my own mind, I'm invisible; that's why I'm
>   dangerous.

This in a poem called **"The Untrustworthy Speaker."** *Ararat,* even more than her earlier great successes, *The House on Marshland* and *Descending Figure* (I thought less well of *The Triumph of Achilles*), is full of a snow-maiden's dry-ice kisses.

It substitutes a knife-edge directness for this poet's redoubtable ability to cast spells. The almost eerily exquisite dream-hushed scenes of the earlier books will be missed by many, but maybe this new, hard tone is something braver, at once more modern and more severely classical. Metaphorical transformations, rippling across whole poems, and rhythmic hypnosis, at which this poet can be so astonishing, and a *remotely* intimate tone—these gifts are kept back. In their place, a Long Island house; a mother brooding over the death of her third child, a girl; another daughter, blond, who crowds the poet at the watering hole of maternal love; a snoozing father practicing for death by covering his face with the *Times*; and the older living daughter, Louise, the dark one, the one who sees all this, the one who counts the short change of love and doesn't say anything, the one whose skin jumps with the truth like a frog even as she simulates being something without nerves, without anger, "Not inert: still. / A piece of wood. A stone" (**"Parodos"**). One summer in Paris, when she sat for her portrait each day after returning from the convent school, only the painter noticed how it really was: "a face already so controlled, so withdrawn, / and too obedient, the clear eyes saying / *If you want me to be a nun, I'll be a nun*" (**"Appearances"**).

*Ararat* is distinguished by a starkly etched grief (in essence, every family's grief, in a cat's cradle geometry of separations and intertwinements) and, in relation to it, a consummate, if not fulfilling, understanding. If depression can speak with wit, intelligence, self-irony, some admiration of others' toughness, maybe even a formal forgiveness that is fortunately never expressed as sentiment, maybe even love, not to mention a pain that is never fingered, but merely put forth, then *Ararat*—named after a cemetery and alluding to the resting place of the ark that saved human life from the deluge and, beyond that, to a covenant between intelligence and love—is articulated depression. Most of the sentences are proddingly narrow and as dry as a doctor's tongue-sticks. Every move that the imagined (thoroughly imagined) voice makes is compelling. No matter that the tone is shackled with neutrality, that it is "so controlled, so withdrawn." Precisely this permits the structures of the poems to say everything. These are structures that (it seems) have been injected with phenobarbital. They are truth's cardiograms.

Glück's powers of mind, her presence, her voice are not self-advertising; they are just there, instantly arresting. There's no fat anywhere in the book. The word-work is all as precise and concentrated as an eye operation. On her son coming home from school: "he knows / I'm watching. That's why / he greets the cat, / to show he's capable / of open affection. / My father used / the dog in the same way." It doesn't occur to the language to be anything other than plain and truthful; it doesn't preen. Is this poetry? Yes, art-speech, however unfussy and free of verbal narcissism; syllable weighted against syllable in a way that is *just so,* all fixed so finally that no accident could dishevel them. Not that it is easy to find the secret of the success. A lifetime of working with words, of paring away at them, of listening is, of course, assumed. And a feeling for the balance of echo and the just off-balance is perhaps crucial, as in these words on her newly widowed mother entertaining visitors:

> In her heart, she wants them to go away.
> She wants to be back in the cemetery,
> back in the sickroom, the hospital. She knows
> it isn't possible. But it's her only hope,
> the wish to move backward. And just a little,
> not so far as the marriage, the first kiss.
>
> ("A Fantasy")

"She wants . . . she wants . . . hospital . . . possible . . . She *knows* . . . it's her only *hope* . . . back . . . back . . . backward"; the foiled longing of the foiled rhyme "away" and "cemetery"; the vein-under-the-skin connection of "sick," "wish," and "kiss," the sibilance that keeps failing yet persisting, like the wanting itself; and still more—a verse centered in itself, after all. Capable, all the same, of sudden still-deeper piercings, as when the last sentence takes up the live fish of pathos and guts it with a furious ambiguity: does it mean, not the whole saga of the marriage again, not *that*? It's no surprise to learn that the poet comes from tough stock: "Now the hero's dead. Like echoes, the women last longer; they're all too tough for their own good" ("A Novel").

Though most of the poems are complete and strong in themselves, it is plain that for the poet they cluster together like wintering bees in a simmering ball, a little organic heater against the cold. The odd-one-out is the poem grandest in itself, **"Celestial Music."** Here, family is replaced by "a friend who still believes in heaven. / Not a stupid person, yet with all she knows, she literally talks

to god." What the poet and her friend agree on, for all their differences, is the necessary peace of composition. The friend says that "when you love the world you hear celestial music" and "She's always trying to make something whole, something beautiful, an image / capable of life apart from her." She has just drawn a circle in the dirt; inside, a dead caterpillar. The two friends are sitting by a road that turns dark, "the rocks shining and glittering": "it's this stillness that we both love. / The love of form is a love of endings." This marks the self-reflexive moment of *Ararat,* the acknowledgment of being bereft of the old celestial register, and at the same time a bow to the elegiac, indeed posthumous spirit of all formal art. Here the book offers itself as an outcropping of hard deposits that shine in the dying light of a family story, and as a circle, in which the torn victim, if brushed free of a few ants, "doesn't move."

I could do without the poet's claim in **"Parados"** that "I was born to a vocation: / to bear witness / to the great mysteries." For me, this direct self-regard is less effective than the snow-cold self-mirroring in **"Celestial Music."** And when Glück says that she and her sister are "like amazons, a tribe without a future," perhaps she confuses patriliny with continuance. But at almost every point *Ararat* is brilliantly hard as both art and understanding (and here the two seem to be one; no axe could split them apart). It is full of, is distinguished by, unshakably final observation and statement. It illustrates what Walter Pater called "the actually aesthetic charm of a cold austerity of mind." With a clarity of language that is next to silence yet that gives up nothing to it, Glück submits herself to what Valéry called "crystal abysses deeper than Erebus." Although feeling is present in the book, it is like a coffin just lowered into the ground; the style repulses all surface displays of emotion—a discipline the poet learned from her father. When she says goodbye to the latter, whom she knows to be dying, there is

> no embrace, nothing dramatic.
> When the taxi came, my parents watched from the
>   front door,
> arm in arm, my mother blowing kisses as she
>   always does,
> because it frightens her when a hand isn't being
>   used.
> But for a change, my father didn't just stand there.
> This time, he waved.
>
> That's what I did, at the door to the taxi.
> Like him, waved to disguise my hand's trembling.

This poem bears the mordant title **"Terminal Resemblance."** But it is clear that the resemblance includes a tense mutual attachment that has been put away in a low-pressure area to keep from shattering. Glück is her father's daughter in already knowing—and requiring—so much separation that death cannot be an outrage. But that doesn't make it speakable, either. The poet is hardened to endure seasons of subtraction, when what goes away nonetheless forms a shadow-pool where a few syllables stop to drink.

The least soft of poets of both maternal and paternal lack, the two lacks most of us neither escape nor cure, Glück looks back on their fatalities, and histories, like a too brilliant moon held in orbit by what has not been concluded—by the trauma of separation itself. The mother, that seductive abyss in which an impossible demand plummets, that weltering paradise—this she rejects as if with the cry, "Not that death, the confused one!" So her father is necessary to her as the hero who goes before her into death, the unemotional one. She emulates paternal strength, Apollo, with every word, making it sting like iodine of light. With her self-denyingly mannerless manner, she is now writing English in its most purified form. She threads passion through pain as if it were a needle's eye, as if it were nothing to rage over but the site, after all, of a joining, the looping point of "time and intelligence" (**"Children Coming Home from School"**).

**Bruce Bond** (essay date 1991)

SOURCE: "The Unfinished Child: Contradictory Desire in Glück's *Ararat*," in *New England Review and Bread Loaf Quarterly,* Vol. 14, No. 1, Fall, 1991, pp. 216-23.

[*In the following review, Bond critiques Glück's fifth book, noting a shift in her use of mythology that illuminates the process through which myth achieves meaning; he concludes that these poems about personal and family history inform the notion of intimacy as crucial to the creative processes of mythology and of poetry.*]

Louise Glück's most recent book, *Ararat,* marks a new and sustained intimacy in her work, the persona of her poems returning to a personally inscribed past, a family circle, so as to offer, more than her other collections, the sense of a narrative whole. But the narrative comes to us in fragments, often jagged and self-contradictory, having a dissonant lyric intensity unsuited to the more modulated pacing of longer narrative structures. As in her earlier books, Glück works in terse, introspective forms, tight spirals of language, as if writing against tremendous psychic resistance, longing for the scrutiny she shuns, gesturing toward the dark context of a larger story. It is in this resistance that Glück comes to demand the most of her language, and in so doing she demands of her readers as well. The result is a precise hesitancy, concealing as it reveals, work which dramatizes and challenges a desire for the clear and intimate.

Although less explicitly mythological in its reference than her third and fourth books, *Descending Figure* and *The Triumph of Achilles, Ararat,* with its recurring fascination for what binds and alienates, makes its focus the very impulse that motivates myth. Not only is this impulse, to use Glück's phrase from her opening poem, the desire "to bear witness to the great mysteries," but also, to borrow from Levi-Strauss's conception of myth, to bring together imaginatively, in pursuit of wholeness, the unsettling dualisms which reason cannot reconcile. Most obviously, Glück's pairings focus on unresolved

personal relationships: daughter and mother, daughter and father, sister and sister, speaker and listener: variations on a primary tension and dependency between self and other—in Glück's language, the "I" and "the world."

To say, however, that what motivates these poems is merely a desire for resolution between self and the other in its many forms would be misleading, trivializing, for desire in Glück's work is characteristically divided against itself. There is a strong counter-impulse to the mythological in Glück's poetry: the personal—that is, the desire for individuation, to be distanced from the world, even though such distance implies pain and longing. The desire for separateness expresses itself by way of the power to say no, to defy one's mother or sister, even, paradoxically, to defy oneself. According to Glück's own analysis, such power finds its dysfunctional extreme in anorexic defiance, an assertiveness that illuminates a weakness, a dependency. Her poetry often dramatizes a self-sacrificing negation, a kind of alienation from oneself, but as revealed a source of wonder: a masochistic sublime.

This tone of wonder becomes disturbingly seductive, contributing to our sense of Glück's persona as divided. The speaker's ruthlessness and generosity of insight both pleases and terrifies, threatening and enlarging her sense of self. Thus the quality of wonder in these poems does not make them any less confrontational. Rather it provides a correlative to the speaker's enduring fascination with irresolvable conflict. The poems enact the sublimity of painful self-discovery, the unveiling, albeit incomplete, of what is denied. In this, they resemble dream disclosures, immediate and mercurial, intimate and remote.

What is revealed is in part the mechanism which motivates testimonial rhetoric. In their tone of intimate distance, Glück's poems self-consciously probe the very issue of intimacy and its limits, of what drives the need to remake and reveal a self through language. In the conflict between the mythological impulse toward reconciliation and the personal impulse toward individuation lies Glück's model for the creative process, a process made possible and desirable by the instability of the self. Although the speaker in *Ararat* may suffer paralyzing idiosyncrasies, Glück's story of jealousy and grieving illuminates something of the unfinished childhood that informs all consciousness—primary conflicts between self and world that motivate speech, replenishing the desire for connectedness and estrangement.

In the poem **"Parodos,"** which opens *Ararat,* Glück creates the sense that her speaker's alienation stems not only from the details of a personal past, but also from an unspecified and thus more generalized affliction. Her wounding resembles an archetypal fall into separateness, that which allows for the compensating gesture of speech:

> Long ago, I was wounded.
> I learned
> to exist, in reaction,
> out of touch
> with the world: I'll tell you

what I meant to be—
a device that listened.
Not inert: still.
A piece of wood. A stone.

The second line of the poem, "I learned," sets us up for the familiar consolations, the idea that suffering makes us wise. But we are soon reminded of the more austere notion: that suffering makes us conscious of existence and of a need to protect it. In coming into existence, the self comes into separateness, a falling away from being—a fact which leads us back to the derivation of the phrase "to exist": "to be outside."

The poem's title alludes both to this distancing and to the vulnerability distance implies. The word "parodos" recalls the "parode," the opening song (or "ode") of a chorus entering from the side ("para") in a Greek drama. Like a parody, it is a kind of adjacent voice, distinguished and thus distanced from its subject by virtue of its role as judge. The poem's title also closely resembles the word "parados," a fortification to protect against attack from the rear. Naturally the self could not exist "in reaction," protecting itself, if it were purely "out of touch." Glück's speaker responds to pain and the threat of pain with extreme, even paralyzing vigilance. The contradictory character of the speaker is focused by the double possibilities of the phrase: "out of touch." In learning to be remote from the world, the speaker reaffirms her dependence on it: she exists "out of" or "as a result of" touch with the world.

The speaker's abrupt testament to an unspecified "you" makes obvious that dependence: "I must tell you," she says, "what I meant to be." (5) Glück's poems frequently invoke the presence of an imaginary listener, as if the speaker were suddenly seized by an anxiety about not being heard. At the same time, the speaker often implicates herself in her own isolation, most obviously in **"Parodos,"** by half-concealing the curious origin of her wound.

Since past affliction appears so generalized as to be associated with mere worldly contact, the act of speech opens that wound. In particular, it is her own confessional speech that the speaker fears and needs most. The paradox of the speaker who confesses to a fear of confession emerges as the focus of the poem entitled **"Confession,"** also from *Ararat*:

> To say I'm without fear—
> it wouldn't be true.
> I'm afraid of sickness, humiliation.
> Like anyone, I have my dreams.
> But I've learned to hide them,
> to protect myself
> from fulfillment: all happiness
> attracts the Fates' anger.

The speaker here, crossed by contradictory desire, takes the risk she fears most, that of revealing her weakness. Her inhibitions testify to the extreme urgency that moti-

vates the confessional act, and in so doing make of the reader an elite witness to something rare.

The reader not only overhears but also makes possible the speaker's confession. In her lecture entitled "Education of the Poet" (*Envoy* 52, 1989: 1-6) Glück voices a conscious preference for a poetry of intimate and urgent address—justifying it, paradoxically, as a means of quieting self-consciousness:

> My preference, from the beginning, has been the poetry that requests or craves a listener. This is Blake's little black boy, Keats' living hand, Eliot's Prufrock, as opposed, say, to Stevens' astonishments. I don't intend, in this, to set up any sort of hierarchy, simply to say that I read to feel addressed, much as the complement, I suppose, to speaking in order to be heeded. . . . The preference for intimacy, of course, makes of the single reader an elite. A practical advantage to this innate preference is that one cares less about the size of an audience. ("Education of the Poet")

Eliot's Prufrock, repelled and seduced by public life, its scrutiny and compromises, provides an illuminating parallel to the speaker in Glück's poems. Both fear the intimacy their rhetoric promotes. The vague referent of their second person pronouns opens up the possibility of the implied auditor as purely imagined, a second self. Given their fears, it is consistent with both Prufrock and Glück's speaker to make of solitude a model for imaginary exchange.

Glück's anxiety at not being heard informs yet another split and irresolution in consciousness: her inclination toward paradox. In her complication of thought and resistance to paraphrase, she demands our closest attention. Glück's love of paradox and the unpredictable utterance has, according to her, its origins in childhood frustrations over not being allowed to complete her sentences:

> Like most of the people in that family, I had a strong desire to speak, but that desire was regularly frustrated: my sentences were, in being cut off, radically changed—transformed, not paraphrased. The sweetness of paradox is that its outcome cannot be anticipated: this ought to insure the attention of the audience. But in my family, all discussion was carried on in that single cooperative voice. ("Education of a Poet")

To defy the so-called "cooperative voice" is, for Glück, to seek a distinctive place within it. We have in Glück's family dynamic a model and motive for poetic creation: in its longing to be revealed, the self becomes assertively enigmatic. Her urge to write poetry, especially in a style that defies preemption, stems from a desire to finish her own sentences and so to clarify the boundary between her voice and the "cooperative" other. The alternative to finishing one's own sentences is assimilation into the "other," a "cutting off" of language and the impulse toward selfhood which drives it. Glück's imaginary listener poses relatively little threat to that selfhood, since the auditor in her poems is without a voice or even the interactive possibilities we might find in a Browning monologue.

Given her love of the unpredictable, Glück takes on an especially difficult challenge in *Ararat,* that of exploring a relatively limited catalogue of family crises with sustained verbal tension and surprise. To further complicate that risk, these family tensions, inspiring as they do states of contradictory desire, of nihilism and denial, often have the effect of paralyzing dramatic action, thus placing the burden of dramatic surprise on speculative rather than narrative events. The poem **"A Novel,"** which comes early in the book, makes explicit the aesthetic and psychological risks to follow:

> No one could write a novel about this family:
> too many similar characters. Besides they're all
>    women;
> there was only one hero.
>
> Now the hero's dead. . . .
> The women can't get moving.
> Oh, they get dressed, they eat, they keep up
>    appearances.
> But there's no action, no development of character.

The success of this poem hinges on how the speaker participates in the denial of the women she describes. She flattens her language, explaining dispassionately how the hero failed, how "his death wasn't moving."

Such distance helps to set up the shock of the poem's closure, in which Glück lifts the mask of daily routine to reveal a piercing anguish, the truth of what it is to be paralyzed by depression, threatened, by denial routine with impoverishment of character:

> Amazing, how they keep busy, these women, the
>    wife and two daughters.
> Setting the table, clearing the dishes away.
> Each heart pierced through with a sword.

Throughout the book, the speaker confesses to paralyzed desire, a repetition compulsion, at times perpetuating adolescent conflicts in spite of the obvious maturity of her insight. Her image of herself as a stone in **"Parodos"** provides a haunting figure for such paralysis. As she claims in the poem **"Appearances,"** "It was something I was good at: sitting still, not moving . . . I'm still the same. The speaker in Glück's poems often finds herself caught between a fear of stasis and one of change.

In **"A Novel,"** change is fearfully denied because it implies loss, the piercing of the sword. To be controlled by a fear of change is to fear the other in the form of life itself, to play, like the father in Glück's tale, the sleeping nihilist.

Glück's image of the pierced heart picks up once again the theme of the deep and permanent wound which appears in **"Parodos"** and resurfaces throughout the book. The effect of the wound is to split the self, as in the poem **"A Novel,"** where the women are split between grief and dispassion. The body, our most obvious and persuasive metaphor for selfhood, takes on the punishment of such self-division. Its wholeness is sacrificed to the demands of the other.

In the poem **"Paradise,"** it is not only the father but also the sister who poses a threat to that wholeness. The poem echoes **"Parodos,"** not only in the sound of its title, a muted pun perhaps, but also in its depiction of a deep, archetypal wound, a fall from the "paradise" of peerlessness:

> But I know. Like Adam,
> I was the firstborn.
> Believe me, you never heal,
> you never forget the ache in your side,
> the place where something was taken away
> to make another person.

Here the banished self is cut clear away from the body. Since that self is not merely divided by but actually becomes the other, the self sees its own image in that other. Glück offers a deeply disturbing figure of polarized desire, a girl torn by the interdependent extremes of alienation and identification. The speaker's body is permanently deprived in the process, its rib "cut off" like a sentence, preempted by the desires of others. The speaker is thus haunted by a kind of Lacanian lack, a sense that some portion of the self is always "out there," exiled into the otherness of the world.

In the poem **"A Fable,"** it is the mother's body and desire that are threatened with division. But rather than let her mother suffer, the child would sacrifice herself. The child preempts the mother's sacrificial role as Glück revises the fable of Solomon and his famous test:

> Let the child be
> cut in half; that way
> no one will go
> empty-handed. He
> drew his sword.
> Then, of the two
> women, one
> renounced her share:
> this was
> the sign, the lesson.
> Suppose you saw your mother
> torn between two daughters:
> what could you do
> to save her but be
> willing to destroy
> yourself—she would know
> who was the rightful child.

In Glück's revised fable, though mother and child exchange roles, the exchange is not absolute. As in the Bible, the child here is mortally threatened, but unlike the Biblical child, Glück's speaker invites destruction upon herself, justifying her actions with a martyr's logic, a faith in the notion that to lose one's soul is to gain it. What motivates the girl to destroy herself is nothing less than the urge to construct a self, to triumph in her battle for the mother's favor, a child's version of salvation.

Frightfully, the logic of the child as martyr resembles the logic of an anorexic. Glück's recollection of her own mid-adolescence helps to clarify what drives the frail, blue-complexioned girl of her poems:

> I couldn't say what I was, what I wanted, in any day to day, practical way. What I could say was no: the way I saw to separate myself, to establish a self with clear boundaries, was to oppose myself to the declared desire of others. . . . The tragedy of anorexia seems to me that its intent is not self-destructive, though its outcome so often is. Its intent is to construct, in the only way possible when means are so limited, a plausible act. But the sustained act, the repudiation, designed to distinguish the self from the other also separates self and body. And, as well, frustrates disdain for flesh, since the spectre of death demonstrates not the soul's superiority but its dependence on flesh.
>
> ("Education of a Poet")

Anorexic repudiation becomes one more form of paralysis, of a failure, or more precisely a refusal, to act. The anorexic seals herself up. And yet that seal betrays a bond, an extreme sensitivity to the judgment and desire of others. To echo the paradox of **"Parodos,"** she exists "in reaction / out of touch / with the world."

Though in her prose reminiscence Glück claims that the intent of the anorexic is not self-destruction, her poems tell the story of a girl whose motives are not so clear. In the poem **"Mirror Image,"** for example, the speaker sees her image superimposed over that of her father and so provokes the suspicion that she too entertains the occasional death-wish:

> Tonight I saw myself in the dark window as
> the image of my father, whose life
> was spent like this
> thinking of death, to the exclusion
> of other sensual matters,
> so in the end that life
> was easy to give up, since
> it contained nothing: even
> my mother's voice couldn't make him
> change or turn back
> as he believed
> that once you can't love another human being
> you have no place in the world.

Death appears here as erotic, all excluding, the dark context of those faces floating in their window. The stark beauty and power of this poem lies in the tension it creates between the speaker's nearness to and distance from her father. The opening enjambment on the word "as" focuses that tension, implying both similarity and difference. The face suspended in darkness suggests that the speaker, like her father, hovers in an absence, a no-place. But the daughter's life clearly contains more than nothing, more than the obsessive thought of nothing. Her face, like her poem, appears as a vessel containing the image of her father. It is the speaker's love for her father, even in his absence, that assures her of being unlike him, of having a place in the world. The will to life is guaranteed by way

of her capacity for identification and emotional investment.

The father in Glück's mirror is thus viewed from an intimate distance, the heightened intimacy strangely accentuating that distance and the degree to which it matters. In this, he resembles not only the entire family cast, but also the sleepers in her opening poem:

> Why should I tire myself, debating, arguing?
> Those people breathing in the other beds
> could hardly follow, being
> uncontrollable
> like any dream. . . .

Though the people here are distanced, sealed away in their wild and hermetic sleep, the poem imagines its way clear to their bedsides, their breath. Like any dream, they are both close and far, private and autonomous. The enjambment at the word "being" foregrounds the sense that these people dramatize conflicts that inform all relations to being. All modes of intimacy carry with them a simultaneous and uncanny sense of what that intimacy cannot overcome.

The sense of wonder in Glück's poems is thus not so much an escapist response as it is the inevitable mark of accurate perception, a response to facts of desire, of "existence" and the strangeness of the near. Perceptual accuracy is challenged by the fact that her subject is so often the formative past, which time both clarifies and blurs. Unlike her father, the speaker in *Ararat* repeatedly gives in to the temptation to look back, though this looking never feels easy, not even entirely desirable. Glück's terse, hesitant language, vertical by virtue of its speed and depth of correspondence, resists narrative flow. Her poems repeatedly encourage us to pause, struck, to gaze at the face in the window. Seated on the threshold of the other, it is in some measure ourselves "out there," vigilant, vulnerable, inhabiting the alien and beloved.

### Charles Berger (essay date 1991)

SOURCE: "Poetry Chronicle: Amy Clampitt, Louise Glück, Mark Strand," in *Raritan: A Quarterly Review*, Vol. X, No. 3, Winter, 1991, pp. 125-33.

[*In the following review excerpt, Berger argues the success of Glück's use of the book-length sequence of short lyric poems in* Ararat, *and finds this approach a good alternative to traditional narrative structures. In addition, Berger favorably assesses Glück's "common language" in the volume.*]

Louise Glück's *Ararat* is a book-length sequence of short lyrics set in the year following the death of the poet's father. Book-length is a phrase I usually recoil from when attached to lyric sequences, since it often serves as a plea for excusing local weaknesses. But *Ararat* truly is a volume of linked poems, a volume operating through laws of accrual where no single poem dominates others or—more remarkably—needs to be salvaged by the work as a whole. One marks each individual poem as it comes along, records slight shifts of focus and form, even while registering a tonal similarity between poems striking enough to make them cognate, but sufficiently flexible to avoid monotone. This is simply to say that strong family resemblances between poems reinforce the guiding obsessiveness of family romance in *Ararat*. The occasion of her father's death forces Glück to rehearse the history of this plain, gray house on Long Island, "the sort of place / you buy to raise a family." Nothing extraordinary happened in this house, except for the quiet failure to sustain that idea of family. The death of an infant girl hardened her mother's heart, her sister's birth inaugurated a sibling rivalry (a "wound") so deep and inexplicable it can only be called ontological, her father's "contempt for emotion" locked the house in a kind of deep freeze—and yet, when her father dies, the "dark nature" of the family plot is revealed to be a "love story":

> Now, the hero's dead. Like echoes, the women last
>     longer;
> they're all too tough for their own good . . .
>
> Amazing, how they keep busy, these women, the
>     wife and
>         two daughters.
> Setting the table, clearing the dishes away.
> Each heart pierced through with a sword.

Reading through *Ararat,* I'm made to think of the failed houses strewn throughout Frost's poetry. (This, too, is a house in earnest.) Philip Roth comes as readily to mind, with his ability to strip away anything extraneous to family combat. But Glück has no flair for Roth's histrionics (not to mention his comedic genius), and the domestic never turns sublimely gothic as it does in Frost. She conducts the narrative of *Ararat* in a deceptively level, sober style, a voice one is tempted to call "plain" but for all the programmatic connotations that have gathered around that term. Though Glück, as always, avoids sumptuous rhetoric, she doesn't go to the opposite extreme of exalting bare-bones minimalism; charged, redemptive symbols in either the high or middle style are not for her, although the vaguely chantlike rhythm of her lines gives a lift to even the simplest words. Above all, she hates distortion and is willing to forgo a certain amount of metaphorical exaggeration. Despite the brevity of her poems, Glück doesn't freeze or still the flow of language in *Ararat*. Instead, she scrutinizes common words as they pass by her, keeping them alive and moving in the stream of discourse, even while wincing at the freight they are made to bear. Part of this burden has to do with the ritual gestures they convey. I will quote **"A Fantasy"** in its entirety because it gives a strong sense of how adroitly Glück takes the measure of common speech and the customs it supports.

> I'll tell you something: every day
> people are dying. And that's just the beginning.
> Every day, in funeral homes, new widows are born,

new orphans. They sit with their hands folded, trying to decide about this new life.

> Then they're in the cemetary, some of them
> for the first time. They're frightened of crying,
> sometimes of not crying. Someone leans over,
> tells them what to do next, which might mean
> saying a few words, sometimes
> throwing dirt in the open grave.
> And after that, everyone goes back to the house,
> which is suddenly full of visitors.
> The widow sits on the couch, very stately,
> so people line up to approach her,
> sometimes take her hand, sometimes embrace her.
> She finds something to say to everybody,
> thanks them, thanks them for coming.
> In her heart, she wants them to go away.
> She wants to be back in the cemetary,
> back in the sickroom, the hospital. She knows
> it isn't possible. But it's her only hope,
> the wish to move backward. And just a little,
> not so far as the marriage, the first kiss.

The nature of Glück's verbal economy—her decisions about what to include and exclude, the value given to words posing as symbols—becomes most apparent when one thinks of *Ararat* alongside the formal decorums of elegy. I say this even though Glück makes little overt use of elegiac machinery and shows even less desire to "subvert" the genre through parodic irony. Part of her saving strangeness as a poet comes from this difficulty in locating her stance toward the institutions of lyric; in this case, she can't be said either to ignore or reinvent the tropes of elegy. The elusive but pervasive strength of the writing in *Ararat* comes instead, I think, from Glück's ability to write about death in the lives of the living, to write about mourning, without immediately assigning herself the elegist's task of turning death into forms of solace or survival. In her last volume, *The Triumph of Achilles,* Glück has a poem on her father's death called **"Metamorphosis."** The title is something of a negative example, pointing to what Glück refuses to do, namely to imagine death as a kind of transformative, visionary odyssey. Of far greater interest to her, especially in the case of her father, is the way the living move toward death in their lives, hardening themselves, emptying themselves out, "so that death, when it came, / wouldn't seem a significant change." This is the frightening ground of resemblance between father and daughter and the basis of the judgment passed in **"Mirror Image"**:

> Tonight I saw myself in the dark window as
> the image of my father, whose life
> was spent like this,
> thinking of death, to the exclusion
> of other sensual matters,
> so in the end that life
> was easy to give up, since
> it contained nothing: even
> my mother's voice couldn't make him
> change or turn back
> as he believed
> that once you can't love another human being
> you have no place in the world.

"Change or turn back," isolated on one line, shorn of syntactical context, almost floats free to become a magical supplication to the dead, but restored to the body of this epitaphlike poem it becomes a formulaic spell Glück will not utter. Spare complexities of this order can be found everywhere in *Ararat*. (This includes the titles of individual poems, easy to overlook.) Glück's art works its secret ministry on the reader: that is what it means to write a version of the common language, a claim often made in American poetry, seldom performed so movingly.

## Lynne McMahon  (essay date 1992)

SOURCE: "The Sexual Swamp: Female Erotics and the Masculine Art," in *The Southern Review,* Louisiana State University, Vol. 28, No. 2, April, 1992, pp. 333-52.

[*In this excerpt, McMahon addresses the issue of the aesthetic differences between men and women. Glück's work, the critic finds, often depicts female sexuality and artistic expression to be at cross-purposes; erotic love has a lack of structure that is the opposite of artistic form. For this reason, the critic concludes, Glück seems to feel that "to be an artist . . . means to adopt the masculine imposition of boundary."*]

For some time now feminist and Marxist and psychoanalytic critics have been exploring the language of patriarchy, trying to unearth a female aesthetic from phallogocentric digs. The lexicon is often funny ("phallocrat" is one of my favorites; another is "phallogocentric," Jacques Derrida's neologism linking phallus, logos, and center, all three of which deconstruction attempts to undo). More often the language is clunky (how many of us doze off at the first assault of Signifier and Signified, or grind our teeth at the torturous infinitive "to privilege"?), or simply and drily obscure. But whatever the failures of the language, the idea behind it is not quite dismissible. The question is an intriguing one: *Is* there an aesthetic difference between women and men? And does that mean it is located in the sexual body? Is a marriage between the masculine art and the female body possible?. . . .

Louise Glück's poems make the most explicit case for the uncrossable chasm between Eros and Art. Her landscape is the bombed-out world after sex. In *The Triumph of Achilles* passion does not unlock art; indeed, it strangles it. The dream of romance—long the province of the feminine—gives way to the "actual flesh" of love, which leads to silence and immobility: "What is a poet / without dreams? / I lie awake; I feel / actual flesh upon me, / meaning to silence me—(**"The Reproach"**); "the man's mouth / sealing my mouth, the man's / paralyzing body" (**"Mock Orange"**); "Then I know what lies behind your silence: / scorn, hatred of me, of marriage. Still, / you want me to touch you; you cry out" (**"Horse"**). The body betrays the mind; the man suffocates the woman; and yet the woman in these poems falls again and again under the affliction of desire, the will paralyzed by sex.

The nine-part poem **"Marathon"** anatomizes desire and paralysis, not in progression—the movement from love to loss, say—but in stasis. The poem begins with **"Last Letter"**; abandonment and betrayal attendant from the inception:

> Without thinking, I knelt in the grass, like
>     someone meaning to pray.
> When I tried to stand again, I couldn't move,
> my legs were utterly rigid. Does grief change you
>     like that?

The poet, betrayed and abandoned, is frozen in an effigy of prayer. Her sexual nature has led to this, a Medusa self-immobilized. Slowly she regains movement, the physical rigor released, but the psychic paralysis is complete:

> I got up finally; I walked down to the pond.
> I stood there, brushing the grass from my skirt,
>     watching myself,
> like a girl after her first lover
> turning slowly at the bathroom mirror, naked,
>     looking for a sign.
> But nakedness in women is always a pose.
> I was not transfigured. I would never be free.

The sexuality in this book loops like a Möbius strip around the twinned notions of death and freedom: the first a search for the father (the birth-right, the patronymic), the second a release from him; both of these in turn tied to the hunger for vision unobscured by physical desire. The erotic longing for the father finds its most acute expression in the sixth poem of **"Marathon,"** titled **"The Beginning."** The poem presents itself as a dream addressed to the father, but the dream occurs outside time—before birth, but after sexual identity. The speaker takes on the sentient aspect of Wordsworth's infant-angels, waiting to be clothed in human flesh. But Glück's speaker knows she is female, knows she is doomed to be divided from the male. She comes, not trailing clouds of glory, but armed with pathetic knowledge:

> I had come to a strange city, without belongings:
> in the dream, it was your city, I was looking for
>     you.
> Then I was lost, on a dark street lined with fruit
>               stands.
>
> There was only one fruit: blood oranges.
> The markets made displays of them, beautiful
>     displays—
> how else could they compete? And each
>     arrangement had,
>       at its center,
> one fruit, cut open.
>
> Then I was on a boulevard, in brilliant sunlight.
> I was running; it was easy to run, since I had
>     nothing.
> In the distance, I could see your house; a woman
>     knelt in the yard.
> There were roses everywhere; in waves, they
>     climbed the high trellis.

Then what began as love for you
became a hunger for structure: I could hear
the woman call to me in common kindness,
   knowing
I wouldn't ask for you anymore—

So it was settled: I could have a childhood there.
Which came to mean being always alone.

The poignance of women, blood oranges, lies in their
defeated similarity: "the markets made displays of them,
beautiful displays—/ how else could they compete?" Then
the terrible, and surgically revealed, heart: "And each
arrangement had, at its center, / one fruit, cut open." This
seems an intentional mixing of the body of the metaphor,
for the heart of this fruit is genital and menstrual, centered
not in the chest but in the womb.

These blood oranges carry a wealth, or burden, of Western poetic tradition as far back as Aristophanes. Anne
Carson's essay in *Before Sexuality,* "Putting Her in Her
Place: Woman, Dirt and Desire," traces the etymology of
"ripeness" and female fruit from its Greek roots in drama
and verse. In Greek society, she writes, a woman went
directly from underripe (virginity) to overripe; there was
no mid-point at all:

> [A] woman's first sexual experience catapults her into
> uncontrolled sexual activity and out of the category of
> desirable sex-object, for she is past her peak the
> moment the ἄγθοs (flower) falls.

A comparable distortion can be seen in Greek usage of
the word ὀπώρα This word means "fruit-time," the
time between the rising of Seirios and of Arktouros
when the fruit ripens, and also the fruit itself. When
used metaphorically of males, ὀπώρα signifies "the
bloom of youth" or "ripe manhood," and does not
exclude the pursuit of sexual fulfillment. But when
used of females, ὀπώρα means virginity and is to be
withheld from all erotic experimentation. . . . When
not guarded, a woman's ὀπώρα becomes blackened
(as an overripe fruit), undesirable and accursed. . . .

Within these usages is operating an identification of
female sexuality with voracious promiscuity and of
virginity with the best moment of female life. Implicit
here is a denial that free sexual activity and "blooming"
are compatible for a woman. There is no such thing as
sexually vigorous ripe womanhood in the Greek view.
At her peak a woman is sexually untried. . . . As soon
as she lets her ἄγθοs (flower) fall, the female is
translated to the slippery slope of overripeness: "A
woman's prime is an inch of time!" wails Lysistrata.

In Louise Glück's poem, there's not even an inch of
time. Each display has one fruit, already cut open. In
ancient Greek verse, Carson says, "a woman who is being compared to an apple on a tree or a flower in a field
can be said to wither the moment she is 'plucked.' Plucking is defloration." But here we haven't even the joy or
erotic drama of plucking; "cut open" insists, in fact, on
the violence of sexuality. "Plucking" summons the rhyme,

of course, but beyond that carries the notion of human
*touch.* "One fruit, cut open" has been removed from the
realm of the human altogether. Some agency has mound-
ed the display, some agency has sliced the center fruit.
This "dark street lined with fruit stands" stretches all the
way back to the earliest examination of sexual difference,
and then forward to the poet's own individual imagining. The "I" descends to a reality already and forever
inscribed by that cut-open fruit. That's the pathos and
power of these poems: that whatever psychic, societal,
legal inroads feminism has made into the depiction of
female sexuality, this "I" remains confined in the reality
of the body. The ancient world is the future world.

And this world belongs to the father; "in the dream, it was
your city, I was looking for you." But erotic longing gives
way to civilized forms; the woman kneeling in the yard,
gardening, will become the mother: "I could hear / the
woman call to me in common kindness, knowing / I
wouldn't ask for you anymore—" The mother can call in
"common kindness" because she knows the child cannot
seriously compete for the father's sexual attention. "So it
was settled: I could have a childhood there." Those are
the prescribed conditions, and the daughter accepts them,
indeed, she *desires* them:

> Then what began as love for you
> became a hunger for structure:

"A hunger for structure" may be the key element in all of
Louise Glück's poems, for the terror of erotic love lies in
its *lack* of structure, its boundarylessness. But the safety
of civilized restraints proves to be illusory. The succeeding poem, **"First Goodbye"** (we're to think back to the
first poem in the sequence, **"Last Letter"**) presents the
display of blood oranges in a new configuration, violent
in its overdetermination. The lover, appropriately, has taken
the place of the father; the proscriptions are in place; the
foundations of civilization are intact. But beneath the order lies self-destruction. The poem begins in betrayal:

> You can join the others now,
> body that wouldn't let my body rest,
> go back to the world, to avenues, the ordered
> depths of the parks, like great terminals
> that never darken: a stranger's waiting for you
> in a hundred rooms. Go back to them,
> to increment and limitation: near the centered rose,
> you watch her peel an orange
> so the dyed rind falls in petals on her plate. This
> is mastery, whose active
> mode is dissection: the enforced light
> shines on the blade.

Go back to the world, back to the displays of oranges,
back to the marketplace of women to choose a new one,
a new hundred of them, what you'll find is . . . incre-
ment and limitation. Odd and unpoetic, the language of
measurement, like the language of society, appears safe.
But near the center of the display ("near the centered
rose"—Dante's celestial flower reduced to this fruit-stand
arrangement) a woman is dissecting herself. "This / is

mastery, whose active / mode is dissection:" How are we to read this? As self-mutilation? As an erotic masochism specifically female? And yet "mastery" remains ironically masculine and dominant, or, in terms of the Medusa legend, Athenian. The mind's will over the body's desire. Athena, sprung from the dry head of Zeus, identifies with the will and intellect of the father; she cannot do otherwise. But Athena knows what it is to be afflicted with desire; the head of Medusa blazes from her shield, both protecting and violating her sexual integrity. She wars with her passionate double. In **"First Goodbye"** the Athenian side of "I" speaks, but only because her other sexual self has suffered betrayal. She has managed to climb back into her head, from which prospect (and vast remove) she can see her former lover and all his subsequent women:

> And the women lying there—who wouldn't pity
>   them,
> the way they turn to you, the way
> they struggle to be visible. They make
> a place for you in bed, a white excavation.
> Then the sacrament: your bodies pieced together,
> churning, churning, till the heat leaves them
>   entirely—

This is indeed a clinical remove, whose active mode is the dissection of analysis. And this analytical vista opens out into Athena's revenge, for she can see into the future:

>       Sooner or later
> you'll begin to dream of me. I don't envy you
> those dreams. I can imagine how my face looks,
> burning like that, afflicted with desire—lowered
> face of your invention—how the mouth betrays
> the isolated greed of the lover
> as it magnifies and then destroys:
> I don't envy you that visitation.

To possess again what one has lost—that's the impossibility of Eros. And it's made doubly impossible by the realization that there never *was* that particular reality. The lover invented the beloved:

> Sooner or later you will call my name,
> cry of loss, mistaken
> cry of recognition, of arrested need
> for someone who exists in memory; no voice
> carries to that kingdom.

What a satisfying revenge: no voice carries to that kingdom. And yet the undertone is unmistakable—this is the kingdom of the dead. The speaker dissects herself even as she coldly dissects the lover's future. Everyone loses.

To dissect one's self means to control one's destiny. Some medical experts say that, like anorexia, this kind of destructive control over the body is a sexual perversion. In societal terms, this "mastery"—ironic and masculine—signals the final female subjugation. In mythic terms, it signals the shifting dominances of female erotics, the duality personified in Athena and Medusa. In Glück's

poetic, the mastery of self-dissection means poetry. Only by conquering the body—the sexuality that blurs distinctions, making poetry impossible—can the mind be free. The body glories in union, in coupling; the mind requires singularity. The body does not write poetry but effaces vision, leaving nothing to describe. **"Song of Invisible Boundaries,"** the penultimate poem in **"Marathon,"** clarifies the derailment effected by Eros:

> Last night I dreamed we were in Venice;
> today, we are in Venice. Now, lying here,
> I think there are no boundaries to my dreams,
> nothing we won't share.
> So there is nothing to describe. We're
>   interchangeable
> with anyone, in joy
> changed to a mute couple.
>
> Then why did we worship clarity,
> to speak, in the end, only each other's names,
> to speak, as now, not even whole words,
> only vowels?

The reduction of speech to mere vowels, the O's of sexual excitement, remind us of the earlier poems of muteness and suffocation, the "man's paralyzing body," the "man's mouth sealing my mouth"; the physical power of the man "meaning to silence me." Yet here the muteness is a "joy," which is why passion is so subversive. The speaker colludes with her own undoing:

> Finally, this is what we craved,
> this lying in the bright light without distinctions—
> we who would leave behind
> exact records.

Exactitude, of course, is impossible without distinctions. The bright light obliterates all boundaries, shapes, contours; it obviates the need or desire to "see." It frees the speaker from the hard, divisive work of poetry. In this aesthetic, the act of poetry belongs to the distinct and bounded world of the masculine, of cerebral Athena. The eros of the female, described as wet and unbounded in some poems, as blurred and lost in others ("The bed was like a raft," the poem **"Summer"** concludes, "I felt us drifting / far from our natures, toward a place where we'd discover nothing"), obscures vision. Glück's "hunger for structure"—which for her makes poetry possible—inclines toward the classical view. Anne Carson summarizes the Platonic model:

> [W]e see that woman is to be differentiated from man, in the ancient view, not only as wet from dry but as content from form, as the unbounded from the bounded, as polluted from pure. . . .

The image of woman as a formless content is one that is expressed explicitly in the philosophers. Plato compares the matter of creation to a mother, in his *Timaios,* for it is a "receptacle," "reservoir," "admission," which is "shapeless," "viewless," "all-receiving" and which "takes its form and activation from whatever shapes enter it." Aristotle accords to the male in the act of procreation the role of active agent, contributing "motion" and "formation" while the female provides the "raw material," as when a bed (the child) is made by a carpenter (the father) out of wood (the mother). Man determines the form, woman contributes the matter. Aristotle expresses a similar view in his *Physics,* and we might note that the Pythagorean table of oppositions sets πέρας ("boundary" or "limit") and ἄρρεν ("masculine") against ἄπεζρ ("the unbounded") and θῆλν ("feminine").

To be an artist, then, means to adopt the masculine imposition of boundary—how else can one survive the extinction of passion? But to take on the masculine notion of form does not mean the banishment of the female eros; nor does it mean an entirely successful self-mastery. In the dissection image of **"First Goodbye"** we're given the cryptic corollary: "the enforced light / shines on the blade." Again Glück points to an extrahuman agency that sets the wheels of destruction circling. Who or what enforces the light? The male dominance we're born into, instituted, as the earliest records attest, from the first structures of civilization? God? Or, in the intimate terms of **"The Beginning,"** is it simply and irrevocably the father? Whatever forces conspire to focus the light on the blade, the *use* of that blade becomes the poem.

Divided from the father, using the tools of the father, succumbing to the father (or the lover that is his proxy)—all this seems to make a case for masculine power that cannot be equaled, or even approached, by the feminine. Analysis appears to win over passion. And yet the last, and most important, poem in **"Marathon"** (called **"Marathon"**) eerily sabotages what we think we have been thinking through these nine stages. Here's the entire poem:

> I was not meant to hear
> the two of them talking.
> But I could feel the light of the torch
> stop trembling, as though it had been
> set on a table. I was not to hear
> the one say to the other
> how best to arouse me,
> with what words, what gestures,
> nor to hear the description of my body,
> how it responded, what
> it would not do. My back was turned.
> I studied the voices, soon distinguishing
> the first, which was deeper, closer,
> from that of the replacement.
> For all I know, this happens
> every night: somebody waking me, then
> the first teaching the second.
> What happens afterward
> occurs far from the world, at a depth
> where only the dream matters
> and the bond with any one soul
> is meaningless; you throw it away.

Beyond the obvious (woman as sex-toy, plaything to be shared between men), lies the poet's astounding decision to remain still and study the voices, to analyze, in effect, her own erotic. And here the significance of the word "marathon" takes on greater dimension. In Greek Olympi-

ads, of course, the marathon runners were men, testing their strength, endurance, prowess, all based on their own knowledge of their own bodies—how they responded, what they would and would not do. They competed against other runners, but they raced against themselves. Louise Glück shifts the grounds of the metaphor. Here the sexual engine is female; the males must run in relay, as they haven't the stamina or endurance to perform singly. The body of the woman (in her sleeping state, the normal one when she is "not supposed to hear" the men discussing her) is presented simply as object, a baton passed between teammates as they run. And therefore we expect the indictment. Socially, politically, psychically, poetically this condition of "object" is unacceptable. Acquiescence is unthinkable. And yet the speaker in the poem does not move: "For all I know, this happens / every night: somebody waking me, then / the first teaching the second." Could it be that we're misreading this phallic relay? That in fact the *men* are objects, mere erotic instruments? The poet doesn't say. "What happens afterward / occurs far from the world," far from our notions of the politically correct, far, even, from the speaker's Athenian ability to analyze and dissect her own sexuality. The world of the father, with its civilizing restraints, its *boundaries,* its specific attachments, recedes; passion takes the "I" to a depth "where only the dream matters / and the bond with any one soul / is meaningless; you throw it away." That's a terrifying conclusion. The anchor of fidelity, marriage, normal sexual response—all lost. The exactitude necessary for art—gone. "The bond with any one soul is meaningless; you throw it away." The nihilism of Eros means social abdication—the death of the Father—but it also means the dissolution of self and thus the death of art. In a way, this marathon races between the poet's two selves, where the line distinguishing male and female, will and genitals, art and passion, is crossed and recrossed, whose only finish is death. "It will run its course," Glück says in **"The Encounter,"**

> the course of fire,
> setting a cold coin on the forehead, between the
>   eyes.
> You lay beside me; your hand moved over my face
> as though you had felt it also—
> you must have known, then, how I wanted you.
> We will always know that, you and I.
> The proof will be my body.

> It is all here,
> luminous water, the imprinted sapling

## Helen Vendler (essay date 1993)

SOURCE: "Flower Power," in *The New Republic,* Vol. 208, No. 21, May 24, 1993, pp. 35-8.

[*In this review of* The Wild Iris, *Vendler explains the poet's use of the metaphors of gardening and flowers to address issues of god, love, and ageing. The critic finds this approach to be reminiscent of previous poets and an interesting development for Glück. Vendler also insists that what has been viewed as the poet's mannered style is an essential poetic gesture.*]

Louise Glück is a poet of strong and haunting presence. Her poems, published in a series of memorable books over the last twenty years, have achieved the unusual distinction of being neither "confessional" nor "intellectual" in the usual senses of those words, which are often thought to represent two camps in the life of poetry. For a long time, Glück refused both the autobiographical and the discursive, in favor of a presentation that some called mythical, some mystical.

The voice in the poems is entirely self-possessed, but it is not possessed by self in a journalistic way. It told tales, rather, of an archetypal man and woman in a garden, of Daphne and Apollo, of mysteriously significant animal visitations. Yet behind those stories there hovered a psychology of the author that lingered, half-seen, in the poems. Glück's language revived the possibilities of high assertion, assertion as from the Delphic tripod. The words of the assertions, though, were often humble, plain, usual; it was their hierarchic and unearthly tone that distinguished them. It was not a voice of social prophecy, but of spiritual prophecy—a tone that not many women had the courage to claim.

It was something of a shock, therefore, when Glück's recent book *Ararat* turned away from symbol to "real life," which was described with a ruthless flatness as though honesty demanded a rock-bottom truth distilled out of years of reflection. In that book Glück restrained her piercing drama of consciousness, and reined in her gift for poetic elaboration. It was clear that some sort of self-chastisement was underway.

**Making contact:**

I thought once that poems were like words inscribed in rock or caught in amber. I thought in these terms so long, so fervently, with such investment in images of preservation and fixity, that the inaccuracies of the metaphor as description of my own experience did not occur to me until very recently. What is left out of these images is the idea of contact, and contact, of the most intimate sort, is what poetry can accomplish. Poems do not endure as objects but as presences. When you read anything worth remembering, you liberate a human voice; you release into the world again a companion spirit.

I read poems to hear that voice. And I write to speak to those I have heard.

*Louise Glück, "Death and Absence," in* Proofs & Theories: Essays on Poetry, *Ecco Press, 1994; essay originally published in 1984.*

Now, reversing course, she has written a very opulent, symbolic book, full—of all things—of talking flowers. The book is really one long poem, framed as a sequence of liturgical rites: the flowers talk to their gardener-poet; the poet, who is mourning the loss of youth, passion and the erotic life, prays to a nameless god (in Matins and Vespers, many times repeated); and the god, in a very tart voice, addresses the poet. As the flowers are to their gardener-poet, so is she to her gardener-god; the flowers, in their stoic biological collectivity, and their pathos, speak to her, sometimes reproachfully, as she speaks, imploringly, to her god. The god has a viewpoint both lofty and ironic, and repeatedly attacks the self-pity or self-centeredness of the poet. These are dangerous risks for a late twentieth-century poem to take, but Glück wins the wager of her premises. The human reader, too, is placed in "this isthmus of a middle state" (Pope) between the vegetatively animate world and the severe spiritual world, and shares the poet's predicament.

She is here returning to an earlier sequence of hers called **"The Garden,"** which rewrote the myth of Eden. As *The Wild Iris* progresses, we see that Eden has collapsed. The opening mood of the book reflects the absolute pointlessness of living when one can think of nothing to hope for. Despair prompts the liturgical addresses to the god (seven Matins by day in the first half of the sequence, ten Vespers by night in the second half). Most of the other titles in the sequence are names of flowers, beginning with the wild iris and ending with the silver lily, the gold lily and the white lilies.

Glück links herself in these flower-poems to her two chief predecessors in using flowers as images of the soul, George Herbert and Emily Dickinson. In spiritual deprivation, the soul is like a bulb hidden underground. In spring, it finds its season of flowering and renewal. Here is Herbert:

> Who would have thought my shriveled heart
> Could have recovered greenness? It was gone
> Quite underground, as flowers depart
> To see their mother root, when they have blown;
> Where they together,
> All the hard weather,
> Dead to the world, keep house unknown. . . .
>
> And now in age I bud again,
> After so many deaths, I live and write;
> I once more smell the dew and rain,
> And relish versing; O my only light,
> It cannot be
> That I am he
> On whom thy tempests fell all night.

And here, to bridge the gap of time between Herbert and Glück, is Dickinson:

> Through the dark Sod—as Education—
> The Lily passes sure—
> Feels her white foot—no trepidation—
> Her faith—no fear—

Afterward—in the Meadow
Swinging her Beryl-Bell—
The Mold-life—all forgotten—now—
In Ecstasy—and Dell—

In a more effortful moment, closer to the more despairing Glück poems, Dickinson wrote about the helpless religious pleading of the seed "That wrestles in the Ground, / Believing if it intercede / It shall at length be found."

But the lessons that the soul was taught in the seventeenth century and the nineteenth century have to be rescripted for the late twentieth century. No longer convinced of the preciousness of each individual soul, are we to grieve over our individual losses? In one of Glück's poems, the bed of scilla reproaches the poet for her focus on the erotic self, and urges her to abandon herself to collective biological being, to be one of an undifferentiated bed of human flowers. The collective wisdom of the scilla bed is one way of looking at one's fate: to say of oneself and others, "We go where we are sent by the wind of Fate, take root by water, and hear the mingled musics of life's current and its songs." Here is **"Scilla,"** as the flowers reprove the poet:

Not I, you idiot, not self, but we, we—waves
of sky blue like
a critique of heaven: why
do you treasure your voice
when to be one thing
is to be next to nothing?
Why do you look up? To hear
an echo like the voice
of god? You are all the same to us,
solitary, standing above us, planning
your silly lives: you go
where you are sent, like all things,
where the wind plants you,
one or another of you forever
looking down and seeing some image
of water, and hearing what? Waves,
and over waves, birds singing.

The poem **"Scilla"** is arranged on a few strings: one is the necklace of "-ing"'s (thing, nothing, standing, planning, things, looking, seeing, hearing, singing)—nine of them in seventeen short lines. The four successive questions comprise another string, and yet another is linked by water: "waves of sky blue," "some image of water," "waves," "waves." Even the word "echo" brings up the myth of Narcissus bending over water; we "look up" to hear the echo, and "look . . . down" to see an image. The sharp reproof of **"Scilla"** asks whether it should not be enough for us to see waves and hear bird-song. What, after all, do we need the post-reproductive erotic life for? And why should we lament its absence so bitterly?

Just when we might begin to believe in the scilla-solution and try to live like plants, Glück's god enters with *his* correction of the scilla's point of view:

Whatever you hoped,
you will not find yourselves in the garden,

among the growing plants.
Your lives are not circular like theirs:

your lives are the bird's flight
which begins and ends in stillness—
which *begins* and *ends,* in form echoing
this arc from the white birch
to the apple tree.

And would the poet want, in any case, to relive the erotic life? Glück answers with a picture of the archetypal young couple in the Garden:

I couldn't do it again,
I can hardly bear to look at it—

in the garden, in light rain
the young couple planting
a row of peas, as though
no one has ever done this before,
the great difficulties have never as yet
been faced and solved.

By the next poem, the garden is being called "the poisonous field," and the couple, fallen into mutual recrimination, are sharply chidden by the god, who reminds them that they suffer equally and should rise in spiritual stature through grief. As the man and the woman sink in self-pity, each saying, *"No one's despair is like my despair,"* the god retorts,

Do you suppose I care
if you speak to one another?
But I mean you to know
I expected better of two creatures
who were given minds: if not
that you would actually care for each other

at least that you would understand
grief is distributed
between you, among all your kind, for me
to know you, as deep blue
marks the wild scilla, white
the wood violet.

Glück's god is here voicing the Keatsian belief that individual grief creates personal identity, the "colors" of character. The ravishing musicality of Glück's ending emphasizes the surprisingly consonant nature of various identities: the *violet* is *white,* the scilla is *wild,* and *wild* and *white* and *violet* in the *woods* make for a phonetic beauty that stands for natural and moral beauty.

I have gone through this much of Glück's narrative simply to show its didactic and dialectical nature, its dimensions, its mythical means. The sequence is constantly surprising as it moves along, since we have no idea who will speak next, in what tone, with what spiritual argument. There is an exquisite defense, for instance, in **"Love in Moonlight,"** of all that the erotic life has meant, could mean, did mean. Outside, we see a summer evening, "a whole world thrown away on the moon":

and in the dark, the gold dome of
    the capitol
converted to an alloy of moonlight, shape
without detail, the myth, the archetype, the soul
filled with fire that is moonlight really, taken
from another source, and briefly
shining as the moon shines: stone or not,
the moon is still that much of a living thing.

Surely this fifteen-line "sonnet" in elegiac memory of the borrowed light of passionate love will hold its own against the strictures of scilla or the scilla's god.

And how does the story end? It has several endings. One is the poet's; she blossoms in spite of herself (the last Vespers). Three are the god's: the tender **"Sunset,"** the stern **"Lullaby"** and the pitiless **"September Twilight,"** as the god erases his work. Two are poems spoken by a single flower: **"The Silver Lily"** reassures the poet about the end, while **"The Gold Lily"** is full of terror and abandonment. Finally **"The White Lilies"** offers a colloquy between two lovers, as one calms the fear of the other with the old paradox that temporal burial is the avenue to imaginative eternity:

Hush, beloved. It doesn't matter to me
how many summers I live to return:
this one summer we have entered eternity.
I felt your two hands
bury me to release its splendor.

These old reciprocals—burial and permanence, mortality and eternity—are lyric standbys. But Glück's white lily, unlike Dickinson's and Herbert's flowers, will not rise from its "mold-life" except on the page.

What a strange book **The Wild Iris** is, appearing in this fin-de-siècle, written in the language of flowers. It is a *lieder* cycle, with all the mournful cadences of that form. It wagers everything on the poetic energy remaining in the old troubadour image of the spring, the Biblical lilies of the field, natural resurrection. It depends, too, on old religious notions of spiritual discipline. It is pre-Raphaelite, theatrical, staged and posed. It is even affected. But then, poetry has a right to these postures. When someone asked Wallace Stevens's wife whether she liked his poems, she answered, "I like Mr. Stevens's poems when they are not affected. But they are so often affected." And so they were. The trouble lay, rather, in Elsie Stevens's mistrust of affectation. It is one of the indispensable genstures in the poet's repertory.

**Stephen Yenser  (essay date 1994)**

SOURCE: "Wild Plots," in *Partisan Review,* Vol. LXI, No. 2, Spring, 1994, pp. 350-55.

[*Yenser is American poet, educator, and critic. Here, he acknowledges that the fifty-four poems in* The Wild Iris *generate a complete sequence; nevertheless, he asserts that the use of many voices is a problematic aspect of her work in the volume.*]

Louise Glück's **The Wild Iris** characteristically contains no poem longer than thirty lines, and many of the poems gleam with the knifing ironies and the burnished paradoxes that have always marked her work, while some show a new visionary fire; but there is a strong sense in which this, her sixth volume, is really a single, rhizomic sequence, a complex structure that we can now see has been evolving at least since her third volume, **Descending Figure,** and which is embodied, in a less integrated form, in her fifth, **Ararat**. Glück wrote these fifty-four poems in ten weeks, a period that lends the book an organizational element: the poems in its first half are set mostly in the spring, while those in its second half occur in deepening summer. At the same time, Glück moves from morning to evening, since the lyrics in the poet's voice in the first half are mostly called **"Matins,"** while the corresponding poems in the last half are **"Vespers."** Taken together, these poems from the poet's point of view constitute one of three kinds of poem in **Wild Iris**. Poems of a second kind see things from the vantage of nature—or, to be more specific, flowers and other vegetation in the family garden. The remaining poems, whose titles usually designate a time of day, a season, or a weather condition, are in the voice of God—here a "father," a "master," a figure of "authority," and primarily Judaic, regardless of the crepuscular Catholic coloring of **"Matins"** and **"Vespers."** The presence of this third point of view puts Glück's compelling sequence in a venerable and recently quite vigorous but ever startling genre that reaches in English from George Herbert through Blake and Yeats to John Berryman and Ted Hughes and James Merrill.

The jacket copy's exigent prose tells us that the volume creates "an impassioned polyphonic exchange among the god 'who disclose[s] / virtually nothing,' human beings who 'leave / signs of feeling / everywhere,' and a garden where 'whatever / returns from oblivion returns / to find a voice.'" In fact, things are both more and less complicated than that. For instance, it is precisely "polyphonic exchange" that never occurs. The different speakers usually don't hear and never truly understand or respond directly to one another, and they rarely (if significantly) speak in unison—and their different isolations give the sequence much of its reverberating pathos. As God puts it in **"Sunset,"** when addressing the poet: "My great happiness / is the sound your voice makes / calling to me even in despair; my sorrow / that I cannot answer you / in speech you accept as mine."

As that passage will suggest, Glück's strategy entails certain nagging epistemological difficulties. For one, God speaks to the poet in words that she cannot understand but can somehow transcribe in the language that she writes and that we read. Or can we elude that paradox by drawing a hard distinction between the "poet" and the human "speaker" of the **"Matins"** and **"Vespers"**—in which case, the invisible "poet" knows the language of God but her "speaker" does not? If so, as the dust jacket puts it mighty casually, we have here a "ventriloquism," whereby the poet throws her voice into God and garden as well as into her own stand-in. Or perhaps we are to infer God as the source of all voices and the rest of the speakers as dummies. But the speaker in one of the **"Matins,"** for *her* part, finds the proposition that God "must be all things" entirely "useless." Maybe we should not posit a source at all; maybe we can know only that we are enmeshed in a network of desiring voices deaf to one another. The possibilities are intriguing—the more so because each of the points of view is contradictory. Thus while God claims transcedent attributes, he is ordinarily all too human (petty, pitying, vindictive, impotent). Similarly, the voices from the garden are sometimes imperious and unfeeling (**"The Hawthorn Tree"** and **"Lanium"**), sometimes wonderfully passionate (**"Trillium"** and **"The Jacob's Ladder"**).

My best guess is that we are dealing with conflicting projections of a single, solipsistic, human sensibility, to which each moment has its own flaring, lyrical life and transitory, dramatic truth. Something like this motivates Berryman's "Homage to Mistress Bradstreet" and Merrill's "From the Cupola" (*The Changing Light at Sandover,* by contrast, resembles *Paradise Lost* in that God is a character in an epic pageant, rather than another importunate lyric presence), but in each of these other poems the conflict is sharply defined and part of the crucial issue from the outset. It is not clear to me that such a psychomachia is sustained in *The Wild Iris*—though I must say that Glück's marvelous final poem brings the different voices together in a fashion reminiscent of the closes of those earlier twentieth-century masterpieces and that it works best for me when I imagine that it springs from and momentarily resolves such a drama. Here is the last stanza:

> Hush, beloved. It doesn't matter to me
> how many summers I live to return:
> this one summer we have entered eternity.
> I felt your two hands
> bury me to release its splendor.

"We," exactly. The title **"The White Lilies"** suggests that this voice is that of the flowers, speaking to the poet/gardener; but the lilies symbolize resurrection and thus blur into the incarnate god, who could be speaking to the poet; while the elated poet herself might deservedly feel that this part of her has been planted like a bulb in the autumn by a gardener/god. In any event, *The Wild Iris* is a perennial.

## Emily Gordon  (essay date 1996)

SOURCE: "Above an Abyss," in *The Nation,* New York, Vol. 262, No. 17, April 29, 1996, pp. 28-30.

[*In this excerpt, Gordon views Glück's* Meadowlands *as a subverted* Odyssey, *telling the story of a voyage away from the ultimate union between Ulysses and Penelope, with the wife in* Meadowlands *being depicted as Penelope unweaving the fabric of the marriage.*]

For Louise Glück in her newest book, divorce is the start awake after the sleep-walking of a bad relationship. As in some of her previous collections, she draws from a mythic source in *Meadowlands,* using central figures and themes from *The Odyssey* to illustrate the dissolution of her marriage. There is abundant proof in *Meadowlands* that Glück has resources to equal those of Odysseus, who says (in Homer's words) "I have a heart that is inured to suffering. . . . So let this new disaster come. It only makes one more."

There are many more in Glück's voyage. The uneasy marital landscape of the Pulitzer Prize-winning *The Wild Iris* has been torn up in *Meadowlands* by frustration and violence. In **"Parable of the Hostages,"** Glück writes of the Greek soldiers that "the world had begun / calling them, an opera beginning with the war's / loud chords and ending with the floating aria of the sirens." *Meadowlands* follows much the same model, the earlier poems sketching apprehension and raw hostility, the final poems succumbing to acceptance. But no one is immune from tragedy, and as foreshadowed in *The Wild Iris's* **"April,"** the "grief is distributed / between you"—as is the tending of this malignant garden. The destruction, as Glück shows us, has been gradual, and has thus done that much more damage.

*Meadowlands* is haunted by voices. Glück speaks in the persona of Penelope, waiting for a husband who will, in this case, never come back. Glück's husband, half of a continuing dialogue, is a frequently cruel Odysseus. (After telling her to wish on a butterfly, he announces smugly, "It doesn't count.") Like Anne Sexton and others, Glück lets traditional villainesses speak for themselves, giving a sympathetic voice to a siren and to Circe, who in **"Circe's Power"** has a refreshing defense: "I never turned anyone into a pig. / Some people are pigs; I make them / look like pigs." A frustrated, perceptive Telemachus has several monologues as well.

As Penelope, Glück addresses many of the poems to the husband/Odysseus. "What can I tell you that you don't know / that will make you tremble again?" she asks. That's just the trouble: Language no longer serves; its purpose is to wound, not to make up or make love, and these two can't talk about anything without being bilious: "Look what you did—/ you made the cat move." "The only time you're totally happy / is when you cut up a chicken." "You'd be a nicer person / if you were a fan of something."

Actually, they're both fans—of the New York Giants, whose home stadium is in—surprise—the Meadowlands. The book is full of sudden juxtapositions of elements from two familiar but disparate worlds, classical Greece and modern America. Why has Glück chosen the location of a football field to frame this tempest? Perhaps because stadiums, the setting of both glory and carnage, are our equivalent of the Homeric battlefield, which here is also the last stand of the heart. As one voice—Glück's, it seems—points out in **"Meadowlands 3,"** the name seems inappropriate: the stadium "has / about as much in common with a pasture / as would the inside of an oven." The husband comes back with "New Jersey / was rural. They want you / to remember that." The same could be said of their marriage: Its origins were green.

Separation can speak for itself: "From this point on," Glück says in **"Quiet Evening,"** "the silence through which you move / is my voice pursuing you." She has arranged *Meadowlands,* full of ocean references, in wave patterns: poems describing hints of reconciliation alternate with accounts of the triggering of the minefields both have been planting for a decade. The knock of waves against pilings is an answer to the perpetual question *Do you love me?* Yes and no and yes and no. And if silence can be speech, absence connives to be presence as well. **"Departure"** is a literalist's word: As Glück's Penelope tells us in **"Ithaca,"** "The beloved doesn't / need to live. The beloved / lives in the head."

If *The Odyssey* is the story of Odysseus's homecoming, *Meadowlands* details its negative: the same ten years journey, but away from Ithaca, toward uncharted waters. As in Homer, Glück's husband and wife suffer separately and without benefit of communication. But in this version, they have to visit treacherous islands together: Bicker, Nostalgia, Regret. Instead of Penelope's nightly unweaving to deceive her suitors, here it is the marriage that is being undone; when all is said and done there is nothing but memory, a poor foundation, to hold them up.

The husband—"a man training himself to avoid the heart"— is no hero here, and in **"Penelope's Song"** the wife says to herself, "you have not been completely / perfect either; with your troublesome body / you have done things you shouldn't / discuss in poems." Conspicuously, Glück avoids specifying what Penelope—she—has done in the absence of the wandering king. She also leaves out the details of the husband's wanderings, though the blame seems principally assigned to him.

The starkness, the lack of filigree, in Glück's lines is a window on her internal pandemonium. Her Siren says, "I think now / if I felt less I would be / a better person." Frequently Glück's characters say things they seem to be trying to convince themselves of, as when she writes, of a flock of birds rising, "You must learn to think of our passion that way. / Each kiss was real, then / each kiss left the face of the earth." The statement is painful and consciously untrue. No kiss that crucial ever leaves the face of the earth; each one lives and dies with us. This husband and wife have a permanent claim on each other.

But in this game's last quarter, bewilderment and blame play very rough. Still Glück emerges as a victorious quarterback, scarred by love: "This is the end, isn't it? / And you are here with me again, listening with me: *the sea / no longer torments me; the self / I wished to be is the self I am.*"

**Vijay Seshadri (essay date 1996)**

SOURCE: "The Woe That Is in Marriage," in *The New Yorker,* May 13, 1996, pp. 93-4.

[*In this review of* Meadowlands, *Seshadri suggests that Glück's considerable lyric expertise and meticulous craft have been tempered by an earthiness and humor.*]

Even before Louise Glück's new volume, **Meadowlands** was published, admirers could be heard describing it, somewhat incongruously, as a "funny" book, with the implication that this represented a significant aesthetic departure. There was something faintly comic in itself about this advance word, which had to do with the inexpert way that people try to generate excitement about a book of poetry. It's a fact that our most accomplished poets can be at least as entertaining as a good "Seinfeld" episode, yet when poetry lovers say as much their claims are often greeted with skepticism. And for readers who are addicted to Glück's ironic inflections, her stern disenchantments, and her capacity to locate the hiding places of a massive, stationary reality, this talk was unsettling for another reason as well. Did we really want a funny Louise Glück? Readers of poetry tend to crave more of the same: they don't like to be excessively surprised by poets whom they've appropriated to their own experience.

*Meadowlands is* surprising and in places very funny (when Glück read from it to a packed house in New York recently, she got lots of laughs), but it's more accurately characterized as an arrival than as a departure. For more than a decade, Glück has been writing books of poems that are meant to be encountered like novels, and has been looking into the difficult problem of finding a structure whereby an essentially lyric gift can be adapted to epic and unifying ambitions. *Meadowlands* gives us her most elaborate and satisfying solution. If her previous book, *The Wild Iris,* was said to resemble a song cycle, this one can be said to resemble a complete cantata, with dramatis personae, recitatives, arias, and instrumental passages. The elements that we have come to associate with her writing—the terse lines over which a diaphanous rhetoric has been carefully laid, the abrupt shifts from romance to hardheadedness and back, the dramatic vocalizations, the flexible use of Greek and Biblical myths—have found a home in a large, baroque edifice.

Much that is authentically new has also been housed here. The vibrant schema of the book, which, in ambiguous counterpoint, employs characters and incidents from the *Odyssey*—a poem of arrivals and reconciliations—to tell the story of a dissolving marriage, accommodates all sorts of fresh feelings and tensions, ranging from the scabrous, such as "I said you could snuggle. That doesn't mean / your cold feet all over my dick," to the naïvely insistent, as in

> If you can hear the music
> you can imagine the party.
> I have it all planned: first
> violent love, then
> sweetness

and the mutely resigned:

> Does it matter where the birds go? Does

it even matter
what species they are?
They leave here, that's the point,
first their bodies, then their sad cries.
And from that moment, cease to exist
   for us.

This schema accommodates a chorus of actual persons, too, from the great dead (Maria Callas, Otis Redding) to next-door neighbors (the Lights, who entertain themselves by playing klezmer music) and figures from current events (Lawrence Taylor and Phil Simms, formerly of the New York Giants). Up to now, Glück volumes have been sparsely populated. *Meadowlands,* by comparison, is a metropolis.

Although Glück is still in the middle of her career, it's clear that she is one of those poets—like Yeats, for example, and unlike Stevens—whose writing is provoked by their unfolding temporal life. Consequently, her work falls naturally into discernible stages. She began by writing what used to be called "deep image" poetry, a variant of the confessional mid-century American lyric in which the otherwise static surface of the poem was enlivened by an infusion of energy from the subconscious:

   As though a voice were saying
   *You should be asleep by now—*
   But there was no one. Nor
   had the air darkened,
   though the moon was there,
   already filled in with marble.

This Celtic-twilight period ended with her third volume, *Descending Figure* (1980)—a perfect book of poetry, but one whose very perfection seemed to exhaust its inherent possibilities. In her next book, *The Triumph of Achilles* (1985), Glück turned away from this earlier work with a vengeance:

   It is not the moon, I tell you.
   It is these flowers
   lighting the yard.

   I hate them.
   I hate them as I hate sex,
   the man's mouth
   sealing my mouth, the man's
   paralyzing body—

The oblique way of working which she had mastered was now brought to bear on sexual and familial politics and on the sensation, always excruciating in this poet, of consciousness trapped in nature. The poems were at once more intimate than confessions and more objective than allegories. They looked slender but were nevertheless monumental; they had sharp edges, and they gleamed with asperity and carefully modulated anger.

Glück hasn't abandoned the edges and the anger in *Meadowlands,* and obliqueness still characterizes her method of operation, though at an angle of incidence considerably less steep. What distinguishes *Meadowlands* from her previous work is the earthiness that she displays and the newfound willingness to let her readers enter the honey-combed quotidian life out of which her poetry is written. This is a brave gesture on her part, and it reflects a supremely rewarded poetic self-confidence.

---

## FURTHER READING

### Criticism

Baker, David. "Kinds of Knowing." *The Kenyon Review* 15, No. 1 (Winter 1993): 184-92.

   In a review of several books of poetry, Baker recognizes the difficulty of presenting intellectual strategies in lyric poetry, declaring that Glück's refusal of image as the essence of poetry is responsible for the success of *The Wild Iris.*

Bonds, Diane S. "Entering Language in Louise Glück's *The House on Marshland*: A Feminist Reading." *Contemporary Literature* XXXI, No. 1 (Spring 1990): 58-75.

   Seeks a feminist resolution to the perceived problem of Glück's immersion in a literary tradition that is primarily male, concluding that Glück's work establishes a much-needed confrontation with androcentric myth.

Cramer, Steven. "Four True Voices of Feeling." *Poetry* CLVII, No. 2 (November 1990): 101-06.

   Recognizes in *Ararat* the elevation of the personal to a tragic level, with Glück using short lyrics to refer to a more inclusive narrative within herself. However, Cramer sees Glück's real risk-taking in her use of metaphor rather than image, of explanation over suggestion.

George, E. Laurie. "The 'harsher figure' of *Descending Figure*: Louise Glück's 'Dive into the Wreck'." *Women's Studies* XVII, No. 3 (1990): 235-47.

   Begins with the alignment of Glück and Adrienne Rich, as George seeks to disclose a radical feminist base for Glück's poetry. George further contends that Glück's primary artistic struggle is against her own raging silence in response to a male-dominated society.

Glück, Louise. "Louise Glück." In *Fifty Contemporary Poets: The Creative Process,* edited by Alberta T. Turner, pp. 110-114. New York: David McKay Company, 1977.

   Discusses the source, composition, and revision of her 1976 poem sequence "The Garden" in response to Turner's questionnaire. Glück notes the departure of these "companion poems" from her typical shorter lyric.

———.*Proofs & Theories: Essays on Poetry.* Hopewell, N.J.: Ecco Press, 1994.

   Collects sixteen of Glück's essays, including critical studies of other poets and commentary on her own work and writing processes.

Hart, Henry. "Story-tellers, Myth-makers, Truth-sayers." *New England Review* XV, No. 4 (Fall 1993): 192-206.

Reviews Glück's *The Wild Iris,* which Hart compares to the poetry of Emily Dickinson and H.D., though he recognizes in Glück's poems her unwavering focus on her own personal archetypes.

Kitchen, Judith. "The Woods Around It." *The Georgia Review* XLVII, No. 1 (Spring 1993): 145-59.
  Applauds Glück's return in *The Wild Iris* to the site of her earlier poem sequence "The Garden." Kitchen asserts, however, that Glück is breaking new ground, cultivating a personal mythology out of which springs a deep spirituality.

Muske, Carol. "Wild Iris." *The American Poetry Review* XX,

No. 1 (January/February 1993): 52-4.
  Views Glück's theme in her sixth book as an argument between the wild and the domestic, observing that once again Glück is in such deep exploration of the conventional world that her work as a poet seems to be dissection.

Vendler, Helen. "Sociable Comets." *The New York Review of Books* XXVIII, No. 12 (16 July 1981): 24-6.
  Compares John Ashbery's *Shadow Train* with Glück's *Descending Figure,* addressing the force of myth in both poets' work, as well as their very different manipulations of lyric. Vendler closes with a refutation of the notion that Glück's work is too pure to be emotionally engaging.

---

**Additional coverage of Glück's life and career is contained in the following sources published by Gale Research:** *Contemporary Authors* **Vols. 33-36 (rev. ed.);** *Contemporary Authors New Revision Series,* **Vol. 40;** *Contemporary Literary Criticism,* **Vols. 7, 22, 44, 81;** *Dictionary of Literary Biography,* **Vol. 5; and** *DISCovering Authors.*

# Jupiter Hammon
## 1711(?)–1800(?)

American poet and essayist.

## INTRODUCTION

Contrary to popular belief, Hammon, not Phillis Wheatley, was America's first published black author. His poem *An Evening Thought: Salvation by Christ, with Penetential Cries* is dated December 25, 1760 and was printed in 1761, preceding Wheatley's verse by at least nine years. All of his writing expresses Christian themes and avoids confrontation with the slaveholding class that governed Hammon's life. Although he is relatively unrenowned, Hammon remains important as the first black American author to appear in print. His verses are considered the forerunners of Negro spirituals and abolitionist dialogues.

### Biographical Information

Hammon's birthdate is believed to be October 11, 1711, though many sources place his birth nearly ten years later. He was born a slave on the estate of Henry Lloyd on Long Island and served the Lloyd family for three generations. As a household slave, Hammon was given many privileges not available to other slaves: he attended primary school with Lloyd's children and learned to read and write. In 1733 Hammon purchased a Bible from Lloyd and began the religious studies that greatly influenced both his poetry and prose. The inspirational hymns of Charles Wesley, John Newton, and William Cowper also profoundly affected Hammon's verse. Hammon's poems were issued on broadsides, large sheets of paper with print on one side only. He published four poems in this manner with his own resources and the financial assistance of his owners. His first poem, *An Evening Thought*, appeared in 1761. After the death of Henry Lloyd in 1763, Hammon became the property of Lloyd's son Joseph, who fled with his family to Connecticut when the British took control of Long Island. In Hartford, Hammon produced several works, the most noteworthy being *An Address to Miss Phillis Wheatly* [sic]. Following the death of Joseph Lloyd, Hammon returned to Long Island as the property of Joseph's nephew, John Lloyd, Jr. Hammon produced only one work, *Address to the Negroes in the State of New-York*, after his return to the Lloyd estate, although it is possible that other pages of manuscript were never discovered. This last work, an essay, became Hammon's most popular piece. The date of Hammon's death is uncertain. The final mention of him in the Lloyd estate records is entered under the year 1790. From eulogistic references to him in the introduction to a later edition of *An Address to the Negroes in the State of New-York*, it is known that Hammon died before the date of publication, 1806.

## Major Works

*An Address to Miss Phillis Wheatly*, Hammon's most significant poem, suggests that Wheatley's enslavement in Ethiopia, arrival in America, and conversion to Christianity were the product of divine will. The poem *An Evening Thought*, which strongly resembles eighteenth-century devotional hymns, reflects Hammon's evangelical preoccupation with salvation, righteousness, and eternal life. *A Poem for Children with Thoughts on Death* consists of seventeen quatrains, each linked to a Biblical verse. Through interpretation of the Biblical passages, the quatrains admonish young people and advise them to follow Scripture. Hammon's last poem, *The Kind Master and Dutiful Servant*, appeared in his essay *An Evening's Improvement: Shewing the Necessity of Beholding the Lamb of God*. A dialogue in verse, it recommends that all slaves show dutiful servitude and reminds them that salvation is available through the love of God.

## Critical Reception

Hammon's work has not been widely discussed. Some commentators criticize Hammon for his repetitive use of themes and language and occasionally weak syntax, while others find his meter and rhymes forced or otherwise imperfect. The primary reason for Hammon's obscurity, however, is most likely what Vernon Loggins called the author's "conciliatory attitude towards slavery." Hammon was not an avid abolitionist, and his seeming acceptance of servitude has made him unpopular with some readers. However, after more than a century of neglect, twentieth-century critics are now beginning to recognize Hammon's important contribution to early black American literature.

---

## PRINCIPAL WORKS

### Poetry

*An Evening Thought: Salvation by Christ, with Penetential* [sic] *Cries* 1761
*An Address to Miss Phillis Wheatly* [sic] 1778
*A Winter Piece: Being a Serious Exhortation, with a Call to the Unconverted, and a Short Contemplation on the Death of Jesus Christ* (essay and poetry) 1782
†*An Evening's Improvement: Shewing the Necessity of Beholding the Lamb of God. The Kind Master and Dutiful Servant* (essay and poetry) 1783
*America's First Negro Poet: The Complete Works of Jupiter Hammon of Long Island* (essays and poetry) 1970

## Other Major Works

*An Essay on the Ten Virgins* (essay) 1779
*An Address to the Negroes in the State of New-York* (essay) 1787

*Includes *A Poem for Children, with Thoughts on Death.*

†The publication date of this work is uncertain.

---

## CRITICISM

### Oscar Wegelin (essay date 1915)

SOURCE: "Biographical Sketch," in *America's First Negro Poet: The Complete Works of Jupiter Hammon of Long Island,* edited by Stanley Austin Ransom, Jr., Kennikat Press, 1970, pp. 29-31.

[*In the following excerpt from an essay originally published in 1915, Wegelin appraises Hammon's poetry as "commonplace" but concludes that his role as America's first black poet is noteworthy.*]

As a poet Hammon will certainly not rank among the "Immortals." His verse is stilted, and while some of his rhymings are fairly even, we can easily comprehend that they were written by one not well versed in the art of poesy. They have a sameness which is wearying to the reader and there is too much reiteration, in some cases the same or nearly the same words being employed again and again.

His verse is saturated with a religious feeling not always well expressed, as he did not possess the ability to use the right word at the proper time. Hammon was undoubtedly deeply religious, but his religion was somewhat tinged with narrowness and superstition, a not uncommon fault of the time in which he lived and wrote.

Although grammatically almost perfect, it seems certain that an abler and more experienced hand than his own was responsible for this.

Compared with the verses of Phillis Wheatley, his lines are commonplace and few would care to read them more than once. When we consider, however, that this poor slave had probably no other learning than what he had been enabled to secure for himself during his hours of relaxation from labor, it is surprising that the results are not more meagre. Although his rhymings can hardly be dignified by the name of poetry, they are certainly not inferior to many of the rhymings of his day and generation.

As before noted, his lines breathe a deep religious feeling and were written with the hope that those who would read them would be led from the ways of sin to righteousness.

His poetical address to Miss Wheatley was written with this end in view and may have had more than a passing effect on that young woman.

He was fond of using certain words, and "Salvation" was one of his favorites, it being made use of twenty-three times in his earliest known publication. . . .

Hammon was also fond of using marginal references from Scripture and in some of his writings they are found at every second line. He was evidently a deep student of the Bible and was inspired by what the Good Book taught him. It seems probable that his effusions were the means of bringing many of his fellow bondmen to the throne of grace.

When we consider that he was probably without any education whatsoever, we marvel that he accomplished as much as he did. Had he had the advantages of learning possessed by Miss Wheatley, it seems possible that as a poet he would have ranked as her equal, if not her superior. His prose writings were also above the mediocre, but from the testimony of one of his printers he was evidently deficient as a speller.

He stands, however, unique in the annals of American poetry and his works must not be too harshly judged. The disadvantages under which he composed them were probably far greater than we can imagine.

It seems, however, too bad that his verse is entirely of a religious nature. Much would have been added to its interest had he written about some of the events that were transpiring all around him during the War for Independence and the years that followed that struggle.

He seems to have been content to sing the praises of the Master whom he longed to serve and whose reward he some day expected to receive, and with that end in view he labored to instill the blessings of religion into his less fortunate brethren.

For this his memory should be honored and let the broken lines which fell from his pen be cherished, if for no other reason than that they were written by the first American Negro who attempted to give expression to his thoughts in verse.

### Kenny J. Williams (essay date 1970)

SOURCE: "A New Home in a New Land," in *They Also Spoke: An Essay on Negro Literature in America, 1787-1930,* Townsend Press, 1970, pp. 3-49.

[*In the following excerpt, Williams compares Hammon's poetry to seventeenth- and eighteenth-century American religious verse.*]

[Hammon's] first publication was a poem of eighty-eight lines entitled *An Evening Thought; Salvation by Christ,*

*With Penetential Cries*. The title page carries his name and asserts that he is a slave "belonging to Mr. Lloyd, of Queen's Village, on Long Island," and the poem is dated December 25, 1760. As the title pages of his publications indicate, Hammon belonged to three different members of the Lloyd family of Long Island. . . .

Apparently the Lloyds were considerate masters who allowed Hammon a great deal of freedom of movement, for he wrote in *An Address to the Negroes in the State of New York* in 1787: "I have good reason to be thankful that my lot is so much better than most slaves have had. I suppose I have had more advantages than most of you who are slaves have ever known, and I believe more than many white people have enjoyed." Among the advantages to which he referred was the granting of the opportunity, elementary though the results might have been, to receive instruction in reading and writing and to attend church freely, where he probably absorbed the doctrines of Calvinism which are an integral part of his poetry.

Stimulated by his religion, Hammon read not only the Bible and the hymn books of his day but also such pious poems as Wigglesworth's then popular *The Day of Doom*. In fact Hammon's **"A Poem for Children with Thoughts on Death"** seems to paraphrase that section of Wigglesworth's poem which describes the fate of children who die in infancy without the benefits of church membership. Hammon's knowledge of both prose and poetic style was probably greatly influenced by his reading. Although it is difficult to determine the extent of Hammon's popularity in his own day, there was a considerable market in America for didactic poetry. Hammon himself said in his *An Address to the Negroes in the State of New York*: "When I was at Hartford, in Connecticut, where I lived during the War, I published several pieces which were well received, not only by those of my own colour, but by a number of white people, who thought they might do good among the servants."

Although most of his poetry was published at Hartford at a time when the Hartford Wits were attempting to aid in the creation of a national literature, there is a great deal of difference between any of their works and the existing poems by Hammon. His poetry was not hampered by the rules of neoclassicism as was the work of the Hartford Wits, neither was his poetry [a] pallid imitation of current English modes. Rather, his poetry is closer in spirit and technique to the poetry of the earlier century of New England, the poetry produced by the New England Puritans of the seventeenth century. Much of this poetry is buried in the annals of New England, but there does exist a tremendous body of it which grew out of the religious fervor of the period. There is in Hammon's poetry a religious feeling which resulted in an intensity which he apparently achieved without conscious effort. From hearing evangelical sermons and from reading the Bible according to his own interpretations, he adapted his ideas regarding salvation, penitence, redeeming grace, God's mercy, death, and judgment day to his poems. He recorded his ideas and impressions in a poetic meter which is designed to be heard. A word which appealed to him is repeated until the

very word itself seems to cast a spell. In *An Evening Thought* . . . the word *salvation* appears so often that the sound of the word becomes far more important than the message of the poem. . . .

Originally the poem was printed without a break between any of the lines; however, Hammon used a variation of the ballad stanza, a verse form which is often found in Methodist and in Baptist hymnals and which is the basic pattern of *The Day of Doom*. This pattern consists of quatrains whose first and third lines are iambic tetrameter and whose second and fourth lines are iambic trimeter; the four-line stanza has a usual rhyme scheme of abcb. Although Hammon followed this pattern in most of his poems, there are instances of irregularities which can be seen in *An Evening Thought.* . . . In addition to his adaptation of the ballad rhyme pattern to abab, there are examples of distorted accents as well as of syncopation which occur most frequently in the iambic trimeter lines. To the twentieth-century reader, Hammon's poetry seems similar to so much of eighteenth-century poetry for his work tends to employ unusual rhyming patterns and combinations, such as: sin/king, ocean/salvation, abode/God, given/heaven, obtain/name, care/fear, here/share. When odd uses of poetic diction occur, they often result because his choice of language is an immediate outgrowth of an apparent need for rhyming patterns.

**"The Kind Master and the Dutiful Servant"** was published in Hartford apparently during the Revolutionary War. It is a dialogue between a master and his servant on such matters as salvation, grace, Heaven, and other subjects bordering on religion. Interestingly enough, the two poetic characters do not mention the inconsistency of the principles of Christianity with the belief in human slavery. Throughout the entire dialogue the two participants manage to keep the affairs of earth and heaven separate. The poem's concluding ideas seem to justify the poet's own belief that both slaveholder and slave can be practicing Christians and both can be considered the children of God. The poem appeared at the end of a sermon by Hammon entitled *An Evening's Improvement* which was issued as a pamphlet, and it was an attempt to summarize the essential meaning of the sermon.

It is apparent that most of Hammon's religious poetry is characterized by a certain naivete, and his art of versification seems little more than spontaneously rhymed doggerel; but this is the same charge which is frequently hurled at Michael Wigglesworth who also used poetry as a means of instruction and as a means of simply stating basic religious concepts. The difference between these two poets, however, rests in the difference between the complexity of the religious dogma of Puritanism which is explained by Wigglesworth and the simplicity of the more primitive forms of Protestantism. In the eighteenth century complexity of dogma and creed was not a characteristic of the Methodist and Baptist movements which appealed to those who wanted their religion unencumbered by the perplexity of an involved or a complicated philosophical system. These more primitive groups stressed "religion by faith" as opposed to the Puritan emphasis on "religion by rea-

son." Wigglesworth—for example—in attempting to simplify Puritanism made its doctrines appear harsh and terrible when he placed them into ballad form; while Hammon, on the other hand, in attempting to capture the tone
of primitive Christianity, seems extremely childlike in his
wonder and in his awe.

---

**From hearing evangelical sermons and
from reading the Bible according to his
own interpretations, Hammon adapted
his ideas regarding salvation, penitence,
redeeming grace, God's mercy, death,
and judgment day to his poems. He
recorded his ideas and impressions in a
poetic meter which is designed to be
heard.**

**—*Kenny J. Williams***

---

In **"A Poem for Children with Thoughts on Death"**
Hammon visualizes the horrors of judgment day very much
as Wigglesworth had done in *The Day of Doom*. While he
includes words of warning to sinful children, Hammon
approaches his subject with a lightness of feeling, unlike
the tone of *The Day of Doom,* which pervades the poem.
The last line of the following two quatrains illustrates
Hammon's technique for making an unpleasant subject at
least palatable.

> Then shall ye hear the trumpet sound,
>   The graves give up their dead,
> Those blessed saints shall quick awake,
>   And leave their dusty beds.
>
> Then shall ye hear the trumpet sound,
>   And rend the native sky,
> Those bodies starting from the ground,
>   In the twinkling of an eye.

One of Hammon's more polished poems was addressed to
Phillis Wheatley in 1778. Five years before this poem
Wheatley had written "On Being Brought From Africa to
America," in which she claims that "mercy" had brought
her to this country and had introduced her to the redemptive powers of Christianity. Hammon repeats the same motif
by asserting:

> God's tender mercy brought thee here;
>   Tost o'er the raging main;
> In Christian faith thou hast a share,
>   Worth all of the gold in Spain.

Hammon concludes his poem by praising divine providence for bringing Phillis Wheatley from Africa to a place
where she could not only know the true religion but also
instruct others in its beneficent ways.

Hammon's two sermons appeared as pamphlets. *A Winter
Piece* was published in Hartford in 1782 and *An Evening's
Improvement* is an undated Hartford publication. Both
works illustrate rather erratic organization and structure.
In each one, however, he did include a poem. **"A Poem
for Children with Thoughts on Death"** appeared in the
former sermon, and **"The Kind Master and The Dutiful
Servant"** appeared in the latter. Both sermons include
admonitions to the unconverted to accept the ways of
Christianity, and both praise the practicing Christian.
Hammon completely minimizes the present in favor of a
future where all shall receive their "just rewards" for life
on earth. . . .

Hammon has been condemned because of his acceptance
of the institution of slavery; yet, it must be remembered
that he was in no position to understand it in its fullest
impact. With his limited experiences in Long Island and
in Hartford and with his own lot being much better than
that of the average workingman of the period, it is no
wonder that he tended to place all of his attention on
matters of religion. While his poems are far superior to
his prose works, his poetry is, after all, eighteenth-century
religious poetry and does not differ too greatly from other
such works of the period. His infrequent references to
slavery and to his race are the only distinguishing marks
of his work. The chaos of the rhythmic structure and the
distortions of rhyme which appear, the sudden bursts of
religious fervor, the sometimes strained poetic diction
coupled with apparent sincerity are characteristics of
religious poetry in America during the seventeenth and
eighteenth centuries.

### Sidney Kaplan   (essay date 1973)

SOURCE: "Jupiter Hammon," in *The Black Presence in
the Era of the American Revolution, 1770-1800,* New
York Graphic Society Ltd., 1973, pp. 171-80.

[*In the following excerpt, Kaplan briefly comments on the
prominence of religion in Hammon's verse.*]

It is altogether possible that Jupiter Hammon was a preacher to the slaves in the communities of Long Island and
Connecticut where he labored for the Lloyds. *An Evening
Thought,* an antiphonal poem echoing the word "Salvation" in twenty-three of its eighty-eight lines, has all the
ringing ecstatic hope for heavenly freedom with "tender
love" that charges the earliest spirituals of the enslaved.
The preacher calls and the flock responds—thus the "Penetential Cries."

> Dear Jesus unto Thee we cry,
>   Give us the Preparation;
> Turn not away thy tender Eye;
>   We seek thy true Salvation. . . .
> Lord hear our penetential Cry:
>   Salvation from above;
> It is the Lord that doth supply
>   With his Redeeming Love.

Jupiter Hammon wrote this hymn on Christmas Day of 1760, and for the next forty years, whenever he cried out in print to his black brothers and sisters, his theme, more or less, was always salvation. Yet there are hints towards the end of his career of a certain impatience, a feeling that freedom was possible—and desirable—in the Here as well as in the After.

It seems significant that his next poem of record, printed as a broadside eighteen years later when he was sixty-seven years old, is *An Address to Miss Phillis Wheatly* in twenty-one scripture-glossed quatrains, "published by the Author, and a number of his friends, who desire to join with him in their best regards" to "the Ethiopian Poetess." Five years after Phillis's *Poems* of 1773, Hammon echoes her sense of miracle in being rescued from pagan Africa.

> God's tender mercy brought thee here;
>    Tost o'er the raging main;
> In Christian faith thou hast a share,
>    Worth all the gold of Spain. . . .
> That thou a pattern still might be,
>    To youth of Boston town,
> The blessed Jesus set thee free,
>    From every sinful wound.

But did Hammon detect in her, at times, a note of frustration, even protest (which he took pains to conceal in his own poems)?

> Thou, Phillis, when thou hunger hast,
>    Or pantest for thy God;
> Jesus Christ is thy relief,
>    Thou hast the holy word.

The "holy word" of this stanza is tagged to Psalm XIII, in which "David complaineth of delay in help."

> How long wilt thou forget me O Lord? for ever? how long wilt thou hide thy face from me?
>
> How long shall I take counsel in my soul, *having* sorrow in my heart daily? how long shall mine enemy be exalted over me?
>
> Consider *and* hear me, O Lord my God: lighten my eyes, lest I sleep the *sleep* of death.

## R. Roderick Palmer (essay date 1974)

SOURCE: "Jupiter Hammon's Poetic Exhortations," in *CLA Journal,* Vol. XVIII, No. 1, September, 1974, pp. 22-8.

*[In the following excerpt, Palmer criticizes Hammon's poetic style and his "intoxication" with religion, suggesting that Hammon could have made a stronger statement against slavery.]*

Throughout his life, Hammon was able to reach remarkable stages of self-awareness and self-assertiveness. In this regard, Hughes and Bontemps state that "Hammon was an intelligent and privileged slave, respected by his master for his skill with tools and by some of his fellow slaves for his power as a preacher" [Langston Hughes and Arna Bontemps, eds., *The Poetry of the Negro,* 1949]. Thus, first as a preacher and later as a published poet, Hammon emerged as one of the foremost and influential shapers of non-militant modes of thinking and of religious preoccupations of his people.

The preaching tradition, along with the saving of souls, caught up in the black experience of slavery and oppression, did not spring into existence suddenly. In the book, *Black Preaching,* Henry Mitchell says that the earliest record of the conversion of blacks in the colonies is that of "Anthony, Negro; Isabel, Negro; William, their child, baptised on February 16, 1623, in Elizabeth City County in Virginia." In his time, Hammon became a moving force in perpetuating this tradition of preaching and saving souls. . . .

Due to his fondness for preaching, the major portion, if not all, of Hammon's poetry is religious in tone and is usually dismissed by critics as being of little aesthetic value. His poetry, however, is filled with didacticisms and aphorisms. Note this fact in selected verses of his first published poem, *An Evening Thought: Salvation by Christ With Penitential Cries.*

> Salvation comes by Jesus Christ alone
>    The only son of God;
> Redemption now to everyone,
>    That love his Holy Word.
>
> We cry as sinners to the Lord,
>    Salvation to obtain;
> It is firmly fixed His Holy Word,
>    Ye shall not cry in vain.
>
> Now is the Day, excepted Time;
>    The Day of Salvation;
> Increase your Faith; do not repine:
>    Awake ye, every Nation.

The reader becomes immediately aware of the contrived and forced rhymes and the poor quality of the verse patterns, which are archetypes of the early Methodist hymns. In fair appraisal, however, the critic simultaneously sees in the poet's crudely penned lines folksy themes that depict the mores of a people who envisioned a life lived righteously "on this side of Jordan" would reap rich rewards on the other side. [Jean] Wagner says that Hammon's verses "represent a halfway stage between the guileless art of the unknown composers of spirituals and the already much wordier manner of the black popular preacher" [*Black Poets of the United States,* 1973].

Eighteen years after Hammon's first verses appeared in print, a poem entitled *A Poetical Address to Phillis Wheat-*

*ly, Ethiopian Poetess*, reached the reading public. From this the following stanza is taken:

> While thousands muse with earthly toys,
>   And range about the street
> Dear Phillis, seek the heaven's joys,
>   Where we do hope to meet.

Throughout this poem, the poet based his theme on the fact that it was divine providence which brought Phillis Wheatley from heathen Africa to a land where she could know the true religion and teach it to others.

---

**Due to his fondness for preaching, the major portion, if not all, of Hammon's poetry is religious in tone and is usually dismissed by critics as being of little aesthetic value.**

*—R. Roderick Palmer*

---

In this and in all of his other poems, there are marked irregularities. The omission at times of one syllable and at other times two seems to mar the poetic line. Yet these profuse examples of syncopation, so characteristic of Negro dance rhythms, are fascinating. The stanzaic form is quatrain and the dominant metrical pattern is iambic tetrameter. Such prosody provides facile reading and almost puerile comprehension.

From **"The Kind Master and the Dutiful Servant,"** part of the dialogue is as follows:

*Master*

> Then will the happy day appear
>   That virtue shall increase;
> Lay up the sword and drop the spear,
>   And nations seek for peace.

*Servant*

> Then shall we see the happy end,
>   Tho' still in some distress;
> That distant foes shall act like friends,
>   And leave their wickedness.

Hammon's style here is conversational in tone. Like others, this poem and especially **"A Poem for Children with Thoughts on Death"** are meant to touch the heart strings with repetitions, predictable rhymes, and uncomplicated structures. All of the subject matter is basically religious with intent to move the heart and spirit, not the mind nor the muscle. It is surprising that in all of his writings the reader is unable to find one statement abhorring slavery and the deprivations of the black people of his era.

Considering the numbers of blacks who listened to Hammon's preachments, one can vividly envision the leadership he could have exerted in apparent struggles for freedom. A pervasive sense of dissatisfaction with American life for blacks in pre-American Revolutionary days had to have its roots in discontent, protest, and rebellion, even in the North. Not so with Hammon! He was content as a "do-gooder", a religious man who believed in and taught the virtue of obedience to oppressed slaves. I must caution, however, that in evaluating Hammon's religiosity, the critic must not just study obvious racial feelings rampant at that time but the religious feelings of Hammon as well. He was thoroughly indoctrinated in the Christian ethic and was truly unable to function otherwise.

In this regard, Wanger disagrees with this premise and concludes his excerpt exclaiming the lack of significance of Hammon's contribution to Afro-American literature with the plausible statement that

> . . . passiveness and resignation obscure the genuineness of Hammon's religiosity, so that today we view his Christian faith as something alien to him. His morality also remains undeveloped, and seemingly restricted to Saint Paul's admonition: "Slaves, obey your masters!" He lets fall not a word that might be taken to criticize slavery, in which he sees only the manifestation of divine foresight and mercy. Thus the deportation of Africans to America becomes a kind of providential pilgrimage toward knowledge of the one true God. [*Black Poets in the United States*]

Today, readers of Hammon's poetry and prose, in their benignancy, will surely admit that the poet possessed a workable knowledge of 18th century writing styles despite the simplistic quality of his productivity. Readers will concur, too, that his emotional involvement with religion, to the point where it approaches intoxication, as one critic puts it, was so intense that the words and the expressions are forced into verse mold almost as a procrustean endeavor.

Personally, I feel, however, that as a product of the uncultivated Negro imagination and temperament, Hammon's writing, sparse as it is and undistinguished, forms an uncommon contribution to American belles-lettres of the 18th century because of its simplicity and its honesty. It is a quaint prelude to the rich and varied songs which were to burst spontaneously from black writers a century later, songs which would make up the great gift from Africa to the art of America.

**Lonnell E. Johnson  (essay date 1992)**

SOURCE: "Dilemma of the Dutiful Servant: The Poetry of Jupiter Hammon," in *Language and Literature in the African American Imagination*, edited by Carol Aisha Blackshire-Belay, Greenwood Press, 1992, pp. 105-17.

[*In the following excerpt, Johnson discusses factors that might have influenced Hammon's writings. These factors include Hammon's religion, his life as a slave, eigh-teenth-century politics and society, and the works of other writers.*]

The poetry of Hammon reveals a devoutly religious man who assimilates the predominant religious views of colonial New England. Because of this he has been accused of being too conciliatory in his attitude toward enslavement. While he does not always speak out against enslavement, he does speak for equality and unity of both the enslaved and master. Upon close examination, the poetry of Hammon reveals his ability to absorb the basic tenets of Christianity, yet use those precepts to mediate a stronger response to enslavement. In his **"A Dialogue Entitled the Kind Master and the Dutiful Servant"** Hammon employs a subtle strategy to unify master and the enslaved before God. The poet's life of service reflects a man totally committed to the cause of Christ. Above all else his works reveal a man trying to resolve the dilemma of being a committed servant of God, yet dutiful servant of a man.

All the works of Hammon mirror a man absorbed in religious matters. His identification as a Christian believer colors his poetry, as [Stanley] Ransom comments on the religious aspect of Hammon's verse: "His poetry is sincere and enthusiastic, and it is primarily religious: Hammon's poetry reflects his great intellectual and emotional involvement with religion to the point where it approaches intoxication" [*America's First Negro Poet: The Complete Works of Jupiter Hammon of Long Island,* 1970].

---

**The poetry of Hammon reveals a devoutly religious man who assimilates the predominant religious views of colonial New England. Because of this he has been accused of being too conciliatory in his attitude toward enslavement.**

**—*Lonnell E. Johnson***

---

With regard to more secular matters, such as the issue of enslavement, Hammon is more moderate in his attitude. His response in "A Winter Piece," however, indicates that while he does not desire freedom for himself, he firmly believes that the young enslaved should be set free. For Hammon true freedom is a spiritual matter: "And ye shall know the truth and the truth shall make you free. If the Son therefore shall make you free, ye shall be free indeed" (John 8:32, 36). In his "Address to the Negroes of New York," Hammon elaborates on the freedom that most concerns him: "But this [earthly freedom], my brethren is by no means the greatest thing we have to be concerned about. Getting our liberty in this world is nothing to our having the liberty of the children of God." It is precisely Hammon's preoccupation with spiritual matters, rather than with his state of bondage, for which he is vehemently criticized.

To more clearly understand Hammon and his development as a poet and proponent of the Bible, it is important to understand the sociocultural background that gave rise to his outpourings in poetry and prose. One must examine the environment out of which his works took root. The portrait of Hammon must be viewed against the backdrop of colonial New York . . . .

[Edgar] McManus points out what was probably the condition of enslavement in New York during Hammon's lifetime: "The slaves lived quietly, enjoyed good treatment, and often looked forward to eventual freedom as a reward for loyal service. All evidence available indicates that master-slave relations were good, often marked by mutual affection and respects" [*A History of Slavery in New York,* 1966]. The mild form of servitude under which most of the colonists lived suggests the privileged state of Hammon, whom Schomburg describes as "the gentleman slave." Hammon describes how well treated he is in his address to the blacks of New York: "I have great reason to be thankful that my lot has been so much better than most slaves have had. I suppose I have had more advantages and privileges than most of you who are slaves, have ever known, and I believe more than many white people have enjoyed."

Hammon's status as an enslaved mirrors that of the household servant as seen in the Old Testament. In eighteenth-century America, perhaps the most effective means of introducing Christianity to the enslaved was by means of participation in religious observances in the master's household. The enslaved, such as Hammon, were part of a household and participated in religious observances, for "family worship was an important feature of the Puritan household. . . . It is probable that most of the Christianized Negroes in colonial New England received their first religious impulse in the family worship of their master's household" [Lorenzo Johnston Greene, *The Negro in Colonial New England, 1620-1776,* 1942].

Because the Puritans based their institutions on the pattern outlined in the patriarchal Old Testament, they drew two classes of bondmen: "Hebrew servants" and "Gentile slaves." Both forms were adopted by the Puritans and changed into an enslaved system where the status of the enslaved was somewhere between the two. Greene mentions, "As such the Negro was considered part of the Puritan family and, in keeping with the custom of the Hebraic family, was usually referred to as a 'servant' rarely as 'slave'."

As the servant of Christian masters who instructed their enslaved in the same religious doctrine of the evangelical movement begun in the Church of England and which spread to America, undoubtedly Hammon was profoundly influenced by the Bible. His poetry and prose reveal a man very knowledgeable of the Scriptures. [Arthur] Schomburg believes him to have been "a missionary and lay preacher" ["Jupiter Hammon, before the New York African Society," *Amsterdam News,* 14, 1930].

Records from the Lloyd estate reveal that Hammon purchased a Bible from his master in 1733. The source of income for such a purchase may have been from hiring out himself to work or from profits from "Jupiter's Orchards." The Lloyds hired out their enslaved for periods of time. Such resourcefulness would have allowed Hammon the financial means and time to learn to read and write and cultivate the impetus to write poetry. That Hammon was a literate household servant in colonial New York was not particularly rare during his lifetime, for [Roger] Whitlow paints this picture of eighteenth-century New England:

> Many blacks, slave and free, were quite well educated . . . blacks were successful artisans and planters, and . . . some themselves owned slaves. In short, blacks were generally better treated in the 18th century than in the 19th, partly because of the influence of religion in the northern colonies, where it was generally held that blacks should be educated at least enough to understand Christianity.

[*Black American Literature: A Critical History,* 1973]

Given the religious climate in New York and New England, it is not surprising that religion dominates the poetry of Hammon. It is also not surprising that Hammon would be literate as a household servant in eighteenth-century New York. Wealthy landowners often maintained private tutors who instructed family members. Conceivably Hammon may have received such tutelage. . . .

The religious convictions of Hammon are most clearly expressed in **"A Dialogue Entitled the Kind Master and the Dutiful Servant."** Written in ballad form, with quatrains of alternate iambic tetrameter and iambic trimeter lines with *a-b-a-b* rhyme scheme, the format is similar to the hymn stanza, often employed eighteenth-century colonial America in the popular hymns of Watts and Wesley. Hammon uses the form to skillfully take the reader on an exercise of "follow the leader." The thirty stanzas open with Master and Servant alternately exchanging remarks for the first fifteen stanzas, with stanzas 16 to 23 offering "A Line on the Present War" and with the Servant closing with the last seven stanzas.

Stanza one opens with an invitation from the Master:

> Come my servant, follow me,
>   According to thy place;
> And surely God will be with thee,
>   And send thee heav'nly grace.

With great irony the Servant is bid to follow "According to thy place," as if he has any choice in the matter. Yet before the poem ends Master and Servant will have changed places.

The Servant responds by pointing out the conditions for following, as he relates the essence of the message of the entire poem:

> Dear Master, I will follow thee,
>   According to thy word,
> And pray that God may be with me
>   And save thee in the Lord.

The poem emphasizes the importance of following, as the term is used or implied in fifteen of the first twenty-four stanzas. The second stanza gives the basis for following "according to thy word." The Master who bids the Servant to follow, likewise, is told to follow by Christ, the Master, who said, "Follow me."

As the dialogue continues, the poet subtly brings Master and Servant to the same level. Beginning in stanza 9, the poem employs the pronouns "our," "us," and "we." Both Master and Servant speak of "King" and the Master acknowledges "My servant, we are sinners all."

MASTER

> My Servant, follow Jesus now,
>   Our great victorious King;
> Who governs all both high and low,
>   And searches things within.

SERVANT

> Dear Master, I will follow thee,
>   When praying to our King;
>   It is the Lamb I plainly see,
>     Invites the sinner in.

MASTER

> My servant, we are sinners all,
>   But follow after grace;
> I pray that God would bless thy soul,
>   And fill thy heart with grace.

The Servant closes the poem, addressing the readers as "friends," a term mindful of Jesus' exhortation to his disciples in John 15:14, 15: "Ye are my friends, if ye do whatsoever I command you. Henceforth I called you not servants . . . but I have called you friends." The poet also uses the term to describe himself and addresses his readers as "Christian friends": "Believe me now my Christian friends, Believe your friend call'd Hammon: You cannot to your God attend, And serve the God of Mammon."

The context of the passage to which Hammon alludes reminds followers of Christ that no man can serve two masters: "No man can serve two masters: For either he will hate the one, and love the other; or else he will hold to the one, and despise the other. Ye cannot serve God and Mammon" (Matthew 6:24).

In referring to himself as "friend," which is an elevated status above a servant, the Servant does not demote his master, but both Master and Servant are placed on the same level as equals before Christ, who is their lord and king (yet also a servant). Matthew 10:24, 25 make clear this position: "The disciple is not above his master, nor the servant above his lord. It is enough that he be as his master, and the servant as his lord."

As the reader progresses through the dialogue, one may ask who follows whom? The Master opens with a call for the Servant to follow him. The Servant responds by establishing the basis for following "according to thy word." Before the poem ends, both Master and Servant are reminded to follow Christ, "our King," thus both become "fellow followers." At the end of the poem Master and Servant have switched places, as the Servant takes the lead and closes the poem. The poet ultimately becomes a good follower by being a good leader as he concludes the dialogue. Although the piece appears to be simple and straightforward, there is a subtle strategy at work whereby Hammon gives a masterful demonstration of "follow the leader.". . .

Inspired by Jonathan Edwards in 1735, The Great Awakening or New Light Movement inaugurated a series of revivals, sweeping America in a wave of great religious emotionalism, touching whites and blacks alike. The powerful sermons of Edwards, Whitefield, and Wesley thundered with the words "regeneration" and "conversion," as thousands of people had deeply personal experiences with God. Such an experience may have been the inspiration for Hammon's *An Evening Thought (Salvation by Christ with Penetential [sic] Cries)*, which opens with:

> Salvation comes by Christ alone,
>     The only Son of God;
> Redemption now to every one
>     That love his holy word.

The poem opens with the word "Salvation," as the poet hammers away with the term twenty-three times throughout the work. *An Evening Thought* is also the only poetic work of Hammon's to use the word "slave."

> Salvation now comes from the Lord,
>     He being thy captive slave.

The poet does not use the term *enslaved* to refer to himself, whom he designates with the milder term *servant*. But the poet reserves the harshest designation of servitude and ladens the couplet with irony and paradox, as he points out the source of salvation, which comes from the Servant of Servants, the Lord, who is not merely enslaved, but "captive slave" to those whom He serves.

Hammon's conscious repetition of the term *salvation* may also have been a means of facilitating memorization, in the same way that Wigglesworth's *Day of Doom* was designed as a didactic tool for Puritan doctrine. [Vernon] Loggins discusses the possible influence of *Day of Doom* upon Hammon's **"A Poem for Children with Thoughts on Death,"** which he describes as a "Methodist Commentary" on the rigid Calvinism expounded in that section of *Day of Doom* describing the Last Judgment of children who died in infancy and who are not God's elect [*The Negro Author in America*, 1931]. Both works are structured the same way, with four-line stanzas followed by the scriptural reference alluded to in that stanza. Because of his use of the same format, conceivably Hammon could have been exposed to Wigglesworth and other such writers.

Hammon undoubtedly had access to some of the noted writers of his day. He speaks of "Mr. Burkitt" [*sic*] in his "Winter Piece," where he also mentions "Bishop Beverage" [*sic*]. Books by Burkitt and Beveridge were part of the extensive library of Henry Lloyd. Conceivably Hammon had the opportunity to read these works and others, for his master not only imported books for sale but lent books to tenants on his property and to the inhabitants of the nearby towns of Huntington and Oyster Bay. Records indicate that Lloyd amassed an impressive collection of "primers, horn books, catechisms, Bibles, Testaments, Psalters, prayer books, a law book, pictures, ink horns, paper, and such titles as *The Twelve Patriarchs, The Young Mans's Companion,* Hodder's *Arithmetic,* Dolittle's *Lord's Supper,* Watt's *Song.*"

Access to the library of the family was undoubtedly a great factor in Hammon's development as a poet. Such exposure, together with diligent reading and study of the Bible and personal devotion, participation in family religious observances, and attendance at church were also factors contributing to the poet's growth. In addition some schooling and catechetical instruction, either from the family tutor or perhaps from the Society for the Propagation of the Gospel, plus the encouragement he probably received from his benefactors also amply account for his degree of intellectual maturity and the literary intensity motivating the poet to write and publish.

Unquestionably numerous influences must have contributed to his writing ability. That he published a poem in colonial America is truly an awesome accomplishment in itself. Not only did he publish poetry but prose as well. Without the assistance of the Lloyds and other supporters, he could not have done this. Relying on such support, Hammon could not offend those whites who encouraged him in his writing endeavors. He assimilates their views; yet he maintains his own integrity, as he attempts to become a dutiful servant who leads his master to the truth. He himself said, "Good servants frequently make good masters."

---

**Hammon's poetry can be described as roughhewn and rugged, rhythmically heavy with at times awkward, forced rhymes. Nevertheless, the poetry does mark a transition leading from the artless beauty of spirituals to the more formal verse of the poets following Hammon.**

**—Lonnell E. Johnson**

---

Examining the cultural background of Hammon's time and recognizing his personal religious commitment, one can sense the dilemma he faced in his efforts to reconcile his position as a servant of God with being a servant of man. Although he contributed to African American literature with the publishing of his first poem, his contribution goes beyond this singular accomplishment. He is a significant figure whose method of composing must have been similar to those who fashioned spirituals from their souls; yet his poetry is original. . . .

Hammon's poetry can be described as roughhewn and rugged, rhythmically heavy with at times awkward, forced rhymes. Nevertheless, the poetry does mark a transition leading from the artless beauty of spirituals to the more formal verse of the poets following Hammon. [Jean] Wagner speaks of *An Evening Thought* as "a halfway stage between the guileless art of the unknown composers of spirituals and the already much wordier manner of the popular preacher" [*Black Poets of the United States*, 1975].

Although Hammon's verse lacks the refinement and fluency of his contemporary, Phillis Wheatley, there are many admirable qualities to be noted in his works. Loggins states that Hammon's verse was composed to be heard with "that peculiar sense of sound, the distinguishing characteristic of Negro folk poetry." [William] Robinson classifies Hammon as an oratorical poet whose works are best suited for oral renderings [*Early Negro Writing*, 1971]. [Dorothy] Porter sees Hammon's verse as "seldom matched by such occasional expressions as hymns, spiritual songs, or didactic verse, however impassioned, on the subjects of freedom, slavery, or worldly bliss" [*Early Negro Writing*, 1971]. Thus in his unrefined yet engaging manner, Hammon strives in his poetry and indeed in his life to resolve the dilemma of being a servant to God, yet a dutiful servant to man.

### Sondra A. O'Neale  (essay date 1993)

SOURCE: "*An Evening Thought: Salvation by Christ, with Penetential Cries*" and others, in *Jupiter Hammon and the Biblical Beginnings of African-American Literature*, The American Theological Library Association and The Scarecrow Press, Inc., 1993, pp. 41-59, 66-75, 134-41, 191-204.

[*In the following excerpt O'Neale argues that Hammon was actually one of this country's first African American protest writers. And given the context of eighteenth century society, and especially the fact that he was a slave, Hammon had to couch his criticism of slavery in religious terminology. O'Neale insists that critics who fault Hammon's poetry for its apparent focus on religious salvation rather that physical emancipation are missing the subtle message of protest in Hammon's work.*]

The essential theme of Hammon's first poem, *An Evening Thought: Salvation by Christ, with Penetential Cries*, is prayer. In any urgent petition such as this one, the petitioner starts with the most crucial needs in the human condition—needs which may not be primarily spiritual. In interceding to God and addressing man in this poem, Hammon therefore has one thought in mind and that is slavery—his own enslavement and that of all Africans in the diaspora. Twentieth-century critics have not recognized this focal point because it is stealthily couched in biblical

language, and readers in this age are less aware of biblical meaning. Hammon's contemporary readers understood him, however, and although he was a slave, they allowed him the latitude to protest his enslavement precisely because he used that biblical rhetoric. . . .

In eighteenth-century theological definitions, the meaning of "salvation" was related to the title of Christ as Savior and to that act of redemption whereby a person was "saved" from sin and Satan. . . . Eighteenth-century readers were quite knowledgeable about Old Testament personages. They understood that the bundle of ideas inculcated in the term "salvation" implied deliverance from slavery in contemporary homiletics. Thus it was impossible for a slave, writing the first literary expression by an African-American, to have penned the term "salvation" without having slavery—his own ubiquitous crucible and that of African fellows—utmost in mind.

For the colonial evangelical clergyman, salvation was effected at that vortex of spiritual vision when one grasped for Christ as the One Absolute God and Savior who could intervene in every earthly circumstance. As a shepherd-priest, the poem's speaker first asks God to give those who read the poem this necessary vision. Then the speaker admonishes his audience to repent. And next he turns to God with pleas that he mercifully accept that repentance. Thus, the persona fulfills the true functions of a pastor-priest who represents God before men, and conversely, men before God. . . .

> It was impossible for a slave, writing the first literary expression by an African-American, to have penned the term "salvation" without having slavery—his own ubiquitous crucible and that of African fellows—utmost in mind.
>
> —*Sondra A. O'Neale*

The phrase "redemption now to every one" is another central refrain of the poem because it expresses the relationship of new contemporary theological thinking (or, as some colonial preachers were calling it, errant theology) to the social practice of slavery. A basic premise of Calvinism—the predominate theological system of the era and the one from which the social mores of slavery in a "Christian" society were derived—was that Christ's atonement was limited, that He died for only that group of people whom God, His Father, had selected for salvation and that all others were doomed to a dismal eternity. This attitude of superior selectivity was a religiously psychological dynamism for the formation of the colonies and was subsequently the "biblical" foundation used to support the enslavement of "unchosen" Blacks.

However, in this his first poem, and as a dominant theme in all of this writing, Hammon is challenging the idea of racial and individual selectiveness. While his work is in some instances influenced by mainstream Calvinism, he seems to have worked out his own brand of Arminianism—namely, that Christ's redemption is available to all who will love and obey Him. The idea that man, and not God, makes the choice about man's eternal status is, of course, Arminian or Methodist doctrine. However, this branch of Protestantism did not come to America until well after Hammon began to formulate and write his doctrinal conclusions. His stance was simply much more compatible with the needs of the disenfranchised and ostracized Africans in American society.

Of equal importance to the concept of "salvation" in the poem's explication is the set of assumptions accompanying religious and social use of the term "redemption" in the eighteenth century. "Redemption" related even more to implications of slavery and emancipation than "salvation.". . .

Hammon uses the terms "redemption," "Redeemer," or "redeemed" in each one of his works. His immediate audience knew exactly what he meant because the term was used interchangeably in a religious sense, and, in the eighteenth-century work force, to establish work agreements between employers and employees particularly for the white indentured-servant class, referred to as "redemptioneers." While a relatively few lower-class Anglo-European redemptioneers were kidnapped for the Atlantic passage, most willingly sold themselves into slavery in order to pay their fares. The purchaser then became part of the financial arrangement between the worker and the captain, and often, when a colonist took over the travel bill, he became known as the worker's redeemer. When the worker's labor had accrued to pay the bill in full, the worker was said to have been redeemed. Thus, when Hammon told the slaves that Christ was "Our Great and Mighty Redeemer," his audience understood that he was ascribing to Christ both the will and the ability to free them from slavery. That these semislaves would be freed after seven years of service because their skin was white, while the African had to remain a slave for perpetuity because his skin was black, must have been a sore boil to Hammon and his fellow slaves. Because the term was so familiar in the society, Hammon therefore knew that his readers—both Black and white—understood that he was speaking of earthly, as well as of heavenly, redemption.

The overriding issue was color—the African's skin color and its supposed connotations of evil. As the first African to publish in America, Hammon thus wrestled with intuitive racial overtones within the English language. Like his contemporary, Phillis Wheatley, he could refer to "our dark benighted Souls" as a description of spiritual death without any regard to the color of the bodies that encased those souls. He knew that in the Bible light and dark referred to the essence of man's spiritual enlightenment, or the lack thereof, not to his physiological hue. His use of the language is metaphorically, not racially, based. His symbolism is no different from that of Dante or Saint John of the Cross who also speak of "the dark night of the soul." Nevertheless, because of the power of the spoken word to create and enforce authority, Hammon knew of the difficult and ironic overtones present when one who is Black, a writer, and a slave uses such color delineations. Thus in his essay, *An Evening's Improvement,* he was able to write that "if we love God, black as we be, and despised as we are, God will love us."

Another one of the poet's recurrent themes steeped in contemporary societal and theological meaning was appropriate nomenclature—assigning a name for God and a name for man. In his dramatic poetry, Hammon has a fictive slaveholder refer to Christ as Master or King, while the corresponding African calls Christ Savior, Redeemer, Servant or, more importantly, Slave. As an example, in the eighth stanza of [*An Evening Thought*] Hammon, speaking to his slave audience, refers to Christ as "thy captive Slave." His purpose is to identify Jesus with American slaves and to make slaves aware that Christ assumed the most humble position among men in order to effect their salvation.

Hammon's reference to Christ as "thy captive Slave" is taken from Mark's Gospel wherein Christ is presented as Servant to God and to man. A contemporary text, Brown's *Dictionary,* lists the Chief of God's Servants as "Christ who, in obedience to His will, assumed our nature . . . and administers the blessings of the convenant to us." Hammon knew that his Christian era accepted such definitions as standard and that his readers likewise recognized Scriptures like Matt. 23:11: "But he that is greatest among you shall be your servant." The poet enforces his premise that the lowly Jesus would have been more at home with the Black colonial slave than with the white puritanical slave owner. . . .

Hammon's emphasis detracts from the idea of a nation or race favored by God. His vision included a spiritual egalitarianism that reached to all the peoples of the world. He knew that America, because of its diversity of races, had the unique opportunity to exhibit that oneness in the Body of Christ. Samson Occom, the renowned Native American evangelist, also lived on Long Island where he converted Montauks to Christianity. Undoubtedly Hammon had heard of his ministry; he perhaps even knew him. Additionally, Hammon observed the hundreds of European immigrants who joined the Englishmen in the New York colony as the melting pot of nations began. He knew that unless slavery was eradicated, the integrated Christian society that he believed the Bible offered to "every one" of "every nation" of "all the world" would be a failure.

Although concerned with racial division and class and color discrimination within the church, Hammon seldom overtly makes Christian love a central homiletic or artistic theme. But in [*An Evening Thought*] ("Salvation doth increase our Love"), he makes an exception. Evoking biblical themes about united Christian fellowship, he voices a evangelical premise that the Godhead cannot come to the earth in its purest essence unless there is love and harmony among Christians. However, within the context of other thematic statements in this work, he is no doubt implying that professing whites, who insisted upon slavery as a necessary economic support, did not experience true salvation because their love was not "increased."

Hammon's continual emphasis on the availability of salvation for "every nation" is, however, like his use of "Ethiopian" as an alternative ethnic distinction, an urgent cry for the inclusion of African-Americans into full, free, and equal Christian fellowship. This plodding not only belies the Western religious psyche's rigid and almost ritualistic tribal separation, it sprang from the poet's longing for a universal, multiracial Church, both in a mystical union and in local assemblies. Such urging undermined the colonial practice of making Blacks substandard Christians in church membership, in communion, and even in baptism. . . .

Throughout his writing, Hammon makes a distinction between individual and corporate sins. He implies that Christ's death on the Cross enables all men to obtain forgiveness for those sins for which they bear a personal responsibility as well as for those sins which they inherit. However, concomitant with his mention of Christ's atonement for man's sins, in this poem (and in his essays *A Winter Piece* and *An Evening's Improvement*) is the underlying suggestion that slaveholders cannot use racial selectivity in calling themselves elect and Blacks condemned. Whites, on the one hand, accept atonement for their personal and inherited (or corporate racial) sins and, on the other hand, cite the Cain/Ham curse, which Blacks supposedly inherited, as justification for enslaving Africans. Either Christ's sacrifice was sufficient to erase all individual or corporate sins for all races or it was insufficient for any.

Additionally, in [*An Evening Thought*], Hammon describes man as triune: that is, as having soul, spirit, and body.

Once departing the body, the soul and spirit would presumably "fly" to God for judgment. Hammon's concepts of a tribunal were multiplicit and derived from his understanding of Scripture that men would stand before God—both as individuals and as members of a group—to answer for life's deeds. In this poem, as in all of his works, Hammon reveals that he saw eschatological judgment as twofold—separate judgments for the unsaved world and for the children of God. His interpretation of Scripture in both of these judgments is that whites will have to answer for their enslavement of Africans and that, because of this corporate sin, white colonists could take part in only the judgment of the wicked, not that of the saints. At this judgment of the wicked, Hammon believed Blacks would be truly vindicated. Other than this indication, he saw no end to slavery. Later he would write that the Revolutionary War represented early punishment for the practice of slavery and was a warning from God of the ultimate judgment which slaveholders faced if they would not end the institution.

Not until the emergence of the Reverend Nat Turner (*Confessions*) and the Reverend David Walker (in Stuckey) in the 1830s did any other contributor to the canon of Black American literature express a vision of violence as an alternative method to end slavery. Just as those early Black American writers who followed him, Hammon hoped that moral persuasion based on Christian principles, such as that in his poetry and essays, would be effective for the eventual eradication of slavery. For instance, in his *Address to the Negroes in the State of New York,* he did not urge Blacks to foment insurrection. He chose instead to express an antislavery statement chiding patriots for their hypocritical bonding of men while they engaged in a war for their own freedom. He tells his Black audience:

> That liberty is a great thing we may know from our own feelings, and we may likewise judge so from the conduct of the white people in the late war. How much money had been spent, and how many lives have been lost to defend their liberty! I must say that I have hoped that God would open their eyes, when they were so much engaged for liberty, to think of the state of the poor blacks, and to pity us.

Other civil rights leaders expressed the same thoughts throughout the Revolutionary era. . . .

[Hammon] was a parttime preacher (when his masters freed him to be) who had not been appointed or ordained by the established church because he was Black and in their eyes not sufficiently educated. Preaching without official sanction was the same charge which the orthodox clergy leveled upon Whitefield, Gilbert Tennent, and other revivalists of the era. Further, orthodox churches especially resisted any preachers who believed in and taught their own brand of doctrine, such as that which Hammon had developed. Thus, Hammon could say in *An Evening's Improvement* that his objectors labeled him "an unlearned Ethiopian," one even unqualified to preach to his fellow slaves. [Joseph] Tracy likewise speaks of an eighteenth-century churchman as saying:

> Private persons of no education and but low attainments in knowledge and in the great doctrine of the gospel, without any regular call, under a pretense of exhorting, taking upon themselves to be preachers of the Word of God, we judge to be a heinous invasion of the ministerial office, offensive to God, and destructive to these churches.
>
> [*The Great Awakening: A History of the Revival of Religion in the Time of Edwards and Whitefield*]

Hammon knew that he surely fit into these definitions of those "rejected of men but called of God." Regardless of attempts to thwart a religious movement among those who were unwelcome in the institutional church, the same exuberant responses which Hammon demanded were burning within burgeoning, underground slave congregations.

Once the congregation attains "true repentance," Hammon, as a faithful and confident priest and shepherd, offers his flock, his audience, to God. As he had asked them to "turn your hearts, accept the Word"—a reference to Christ himself as in John 1:1—and as they had shown true repentance, there is no other step or additive to the spiritual process. [*An Evening Thought*] moves to the heavenly descent of the Holy Spirit and man's worshipful entrance before God's throne. The pastor-priest has completed his task. His flock has been reconciled to God.

. . . . .

[*An Address to Miss Phillis Wheatly*] makes it clear that Hammon saw himself as the elder statesman of Black American poets and that, as such, he bequeathed a heritage and a charge to this next-generation writer.

Hammon establishes quite early in the missive that they are both outcast Africans living in America by God's predestined allowance and that He permitted this arduous circumstance so that they might hear and receive the Gospel. The poet enjoins Wheatley to the highest moral behavior befitting her status as America's first Black female spokesperson. The times call for such decorum, he reminds her, because God will hold them accountable as among those who have been called to lead a defenseless people for whom there is little other temporal "light.". . . He also wants her to resist the seduction of temporal fame, which is a dangerous illusion for one trapped by the same society that lauds her as an eminent poet.

The subscription of stanza 1, taken from Ecclesiastes 12, sets the fatherly tone and theme for this entire poem. After the injunction to youth in the first verse of this famous chapter—"Remember now thy Creator in the days of thy youth"—King Solomon identifies himself as the narrator of Ecclesiastes and continues the chapter with admonitions to the young that life is fleeting and that life's most important charge is to remember one's commitment to God. Hammon patterns his poem with the same injunctions and thematic imagery with which Solomon completes his poetic didactics. The king-poet continues the Ecclesiastes chapter with a symbolic description of the disintegration of the physical body in aging and in death. However, rather than dwelling on bodily degeneration in the grave, Hammon looks forward in hope to the "translation" of Christian saints at the Second Coming of Christ.

Like Solomon, Hammon is concerned that Christian young people, especially Black ones, know the meaning of life, death, and resurrection. His **"Poem for Children with Thoughts on Death"** reflects that concern, but only in this address does he stretch his eschatology to include God's judgment and rewards. Thus, Hammon advises Wheatley of her special calling to serve God as a writer, as an intellectual who has survived not only the Middle Passage but also the continuing dangers of eighteenth-century slavery, and as one whose responsibility is to leave a record of Black existence, no matter how surreptitious that record may have to be. The senior poet indicates his awareness of the painful realities of slavery which he and Wheatley observe and endure on a daily basis. However, he tells her, she must not despair about her own enslavement or about the miserable conditions of their people in America. She is to keep Christ and his ultimate purposes utmost in mind. Thus, he instructs her—in stanzas 2, 4, 11, and 21—that, in order to develop a character of joy in

the midst of this tribulation, she must appropriate a power which is beyond the reach of their captors. That power, he surmises, would come from God and from faith in his word.

Stanza 5 represents the vortex of two of the poem's main themes. First, like all eighteenth-century Christians, Hammon wrestled with the sovereignty of God in the affairs of men. The haunting theme of the deaths of millions of Africans during the Atlantic passage is introduced early in the work. He reminds the young poetess that this holocaust left few Blacks who were schooled enough in the language and iconography of the Western world to use literary talent in order to raise a cry against slavery and the slave trade. When Hammon wrote this poem, as far as he knew, he and Wheatley were the only ones with public accessibility to do so. In the lines "While thousands tossed by the sea, / And others settled down, / God's tender mercy set thee free, / From dangers that come down," Hammon expressed as much anguish over African genocide as the eighteenth-century fourth estate would allow.

For Hammon, as well as for Wheatley, the words "that thou a pattern still might be / to youth of Boston town," does not address the issue of predestination, but does speak of the burden to report the truth while in throes of constraining circumstances. Like those Africans who did not survive the passage, Hammon is reminding Wheatley that they too must die. However, considering the Christian context of death and judgment, he insists that they must answer to God for their unique mission to disclose the evils of slavery.

Hammon was not unconcerned with slavery, as his critics have charged. In his view of eighteenth-century political realities and in his studied eschatology, he simply had no hope that the slave institution would end through the voluntary and merciful intentions of the slaveholding society. In all of his essays, particularly in *An Address to the Negroes in the State of New York,* Hammon presents the same plan to his AfricanAmerican audience that he presents to Wheatley in this poem. They are to endure slavery and to trust God to judge the slaveholders with both temporal (that is, the Revolutionary War) and eternal judgment.

In **"An Address to Miss Phillis Wheatly"** Hammon seems to posit that God placed him and Wheatley in America and that he ordained them to be both writers and slaves:

> O come you pious youth! adore
>   The wisdom of thy God,
> In bringing thee from distant shore,
>   To learn his holy word.
> Thou mightst been left behind,
>   Amidst a dark abode;
> God's tender mercy still combin'd,
>   Thou hast the holy word.
>         . . . . .
> Thou hast left the heathen shore,
>   Thro' mercy of the Lord;
> Among the heathen live no more,
>   Come magnify thy God.

But elsewhere in his writing, Hammon is ambivalent about whether God sanctions slavery, or if the institution is simply in his "permitted" will. The elder poet wrestles with the Calvinist doctrines of predestination, election, and prevenient grace and replaces them with his own doctrinal understanding that men and women are liable for their own actions and decisions and that they will be held fully accountable for what they do to their fellowmen. In the Calvinist view, although all people are seen as totally depraved sinners with no hope of self-deliverance, God, in his own will and purpose, directs certain chosen sinners into pathways of salvation. And slavery itself could be seen as part of that direction. Wheatley seems to agree that she came to America through God's intervention. In her poem "On Being Brought from Africa to America" she writes:

> 'T'was mercy brought me from my *Pagan* land,
> Taught my benighted soul to understand
> That there's a God, that there's a Saviour too.

[Oscar Ronald] Dathorne is quite critical of early Black American writers because they refer to Africans as heathens ["Africa Their Africa," *NeoAfrican Literature and Culture,* Bernth Lindfors and Ulla Schild, eds., 1976]. However, Hammon and Wheatley considered any persons outside of Christ to be heathens, as evidenced in her attack against the atheistic students at Cambridge and his repeated referrals to white slaveholders as being unsaved. In both cases the heathens were but in this instance the poets speak through spiritual perspectives, without considerations of race or color. . . .

Wheatley's volume of poetry appeared in 1773, giving her an international reputation. But to Hammon she was a vulnerable young African who needed his fatherly advice. The shephered-pastor symbolism of stanza 12 and its subscript follows the theme of Psalm 23. Christ is the Shepherd and believers are his sheep. Hammon cautions Wheatley that she is to depend on God alone for all the affairs of life, but he also speaks of the slaves' insecurities. Slaves in eighteenth-century America, despite any intellectual accomplishments that they may have achieved, were still on the margins of national, social, and religious life. Thus, as early as Black American literature indicates, Blacks maintained their own loose religious and social structures. Just as the early literature transfers information through coded inferences, those community structures likewise existed in spasmodic, underground, and unannounced relationship to the white world. But they existed nevertheless. As third-class members of white congregations—often denied baptism and communion and always denied a role in church leadership—Black Christians could not go to white pastors for consolation about slavery because most of those pastors supported the slave system. Therefore, these pastors would report any rumors of resistance—topics which began quite naturally in church or any other of the few social settings where servants could congregate—to owners as well as to the state. Just as illegal in the eighteenth-century North as in the nineteenth-century South, such resistance resulted in the death penalty. Thus, even the church was not a relief from the alienations of slave life.

Hammon uses the narrative of the woman of Samaria from John 4 as his best illustration of that alienation. For him, the parable of this Samaritan, along with stories about publicans and the poor in Christ's day, served as a very necessary biblical text for a slave audience because it showed Christ's love for the utmost of community pariahs. . . .

In most of his seven extant works, Hammon sets the text of the Samaritan woman before his slave audience to identify the African with the Samaritan and to illustrate Christ's primary concern for those rejected and oppressed by a hypocritical society. Hammon implies here and in his other works that, for slaves, a true pastor—one who devotedly serves his people as Christ's undershepherd—can only be one who understands and commiserates with the sufferings of his sheep. While scholarship proves that Hammon was a preacher of considerable experience whom slaveholders invited to preach among Blacks on their plantations, I also suspect that he was an early pastor of an underground Black church, although the first open Black congregation did not emerge until the end of the eighteenth century, some twenty years after [*An Address to Miss Phillis Wheatly*] was written.

The theme of judgment with which Hammon completes the poem is not only personal but he envisions adjudication on multiple and corporate levels: "When God shall send his summons down, / And number saints together." In addition to the individual—in this poem, a **"A Poem for Children with Thoughts on Death,"** and in his essay-sermons—both church and society will be judged. . . . In addition, Hammon believed that the church, as the smaller but more moral body within the society, must with even more severity answer for its deeds. . . .

Thus, the tone of [*An Address to Miss Phillis Wheatly*] is one of urgency. Hammon urges that Wheatley must conform her art to the needs of Africans confined in a Christian land, and that she must do so while conducting her life with a moral standard which their professing Christian society itself ignores. Her writing should always include both a sense of African history (particularly the immediacy of the Atlantic passage and the century and a half that the race had been enslaved on America's shores) and the knowledge that they must answer for their art in death and judgment. He renders this crucial testament because of his own age ("Blest angels chant, [triumphant sound] / Come live with me forever")—that is, his time to herald the unique message of a Black American writer to his people is almost over—and because opportunity to end the slave institution in a peaceful manner is almost over. He also writes because, as far as he knew, Wheatley was the only one who could perpetuate the witness of Black American Christian intellect.

With his ending anthem, the poet moves the work beyond race or any other temporal consideration. God, who alone shall rescue Wheatley and the rest of Hammon's literary congregation from the evils of their present circumstance, must finally and forevermore be praised:

Now glory be to the Most High,
  United praises given,
By all on earth, incessantly,
  And all the host of heav'n.


. . . . .


Hammon draws the structure, symbolism, and theme of this elegiac poem 4. ["**A Poem for Children with Thoughts on Death**"] from the Wisdom Books of the Bible—Ecclesiastes and Proverbs. Like the Old Testament Hebrew monarch, King Solomon, the author of those works, Hammon would have young people live a life of piety because of the imminence of death, resurrection, and judgment. The poet's concern for young Africans becomes particularly evident in this work. . . .

Because his masters wanted him trained enough to work as a clerk in their local store, Hammon received a minimal, elementary education through the SPG [Society for the Propagation of the Gospel in Foreign Parts] system. He desired that all Black children would receive enough schooling at least to read the Bible, the SPG's major textbook. However, he desired for the African child not just education and evangelization but emancipation as well. Whenever he argued for the freedom of slaves, Hammon primarily pleaded for the manumission of young people. Thus, he contributed to the eventual release of young men and women both in the Lloyd Manor and in New York province. At the turn of the century, one member of the Lloyd family freed his slaves when they reached twenty-one, and in 1799 the State of New York passed a law manumitting all young and unborn slaves when they reached adulthood. . . .

Hammon's concern for young Africans resulted directly from the SPG's zeal to reach enslaved children earlier in the century. Those SPG ministers who came to Oyster Bay to teach not only the Lloyds' sons but also their young slave Jupiter gave America's first African writer a basic understanding of biblical symbolism. On his own, he then acquired enough proficiency to turn the Bible, the most widely read book in the colonies, into both a vehicle and a framework for his artistic protests against slavery. The whole thrust of this poem (and of *An Address to Miss Phillis Wheatly*)—that youth must gain wisdom to succeed on earth and to prepare for heaven—is a reflection of the evangelical outreach that touched Hammon's life.

Writers produced much popular poetry in the eighteenth century for children of Christianized parents. Of special interest to most white colonists was the question of children's predetermined state, based on the election or rejection of the parent. The procedure for determining the spiritual state of either was a major theological debate, one especially surrounding a child's eternal destiny, if death occurred before adulthood. Most of those in established traditional denominations believed that the parents' election assured their offspring's salvation. Similarly, the doctrines of original sin and total depravity condemned the children of the unsaved to perdition with their parents. In the same choiceless manner, this eternal death warrant applied to unsaved lower-caste British colonists, and much more to the African slave. The children of Africans had not been considered seriously in the debate since the early commitment of the SPG to educate and evangelize them in the first quarter of the century. Hammon, angered by the oversight, castigated whites in some of his most unsubtle remarks for their sinful neglect of slave children. Attached to *A Winter Piece,* an essay which Hammon directed to his fellow slaves, this poem has slave children as its object.

A guideline based on racial selectivity transformed for social and cultural uses, the very psychology of the doctrine of election embodied a cultural rejection of Africans. Thus, while his more famous contemporary, Michael Wigglesworth, says plainly in *Day of Doom* that innocent infants of non-Christian parents cannot possibly be saved, Hammon, in this treatise on death directed toward children, makes no such reference, primarily because he is speaking to children of African descent whose parents had no opportunity to become Christians. In subscriptional entries for verse 166, Wigglesworth predicts that "reprobate Infants plead for themselves." Then he has his God turn down their pleas: "Hence you were born in a state forlorn, / with Natures so deprav'd." Wigglesworth's well-known epic was published eleven times in the eighteenth century. Undoubtedly Hammon read it, but he refuses to make such a distinction about children of unchurched parents. In the fourth and fifth verses of this poem, the African poet has Jesus call all children to heaven. Slater's study, *Children in the New England Mind in Death and in Life,* gives background to illuminate the gracious, compassionate universality of Hammon's stand. Slater says that the colonial period was an age when the realities of early death, discussions of inescapable sin and of inevitable judgment made a child's life full of unrelenting fears. Thus the poem's theme would have brought hope to all children, including those of underprivileged whites and enslaved Blacks, not just the offspring of the elect. . . .

In the poem's final verses, Hammon brings his theological thrust back to the orthodox mainstream. He asserts that the soul which inhabited the body of a deceased Christian before the corporate resurrection of the Body of Christ (that is, all Christians who have lived since Christ's resurrection) will at the return of Christ rise from the grave in a reformed physical state. . . .

[The] preacher concludes the poem with the finality of unity on three levels. First, the child's body will be reunited with his soul and spirit at death. Second, the child is assured that he or she will indeed rejoin a Christian family either in heaven or at a corporate resurrection. And third, as depicted in the "angelic train" idiom, the child will then join an extended and authentic Christian community. This ultimate union will obviate the racial, class, and age division existing among professing Christians on earth. Thus, Hammon assures children, death becomes the ultimate victory, the final and eternal glorious life.


. . . . .

This poem ["**A Dialogue, Entitled, The Kind Master and Dutiful Servant**"] is Jupiter Hammon's artistic zenith. It is a dramatic exchange between a dictatorial slaveholder and a clever Servant whom the Master thinks he owns. Hammon created personae who were stereotypical of the eighteenth-century slaveholder and slave. On the surface, the slave feigns placid obedience to the Master. Yet beneath the poetic line, the slave (or "Servant," as Hammon prefers to call him) articulates subtle rebellion against the Master's position. The Master, on the other hand, overtly represents the typical interests and beliefs of his aristocratic class. Both profess Christianity, but their views of God and theology differ vastly. . . .

The Master in Hammon's play is a pragmatic religionist. Like his seventeenth-century counterpart John Saffin, an ardent slave apologist, the Master perceives slavery as an earthly, economic venture, one needed for society's survival. In accordance with the doctrine of all contemporary colonial denominations (except the Quakers), missionary teachers were to instruct Africans on the love of God so that they could be better servants. The Master travels a one-way street of personal insecurity beneath a facade of aristocratic confidence. He wants the slave to love him with wholehearted devotion, but it never occurs to him to love the slave with the same zeal. . . .

When he has the Master remind the Servant of "thy place," Hammon makes his character utter the standard religious-jargon that establishment ministers like Mather preached to their congregations continually. One could say that in his own writing Jupiter Hammon advocated the same moral "righteousness" for slaves, but several differences exist. Men like Mather believed that they were morally perfect. But, because of slavery, Hammon had already judged their morality to be a facade to true Christianity. He could therefore tell his readers to establish a relationship with God that transcended the example or advice of Cotton Mather or any other slave master. Secondly, Hammon had no vested interest in having good slaves. He had no power to ingratiate and no rewards to give. As a Black leader, he desired to channel his people through the quagmire of slavery by directing their view to Christ, whom he believed would eventually lead them out of it.

Hammon's choice of the word "grace" to end stanza 1 is fitting. The Master's view of grace inculcates an ironic twist of Christian dogma. A contemporary theologian defined grace as that love of God which comes with salvation and is free for all. The Master assumes that definition for himself. He never mentions any condition that he must meet for his own salvation, but he demands obedience and subservience as conditions for the slave's salvation. One view is based on grace as a free gift; the other is based on grace as attained by works.

Tradition, church dogma, and political and economic expediency inform the Master's vision. He is not influenced by urgent personal need or spiritual experience. But the Servant charts a new course. In his walk of revelation, he must not trust man's guidance but have "grace and truth's insight." Thus, throughout the poem, the Servant tells the Master that, while he may appear to be a "normal," dutiful, and obedient slave, in actuality, he seeks solely to please God, to whom he looks for vindication and judgment. The Servant says that his "whole delight" in serving the Master is sustained by his ultimate faith, not in the Master's righteousness but in God's goodness and reward.

---

**As a Black leader, Hammon desired to channel his people through the quagmire of slavery by directing their view to Christ, whom he believed would eventually lead them out of it.**

*—Sondra A. O'Neale*

---

The Master represents a classic Anglican-Puritan speaker. Very much like him, Hammon's "owners" were loyal Anglicans, but as this British denomination did not have a parish in their nearby hamlet, they worshiped with a Puritan congregation. Both denominations staunchly adhered to Calvinism. The Master uses these doctrines variously in the poem to explain the cosmology of slavery. His theological phraseology, "we are sinners all," represents the first principle of Calvinism: total depravity, or man's inability to save himself or reorient his fate without divine intervention. However, illustrating typical eighteenth-century slave psychology, the Master assumes that the slave's depravity carries more weight than his own. This assumption is then merged into Great Chain's scientific and religious thought. These and other interdependent theories of race and color allowed the Master, and other members of his class, to excuse the practice of slavery while ostensibly building a Christian society.

When the Servant, who earnestly prays for the Master's salvation, persists in bringing the "Dialogue" back to issues of death and judgment, the Master acknowledges that he must one day stand before God and answer for his sins. The issue, though, is whether he will be judged with repentant saints or hardened sinners. In his essays, Hammon implies that unrepentant slaveholders, regardless of their professions of Christianity, inevitably will be condemned at the Great White Throne Judgment, the final reckoning for sinners, and that they will be sentenced to a degree of punishment in hell appropriate for injustices against African slaves.

The Master is myopic. He insists that the Servant's salvation, indeed the whole social order ("that Christ may love us all"), precariously depends upon the Servant's obedience. Yet without compunction, he himself willingly belongs to a social stratum presently rebelling against its British king. In his essays, Hammon lambastes this moral blindness—the irony of slavery during the zeal for Revolution—and he tells his African readers that they must seek a freedom of more lasting integrity: "when the Son shall set you free you are free indeed."

Toward the end of the poem, the Master slightly repents of his caustic stand. He had previously acknowledged (stanza 13) that both he and the Servant had to face the heavenly King together in judgment. But in stanza 19 he admits that if God does have sovereign power, then the Almighty may have permitted the war's fervor to humble proud America. But his general advice that all nations pray for peace, rather than any specific sorrow over his own failures and those of his nation, makes the Master's call for repentance a hollow one. His perspective, however, is taken from another Calvinist doctrine prevalent in mid-eighteenth-century theology—that God holds sovereign responsibility for all events in the world of men. Thus when he says, "This is the work of God's own hand, / We see by precepts given; / To relieve distress and save the land, / Must be the pow'r of heav'n," the speaker assumes no accountability for what he or those members of his class may have done to precipitate the war.

When the Servant answer the Master the first time, he attempts to move the relationship from one of manipulation and guilt to one wherein he, although a slave, can somewhat control his own motives and actions. That does not mean that he acquiesces to slavery; he merely bides his time until emancipation, and attempts to create an atmosphere that allows him to deal with the Master on a man-to-man, not a man-to-slave, basis. Because of both his slave state and his Christian commitment, Hammon could not advocate violent insurrection to end slavery. However, as the first published Black preacher in America, he was the progenitor of such Black churchmen as Dr. Martin Luther King, Jr., who advocated nonviolent change through faith and a sense of self that transcended immediate circumstances. Throughout national history this political psychology has forced the dominant class to negotiate agreement whether its leaders wanted to or not. In both religious and civil terms, such a negotiated settlement was called a "covenant" in colonial society. . . .

This inherent meaning of "covenant"—peace and reward as a result of fulfilled agreement—does not suggest that the Servant in the poem must approve of his own enslavement. Rather, Hammon's speaker tries to renegotiate the circumstances of an otherwise choiceless existence and to convince the Master that his submission to service fulfills motives far different than those the Master has in mind.

When the Servant says, "I will follow thee, / According to thy word," he uses covenant language which the society, and the Master, deem acceptable in work agreements with indentured servants. . . .

But, as the Servant does not share the Master's cosmological vision of heaven or of God, the proposed agreement would be strictly a temporary accommodation because of the undeniable presence of slavery. Of paramount importance to the Servant, the Master, and more importantly the poet's larger audience, one must correctly identify the person and function of God even in the midst of these temporal situations. To the Servant, Christ is primarily the Lamb of God: the Great Sacrificer, God, King of all, who himself gave up his life for all mankind. For the Servant that is true kingship: the gracious act of a heavenly aristocrat coming down to the level of common men, becoming one with them, and shedding his life's blood to create a new brotherhood in his image. The Master in Hammon's poem never accepted that kind of royal condescension as an example that he should follow.

The Servant's image of a heavenly abode is one where Christ welcomes penitents in an attitude that New World missionaries, visitors to the continent themselves, should have offered to Native Americans and Africans. Hammon's reference to Christ as the welcoming "King / . . . standing on some distant land, / Inviting sinners in" (stanza 12) imbues his vision with deep implications for Africans abducted to the colonies, their own "distant land" from where they yet hoped to be rescued.

In stanza 24, the Servant becomes the main speaker and remains so until the poem's end. He asserts that all professing Christians, not just servants, must obey God's word. Ironically, the Servant now is the one in the controlling position: as the narrator he has the last word. In this reversal of the Chain of Being structure, where supposedly only whites are intellectually competent enough to create art, Hammon posits that the Master's hierarchical position—and the psyche that lends credence to his "Great Chain" scale—is suspect.

There is a definite pattern in each of the first fifteen stanzas of the poem. In the first two lines each speaker relates to the other, while in the next two lines he speaks of his, or sometimes their, relationship with God. In stanza 2 the Servant tells the Master that as slaveholder, he is not saved: "And pray that God may be with me, / And save thee in the Lord." In stanza 6 the Servant tells the Master that he is praying that the latter will even see inside heaven: "And pray that God would bless thy soul, / His heav'nly place to see." After telling the Master politely that he may follow him on earth, "According to thy word" (stanza 2), the Servant cries that really, "The only safety that I see, / Is Jesus' holy word" (stanza 8). The implication here of course is that while the Servant does have a trustworthy covenant with God, he does not have such an assurance or covenant with the Master.

Finally, in stanza 12, the Servant simply tells the Master that in reality he, the slave, is not listening to the voice of the Master at all; he is in reality listening only to God: "Dear Master. I shall follow then, / The voice of my great King." This faith in his unseen Master is the thrust of Jupiter Hammon's work. He dismisses slavery as evil, temporal, and under the harsh sentence of God's judgment. The crucial purpose of his art is that his readers would join him in this assessment and go about reordering the priorities of their lives. If those readers were white, they would work to end the institution. If those readers were Black, they would follow him in this biblical knowledge that led at once to the freedom of the soul and that would lead ultimately to freedom from earthly bondage.

## FURTHER READING

### Bibliographies

Klinkowitz, Jerome. "Early Writers: Jupiter Hammon, Phillis Wheatley, and Benjamin Banneker." In *Black American Writers: Bibliographical Essays. Volume 1: The Beginnings through the Harlem Renaissance and Langston Hughes*, edited by M. Thomas Inge, Maurice Duke, and Jackson R. Bryer, pp. 1-20. New York: St. Martin's Press, 1978.

> Identifies sources of information about Hammon's works, manuscripts, letters, biography, and critical reaction to the author.

Wegelin, Oscar. "Bibliography." In his *Jupiter Hammon, American Negro Poet: Selections from His Writings and a Bibliography*, pp. 47-51. Reprint. 1915. Freeport, N.Y.: Books for Libraries Press, 1970.

> Annotated bibliography of Hammon's poetry and essays.

### Criticism

Baker, Houston A., Jr. "Terms for Order: Acculturation, Meaning, and the Early Record of the Journey." In his *Journey Back: Issues in Black Literature and Criticism*, pp. 1-26. Chicago: The University of Chicago Press, 1980.

> Addresses the role of religion in Hammon's poetry. Baker maintains that religion is used by Hammon as a means of conforming with and surviving in eighteenth-century white society.

Bell, Bernard W. "African-American Writers." In *American Literature, 1764-1789: The Revolutionary Years*, edited by Everett Emerson, pp. 171-94. Madison: University of Wisconsin Press, 1977.

> Faults Hammon for his "negative image of Africa and conciliatory tone" and for his emphasis on hymnal form. Bell finds Hammon's poetry lacking in those qualities that elevate the early African-American spiritual.

Ransom, Stanley Austin, Jr., ed. *America's First Negro Poet: The Complete Works of Jupiter Hammon of Long Island*, by Jupiter Hammon. Port Washington, N.Y.: Kennikat Press, 1970.

> Includes an introduction by Ransom to the author's life and works, a biographical sketch by Oscar Wegelin, a critical analysis of the poems and essays by Vernon Loggins, and a bibliography of Hammon's works.

Redding, J. Saunders. "The Forerunners: Jupiter Hammon, Phillis Wheatley, George Moses Horton." In *To Make a Poet Black*, pp. 3-18. College Park, Md.: McGrath Publishing, 1939.

> Finds fault with Hammon's poetic style and themes, arguing that his poems do not speak out strongly enough against slavery.

Vertanes, Charles A. "Jupiter Hammon: Early Negro Poet of Long Island." *The Nassau County Historical Journal* XVIII, No. 1 (Winter 1957): 1-17.

> Discusses Hammon's education, the social setting that shaped his poetry, and the manner in which Hammon voiced his opinions about slavery.

---

Additional coverage of Hammon's life and career is contained in the following sources published by Gale Research: *Black Literature Criticism*, Vol. 2; *Dictionary of Literary Biography*, Vols. 31, 50; *DISCovering Authors: Multicultural Authors Module* and *Poets Module*; and *Nineteenth-Century Literature Criticism*, Vol. 5.

# Robert Hass
## 1941–

American poet, translator, and critic.

### INTRODUCTION

A respected critic and translator of works by Czeslaw Milosz and Japan's masters of haiku, Hass is also a renowned poet in his own right, and has garnered recognition for the breadth of his facility with poetic forms. Rich in allusion and abounding in nature imagery, Hass's poems often appear as discursive meditations illuminated by a richness of sensory experience and human feeling. Although his frequent references to books, music, paintings, films, and prominent figures of the *belles-lettres* have caused Hass to be labeled an "intellectual" writer, many critics counter what might be seen as a fault by pointing to his agility in his craft. Accordingly, most observe that his conversational style and use of traditional poetic images in a refreshing manner combine to make his verse highly accessible to readers. His essays are, likewise, personal and thoughtful, and provide engaging insights for readers of haiku, Milosz, and Hass's literary contemporaries.

### Biographical Information

A native of California, Hass has lived in the San Francisco Bay Area for most of his life, graduating from St. Mary's College and Stanford University, the latter of which is also the source of his master's and doctorate degrees. He studied briefly with Yvor Winters, a proponent of New Criticism and a noted champion of the moral value of poetry. Hass has been influenced by Kenneth Rexroth and the "San Francisco Renaissance" of American poetry that originated with the Beat movement, and his work is often compared with that of Gary Snyder and John Ashbery. "I think very much the influence for me in poetry is poetry," Hass said in a 1981 interview. "Specifically Wordsworth and Pound and through them Snyder and Whitman and others. . . . I guess there is not one model. What I seem to return to most is Pound in the late *Cantos*, and Wordsworth's blank verse." Having lectured at the University of Virginia, Goddard College, Columbia University, and the University of California at Berkeley, Hass taught at SUNY Buffalo before returning to his alma mater, St. Mary's College, where he has been a professor of English since 1971. His first volume of poetry, *Field Guide*, was honored with the Yale Series of Younger Poets Award in the year of its publication, while his first collection of criticism, *Twentieth Century Pleasures: Prose on Poetry*, received the National Book Critics Circle Award in 1984.

### Major Works

With *Field Guide* and *Praise*, his third volume of poetry, Hass established himself as a naturist, and a meditative

and imagistic poet. In these works he creates catalogues, as a naturalist would, and demonstrates his ability to provide a "name" for the elements of everyday experience. Both works also display Hass's characteristically historical and geographic consciousness. The former is rife with descriptions and evocations of California flora and fauna, and contains musings on themes of desire and despair, nature and imagination, life and death. In many ways *Praise* continues with the work of *Field Guide*, exploring the act of naming as a movement toward closing the gap between subject and object and as a gesture of praise. *Human Wishes*, Hass's fourth collection, was originally titled *The Apple Trees at Olema*, but was changed before printing. The word "I" is absent from this work, reflecting Hass's concern with all of humanity as his subject. In keeping with this free-ranging and inclusive spirit, Hass experiments with the limits of free verse and the form of poetry. For example, he adapts Ezra Pound's spondaic style in "Late Spring" to prose narrative, from which Hass eventually shifts into the lyric mode. The second section of the volume, comprised of prose poems, uses formal diction and cadenced lines to heighten the tension between the seemingly prosaic and the poetic. Hass's collection of ten essays and four reviews, *Twentieth Century Pleasures:*

*Prose on Poetry*, treats the work of Robert Lowell, Rainier Maria Rilke, James Wright, and Stanley Kunitz, as well as the Slavic poetry of Milosz and Tomas Tranströmer. Three of the essays discuss poetic form; prosody and rhythm; and images, respectively, the latter focusing on the imagery of haiku and its use by contemporary American poets.

## Critical Reception

Hass's work has most often been greeted with praise. His first published volume of verse, *Field Guide*, was acclaimed by Stanley Kunitz, who commented that "Hass's poetry is permeated with the awareness of his creature self, his affinity with the animal and vegetable kingdoms, with the whole chain of being. . . . Natural universe and moral universe coincide for him, centered in a nexus of personal affections, his stay against what he describes as 'the wilderness of history and political violence.'" Likewise, his third volume, *Praise*, earned Hass the William Carlos Williams Award and high critical favor: "[Hass is] an important, . . . pivotal young poet," remarked Ira Sadoff, and Hayden Carruth concurred in his review for the *New York Times Book Review*. His most recent poems, collected as *Human Wishes*, were seen as "swollen with abundance and perception . . . never ending, or at least as long as a list of human wishes. . ." by the *Village Voice Literary Supplement*. For *Twentieth Century Pleasures: Prose on Poetry* Hass was lauded by the National Book Critics Circle for bringing "a poet's sensibility to powerful readings of Lowell, Rilke, . . . combining deep learning with passionate conviction. The criticism, like Hass's poetry, is robust, engaged, and utterly lucid." His relaxed, refreshing prose style, peppered by anecdote, inviting and engaging, is said to affect in the reader Hass's deep faith in the power of poetry. His translations of Basho, Buson, and Issa, on which he worked for over two decades, are hailed as "the standard versions for at least as long again," as Hass "wisely resists attempting to re-create the multiple puns and allusions that reveal the occasion and further meanings of a particular haiku. . . ." Hass has also been recognized as a Woodrow Wilson, Danforth and Guggenheim fellow and has received Belles Lettres and American Academy of Art and Letters awards.

## PRINCIPAL WORKS

### Poetry

*Field Guide*  1973
*Winter Morning in Charlottesville*  1977
*Praise*  1979
*Human Wishes*  1989

### Other Major Works

*The Separate Notebooks* [by Czeslaw Milosz; translator, with Robert Pinsky] (notebooks)  1983
*Twentieth Century Pleasures: Prose on Poetry* (criticism) 1984
*Unattainable Earth* [by Czeslaw Milosz; translator, with Czeslaw Milosz] (poetry)  1986
*Collected Poems, 1931-1987* [by Czeslaw Milosz; translator, with Louis Iribarne and Peter Scott] (poetry) 1988
*The Essential Haiku: Versions of Basho, Buson, and Issa* [editor, translator] (poetry)  1994

---

## CRITICISM

### James Fahey  (essay date 1973)

SOURCE: A review of *Field Guide,* in *Best Sellers,* Vol. 33, No. 8, July 15, 1973, pp. 178-79.

[*In the following review, Fahey criticizes* Field Guide *as self-consciously poetic, grounded in "ideas" and not in "words."*]

The Yale Series of Younger Poets (e.g. anyone under forty and not yet published) has discovered some fine poets; most notably James Tate and recently Judith Johnson Sherwin for *Uranium Poems,* and Michael Casy for his acclaimed work, *Obscenities.* This year's winning volume has been described by Stanley Kunitz, the judge of the competition, as like "stepping into the ocean when the temperature of the water is not much different from the air." I find this compliment for Robert Hass's **Field Guide** accurate but in the pejorative sense.

One can easily fall into Robert Hass's poems and land not knowing what went by, and that, I feel is not an admirable quality. The work is deceptive. If one is skimming through the pages, the lines appear full of image; yet, after a closer look, the images are always a blur:

> Casting, up a salt creek in the sea-rank air,
> fragrance of the ferny anise, crackle of field grass
> in the summer heat. Under this sun vision blurs
> Blue air rises, the horizon weaves above the leaden
>    bay
> Rock crabs scuttle from my shadow in the silt.

These lines sound like a rather poor imitation of Dylan Thomas, while the jacket cover and foreword boast that the work is "earthy" and in the "American epic tradition." The author seems to be concentrating on ideas not words. Too often the stanzas appear to be consciously poetic. It doesn't work. Word arrangements behave as foreign bodies sitting next to each other, and quite uncomfortably at that. If one notices the relation of the title to the work it would seem to be a sophisticated directory of nature; that is to say that the descriptions are of "eucalyptus groves, aromatic fungi, pointillist look of laurels, slime of a saffron milkcap, fruity warmth of zinfandel, ornamental oranges, reedy onion grass" and on into "your acacia grove" folks! I reckon that to go through Mr. Hass' garden of thought I better fetch my Oxford English Dictionary.

Ironically the best lines in the entire volume are the most simple and representative of the fault in this work:

> But I had the odd
> feeling, walking to the house
> to write this down, that I had left
> the birds and flowers in the field,
> rooted or feeding. They are not in my
> head, are not now on this page.
> It was very strange to me, but I think
> their loss was your absence

I should have liked to be there.

## Vernon Young (essay date 1973–1974)

SOURCE: "Fool, Thou Poet," in *Hudson Review,* Vol. XXVI, No. 4, Winter, 1973–74, pp. 717-34.

*[In the following excerpt, Young comments on Hass's use of "naming," or providing a catalogue of nature, in* Field Guide.*]*

With no gods all their own and with the total breakdown of their civic world as a vehicle of continuing aspiration (or even as a consolatory place to live out the day), American writers in greater number are turning to the wilderness as their one great external source of unadulterated poetry. Joyce Carol Oates . . . asks, in one of her intelligent and lovely poems, "Is all space so empty? / must we fill it with ourselves?" Of course: only so it can be habitable. To *fill* it, you'd need a heap of majesty; to inhabit it, with any hope of definition as poet, you begin by finding names for its manifestations. This is what Robert Hass is doing in *Field Guide,* finding names; if he succeeds as abundantly as he promises in his first bookful of poems, he will soon be a "name," himself, in the growing company of American naturists. Readers of *The Hudson Review* may better remember him from **"Book Buying in the Tenderloin,"** an acrimonious, headlong poem of another sort. In the context of this admirable collection it has more recognizably the sound of another poet, perhaps Robert Lowell. Hass can be vehement, with political edge, in his own way (cf. **"Assassin"** and **"The Failure of Buffalo to Levitate"**); on balance, however, the landscape pieces are those that strike roots. Here is his domain: ". . . calligraphies of pheasant tracks / in the last crisp snow around the soggy fields. / Some buds, magenta-colored, green-veined, / sap rising. . . ." He is not yet out of the woods; literally he's safest when in them. Flower-power and injustice-hunting have left their marks. He professes wonder (**"Lament for the Poles of Buffalo"**) that there is no monument to a drunken Seneca who stabbed two defenseless whittlers (in 1802) and was hanged. Under frontier conditions, what could have been a likelier outcome?

In **"The Return of Robinson Jeffers"** he wants to reclaim Jeffers for "An awkward brotherhood with the world's numb poor" and make his ghost see "finally, / that though rock stands, it does not breed." These are sentimental condescensions that refute the whole nature of Jeffers' poetry. At the storm center of his work stands the modern heresy he hunted down and for which he shaped his powerful and recurrent incest-symbol: the dependence of contemporary man on social (i.e. sexual) reflections of himself, "the woman, the serpent: the man, the rose-red cavern," and the narcissism of "falling in love inward" . . . "he had given himself to stone gods," says Hass. No. Let's not confuse metaphor with man. If Hass has read Jeffers' letters, he must see that the man was sympathetically *involved* that he had an informed political intelligence, that it was he who said of another, "I think even poets should read the newspapers," that he busily served on prize-giving juries and addressed himself with conscience to the hard choice of rewarding talent or meeting financial need. And let's be real: he married and had two sons; today, one is a National Park ranger, the other a CPA—"rock . . . does not breed." Mr. Hass said that. Since Jeffers casts the longest shadow over his shoulder, Hass is no doubt performing a ritual-murder of the father. That's to be expected. I simply feel that Jeffers' ghost should not be burdened with even more misunderstanding than its owner took to the grave. (Since no one in America has written poetry more sensual, I'm surprised Jeffers isn't now fashionable!) Hass needs no self-aggrandizement. His purest poetry here (not perhaps his richest but his purest) is in the **"Pornographer"** quartet. As I read it, the motive is not far from that of Jeffers' "Love the Wild Swan": the fragility of *art* (pornography, for the instance) when tested against the reverberations of history or "the two-note whistles from a cardinal." In these formally perfect verses, beginnings and endings harmonize, revealing themes at a glance, like a sheet of music. Here are two examples.

> He had thought March was the blackbird's month.
>   April is the blackbird's month. . . .
> All around him is the gravel music
>   of the blackbirds' cries.
>
> Like America, his art consists
> in the absence of scale. . . .
> There is no walled city come to.
> The sphinx proposes nothing.
> There is no plague . . .

## Michael Waters (essay date 1975)

SOURCE: A review of *Field Guide*, in *Southwest Review*, Summer, 1975 , pp. 307-11.

*[In the following review, Waters praises Hass's deft "translation" of both nature and personal history in* Field Guide.*]*

*Field Guide* is both the poet and his remarkable volume of poems, a tour through the America of his historical and political consciousness, his vast privacy of landscape. In a "**Letter**" to his wife he states: "I have believed so long / in the magic of names and poems." This belief extends his geography past any coastal boundary, and his vision telescopes through love for his family to focus with "an ancient / imagination" on "what is familiar / felt along the flesh."

The purpose of the book, then, is to name these feelings, the undercurrent that flashes through "the pulse / that forms these lines." There are three sections. The first, **"The Coast,"** is set in California, the last frontier. Hass is fascinated by his woman and the land, and his marriage to both evokes a timelessness, a sense of ancestral memory. In the opening poem, **"On the Coast near Sausalito,"** the poet catches "an ugly, atavistic fish" and holds it before him:

> Creature and creature,
> we stared down centuries.

While Hass and his wife struggle through their early years together, he places himself in a historical context with the men of his land, as varied as Kit Carson and Ishi, the last wild Indian. He dwells on the beauty of the Spanish and Indian names surrounding him, yet feels the violence associated with them: "Death shook us more than once / those days and floating back / it felt like life." He is always drifting through the landscape like a ghost, trying to transform (or, through his concern with language, *translate*) that past into something relevant and useful in his own life. In a **"Graveyard at Bolinas"** he sees lettuce growing on an early settler's grave and picks "a bunch / thinking to make / a salad of Eliza Binns."

Still, that violence, "the old fury of land grants, maps, / and deeds of trust," is ever present as a "tanker lugs silver / bomb-shaped napalm tins toward / port at Redwood City." This evidence of man's abusing the land is now reciprocated:

> A furious dun-
> colored mallard knows my kind
> and skims across the edges of the marsh
> where the dead bass surface
> and their flaccid bellies bob.

Nature shuns us, and the loss activates a bitterness charged with a personal identification with this diseased land: "My God, it is a test, / this riding out the dying of the West." Hass, as a poet, feels this self-denial deeply:

> Some days it's not so hard to say
> the quick pulse of blood
> through living flesh
> is all there is.

Yet it is this same pulse that creates a beauty by working the language of the land, by preserving through his own life the perfect details of natural landscape.

The poems in **"A Pencil"** deal with writers and are necessarily self-conscious. Hass feels a brotherhood with all poets through history, through "the peace / of the writing desk / and the habitual peace / of writing." One poem, **"After the Gentle Poet Kobayashi Issa,"** is an extended form of linked haiku. In the earlier section, Hass noted the sensual exoticism of food:

> On the oak table
> filets of sole
> stewing in the juice of tangerines,
> slices of green pepper
> on a bone-white dish.

Here he relaxes and laughs:

> These sea slugs,
> they just don't seem
> *Japanese.*

Other poems in this section deal with Basho, Baudelaire, Chekhov, and Jeffers. This group ends with a series of "pornographer poems" that try to settle a difference, at least in the poet's mind, between physical reality and creative imagination. The pornographer keeps a pencil "in a marmalade jar / which is colored the soft grey / of a crumbling Chinese wall / in a Sierra meadow." This confusion of images suspends a sense of time, and the poet and his landscape often become one. The pornographer finds that nature is much more interesting than anything he can create, and in this sense the poet, in the act of writing, confesses his failure to express his loves with honesty. His role remains that of the guide.

The poems in the last section, **"In Weather,"** are set in the east, in Buffalo, N.Y. Hass thinks of himself here as a contemporary settler, starting a new life away from his home- and heartland, the California coast. He feels himself, for the first time, taking root in his experience: "I am conscious of being / myself the inhabitant / of certain premises." He is becoming history now, and his concern still remains in reshaping that sense into something useful, in gathering the past and its violence into something approaching beauty:

> Counterpane:
> Grandfather's Death
>
> On the pillow
> the embroidered flowers ·
> are fading
> fading that patient spider
> my grandmother
>
> who made the best
> of losses
> bright quilts from rags
> that are every bird
> Audubon ever killed
> in America.

He sews a new landscape from the ragged remains of the past.

The best poem in the volume, **"In Weather,"** deals with his loss of place, his adaptation to a new geographical location and its history, its role in his poetry. His ability to use the past of his forebears, to "kindle from their death / an evening's warmth," mellows him. He misses the West, and the wasteland of the industrial city sets him writing, turns him inward: "The refuse of my life / surrounds me and the sense of waste / in the dreary gathering of it / compels me. . . ." Still, even in such desolation, in the scraps of his own refuse, he finds some worth:

> I was rewarded. A thaw turned up
> the lobster shells from Christmas eve.
> They rotted in the yard
> and standing in the muddy field I caught,
> as if across great distances,
> a faint rank fragrance of the sea.

In his isolation he identifies more with animals, with a male sea-worm who lives inside the female, as he lives inside the solitude of his family. In bed at night, hearing an owl, he imitates its *twoo* sound and experiences the small pleasure of simple life:

> I drew long breaths.
> My wife stirred in our bed.
> Joy seized me.

His darkness is one of constant self-discovery, the desire to fulfill himself in his time:

> I know that I know myself
> no more than a seed
> curled in the dark of a winged pod
> knows flourishing.

---

**Field Guide is a means of naming things, of establishing an identity through one's surroundings, of translating the natural world into one's private history.**

—*Michael Waters*

---

The final poem, **"Lament for the Poles of Buffalo,"** echoes Lowell in its attempt to take historical situations and place them directly in his own experience. He addresses the Polish people in their isolation from their homeland and attempts to give them a sense of the history of upstate New York, something as rugged and private as their own proud past. He makes them see their sons, more

Americanized and politically conscious, as extensions of that heritage. He compares their languages, the "buckshot / on the tongues of your grandfathers" to the "pellets doctors dug / out of students' skulls last spring." As these people have lost their dream of America, Hass too has seen his dream of their heritage, culled from books, grow less romantic, less healthy and rustic. He sees them all united in this desolation, "married in dead salmon." Yet he compares their sons, in their concern for the land and the way it shapes and changes a man, to the Indians as well as their rugged Polish ancestors. This "ancient imagination" holds sway, draws them together in a sense of continuing grace, a spirit of loving survival. This past "translates easily" into their own lives.

*Field Guide* is a means of naming things, of establishing an identity through one's surroundings, of translating the natural world into one's private history. This is a lot to accomplish, yet Robert Hass manages it with clarity and compassion. He is a fine poet, and his book is one of the very best to appear in a long time.

**Hayden Carruth (essay date 1979)**

SOURCE: "Impetus and Invention: Poetic Tradition and the Individual Talent," in *Harper's,* Vol. 258, No. 1548, May, 1979, pp. 88-90.

[*In the following excerpt, Carruth reviews* Praise *favorably and includes Hass among the many individual talents "inventing" poetry today.*]

When we open a book at random and read this:

> Ah, love, this is fear. This is fear and syllables
> and the beginnings of beauty. We have walked the
>   city,
> a flayed animal signifying death, a hybrid god
> who sings in the desolation of filth and money
> a song the heart is heavy to receive. We mourn
> otherwise. Otherwise the ranked monochromes,
> the death-teeth of that horizon, survive us
> as we survive pleasure. What a small hope.
> What a fierce small privacy of consolation.
> What a dazzle of petals for the poor meat . . .

we have found a poet who knows, loves, and uses the great tradition, knowing, too, that it is never pedantic, never self-imitative, but always moving its huge chords through the modulations of individual sensibilities. This is the first stanza of a poem by Robert Haas, whose first book won the Yale Younger Poets competition several years ago, and whose new and second book, *Praise,* is a notable advance. My quotation gives only an inkling of what he can do; he writes in many shapes, moods, even styles. Yet everywhere one recognizes this reverence for the power of language, words in their gull-flight of syntax, what we—or our ancestors—used to call eloquence. There are many pleasures in poetry, and for my part, being incorrigibly maverick, I'd lose none of them. One of the greatest is discovering that the language of one's youth, Shakespeare's or Yeats's (and of course it is both), is not dead, has not been refined out of existence. The mainstream does not dry up; it deepens and widens. Think of jazz. Charlie Parker was a revolution, not to say revelation, from whom sprang the line of Rollins, Coltrane, Shepp, whom we would be loath to do without; but long after Parker such men as Ben Webster and Paul Gonsalvez were finding *impetus* and *invention* in the central evolution of jazz; and today we have Scott Hamilton. Yes, many pleasures. And in this review I have been lucky enough to catch poets who give us a broad sampling of them. I hope readers will take to them all—always acknowledging the prerogatives of taste—and to Robert Haas as much as the others.

**Peter Stitt   (essay date 1980)**

SOURCE: "Summer Birds and Haunch of Winter," in *Poetry,* Vol. CXXXV, No. 4, January, 1980, pp. 229-37.

[*In the following excerpt, Stitt argues that* Praise *illustrates the development of the American poem in terms of organic structure and ingenuity.*]

In *Praise,* Robert Hass combines rather radically two complementary trends present in the progress of American poetry since the nineteenth century. In terms of imagery and statement, he is willing to include anything demanded by the poem, no matter its source, no matter how subtle or tenuous its relevance. In terms of structure, he is carrying the idea of the organic poem to ever-increasing degrees of linearity. The idea of a well-made poem generally includes the concept of circularity; all is preconceived, blue-printed, nothing enters by happenstance; the end refers to the beginning, all questions are answered, nothing is left dangling, a circle is formed. The organic poem, by contrast, grows as a tree grows, responding to the necessities of environment; its logic is internal, discovered along the way, never preconceived. When the organic poem achieves linearity, as is often the case in Hass, its end may neither resemble nor remember nor refer to its beginning; questions may go unanswered, all things may be left dangling; we stop at the end of the line on a one-way trip to somewhere.

Probably the best poem of this sort in *Praise* is **"Not Going to New York: A Letter."** The poem is a kind of linear, internal meditation; whatever occurs to the mind of the poet along the way is integrated into the flow. Memory and present observation combine to assist in explaining why the speaker is staying at home. His childhood comes into it, and his grandmother, recently dead—for whom the poem is a kind of elegy. Towards the end these elements come together in a surprising way to produce a

superb comment on the nature of poetry. Given the character of this form, its dense unity, my quotation must of necessity be long; we enter as the speaker's son touches the "Withered cheek" of his father's grandmother:

she looked at him awhile and patted his cheek back and
    winked
and said to me, askance: "Old age ain't for sissies."
This has nothing to do with the odd terror in my memory.
It only explains it—the way this early winter weather
makes life seem more commonplace and—at a certain
    angle—
more intense. It is not poetry where decay and a created
radiance lie hidden inside words the way that memory
folds them into living. "O Westmoreland thou art a
    summer bird
that ever in the haunch of winter sings the lifting up of
    day."
Pasternak translated those lines. I imagine Russian
    summer,
the smell of jasmine drifting toward the porch. I would
    like
to get on a plane, but I would also like to sit on the porch
and watch one shrink to the hovering of gulls and glint
in the distance, circle east toward snow and disappear.
He would have noticed the articles as a native speaker
    wouldn't:
*a* bird, *the* haunch; and understood a little what persists
when eyes half-closed, lattice-shadow on his face,
he murmured the phrase in the dark vowels of his mother
    tongue.

I don't intend to interpret these remarkable lines, but want only to point out their linear, flowing, organic, inclusive structure.

> **Hass is at his best when the complexity of his themes and the density of his language and imagery combine to help him attain a heightened form of expression.**
>
> **—Peter Stitt**

Hass is not the only poet who has tried this kind of thing, but is remarkable for the extent to which he has done it. And yet the book is far from a consistent success. Hass is at his best when the complexity of his theme and the density of his language and imagery combine to help him attain a heightened form of expression. In the poems where this happens—among them are **"Heroic Simile," "Against Botticelli," "The Pure Ones,"** and **"Old Dominion"**—he is very good indeed. In other poems he seems content to accumulate commonplace images and ideas; the result, as in **"The Beginning of September"** and **"Songs to Survive the Summer,"** is a chatty, low-key, unengaging linearity. The book is a strange disappointment on the whole, but only because some of its parts are so surpassingly good. In the future let us hope that Hass will keep the pressure on, in all his poems.

### David Kalstone  (essay date 1980)

SOURCE: A review of *Praise,* in the *New York Times Book Review,* May 4, 1980, pp. 15, 43.

[*In the following excerpt, Kalstone comments favorably on the sequence "Songs to Survive the Summer" but observes that* Praise *as a whole is an uneven work.*]

One of the tests for good poets these days seems to be whether they can take the leap from writing accomplished short poems to building longer structures, refigure their isolated lyric discoveries as part of a larger tissue of inquiry. . . . Robert Hass—though on a small scale— [does so successfully] in the sequence, **"Songs to Survive the Summer"** that closes his new book, *Praise.* Perhaps it's no accident that the poem . . . is addressed to a young daughter in whose presence her father is made to feel "This is my life, / time islanded / in poems of dwindled time." The songs are triggered by what he and his daughter hear from the child next door: "Let's play / in my yard. It's OK, / my mother's dead." The dead woman, 31, had been a friend of his daughter, had taught her to weave. The set of poems, obliquely related to one another, is an attempt to forestall her nightmares and fears. One section was in fact a separate poem, **"For Chekhov,"** in Mr. Hass's first book, where it seemed orphaned; here it is truer because more tentative, only one among a number of views of suffering. The sequence is invigorated by its variety: youthful memories, a recipe, tales, even an unexpected revelation in the story of Wilhelm Steller, whose discovery of the jay later named after him led to the fortuitous, almost overlooked discovery of Alaska. The **"Songs"** emerge as a chap-book of bitter pleasures in which death is "all things lustered / by the steady thoughtlessness / of human use."

This is the best poem in a generally unsettled book. Mr. Hass's first collection, *Field Guide,* the Yale Younger Poets selection in 1972, was a set of fine, troubled lyrics by a wary naturalist. It took its title from the "terrifying field guide" that teaches us to identify poisonous mushrooms. Its encounters were alive to evolutionary detail ("Creature and creature, / we stared down centuries"), and its historical curiosity reawakened buried presences in California life. In *Praise* Mr. Hass suffers a crisis of confidence in his early style. Structuralism seems to have gotten to him too noticeably, though he silences with blackberries the **"Friend Who Has Been Reading Jacques Lacan."** "A word is elegy to what it signifies," he tells us; but it is disconcerting to find whole poems cast as elegies for the lost immediacy of his earlier writing: "I used to name the flowers."

Mr. Hass is tempted to give up Roethke for Merwin, the minutiae of growth for the thresholds of eternity:

I am outside a door and inside
the words do not fumble
as I fumble saying this.

These are the first lines of a successful effort in his new style, **"Like Three Fair Branches From One Root Deriv'd,"** a poem that symbolically stills, even fuses the warring elements in love. Other attempts at *vision*— **"Transparent Garments,"** for example—do not work so well. In a mixed and more congenial style, **"The Origin of Cities"** and **"Not Going to New York: A Letter"** are particularly appealing. But *Praise* as a whole is uneasy.

### Robert Hass with David Remnick  (interview date 1981)

SOURCE: An interview in *Chicago Review,* Vol. 32, No. 4, Spring, 1981, pp. 17-26.

[*In the following interview, Remnick questions Hass about his own work in light of his influences.*]

[Remnick]: *What was the original impulse to begin writing?*

[Hass]: I just liked the sound of it, I think.

*Do you remember what those early efforts were like?*

They were all rhymed imitations of Robert Service or Vachel Lindsay. They were very often narratives about my friends.

*Was there a point at which you realized that you didn't really have to use traditional forms?*

I sort of knew that early on. I mean I had seen e.e. cummings in anthologies, but I didn't know how to hear the music of poetry without rhyme until I was in high school. City Lights Bookstore in San Francisco published Allen Ginsberg's *Howl* around that time. I think the Chief of Police banned it as a dirty book so, naturally, we went out and bought it and read it. The music of *Howl* and then Kerouac's novels, which were appearing then, sent me to writers they mentioned, Whitman and Pound, and I began to get a feeling, a very primitive feeling, for free verse.

*What was it about* Howl *that was particularly inspiring?*

Really just the sound of it. No, that's not true. The promise of adventure and intensity. And sex, I guess. Reading was always a little erotic; it carried information of the great world, right. But the actual experience in *Howl* was so different from mine. I was just a kid and I felt I guess the way high school kids do, sort of alienated from the mob-ethic of high school. So it was attractive, but Ginsberg's experience, the East Coast experience that he described as "vomiting paranoia," of desperation and hysteria, was not mine. In lots of ways the world seemed good to me, and I don't think I understood those poems very well.

*Did anyone help you with your writing while you were in college? I find often in high schools and colleges there is a shyness about showing work to authorities like teachers or parents, and what develops is a kind of peer-reading group.*

Exactly. There was a bunch of us at St. Mary's who wrote and showed each other the work. I was writing mostly prose. We all wrote both poetry and prose. I had two friends who were very conscious of being poets and whose ambitions were to be poets. Anything that conscious was a million miles from my mind. Anyway, it was a situation in which there were a lot of people in love with writing, and everybody showed each other their work.

*What about the value of writing in imitation of other poets in order to learn how in a sense to read and write?*

We read a lot of other people and then wrote imitations of them and of each other. You know, this was a random, intermittent activity. We weren't in training or anything. One guy imitated Pound and Hart Crane a lot but they were both too hard for me. I had read a lot of the body of traditional English poetry and, of course, Robinson Jeffers. I had a lot of it in my head memorized and . . . the poet who mattered to me most was probably Wordsworth, whom I really loved. At the same time, I was taking a course in this great books program in which, instead of the usual course in biology or botany, they gave us a pair of binoculars and turned us loose to watch birds for a semester. They gave us an essay by Darwin and an essay by Aristotle. At the end of the term, we had to turn in our notebooks of observation and an essay on whether looking at things and classifying them was real knowledge or not . . . In the meantime, I kept huge notebooks full of soul-searching and things like that. Strangely, it never occurred to me to put the two things, the notebook of creatures and plants and the notebook of interior warm-ups and practice to be a writer, together.

*I think it might be fair to say that in **Field Guide** you've put the two together. And in many of the poems there seems to be a fascination with the names of birds and fish and so on, the very kinds of observation and classification that you did in that notebook.*

When I started doing botany and natural history in college, part of it consisted of learning the names of things I already knew, sensually, as familiars of childhood, and there was a kind of power I felt from learning the names. I felt like I was the secret owner of everything that I had come to see carefully enough to be able to give a name to. It wasn't merely a matter of having a label for something, because in order to name it, you had to know it in its uniqueness. And the other thing, I suppose, to return to the theme of California, was that everything was changing so fast. The whole post-war explosion in America was

going on, and my study was a way of holding on, a way of making things that I valued stay put. By getting to know one species of grass from another, one species of bird from another, and by knowing the names, they could stay put. I thought.

*There is a terrific poem in **Praise**, "Mediation at Lagunitas," that among other things plays with this idea of names and naming.*

Yeah. I think that poem came out of a sudden realization that the word was not the thing. It was something that dawned on me very slowly even though it is the most obvious thing in the world. I always got things like that confused. I read *War and Peace* and wanted to be a writer because Pierre and Andre had such interesting lives. Somehow I didn't realize that Tolstoy spent all of his time sitting on his ass writing *War and Peace*—you know the confusion? The poem really came about because a friend came over and was explaining to me ideas in contemporary philosophy about how man uses words because he is alienated from his environment, that we use words because we don't have what we want and that, in fact, language emerges from the difference between here and there. So all language is an expression—not of what I took it to be in my experience of naming and calling the world into being—but rather of saying goodbye to it or come here to it.

*Do you recall the composition of the poem?*

It took me a very long time to write it because what I first wrote did not seem a poem to me. "All the new thinking is about loss. / In this it resembles all the old thinking . . ." That kind of philosophical, or general, language didn't belong to my notions of what you could do in a poem. All right, I thought you could do it, you can do anything in a poem, but it made me uneasy. A version of it sat for a very long time unfinished, for two or three months or so, and then I picked it up and finished it in a different version than this and was very unhappy with it. I felt uneasy about it and set it aside. That was three or four years ago. About two years later I was going through some poems and thought, "Actually this is kind of interesting," and saw what the problem had been.

*Can you say what the problem was?*

It's hard for me to talk about it. I write, "There was a woman/I made love with and I remembered how, holding / her small shoulders in my hands sometimes . . ." I don't know exactly what I had there before, but I knew the issues in the poem had for me to do with the power, the ferocity of the impulse to be merged with someone. With violence. And it troubled me, coming up against this. I had written another poem, **"In Weather,"** that contained images of violence against women and I thought, "Wait a minute, what am I? A vampire? Why is this coming up again." But I was pretty sure it wasn't the same thing. I thought **"In Weather"** was about nature-hating, insofar as a poem is "about" something. I had sensed a connection between nature-hating and woman-hating in somebody else, in a poem I heard read, and was trying to feel my way into the poem, and I found it was very easy to feel my way into it, and that shocked me. This poem felt different. I was trying to think about aggression against women, on the one hand, which is real and all around us, and a different and absolutely necessary kind of violence in sexual desire itself. Most of this wasn't very conscious. I was grouping for a phrasing or a music. At just about that time, two things happened: a friend of mine killed himself and a young sculptress whom I had met was murdered. It was one of those times in life when you feel like getting through it is wading through blood. I couldn't think about small distinctions anymore. I just felt sick, so I set the poem aside again. Then one day about a year later I found myself, because I remember what I've written, reciting the poem aloud to myself as I was taking a walk, and the phrasing came to me. So went home and dug out the poem and finished it. That was four years after the first writing. The last lines had to be altered slightly, and then I felt the poem was done. I don't usually work quite that way.

*Usually a little quicker?*

Oh yes, because after a while it becomes a question of how long are you the same person working on a poem.

*Do you think any kind of non-poetic music, real music, has influenced your work at all?*

No, I don't think so really. I think very much the influence for me in poetry is poetry. Specifically Wordsworth and Pound and through them Snyder and Whitman and others. A lot of people. Another poet I admire a lot is a sixteenth-century poet, Sir Thomas Wyatt, who wrote songs to be sung to the lute. Those songs are a lot like George Oppen's poems. They are very tough, austere poems with plain, rough rhythms, and an enormously subtle discrimination. I go to Wyatt to hear his music a lot because there is no bullshit about it. On the other hand, I love the music of people like Hart Crane and Roethke. I guess there is not one model. What I seem to return to most is Pound in the late *Cantos,* and Wordsworth's blank verse.

*Certain poetic communities like the Beats or the Black Mountain group not only consisted of outstanding poets and poems but also seemed to show the value and sometimes the dangers of such a community. Do you find correspondence with fellow poets about your work to be useful?*

Sure. Though after college, when I began to write most intensely, I felt very isolated, and I don't have the habit of a community of writers. That sort of first publication that comes from showing poems to friends is not deeply a habit of mine, and I feel it sometimes as a lack. But I do find it very useful to correspond with friends, and with different people for different things. John Peck is an old friend and, though he knows the experimental tradition better than I do, I think his attitude toward poetry is more formal and more austere. So we get into arguments that are very helpful to me. I remember he said to me in one letter, "I'm not interested in passion; I'm interested in affections. I'm not interested in vision; I'm interested in attention." At that time, working on the poems in *Praise,* passion and vision were what interested me. I think in *Field Guide* it might have been affections and attention. I was in a bad way and was trying to probe sources but I felt very unsure of myself. So I wrote back, "How can you sustain attention or affection if they don't come from some vision or some deep passion?" He himself had a kind of Augustinian passion for accuracy, for real clues, you know. I think he was writing "The March Eclogues" at that time and his attitude was that American romanticism was bloated and in its death throes. The fashion was to freight poems with poeticisms, call them archetypes, and ego exaltation. I think he would just as soon have killed it off. I found the problem as he posed it helpful.

*In the "Songs to Survive the Summer," there is a section that delineates an entire recipe for onion soup, and as a whole that kind of simplicity, naturalness and directness seems almost Oriental to me. In fact, you have written an imitation of Basho, and Stanley Kunitz has pointed out other poems in which you write either in imitation or celebration of Oriental forms. Have you studied Oriental languages or culture?*

I've studied Japanese a little but haven't studied Chinese at all. My interest in Asian poetry comes through what was in the air on the West Coast, Kenneth Rexroth and Gary Snyder, and then it's central to modernism, anyway, in Pound and Arthur Waley's translations. For a long time I didn't understand haiku. My friend Phil Dow finally thrust it at me. To my eternal gratitude. The attractiveness of it is in the clarity, and the clarity of it is like having a clear head. What you sense about John Ashbery, for example, is that he is really trying to protect himself against all the brain-roof chatter by *becoming* the brain-roof chatter and by just letting the mind move the way the mind moves when it's doing that. Another tactic for dealing with the same thing is to try to sink into the place where all that noise stops, and that was traditionally the way of the Japanese poet. It is very attractive to me, not so much as a way of writing poetry but as a way of being and of clearing my head of distraction.

*A contemporary of yours, Charles Wright, described a certain distance he required of himself in his poems as a kind of invisible pane of glass, a situation that, in effect, allowed everything to be seen but prevented total self-involvement as in so-called confessional poetry. Is there any thought of distance in your attitude toward your poems?*

I'm not sure I understand what he meant, but the idea of lacquering the poem, even transparently, and putting it on the wall in a museum so it is a poem, and not an extension of yourself, bothers me. I dislike that idea of art a whole lot. Poetry is a way of living, I think. It's a human activity like baking bread or playing basketball. At least I think it should be. It ought to have that quality. What ought to distinguish it in that way is craftsmanship which is not distancing, though it does throw your attention off yourself and onto the work to be done.

*I think his idea is that in some, say, of Anne Sexton's lesser poems, there is too much bleeding directly onto the page, and that is a problem.*

I think that's not true. I think the problem with those poems is that they are not close *enough* to Anne Sexton, not that they are *too* close. They are bad fictions of being personal. But every poet has his or her own tactic to get to the place where you need to get to write poetry.

*Is the self in your poems never a persona?*

I think that you never get your whole self into a poem. If there is such a thing as "the whole self." As soon as you say "I" on the page, it is a persona. But every time we speak, it is to some extent a persona: it's not the whole person— at the level of *content.* At the level of *act,* the whole person can be speaking. In a good poem, for that reason, this shouldn't be an issue. Basho says that the trouble with most poetry is that it is either subjective or objective.

*It should be both?*

It should be neither. It should get past the place where those words have any meaning.

*Like most other poets, you have in various poems made allusions to other poets and poems. I think one of the things that seems to scare a new reader of a poet like Eliot, whose work asks for quite a bit of previous reading, is this idea of prerequisite reading. Do you sympathize with that fear at all?*

Sure, and I felt the same way. When I started reading modern poets, the difficulty of certain poems, not the difficulty created by grammar and things like that but the difficulty created by work I hadn't read, annoyed me. In fact I just wouldn't read them. I'd pick up a poem and it would have an epigraph in Greek and a title in Italian and that was it, I never read it. I had a strong feeling when I began writing that I wanted to write poems that at the level of reference were simpler, though not necessarily at the level of grammar. If it is a hard thing to say, then it's hard to say it and it is not going to come out easy. Poetry is hard in some ways and the society it makes its way in is too goddamn easy.

*In what way is it easy?*

A terrific example is "Star Wars." In "Star Wars" Luke Skywalker at the end of the movie, which kids have seen 50 or 60 times, is told to trust his feelings and shoot a torpedo, while he is going 600 mph, into a target of around a quarter of an inch. The training that prepared him to do this, in the structure of the movie, was to wave a light beam for a minute and a half. In the traditional hero tales, like the tales of the samurai or the story of Odysseus, the hero goes through a prolonged period of training and then maybe he can trust himself. Chuang Tzu said in the Emperor's court: "I don't want to rule other people. I am going to do something much harder, I am going to learn how to rule myself." And he spent his life working at it.

*I'd like to turn now to one of your long poems, "In Weather," and ask about the history of its writing.*

The writing of the poem is interesting to me, because I wrote the first section of it, which is no longer the first section, and thought I had written a poem—and liked it. I called it **"In Weather."** I was living in western New York and I went to the university to teach the next morning and I came back the next evening, read it, wrote a second section, and again thought I was finished. The third day I read the first two sections and wrote a third, the fourth day a fourth, and so on, for eight days. It was mostly written without revision. A couple of weeks before I had been reading a long poem by a Kentucky poet, Wendell Berry, called "The Window Poems," which I admired a lot, and I think the versification of my poem, its way of moving in its lines, came from that. Originally I wrote it in the third person, so it began, "What he wanted / in the pearly repetitions of February / was vision . . ." which I guess is something that Charles Wright would call a distancing tactic. At first I didn't understand why I did that; it turned out the reason was that the poem was going to deal with some frightening material for me. When I finished it, I saw that it should really be in the first person—mainly so that it owned up to the material in the fourth section—and that involved some small rewriting. I also felt that the first poem or the first section was really a warm-up, it wasn't necessary, so I lopped it off.

*Does that happen very often, that the first lines or stanzas or even sections turn out to be a warm-up or slow arrival at the real poem?*

Yes.

*Is it ever used later?*

Well, I never throw anything away.

*Much of the impact of the poem comes from the juxtaposition of the various sections. Generally, what is your view of numbered sections in a long poem, how do you want that to work for the poem?*

Think of it as a digging with interconnected passages. Some of them are used a lot, some are there if you want to use them, some have been sealed off. One of the impulses I have is to mine the abandoned rifts. Setting things against each other is a way of doing that, and numbered sections is a way of indicating it.

I think the first important poem I know of that uses numbered sections in that way is Wallace Stevens's "Thirteen Ways of Looking at a Blackbird." It's possible that Pound did it earlier. It comes from cubism. What Picasso did was to take all the pieces of a person and reassemble them so that there was a feeling of things being held together under duress in some painting or, by the addition of some fantastic or grotesque dream-element, of falling together in some weird way that seems shockingly natural. Not normal, but natural. Anyway, the technique is by now a sixty-year-old way of indicating this kind of exploration.

It's probably also, less grandly, a device like the chapters, to mark a pause and keep the attention from flagging.

A women said to me that she felt **"In Weather"** was like a Chinese screen, that the different faces of the poem commented on each other, and that pleased me. I had the feeling that a metaphor in one poem was equivalent to a metaphor in another poem on another subject. These aren't things I was entirely aware of while I was writing. To take an obvious example, the way that my life seemed to be a matter of picking up garbage and tending to things that didn't give a damn about me one way or the other in the second section is a little bit like the life of the male part of the innkeeper worm in the third section. There are a lot more. It felt dense with connection.

*And you say that you didn't think in terms of these connections while writing the poem?*

No, I wasn't thinking, now I am going to write a section. They came one day after another at the bidding of what went before . . . I would get a feeling that it wasn't finished and would feel the next thing happening.

*Do you feel there is something magical or awesome about that?*

I sure do. Yes. What I think is that "the imagination is shapely." It's the ordinary miracle. And artists make themselves available to it. Maybe one of the things that is true about language is that it is our function to be the consciousness of things.

*When you sit down to write a poem do you usually begin with an overall narrative or theme or a rhythm or phrase?*

Usually a rhythm or a phrase, hardly ever a thematic notion.

*How did that happen with "In Weather"?*

I had never lived in snow, and I think that the poem originally began "Never having lived in snow / I had not known how it harbored / death in its absences." Something like that. It was the phrase "how it harbored death in its absences" that came into my head, and a feeling having to do with snowfall and skin in the moonlight.

*The length of your line in "In Weather" is pretty consistent; it is a short often trimeter line that was used often by Yeats and contemporaries like Philip Levine.*

But I vary the line length a lot. **"The Return of Robinson Jeffers"** had a really long line and then in my later poems I have consciously tried to write a longer line.

*Why?*

Because the poems started to look like a riddle about how did the moron get to the bottom of the ladder. It was one perception per line going down the page. When I first started reading poets like Creeley, James Wright in *The*

*Branch Will Not Break,* Galway Kinnell, and Williams, one of the things that seemed terrifically fresh and attractive about them was that there was that one clear perception on each line or broken very plainly across two lines; it was unlike the packed, complicated modern poets—Eliot, Pound, and Hart Crane. It was like a first icy taste of something. That was very appealing to me. It was also characteristic of the Chinese poems. Each line is a clear unit of meaning with one clear image in it. Then, after a while, I felt impatient with it. I began to feel that there were kinds of richness that just couldn't be touched if that was the only way you rendered perception.

Also, once you start to hear a music, you can become a slave to the way you write. You might begin writing in a certain way because it feels right for the way you experience the world. After you do it for a while, you might find yourself experiencing the world in a certain way in order to write about it in the way that you know how to write. And that's boring, and pretty soon you'll start jazzing it up, writing from your will. That's happened with the one line one image thing. The image has gotten more and more bizarre and inflated in the effort to make the perception seem original. When a good style starts to feel like necrophilia, it's best to walk away from it. You know: glitter rock, punk rock, post-punk rock. It's time to try something else.

In order not to get trapped, I think an artist has to keep trying to enrich his means so that all the different ways he or she feels about things are available as materials for the art they practice. (Bad grammar. I'm trying to deal with gender in the language.) Otherwise, you just get locked into a particular way of seeing and speaking and feeling.

*When you go back over your poems in the process of revising, do you ever count syllables or work out the metrics?*

With some poems I do. Mostly I go by instinct these days. There are really two main elements of music for me, stress, which governs the line, and the rhythm of phrases, which governs the building of the larger structure. Though it's not metrical, the kind of poem we were talking about, plain and clear, relies on stress because there are a lot of pauses while the things presented sink in. If you speed things up and lengthen the line, stress becomes relatively less crucial. And since we have ways of talking about stress rhythm and don't have systematic ways of talking about phrase rhythm, you have to go by instinct pretty much. I mean, you would anyway, but you can't mumble to yourself, I think I'm going wrong here because of such and such, in the way that you can, thinking about stresses. Sometimes I can feel in my own work, or in student work when I've taught, that the powerful part of the writing has a certain kind of rhythm, and when I've gone away from that rhythm I've lost it. I'll maybe call myself back by analyzing the parts of the poem where it seems powerful or interesting to see if I can get back into that music and stay with it until it plays itself out.

**Robert Hass** (essay date 1982)

SOURCE: "One Body: Some Notes on Form, 1978," in *Claims for Poetry*, University of Michigan Press, 1982, pp. 151-64.

[*In the following essay, Hass traces the development of poetic forms from the human hunger for repetition, for mother, and for myth, to its present use as an expression of the poet's personality.*]

I've been trying to think about form in poetry and my mind keeps returning to a time in the country in New York when I was puzzled that my son Leif was getting up a little earlier every morning. I had to get up with him, so it exasperated me. I wondered about it until I slept in his bed one night. His window faced east. At six-thirty I woke to brilliant sunlight. The sun had risen.

Wonder and repetition. Another morning I was walking Kristin to her bus stop—a light blanket of snow after thaw, the air thick with the rusty croaking of blackbirds so that I remembered, in the interminable winter, the windy feel of June on that hill. Kristin, standing on a snowbank in the cold air, her eyes alert, her face rosy with cold and with some purity of expectation, was looking down the road. It was eight-fifteen. Her bus always arrived at eight-fifteen. She looked down the road and it was coming.

The first fact of the world is that it repeats itself. I had been taught to believe that the freshness of children lay in their capacity for wonder at the vividness and strangeness of the particular, but what is fresh in them is that they still experience the power of repetition, from which our first sense of the power of mastery comes. Though *predictable* is an ugly little word in daily life, in our first experience of it we are clued to the hope of a shapeliness in things. To see that power working on adults, you have to catch them out: the look of foolish happiness on the faces of people who have just sat down to dinner is their knowledge that dinner will be served.

Probably, that is the psychological basis for the power and the necessity of artistic form. I think of our children when they first came home from the hospital, wide, staring eyes, wet mouths, fat, uncontrollable tongues. I thought they responded when I bent over their cribs because they were beginning to recognize me. Now I think it was because they were coming to recognize themselves. They were experiencing in the fluidity of things a certain orderliness: footsteps, a face, the smell of hair and tobacco, cooing syllables. One would gradually have the sense that looking-out-of-the-eyes was a point around which phenomena organized themselves; thinking *this is going to happen* and having it happen might be, then, the authentic source of the experience of being, of identity, that word which implies that a lot of different things are the same thing.

Being and being seen. R. D. Laing says somewhere that small children don't get up at night to see if you're there, they get up to see if *they're* there. It helps me to understand that my first delighted mistaking of the situation—they know who I am!—was natural because I had the same experience as my children. Maybe our first experience of form is the experience of our own formation.

And we have that experience mainly with our mothers. Its roots are in hunger. The infant wants to know that his hunger is going to be satisfied. He cries out, there is a stirring of sensations that begin to be a pattern, and he is fed. The lovely greed of babies: so that the later experience of cognition, of the apprehension of form, carries within it the experience of animal pleasure and the first caressing experience of human affection.

This is clearest in poems of disintegration and return. In Rimbaud's "The Drunken Boat," there is the power of the moment when, in the exhaustion of the impulse of flight, he says: "I dream of Europe and her ancient quays." And Roethke in "The Lost Son"—

> The weeds whined,
> The snakes cried,
> The cows and briars
> Said to me: Die
>
> What a small song. What slow clouds. What dark
>     water.
> Hath the rain a father? All the caves are ice. . . .

—returns: "A lively understandable spirit once entertained you." It feels like the first moment after a hard rain. And Pound: "Soshu churned in the sea." The return is so powerful we are cradled entirely in the form of things, as in that poem when Gary Snyder's mind leaps from his small fire in the mountains to the little fires of the summer stars:

> Burning the small dead
>     branches
> broke from beneath
>   thick spreading
>         whitebark pine
>         a hundred summers
> snowmelt rock and air
> hiss in a twisted bough
>   sierra granite:
>         Mt. Ritter—
>         black rock twice as old
> Deneb, Altair
> windy fire

But I am not thinking mainly of poems about form; I'm thinking of the form of a poem, the shape of its understanding. The presence of that shaping constitutes the presence of poetry. Not tone, not imagery, however deep or subtle, not particular qualities of content. It is easiest to say what I mean by way of example, but almost all the bad examples seem unfair. This, from last night's reading. "The Sphinx's Riddle to Oedipus" by Randall Jarrell:

> Not to have guessed is better: what is, ends,
> But among fellows, with reluctance,
> Clasped by the Woman-Breasted, Lion-Pawed.

To have clasped in one's own arms a mother,
To have killed with one's own hands a father
—Is not this, Lame One, to have been alone?

The seer is doomed for seeing; and to understand
Is to pluck out one's own eyes with one's own
    hands.
But speak: what has a woman's breasts, a lion's
    paws?

You stand at midday in the marketplace
Before your life: to see is to have spoken.
—Yet to see, Blind One, is to be alone.

The intentions of this poem are completely real. And I learn things from it: learn from its verbs why Oedipus blinds himself with Jocasta's clasp, for example. And I see that the sphinx is herself death. But the poem never quite occurs. It can't find its way to its rhythm. In the first line, in the fourth, in the sixth, in the seventh, in the ninth, Jarrell tries, each time in a different way, to find a rhythm. You can feel the poem groping for it, like someone trying to gain admittance to a dance and being each time rebuffed by centrifugal force because he has not got the feel of the center. The last stanza, in his craftsman's hands, gives the poem a structure, but I do not feel the presence of form. That's why the last line sounds portentous and hollow. He has not entered the dance. My guesses about the reasons for this have to do with my reading of the rest of Jarrell's work. He is *sympathizing* with Oedipus and that is a characteristic stance of his poems, to be slightly outside the process sympathizing with someone else, soldiers in the early work, lonely women in the later work. In this poem, he has found an interesting perception, an important perception, but the stance has thrown him off himself. He has not found for himself the form of being in the idea.

Criticism is not especially alert to this matter. It talks about a poet's ideas or themes or imagery and so it treats all the poems of Stevens or Williams equally when they are not equally poems. The result is the curiosity of a huge body of commentary which has very little to do with the art of poetry. And this spills over into university instruction—where, whether we like it or not, an awful lot of the reading and buying of poetry goes on. Students are trained to come away from that poem of Jarrell's thinking they have had an experience of poetry if they can write a four-page essay answering the question. "What has a woman's breasts, a lion's paws?" What gets lost is just the thing that makes art as humanly necessary as bread. Art is an activity of the spirit and when we lose track of what makes an art an art, we lose track of the spirit. It is the form of "Western Wind"—

Western wind, when wilt thou blow,
The small rain down can rain.
Christ, if my love were in my arms
And I in my bed again!

—that makes life seem lucky, and intense. It is the form of "The White Horse"—

The youth walks up to the white horse to put its
    halter on,
and the horse looks at him in silence.
They are so silent they are in another world.

—that makes it seem wonderful and solemn.

The connection between gazing and grazing in the Lawrence poem brings us back to the connection between form, being, and looking. The best account of this that I know is in the 1805 *Prelude.* Wordsworth writes:

Blessed the infant babe
(For with my best conjectures I would trace
The progress of our being) blest the babe,
Nurs'd in his mother's arms, the babe who sleeps
Upon his mother's breast, who, when his soul
Claims manifest kindred with an earthly soul,
Doth gather passion from his mother's eye!
Such feelings pass into his torpid life
Like an awakening breeze, and hence his mind
Even in the first trial of its powers
Is prompt and watchful, eager to combine
In one appearance, all the elements
And parts of the same object, else detached
And loth to coalesce.

*Loth to coalesce.* The phrase seems to speak particularly to the twentieth century, to our experience of fragmentation, of making form against all odds. It explains something of Picasso's cubist nudes which come to form in the insistence of some previous and violent dismemberment; it glosses Bergman's borrowings from Picasso in the haunting visualizations of films like *Persona* and the savage dismemberments of Sylvia Plath, the strange rachitic birds Charles Simic is likely to see arising from the shape of a fork. We have been obsessed with the difficulty of form, of any coherent sense of being, so one of the values of this passage is that it takes us back to a source:

Thus, day by day,
Subjected to the discipline of love,
His organs and recipient faculties
Are quickened, are more vigorous, his mind spreads
Tenacious of the forms which it receives,
In one beloved presence, nay and more,
In that most apprehensive habitude
And those sensations which have been derived
From this beloved presence, there exists
A virtue which irradiates and exalts
All objects through all intercourse of sense.
No outcast he, bewilder'd and depressed;
Along his infant veins are interfused
The gravitation and the filial bond
Of nature, that connects him with the world.
Emphatically, such a being lives,
An inmate of this *active* universe . . .

It is this forming, this coming into existence of imagination as a shaping power, that "irradiates and exalts all being" and makes the forms of nature both an echo of that experience and a clue to the larger rhythms of a possible order in which the human mind shares or which it can make. This is also the force of that passage, early in the *Cantos,* when Pound reaches back through a scrap of Chaucer to the origins of poetry in European consciousness:

> Betuene Aprile and Merche
>           with sap new in the bough
> With plum flowers above them
>           with almond on the black bough
> With jasmine and olive leaf
> To the beat of the measure
> From star up to the half-dark
> From half-dark to half-dark
>           Unceasing the measure
> Flank by flank on the headland
>           with the Goddess' eyes to seaward
> By Circeo, by Terracina, with the stone eyes
>           white toward the sea
> With one measure, unceasing:
>           "Fac deum!" "Est factus."
> Ver novum!
>   ver novum!
> Thus made the spring. . . .

And I might just as well summon Stevens on "our old dependency of day and night," on the power of the knowledge that the world is out there:

> Deer walk upon our mountains, and the quail
> Whistle about us their spontaneous cries;
> Sweet berries ripen in the wilderness . . .

It amazes me, the way Wordsworth has come to it:

> From nature largely he receives; nor so
> Is satisfied, but largely gives again,
> For feeling has to him imparted strength,
> And powerful in all sentiments of grief,
> Of exultation, fear and joy, his mind,
> Even as the agent of the one great mind,
> Creates, creator and receiver both,
> Working but in alliance with the works
> Which it beholds—Such, verily, is the first
> Poetic spirit of our human life . . .

though I have none of this assurance, either about the sources of the order of nature or about the absolute continuity between that first nurturing and the form-making activity of the mind. It seems to me, rather, that we make our forms because there is no absolute continuity, because those first assurances are broken. The mind, in the act of recovery, creates.

Louise Glück's "To My Mother" explores this territory and it registers a shock that Wordsworth doesn't:

> It was better when we were
> together in one body.
> Thirty years. Screened
> through the green glass
> of your eye, moonlight

> filtered into my bones
> as we lay
> in the big bed, in the dark,
> waiting for my father.
> Thirty years. He closed
> your eyelids with
> two kisses. And then spring
> came and withdrew from me
> the absolute
> knowledge of the unborn,
> leaving the brick stoop
> where you stand, shading
> your eyes, but it is
> night, the moon
> is stationed in the beech tree
> round and white among
> the small tin markers of the stars:
> Thirty years. A marsh
> grows up around the house.
> Schools of spores circulate
> behind the shades, drift through
> gauze flutterings of vegetation.

The power of this poem has to do with the intensity of the sense of loss, the breaking of myth. The fabulous mother has become an ordinary woman on a brick stoop, squinting into the sun. And the assurance of natural process breaks down: day becomes night, the moon is stationed in the beech, the stars are tin. There is a strange veering definiteness to the syntax which moves us from a world of romance to a lost Chagall-like memory of it. The repeated phrase does not have the magic of recurrence; it is spoken with a kind of wonder, but it has the relentlessness of time, of the ways in which time excludes our own lives and deaths from the magic of recurrence. "It is spring!" she says, in another poem, "We are going to die!" But already something else is at work in the movement; the deliberate writing and the articulation of the syntax are making a form. When we come to the phrase, "A marsh grows up around the house," we feel both house and marsh, the formed and the unformed thing, with equal intensity. In the title of the book from which the poem comes, the nouns have been reversed to make an aesthetic commitment: *The House on Marshland.* The marsh, the shifting ground, gives the image a terrible pathos. This is a poem about growing up and it is the marsh, not the house, that grows up. *The mind creates,* Wordsworth says. The final image is a creation. It makes a form from all the pathos of loss and dispersal. Spores, gauze curtains, window, the vegetable world beyond the window are gathered into a seeing, into the one body of the poem.

One body: it's an illuminating metaphor, and so is the house, the human indwelling which art makes possible when it makes forms the imagination can inhabit. I don't think we have thought about the issue very well. What passes for discussion of it among younger poets has been an orgy of self-congratulation because they are not writing metrical poems. A marginal achievement, since many of us, not having worked at it, couldn't write them competently if we wanted to. The nature of the music of poetry has become an open question and music, the rhythm of poetry, is crucial to its form. Thinking about poetic form has also been complicated by the way we use the word. We speak of the sonnet as "a form," when no two sonnets, however similar their structures, have the same form.

The form of a poem exists in the relation between its music and its seeing; form is not the number or kind of restrictions, conscious or unconscious, many or few, with which a piece of writing begins. A sonnet imposes one set of restrictions and a poem by Robert Creeley with relatively short lines and three-or four-line stanzas imposes another. There are always restrictions because, as Creeley says, quoting Pound, "Verse consists of a constant and a variant." That is, the music of the poem as it develops imposes its own restrictions. That is how it comes to form. When Robert Duncan, in "A Poem Beginning with a Line from Pindar," comes upon all those trochees and dactyls in the names of the presidents—

> Hoover, Roosevelt, Truman, Eisenhower—
> where among these does the power reside
> that moves the heart? What flower of the nation
> bride-sweet broke to the whole rapture?
> Hoover, Coolidge, Harding, Wilson
> hear the factories of human misery turning out
>     commodities

—he has to go with it and then find his way out of that music, which he does, beautifully:

> Garfield, Hayes, Grant, Johnson
> dwell in the roots of the heart's rancor
> How sad "amid lanes and through old woods"
>     echoes Whitman's love for Lincoln!

This is a matter of bodily rhythm and the mind's hunger for intelligible recurrence. It applies equally to all verbal music.

I don't think we are in a position yet to understand the reaction against metrical poetry that began in the middle of the nineteenth century. It's an astonishing psychological fact, as if a huge underpinning in the order of things had given way and where men had heard the power of incantatory repetition before, they now heard its monotony. Or worse. Frost's rhythms use meter in a way that is full of dark, uneasy irony:

> And I keep hearing from the cellar bin
> The rumbling sound
> Of load on load of apples coming in.

And irony, the stresses falling like chains clanking, is very often Robert Lowell's way with meter:

> Our fathers made their world with sticks and stones
> And fenced their gardens with the red man's
>     bones.

The writing seems to accuse not only the fathers but the culture that produced meter and rhyme.

It has always interested me that, if you define meter as the constant, and the rhythmic play of different sounds through meter as the variant, then meter itself can never be heard. Every embodiment is a variation on the meter. One-TWO is a rhythmic variant on the pure iamb and three-FOUR is another. The pure iamb in fact can't be rendered; it only exists as a felt principle of order, beneath all possible embodiments, in the mind of the listener. It exists in silence, is invisible, unspeakable. An imagination of order. A music of the spheres.

Which is how the Renaissance conceived it. All through the Elizabethan period the dance of the order of things is associated with music. And this was the period of the other momentous event in the history of the sound of English-language poetry, the invention of the printing press. In the course of about a hundred years, the printing press tore the lyric poem away from music and left the poet with the sound of his own voice. I think that's why, in the freshness of those writers, in the satires of Wyatt, for example—

> My mother's maids when they do sew and spin,
> They sing a song made of the fieldish mouse . . .

or in a prayer in Ben Jonson—

> Good and great God, can I not think on thee,
> But it must straight my melancholy be . . .

—meter has the authority of a profound formal order. I think the human voice without music required it; otherwise it was just individual noise in the universe.

Herrick is a fascinating figure in this way. He seems to be a maker of Elizabethan songs, but really he was living by himself fifty years past that time in a country priory in Devonshire, making that music out of his own head. The public occasions of Campion—

> When to her lute Corinna sings

—have become a private music in the mind, a small imagined ordering dance of things. Meter has replaced the lute and become a way of imagining experience, a private artistic vision. It has become form:

> Whenas in silks my Julia goes,
> Then, then, methinks . . .

And meanwhile in London, Denham and Waller were tuning up the new, print-conscious and social sounds of the heroic couplet.

Another clue is the response to Wordsworth's poetry. When he sent one of his books to Charles James Fox, the leader of the liberal faction in Parliament, Fox wrote him a note saying he loved "Goody Blake and Harry Gill" but that he didn't like "Michael" and "The Brothers" because he felt "blank verse inappropriate for such simple subjects." You could write about working people in ballad meters, but not in the lofty riverrun sound of blank verse. That was what bothered people about those poems. They democratized the imagination of spiritual order inside meter.

That's why it's a short leap from Wordsworth to Whitman—or one of the reasons why. It is why free verse appears as part of a consciously democratic poetic program. As long as the feudal class system was a series of mutual obligations, a viable economy, it seemed a natural principle of order. By the time of the French revolution, it had stopped working and society seemed class-ridden. So meter seemed class-ridden. Only it took someone as stubborn as Wordsworth to demonstrate it by introducing the Cumberland beggar to his readers in the spiritual dress of blank verse:

> In the sun,
> Upon the second step of that small pile,
> Surrounded by those wild unpeopled hills,
> He sat, and ate his food in solitude:
> And ever, scattered from his palsied hands,
> That, still attempting to prevent the waste,
> Was baffled still, the crumbs in little showers
> Fell on the ground; and the small mountain birds,
> Not venturing yet to peck the destined meal,
> Approached within the length of half his staff.

Once this gesture, or the swollen ankles of a shepherd, was included in the music of the spheres, that music had ceased to have the same function and the ear was prepared for the explosion of "Crossing Brooklyn Ferry":

> I too lived, Brooklyn of ample hills was mine,
> I too walked the streets of Manhattan Island, and
>     bathed in the waters around it,
> I too felt the curious abrupt questionings stir
>     within me,
> In my walks home late at night or as I lay in my
>     bed they came upon me,
> I too had been struck from the float held forever
>     in solution,
> I too received identity by my body

And after this moment in the history of the race, in the history of the race's relation to the magic of language, the godhead was scattered and we were its fragments.

So Frost was wrong to say that free verse was like playing tennis without a net. The net was the insistence of the iamb. A lot of William Carlos Williams's individual perceptions are a form of iambic music, but he has rearranged them so that the eye breaks the iambic habit. The phrase—"a dust of snow in the wheeltracks"—becomes

> a dust of
> snow in
> the wheeltracks

and people must have felt: "yes, that is what it is like; not one-TWO, one-TWO. A dust of / snow in / the wheeltracks. That is how perception is. It is that light and quick." The effect depends largely on traditional expectation. The reader had to be able to hear what he was not hearing.

That's probably why Eliot and Pound were so alarmed when Amy Lowell moved in on imagism. Pound records the moment in one of his essays: "At a particular date in a particular room, two authors, neither engaged in picking one another's pocket, decided that the dilution of *vers libre,* Amygism, Lee Masterism, general floppiness, had gone too far and that some countercurrent must be set going. Parallel situation centuries ago in China. Remedy prescribed *Emaux et Camées.* (Or the Bay State Hymnbook). Rhyme and regular strophes. Results: poems in Mr. Eliot's *second* volume . . . also 'H. S. Mauberly.' Divergence later."

It does seem to be the case that the power of free verse has had something to do with its revolt against some alternative formal principle that feels fictitious. That was certainly part of the excitement of first reading Creeley and Ginsberg, Duncan and Dorn. They had come back, passionately, to the task of discovering forms of perception. In what Gary Snyder describes as "the spiritual loneliness of the nineteen-fifties," there were all these voices finding their way. And a decade later, when I read them, they still had that intensity.

Now, I think, free verse has lost its edge, become neutral, the given instument. An analogy occurs to me. Maybe it is a little farfetched. I'm thinking of balloon frame construction in housing. According to Gideon, it was invented by a man named George Washington Snow in the 1850s and 1860s, about the same time as *Leaves of Grass.* "In America materials were plentiful and skilled labor scarce; in Europe skilled labor was plentiful and materials scarce. It is this difference which accounts for the differences in the structure of American and European industry from the fifties on." The principle of the balloon frame was simply to replace the ancient method of mortise and tenon—heavy framing timbers carved at the joints so that they locked heavily together—with construction of a frame by using thin studs and nails. It made possible a light, quick, elegant construction with great formal variability and suppleness. For better or worse. "If it had not been for the balloon frame, Chicago and San Francisco could never have arisen, as they did, from little villages to great cities in a single year." The balloon frame, the clapboard house and the Windsor chair. American forms, and *Leaves of Grass* which abandoned the mortise and tenon of meter and rhyme. Suburban tracts and the proliferation of poetry magazines. The difference between a democratic society and a consumer society.

Stanley Plumly has written a very shrewd essay in which he argues that, in contemporary verse, tone has become important in the way that it is important in the dramatic monologues of Browning. Only the poems aren't dramatic monologues, they are spoken by the poets out of their own lives. That is, instead of being an instrument to establish person, tone has become an instrument to establish personality. And the establishment of distinctions of personality by peripheral means is just what consumer society is about. Instead of real differences emanating from the life of the spirit, we are offered specious symbols of it, fantasies of our separateness by way of brands of cigarettes, jogging shoes, exotic food. Once free verse has become neutral, there must be an enormous impulse to use it in this way, to establish tone rather than to make form. Because it has no specific character, we make a character in it. And metrical poetry is used in the same way. When it is strong, it becomes, as it did for Eliot and Pound in the twenties, a personal reaction against cultural formlessness. When it is graceful and elegant, it becomes, as it was in Herrick, a private fiction of civility with no particular relation to the actual social life we live.

## Alan Shapiro  (essay date 1983)

SOURCE: "'And There Are Always Melons,' Some Thoughts on Robert Hass," in *Chicago Review,* Vol. 33, No. 3, Winter, 1983, pp. 84-90.

[*In the following essay, Shapiro illustrates how Hass's strengths—his intellectuality and his ability to render experience—are often at odds with each other in his poetry.*]

One of the strengths of Robert Hass's work is his great ability to describe the world around him. Yet much of his interest in description proceeds from a disturbing desire (which gets complicated in his later work) to live wholly in a world of sensory experience and from a concomitant distrust of intellectuality. This distrust may seem surprising, as Hass is a plainly intellectual writer. His poems abound with references to books, films, paintings and music: his great temptation is to prefer representations of experience to experience itself, a temptation for which description serves as an antidote. Take, for instance, **"Spring,"** a poem from his first book, *Field Guide*:

> We bought great ornamental oranges,
> Mexican cookies, a fragrant yellow tea.
> Browsed the bookstores, You
> asked mildly, "Bob, who is Uggo Betti?"
> A bearded bird-like man
> (he looked like a Russian priest
> with imperial bearing
> and a black ransacked raincoat)
> turned to us, cleared
> his cultural throat, and
> told us both interminably
> who Uggo Betti was. The slow
> filtering of sun through windows
> glazed to gold the silky hair
> along your arms. Dusk was
> a huge weird phosphorescent beast
> dying slowly out across the bay.
> Our house waited and our books,
> the skinny little soldiers on the shelves.
> After dinner I read one anyway.
> You chanted, "Uggo Betti has no bones,"
> and when I said, "The limits of my language
> are the limits of my world," you laughed.
> We spoke all night in tongues,
> in fingertips, in teeth.

The poem turns on the illusion in line five that the "bearded bird-like man" is the answer to the question, who is Uggo Betti. Not until line nine do we realize that he's only someone who can explain who Uggo Betti is. This ambiguity reflects Hass's uneasy sense of culture—which this man embodies—as a kind of second-hand experience. Sensuously forbidding ("priestly") and wearing a raincoat on a sunny day, this explainer is cut off from the physical world, but also metaphorically protected from its weirdness, its evanescence, in part the source of its beauty. The implication is that art not only compensates us for the change on which the brute world is predicated, but is also a prophylactic against sensuality. And Hass indicates the insufficiency of art's compensation by characterizing his books as "skinny little soldiers" opposing the "huge beast" of evening, and by frankly characterizing the man's words about Uggo Betti and his own about language as tiresome, especially when set next to the attractive "slow dying" of the dusk, and the sexual talk that concludes the poem.

The poem shows rhetorical skill: Hass draws the syntax through the free-verse lines expressively, and the contrast between the man and the evening is nicely balanced. But the thinking that animates the poem warrants skepticism: to set sex against reading is like Yeats' specious proposition that one must choose between perfection of the art, or of the life. Devotion to the artifacts of consciousness does not necessarily limit or impair our sensuality. If it did, Paola and Francesca would not have gotten into such hot water.

But this is Hass's difficulty. He is tempted toward an excess of thought, not feeling. It's not surprising that he should be aware of the dangerous (and in some respects inevitable) limitations too much reflection can impose. This awareness, though, too often leads to an equally limiting and formulaic glorification of immediacy, as at the end of **"Graveyard Near Bolinas"**:

> . . . The sun was on my neck.
> Some days it's not so hard to say
> the quick pulse of blood
> through living flesh
> is all there is.

"Some days" implies that most days it's damn hard to say there's nothing more permanent or meaningful than the blood's pulse. But this implied struggle is only vaguely gestured at. The speaker gives an amusing account of some of the grave markers ("Eliza Binns is with Christ, which is better"), and some good description. But the details and the humor indicate little of the struggle which the conclusion suggests and from which the poem draws its power. Consequently, that power comes across as unearned and inflated, a product of the rhetoric only.

Hass employs a similar rhetorical strategy (with more success) at the end of **"Meditation at Lagunita,"** a later poem and perhaps his very best. The poem, impressive for the terrain it covers in so few lines, has all the provisional feel of an ongoing meditation, of a mind making discoveries as it goes from thought to thought, forcing each proposition toward the exception that informs and qualifies it. Yet Hass's qualifications emerge less from rhetoric than from a desire to keep an honest account as he moves over his subject:

> All the new thinking is about loss.
> In this it resembles all the old thinking.
> The idea, for example, that each particular erases
> the luminous clarity of a general idea. That the clown-
> faced woodpecker probing the dead sculpted trunk
> of that black birch is, by his presence,
> some tragic falling off from a first world of
> undivided light. Or the other notion that,
> because there is in this world no one thing
> to which the bramble of blackberry corresponds
> a word is elegy to what it signifies. . . .

He opens wryly with two examples of "the new thinking": the first derives from the scholastic notion of haecceity—that each particular, by its presence, represents a falling away from a realm of seamless purity, of "undivided light"; the second, also derived from scholasticism, is the nominalist notion that in the representation of the thing the word is, at best, "elegy to what it signifies." What we have then is a double erasure—the general truth erased by each particular, and each particular erased by the word that refers to it.

So far the thinking, abstracted from the particulars of actual experience, has been archly academic, just the kind of thinking Hass indulges in often and consequently so distrusts. What he is really commenting on here is just this tendency in himself toward a rarefied intellectuality, a kind of talking so removed from experience (even when experience is the subject) that the word, indeed, becomes elegy to what it signifies. And he goes on to say:

> . . . After a while I understood that,
> talking this way, everything dissolves: *justice,*
> *pine, hair, woman, you* and *I.*

In moving from the general concept to the particular pronouns, the list of words recapitulates the movement of the whole poem, and it enables him to turn associatively to a personal experience, to rethink the same problems in terms more integral to his life:

> . . . There was a woman
> I made love to and I remembered how, holding
> her small shoulders in my hands sometimes,
> I felt a violent wonder at her presence
> Like a thirst for salt, for my childhood river . . .
>        . . . It hardly had to do with her.
> Longing, we say, because desire is full
> of endless distances. I must have been the same to
>        her.

Testing the philosophical assumptions about loss against his own experience, he realizes that the woman was in many ways incidental to the associations she evoked. Yet the associations are problematic: what are we to make of "a thirst for salt, for my childhood river"? If she arouses

in him a desire to return to some preconscious state, then perhaps these details are related in terms of water: the fresh water of the river, the salt water of the embryonic fluid. "A thirst for salt" may also express a thirst for thirst, a desire for desire. In either case, this woman arouses in him a longing for some inaccessible state where there are no divisions between word and thing, "you" and "I," and where there is, therefore, no loss. This test-case, then, would seem to support the assumptions on which the poem began. But, determined to prevent these assumptions from simplifying his recollection, he keeps pushing his thought toward the exceptions:

> But I remember so much, the way her hands
>        dismantled bread,
> the thing her father said that hurt her, what
> she dreamed. There are moments when the body is
>        numinous
> as words, days that are the good flesh continuing,
> such tenderness, those afternoons and evenings,
> saying blackberry, blackberry, blackberry.

Although the intimate details he now recalls "the thing her father said," "what she dreamed"—are representations of other experiences, the representations are particular experiences themselves (he makes a similar perception in **"The Beginning of September"** when he says "Words are abstract, but *words are abstract* is a dance, car crash, heart's delight"). There are times, he realizes, when the divisions we assume between experience and representations of experience, self and other, word and thing, do not matter; instead of longing, which implies distance and privation, at such times the good flesh can continue.

Throughout **Praise,** his second book, Hass's distrust, which in his earlier work takes a decidedly anti-intellectual turn, now deepens to become a habit of feeling. What he fears and is now drawn to is desire as longing, as privation. And this, he knows, is not restricted to any one realm of experience. In art, it manifests itself as the desire to sieve out of process some object that will point to a transcendent meaning, to an undivided light; in strictly intellectual matters, it is the desire to escape from the ambiguities and complexities of experience through some single principle or absolute; in love, it is the impossible desire to get out of the self.

Hass now sets as a kind of ideal those experiences associated with "continuing pleasure" rather than epiphanic ones. He seeks to confide in experiences that are larger and more inclusive than the unique occasion. For instance, in **"The Beginning of September,"** it is the mastery of setting the table: "Spoon, knife, folded napkin, fork; glasses all around. The place for the plate is wholly imagined." In **"Transparent Garments,"** in which he rejects the romantic pursuit of darkness (inanimate being) on the one hand, and light (pure spirituality) on the other, he desires to emerge in a non-symbolic landscape where "the juniper is simply juniper." Likewise, in **"Songs to Survive the Summer,"** the light he's drawn to is terrestrial, it is the light "of all things lustered by the steady thoughtlessness of human use," not the undivided light of **"Meditation at Lagunitas"**; and in **"Santa Lucia,"** what he or rather what his speaker wants "happens not when the deer freezes," that is, not at the revelatory moment isolated from time, but "when she flicks her ears and starts to feed again," returning to the continuous, normative act.

---

**Throughout *Praise*, his second book, Hass's distrust, which in his earlier work takes a decidedly anti-intellectual turn, now deepens to become a habit of feeling. What he fears and is now drawn to is desire as longing, as privation.**

—*Alan Shapiro*

---

But continuity is an ideal Hass will have trouble realizing. As he says in **"Songs to Survive the Summer,"** he's caught in the war between "Dailiness and desire," between a craving for the intensity of the climactic moment and an equally strong desire to repose in traditions—continuous, time-honored practices—that embrace more of life than the discrete occasion. This ambivalence produces a curious stylistic mix, tending on the one hand toward a prose inclusiveness, and on the other, within the framework of that inclusiveness, toward a reliance upon the fragment and the list as primary organizing principles. Even when he argues for the continuous and ordinary . . . the argument takes the form of fragmentary impressions. But impressions are not traditions. And this impressionistic method pushes the poem toward the very isolation Hass is attempting to reject. It tends toward the unique and isolated occasion, not the normative one which, by definition, depends on recurrence, on the connections between things in addition to the things themselves. In other words, there seems to be an essential disjunction between his method and what he wants that method to accomplish. And it is this disjunction that accounts for the uncertainty and confusion that one meets on almost every page of ***Praise***.

A thoughtful and often moving writer, and an immediately appealing one too, Hass is traditional insofar as he is willing to draw upon resources that the past (non-literary as well as literary) makes available. Works of art, history, philosophy, are joined to personal details in order to make sense of his own experience. And to accommodate this eclectic interest, he has been gravitating toward an inclusive proselike style of composition. But within this style he relies principally on impression and on the juxtaposition of fragmentary details (literary techniques associated with imagist and post-imagist practices). And this I think not only limits the effectiveness of his eclecticism, it frustrates and defeats at times the intentions that lead him to the inclusive style. If he truly desires to bring his art closer to the center of life where "the good flesh continues," he will have to develop a

method of composition that is not so inextricably bound up with the intensity of the marginal and momentary, a method that is not, in other words, a kind of formalization of longing itself.

## Bo Gustavsson (essay date 1989)

SOURCE: "The Discursive Muse: Robert Hass's 'Songs to Survive the Summer'," in *Studia Neophilologica,* Vol. 61, No. 2, 1989, pp. 193-201.

[*In the following excerpt, Gustavsson explicates "Songs to Survive the Summer," while observing that the poem is Hass's most successful work using a new discourse that breaks with the aesthetics of modernist lyric poetry.*]

In the 1970s a group of American poets emerged who shared the common ambition to write a new discursive poetry. These poets, among others Robert Pinsky, Stanley Plumly, and Robert Hass, perhaps the best poet of the group, all reacted against the conventions of modernist lyric poetry and instead they wanted to recover for poetry the virtues of good, expository prose. Rejecting the esthetics of modernist lyric poetry they wanted to write a poetry of the mind that explored the discursive resources of statement and argumentation. The goal was to "have a mind of winter," in Wallace Stevens's terminology: to go beyond the lyric self and to speak about the facts of our common existence in the world. Thus these poets sought in their own individual ways to develop the possibilities of discourse in contemporary poetry. . . .

Among the poets of his generation, Robert Hass best succeeds in his ambition to write a new poetry of discourse. Instead of limiting discourse to didactic reflection or mastery of tone, as Pinsky and Plumly seem to do, Hass wants to realize the full possibilities of discourse by using it as a means of meditating on our human condition. Hass is also a perceptive theorist who in his essays, collected in the volume *Twentieth Century Pleasures* published in 1984, sketches an esthetics of discourse that both illuminates his own practice and points to the shared assumptions of the poets of the seventies.

Outlining his esthetics of discourse Hass begins by criticizing the lyric poetry of the sixties. The poets of the sixties, he argues, all courted in one way or another extreme states of mind. They wrote a poetry derived from a sharp division between inner and outer experience; the outer world was rejected in favor of an extreme inwardness, as for example in the case of the confessional poets and the deep imagists. Interestingly enough, in his review-essay on Tomas Tranströmer's *Baltics,* Hass places Tranströmer in the category of the lyric poet who, faced by a threatening world, chooses to retreat into his own subjectivity. According to Hass, the lyric poetry of the sixties was then built on a strong sense of alienation, a reaction against our modern, materialistic civilization, and it often resulted in some form of solipsism since the lyric poet tended to get lost in the labyrinth of the self.

Hass here draws attention to the problematic nature of all lyric poetry: the fact that the lyric poet's chief concern is not with the larger reality of our common existence but with the emotional states of the self.

The impetus behind the poetry of the sixties was a yearning for the absolute, a yearning for visionary states of mind, accompanied by a disgust with the drabness and emptiness of daily life. However, this yearning for the absolute, this preoccupation with the poet's own subjectivity, severely limits the subject matter of poetry while robbing poetry of any larger relevance for the lives people actually live. Moreover, Hass observes, the lyric poet is doomed to his sense of alienation by the mere fact that he dwells exclusively in his own subjectivity. The task for the discursive poet, on the other hand, is precisely to overcome the modern disease of alienation by anchoring his sensibility in our common everyday life. If the lyric poet distrusts the mind and thought seeking to leap out of time and the world into visionary states, the discursive poet on the contrary relies on thinking in his attempt to understand the world as we really know it. The discursive poet does not want to leap out of the world, he wants to be part of the world meditating on our common life in time. Thus he broadens the subject matter of poetry while making poetry once again a matter of public concern. It must be emphasized that Hass's ideal poet is not primarily concerned with social or political issues but rather with the only permanence we can perhaps know: daily life. The imagination of the discursive poet works within the things of this world instead of becoming a vehicle of inwardness; in other words, imagination works in the service of patient, thoughtful understanding rather than ecstatic vision. Hass can therefore condemn the lyric poetry of the sixties as a symptom of decadence observing that "the artists of decadence turn away from a degraded social world and what they cling to, in their privacy, is beauty or pleasure. The pleasures are esoteric; the beauty is almost always gentle, melancholy, tinged with the erotic, tinged with self-pity." He proposes as a remedy a poetry of discourse that can speak out of an engagement with our "world of days and habits," as he expresses it. Poetry becomes a way of being fully alive to our existence in the world, with one's whole mind and imagination, and the goal is to understand our true place in the scheme of things.

The inclusiveness of the discursive mode arises from the fact that the mind of the poet is free to move in and out of experience. Moments of lyric intensity do of course occur, as do moments of narrative or pure fantasy, but they are swept along and incorporated into the flow of discourse. Hass's model for this kind of poetry is probably Wallace Stevens, the master of discourse in this century. Stevens can be said to be the metaphysician of daily life in that he spent his whole life as a poet meditating on the nature of reality. A typical poem by Stevens consists of a series of statements undergoing endless qualifications and modifications. His poetry records the twists and turns of a mind moving about in the world. Another side of Stevens is his sensuousness, his delight in the life of the senses, and this is also something Hass

shares with him. Both poets, then, are firmly anchored in the world of their own experience and both are meditative poets of time using the conversational mode as a means of meditating on our life in time. According to Hass, discourse is a "form of time" imitating life in time, and that is why discourse plays such an important role in his poetry. Discourse enables him to fulfill the dual task he sets himself as a poet: both to record and to understand our life in time.

Hass's attitude to life has much in common with Zen Buddhism, particularly with the haiku poets of Japan. In his essay "Images" he has written perceptively on the Japanese haiku poets and especially Buson seems to be a favorite of his. Hass praises Buson for his alertness to the things of this world and for his freshness of observation. However, this freshness of observation is suffused with a meditative attitude of mind; the act of seeing thus becomes an act of meditation. Buson has a transparent mind purged of all lyric egotism and the amazing thing is that his transparent mind somehow functions as a sixth sense illuminating the world. This also explains Buson's emotional range: he can write about suffering, grief, and joy with the same kind of clarity and quiet intensity. Hass is of course not a haiku poet, nor is he a Zen Buddhist, still in his poetry of discourse he seeks to inform his own some illuminating insight into our human condition.

**"Songs to Survive the Summer"** is at once Hass's longest and most successful poem. Standing as it does at the end of his second book *Praise,* published in 1979, this poem in many ways represents the culmination of his development as a poet. In his first book of poems, *Field Guide* published in 1973, Hass is mainly concerned with the naming of things. Poetry here serves as a kind of field guide helping the poet to take possession of his own world, to stake out, so to speak, the territory of his own sensibility. Hass wanders about in his native Californian landscape observing with sensual delight what goes on around him. He seems to be particularly fond of the fruits and berries that grow in California; many poems also express a quiet celebration of domestic love. Temperamentally Hass is above all a poet of joy who gives his heart to the good things in this life, yet he is very much aware of the presence of darker forces.

The naming of things in *Field Guide* appears almost programmatic on Hass's part: it is his way of keeping his own sanity in an insane world characterized by war and violence. It must be remembered that most of these poems were written at the time of the Vietnam war. By going back to the essentials of life, by keeping close to the facts of his own existence, Hass seeks in the manner of the Japanese haiku poets to preserve his clarity of mind. It is therefore no coincidence that a group of poems invokes Buson, Issa, and Basho, the three great masters of the haiku tradition. Hass also needs that clarity of mind when meditating on the contradictions of our human condition. The project in his second book, *Praise,* is precisely to somehow exorcise the terror at the heart of things by giving it a name and a place in human consciousness. Discourse acquires as a result a new urgency and inventiveness; facing the inescapable Medusa-head of human existence, the specter of loss and death lurking within all things, Hass draws on the full resources of his art and imagination. And catharsis now becomes the goal of his art: the purgation of the fears and anxiety inhering in our mortal condition. Hass's development as a poet can then be summarized in this way: first he names the world as it is, then he goes into the crucible of loss, and finally he is able to celebrate the world as it is. **"Songs to Survive the Summer"** exemplifies above all the last two stages of his development while fully orchestrating the thematics of loss.

To give one's "fears a shape," in Hass's own terminology, becomes both the subject and the goal of **"Songs to Survive the Summer."** The question of form therefore assumes thematic significance since form is what enables the poet to come to terms with our mortal predicament. In his long sequence Hass uses a fixed form, a three-line stanza, which is quite unusual for him. As most free-verse writers he lets each poem assume its own particular form, but here in **"Songs to Survive the Summer"** he adopts a given, fixed form. The triplet is then the "shape" he employs in order to organize his "fears." Within the unit of the triplet, a quite simple form, Hass can vary his line length from one to four stresses whereby he achieves a new freedom and flexibility of rhythm. Perhaps Wallace Stevens serves as his model here; Stevens is very much "form's hero," as Hass calls the Arctic explorer Wilhelm Steller, the persona of his sequence. What Steller accomplishes as a scientist, Stevens manages to do as an artist: by means of his craft he gives shape to the formlessness of experience walking around with a "pure exclusive music / in his mind," in Hass's own words.

Hass is very much aware of the need to revitalize free verse as a medium of writing and in his collection of essays he devotes two important essays to this subject. He thinks that free verse: the creative sense of form. Rhythm, Hass insists, constitutes the basis of free verse. The revolution of the fifties, initiated by such poets as Allen Ginsberg, Charles Olson, and Robert Lowell, has degenerated into an orthodoxy of conventional free verse. In order to revitalize free verse, young poets must regain a creative sense of form because without a vital, living sense of form free verse loses its special energy and strength. If a young poet wants to make it new, to use Pound's famous dictum, he must recapture the very pulse of free verse: the creative sense of form. Rhythm, Hass insists, constitutes the basis of free verse, not diction, imagery, or tone; rhythm alone is the revolutionary ground of poetry. One solution to the crisis of free verse is to do what Hass himself does in **"Songs to Survive the Summer"**: to fall back on a rather simple form, in his case the triplet, and to use this form as the basis for writing free verse. Another solution would be to rely on the shapeliness of discourse, a discourse governed by a meditative act of mind, as Hass's own poetry so well illustrates. That Hass holds strong views about the importance of a shaping principle in free verse is borne out by his comment on Stanley Plumly's notion of tone. To exclusively rely on tone, Hass observes, is yet another sign of the degeneration of free verse adding that because "it has no specific character, we make a

character in it." The formal principle for a vital free verse on the other hand derives from what he calls "the shape of its understanding": the movements of a mind weaving a pattern or design out of the particulars of experience. It is appropriate to use the metaphor of weaving here for the form-creating activity of art since Hass himself adopts this metaphor in **"Songs to Survive the Summer."**

> **Hass's development as a poet can then be summarized in this way: first he names the world as it is, then he goes into the crucible of loss, and finally he is able to celebrate the world as it is.**
>
> —*Bo Gustavsson*

**"Songs to Survive the Summer"** can be seen as a long meditation on the ever-present fact of death. The situation of the poem is announced at the very beginning: the mother of a neighbor child suddenly dies of an allergic swelling in the throat. The dead mother was a close friend of Hass's daughter who now is unable to sleep because of the shock of this sudden death. The motivation of the poem is then urgently and deeply personal: it is addressed to Hass's own daughter to somehow help her come to terms with the inescapable fact of death. Hass sympathizes with his daughter's fears because, as he tells us in one of his essays, he himself once barely escaped dying of an allergic swelling in the throat. **"Songs to Survive the Summer"** therefore constitutes his attempt to give his fears a shape through art, or through weaving, the key image of the poem. His daughter has been taught how to weave by her friend who died so unexpectedly, and throughout the poem she occupies herself with weaving. The key image of weaving brings together the notions of death, art, and consciousness; in other words, as so often is the case, death turns out to be the mother both of art and consciousness.

The idea that loss and grief form part of our very lives is emphasized by the epigraph to **"Songs to Survive the Summer"** taken from Fyodor Dostoyevsky's *The Brothers Karamazov*: "It's funny, isn't it, Karamazov, / all this grief and pancakes afterwards." In his long poem Hass seeks to elucidate this central paradox of our lives by drawing on the full resources of his discursive art, adopting "a collage of different attitudes towards experience," to use his own description of the method that Czeslaw Milosz employs in his late poetry. According to Hass, Milosz's aim in his late poetry is to fully render the contradictions of life speaking through a series of personae in search of abiding truths. In a similar manner Hass adopts different attitudes or approaches toward the central enigma of death in his own long sequence.

Hass opens his sequence by recalling an intriguing memory from childhood. Once, standing under the loquat tree outside his bedroom window, his grandfather gave him a wooden nickel saying: "Don't / take any wooden nickels, / kid." He never understood his grandfather's joke or advice never to let himself be deceived and, even as a grown-up, he still carries around that wooden nickel in his pocket as a kind of talisman. The implication of this anecdote seems to be that there are things in life that cannot be understood but must simply be lived with, such as time, the arch-deceiver and thief, who robs us of every paradise we have; "every paradise is lost," Hass observes in another poem. And finally time will rob us of life itself. Standing under the loquat tree, the tree of life in his childhood world, Hass received his first initiation into the secrets of life. Later on in the sequence, this same loquat tree will figure in another charged memory from childhood.

In order to exorcise their fears, caused by the specter of loss and death, Hass and his daughter sing old country songs together. They try out recipes for soup, the "herbal magic," and Hass even includes an appetizing recipe for onion soup in his poem. He seems especially to enjoy cooking, and eating represents of course the central ritual of our daily lives, a celebration at once of love and permanence. Hass and his daughter also read fairly tales about "spindly orphan / girls" who, although lost and lonely in the world, always manage to overcome their difficulties. However, adult life is very different indeed since the world is full of lost and lonely people. At this point Hass is reminded of a short story by Anton Chekhov: the story is about the widow Maryushka who goes mad when her only son leaves her. Every day she writes a letter to her son where she gives vent to her troubled mind.

> "When it is bad, Vanya,
> I go into the night
> and the night eats me."

In fact the section about the unhappy widow Maryushka is lifted verbatim from the poem **"For Chekhov"** in *Field Guide*. Hass, by the way, has a special liking for Chekhov; he refers to him repeatedly both in his prose and poetry. In world literature Chekhov stands as the undisputed master of the pathos of human loss. He writes about lonely and lost characters who are all defeated by life and forced to retreat into their own dreams. An atmosphere of sadness and melancholy saturates Chekhov's work; it is the sadness and melancholy of the universal human experience of loss.

As a counterpoint to the previous section's hysterical reaction to loss, Hass now inserts a haiku to right the emotional balance of his sequence.

> What a strange thing!
> To be alive
> beneath plum blossoms.

This haiku expresses the wonder of merely being alive and in this it resembles many of Buson's haikus. Hass's haiku seems in fact to be inspired by one of Buson's most famous haikus, his death-bed poem (in Hass's own rendering):

> In the white plum tree,
> night to next day just
> turning.

The plum blossoms in Hass's haiku add to the poignancy of his sense of wonder since the plum tree blossoms during such a fleetingly short period of time. Still he is not content with expressing an ecstatic moment of wonder; he also notes wryly that the "black-headed / Steller's jay is squawking / in our plum." The jay occupies a special place in Hass's imagination since it keeps reappearing throughout his writings. To Hass the jay has an almost emblematic value: it represents for him the bird of death. His sense of wonder standing under the plum blossoms is then severely undercut by the squawkings of the bird of death, and he muses to himself: "A hard, indifferent bird, / he'd snatch your life."

Still moments of ecstacy, though transient, are very real indeed; perhaps it is during these moments that we glimpse our true nature and destiny. Hass remembers a vision of transcendence that he once had in the Palo Alto marsh: "sea-birds rose in the early light // and took me with them." Another time he dreamt that river-birds lifted nd carried him away. Visions and dreams are the very stuff of our spiritual lives; they are what satisfies the spirit's hunger for transcendence. Hass now turns to sexual desire, the hunger of our flesh. Sexual desire resembles spiritual longing in that neither can be wholly satisfied. He presents sexual desire as a kind of affliction or sickness that is disturbingly alike the allergic swelling that suddenly killed his neighbor. . . .

His sense of sexual revulsion is associated with the oppressive heat of July when flies drone "in the juice of rotten quince," an oblique allusion to the sexual act. At the end of **"Songs to Survive the Summer"** he will return once again to the knot of sexual and spiritual desire.

Hass now approaches a decisive crisis in his long meditation on death. He almost touches the despair of the widow Maryushka in Chekhov's short story, feeling the intense loneliness of the human heart in the face of pain and frustration. . . .

[In the poem speed or restlessness represents] the modern way of life; it is, in a sense, restlessness that saves us from the anxiety of death. Yet, properly understood, restlessness is the perverted form that the anxiety of death has taken in our time. However, Hass manages to break out of his spell of despair by recalling the achievement of the Arctic explorer Wilhelm Steller, "form's hero" who "made / a healing broth." Steller becomes his persona through whom he can finally arrive at an affirmation of life as an art of survival.

Wilhelm Steller was a German naturalist who accompanied Bering on his second Arctic expedition in 1741-42. This expedition led to the discovery of Alaska and Steller's task was to observe the fauna and flora of the Arctic region. During his voyage to the North he kept a journal where he carefully noted down his observations; the epigraph to *Praise* is probably a quotation from this journal. Because of his intractable and quarrelsome temperament Steller soon attracted the enmity of the crew, but he was a dedicated scientist who never lost an opportunity to study the wildlife of the Arctic. The voyage was very difficult, full of hardships and troubles, and it nearly ended in disaster when the ship went aground on Bering Island. Most of the crew had already died of scurvy by then and now Bering himself died and was buried on the island. However, in spite of all the hardships, Steller succeeded in naming "all the beasts / and flowers of the north," in Hass's own words. As a matter of fact, Hass's emblematic bird of death is actually named after the German naturalist: Steller's jay. In **"Songs to Survive the Summer"** Steller's voyage of exploration into the Arctic North becomes a metaphor for the difficult voyage into the great unknown: death. Like his persona, Hass observes and names the great unknown, death, and by so doing he learns the difficult art of survival. The goal is to acknowledge the ever-present reality of death, to see it as part of our very lives. As a final gesture of acceptance Hass imagines that after death all the dead will be saved; after the sufferings and grief of time all the dead will be made whole again outside time. . . .

The dead have a feast, a kind of thanksgiving feast curiously alike the American thanksgiving dinner, before taking possession of their new-found land.

In the next section of **"Songs to Survive the Summer"** Hass yet again shifts the scene of his poem, this time to a memory from childhood. He remembers how, when he was just the age of his daughter, he sat in the loquat tree eating figs while watching the Pentecostal meetings at a neighbor's house. He sat there in the moonlight eating the first fruits of knowledge, listening to the bewildering songs of spiritual longing, "half / pleasure and half pain." Spiritual longing here appears mixed in a strange way with sexual desire; where there is human desire of any kind there is also pain and frustration. In fact frustration and pain add strength and depth to our desires; in other words, death intensifies life, it is ultimately what gives meaning to life. Yet death is also the great enigma or the mysterious Other of our lives. **"Songs to Survive the Summer"** can therefore be seen as a wisdom poem; Hass uses this term himself in his essay on Tranströmer. It is a wisdom poem moving towards some kind of healing knowledge. And Hass closes his sequence by summarizing both for his own and his daughter's benefit the chief insight of his long poem. . . .

If we are the children of death, if death sings us, then death is the way we use our lives. Paradoxically, death is at once our fate, and what constitutes our true freedom. To be aware of death, to use our lives with this awareness in mind, is to be fully human: the true children of death. Thus death breathes on us an awareness of our proper destiny in time. Such then is the insight that Hass has wrestled from the Angel of Death in **"Songs to Survive the Summer."** After his long struggle with the Angel of Death he has received a liberating benediction: to finally enter the only paradise left to us, that is, to

enter our transient and imperfect lives celebrating "the steady thoughtlessness / of human use." A curious thing to celebrate perhaps, "the steady thoughtlessness / of human use," yet deeply meaningful for a poet whose central impulse has always been to joyfully affirm our common everyday life.

### Carolyn Kizer (essay date 1989)

SOURCE: "Necessities of Life and Death," in the *The New York Times Book Review,* November 12, 1989, p. 63.

[*In the following review, Kizer provides a favorable assessment of* Human Wishes.]

Robert Hass is so intelligent that to read his poetry or prose, or to hear him speak, gives one an almost visceral pleasure. He is the master of what I call the reticule poem. A reticule is a capacious bag carried by some of our grandmothers, which might contain knitting, cough drops, gloves, a tin of cookies, a volume of Wordsworth or Jane Austen or a missal, coin purse, shopping list, makeup and a folder of family snapshots. In short, necessities of life. One can say that all these articles go together because they are together, in one bag. But it is Mr. Hass's associative processes, his associated sounds and his strategies that enhance, combine and weave together these elements to give his poems their rich and singular flavor:

> When Luke was four or five
> he would go out . . . still in his dandelion-
> yellow pajamas on May mornings
> and lie down on the first warm stone. . . .
>
> Later, on street corners,
> you can hardly see the children, chirping
> and shivering, each shrill voice climbing over
> the next in an ascending chorus. "Wait, you guys,"
> one little girl says, trying to be heard.
> "Wait, wait, wait, wait, wait." . . .
>
> Richard, who had recently divorced,
> idly rolling a ball with someone else's child,
> healing slowly, as the neighbor's silky mare
> who had had a hard birth in the early spring,
> stood quiet in the field as May grew sweet,
> her torn vagina healing

[*Human Wishes* needs] to be heard, spoken: resonances, pauses, intonations, the vocal music. Mr. Hass is a poet of domestic passion—for children, friends, the household, the neighborhood, for women as lovers, women as friends. His publisher speaks of his work as poems of loss, of mutilation. Rather, he is a poet of abundance, a romantic of the breakfast table, of a companionable walk in his California hills. Perhaps his publisher was bemused—as well she might be—by his elegy to a vanished life, a miscarried child, called **"Thin Air."** This noble poem, which defies paraphrase and should not be amputated by quotation, is the keystone of a remarkable book.

**Don Bogen  (essay date 1989)**

SOURCE: "A Student of Desire," in *The Nation,* New York, Vol. CCXXXXIX, No. 20, December 11, 1989, pp. 722-23.

*[In the following review, Bogen lauds Hass for his ability to evoke and explore the complexity of desire in* Human Wishes.]

What's immediately striking in Robert Hass's work is the sheer abundance of pleasures. Who else among our poets would bring together the delights of landscape, climate and food in a salad "with chunks of cooked chicken in a creamy basil mayonnaise a shade lighter than the Coast Range in August" (**"Vintage"**) or include a recipe for onion soup—complete with shredded Samsoe and advice on how to eat it with friends—as a **"Song to Survive the Summer"**? In his incisive collection of essays, *Twentieth Century Pleasures,* Hass set our engagement with poetry squarely in the context of other forms of satisfaction—in domestic life, in nature, in the senses. The title of his new book of poetry, **Human Wishes,** reveals his basic concerns: He is a student of desire, of what we want and how likely we are to get it.

If one pleasure of poetry is the evocation of beautiful things, Hass's work definitely satisfies. From his first book, **Field Guide,** which won the Yale Series of Younger Poets Award in 1973, through **Praise** in 1979 and now **Human Wishes,** he has shown a mastery of sensory description, combining the light touch of a calligrapher with the specificity of a botanist. Place—particularly northern California, where he grew up and now lives—has always been central in Hass's poetry, and few writers capture the special qualities of this environment as well. **"January"** gives a fine sense of that gorgeous oddity, a Bay Area winter:

> Back at my desk: no birds, no rain,
> but light—the white of Shasta daisies,
> and two red geraniums against the fence,
> and the dark brown of wet wood,
> glistening a little as it dries.

Hass's continuing engagement with Japanese poetry is evident here. Casual in tone, the lines seem almost transparent, as if they were just a moment's observation. Yet their arrangement is exquisite. The contrast between the blank monosyllables of the first line and a half—"no birds, no rain"—and the sudden appearance of those specific, polysyllabic Shasta daisies; the step-by-step expansion of the color scheme—"white," "red," then "dark brown"; the subtle echoes of sound in "red" and "wet," "daisies" and "dries"; and the hint of blank verse for closure in the last line show a rigorous and self-effacing craftsmanship. The lines have been written so well they hardly seem "written" at all.

With his California subjects and his skill at evocation, Hass could easily have settled for the reproduction of a

predictable and popular verse "product." Indeed, a few years after *Field Guide* came out, a small fad for poems with references to food, accounts of hikes and other surface elements of his work flourished in the literary magazines. But Hass is after something more than sensuous word painting. The mind behind the description is analytical, probing, unsatisfied with the conventional stances language often provides. The poems in **Human Wishes** are energetic and full of surprises. They turn on themselves suddenly, breaking into self-consciousness or rejecting their initial visions, as when the idyllic reverie of **"Late Spring"** is revealed to be a fabrication that keeps the poet awake at night, or the list of pretty images at the start of **"Spring Drawing"** and again in **"Spring Drawing 2"** implies but then fails to generate a sentence.

Hass's awareness of the limits of language helps fuel his restless exploration of different poetic strategies. Each of his books makes use of a range of approaches and forms, from rhymed iambic pentameter to haiku, from brief lyrics to sequences of fragments to long discursive meditations. In **Human Wishes** he consolidates the strengths of his earlier work while pushing on into fresh territory. The first section of the book, for example, develops a new kind of line: lengthy, proselike in its rhythms and set off in a stanza by itself. These lines function as independent postulates in an argument, some plush and physical like the one about chicken salad, others gnarled with abstraction like these from the first poem in the book, **"Spring Drawing"**:

> as if spirit attended to plainness only,
>   the more complicated forms ex-
>   hausting it, tossed-off grapestems
>   becoming crystal chandeliers,
>
> as if radiance were the meaning of
>   meaning, and justice responsible to
>   daydream not only for the strict
>   beauty of denial,
>
> but as a felt need to reinvent the inner
>   form of wishing.

Hass has never shied away from the language of theoretical discourse. In fact, he finds a rarefied music in the polysyllabic abstractions, long clauses and parallel constructions of his argument. This is not a music everyone will enjoy. It can be daunting to encounter a passage like the one above on the first page of a book of poetry. But if the demands on a reader are high, they signal Hass's commitment to his enterprise: an art that can both evoke and analyze the complexity of human desires.

The second section of **Human Wishes** consists of prose poems, a form prefigured in some of the work in **Praise** but not developed consistently until now. Rimbaud is the father of this type of poem, and much American work in the genre still reads like a bad translation from the French. Hass has avoided the portentousness and easy surrealism that can afflict paragraphs trying too hard to be poetic. Instead, he looks to narrative models—the short story, the anecdote—as well as to allegory and the personal essay as guideposts. A few of the shorter prose poems—**"Duck Blind," "In the Bahamas"**—can seem a little thin, but the longer pieces give him room to juxtapose scenes and events, building up a constellation of meaning. **"The Harbor at Seattle,"** for example, looks at friendship and personal tragedy within different contexts of history, art and work. Each paragraph in this beautifully structured poem works like a controlled reaction as the poet puts two elements together, notes the effects, then moves on to the next step. In the title poem of *Human Wishes,* Hass achieves a more dense interactive texture. This page-long paragraph uses rapid shifts of focus, from the Up-anishads to a Cambridge pub, to expose a web of varied individual desires—for beauty, for understanding, for wealth, for a good time with friends—in all its intricacy and imperfection.

The unspoken element in all "human wishes" is, of course, vanity. Hass may not be as explicit as Juvenal on this point—he finds beauty in some of these wishes, flawed as they are—but he's well aware of the devastating power of time and human failings. In the extended meditations that make up the last two sections of *Human Wishes,* he traces pleasures and their loss—in love, in family life, in the living world—with intelligence and a deft control of tone. Despite the wealth of personal detail in these poems, there is little overt self-dramatization. The poet is not set up as the tragic hero of his own life. His presence in the work is rather that of a man *thinking*: remembering, describing, defining, comparing, imagining.

As in the prose poems, the strength of these meditations lies in Hass's ability to handle several themes at the same time and his exploration of the range of possibilities the form presents. In one of the most intriguing, **"Berkeley Eclogue,"** he takes on the hoary literary convention of the pastoral dialogue. The decorous speech of stylized shepherds becomes an internal argument, with a harsh second voice—a kind of nagging muse—prodding the poet toward more clarity and depth with italicized comments such as *"You can skip this part"* and *"Do you believe in that?"* Other meditations are symphonic in structure. **"Santa Barbara Road"** introduces, repeats and varies several different motifs—the poet building a bench, children and their parents, classical Chinese thought, June weather, various walks—in an extended reflection on the abundance and impermanence of family life.

Hass's sense of the interrelatedness of all human endeavor gives his book a breadth of perspective and a distinct focus. Even the man brewing one cup of tea and immersing himself in his own memories at the end of **"Thin Air"** is connected to the frustrated warehouse worker who packed the tea leaves. This is not liberal sympathy but a recognition of how things work, of the context of suffering and loss in which we live. It is a mark of Hass's integrity as a poet that he rejects the usual consolations here. Art, nature, love—these are certainly pleasures but not solutions. They are parts of what he calls in **"On Squaw Peak"**

> . . . the abundance
> the world gives, the more-than-you-bargained-for
> surprise of it, waves breaking,
> the sudden fragrance of the mimulus at creekside
> sharpened by the summer dust.
> Things bloom up there. They are
> for their season alive in those bright vanishings
> of air we ran through.

If the first half of the passage is as rich and surprising as its subject, the last sentence stumbles on the perfect awkward placement of "for their season." In *Human Wishes* Robert Hass captures both the brightness of the world and its vanishing.

## Michael Davidson    (essay date 1989)

SOURCE: "Approaching the Fin de Siècle," in *The San Francisco Renaissance: Poetics and Community at Mid-Century,* Cambridge University Press, 1989, pp. 200-18.

[*In the following excerpt, Davidson evaluates Hass's use of the scenic mode in his poetry, commenting on his skill in evoking the natural landscape and describing its allegorical relationship to a cognitive act.*]

The most obvious change that has occurred in the past twenty years (the perennial Beat revival notwithstanding) has been a growing skepticism about the more expressive or visionary claims of neoromantics like Duncan, McClure, and Ginsberg. The elegiac rhetoric of the 1940s and the bardic chant of the late 1950s have given way to a considerably cooler tone and chastened rhetoric. At times, as in the case of "language writing," this skepticism has been embodied in formal procedures (the use of Fibonacci number series, collaboration, the "new sentence," etc.) that limit the role of personal expression. And where a process- or action-oriented aesthetics dominated much of the poetry that we have seen so far, poets of the 1980s have developed more subtle modulations of tone that return a degree of irony and self-effacement to poetry. Though these characteristics are by no means limited to Bay Area writers, they have been nurtured by and in response to many of the issues raised by the expressivist poetics that dominated the San Francisco Renaissance.

Recent writers have taken two directions in addressing the crisis of expressivity. The first, epitomized by the work of Robert Hass (and evident in other local writers like Robert Pinsky, Jack Gilbert, Denise Levertov, Diana O'Hehir, Joseph Stroud, and Gary Soto), derives from Kenneth Rexroth and Gary Snyder and emphasizes an allegorical relationship between the natural landscape and cognitive acts. The second, embodied in the work of Lyn Hejinian and others of the so-called language movement, extends from linguistically self-reflexive tendencies in Jack Spicer and Robert Duncan that stress the productive nature of language in forming the subject. Although these two tendencics have a common emancipatory goal for poetic language with respect to social practices, they differ in the specific ways that language functions in relation to those goals.

Charles Altieri [in *Self and Sensibility in Contemporory American Poetry*, 1984] has characterized the work of Hass and many of his contemporaries in terms of the "scenic mode." In such poetry (his example here is William Stafford),

> [the] work places a reticent, plain-speaking, and self-reflected speaker within a narratively presented scene evoking a sense of loss. Then the poet tries to resolve the loss in a moment of emotional poignance or wry acceptance that renders the entire lyric event an evocative metaphor for some general sense of mystery about the human condition.

Altieri is not entirely happy with the scenic mode in its pure form and sees in a poet like Hass a more subtle working-out of its major presuppositions. Hass is particularly valued for refining the dramatic and emotional features of that "lyric event" so that the "mystery" is grounded in specific properties of voice.

If one of the principles of the scenic mode is its dependence on evocation of scene, one could hardly find a better example than Hass. His work often describes the natural landscape, particularly that of the coast. Hass comments on the importance of this landscape to his poetry in "Some Notes on the San Francisco Bar Area as a Culture Region." It is partly an homage to Kenneth Rexroth, who inspired the younger poet to write a poetry of place, but the debt is acknowledged in a rather roundabout way. In the essay, Hass describes growing up in San Rafael, his Portuguese babysitter, life in Catholic school, playing Little League baseball, the beginnings of his literary career in an essay contest, and his discovery of poetry in an anthology bought with his prize money. In the midst of these reflections he provides a terse statement of poetics:

> Art hardly ever does seem to come to us at first as something connected to our own world; it always seems, in fact, to announce the existence of another, different one, which is what it shares with gnostic insight. That is why, I suppose, the next thing that artists have to learn is that this world is the other world.

The essay complements this remark by its meandering, anecdotal quality. Just as Hass wanders among his memories of childhood that led him to Kenneth Rexroth's poetry, so we as readers are invited to discover Hass's poetics along the way. The daily world of a familiar landscape and the exotic world encountered in literature are one and the same, though the former is often invisible without the latter.

The unifying image that holds landscape and art together is the creek that flowed next to the poet's Little League field. The same creek appears in a poem by Kenneth Rexroth that Hass quotes:

> Under the second moon the
> Salmon come, up Tomales
> Bay, up Papermill Creek, up
> The narrow gorges to their spawning
> Beds in Devil's Gulch.

Rexroth's poem, so active in rendering the specific California locale, links Hass to his past and to the "other world" immanent in this one. This world within the world is not a mystical quotient but something constitutive in the "culture of the West Coast"—a synthesis of place and propositions about the place. It is a synthesis that is fully developed in the work of Wallace Stevens, another poet Hass quotes in the essay. The fish that return to spawn in Papermill Creek are obeying a primitive rite of return, which the essay, in its memorial tribute to Rexroth, imitates. Poetry, landscape, and sexual imperative merge and follow their own instincts, though Hass's procedure is anything but arbitrary.

The essay I have been describing appears in an anthology called *19 New American Poets of the Golden Gate*, the title including an obvious reference to Donald Allen's earlier anthology in which the San Francisco Renaissance was first acknowledged as a literary force. Hass follows his essay with a poem, **"Palo Alto: The Marshes,"** that dramatically underscores the influence of Rexroth on his work:

> She dreamed along the beaches of this coast.
> Here where the tide rides in to desolate
> the sluggish margins of the bay,
> sea grass sheens copper into distances.
> Walking, I recite the hard
> explosive names of birds:
> egret, killdeer, bittern, tern.
> Dull in the wind and early morning light,
> the striped shadows of the cattails
> twitch like nerves.

This first section of the poem establishes an identity of two sorts: a temporal one between the speaker and the absent "She" (Mariana Richardson, whose father owned the San Rafael land grant in the late 1890s) and a spatial one between both speakers and the tidal landscape. The spatial bond between speaker and addressee is not only geographic—their shared concern for a common landscape—but psychological in that this same tidal region provides the backdrop for troubled dreams of natural destruction and human cupidity. In establishing the literal as well as psychic landscape, Hass acknowledges his close links to Rexroth and Everson, who . . . read social and theological meanings in the text of nature. And in rehearsing "the hard / explosive names of birds" he continues an imperative in Gary Snyder. But whereas for Snyder naming offers a healthy antidote to human exploitation of nature, Hass recognizes a fatal complicity between the desire to name and the desire to control.

Hass views the historical transformation of the California landscape by invoking the eyes of Mariana, once glimpsed in a picture:

Black as her hair
the unreflecting venom of those eyes
in an aftermath I know, like these brackish,
russet pools a strange life feeds in
or the old fury of land grants, maps,
and deeds of trust. A furious dun-
colored mallard knows my kind
and skims across the edges of the marsh
where the dead bass surface
and their flaccid bellies bob.

Hass's obvious pleasure in naming birds, plants, and animals is gradually qualified as he realizes his own role in the history he describes, a history that disempowered the native inhabitants of the region, and ultimately, turned the marshes into "brackish, / russet pools" where only "dead bass surface / and their flaccid bellies bob."

The poem quietly chronicles this usurpation of land from the period of land grants and settlement through the Bear Flag War and Kit Carson's raids on Indian villages. By the end, this history (Hass continues to call it a "dream") includes American adventurism in Vietnam:

Here everything seems clear,
firmly etched against the pale
smoky sky: sedge, flag, owl's clover.
rotting wharves. A tanker lugs silver
bomb-shaped napalm tins toward
port at Redwood City. Again,
my eye performs
the lobotomy of description
Again, almost with yearning,
I see the malice of her ancient eyes

Hass recognizes that the desire to describe the landscape in such detail is part of the problem. The writer performs "the lobotomy of description" and feels the "malice" of historical judgment. When he claims that "Here everything seems clear," he refers to the time and place but also to the clarity of historical contradictions that emerge through the speaker's desultory meditation. What began as an attempt to remember the "explosive names of birds" rebounds as a mockery of that adjective when set beside "bomb-shaped napalm tins." What establishes itself, what is "etched against the pale / smoky sky" may be clear to the physical eye, but to the conscious intellect that must negotiate phenomenological claims against historical reality, the scene is quite murky.

Hass concludes by leaving many of the rhetorical tensions in place, much as he sees California as a conflicted dream of natural beauty and human despoilment:

The otters are gone from the bay
and I have seen five horses
easy in the grassy marsh
beside three snowy egrets.
Bird cries and the unembittered sun,
wings and the white bodies of birds,
it is morning. Citizens are rising
to murder in their moral dreams.

These last two quatrains are reminiscent of two other poets of place, James Wright and Robert Bly (although the ghost of Theodore Roethke hovers over the entire poem), in the way that they merge precise description with generalized statement. The final image, in its rather heavy-handed moralism, attempts to transcend the natural hieroglyph of "five horses" "beside three snowy egrets." Of course this heavy-handedness is part of Hass's method—as it is in Wright's "Lying in a Hammock at William Duffy's Farm in Pine Island, Minnesota." Hass deliberately scuttles his own tendencies toward refined imagistic clarity in a moment of apotheosis and bald declaration. It is a sign of impatience, much like the famous "blackberry, blackberry, blackberry" conclusion of **"Meditation at Lagunitas,"** a refusal of equivocation in the face of a palpable sense of loss and contradiction.

In Hass's work, craft is everywhere present yet nowhere evident, a value inherited from his former Stanford teacher Yvor Winters. Where Everson's rocking iambic cadences or Snyder's pared-down imagism foreground the materiality of language, Hass modulates his voice to attempt various dramatic responses to a crisis that is both historical and existential. We "seem" to be hearing a person talking to himself ("Well, I have dreamed this coast myself"), but the discursive tone is constantly modified by lyric compression: "The star thistles: erect, surprised, / and blooming / violet caterpillar hairs." Repetition, though unenforced, is operative in producing historical ironies that undergird the poem. The "silver" salmon that Kit Carson finds upon entering an Indian Village return as the "silver" napalm tins; the "dream" of bay marshes shared by speaker and subject returns as the "moral dreams" of a civic mandate. Throughout the poem, the speaker's outrage is tempered by rhetorical balance, a balance that ultimately recognizes its own will to power.

## Robert Hass with Linda Gregg (interview date 1991)

SOURCE: An interview in *Iowa Review,* Vol. 21, No. 3, Fall, 1991, pp. 126-45.

[*In the following interview, Hass discusses prose poetry and explains his views on the poet in relation to politics.*]

Unfortunately, not all of the questions that arose during this session held in November 1989 were preserved on tape, and so we leave some of them to your imagination.

[Gregg]: *Why a prose poem, and what is a prose poem?*

[Hass]: I haven't arrived for myself at any very satisfactory formulation of what a prose poem is. Certainly it has something to do with condensation. If it's narrative in form and gets to a certain length, it's probably a story; if it's very short and in a book by a fiction writer, it's a sudden fiction; if it's in a book by a poet, it's a prose poem; and if it gets to a certain length, it's an essay, or a sketch, or something like that. So I suppose condensation has something to do with it.

I don't know how to define it in terms of genre, and when I was working, I guess I just stopped trying to think about that. What I *did* think about was what the conventions of the prose poem were. At the time that I was starting to write them, the prose poem, as it had been revived in America, was used almost entirely for a kind of wacky surrealist work, and I think that nervousness about using prose was that then you had to put a lot of what people *thought* was poetic—that is to say, wildness and imagination and free association—into it to make sure that it was poetry, because if it got too near the conventions and sentence sounds of expository prose or narrative prose or something like that, then it really wasn't poetry. So almost as soon as I started working, I got interested in those boundaries: what the prose poem *wasn't* supposed to sound like.

I think I came on it in the first place from writing prose. When I was writing essays, I found that there would be a passage where I wanted to give an example, or tell a short anecdote to make a point, and that I would find myself laboring over the making of that paragraph with the kind of pleasure I get from working on a poem. So that was in my mind with "Museum"—the prose poem about the young man and woman handling their baby back and forth in the restaurant. It was very hard to . . . I had *seen* it and I was very moved by it, but I couldn't find a rhythm for it. Each time I got into it there was some prosodic problem with the business of people handling each other the baby, back and forth. If I wrote it sort of contrapuntally, it had an elegance that I didn't want. And if I enjambed the line so that it wasn't one line playing off another, it had a jaggedness I didn't want. I could not find a way to do it, and at one point, in frustration, I turned to the side and wrote out as clearly as I could—you must have done this—in pencil, exactly what I was trying to get at. And then I realized . . . why then, convert it into something else? So then I went to work on that, and thought that I had written a prose poem. And also for me it was a little narrative. It almost seemed like photography to me, and it gave me a feeling that I wanted to experiment with the form, and so I started doing it.

I wrote a whole lot of them, and I got interested in textures, the way that you would with a given palette. Every time I picked up a piece of prose, the sound of it was like a color. I mean, I picked up a John Le Carré novel, and I suddenly noticed that all of his sentences are terrifically suspended, because suspense is what he's thinking about. So a sentence would go, "In Prague, on a gray afternoon, an old woman—she was not as old as she seemed, the streets were not as old as they seemed, and they seemed ancient—was making her way, however fitfully, the rains are always difficult . . ." That kind of almost Jamesian sentence has to do, in his case, with these labyrinth- and maze-like mysteries that are always in his books. Anyway, I loved that tonality of sentence, so I wanted to sit down and do something in that tonality of sentence. It would be like the color on a palette. So I began **"Churchyard"** with the sentence: "Somerset Maugham said a professional was someone who could do his best work when he didn't particularly feel like it." I had read that sentence in the paper the day before, and

it was in my head, and I was wondering if it were true (wouldn't it be great if that were true!), and thinking I'll never be a real writer because I can't do that. And so I sat down to the sentence, and as soon as I wrote it—I don't know if the poem is any good—I felt excited because I knew it was exactly what the prose poem wasn't supposed to be. It was too much like the sound of expository prose.

So for a while, it seemed to me that this opened up everything. I'd sit at a dinner party and people would start telling their anecdotes, and the shop door would open, and I would sit there with a smile, listening, waiting for something I could use. And all the stories that *I* had told, that I wanted to write down before I died, or they would be gone—I thought I could do it with this form. Then I found out that it didn't work, that it was very complicated, that some of them wouldn't accommodate themselves to this form: they took too much telling, or they weren't my story.

Later, something else occurred to me: I was working in these forms because they had a certain outwardness that verse didn't have. I think I was at a time—I mean *I know*—when things were going on in my life that I didn't want to look at, didn't want to feel. And I wanted to keep writing, so I unconsciously started writing prose to avoid the stricter demands of incantation. When I was doing it, it seemed to be exploratory; in retrospect, it seems a sort of long escape.

. . . . .

William Stafford's conversational naturalness is not an ideal for me. I like a certain kind of appearance of naturalness in a poem, and in writing, I love plainness. It seems to me, a lot of the great lines of poems that I love are very simple. I love Wordsworth's line, "All things that love the sun are out of doors." [Frost's] "Nature's first green is gold." [Stevens's] "Among twenty snowy mountains, / The only moving thing / Was the eye of the blackbird." Much of what's in my head, what appeals to me, is not [Crane's] "How many dawns, chill from his rippling rest / the seagull's wings shall dip and pivot him." I love that language too, but I'm always most amazed by great plainness in language.

I became aware of a bunch of possibilities. One had to do with a poem I absolutely love by Robert Duncan. It's the second poem in his book *The Opening of the Field,* and it's called "The Dance." It's written in his high, ecstatic style, and it addresses some of the characters in his Victorian fairy tale mythology: the lady under the hill, and the voice that tells him to dance. Then suddenly, toward the end of the poem, this prose voice breaks in, and says, "That was the summer I had the job sweeping on Saturday mornings," and it describes just briefly in prose this memory of having a job sweeping the dance floor in Larkspur. [Turns to Linda Gregg] Do you remember the name of the place? They used to have the dances? My older brother went, then it closed, just at the time I was old enough to get to go. It's one of those things I'm never going to get to do in my life. So Duncan, in the forties, had the job of sweeping this place on Saturday mornings, and he breaks in with the story of it, and a memory of being taught to dance by the family's German maid, and then he comes out of it again, and the voice says to him—it's partly the German maid's voice and it's back in the language of verse—"You have entered the dance—dancer." The juxtaposition of the prose of the memory with the higher mythic voice is incredibly beautiful to me. I would like to get that.

There's another place in a poem by George Oppen called "Route" which is one of his two or three greatest poems, I think. He's musing along in that sculpted, difficult, austere, beautiful verse, and suddenly he breaks off and there's a prose passage: a young Alsatian in World War II was conscripted by the Nazis to fight. If he did fight, some terrible consequence followed for his family, besides the fact that he had to do a dishonorable thing; and if he didn't, and went into hiding, they were arresting and deporting the families of the deserters who failed to report. So he had a buckdancer's choice. What he did was kiss his wife goodbye, kiss his kids goodbye, and get on a bicycle and ride downhill very fast into a tree and kill himself. That way he guessed his wife and children would not suffer German reprisals. It was a solution to their problem. And Oppen just tells the story in the plainest way, in the plainest language, and then moves back into the musing, austere music of verse again.

I didn't know how to get to either of those things, but the whole time I was working on the prose poem I knew that somehow I never particularly loved the *idea* of the prose poem. But it was interesting to me to think about a larger form that might mix verse and prose.

Two formal models of mixing verse and prose have occurred to me since. One is Shakespeare's comedies, which are just amazing—a totally delicious mixture of verse and prose. I don't know who you would imagine putting together—I was going to say Milan Kundera, but he's not earthy enough. I don't know whose prose . . . Faulkner's storytelling side, mixed with James Merrill, all into one large form, or something like that. So I began to imagine that, and then of course Japanese haiku journals are another example of that kind of thing. At that time, I had already begun to work on Milosz's poems, but I hadn't yet seen him working in some of these longer forms where he had experimented with verse and prose.

There are lots of convergences going on right now with poetry and prose, and lots of different kinds of writing working the boundaries between the two, but it seems to me that, as a form to be figured out and exploited, we haven't even begun. The next great epic work, I would guess, is likely to be a mixture of the two. We haven't started to tap the possibilities. We were talking about Carver and Barthelme both dying. Barthelme's stories always seemed to me to have been written essentially by a poet, as if they're an extension of the early work of Wallace Stevens in their formal imagination, and Ray, of course, worked in both media and at the end began to blend them. There's that on the one hand. There are the strategies of Kundera's prose on the other hand which introduce other kinds of prose—expository, critical—into the narrative. And then there are intensities in verse that just aren't available to prose. This is not where I am working right now, but it's certainly there for me, and it's there for you, God knows.

I think this is a very interesting time to be working, because lots of formal options are open. There's a kind of rawness and questioning in the political and social world, as well as some peculiar urgency because of the century coming to an end. And there's no proposition of a form for a long ambitious poem. I mean, I don't think anybody wants to try the cantos again—another modernist epic doesn't seem to me just the ticket. That's how this prose thing—how the revival of realism in the other arts—plays into this in fiction and in painting. I mean, for example, a kind of expressionist representative painting, melody coming back into music.

*Are the "Spring Drawing" poems at the beginning of* **Human Wishes** *prose poems?*

I thought of those poems absolutely as verse when I was working on them. They began actually with fooling around and sketching. I had been reading Michael Palmer's *Notes for Echo Lake*—and particularly *that* poem I love—and in the way that you might sit down and try to imitate Roethke or something like that, I sat down and tried to see what would happen if I worked in a mode something like that. As I was working on one of them, I was playing the line out to the end, and the first one that I wrote ended up being twelve lines long. The fun of it was that almost immediately I realized that it was going to have a formal shape, and that the form would probably be a certain number of lines, but also that if you used these long looping lines and then stopped, it was like long oar strokes, and then you stood for a while, and then another long oar stroke, and so on. It created that kind of formal measure in which you could fool around a lot. So you could have long lines and short ones. So then I just made a rule: that it was a new kind of sonnet I had invented, and it was twelve lines long. But the other rule was that each line could be any length, up to *Paradise Regained,* that you could just go on forever. But the poem would have this series of strokes, so the rhythm would be something like:

> Now the rain is falling, freshly, in the intervals
>     between sunlight,
>
> a Pacific squall started no one knows where, and
>     drawn east as the
> drifts of warm air make a channel;
>
> it moves its own way, like water or the mind,
>                   **"Spring Rain"**

—a relatively short line to vary it, then—

> and spills this rain passing over. The Sierras will
>     catch it as last snow

flurries before summer, observed only by the
   wakened marmots at ten thousand feet,

and we will come across it again. . . .

                              **"Spring Rain"**

You see? Then it was like a territory to play in, and I
could alter the rhythms:

   And then in mid-May the first morning of steady
      heat,

   the morning, Leif says, when you wake up, put on
      shorts, and that's it for the day,

   when you pour coffee and walk outside, blinking in
      the sun.
   Strawberries have appeared in the markets, and
      peaches will soon;

   squid is so cheap in the fishstores you begin to
      consult Japanese and Italian cookbooks. . . .

                              **"Late Spring"**

For me it was absolutely verse, utterly verse, in the sense
that it had everything to do with rhythm, and when I sent
them to magazines, right away they said, "These are in
your new 'prose poems period,'" and I thought, "Oh, shit."

*I tried to discover a formal rule for where your lines are
divided. They seemed to me to do what Williams does
sometimes, that there is a gesture of thought. In Williams
they tend to be very small, two or four words, but there's
one gesture of thought, and as soon as the gesture of
thought ends, even if it's very short, then the next line
begins. So they seem to me to have that rhythm.*

I wasn't aware of it before, but afterwards I thought, that's
exactly right, it's like Williams's variable foot. That's what
I had in mind, though I didn't know it. The same analogy
occurred to me. Again, working, it was my experience that
almost everything I've done in the last few years, I would
turn to another phase of Milosz's life and find that he had
already done it. Then it seemed to me that dithyrambic
verse, longish rhythmic verse, strophes, or whatever you
want to call it, was completely typical of European poetry
all through the twentieth century. St. John Perse is the
great example, but there are a lot of others. Let's see if
there's an example in [Milosz]. It's a form he uses . . . not
quite the way I did. Of course my Polish is nonexistent, so
I can't tell. I mean I could begin to pick it out with a
dictionary, but I can't tell what kinds of formal stringencies are in the sound of his poetry. The Polish language
tends to sprawl anyway because it has a Latinate syntax.
It would seem that all you could do is make a comedy of
the sprawl, but he does something else here: this is a three-
line poem, each line very long. It's not the same thing, but
it's near to it.

   I looked out the window at dawn and saw a young
      apple tree translucent in brightness,

And when I looked out at dawn once again, an
   apple tree laden with fruit stood there.

Many years had probably gone by but I remember
   nothing of what happened in my sleep.

                              **"Window"**

That's a kind of long epigram, but its rhythmic idea is to
play with a very long line. And it's verse, you know? As
you say, take each one in as one measured unit of thought
or perception.

*I wonder what your thoughts are about being a poet in
America in the '90s, and particularly in terms of politics.*

Well, it's a dilemma to know how to be political now
and also how to think about politics, but it's a dilemma
whatever you are. It would be a dilemma if you were an
engineer—what am I doing, pissing my life away being
a traffic engineer? When I was in graduate school, I was
very involved in politics. In Palo Alto, a group of us
started a newspaper, a community self-help organization,
and a free university, and there was a political organization that went with all of this. When I finished all my
graduate work, I had to make a decision, whether to stay
there and figure out somehow to make a living while
continuing this work, or go be a professor and get on
with my life as a writer. I thought I could be a writer
doing either thing, but I knew that I couldn't give myself
wholly to both things. And I hated meetings. You know,
so much of politics is going to meetings; you have to be
patient, listening to people who are completely full of
bullshit. Everybody has to get their turn saying their thing,
you know. Oscar Wilde said, "Socialism takes too many
evenings!" A guy gets up and has to give a long talk on
why Ho Chi Minh was a deviationist because he had all
the Trotskyists eliminated from the labor movement in
Hanoi in 1945 before taking over, just as a preface to
some remark about whether we should go from door to
door leafletting. I absolutely couldn't stand it; I'm not a
methodical person and I wasn't good at it. A person who
was a big influence on me at that time was Paul Goodman, who, when I talked to him about this, said, "Do
what you love, and it will take you into a job and a way
of life—change *that* so it's a human place." So hating
politics, I ended up teaching at this little college where
I was captive to meetings because my friends' jobs were
on the line. Any form of life you get into is political in
that way.

The job itself, my own writing, and the kind of emotional issues I deal with in the writing all took me away from
politics outside my immediate community. *Field Guide*
is in some ways a political book; *Praise* is, it seems to
me, a mostly apolitical book, because I was so concerned
with my erotic and epistemological agonies. The social
world returns a bit in *Human Wishes,* and I think it will
be there in the things I'm working on now. I think that
if you're somebody who thinks about that stuff, it enters
your writing. And for some writers—if you're South African or something like that—it's an inescapable subject.
The problem for American writers, particularly for white

male American writers, is that it is an escapable subject. There are subjects that are not escapable, but for me, it is escapable.

It's one of the reasons why the writing on the peripheries seems so interesting now. John Coetzee and V. S. Naipaul, people who testify out of explicitly political situations, seem terrifically attractive to me and at the same time I'm suspicious of my attraction. I think we're all haunted by the martyrdom of Mandelstam out of a kind of bad conscience. Seamus Heaney's book *The Government of the Tongue* is a disturbing book to me, because as much as I admire him, and admire his work, and find his critical prose delicious, I'm bothered by something I recognize in myself: the—what's the word—longing in his attitude toward Eastern European poetry—where poetry really mattered. It made me uneasy about that book. I'm not quite sure I understand the Irish context, the problem of what poetry can do in the face of intransigent tribal fury, but I know that there's something a little bad-conscience and voyeuristic about an American reading of those materials.

Poetry is a phenomenon of the urban middle class: a phenomenon of the urban middle class in Korea, a phenomenon of the urban middle class in New Zealand. It's an urban middle class that doesn't particularly want to be urban and middle class, and often, if it has roots in the country, it draws strongly on those roots and is the place that articulates them. But really, since Alexandrian Rome and Athens, poets came to the city, poetry was preserved and disseminated through the cities, and consumers of poetry were the citizens of the cities. It's the problem of displacement—by the time people are comfortable enough to be in a situation to study and write poetry, the situation has been displaced. It's amazing how a young Indonesian poet, who you would think would live among the sweat shops and see, is just as blind, just as cut off from those things by class, habit, roads through town, as we are. So displacement becomes the great subject in a certain way. That's why I think V. S. Naipaul, however odious his politics can sometimes be, is a great political writer, because he writes so brilliantly about displacement.

Anyway, I think about politics a lot; I go through periods when I don't think about it at all, but then at other times I think about it a lot, and I've written about how one thinks about it. I don't think that there's an easy solution to the present retreat. The nineteen-eighties was culturally and politically a sink of a decade, the worst in America in this century, and I think we all feel somewhat defeated by it, by Reagan's popularity, by the unconsciousness and greed.

You all know the story about George Oppen? In 1931, '32, whenever it was, he went to New York and met Williams and Zukofsky. He had a little bit of money, a family inheritance, and started a press, The Objectivist Press. He published some Williams, published some Pound, and was going to be their younger protégé with a little money starting a press along their lines and get-

ting something going. Pound was always enthusiastic about these things, especially having a rich young Jewish guy from San Francisco set up a press where he could print his "funny money" pamphlets. Anyway, Oppen wrote one book of poems while he and his wife Mary were living in Brooklyn. The Depression was devastating in New York City, so he made a conscious decision to organize rent strikes, and to not write poetry. Since he didn't want to be torn between the two, he set poetry aside, and he and Mary joined the Communist Party. He spent four or five years organizing rent strikes in Brooklyn, helping the people with housing, and so on. Then later he worked in factories and served in the Army, and after the war, having fled to Mexico to avoid the McCarthy thing, he suddenly started writing again. It was 1954, I think, and he was reading Jacques Maritain's book *Creative Intuition in Art and Poetry,* a wonderful book, and he started writing poetry, twenty-five years after he set it aside. What's so wonderful for me about his poetry of the later years is that he's not trying to prove he's a really good person in the poems. He'd absolutely done his work of conscience, and set it aside, so that when he came back, he wrote a kind of Heideggerian poetry. It's also a social poetry of curiosity, a phenomenological poetry, full of tender but suspicious and absolute curiosity about being. It's authentic in part because he doesn't ever have to demonstrate that he's political—he's already done that.

I think political writing is problematic. Neruda wrote a lot of bullshit, because he wrote political poetry, and a lot of it is gesturing and posturing. It made possible "The Heights of Macchu Picchu," which is very great and actually a kind of politically confused poem, I think, in the way that Ginsberg's *Howl* is a politically confused poem. But the confusions don't matter in certain ways.

It makes me think of Polish poetry, of the poetry written by writers of my generation in the sixties—it's not readable much now. They all wrote a consciously political poetry that's very clever. I mean they would take the language of the media and the broadcasters and turn it on its ear. They did a reportorial and a documentary poetry, but it was stuck in the outward world in a certain way. And when they became dissatisfied with it—Baranczak, Zagajewski, Krynicki, and others—each of them at some point made a decision not to let Polish politics so dominate their imaginations that they didn't write about everything else that was inside them. Then the poetry took off, and in the Eastern European context, it became more political to be antipolitical than to be political. The Hungarian novelist Gyorgy Konrad's very interesting book *Antipolitics* is another instance of that.

In the United States, in the center of the empire, this same freedom can be problematic. During the sixties, some people were furious at Ashbery and O'Hara; O'Hara in particular seemed maddeningly narcissistic. There was this stuff going on, American tax money was being spent on incinerating a whole culture, and he was writing about what color belt to buy on his lunch hour, and it pissed people off. People say that being antipolitical is ultimately subversive, but there's always Oppen's example hovering over one's head, saying that subversive is a dime a dozen, all artists think they're subversive. Don't flatter yourself. *Howl* seems to me the nearest thing. There are two things besides the invention in the language that make *Howl* a great poem, I think. One is the vision of Moloch. Milosz says American poets are juvenile, mainly because they have a vision of bad guys but they don't have a vision of evil—but Moloch is a vision of evil. The poem names the soullessness and fear in all of us that produces the horror, and really does it in a powerful way. But the other thing that makes it a great poem is that it's ultimately about his mother. When you get to the the asterisks at the end of the first section, the final image of the poem is "down to the last piece of mental furniture, a yellow paper rose twisted on a wire hanger in the closet, and even that imaginary . . ." It's his image of Naomi, his fury at his mother's madness that's at the core of that poem. That's the great thing about Ginsberg—it would have been easy for him to write a poem in which American society did that to Naomi, but he's not sure what did it to her. So there is this personal lyrical agenda, this elegiac agenda, this ontological agenda of grief and rage that is anchored in the absolutely personal. That's why I'm slightly suspicious of the term "rhythm of the streets," as applied to Ginsberg, because the rhythm that artists are ultimately responsible for is the one that the rhythm of the streets produces in them.

. . . . .

Recently I've been listening to the graduate students give talks, and to some of the lecturers who come through Berkely. It fascinates me that all of the criticism is written from the point of view of a total superciliousness toward literature. It's really the old French thing: it's a new language, but they pull the same rabbit of bourgeois ideology out of the same hat of literary analysis. Which is okay—I think disenchantment is an important work of the mind, but it's their position of superiority that puzzles me because it's based on the implicit, usually Marxist, idea that they have a superior vision of social and political economy. But they fail to acknowledge that something has collapsed in Eastern Europe, that began, as Kundera's books say, in Utopian joy. As a result, the position which this criticism is based on has collapsed, and you'd never know it from the viewpoint of the academics, who still get up there in their Italian suits and give these incredibly witty contemptuous lectures on how the poets and the novelists don't understand the bourgeois ideology of what they're writing. It enrages me.

Meanwhile the whole world is being sold the bill of goods that somehow this system has triumphed, a country whose cities have something like two-thirds unemployment of non-white males between the ages of eighteen and thirty, and half of the country, especially white, white-collar workers, addicted to crack or cocaine. I mean—leave alone the question of homelessness—this country is in catastrophic condition, and the media's got everybody convinced that we've found the victorious solution—and I mean, if *this* is the solution . . .

So, all political questions seem to me open and really puzzling. It looks like it's going to turn out that the intellectuals of the 19th and 20th centuries who didn't favor the market system were wrong about it—the same system the jocks and the cheerleaders we went to school with loved, and went out to be part of, and get the goods in. *We* went off to talk about how terrible it was and about what kind of rules we'd set up for a government that was fair to poor people—which meant that we were in favor of imposing moral authority on the economy from above—and it hasn't worked anywhere. So it turns out that all the people I hated in high school might have been more right than I was about this stuff. And every time one of the people like me got into power—Ho Chi Minh or Ortega or someone like that—he turns out to be another moralistic authoritarian. Or something else: Castro may not be a moralistic authoritarian, but at the least, he's a king.

So it's puzzling. I know what I hate, but I know less and less about how to change it. That's why I said in **"Rusia en 1931"**:

> Poetry proposes no solutions: it says justice is the
> well water of the city of Novgorod, black and
> sweet.

Mandelstam's great political ideal was the Italian city-state, and the most Italian city-state in the Russia of the Middle Ages was Nizhni Novgorod, and it was famous for being a free place because they didn't tax you for the well water. Anybody, citizen or not, had access to the well water at any time. It was his image of a just, small society. And I think that's right; I think the task of art is to over and over again make images of a livable common life. How do you retranslate "Crossing Brooklyn Ferry" into the 20th century? Alfred Corn tried to do it—it's really a noble experiment, I think, in *A Cry in the Midst of the Crowd*. I so admire the impulse of it, especially from him who's such an elegant poet. He tried to do it. O'Hara in his way—in *Lunch Poems* especially—tried to do it. You know, it's not everybody's world, the art scene in mid-town Manhattan, but he tried to get some of common life into his work. So that's one task.

Another task is to make images of justice: make ideal images or make outraged images or just do witness. There are all the usual tasks. You'll always feel a bit of a tourist in them, you know, as in Linda Gregg's wonderful poem about visiting the women's shelter. It's part of the job of being a poet, but I think you'll always feel a little bit like a voyeur and a tourist writing those poems. And a little uneasy reading them. But the choice is that or silence, and so you do it. Or Jorie Graham's poem about Paris in '68— when political experience comes your way, you write about it. The trick—I've seen it in Milosz's work especially—is to write very honestly about the actual dilemmas, which means thinking about them clearly, which means not flattering yourself that you know what the solutions are. At some point, somebody's going to see things truthfully, as with "Howl." There are just moments when somebody finds a way to say it, you know, stumbles on it. I've just been reading that biography of Ginsberg, who had sort of an unpromising start. He went to an Ivy League college and got taught by Lionel Trilling and had a lot of his classmates become editors and stuff like that. So he had access to and understood very well the publicity mechanisms of American writing, but he had such a miserable family life and terrible personal dilemmas. And out of some combination of guts and talent, he stumbled into telling the truth in some powerful way, raggedly and imperfectly. And I feel that will happen again. Certainly everybody would like to do it, or at least have their writing be part of the writing that leads to it, and I think of Milosz's example, and in a way of Ginsberg's example, of not writing from knowing the answers.

I don't know if any of you have read *Coming to Jakarta* yet. Peter Dale Scott is my colleague at Berkeley; he's a Canadian poet in his late fifties and his father's a very distinguished Canadian poet who was one of the founders of the Canadian Socialist Party. And Peter went through traditional Canadian upper-middle-class education—McGill and Cambridge, or whatever—and then he joined the diplomatic corps. He worked in Poland, then in Indonesia, then at the UN, and then he quit and became a high school classics teacher, and somehow he ended up teaching Latin to English medievalists at Berkeley. During the Vietnam years, trying to figure out what started that war, he began doing research on the cocaine traffic and the CIA involvement in Central America and Southeast Asia, and wrote a couple of books about these subjects. He's a very interesting guy; he spends his time in the English department and in Washington think tanks. He's developed into somebody who has a way of putting all of his previous political stuff together, and it's finally erupted into this Poundian poem.

At some point when he was doing research, it dawned on him that Lake Massawippi, where he'd summered as a kid, had these genteel academic cabins on the Canadian side—you know, Pendleton shirts and rowboats and minnows and fishing for pike—while on the other side, the whole American ruling class had these incredible, elegant places where they mingled. So as he read with outrage about the founding of the CIA, and the founding of the Council on Foreign Relations, and how all of these people had taken it upon themselves to police the world, it dawned on him that Lily Dulles, whose house they'd always picnicked at on Sundays, was in fact the sister of Allen and John Foster Dulles. So what emerges in the poem is both a reconstruction of his own childhood and a realization that he was spying on the set of social connections that created the CIA and the Council on Foreign Relations.

The Council on Foreign Relations was the group of interested businessmen and intellectuals and bankers from John McCone to David Rockefeller who have dominated American foreign policy—really created it—since the Truman administration. The poem is about all of that, and it aims toward trying to figure out what brought about the counter-revolutionary massacre in Indonesia in 1962 that killed an estimated one million people. It started as a purge of radical elements in Indonesia and ended up as the slaughter of the Chinese in Indonesia. It was partly just a racial pogrom, but it also wiped out almost every communist, which is to say almost every schoolteacher and incipient middle-class person in a peasant society. It was a horrible slaughter and the CIA was—unquestionably—implicated. From their point of view it got out of hand, but it's one of the real horrors of the twentieth century, equal in horror to other more infamous events. And what Scott has done is construct this poem that begins with flickering memories of looking into the water, into the reeds, and getting a creepy feeling at Massawippi. Then it moves to a series of images: little bits of Indonesian shadow dance with violence and destruction emerging in it, stuff about the drug traffic as it was formed in the 1950s, stuff about the parties at which John Foster Dulles and Allen Dulles connected with the bankers, and so on. . . . It's a political poem that actually tries to be informed by a knowledge of how the horrible events of the twentieth century have come about, and it's an amazingly interesting poem, a very ambitious poem. Which is to say you should read it.

I guess a lot of the questions in poetry can only be answered by poetry. That is, they can only be answered by dramatizing and intensifying the contradictions which we suppress in everyday life in order to get on with it. We suppress what we don't know, what we can't say—you know, Jorie Graham's notorious blanks that everybody's trying to figure out. That has to be brought forward with what you do know, with what you witness, with the kinds of knowledge that aren't public knowledge. It would be something to write a great poem about the CIA training the Savak, the Shah's secret police, who tortured the Ayatollah Khomeni's son to death. Why hasn't any American written *that* poem?

Clearly, to write a political poetry is complicated. Neruda, in writing "The Heights of Macchu Picchu," wanted to write a poem that was mainly on the side of the working class, but was also about the Spanish destruction of Indian culture—a culture that had its own slaves and its own oppressed class who built its sacred temples. So there's no cause for sentimental opposition between good Indian and bad Spaniard, or for that matter, between good proletariat and bad ruling class. His very language implicates him, so that there can be no luxury of simply being on the right side. So often when writing about history, the temptation is to look at the thing and say these stupidities and evils repeat themselves endlessly—so what else is new. And then you end up with a shrug of irony and a commitment to singularity in art and intelligence. Or you simplify, strike poses—deeply felt probably, but poses. In order to rise above that, you have to be smart, otherwise you end up writing stupid sentimental poems. By smart, I don't mean IQ smart, I mean reflective—you have to have thought some of this stuff out. But finally, I don't think knowledge—either kind—gets you there. Then what does get you there? It would seem, from the example of the artists who have done it, that among the things that get you there are fidelity to your craft, stubbornly practicing it against all odds, measuring yourself against great examples, against the noblest stuff of art. I want to write, "*Am-*

*bition,* high ambition, for your art,"—that actually *does* seem to help. Brecht had it, Rilke had it, Neruda had it, Whitman had it, Ginsberg has it.

*There's a political vision in the prose poem "The Harbor at Seattle" that seems to combine political and historical knowledge with a sense that knowing doesn't get you anywhere.* **Praise,** *for example, had a lot of poems that suggest that you can travel and travel and travel but ultimately you'll get to a radiant state, not a final knowing. The two suicides in "The Harbor at Seattle" that are never resolved suggest to me that you have a sense that knowing doesn't save things: it doesn't save a political system, it doesn't save Telegraph Hill, it doesn't save the two suicides in that poem, and it doesn't save the fragile relationships among the four people who were the study group in the beginning of the poem. How can you bring that into play with the rest of what we've talked about?*

It does seem like a theme of mine; I had never seen it before. Once, I showed something I wrote to a woman who had been studying Charles Olson and Ezra Pound with Hayden Carruth, and she said, "I kind of like that. I kind of like the male ecstatic knowledge trip," which I thought was very funny. I felt incredibly deflated. I think I overvalue knowing, and I think I overvalue knowing because I think my parents would have done better if they had known more. I think it's completely delusory, but knowledge really was power for me in a certain way, because I thought that everything that was out of control in my childhood could be controlled if I just knew more, somehow. So I've probably just been unlearning an obviously wrong thing my whole life.

*You've always acknowledged at least in your writing that the knowledge looks like power, but doesn't wind up being power. There are a couple of places where it seems crystalized, where there's an impulse to join the erotic and the knowledgeable and the political lives. "The Harbor at Seattle" posits the suicides and the eating away of Telegraph Hill. The poem knows all, and loves all—I mean there's all this intimacy for these things—loves the photograph of one of the women who committed suicide, and loves the man who committed suicide. And it knows a lot about them, but ultimately Telegraph Hill winds up being destroyed. It seems like a kind of a tragic formulation of how all of the worlds work: the personal world, the political world, and the world of knowledge.*

The question of what *does* save seems to turn on the question also of where politics leaves off. There's the famous story about the First International Congress of Soviet Writers in Moscow in 1934. After three or four long speeches by writers about the socialist future, someone raised his hand and asked, "Mr. Chairman, I would like to know what would happen in the socialist state when a beautiful young person got run over by a trolley car." And everybody burst out laughing. On the last day they got Maxim Gorki out of his death bed and propped him up in front of the podium to say that in the perfect socialist state, beautiful young people wouldn't be run

over by trolley cars. But the fact is, they *would.* So it seems to me that without wanting to, I have a slightly dualistic attitude toward politics and whatever other thing art is involved with—maybe religion is the word for it. A task of poetry is to make an image of the common life and of justice. It can make an image of the best possible life that you could intelligently imagine, reasonably imagine. But that life wouldn't satisfy us, because we would still be outraged by nature: early death, AIDS, late death. . . . Milosz was once asked to give a talk at a demonstration against nuclear power plants, and he said, "Why don't they ever demonstrate against old age? It kills far more people." So he's an unrepentant anti-nature dualist who thinks that it's an affront that our individual consciousnesses, with everything they carry, are to perish. He takes a stance against the casual acceptance of death—but does make an effort to have some humility before natural process. It's nevertheless the case that there are all kinds of awful things that are awful not because anybody's done anything stupid or anything bad to anybody else, they're just awful. And so there's a huge part of the human spirit that's wrestling with that. I'm not saying it's not political, because everything that gets cast in this world automatically has a political aspect. But there are things that are not fundamentally political: the problem of suffering, the problem of evil. . . . So in both cases, whether fundamentally political or not, knowledge comes into place mainly in the sense of knowing what it helps to know and what it doesn't help to know.

. . . . .

We were talking last night about Edmond Jabès, a great contemporary French poet and essayist who was born a French-speaking Jew in Cairo and moved to Paris. He took a certain Talmudic training, with its accompanying interest in symbol systems, and married it to a sense of the complete disintegration of the kind of community of symbols that language represents, which includes some feeling that the Holocaust disintegrated the social contract. So really he anticipated, as Paul Celan did—though he's a few years older than Celan—all the notions of Derrida and Lacan and post-structuralist French thought ten or fifteen years before they were even warmed up. And he did it through his writing practice. He had Emily Dickinson's kind of ambition—I don't know how to describe it exactly—he certainly wasn't ambitious to be famous. . . . But some of those books are such sustained acts of imagination, it takes a certain will to have produced them, I think, which instances that kind of commitment, or obsession.

. . . . .

It's interesting to talk about what's happening in writing right now and where it's going. It's clear that the writing which I grew up with (along with Jim Galvin and Linda Gregg to some extent—Jorie Graham's formation was somewhat different), the writing of the late fifties and early sixties, was a reaction to the writing of the thirties and forties. That whole series of writers of the Ginsberg/ O'Hara generation was writing furiously against the new critical formation that came out of Eliot's prose, and the examples of Auden, Yeats, Ransom, and so on. So there was that explosion of energy. But it does seem that in writers younger than I, there has been, among other things, a reawakening interest in formality. One of the signs of it is the so-called new formalism on the right, and language poetry, which has other kinds of formal propositions, on the left. So in general there's some hunger to start wearing starched shirts and blouses again. There's a phrase that comes to mind. Somebody reported to me that coming out of a reading—I don't know who was reading, if it was Robert Bly or Allen Ginsberg—a young woman with shimmery peach and black hair turned to someone and said, "I'm just not interested in the cliché of intensity." I thought, my God, you know, such withdrawal from what has certainly been one of my touchstones. I don't know exactly what the opposite would be—I mean, there *are* opposites of intensity, like the telephone book, that some of the new poetry puts me in mind of. Dryness and austerity are not the opposite, by the way. Zbigniew Herbert is an intense writer, and in fact dryness can be a sign of intensity in poetry. But there is something going on, and it's related to the question of where we are in history, where our experience is, and what's been done with personal and psychological experience in poetry since 1955. How can you do anything new with this material, but how can you *not* write about it? It used to knock me out that Charles Olson's wife died in an automobile accident and he didn't miss a beat in writing *The Maximus Poems*—it didn't enter them, it just didn't enter them, you know, because it wasn't part of that project. For most who began writing, with very few exceptions, since the early sixties, it would be unthinkable that you wouldn't have to somehow deal with that material in your writing. There's so much to get down, so much to express, inside and outside—all religious questions are up for grabs.

My friend Brenda Hillman just finished this long poem about the death of a teacher, a friend, an older woman, and I heard her read a bit of it the other night. Somebody said afterwards that they were hearing something like a feminist—or, not a feminist, a woman's—rewriting of Tennyson's "In Memoriam." But one of the haunting questions in the poem is, *where did she go?* I mean, we have a common society, but we don't have a common idea about what happens to the dead. We have no common imagination of it. It's a religious matter, it's a private matter, so you don't talk about it, because it'll only start arguments. And therefore, about the fundamental mysteries of life, we have no agreement; in fact, we have an agreement not to talk about it. You not only don't know what's going to happen to you when you die, you don't know what the person you're talking to thinks about it. In my case, you don't know what you think yourself. There was a period when it was just in bad taste to talk about it, because you looked like such a naive person. Certain post-Startre intellectuals talked as if it were not an interesting question—embarrassing poetry of that kind was something the Victorians did. The thing I love about C. K. Williams's elegy for Paul Zweig is its philosophical embarrassment. It just opens that question again, like a Victorian poem, as if it were not embarrassing to admit that you don't know what death means, and you

don't know how to think about it. You've read a lot of books of philosophy and considered a lot of different answers and the set of prejudices about it—whether you hate the religion or like the religion that you grew up with—none of which may be relevant. And I really do think this is work no art form does the way poetry does it. Nothing gets as close to the absolute feel of the inner life as it asks these questions, because they're questions that have to be answered in words.

## Louise Glück   (essay date 1994)

SOURCE: "Obstinate Humanity," in *Proofs & Theories: Essays on Poetry,* The Ecco Press, 1994, pp. 65-71.

[*In the following excerpt, Glück discusses Hass's work in relation to that of Robinson Jeffers and Czeslaw Milosz.*]

Robinson Jeffers appears to be a poet other poets chastize eloquently. That is: the inducement to literary reprimand is in proportion to the stakes: the grander, the more fundamental the objection, the more inviting the project. The remarkable poems of this little genre, Milosz's and Hass's, are devoid of flamboyant condescension, at least insofar as the living can avoid flaunting their ongoing development at the immobile dead. "So brave in a void / you offered sacrifices to demons": so Milosz addresses Jeffers. If not exactly tribute, this is nevertheless a particular species of reproach: giant to giant.

The reprimand is moral: at issue is humanity, the definition thereof. And Jeffers' crime, in Milosz's poem, "to proclaim . . . an inhuman thing." Hass concurs, pretty much, though his formulation changes the emphasis, focusing on causes: "human anguish made him cold."

What's odd to me is that Jeffers in all his hardness and obstinate fixity and dogmatic revulsions is, of the three, the most poignantly, albeit cheerlessly, human.

I read Milosz in translation, which makes discussion of tone problematic. And yet, at issue in his poem to Jeffers is the placement of the speaker relative to his subjects and, in fact, Milosz speaks as a diplomat, an envoy, his mission being to explain, or represent, one form of paganism to another.

The paganism he defends is maternal. Earth centered. Moon centered. Fruitful. Predictable. Cyclical. This is the same fecund earth Hass reveres. Both approve it as the wise man approves woman, radiant in otherness. Homage to the source, the root, but homage paid, in Milosz, by someone well beyond primitive gesturing.

The mathematical equivalent of feminine earth is multiplication: increase, whatever its metaphoric manifestation, seems inherently life-affirming. Whereas the corresponding, the declared metaphor for Jeffers' earth, the "massive mysticism of stone," is elimination: a dead end, presumably.

Hass puts all this more eloquently: "though rock stands it does not breed." He sees the lure of rock but names its spiritual danger: sterility. To stand, to not breed, is to be finally inhuman, and, pragmatically, *not* lasting: the future of the species is more profitably assured through reproduction than through endurance. In Hass's mind, mutability, not fixity, sponsors ongoing existence. And yet the manner in which Jeffers espouses rock is immensely human: exposed, rash, extreme, vulnerable. Rigid, where Hass and Milosz are lithe-minded, evolved.

Jeffers writes out of enraged, disappointed romanticism: civilized in his expectations, he cannot forgive civilization in that it wasn't worth his faith. This can seem, to a reader, cumulatively trying: repetition deprives a last stand of its dramatic force.

Whereas Hass characteristically resists resolution: a mark of intellect, but also a temperamental inclination which can create its own form of stasis, in that it lacks not motion but momentum.

Hass hates disappointment, hates being imprisoned in its continuing and limited range of attitudes, of tones: rue, regret, plangent lament. When Hass *sighs* in *Praise* he does so with a kind of savage fury, constrained by perspective, by habitual poise; in these moments, he comes closest to being what Milosz has always been, since to write as an ancient soul is to write as an ironist (the alternative, I suppose, being to sing the purest and briefest of lyrics—).

Hass's method of poetic development has always been exposure: he uses his empathetic capacity to extend his range. Though he is not, I think, at home in irony (unless there is irony in the Buddha's composure), he has most certainly, as Milosz's translator, been exposed to its most subtle and resourceful practitioner.

Hass and Milosz have in common astounding intellectual gifts and the virtuoso's mastery of tone which contrives to endow natural speech with a sometimes unbelievable subtext of resonances. But the sources of flexibility differ: Milosz's detachment differs from Hass's empathy, as irony is distinct from ambivalence.

It will be interesting to see whether Hass ripens into the sort of poet Milosz is: ironic, but with an irony by turns delicate, malicious, passionate, judgmental, tender. He already has Milosz's 360-degree gaze, as opposed to Jeffers' fixity.

Jeffers' ferocity is alien to Hass; his landscapes less so. Like Jeffers, Hass is attracted to the absence of the human. There have been, from the first, counterparts in Hass to Jeffers' harsh, unpopulated world. And this is an aspect of the work even in *Field Guide,* even before human presence or human agency come to be characterized as that contaminating "steady thoughtlessness." But where Jeffers' imagination settles on rock and hawk, Hass gives us frog and pond, a bowl of oranges. Into these worlds, human beings, men and women, come as intrusions.

Most poets are, in Frost's phrase, acquainted with the night. Hass is unique in having inhabited, as an adult, a sunlit world. Exiled from Eden, he's like the man who's always been healthy and gets sick: when the amazement passes, he simply can't stand feeling this way. And the tonal problem of *Praise,* the collection that registers this change, is to avoid petulant irritability.

The earlier work, **"The Return of Robinson Jeffers,"** is built around a move typical of Hass's work, early and late, an extended enactment of empathy. Hass imagines Jeffers' return from death: "I imagine him thinking . . .": so the meditation starts. Hass's projected epiphany duplicates Milosz's bias; this is not curious, since they address the same figure, the same perceived limitation. Jeffers, in Hass's imagination, ". . . feels pain as rounding at the hips, as breasts." And the form reeducation takes is the birth of feminine empathy and suffering to replace male arrogance.

It is either very touching, very feminine (on this grid) or extremely arrogant that Hass prefers to imagine these revelations as occurring to Jeffers himself, while at the same time refusing to abandon his own position as narrating, as sponsoring intelligence: the epiphany occurs in Hass's imagination. The fact is, Hass has learned much from Jeffers. There are tastes in common: the long, rhythmic, complicated sentences, with subsequent sentences beginning on a repeated phrase, like a thread picked up in a complex tapestry, so that one is always aware of, always hearing the human voice (the danger of complex syntax being that voice will be lost and, with it, intimacy, directness). The similarities are, in any case, easy to hear, for all the difference in ambiance: ". . . . what a festival for the seafowl. / What a witches' sabbath of wings / Hides the water." That's Jeffers, but Hass has moments very like.

What Hass does, what no one else now writing does with such skill, is a kind of spiritual ventriloquism: he is able to project not merely voice but a whole sensibility. On the surface, this resembles Keats's ideas of negative capability; in fact, it differs profoundly from Keats, in motive and effect. Always Keats's excursions conclude, and the act of conclusion marks a restoration of self. This is the romantic journey: it might be, it can be imagined, it is not. Hass may assert the fact of limitation, but limitation does not seem to be an attribute of the voice. And the romantic sound is not one Hass seems especially eager to make. His poems are, regularly, a flight from self; what they lack, when they lack anything, is a sense of the restrictions of self, of singleness, which perception necessitates acts of judgment, decision, assertion of priorities. His poems repudiate self in its romantic role: bedrock, shaping principle.

---

## FURTHER READING

### Criticism

Aldan, Daisy. Review of *Human Wishes. World Literature Today* (Spring 1990): 313.

Examines the four parts of the volume in order, praising Hass's imagery and prose poems in particular.

Berger, Charles. "Dan Pagis and Robert Hass." *Raritan* 10, No. 1 (Summer 1990): 126-38.
Explores *Human Wishes*, focusing on Hass's lyrical pieces and prose poems.

Florby, Gunilla. "Holding Out Against Loss and Jacques Lacan: Some Reflections on Robert Hass's Sensuous Line." *Studia Neophilologica* 63, No. 2 (1991): 189-95.

Discusses Hass's poems as adumbrations of Saussurean and Lacanian theories of language.

Lea, Sydney. "A Matter of Conscience." *The Nation* (19 May 1979): 574-75.
Reviews *Praise*, finding Hass's distinctive voice as the vehicle that successfully balances the volume's aesthetic and moral conflicts.

Selman, Robyn. Review of *Human Wishes*. *Village Voice Literary Supplement* (December 1989): 5-6.
Delivers unqualified approval of Hass's fourth collection of verse.

---

Additional coverage of Hass's life and career is contained in the following sources published by Gale Research: *Contemporary Authors*, Vol. 111; *Contemporary Authors New Revision Series*, Vol. 30; *Contemporary Literary Criticism*, Vols. 18, 39; and *Dictionary of Literary Biography*, Vol. 105.

# Gyula Illyés
## 1902–1983

Hungarian poet, novelist, essayist, short story writer, dramatist, and political activist.

## INTRODUCTION

For the quality of his writing and political activism through that writing, Illyés is generally considered the greatest Hungarian poet of his time. In a country where the inhabitants have historically turned to their artists for support in times of crisis, Illyés is accepted as the greatest spokesperson for the common people. Regardless of genre, his works are marked by a simplicity of language and stark immediacy that compound its stirring nature. Illyés's work can never be discussed without placing it in the context of Hungary during his lifetime—a period marked by great political upheaval—because, as he himself admitted, "With all the literary genres with which I experimented I wanted to serve one single cause: that of a unified people and the eradication of exploitation and misery. I always held literature to be only a tool."

### Biographical Information

Illyés was born in Rácegres, on the Hungarian *puszta*, or plains, at the estate where his parents were servants. His people were landless agricultural workers in this feudal society. The efforts of his family allowed him to attend school in Budapest, but after his participation in the unsuccessful Hungarian Communist Revolution of 1919, he was forced to flee the country and finish his education at the Sorbonne in Paris, France. Illyés's time in Paris had a profound effect on his work in that his experiences outside of Hungary gave him a better understanding of his homeland. At that time he also associated with dadaists and surrealists Paul Eluard, Louis Aragon, and Tristan Tzara, although their influence did not have a lasting effect on his style. He began his writing career in Paris but returned to Hungary in 1926. With his first novel, *Puszták népe (People of the Puszta)* in 1936, Illyés established himself as an influential writer on the scene, and he continued to gain esteem as his career progressed. In 1937 he became an editor of *Nyugat (West)*, a well-respected literary magazine, and eventually began his own magazine, *Magyar Csillag (Hungarian Star)*. At the onset of World War II, Illyés's writing became increasingly political and he was censored for it. When Nazi oppression ended, Hungary enjoyed a brief period of independence during which Illyés served in parliament. When Communists came to power, Illyés was allowed some freedoms because of his position among the people, despite his constant denunciation of the government. His work continued to champion the people even after his death in 1983.

## Major Works

Although most widely known as a poet, Illyés is renowned for his prose masterpiece, *People of the Puszta*, a mostly autobiographical tale of peasants and poverty. Its objective and detached descriptions helped expose the horror of that life, spurring on other social commentators and fledgling acts of reform. Illyés's next work, *Petöfi* (1937), a critical biography of the nineteenth-century poet Sandor Petöfi, is held as the greatest work on that subject. Illyés was extremely prolific throughout his life and was known for the complete body of his work, especially his poetry. Without objection, however, critics consider his most famous poem to be "Egy mondat a zsarnoksagrol" ("One Sentence on Tyranny"), a simply stated and profoundly moving piece on the causes of tyranny published in 1956.

## Critical Reception

Gyula Illyés was universally lauded throughout his long career by critics and, more importantly, the people of Hungary. He was loved and read not simply for his writing skills, but for his constant support of the people through his works. Because a good part of his work has not been translated, nor has there been an adequately detailed study, Illyés remains relatively unknown to the English-speaking world. But as French critic Alain Bosquet noted, "There are only three or four . . . poets in the world who could gradually absorb the spirit of the century in the widest sense of the word. . . . In Gyula Illyés their genius is present. . . . His famous poem 'One Sentence on Tyranny' will survive as one of the purest cries of a generation's pain."

---

## PRINCIPAL WORKS

### Poetry

*Nehéz föld* [*A Hard Land*]  1928
*Ifjusag* [*Youth*]  1934
*A kacsalaba forgo var* [*The Wonder Castle*] (epic poem) 1936
*Egy mondat a zsarnoksagrol* [*One Sentence on Tyranny*] (epic poem) 1956
*Kézfogások* [*Handshakes*]  1956
*Fekete fehér* [*Black White*]  1967
*Hommage à Gyula Illyés* [*Homage to Gyula Illyés*] 1963
*Összegyüjtött versei*  1977

### Other Major Works

*Puszták népe* [*People of the Puszta*] (novel) 1936
*Petöfi* (biography) 1937
*Hunok Parisban* [*Huns in Paris*] (novel) 1946

## CRITICISM

### László Ferenczi  (essay date 1977)

SOURCE: "Gyula Illyés, Poet of a Nation," in *The New Hungarian Quarterly,* Vol. 18, No. 68, Winter, 1977, pp. 54-65.

[*In the following essay, Ferenczi muses on Illyés's "open door" policy concerning creativity and his promotion of that openness.*]

There are some magic titles, or metaphors, which give a true description of the attitudes or philosophy of a poet. How revealing Paul Éluard's *L'amour de la poésie!* How much we know about Robert Goffin from *A bout portant,* or about W. H. Auden when he says *Another Time,* or about Stephen Spender when he writes *The Still Centre,* or about André Frénaud when he argues *Il n'y a pas de paradis.* Gyula Illyés, poet, writer of prose, dramatist, essayist, translator, announces to the world *Nyitott ajtó* (*Open door*), *Ingyen lakoma* (*Free feast*), and *Kézfogások* (*Handshakes*).

Illyés published a selection of his verse translations of *Open door* in 1963. Almost every European literature is present in this volume, and Chinese and Japanese poems to boot. Medieval French poetry and modern European poetry are especially well represented; among the contemporaries we find his personal friends, Tristan Tzara, Jean Follain, André Frénaud, as well as Boris Pasternak and Nezval. This son of the Hungarian *puszta* became acquainted with the medieval French, the dadaists, and the surrealists, all at the same time, in the early twenties in Paris; and that was when he undertook to translate them.

*Free feast* is a selective anthology of essays published in 1964; it includes the work of several decades. The subjects are Hungarians and foreigners; Racine, Éluard, the Soviet G. Martinov, or Eastern poetry. The expanded edition of 1975, *Iránytűvel* ("With a compass") includes, in addition, an essay on Tzara, a record of the poet's creed regarding loyalty to friends and responsibility. In the course of half a century Illyés has returned again and again to Tzara in translations, in essays, or in quotations throughout his autobiography. Even now, looking back from the seventies, Illyés considers dadaism a serious and noble movement, whereas Tzara is regarded not as a curio of literary history, but as a poet whose qualities will be discovered by future generations.

What Illyés himself had accomplished, however, is radically different from Tzara's work. Illyés is the poet of the landless peasant; he is the classicist poet of Hungarian national consciousness. Yet he feels we can better grasp, and become more aware of, folk poetry under the effect of surrealism.

*Handshakes* (1956) is one of Illyés's twenty volumes of poetry. Perhaps no more important than the others, it is nevertheless my favourite; it was in some of these poems,

published in reviews (and eventually included in this volume) that I discovered the poet for myself during my high school days, and began to suspect something that Jean Follain had formulated so perfectly:

> Faced with (this) mystery of Time and that of death, Illyés wants to preserve—in spite of all the evil deeds of history and its troublesome ambiguities a certain innocent view of the world. He knows how to keep alive all the great frontiers of the unknown. (From *A Tribute to Gyula Illyés,* eds. Thomas Kabdebo and Paul Tabori, preface by Jean Follain, Washington: Occidental Press, 1968).

One of these poems that had appeared in a periodical first was titled **"Bartók."** Not quite a quarter of a century after its appearance it became a classic, nowadays it is taught at school. The poem is passionate, meaningful, thought-provoking, and has a quieting effect—like all good poetry. But what passions it provoked at the time of its appearance! I had not read such liberating verse by a living poet during my schooldays. The dogmatic cultural policy of the first half of the fifties held that Bartók was alien to socialism and humanism, as were so many other great artists of the past and present. This was also the poem which mentioned the name of Pablo Picasso, likewise rejected until then; in other words, the poem rehabilitated the Hungarian composer and the Spanish artist, rehabilitated true universality.

It was an occasional poem in the true sense of the word, an artistic programme of liberation and of enthusiasm and, of course, a political poem as well; and from the distance of almost a quarter of a century it is obviously a masterpiece. Of course we, enthusiastic students (and I believe others as well) already suspected it, but at 17 and 18 we could not have known Illyés's secret, that potential immortality lies concealed even in his most occasional work, because of the extremely demanding form, his incredible respect for artistic principles, and his honesty as a thinker. To put it differently, he prepares the most topical texts from durable matter. He is master of lasting political verse.

After his **"Bartók"** poem, after the volume **Handshakes** neither *Open door* nor *Free feast* were surprising titles. How pertinent the preface to the latter:

> It is good to eat, but people have to be taught and encouraged to do even that. They must be educated constantly in order to eat what is tasty, what is good, what is healthy; they must overcome their prejudices in this domain as well. There is so much great food— varying from country to country—that people will not take a bite of, or sip, out of superstition. The same goes for intellectual food. This is where appetite has to be fostered, tastes analysed, vitamins and calories recommended: to beg that at least a spoonful of the unfamiliar dish be introduced into the guzzle.

*Open door* is the opportunity to defeat superstition and prejudice. It is only through the open door that the offering of the free feast and the act of shaking hands become possible.

In his volume of translations he docs not print the poets according to nationality: "I thought it would be more instructive if I arranged them in the order of their birth. Since their development is along different lines, this mingling—though the oriental poets remain separate—may lead to the clarification of that which is essential. How much more significant it is within a given civilization, when he lived, than where! How similar the language of poets in a given era is; they transcend the hedges of their mother tongue, the ramparts of their fatherland! How well they understand one another even in their debates, even in their misunderstandings!"

The poet who wrote this is the same who in the 1930s, in his brief and grotesque epic *Hősökről beszélek* (*I speak of heroes*) revealed to us the world of the large estates, and of the field-hands living under conditions of semi-serfdom servitude on those estates. I mean, in particular, *The People of the Puszta,* this sociological description permeated with autobiographical elements, by now a classic. The poet became the spokesman of landless peasants and also in the early thirties of national consciousness, tortured as he was by the nightmare of the death of the nation. (Visions of the death of the nation Illyés reminds us, has been a theme of Hungarian poetry ever since the 17th century.)

It is about this national poet, sometimes accused of being overly national, that his younger contemporary Alain Bosquet said: "Only three or four living poets have been able to identify themselves with the soul of the century, in the widest sense of the term . . . Their genius burns in the Hungarian poet Gyula Illyés . . ." (Quoted in *A Tribute to Gyula Illyés,* inside jacket).

I believe so myself, but I was happy to quote Alain Bosquet. I think it would be the worst kind of hypocrisy if, while addressing a foreign public, I would not admit that we in Hungary believe Illyés to be one of the greatest, most universal poets and educators of our century.

I don't know Illyés personally. Two or three superficial meetings cannot be considered a personal acquaintance. But I owe him friendship, important conversations, significant reading experiences. If I managed to exchange meaningful words with ten or fifteen European, Asian, or African poets, if I have an inkling of what my interlocutors said about the land problem, the way of life of the peasant, the significance of national being and tradition, the function of literature in their respective countries, if they felt they were not talking to the walls or to the tape-recorder, then I owe it, at least in part, to the fact that I am a reader of Gyula Illyés.

I speak about myself shamelessly: but I received authorization for it from Illyés himself. He was once asked, during an interview: "What is poetry good for, all things considered?" And Illyés answered:

> I can give you an answer only by telling you what it is that the poems and literature as such gave me. Poems have taught me how to speak. It is through

poetry that unconscious feelings, intuitions, concepts have touched me first. I would be unable to formulate exactly the plus-value I may have received from a specific poem, but I know that poetry taught me a whole scale of inexpressible, and perhaps as yet unexpressed feelings, just as my mother had taught me what is a cup, a table, a pair of plyers, a knife. People who have been raised in the same literary environment can understand one another practically at a glance; they approach each other with ease. Hence poetry has a practical effect, that is what I would tell a social scientist. As for subconscious, transcendent experiences, these should be discussed in a psychological essay.

And in the preface to his volume of poetry **Fekete fehér** (**Black white**), in 1967, he wrote: "It is not his own business the writer has to investigate but that of his readers."

Illyés, this lonely man, often prone to despair, who neither offers nor accepts easy solutions, is a true citizen of the *république des lettres.* He respects the work of art, the artist, the real or potential reader, in sacred earnest. In this century didactic poetry is not what it used to be in the 17th or 18th centuries. The best didactic poetry of the 20th century, to mention but a few examples, was written by poets like Pessoa, Auden, Léopold Sanghor, or Éluard. And Gyula Illyés. True enough, the others wrote theirs mostly in the first half of the century.

Illyés is the poet of the creation of values, the preservation of values, the making aware of values. And not only the values of poetry; rather the values of the individual, of particular classes, of particular nations. No one appreciates poetry more highly than he does. But there is no one who knows better to appreciate products other than poetic, whether it be that of the peasant, of the artisan, or of the industrial worker. More accurately, perhaps, he includes all true creativity within the category of poetry.

He was born in 1902 at Rácegres, on a large estate in Western Hungary, on a *puszta* (this is nothing like the stepps called *puszta* and found by the tourist seeking exotic sites—the pseudoromantic *puszta* promoted in such a theatrical, hence false way, in the Great Plains, by the Hungarian tourist organizations). His father was an engineer on the estate. Gyula was not the first in the family to receive an education. He became an avid reader early in life. In one of his reminiscences he describes the frenetic, formative influence exerted on him as a schoolboy by one of the great classics of 19th-century Hungarian literature, the epic poem *Toldi* by János Arany. Thanks to a teacher uncle he became acquainted, at the time of the First World War, with the best series of publications of the times; thus he reads Guglielmo Ferrero, Kropotkin, and Darwin. He read Marx for the first time, and studied French enthusiastically:

"I learnt to speak my mother tongue in a heavy dialect. The way I said 'yes' betrayed not only my provincial origin but also that I grew up on a *puszta*: that my world was the lowest stratum even among the peasantry. It was some kind of negro skin I was wearing, a yellow star. I started to learn French in order to be able to speak. For my dialect bore this stamp, which gradually deprived me of speech altogether. So it occurred to me that when I speak French nobody would notice I came from a *puszta*. At most, they might notice that I am Hungarian. And as such I would blend into equality with the millions who speak French with a foreign accent. Hence, unlike others, it is not national but class isolation that I wanted to break away from," he wrote in 1963 in his essay "Hála a második anyanyelvért" ("Thanks to the second mother-tongue") dealing with French language and literature.

He was sixteen when the Austro-Hungarian Monarchy collapsed at the end of October 1918; in the next three-quarters of a year he witnessed the failure of the bourgeois revolution, and the fall of the Republic of Councils. He was there, arms in hand, when the eastern front of the Republic collapsed, and he participated in the support action on behalf of the relatives of the political prisoners. He had to emigrate.

He lived in Paris for five years, until 1926.

"Paris was freely and refreshingly infinite, like the puszta itself. It was not merely a matter of French civilization. There was even a Parisian civilization. Its main accomplishment is that even in crowd one has the right to be alone. My self-confidence was enhanced by my belief that one could step into the apartment of a writer as one would into a museum, into an old church, into other public places . . . And they received me at all hours with exemplary self-control . . . In his flat in Montmartre . . . (Paul) Reverdy lit a slice of paper from a small oil lamp at a picture of the Virgin between two Picasso masterpieces, and then lit the wick under the samovar to make tea. He talked to me, and made me talk" ("Thanks to the second mother-tongue.")

In his autobiographical narrative *Hunok Párizsban* (*Huns in Paris,* 1946) Illyés describes Tristan Tzara's moving kindness and attentiveness. He was also witness to the production of the pamphlet "The Carrion" by young surrealists at the time of the death of Anatole France.

"It was Paris that made me Hungarian," he wrote elsewhere.

In 1934, in *The People of the Puszta,* he wrote: "Those who set out from the farm servants' dwellings to become human beings regularly cast aside and forget their origins at first, like tadpoles becoming frogs. This is the road of progress and there is no other. Those who desert the air of the pusztas must acquire new hearts and lungs, otherwise they die in their new environment. And if they ever want to get back there, they must compass the world to do so."

"I myself went through the stages of this agonizing metamorphosis and only after the sixth or seventh stage did I become enough of a man to tackle the puszta."

The work of his life since his return home or, if we need pinpoint a date, since the publication of his first volume of poems, *Nehéz föld* (*A hard land*) in 1928, is a record of this undertaking.

The metamorphosis described by Illyés, the leaving and returning, and later the process of undertaking, are all well known psychological phenomena; the confessions of a number of artists, scientists, and politicians bear it out. Illyés was not the only one who did not slam the door behind himself after the metamorphosis. But every kind of fidelity is unique and indivisible, and even in the most difficult times Illyés remained faithful to his French experience, to the spirit of the *république des lettres* which he seems to have acquired in the company of dadaists and surrealists.

In 1942, when Hungary was an ally of Fascist Germany, it was he who edited (and translated in part) the anthology *A francia irodalom kincsesháza* (*The treasure-house of French literature.*) He wrote in the preface:

"How can one express gratitude to an entire nation? Since Bessenyei and Petőfi how many Hungarians have become richer from the wealth of the French spirit? Translation work is a mark of homage. I would like to present this collection of homages as the expression of our gratitude at this difficult moment of the French nation."

The anthology introduced French literature from the first text in verse in the vernacular, the Cantilène of Sainte Eulalie (881) to Péguy and Apollinaire, including the works of poets, prosewriters, and moralists. Although part of a series, it was an occasional collection: a political and artistic programme, the praise of the French spirit, the defence of the "open door", in the third year of the Second World War. And, like the Bartók poem, it stood the test of time, and remains to this day among the best, the most stimulating introduction to French thought in the Hungarian language.

Between 1942 and March 1944 Illyés was a literary power, the editor, of the periodical *Magyar Csillag*. This was the most prestigious literary periodical of the time in Hungary. Illyés believed, quite consciously, the periodical to be an arm of resistance, a "corrall" into which all values could be collected and preserved. When, as a result of the Race Law (à la Nürnberg) the Hungarian writers of Jewish descent found themselves excluded from literature, Illyés opened up the periodical to them in spite of attacks from the extreme right. Not Illyés, but the interested parties testify that he saved lives in this manner. Incidentally, his youthful experiences with the workers' movement and the reminiscences about his contacts with French writers recorded in *Huns in Paris* began to appear in *Magyar Csillag*. This too required some courage. The German occupation of the country on March 19, 1944, forced him into hiding.

The leading periodical of the great literary renaissance at the beginning of the century was *Nyugat* (1908–1941), often referred to as a Hungarian version of the *Nouvelle Revue Française*. One of the respected collaborators of *Nyugat* from the very start, and its editor during the last decade was Mihály Babits (1883–1941), the liberal Catholic poet, novelist, essayist, and translator. One of his most significant works was the *Európai irodalom története* (*The history of European literature*); and it was precisely Illyés who wrote the preface to its German edition. In the introduction to the *Open door* Illyés proved again a disciple of Babits: "Supra-national literature, read everywhere alike, preceded national literatures", he argued.

Among those who began writing between the two world wars there were barely any who did not learn one thing or another from Babits; likewise there were but few who did not turn on Babits passionately for a longer or shorter period of time. Perhaps there never has been a writer so fiercely berated by friends and opponents of merit.

Soon after his return from Paris Illyés became a close and faithful friend to Babits, by fifteen years his senior; he also became one of the main contributors of *Nyugat*. After the death of Babits, when the officials of the Horthy regime made the continuation of the "liberal-destructive" periodical impossible, Illyés received permission to launch *Magyar Csillag*. This review became a rallying point for the most diverse views; it became the mouthpiece of progressive creative artists and writers, including the "populists."

It is possible to date the beginnings of the "populist" movement with fair accuracy by the publication of a certain article. In 1933, Illyés published in *Nyugat* a warning about the destruction threatening the peasantry of Western Hungary. The article elicited a considerable response, and soon led to the formation of a group of writers who were wont to identify the peasantry with the nation (or, to be more exact, the nation with the peasants). The members of the populist movement, however, were not exclusively of peasant origin, as Illyés reminds us. For instance, their periodical was edited by György Sárközi, who started under the influence of Neo-Catholicism somewhere close to Babits and who, because of his Jewish descent, fell victim to the National Socialist terror.

It is not my task to write about the populists here, although I feel justified in regarding them as the most significant Hungarian intellectual movement between the two world wars. I need only mention that we are not dealing with a unified movement at all; that its own semiofficial historian excluded precisely Illyés and László Németh, preferring to describe Illyés as a disciple of Babits, and Németh as a "loner." This ostracism, however, did not prevent Illyés either then or now, from identifying himself with the attitudes of the populists. And something else. Those conversations I owe to Illyés, to which I had referred above, have convinced me that the "populist" movement was not as peculiarly Hungarian as its opponents, or its biased supporters, would often have it. The social and national problems of the peasantry, the problem of national identification, the relationship of rural and urban, from the turn of the century to our days, in Europe and beyond Europe, in this century or that, at this time or that, have become topical issues. Illyés himself had always said so himself.

It is characteristic of Illyés after his metamorphosis, after he found his calling, that he stood up for his views on the "open door" not only in the sixties and seventies, but also during the decade and a half before 1945, when it was most dangerous. He has always remained faithful to Babits, although several of his companions among the populists had attacked the great poet, considering him as just about the enemy number one; and Illyés has always remained faithful to the populists as well, even during the most diverse attacks against them, before 1945 and after, from the right and from the left; and he has remained always faithful to the dadaists and surrealists, although this faith was likewise not without peril either before 1945, during the Fascist period, or after, in the years of dogmatism. Almost alone among the thinkers of our century Illyés deems that we can only be faithful to the principles of social progress and to universal culture, by leaning on national culture and traditions.

This triple faith, in the populists, in Babits, and in the surrealists, is embodied in masterpieces such as *The People of the Puszta* (1936), his biography of *Petőfi* (1936), or *Magyarok* (*Hungarians*), a collection of essays and diary notes published in 1939, and in hundreds of poems as well (but I would also refer to his plays). *The People of the Puszta* is actually an overture to the sociological and literary movement by means of which the populists sought to uncover, document, and change the life of the peasantry. His Petőfi biography of 1936 asserts in a straightforward and provocative way, in contrast to the conservative, official interpretation of the time, that Petőfi was a poet of the revolution, and that this revolution had become, if possible, more timely than ever. This piece of writing was also incidental, just like his *People of the Puszta*, and it too became a classic; both dealt with the most burning daily problems. And their increasing effect at home and abroad proves, after more than forty years, that Illyés had been using lasting materials and created lasting works. Incidentally, this also applies to the far less familiar *Hungarians* in which we find side by side essays dealing with the misery of the peasant, the threat to the nation, and Tzara.

Furthermore, all this is particularly characteristic of his poetry. One of his poems of more than forty years ago, one of the most important pertaining to the populist movement, was described as follows by the English poet Eric Mottram in *The New Hungarian Quarterly*: "Illyés **'The Wonder Castle'** is a major example of how to get explicitly social consciousness into a poem, without turning the work into a documentary or a form of propaganda."

This lengthy lyrical work is practically a summing-up of everything that has preoccupied Illyés in *The People of the Puszta, Petőfi,* and *Hungarians*. I will quote two excerpts. An invitation to a dinner in a swanky residential area of Budapest gives the poet the occasion to talk about contrasts and confrontations. Thus, he meditates while the cog-wheel railway climbs the hill:

> . . . I felt I was climbing
> up the Hill straight from the puszta's

evening fields, where many times
I'd written out day-labourer's schedules.

I'll tell you why I thought that way,
looking at the ticket in my hand
in my seat on the Cog-Wheel Railway:
for should a peasant have a mind
to take the self-same ride,
he'd dig for his ticket an entire working day.
At home seventy fillérs is a whole day's pay.

And this was how he saw the upper-class neighbourhood:

. . . With the old look-out tower
it was like a magic castle,
the terrifying or happy
seat of some Asiatic deity
found only in Hungarian or Vogul folk-tale,
called Castle Spinning on a Duck's Leg: Wonder
                                                            Castle.

In 1934 he met Malraux in Moscow, at the first congress of Soviet writers. (By the way, Illyés had written an excellent account of his trip, acceptable even now, in fact, reissued under the title *Oroszország* [*Russia*].) During the sixties, Malraux, as a member of the Government, received a delegation of Hungarian writers, of which Illyés was a member; the meeting was recorded by Illyés in one of his most memorable essays.

On the day of the burial I was reading Malraux's *Lazare* which had just seen print; and I also happened to pick up the book Illyés had written seven years earlier, and which exists in French and a number of other languages. *Kháron ladikján* (*Charon's ferry*). Was it the time and the place? The two books frightfully resembled each other. Not because of the style, and not because of their topic taken in the narrow sense. Rather because of the passion with which both authors interrogate death; because of the ruthless objectivity with which they look at themselves; because of their rejection of every form of cheap consolation. And because both appeal to human solidarity. For decades, both had been preoccupied with the problems of death and of creation. Illyés writes in "Charon's ferry": "Actually old age is the only worthwhile question any imaginable philosophy may ask."

In 1926, as he returned from Paris, Illyés met the problem of death. He was concerned with the nightmare of national death, as were many Hungarian writers before him, and the problem of human death, the death of the individual without the shelter of religious faith—actually for the first time in Hungarian literature. During four decades, varying according to place, time, occasion, age, Illyés had written about death unflinchingly. To resort once again to the metaphor I have used many times already, here too Illyés opened doors: he joined, without appeal, the individual being to the social being. When he pays attention to a class, to a nation, and to nations in general (since even geographically speaking his interests become ever more catholic, the years having only enhanced his curiosity and his worries), he never forgets about the individual human

being, and vice versa. And he formulates this unity, in the spirit of the *Open door* of the *Free feast,* and of the **Handshakes** in the epilogue to his poem **"The Maker"** (**"Teremteni"**):

With these mortal eyes
to learn what I am here to do,
the job that waits for me to do it,
for which, somewhere,
a peasant, hoeing, sends me this
glass of wine,
a worker touching down his soldering-iron
sent light
into my room,
to find with mortal eyes
the eternal task:
Make the future speak!
—already it is quarreling with death,

skillfully, intelligent,
bustling, with
authority.

To do the job
well, to our liking
—yes, like good
love-making.

Almost stroking its face
in gratitude.

To leave it there,
to look back a few times
on the one who lies there satisfied;
she keeps my riches,
conceiving my future,
the meaning, maybe forever, of all
I was here for,

Mortal, imperishable.

Thus wrote Illyés in 1968, almost a decade ago, when he was 66.

*Teremteni*—(literally: "to create") the title of the poem and of the volume, the title of the second volume of his collected verse, covering the period 1946 to 1968. It is a key word, sibling to *Open door, Free feast,* and **Handshakes**. At 75 Illyés continues to work, to create, faithful to himself, and without repeating himself. The work shapes him and he shapes with his work. To despair, illness, old age, nightmares he replies with work that has become a ceremonial act. Jean Follain knew about him that "he offers us communion without reservations or literary artifices with the joys and sorrows of the present; but he is always caught again by amazements that bear witness to hope."

**Mátyás Domokos  (essay date 1982)**

SOURCE: "Gyula Illyés, A Living Classic," in *The New Hungarian Quarterly,* Vol. 23, No. 88, Winter, 1982, pp. 9-22.

[*In the following essay, Domokos defines Illyés's "clas-sicism"—the strength of his poetry due to its complete integration with the Europe in which it was created.*]

Gyula Illyés's first pieces were published in the begin-ning of the twenties in Hungarian and international clas-sical avant-garde magazines. Since then, from over fifty published volumes and innumerable other writings as yet unpublished in book form, a many-sided artistic world emerges, whose every individual manifestation must al-ways have been found astonishingly new, disturbingly original and exciting by his readers—to borrow the title of one of his late poems, each piece belongs to "the world of eternal works of art." The author himself is considered one of the truest, one of the most representa-tive of Hungarian writers. His great fellow-poet and friend, L őrinc Szabó, justly wrote of him in 1956: "All the citizens of Hungary—no, even the whole of our cultural life of the future, shall forever remain in his debt." He is instinctively and naturally thought of as a living classic by the literary and intellectual Hungarian public.

Illyés's pen does not bind him to any one particular lit-erary genre. He has been writing poetry and prose, essays and drama, polemical pamphlets and literary sociology for six decades, expressing himself with the same pas-sionate clarity in short newspaper articles, many-tomed biographically inspired novels, diaries and philosophical treatises alike. It would be hard to determine which part of his own writing he considers the most important: the essays that celebrate the spirit, the variety, the expres-siveness, the vividness of the Hungarian language; the journalistic pieces intended to shape, analyse or redress the historical consciousness of the Hungarian people while illuminating current questions of vital importance; the translations, the artistic virtuosity of interpreting, with unfaithful fidelity, the messages of foreign poetic worlds; or that which we consider after the French as the "at-tempting of the impossible," the expression of that which cannot be told except in verse. In other words, his is a universal literary spirit, continually inspired, active in all literary fields, and producing work of lasting validity.

But what is the meaning of this *epitheton ornans,* on what is it based? It is based on the unity of the life and the work, on the artistic realisation of this unity. Yet is it right, is one entitled, in an aesthetic sense, to judge a work in the light of our knowledge of the facts of the personal life of the author, to place the facts of that life upon the precision-scales of the ideas professed in the work of art? T. S. Eliot, in his essay *Tradition and the Individual Talent,* emphatically declares that "the honest critic and the sensitive judge is not interested in the poet as a person, but in his poetry." Illyés himself is among those who object to a critic's vivisection of the personal life of the artist (he usually cites Maupassant, who wrote in a letter to a friend: "I don't like the public barging in on my life . . . My life is my own . . . Everything I have written belongs to the public, to the critics, is open to discussion and curiosity, but I do not want anything that relates to my way of living or my person to be cried from the housetops."

Illyés himself knows that the biography of a poet has always more to offer, is always richer and thus more enlightening than an ordinary, everyday biography, and is necessary for a deeper, more complete understanding of the poet's work—if he did not know it he would not have sown his œuvre with biographical references, ex-amples and allusions. In art, as in life, experience lived is the most irrefutable argument if it has undergone a metamorphosis of sorts. Eliot knew this well, writing in his study of *Hamlet,* as if continuing the above-cited thought: "*Qua* work of art, the work of art cannot be interpreted; there is nothing to interpret; we can only criticize it according to standards, in comparison to oth-er works of art; and for 'interpretation' the chief task is the presentation of relevant historical facts which the reader is not assumed to know." Which seems an insol-uble task within the limits of an essay of determined length, since in the case of a Hungarian poet, because of linguistic and other barriers, almost every historical fact can be considered as unfamiliar to the foreign reader. This is why I am taking the liberty of outlining a rudi-mentary biography in order to characterize the nature of Illyés's classicism from the personal side as well.

Gyula Illyés is known throughout the world primarily as the author of *The People of the Puszta (Puszták népe,* 1936) since this, invariably moving autobiographical novel appearing in the guise of literary sociology is the work which has been translated into the most languages. (In New Zealand it became compulsory reading material as a guide to the true nature of European feudalism.) He was in actual fact born on a "puszta," on the 2nd of November in 1902 in Felső-Rácegres, at a time when Hungary was still part of the Dual Monarchy. Though his mother had rocked his cradle in front of a mechanic's house, a large step away from a farm labourer's dwell-ings, they were nevertheless inhabitants of the Trans-danubian countryside, a bleak and dreary wilderness which, though Illyés has called it the "fairy valley" of his childhood, bears in reality little resemblance to the pho-tographs found in travel agencies, embellished by com-mercial romanticism. (The Transdanubian *puszta* means the miserable dwellings of farmhands and labourers on big estates, while on the Great Plains it means the infi-nite flat steppe.) As a "young dog" his spirit and intellect were matured by the agitated years and bloody events of the First World War, and the self-imposed study of the French language was a first sign of that longing, that yearning after education, enlightenment, the radiance of European culture, which was to characterize his life. During the age of revolutions and counter-revolutions following the "golden age" of Francis Joseph, his Beat-rice was the Goddess of Revolution, unattainable through-out the history of mankind, and as her romantically ar-duous teen-age knight he came into contact with the struggling Hungarian labour movement—as a consequence of which he had to escape to Paris when he was barely twenty, and remained there in exile for five years. After his return in 1926 he became one of the mainstays of the last significant Hungarian avant-garde magazine, the *Do-kumentum,* founded by Kassák; then he joined the ranks of the leading contributors to *Nyugat,* a literary magazine of the highest standard, which revived Hungarian literature from the beginning of the century, expressing the direction, the spirit, the atmosphere of this revival in its chosen title—West. After the death of Mihály Babits, the editor of the magazine, Illyés became editor-in-chief of *Magyar Csillag,* which continued in the *Nyugat* tradition and became in turn a stronghold of European left-wing humanism, until forced to cease publication when German troops occupied Hungary. Illyés spent the last months of the war in hiding. In the post-war world he reorganized and edited the magazine *Válasz,* which was devoted to the cause of the village proletariat. Since *Válasz* ceased publication on official orders at the end of the forties, he has lived for his writing only, but his work, ideals and behaviour have always been the subject of invariably passionate debate.

This much should have become clear from this bird's-eye view of the author's life (which is also the reason why I thought it worth giving): though Illyés has lived through seven forms of government, which, in historical terms, can be divided into at least a dozen extremely distinct, at times sharply contradictory periods, he is among those who can have the rare satisfaction of never having had to rewrite or disclaim a single line of his life-work in this ever-moving, ever-changing East-Central European world. This is the constant moral co-ordinate of his living classicism; to this he owes his permanent, large reading public—and to this consistent moral attitude, characteristic of the whole of his œuvre, he has owed the outbursts of jealousy and "foaming hatred." His œuvre has thus weathered the storms of changing opinions and turbulent passions, from which it would appear that he has found a conscientious solution to the objective moral dilemma which haunts the modern artist (and not only in Hungary). Thanks to the moral integrity of his personal life his work bears the stamp of authenticity without having to resort to spectacular-romantic gestures or wild heroic scenes; it nevertheless safeguards his work from moral wear and tear.

However, Gyula Illyés is originally and ultimately a poet; moreover, a poet of avant-garde instigations. In Paris as a young man he had been part of that company of poets who had begun to form a new French avant-garde which counted among its members Aragon, Eluard, Crevel, Max Jacob, Breton, Cocteau, Desnos, Vaillant-Couturier, Malraux, Supervielle, and the pope: Tristan Tzara. Not only had he been part of the company, he had also written and published hair-raisingly modern poems in French. Is it not sacrilegious, or to look upon things from another angle, can it not be thought old-fashioned pedantry to speak of "classicism" in the case of a poetic œuvre emerging from the cascade of the permanent revolution of modern poetry—a poetic œuvre which has remained loyal to certain fundamental laws of that poetic revolution? And what can, after all, be considered the criterion and possibility of classicism, in a process whose single invariable trait is undefinability and permanent uncertainty, a trait which, to all intents and purposes, connects modern poetry with quantum physics?

Let us imagine (if we can) that an unprejudiced, uncommitted, critical mind sets out to write the precise and true history of the newest epoch of European poetry. It is clear that we must imagine the impossible: the "perfect critic," who, with infinite knowledge and an all-encompassing gaze, is capable of bringing order and method into the chaos which began in the middle of the last century, in the summer of 1857, when Baudelaire's *Les Fleurs du Mal* was published. This chaos dates back more than a hundred years and is invariably called "modern poetry" by general agreement throughout the world (as if its inspiring Muse were related to those beautiful ladies who have a past but are ageless). If this ideal critic wished to penetrate the theoretical clouds surrounding this chaotically swirling modern poetical world from its cradle, his pragmatic passions will find that the process originates—paradoxically—in Hegel's aesthetics, who predicted the death of poetry from his professor's desk at the Berlin university, irrefutably asserting that art shall step "from the poetry of the imagination into the prose of thought," because poetry is "that strange art in which art itself begins to disintegrate," to be replaced by the prose of scientific thought.

> **Thanks to the moral integrity of his personal life his work bears the stamp of authenticity without having to resort to spectacular-romantic gestures or wild heroic scenes; it nevertheless safeguards his work from moral wear and tear.**
>
> —*Mátyás Domokos*

The outcome (which seems to be a malicious trick that history plays to demonstrate how unsuccessful futurologists and theoretical soothsayers and prophets of the spirit are) is well-known by all. Contrary to Hegel's gloomy prophecy (and probably without his knowledge) Rimbaud completed the revolution in contemporary poetry within the "inner age of imagination and sensibility" (Hegel) with the categoric imperative of *Il faut être absolument modernel.* Instead of decaying, poetry began to flourish, a phenomenon which we can bear witness to even today. Bear witness to—and endure. Because parallel with the birth of never before experienced, gloriously new poetic worlds, a symptomatic Badness is becoming ever more apparent, a badness more ignominious than the predicted painless death: it is the general, almost irredeemable discrediting of the modern poetic word, of modern poetry. To be aware of this it is unnecessary to attend the arrival of the ideal critic of one's imagination. No humble but honest commentator of modern poetry can turn a deaf ear to the loud complaints of the reading public (complaints whose validity, if he is not tone-deaf, and if his honesty is stronger than his snobbishness, his own reading experience will affirm). Our contemporary poetry, especially its neo-avant-garde, reflects to a lesser and lesser extent those vital historical, social, moral, and metaphysical problems of our age that fill human existence with almost unbearable tension and anguish and upon whose precise artistic description and implacably truthful artistic interpretation the spiritual life, the future—the very existence of humanity—may depend.

It is not so long ago that Fernand Léger, the man who transformed the everyday mythology of the twentieth century into modern yet timelessly universal images, the brilliant painter friend of Apollinaire, Max Jacob, Reverdy, Cendrars, Cézanne, Henri Rousseau, Picasso, and Braque, defined the fundamental problem and test of modern art as that of "being free yet not losing contact with reality." It is this, the contact with reality, that seems to have been lost in the all-inundating silt of contemporary modern poetry; this is why it leaves unanswered the agonizing questions of contemporary man, why it remains silent in the face of the agonizing emptiness. For how can it give heed to Max Jacob's counsel, according to which "modern poetry is the world in man," if it is unable to retain its contact with these two fundamental realities? If its aimlessness must be compensated for by fashions, fads and theories, if it has lost the significance of its freedom by not knowing what to do with these two realities, with man and the world in the widest sense of the word, in which the surrealism of dreams is as real as history, politics, or love, or the facts, passions, interior and exterior excitements of the intellect which the human heart can still wish to see as the possible material of modern poetry, as in the times of Virgil, Dante, or Baudelaire . . .

Artistic freedom perceiving reality in a new way: classicism cannot be imagined without it. But what is the hormone of this classicism? For simplicity allow me to quote Eliot once again: "If there is one word on which we can fix, which will suggest the maximum of what I mean by the term 'a classic,' it is the word *maturity*." This maturity, one must add, is the artistic method of handling, of manipulating, reality and all poetry incapable of attaining that maturity with creative originality within the historical period of the language and civilisation in which it appears is unavoidably devalued and discredited in the eyes of humanity. "Maturity of mind: this needs history, and the consciousness of history," adds the author of *The Waste Land* in *What is a Classic*. "Consciousness of history cannot be fully awake, except where there is other history than the history of the poet's own people. We need this in order to see our own place in history. There must be the knowledge of the history of at least one other highly civilized people . . ."

For Gyula Illyés this maturity of the spirit, the original artistic contact with reality and the consciousness of history in Eliot's sense of the word, was achieved during the five years of exile in Paris between 1921 and 1926. The weekdays spent in physical labour and as a trade union activist, the holidays spent on the terraces of the Dôme, the Coupole and the Flore in the company of the young revolutionaries in art made him familiar with the history of another, widely cultured people, made it part of his destiny. And the history of France, according to

Illyés, "is principally characterized by striving for lucidity." It was through this lucidity that he was able to recognize his poetic material and his own place in history. It is almost symbolical that the most significant pieces of his first volume of verse, *Tough Land* (*Nehéz Föld*), published in 1928, which attracted immediate attention for its originality and modernity, the pieces which reflected Hungarian conditions according to the harmonics of the most modern French poetry, were all written in Paris. Bewitched by the surrealist word-cinema, it was nevertheless without volition or intention that the image of **"The Sad Field-hand"** (**"Szomorú béres"**) arose in his mind and was put to paper immediately—on a bench on the Ile Saint Louis, opposite the Palace Lambert.

"Actually, the reason why I am grateful to Paris," declared the eighty-year-old poet recently, "is because it was upon my return from there that I discovered—the world. I could have gone back, I had the opportunity. But it was with my Paris mind that I realised that this material, this place was mine; that if anywhere, this is where I must work . . . If I hadn't have gone to Paris, I would never have understood it." And however strange it may sound, this is how the "Hungarian abyss," *The People of the Puszta,* the awe-inspiring, incendiary book dealing with the life of the field-hands, enriched by biographical elements, was born—and could only have been born—out of the most typical avant-garde gesture and passion. Gide's *Voyage au Congo,* published a little earlier, encouraged and stimulated him to describe the "natives" of Central Europe, the suffocatingly hopeless life of tens of thousands living from hand to mouth in virtual serfdom: the life of those who "are to suffer corporeal punishment only until the age of forty," because, later, a telling off was enough to bring tears to their eyes. (Let me repeat that this was in the first third of the twentieth century, in the centre of Europe!) "I am more or less Gyula Illyés's fellow-countryman," wrote Mihály Babits, one of the leading figures of the artistic revolution which revived Hungarian literature. "But I read this book, full of incomparably rich and authentic experiences, as if I was reading an exciting travelogue about a so-far undiscovered continent and its natives, as if I myself were part of the expedition—all the more sensational and exciting as the continent chances to be the land of my birth." And the most shocking discovery—one may safely say its avantgarde novelty—for Babits as for every reader was that the people of the puszta are—servants; since "the puszta," writes Babits, "exists in our imagination as the idyllic land of freedom."

In Illyés's case the moment of creating modern poetical contact with reality coincided with the historical moment in Hungarian poetry when, to quote Babits, "the phoenix of Hungarian populist poetry was reborn." This same moment arrived throughout Europe, in the lyrical poetry of the twenties and thirties from Esenin to Lorca, as though poets from Leningrad to Granada had suddenly become aware, through the secret channels of inspiration (originating in Burns perhaps) that twentieth century civilisation would efface the old, traditional peasant way of life from the sociological map of Europe. The poets who belonged to this layer of society by birth felt it their mission to sing the swan-song of this disappearing world and human culture. Illyés himself wrote his poems in awareness of this: "A hundred dead peasants had to sing | furrowed brows bent over ploughs | that I should one day join their host | and open my mouth in song. | Fly high, my words, cry loud, my memories, | shout out, my people | I am singing your song." (**"Three old men"**, **"Három öreg"**, 1931. Prose translation.)

The most general "material" co-ordinate of Illyés's living classicism, of the maturity of his handling of his poetic material is this sociological reality. It is from this that he derives the concreteness of his poetic language, images and perception, whose inspiring sentiments and passions are fed by the primary human experiences of childhood: the continuous, nostalgic attachment to the world of the poor. "We were simple poor people" he wrote, describing this attachment in the prose volume *Like the Cranes* (*Mint a Darvak,* 1942) in an almost biblical idiom in the beginning of the forties, "and like the sage wanted nothing from life except simple living . . . My childhood in the puszta—with its mysteries and hardships—was more unhappy than happy . . . but if we were happy sometimes, it was because we were poor, because all the people around us were poor, that is, workers; that is, manual labourers . . . The secret of what life was could only be discovered through them. They are still in contact with what creation was for. Contrary to all appearances, I must maintain that only the poor know how to live, they alone know what life is, they alone can identify themselves with it . . . The most valuable spiritual part of humanity can be found in the infinite host of the poor." Stronger than the determination of his origins, stronger than the recognition of his poetic material, it was this conviction that led Illyés to join the ranks of those writers who acted as the spokesmen for the poor, for the Hungarian village proletariat. From the middle of the thirties he was one of those writers who ruthlessly and realistically depicted village conditions between the two world wars. What they did, politically speaking, was to defend human rights with the devices of art, in the spirit of Helsinki, but preceding it by forty years.

The unbroken contact with social reality and his own Voltairean spirit luckily safeguarded Illyés from treating the "divine" people or its synonym, the poor, as a myth. "It was not poverty, but the poor | that I praised to my heart's content," wrote Illyés at the end of the Second World War, on the eve of the great changes which would radically transform the aspect, the structure and the hierarchy of Hungarian society. "I profess—let there be an end to poverty!" writes Illyés in **"One Year"** (**"Egy év,"** 1945); but also "Change, but without changing"—in other words, let the poor preserve the "most valuable part of their spiritual selves," their old, high moral standards in spite of the temptations that are the trappings of power.

Once again he recognized the impending dangers as a revolutionary poet, as the avant-garde, the "vanguard" of artistic and social revolutions should. He recognised the impending dangers of the preconditional interdependence

of the instinct to tyranny and the instinct to servility which resulted in the numerous human, political and historical dramas of the fifties—and which provided him with material for his plays. *The Minion* (*A kegyenc*), an adaptation of a nineteenth century play, for example, clothed this century's lust for power in the garb of Roman history. It was first presented at the Vieux Colombier theatre in Paris at the beginning of the sixties. And if the classicism of Illyés has a political co-ordinate, more complex than that which is concerned with the tactics of everyday politics, it must be looked for he resolves the dilemma of political action and morality. It can be found in the conviction that man cannot be disloyal to the moral inheritance which entitled him to take part in the formation of history, an inheritance acquired and created through much suffering and pain. To this he cannot be disloyal even if his social circumstances change, even if he is under the spell of a certain goal.

Through the unrestrained contact with the realities of the century, Gyula Illyés's life-work, especially his poetry, is capable of dealing with subjects which resolve the schisms apparent in modern lyrical poetry since Mallarmé. His is the poetic synthesis of all the opportunities offered by European avant-garde and Hungarian classical traditions and it presents, in poems, be they in prose or in classical form, that philosophical reality or awareness of life that was brought to light by the end of the twentieth century. It is perhaps unnecessary to say that in our days it is to this that Illyés's classicism, his artistic, moral and intellectual maturity owes its most exciting results. But this was inherent in his poetic nature from the beginnings in Paris. Because Illyés has always been "a poet of many instincts," as his contemporary, László Németh diagnosed him. "There are some poems of Illyés which make me say that folk-songs shall never grow out of date," he wrote of **Tough Land** (**Nehéz föld**) in 1928, in a review of Illyés's first volume. But folk-poetry is only one of his impulses. Another is Horace and Virgil, via the poems of Hungarian romanticism. He can diffuse the atmosphere, the enthusiasm of Latin lyrical poetry in the form of avant-garde vers libre. The third poetic impulse of this rational poet, Voltaire-like in spirit, against all obscurity in poetry, was that faculty of abstraction of which László Németh wrote: "his most concrete images are somehow full of intimations of metaphysics." Over and above the images, his poetry on the whole—in fact, his inspiration—is full of "metaphysical intimations" and since the end of the fifties he too has been leading (as his master, Babits did "as the fisherman of an eternal current") a new poetic crusade into "Nothingness." These existentialist poems are naturally not the revelations of a dogmatic philosophy: they express the mysteries of philosophy, the agonizing ecstasy and drama of thinking. The single worthy—or, if you like, distressing—metaphysical question for Illyés, the question which emanates the atmosphere of philosophy in recent poems, is the question of Non-Existence. In point of fact it is a question that almost corresponds to the problem of suicide raised in the essays of Camus. But the difference is enormous. Illyés does not wish to provide the unavoidable metaphysical questions of existence with solutions of a metaphysical nature. He prefers to give earthly—materi-alistic—answers. Illyés's crusade into Heidegger's Noth-ingness, his struggles with the thought of death, with the agonizingly absurd question—Can death be defeated?—are concluded, through his original approach to the prob-lem, in a manner new to modern Hungarian and Europe-an poetry. His materialistic conception of the universe leaves him without a God, without transcendence—with-out the possibility of belief in survival which gave solace to Christian humanity through hundreds of years, provid-ing them with the final meaning of life, a recipe written on the pages of the Bible. Illyés, however, does not worship the idols of his own materialistic convictions. He asks his own questions, starting from the premises of a new state of existence. He is capable of discerning the changes wrought in the collective consciousness—and the collective subconscious—of humanity towards the end of this century, the consequences of which are evident: the world has lost its gods, the world has lost transcen-dence. But the consequences of this loss are not as ob-vious, as if we were afraid to reflect upon the life we are living. Yet if there is no God, if transcendence has gone like a dream, then the new, non-metaphysical interpreta-tion of death lays the duty of giving an entirely new interpretation of life on the poet. The mission of the poet, as the late poems of Illyés affirm, is to keep these questions alive—to help man find his new place, his new "consciousness of existence" in a life without God.

What is the meaning of life, and can it have any mean-ing if death awaits us as the end, inevitably but totally senselessly? This question was planted in the conscious-ness of ontologically orphaned man with unbearable poignancy by the existentialists. Illyés does not accept the question as a starting point because he is an existen-tialist; he feels with an acute poetic instinct that the existentialists, Camus among them, have simply given a definition to that distressing, instinctive feeling which in the absence of a rational, that is, an acceptable and re-assuring answer, can lead to the most varied excesses in the practical and moral—and historical—way of contem-porary living; all this is due to the devaluation of moral norms and restraints based on old metaphysical illusions. Life has become dull, mass-produced, hopelessly manip-ulated. "Life is not worth the effort it takes to sustain it"—this is perhaps Georg Büchner's most bitter thought, voiced by the disenchanted Camille Desmoulins in a play (*The Death of Danton*) written some hundred and fifty years ago. Georg Büchner's bitterness today is a general experience and a general item of evidence. Yet it is this degraded, defenceless, pointlessly but skillfully tortured and subdued life that seems the most important, the only value in the eyes and consciousness of the world, a value whose hedonistic sustenance thus justifies any means. "Only the apes suffer" in front of the mirrors of their conscience, says Büchner.

Illyés knows that this question—which on a philosoph-ical level cannot be considered the concern of many—is at the same time an ever more absurd practical contra-diction. For the most part it is unformulated or uncon-scious, but nevertheless poisons every minute of our lives in the form of mass anxiety, and is thus one of the most vital problems of our life today. This is the reason why Illyés the poet accepts the superhuman and absurd chal-lenge of the question. The intellectual poems of his most recent period indicate that his answers are not limited to metaphysical solace, nor to the moving expression of the sufferings of the solitary Self under the depression of passing time, as often happens in the better examples of modern lyrical poetry. Illyés would like to find a com-munal answer to this most personal, yet most general question, an answer which counteracts the consciousness of certain defeat—of death—by-passing the earlier meta-physical beliefs and illusions of historical man.

At all events, this is the most delicate question of poetry and of Existence, and it is a sure sign of Illyés's matu-rity—of his classicism—that to deal with this most ago-nizing and most harsh reality of our time, he is coura-geous enough to be a modern poet who is not ashamed of being intelligible. That which cannot be expressed by human words, which, as Montaigne wrote, is "as hard to perceive as a flash of lightning"—that is where Illyés is at his clearest. This poet, who at a certain point in time incited a whole class to find a new place in society, who later urged a whole nation to a new conquest, would now, in the most personal and most deeply concerned messages of his latest poems, urge the whole of human-ity to create a new kind of domesticity for themselves—he urges on humanity which, he says, is always "on the road," its mode of existence being a procession of car-avans. "The host of humanity marches on," he writes, unfolding one of the basic metaphors of his œuvre, "marching since the beginnings of time. It drags itself along jungle paths and in marshes, then invents the wheel and travels in waggons, and soon the waggon can roll without its team of oxen. And at all times there are some who travel above the procession; they are those who seem to fly. They are conscious of something, of a certain goal. I am not thinking of the 'vanguard,' or the 'pio-neers,' nor of the 'leaders.' Those whom I am thinking of rarely voice their thoughts; they can be seen only in rare lucky moments. Nevertheless, they are the true lead-ers. There are but a few of them and are to humanity what salt is to goulash: without them the whole world would be just about bearable."

The instigator of Illyés's continual attraction to the no-tion of the road is probably the recognition of a primeval modelling principle. The *story* of art has portrayed hu-man life, the realization of human destinies from the be-ginnings of time—from Homer to the Gospels and the various legends on the quest of the Grail—always on the road. Cervantes sends his hero on a journey, as do the authors of the great epics, as does Goethe his Faust, as do the authors of Bildungsroman and the great Russian, English and French novels of the last century and this. (Kerouac's *On the Road* even emphasizes the conscious return to the myth and metaphor of the road in its title.) Literature expresses and realizes the "space-time" of human destiny in the metaphor of the road. But who is Illyés thinking of when he speaks about the true leaders of the procession? The fact that anyone who can offer a worthwhile human goal, belief—or at least a hope—may become a leader of the procession adds to the mystery, the beauty but also to the truth of the metaphor. And at least a volume of Illyés poems render probable the assumption that "surveyor" poets who bear the true knowledge of the meaning of the journey, of the relation between road and destination, are also among the leaders.

To be the vanguard of the procession as an intellectual, to be a true leader—this characteristically avant-garde virtue has been the historical role and tradition of Hungarian literature for centuries. To understand this the foreign reader must be aware of the historical fact—or, rather, of that series of events—which led authors from the sixteenth century onwards to sound another note on the lyre of Hungarian poetry, a note that is rarely heard in the poetry of other, luckier nations. (There are exceptional situations, such as that which made Aragon feel it his self-evident poetic duty to write on *La Nuit de Dunkerque* instead of on Elsa's eyes.) This note is the voice of the poet deeply concerned about the fate, the future, the survival, the existence of his nation, of those who speak the same mother-tongue. During the Middle Ages Hungary was a flourishing, prosperous, militarily efficient nation; which began to decline in consequence of the defeat at Mohács and the Turkish invasion. No longer self-governed, broken up into three large areas, the nation was left to fend for itself with no institutions of its own and its people lived in a perpetual awareness of death, ready to fight for survival, against annihilation. There were many periods during this decline when the maxim of Count Széchenyi, the most significant figure of Hungarian romanticism, pointed to the single perceptible manifestation, the single historical form of Hungarian national existence. The maxim was: "In its language a nation lives." During the Turkish occupation of Hungary the poetry of Balassi, Zrinyi, the romances and lays of protestant preachers, the university plays and the encyclopedias all served to preserve the national consciousness of the Hungarian people from the strongholds of the language. After the Turks had been driven out, the literature of the Hungarian enlightenment and romanticism performed the same role, counteracting the Germanizing politics of the Habsburgs. But this poetical role did not end with the appearance of Endre Ady and his companions, the founders of modern Hungarian lyrical poetry. In a sense it culminated in their work, in Ady's prophecies about the future of the Hungarian people, about their dispersion, the forced Diaspora, which history confirmed with terrible force after the fall of the Monarchy. Every third Hungarian-born person out of fifteen or sixteen million now lives anywhere in the world, from Alaska to the Cape Province.

In one of his studies Ortega writes that life is "continual endangerment, foundering on the open sea." The fundamental historical experience of the Hungarian people until the most recent times has been a series of shipwrecks upon the always stormy seas of East-Central Europe. The historical role of Hungarian lyrical poetry was not only determined by the fact that poets were existentially bound to the collective historical destiny of the nation, but was determined to the same extent and with the same intensity by the fact that the consciousness of the Hungarian people was existentially linked to the life-boats of its literature and poetry. This defined the spiritual and moral character of Hungarian lyrical poetry for centuries; this is what made Hungarian lyrical poetry sensitive towards national, social and political problems. An interest like this can only exist in countries where literature was forced into "résistance" for some length of time. This is one of the central "nerves" of the historical Hungarian lyrical sensibility. And it can be dissected out of four lines of Kölcsey's poem, now our national anthem, with the precision of anatomical sections: "The hunted hid, but in his den | a sword was tended to pierce him. | He looked around, but could not find | a home within his country." (Prose translation.)

This *poesis hungarica* nerve running through Illyés's poetry also developed through his meeting with a European mentality and art in his youth. Towards the end of the sixties he wrote: "The outlook, the artistic and social attitude that gave new colour, a new appearance to the conditions that I found at home was formed in the environs of the Sorbonne, in the literary cafés, at student debates and lectures for workers . . . This was why I was capable of seeing clearly the tragedy of Hungary and later of portraying it with the scope that Western artistic and political views had given me . . . and it was then that I recognized the true voice of Hungarian literature. The greatness of the language, its force of expression, but also its difficulties, which brought home to me with benumbing forcefulness the duty of the Hungarian poet, the duty of all humanists in this country. Above all the duty of those who are able to see local problems with the lucidity of a whole world. This is why, though I have always tried to express my thoughts as clearly as possible with the most modern devices, these thoughts were in point of fact the thoughts that had always haunted the authors of classical Hungarian literature. This may seem contradictory to some. But if I can throw a light upon the two influences that have governed me, I believe I can clarify my 'spiritual image.'"

This is the historical co-ordinate of his maturity, of his classicism and because of this there are some who (with the emphasis given to what is a little out of date) speak of him as "the last bard," the "last European national poet." Yet Illyés's poetry is in fact one of the most magnificent examples in modern art of the fact that personal problems, the problems of a nation and the problems of the world may easily be reconciled within a single poetic œuvre, since their conciliation is not simply a question of content but also of poetic attitude, and is realized according to the extent and quality of the poet's talent. Especially in an age which, one must admit, has not drawn a lesson from Voltaire's *Candide,* an age in which persecution, oppression and discrimination are not confined to politics, be they evoked by racial, national, religious or intellectual prejudice: they have become a general, universal state of existence. And they are what, if one is to preserve the vestiges of one's self-respect, poetry must exercise its right of veto against.

## Mátyás Domokos (interview date 1983)

SOURCE: "A Poet Taking Sides, " in *The New Hungarian Quarterly,* Vol. 24, No. 91, Autumn, 1983, pp. 14-26.

[*In the following interview, Illyés reveals his philosophies and opinions regarding a poet's beliefs and poetic responsibilities to the nation.*]

[Domokos]: *Gyula Illyés is 80 years old. Perhaps it would not be inopportune to talk with him on this day on the same topics as usual. Of poetry and ideas, on the position and opportunities for poetry today, its destiny and mission for man as the end of our century approaches. Perhaps it will not be inopportune to go directly into these topics and refer to something typical of what writers and artists have to face. I mean that more and more we hear that poets, literature and art are unable to answer the crucial historical, social and moral questions—the troubling questions of our time: on existence, on history, on society, and ethics. The questions on which will depend the life, the future of mankind, of Hungary. Even if there will be one. During a career now stretching over more than half a century, Gyula Illyés has believed and proclaimed that the primary duty of a poet is to answer these very questions with "a courageous tongue" and with "an ear listening into the future." So, what do you, Gyula Illyés, think of this devaluation of poetry in the public mind?*

[Illyés]: Readers resent poets because they cannot understand what they are reading, and poets resent readers even more for not treating properly what the poets are saying from the depths of their hearts. A reader today is certain to expect from poetry something rather different from what he actually gets. Poetry has become too enswaddled in too great a particularity and at the same time people have become less interested in particular destinies and more in public issues in art. These public issues have been expressed in poetry ever since the world began. Sometimes it is extremely difficult to give them a proper expression but that is when poets should in fact make a great effort to approach—not what their readers expect!—the artistic expression of truth. I do believe that there are no issues which cannot be effectively implanted in readers through art. People, and this is something else which cannot be denied, often expect the ready-made, they expect the poet to speak like a politician. But the voice of poetry can only be directed at eternity. It was no easier for Sándor Petőfi or Dániel Berzsenyi to write on public affairs than it is for a poet today. Well . . . in a way it was easier for them since they were both geniuses but in art genius is not the only . . . I mean, you have to actually begin . . . This is not to condemn, say, abstract poets who claim a little too loudly that it is they who are producing real poetry. Valéry's views on *la poésie pure* are well known. These are expropriated by everyone now, saying that the more the artistic elements are concealed, the superior the work is.

*You are saying that the poetic deed, the act of poetry, is to deal with public issues not in the manner of a politician but in the manner of a poet?*

No! The task of a poet is to express feelings and thoughts with a force that has the same impact on society as a victory on a battlefield. People are not sufficiently aware of this? . . . Because the poet's act is primarily an artistic act? I am not saying that a poet should not engage in politics. Today many poets say that they detest politics. But nobody detests politics: we all live in a community and we cannot deny this fact. I only try to keep a distance between myself and the low aspects of politics. But we *do* live in the *polis,* the community, and the poet has to be aware of this too.

*But whether through spite or lack of talent or the sense of restriction or even through the flippancy of the injured, we see in certain of the arts in this century that some writers have forgone public issues.*

I'll be direct: it is not merely a question of self-esteem or of being hurt, it is one of talent too. It is impossible to write poetry, to produce art, without inspiration or training. The less care we take over saying what art is, then the greater currency of the view that as an artist you must be absolutely an individual . . . I would go so far as to say that my own person, important though it is as a subject for poetry, is of little interest to me. Of course pleasure is an essential attribute of art. Art cannot exist if there is no pleasure, true. But this is only a short step away from affectation and another short step from self-content and from a mincing display of yourself. At the turn of the century it was also fashionable to proclaim that a poet should strive for self-realization. So every little Johnny Kovács from Kiskundorozsma or wherever wanted for this reason to realize himself in poetry. Though of course . . . In realizing yourself you should also realize human values of common interest! The reason why Petőfi was great was not because he was the son of an innkeeper or of the people but because of what he expressed out of this given fact and through his own destiny.

*Finding a task through which one also realizes oneself is not self-evident. How does one go about it?*

The boastful separation of ethics and aesthetics was another fatal mistake of many nineteenth century artists of talent. In this sense it was Oscar Wilde who went furthest. Every single artist without exception has two beings, one ethical, the other aesthetic. One always takes sides as between the ugly and the beautiful, even unconsciously just as one does between good and evil. Can it be possible then to push aside social injustice, social ugliness by saying "it's none of my business?" It is the greatest artists who have been very sensitive indeed to what is good and bad in society, and they expressed injustice. There is a great tradition for this and not only in Hungarian poetry. It is part of all poetries, although it has been especially rooted in Hungarian poetry. In my simple view, to sum up my poetic principles, a good society advances in the same way as a Roman war chariot. There are two wheels, one of which is politics, public life and the other is the intellectual—including the artistic—life. If one of the two doesn't turn or falls out of rhythm, then the chariot is thrown off-balance. The problem is enormous when politics takes up the task of art and dictates to art what it should say—and it is also a problem of the same magnitude if art has to take on the task of politics. This has happened in Hungary very frequently and not only here but in every country which has not achieved or has lost its statehood. We know full well that the Hungarian people lost their statehood in the sixteenth century at Mohács and our life of intellect reverted to the priest, the poet and the folksong. It was Hungarian poetry which accepted this with the greatest tenacity and talent: this is what we are proud of and this is our national characteristic in poetry. This is what I grew up with and among the immortals those are my masters who served this cause.

*Memory can be very ungrateful, very forgetful where history is concerned, even when memory ought to recall suffering. At the same time there is always a feeling of disappointment in the actual course of history. Is this inevitable? You had a longish poem in* Nyugat *in 1935, deliberately reminiscent in form of Apollinaire's* La chanson du mal-aimé. *There is hardly a more accurate way of expressing this feeling than you did in this poem, so let us have some lines from it.*

### FALLEN LEAVES

There is silence in me. It flows.
Like a raging epidemic, wherever I go
I infect that region with silence.
There in my heart ferments
enough poison for a continent.

You can change a shirt, a lover,
your faith but not your hopes,
nor the hopes of youth in your heart,
which made a man of you.
But what, then, were my hopes?

I have no regrets for my life,
but for the lives of those who accompanied me:
sometimes they stopped, they stumbled
halfway they fell onto their faces,
those brave passions of youth.

What was I given, do you know?
After the dreadful sorrow at the funeral feast
what did I drink more and more eagerly,
what maddening, distilled
frenzy to bring me comfort?

What images, what dazzling
lights flared up in my brain:
I recited with drunken lips:
Man can be changed for the better!
That's what I believed that spring.

Springs do come, which call
up his face, like the child does of
the old lover and the love.

But that intensity, that Future
which was mine refuses to come back to life.

*What should poetry do about this feeling? What about the accusation that the poet who expresses this frustration, out of a sense of the truth, is a pessimist?*

I don't think that is true. All sorts of different things are being thrown together here. To sum it all up very simply: one must get back again to the idea that the subject presented—the subject of a picture—differs from the artistic force it contains. Artistic accomplishment is always soothing . . .

### REPORT

It was easy to describe the
streams in their freshness, they rustled
into the beating meter of our poems.
And the hill, the meadow—all that
our words could reach became human.
    But then followed
The desert land of slag-Alps.
The setting of mining districts, bare of grass,
grey and moonlike.
And brooks from tanneries, black as Styx
rising from hell.
Red brick barracks
from which suddenly came
like mad clocks striking
the sound of a firing squad.
    That's what life has brought now. Crimson
smoke and ash floated
over a country of chimneys
more crowded than the vine-props
instead of across the sky.
    We described this too. Because
now across here marched the host,
drawing after it dogs, children
weighed down by heavier and heavier
less and less necessary burdens and bundles.

. . . poets and artists, with Tolstoy leading them, always have been angered by social injustice and rightly so. I hope that these old injustices are over with now. But it is not only Tolstoy's work which remains with us, his attitude does too. And if we do not retain this, if we do not keep on looking at the world in this way then we reject art itself. The most optimistic cry is: "I'm suffocating! I can't bear it anymore!" As long as someone can and wants to cry out how poor is his lot, he is actually searching for the most optimistic form of expression. Not only ours, but every generation of poets and artists has identified the most painful problem in its society and if they were able to find the material to express it through, so that it still remains effective, then we have something of permanent validity. We, the populist writers, recognized the situation Hungarian peasants found themselves in, drew attention to it, moved the conscience of many people. So I think we carried out an historical duty, not just a literary duty. And don't we have some similar problems today? The oppression of national minorities, the persecution of minority languages is rampant. People have never suffered or been despised so much for their religion, their race or the colour of their skin as today . . .

*. . . starvation and poverty on a world wide scale . . .*

. . . here we aren't starving now, thank God! But when I see the problems we've mentioned around us, then it's not because India is overpopulated that I am grieving. Our population isn't increasing! For us, this is the "problem" and it is here. There is always and everywhere a reality to deal with. That it isn't easy?

*Just recently an old piece of yours came out again,* Ki a magyar? *(Who is Hungarian?) This is a question your work continuously answers; indeed, the question itself is continuous, demanding fresh answers from each generation. In 1939, when you wrote the piece, this is what you had to say: "It is not physical similarity, but a shared past, common problems and the sense of a home which unite a nation and separate it from another with a separate past and present." And in the preface to your 1960 play* Malom a Séden *(Mill on the Séd) you say: "Who or what is Hungarian? Anyone who accepts being so."*

—Right!

*Let me put it another way—what does being Hungarian mean today? What does someone who accepts his Hungarianness have to do?*

Well, that's no elementary school question either. There is a great line in Petőfi which I always quote: "If I hadn't been born Hungarian, I would now join this nation. Because it is forlorn, the most forlorn of all the nations of this world." It was not exactly so, but the main thing here is the poetic attitude behind the words. The depths of the issues of internationalism and nationalism can be reached through it. I can also answer your question by saying that I have been called a nationalist, and even at one time, a racialist. I want to see the man who would demand as consistently as I do a human existence for every people, without exception, but including the Hungarian people. Whoever is an internationalist in Hungary has first of all to win for the Hungarian people those rights which have been so much contested up to this day. I don't want to elaborate on *Ki a magyar?*: it was in fact a propaganda piece written against the impact of German Hitlerian racism. Today I would probably formulate it by saying that there are fifteen million Hungarians living in the Danube basin. Ten million of them within the borders of the country. Every third Hungarian is outside, that is. A responsible politician can—properly—speak only on behalf of this ten million. But the country of a poet is his mother tongue and my country is those fifteen million Hungarians who are also my readers, who can understand what I say. Thus the borders of my country are more flexible. Even the emigré Hungarian living in a Western city who reads Hungarian poetry can be closer

in spirit to me than many of those who belong here. So there is a Hungary of the mother tongue which is being persecuted, not because someone is being put in prison but because, say, one cannot go to a Hungarian school in New York . . . To think of these citizens of the mother tongue, compatriots of the language, is an especially important duty of the poet. It is a duty poetry has always undertaken involuntarily: and I am stressing deliberately that it *is* a duty, if there is such a thing for poetry. Lenin went even further—he said that the people of an oppressed nation have a greater right to decent treatment than the people of great nations—preferential treatment, in fact, is their due. And this is very true, this is what morality and justice demand.

*Why is it useful and important especially for those who come from small nations to encounter the more advanced cultures of Europe, even through actually living abroad for a time?*

The results answer the question straight away: without exception this has always proved advantageous to those small nations whose people have, whether as trail-blazers or of their own desire, got to know a society on a different—I'm not saying higher—level of development. These people returned with different eyes. It was the great good fortune of the Hungarian people that throughout their history so many of its spiritual leaders were educated abroad. Protestant ministers of old, as you know, were educated in protestant countries. Catholic priests had to make themselves familiar with the culture of Rome. Hungary's attachment to the West rather than to Byzantium entailed the bringing up of generations with a European outlook. At the same time they also passed a worthy test of character. Those Calvinist students for the ministry who had their education in Holland or England or elsewhere, or those Hungarians who lived in Paris or in Rome could well have stayed there for good. If a preacher of the seventeenth century spent some time in Holland and then returned to the bogs of Hungary and started preaching morality, he was also himself giving a credible example. And to some extent this happened in literature too. There have been and there are many gifted Hungarians who really could have easily stayed abroad and been successful. But they came home. It is our great fortune that Hungarianness has always exercised such a force of attraction and "re-attraction." There is no need to list the names of all those Hungarian thinkers who have been able to take stock of the Hungarian condition through the education and outlook they acquired abroad. I must confess that the reason why I am grateful for my five years in Paris is that when I returned I was able to discover the world. I could have gone back to Paris— there was the opportunity—but it was my Parisian mind which made me grasp that this is my *material,* that this place is mine, that this is where I must do something . . . If I had not been in Paris, I would never have understood this. This has happened too even to those who didn't actually spend much time abroad. For instance, László Németh, whose European or world culture helped him to refine his vision so that he was able to see things at home all the more clearly. It was the case for others too, Babits included. This is how the Hungarians, at least in ambition, have become a West European nation. Ever since, in fact, the time a thousand years ago when King Saint Stephen joined that horde of barbarians we used to be with the West.

*There is no history of Hungarian literature written or to be written or even to be imagined which would not devote at least a chapter to the work of Gyula Illyés. Nor is there a literary historian who would not stress that the poet of* **Nehéz föld** *(Tough Land), the writer of* Puszták népe *(People of the Puszta) undertook from the beginning of his career to formulate those "bolder truths" and that he also accepted the role which expressing those bolder truths has compelled or forced him into. Yet it is still said of you that you are a poet "in hiding," someone whose work is always in the arena of literature, of public life, but whose life is one of a poet in hiding.*

### MASK

Whatever I say, it covers, it conceals,
Like a mask dangles between you and me.
I smile, while, with its distorted grimaces,
Whatever I don't speak about, pants like a
   murderer,
Bares its teeth, rattles, wants just blood, just pain.
I wait with irony for the moment when you will
   shoot me in the head.

*To what extent are we to take this poem seriously? You wrote it in 1934, the year* People of the Puszta *appeared? Is there such a thing as a mask? If so, what does it conceal?*

Well, again, this is a many-layered thing. There are indeed poets who like to display themselves. I have already said that trying to please in art, which with some doesn't always stop short of mincing, is far from rare. That's why there are poets whose private lives are more successful works than those they have actually written. Very often chance has an important part in this. But, I'd prefer to read a Petőfi, to come back to him again, who was still writing as a man of eighty rather than being haunted constantly by the terrible image of him impaled on a lance on a battlefield at the age of twenty-six. Of course it made him into a Romantic hero, but if only he could have used a pen as a sage! There are poets, however, who want to lead a withdrawn life. To themselves, without any role or fame. In my case this was a kind of inheritance. I was brought up on the *puszta* in a smallish family circle and I can still remember my father's words, his parting advice, when I went away to secondary school. He said: "And I don't want to hear anything about you!" This is not really hiding . . . This is what a man should be—modest. Even young maidens can be immodest but it is unbecoming in a man. For me, it is something of a contradiction that a man can be an artist: that he conceives, that he goes into labour, that he gives birth. . . .

I've never been able to be happy with this coincidence of usage in the language. Serious creators, Michelangelo and his like, have never gone in for this kind of thing. It's none of the audience's business to know how someone works. It really is difficult to create something which is good. Someone who doesn't tear up work, five times if necessary, and presents it in its napkin stage and boasting "look, I can do it!," someone like that is, at least, over-hasty in his work.

*There's a well known saying of yours that in a way an artist signs and authenticates his work with his life. How is this so in the case of a modest poet?*

Again a matter of geography. There are countries whose writers inevitably have to acquire some public role. In the West, though I might add, in every country where the practice of art is healthy, a poet as an individual can be dishonest, a cheat, a man of no moral character, this would have no effect on his work. I'm not saying that this would be absolutely impossible here either. But here the poet is normally expected to tell the truth, even to live a "life of truth" as an individual. I repeat that the reason for this is that often in this part of the world intellectual and public life go their seperate ways; this is what every real artist has always felt even if he does put on a show of being untouched by "bourgeois" morality. This is not exclusively Hungarian either—poets from ill-fated nations have always been forced to this. I don't like the term *vates,* it's an empty cliché with a hollow sound to it. Still, there was a time when men of letters and such did play the role of Tyrtaeus—something taken as given here. You cannot avoid it; or if you try to, you end up in a different blind alley.

### Béla Köpeczi   (essay date 1983)

SOURCE: "At the Graveside," in *The New Hungarian Quarterly,* Vol. 24, No. 91, Autumn, 1983, pp. 27-34.

[*In the following eulogy, Köpeczi describes the ideals, both social and political, that fed Illyés's work and their lasting effect on Hungary.*]

Gyula Illyés, the great poet, lived in an age in which the world and Hungary underwent epochal changes which were accompanied with anguish and sacrifice but which had their historic results, too. Illyés faced this age together with its contradictions and its aspirations to build the future. He was active in the working-class movement at the time of the Republic of Councils, he was all his life an advocate of the peasantry and of the entire nation, one who wanted and succeeded not only in writing but in acting in the interests of progress.

In 1939 he wrote that: "Man's business in this world is to be as perfect and as humane as possible, to be all the more sensible, the better and the more honest, to be all the freer without infringing upon the right of his fellow-beings to freedom. It is the nation's business also steadily to become perfect."

"Becoming perfect" meant to him first of all that he unhesitatingly struggled to see that social justice prevailed. As he himself said, "peasant experience" led him to seek "honesty" where the oppressed, the defenceless, the exploited were concerned. The writer of *People of the Puszta* described the pauperism of the Hungarian peasantry between the two wars with such force and such fervour of protest that he will for ever be remembered for his condemnation of an unjust social system and will set an example in the neverending struggle for the new. He cited also the revolutionary and literary example of his great predecessor Petőfi because he expected a radical social change to bring improvement in the lot of the people. This realization led the author of *Ebéd a kastélyban* (*Luncheon at the Mansion*) to identify himself with the historical judgement which socialism has passed on the capitalist Hungary encumbered with feudal vestiges. In *Beatrice apródjai* (*Beatrice's Pages*) he traversed with deep moral conviction the revolutionary path that has led to a change in the world and he remained—until death—true to the idea of social progress even though many things failed to come about as he had expected, even though he met with disappointments.

To him society was inseparable from the nation. He saw the nation as the community of working people who speak the same language, a community whose feature is the common work of shaping the future and to which language and culture also signify bonds which link even beyond the frontiers. His interpretation of the national idea was controversial even among his friends and companions-in-arms; his intention and the substance of his message, however, were unequivocal: he wanted equal rights and cooperation to prevail among nations. In 1959 he concluded an autobiographical piece thus: "I am sure that the peoples of this earth are travelling towards a classless society. The first stage of their organic union is full equality of rights. It is an absurdity to create equality of rights between parties showing mutual respect other than through understanding, that is in peace; indeed it is a contradiction in terms." Equality of rights through understanding and peace—this was the national and international programme of Gyula Illyés.

When taking stock of the national and national minority problems he always linked together his uneasiness and the idea of cooperation with neighbouring nations—in the 1930s as in the last years of his life.

Illyés did not lock himself up in the Hungarian microcosm, his experience as an exile helped him to see in politics and literature the whole world as well as his country. *A hunok Párizsban* (*The Huns in Paris*) shows the unparalleled comprehension of the fusion of national and international. All his work as a poet, but particularly his many literary translations, demonstrates time and again his search for universal connections.

These ideas are characteristic of all of his remarkably rich and many-sided lifework. He himself professed: "Without a good world-view . . . there is no kind of piercing the essence, stimulating action, namely 'genuine, great' poetry." "The surrealist of clarity" thought that literature ought to deal with everything of interest to man and the nation, and indeed he used his great poetic sensitivity to answer the questions which preoccupied the world and his homeland. This everyday commitment moved him also to profess a programme of poetic realism and of genuine artistic democracy. He knew all there was to know about literature, especially poetry, he knew every innovation of the avant-garde, yet by drawing on popular sources he became a modern classic who held that it was worth one's while writing only to be able to mould oneself and shape others as well, to stimulate to action.

Mihály Babits wrote of Illyés: "To resuscitate Hungarian and popular forms and to make them up-to-date, as the most essential possibility, the most difficult and most imperative of all tasks . . . With the people's verse, out of the people's soul, something comes in literature: greater simplicity, greater clarity, the spirit of 'meek poverty lasting for centuries'. Illyés is the poet of this spirit, who can belong to the people without repudiating culture, and to culture without repudiating the people . . ."

All his life Illyés wanted to tell the general public—and not the élite—what was "beautiful, good and useful" in plain, clear and succinct terms, in the finest and most informal language. His œuvre was and remains our companion, it makes us conscious of our thoughts and feelings, it prompts us to self examination by its high intelligence and by the simplicity of great truths.

Despite doubts, inner struggles and contradictions he professed historical optimism: "I have confidence in the Hungarian people's strength, I am certain that this nation progresses not towards its ruin but towards its improvement, no matter what trials it has been exposed to . . ." This was how he formulated the experience of the people to whom he always remained loyal and whose thoughts and feelings he expressed. The writer of the community made greater the chances of national and human advancement not only by what he produced but by creating around himself and his œuvre, with an unbroken consistency of ideas, a lively and constructive atmosphere for communal life. This is where poetry and politics meet, and this happened during the past twenty-five years or so in such a way that the creative energies in both spheres served the progress of the people. Illyés is a great artistic ally of socialist construction, which does not mean that politics or any person would or might make a claim to him. He is a writer of the Hungarian people, his œuvre belongs to the people, but any consistent policy or rather social activity imbued with the intention, the sense and loyalty serving the people can find in it a source of intellectual power.

Awe and pain fills us, taking leave of a great Hungarian author. To quote Horace his work is more lasting than brass. It is our responsibility to make common property of what he has bequeathed us, and to ensure that the generations after us will know it and be able to draw from it ideals, thoughts and feelings to the edification of the individual and the community.

May the poet's memory and works be surrounded, for the centuries to come, with the halo of the devoted affection of the Hungarian people, of the profound respect of the followers of socialism, and of the everlasting esteem of progressive men.

**William Jay Smith  (essay date 1984)**

SOURCE: "Gyula Illyés: Lyric Realist," in *The Hollins Critic*, Vol. XXI, No. 1, February, 1984, pp. 1-12.

[*In the following essay, Smith shows that Illyés is a lyric realist who eschews theory and involves himself directly in the view of humanity.*]

I

Gyula Illyés, long considered Hungary's national poet, throughout his lifetime drew inspiration, like Bela Bartók in music, from Hungary's deepest roots. In his introduction to *Once Upon a Time: Forty Hungarian Folk-Tales* (1964) he says:

> The Hungarian folk-tales, clothing the peasantry's confessions in pure poetry and expressing its aspirations to a higher, freer and purer life, do more than amuse us. It was over vast distances and at the cost of untold sufferings that the Hungarians reached their country. The Hungarian folk-tale—in which the heroes embark on incredible adventures, fight with dragons, and outwit the devil—has preserved, in its fairy-like language, the ancient treasures; it has preserved an ancient Hungarian view of the world.

That ancient Hungarian view of the world is preserved not only in the folk-tales but also in the anonymous poets of the Hungarian countryside. Gyula Illyés was inspired by them both in his poetry and in his autobiographical volume *People of the Puszta*. In all his work he avoids theories and concerns himself directly and particularly with basic humanity. "For him," Jean Follain has said, "the poet remains the foremost pioneer: he alone can say at which instant man turns assassin and hangman—when originally he had been a hero. The poetry of Illyés shows us the closeness of the infinite, and of childhood, the proximity of peace and death, while it brands and denounces the tyranny bent on leading human beings astray and provoking their miserable fears and stifling the fraternity of mankind."

Gyula Illyés, who died in 1983 a few months after his eightieth birthday, was born at Ráczegrespuszta in Western Hungary. His forebears had been indentured servants, shepherds and agricultural workmen, on a large estate; his father had risen to the position of village mechanic,

and through the combined efforts of various members of his family Illyés was sent to school in the neighboring village and afterwards to high school in Budapest. He interrupted his university education to enlist in the army of the Republic of Councils in 1919, and when the republic fell, to escape arrest, he fled in 1921 to Paris, where he lived for the next five years. While working as a bookbinder, he attended courses at the Sorbonne. He published poems in French, and became the friend of Eluard, Cocteau, Aragon, and Tzara, gaining an intimate knowledge of Dadaism and Surrealism. He could easily have stayed on in Paris and earned a reputation as a poet writing in French, but he chose to return to Hungary. This decision was the turning point in his life: he separated himself from modernist literary movements, and, inspired by the ideals of the Hungarian poet Petőfi, a brilliant biography of whom he was later to write, he set out on a conscious mission to speak for the masses of his people. On the Ile Saint-Louis in Paris, opposite the Palais Lambert, Illyés sat on a bench in 1926 to set down his poem **"The Sad Field-Hand"**:

> The sun has hardened my crust of bread;
> Tepid is my flask
> And heavy and slow my sun-warmed blood.
> Seated amid the steam of my worry and my sweat,
> I watch the silent fields pitch around me.
> It is noon.
> Deep in the woods the wind and the future repose.
>
> The overseer passes in his carriage.
> My weary hand lifts my hat;
> I am covered with ash and grime,
> The gaze of my cattle refreshes my heart.
>
> Beyond the dust, beyond the trees,
> Beyond the spread of clouds, the fronded dust,
> There where the indifferent sun reels on its way
> Lie distant cities with illuminated squares wheeling
>   beneath the stars,
> And seas, floating islands, and flaming mountains
>   of gold,
> Of all these I have heard—
> Of heaven and earth bursting with riches, and yet
> I remain here, irresolute, at the center of an alien
>   field,
> A stranger for whom no one waits, and who, in the
>   autumn,
> His work completed, in the shade of a haystack,
> Will without a word sink down to join the
>   impassive earth.

In spirit the poet had never left his native heath, and he never would.

The position of the peasantry, from which he came, was always foremost in Illyés's mind. Miklós Vajda describes visiting him some years ago: "I casually mentioned that an experimental theater company was to be formed in Budapest. He looked at me sharply, and said abruptly, '[Damn, that will cost the peasant another two eggs.]' And then he broke into an impish smile. He still instinctively measures everything in terms of cost to the people, and rightly so, because this has always been a country where everything has to be done at the expense of something else; priorities are of supreme importance."

When Illyés returned from France, the poet Mihály Babits, the editor of *Nyugat* (*West*), took him under his wing, and Illyés became a regular contributor to the magazine. He published several volumes of poems in the late twenties and early thirties, all dealing with the plight of the poor villagers. With the publication of his two distinguished prose works, *People of the Puszta* and *Petőfi* in 1936, he became one of the leaders of the Populist writers who sought to give expression to the feelings of the people. When *Nyugat* was closed down by the authorities and Babits died in 1941, Illyés took over as editor of *Magyar Csillag* (*Hungarian Star*), and remained as its editor until the Germans came in March 1944. In several volumes of poetry and prose in the late thirties and early forties he wrote again of his childhood, but with less of his youthful enthusiasm. *The Huns in Paris* (1944) is a witty prose account of his years in France. After World War II Illyés planned to take over the editorship of a new review, *Valasz,* but when the authorities forbade him to do so, he retired and spent most of his time in his little house jutting into Lake Balaton at Tihany.

Always in the front ranks of literary movements, Illyés was even in his periods of enforced silence somehow eloquent. Because of his ability to survive and to express himself under the most difficult circumstances, some critics have remarked on his cunning and have compared him to a fox. His cunning apparently comes from an awareness of the contradictions within himself. In his youth he experienced the double influences of Catholicism and Calvinism, and in his education he was disciplined in Gallic clarity. (The history of France, he said, is "principally characterized by striving for lucidity.") During the Stalinist period in Hungary Illyés refused to publish, but because of his eminence as a writer the pressure on him was so great that he could not remain completely silent. He wrote at this time a poem titled **"Roofers,"** which on the surface seems to praise people for rebuilding their houses but in reality is about the difficulty of writing in such a period. Illyés's most famous poem, **"A Sentence for Tyranny,"** was written during the Stalinist era but was first published in 1956. It has still not been published in Hungary. Its concluding stanzas, brilliantly rendered into English by Vernon Watkins, demonstrate its appeal to so many people (it has been translated into more than forty languages):

Where seek tyranny? Think again:
Everyone is a link in the chain;
Of tyranny's stench you are not free:
You yourself are tyranny.

Like a mole on a sunny day
Walking in his blind, dark way,
We walk and fidget in our rooms,
Making a Sahara of our homes;

All this because, where tyranny is
Everything is in vain,
Every creation, even this
Poem I sing turns vain:

Vain, because it is standing
From the very first at your grave,
Your own biography branding,
And even your ashes are its slave.

II

. . . . In both his poetry and his prose Gyula Illyés might be termed a lyric realist. Edwin Morgan has called him one who like Robert Burns "gave the land a voice." In 1928 he wrote:

What you have almost forgotten—
The speech of your quiet people—learn again!
More reviving than a glass of fresh water
Is their hearty welcome to the tired traveller,
A welcome that brims with friendly warmth.
See how here among the villagers waiting to be
  paid
You too nod agreement when they speak, as they
Tell of their destiny in their own rough words,
Give reasons for their poverty.
Eager life flutters birdlike
In the difficult movements of their lips.
                    (translated by Gavin Ewart)

If, as some critics have found, his poetry at times appears to be lacking in mystery, it may be that he tries too strongly to adopt the speech of his "quiet people," to speak directly, and to disguise nothing.

What is immediately striking in the poetry of Illyés is its immense variety. He makes use of every kind of stanza form and every line length; he is equally at home in very formal stanzas and in impressionistic prose poems. In the couplets of **"Aboard the Santa Maria"** the poet, on his misty ledge overlooking Lake Balaton at Tihany, pictures himself as Columbus aboard the Santa Maria:

Buttressed forth, a hanging garden there,
the terrace like a ship divides the air.

A table of stone, a rickety chicken coop
emerge through holes within the shifting fog . . .

And now when the pounding waves reach up to me,
I feel I am centuries ago at sea . . .

Always in his poetry, as in *People of the Puszta,* he has an eye for precise, concrete detail. That detail can be exquisite and delicate as in **"The Approaching Silence"**:

Lightly clad, on tiptoe, the little rain has just
  run into the garden
through the gate. Is the sunlight here? The rain
  stops, listens, gazing at itself

in the glass balls, shifts its weight; draws away.
　　But it is still here; now and
then its drops continue to fall.

or in the Mozartian final stanzas of **"A World in Crystal"**:

　　Now furtively I stroll
　　　　among the cherry trees
　　with their Japanese red tea
　　　　service of porcelain.
　　All detachable beauty
　　　　causes me pain. I live
　　in fear for all the fragile
　　　　values of this earth.

　　A transparency of crystal
　　　　exists not just in trees,
　　transparency is all:
　　　　faces, hearts of air—
　　all transparency—
　　　　tell me, will you, how
　　well in autumn wind
　　　　will fragile being fare?

　　The wind has not yet risen:
　　　　creation and the garden
　　stand clearly in the light.
　　　　All the more painful now
　　to watch, as here and there,
　　　　from high in a still tree
　　—and in what deathly silence—
　　　　a crystal leaf drifts down.

or terrifying, as in **"While the Record Plays:"**

　　They heated hatchet blades over gas fires in roadside
　　　　workshops and hammered them into cleavers.

　　They brought wooden blocks on trucks and carried
　　　　them across
　　　　　　these new provinces grimly, quickly, and
　　steadily: almost
　　　　　　according to ritual.

　　Because at any time—at noon or midnight—they
　　　　would arrive
　　　　　　at one of these impure settlements,

　　where women did not cook nor make beds as theirs
　　　　did, where men
　　　　　　did not greet one another as they did, where
　　children and
　　　　　　the whole damned company did not pronounce
　　words as they did,
　　　　　　and where the girls kept apart from them.

　　They would select from these insolent and
　　　　intolerable people
　　　　　　twelve men, preferably young ones, to take to
　　the marketplace,

and there—because of *blah-blah-blah* and moreover
　　*quack-quack-quack*
　　　　and likewise *quack-blah-quack*—would beat
　　and behead them,

of historical necessity—because of *twaddle-twiddle*
　　and *twiddle-diddle,* and
　　　　expertly, for their occupations would be
　　different one from the other. . . .

Although he was able as a boy to take the killing of pigs
and chickens on the *puszta* in stride, he tells us in
**"Work"**, his first "really shattering experience" came
when watching the hooping of a cartwheel. The lesson of
the craftsmen he witnessed he retained for a lifetime:

　　From the huge coal fire, with pincers at least a yard
　　long, the apprentices grabbed the iron hoop, which by
　　then was red hot up and down. They ran with it to the
　　fresh-smelling oak wheel that had been fixed in place
　　in the front of the blacksmith's shop. The flesh-colored
　　wooden wheel was my grandfather's work; the iron
　　hoop, which gave off a shower of sparks in its fiery
　　agony, was my father's. One of the apprentices held
　　the sledge hammer, the other the buckets. Places,
　　everyone. As on shipboard. As at an execution. The
　　hoop, which in its white-hot state had just expanded
　　to the size of the wheel, was quickly placed on it; and
　　they began to pry it out with their tongs. My father
　　swung the hammer with lightning speed, giving orders
　　all the while. The wood caught fire; they poured a
　　bucket of water on it. The wheel sent up steam and
　　smoke so thick you couldn't see it. But still the
　　hammer pounded on, and still came the "Press hard"!
　　uttered breathlessly from the corner of the mouth.
　　The fire blazed up again. Water flung again as on a
　　tortured man who has sunk into a coma. Then the last
　　flourishing bush of steam evaporated while the
　　apprentices poured a thin trickle from a can on the
　　cooling iron which, in congealing, gripped lovingly
　　its life-long companion to be. The men wiped the
　　sweat from their brows, spat, shook their heads,
　　satisfied. Nothing—not the slightest flicker of a
　　movement—could have been executed differently.

Like his father and his grandfather before him, Illyés
had a deep respect for his craft. At the end of many of
his poems one can almost sense the poet, like his peasant
forebears, wiping the sweat from his brow, satisfied with
the artifact that he has created, for which nothing "could
have been executed differently."

This sense of craft is carried to a point of extreme sophistication and subtlety in **"The Maker,"** which might
have come from the pen of Paul Valéry:

　　More ardent
　　than two lithe bodies dancing
　　together, embracing
　　those two
　　thoughts so different from each other
　　frolicked and turned
　　struggling
　　for life, for death,

finding their fulfilment
in a third.

As a babe in the hands of a midwife
begins to live, a success,
tiny, naked,
powerful,
it kicked among the wheels and springs,
a deed that has been given
life and body almost
like our own.
It came with me,
came as my perpetual
dog, my master
on my leash,
myself on leash. . . .

(translated by Daniel Hoffman)

For all the autobiographical detail in Illyés's poems, he always maintains a classical distance. Not long before his death Illyés was asked about these lines which he wrote in 1934 at the same time that *People of the Puszta* appeared:

### MASK

Whatever I say, it covers, it conceals,
Like a mask dangles between you and me.
I smile, while, with its distorted grimaces,
Whatever I don't speak about, pants like a
    murderer,
Bares its teeth, rattles, wants just blood, just pain.
I wait with irony for the moment when you will
    shoot me in the head.

(translated by Miklós Vajda)

To what extent, he was asked, could this poem be taken seriously and if there were for him such a thing as a mask, what indeed did it conceal. Illyés's answer tells a great deal about the nature of his poetry: "This is a many-layered thing. There are indeed poets who like to display themselves. I have already said that trying to please in art, which with some doesn't always stop short of mincing, is far from rare. That's why there are poets whose private lives are more successful works than those they have actually written . . . I was brought up on the *puszta* in a smallish family circle and I can still remember my father's words, his parting advice, when I went away to secondary school. He said: 'And I don't want to hear anything about you!' This is not really hiding . . . This is what a man should be—modest. Even young maidens can be immodest but it is unbecoming in a man. For me, it is something of a contradiction that a man can be an artist: that he conceives, that he goes into labor, that he gives birth . . . I've never been able to be happy with this coincidence of usage in the language. Serious creators, Michelangelo and his like, have never gone in for this kind of thing. It's none of the audience's business to know how someone works. It really is difficult to create something which is good."

Even when speaking of social injustice, as he does eloquently in one of his finest poems, **"Wonder Castle,"** he maintains a certain reserve. In this poem, written in 1937, he tells of arriving in Budapest from the country and of taking the funicular up the Buda hills to the more affluent section of the city:

It was as if, from the hell of the plain below us,
we were borne up from circle to circle
into some present-day Turkish heaven.
Or, with the old look-out tower
it was like a magic castle,
the terrifying or happy
seat of some Asiatic deity
found only in Hungarian and Vogul folk-tale,
called Castle Spinning on a Duck's Leg: Wonder
    Castle.

(translated by Kenneth McRobbie)

But he finds little wonder on the faces of the high-society figures he encounters in this wonder castle. He examines them closely and records their true lineaments with savage satire. At the end of the poem he has a vision of the plain from which he has come rising up, as it does in the folk-tale, and bringing down the towers on the hill. But even if such a revolution were to occur, the poet affirms that he would still want to retain his objective posture as a dispassionate observer:

I would even then
stand aside, still play the quiet man,
so that when all came tumbling down
order might be kept,
and calmly, impartially, I should
be able to give account
of how life was before the flood
in this pre-historic period.

(translated by Kenneth McRobbie)

In his introduction to the anthology *Modern Hungarian Poetry,* Miklós Vajda points out that poetry in Hungary has had through the centuries a special position never equalled by the other arts: "Poetry, which cannot be shelled like a city, or whitewashed like murals, crushed like sculpture, closed like theaters, or even banned and censored as easily as novels and journals, can spread and be influential even without print or manuscript. And so it dominated the literature of a people that had to live under difficult conditions, luring the best talents and forcing them to lead dangerous lives and produce extraordinary achievements." Gyula Illyés was the living embodiment of this poetic tradition. In one of his later poems, **"A Wreath,"** he pays tribute to the Hungarian language, which is spoken by no more than fifteen million people, a third of whom live outside the country. The poem is a passionate statement addressed to his mother tongue, evoking those who have struggled to keep it alive:

You can no longer
soar. And yet you blaze,
wind-slit Hungarian tongue, sending
your snakelike flames along the ground, hissing
at times with pain,

more often with the helpless rage of the
   humiliated,
your guardian angels forsaking you.
Again in grass,
in weeds, in slime.
As through all those centuries, among
the stooped peasants. Among
the tight-lipped old, keeping their counsel. Among
girls trembling under coned reeds as
the Tartar hordes swept past. Among
children lashed together
while mute lips shaped their words,
for the Turks, if they heard a sound,
would bring whips down in their faces.
Now you show forth
truly—and to me as well—your use,
your pedigree, your coat-of-arms, the stone-biting
strength in your veins.

Language of furtive smiles,
of bright tears shared in secret, language
of loyalty, lingo
of never-surrendered faith, password of hope,
   language
of freedom, briefly-snatched freedom, behind-the-
   prison-guard's-back-freedom,
language of master-mocked schoolboy, sergeant-
   abused rookie,
dressed-down plaintiff, of little old ladies boring
   clerks,
language of porters, odd-job hired men, being a
   language
of the no-good-for-the-factory, no-good-for-test-
   passing proletariat,
language of the veteran stammering before his
young boss; testimony—
rising from depths even greater
than Luther's—of the suspect
beaten up on arrival at the station;
language of the Kassa black marketeer, the
   Bucharest servant girl,
the Beirut whore, all calling
for mother, behold your son, spittle
on his rage-reddened face,
master of many tongues,
held worthy of attention by other nations
for what, as a loyal European,
he has to say:
he cannot mount any festive platform,
cannot accept any wreath,
however glorious, which he would not, stepping
   quickly down,
carry over to lay at your feet, and with his smile
   draw forth
on your agonizing lips,
your smile, my beloved, ever-nurturing mother.

The reference to the Bucharest servant girl reminds us
that in the last decade of his life Illyés spoke out in a
series of articles against what he called the cultural genocide of the two million Hungarians residing in Transyl-
vania. He had treated the subject years before, in its full

brutality, in **"While the Record Plays."** Illyés was not
an apologist for socialism nor a public defender of any
system or theory. He continued, a literary giant, throughout his life to attack injustice wherever he found it, and
to promote passionately, and with the power and balance
of his art, a civilized view of man:

### Tilting Sail

The tilting sail careens;
   scything the foam,
the tall mast creaks and leans—
   the boat plows on.

Look—when do mast and sail
   fly forward most
triumphantly? When tilted
   lowest.

---

## FURTHER READING

### Criticism

Béládi, Miklós. "The Seventy Years of Gyula Illyés." *New Hungarian Quarterly* 13, No. 48 (Winter 1972): 83-9.
   Attempts to answer the philosophical question: Who is Gyula Illyés?

Csicsery-Rónay, István. "Gyula Illyés: Grand Prix for Poetry." *Book Abroad* 40, No. 2 (Spring 1966): 156-7.
   Summarizes Illyés's life and importance.

Cushing, George F. "The Role of the National Poet." *Review of National Literatures* 17 (1993): 59-80.
   Discusses the history of national literature in Hungary, with emphasis on Petöfi and Illyés.

Gömöri, George. "Gyula Illyés (1902-1983): An Appraisal." *World Literature Today* (Summer 1984): 344-47.
   Assesses Illyés's life and works on the occasion of his death.

Illyés, Gyula. "The Business of Poets (Brief notes)." *New Hungarian Quarterly* 16, No. 57 (Spring 1975): 72-7.
   Collection of thoughts on the job of the poet.

Remenyi, Joseph. *Hungarian Writers and Literature.* New Brunswick: Rutgers University Press, 1964.
   Critical analysis of Hungarian literature.

Szabó, Peter Szentmihályi. A review of *Összegyüjtött versei,* by *Összegyüjtött versei. World Literature Today* (Spring 1978): 316-17.
   Positive review of the two-volume edition of collected poems by Illyés.

Additional coverage of Illyés's life and career is contained in the following sources published by Gale Research: *Contemporary Authors*, Vols. 109, 114.

# Alphonse de Lamartine
## 1790–1869

(Full name Alphonse Marie Louis Prat de Lamartine)
French poet, novelist, historian, and essayist.

### INTRODUCTION

Lamartine, a pioneer of the French Romantic movement, is considered one of the greatest French poets of the nineteenth century. He is best known for his collection of verse entitled *Méditations poétiques* (*The Poetical Meditations*), in which he stressed emotion, mysticism, and nature. Lamartine was also a prominent statesman who wrote a number of historical works, including *Histoire des girondins* (*History of the Girondists*). Though popular during his life, Lamartine's histories are largely overlooked today. He is now remembered as a significant figure in the history of French literature whose poetry marked the transition from the restraints of the Neoclassical era to the passion and lyricism of the Romantic period.

### Biographical Information

Descended from the minor French nobility, Lamartine was born in Mâcon, France. He was raised on his family's country estate in nearby Milly, where he devoted himself to the study of Greek and Roman classics as well as contemporary French works. In 1811 he visited Italy, where he fell in love with a young Neapolitan woman who eventually became the subject of *Graziella* (*Graziella; or, My First Sorrow*), an idyll included in his novel *Les confidences* (*Les confidences: Confidential Disclosures*); several years later, his passion for Julie Charles, the wife of the famous French physicist Jacques Charles, inspired many of the poems comprising *The Poetical Meditations*. In 1815 Lamartine served for several months as a personal guard to King Charles X. However, he found the life of a soldier dull and aspired to a diplomatic career. Shortly after the appearance of *The Poetical Meditations*, which was greeted with tremendous critical and popular acclaim upon its publication in 1820, Lamartine obtained an appointment to a French embassy in Italy, where he spent the next ten years. This proved to be a period of sustained creative activity, for Lamartine's minor diplomatic duties afforded him ample time to write. In addition to several lesser-known works, Lamartine published *Nouvelles méditations poétiques*, a collection of verse that enhanced his already substantial reputation. Soon after his return to France in 1828, Lamartine was defeated in his bid for a seat in the national parliament. He then toured the Middle East. His recollections of this journey are preserved in *Souvenirs, impressions, pensées, et paysages pendant un voyage en Orient, 1832-1833* (*A Pilgrimage to the*

*Holy Land*), a collection of travel sketches that was mildly successful. After leaving the Middle East in 1833, Lamartine moved to Paris, where he served as a member of the Chamber of Deputies until 1851. Lamartine's career as a statesman reached its apex in 1848 when Louis-Philippe was ousted in the Revolution and Lamartine became the president of the Second Republic's provisional government. He proved an ineffective leader during this volatile time, and his popularity diminished to such an extent that he was soundly defeated by Napoléon III in the presidential election held later that year. Lamartine retired from politics in 1851 and wrote prolifically until his death in 1869 to support himself and his family.

### Major Works

In two sets of poems in *The Poetical Meditations*—those inspired by Julie Charles and those addressed to Elvire, his evocation of the universal woman—Lamartine wrote of ideal love and the grief experienced at its loss. In other poems he described his religious beliefs and emotional reaction to nature. Lamartine viewed nature as a manifestation of divine grandeur and believed that its contemplation could inspire religious faith. At this time, Lamartine's religious views were those of an orthodox Catholic: he affirmed the existence of an afterlife and exhorted his readers to accept divine will. *The Poetical Meditations* includes Lamartine's most famous single work, "Le lac." In this poem, based on a boat ride with Julie Charles, Lamartine treats the ephemeral nature of life and love. Written in highly melodious and emotional verse, "Le lac" epitomizes the lyrical qualities of Lamartine's poetry. *Nouvelles méditations poétiques*, similar in subject and tone to *The Poetical Meditations*, includes poems that combine religious topics and idyllic natural settings. Lamartine long envisioned an *épopée humanitaire*, or universal epic, in which he would express his religious and social views. The work *Jocelyn* forms the first segment of *Les visions*, the title of his projected epic. In *Jocelyn*, Lamartine depicted a young priest's struggle with temptation and ultimate renunciation of forbidden love. While popular for its sensational subject, the work received varied critical estimates. *La chute d'un ange*, the only other completed segment of the projected epic, describes the earthly trials of a fallen angel in his quest for redemption. During his travels in the Middle East, Lamartine had become interested in Eastern religions, and *La chute d'un ange* reflects his fascination with reincarnation and pantheism. Although he had been regarded previously as a deeply religious poet, both *Jocelyn* and *La chute d'un ange* were banned by the Catholic church, which considered them a refutation of traditional faith in favor of rationalism and deism.

## Critical Reception

*The Poetical Meditations* is considered a transitional work that helped pave the way for the French Romantic movement, and critics have pointed out both Neoclassical and Romantic elements. Adopting forms common to eighteenth-century poetry, Lamartine made use of the elegy and ode; reflecting the new spirit of nineteenth-century verse, he used the themes of love and death. *The Poetical Meditations* differs markedly from the emotionally restrained verse of the Neoclassical era in its sincere tone, lyric effusiveness, emotionality, and religious content. Now regarded as the first document of French Romanticism, *The Poetical Meditations* firmly established Lamartine's reputation as both a Romantic and Catholic poet. By his death his reputation had waned significantly: his prose works were seldom read, and his verse lost favor with an audience that preferred the more passionate lyrics of the late Romantics. Lamartine's work has received consistent notice in France, but little twentieth-century commentary in English. Modern scholars have focused their attention on the two completed parts of Lamartine's epic, *Jocelyn* and *La chute d'un ange*, and many individual poems, particularly "Le lac," have been the subject of close textual analyses. Critics have also demonstrated an increasing interest in Lamartine's role as a social reformer and his importance to the history of French literature. Today, Lamartine is renowned for his emotionally evocative verse that contributed to the development of the French Romantic movement.

## PRINCIPAL WORKS

### Poetry

*Méditations poétiques* [*The Poetical Meditations of M. Alphonse de Lamartine*] 1820
*Nouvelles méditations poétiques* [*New Poetical Meditations*] 1823
*Harmonies poétiques et religieuses* [*Poetic and Religious Harmonies*] 1830
*Jocelyn: Épisode; Journal trouvé chez un curé de village* [*Jocelyn*] 1836
*La chute d'un ange* [*The Fall of an Angel*] 1838
*Recueillements poétiques* 1839
*Oeuvres poétiques* (poetry and drama) 1873-74

### Other Major Works

*Souvenirs, impressions, pensées, et paysages pendant un voyage en Orient, 1832-1833; ou, Notes d'un voyageur* [*A Pilgrimage to the Holy Land*] (travel sketches) 1835
*Histoire des girondins* [*History of the Girondists; or, Personal Memoirs of the Patriots of the French Revolution*] (history) 1847
*Les confidences* [*Les confidences: Confidential Disclosures*] (novel) 1849
*Le conseiller du peuple. 2 vols. (essays) 1849-50
*Histoire de la révolution de 1848* [*History of the French Revolution of 1848*] (history) 1849
*Raphaël: Pages de la vingtième année* [*Raphael; or, Pages of the Book of Life at Twenty*] (novel) 1849
*Le civilisateur: Histoire de l'humanité par les grands hommes. 3 vols. [*Memoirs of Celebrated Characters*] (biographical sketches) 1852-54; also published as *Vie des grands hommes* (enlarged edition), 1855-56
*Cours familier de littérature: Un entretien par mois. 28 vols. (essays) 1856-59
*Oeuvres complètes de Lamartine publiées et inédites. 41 vols. (poetry, histories, biographical sketches, travel sketches, and novels) 1860-66
*Les foyers du peuple. 2 vols. (essays) 1866
*Correspondance de Lamartine. 6 vols. (letters) 1873-74

*These works were published in monthly installments prior to their publication in book form.

---

## CRITICISM

### D. N. (essay date 1836-37)

SOURCE: "Lamartine," in *Westminster Review*, October-January, 1836-37, pp. 501-41.

[*In the following excerpt, a contemporary of Lamartine comments on the themes and style of the poet's works. The essay was signed only with the author's initials, D. N.*]

The poetry of M. de Lamartine does not properly belong to the department of practical truths. Not but that we may find in his poems traits of real life, such as the epic, dramatic, and philosophic poets present at every page; but these traits are wanting in definiteness, or exaggerated out of all proportion by the habit of idealizing everything, which is the particular turn of mind of M. de Lamartine. The earth, which is the theatre of the life of man—that earth which Dante painted in such sombre colours—resembles, in M. de Lamartine's verses, some planet inhabited by beings more perfect than we, lighted by a softer sun, washed by more pacific seas, watered by more murmuring rivulets, caressed and not ravaged by the winds—the abode of creatures intermediate between man and the angels. Even his shepherds are so beautiful, that one might take them for the angels of Thomas Moore, come down under that form to make love to our peasant-girls. These last, worthy of such shepherds, have 'fingers of ivory;' a greyhound has qualities and graces, such as the most enamoured lover sees in his mistress, or as the most ambitious mother would desire for her daughter; a hind has movements more voluptuous than an odalisque—looks more tender than those of a young wife, when she beholds her long-absent husband returning from afar—has thoughts more subtle than those in a sonnet of Voiture. All things are magnified, purified, embellished, in the same proportion; the smallest landscape has all climates and all suns at once; the smallest piece of water is a lake, a lake is a sea. Who would not fancy that the subject of the following line was a bird?—

A surprendre en son nid le faon qui vient d'éclore.

*Nid* (*nest*) is not used for quadrupeds; *éclore* is strictly applied only to the young of oviparous animals, particularly of birds, for whom this graceful word seems to have been expressly formed. The passage is as incorrect, though not as ludicrous, as if we said in English, 'to surprise in its nest a fawn just hatched.' But M. de Lamartine wished to give his fawn a dwelling more noble than a thicket in a wood, and an origin more poetical than the littering of the hind.

It is thus that he elevates and transfigures all things; and if we cite this verse, it is less to criticise the expressions than to give one instance among a thousand of M. de Lamartine's manner of seeing and representing real objects. It is not, therefore, in this department that we must look for his merits; it must be in the metaphysical ideas or truths which his poetry embodies.

The first poems of M. de Lamartine, besides the charm of his verse, had the attraction of complete novelty. Till then the poet in France had only been the describer and personifier of the common feelings of mankind; his poetry was not the expression of his own individuality. There lay behind the works of a poet an entire man quite unknown to the crowd, and who published those only of his private thoughts and feelings, in which his reason and his taste assured him that the rest of mankind could meet him on common ground—could comprehend and sympathise with him. This, we conceive, is the just conception of the character of the poet. The ancients had recognised it, and personified it in Homer singing to the nations of Greece the gods and heroes of their common country. The poet was conceived as the man to whom the gods had accorded the gift of expressing the thoughts of all in passionate and harmonious words. Modern times, while their more austere creeds deprived the poet of the attributes ascribed to him by the nations of antiquity, his melodious lyre, his crown of laurels, his mysterious communication with the muses, left him his character and function of a public man—an inspired teacher and singer of ideas and feelings recognised by the mass.

Such was still in France the received creed when M. de Lamartine made his appearance. The poets who had preceded him had more or less abridged and lowered that function of poetry, whether from the humbleness of the class of composition to which they devoted themselves, or for want of the talents necessary to render them fully equal to the office, or because, by the fault of their age as well as by their own, the feelings they embodied were only passing through general caprices, instead of the durable tastes and sentiments of humanity. The public demanded novelty: it was sought for at any price—at whatever price the looked-for poet might choose to put upon it. This poet was M. de Lamartine. It was the first time that the poet was seen to be the hero of his own poetry. The success was immense. All imaginations were captivated with a young poet giving the history of some years of a life perfectly unknown, of which the most stirring incidents were doubts and speculations about the things of the invisible world, and of which the principal event was a love-affair.

But even the success of M. de Lamartine, instead of proving, as might at first appear, that the old opinion had changed respecting the character and office of the poet, was a confirmation of that old opinion. M. de Lamartine pleased all only because he was the poet of all. His history was more or less the history of all the delicate and cultivated minds of his time. They all had the same doubts, took pleasure in the same sort of speculations; and those who loved, as well as all those who wished to love, gave, or aspired to give to their passion the very same form and character as the lover of Elvire. M. de Lamartine had not, properly speaking, invented anything: what he produced was nothing new. Since the commencement of the century, but particularly since the fall of the empire, all imaginations were prepared for this kind of poetry. [Johann Wolfgang von Goethe's] *Werther* had almost exhausted the subject of the *malaise* of superior characters in the midst of a society which does not comprehend them, and of that sort of susceptibility of heart which is in fact one of the forms of pride. Byron had placed scepticism on a triumphal car. M. de Chateaubriand had described the malady of Réné, which soon became contagious, and had turned once more the general imagination into the direction of religious faith. Madame de Stael had contributed her sex's share towards these influences, half social, half literary—the natural fruit of a revolution which, by sweeping away all the most eminent of the intermediate generation, and charging the young with the undivided weight of the present and the future, had implanted in them the doubts of age beside the illusions of youth, and along with a great *besoin* of reverence, a great disgust with all known objects of it. There were already in the French language fine models in prose for the expression of these feelings. There were ingenious and eloquent formulæ for insolent doubt, which glories in its own sagacity, as well as for desponding doubt, which would be happy to believe. There were the like formulæ for the gloomy mystery of death, for the frailty of human wisdom, for the irreparable wasting away of life, for the littleness of glory. There were also such for external nature, fitted to the excessive nervous sensibility of the new philosophers who were about to fill it with emotions, with murmurs, with songs, with harmonies, and make it the visible aspect of the divinity: there were such for love—no longer the gallant and chivalrous love of our fathers (somewhat less subtle than we in that matter), but a restless love, full of vapours and *ennui,* ending before it was fairly begun, and lamenting over its own extinction: a love stormy without motive, greedy of sufferings and tears, and which, still seeking to gratify itself in the old-fashioned mode, clothed the pursuit with a most copious drapery of susceptibilities and despairs. M. de Lamartine's originality was that of being the first to put into fine verse the most delicate and the most durable of those ideas and feelings, and to express the metaphysics of them with a peculiar charm of sweetness and facility of numbers, which till then had been deemed incompatible with the severe laws of French poetry.

His first **Meditations** (though new in French poetry as to the *fonds* of the ideas), considered as a work of art and of language, remained true to those laws; he innovated, but it was within the limits of established principles. Very fortunately for the young poet, the systematic prefaces, the resuscitation of the poetry of the sixteenth century, the theories of 'art for art's sake,' the projects of renovation in the language of poetry, were still dormant in the heads whence they were afterwards to issue armed, in the costume of barons of the middle ages. Such poetry and poets, *soi-disant* classical, as there still were, if they took but a low rank according to the standard fixed by the great authorities, at least kept up the respect for that standard, and confirmed its excellence by their very inability to come up to its austere precepts. No one had yet ventured to deny that French verse should be like French prose, precise, energetic, without slovenliness of expression, without inconsistent metaphors or false images, and that the reason should, as in the time of Boileau, govern the imagination. M. de Lamartine had made his first verses under this discipline; not perhaps with a very strong and clear sense of the durability which it alone gives to the productions of genius, but at least with a happy natural sense of what was suited to the French language, and probably with good habits, derived from early instruction. He then thought more of the advantages which followed the observance of the precepts of his art than of the restraints which that observance imposed. He was unknown, solitary, without that sort of friends who make a poet in love with his defects, and even make them more dear to him than his good qualities, by becoming the apologists and champions

of them to the public without. It is even said that he had found, what poets never find unless they seek him with great sincerity, the Aristarchus of Horace, the 'ami prompt à vous censurer' of Boileau; a man of taste and *esprit,* to whose scruples, it is said, he sacrificed verses which might be beautiful, but were not so in a good style. That friend must even then have sought to strengthen him on the side on which he was destined to be always weak, that of critical discrimination; and must have warned him against the snare of mere facility of versification—a miserable talent, which should be left to improvisatores.

M. de Lamartine had, from the beginning, two sorts of admirers: the one sort were partisans of the old classical traditions; the other belonged to a younger generation, which already carried all the feelings and all the restlessness of the age to extremes, and were destined soon to exhibit the very caricature of it. The former, reserved and prudent, almost more uneasy about what still remained for the young poet to do than pleased with what he had already done, accompanied their admiration with advice; told him to watch himself, to make his verses more terse, to guard against his own facility, to fear it. The latter, seizing on his defects as the part of him which could most easily be imitated, called upon him to give himself free scope, to yield to the inspirations of his genius, to drink deep of his own music, to take the golden lyre and touch all its chords at hazard; in plain prose, to multiply his faults, that he might more and more resemble *their* miserable imitations of him, and that his authority might protect them from criticism: the natural tactics of the imitator— that evil genius of all poets.

When the second **Meditations** appeared, the same conflicting counsels were repeated, which had greeted the first; and, as usually happens each side went greater lengths in its opinion. The partisans of tradition exhorted M. de Lamartine to vary himself; his imitators, and their theorists, to exaggerate himself: the former, to think more of his reader than of himself; the latter, to think more of himself than of his reader: the first, to remain true to the language and its laws; the last, to create a language for himself, by his sovereign right as a poet, and to commence an era of new laws: the first, to study the Georgics of Virgil, [Jean Racine's] *Athalie,* La Fontaine, even Boileau, whose austere art it would have been so glorious to apply to more poetical and more interesting ideas; the last, not to go higher than André Chénier, (unless it were to dip into Ronsard), but to read sedulously those English and German poets whose poetry is most exclusively the subtle expression of their own idiosyncracies.

The eulogiums of the new school prevailed over the counsels of the partisans of tradition. Their praises were without condition and without reserve: they came from young men and beautiful women, whose applause has greater charms than the calm approbation of mature years and solid understandings. There were woven for him chaplets of verses and of flowers: young men dedicated their poems to him—poor echoes of his: young women made love to him, and sued for some beatings of the heart that had sighed for Elvire. M. de Lamartine was carried away by

the stream: he submitted to the new influences; he adopted the language of his chosen audience, and began to feel
himself fettered in that of the first **Meditations**: he wrote
hastily, and without study. It was the time of the famous
theory of *l'art pour l'art:* M. de Lamartine gave in his
adhesion to the theory. The two volumes of the **Harmonies Religieuses** were the result.

The **Harmonies,** which appeared in 1830, present more
fine verses, perhaps, but fewer fine poems than the collection of the **Meditations**; and they are more marked with
the faults of readiness and facility, which was destined to
be the besetting sin of M. de Lamartine's talent.

We now lose almost every trace of practical life. In the
**Meditations** the most humble reader might sometimes
recognise his own feelings in the poet's reveries, in his
sorrows, in his pleasures; but in the **Harmonies** the poet
isolated himself more and more, withdrew himself from
the observation of men, and made himself visible but to
God, in a cloud of vapoury poetry. He was no longer the
poet of the epoch, of which a great prose writer, M. de
Chateaubriand, had observed with accuracy and characterised with precision the more serious instincts, and all those
of its uneasinesses which were the least remote from the
general constitution of man. M. de Lamartine had transported thought into the realms of vague and recondite
speculations; into regions whither we could no longer
follow him, for want of wings; into a world where there
was not the smallest corner for us. Many readers who dare
not yet say so, and many who loudly proclaim it, quitted
M. de Lamartine at his **Harmonies**; either because they
found that one-half of the book merely repeated, weaken-
ing them by diffusion, the most melodious notes of the
**Meditations**; or because the reader cares to follow the
poet no further than he can carry with him his right of
judgment; or because we only like the things on which our
own thoughts, although more humble than those of the
poet, have nevertheless touched.

An analysis of the **Religious Harmonies** is scarcely possible; for if it were clear it would be more so than the
work which it professed to analyse; and, according to the
admirers of the **Harmonies,** to desire to see clearly in
them is to show ourselves incapable of comprehending
them. We will, however, attempt to describe those of the
thoughts contained in them which are the least evanescent
and untangible.

The title of these poems indicates their leading idea; which
is, or at least seems to be, that of displaying all the physical and moral harmonies which connect the world with
God. The poet continually ascends from the visible to the
invisible, and interrogates all creation on the subject of its
relations with the Creator. He asks the oak, how, from an
acorn dropped by the beak of an eagle on some arid sand,
it became an oak, and spread out those vast branches which
suffice to shelter against the tempest the shepherd and his
flock. He asks of the morning, whence it has its freshness
and its beauty; what makes the forests shiver before the
coming of the storm; what raises the cups of the flowers
bent down by the dews of the night; what awakens the

winds from their mysterious slumber. He asks the night,
who gave it that mute language understood only by poets, by lovers, and by those who suffer; and why man is
afraid of a dark night, though all is sleeping around him,
even crime. And to each of these, and of other and stranger
questions, he answers—it is God.

Sometimes he loses himself in sublime extacies: he mounts
from thought to thought up to the throne of God; and there
his voice has no longer anything human in it; his song is
a mystical and inarticulate hymn, into which the souls who
are prepared by meditations of a similar character can
alone follow the poet; we seem to hear the distant echo of
a chorus of angels, in which we join without understanding it. The soul of the poet seems to melt away in the light
of the divine presence, and he can no longer utter anything but confused and harmonious sighs. At other times
he renews his flight towards the empyrean, still burning to
see and to know; but this time, his faith being less abundant, the Deity eludes his sight; he still tries to soar, but
with a wing weakened by doubt, until, exhausted by his
efforts, he falls from weariness upon the earth, and bruises
his wings against the rocks.

All creation is ennobled by the pen of the poet, to be
worthy of this direct communion with God. His descriptions are those of a world of which ours is only a rude
sketch. There exists not a country so favoured of heaven
that M. de Lamartine does not embellish and idealize.
Even Italy is something more than that privileged land
where the breezes are so soft, the shade so soothing, and
the hours glide past so gently; something more than that
marvellous soil where all is beautiful, even destruction.
With M. de Lamartine the breezes of Italy have a voice,
and sing melodies as they glide among the branches: the
sound of her tempests is a voice rising from the sea in
solemn adoration of the Almighty; her bays, sprinkled with
white sails, are second skies gleaming with stars, or vast
azure mirrors on which reposes the great shadow of God.
If M. de Lamartine ever approaches the things of common
life, it is to cast upon them a careless look, or to borrow
from them, in passing, some image which he magnifies. If
he descends to speak of our miseries, it is in the style of
one who cannot touch even a sore without ennobling it.
The poet of the **Harmonies** is endowed with senses which
we have not: what is to us silence is to him a concert of
unutterable melody; in the flowers which we trample under our feet he finds intoxicating perfume. In his first
poems we could follow him into a world of thoughts,
superior, but still analogous to ours; we were below him,
but we beheld him beckoning to us from on high. But in
the **Harmonies** we have lost sight of him; he has veiled
himself from us; he has soared beyond the reach of our
vision; and those who profess that theirs has followed him
to the footstool of the throne of God, have seen him, we
fear, only with the eyes of faith.

The poem of **Jocelyn** is a return to ideas of the practical
sort. M. de Lamartine has descended from the empyrean
into the everyday world. **Jocelyn** is a novel in verse. The
**Harmonies** had been written in the time of *l'art pour
l'art,* when so many poets, some of whom have remained

men of talent, were bitten with the mania of not being understood; some in good faith and with candour; others, by one of those thousand artifices of vanity, which provide, by anticipation, apologies in the event of failure. For, was it not clear that, if the crowd did not understand them, they resembled those poets whose glory has been posthumous? It was therefore necessary to envelop themselves in sufficient darkness to be able to disown the jurisdiction of the critics on the ground of incompetence, and to console themselves for not being admired in their life-time. The theory of *l'art pour l'art* was a mere paradox of vanity. M. de Lamartine, ill-protected by critical discrimination, laid open, besides, to all new ideas by his benevolent nature, was caught in the snare, and ranged himself among those who disowned all discipline; but, like every fertile and elevated intellect which falls into a sophism, he carried into it his natural qualities, and endowed his erroneous system with beauties which belonged to the poetry of all times and all countries. Nevertheless, making allowance to the **Harmonies,** published in 1830, for the unfavourable moment at which they appeared, and for the interference of the more stirring emotions of politics with the interest they might have excited, it must still be confessed that they were less relished than the **Meditations.** M. de Lamartine felt that he had gone too far. The poets who soar highest above our heads, and even those who in their theories exclude the public at large from the capacity of understanding their works, do not like to see their readers dwindle or grow cool. His poems in the style of the new school, had driven his readers away; the form of a romance, on the contrary, might bring them back; popularity was on that side—M. de Lamartine wrote **Jocelyn.**

The story of Jocelyn is very romantic. Jocelyn is the son of an honest man, who lived in a humble style in the neighbourhood of Grenoble, on a small fortune, which was to be divided between this son and a sister. This sister loves a young man of the country, and is loved by him; but with only her own half of her father's fortune, she is too poor for the relations of the young man. Jocelyn gives up to her his half, renounces the world, and enters a *séminaire.* The revolution of 1789 breaks out; crimes increase rapidly; France is covered with scaffolds. Jocelyn, threatened with death, flies from the *séminaire,* and with great difficulty escapes to the Alps. He buries himself in an inaccessible retreat, where an old shepherd supports him, by depositing daily in the hollow of a rock a portion of his loaf of bread.

After some weeks, Jocelyn sees two men flying in the direction of his retreat—one very young, the other of mature age—pursued by soldiers. They reach the brink of the torrent which protects Jocelyn's retreat. The young man prefers the call of humanity to that of safety: he points out to the two fugitives the bridge by which he is accustomed to pass the torrent, and assists them to cross it. The soldiers, slain by two gun-shots from the more aged of the fugitives, fall, and are precipitated into the abyss. But the man himself is mortally wounded;—Jocelyn assists him in his last moments;—he dies.

Jocelyn is now left alone with the younger, Laurence, who has been recommended to his care by the dying man. A warm friendship grows up between them. On the part of Jocelyn, the elder of the two, that friendship is mixed with a sentiment of protection; on that of Laurence, with one of obedience. They become inseparable; but something is always wanting to their unreserved intimacy. A winter and a summer pass away, and their friendship is increased, but along with it the uneasy consciousness that there is something which they are concealing from each other. They are happy, nevertheless; for who can be happier than two friends, pure of heart, in a solitude laid out for them by M. de Lamartine? The poet provides abundantly for their wants, making them live on pigeons' eggs, fishes who let themselves be caught by hand, and wild fruits which he makes ripen at elevations where even the elder-tree cannot flower. He tempers for them the rude blasts of winter; he withholds the snow, which in those solitudes falls incessantly from autumn till spring; and he tames for them, and endows with superior intelligence, a hind, who dwells with them as a companion, and who testifies by the tenderness of her looks, and the intelligent motions of her ears, that she understands their conversation—albeit somewhat mystical.

One day, when a storm, by rendering the paths impassable, had prolonged for some hours the absence of Jocelyn, who had gone out, according to his custom, to receive the bread of the old shepherd, on his return he finds the cave deserted. Neither Laurence nor the hind are there. He wanders far and long among the mountains, vainly crying out for his friend. At length the hind comes to him, and—thanks to the gift of language with which the poet has endowed her—contrives to apprize him where Laurence is. Jocelyn follows the faithful animal; he descends to the bottom of a ravine, and perceives, half buried in blood-stained snow, a human form. It is Laurence. He takes him in his arms—warms him with his breath and his tears—hurries with him to the cave—uncovers his bosom to dress his wounds.—Laurence is a woman!

The secret is revealed which hindered their mutual confidence from being complete, and love takes the place of friendship between Jocelyn and Laurence, restored to life and health. But a new uneasiness springs up. Jocelyn is devoted to the altar: and though the Church has not yet ordained him priest, he has inwardly vowed to consecrate himself to religion. While he is distracted between his scruples of conscience and his irresistible wishes, he is sent for to the town, to receive the confession of the old Bishop of Grenoble, who is to die the following day on the revolutionary scaffold. Jocelyn is introduced into the prison; the old man demands of him the prayers which remit the sins of those who are about to die. 'I have no right to pronounce them,' said Jocelyn, 'I am not a priest.'—'You shall be made one by my hand,' replied the bishop. Jocelyn resists. The sacrament is about to deprive him of Laurence for ever. But the unpitying bishop places before him the alternative of being consecrated or receiving his curse. Jocelyn suffers the imposition of hands: all is over.

We find him, some time after, a *curé* of a small village among the Alps, with his aged servant, his pigeons, his dog, and a few books—sharing his bread with the poor, offering hospitality to travellers, burying the dead without fee, and sometimes providing them with a coffin and a winding-sheet—mediating in the quarrels of the villagers, and reconciling them by means of parables—sometimes explaining to them the course of the stars, some times the wonders of vegetation: gentle, pious, humble of heart, having given to God all that he had to give—all but the chaste and mournful recollection of Laurence. As for her, she has been first married against her will to a man who has not her heart, and who dies for grief that he has not. A widow at twenty, she seeks forgetfulness in *coquetterie*—she allows many adorers to sigh for her in vain:—

> Je les laissai m'aimer, mais, moi, je n'aimai pas:
> L'ombre de mon ami *m'entourant d'un nuage,*
> Toujours entre eux et moi jettait sa chère image.

At length her feeble health has given way: afflicted with an incurable malady, she has been advised to travel into Italy. At the end of the story we see her on the pallet of a village-inn, confessing to a priest, who listens to her with downcast eyes and irrepressible emotion. That priest is Jocelyn.

Laurence dies; Jocelyn follows her some years after. Not far from the cave which had been the scene of their loves, one cross covers three graves—those of Laurence's father, of Laurence, and of Jocelyn. Thus ends the romance.

Such is a historical sketch of the principal poems of M. de Lamartine. Such have been the three principal phases of his poetical career.

The success of these three works has been unequal; but the success of the whole has been immense. The reason is, that M. de Lamartine has been the poet not only of the serious feelings of the epoch, but also of its caprices of imagination and its passing fashions in literature.

The *Meditations,* the first and most genuine of his productions, appeared before fashion and imitation had exaggerated those serious feelings: that return of religious emotions and aspirations in the midst of doubt; that vague melancholy of a generation *blasé* from the cradle; that languidness of character in the age of vigour; that discouragement in the age of hope; that weariness without having struggled, and disenchantment without having enjoyed; that morbid sensitiveness of heart, that unquiet self-questioning and self-analysing of a soul which retires into itself, and dares not manifest its feelings to a world too cold and repulsive for it; those thousand delicate griefs and painful pleasures, the nice shades of which are described in the *Meditations* in so attractive a manner, and occasionally with a purity of style which would have satisfied the great intellects of the seventeenth century. Imitation and fashion had not yet brought this class of subjects into disrepute, by multiplying feeble and exaggerated delineations of them, or by copying with the head what originally came from the heart.

The *Harmonies* represent another of the tendencies of the time, also serious, but already mixed with phantasy. It is

that belief (viewed as one of the worst of heresies by all established religions) in a God half personal, like that of the Hebrew Scriptures, half pantheistical, like that of Virgil,—

> Mens agitat molem,

and of the freethinking philosophers of Germany. The God of the *Harmonies* is at once the God of the great scholastic poem of Dante, the God of St. Thomas Aquinas, and the God 'Soul of the World' who breathes in the winds, murmurs in the waves, flutters in the foliage, is unfolded in the flowers—whose voice is heard in all the varying sounds of Nature. The religion of the *Harmonies* is, in fact, the real religion of the age in France: a religion sprung from that weariness of doubt which is depicted in the *Meditations,* and greatly promoted by the revival, at that time, of a taste for the productions of the middle ages. The *Harmonies* represented the Deity with the same grandeur, the same multiplicity, and with as contradictory attributes, as constituted the vague idea already floating in the imagination of the public. So far, therefore, their success was natural, independently of the aid they derived from their connection with the theory of 'l'art pour l'art,' a passing caprice which the three days of July swept away, along with many other things which seemed far more solid.

In *Jocelyn* the religious tendencies are a little more definite than in the *Harmonies;* and as the doubt, anxious to believe, of the *Meditations* had been succeeded by the biblico-pantheistical God of the *Harmonies,* so this rather shadowy divinity was gradually to assume a more distinct shape, and to put on the characteristics of the orthodox God—the God of the received view of Christianity. The God of Jocelyn, a Catholic priest, is, in fact, the God of the established religion. The age, or rather that crowd of impatient and forward-pressing spirits who are personified under that name, fancy that they too have returned to the God of Jocelyn. In less than twenty years these spirits have passed, like M. de Lamartine, from doubt to a rather confused belief, and from that belief to a sort of Catholicism, without ceremonial observances and without works. Jocelyn consequently has been successful: first, because the hero of the poem is a priest according to the Catholic ritual (although the orthodox have exclaimed against the rather summary form of his ordination in the prison of the old bishop), and next, because the poem conformed to a caprice of fashion of a less serious kind, but sufficient to be decisive of its success— we mean the general taste for the romance form. Thus, while in the *Harmonies* M. de Lamartine, so far as thoughts were concerned, made himself the organ of one of the serious and elevated tendencies of his times, and, by the style, flattered the caprice of *l'art pour l'art;* so, in *Jocelyn,* by making a Catholic priest the hero of his tale, he satisfied the religious and those who aspired to religion, without offending any unbeliever of a tolerant disposition; while, by the adoption of the romantic form, he made himself be read by all the light readers.

It is thus that M. de Lamartine has gained the applause of his contemporaries; by always falling in with the prevailing temper of their minds, if not through the strength of his penetration, at least through the similarity of his own nature and personal tendencies. It must however be said to his honour, that he has always been sincere and in earnest, whether he expressed the more serious and deeper feelings of his age, or, in ephemeral verse, represented only its frivolous side. He has too often yielded to the literary caprices, the mere fashions of the time; but he has never flattered its licentiousness, nor sought success beyond the limits of morality. It is, above all, from this high characteristic, that the impression he has made has gone deeper into the heart of society than that of any contemporary poet. His success has been a fire-side success—his glory a domestic glory. He has given to voluptuousness itself a modesty of mien and a chastity of language which retains the mind within the circle of the thoughts which a pure mind may permit to itself. He has, besides, adopted all the household traditions, all the good and simple lessons of forbearance, of moderation, and of kindness, which the mother has received from her parents, and transmits to her children. He has made fresh and attractive, with his charming pen, all that every-day morality without which there is no happiness for man; in a word, he has desired to be a poet such as parents would put into the hands of their children; and he has succeeded, as his publisher could testify, who is at this moment piling up copies of his works for the *étrennes* (new year's gifts) of 1837.

It remains to inquire how much of this popularity will last, and how much will pass away; to estimate M. de Lamartine's poems by the standard of absolute excellence, and attempt to foretel what, with respect to him, will be the decree of posterity. . . .

In all his works posterior to the **Meditations,** M. de Lamartine has departed from the essential conditions of French poetry, and of all poetry which is not abandoned to individual fantasy. We will not dispute with him about expressions; the time is long gone by when the battle could be fought on that field. As Christianity is no longer fighting against scepticism for its minor ceremonial, but has been put upon the defence of its essentials—of its very existence; so good taste, in our day, has a very different task to perform from that of defending correctness of language: the controversy has fallen back upon the very nature and essence of poetry itself: what has now to be contended for is, that Molière, Racine, Boileau, La Fontaine, Corneille, in the durable part of their works, shall still continue to be considered the best poets of France, and great poets for all times and all countries. It is upon this ground that French poetry has to be protected against the errors of M. de Lamartine. It is the main body itself of poetical imagery and diction that we should beg of him to spare.

The **Harmonies** already presented too many examples of those immense periods in which the phrase perpetually commences, and never ends. *Jocelyn* carried this licence to still greater extravagance; there is scarcely a trace left of the structure of the poetical sentence. Where is that variety of rhythm—those sentences of unequal length, imitating the natural movement of the mind, and which

seem the very breath of thought? A period, without shape, and without limits, has absorbed all those forms, and drowned all those *nuances*. Rarely, with M. de Lamartine, does the thought form a whole, detached, complete, artfully divided, and having none of its members languid or superfluous. Either the words come before the thought, or they continue after the thought is ended. Sometimes the thought, or rather what ought to be such, begins confusedly, under the vague forms of a prelude, resembling the scattered chords of a musician who is trying his instrument. By degrees the poet becomes animated; his thought attempts to disengage itself; the verse flows, the images crowd in; but, as they proceed, they raise up other thoughts, which take the place of the first; then others still, by which these are in their turn put to flight. At other times, on the contrary, the thought announces itself freely from the commencement, and, like a well-touched string, gives forth the sound in all its fulness. But it gradually dwindles as it goes on; it becomes more and more uncertain and vapoury, like a sound which, as it becomes distant, loses its original clearness, and can searcely be distinguished from any other sound which is dying away; in short, after the thought is exhausted, there still remain verses and numbers which are, as it were, the distant echo of it; as, after the sound has ceased, there is not yet silence; though the ear no longer hears, the mind may still fancy that it has not yet ceased to hear. But this, which is no fault in music, is inexcusable in verse: the words ought to begin and end with the thoughts which they express.

The consequence is, that the mind skips those preludes of the commencing thought, or glides over those last vibrations of the finishing thought; it runs to the substance of the subject. No new theory of criticism, no education, can prevent this. If it is in a description that the poet thus lingers, thinking little and writing much, the mind does, like Boileau reading the descriptions of Scudéry—

'Il saute vingt feuillets pour aller à la fin.'

The humblest reader, as well as the most intelligent, has that rapidity of *coup d'œil* which makes him see from a distance what there is in a book which suits him. Is it in the narrative parts that the poet flags? Then the reader's fault of reading fast, and hastening to what he wants, augments in proportion to the writer's diffuseness. He loses all respect for the poet. His curiosity pushes him forward: woe to the poet who, not having the same impatience, as he knows his own *denouement* before-hand, has taken too much time to reach it. The story is become the property of the reader; he disposes of it as a master; he abridges and mutilates it at his pleasure. According as he is more or less impatient, he tolerates more or less of the mere accessaries; but even the most indulgent is not much so. We are sure that among the pledged admirers of M. de Lamartine, among those who have moistened the book with preengaged tears, there are few who could give their word of honour that they have always read but one verse at a time; and that their mind has never moved faster than their eyes. So rapid is the declivity on which we are placed by an absorbing story, or a well-planned dramatic action, that we scarcely have patience even for great beauties of language; which, rather than stop, we like to return to, as to a pleasure of a different order, after our curiosity has been satisfied. What then, if the story or the drama is only retarded by *hors d'œuvres* carelessly written, towards which we believe ourselves to have sufficiently done our part by reading them as they have been written, that is, a first time only! It is thus that more than half of *Jocelyn* has been read. It is thus that the most popular novels are read. *Jocelyn* has over them only the advantage of being as amusing in a more difficult art. The public has taken the author at his word: he called the story an episode, and it has been treated as an episode, of which the scanty incidents are lost in the lengthy developments of a poem. The reader has rescued the episode from the midst of the developments, and has forgiven him the rest of the book, as a licence justified by popularity; just as a novelist in vogue is forgiven the interminable descriptions in which he wraps up a very minute thought,—because a man must live by his talent.

*Jocelyn* has, then, had the success of a novel! 'The descriptions in *Jocelyn* are very long and very numerous,' said in our presence an admirer of M. de Lamartine, who, perhaps, complained to the poet that he had made them too short and too few, and who will be very indignant with those who dare to say what he thinks. 'For my part,' replied a lady, 'I have skipped them, and have read my *Jocelyn* in two hours!' Eight thousand verses in two hours! It is true, the lady boasted of having moistened with her tears every page 'in which there is any story.' Is this success? Is it not rather the most cruel affront which French poetry has ever received? The great Condé listened patiently for hours to the miserable verses of Chapelain, solely out of respect for that poetry!

As there is no poetical style possible in France, of which the ordinary sentences are periods of thirty or forty verses each, without a pause, so there is no poem possible with episodes of eight thousand verses. If the poem *On Mankind,* promised us by M. de Lamartine, and of which *Jocelyn* is an episode, is to be on a corresponding scale, it is not forty thousand verses (which are said to be the number he announces), it is not a hundred thousand, which will bring the entire poem into a just proportion. It must resemble the Hindoo poems, each of which is a library in itself. We know not how, in this busy age, after terminating all the other labours of the day, we can find time to read the *Poème Humanitaire.* There would be only one mode of getting it read (and that only in the same summary manner as *Jocelyn*), by publishing it in the form of a daily newspaper. At a few hundred verses per day, one might get through it in a year.

When we have such errors of judgment to expect from a popular poet, to what purpose is it to criticise mere faults of execution? What need to comment upon that false poetical refinement which consists in avoiding the proper word whenever it seems in the slightest degree *bourgeois,* and replacing it by pretended equivalents which

change the meaning; and that habit of idealizing everything, which takes from objects their own form and nature, either by ornamenting them so richly that the dress is substituted for the object, or frittering them away into such vagueness that we lose all sense of reality? Why should wc reckon up all those faults of facility in composition, and want of critical perception,—those imitations of all possible styles,—sometimes circumlocutions after Delille, sometimes trivialities in the manner of the new school, according as the one or the other imitation gives least trouble and takes least time; those constant repetitions of certain turns of expression, as a musician of little originality returns continually to a *motivo* which he has accidentally hit upon; and a thousand other faults, which can scarcely move us now that we are threatened with a poem of the length of the Mahabarat or the Ramayan?

What, then, in M. de Lamartine's productions, is destined to survive? The **Meditations,** some poems in the **Harmonies Réligieuses,** and some passages of *Jocelyn.* There will survive a great many of those admirable verses, which do not redeem the poems containing them from mediocrity, and which are the last flowers with which dying poetry adorns itself. There will survive the memory of great poetical powers, very superior to what they will have produced; and the harmonious and sonorous name of a poet, to whom his age will have been too indulgent, and glory too easy, and in whom his contemporaries will have loved too well the reflection of their own infirmities.

There might survive much more, if our anticipations deceive us; if M. de Lamartine *is* endowed with that critical faculty which his latter works do not permit us to acknowledge in him; if, instead of that placid self-satisfaction which we have imputed to him he has the quality of all great minds, that dissatisfaction with their works which excited while it restrained them; if, superior to his own successes, more severe towards himself than his age, he would give us, instead of some still worse specimen of the negligences of *Jocelyn,* new poems, sweet, tender, profound, like the **Meditations**; rich in language, like the fine passages in the **Harmonies,** and somewhat more terse in style than all he has yet done.

It the good fortune of M. de Lamartine, or, to speak his own neo-Christian language, if his good angel, bring him back into the first paths which conducted him so rapidly to a glory that has become perilous, would it not be a considerable honour for criticism to have been an auxiliary, though a somewhat rough one, of the poet's own judgment?

But if he yields to that ephemeral popularity which already demands of him Indian poems, it ought to be some consolation for criticism not to have to answer to its country and posterity (before whom the illustrious poet always drags his humble judge) for the foolish applauses which retained in the inferior region of the second order of talent a poet who possessed sufficient natural capacity to have elevated him to the rank of men of genius.

---

**An early reaction to Lamartine's poetry:**

The success of the *Meditations* was prodigious,—not greater than they deserved, but still prodigious; after the sallies of the empire, after the tame and almost insipid, but amiable literature of De Jouey and Abbé De Lille, and after the correct M. De Fontanes, it was prodigious to see a serious poet—indeed, a religious poet—read with enthusiasm, and raised to honour and fame. It was a sort of poetry which only addressed itself to highly cultivated minds. Sister of the poetry of Manzoni and of Pellico, sister of the poetry of Tasso, as of that of the Hebrews, it showed itself calm and *suave,* greatly simple, and surrounded with all the charms of Christian beauty and truth. Sometimes his *Meditations* resembled the poor sick daughter of love, and were elegiac in the style of Sappho. Sometimes the voice was of a different tone; and the cry of grief was heard, and the hymn of expiation was chanted, and his sacred lyre riveted all attentions and gained all hearts. . . .

Between the *Meditations* and the *Harmonies* of De Lamartine there is a vast difference, but it is that resulting from the lapse of time and from mental suffering. The *Harmonies,* like the *Meditations,* are the production of an enthusiastic mind and a believing and pious soul. But sorrow has his young days shaded—suffering had left its impress upon his heart; and there is all the difference between the two works that there is between tears and joy, or the poetical forebodings of evil, and evil actually realized. He who was tender as Tasso and sensitive as Schiller in his *Meditations,* is in his *Harmonies* sublime as Klopstock in his *Messiah,* and religious as Fenelon. There are *four* elements in the poetry of the *Harmonies:*— the recollections of his childhood—the life of an orderly, pious, and happy family—the political transformation of his mind from a secluded provincial royalist to that of one who even then dreamt of forming a "social party"—and, finally, real, genuine, heartfelt piety.

*"De Lamartine," in* Blackwood's Edinburgh Magazine, *January, 1839.*

---

**Albert Joseph George (essay date 1940)**

SOURCE: "The Vision of 1821 and Lamartine's Philosophy" and "Unanimism and Lamartine's Metaphysics (1821-1830)," in *Lamartine and Romantic Unanimism,* Columbia University Press, 1940, pp. 12-29, pp. 30-66.

[*In the following excerpt from his study of Lamartine's belief in the oneness of the universe, George finds evidence of Lamartine's mystical outlook in his poetic works and aesthetic principles.*]

It happened on January 10, 1821, near Naples, while Lamartine was strolling down the streets of his beloved Italy. Head bowed, he was mulling over plans for an immortal work, the great Christian epic that the centuries had so far failed to produce. As he thought about God and the purpose of Creation, his pace slackened and, suddenly, the divine grace descended on him as it had on Descartes and Pascal. A hand seemed to brush aside a curtain from the night sky, and an intense vision transported him beyond reality. . . .

During this moment of inspiration, the drama of existence was reënacted upon the stage of his imagination. Before his eyes matter came to life, each atom revealing itself the possessor of a soul. Following a mathematical pattern, these particles separated into two great divisions, the material and the spiritual, then spread across the sky in an infinite hierarchy. At the top of the scale stood God; at the bottom, the condemned. Between these two extremes stretched intermediary links whose relative spiritual status was indicated by the comparative darkness of their surroundings. Up and down the ladder moved the myriads of souls, perpetually undergoing tests of their fitness, continually metamorphosing into new forms. Some rose when merit earned them a reward; others fell when a transgression brought retribution. But with patient efforts each struggled to mount to the top and rejoin the Creator. Before the astounded poet, the parts of this living universe rehearsed in miniature their preordained function, demonstrating in the space of two hours the shifting relationships of progressing souls. All matter lived, he learned, all matter covered a soul, and each of these souls existed only to reach the source from whence it came. Before the vision faded, Lamartine believed that he had been granted an insight into the divine plan. Exultation swept over him when, in *Les Harmonies,* he recalled this revelation:

> O Dieu! tu m'as donné d'entendre
> Ce verbe, ou plutôt cet accord,
> Tantôt majestueux et tendre,
> Tantôt triste comme la mort!
> Depuis ce jour, Seigneur, mon âme
> Converse avec l'onde et la flamme,
> Avec la tempête et la nuit!
> Ces choeurs étincelants que ton doigt seul conduit,
> Ces choeurs d'azur où leur foule s'élance,
>
> ["**Poésie**"]

> Je les comprends, Seigneur! tout chante, tout m'instruit
> Que l'abîme est comblé par ta magnificence,
> Que les cieux sont vivants, et que la providence
> Remplit de sa vertu tout ce qu'elle a produit!
>
> ["**Hymne de la nuit**"]

This was the dazzling vision which furnished Lamartine with the schema of his philosophy. Later, as time and criticism disclosed gaps in his cosmology, he developed it by borrowing indiscriminately from predecessor and contemporary. In this fashion he absorbed by the end of his life a doctrine sufficiently profound to satisfy all his intellectual needs, although it had not been systematically constructed.

Vague though it seems, the apparition of 1821 reorientated his life along lines from which he never departed. In the first place, it left its mark on his literary and his political career. During his youth, when Lamartine was conceiving his system, preoccupation with it colored his verse. **Les Harmonies** and the **Mort de Socrate** revealed cautious attempts to poetize metaphysics; **Jocelyn** and **La Chute d'un ange,** bolder efforts to portray a philosophy in action. Even the *Voyage en Orient,* ostensibly designed as a travel book, developed into a strange mixture of metaphysical, political, and social digressions. It may well be said that, prior to 1848, most, if not all, of Lamartine's prose and poetry originated from a desire to prove to himself and to France that his vision had actually solved the enigma of life. From 1843 to the time of his retirement from public office, Lamartine attempted to apply to politics precepts deduced from the philosophy he had found in Italy; then, in 1852, he turned back with his dream to writing.

In the second place, his mystic experience swayed Lamartine from his past religious life. Born and educated in the Catholic Church, a pupil of the Jesuits, and the son of an extremely devout mother, he had hitherto accepted Catholicism unconditionally. But after 1821, with the memory of his revelation continually before him, he passed rapidly to doubt, then denied his faith for a new religion. To cross this Rubicon was a momentous step for Lamartine.

Interwoven in Lamartine's works lies the philosophy of which he often proudly spoke. Essentially it concerned the same chain of beings he had seen intuitively near Naples, and, as such, represents the nucleus of romantic thought. Consciously he recognized the disparity and fluidity of the universe, admitted the existence of differences and separations, but at the same time he tried to find a harmony and a oneness beneath what he considered a veneer of contradictions.

On the basis of an instinctive love for all that surrounded him, Lamartine formulated the group of concepts which welded into a whole the apparently unrelated or opposed aspects of the universe. Like Lamennais, Michelet, and countless others, he felt that this sentiment gave the world coherence and purpose. It held men together, transcending any political boundary:

> Un seul culte enchaîne le monde
> Qui vivifie un seul amour:
>
> . . . . .
>
> Cette loi qui dit à tous "Frère",
> A brisé ces divisions
> Qui séparaient les fils du père
> En royaumes et nations.
>            ["**Utopie**," *Recueillements poétiques*]

Lamartine pictured humanity from the artist's point of view, seeking balance and perspective in fitting all its parts into a clear design. For him, the significance of the individual lay not in his isolated personality but in his social relationships. . . .

*A photograph by Nadar of Lamartine in his sixties.*

The family. . . was the lowest common denominator of society that excluded the anarchy of irresponsible individualism and offered a solid basis for peaceful human intercourse. . . .

Once Lamartine had interpreted the role of man as an intrinsic part of a group, he described a broader conception of unity, the nation. Since the union of one family with another to produce a third molded all three into the same likeness, the continuation of this process resulted in the fusion of the families of any one nation.

Although barriers of religion and tradition stand between nations and races, he pointed out that a greater force ["la sympathie de la civilisation"] acts to level these obstacles. . . . The proof of this "sympathy of civilization," he was convinced, lay in the testimony of history that man is progressively attaining peace with himself and with society. . . .

The picture was cleverly constructed to suit Lamartine's aesthetic taste. By negating the importance of the individual and accepting the family as a nucleus, he drew a design of life consisting of a series of concentric circles. Thus, as he saw it, this symbol imposed on the world a unique loyalty and devotion to all men without regard for the vagaries of birth. . . . For this reason Lamartine sympathized with Claude des Huttes, the stonemason of Saint-Point, in his all-embracing love. Both felt themselves integral parts of a collectivity rather than individuals.

But not content with imagining humanity as closely knit at any one time, Lamartine followed the example of Joseph de Maistre and Ballanche in considering its unity from a historical point of view as well. . . . Collectively and separately, he remarked, the family, the nation, and the race survive the individual to perpetuate their best qualities. . . . One generation yields to another, each leaving a richer heritage than it received. . . .

> Et la famille, enracinée
> Sur le coteau qu'elle a planté,
> Refleurit d'année en année,
> Collective immortalité.

[*Jocelyn*]

Thus, from any point of view, at any time

> Le genre humain n'est qu'un seul être
> Formé de générations. . .

["A l'esprit saint," *Harmonies*]

Although, in the eyes of Lamartine, humanity formed an entity, he could not prevail upon himself to isolate man from his environment. Life was universal; and man was invisibly connected to other worlds. . . .

Lamartine had been brought up in Mâcon, surrounded by pets and domestic animals; horses and dogs were always his favorites. Therefore, it was essential for him to include them in the scheme of things. The ninth epoch of *Jocelyn,* wherein Lamartine apostrophizes his dog, clearly demonstrates the affinities which the poet felt related them: man and dog merely represented differing degrees of the same creation.

In the final version of *Jocelyn,* Lamartine renounced affirming too categorically the existence of a soul in animals lest he offend orthodox friends and, more especially, his father and his wife. The manuscript, however, reveals that the reference to his pet in the line

> Révèle en toi le coeur avec tant d'évidence

had originally read

> L'âme en toi se lève avec tant d'évidence.

His dog possessed the same right to immortality as its master, even shared in the enjoyment of a soul. This so impressed Lamartine that, many years later, he digressed in the *Cours familier* to express the conviction that eventually someone would reveal the physical and spiritual harmony between man and beast.

The same unity encompassing these two orders he extended to plants. Just as a love for animals had persuaded him

to enlarge his system, so did an interest in nature demand an explanation of the significance of plant life. . . .

So keenly did he sense his alliance to the world that he recognized a close tie with even more than the trees and the grass:

> Au sillon, au rocher j'attachais ma paupière,
> Et ce regard disait: A la brute, à la pierre,
> Au moins, que ne suis-je pareil?

["Le tombeau d'une mère," *Harmonies*]

He discovered new relationships in the soil. The very dust lived; every globule of air comprehended an inhabited planet. Each microcosm lived its days and nights in its drop of space; and through it life and thought circulated as millions of minute, unseen universes pursued their destinies:

> Comme ils gravitent en cadence,
> Nouant et dénouant leurs vols harmonieux!
> Des mondes de Platon on croirait voir la danse
> S'accomplissant au son des musiques des cieux.
> L'oeil ébloui se perd dans leur foule innombrable;
> Il en faudrait un monde à faire un grain de sable,
> Le regard infini pourrait seul les compter:
> Chaque parcelle encor s'y poudroie en parcelle.
> Ah! c'est ici le pied de l'éclatante échelle
> Que de l'atome à Dieu l'infini voit monter.
>
> Pourtant chaque atome est un être!
> Chaque globule d'air est un monde habité!
> Chaque monde y régit d'autres mondes peut-être,
> Pour qui l'éclair qui passe est une éternité!
> Dans leur lueur de temps, dans leur goutte d'espace
> Ils ont leurs jours, leurs nuits, leurs destins, et leur
>   place
> La pensée et la vie y circulent à flot;
> Et, pendant que notre oeil se perd dans ces extases,
> Des milliers d'univers ont accompli leurs phases
> Entre la pensée et le mot!

[*Jocelyn*, "4ᵉ époque"]

All these atoms held with man an equal dignity before God. Since reason had been granted them in proportion to their significance in the universe, the sole respect in which they differed from each other and from the rest of the world was in degree of intelligence.

Thus, there arose in Lamartine's mind a picture of life as a chain of beings that stretched from the smallest possible entity to man. The mineral, plant, and animal kingdoms were but extensions of each other. The plant represented a more advanced stage of reason than the stone; the animal was superior to the plant; and man marked the culmination of the evolution of the visible creation. Yet each realm remained in close contact with the others, linked by shadowy borderlands consisting of forms of being that were not of one species, but of two. Nowhere did a gap open the chain, for God had allowed neither incompleteness nor death in his work. Man, then, manifested the highest form of the material world by virtue of an advanced intelligence, and he existed only as a fraction of the great unity into which all things are shaped. . . .

Meditation [on the nature of existence] brought Lamartine, like Pascal, to the discovery that man constitutes the *trait d'union* between two infinities:

> L'homme est le point fatal où les deux infinis
> Par la toute-puissance on été réunis.
> > [**"Isolement,"** *Les méditations*]

From humanity to the Creator stretches another endless progression of unperceived beings, connecting man to the angel, the angel to the seraph, and peopling space with spiritual life. The chain, then, as Lamartine wrote in a plan for *La Chute d'un ange,* continues upward through infinity without interruption, a notion already present in *Les Harmonies*:

> Et quelle vaste intelligence
> S'élevait par degrés de la terre au seigneur
> Depuis l'instinct de la brute existence,
> Jusqu'à l'âme qui loue, et qui prie, et qui pense
> Jusqu'au soupir d'un coeur,
> Qu'emporte d'un seul trait l'immortelle espérance
> Au sein de son auteur!
> > [**"Hymne de l'ange de la terre,"** *Harmonies*]

This conception filled Lamartine with the joy of having discovered the design of the world. It enabled him to visualize metaphysical existence:

> Qu'il est doux pour l'âme qui pense
> Et flotte dans l'immensité
> Entre le doute et l'espérance,
> La lumière et l'obscurité,
> De voir cette idée éternelle
> Luire sans cesse au-dessus d'elle.
> > [**"L'idée de Dieu,"** *Harmonies*]

Far removed from the creation, listening to the adoration of his creatures, the God of Lamartine exists in timeless perfection. He is the supreme individuality, universal and eternal. As in the Gospel according to Saint John, the poet's God is the source of life, the beginning and end of all things. Around God, the Father and Creator, revolves the infinite soul; power, beauty, love, intelligence, and law are his accomplishments.

Lamartine believed that this all-comprehensive God, bringing forth diversity from one idea, had willed the universe in order to admire his own image.

> Or le ciel et la terre, et ce que Dieu renferme
> Dans un jour éternel, tout est né d'un seul germe:
> Et ce germe est de Dieu la pensée et la loi,
> Qui porte toute chose avec sa forme en soi.
> > [*Chute d'un ange*]

A single wish animated space with beings, each of which shared in the soul of the Maker. From one *germe* all else

was born through a process whereby the original thought transformed itself into matter and multiplied indefinitely:

> De sorte qu'à la fois tout est vieux, tout est neuf,
> Qu'un monde décrépit d'un autre monde est l'oeuf,
> Qu'une chose accomplie enfante une autre chose,
> Et que chaque existence est une apothéose
> Où l'autre produit l'être en se décomposant,
> Où tout se perpétue en se divinisant!
> Et l'homme est ainsi né, fruit vivant de la terre;
> Non, comme Jéhovah, complet et solitaire,
> Mais de deux composé, mâle et femelle, afin
> Que sa dualité lui révélât sa fin
> Et que cette union de l'homme et de la femme,
> Qui féconde le corps et qui complète l'âme,
> Fût le symbole en lui de la divine loi
> D'amour et d'unité qui doit tout fondre en soi!
> > [*Chute d'un ange,* "8ᵉ vision"]

However, to maintain his conception of a God aloof who, at the same time, watched anxiously over the world, Lamartine was forced to establish the existence of demigods, numerically equal to the visible beings, who were charged with the welfare of some member of that part of the hierarchy which ends in man. On each of them, as guardian angels, rested the responsibility for a lesser creature. They undertook, he claimed, to fulfill the function of connecting the two realms of creation.

Despite the impression Lamartine gives that his vision had descended on him unexpectedly, it is obvious that the revelation had been prepared, first, by a desire for a personal religion, to be found in the *Méditations*; and, second, by his dissatisfaction with Catholicism.

To those who carefully scrutinized the *Méditations,* Lamartine's first collection of verse betrayed a curious mixture of religious aspirations, both orthodox and heretical. Had they but known the dates of composition of the individual poems, they would have been able to discern a distinct tendency toward a personal religion, for, as far back as August, 1817, when **"Le Lac"** was composed, there had appeared a desire to seek proof of the existence of God in the manifestations of nature:

> Ma pensée, embrassant tes attributs divers,
> Partout autour de soi te découvre et t'adore,
> Se contemple soi-même et t'y découvre encore:
>  . . . . .
> C'est toi que je découvre au fond de la nature,
> C'est toi que je bénis dans toute créature.

A year and a half later, Lamartine had discovered the concept of a chain of beings, when in May, 1819, he began his poem, **"Dieu."** Writing to Lamennais, he aired his recently acquired views on the personality of the Deity and his relationship to the universe:

> Le néant jusqu'à lui s'élève par degrés:
>  . . . . .
> Et comblant le néant de ses dons précieux,
> Des derniers rangs de l'être il peut tirer des dieux!

Mais ces dieux de sa main, ces fils de sa puissance,
Mesurent d'eux à lui l'éternelle distance,
Tendant par leur nature à l'être qui les fit;
Il est leur fin à tous, et lui seul se suffit!

["Dieu"]

Thus, by 1820, Lamartine hung on the verge of discarding Catholicism in favor of a more individual doctrine. He needed but little to push him over the edge, and the impetus came from his dissatisfaction with Catholic dogma.

. . . . .

Though still paying lip service to the Church, Lamartine had evidently ceased to be a Catholic after his vision of 1821. He stood now on the threshold of another period of his life, that in which he versified the metaphysics of his mystic experience. Little by little he had summoned enough courage to maintain his new position. Then, on the occasion of the publication of the *Nouvelles Méditations* in 1823, the poet definitely announced his adherence to the fundamentals of *unanimism* by clarifying and continuing certain ideas contained in the *Méditations*:

Tout me dit que la terre un moment m'a prêté
De ce feu qui l'anime une faible étincelle,
Que ma tombe lui rend ce que j'empruntai d'elle;
Que ce souffle de vie, exhalé sans retour,
Dans ces êtres sans fin circule tour à tour;
Que, sans pouvoir jamais se joindre et se
    connaître,
De ce MOI qui n'est plus d'autres MOI vont
    renaître,
Qui, subissant ainsi l'unique loi du sort,
Passeront du néant à la mort.

["Réflexion"]

To this doctrine of the transmigration of souls he added the notion of a hierarchy of beings to form the basis of the metaphysics he was later to preach:

C'est ainsi qu'entre l'homme et Jéhovah lui-même,
Entre le pur néant et la grandeur suprême,
D'êtres inaperçus une chaîne sans fin
Réunit l'homme à l'ange et l'ange au séraphim;
C'est ainsi que, peuplant l'étendue infinie,
Dieu répandit partout l'esprit, l'âme et la vie.

["L'ange," *Les nouvelles méditations*]

And in each of the poems he composed at this time he expressed the same thoughts, continuing in *Les Harmonies* and *Les Visions* the formation of the theology he had found in Italy. . . .

One of Lamartine's last connections with the Church snapped in 1829, when his mother died. To her he owed his religious training; for her sake he had withheld deserting Catholicism. But once her restraining influence was removed, he felt free to express his personal opinions. Now he need no longer refrain from writing what might hurt her. Each departure from what she had taught left a wake of bitterness, but his path lay clearly mapped.

He took advantage of this freedom when he published *Les Harmonies* (1830). More and more his verses concerned themselves with emphasizing the fundamental unity of creation, the harmony of the numberless parts that form the Whole. They were, he explained, "destinées, dans la pensée de l'auteur, à reproduire un grand nombre des impressions de la nature et de la vie sur l'âme humaine," and were printed for the chosen few who sought "des degrés pour monter à Dieu" [Foreword to *Harmonies*].

With few exceptions, the very titles of the poems betrayed the power of the mysticism into which Lamartine had plunged. He wrote hymns to the spirits that govern the parts of the day, discussed **"L'Infini dans les cieux,"** **"L'Humanité,"** **"L'Idée de Dieu,"** and listened to **"Le Cri de l'âme."** And all this he set forth in tones that recalled the teachings of the cabalists and the illuminists:

A toi, grand Tout! dont l'astre est la pâle étincelle
En qui la nuit, le jour, l'esprit, vont aboutir!
Flux et reflux divin de vie universelle,
Vaste océan de l'Etre où tout va s'engloutir!

["L'occident," Harmonies]

The unity of *Les Harmonies* lay, as Lamartine warned, in their very diversity. In *Les Visions* he had tried vainly to fit his philosophy into one long poem, and, when that seemed impossible, adopted the opposite course. By distributing throughout many poems the gist of his revelation, he believed he could succeed in teaching his metaphysics to his friends through a series of interpretations of nature. This method also claimed the advantage that most sceptical readers would overlook his theology, the significance of which could be grasped only by a few kindred spirits. After all, he had written, "ces vers ne s'adressent qu'à un petit nombre" [Foreword to *Harmonies*].

Through the collection of *Les Harmonies* ran a series of philosophical observations that recapitulated Lamartine's metaphysical discoveries since 1821. For the most part they reproduced poetically all he had attempted to put into the ill-fated *Visions* and reaffirmed the poet's gratitude to God:

O Dieu! tu m'as donné d'entendre
Ce verbe, ou plutôt cet accord,
Tantôt majestueux et tendre,
Tantôt triste comme la mort!

. . . . .

Mon âme sans chagrin gémit-elle en moi-même,

. . . . .

C'est que de tes gradeurs l'ineffable harmonie
N'est qu'un premier degré de l'échelle infinie.

["Le golfe de Gênes," Harmonies]

But, in one respect, Lamartine's philosophizing differed from his previous attempts at metaphysical poetry. With *Les Harmonies* he lost the hesitation that marked *Les Méditations* and *La Mort de Socrate*. He now passed from the role of neophyte to that of instructor. "Savez-vous son nom," he asked in **"L'Hymne de la Nuit,"** "quel Dieu nous imposa nos lois?" And thereupon he began preaching the fundamentals of a new religion:

La vie est un degré de l'échelle des mondes
Que nous devons franchir pour arriver ailleurs!

. . . . .

On s'arrête, on s'assied, on voit passer la foule,

. . . . .

On reconnaît de l'oeil et du coeur ses amis,
Les uns par le courage et l'espoir affermis,
Montant d'un pas léger que rien ne peut suspendre,
Les autres chancelants et prêts à redescendre.
                 [**"Epître à M. de Sainte-Beuve,"** *Harmonies*]

En vain le coeur vous manque et votre pied se
    lasse,

. . . . .

Marche! sa voix le dit à la nature entière,
Ce n'est pas pour croupir sur ses champs de
    lumière
Que le soleil s'allume et s'étient dans ses mains!
Dans cette oeuvre de vie où son âme palpite,
Tout respire, tout croît, tout grandit, tout gravite!
Les cieux, les astres, les humains!
                 [**"Les révolutions,"** *Harmonies*]

Patiently Lamartine sought to convince France of what he had seen, to demonstrate that behind all change there existed a unity that he knew to be eternal. The passage of time, the sequence of events, life and death, were but parts of an infinite whole. Or, as Lamartine gracefully stated it:

Dans l'hymne de la nature,
Seigneur, chaque créature
Forme à son heure en mesure
Un son du concert divin . . .
                 [**"Hymne du matin,"** *Harmonies*]

***

***The Times Literary Supplement***  (essay date 1964)

SOURCE: "Lamartine Steps Down," in *The Times Literary Supplement*, No. 3266, October 1, 1964, pp. 889-90.

[*In the following excert from a review of an edition of Lamartine's complete poetry, the critic delivers a harsh assessment of Lamartine's appeal for modern readers, identifying his central weaknesses as "the poverty of imagination, the crippling inability to explore the particular, the readiness to vamp."*]

One of the few funny poems that Lamartine wrote is styled simply **"Au Comte d'Orsay."** Alfred d'Orsay had modelled a statue of his illustrious cousin; he is thanked in verse for his labours, but advised to throw them into the river; otherwise posterity will look on the throbbing brow, the fiery lips, the ecstatic flank, the masterful arm, the dreaming eye, the heaving heart, the stubborn foot ("Phidias a pétri sept âmes dans l'airain")—will look on all this and be struck dumb by the thought that the world has rejected so much genius. Better that posterity should be

**On the limits of Lamartine's talent:**

The lyrics of M. de Lamartine commanded attention and admiration both in his own and other countries. The vigor and purity of thought and feeling, the richness and graphic beauty of imagery, and the mastery of versification, they displayed, secured at once for the author the first place among the living poets of France. He embodied the highest, the most serious, feelings of his age, and every cultivated mind acknowledged the truth of his sentiments. Unfortunate enough, however, to have few worthy rivals, the adulation lavished upon him, if it did not wholly blind him to his faults, incapacitated him for that high perception of excellence in his art, so indispensable to improvement. Nor was this all. He was essentially deficient in the loftiest attributes of genius. He possessed a pure heart, an active fancy, a ready apprehension of the beautiful, and an almost unbounded command of language. But not to him belonged the original faculty, that "bodies forth the forms of things unknown"; that penetrates the hidden recesses of nature, and brings us thence new objects of delight, new themes for meditation. Nor had he the overwhelming passion, that leads the soul captive, and is inferior only to the inventive power. His genius was imitative. It received its impulse, perhaps unconsciously, from the writers of other countries, though the novelty of his sentiments and his style gave him an ascendency over those of his own.

*Elizabeth Fries Ellet, in* The North American Review, *Vol. 48, April, 1839.*

spared an example so liable to discourage it. Is it necessary to add that this poem, which Lamartine called his "sublime va te faire f. . .lancé au peuple", dates from October, 1850, and marks his withdrawal from public life?

Seven souls may be considered an inflated number. Lamartine began his public career in embassies in Italy; then for a decade and a half he made speeches in the Chambre des Députés, took an interest in the sugar-beet lobby and foreign affairs, became highly idealistic and democratic, in 1848 turned his oratory on a revolutionary populace, became Foreign Minister in the Executive Committee of the Republic, was abandoned after the June days by the professionals, stood for President and received 17,910 votes. At no other moment in history perhaps would this adventure have been open to soul number one. Soul number two inhabited a prolix and affable journalist who for the last thirteen years of his life assembled from his memories a gossipy and unreliable *Cours familier de Littérature*, and before that a series of pot-boiler histories (the 1848 Revolution, the Restoration, the Constituent Assembly, Turkey, Russia) in an attempt to repeat the success-story of the *Histoire des Girondins*, published on a rising tide of democratic fervour; to say nothing of sundry *Confidences, Nouvelles Confidences,* and other self-advertisements. We may include under its action a handful of sentimental narratives (*Raphaël, Graziella, Le Trailleur de pierres de Saint Point*) which adorned a good many drawing-room tables 100 years ago.

Soul number three belonged to a propertied gentleman with aristocratic pretensions. . . . Soul number four was subject to poetic inspiration—very freely from early years down to about 1840, thereafter only fitfully.

The new Pléiade volume of Lamartine [*Oeuvres poétiques complètes*] is strictly limited to soul number four, minus the narratives. It is admirably produced and scrupulously edited by Professor M.-F. Guyard, who by his earlier work on the poet has already shown himself to be a leading authority. The principles upon which the text is established are lucid and logical: everything in verse is there, presented in a chronological sequence which is waived only for good reason, and there is no prose—not even Lamartine's prefaces or the voluminous commentaries he supplied for some of the *recueils*. The notes are economical, the references to critical works are discriminating, the misprints relatively few. In all, a volume which comes up to the highest standards of a distinguished series, and invites a reappraisal of this fallen idol of the nineteenth century.

Whatever the outcome of such an appraisal, it must be recognized that the basis offered by this edition is not one that Lamartine would have approved of, or even understood. For him all the souls depicted by Comte d'Orsay were one. Thus although, as Professor Guyard points out, the Elvire of the poems is a highly composite lady, in Lamartine's public image she is associated deliberately with the heroine of *Raphaël,* and most of the school anthologies are content to say she was Mme. Julie Charles. So, too, with Graziella; or the peace-loving hero he pictured himself as, "un tribun de la paix soulevé par la houle". Lamartine put the manufacture of a legend above other considerations in his writing, and in consequence was not much concerned to give pre-eminence to one medium rather than another.

At times he may address the world, at other times chat amiably, or again sing: "Je chantais, mes amis, comme l'homme respire". But what he sang was no more decisively him, or his legend, no more attentively composed, even, than what he spoke. Some stanzas are indisputably unique, in the conjunction of a vaporous tonality, a chastely archaic range of image, an easy control of strophic form, a natural overall rhythmic pattern. They define the musical resources of the French language around 1820 even where they were written much later; they are in all the anthologies and in consequence need not be quoted here (**"Le Vallon," "Le Lac," "La Vigne et la Maison"**). But they break no new ground, they in no way transcend those resources; their merits are the merits of Mendelssohn in his duller chamber music, or better, of Moschelès. For sustained control, Professor Guyard invites us to read through **"Novissima Verba"** without interruption—not an easy task, but one which reveals that these qualities, while satisfying the requirements of formal eloquence, in no way

excite or arrest the attention. *Les Préludes,* another central piece with a characteristically romantic title (what exactly is all this a prelude *to*?), does no more than conflate into a vague magma reflections on life, death, love, war, peace, bliss, suffering, country life, resignation . . . and the end result to the reader is an odd impression of complacency. Liszt for all his vulgarity, was more adventurous.

Even to those contemporaries for whom Lamartine's music was a revelation, the looseness and carelessness of it all was a matter for regret. Sainte-Beuve drew the line at **Les Recueillements,** on which he pronounced severely and pointedly. Lamartine was unrepentant: how, after all, does one criticize breathing? But the vice lies deeper; the incontinence which makes three-quarters of this volume unreadable is not simply to be explained by the fact that Lamartine was unable to criticize his own work. Or rather, this fact itself may be explained in the larger context of souls one, two and three. For each of these facets of a *persona,* the manufacture of a legend was integral to the man, and this legend had no place for the critic, only for the creator; no place for the artisan of words, only for the born leader of men; no place for terseness, for the kind of poetry—or thought processes—which impose demands on the reader, only for the lofty common-place. *Les Méditations* having made their hit, the journalist, the public figure, and the gentleman enter into a conspiracy to ensure that the poet should go no further. "Etranglé par la vieille forme", said the adolescent Rimbaud—not a bit of it. Lamartine was at no point aware of a linguistic hindrance: it was not the language but the legend which dictated the poet's career—and from an early date.

Lamartine, for example, thought of himself as on a level with that other legendary figure, Byron. Inspired by the latter's death he wrote **Le dernier chant du Pélerinage d'Harold,** speaking from height to height and over the heads of the multitude, and in this interminable meditation we sense nothing like the distancing which the original Childe had put between himself and his rhetorical exercises. The admiring identification with a legend is complete, authenticated with a sob:

> Si ses chants quelquefois ont élevé votre âme,
> Donnez-lui . . . donnez-lui . . . ce qu'une ombre réclame.
> Une larme!

—the same tear, it may be added without malice, which Lamartine so insistently invokes on all relevant occasions for soul number four: but also for number three, faced with the painful necessity of parting with successive slices of the ancestral home, the family nest (the preface to *Mes Confidences* describes graphically, as they say, the scene with the notary when the alternative was presented of selling some pasture outside the drawing-room window or signing a contract to reveal these cherished personal secrets). Lamartine, who never met Byron, could not have suspected the intelligence which he so conspicuously possessed; lacking acerbity and wit also, it is only natural that once imprisoned within the legend started by the **Méditations** Lamartine should never escape, or even seek to escape.

The tears, the lack of intelligence, the **Méditations** and the legend combine then, as his latest editor says, to make Lamartine's poetry almost unapproachable to the reader of today. Over about six generations he has offered—by his own choice—an easy stereotype of the Poet for middle-class consumption: interesting, unhappy, sincere, refined in feeling, aristocratic in the disinterested quality of his actions, aristocratic, too, in the propensity to fix his gaze on eternal things like Liberty and Love, to rise above particularity and soar into the sky like his own **Jocelyn**. Lamartine has flattered tens of thousands by letting them share the feeling of being a little bit more upper-class than most of them were; reading his poems is in two ways an ennobling experience—because they are (usually) edifying and because they are part of a lofty view of things appropriate to people not under the necessity of earning tomorrow's bread (the revelations from time to time of money troubles give, however, a reassuring sense of fraternity). If we ask, innocently, why Lamartine is so famous as a poet, part of the answer must be that the stereotype was in demand for a long time, cherished first among right-thinking and genteel (but of course not stuffy) persons, and then taken over by schoolmasters and other custodians of the national treasure. For three or four generations the piety has waxed, and for two or three now it has waned: fewer genteel persons, no doubt, and many more custodians.

What is left? Of the poetry, not much. The anthologies are less unfair to him than to Victor Hugo. Professor Guyard seems hardly to wish to make a case for the complete poetical works other than on grounds of scholarly piety. He observes that the lyrical idiom is faded and unremarkable, though the virtuosity in dealing with strophic forms is considerable; that at best "le support intellectuel et matériel est réduit à presque nien; ne reste qu'une mélodie suggestive"; "la pensée est d'un flou inquiétant". To this something must be added on Lamartine's epic vision. At a time when so many English parsons in the provinces dreamt of being a second Milton, in Paris uncrowned legislators dreamt of being Dante, Milton and Napoleon all in one; and Lamartine was no exception. Indeed his nebulous philosophic excursions are part and parcel of the whole sensibility. The fragmentary **Visions, Les Chevaliers, Jocelyn,** above all the interminable, **La Chute d'un ange,** show him in full cry after the epic of humanity—the epic which only Hugo, among contemporaries, was able to show to be anything but a mirage. Here Lamartine's verse fails to do him justice.

The best things in **La Chute** are the voluble raptures on antediluvian scenery, lacking colour, no doubt, but indicative at least of effort on his part to go beyond the habitual scenic platitude; and the canticle of the cedars of Lebanon, which has a soaring grandeur achieved nowhere else. But the rest of the long fantasy, from the Tarzan-type adventures of the fallen angel to the sadistic orgies of the giants, told in a manner which recalls John Martin, has little but oddity to commend it; and the evocations of an early syncretist religion, in spite of the poet's valiant efforts to impress, carry neither theological conviction nor poetic fervour. Lamartine is a conspicuous instance of a

man filled with pretentious cosmic intuitions, often reflected in a lyric *épanchement* (Alors dans ce grand tout mon âme répandue/A fondu . . . ), sometimes trailing after a more distinct symbol; always so vague in its mellifluousness, however, that the very convention of verse appears to mask a possible incisiveness. With the Pléiade Lamartine available, there is no excuse now for not sampling these extended poems—though every excuse for not prolonging the experience. If the reader remains intrigued by hints about the Maronites, speculative philosophy, or cosmic intuitions, he may care to turn from the epic plane to the prosaic level of the *Voyage en Orient,* where Lamartine looks outwards instead of inwards, discusses what he sees or is told, keeps away from the vaticinatory tripod, and writes with an informality which is far more natural to him.

The *Voyage en Orient* is, of course, a scrapbook, easily written, easily read, and (much of it) easily forgotten. It was the prototype of a genre in which both Hugo and Nerval far surpassed their model; a comparison with *Le Rhin* and with Nerval's *Voyage en Orient* makes very clear the central weakness of Lamartine, the poverty of imagination, the crippling inability to explore the particular, the readiness to vamp. Nevertheless, it is in this lengthy scrapbook that one finds Lamartine at his best, in a few sequences where from time to time affectation is happily blended with a naive enthusiasm for the matter in hand—for example, some excellent descriptive writing in the visit to the famous cedars of Lebanon. In their shade Lamartine was anxious to offer up a prayer (unfortunately the ride proved more difficult than expected, the horses floundered in snow up to the saddle-girths, and the intrepid voyager was obliged to sit on a rock and meditate from a distance on the sacred relics—"le vent harmonieux qui résonnait dans leurs rameaux sonores jouait dans mes cheveux, et glaçait sur ma paupière des larmes de douleur et d'adoration . . ." and the aeons again unfolded before his mind's eye).

Or better, there is the visit to Lady Hester Stanhope: the sublime mountainous setting, the dwelling-place of the hermit suitably austere, though exotic. Lady Hester discerned his character by his footfall outside, though she had never heard of him (such is *la gloire!*); she discoursed on lost sciences of the east and on the second coming of the Messiah for which she had ready two horses; he expounded his own social creed, humanitarian and vaguely religious; she praised his noble character; he admired her conversation, "élevée, mystique, nuageuse"; they found themselves in agreement on many things. The encounter was for the romantic *publiciste* in him a scoop, an historic occasion; and its leisurely description is a delightful compound of awe, incredulity, fatuity, and talking to the gallery. How much of what he records was actually said is of course anybody's guess. But the "Visit to Lady Hester Stanhope" is without doubt an important paper in the Lamartine dossier; and papers of this kind are not without their relevance to the poetic oeuvre, and much more palatable than **La Chute d'un Ange**.

"Le Cas Lamartine" is in the last resort to be treated as a social phenomenon: in this case the poet without his public is apt to look too foolish. Lamartine provided the safe heart-throbs for an age; in both prose and verse he knew how far to go. The story *Graziella,* based on a squalid affair on Ischia in 1811, is a case in point. In reality, he picked up a young Neapolitan fisher-girl, amused himself for a few months, and then abandoned her. In the tale, the situation is heavily disguised, with a dying mother calling her wayward son home and tears and remorse poured out for an apparently innocent relationship: a fantasy as implausible and mawkish as the atmosphere of it is poetic. *Graziella* was however a best-seller; the watchful paterfamilias saw no danger in it; almost the only adult reaction of the century was that of Tristan Corbiére, who wrote a sly parody called *Le Fils de Lamartine et de Graziella* in which the putative offspring is met scrounging from tourists on Procida. No doubt *Graziella* is not even read now in schools. But Corbiére's instinct was right in one particular. To this day Lamartine's little caper is piously commemorated on the island of Procida by a beauty contest; the year's Miss Graziella is selected, fisher-girl costume and all, with appropriate publicity; her prize is, curiously, a wedding trousseau; clearly the promoters of this event reveal due awareness of a modern tourist public's regard for the poetic. As Lamartine said to Lady Hester Stanhope, "Voilá ce que c'est que la gloire!" But the reflective reader might on this occasion shed a tear.

---

**On Lamartine's accomplishment:**

[Lamartine's] popularity as a poet has been unequalled during his day in France. De Vigny has given some fine specimens of both taste and feeling; Victor Hugo's political lyrics and *Orientales* show spirit and imagination; Beranger's lyrics are written *ad populum,* and will live forever; but Lamartine appeals more variously and profoundly to the sensibilities of the heart. The religious sentiment, with its deep anxieties, the remorse of guilt, the felicity of virtue, manful indignation at wrong, however consecrated, brave vindication of the right, however despised, the aspirations and sufferings of genius, the domestic affections, the love of country, the heroic in character, the picturesque in nature, the sentimentality of love,—all subjects indeed which are susceptible of the idealism of poetry,—have kindled his inspiration. Herein is the security of his poetical fame. He has sung of subjects which have not an adventitious, but an abiding relation to the sympathies of human nature, and he has sung of them in a style defective in many respects, but always earnest, solemn, and thrilling—the true style of the true bard and seer.

"*Lamartine,*" *in* Methodist Quarterly Review, *Vol. 31, 1849.*

---

**J. C. Ireson (essay date 1969)**

SOURCE: "'Poète véritable'," "Personal Philosophy," and "The Lamartinian Aesthetic," in *Lamartine: A Revalua-* *tion,* University of Hull Press, 1969, pp. 7-15, pp. 16-25, pp. 30-37.

[*In this excerpt, Ireson examines the relationship between Lamartine's personal beliefs and his poetry.*]

We have in our time a complex image of Lamartine as he emerges judged from many stand-points. His contemporaries have seen him through various lenses. Traditionalists have reproved what might have appeared to be dangerous innovations or lapses. Journalists have fastened on the abundant material of his life in all its forms, domestic, sentimental, political, seignorial. Scholars have performed the necessary *labeur de bénédictin,* with growing precision and confidence.

Out of this tangle of concentrated attention a number of clear threads may be drawn. Lamartine has never left his public indifferent, though the nature of the response he arouses varies considerably from period to period. We have seen the usual manifestations of reverence from those for whom whitewash is the natural substance of criticism. We have long heard the cries of the persecutors and denigrators. In recent years, with the ebbing of the tide for Lamartine, we have seen the emergence of scholars whose methods are impeccable, whose knowledge is laudable, who probably know the work of their author better than any of their predecessors, and who resolutely sit on the fence where matters of judgment are concerned, either out of deference to the prevailing fashion, which is anti-Lamartine, or possibly because of the difficulty of fitting into the framework of catholic orthodoxy an author, three of whose works were put on the Index [*Voyage en Orient* and *Jocelyn* in 1836; *La chute d'un ange* in 1838].

Lamartine has often been harshly judged by his fellow writers. Balzac pillories him in *Modeste Mignon* in the person of the precious and dilletantish poet Canalis. It is well known that Flaubert had no great love for him. Dostoievsky appears to have had the same difficulty in adjusting his sights to him as Tolstoy had with Shakespeare, evoking as he does, in his *journal d'un écrivain,* the *Méditations poétiques* as a kind of opium of the bourgeois classes. . . . Dostoievsky's judgment at least underlines the fact that the *Méditations poétiques* have been something of a best-seller in France, not far short of 100,000 copies of the editions published in France being sold up to 1914. Renan underlines the egregious and apparently unlearned quality of the poet when he observes that 'l'université aurait été incapable de former un Lamartine'. It is tempting to think that the great nineteenth-century critic was formulating an opinion set up by a gallop through the *Cours familier de littérature* or through some of the volumes of popular history, the history of Russia, for example, or of Turkey.

In our own country, where for a long time the attitude towards Lamartine was one of perhaps strained respect, a curious article appeared a few years ago on the front page of the *Times Literary Supplement,* under the title of "Lamartine Steps Down," marking the publication of Professor Guyard's edition of the collected poems in the

Pléiade series. The date of the article was October 1, 1964. The title indicates very accurately a familiar current attitude towards Lamartine. I take it that a person who steps down is in the act of relinquishing a function as a member of the Establishment and accepting a not altogether glorious return to the condition of a private man. The terse and unequivocal tone of the caption reflects very clearly the attitude and quality of the article itself, and I am inclined to think that they may both have served to cook Lamartine's goose for the foreseeable future as far as the contemporary generation of general readers is concerned. The article itself represents a number of the features of modern British journalism of the intellectual sort. The writing is lively, sharp, oddly informed, partial, sophisticated, sometimes showing an interesting tendency to misinterpret the sense of texts that are touched on in passing.

At its beginning, the article makes play with the seven souls which Lamartine arrogates to himself, though its author, in the course of a lively commentary, does not advance beyond soul number four. . . . Readers of Lamartine can make up their own list: soldier, writer, diplomat, statesman, landowner, orator, family man—the mere attempt recalls a familiar counting-out game. The serious business for Lamartine was probably the sense of possessing, or being possessed by, a multiplicity of talents, a cluster of qualities, septenate as far as they could be counted. . . .

Thereafter, the writer makes a number of traditional points about Lamartine's shortcomings, his inability to 'excite or arrest the attention', the absence of real innovations, as evidenced by the anthology pieces, the substitution of a legend for real lyrical force. The conclusion, foregone, since it emerges already towards the bottom of the first page, is that 'three-quarters of this volume [is] unreadable'.

In one way the writer of the *Times Literary Supplement* article is abundantly right. Lamartine is smothered by legend, and to such an extent that any reconnaissance party sent out to discover the real Lamartine finds itself reconnoitring in the middle of a jungle in which unorganized guerilla warfare is carried on, with comouflaged snipers behind trees, booby-traps underfoot (for example, the temptation to attribute a real-life identity to all the female characters of the long and complex Lamartine romance) and with over-kill experts attempting defoliation operations from a safe height.

The Lamartine phenomenon offers a rich assortment of problems. A few may be provided with answers, many more might well be better left without answers. His chastity has been a source of enthusiastic speculations. To the question, 'Lamartine fut-il un Don Juan?' the writer of an article in a pro-Lamartine revue published in Lyon, provided, thirty or forty years ago, a firm and negative answer [Germain Trezel, "Lamartine fut-il un Don Juan," *La flamme,* November, 1933]. The romantic and sentimental myth could not, must not, be dispelled. Lamartine's health has been the subject of detailed scrutiny.

René Tatin devotes a thesis to the poet's symptoms and syndromes (*Essai médico-psychologique sur Lamartine,* 1929). Did the author of **"Le Lac"** ever relinquish amateur status as a poet? Did he write mainly 'beautiful nonsense'? Or, at any rate, did he really write, as we might believe from some of his verses, 'as man breathes, as the bird moans, as the wind sighs, as water murmurs while it flows along'? [**"Le poète mourant,"** *Nouvelles méditations poétiques*].

Small wonder that the image which emerges from the crosstalk of the critics is a confused one. What is worse, the image which emerges from Lamartine's own statements is not noticeably clearer, nor is it, at first sight, unduly appealing to the contemporary eye. Alphonse is always right. He appears in his work always too noble and too upright to be true. He certainly makes little appeal to trend-following people nowadays. He is not in the least anti-Establishment. He does not found or lead any literature of protest. Worst of all, he is consistent and has little sense of humour. . . .

Can we, out of this unpromising magma, crystallize an individuality? Two things, in my view, chiefly characterize Lamartine and unfailingly motivate his actions.

First, he is fundamentally a rational and a religious man. . . . Lamartine's view of poetry, . . . though borrowing analogies that frequently appear to a modern sensibility to be in the worst Romantic taste, or founded on the more naïve forms of the pathetic fallacy, remains consistent and covers most of the area within which all the poets coming after him have manoeuvred. His political creed raised him to the heights of power because of its simplicity and incorruptibility and cast him down very swiftly because it was undeviating and unable to fall into compromise or to accommodate itself to threatening situations by acts of lifemanship. His religion took its energy from a quest for certitude that went on within the vast limits of intuitions of a transcendental character. His renunciation of Catholic orthodoxy was not a vagary or a wilful excursion into an easy Platonism. With him all forms of action are religious. He constantly sought for ways of life, patterns of event, signs or symbols capable of interpreting his conviction that a purposeful intelligence permeates the world. The acts and choices he most admired were those which were dedicated to the affirmation of these convictions. Whatever may be said about his lack of direction in earlier life and of the bathos of some of his sexual relationships, his ambitions were always directed towards tasks and responsibilities which would justify his beliefs. His poetry is in one sense an extended psalm, a lengthy series of variations on a religious theme which, despite passing periods of doubt, remains a song of praise. Quest, affirmation, justification, praise, these are not only the preoccupations of his writing, they are also the themes of his life.

Secondly, Lamartine is activated by a constant need to communicate improvingly with his fellow men. Poetry may have been for him, in the first instance, an absorbing exercise, the mastery of which was guaranteed to take him

*A caricature of Lamartine by Nadar, a member of the extreme left, who accused Lamartine of attempting to prevent a socialist revolution in 1848.*

into the front ranks of the catholic and monarchist society of the eighteen-twenties, but the exercise never succeeded in captivating him to the extent of involving his whole energies and aspirations in an aesthetic. Despite the ready success of the *Méditations poétiques,* there is no doubt that Lamartine became, quite early on, aware that these verses, whatever fashionable chords they may have set vibrating, were far from achieving the universal communication which for him was the ultimate need of expression. Hence the attempts at the *"Grand Poème,"* which was the highest reach of his ambition.

. . . . .

These two main features, the presence of qualities fundamentally rational and fundamentally religious, together with the constant need to communicate improvingly with his fellow men, are found at all times in Lamartine's speculative thought. . . .

Speculation for Lamartine is not possible outside a religious context. This context is wide and varies from time to time, though Lamartine never denies the primacy of the native climate of Christianity in which his spirit is nurtured.

A poem such as **"Dieu,"** in the *Méditations poétiques,* after preliminary flourishes and precautions, attempts what

we assume to be impossible, to define God. The attempt is made first within the limits of a rhetorical convention. The poet postulates attributes of God in a careful order, (i) existence and self-consciousness, (ii) an inclusive eternity of space and time, (iii) a steady creativity through which a primal intelligence manifests itself, (iv) an imperfect creation bearing the mark of archetypal qualities (*puissance, ordre, équité, sagesse*), (v) a self-sufficient identity. The analysis is developed within an anthropomorphic convention: God is represented as a being whose organs and members are identified with aspects of the cosmos and of perceptible reality. The ontological argument proceeds according to a poetic convention, the Alexandrine form and the language of neo-classical speculative poetry being used to express a personal and synthetic religious doctrine. But it cannot be said that the concept is developed within any clearly noticeable Christian convention. Indeed, in the section of the poem which follows immediately after the representation of God, the poet develops the idea of the essential unity of religions, the God represented in his own verses presumably being the culmination of an evolving religious idea, which reaches its apogee with the advent of Christianity. . . . The poem **"Dieu"** is, of course, relatively early. As time goes on, Lamartine's advocacy of the Christian view of existence takes on more of the relativist quality which characterizes most of the literature of the middle third of the nineteenth century. . . .

As in the case of almost all the great poets of the nineteenth century, Lamartine's ideas are in their general tendency spiritualistic, strongly flowing towards forms of Platonism, particularly in the theory of art, brought up sharply against the existential problems, affected by the growing currents of deterministic and scientific doctrines with which they often conflict sharply. Unlike Hugo, much of whose mature poetic effort is concerned with the elaboration of a *credo,* Lamartine does not attempt a synthesis of the principal philosophical and religious attitudes. Unlike Vigny, he does not consciously set out to redeem a comfortless planetary and social situation by the construction of works of art which will vindicate human life by lighting the stages of a long and painful progress towards a condition controlled by *l'Esprit pur.* Unlike Leconte de Lisle and Mallarmé, he does not balance a metaphysic of despair by an idealist aesthetic. . . . Lamartine interprets for his own religious purposes the transformist and evolutionist doctrines of his time. On occasions, he flies flat in the face of these doctrines as, for example, when he extols the religious perceptions of human beings and human societies in the earlier ages of this globe and points to the span of recorded history as a period of relative degeneracy. Occasionally he enunciates ideas that are simply untenable. . . .

Of the three prime faculties, intelligence, sentiment, conscience, he firmly picks the last as being the highest, the controlling force, determining the stages of morality and the merit of individual lives. Taken together in their combined action, action frequently disrupted by defects of lucidity or by the effect of the passions, they form the entity (*l'âme*) whose instinctive function is to scan the world in order to sound and probe it and pass beyond for intimations of its authorship.

In Lamartine's view, intelligence has the limits of an unfeeling instrument. Sentiment reflects aspiration, passion, the perceptions of individual existence, the sense of suffering inflicted by material conditions. Though it may be a precious instrument for determining individual reaction and the expression of this reaction, sentiment is essentially passive. There remains conscience, the function of which for Lamartine is to illuminate and reflect, to guide conduct, to evaluate experience.

These notions, which inform the whole of Lamartine's work . . . have one peculiar and interesting aspect. They are steadily orientated towards action, towards conduct, private and public, individual and social. A great part of Lamartine's ideas is concerned with society, with the evolution of contemporary social patterns, with the political ordering of society.

. . . . .

Art for Lamartine is the highest exercise of the reason, where reason is assumed to be the power in control of the intuitive, sentimental and imaginative faculties. . . .

The power of the vision and the expressive quality of the art presumably come within the scope of reason. The spiritualistic, celebrative function of art is for Lamartine its essential function, all others falling within that category of form and procedure to which Verlaine refers pejoratively in his *Art poétique* as *littérature*.

Poetry is therefore divorced at the outset from language. Poetry does not grow out of language. It is a state or quality before it becomes an activity. It exists primally in the religious experience, where religious experience is understood to mean a deepened and heightened awareness of the area of human consciousness and a deepened imaginative awareness of the outside world. This means that Lamartine is unlikely to have been much concerned during most of his lifetime about elaborating a theory of poetry. . . .

Lamartine's personal views on poetry emerge forcefully from [his Foreword to *La mort de Socrate*], particularly his views on the *properties* of poetry, which may be listed as follows: sublimity, music, harmony, elevation, energy. It is most interesting to see this poet of reverie and nostalgic reminiscence insisting on energy as an essential property of poetry. Lamartine elaborates this notion by indicating the double action of poetry, on the senses and on the spirit alike. We may observe that Baudelaire uses the same components to elaborate his doctrine of *surnaturalisme* in his prose writings. In his definition of modern, that is to say, Romantic art, Baudelaire divides the emphasis between elevation and suggestive power; and the insistence on the use of sensory elements to project intuitions about private experience is, in his theoretical writings, associated with a vocabulary similar to that used by Lamartine.

The poet of the *Méditations,* however, adheres to a convention well established in the ancient and modern literatures of Europe, by which poetry becomes an instrument for writing about poetry, a convention probably carried to its furthest point by Mallarmé. In Lamartine, the procedure seems at first sight both hieratical and casual. If we read, for example, the two poems of the *Nouvelles Méditations poétiques,* "**Le Poète mourant,**" and "**Adieux à la poésie,**" we find that the ideas are set within rigid classical terms of reference: the lyre and the harp representing the expressive medium, a limited range of images (birds, water, tears, the tomb) representing the life and death of the poet. We find as well that these conventional figures are used quite loosely within the rhetorical structure of the poem; and that the general purport of both poems is an apology for untutored lyricism. There are, in fact, four main ideas expressed in these pieces. The first, which, viewed superficially, appears to dominate, is the Æolian quality of lyricism, that is, the instinctive and innate propensity of the poet to exteriorize experience in regular and harmonious forms of language. The second is the stress laid on elegiac inspiration, which is one of Lamartine's favourite modes and which uses grief and melancholy as poetic sources. The third is the representation of the poet as a despiser of reality, with no attachment to the world. . . . The fourth is the idea of poetry as the vehicle for some existential intuitions: the sense of exile accompanying individuation; the heightened consciousness of the artist, inimical to his personality and personal field of action; the sense of fall from a former privileged state. . . . These latter themes, sown about the two poems with a liberal hand and with little regard for constructive effect, are those which led in the course of the following century to the composition of some of the most distinguished poetry of France, themes which have taxed the scope and strength of Parnassians, Symbolists and moderns.

Other verse passages throw light on the extensions of Lamartine's ideas. We have already, in two separate contexts, come across the image of the priest, used by Lamartine to represent man in his artistic and interpretative functions. This is one of the central symbols in Lamartine's reflective writing. With him the poetic impulse is never dissociated from the religious impulse, and both merge into the elevation induced by sexual love in its exalted sentimental forms. The following passage, taken from *Jocelyn,* relatively little quoted, achieves a typical extension of ideas:

> Le prêtre est l'urne sainte au dôme suspendue,
> Où l'eau trouble du puits n'est jamais répandue,
> Que ne rougit jamais le nectar des humains,
> Qu'ils ne se passent pas pleine de mains en mains,
> Mais où l'herbe odorante, où l'encens de l'aurore
> Au feu du sacrifice en tout temps s'évapore;
> Il est dans son silence au reste des mortels
> Ce qu'est aux instruments l'orgue des saints autels:
> On n'entend pas sa voix profonde et solitaire
> Se mêler hors du temple aux vains bruits de la terre;
> Les vierges à ses sons n'enchaînent point leurs pas,

Et le profane écho ne les répète pas;
Mais il élève à Dieu, dans l'ombre de l'église,
Sa grande voix qui s'enfle et court comme une
   brise,
Et porte, en saints élans, à la divinité
L'hymne de la nature et de l'humanité.

This passage in its tone and movement is not very different from **"Le Poète mourant"**; and the definition of the priest given here overlaps to a considerable extent the typical Lamartinian evocation of the function of the poet. More interesting still is the fact that the passage, in its theme as in its movement, is not very different from Baudelaire's "Bénédiction" at the beginning of *Les Fleurs du mal,* at any rate in the second part of that poem, where Baudelaire celebrates the ultimate benediction of the poet, transcending the triple malediction under which he suffers socially, sexually and filially. What is more, the essential vocabulary of the passage: *urne, dôme, nectar, odorante, encens, s'évapore, orgue, temple, hymne,* anticipates very closely the vocabulary of Baudelaire's spiritualistic pieces. And this notion of the priest-oracle acting as a focus of sonority for the two great nineteenth-century themes of adoration—nature and humanity—anticipates likewise Hugo's "Fonction du poète," which appears in *Les Rayons et les ombres* (1840), and "Les Mages," which takes its place in the remorseless eloquence of the final book of *Les Contemplations* (1856).

Again, like Baudelaire, Lamartine speculates, though without the Satanic overtones of *Les Fleurs du mal,* on Beauty as a principle and on its effects on the senses and the conscience:

Beauté! secret d'en haut, rayon, divin emblème,
Qui sait d'où tu descends? qui sait pourquoi l'on
   t'aime?
Pourquoi l'œil te poursuit, pourquoi le cœur aimant
Se précipite à toi comme un fer à l'aimant,
D'une invincible étreinte à ton ombre s'attache,
S'embrase à ton approche et meurt quand on
   l'arrache?

To the first two lines we shall have, twenty years later, the Baudelairian antiphon:

Viens-tu du ciel profond ou sors-tu de l'abîme
O Beauté?
      ["Hymne à la beauté," *Les fleurs du mal*]

The whole of this passage by Lamartine, fifty-six lines in length, found in the "Troisième Epoque" of *Jocelyn,* merits commentary. In the lines I have quoted, Lamartine is speculating not only on the origins of a power whose existence confirms intuitions about the descent of the immediately perceptible world from an invisible source, but on the dynamism of that power. It is this aspect that is developed in the lines which follow. Beauty is represented conjecturally as 'a primary or fifth element', and endowed with the physical properties of an element. But such an element would presumably be unique in the multiplicity of forms it engenders. The examples furnished by

Lamartine are all characterized by movement and vigour, deriving in each case from the force and substance of the planet or the firmament in which the planet circulates. The highest point of the examples is reached with the finest qualities of the human face, which poses the enigma of a symbolical representation of a higher personalized form of being. Above all, it is the fascination of Beauty which arrests Lamartine's attention, from which he derives a notion of reciprocity of energy between perceived and percipient. . . .

Lamartine's speculations on Beauty never stay for answers to sophisticated problems. They sweep him towards a Wordsworthian rapture, and beyond, towards experiences that transcend language. These are moments of plenitude, often found through prayer, where the poet, in Eliot's phrase, finds himself 'looking into the heart of light, the silence' [*The Waste Land,* Part I]. He constructs an idea, expressed, for example, in **"Dieu,"** based on the existence of ideal forms of communication, wordless and soundless, to which existing languages may only aspire. . . . Elsewhere, in *Jocelyn,* we see how the exercise of prayer puts the monk into a state of inspiration identical to that described in **"Dieu."**

It might be thought that much of Lamartine's apparent indifference to poetic achievement lies here, in his recognition of the limitations of poetic language and poetic forms. He consistently maintains that poetry lies elsewhere. But if by indifference we mean an easy negligence towards expression, then this is incorrect. There is almost certainly a hierarchy of forms for Lamartine. The symbolical farewells to poetry in the *Nouvelles Méditations poétiques* are a reflection of this, being disclaimers of what to him at the time were the relatively lightweight *genres,* the lyric and the elegy, which had kept him from the "Grand Poème," the *Epopée de l'âme* which he was never properly to achieve. In any case, the legend of a dilettante toying with the Muse is not one that can be seriously sustained.

### Charles M. Lombard   (essay date 1973)

SOURCE: "From the *Méditations* to the *Harmonies,*" in *Lamartine,* Twayne Publishers, 1973, pp. 20-40.

[*An American educator and critic, Lombard is the author of* French Romanticism on the Frontier *(1972) and a study of the French polemical writer Joseph de Maistre. In the following excerpt, Lombard provides an overview of Lamartine's poetic works through* Harmonies poétiques et religieuses *and examines the evolution of his religious thought.*]

The *Méditations poétiques* was published in March, 1820, by Didot. Twenty-four poems made up the collection whose contents justified the title. From the first poem, **"L'Isolement"** to the last, **"La Poésie sacrée,"** a general plan was discernible. Starting on a reflective tone, the work depicted various stages of religious feelings and

**On the appeal of Lamartine's verse**:

Lamartine's influence was due to the fact that he uttered, now the sad, now the comforting, now the inspiring words which thousands craved to hear. They did not feel the want of new thoughts in his utterances; they were moved by the sound of his sympathetic voice. They felt once more vibrating within them fibres which, during the period of universal depression, had been completely benumbed; he conjured tones from strings which had long given forth no sound; and men delighted in the novelty which consisted in a revival of old memories. But, besides all this, there was one really new element. For Lamartine the ugly and the bad, nay, even the petty and the mean, did not exist. He clothed everything in a garment of shining light. There was a heavenly radiance over his poetry. For the first time for long years, a wealth of beautiful feeling found expression in melodious verse.

*George Brandes, "Lyric Poetry: Lamartine and Hugo," in* Main Currents in Nineteenth Century Literature, *1903.*

attitudes and ended in a hymn of praise. Lamartine preached to the skeptical Byron, underwent momentary doubts followed by a rebirth of faith, presented his own version of mystical experience, and pondered on various aspects of nature, humanity, and the universe.

Throughout the *Méditations* Lamartine assumed a personalized tone. Yet structurally his work represented no sharp break with Classicism. The Alexandrine or twelve-syllable line divided into hemistichs, or divisions of six lines with a caesura, was preserved in the main. Nor was the imagery calculated to startle contemporary readers used to the poetry of Jacques Delille and Charles Chênedollé. Much of the *Méditations* smacked of the Neo-Classical vogue of the Empire with a fresh element injected. The *Génie du Christianisme* had unmistakably left its mark on Lamartine, and many lines recalled the cadenced prose of Chateaubriand. Fondness for the natural world, its trees, hills, lakes, and forests, represented nothing surprisingly new. Lamartine, however, made use of this background to insert an intensely personal note into his lyrics in which nature literally seemed to vibrate in sympathy with the poet. The *Méditations* was especially relevant to the younger generation of the 1820's, reared in the tradition of Rousseau's sentimentalism and the religious emotionalism of Chateaubriand. Lamartine's brand of poetry and mysticism blended admirably with the scheme of things. Little wonder then that his poems were read passionately to hushed audiences in the refined salons of the Romantic period.

Foreign sources were noticeably present in the *Méditations*. Brooding about man's existence, the origin of the soul, and other weighty questions brings to mind similar observations in Young's *Night Thoughts,* Gray's "Elegy," and Pope's *Essay on Man*. Ossian and Petrarch also furnished themes employed by the poet, and there was a Byronic cast to many lines.

The opening poem, **"L'Isolement,"** communicates to the reader the basic mood of the *Méditations*:

> However, coming forth from the gothic spire, a religious sound is spread in the air; the wayfarer stops, and the rustic bell mingles holy music with the last sounds of the day.

Lamartine subtly blends a natural setting with a religious motif in the manner of Chateaubriand without accumulating a series of concrete terms the Classicist would judge in bad taste. The soft, flowing quality of Lamartine's verse marked its freshness despite its Neo-Classical form.

In **"L'Homme"** Lamartine took on the task of reminding his cynical colleague, Byron, of man's sublime destiny: "Limited in his nature, infinite in his aspirations, man is a fallen god who recalls the heavens."

The Platonic commonplace of the soul's preexistence supplies a transcendental concept of man's immortality based on a spiritual destination beyond this earth where after death the soul will be reunited with the perfection that is God. Christianizing a Platonic notion dates back to Augustine, but Lamartine reintroduces it here in the context of Romantic individualism and the quest of an ideal order. Lecturing to Byron on the necessity of leading a Christian life impressed Catholic readers, but the English poet cursed the French writer's presumptuousness.

With the remonstrance to Byron out of the way, he again invokes a reflective mood in **"Le Soir"**: "The evening brings back silence. Seated upon these forsaken rocks, I follow in the open sky the nocturnal chariot that is approaching."

The octosyllabic quatrain, a standard form in the eighteenth century, denotes the extent of Lamartine's Classical roots. In this type of stanza there was greater freedom in placing the caesura. Ossianic themes, the starlight night and the invocation to the evening star, are present in **"Le Soir."** Lamartine belonged to a generation in which many still did not question the authenticity of Macpherson's translations of the Celtic bard.

**"L'Immortalité"** touches upon the subject of earthly love and asks whether two lovers separated in this life will be reunited in the next:

> After a vain sigh, after the last farewell from all that [once] loved you, is there [now] no longer anything that does love you? Ah! only question yourself about this great secret! Behold the one who loves you dying, Elvire, and answer me!

Deprived of this theme, Romanticism would lack a vital element, one that permitted poets to unite the profane and the divine. Did not God, the exemplar of celestial love, smile upon its human manifestations? Lamartine asks this question of Elvire, a composite of Julie and Graziella who represented to Lamartine a latter-day version of Dante's Beatrice.

"**Le Vallon**," written in the same vein as "**L'Isolement**" and "**Le Soir**," affords a quiet broken by "**Le Désespoir**." Here Lamartine complains of a cruel and indifferent deity:

> Heirs of sufferings, victims of life, no, don't expect
> His appeased rage to deaden [the pain of] Misfortune,
> until death, unfolding her enormous wing, swallows
> up forever eternal suffering in everlasting silence!

Seemingly Voltairean in tone, "**Le Désespoir**" has been a convenient point of departure for critics bent on making an agnostic out of Lamartine. Nothing could be further from the truth. The underlying motif, despite Voltairean rhetoric, is Jobean. Chateaubriand popularized the Bible, and the Book of Job with its strains of despair and melancholy was a favorite of the French Romantics. "**Le Désespoir**" is simply a literary convention and expresses the momentary doubts experienced by many believers. The next poem, "**La Providence à l'homme**," supplies a rebuttal by God Himself to the blasphemy of "**Le Désespoir**":

> What! the son of the void has cursed existence! What!
> You can accuse me of my own good deeds. You can
> close your eyes to the magnificence of the gifts I have
> bestowed on you!

From this point on in the *Méditations* Lamartine no longer questions God's will and returns to more tranquil themes. "**Souvenir**" is another graceful poem striking a meditative mood in which the poet muses on the passage of time. The calmness of "**Souvenir**" yields to a more vigorous tempo in "**L'Enthousiasme**" and the expressed desire to love in the present rather than indulge in a fruitless quest for fame:

> Glory is the dream of a shadow. It has reduced too
> much the number of days on which it should cast its
> spell. You want me to sacrifice to it this last breath of
> my life! I wish to keep it in order to love.

The motif of the preceding lines supplies a fitting introduction to "**Le Lac**," the most popular and best-known poem of the *Méditations*. Scenes from *Atala* and the *Nouvelle Héloïse* are recalled more than once in the description of two lovers enthralled by the beauty of the lake and the forest. The passage of time is a phenomenon that perplexes Lamartine and Elvire:

> Eternity, nothingness, past, sombre abysses, what do
> you do with the days you engulf? Speak, will you give
> back to us these sublime ecstasies that you snatch from
> us?

There is little question that "**Le Lac**" records the poet's vivid recollections of moments spent with Julie Charles in a similar setting. Rousseau had already popularized the theme of "**Le Lac**," namely, the return to a spot that recalls passionate and tender memories of bygone days. Sénancour in *Obermann* and Byron in *Childe Harold* employed a similar technique. Lamartine was acquainted with these sources as well as with Rousseau. In fact, this particular theme can be traced back to the pastoral novel of the seventeenth century.

Joined to the motif of a return to a place where love knew brighter moments is the concept of the impermanence of time, its fleeting character and instability. Besides Rousseau, Mme de Staël also favored this notion of the passage of time as a poetic theme which was counterbalanced by the knowledge that eternity would provide the repose incapable of realization in this life. Ossian, as interpreted by Macpherson, would have furnished Lamartine the idea of the appeal to nature to perpetuate the memory of his love for Julie.

At the time "**Le Lac**" was composed Julie was still alive. Her subsequent death gave an entirely different meaning to the original lines, which understandably became more touching and tragic. Even in reading the poem with the knowledge it was written before Julie had died many still receive the impression that Lamartine somehow had a premonition of impending tragedy.

In the ephemeral aspect of time the poet also touches upon a theme familiar to the great writers of French Classicism. Certainly Pascal dwelt upon the transitory character of earthly existence in stressing the need for man to focus his thoughts on eternity. Bossuet, for that matter, frequently referred to the same theme in his sermons. An admirer of the Classicists, Lamartine learned many a valuable lesson from them. By that token "**Le Lac**," then, embraces themes common to several literary schools. It is consequently all the more remarkable that Lamartine gave fresh life to what was by 1820 a literary convention.

With an abrupt switch in tempo and subject Lamartine dedicates the eleventh meditation, "**La Gloire**," to a Portuguese writer, Manuel do Nascimento. It is a sober piece written with a Neo-Classical flourish possibly intended to please conservative readers who would not quite condone the passionate emotions in "**Le Lac**."

The twelfth meditation, "**La Prière**," has not always received the attention it deserves. Lamartine prized it highly as an expression of poetry in the highest sense of the term. All nature joins the poet in adoration of God:

> Behold the immense, universal sacrifice! The universe
> is the temple and the earth is the altar. The heavens are
> the dome, and these stars without number, pale ornament
> of the shadow, sown with order in the azure archway,
> are the sacred candles lit for this temple. . . .

This passage has Martinist overtones with its comparison of a natural setting to a cathedral. As in the Catholic mass the candles are lit and the altar ready. The poet himself acts as priest, thus completing Louis-Claude de Saint-

Martin's prescription for worship of God in nature. According to Martinist teaching a select group, the *hommes de désir* (men of desire), possessed extraordinary insights into the divine will and plan. Their duty was to make this revelation known to other men. Lamartine adapted this concept to the Romantic notion of the poet's lofty mission. The *homme de désir* of Saint-Martin becomes the poet in his exercise of a sacerdotal function. As the poet-priest Lamartine communicates with a deity who transcends sectarian bounds: "Soul of the universe, God, Father, Creator. Under these divine names, I believe in you, Lord. . . ."

In the performance of his priestly office, Lamartine composes a prayer embracing some of the major religious beliefs held by mankind—deistic, pantheistic, and Christian. With his easygoing approach to theology, the poet probably felt the prayer was sufficiently Christianized by using *Seigneur* (Lord) as a common denominator. It is also a reflection of Eclecticism, the school established by Victor Cousin, and a trend that affected Lamartine's thinking.

**"La Prière"** was for the author the high point of the *Méditations* although readers undoubtedly enjoyed shorter selections like **"Invocation"** where the poet dreamed of a Platonic reunion in the next world with Elvire.

**"La Foi"** rejects all obstacles to belief and, putting aside rationalistic arguments on God's existence, relies on intuition to attain knowledge of the deity . . . : "This proud reason, an insufficient light, is extinguished, as life is, at the doors of the tomb. . . ."

The **"Golfe de Baïa"** relieves the reader temporarily of theological concerns as Lamartine gives vent to his antiquarian interests by singing the praises of ancient Rome's architectural achievements. Then **"Le Temple"** marks a return to Catholic motifs, the Church and its spiritual consolation being detailed in the best Chateaubriandesque fashion.

The **"Chants lyriques de Saül"** represents Lamartine's effort to capture some of the solemnity of the Psalms. At times he has fair success in simulating the psalmist's loftiness of tone: "God! How sweet the air is! How pure the light! You reign as victor over all nature."

The **"Hymne au soleil"** and **"Adieu"** recapitulate, respectively, the reunion of lovers in a Platonic paradise and the poet's farewell to the world. Lamartine handles such themes well but is more at home in **"La Semaine sainte"** recording his impressions of worshipers during the final week of Lent:

> All these bowed foreheads, this fire which sets them aglow, these perfumes, these sighs being exhaled from the holy place, this passionate enthusiasm, these tears of ecstasy, all reply to me that there is a God.

Quite fittingly the **"Chrétien mourant"** enlarges on the message of **"La Semaine sainte"** since the devout Christian must eventually resign himself to death. Much of the poem has a ring of sincerity because Lamartine wrote it when he was very ill. The same quality is discernible in **"Dieu"** as the poet makes another Platonic analysis of the soul's origin and destiny.

For an indication of Lamartine's attitude toward nature, **"L'Automne"** furnishes a handy example. Under his pen the scene acquires some of the light and color imparted by eighteenth-century landscapists to their paintings:

> Earth, sun, valleys, beautiful and sweet nature, I owe you a tear at the edge of my grave. The air is so fragrant, the light is so pure! The sun is so beautiful to the eyes of a dying man.

From the serenity of **"L'Automne"** Lamartine moves on to the final poem, **"La Poesie sacrée."** Having sung the divine praises, the poet bids his muse be still as he awaits the coming of the Lord:

> Silence, o lyre, [be] you silent, prophets, voices of the future! All the universe in advance grows still before the one who is to come!

Thus the *Méditations* opens and closes with a note of prayer and contemplation which outwardly at least justified the title of a work that created a sensation on the Paris bookmarket. Lamartine managed to combine various elements that would guarantee a wide readership during the Restoration. Devotees of Chateaubriand and Rousseau could not fail to be moved by the sentimental mixture of profane and divine love set against a backdrop of beautiful, placid lakes and majestic forests. The Christian cast of many of the poems convinced all but the most scrupulous theologians that the *Méditations* was the poetic counterpart of the prose masterpiece, the *Génie du Christianisme*. Without offending Neo-Classical sensibilities, Lamartine brought a new spirit to the French lyric. No radical departure from standard versification, subject matter, and vocabulary was necessary to allow a poet with a fresh view of God and nature to instill new life into French poetry. The *Méditations* remains today—despite changing literary fads—one of the landmarks in French literature. Unquestionably, modern poetry owes much to Lamartine, the first widely read poet since the Pléiade to restore personalism as a necessary component of the lyric. Debates may continue on the significance and merits of that contribution, but the issue seems to narrow down to whether Lamartine was a great poet or just a good one. In view of his mastery of the idyllic setting and the sheer musicality of poems like **"Le Lac,"** he does not deserve neglect.

The *Nouvelles Méditations* was published in 1823 by Canel. Many of the poems repeated themes of the *Premières Méditations*. **"L'Esprit de Dieu"** resembled **"La Foi."** **"Sapho"** bore a Classical stamp, and **"La Solitude"** was reminiscent of **"L'Isolement."**

One of the most widely read poems, not only in France but in England and America, was **"Bonaparte."** In reviewing Napoleon's career the poet in spite of Bourbonist leanings left final judgment of the erstwhile usurper to God:

His coffin is closed. God judged him. Silence! His crime and his exploits weigh in the balance. Let the hand of weak mortals touch it no more! Who can fathom, Lord, your infinite clemency? And you, scourges of God, who knows whether genius is not one of your virtues?

For the first time in his writing Lamartine openly touched upon political and social issues. The Bonapartist cause was not dead, and Lamartine might well be addressing Napoleon's sympathizers when he describes how peaceful France would have been if their hero had restored the Bourbons to power. Tyrants, however, forget how they will ultimately appear in God's eyes.

Similarly in **"La Liberte"** when he considers Rome's past he reflects on the dangers of anarchy: "When the people are the tyrant, they insult kings!" Without doubt, the poet was thinking of the violence of the French Revolution and may have sensed he would one day be in a similar position.

One short poem, **"Le Papillon,"** provided a pleasant contrast to Lamartine's customary lyrics. The butterfly flitting about becomes a symbol of the poet seeking eternal truth:

> To be intoxicated with fragrance, light and the azure sky shaking, still young, the powder from its wings. To take flight like a breath of air towards the eternal heavens. Behold the enchanted destiny of the butterfly.

Lamartine's occasional use of one symbol as the central motif of a poem suggests that in some way he foreshadowed the more sophisticated techniques of the Symbolists. **"La Branche d'amandier,"** for example, centers the reader's attention on a flower signifying the fleeting delights of life here on earth:

> Blossoming trunk of the almond-tree, symbol, alas, of beauty. Like you the flower of life blossoms and falls before summer.

The writer compares himself in **"Le Poète mourant"** to migratory birds who never linger long enough in one spot to make a lasting impression on those who have heard their song:

> The poet is like the migratory birds, who do not build their nests on the shore, who do not place themselves on the branches of the trees. Nonchalantly cradled on the current of the wave, they pass singing far from the shores and the world knows nothing about them except their voice.

If Lamartine dealt on occasion with art and life in simple direct symbols unobscured by literary artifices, he was equally forthright in acknowledging, as he does in **"Les Préludes,"** his basically rural orientation:

> Yes, I return to you, cradle of my childhood, to embrace forever your protecting hearths. [Keep] far from me cities and their vain opulence. I was born among the shepherds.

The Lamartine who wrote these lines was a lover of the outdoors and numbered many dogs and horses among his pets. He was a man of action still capable of reflections almost feminine in their sensitivity in **"Le Crucifix"** such as the scene where the priest administers the Last Sacrament to Julie Charles:

> The holy candles cast a final glow. The priest murmured these soft chants of the dead similar to the plaintive songs which a woman whispers to the child who is falling asleep.

All the familiar ingredients used so well by Lamartine are here, the moving ceremonial of the Church, the paternal figure of the priest, and the prayers for the dying. He combines them effectively in commemorating the death of Julie Charles. Although the poet exalts an adulterous love, readers at the time applauded this deft mixture of the profane and divine. In heaven lovers, married or not, would be reunited. Many concurred with Lamartine in this belief that love would be thus raised to a higher level. In no other poem did he blend so successfully current secular and religious tastes. Sentimental Christianity was present, and the poet like Chactas mourned the death of his sweetheart. For popular consumption it was a most workable formula. Lamartine enjoyed a reputation with the public as a Christian poet. The opinion of theologians in the seminaries, therefore, mattered little.

Besides the continued use of devices that assured the initial success of the *Méditations,* the *Nouvelles Méditations* introduces new features in Lamartine's writing. Political and social issues begin to form part of his perspective and he utilizes on occasion a central image in a poem. His verse was still basically Neo-Classical in structure, and he desired no rupture with standard verse form. Equally concerned about traditional religious ties, he had no quarrel with the Church although he was by no means a dogmatist as is borne out by the profane spirit of **"Le Crucifix."** Even here he was not an intractable rebel. Catholic poets before him had freely intermingled the theme of love of God and that of comely lasses without being excommunicated.

*La Mort de Socrate* was published in 1823 by Hatier. The subject, a popular one in the eighteenth century, attracted Rousseau who compared Socrates' death to the crucifixion of Christ. Lamartine also likens the demise of Socrates to Jesus' sacrifice and in so doing has him foretell to his pagan brethren the advent of the one true God:

> Just a little while longer, and your great crowd receding with the error of your crumbling olympus will give way to the one, holy, universal God, the only God I adore and who has no altar.

The last line has been interpreted by some as a rationalistic remark, although, since Lamartine sees Socrates here as an ally of Christ, emphasis is probably being placed on the nonpagan manner in which the new, unknown god is to be worshiped. The poet was more concerned with finding a common ground for Platonism and Christianity. Accordingly, he pictures the soul of Socrates in a place where the Platonic World of Ideas and the Christian heaven are one and the same:

> Seeking these great spirits it had formerly loved, from sun to sun, from system to system it flies and loses itself with the soul that it loves, follows the vast detours of infinite space, and in the bosom of God always finds itself again!

Lamartine's Socrates is also a true Romantic in the nineteenth-century sense. Life to him seems at best a melancholy affair on this earth and serves largely as a form of expiation: "Life is the struggle, death is the victory and earth is for us the expiatory altar. . . ."

*La Mort de Socrate,* in a period when Platonism and Eclecticism were in vogue, catered to contemporary tastes and enhanced Lamartine's status as poet-philosopher. Academicians would dispute this claim, but their opinion had little effect on the sale of Lamartine's works. Not read much today, *La Mort de Socrate* is merely a mediocre piece of poetry of interest only as an indication of the range of the poet's subject matter.

*Le Chant du sacre,* published in 1825 by Baudouin, gave Lamartine an opportunity to air his Bourbonist views. Written on the occasion of Charles X's coronation, it depicted the new king as a successor to the ancient paladins of France. In the poem Charles X keeps vigil through the night awaiting the solemn moment of coronation. After placing the crown upon Charles' head the archbishop tells him that, unlike people in medieval times, no one expected supernatural manifestations to accompany great events. Instead the modern era looks upon great men as a sign from heaven:

> But the times are no more! The past removes them. Heaven speaks to the earth a stronger language. It is reason alone which explains it to faith. Great events, there are the great wonders!

More than likely Lamartine was merely toadying to the newly crowned king and not making a disparaging remark about Church teaching on miracles. Catholicism still satisfied his emotional needs; moreover, he had other preoccupations, chief of which was a contemplated career as diplomat and statesman. A role as singer of royal praises would not diminish his chances. Certainly *Le Chant du sacre* had to serve some purpose. It did nothing for his literary reputation.

*Le Dernier Chant du pèlerinage d'Harold* was published in 1825 by Dondey-Dupré. Byron had died in Greece the previous year, and Lamartine felt impelled to write another poem like **"L'Immortalité"** dedicated to the English poet and which would narrate the final events in Byron's life. Harold's skepticism is in reality Byron's own cynicism about religion in general: "Jupiter, Mohammed, heroes, great men, gods, O Christ, pardon him, are nothing in his eyes. . . ."

Always fond of listing the major world religions, Lamartine has a field day in treating Harold's peculiar system of metaphysics, which takes a rather cold view of the world and its Creator:

> The God that Harold adores is this supreme agent, this mysterious Pan, an insoluble problem, great, limited, good, bad, which this vast universe reveals to his eyes under a thousand different aspects. A being without attributes, a force without providence, exercising by chance a blind power. . . .

A penchant for involvement with philosophical concepts when writing poetry makes Lamartine subject to various interpretations at times. Harold's lack of a firm belief in a divinity as described here by Lamartine does not signify a continuation of the skepticism of **"Le Désespoir."** The poet simply sets the mood for the final phase of the poem where Harold, after wandering through the world, dies, meets Christ face to face, and fails to pass the test necessary to achieve salvation. Lamartine valued a belief in a personal God and the hereafter. He somehow wished Byron would share that belief. *Le Dernier Chant* was a vehicle for Lamartine's religious notions as well as a means to take advantage of the current Byronic craze in France. Having achieved fame with the *Méditations poétiques* and the *Nouvelles Méditations,* Lamartine temporarily lapsed into mediocrity. *Le Chant du sacre, Le Mort de Socrate* and *Le Dernier Chant* attest to that.

The *Harmonies poétiques et religieuses* was published in 1830 in Brussels by Michel. Since then there have been several editions. Observing in the preface that some people by temperament were better suited to contemplation, Lamartine hinted strongly he was one of the favored few and promised to depict in the *Harmonies* the various mental and emotional states experienced in meditating on God and the wonders of the universe.

One of the first selections, **"Invocation,"** a description of the poet's role in offering to God his own homage and that of nature, tells how his whole being trembles in the realization the poetic gift is of divine origin:

> But above all it is your name, O King of nature, which causes this divine instrument to vibrate in me; when I invoke this name, my heart filled with murmuring resounds like a temple where people sing endlessly.

In fulfilling his function—the singing of the divine praises—Lamartine contemplates the cosmos and is overwhelmed by the evidence of God's omnipotence and omnipresence. He bids all nature worship Him: "Carry back to the heavens the homage of the dawn. Ascend, He is on high, descend, He is all!" (**"Hymne du Matin"**).

The poet's perspective is pantheistic in a general sense. Everything is a reflection of God inasmuch as He exists everywhere. Lamartine does not speak of individual identity being merged with a transcendent force in the world. Like most Romantics, Lamartine is awed by the fact of divine ubiquity, and any expression of his wonderment is purely a literary tour de force; no metaphysical probing into God's nature is intended.

It was a different matter when a question of the believer's personal relationship with God. Every seeker after truth obtained a hearing from God whether Christian or Moslem:

> In the absence of enlightenment, He credits us with a wish. The voice that cries "Allah!" the voice that says "My father!" bring to Him pure incense and false incense. [It is] for Him alone to choose. (**"Aux Chrétiens"**)

Basically nonsectarian in outlook, Lamartine went beyond doctrinal differences to embrace all believers in his world view. The preceding lines, often misread, do not reveal at an early date Lamartine's preference for Islamism, as some critics feel. They merely represent the poet's plea for tolerance on the part of fellow Christians.

If open-mindedness is necessary in assessing the sincerity of contemporary world religions, then it is even more so in any judgment of past theologies. The remains of great faiths of antiquity bear witness to man's endless desire to honor the deity:

> Uncertain relics of an unremembered past. Mysteries of an old world written in mysteries. And you temples [still] standing, superb basilicas whose squares are animated by a divine breath! (**"Jéhova"**)

Man's religious thinking is in a state of flux because truth by its very nature is constantly evolving:

> Behold the truth! Each century in turn believes it lifts its veil and walks by its light, but the one that our ignorance worships today is tomorrow only a cloud; another is ready to shine forth! (**"Novissima verba"**)

Central to many poems of the *Harmonies* is the notion of a timeless religious drive in man. Lamartine repeatedly asserts various aspects of his relation to God. Creeds may be changed and modified, but one factor remains constant—an instinct in man that directs his thoughts and aspirations to the Creator: "Everywhere I sought the God that I adore wherever the instinct led me . . ." (**"Pourquoi mon âme est-elle triste?"**)

Such searching may cause the soul to despair, but Lamartine finds solace in prayer, a logical solution for a poet to whom poetry and prayer are one. Toward the close of the **"Hymne au Christ"** and after reflections on Jesus' sublime message Lamartine reverts to childhood remembrances and longs for the consolations of the simple unquestioning faith he once knew: "For me, whether your name revives or succumbs, O God of my cradle be the God of my tomb!" (**"Hymne au Christ"**).

Two characteristics of Lamartine are the cherished notion of a childhood faith and an impulse to return to an earlier pattern of feeling when life was less complex and he enjoyed the heartwarming experience of everyday life at Milly. Regression was typical of other French Romantics when recalling their youth and early loves. In Lamartine

this inclination expresses itself in some of his finest and most moving verse.

A true picture of what Lamartine actually thought and felt about nature, the physical world around him, may be read in those lines when he recalls the scenes of boyhood and adolescence at Milly. There he spent his happiest years and there he wishes to be buried:

> Dig for me in these fields the grave that I long for and this last furrow from which another life will spring. (**"Milly, ou la Terre natale"**)

There is nothing artificial in the poet's spontaneous reaction to a swallow gliding gracefully over the water, and he is capable of depicting such moments honestly and without affectation:

> Behold the wandering swallow which skims with the end of its wing the sleeping waters of the marsh. Behold the child from the huts who gathers on the heath the fallen wood of the forests. (**"Pensée des morts"**)

The song of another bird, the nightingale, will unite, he hopes, with his own prayer in order that all God's creatures may join in praise of Him:

> Oh! Combine your voice with mine! The same ear hears us, but your airborne prayer rises better to the heaven that awaits us. (**"Au Rossignol"**)

This closeness to nature makes the poet aware of its dynamism:

> And I hear buzzing under the grass that I trample upon these waves of living beings that each furrow unfolds. Atoms animated by the divine breath! Each ray of daylight rises from it without end. (**"L'infini dans les cieux"**)

More expansive in conceiving nature than the *Méditations,* the *Harmonies* discloses Lamartine's response to the physical forces at work about him. Basically an unabashed lover of the outdoors, he has a fierce devotion to his native soil. He can capture the mood of a quiet moment in the wilderness or use a lone bird as the central image of a poem. Lamartine is attuned as well to the vitality he senses in the smallest blade of grass. Too often dismissed as an effeminate poet, he had a virile temperament beneath the deceptive softness of his style.

Vigor and virility characterize **"Les Révolutions"** as Lamartine, after reviewing outmoded religious and social institutions, proclaims the need for mankind to be constantly on the march to better the human condition:

> March! Humanity does not live by one idea! It extinguishes each evening the one that has guided it, it lights another from the inextinguishable torch; like these dead dressed in their soiled attire, the [passing] generations take along from this world their clothing into the tomb! (**"Les Révolutions"**)

The eighteenth-century notion of indefinite progress is insufficient for man's needs without the moral strength of Christianity. It is for Christians to combine progress with their religious heritage in leading mankind forward under their banner: "Under yours, O Christians! Man in whom God works constantly changes in form and size" (**"Les Révolutions"**).

To readers of the *Harmonies,* Lamartine's increasing awareness of life about him is readily discernible. The poet has not only developed a greater appreciation of God and nature; he has also become more responsive to political and social issues. **"Les Révolutions"** reveals the writer's outlook on the eve of his formal entry into politics. Up to this point he has only enunciated general principles. The time is not far off when he will have to furnish specific answers to some perplexing problems.

Just as every aspect of human endeavor corresponds to the universal search for religious truth, nature too discloses a unifying principle which Lamartine detects in the felicitous arrangement of the various levels of creation:

> Holy and mysterious law! A melodious soul animates the whole universe; each being has its harmony, each star its spirit, each element its concerts. (**"Désir"**)

As a result of the infinite harmony perceived in the cosmos Lamartine feels the urge to proclaim the wonders of creation. A faculty within the poet directs him to laud the deity whose omnipotence is so apparent:

> But the instinct that adores you has grown in my soul; henceforth it is the only one my life needs; it sees, it senses, it touches, it hears, it proclaims things from on high and its God from afar! (**"Le Solitaire"**)

A by-product of this perception of universal harmony is an arresting image emphasizing the essential unity of the world:

> It was this great spirit, this universal soul which lived, which felt, which vegetated for it. A being almost divine for which it was the body, that activated all the springs of its inert mass . . . (**"Hymne de l'ange de la terre après la destruction du globe"**)

The oneness of the world had long been a tenet of Indic philosophy, and Lamartine by his use of the preceding figure shows a probable borrowing from an early work on Hinduism, Friedrich Creuzer's *Symbolik* translated in French by Joseph Guigniaut as *Religions de l'Antiquité. . . .*

Nor is there likewise any risk in presuming Lamartine's acquaintance with Louis-Claude de Saint-Martin, traces of whose theosophy already appear in the *Méditations.* Martinism and Hinduism would provide the poet with apt metaphors to describe a mystical encounter with divine secrets hidden from ordinary mortals:

> If the letter of the great book of nature, imperceptible to your eyes, does not disclose it everywhere, ah! man

*Lamartine in 1825, in a lithograph by Ratier.*

is the supreme book. In the fibers of his very heart read mortals! there is a God! (**"L'Humanité"**)

In the theosophic jargon of Saint-Martin, the person initiated into celestial mysteries was the divine book revealing God's secrets to the rest of mankind. Such a person in contact with the deity could aspire to a fuller knowledge of the universe. Lamartine would naturally limit such a privilege to the poet already favored with this preternatural talent.

While Lamartine's preoccupations in the *Harmonies* were often religious and philosophical, he could also turn his attention to the dispassionate contemplation of beauty. Take, for example, a passage depicting the sculptural grace of a young maid, her body covered by long, flowing hair:

> It is entwined like a necklace about the white neck it embraces. (It) comes down, winds, and proceeds to unfold upon a bosom where scarcely swell up two sources from which life is to flow in streams of love.
>
> (**"L'Humanité"**)

Through a concern with the plastic aspects of his word painting the poet anticipates the Parnassians. Usually not associated with that school, Lamartine was capable at times of achieving some of the same effects. The poet's scope was not necessarily limited to the poetry of ideas.

To a greater extent than preceding works the *Harmonies* supplies readers with a well-rounded picture of Lamartine's versatility and the central religious and philosophical themes of Lamartine's poetry. Many elements represent a carryover from the *Méditations,* the emotional states characteristic of prayer, alternate moods of hope and despair, worship of God in the great outdoors, a nostalgic longing for the homestead, and an eclectic view of religion. Lamartine explores further the diversity of creation. Besides observing the flora and fauna around him, he focuses his attention on a historical perspective of man. Christianity is a sublime exemplar of truth but not its sole possessor. Involvement in the dynamic nature of religious truth leads directly into a consideration of man's social progress. Faced with complexity on all levels of creation, the poet finds a solution in the realization everything is animated by one principle. Without becoming openly pantheistic, Lamartine depicts the oneness of a multifaceted world in terms borrowed from Hinduism and Martinism. He thus persists in and enlarges upon his eclectic view of the world.

---

**Reception of Lamartine by foreign contemporaries:**

Lamartine's esthetic theories and philosophy may seem outmoded and trite at present in light of our more complex problems and sophisticated literary tastes. However, Anglo-American readers of the last century, including those who were not enthusiastic admirers of the poet-statesman, considered him an important figure in both the world of letters and politics. British critics were delighted by the extent to which the *Méditations* reflected the French writer's acquaintance with Pope, Gray, and Byron. In America the unbounded faith in human progress expressed in the *Méditations* and the *Harmonies* was warmly received in a pioneer culture as yet unaffected by the skepticism of older and more experienced European civilizations. Protestants in England and the United States generally acclaimed the religious tone prevalent in his works. At a time in America when French writers were frequently suspected of immorality Lamartine was one of the first of his countrymen to win a considerable measure of acceptance and approval.

*C. M. Lombard, "Lamartine in America and England (1820-1876): A Check List," in* Bulletin of Bibliography, *May-August, 1961.*

---

## Norman Araujo (essay date 1976)

SOURCE: "People, Prisons, and Palaces," "The Terrestrial Eden," and "Conclusion," in *In Search of Eden: Lamartine's Symbols of Despair and Deliverance*, Classical Folia Editions, 1976, pp. 15-66, pp. 199-232, pp. 307-10.

[*In this excerpt, Araujo examines the significance of Lamartine's religious symbolism in his major poetical works.*]

The point of departure in Lamartine's quest for Eden is a shattering sense of man's nothingness. No figure in human history more tragically and more meaningfully symbolizes that nothingness, in his view, than Job, whom he quotes in

his *Cours familier de littérature* (1856-1869). This work of his mature years, presumably designed to educate the masses to the moral beauties of world literature but more significant as a depository of some of Lamartine's fundamental philosophic and literary tenets, records the essential and unanswered question which the anguished victim of divine wrath puts to God:

> L'insensible néant t'a-t-il demandé l'être,
> Ou l'a-t-il accepté?

An initial assumption might be that Lamartine registers this query and meditates on it because he is an aged, moneyless writer traversing the inglorious twilight period of his life. The author's comparison of himself with Job during these difficult years—in the poem *Le Désert* (1832-1856) and in other texts—and the same analogy drawn by friends like Charles Alexandre would appear to support this interpretation. Moreover, critics possessing no direct personal ties with Lamartine, such as Ethel Harris [*Lamartine et le peuple*, 1932] and Jean des Cognets [*La vie intérieure de Lamartine*, 1912], tend to perpetuate the image of the elderly poet as a tormented Job.

But the selfsame words of Lamartine's Job, which are inspired by the *Book of Job* and do not differ greatly from the words attributed to the Old Testament figure by Milton in *Paradise Lost* or Young in *Night Thoughts*, are already to be found in a poem of the *Méditations poétiques* (1820), "Le Désespoir" (1818). Their presence indicates that, at an early point in his literary production, Lamartine marks what is to be a lifelong fluctuation between optimistic faith and haunting doubt, a fluctuation observed by several researchers and aptly conveyed in Henri Guillemin's phrase, *balancement tragique* [*Connaissance de Lamartine*, 1942].

In the *Cours familier de littérature*, Lamartine's solidarity with Job—a solidarity shared in varying degrees with Goethe, Byron, Chateaubriand, and Hugo, who placed Job among his *mages*—is strongly reinforced. Lamartine expresses a persistent desire, only temporarily suspended in the past during rare moments of fleeting happiness, to return the gift of life to his Creator and enjoy once again the peace of nothingness:

> . . . there have been few moments in my life when, if the Almighty had consulted me, I would not have returned to Him with horror the gift of life and told Him, like Job: Take back your fatal present; leave me in peace in my void. In your incomprehensible creation the only happy people are the dead! . . .

Special importance attaches to the word "void," which renders the original French *néant*. . . .Lamartine employs the word in both these senses, which he sees as complementary. In his thinking, the meaninglessness of human existence, the *néant* of the world which we know, only creates, unless counterpoised by religious beliefs, an irrepressible urge to embrace the absolute *néant*, that of nonexistence. Here the splendid virtue of the negative absolute is the liberation which it promises from the folly of human hopes and illusions.

A study of some of the frequent allusions to the *néant* in Lamartine's writings will both demonstrate the coherence of his reflections in this regard and establish a proper framework for the further examination of his symbols of despair. . . . The extoller of rustic beauty and serenity who pens **"Le Vallon"** (1819), the sentimental lover who addresses the lake as a confidant in **"Le Lac"** (1817), is likewise capable of discerning in nature the reflection of human wretchedness. The sea can produce an effect similar to that of the mountain, as in **"Éternité de la nature, brièveté de l'homme"** (1828), where Lamartine seems to anticipate Gaston Bachelard's qualification of water as "un néant substantiel," [*L'eau et les rêves—essais sur l'imagination de la matière,* 1942]. Life is but a drop of water in the basins of the ocean. . . .

More devastating in this connection than the contemplation of nature is the philosophical self-evaluation which is prompted by the imminence of death. In **"Hymne de la mort"** (1829), the soul is about to cast away its mortal coil, and the poet wonders rhetorically about the final implications of its habitation of this globe. He asks whether it sensed, in the course of its terrestrial sojourn, "ce néant de l'existence." The ramifications of Lamartine's question are manifest in **"Novissima Verba"** (1829), where the nearness of death once again stirs a frightening sensitivity to the total uselessness of life. . . . Man has no real consolation in the face of such nothingness, unless it be the tombstone. In another section of the poem, Lamartine alludes to this lonely and mute testimony to man's transient presence on earth.

With the recognition of man's insignificance comes also that of the perishable character of everything which results from his worldly activity. While this enlargement of Lamartine's view is not without parallel in Pascal and Blake and surely not unexpected in the light of the Romantic conception of life, what lends interest to his particular outlook is the constant, almost obsessive, concern with the *néant*. The **"Réponse aux adieux de Sir Walter Scott"** (1832) calls attention to the ephemerality of our most grandiose creations and condemns at once our vain pursuit of immortality through the ready inscription of our names on these proud monuments. But however phrenetic our creative efforts and insistent our glory-hungry design to inscribe them, the result is always nil. Wherever we leave our names, they still translate only *néant*. As if further to debunk the vainglorious ambitions which impel man to create, Lamartine places in the mouth of Jocelyn a ringing rejection of the futile human attempt to escape the law of the universe, which is one of eternal shift and change. The poet has not modified, in the meantime, his evaluation of the fruits of mortal achievement. The same term already employed to characterize that achievement reappears:

> En vain l'homme, orgueilleux de ce néant qu'il fonde,
> Croit échapper lui seul à cette loi du monde,

Clôt son symbole, et dit, pour la millième fois:
Ce Dieu sera ton Dieu, ces lois seront tes lois!

[*Jocelyn*]

Overwhelmed by what he considers the irrefutable evidence of the *néant* of man's earthly accomplishments, Lamartine yields in moments of depression to the beckoning desire to be reabsorbed in the larger *néant* of nonexistence. The symbol of Job, introduced at the beginning of this [essay] becomes, therefore, a very real expression of Lamartine's spiritual plight and not merely a random literary device. But whereas Job clings desperately to the idea of a vengeful but just God, the French writer is driven, at the height of his doubt and despair, almost entirely to repudiate the notion of divine justice. The *néant* is at least comprehensible to him. It is actually, he tells us in one instance, as he recoils from the impact of Lamennais' *Essai sur l'indifférence en matière de religion,* the only god which he is capable of understanding. In a darker mood of despondency, Lamartine generalizes his particular case and views all humanity and all creation as propelled by the same yearning for a reintegration with the *néant*. This yearning is articulated in **"Le Désespoir,"** a poem which apparently impressed the Italian composer Rossini but whose pessimism shocked the poet's mother and caused Lamartine to counter with **"La Providence à l'homme"** (1819), specifically written to please her—or so he says in his "commentaire." **"Le Désespoir"** contains an affirmation which echoes the despairing tones of Young's eleventh "Night." Lamartine asserts that every living organism, from the very start of creation, has only wished to be assimilated into the *néant* from which it originally sprang.

Mention was made above of the constant vacillation in Lamartine's thought between religious fervor and gnawing uncertainty. One need look no further, for a different vantage point on the subject of the *néant,* than the professed disavowal of **"Le Désespoir"**—**"La Providence à l'homme."** This poem, while incorporating the language of Job and Young, purports to castigate the pessimism formulated in other places of the author's work. . . .

But in spite of such divine reassurance, and even in the face of the occasional fear that the *néant* is to be dreaded as much as life itself, Lamartine does not easily neutralize the urge to end the agony of his terrestrial existence. It is the expectant emancipation from this very suffering that in **"Novissima Verba"** strips from death the integument of horror and sadness which traditionally envelops it:

> Triste comme la mort? Et la mort souffre-t-elle?
> Le néant se plaint-il à la nuit éternelle?
> Ah! plus triste cent fois que cet heureux néant
> Qui n'a point à mourir et ne meurt pas vivant!

One may speculate for a moment on the meaning of this "heureux néant." Clearly, happiness is no longer conceived in the finest Epicurean sense as the absence of pain. Rather it is to be construed as that cosmic nothingness and anonymity which are the very negation of life itself. Lamartine lays further stress on the worthlessness of human existence by characterizing it as merely a few minutes stolen insignificantly from the *néant*.

Against the back cloth of his dual perspective on the *néant*, seen as nonexistence or as the perishability of man and all his creation, the concrete symbols which Lamartine utilizes to dramatize the wretchedness of man's lot on earth assume a particular significance. They are designed to deflate our ego by associating us symbolically with all those phenomena about us, animate and inanimate, which we regard with scorn or repugnance. Among these is the insect, which Lamartine selects as the symbol of man himself. Despite his pretensions to grandeur, man cannot escape from the truth of his inconsequential being as measured against the universal standard. . . . [His mother's view of life] impressed Lamartine with the trifling role of man in the universe. Extremely revelatory, in the context of our present discussion, is the fact that the comparison used by Madame de Lamartine to translate her thought involved the insect: she observed that God could crush man as if he were an insect. The comparison must have remained indelibly etched in Lamartine's memory. He was frequently to have recourse to it.

Madame de Lamartine's teachings must not be simplified, and it cannot be maintained that all Lamartine's references to the insect are deprecatory to man. Penetrated by the concept of the chain of being, which he discovers in Pope and other writers of the eighteenth century, Lamartine sometimes marvels at the endless compassion of a Creator Who can look with equal love on all links of **"La chaîne à mille anneaux"** going from man to the insect. But by and large his use of the symbol of the insect to represent man, a symbol the offshoots of which Louis Racine had traced far back into classical antiquity, reflects despair rather than joy. Lamartine derives no permanent sense of comfort from the harmonious order of the chain of being theory. . . .

Is man not saved from the demeaning implications of comparison with the insect by his rational powers? Such an argument ostensibly finds favor with Lamartine as he advises Hugo to leave the city for the physically and spiritually refreshing countryside, a welcome refuge against the constant embattlement of urban life. Adopting a phrase reminiscent of Pascal's *roseau pensant*, Lamartine admonishes his literary comrade-in-arms to flee the "champs de bataille" where the passers-by crush the "insecte pensant." This example and a few others like it notwithstanding, Lamartine is not one, in the final analysis, to glorify human reason. As Citoleux has convincingly established [in *La poésie philosophique au XIXᵉ siècle: Lamartine*, 1906], not only the **Méditations poétiques** but other works of Lamartine as well advance the notion that man's rational faculties are weak and incapable by themselves of creating a secure basis for belief in God. It is not really surprising, then, that Lamartine should compare man's rational attempts to capture the image of God with the buzzing or "bourdonnement" of the insect. *Le Désert* features verses in which God, explaining to man that He is accessible to man's mind but only through His attributes, affirms the uselessness of mortal endeavors to depict Him. Such en-

deavors are but the vain efforts of "Insectes bourdonnants," since man is unable to reproduce or measure God. Of like inadequacy is the human ambition to enclose the essence of God in sacred books. Again mention is made of the pointless buzzing of mankind, as Lamartine emphasizes that if God were in sounds, He still could not be encompassed by "Les langues que bourdonne un insecte ici-bas." If there is some fragile human hope to suggest, however imperfectly, the sublime splendor of God, that hope rests not with the *insecte pensant*, nor the *insecte bourdonnant*, but with the poet, or the *insecte chantant* of **"Le Cachot."**

The symbol of the insect is one of extreme fecundity for Lamartine: it indicates both man's puny potential in physical and verbal terms and his all-too-brief life span. At best, such a life span is totally dependent on the support of man's environment. . . .

The word used repeatedly to mark the brevity of our stay on this planet is *éphémère*. At times, Lamartine applies the term literally to actual insects [cf. **"L'infini dans les cieux"**], and he does so appropriately, given the literal meaning and derivation of the word. But there is a more important application of *éphémère* in regard to human beings. Lamartine is speaking quite clearly of himself and of humanity in general when he introduces the symbol of the "insecte éphémère" in **"A la croix"** (1830):

> Je fus homme: insecte éphémère
> Pétri de misère et d'orgueil,
> Pécheur dès le sein de ma mère,
> Et chancelant jusqu'au cercueil;
> Entre la lumière et le doute
> Perdant et retrouvant ma route. . .

These verses go beyond a mere reminder of man's transitory presence on this globe. They dramatize the double affliction of misery and pride which torments him in his sinful state and highlight, once again, the incessant fluctuations of the author between faith and uncertainty. . . .

A substitute for the word *insecte* in Lamartine's symbolic vocabulary is the term *atome*. Sometimes, as in the case of the *insecte*, the *atome* is presented as a part of the great chain of being linking man to God and thereby the object of the Creator's concern. In other instances, the *atome* is a Pascalian, or perhaps more precisely, a Voltairian *atome pensant*. But in many texts, the symbolism of the atom is far less flattering and patently designed to underline the unimportance and weakness of man. In the **Recueillements poétiques** (1839), which attests Lamartine's humble acceptance of the social aspect of the poet's Orphic mission—to civilize man by pointing the way to progress— the atom stands for the presumptuous bard. Only now, after the vanity of his first lyrical outbursts, does Lamartine take stock of his minute function in the overall plan of the universe. **"A M. Félix Guillemardet"** (1837) equates him with an "atome insaisissable" which had the egocentrism to think itself capable of sheltering "un monde." Although consumed by a spark of creativity, Lamartine continues, in **"Utopie"** (1837), to reduce himself symbolically to the status of a being shaded by an atom.

While the *Recueillements poétiques* looms initially as a poetic repudiation of the nostalgic self-aggrandizement characteristic of Lamartine's attitude in thc *Méditations poétiques,* certain poems of the 1820 publication fore-shadow the subsequent change of perspective. One of these is **"L'Homme"** (1819), in which Lamartine's praise of Byron is mingled with more humbling observations about the latter's cosmic role of "faible atome":

> Mais pourquoi reculer devant la vérité?
> Ton titre devant Dieu c'est d'être son ouvrage!
> De sentir, d'adorer ton divin esclavage;
> Dans l'ordre universel, faible atome emporté,
> D'unir à ses desseins ta libre volonté,
> D'avoir été conçu par son intelligence,
> De le glorifier par ta seule existence!

Clearly, the lowly station of the atom is spiritually compensated by the divine purpose to which it is subordinated. But poetic glorification of God must still proceed from a basis—Christian in essence and restated by Lamennais—of "esclavage." This deflationary appraisal of man's position in God's grand design and the symbol which translates it reappear in the *Harmonies poétiques et religieuses* (1830). Lamartine asks his own version of the rhetorical-philosophical question so strikingly put by Montaigne in his *Essais.* Not "Que sais-je?" but rather "Que suis-je?" is the formula adopted by the poet of **"L'Infini dans les cieux."** The response, measured against the infinity of the skies, is as anticipated: "grain de sable," "atome," "insecte invisible." In order to place man in truer perspective, compared with the celestial expanses, Lamartine intersperses an alternate term of comparison, the earth itself. The skies dwarf man; they dwarf his globe as well. His claim to immortality is akin to an echo which lasts but a second on "cet atome obscur que nous nommons un monde."

. . . . .

As Lamartine understands it, man's state of exile is a direct result of Adam's expulsion from the Garden of Eden. The Christian underpinnings of this relationship and its coloration by an eighteenth-century preoccupation with the Edenic theme in exotic literature are too well known to deserve comment here. What marks the originality of Lamartine's perception is its symbolic application in so many of his works. One reason why the author of the *Cours familier de littérature* is attracted to Indian philosophy is that philosophy's incorporation of the notion of a lost Eden, a haven from sin and misfortune which man should strive to relocate. In his poetry, Lamartine stresses the universality of this quest, since all mortals are in the position of Adam, banished like him from the blissful Garden. . . . The nostalgic regret embodied in [**"L'homme"**] is ever present in Lamartine's vision of man's dcspair. That vision is continually founded on the awareness of man's Adamic descendance, but still more so on the banishment from Paradise. The first man to walk the earth is characteristically labeled the "enfant d'Éden." Furthermore, Lamartine is haunted by the loss of that intimate communion between God and man which, to a greater degree than the innocent and luxuriant natural setting, endowed Eden with its truly paradisiacal character. In **"Réflexion,"** as he is in the process of enumerating those ways in which we can know God—how He is manifest in His works, how our conscience is His second voice, how His laws are engraved in our hearts—Lamartine does not neglect to mention that God spoke "dans Éden au père des mortels." All man's subsequent activity, one would surmise from the poet's words, should be directed to the eventual resumption of that interrupted dialogue.

It is difficult, moreover, to avoid the conclusion that in moments of metaphysical nostalgia Lamartine wishes that he had been an immediate descendant of Adam, or possibly Adam himself. The conclusion proposes itself quite definitely in **"Dieu."**. . . Lamartine regrets not having been a part of the first Biblical generation, which was able to converse with God . . . In *La Chute d'un ange,* the same regret is transparent in the poet's allusion to the first people coming after Eden, who vividly remembered it still. Lamartine envies the men of those times, full of God and seeing the whole of creation as a hymn to His greatness. Lamartine's great epic poem, the poem that he dreamed all his life of composing, the poem of which he speaks so often in his *Correspondence,* would have begun with Eden. . . .

In spite of his sturdy conviction that man's impulsion on this earth—as dictated by his spiritual history and whatever naturally good impulses have escaped the corruption of sin—is to look for the route to a terrestrial Eden while waiting for his liberated soul to rise to the heavenly paradise, Lamartine is sometimes disheartened by the present-day world's extreme dissimilarity with the original Eden in literal and symbolic terms. Instead of bucolic beauty and total innocence, the hapless mortal of modern times encounters dirt—both real and symbolic—noise, confusion, derisive laughter, and a multiplicity of roads, which are also both real and symbolic. Only a few of these lead back to God and Eden. There is, of course, the release of death, but, in the final analysis, Lamartine is not attracted to suicide as a solution: one must live out one's life as best one can before the emancipation of the final hour.

Like his fellow Romantics, primarily Musset and Hugo, Lamartine yields somewhat to the temptation to transpose his quest for Eden into the framework of his childhood. It turns out consequently that he, like them, has known his earthly Eden as an innocent child, in a manner of speaking like the "child" Adam before the desire of "adult" knowledge corrupted the latter. This road to Eden is then the road of reverie, the road of meditation on the irretrievable Edenic quality of one's early years on this planet, years which one writer has termed "the archetype of simple happiness" and "innocence incarnate." Because his family created this quality of life for him, Lamartine will always remain sensitive to the joys and beauties of family life. . . . In the Lamartinian reverie, Edenic childhood is linked indissolubly with friends as well as with homeland and family. Lamartine wonders aloud, in his *Correspondence,* whether one can meaningfully talk of paradise, after the age of twenty-one, away from the homeland:

> Is it a paradise? Is there any far from our country and our friends, when we have passed twenty-one? No, no, no; we must live, see each other, love each other, and not be separated from each other, at least not by seas.

The above text implies not so much that paradise away from one's homeland is imaginable before the age of twenty-one, as that the homeland continues, even in adulthood, to exercise an invincible attraction. **"Milly ou la terre natale"** maintains that, for all the excitement which they are capable of generating, the native lands of great literary figures cannot rival the charm of Lamartine's— a charm largely responsible, incidentally, for the poet's refusal to part with the family property and for the consequent incurrence of heavy debts. The same sentiment pervades **"Le Retour"** of the *Harmonies poétiques et religieuses,* where, at that psychological juncture which Bachelard calls "the fusion of the poetry of remembrance and the truth of illusions," Lamartine proclaims the deep satisfaction of being able to breathe once again the air of one's homeland, that air "embaumé d'antiques souvenirs." A third poem filled with Lamartine's ardent love for his own native soil is **"Ressouvenir du lac Léman."** No more beautiful name exists on earth for mankind, writes the poet, than *patrie.* . . .

Just as his memories of childhood are memories of purity and innocence in a pastoral environment, reminiscent of the terrestrial Eden, so Lamartine's perceptions of modern urban life are perceptions of physical and moral degradation indicative of the downward path of humanity since the Biblical Paradise. From the very outset, the big industrial city looms in the writer's eyes as the extreme antithesis of Eden. . . .

Evidence of the city's corruptive influence is abundant in Lamartine's works. The Paris of *Jocelyn* is inescapably associated with the suffering of the mother of the protagonist: her residence in this "ville banale" was a second period of exile. *Le Désert* extols the desert life not only because of its liberation from noise but also because of its freedom from the spiritual decay of the city. In *Geneviève,* the moral insufficiency of the city assumes a more direct and personal form. Geneviève learns through painful experience that it is better to rely on the generosity of the people of the country than on that of the people of the city. The latter, in spite of their riches, are less likely to give. *La Chute d'un ange* involves an extreme case of the city's capacity to foster vice and viciousness. The evil is discernible in the very architecture of the giants' creation, which is at once a sign of colossal vanity and an indication of their total indifference to the humanity under their rule. The fact that the heart of the city is its sinister subterranean development must be interpreted as something more than an ironic prophecy regarding the future downward expansion of the sprawling metropolis: this "flight from light" is to be construed symbolically as a flight from the good and the pure.

The mammoth city of *La Chute d'un ange* has many flaws in common with other real cities that Lamartine has appreciated. But these flaws are magnified and compounded beyond belief in that epic of evil. The noise is not simply that of the city's brisk activity but in large part the horrible screams of the many persons being tortured or molested. It was to escape this massive oppression and preserve his faith that Adonaï fled into the countryside, taking refuge in the grotto where Cédar and Daïdha come upon him. . . .

It would be a simplification of Lamartine's thought to suggest that all his terrestrial Edens were havens of verdant vegetation or high mountains. He does not directly assign traditional Edenic characteristics to the desert in *Le Désert.* But it is evident that this arid refuge . . . permits man to reestablish at least some of the earlier communication with God. This communication is possible because the desert brings man the liberty of mind—or what Bachelard might call "an intensity of the inner being" [*La poétique de l'espace*]—which is the first "terre promise" and without which knowledge of God is unattainable. . . .

An examination of Lamartine's other works reveals that the quest for Eden on earth permeates, in one form or another, all his literary production. . . .

*La Chute d'un ange,* like *Jocelyn,* is bound up with the search for and enjoyment of an Eden on earth. As the tracked lovers head for the sea, they are impelled onward by the exhilarating hope of soon beholding "Mille fruits inconnus" and smelling "les plus doux parfums.". . . The Edenic theme is more explicitly etched when the *chœur des cendres* likens the patch of cedar trees to a "vert diadème" which God created "aux sommets d'Éden." But these details are episodic and peripheral when compared to the fuller symbolism attaching to the places—also boasting their grottoes—inhabited by the old man who relates the story of Cédar and Daïdha and the venerable keeper of the *Fragment du livre primitif.* Both these servants of God—who are in a long line of wise old men found in Ariosto, Fénelon, Voltaire, and Chateaubriand—live in havens approximating Eden to a greater or lesser extent. The gigantic stems visible at the site of the first of these holy figures are the "sacrés vestiges" of the trees of Eden. When the other, Adonaï, takes Cédar and Daïdha through his home, he proceeds like one who is conducting a tour of Eden itself. . . . The whole experience of the young couple and their aged host, a spiritually exalting experience, is reported in Edenic terms. Cédar and Daïdha decide to remain for a while with their religious mentor, with whom they spend "Leurs jours délicieux" in "cet Éden céleste."

If Eden were symbolically represented in Lamartine's works only as a place of breathtaking natural beauty, its spiritual value would be thereby diminished. The Eden which Lamartine contemplates is a haven of love as well as a scenic wonder. That is why in most cases it is a backdrop for a love experience. The association derives from the Bible, and Adam and Eve. In **"A Guichard,"** the Biblical background is very much present in the poet's memory as he descants for Bienassis on the characteristics of the god *Amour.* The poem is dated 1808, or twelve years before the publication of the *Méditations poétiques*. But the identification of lovers with Adam and Eve, persistent in his later works, is already a prominent feature of Lamartine's approach. So is his religious syncretism. . . . It is of further significance that in . . . this poem Lamartine deals with the history of love, a history marked by the loss of love's innocence and purity.

"Ischia" (1820-1822) in the *Nouvelles Méditations poétiques* furnishes more evidence regarding the fusion of the ideal of Eden with that of love. Commenting on the beauty of a natural setting which in his eyes combines the enchantment of Biblical Paradise with that of the pagan Elysian fields, Lamartine can think of no finer encomium than to declare that the site is one in which love would have been happy to hide its Eden. . . . Linked are not simply nature and love but nature, love, and God. *Les Visions* proposes the same essential connection between love and nature. Enamored of Hermine, Tristan dreams of living only for their passion and thus transforming the nature that serves as its back cloth into an Eden. . . . In *La Chute d'un ange,* being in love is again symbolically synonymous with being in Eden. Cédar, who has beheld the celestial Eden and is thus in a position to make a valid comparison, exclaims that Daïdha and his attachment to her have changed the world into a paradise for him. Daïdha's hair shades the flower of his terrestrial Eden, as he lyrically puts it: "De mon terrestre Éden vous ombragez la fleur."

*Jocelyn* extends this love symbolism. As he meditates on his devotion to Laurence and on the happiness which he has known in the *grotte des aigles,* Jocelyn realizes that this place of exile has been the background for his "première innocence" and "céleste amour." To be sure, the specific idea of Eden is not formulated here. But it is implicit if one recollects an earlier section of the poem, where Jocelyn leaves his mountain grotto for an exploratory trip into the countryside. The charm of the pastoral existence which he discovers reawakens in him an Edenic nostalgia that will explain later his exalted perception of his love for Laurence. . . . The notion of genuine love as possessing both the intensity and the innocence of the love binding Adam and Eve before the fall is set forth also in *La Chute d'un ange*. Adonaï is delighted with the innocence of Cédar and Daïdha; he thinks to discern in it a vestige of the innocence of Eden. . . .

The relative abundance in his works of allusions to Adam, and even more so to Eve, establishes an additional basis for the inference that ideal love, as imagined by Lamartine, retains the basic qualities of Edenic love. "Hymne de l'ange de la terre" testifies to the nostalgic substance of Lamartine's meditations on Adam. The angel depicted in the poem is reminiscent of the first man on earth. He is a harmonious composite of the celestial and the human, "De cet être déchu type primordial." In *Jocelyn,* the relationship is more direct. Having located Laurence after her degradation, Jocelyn is attracted irresistibly, each time he goes out, to her hotel, where he listens at the door for a voice from heaven or earth. He compares his plight

with that of Adam, who, "exilé des jardins du Seigneur," listened to the voices of his happiness fade away. But Lamartine's thoughts are mostly of Eve. The Daïdha of *La Chute d'un ange* is much like Eve in her impeccable loveliness and simplicity. Lamartine is explicit on this point: his heroine is in the presence of Cédar like Eve in the company of Adam. . . . Throughout his works, in fact, Lamartine casts the ideal woman in the image of Eve. All women, he insists in one poem, are "filles de l'Éden" adored by men. . . . Perhaps the most striking association of love, innocence, and Eden is to be encountered in another poem, whose meaning specialists have endeavored with questionable success to penetrate in order to determine whether it implies a dubious relationship between Lamartine and his niece Valentine. . . . [In "Un nom"], what is conveyed is not so much the figure of Eve as the Edenic bliss caused by deep love for a woman. . . .

By themselves, a beautiful natural setting and pure, innocent love—or just the latter—can bring into being Lamartine's terrestrial Eden. But animals sometimes play a part in his symbolism. The placidity of his fauna is like that of Eden's animal life before the fall. In *Les Visions,* Lamartine suggests that the animals of Eden come readily to his mind when he recognizes in their descendants the same gentleness of comportment. He describes—in language which accords with the feminist persuasion of Toussenel regarding the particular attachment of the animals of Eden to Eve rather than to Adam—a young girl being followed by two lambs. . . .

If one can put out of one's thoughts for a moment the absurdly periphrastic portrayal of the chicken in the "Troisième Vision"—which is an illustration of the stylistic inadequacies at the root of the exasperation of so many critics of Lamartine from Vigny to Guitton—one can appreciate that the animals of *La Chute d'un ange* are conceived in a similar light. For Lamartine, they revive the instinct of love which pervaded the atmosphere of the Biblical Paradise. When Cédar and Daïdha lie among the animals, the latter remain peaceful. The purity and innocence of the two lovers seem to tame them. The poet draws a more general conclusion from the absolute peace of this scene, which is that man must endeavor to recapture the "première harmonie" of Eden as it is reproduced in the untroubled co-existence of the lovers and their neighbors from the animal kingdom. . . . Lamartine's employment of the symbol of Eden in the abstract sense is generally designed to translate his yearning for a heavenly abode which is not simply the reproduction of Adam's initial place of residence but rather the final destination of the soul. Even as he persists in his search for a terrestrial Eden, Lamartine knows that such an earthbound haven is not his ultimate goal. He ends up yielding, at times inadvertently, to those flights of the imagination which conjure up the longed-for celestial home; he finds himself encouraging others to indulge the same aspiration. In the midst of an argumentation to dramatize the misery of man, Lamartine ironically invites the foolhardy dreamer to maximize his fantasies: "Dream then the Eden of your dreams with this chaos of organic infirmities. Make then gods with this grain of intelligence imprisoned in this bit of mud . . ."

*An illustration for "Le lac" from the 1855 edition of* The Poetical Meditations.

Its intended irony notwithstanding, this text brings together three of the central concepts underlying Lamartine's symbolism . . . : the perishable substance of man and his thought, the imprisonment of the human spirit, and the divine essence which impels that spirit to aspire in dream to an ethereal Eden. . . .

If an exploration of Lamartine's religious symbolism proves anything, it proves his constant preoccupation with spiritual matters: for the symbolism is everywhere, its vibrancy noticeable in his novels as well as in his poetry, in his discourses on literature as well as in his confessional writings, in his historical works as well as in his letters. But the constant preoccupation is also a coherent one: Lamartine's symbolic mode of expression is as stable as it is ubiquitous, there being no essential difference between his historical symbols and his poetic ones, between the symbols of his novels and those of his correspondence. . . . The constancy and coherence of Lamartine's spiritual preoccupation stem from the relentlessness of his quest for some kind of metaphysical certainty and his ardent need to know and adore his Creator. Whatever the sexual overtones of some of his pages, whatever the excessive poetic distortion of others, whatever the self-glorification of many, the irre-

pressible motif of nearly all is this consuming quest and need. No matter that the search is never ended, the absolute truth never found, the doubt-free adoration never articulated. That Lamartine should have undertaken the endeavor in the first place and sustained it through thousands of pages and myriad subjects evinces that Pascalian *inquiétude* symptomatic of the soul longing for God.

To determine from his religious symbolism that Lamartine's principal orientation is spiritual is not, however, to reach a precise conclusion with regard to the quality and value of his spirituality. Much was made above of the obsessive presence of Edenic images in Lamartine's meditations on this life and the next. The vision of Eden, whatever its ideological substructure or aesthetic form, is a vision of the past, and not one of the future. It is the vision of a "nostalgist," who wishes to recapture the quintessence of what has gone before, and not the vision of a meliorist or progressive, who looks ahead to something better than what is today, or was yesterday. In a word, the vision of Eden is a vision of lost innocence. . . .

The skeptical might existentially view this state of affairs, this permanent Edenic hallucination, as simply a failure to grow up. Surely, Lamartine regrets the past purity of his childhood and associates that purity, as seen above, with an Edenic innocence. But he does not really want to become a child again in any sense save the metaphysical. Although he cannot summon the sophisticated language for its expression which his twentieth-century successors command, Lamartine perceives the unavoidable antagonism between innocence and experience, the incompatibility of the ideal with reality. He knows that to live is to sully the soul. Admittedly, he is incapable, on a sustained basis, of the fusion of innocence and experience in a new synthesis transcending both. His heaven is Eden, a spiritual relic from the past. Nevertheless, his Edenic vision has an appeal which is spiritually salutary. One is sometimes distracted from this vision by more than a few suggestions of the Romantic pose, and a tendency, still unmistakable in his supposedly confessional writings, to put himself in the best possible light. Over all these distortions, however, there hovers a nagging conscience, a persistent propensity to comparison with the innocence which once was. If Hugo is the active, intrepid knight of French Romanticism, Lamartine is its more introspective, contrite conscience. The role is limited, naturally; but it does not lack spiritual merit.

**William Fortescue   (essay date 1983)**

SOURCE: "Conclusion," in *Alphonse de Lamartine: A Political Biography,* St. Martin's Press, 1983, pp. 281-88.

[*An English historian, Fortescue is the author of* Revolution and Counter-Revolution in France, 1815-1852 *(1988). In the following excerpt, he discusses the relationship between Lamartine's literary career and his public life.*]

[Lamartine] was always one of the most prominent and controversial speakers, while **Méditations Poétiques** and the *Histoire des Girondins* were two of the most sensational publications of his generation. He owed his success as a writer to a remarkable facility for literary composition in the Romantic manner. He played on his readers' emotions; he aroused their enthusiasms by the use of colourful imagery and lavish description; he overwhelmed them with words—chosen as much for sound and effect as for precise meaning. . . . [His] popular success in both literature and politics depended on the extent to which his emotive appeal and individual style coincided with the mood and sympathies of his audience: such a coincidence was frequently not achieved. Too often he was over-ambitious, too often he failed to understand, and respond to, other people's mentalities.

Lamartine invariably worked with prodigious speed. . . . The achievement of such speed, however, entailed sacrifices. Lamartine once asked a friend: 'What are you doing there, my friend, with your head in your hands?'—'I am thinking.'—'Extraordinary! I never think, my ideas think for me!' [Ernest Legouvé, *Lamartine*]. Whether this exchange took place or not, Lamartine was certainly not given to original thought, painstaking research, careful analysis or concise argument. . . .

Although rarely hated, Lamartine was often criticised. One criticism, made by hostile commentators such as Odilon Barrot and the comte de Falloux, was that he was merely a poet with the delusion that he was also a politician. He tried very hard to refute such views. He would stress that he attached little importance to his poetic achievements, that poetry had been for him merely a passing phase, and that he was not a poet but a serious and practical man of affairs. He would also assert that no essential conflict existed between the roles of poet and politician. 'Do you know what a great statesman is?' he once asked Ernest Legouvé. 'A great poet . . . in action!' The links between Lamartine's poetry and politics were indeed quite tangible. His poetry had been an invaluable aid to his success in the Paris *salons,* his diplomatic appointment at Naples, his subsequent posting to Florence, and his establishment as a national public figure. Fully aware of this, Lamartine took care to present copies of his published poetry to influential individuals such as Chateaubriand; and clearly he was convinced that through his poetry, as well as his other writings, he could influence public opinion to his own political advantage. Consequently he early acquired a lively interest in publicity. Always very concerned with the critical reception of his poetry, he resented hostile reviews, complained if his poems were ignored, and cultivated favourable reviewers. This interest in publicity encouraged an equally early appreciation of the importance of the newspaper and periodical press: he had individual poems published in newspapers and journals, and seems to have cultivated newspapers which published, and favourably reviewed, his poetry. . . . In addition, a concern for the sound of words, so pronounced in his poetry, characterised the style of his political speeches and writings; a belief in the need for harmony influenced both his poetry and his social and political thought; and a number of the subjects which interested him as a politician, such as railway construction or the fate of orphans and abandoned children, had, at least so far as he was concerned, a poëtic character.

This relationship between poetry and politics was a source of strength as well as of weakness. Poetry launched him on his public career, contributed towards his success as an orator, and helped to give him a Romantic image which, on such occasions as the February Days, could be a major political asset. But in more normal times, because he had first made his reputation as a poet and subsequently written so much poetry, both parliament and public found it difficult to take him seriously. As a worker bluntly put it, having been asked why he was not going to vote for Lamartine in the presidential election: 'M. Lamartine is a poet. We are told that poets cannot cope with public affairs' [*L'eclaireur des Pyrénées,* December 3, 1848]. He did in fact possess a number of attributes often associated with poets but usually disastrous in politicians: a tendency to absent-mindedness, a certain lack of realism, a weakness for reckless gambles, and a total inability to manage his own finances. . . .

[Fundamental] conflicts and inconsistencies can be found in his thought and actions. He believed in human reason and in human instincts, in the virtues of solitude and in the value of popularity, in the will of Providence and in Rousseau's 'general will', in the omnipresence of God and in the secularisation of education, in the universal application of Christian principles and in the official separation of Church and State. About his objectives he was invariably uncertain: whether to be a poet or a politician, a private individual or a public figure. . . .

[But there] were a number of beliefs and principles he constantly retained. He always tried to preserve his independence. He always supported the institutions of the family and private property. He always believed in personal liberty, some form of political democracy, the ideals of 1789, and their continuing relevance to the development of France. He always remained fully convinced that Christian morality lay at the heart of civilisation, and that the supreme duty of writers and politicians was to make Christian morality the foundation of their societies.

## J. C. Ireson  (essay date 1984)

SOURCE: "Poetry," in *The French Romantics,* Vol. 1, edited by D. G. Charlton, Cambridge University Press, 1984, pp. 113-62.

*[In this excerpt, Ireson assesses Lamartine's contribution to French Romanticism.]*

Two dates effectively mark the period of the Romantic movement in French poetry. These are 1820, which saw the publication of Lamartine's **Méditations poétiques,** and 1840, which marks a point of termination and a clear divide in the poetry of the nineteenth century. Within these two decades, the values and procedures of French poetry were revolutionised. . . .

Lamartine was the first poet to break through into the new period. The twenty-four poems of the original edition of his *Méditations poétiques* mark a departure from previous poetry, not in the form or language, for both of these clearly follow the models presented by the eighteenth century, but in the range and treatment of themes and in the sensibility which they express. With two exceptions (**'Chants lyriques de Saül'** and **'La Poésie sacrée'**), which are adaptations into French verse of lyrical passages from the Old Testament, the themes are contemporary and are brought into a sharp focus by being apparently related to the direct experience of the poet himself, experience which is, however, held within an ambivalent perspective, so that it is not clear whether imagination or memory is at work. Revelations by Lamartine himself, in the form of commentaries published with the 1849 edition (which includes the subsequent volume, *Nouvelles Méditations poétiques*), throw a discreet light on the circumstances which gave rise to individual poems, but are subject to caution in many cases over precise questions of fact. Popular imagination has fastened on a few poems where elevated passion and grief at separation or bereavement are expressed lyrically against allusions to events personally experienced (**'Invocation'**, **'L'Isolement'**, **'Le Lac'**, etc.), and biographical details have been made to obtrude upon the text. The main facts concerned refer to the liaison between Lamartine and Julie Charles, the wife of the President of the Académie des Sciences. Meeting at Aix-les-Bains in Savoy, a little more than a year before her death, the two lived out an idyll which passed rapidly from sensual love to a deep, spiritualised passion, thwarted by convention and separation. 'Ma vie est liée à celle d'une femme que je crois mourante!' wrote Lamartine to his friend de Virieu on 16 December 1816, and Mme Charles was indeed moving into the terminal stages of tuberculosis. News of her death in Paris, following a year of frequent meetings while the illness visibly grew upon her, reached Lamartine at his family's house in Mâcon in late December 1817. This event, the first major crisis in his life, marked a rapid change in his poetry, deepening and widening the range, linked, as it immediately became, with the problem of religious faith and doubt.

It also intensified the special quality of his verse, the sense of immediacy with which he appeared able to communicate with his reader through the formality of the verse instrument which he used. Looking back in 1849, in the first detailed preface which he added to his *Méditations,* he wrote: 'Je suis le premier qui ait fait descendre la poésie du Parnasse et qui ait donné à ce qu'on nommait la muse, au lieu d'une lyre à sept cordes de convention, les fibres mêmes du coeur de l'homme, touchées et émues par les innombrables frissons de l'âme et de la nature.' This quest for a new power of directness in poetic language will be at the centre of most developments in French poetry in the nineteenth century. Lamartine's formulation is significant. It shows the extent to which he himself is constrained to work within the limits of the old conventions and style; and it also shows his personal sense of the

transposition achieved through poetry: a resonance set up by inward and outward events and seeking its equivalents in language. He notes, in the same preface, the two main ways in which poetic language makes its impact: through images and through verbal harmony, leaving aside the ratiocinative function, perhaps as an unwanted legacy from the previous century. The image he sees as deriving from imagination, and imagination as inseparable from memory ('l'*imagination,* c'est-à-dire la mémoire qui revoit et qui repeint en nous'). The recalled image arouses associated feelings, and the play of such images enlivens the field of ideas set up by the poem. The primary quality of poetry appears, however, to have been, for Lamartine, its verbal harmony, a pre-cognitive feature which he himself exploits with great facility.

This facility, which becomes a fault in the later poetry, is not too readily apparent in the *Méditations poétiques* of 1820. Lamartine claims (also in his preface of 1849) that these first published poems were the result of several years of preparation. The earliest go back to about 1814 (**'A Elvire'**, **'Le Golfe de Baya'**). The lyrical extracts from *Saül* recall the relative success, through readings in the salons, of a tragedy turned down by Talma in 1817. In his search for a form and style adapted to his needs (what he calls 'la voix'), he was particularly affected by the writings attributed to Ossian (read, presumably in Letourneur's translation of 1777, or Baour-Lormian's of 1801), and ascribed some of the melancholy of his descriptions of natural scenes to the example of the Gaelic bard. But, in the first instance, he turned his hand to the composition of elegies in the manner of Bertin (*Les Amours,* 1780) and Parny (*Poésies érotiques,* n.d.; in *Euvres complètes,* 1808), who wrote short, amatory pieces, without the necessary inclusion of the theme of grief or melancholy. Millevoye (*Élégies,* 1814) had recently provided examples of the latter kind. Out of these exercises Lamartine developed his own form of lyrical poem. He acquired, probably from Parny, the technique of increasing the impact of a poem by bringing together two opposed themes within a single piece in order to produce a heightened emotional intensity and, by an original handling of the internal structure of the poem, created the characteristic tone and movement of the *méditation poétique,* which was virtually a new form of the lyric in France. The external forms of the poem have not changed. Lamartine uses short sequences of quatrains to form what are recognisably elegies (**'L'Automne'**, **'Le Vallon'**, **'L'Isolement'**). He constructs odes in the ten-line and six-line stanzas used by J.-B. Rousseau (**'Le Génie'**, **'L'Enthousiasme'**, **'Le Désespoir'**), an epistle to Byron (**'L'Homme'**) and a *discours en vers* (**'Dieu'**) in the traditional alexandrine. **'Le Lac'** was originally titled 'Ode au lac du Bourget', and is in fact an ode to time, apostrophising the lake and the landscape around it, while other formal devices, such as the rhetorical recall of an episode, antiphone, syntactical repetition, are used to provide a clear structure, without inhibiting a freer movement suggesting intuitions about time and the personal experience which has induced them.

This capacity to combine reflections on universal themes with notations of personal feeling, without departing from accepted conventions of form and expression, is an essential part of the formula developed by Lamartine. The *méditation* is thus a personal construction, and could hardly exist independently of the poet who conceived it. Isolated yet confidential, deeply involved with the life of his time, as well as with the universal questions, the spirit of Lamartine engaged the feelings of his readers as no poet had done for a century or more. Something aloof and intangible in his personality kept his poetry from becoming a confession, while the sense of vulnerability and world-weariness impinged larger than life on the sensibility of his contemporaries. Episodes and figures from his private life, where they occur in his poems, are transposed to a level of imagination which enables him, for example, to bring together references to mistresses other than Julie and to use the faintly surprising designation of 'Elvire'.

But the personal *méditations* are relatively few in number in the original volume. Lamartine is at pains to extend the range of his poetry to include public themes and fundamental questions of religion. In **'L'Homme'**, he is able to combine familiar references to the fashionable poet of the English Satanic School (he was unknown to Byron at this time) with references to his own life, which he uses as an exemplar of the human condition, and with a passionate plea for faith and confidence in the unseen divine purpose. Public themes become more numerous after his appointment to the Embassy at Naples in 1820 (**'Ode sur la naissance du duc de Bordeaux'** and the **'Ode'** written to the French people were included in later editions of the *Méditations poétiques*, while **'Bonaparte'** and **'La Liberté, ou Une Nuit à Rome'**, showing an evolved technique, were written for the *Nouvelles Méditations* of 1823). But the strongest theme, whether considered in the original collection or in the collected editions, is the theme of conflict between doubt and faith.

Concerned as he was to present himself as the new poet of a royalist and Catholic period, Lamartine hardly comes across in his religious poetry as orthodox in the matter of religion. **'Le Désespoir'** and **'La Providence à l'homme'**, placed together in all editions, form a diptych, in which sentiments of revolt against a fallen and suffering world are countered and, supposedly, overwhelmed by the certitude that can be derived from the order of the universe and the magnificence of the earth and the heavens, symbols of a higher glory. The poem of revolt, originally called 'Ode au Malheur', is spoken according to a human perspective on creation. The reply is, supposedly, given by the Creator and is spoken in the first person, in the manner of the words of Jehovah in the Old Testament. These two pieces, the first of which gives a powerful, lyrical tone to an attitude of scepticism, were probably brought together in order to maintain, or perhaps to summarise in more dramatic form, the theme of conflicting forces in the poet's mind. In the poem to Byron, Lamartine concludes with what he calls 'l'hymne de la raison', in which reason is used to look beyond the discouraging realities of individual life towards the universal order in which existence has its context. The limitations of this same reason are asserted in **'L'Immortalité'**, where an idealism based on a symbolistic view of the world, attributed to Elvire,

reverses the poet's pessimism and counters the view of materialist philosophers, the 'troupeau d'Épicure'. This view of nature as a symbolic temple forms much of the substance of **'La Prière'**, human intelligence being presented as the means whereby intuitions of a divine presence may be sought in the solitude of remote places. In **'La Foi'**, developing this theme of quest, he sets beyond death the stage of full revelation:

> Cette raison superbe, insuffisant flambeau,
> S'éteint comme la vie aux portes du tombeau,

And beyond death, too, the idealised presence of the lost mistress remains, still sensually apprehended. Flight into the 'pures régions' is evoked, in **'Dieu'**, as a natural movement of the poet's mind, bringing him, at privileged moments, 'face à face avec la réalité'. This 'reality' Lamartine attempts to convey by a description of God, represented in what appears to be a generally pantheistic view, as coextensive with the universe, sustaining and controlling it with His material being. . . . Lamartine's aim is to give a universalised vision of a God perceptible to human reason and freed from credulity and superstition, capable of intervening in the history of the world.

Successive and expanded editions of the *Méditations poétiques,* and the publication of the *Nouvelles Méditations poétiques,* added variations to the themes of the initial volume: **'Ischia'** and **'Chant d'Amour'**, both from the 1823 collection, parallel the sublimated love poetry of 1816-20 with lyrical stanzas on shared happiness and amorous pleasure, prudently controlled by the conventions of decorum of the time; **'Les Étoiles'**, again from the second volume, adds a range of cosmic imagery to the lyrical, highly personalised treatment of the theme of individual consciousness; **'Bonaparte'**, begun at some point after the death of the Emperor in 1821 and completed in 1823, is a solidly constructed ode in which each stanza is marked by a dominant image accompanying the argument of the poem. But the vital contribution of Lamartine to the development of French poetry was made in 1820. Though in some respects the *Nouvelles Méditations* show a maturing of his talent, they are more uneven in quality, and the pressure of demand from his publishers to produce a second volume following the great success of the first, at a time when the style and condition of his life had changed considerably with his marriage and the beginnings of his diplomatic career in Italy, meant that he was obliged to return to earlier material, passed over for the first volume, in order to fill out the second.

*La Mort de Socrate,* also published in 1823, is an experimental poem of another type: longer than the *méditation,* which rarely extends to 200 lines, it develops, over approximately 800 lines, the themes of idealism and religious syncretism already seen in **'Dieu'**, but uses an episodic framework, based on Plato's *Phaedo,* in which Lamartine invests the final message of Socrates with his own lyrical view of death and immortality. Perhaps the return to classical sources and the narrative and descriptive form of the poem account for the relative lack of enthusiasm with which it was greeted on publication. It should nevertheless be said that in the main lines of its technique, the projection of ideas through a figure engaged in heroic or tragic action, it offers interesting points of comparison with some of Vigny's early pieces and that some of the descriptive effects already anticipate the manner of the Parnassians. A fourth work, *Dernier Chant du Pèlerinage d'Harold* (1825), was written after the death of Byron as an additional episode to those recounted in Byron's four cantos. Lamartine divides his "Chant" into forty-nine sections, all but one composed as a short sequence of alexandrine couplets, in place of the Spenserian stanzas used by Byron. The manner is grandiloquent and, in its superficial mannerisms, classical, with a more modern technique used in some of the descriptive and narrative passages. The soliloquies are used to present thinly disguised aspects of Lamartine's opinions and attitudes at a restless and perplexed period of his development.

Throughout the 1820s Lamartine had intuitions of a great poetic work to be accomplished, and ideas for a form of lyricism which would express, and possibly resolve, the religious problem which dominated his private thoughts at a time when his reputation and career were beginning to take him towards public life. These plans were to form the second half of his work as a poet and, historically, form part of the second decade of Romantic poetry. Lamartine's major contribution was already made, however, with the *Méditations poétiques*. . . .

Lamartine, from the end of 1825 on diplomatic service in Florence, and back in France on indefinite leave in 1828, the star of the salons when he appeared in Paris, was . . . passing through a crucial stage in his relationship with his art. The epic poem, the 'Grand Poème' that he longed to write, while fearing that his time and his powers would not permit him to complete the vast design—the slow movement of a spirit towards redemption through many incarnations—was hardly taking shape. He fell back on a less ambitious enterprise, the composition, from about the spring of 1826, of a series of religious lyrics which he first called 'modern psalms'. A volume of these lyrics took shape over four years, appearing in 1830 under the title of *Harmonies poétiques et religieuses*. About half were written in a period of relative tranquillity in Italy, the others in the two years preceding the abdication of Charles X. The 'harmonies toscanes' were of more purely religious inspiration, those written in France reflect some of the unrest of the second crisis of his life. His political views were changing, and with the change the direction of his life was called into question. In his speech to the Académie Française on his reception in 1829, he publicly underlined his growing liberalism. During 1830, his decision was probably made to seek election as a *député* in the new government. But before this, a more immediate ambition remained: a grand tour of the Middle East and the Holy Land, where perhaps his religious doubts might be resolved. His mother's death in 1829 had deprived him of the strongest influence inclining him to Christian belief. He undertook the journey in 1831.

The principal motive for the composition of the *Harmonies* was, however, ambition. The title shows the continu-

ing quest for artistic discovery, a stage beyond the *Méditations*. In a postscript to the Letter introducing his *Harmonies* in the 1849 edition, Lamartine gives a tentative definition in the form of a list of themes virtually coextensive with individual human life, and concludes with the following: 'tous les bruits de la vie dans un cœur sonore, ce sont ces harmonies . . . ' Lamartine's *harmonies* appear to be the transcription of the affective life of an individual and not concerned with external events in themselves. The realities on which they are based are the inner realities of the poet's mind, whether musing on the past, or on the prompting of impressions from the outside world, or (which is most often the case) on the disproportion between the evidence of life as lived in the world and the desire to savour the assurance of an unseen divine order. No clear sense of the term *harmonies* emerges from Lamartine's explanation, but the poems themselves suggest two levels of interpretation, corresponding respectively to the thought and the technique. At the first level, the poems invite interpretation as the blending of dissonant themes to achieve a final expression of elevation and hope. At the second, they can be taken, by virtue of their form, as analogous to musical compositions. In using the word 'psalm' to describe them, Lamartine was presumably thinking of the musical nature of the psalm, as well as of its inspiration, guided between songs of distress and paeans of praise and deliverance. In style and imagery, as well as in the handling of this great double theme, Lamartine follows the manner of the Psalms, but prefers labels such as *hymne* and *cantate*. These *hymnes* usually have the strophic variety of the ode, but the term is no doubt used by Lamartine to indicate a less complicated form, adapted to the celebrating of one theme, without the ornamental devices of the ode. Not all the poems follow this formula. The religious tension is relieved by shorter pieces developing immediate impressions: on sadness; to a nightingale; a woman singer. One great poem (**'Novissima Verba'**) is a development of the *méditation,* moving retrospectively over the surface of the poet's life and illustrating the transient beauty and inconclusiveness of man's passage through the world.

In the *Avertissement* to the 1830 edition, Lamartine, in stressing the naturalness of his process of composition, describes his *Harmonies* as 'quatre livres de poésies écrites comme elles ont été senties, sans liaison et sans suite, sans transition apparente'. The mastery of form and the appearance of effortless development do indeed suggest the presence of a natural poet. But the volume is carefully prepared and carefully ordered. The seventy-two poems of the original edition are distributed more or less equally over the four books referred to. Books i and ii are forms of reflection on a missing reality and on the means of stirring the human consciousness to awareness of the Creator. These are suggested through symbols, subjects of meditation for the solitary mind: the solar cycle (**'Hymne de la nuit'; 'Hymne du matin'**); the lamp in the sanctuary (**'La Lampe du temple'**); a moonlit landscape (**'Poésie, ou Paysage dans le Golfe de Gênes'**); the destruction of a famous Roman landscape (**'La Perte de l'Anio'**); images of time and change (**'La Source dans les bois d'***'**). A sequence of four powerful odes on the idea of God conveys, through sets of images, a historical and, in some respects, evolutionary view of religious consciousness, combining modern attitudes with a range of poetic effect, from recitative based on the Old Testament ('**Jehova**'), to the demonstrative stanza of the traditional ode ('**Le Chêne**'), and to a more personal lyrical style ('**L'Humanité**', '**L'Idée de Dieu**'). These four poems, presenting a view of the progressive nature of religions and a vision of man caught between two mysteries, mortality and immortality, form the centre of the first two books. In Books III and IV, Lamartine concentrates pieces in a more familiar style, tracing reminiscences and impressions of his personal life ('**Milly, ou La Terre natale**' is one of his best-known poems in this descriptive and reflective register). These are grouped round two poems, in each of which the poet sets down an aspect of his credo. '**Hymne au Christ**' is an affirmation of his attachment to the Christian faith in an age of doubt and conflicting doctrines. '**Novissima Verba**' is a survey of the values of his life, now seen as dominated by tokens of mortality and fragments of truth. Such tokens and fragments are the substance of short pieces of Books III and IV ('**Le Tombeau d'une mère**' is written on the death of his mother; '**Le Premier Regret**' evokes memories of Graziella and Italy more than fifteen years before).

The religious theme, basically the conflict of doubt and faith and the quest for evidence from human experience that might abolish doubt, is continued from the *Méditations,* where it had found its most dramatic expression in '**Le Désespoir**' and '**La Providence à l'homme**'. The central conflict is no nearer resolution in the *Harmonies*. The '**Hymne au Christ**' is largely about the growing challenge to the values brought to the world by Christ. The religious elevation of Books I and II is a form of idealism whose associations range over religions in general. In Lamartine's eyes, no doubt, this poetry was modern and original in that it brought the historical perspectives of contemporary thought into the same lyrical framework as the sacred songs of the Old Testament. It also marked a stage in the development of the long tradition of biblical paraphrase by French poets. Further, the adaptation of techniques and style to the variations which the religious theme demands is at a level probably not reached before. The fixed forms of individual poems keep largely to the alexandrine or octosyllabic line; but there are also short experimental pieces in a melodic style ('**La Tristesse**', '**Le Rossignol**'), in which already something of the tone of Verlaine is heard. But it is in the *hymnes* and the odes that the control of form is at its finest. Within the long poems of free construction, the modulations are obtained by striking metrical variety (lines of seven or five syllables are used to particular effect) marking the stages of the theme.

This inventiveness is part of the Romantic renewal of poetry, and has its counterpart, at another level, in Hugo's *Orientales*. But Hugo's verse marks also an advance towards modernity in the enlargement of poetic vocabulary for greater precision in pictorial effect. Lamartine, despite his awareness of the need for change, did not follow in this direction. While his syntax is mainly free from the inversion and periphrasis of the style of the previous century, his vocabulary is marked by influences from the Old Testament and by the persistence of stylised classical elements.

This is one reason why his *Harmonies,* where his artistic powers are at their height, did not have any decisive effect on the course of lyrical poetry in France. Another, and more cogent, reason is that attitudes were changing. Liberalism and scepticism were replacing, among the literary generation of 1830, the Catholicism and royalism that Hugo had confidently predicted for the society of the Restoration. . . . Lamartine himself saw fit to orientate his book more closely towards the contemporary world by adding to the 1832 edition an important ode: '**Les Révolutions**', on the theme of progress, and in which he castigates the instinct of peoples and rulers to perpetuate an existing order, and summons them to accept change, however violent or unpredictable, as part of an ordained movement towards a more perfect state. But other issues occupied the minds of younger writers in 1830, and Lamartine's lessons of idealism and lyricism, appreciated as they were by the public of the time, drew him few disciples. . . .

By 1833 the Romantic movement in French poetry had done its work. Starting with the regeneration of poetic forms, the search for a new immediacy of expression and the adaptation of verse to public as well as private themes, it had produced, in something over a decade, an enlargement of poetry which enabled it to cover religious, philosophical and historical subjects in a highly individual manner, largely free from didacticism. This was made possible by three developments of technique. First, discoveries were made, principally by Lamartine and Hugo, about the increased impact of imagery once freed from the formality of classical reference and made a necessary part of the poet's invention. Secondly, by exploiting areas of familiar and technical language hitherto closed to writers of verse, the Romantics greatly increased the scope of poetry by putting it on a direct footing with contemporary life. . . . Thirdly, the renewal of the expressive power of poetry needed a wealth of stanza forms and a verse instrument better attuned to modern syntax and language. The modifications brought to the alexandrine, discrete enough in themselves, provoked much opposition in their time but, once accepted and integrated, lasted without much further change until the Symbolist experiments of 1886. . . .

Lamartine's concern with the epic has already been noted. His 'Grand Poème', conceived in a burst of visionary fervour as early as 1821, was to have been an immense work providing a scenario of human progress. Preliminary fragments written between 1823 and 1829, and partially published by Lamartine in 1851 in his *Nouvelles Confidences,* indicate something of the visionary and episodic intentions of the work. The theme was to be one already treated, notably by Byron and Vigny, and the line of the narrative was to be determined by the stages of the redemption of the spirit of a fallen angel through successive reincarnations. The ending of *La Chute d'un ange* indicates that nine such episodes were envisaged.

In the event, only two were carried through as far as publication: *Jocelyn* (1836) and *La Chute d'un ange* (1838). Published in this order, as separate volumes, the two works could have given little idea of the plan on which they were based. *Jocelyn,* deliberately pitched at the human level, recounts the sacrifice of the life's happiness of two beings thrown together in the solitude of a mountain refuge during the Revolution. The plot, straining credibility at times, follows the movement of the poem over nine *époques* covering seventeen years (1786–1803): a love idyll (*époques* 1–4); a crucial event (*époque* 5—Jocelyn's enforced ordination before the execution of his bishop); the years of austere and humble dedication (*époques* 6–9), with the theme of the embittered and fallen life of Laurence as counterpoint, but redeemed by religion and by the hope also of the spiritual union after death of the soul-mates, separated in their lives. The poem is given further amplitude by passages of religious lyricism, descriptions of the changing seasons in the mountainous region of France known to Lamartine, and evocations of the humble rustic life shared by the priest.

The episode of redemption therefore precedes the initial account of the Fall. *La Chute d'un ange* is a fictionalised interpretation of the verses of Genesis describing the world before the Flood. Lamartine's angle, Cédar, obsessed by the human beauty of Daïdha, assumes human shape to rescue her from a group of giant pillaging barbarians. The fifteen *visions* into which the poem is divided recount the doomed idyll of this pair, a girl of the race of Cain and a semi-divine but primitive being unversed in human lore. Their wanderings take them to the cave of a prophet who, in the seventh and eighth *visions,* reveals to them the fundamentals of a divine code set down in a 'fragment du Livre primitif'. The doctrine is drawn from Lamartine's own brand of deism, idealism and enlightened rationalism, which is presented as the essential basis of true religious belief. The tribulations of the pair continue in Nemphed's city of giants and demi-gods, from whose barbaric violence they eventually escape only to perish in the desert, Cédar burning on a pyre of his own making, with the bodies of Daïdha and their twin children.

Epic in its conception and in the main lines of its action, *La Chute d'un ange* is a sadly imperfect work, largely through the haste and inattention with which it was composed, partly through the incongruities occurring in the attempt to prepare a biblical epic for popular consumption. The level of the action is mainly that of a sensational adventure story. Cédar's Homeric combat with the six giant cavemen in the second *vision* has all the ingredients of a Hollywood fight sequence. Yet there is a ferocity of imagination, in the monstrous prison scenes for example, which surprises and suggests a range of resources never exploited in any measure by Lamartine. In any case, the 'épopée métaphysique' was a forlorn venture at this stage of his life. His ideas on progress based on a religious rationalism, which he had hoped to communicate to a large section of the French people, were absorbed into his political life, or diverted into works of fiction. . . .

## Margurite Iknayan (essay date 1985)

SOURCE: "*La chute d'un ange*: Heaven and Hell on Earth," in *Nineteenth-Century French Studies*, Vol. XIII, No. 4, Summer, 1985, pp. 191-99.

[*In the following excerpt, the critic explicates* La chute d'un ange, *focusing on humankind's relationship to God, suffering, and evil as presented in the poem.*]

*La Chute d'un ange* brings us into a world where men have forgotten Heaven. The nomadic tribesmen who figure in the first part of the narration are thus doubly fallen, for they have not only been excluded from Eden, they have no recollection of God and have lost the power to see the signs of His presence which are visible in the universe. The central narrator, who is a holy man, has told us that in the antediluvian natural universe, still in its original state of perfection, all things are "pleins de Dieu." But when the cedars of Lebanon sing their hymn of adoration to God, it is before an audience of angels; men do not hear them. Nature has not lost all sacred meaning, however, for, as Daïdha tells Cédar, pagan gods who have fallen to earth after being defeated in wars with other gods (pagans too have their myths of fallen gods) sometimes hide in natural objects such as a stone or a piece of wood, and there the nomads hold them by charms, threats, or tears. These are the gods they carry with them and often trade or break and which they worship or insult as their fortunes vary. The tribesmen also have a privileged place to which they return each year and which they consider their fatherland. Here are caves where they and their ancestors have lived, full of memories and mysteries; they place them under the care of their gods. Here too is the burial ground, where the nomads speak to their dead relatives' souls and leave gifts for them. The caves, which should be considered their holiest places, are hollowed out of the earth and rock and have no vertical opening to the sky to communicate with transcendent forces.

The nomads' religion does not occupy them for long after they settle into their daily pastoral life. The narrator views their practices with contempt because they are pagan; to the reader they appear minimal as religious observances, whether pagan or not. However, if these primitive tribes do not worship the fertility of Mother Earth as an agricultural society would, but live rather heedlessly off her abundance, this cult is replaced symbolically to some extent by the honor given to the family; and the mothers, with their nourishing milk, are a human expression of nature's great richness and generosity. The nomads live contentedly in a benevolent but weakly sacralized universe.

The one solid structure that the nomads build is the *Tour de la Faim,* made of stones and mud, where Daïdha and her children are placed to await death by starvation. It is open to the sky, so that the gods may accuse no one of her death. Stars look down and a swallow visits her, but no gods intervene. It is Cédar, now only a man, who appears at the top of the walls to save his wife and children; profane love is here the effective force. Such heroic rescues still belong to the repertory of motifs of the modern mythology we observe today in desacralized society.

Babel (or Balbeck: Lamartine uses both names), the other society depicted in *La Chute d'un ange,* is more than desacralized, it is the extreme of the wicked society, not just of the profane but of profanation itself. Kindly Moth-

**The value of Lamartine's poetry:**

Lamartine's only consistent 'philosophy' was a kind of Christian pantheism: the whole universe is an expression of the deity—the same deity, it may be added, whose image had been formed by the gentle Madame de Lamartine and the kindly fathers of the Collège de Belley, and so was beneficent. Beyond that, he is the poet of the great commonplaces—using the word in its most favourable sense. The melancholy of autumn, the exaltation of a windy day, the calm of evening inducing worship, the vigour of morning evoking praise—these universal and primarily physical experiences are rendered in verse so entirely appropriate in its music and texture that it often does seem to be the voice of the thing itself. Lamartine's strongest claims as a poet rest on this quality.

*Geoffrey Brereton, "Alphonse de Lamartine," in* An Introduction to the French Poets, *1956.*

er Nature is replaced with an artificial world of towers, walls, and man-made trees. The giants who rule there have not just forgotten God; they have denied and banished Him and put themselves in His place. All values are reversed and symbols of the sacred are perverted: the city is not a holy city but Hell on earth; the holy mountains are replaced by the heights on which the city is built, not so that the giants may be nearer to God, but so that they may supplant Him. The polluted air forms a miasma above the city which cuts off contact with Heaven, and in this atmosphere airships fly about like desecrated angels. One does not descend into this Hell, since the demons who rule it are passing themselves off as gods, but within the city the giants maintain their power and enjoy their cruel pleasures on the heights, while relegating their dehumanized slaves to deep dungeons.

It is in these two milieus that Cédar, the fallen angel, will pass his first sojourn on earth, with a brief stay in an earthly paradise between the two. Cédar, like the nomads, is doubly fallen: not only has he become a man, but he has forgotten Heaven and no longer knows that he was ever an angel. Thus God has punished him for preferring the promise of profane love to sacred love. Since he is a newborn man, a clean slate, he will follow the example of the nomads among whom he has fallen and will become vaguely pagan. He suffers from his mental blank, but the narrator tells us that he has the instinct for God, though he lacks the idea. It is no doubt because of this instinct which he still retains, that Cédar is closer to nature than the tribesmen. Besides, he is excluded from human society and forced to live in isolation in the wild. His intellectual development takes place in contact with nature and

with Daïdha. When he is sad or in danger, nature befriends him. Fountains in the woods assuage his sorrow; the river Oronte, where he is thrown for dead, revives him, and the log to which he is shackled floats and saves him. He discovers a wonderful hiding place were he will take Daïdha to make her his bride. There they spend the night on a vast hammock made of vines, flowers, and bird feathers, a nuptial bed which by its height above the ground is brought a bit closer to Heaven. This paradise on earth, by the beauty and luxuriance of its vegetation, recalls the bower of Adam and Eve in Milton's *Paradise Lost* (Book IV), but Cédar and Daïdha do not, of course, stop to worship God, and the angels are not vigilant, as in Milton, but stop in envy as they listen to the earthly couple.

Some of the sacredness of nature begins to penetrate Cédar's consciousness. When during a happy moment of reunion with his family he wishes to share his joy with someone, he turns to nature: this is his instinctive way of thanking God. He marvels at the glories of the infinite sky and the elements of nature which he studies, and later, when he and Daïdha follow the coast, the sight of the sea fills them with rapture and they seem to discover the perfect original communion: "Avec leurs sens ravis tout semblait converser." The instinct is developing, but the idea is yet to be revealed.

Up to now, being cut off from God does not matter much to Cédar, for he is entirely preoccupied with what brought him to earth in the first place, his love for Daïdha. Conceived in Heaven, it is a perfect love and will be completely realized on earth. Cédar knew before his fall that earth was an "enfer des larmes" where true love is the one happiness. And so it turns out: love brings to Cédar an ecstasy unknown in Heaven. The true Heaven is where Daïdha is: "Et Cédar aspirant le ciel dans son [Daïdha's] sourire, / Crut que le ciel entier n'était que ce délire." As long as he has Daïdha and the children, he does not feel in exile on earth, though in many places it is impossible for him to live. But since his love is unsanctioned by Heaven, its happiness must be fleeting. At the moment of his fall, Heaven cries out threateningly: "Savoure jusqu'au sang le bonheur des humains." So from the very beginning of his human life, Cédar is under sentence, though unaware of it.

It is altogether fitting that in societies largely devoid of a sense of the sacred, divine or diabolical forces should be incarnated in men, Cédar and his family on one side, the barbaric tribes or individuals like Nemphed and Stagyr on the other. As a transcendent being, God is remote; in nature he is a source of good, but he has abandoned men to evil. However, these wicked men will serve as His agents, and it is through them that divine wrath will be visited on Cédar. His punishment throughout most of the poem will be meted out by men and their societies, by the barbarous nomads and the unspeakably cruel giants. From his very first moment on earth he has to fight to save Daïdha and himself; they are forced constantly to be on the run to escape man's malevolence. On several occasions, we see that Cédar's good deeds do not go unpunished. His reward for saving Daïdha at the beginning of his life on earth is to be shackled as a slave. Later when he leads the oppressed city-dwellers to revolt and freedom, they become as cruel as their former masters. And his last and fatal mistake is to be magnanimous to a surviving giant/god whose betrayal will bring about the death of the family. In the first part, the only time when a non-human power seems to intervene to make Cédar suffer is in the incident when by mistake he kills his dog, his only friend.

In general, Cédar's life in this section of the poem alternates between the joy of love and the sufferings of persecution, danger, and threatened loss in a series of suspenseful episodes. The recurring image of being thrown over a cliff into water or into the abyss shows the precariousness of his existence and his love.

The visit to the earthly paradise in the mountains serves several functions besides giving Lamartine a place for his major philosophical poem. It is a utopia in the midst of a world of disorder and danger, where the young family meets the only good man of the poem and where they find a well-ordered agricultural environment, with rich wheat fields, orchards, vegetable gardens, and domestic animals. In this peaceable kingdom all creatures exist in harmony, and the wild beasts are so friendly that they allow the children to pet them. If there are no other men there, at least the *Livre primitif* gives a theoretical base for the good society. But most of all, the existence of God is revealed to Cédar and Daïdha. The narrator tells us that under Adonaï's tutelage, Cédar's memory is awakened and he begins to find God again in his soul, and the thankfulness he and Daïdha once in a happy moment felt to "je ne sais quel dieu" is replaced by the first attempts at prayer. Adonaï's realm is the one place where the sacred retains its power.

The family's sudden capture and transfer to Balbeck is for Cédar a second fall from Heaven, cruel as the first one was not, for now he finds himself in a real Hell where he risks losing all that he loves. Balbeck is horrible at any time, but Hell seems worse when you have just come from Heaven. This time Cédar will not forget God, but the revelation of His existence brings him no comfort, it only makes him more conscious of the profanation of all that is good. He leads the oppressed people of Balbeck to revolt in the name of Adonaï and of God, but the revolt becomes carnage.

In this section and up to the end the demonic imagery is intensified. Evil is the dominant power on earth, and it is manifested in men and their works, which have a nightmarish quality that they would not have if they did not indicate some fiendish power at work. Of the examples of demonic imagery given by Northrop Frye in his *Anatomy of Criticism,* most appear in *La Chute d'un ange*. Those found in the first part are magnified in Balbeck: Cédar, enslaved and bound with lianas by the nomads but still living relatively free in the open air, is now in irons in a dungeon; aimless flight through the forests and across the mountains will be followed at the end by lost wandering in the desert; the *Tour de la Faim* will be multiplied a hundredfold by the sinister towers of Balbeck. And now

some other elements are added: the tyrant, the mob, the harlot, cannibalism, the burning city. At the end the verdant nature friendly to Cédar has become a demonic wasteland.

When nature turns against Cédar, we know that the time of reckoning has come. Maddened by grief, he looks upward but it is to throw a handful of sand against cruel Heaven, then he curses stepmother earth for having brought forth man only to let him suffer and die. Horrified by the ultimate cruelty of the giants' sadistic pleasure, he revolts against God Himself and prepares the funeral-suicide pyre.

Cédar, who remains a simple man and to some extent a *naïf* up to the end, is in many ways an unlikely epic hero. By his isolation from the social group, by his pursual of his own survival and that of his immediate family rather than representing the moral values and aspirations of the tribe or nation, he fails to live up to the traditional role of the hero of epic. Being a former angel, he does not, like Adam, represent the human race. He does not advance toward the accomplishment of a mission but flees from the danger of death. His athletic feats and hairbreadth escapes have reminded some critics (H. J. Hunt, Léon Cellier) of Tarzan, and his exploits, such as the rescue from the *Tour de la Faim* alluded to earlier, belong to the corpus of modern popular myth. According to Cellier, "Cédar comme Tarzan matérialise le rêve d'un surhomme, situé dans le passé, et se présentant sous les traits d'un homme jeune, beau, athlétique et nu" [*L'epopée romantique,* 1954]. He climbs perilous heights and swings across a river on vines, but this "superman" is very vulnerable. In this respect, as in some others, Cédar resembles a hero of melodrama, a genre which often encompasses these modern myths: he is constantly beset by external obstacles; he passes from the extreme of one emotion to its opposite and back again; he is the strongest, bravest, and most handsome of men but not the most astute. Like the hero of melodrama, he engages our sympathy and arouses our pity.

Indeed, *La Chute d'un ange* shares many characteristics of melodrama, not just the polarization of emotions but also the polarization of good and evil, the persecution and humiliation of the innocent by sinister dark villains, a rapid succession of sensational peripeties, and fascination with lurid scenes of crime, sadism, and horror. The *topos* of the abyss is a suitable one for melodrama, with its frantic movement indicative of a universal instability and unease. It yawns beneath the evil as well as the good. In Balbeck we see Nemphed, who represents the extreme point of the loss of the human soul, looking down with dread from the "faîte escarpée" where he has arrived, feeling himself morally suspended over the abyss.

However, Lamartine violates one of the most important conditions of melodrama, the happy ending. Cédar must be punished: God has so decreed, the narrator knows it and has told us to expect the punishment. Cédar, himself being ignorant of it, keeps hoping and striving up to the end, and when the terrible loss comes, does not know what he is being punished for. Thus the use of the omniscient narrator gives a strong tragic irony to Cédar's story. In this poem we have not only the outlook of the good man struggling for happiness on earth; we also have the point of view of Heaven represented by the narrator and, within the central story, Adonaï and the *Livre primitif,* which is the revealed word of God.

It is true that the narrator is so moved by the poignancy of the story he is telling that he interrupts his recital to ask the stars if God enjoys seeing men suffer: "Pour l'incompréhensible et sainte volonté, / La ruine de l'homme est-elle volupté?" If so, God would be the ulti- mate sadist, not so different from the giants or from some barbarous pagan Moloch. But the old man imme- diately imposes silence upon himself, for "envers Dieu la plainte est une offense," and his last words are "Gloire à Dieu!" The listener who, as the narrator of the first and last sections is the poet's persona, seems to concur in this point of view, for he kneels contritely and accepts the old man's summation. The *Livre primitif* had set forth the guiding principle, which Cédar might have accepted if he had been given time to absorb it rather than being snatched away from Eden. . . .

It is the long view that we must take, with its hope for an often distant future, and not on earth but in Heaven. When the constellations wonder why God permits such evil as the orgies of the giants to exist on earth, the angels reply: "Patient! car il est éternel." Moreover, in two passages the narrator assures us that some good will eventually rise again out of the destruction wrought by evil: the ashes of the *Livre primitif* will bear fruit later, and the ashes of the final funeral pyre are scattered by the wind, like seed. Thus it is indicated at intervals in *La Chute d'un ange* that in the long run God is just. At the end of the narration He is about to punish wicked men by engulfing them in the Flood. But He has already pun- ished the innocent, Daïdha and the children, along with Cédar. The vague promises of eventual justice are not communicated to Cédar; even if they were, they would not alleviate his pain.

God has certainly made life on earth impossible for Cédar after the loss of love, for there is no salvation to be sought in human society. The constant tenor of the poem is that men in organized society are wicked and intractable. The just man must always be an outsider, living in isolation and often fearing for his life. Jocelyn, forced to sacrifice his love for Laurence, can find a reason for existence in serving his fellow-men. For Cédar, pariah that he is, no such alternative exists.

*La Chute d'un ange* is a strange and disconcerting work, as much melodrama as epic, with its combination of the primitive and the technologically advanced, with its hero who is both a man and not a man, and especially with its double point of view: revolt or acceptance, the pursuit of happiness or submission to incomprehensible suffering. Lamartine has left the possibility open for readers to re- spond according to their own lights. They may find that what the old seer narrates is more persuasive than his comments on his own story; while deferring to his mature

wisdom, they may give preference to Cédar's "tête insen- sée." Unlike other fallen angels of myth and literature, the man Cédar remains angelic. The very impulse which leads to his fall, forgetting onself to go to the aid of another, is deemed admirable among men. He is as nearly perfect as a man can be (his desire for vengeance cannot be held against him), and his love is as tender and exalted as one could desire. He might have lived happily on earth even without the returning memory of God's existence; he is not a better man for it, and certainly not a happier one. Presumably, if the nomads and the giants had not turned away from God, they would not be so wicked and Cédar would fare better among them. But in that case God would have found some other way to punish him. At the end, virtue does not triumph, God does, in all His implacabil- ity.

The conclusion, "Gloire à Dieu!" sounds hollow, just as the last two lines of **"Gethsémani,"** "Mais c'est Dieu qui t'écrase, ô mon âme, sois forte: / Baise sa main sous la douleur!" seem forced at the end of the long despairing poem on the death of Lamartine's daughter Julia. Where is the comforting faith of **"L'Homme"**? Jocelyn achieves a heroic resignation; it is presented as the culmination of the long process of reintegration with God which begins with Cédar's unrelieved despair. But *La Chute d'un ange* coming after *Jocelyn* bears witness to the anguish of the poet as he moves away from Christian faith toward deism.

The poem exalts above all the love of woman, who is not compared to angels, as in **"Novissima verba,"** but who, as represented by Daïdha, is purely human. What does Cédar's eventual return to the "heureux néant" of Heaven mean if earthly love is the greatest joy of all, "la volupté suprême," and it is forever lost, forbidden and destroyed by a jealous God? When God receives Cédar back into Heaven, He would be cruel indeed if He did not again erase his memory and wipe out all recollection of his earthly loves.

### Clive Scott  (essay date 1986)

SOURCE: "Theme and Syllabic Position: Lamartine's *Méditations poétiques,*" in *A Question of Syllables: Es- says in Nineteenth-Century French Verse,* Cambridge University Press, 1986, pp. 1-30.

[*In the following excerpt, Scott contends that the flexibil- ity of Lamartine's poetic language enabled him to reveal "two worlds—a world of contingent existence, an unin- habited, purely natural, unregenerate world on the one hand, and, on the other, a world informed and visited by divinity, a world which may equally encompass the nat- ural world."*]

What is the nature of Lamartine's existential struggle? It is primarily, I suppose, a struggle with time, with time's passage. It is easy to assimilate this to the great poetic commonplaces of man's mortality, the fleetingness of beauty, happiness and so on. But this is to mask something unique about Lamartine. Lamartine is subject to time's cruelty *in the very fabric of his verse*: he experiences the passage of time directly, in the fluency of his own utterance, which carries him unrelentingly through and away from his experiences and memories. And this hand-to-hand struggle with time comes into its sharpest focus as a clash between 'encore'—the still there—and 'déjà'—the already gone:

> Au sommet de ces monts couronnés de bois
>     sombres,
> Le crépuscule encor jette un dernier rayon;
> Et le char vaporeux de la reine des ombres
> Monte et blanchit déjà les bords de l'horizon.
>
> ('**L'Isolement**')

Lamartine's poetry is an attempt to prolong this slightest of moments between the still there and the already gone. But the suavity of his writing is his own worst enemy. And it would perhaps not be too fanciful to see the short last line of the stanza used, for example, in '**La Gloire**' or '**Le Lac**' as a form of exquisite self-torture:

> Eternité, néant, passé, sombres abîmes,
> Que faites-vous des jours que vous engloutissez?
> Parlez: nous rendrez-vous ces extases sublimes
>     Que vous nous ravissez?
>
> ('**Le Lac**')

The abrupt finality of this last line is like time accelerated or abbreviated, like an exasperated reaching for an end that spells irrevocability. Ultimately the poet gives up trying to postpone the awful moment when all will be gone and, suicidally almost, accedes to time's consummation.

Another factor which makes Lamartine's world peculiarly elusive, slipping through the poet's fingers, dissolving, is the lack of resistance in his landscapes. If we look at the opening of '**L'Isolement**', we find the characteristic situation:

> Souvent sur la montagne, à l'ombre du vieux
>     chêne,
> Au coucher du soleil, tristement je m'assieds;
> Je promène au hasard mes regards sur la plaine,
> Dont le tableau changeant se déroule à mes pieds.

Not only is the world itself in a state of constant change, but the poet looks at it in a gliding, glancing, drifting way. The passive randomness of his gaze echoes the passivity of his stance, seated as he is beneath a tree. '**Le Soir**' opens in a similar fashion:

> Le soir ramène le silence.
> Assis sur ces rochers déserts,
> Je suis dans le vague des airs
> Le char de la nuit qui s'avance.

The objects in Lamartine's world are not obstacles, do not detain the eye. They are, rather, transparent, or dissolved and rendered uniform by surrounding atmospheres, mists, twilight.

The instant, the precious moment between 'encore' and 'déjà' cannot, it seems, be arrested. But it is certainly not for want of trying. The poet's chief resources in this desperate attempt are rhetorical. By means of apostrophe, invocation, rhetorical question, he seeks to distract the elements of his environment from their single-minded preoccupation with moving on or moving away; he tries to engage them in his predicament, to create pauses in process, to find respite in the very request for answers, reasons, probabilities. These rhetorical devices usually have the ironic effect of further isolating the poet, leaving him to supply answers he has no access to, making his *recueillement a recueillement* of time-wasting speculation. But the poet frequently resorts to much more direct and unashamed methods, to the kind of plea that we find in '**Le Vallon**':

> Prêtez-moi seulement, vallons de mon enfance,
> Un asile d'un jour pour attendre la mort.

What is noticeable about the plea is its eminent reasonableness; he wants the respite of only a day, where 'jour' is not to be understood strictly as twenty-four hours, but as a very limited period of time nonetheless. This is perhaps no more than a ploy to intensify the pathos of the situation and helps, of course, to emphasise time's intransigence. But the poet always makes apparently modest pleas like this—we have only to remind ourselves of the final line of the first stanza of '**Le Lac**': 'Jeter l'ancre un seul jour'. 'Just one more moment, please' and after that 'Just one more moment, please'; Lamartine is the poet of patient prevarication.

But it is also true that no moment has any value for Lamartine unless it is, precisely, the last moment. The last moment is, of course, always the richest, because it is only when things threaten to leave us that we know how to treasure them, and this treasuring is imbued with the poignancy of its inevitably being too late. The last moment is the moment of the availability of all memories and the moment when the pressures of aspiration beyond the moment and beyond time are at their greatest. In '**L'Homme**', the poet looks back to Elvire's passing away—and the notion of passage is certainly more suitable than that of death:

> Je voulais retenir l'âme qui s'évapore,
> Dans son dernier regard je la cherchais encore!
> Ce soupir, ô mon Dieu! dans ton sein s'exhala;
> Hors du monde avec lui mon espoir s'envola!

In true Lamartinian style, he has each day begged 'Soleil! encore un jour!', but to no avail. Elvire passes away, the last moment is lost and the world is of no more interest to the poet. Lamartine is a connoisseur in both the anticipation and enjoyment of last rites.

Some moments really are the final ones. But Lamartine also takes pleasure in savouring last moments which do not have the seal of finality, because they are part of the natural cycle, as in '**L'Automne**':

> J'aime à revoir encor, pour la dernière fois,
> Ce soleil pâlissant, dont la faible lumière
> Perce à peine à mes pieds l'obscurité des bois!

This is an enjoyment of the peculiar piquancy of last moments under false pretences, a vicarious last-moment experience. Lamartine cannot escape the paradoxical truth that things only really begin to exist when they are on the point of ceasing to exist; he has to push things to the very brink of their extinction before he can enter into a rich sensory relationship with them.

Lamartine clings to the light, but it fades from him; he tries to encompass the landscape, but his eye slips over it in such a way that the horizon seems to recede from him, to draw him away, annihilating objects as it goes; he follows without resistance towards a world that has a monotonous neutrality. This is a dismal picture, but one which has its brighter side. Built into Lamartine's understanding that he cannot arrest the world around him, cannot prevent the loved one and a topography slipping away from him, is a concomitant and conflicting understanding that this very process of effacement is the means by which access may be gained to the higher world. Lamartine is a transcendentalist; his desire is to rise above his surroundings, not to lose himself in them, however consoling nature manages to be for him.

With the instant gone, the last moment irrevocably taken from him, Lamartine must seek to preserve its vestige, its trace, its memory. How is he to do this? Simply by *recueillement,* by an ingathering of his intellectual and emotional impulses, by a quiet collection of his spiritual longing, by a special intimacy. As he puts it in **'Le Vallon'**:

> Mon cœur est en repos, mon âme est en silence!
> Le bruit lointain du monde expire en arrivant,
> Comme un son éloigné qu'affaiblit la distance,
> A l'oreille incertaine apporté par le vent.
>
> D'ici je vois la vie, à travers un nuage,
> S'évanouir pour moi dans l'ombre du passé;
> L'amour seul est resté: comme une grande image
> Survit seule au réveil dans un songe effacé.

The lure of surrounding space inviting the poet to try and make sense of himself in relation to its diversity, is shown to be, precisely, a *lure,* a dangerous seduction. The erasure of reality is not now seen as a loss, but as a necessary process of spiritualisation and disembodiment. Lamartine has forsaken the commanding view which led to such inner distress in **'L'Isolement',** and taken up his position in a valley, a locality that denies external space in favour of the development of an inner space, a place of refuge, a womb at the heart of the created world which promises a new kind of birth (compare with the valley of **'Adieu'** and the subterranean chapel of **'La Semaine Sainte'**). Liberated from the interference of sense-data, Lamartine can concentrate all his being on forcing a passage into the super-terrestrial realm.

Hitherto Lamartine has used language to do battle against the flowing, elusive world only to find that language itself is fluid, runs away, confirms that which it sets out to gainsay. He has used language to try to revive the past, to

*An engraving by Tony Johannot depicting a scene from* Jocelyn.

voice his sense of abandonment, only to find that language is not strong enough to resurrect, is only a self-indulgent release of frustrations. But in the valley, in his new realisation of redemption, isolation is beneficent and language is no longer necessary. As the twilight creeps on, as sounds die down and sights become obscured, with the elimination of all distraction, Lamartine can cast off the exasperations that language encourages, and communicate in a soundless spiritual fashion, in prayerfulness, in fact. This is how he puts it in the last stanza of **'Le Vallon'**:

> Dieu, pour le concevoir, a fait l'intelligence:
> Sous la nature enfin découvre son auteur!
> Une voix à l'esprit parle dans son silence,
> Qui n'a pas entendu cette voix dans son cœur?

and in **'La Prière'**:

> Tout se tait: mon cœur seul parle dans ce silence.
> La voix de l'univers, c'est mon intelligence.

How does this state of communication with the transcendental world manifest itself? It manifests itself in the 'rayon', the shaft of light which breaks through the clouds and acts as a corridor of release. Addressing the deceased Elvire in **'Le Soir',** the poet describes the visitation of an Elvire-bearing light:

Tout à coup, détaché des cieux,
Un rayon de l'astre nocturne,
Glissant sur mon front taciturne,
Vient mollement toucher mes yeux.
Doux reflet d'un globe de flamme,
Charmant rayon, que me veux-tu?
Viens-tu dans mon sein abattu
Porter la lumière à mon âme?

It is perhaps worth noticing the gentle sensuality of this contact, expressed in 'mollement'.". . . It is worth noticing, too, not only that the poet is again absolutely silent— 'sur mon front taciturne'—but also that 'glisser' here has a positive charge: it does not describe that quicksilver quality of time, that awful, because imperceptible, leaking away of life into an anonymous void, which we find expressed at the beginning of **'Souvenir'**:

En vain le jour succède au jour,
Ils glissent sans laisser de trace

On the contrary, it is like a gesture of blessing, a soothing therapeutic caress of light, the holier, the more healing, for its being slight and insubstantial. This connection between the verb 'glisser' and the 'rayon' is to be found again in the penultimate stanza of **'Le Vallon'**.

Avec le doux rayon de l'astre du mystère
Glisse à travers les bois dans l'ombre du vallon.

As we have intimated, the movement through the 'rayon' is not exclusively a downward movement; the 'rayon' is something like a pneumatic chute for the poet, along which his yearning soul can thrust itself ('s'élancer', 's'élever', 's'envoler' are the characteristic verbs of this movement). The dawn, the rising sun offer the poet explicitly upward-thrusting rays [in **'L'Isolement'**]:

Que ne puis-je, porté sur le char de l'aurore,
Vague object de mes vœux, m'élancer jusqu'à toi! . . .

The word 'rayon' suggests a single, bright, focussed ray of light, cutting like a knife through the intervening space and alighting like a spotlight on the souls of the elect. One only has to change the noun 'rayon' to the verb 'rayonner' to multiply the rays and provide a more diffused kind of light: we find in **'Souvenir'** for instance:

Tes yeux, où s'éteignait la vie,
Rayonnent d'immortalité!

The verbs which most typically describe this diffused light are 'inonder' and 'répandre'. The former appears, for example, in **'L'Immortalité',** a poem once again addressed to Elvire:

Tu viens d'un jour plus pur inonder ma paupière

and the latter in **'La Prière'**:

Pour moi, c'est ton regard qui, du divin séjour,
S'entr'ouvre sur le monde et lui répand le jour

In both cases the verb is not accompanied by 'rayon' at all, but by the generalised 'jour'. But it would be wrong to dissociate this more widespread light from the sharp light of 'rayon', for two reasons. First, because Lamartine does, in some images, attempt to reconcile the two, to use the 'rayon' idea to give light a direction, an urgency, an intensity, and to combine this with the process of diffusion, to convey the universal beneficence of an Elvire who has become something more than the poet's personal possession; thus the 'rayon' is endowed with a gentleness, a power of tender encompassment which generates a feeling of the warm solicitude of the divine, rather than of its authoritarian summariness. The unambiguous ray of light must somehow be allowed to invest the whole of existence. One of the examples of this effort towards combination concerns not a visual perception of light, but a visual perception which shades into an aural one; it is the image of the church in the fourth stanza of **'L'Isolement'**:

Cependant, s'élançant de la flèche gothique
Un son religieux se répand dans les airs

Here the spire stands in, as it were, for the upward ray of light, but the sharp thrust of the building disperses in a vague haze of sound; the verticality of the spire is countered by the horizontality of the spreading religious note. In fact, there is a sense in which the image is quite literally a contradiction: how can 's'élancer' really be applied to a sound as diffuse as this? The image we are left with is as of a fountain, the jet of water breaking at its zenith and scattering in a fine mist of drops.

And this leads to our second reason for not dissociating diffused light from the concentrated light of the ray. What we find in the example from **'L'Isolement'** is the association of two different sense-impressions, one visual, one aural, one specific, one generalised. The invasion of the poet's being by a vague, self-insinuating but balm-giving force involves other senses too, smell and touch, because Lamartine uses perfumes and light winds to fulfil the same function as diffused light. Here again are sensations which, at one and the same time, have a high degree of insubstantiality and a certain voluptuous charge. We find perfume and breeze fused in a single complex in a stanza added to **'Souvenir'** in the second edition:

Et si le souffle du zéphyre
M'enivre du parfum des fleurs,
Dans ses plus suaves odeurs
C'est ton souffle que je respire.

Here is a much more pantheistic picture of Elvire's benign influence, coming from the immediate environment, which does much to restore the intimate and terrestrial side of the relationship, so necessary to the efficacy of the transcendental projection of it. And it does seem that the energy of Lamartine's spiritual longing depends on the impetus of a sensual experience, however masked this may be. We learn next to nothing about Elvire's physical appearance, it is true—apart from Ossianic commonplaces like her 'tresses d'ébène'—but the poetry exudes a kind of light-headed and pleasurable intoxication, conveyed in great part, perhaps, by the caressing melodiousness of the verse itself. Fine spiritual ecstasies often turn out to have solid physical sources, and Lamartine's are no exception; one of the stanzas excised from **'Le Lac'** makes this abundantly clear:

> Nous ne pûmes parler: nos âmes affaiblies
> Succombaient sous le poids de leur félicité;
> Nos cœurs battaient ensemble, et nos bouches unies
> 　　　　Disaient: Eternité.

The final word of this stanza, 'Eternité' looks like a last-ditch justification for, and rendering respectable of, an embrace so pleasurable as to need no moral support.

At all events, the benign light wind, the 'zéphyr', as opposed to the harsher 'acquilon', is like an exhalation, carrying the last breath, the perfume, of the dying beauty, rose or woman. The wind is also that part of the natural scene that can exist without the landscape, that profits by Lamartinian evanescence. Lamartine is no stranger to synaesthetic experience; we may have suspected this in the church spire example, we see it at the end of **'L'Automne'**, where while the flower expires in perfume, the poet expires in sound, the swan-song of his own verse. But more pertinently to our purpose, we might quote lines from **'La Prière'**:

> Sur les rayons du soir, sur les ailes du vent,
> Elle s'élève à Dieu comme un parfum vivant.

The 'elle' referred to here is the voice of the universe, the poet's 'intelligence'. Again we feel not only the will to fuse together different types of sensory perception, to create a spirituality which is connected with a total sentience, a total availability to the bodiless communications of a higher principle both beyond and within the natural world; we feel also the will to reconcile the 'rayon', now in a more amenable plural form, with more dispersive agents of communication.

There is one final form of contact between the terrestrial and transcendental worlds, which I would briefly mention, and that is reflection. This world reflects the other world. This is again an extremely vague and diffuse kind of contact, but unlike breeze and perfume it is utterly passive: it simply exists or does not exist, depending on symbolic atmospheric conditions. The advantage of the reflection system is obvious: reflections can multiply themselves, create a chorus of reflections, create a form of involvement, out of their very passivity, an involvement in which all contributors are put on an equal footing and thus more meaningfully conjoined; as Lamartine puts it in **'La Prière'**.

> L'univers tout entier réfléchit ton image,
> Et mon âme à son tour réfléchit l'univers.

where 'tu' is God.

The idea of reflection naturally suggests images of water, because it is the stretches of water which are the real mirrors of nature. Of course Lamartine's primary concern is whether the water is clear and smooth-surfaced or not, whether it is a good reflector or not, and this question naturally attaches to the concomitant emotional or temperamental condition of the poet. In **'Le Vallon'**, for instance, the poet has come in search of inner peace, to reconcile himself to his life of disappointment, to set his love in its right, celestial perspective. In the opening description of the valley, his eye alights on two streams:

> Là, deux ruisseaux cachés sous des ponts de
> 　verdure,
> Tracent en serpentant les contours du vallon;
> Ils mêlent un moment leur onde et leur murmure,
> Et non loin de leur source ils se perdent sans nom.

These lines would seem to allude to the poet's relationship with Elvire, its hiddenness, its gentle sensuality ('serpentant'), the moment of fulfilment and the subsequent return to oblivion. In the following stanza, the poet makes these streams explicitly significant to his own situation, but in another direction:

> Mais leur onde est limpide, et mon âme troublée
> N'aura pas réfléchi les clartés d'un beau jour.

The poet presents his doubts about his ultimate redemption as a fear that his soul, rendered turgid, no doubt by his hesitation and diffidence, will never have the ability to reflect the divine light. This contrast of limpidity or turgidity is to be found again, and perhaps more interestingly, in the second stanza of **'L'Isolement'**:

> Ici gronde le fleuve aux vagues écumantes,
> Il serpente, et s'enfonce en un lointain obscur;
> Là, le lac immobile étend ses eaux dormantes
> Où l'étoile du soir se lève dans l'azur.

Here the contrast is what one would expect: the flowing river is a destiny that cannot be guessed at, the troubled water of passing time, while the lake is the still, but not stagnant, surface, the achieved spiritual plateau and site of regeneration by reflection. Here, dramatically juxtaposed, are the two worlds of which we have been speaking all along, but we can begin to see how the one is a necessary condition or complement of the other. The lake is a kind of abstraction of the river, the river, like the disappearing landscape, a necessary preamble to spiritual quietude and self-realisation. Strangely perhaps the serpentine movement is here connected with the troubled water rather than the limpid. But we should recognise the essential ambiguity of much of Lamartine's lexicon, or rather his own ambiguity and temperamental changeability. 'Serpenter' may in one context indicate elusiveness, even deviousness, in another sensuality or integration, depending upon what principle of the poet's existence it is applied to.

One of the other factors to which these last quotations draw attention is the acoustic property of water. This is perhaps the more necessary, since many Lamartinian events take place in the fading light when water surfaces are difficult to make out. **'Le Lac'** is remarkable for its absence of visual impressions. The concord of the lovers is answered by the regular, rhythmic striking of the oars, and the sweet tones of Elvire's voice are answered by the echoes of the spell-bound shore. Echoes like these might be considered as the acoustic equivalent of reflections (see also **'Le Golfe de Baya'**).

These quotations point up the connection between the water and the light. The still water not only reflects the diffused brightness of the day, but also, by implication, the sharper, focussed image of the moon. The water is also connected with light in a verb we have already encountered in a line from **'L'Immortalité'**, namely 'inonder'. But most important of all, by way of rounding off this brief thematic exploration, the ray of light itself, the nocturnal ray, is equally a reflection, as a stanza from **'Le Soir'**, already quoted, affirms: the rays of the moon are reflections of the sun:

> Doux reflet d'un globe de flamme,
> Charmant rayon, que me veux-tu?
> Viens-tu dans mon sein abattu
> Porter la lumière à mon âme?

This thematic outline is certainly far from comprehensive. There is much, particularly relating to Lamartine's mystical experiences and to the processes of memory, which is lacking. There are large tracts of Lamartine's lexicon which are overlooked—one might, for example, with equal profit study the lives of 'déserts', 'concerts', 'séjour', 'regard'; and the words/themes which have been selected are by no means treated exhaustively. But we have sufficient evidence to make some general observations about Lamartine's lexicon, and sufficient material for a prosodic project.

Lamartine may have taken over a diction all but exhausted by the eighteenth century; his poetry may have acquired the reputation of being almost exclusively intertextual, with its sources in the Bible, Milton, Ossian, Rousseau, Parny, Gray and Chateaubriand among others. But in many instances, Lamartine may be as much quoting himself as drawing on others, and besides, read as we have read it, his verse gives no hint of its genealogy: refreshed by its immersion in an existential condition, his vocabulary acts as a gravitational centre for a multiplicity of private impulses; this vocabulary is as limited as it is apparently conventional, but its limitedness has the same kind of virtues as the limited vocabulary of Racine's theatre: that is to say an unflagging pertinence and an ability to encompass and highlight the changing and contradictory impulses of the speaker—hence the multiple value of so many of the words. Although critics may point to the heterogeneity of these twenty-four *Méditations,* both in tone and form, they are all essentially about the same thing, but with so much variation in mood, emphasis and formal context, that there is no repetition, only an engrossing exploration.

Lamartine's landscapes do not belong to a specific time and specific place; they are accumulated landscapes, the products of superimposed images of the same thing (**'Souvent sur la montagne . . . '**), of superimposed images of different places, of superimposed literary topographies,

all sifted through the colorations of interiority; literarisation is indeed a cause or symptom of the general dematerialising tendency in Lamartine's work. All this produces a certain destabilisation of language. In Lamartine's poetry two worlds—a world of contingent existence, an uninhabited, purely natural, unregenerate world on the one hand, and, on the other, a world informed and visited by divinity, a world which may equally encompass the natural world—are served by the same vocabulary; as a result, the same word in different contexts may oscillate between opposing poles of value. Moreover, any word may flicker uncertainly between the literal and the figurative, for if God may inhabit anything at any time, then any object may at any time cease to be object and become a particular manifestation of His power, or solicitude, or mere presence. The evanescence of the landscape, encoding the passage of time, is a direct challenge to persistence and memory, a constant urge towards oblivion, a threat to all relationship, all sense of identity and purpose. At the same time, that same evanescence may be an exciting prelude to the fruitful hiatus between evening and morning, when the individual enters a purely spiritual space and establishes contact with a higher order of being; in these circumstances, evanescence becomes itself a form of concentration of the self in the self. Correspondingly, as we have seen, a verb like 'glisser' can belong to either world and derive from each a different emotional charge. Similarly, 's'envoler', which in relation to the spiritual world expresses release from mortality and flight to the stars, can, when used of the contingent world, just as well express a centrifugal movement of dispersal. 'Aurore' can refer either to the dawn that comes too soon and disturbs the quiet rapture of the poet communing with the night sky or indeed with the living Elvire (**'Le Lac'**), or, alternatively, to a mystic dawn, a dawn of birth to eternal life, a dawn of reunion with the deceased Elvire (**'Souvenir'**, **'Le Soir'**). It is with this sense of the mobility of Lamartine's language in mind, that we should approach the operations of his lexicon in verse-structure.

---

## FURTHER READING

### Bibliography

Lombard, C. M. "Lamartine in America and England (1820-1876): A Check List." *Bulletin of Bibliography* 23, No. 5 (May-August 1961): 103-06.

> Identifies sources of poem translations, book reviews, and critical and biographical articles published in English between 1820 and 1876. All items are listed under the periodicals in which they appear.

### Biography

Kelly, George Armstrong. "Alphonse de Lamartine: The Poet in Politics." *Daedalus* 116, No. 2 (Spring 1987): 157-80.

> Assesses the effect of Lamartine's poetic avocation upon his success as a politician, noting "modern society is hospitable to opinion, but not to poetry."

Robinson, A. Mary F. "Lamartine and Elvire." In her *The French Ideal: Pascal, Fénelon, and Other Essays,* pp. 277-312. New York: E. P. Dutton & Co., 1911.

> Portrays the relationship of Lamartine and Julie Charles, whom Robinson presumes to be the inspiration for the idealized woman "Elvire" in Lamartine's poetry and prose. The critic, Mary Robinson, is also known as Madame Duclaux.

Whitehouse, Henry Remsen. *The Life of Lamartine.* 2 vols. Select Bibliographies Reprint Series. 1918. Reprint. Freeport, N.Y.: Books for Libraries Press, 1969.

> The standard English-language biography.

Whitridge, Arnold. "The Revolution in France: Lamartine." In his *Men in Crisis: The Revolutions of 1848,* pp. 39-78. New York: Charles Scribner's Sons, 1949.

> Presents Lamartine as perhaps the most significant figure in the events immediately following the overthrow of the French monarchy in 1848.

Winegarten, Renee. "In Quest of Lamartine: A Poet in Politics." *Encounter* 59, No. 2 (August 1982): 22-9.

> Sketch of Lamartine's life, focusing on the evolution of his political beliefs and his role in French politics.

## Criticism

Ages, Arnold. "Lamartine and the *Philosophes*." In his *Literature and History in the Age of Ideas: Essays on the French Enlightenment Presented to George R. Havens,* edited by Charles G. S. Williams, pp. 321-40. Columbus: Ohio State University Press, 1975.

> Studies the influence of the French philosophers Voltaire and Jean Jacques Rousseau on Lamartine's thought and work.

Birkett, Mary Ellen. *Lamartine and the Poetics of Landscape.* Lexington, Ky.: French Forum Publishers, 1982, 105 p.

> Focuses on Lamartine's contribution to French landscape poetry. Birkett maintains that Lamartine considered the creative process and poetic diction more important than the actual landscape depicted. In addition, the critic contends that Lamartine anticipated surrealist diction in his emphasis on the musical evocativeness of words rather than on their descriptive power.

Bishop, Lloyd. "'Le lac' as Exemplar of the Greater Romantic Lyric." *Romance Quarterly* 34, No. 4 (November 1987): 403-13.

> Argues that "Le lac" merits consideration with "Tintern Abbey" by the English poet William Wordsworth as an archetype of the Romantic lyric.

Brereton, Geoffrey. "Alphonse de Lamartine." In his *An Introduction to the French Poets: Villon to the Present Day,* Methuen and Co., Ltd., 1956, pp. 93-106.

> Assesses Lamartine's literary achievement. Brereton provides biographical information for a fuller understanding of the poet's work.

Denommé, Robert T. "Alphonse de Lamartine and the Neo-Classical Inheritance." In his *Nineteenth-Century French Romantic Poets,* pp. 422-62. Carbondale, Ill.: Southern Illinois University Press, 1969.

> Considers evidence of Neoclassicism in Lamartine's poetry, concluding: "His ability to adapt and adjust his form and his ideas to the shifting moods of a difficult era explains why his writing gave the impression of being dictated by a lingering sense of neo-Classicism and a vibrant conception of Romanticism."

Goddard, Eunice. "Color in Lamartine's *Jocelyn.*" *Modern Language Notes* XXXVI, No. 4 (April 1921): 221-25.

> An analysis of Lamartine's use of color in the landscape descriptions of *Jocelyn.*

Gosse, Edmund. "Lamartine and the English Poets." In his *More Books on the Table,* pp. 315-23. New York: Charles Scribner's Sons, 1923.

> Suggests that Lamartine was influenced by the works of eighteenth- and nineteenth-century English poets, particularly Lord Byron, Thomas Gray, and Edward Young.

Harms, Alvin. "Lamartine and the Problem of the Ineffable." *Romanistisches Jahrbuch* XXIII (1972): 130-36.

> A discussion of Lamartine's aesthetic theories.

Hastings, Hester. "Man and Beast: Lamartine's Contribution to French Animal Literature." *PMLA* LXI, No. 4 (December 1946): 1109-25.

> A study of Lamartine's attitude toward animals and their representation in his works, particularly in *Harmonies poétiques et religieuses* and *Jocelyn.*

Lombard, Charles M. "The Influence of Saint-Martin on Lamartine." *Modern Language Notes* LXX, No. 1 (January 1955): 42-4.

> Describes the influence of the leading eighteenth-century French philosopher Louis-Claude de Saint-Martin on Lamartine's verse, especially as evidenced in *The Poetical Meditations.*

———. "Portrait of Lamartine in the English Periodical (1820-70)." *Modern Language Review* LVI, No. 3 (July 1961): 335-38.

> Discusses the reception of Lamartine's writings in England over a fifty-year span.

———. "Anglo-American Protestantism and Lamartine." *Revue de littérature comparée* XXXVII, No. 4 (October-December 1963): 540-49.

> A survey of criticism on Lamartine by American and English Protestants.

Pirazzini, Agide. *The Influence of Italy on the Literary Career of Alphonse de Lamartine.* New York: Columbia University Press, 1917, 160 p.

> A biographical and critical study tracing the influence of Italian literature and culture on Lamartine's works.

Porter, Laurence M. "Appeal and Response in Lamartine's

Elegies." In his *The Renaissance of the Lyric in French Romanticism: Elegy, "Poëme," and Ode*, pp. 19-46. Lexington, Ky.: French Forum, 1978.

>    Discusses Lamartine's verse within the context of the elegy in nineteenth-century French poetry. Porter concentrates on Lamartine's use of such poetic devices as mirror imagery, personification, and apostrophe.

Pugh, Anthony. "On Analysing Poetry: 'Le lac.'" *Modern Languages* 51, No. 1 (March 1970): 20-4.

>    A detailed interpretation of the poem "Le lac" from *The Poetical Meditations*.

Shields, John. "Three Elegies." *Studies in Philology* XL, No. 4 (October 1943): 576-82.

>    Compares Le lac" with the poems "Tristesse d'Olympio" by Victor Hugo and "Souvenir" by Alfred de Musset.

Smith, Maxwell Austin. "The Intimate Poetry of Lamartine and Sainte-Beuve: A Contrast." In *Studies by Members of the Department of Romance Languages,* pp. 152-62. University of Wisconsin Studies in Language and Literature, No. 20. Madison: University of Wisconsin, 1924.

>    Contrasts the *poésie intime*, verse representing the joys of everyday life, of Charles Augustin Sainte-Beuve and Lamartine.

Tilley, A. "Lamartine's *Méditations poétiques*." *Modern Language Review* XXVI, No. 3 (July 1931): 288-314.

>    A survey of *The Poetical Meditations*. Tilley describes the genesis of these poems and provides brief interpretations of each.

# Mina Loy
## 1882–1966

(Born Mina Gertrude Lowy) English poet and artist.

## INTRODUCTION

Loy is closely associated with the modernist movement in American and English poetry in the early twentieth century. She is noted for her innovative experimentation with free verse and her use of such themes as sexuality and female experience. Her work is often autobiographical and reflects her association with the Italian Futurist movement, French metaphysics, and with other avant-garde writers such as Gertrude Stein, Ezra Pound, and Marianne Moore.

### Biographical Information

Loy was born into a conventional English Victorian family of Hungarian descent. She started writing poetry and painting early, and as a young woman, she travelled to Germany and Paris to study art. In 1903 she married the artist Hugh Oscar William Haweis (known as Stephen) in Paris. She had some early artistic successes at the Salon D'Automne, after which Haweis moved the family to Florence. She had three children with Haweis, who abandoned her in 1913. After becoming enamored of the Futurist movement in Italy, she began writing verse extolling the Futurist philosophy. She eventually became disillusioned with the fascist and misogynist tendencies of the movement and abandoned Europe for New York. After being published in avant-garde journals such as *Others*, the *Dial*, and *Camera Work*, Loy's poetry began to garner critical attention. In 1918 she married Dadaist Arthur Cravan, who disappeared and was presumably found dead in the Mexican desert in 1919. She published her first collection of poetry, *Lunar Baedecker* in 1923. That same year she settled in Paris with her children and worked as a lampshade designer and artist's agent to support her family. She returned to New York in 1936 and continued to write poetry sporadically. Loy died in Aspen, Colorado, in 1966.

### Major Works

Loy's importance as a poet is based largely on her early work, which reflected her concerns with the role of women in a modern world. Her *Love Songs* (1981), "Parturition," "Three Moments in Paris," and "Italian Pictures" are unsentimental explorations of a woman's experience of childbirth, love, sex and its aftermath which reflect the modern artist's use of collage and other stylistic techniques. Loy's political philosophy is manifest in her "Aphorisms on Futurism," a prose poem that celebrated

the Futurist movement and "Feminist Manifesto," a call for economic and social reform in the lives of women.

### Critical Reception

Loy's early work was favorably received by the influential modernist poets Ezra Pound and T. S. Eliot, both of whom admired her innovative and autobiographical verse. Yet the modernist aspects of Loy's poetry alienated most commentators, in particular the unconventional structure and the overlapping characters and images in her work. Her frank treatment of sexual themes shocked mainstream audiences and prevented her poetry from being published in major journals of the period. Today she is the focus of critics who examine her work within the context of feminist and modernist poetry.

---

## PRINCIPAL WORKS

**Poetry**
*Songs to Joannes, Others*   1917

*Republished as *Love Songs*, 1981.

--------

## CRITICISM

### Kenneth Fields   (essay date 1967)

SOURCE: "The Poetry of Mina Loy," in *The Southern Review,* Vol. 3, Summer, 1967, pp. 597-607.

[*In the following essay, Fields provides a thematic and stylistic analysis of Loy's poetry.*]

Mina Loy was a contemporary of Williams and Pound, and although she was born in England, her poems are an important part of the American free verse movement. She published her first poems in Alfred Stieglitz's *Camera Work,* and later appeared in *Little Review, Others, The Dial,* and other prominent American magazines. Like the work of most first-rate writers, her poems were controversial, but she was held in high regard by her contemporaries. In 1921, Pound writes to Marianne Moore: "Also, entre nooz: is there anyone in America except you, Bill and Mina Loy who can write anything of interest in verse?" ***Lunar Baedecker*** [*sic*], containing 31 poems, was published in 1923, and Jonathan Williams, in 1958, published ***Lunar Baedecker and Time-tables,*** unfortunately, on his small and little-known press. This book went out of print almost immediately, and today Mina Loy's poems are virtually unobtainable. One of the best poets of the period, she is now scarcely read, and her name appears only in the midst of semischolarly lists compiled by men more interested in history than in distinguished poets.

Everyone knows that the tens and twenties were a difficult period for writers, and the fragmentary and obscure details of Mina Loy's private life which emerge are anything but happy. Her attitude toward her experience and much of her poetic subject matter is one of detached irony of an unusual directness. "Mina Loy," recalls William Carlos Williams in his *Autobiography,*

> was very English, very skittish, an evasive, long-limbed woman too smart to involve herself . . . with any of us . . .

And from the questionnaire in the final issue of the *Little Review* (May 1929) we learn that she considered her weakest characteristic to be her "compassion," and her strongest, her "capacity for isolation." These answers tell us something about her poetry. She does not mean that her compassion is deficient; but rather, that compassion, inescapable and human, causes her so much pain that isolation seems a virtue. And we find both characteristics in her poems.

I have said that her attitude is one of detached irony of unusual directness. This may appear contradictory, but it is not. Let me illustrate what I mean by quoting the final lines of **"Lunar Baedecker,"** in which she describes the moon ("Crystal concubine") in terms of its excessive use as a poetic property. The irony permits her to achieve objective distance, but the lines are impressive for their straightforwardness:

> Pocked with personification
> the fossil virgin of the skies
> waxes and wanes.

Such directness may be disconcerting to some, but it is the source of her power. At a time when "cerebral" was a pejorative term, Mina Loy was dealing with ideas. Pound's genius lay in other directions; his importance is his diversity: his mastery of various styles, his influence on the little magazines, and the fragments of a curious sort of scholarship. It may be that Williams, in a few poems only, surpasses Mina Loy stylistically, because of his extraordinary finish and precision, but the body of his work does not compare with her poems; his subjects are frequently trivial, and hers are not. And where Marianne Moore is clever and superficial, Mina Loy is profound; where Miss Moore is amusing, Miss Loy is bitterly satirical. The poets of this period tended toward a narrowness which was concerned with the image, "the thing itself," and with the technical aspects of free verse. This sort of brilliant specialization is always beneficial for the sophistication of poetic style, but it may prevent the writer from dealing with broader and more permanent areas of human experience. Thus Williams, because of his scepticism, his desire for communication, and his personal limitations, narrowly restricts his subject in his best poems and presents the isolated object with great clarity. While Pound, who lacks nothing in depth of subject, breaks his material into intractable fragments, resulting in an incoherence of which Pound is most aware. And in the poems of H.D., who cultivates effects of rhythm and sound to a high degree, subject gives way to a monotonous and private ecstasy.

Mina Loy's intelligence enables her to deal with matters of more general concern than those of her contemporaries, while her sharp perceptions and style always render the experience unique. Frequently with great brevity, she handles many of the sentimental stereotypes which had been too easily accepted for some time; and this refusal to accept the merely conventional involves a rigorous examination of states of mind and feeling, and gives to her poems a very personal quality. Perhaps the most famous example of this sort of thing is, from **"Love Songs I,"**

> Pig Cupid      his rosy snout
> Rooting erotic garbage,

but a better example is the brief **"Love Songs VI"**:

> Let Joy go solace-winged
> To flutter whom she may concern.

Miss Loy has written poems on D'Annunzio, Brancusi, Wyndham Lewis, and Joyce, and much of her subject matter involves a critique of many of the aesthetic commonplaces of the period and of the preceding "nineties." One of these commonplaces was the artist-as-clown, a notion which relegates art to the skillful pose and derives from an aesthetic such as Wilde's which declares that "All art is quite useless." It is art for art's sake, or art specialized to the point of excluding life. She may sympathize with the despair which is usually found behind the dandy's pose, but she satirizes the attitude which undermines artistic integrity. For style, if one takes the notion in its extreme sense, may become simply a game, and all art, a fraudulent discourse. Here are the opening lines from **"Crab-Angel,"** which treats the subject:

> An atomic sprite
> perched on a polished
>     monster-stallion
> reigns over Ringling's     revolving
> trinity of circus attractions
>
> Something the contour
> of a captured crab
> waving its useless pearly claws.

In **"Lunar Baedecker,"** the moon at first emerges as a nineties effigy, the superficial artists "draped / in satirical draperies." The irony in phrases such as "posthumous parvenues" is consistent and cannot be summarized. Moreover, the figurative language of the poem controls several areas of experience, and a good deal of careful reading is required to keep them in mind. The language, for example, evokes, not only the sterile poetic commonplaces ("Eros obsolete"), but also the effete, superficially dazzling life of (presumably) New York of the period. Both aspects are brought into juxtaposition by very forceful imagery. I quote the entire poem:

> A silver Lucifer
> serves
> cocaine in cornucopia
>
> To some somnambulists
> of adolescent thighs
> draped
> in satirical draperies
>
> Peris in livery
> prepare
> Lethe
> for posthumous parvenues
>
> Delirious avenues
> lit
> with the chandelier souls
> of infusoria

> from Pharoah's tombstones
>
> lead
> to mercurial doomsdays
> Odious oasis
> in furrowed phosphorous
>
> the eye-white sky-light
> white-light district
> of lunar lusts
>
>         Stellectric signs
> "Wing shows on Starway"
> "Zodiac carrousel"
>
> Cyclones
> of ecstatic dust
> and ashes whirl
> crusaders
> from hallucinatory citadels
> of shattered glass
> into evacuate craters
>
> A flock of dreams
> browse on Necropolis
>
> From the shores
> of oval oceans
> in the oxidized Orient
>
> Onyx-eyed Odalisques
> and ornithologists
> observe
> the flight
> of Eros obsolete
>
> And "Immortality"
> mildews . . .
> in the museums of the moon
>
> "Nocturnal cyclops"
> "Crystal concubine"
>
> Pocked with personification
> the fossil virgin of the skies
> waxes and wanes.

The infusoria (lines 12-18) are marvelous. A certain species of these microscopic organisms is shaped something like a chandelier and, seen through a microscope, appears to be tremulously glowing with light. The image describes both the neon lights of Broadway ("Stellectric signs") and the stars of this **"Lunar Baedecker"**; it is a controlled vision of decay in which macrocosm and microcosm, the telescopic and the microscopic, are united. It is this compression by way of imagery which is peculiar to Mina Loy. It is her own special brilliance.

Mina Loy's versification is unsophisticated and sometimes awkward. Her line resembles neither the quick, nervous line of Williams and H.D., nor the smooth, longer line of Pound, sometimes Stevens, and John Gould Fletcher. Her most serious rhythmic deficiency is a lack of unity from beginning to end of many of her poems. In **"Lunar Bae-decker,"** for example, she stops and starts, moving from one subject to the next, the individual stanzas nearly becoming separable sections in themselves. Her rhythms vary in speed, but the movement of most of her verse is slow; if it is uncomplicated, it is nevertheless unpretentious. What is most impressive about her verse, finally, is the incredible energy of her language—and her intelligence. The simple movement is often accentuated by the use of unusual and unexpected rhymes and effects of alliteration (for example, the first twelve lines); note the striking use of assonance in the following lines:

> Onyx-eyed Odalisques
> and ornithologists
> observe
> the flight
> of Eros obsolete

But these devices may be used excessively, and **"Lunar Baedecker"** comes short of her best work because of the awkwardness and obvious redundancy of lines such as 24-26 and 44-48.

---

**Loy's poetry will be slow work for the curious, carried out in rare book rooms and magazine files. But I know of no poetry in English which resembles hers; she is unique. This is the distinction, and, I suppose, the despair of the great.**

*—Kenneth Fields*

---

**"Apology of Genius"** is better. The theme of the artist's isolation grew increasingly more common toward the end of the nineteenth century as a result of very narrow ideas about art and epistemology. Here, the experience is more universal. If poetry is a function of the intelligence, and if great poets are to be persons of genius, then their poems will be largely unintelligible to the majority of the people. I am not speaking about technical features only; many poets, I suspect, would be satisfied if the simple content of their poems were understood. This is not to say that great poems are obscure; but poetry, contrary to popular notions, is not for the enlightenment of the masses; it is available to those who possess the talent and the energy to acquire a rather specialized knowledge, and who, additionally, are willing to respect the mind of the poet of genius. Consequently, those who lack this respect are often the cause of unpleasantness for the poet; at best, his poems are misconstrued. But poets wish to have their poems understood, and the isolation, increasingly more modern as fewer ideas are commonly shared, is painful and desperate.

To the first number of *The Blind Man,* dedicated to the Independents, Mina Loy contributes a short note, evidently the transcript of a public address, on the subject of educating the public. "*The Public* likes to be jolly; *The Artist* is jolly and quite irresponsible. Art is *The Divine Joke,* and any *Public,* and any *Artist* can see a nice, easy, simple joke, such as the sun . . ." She presents ironically the split between the artist and the public and concludes the note:

> So *The Public* and *The Artist* can meet at every point except the—for *The Artist*—vital one, that of pure, uneducated *seeing.* They like the same drinks, can fight in the same trenches, pretend to the same women; but never see the same thing ONCE.

> You might, at least, keep quiet while I am talking.

In **"Apology of Genius,"** we get the public view of the artist ("Lepers of the moon" and "sacerdotal clowns") along with the poet's view, stated with the force which illustrates her genius:

> unknowing
> how perturbing lights
> our spirit
> on the passion of Man
> until you turn on us your smooth fools' faces
> like buttocks bared in aboriginal mockeries.

The procedure differs from that of a "compensatory ironist" such as Laforgue in this way: while Laforgue vacillates between the sentimental cliché and its hard-boiled reverse (this is essentially the method of Cummings), Mina Loy presents the double view while maintaining the integrity of her art. The result is an unsentimental poem of great irony and satiric force, in which the bitterness is stated in precise terms.

### Apology of Genius

> Ostracized as we are with God—
>> The watchers of the civilized wastes
>> reverse their signals on our track
>
>> Lepers of the moon
>> all magically diseased
>> we come among you
>> innocent
>> of our luminous sores
>
>> unknowing
>> how perturbing lights
>> our spirit
>> on the passion of Man
>> until you turn on us your smooth fools' faces
>> like buttocks bared in aboriginal mockeries
>
>> We are the sacerdotal clowns
>> who feed upon the wind and stars
>> and pulverous pastures of poverty
>
>> Our wills are formed
>> by curious disciplines
>> beyond your laws

You may give birth to us
or marry us
the chances of your flesh
are not our destiny

The cuirass of the soul
still shines
And we are unaware
if you confuse
such brief
corrosion with possession

In the raw caverns of the Increate
we forge the dusk of Chaos
to that imperious jewelry of the Universe
—the Beautiful

While to your eyes
    A delicate crop
of criminal mystic immortelles
stands to the censor's scythe.

The use of "lights" as a verb in line 10 is at first ambiguous, but the writing everywhere else seems distinguished.
Lines 28-31 are very powerful; the slow movement, with
the repetition of vowel and consonant sounds in the heavily stressed words, gives peculiar force to the abstract
statement. Lines 32-35 may seem a little grandiose, for
they are an elaboration of an aesthetic commonplace of
the *fin de siècle*. But the lines serve to set up the irony
of the contrasting final lines, in which poetry, immortal
art, becomes, "to your eyes," nothing more than a crop
of "immortelles"—merely dried flowers.

**"Der Blinde Junge"** is, I think, her best poem (Jonathan
Williams does not reprint it in his 1958 edition). There
is no awkwardness here. The poem has a thematic and
rhythmic coherence which many of her poems lack, and
its conclusion is, for me, as moving as anything in the
period. Here, she deals with another, more absolute sort
of isolation, in which feeling, cut off from its object,
becomes a "centripetal sentience" of unfulfilled craving,
objective values having been lost which might accurately
inform experience. The treatment of vision in religious
terminology is another example of the density of her
figurative language. The black lightning of war has desecrated the retinal altar of the young boy, the purposeless eremite. By virtue of this compressed diction, she
can keep before us the general and the particular situations at once, both of which are equally terrifying. The
motive is World War I, and the blind youth is "Kriegsopfer," war's offering, of Bellona, the goddess of war.
Though the poem may be an analogue for the bleakness
of much of modern experience, and though Mina Loy is
in sympathy with the blind anguish of the youth, her
statement is more than the effusion of "concussive dark";
for the poem is written with great precision:

The dam Bellona
littered
her eyeless offspring
Kriegsopfer

upon the pavements of Vienna

Sparkling precipitate
the spectral day
involves
the visionless obstacle

this slow blind face
pushing
its virginal nonentity
against the light

Pure purposeless eremite
of centripetal sentience

Upon the carnose horologe of the ego
the vibrant tendon index moves not

since the black lightning desecrated
the retinal altar

Void and extinct
this planet of the soul
strains from the craving throat
in static flight upslanting

A downy youth's snout
nozzling the sun
drowned in dumfounded instinct

Listen!
illuminati of the coloured earth
How this expressionless "thing"
blows out damnation and concussive dark

Upon a mouth-organ.

There is the suggestion of a tenuously restrained violence in **"Der Blinde Junge"** in regard to both diction
and rhythm. The heavy stresses (') occur generally in an
iambic environment (upón the pàvements óf Vièrnna) and
account for the slow and deliberate movement of the
poem. But in lines 16 and 17, in which the diction for a
moment reaches a peak of abstraction and violence, the
rhythm becomes much quicker and lighter. The lines
contain rapid trochaic words of very short stress ("vibrant tendon index"). Line 17 runs over into a more
heavily stressed line in which the rhythm is resumed.
And the complexity of diction and rhythm in lines 27-30
concludes in the final short line ("Upon a mouth-organ")
with stunning plainness, the movement of the passage
nearly suggesting that furious music.

The purpose of this essay has been to acquaint the reader
with a few facts about Mina Loy and to provide him with
the texts of three of her poems. She is one of the great
modern poets and, in spite of her faults, should be read
in bulk. It will be slow work for the curious, carried out
in rare book rooms and magazine files. But I know of no
poetry in English which resembles hers; she is unique.
This is the distinction, and, I suppose, the despair of the
great.

## Carolyn Burke (essay date 1980)

SOURCE: "Becoming Mina Loy," in *Women's Studies,* Vol. 7, Nos. 1-2, 1980, pp. 136-50.

[*In the following essay, Burke analyzes several of Loy's poems from the years 1914 and 1915 in order to show the poet "examining the traditional spaces in which women live their lives, defining her own place within the 'spatiality' of poetry, and shaping the contours of a new psychic terrain."*]

"images            for the relief of the body and the reconstruction of the mind."

—Adrienne Rich

Mina Loy was an early explorer of that uncharted territory, the "new psychic geography" of women's poetry. Writing just before World War One, she felt the urgency of learning new ways to speak as a woman. Her poems are born of the desire to enter into a terrain where physicality embodies the spirit, where the body is animated by the mind. Appearing at the height of the first Women's Movement, her earliest work was informed by her sympathetic awareness of other women's efforts to free themselves from the constraints of tradition. Yet though her poetry appeals to contemporary readers, it is all but unavailable to us today: *Lunar Baedeker* has long been out of print, and only a handful of poems have appeared in recent anthologies. In this essay, part of a longer project that will result in a critical biography of Mina Loy, I shall discuss a group of poems published in New York in 1914 and 1915, when she was still living in Florence. They show her examining the traditional spaces in which women live their lives, defining her own place within the "spatiality" of poetry, and shaping the contours of a new psychic terrain.

When Loy arrived in New York late in 1916, she was surprised to learn that she was already known as a daringly modern poet. Her poems had preceded her, making her name familiar to the sophisticated readers of *Camera Work, Rogue, The Trend,* and *Others,* where they appeared with the work of William Carlos Williams, Marianne Moore, Gertrude Stein, and Wallace Stevens. The general public, however, took her to be a specimen of the infamous "new woman." Newspaper critics derided her lack of punctuation, audacious spacing, and unladylike subject matter. When she analyzed sexual love from a woman's perspective in *Love Songs,* a free verse sequence of considerable frankness, readers took the sequence as confirmation of the popular view that free verse did indeed lead to free love. The deliberately unsentimental voice of her poetry seemed to announce the end of an age. Her work implied that women were no longer to appear in verse as muses, mothers or mistresses, that they had become articulate interpreters of their own experience. And indeed, poetry did give Mina Loy the means to explore new territory and the freedom to speak as herself. To realize the significance of this moment in her development, we must look into what she called the subconscious archives, those lay-ers of interwoven memories that define the boundaries of the past.

Born in London in 1882, the same year as Virginia Woolf, Mina Loy grew up in a middle-class family of limited cultural aspirations and little tolerance for poets. In her mother's view, a young lady should not contaminate her mind with intellectual matters: she was expected to have no vocation other than marriage. Her father, however, had greater tolerance for Mina's independent ways and recognized her artistic talent. Although he didn't think much of artists, he allowed his daughter to attend art school in London, Munich, and later in Paris, once it had been decided that, in spite of her beauty, she was too unconventional to make a good marriage. In Paris Mina shortened the family name, Lowy, to Loy, thus adding emotional distance to the geographical separation. This act of self-naming was surely an important step toward becoming her own woman. She used Loy professionally throughout her life, for both painting and poetry.

Mina had written poetry as a child but soon learned to her dismay that this activity irritated her mother. Her favorite poets were Christina and Dante Gabriel Rossetti, both painters like herself. As a young woman, she dressed "aesthetically," in the pre-Raphaelite manner or in Liberty fabrics inspired by William Morris' designs. Although the doomed glamor of the Rossetti circle colored her ideas of the artist's life, Loy was too skeptical about the truths of the Church of England to imitate Christina Rossetti's self-deprivation and eroticized piety. She responded instead to the undercurrent of Rossetti's poetry, its quiet anger and barely repressed sensuality. She knew "Goblin Market," that most startling of Victorian children's poems, and for many years Christina Rossetti remained in some ways the negative image of the poet that she wanted to become.

During her twenties, before she began to publish her poetry, Mina Loy found herself caught between the conflicting demands of an artistic career and what she understood to be her role as a woman. Her very beauty got in her way, since most people she knew thought that an aesthetic young lady should inspire a painting rather than paint one. Christina Rossetti's sonnet "In an Artist's Studio" describes the artist's muse as the woman whose "face looks out from all his canvases" yet who is present in them "Not as she is, but as she fills his dream." The poem alludes to the ironies of Lizzie Siddal's role in Dante Gabriel's painting. Loy knew of the disastrous consequences of that marriage, but she could not have anticipated that her own would also sap her creative energies and divest her of a professional identity.

In 1904 she married Stephen Haweis, an English painter. They lived and worked together in his Montparnasse studio until 1907. During these years Loy showed her paintings and drawings at the Salon d'Automne, where she was elected to membership although Haweis was not. Her contacts with new currents in the Paris art world were abruptly broken off, however, when the couple moved to Florence. As she and her husband were taken up by the American and English residents with artistic interests, what had seemed like a promising career in Paris gradually dwindled to a round of social visits. Contemporary memoirs recall Mina Loy as "Ducie," Stephen Haweis' name for her. Her own memoirs convey both regret and resentment, for she found herself becoming an attractive appendage to her husband. Although she continued to paint in Florence, Mina Loy lost touch with the artistic vitality of her earlier years. As Ducie Haweis, she seemed "perpetually dissatisfied" according to Mabel Dodge, in whom Stephen Haweis confided his own dissatisfactions. He began an extended painting trip to the South Seas in 1913, leaving his wife to their children and the Florentine expatriate colony.

Mina Loy later said that she "woke up" from the enervating gentility of these years when she met Filippo Tommaso Marinetti. This aesthetic prophet arrived in Florence with his fellow Futurists in 1913, and they proceeded to shock the town with a series of provocative declarations and energetic happenings. Calling noisily for a complete break with the standards of the past, they claimed to have created dynamic modes of artistic expression to convey the tempo and feel of modern life. Mina Loy was intrigued by the inflammatory language of their manifestos and their deliberately outrageous behaviour at public events. Since she too had many reasons to wish for a break with the past, she found their rhetoric invigorating. For a time she was personally associated with their movement, but she never officially joined their ranks. Yet although Mina Loy soon found much to criticize in Futurist disdain for women, her brief contact with this group revived her energies.

In the same year—1913—Loy was writing of "the crisis in consciousness," her increasingly acute awareness of the need for a transformation of personal consciousness and artistic vision. Futurist theory stimulated her to reconsider her role, as a woman and as an artist, in relation to the worlds that she created on canvas and on the page. In a series of poems from this period, she reflected upon her situation as a spectator, a woman of privileged status in a culture that afforded little autonomy to women; at the same time, she examined her position "inside" and "outside" the frame of her creations. Entering into the scene presented in a poem, she sought to reimagine her own experience. Writing her way out of the past, she reemerged as Mina Loy.

Although Futurism was largely an unknown quantity in the New York of 1913, everyone knew that it claimed to express the quintessence of the modern spirit. The following year, therefore, Alfred Steiglitz presented Mina Loy's first published work, **"Aphorisms on Futurism,"** in the January issue of *Camera Work,* a review of the modern in all its manifestations. Her **"Aphorisms,"** a prose-poem in the form of a manifesto, is in fact the central literary text in the issue: Mina Loy seems to burst upon the scene in the radical posture of a Futurist, compelling the attention of her audience through her use of "the new form . . . that moulds consciousness." Her aphorisms are highly charged containers of awareness in an explosive sequence:

> YOU prefer to observe the past on which your eyes
> are already opened.

But the Future is only dark from outside.
*Leap* into it—and it EXPLODES with *Light.*
FORGET that you live in houses, that you may live
   in yourself—

     . . . . .

WHAT can you know of expansion, who limit
   yourselves to compromise?

     . . . . .

THE Futurist can live a thousand years in one
   poem.
HE can compress every aesthetic principle in one
   line.
THE mind is a magician bound by assimilations; let
   him loose and the
smallest idea conceived in freedom will suffice to
   negate the wisdom of all forefathers.

The whole sequence works according to principles of compression and expansion, as the lines imitate the mind's intensification of focus and the sudden psychic enlargement of release.

Loy's aphorisms are equally concerned with the urgency of clearing the "fallow-lands of mental spatiality" in order to create what we might call a personal space. The care with which they are set on the page suggests that writing can itself create this new space through a subtle attention to the spatial relations of typography. Initial words are printed in capitals to give greater emphasis: they shout at the reader in the declamatory tones of the Futurists' public readings. Sentences are printed in one line to stress the force of the final, climactic word, or they may be run over so that both the final word of the first line and the initial word of the next are prominent, standing out in the white space surrounding them. Loy uses hyphens functionally, to create at appropriate points within the line the pauses of intuition that Marinetti advocated. Between the aphorisms there are no connectives, only the white space of the page, which gradually comes to assume metaphorical significance as the newly cleared "mental spatiality." Accustomed to visual thinking, Mina Loy saw the page as a new realm for creative action.

For the feminist reader, however, this new space has a resolutely masculine character. Loy's speaker uses the generic "he" to refer to the mind and the Futurist; derides "you," that part of the self that is weak or subservient, as well as the reactionary public; and identifies with the Futurist campaign to "arrive at respect for man as he shall be." Yet if we are struck by the aggressive tone of Loy's "aphorisms" and sometimes feel the lack of a female consciousness in this piece, we must remember that virtually all the powerful figures in her professional life were men. She was brought up in the belief that artistic expression, like other activities requiring courage and self-assertion, would be tolerated in female artists only as long as such women didn't take themselves seriously. Going beyond the conventions of womanly feeling in **"Aphorisms,"** Loy's speaker identifies with those who possess the power to risk being outrageous: few women could forget that they lived in houses in order to live in themselves, and few could dare express "egotism . . . so gigantic that you comprise mankind in your self-sympathy." In other poems of this period, Loy's speaker chooses to identify the self as female when she reflects upon those experiences in which identification with male power is problematic for women. The self-assertive **"Aphorisms on Futurism"** is another face of the more self-reflective poems of this period: they represent related phases in a process of self-discovery and self-naming.

Mina Loy had to exhume and examine her subconscious archives before she could reinvent a first-person singular that was also female. Earlier poetic models were useless to her in the "crisis of consciousness": she came gradually to her distinctive voice in a kind of dialogue with Futurism. In the painters' manifestos, she found prescriptions for the artist's participation in his work that stimulated her to embody her own experience within her poems. Their central concept of dynamism posited "an equation between the activity of the outside world and the activity of the mind." This revitalized connection with exterior reality "released their imprisoned sense of self and gave them a new confidence in their creative powers." Mina Loy greatly admired the painting of Carlo Carrà, who explained, "We Futurists strive with the force of intuition to insert ourselves into the midst of things in such a fashion that our 'self' forms a single complex with their identities." Futurist painting would reproduce "stati di animi" (states of mind) through a process of active intuition, and the revivified quality of the painter's own experience of his subject would animate his painting. When the flow and bustle of modern life were recreated on canvas, the viewer could then, in turn, experience the emotional force of the original scene. Symbolist aesthetics had required both the artist and his audience to stand outside the frame as observers, gazing into a dream world; Futurist dynamism urged them to throw open the window to modern life.

What one saw, however, depended on one's ability to participate fully in modern life. It did not concern the Futurists that a woman's expectations might be more limited in this respect. Nor did they suggest that liberation from the past and commitment to the future could not occur in an instant, that the psychic processes required for taking such steps involved a slow and often painful analysis of one's own past. In a poem published in 1915, Mina Loy suggests something of the self-analysis necessary to enact the changes envisioned in **"Aphorisms."** **"Café du Néant"** shows affinities with early Futurist painting, in which the painter invokes Symbolist themes in order to criticize, revivify, or discard them. Loy composes a café interior with the acid colors of a Toulouse-Lautrec only to suggest how destructive its Symbolist ambience is for her own sex. In this artificial atmosphere, flickering lights seem to illuminate groups of couples, but seeing is not necessarily believing: "Eyes that are full of love/ And eyes that are full of kohl/ Projecting light across the fulsome ambiente." Self-deceived lovers tell each other "lies of no consequence" in their mutually sustained illusion of romance. The Café du Néant closes in upon itself, a decadent dream.

> It is important that we learn more about Loy's struggle to create an authentically modern woman's voice, one that speaks from the body to articulate the urgent needs of the spirit.
>
> —*Carolyn Burke*

Loy evokes "this factitious chamber" in order to set it within a verbal frame. Significantly, she analyzes her own composition by focusing upon the attitude of the central figure, a woman, who acquiesces in her lover's cruelty. Enthralled by the myth of love as suffering, this mysterious female smiles "as bravely/ As it is given to her to be brave." Her love potion (cherries in brandy, traditionally a "woman's drink") recalls the forbidden fruits of the goblins' market, just as her melancholy sensuality reminds us of a Rossetti heroine. Similarly, her languid acceptance of passivity and self-destruction mark her as a Symbolist ideal. The heavy irony of the speaker suggests, however, that there are alternatives to this morbid aestheticism. In fact, through the speaker, we acquire the distance necessary to realize that it is possible to wake from such a dream; in Mina Loy's analysis, one must quit the Café du Néant to gain the perspective that Futurism could provide.

This poem should be reread with its companion poems in Loy's sequence, **"Three Moments in Paris."** Together, these three poems depict a world in which women are defined by their dependence upon men, even though they have begun to question this definition. Loy's speakers are aware of the ironies involved in even the most tentative analysis of relations between the sexes. In the first poem, **"One O'Clock at Night,"** the speaker is bemused by her relations with a man in whose presence she becomes "a mere woman" and puts aside any "personal mental attitude" in admiration of his "cerebral gymnastics." She admits the force of his physical mastery but reflects ironically upon his verbal sparring with another man: is their argumentativeness ". . . the self-indulgent play of children/ Or the thunder of alien gods"? Rereading **"Café du Néant"** in sequence, we feel that the speaker has resumed her personal mental attitude and gone beyond the ironic complicity of the first poem. In the final poem, **"Magasins du Louvre,"** the speaker appears as a spectator who is both like and unlike other women. Her intelligent perceptions set her apart from the shop-girls and cocottes of the Louvre department store, but in her superior isolation, she regrets the loss of innocence that such lucidity entails. In this Paris of the mind, feminity is all but incompatible with vision and comprehension, which have traditionally been seen as masculine prerogatives. The woman with a personal mental attitude sets herself apart from others, and she is uncertain whether she has lost or gained thereby. Both the interest of these poems and their unevenness derive from the speaker's unsettled attitude toward her own abilities. Educated to a polarized view of sexual roles,

Mina Loy could be disquieted by her analytic and creative powers, even as she was using them to break with the past.

In **"Three Italian Pictures,"** another sequence from the same period, Loy writes as an expatriate English woman in a country where women are thought "to exist for only one purpose." From her isolated position as cultural spectator, a consequence of her foreign status, she observes her Italian neighbors with compassion and melancholy irony. Circumscribed by marriage, the Italian women's concerns focus narrowly upon the marriage-bed; the speaker, nevertheless, prefers the vitality of their predictable passions to the tepidness of the resident English colony. The first poem of the sequence, **"July in Vallombrosa,"** contrasts the spiritual dessication of English convalescents with the sensuality of Italian matrons who "discuss the better business of bed-linen." The English visitors are dying of their indecent chastity, a festering abstention from the life of the senses. As critical of her compatriots as E. M. Forster in his Italian novels, Loy nevertheless identifies with them in **"The Costa San Giorgio,"** the second poem of the sequence: "We English make a tepid blot/ On the messiness/ Of the passionate Italian life-traffic." Beginning as an outsider, she enters into the scene in the course of transcribing a stroll up the Costa San Giorgio.

If the **"Café du Néant"** is composed as an interior, **"The Costa San Giorgio"** is a street scene, a poem that shows affinities to Futurist paintings which aim to create the plastic equivalent of the sounds, sights and smells of public life. Thus Loy's irregular verse and unusual spacing in this work are visual and kinaesthetic transcriptions of the city's pulsing "life-traffic."

> Throbbing the street     up     steep
> Up          up          to the porta
> Culminating
> In the stained fresco of the dragon-slayer

Capital letters appear from nowhere to suggest street signs, snatches of conversation mingle with vendors' calls, and cooking smells waft out onto the Costa. Life is imported whole into the body of the poem through the poet's imitation of its flow in the structure and rhythms of her own creation.

This scene has not been composed in a random manner: elements selected from the street lead us to ". . . all the green shutters/ From which/ Bits of bodies/ Variously leaning/ Mingle eyes with the commotion." Behind the shutters women dwell in uncontaminated intimacy, with little to do once they have finished shopping, adjusted bed-pillows initialed with the family name, and dusted china. Yet the tone and imagery of Loy's conclusion imply that the inner world of these women is full of pretense. Their pillow-shams are false—sham—their initials exaggerated. Self knowledge is not easily won in such a setting. Similarly, the barber's mirror is only an imitation, and women pray to the Virgin to maintain the deception: "Mary preserve our mistresses from seeing us as we see ourselves." Drawn into sympathetic observation of her

neighbors, the speaker reflects upon the interiors where such women pass the better part of their lives shut away from the vitality of the street: although these lives can not be said to be tepid, they are lived within the narrow boundaries of social and sexual conventions.

The third poem of this Italian tryptich, **"Costa Magic,"** relates the tale of a father who, "indisposed" to approve of his daughter's marriage, bewitches her and brings about her death. Entering into the story as an active participant in her efforts to help the girl, the speaker compares the "unnatural" father to her own husband: both men have the power to control the lives of their female kin. Thus although Loy's awareness of the cost of sexual subordination is not entirely explicit in the first two poems of the sequence, it emerges here on the surface of consciousness. Not long after the publication of **"Aphorisms on Futurism,"** Mina Loy's poems recreated the immediacy of her own experience, however disturbing, and took on the responsibility of speaking with an articulate woman's voice.

In the same year, Loy published a remarkable work of self-creation, **"Parturition."** The poem renames and remakes the experience from the inside out, with the poet as her own midwife.

> I am the centre
> Of a circle of pain
> Exceeding its boundaries in every direction
>
> The business of the bland sun
> Has no affair with me
> In my congested cosmos of agony
> From which there is no escape
> On infinitely prolonged nerve-vibrations
> Or in contraction
> To the pin-point nucleus of being
> Locate an irritation     without
> It is                    within
> Within
> It is without.

Here Loy's lines imitate the contractions and expansions of labor and mime its rhythm of pain and relaxation: "I reach the summit/ And gradually subside into anticipation of/ Repose/ Which never comes." The white page around the poem functions as the outer boundaries of existence; the space at the center, between the contractions of "within" and "without," suggests the inner space from which the birth is issuing. As in **"Aphorisms on Futurism,"** words receive final or initial positions to reinforce their meaning. But in this poem, the impersonal attitude of **"Aphorisms"** has been personalized, and the unrealized urgency of the manifesto has engendered self-knowledge of a new kind.

The "spatial contours" that concern Mina Loy in most of her writing merge with the personal boundaries of existence in **"Parturition."** In her efforts to become "consonant" with the pattern of labor, the speaker achieves a sensuous revelation of her own identity, in which the contradictory aspects of mind and body are unified: "There is a climax in sensibility/ When pain surpassing itself/ Becomes exotic." At the moment of birth, the self is co-equal with the universe, yet the mind retains the ability to comprehend its experience.

> Mother I am
> Identical
> With infinite Maternity
> Indivisible
> Acutely
> I am absorbed
> Into
> The was—is—ever—shall be

Returning to a separate identity by stages, she keeps the knowledge that "I am knowing/ All about/ Unfolding." She has become consonant with herself in this new dimension.

At the conclusion of **"Parturition"**, the self-knowledge of Loy's speaker expands to include identification with the "undulation of living" in all forms, as well as sympathy with the "woman-of-the-people" who arrives on the scene to offer comfort. Significantly men are all but excluded from this world, except for the "fashionable portrait painter" (probably a glance at Haweis) who runs callously up the stairs to an amorous rendez-vous while the woman enters into hard labor. Yet, laboring, this woman reflects coolly enough that "the irresponsibility of the male/ Leaves woman her superior Inferiority." Loy's irony demystifies an ideology: woman is neither superior nor inferior, once she can define her experience in her own terms. Such moments of self-knowledge—however temporary—can indeed provide relief for the body and the reconstruction of the mind.

With this poem, an entire mode of female consciousness breaks out of the confinement to which convention had relegated it. When Mina Loy spoke of a woman's bodily sensations and her "lascivious revelation" of being, the poem shattered a taboo. It has been a well-kept secret even into our own time that the most intense moments of childbirth may result in an orgasmic experience of self. When a woman dared to voice the sexualization of her body, it shocked even "modern" readers in Mina Loy's day. Amy Lowell, for one, wrote some moving poems in praise of the female body but found Loy's very different assertion of her sexuality offensive, and many readers were outraged by Loy's even franker *Love Songs,* which begin by alluding to the male principle as **"Pig Cupid"** and describe his "rosy snout/ Rooting erotic garbage." Few were ready for the exploration of sexual experience in so unsentimental a manner when these poems were published in 1915. It was not supposed that women ever thought in such terms.

In the afterword of her remarkable study, *Of Woman Born,* Adrienne Rich calls on us "to imagine a world in which every woman is the presiding genius of her own body." She asks

> whether women cannot begin, at last, to think through
> the body, to connect what has been so cruelly

disorganized—our great mental capacities, hardly used; our highly developed tactile sense; our genius for close observation; our complicated, pain enduring, multi-pleasured physicality.

In spite of its unevenness, Mina Loy's early poetry shows her trying to think through the body and write from within its spatial contours. This kind of thinking does not come easily in our culture, and its translation into poetic form requires unusual ability. It is important, therefore, that we learn more about Loy's struggle to create an authentically modern woman's voice, one that speaks from the body to articulate the urgent needs of the spirit.

**Virginia M. Kouidis  (essay date 1980)**

SOURCE: "Rediscovering Our Sources: The Poetry of Mina Loy," in *Boundary 2,* Vol. VIII, No. 3, Spring, 1980, pp. 167-88.

[*In the following essay, Kouidis discusses Loy's involvement with feminism, futurism, French metaphysics, and the free verse movement through a reading of several of her major works.*]

Although British by birth, Mina Loy (1882-1966) has been considered an American modernist poet since her arrival in New York in 1916. One of the European expatriates from World War I, she shared the glamour and notoriety accompanying this group's pursuit of artistic and personal freedom, and her exceptional beauty, cerebral disposition, and cosmopolitan background distinguished her among the artists surrounding avant garde impresarios Alfred Stieglitz, Walter Conrad Arensberg, and Alfred Kreymborg. This milieu provided a sympathetic audience for her daringly innovative poetry, and to its writers' experiments in word, line, and image she contributed her firsthand knowledge of European modernism. The American little magazines were her publishers. Even before she arrived in the States her poems (and experimental plays) had appeared in *Camera Work, The Trend, The International, Rogue,* and *Others*; and in the late 1910s she moved with the experimentalists to *The Little Review* and *The Dial.*

Mina Loy's seminal place in the American poetry revolution is suggested by the appreciations of Ezra Pound and William Carlos Williams. Pound crowed from London in 1918: "Mi credo, Masters, Frost, Lindsay are out of the Wild Young American gaze already. Williams, Loy, Moore, and the worser phenomena of *Others* . . . are much more in the 'news.'" A more subdued letter to Marianne Moore (1921) made the same point: "entre nooz: is there anyone in America except you, Bill and Mina Loy who can write anything of interest in verse" [*The Letters of Ezra Pound,* 1950]. In the Prologue to *Kora in Hell* (1920) Williams established Mina Loy and Marianne Moore as the polarities of the avant garde landscape. Marianne Moore, carefully avoiding everything she "detests," represented the North; Mina Loy and her associates on *The Blind Man,* tolerating, Williams implied, experiment tinged with the absurd, the obscene, the nihilistic, represented the South.

Following the lead of Williams and Pound, literary history remembers Mina Loy—when it has bothered to remember—as an American modernist. But readers have generally overlooked her contributions to poetry, partly because she did not sustain the quality or quantity of her early work. She wrote most of her poetry from 1913-1925 with a small second effort in the 1940s. Significantly, the gradual recovery of her poetry begun by Kenneth Rexroth's "Les Lauriers Sont Coupés" (1944) coincides with the emergence of the postmodern poets of the 1950s and 1960s. In Rexroth's initial estimation, "She is tough, forthright, very witty, atypical, anti-rhetorical, devoid of chi-chi," an erotic poet who is "elegiac and satirical" rather than lyric [*Circle,* 1944]. Thirty years later [in his *American Poetry in the Twentieth Century,* 1971] Rexroth distinguishes Mina Loy from the "classic American modernists," placing her among the "American representatives of the international avant-garde" (Gertrude Stein, Arensberg, Laura Riding, Eugene Jolas). Other of her postmodern admirers include Jonathan Williams (her publisher), Denise Levertov, and Jerome Rothenberg. Rothenberg's recognition, especially, clarifies Mina Loy's significance. Like Rexroth he praises her vigorous defense and practice of artistic freedom and deplores her submergence by the reactionary modernism of mid-century. He situates her among the first, "circa 1914," to awaken to the "revolution in consciousness" and subsequently to explore "the relationship between consciousness, language & poetic structure: what is seen, said & made." Rothenberg joins the few critics, historians, and anthologists who have discovered in Mina Loy's oeuvre many individually exciting poems and a body of poetry important to an understanding of the modernist vortex. Her poetry aligns itself with that of Stein-Pound-Williams to form a "counter-poetics" that by generating postmodern poetry is emerging as the most vital force in twentieth-century American poetry.

Pursuing these appreciations, this [essay] will attempt to place Mina Loy in her cultural and literary milieu and, most important, to suggest the achievement of her poetry.

I

Mina Loy's modernist education began with an interest in painting. Raised in an English middle-class Victorian family which did not consider it necessary to prepare women for living by a formal education, she was nevertheless encouraged in her artistic talent by an indulgent father. Studies with Augustus John in England and Angelo Jank in Munich preceded her convergence with her generation in Paris, where she and her first husband, Englishman Stephen Haweis, exhibited in the Autumn Salon for 1906 (a reviewer described her painting as a combination of Guys, Rops, and Beardsley; his as "pur whistlérien"). Her Paris sojourn ended in 1907 when she, her husband, and a daughter (the Haweises had two other

children, one of whom died in infancy) moved to Florence.

During the Florence years (1907-1916) Mina Loy seems to have begun to write poetry. The reason for the new interest can only be conjectured; the failure of her marriage and her disillusion with woman's traditional roles are probably significant. Certainly her muse is **"Pig Cupid,"** the grotesque god who presides over the *Loves Songs,* or *Songs to Joannes* (1915-1917), a thirty-four poem-collage of the failure of romantic, religious, and sexual love. Pig Cupid embodies male carelessness and arrogance (the irresponsibility of Don Juan, or Joannes), as well as female disillusion and guilt. A product of the subconscious, he has destroyed the dreams of youth and swills the wastage of his victim's "star-topped" aspirations:

> Spawn of Fantasies
> Silting the appraisable
> Pig Cupid    his rosy snout
> Rooting erotic garbage
> "Once upon a time"
> Pulls a weed    white and star-topped
> Among wild oats    sewn in mucous-membrane

To convey despair and the shocked recognition of the body-mind interdependence, Mina Loy employs an imagery that looks back to the blasphemies of her Decadent heritage and forward to the grotesque psychic disfigurations of Surrealism. Such is poem III:

> We might have coupled
> In the bed-ridden monopoly of a moment
> Or broken flesh with one another
> At the profane communion table
> Where wine is spill't on promiscuous lips
> We might have given birth to a butterfly
> With the daily-news
> Printed in blood on its wings.

What in its time seemed excessive attention to sexuality sprang from Mina Loy's belief that to be modern was to open this "proscribed psychic area" so carefully avoided by her English ancestors and contemporaries. She characterized this first period of her writing as a working through of the sexual problem so that she could "develop some other vision of things." On a personal level she was attacking her Victorian heritage which calculated the marriage value of women according to their purity and ignorance, and imprisoned their spiritual vitality in busks as rigid as those which molded and suppressed their bodies. Artistically she was fighting the failure of literature to treat life honestly.

Mina Loy's familiarity with the artistic circles of London, Munich, and Paris suggests that she early had exceptional opportunities to break her ties to the past. However, letters and poems indicate that liberation from restrictive expectations for women awaited her friendship with the Futurists. In 1914, writing with skepticism as to the outcome, she says that she is being converted to Futurism. Later she writes that she was not a Futurist nor considered one by them, although she credits F. T. Marinetti, their leader, with "waking me up." Futurism seems to have awakened Mina Loy to the potentialities of the self, the need to reject the strictures of the past, and the availability of new poetic forms for discovering and expressing her freedom; thus it joins female self-consciousness as the wellspring of her poetry.

Florence also brought friendships with Mabel Dodge and her guest at the Villa Curonia, Carl Van Vechten. Returned to New York in 1913, they served as agents for Mina Loy's poetry and confirmed her desire to visit America. She arrived late in 1916, hoping to market her skills as a designer of clothing and to have her children, left with a nurse in Florence, join her as soon as she was settled. As an artist, she saw herself a Columbus drawn to the emerging center of the present, like him to be discovered by America. "'No one,'" she told an *Evening Sun* reporter in 1917, "'who has not lived in New York has lived in the Modern world.'"

Mina Loy's expectations were not disappointed. While New York did not bring prosperity, it did supply a community of like-minded artists and a moment of personal happiness. Among the city's expatriates she met Arthur Cravan, world vagabond and forerunner of Dada, who defied convention in a thoroughgoing manner that Mina Loy admired but could not emulate. The athletic, handsome Cravan, whose nonconformist bravado masked extreme sensitivity, became the great love of Mina Loy's life and they were married in Mexico in January 1918. They lived for a while in Mexico City where Cravan ran a boxing school and lectured on Egyptian art. Then, ten months after the marriage, Cravan, intending to join Mina Loy who had preceded him to Buenos Aires, vanished. The United States Department of State eventually reported that his body, beaten and robbed, [had] been found in the Mexican desert.

After Cravan's disappearance and the birth of their daughter, Mina Loy searched for her missing husband in Europe and America, briefly joining the Greenwich Village scene of the early 1920s. She settled in Paris in 1923, at the center of the American and European artists who shaped the legendary post-war era. The Twenties brought *Lunar Baedeker* (1923), her first volume of poetry, published by Robert McAlmon's Contact Editions, and the semi-autobiographical *Anglo-Mongrels and the Rose*, published in *The Little Review* (1923-1924) and in McAlmon's *Contact Collection of Contemporary Writers* (1925). In the next decade little of Mina Loy's work appeared, and by 1936 when she followed her daughters to New York she had faded into obscurity. But she wrote poetry and prose at least into the 1950s, and her work occasionally appeared in the little magazines until 1962. A second volume of poetry, *Lunar Baedeker & Time-Tables* (1958), went unnoticed. She continued to paint and was honored in 1959 by an exhibit of her collages, titled **"Constructions,"** at New York's Bodley Gallery, and by the receipt of the Copley Foundation Award for her painting. However, when she died in Aspen, Colo-

rado, where she had lived with her daughters since 1954, her poetry and painting were largely forgotten.

II

Mina Loy incorporated much of this exceptional biography in her poetry. Her first poems, examinations of the injustices of woman's life, are rooted in her effort to break with her repressive Victorian heritage; and the child-heroine Ova of *Anglo-Mongrels* enacts the female-artist's search for self-and-world understanding. Poems on art and artists are drawn from Mina Loy's friendships with the Decadents, the Futurists, James Joyce, Constantin Brancusi, and Jules Pascin. Her many poems on society's misfits—bums, the physically deformed, the poor—issue from the lifelong fascination with failure that drew her into the Bowery to live from 1951 to 1954. But the dominant biographical influence is Mina Loy's metaphysical (her label) preoccupation with the self, "a covered entrance to infinity / Choked with the tatters of tradition" (**"O Hell,"** 1920). The basis of her metaphysics is the **"Aphorisms on Futurism"** (1914), fifty-one prescriptions for selfhood that were among the first modernist credentials she sent to America. The **"Aphorisms"** dismiss the past—"DIE in the Past / Live in the Future," and proclaim the individual's ability to shape the universe after a self-image—"NOT to be a cipher in your ambient, / But to color your ambient with your preferences." Central is the call to awakening—"TODAY is the crisis in consciousness."

In answer to the challenge of the **"Aphorisms"** Mina Loy analyzes the self-world relationship and explores obstacles to self-fulfilment. If her poetry emits a cerebral chill, the reason is that she perceives the struggle and failure of her subjects not so much as personal suffering, but as illustrations of her metaphysics. The cosmos she constructs is chaotic, purposeless, and indifferent to humanity. At its center burns the life-giving sun of reality that illuminates life's beauty and harshness without bias. Within this vast indifference the self, symbolized by the eye, affirms its humanity by a relentless probing of time's shifting images for clues to elusive cosmic purpose: as **"Ephemerid"** (1946) explains, "The Eternal is sustained by serial metamorphosis."

Emblematic of the spiritual atrophy that accompanies the failure to exercise vision is the war-blinded youth of **"Der Blinde Junge"** (1923). Descendant of Charles Baudelaire's "Les Aveugles" and Théophile Gautier's "L'Aveugle," he is a victim of war and fate:

> The dam Bellona
> littered
> her eyeless offspring
> Kriegsopfer
> upon the pavements of Vienna
>
> This slow blind face
> pushing
> its virginal nonentity
> against the light

> Void and extinct
> this planet of the soul
> strains from the craving throat
> in static flight upslanting

Most of Mina Loy's subjects bear greater responsibility for their blindness. Desiring to escape the challenge of a constantly changing world, they seek a blissful Nirvana, also called Elysium and Ecstasia, beyond the painful processes of life. That is, they flee vision-in-time for the false refuge of a static absolute.

In the later poetry Mina Loy mostly records acts of failed vision. But at the outset of her metaphysical exploration she involves the I-narrator in a struggle for clear vision that is embodied in word, line, and image: the depiction, as Rothenberg says, of "the relationship between consciousness, language & poetic structure." The results, along with a proto-existentialist insistence on unremitting effort, place Mina Loy among the optimists of poetic modernism who, seeking better to comprehend and express the human situation, leave the individual open to discovery and growth.

III

Mina Loy bases her depiction of consciousness on the word. As her contribution to the "generation of the word," seeking in Europe and America to rejuvenate desiccated poetic language, she developed a sound-vibrant, sharp-edged diction that often saves her metaphysics from the mists of speculation or the sloughs of free verse exercise. When language becomes the word, not just the repetition of old visions, it liberates consciousness. This accomplishment, Mina Loy explains, is Gertrude Stein's:

> Curie
> of the laboratory
> of vocabulary
>   she crushed
> the tonnage
> of consciousness
> congealed to phrases
>   to extract
> a radium of the word

As for the technique Mina Loy used to implement her theory of the word, Ezra Pound's early explanation is still useful. In Pound's view Mina Loy writes "logopoeia or poetry that is akin to nothing but language, which is a dance of the intelligence among words and ideas and modification of ideas and characters." He cites Jules Laforgue as the forerunner and singles out Marianne Moore and T. S. Eliot as other practitioners of the mode. Pound elaborates his definition by distinguishing logopoeia from melapoeia, "poetry which moves by its music" and from imagism (later phanopoeia), poetry dependent on the image [*Little Review,* No. 4, 1918]. Logopoeia, he says, "employs words not only for their direct meaning, but it takes count in a special way of habits of usage, of the context we *expect* to find with the word, its usual concomitants, of its known acceptances, and of ironical play" [*How to Read,* 1931].

Mina Loy does write a poetry of ideas that makes the reader exceptionally aware of individual words. She likes the shocking sexual-scientific words of Laforgue as well as his exoticisms and dry abstractions, colloquialisms and puns. A diction compressed to the point of fragmentation is common, and juxtaposition and typographical fragmentation add visual and tactile dimensions to the word's referential power. But the use of sound dominates these means of emphasizing the word and setting it to the dance of ideas or, more accurately, the dance of consciousness. Always the poetry reverberates with sound, often to underscore satire, sometimes to delineate an image. Usually sound patterns replace meter as the regulating device of the poetry. Denise Levertov's appreciation focuses on the importance of sound: "An appetite for sounds—for words as sounds—which results in a scintillating precision. And it's this that makes for—IS—the close reasoning: it's there IN the words! Here's a virtue! There in words, which are sounds, which once were made up experimentally by our forebears—don't we live in a daily forgetting of that?"

IV

For the movement of words within the line and image Mina Loy drew upon French philosopher Henri Bergson, with whom she shares the theme of self-liberation, and Bergson's belligerent disciples the Futurists. She substantiates her familiarity with Bergson in a two-part article on Gertrude Stein. Of Stein's "Galeries Lafayette" (1915) she says, "This was when Bergson was in the air, and his beads of Time strung on the continuous flux of Being, seemed to have found a literary conclusion in the austere verity of Gertrude Stein's theme—'Being' as the absolute occupation" [*Transatlantic Review,* 2, No. 3, 1924].

Mina Loy also strives to incorporate the Bergsonian flux of Being (or consciousness) in language but her means differ. Stein abandons traditional syntax and employs repetition to record the subtle alteration, from moment to moment, in the object observed and the consciousness observing it. Mina Loy describes the result: "by the inter-varied rhythm of this monotone mechanism she uses for inducing a continuity of awareness of her subject, I was connected up with the very pulse of duration. // The core of a 'Being' was revealed to me with uninterrupted insistence. // The plastic static of the ultimate presence of an entity." Consciousness as Mina Loy shapes it is more dynamic. She structures its movement as the alternation of the Bergsonian states of intellect and intuition, interdependent aspects of consciousness that she embodies in abstraction and image. In the abstractions the mind comprehends the external forms of existence, whereas images plunge to the essence of existence and—if not intuitions themselves—carry the speaker to the brink of intuition. "No image," says Bergson, "will replace the intuition of duration, but many different images, taken from a quite different order of things, will be able, through the convergence of their action, to direct the consciousness to the precise point where there is a certain intuition to seize on" [in *Introduction to Metaphysics,* 1961]. Mina Loy alternates abstraction and image to depict the movement of consciousness inward to discover the essence of self and outward to place the self in cosmic becoming. She desires to transcend the fragmentations of earthly time and merge with Bergsonian *durée*: a "pure duration . . . in which the past, always moving on, is swelling unceasingly with a present that is absolutely new" [*Creative Evolution*, 1944].

This movement of consciousness shapes **"Parturition"** (1914), a poem alternating abstraction and image to convey the metaphysical quest of a woman in childbirth. Within this alternation irregular line length and internal spacing embody mental fluctuations and intuitional pauses, and are extensions of the spasms of pain. Typically, the self—cut off from unity with the "bland sun" of reality—strives to break its boundaries and merge with cosmic becoming:

> I am the centre
> Of a circle of pain
> Exceeding its boundaries in every direction
>
> The business of the bland sun
> Has no affair with me
> In my congested cosmos of agony
> From which there is no escape
> On infinitely prolonged nerve-vibrations
> Or in contraction
> To the pin-point nucleus of being
> Locate an irritation                without
> It is                                          within
>                                                     Within
> It is without.
>
> I am the false quantity
> In the harmony of physiological potentially
> To which
> Gaining self-control
> I should be consonant
> In time

Interspersed among these abstractions are vivid naturalistic images:

> Have I  not
> Somewhere
> Scrutinized
> A dead white feathered moth
> Laying eggs?
> Rises from the subconscious
> Impression of a cat
> With blind kittens
> Among her legs
> Same undulating life—stir
> I am that cat
>
> Rises from the subconscious
> Impression of small animal carcass
> Covered with blue-bottles

On this flux of image and abstraction the speaker attains the desired intuitive identification with cosmic becoming. Although her intuition is not all she hoped it would be—

her Being is one with "evolutionary processes," she briefly transcends earthly time:

> Mother I am
> Identical
> With infinite Maternity

The final image, however, returns the speaker to the meager but necessary consolations of humanity:

> The next morning
> Each woman-of-the-people
> Tip-toeing the red pile of the carpet
> Doing hushed service
> Each woman-of-the-people
> Wearing a halo
> A ludicrous little halo
> Of which she is sublimely unaware

In experimenting with structures of consciousness Mina Loy elsewhere combines the alternation of abstraction and image with series of vivid, disconnected, and sometimes fragmented images. Bergson's theory of the image as a means to intuition is relevant, but the Futurists are probably the more direct influence. Marinetti called for a poetry that is "an entire freedom of images and analogies, expressed by disjointed words and without the connecting wires of syntax. . . . Poetry must be an uninterrupted sequence of new images" [*Poetry & Drama*, 1913]. He wished to express the dynamism of the technological age, and these fragmented images were intended to carry the reader to an intuition of the essence of dehumanized matter.

Unconcerned with technology, Mina Loy adapted the aggressive tone and the technical innovations of the Futurist painters and poets to the purpose of depicting consciousness. These adaptations account for her classification as a genuinely radical, hence still instructive, modernist. She used the Futurist collage structure (Bergson and Marinetti's series of disconnected images) and typographical fragmentation, a corollary of collage. In collage the sequential relation of images and words is diminished in favor of spatialization: a simultaneous rather than linear arrangement of parts resembling the abandonment of three-dimensionality in modern painting.

Mina Loy most successfully implements Futurist techniques in **"The Costa San Giorgio"** (1914), an evocation of the dynamism of Italian street life. As part of her metaphysics the poem implies that ideal selfhood would balance excessive refinement, here associated with the English tourists, with the unreflective vitality of the Italians. The poem also links the poetry of Mina Loy and William Carlos Williams. In **"The Costa San Giorgio"** she strives as he does in "Spring Strains" to turn the poem into the two-dimensional plane of a modernist canvas. Her poem addresses Williams' theme of the necessary "contact" between the soul of a people and the soil of their habitation:

> We English make a tepid blot
> On the messiness
> Of the passionate Italian life-traffic

Throbbing the street   up    steep
Up   up   to the porta
culminating
In the stained fresco of the dragon-slayer

The hips of women sway
Among the crawling children they produce
And the church hits the barracks
Where
The greyness of marching men
Falls through the greyness of stone

Oranges half-rotten are sold at a reduction
Hoarsely advertised as broken heads
BROKEN HEADS    and the barber
Has an imitation mirror
And Mary preserve our mistresses from
   seeing us as we see ourselves
Shaving
ICE CREAM
Licking is larger than mouths
Boots than feet
Slip    Slap    and the string dragging
And the angle of the sun
Cuts the whole lot in half

And warms the folded hands
Of a consumptive
Left outside her chair is broken
And she wonders how we feel
For we walk very quickly
The noonday cannon
Having scattered the neighbour's pigeons

The smell of small cooking
From luckier houses
Is cruel to the maimed cat
Hiding
Among carpenter's shavings
From three boys
—One holding a bar—
Who nevertheless
Born of human parents
Cry when locked in the dark

Fluidic blots of sky
Shift among roofs
Between bandy legs
Jerk patches of street
Interrupted by clacking
Of all the green shutters
From which
Bits of bodies
Variously leaning
Mingle eyes with the commotion

For there is little to do
The false pillow-spreads
Hugely initialed
Already adjusted
On matrimonial beds
And the glint on the china virgin

Consummately dusted

Having been thrown
Anything or something
That might have contaminated intimacy
OUT
Onto the middle of the street

The heading *Italian Pictures* under which **"The Costa San Giorgio"** appears suggests the poem's painterly aspirations. Mina Loy's goal is not the superficially realistic reproduction of one scene at one moment, but the creation of the vibrant movement of the street and thereby of the energy of life. She has adopted the Futurist imperative "THAT UNIVERSAL DYNAMISM MUST BE RENDERED AS DYNAMIC SENSATION. . . ."

To structure **"The Costa San Giorgio"** as a dynamic two-dimensional canvas Mina Loy employs Futurist techniques such as overlapping planes, juxtaposition, signs, and fractured images. The transformation from narrative to canvas begins in the first line. Linear narrative yields to a spatial composition as the speaker and her English fellows become a "tepid blot" on the messy Italian landscape, an abstract element of form, color, and motion compositionally related to "Fluidic blots of sky," "green shutters," "Bits of bodies," and "eyes." Blots of paint signifying the sky destroys the illusion of atmospheric depth. Similarly, the sun at the end of stanza three is reduced to a geometric angle, a frequent sign on Futurist canvases for atmospheric light which provides dynamic thrust and, like the light of the Impressionists, shapes reality. In stanza two Cézanne's technique of *passage,* "the running together of planes otherwise separated in space," is employed in "falls through" to make one dimension of the greyness of war, men, church, and stones—the extensions and opposites of the women-and-children. In stanza six the verbs "shift" and "jerk" energize the atmosphere into moving shapes on the poem-canvas. Pictorial realism is also distorted by the exaggeration of visual and auditory fragments so that they dominate the wholes to which they belong. "BROKEN HEADS," "ICE CREAM," and "OUT" balloon above the poem; and "shutters," "Bits of bodies," and "eyes" protrude surrealistically. As the speaker recedes to a minor compositional element in the opening line, she merges with the chaotic vitality of the street. The Futurists explained this shift in perspective: "Painters have always shown persons and objects as if arranged in front of us. We shall place the spectator in the centre of the painting."

To depict the dynamism of the scene Mina Loy juxtaposes activity and stasis, just as a Futurist might juxtapose a sphere and cone to "give the impression of a dynamic force beside a static force." Stanza three, for example, explodes with movement and sound: the selling of oranges, shaving, licking ice cream, the slip-slapping of shoes. In contrast, stanza four contains an immobile invalid whose sole activity is mental: she "wonders."

Dynamism does not cease with the tension between movement and stasis. Colloquial speech enlivens language and evokes the inner rhythms of the participants. Introduced in

"We English," it continues throughout the poem and is punctuated by irregular line length, capitalization, and internal spacing. These devices also convey the rhythms of the street, just as in "Parturition" they echo the mental and physical rhythms of a woman in labor. Small scale juxtapositions reflect the movement of the eye and make visual puns. In stanza three syntax lapses as the eye jumps from the "BROKEN HEADS" of the orange vendor to heads shaved by the barber, and the shaving cream of the latter becomes "ICE CREAM"; the licking of "ICE CREAM" and the wearing of over-sized shoes are joined as disproportions between need and means that suggest the Italians are oblivious to the required symmetries of refinement.

Verbs also create movement. The present participle dominates the poem and surely "anything" and "something"— the troublesome vitality tossed into the street—were selected for their relation to the participle. Verbs and verb forms are positioned for emphasis; and the juxtaposition of movement and stasis continues in the contrast of present tense verbs and participles to past participles. The latter depict the finished, the hopeless, the non-vital: the fresco is "stained"; the consumptive sits with "folded" hands and she has been "left" in a "broken" chair, like the "maimed" cat she is defenseless; the boys cry when "locked" in the dark; and inside quiet homes pillow spreads are "initialed" and "adjusted," the china virgin "dusted."

---

**The connection Loy forges in her imagery between (female) sexuality and consciouness looks to Surrealist, confessional, and feminist poetry. . . . Her use of language fulfills the poet's responsibility, as she defines it, to make the world a radioactive particle that penetrates and shatters the clichés of experience.**

**—Virginia M. Kouidis**

---

The collage fragmentation Mina Loy learned from the Futurists becomes more complex in the *Love Songs*, a group of poems whose innovative structuring of consciousness merits consideration with Guillaume Apollinaire's *Zone* (1912), Stein's *Tender Buttons* (1913), Eliot's *Prufrock* (1915) and *The Waste Land* (1922), Williams' *Kora in Hell* (1920), Pound's *Hugh Selwyn Mauberley* (1920), and Moore's "Marriage" (1923). The *Love Songs* are too long to consider in their entirety but poem I illustrates the shape of the whole:

> Spawn      of      Fantasies
> Silting the appraisable
> Pig Cupid   his rosy snout
> Rooting erotic garbage

"Once upon a time"
Pulls a weed    white and star-topped
Among wild oats    sewn in mucous-membrane

I would an     eye in a Bengal light
Eternity in a sky-rocket
Constellations in an ocean
Whose rivers run no fresher
Than a trickle of saliva

These    are suspect places
I must live in my lantern
Trimming subliminal flicker
Virginal    to the bellows
Of Experience
*Coloured glass*

The juxtaposition of heterogeneous images forms a collage of biological, romantic, religious, and cosmological fragments, as well as past, present and future times, to depict the disintegration of an ordered, purposeful existence. Combined with these juxtapositions is a typographical breaking up of the poem that forecasts composition by field. The internal spaces reflect pauses of the intuition and leaps into the subconscious. The poem alludes to the Cupid and Psyche myth and the parable of the virgins (Matthew 25:1-13), and it borrows images from Bergson and Laforgue. As in "Parturition" the speaker merges with cosmic process; but in the dissipation of the skyrocket (Bergson's image of supra-consciousness, and a phallic symbol that complements the feminine ocean) to a trickle of saliva, the disillusioned speaker mocks the optimism of Bergson and the Futurists. The dissipation conveys the fall from ecstatic, orgasmic transcendence to a spatialized chaos where varieties of conscious and subconscious awareness are simultaneously present. The collage pattern is repeated in the overall structure of the thirty-four poems. Each poem is a kaleidoscopic reshifting of the fragments and colors of failed love. A vague narrative runs throughout and each poem is somewhat autonomous; however, poem I contains the entire narrative and subsequent poems, using an exaggerated self-reflexive imagery, merely complete the fragments introduced here.

Both "The Costa San Giorgio" and the *Love Songs* employ collage spatialization to step outside of time. In the former, abandonment of time progression involves an effort to experience the world in its rich immediacy. In the *Love Songs,* on the other hand, spatialization depicts a mental confusion that offers no escape into time and the healing processes of change and rational explanation. Seeking to transcend time in a Nirvana of romantic-sexual love, the I falls back not into time but into a negative space of unending torment. Poem XXXI images this condition as "Crucifixion / Wracked arms / Index extremities / In vacuum / To the unbroken fall." Thus the *Love Songs* fit the modern mold defined by Joseph Frank in "Spatial Form in Modern Literature." In disequilibrium with the cosmos, the modern, says Frank, escapes historical time through the creation of a non-naturalistic spatial composition that juxtaposes past and present to mythicize experience. Accordingly, in the *Love Songs* allusions to Cupid and Psyche, the fairy tale "'Once upon a time,'" and the Biblical virgins place this modern love story within the larger unchanging pattern of human experience wherein the self finds divinity through earthly love. Ironically, of course, the modern Psyche is unredeemed; the *Love Songs* are Mina Loy's flirtation with the modernism of despair associated with the early Eliot.

v

In *Lunar Baedeker* Mina Loy abandons radical fragmentation and collage in favor of series of vivid abstract-concrete images that unite intellect and intuition in a clearly crafted moment of vision. Short image-stanzas follow each other in a series that can be construed as a collage, even though a conventional syntax unites the images. Many of these poems praise the artist and, appropriately for this subject, consciousness is not depicted as a process but acts as form giver. The artist alone, in Mina Loy's metaphysics, possesses the vision to discover meaning in the flux of time. The tradition is Art for Art's Sake as it evolves from Gautier through Baudelaire, the Parnassians, and the *fin de siècle*. **"Apology of Genius"** (1922), a gloss of the tradition, equates the artist's form-giving genius to God's:

> In the raw caverns of the Increate
> We forge the dusk of Chaos
> To that imperious jewelry of the Universe
> —*the Beautiful*—

The same analogy informs **"Brancusi's Golden Bird"** (1922), a defense of abstract art and one of several poems on individual artists. Brancusi has penetrated the chaos of nature—of time—to fix an intuition of "the nucleus of flight":

> The toy
> become the aesthetic archetype
>
> *As if*
> some patient peasant God
> had rubbed and rubbed
> the Alpha and Omega
> of Form
> into a lump of metal

As Brancusi shaped in brass, so Mina Loy in the poems on art shapes and polishes language to achieve exquisite verbal sculptures. To a considerable extent these poems possess the economy and concreteness of the Imagist poem, except that Mina Loy remains too discursive to be an Imagist. Typically, an exotic vocabulary unites with sound to carve dazzling epigrammatic images. **"Lunar Baedeker"** epitomizes the technique. A satire of idealistic escapists, especially the Decadents, the poem creates a decor of Decadence using exotic words and images and lush patterns of sound. (The influence of Laforgue, evident in the irony, imagery, and logopoeia of other poems, is substantiated by this poem's borrowings from Laforgue's "Climat, Faune et Flore de la Lune.") In addition to the excessive opulence of word, image, and sound, the satire de-

rives from the motif of death that is woven into the glittering lunar landscape. Each stanza is a meticulously constructed sound-unified image that is usually centered on a strategically located verb:

> A silver Lucifer
> serves
> cocaine in cornucopia
>
> To some somnambulists
> of adolescent thighs
> draped
> in satirical draperies
>
> Peris in livery
> prepare
> Lethe
> for posthumous parvenues
>
> Delirious Avenues
> lit
> with the chandelier souls
> of infusoria
> from Pharoah's tombstones
>
> lead
> to mercurial doomsdays
> Odious oasis
> in furrowed phosphorous———
>
> The eye-white sky-light
> white-light district
> of lunar lusts
>
> ———Stellectric signs
> "Wing shows on Starway"
> "Zodiac carrousel"
>
> Cyclones
> of ecstatic dust
> and ashes whirl
>
> crusaders
> from hallucinatory citadels
> of shattered glass
> into evacuate craters
>
> A flock of dreams
> browse on Necropolis
>
> From the shores
> of oval oceans
> in the oxidised Orient
>
> Onyx-eyed Odalisques
> and ornithologists
> observe
> the flight
> of Eros obsolete
>
> And "Immortality"
> mildews

in the museums of the moon

"nocturnal cyclops"
"Crystal concubine"

———

Pocked with personification
the fossil virgin of the skies
waxes and wanes

VI

This satire of the dishonest artist who seeks through art to escape the responsibility of vision-in-time provides Mina Loy's critique of absolutes: they are death to the self. Even the legitimate transcendence of time offered by the beautiful forms of exemplary artists like Brancusi are tentative and temporary; they are meaningful orderings of life but not substitutes for it. The **"Aphorisms"** early reject absolutes—"THERE are no excrescences on the absolute, to which man may pin his faith"; and several poems are equally didactic. **"The Black Virginity"** (1918) satirizes religious absolutes, using priestly novitiates who have entombed their souls in the 2000-year-old Christian vision:

Baby Priests
On green sward
Yew-closed
Scuttle to sunbeams
Silk Beaver
Rhythm of redemption
Fluttering of Breviaries

Fluted black silk cloaks
Hung square from shoulders
Truncated juvenility
Uniform segregation
Union in severity
Modulation
Intimidation

Pride of misapprehended preparation
Ebony statues training for immobility
Anaemic jawed
Wise saw to one another

Similarly, **"Human Cylinders"** (1917) instructs us that to accept an absolute is to "Destroy the Universe/With a solution."

The importance for Mina Loy of this tension between doubt and certainty, between time and space, is reflected in the fact that she makes an awareness of it a formative experience for her fictional surrogate, the child Ova in *Anglo-Mongrels and the Rose*. Having been unjustly punished by her parents, Ova flees to the garden where she has an "illumination":

The high—skies
have come gently upon her
and all their
steadfast light is shining out of her

She is conscious
not through her body    but through space

Because Ova is human her bliss is short-lived: a chicken egg breaks on the garden path, "a horrible / aborted contour / a yellow murder / in a viscous pool." Ova does not comprehend the broken egg, but she feels a "contraction" to the "uneasiness" of the world's processes. Henceforth, Ova and the mature narrator of Mina Loy's poems involve themselves in the Sisyphean struggle for clear vision. The long Ova poem depicts the growth of the child's consciousness, and the poems of 1931-1962 are devoted to the need for clear vision and to the flight of most individuals from this responsibility.

But while these later poems remain loyal to the original metaphysics—an assertion of human responsibility amidst cosmic chaos, they lack the structural innovations that distinguish the early poetry. Among the first to respond to the "crisis in consciousness" of the new century, Mina Loy lacked the discipline, or desire, to carry her innovations much beyond their culmination in *Lunar Baedeker*. Later poems do not break through to new means of conveying the I-eye's relation to existence; in fact, they abandon some early achievements. Rather than depicting the process of vision, the poem is usually a vignette of failed vision. Imagery is less vibrant, although sometimes possessed of a delicate loveliness. Diction is less vigorous, and sound interplays tend to be hackneyed. Abstraction and image separate without the vigorous alternation of earlier poems. Forceful satire gives way to a more reflective and discursive tone, the cynical wordly wisdom of an observer remarking the persistence of humanity's evasions.

However, the lessened vigor of the late poems should not obscure Mina Loy's significant contributions to the modernist sources that feed the present of American poetry. While her proto-existentialist theme parallels one strain of contemporary literature, her early experiments in depicting consciousness and her insistence on poetic honesty are probably her more important contributions to the poetic present. The connection she forges in her imagery between (female) sexuality and consciousness looks to Surrealist, confessional, and feminist poetry. Her use of collage, fragmentation, and free verse anticipates the composition by field proposed in Charles Olson's "Projective Verse"; and although she usually deifies the self, **"The Costa San Giorgio"** anticipates the Projectivist depiction of a world in flux with the I become part of the world's thingness. Most important, her use of language fulfills the poet's responsibility, as she defines it, to make the world a radioactive particle that penetrates and shatters the clichés of experience.

**Carolyn Burke  (essay date 1985)**

SOURCE: "The New Poetry and the New Woman: Mina Loy," in *Coming to Light: American Women Poets in the Twentieth Century*, edited by Diane Wood Middlebrook and Marilyn Yalom, The University of Michigan Press, 1985, pp. 37-57.

[*In the following excerpt, Burke places Loy's poetry, in particular her "Three Moments in Paris" and* Love Songs, *within the American feminist movement.*]

Soon after her arrival in New York for the first time (1916), Mina Loy was contacted by a newspaper reporter who wanted to interview a representative "new woman." The reporter began her article by asking, "Who is . . . this 'modern woman' that people are always talking about," then reflected, "Some people think that women are the cause of modernism, whatever that is." Loy's name had been suggested because of her radically modern poetry: already published in such avant-garde magazines as *Camera Work, Rogue,* and *The Trend,* she was known as the author of the most widely quoted poems in *Others, A Magazine of the New Verse,* the scandalous new rival to Harriet Monroe's *Poetry.* For the average reader, Loy's writing was of a piece with the baffling artistic projects of Alfred Steiglitz, Gertrude Stein, and the Italian Futurists, and her subject matter with the public soul-searching and lawbreaking of the new woman. The reporter remembered her poems as "the kind that people kept around for months and dug out of corners to read to each other." Not only were they written in an original kind of free verse, but they also presented a new female perspective. The reporter came away from the interview with the impression that this new woman believed it out-of-date to write or live according to the rules and thought it necessary "to fling yourself at life" in order to discover new forms of self-expression. Loy's art was modernist (whatever that was) because she threw the rule book out the window and wrote direct from life.

The interview is of interest because it makes explicit the connection between the politics of the new woman and the principles of the new poetry. Although Mina Loy's name is no longer familiar, in 1916 it was synonymous with the most daring poetic experimentation. Until very recently, however, historians of American poetry have tended to ignore the importance of *Others,* unless it is to observe that Marianne Moore, Wallace Stevens, and William Carlos Williams got their start in its pages. Yet Harriet Monroe thought it wise to stake out her own territory by observing that *Others* stood for "a rather more youthful effervescence than I am quite ready to endorse publicly [*Horriet Monroe and the Poetry Rennaissance,* 1977], and Ezra Pound described the new magazine as "a harum scarum vers libre American product, . . . useful because it keeps 'Arriet from relapsing back into the Nineties" [*The Letters of Ezra Pound,* 1950]. Among anthologists, William S. Braithewaite categorized *Others* poets as disciples of Pound in order to distinguish them from his more sedate former associates, the Imagists, while the influential Louis Untermeyer dismissed them as "crank insurgents," offering Loy's *Love Songs* as Exhibit A in what reads like an attempt to have the whole group indicted for poetic rebellion [*American Poetry since 1900,* 1923]. Although Loy's radicalism was obviously disconcerting in her own time, contemporary readers are rediscovering her ellipti-

cal, fragmented images of a modern woman's psychosexual experience as the revisionary histories of both modernism and feminism are gradually pieced together.

Although many women continued to publish traditional lyric poetry during the 1910s, poets like Loy, H. D., and Marianne Moore were writing poems that spoke from the brain as well as from the heart. Critical response to these intellectual poets depended upon the individual's opinion of the modern woman as well as personal aesthetics. When Untermeyer called Loy and her contemporaries "cerebralists" and complained of their "eroticism gone to seed," Pound praised them for their obvious intelligence. Opting for a Poundian version of modernism (in *Revolution of the Word: A New Gathering of American Avant-Garde Poetry*), Jerome Rothenberg recently resituated Loy at the center of her peers' attempts to articulate what she called "the crisis in consciousness" (1914). Similarly, David Perkins's characterization of Loy's best poetry [in the *Revolution of the Word,* 1974] as "witty, physical, philosophical, antisentimental and vigorously phrased" places her once again in the context of the New York avant-garde and the *Others* poets. Rothenberg and Perkins both fail, however, to speculate upon the convergence of Modernism and feminism in her (and her generation's) writing. I intend to reconstruct the climate of opinion in the explosive prewar years, first in relation to feminist issues of the period, and next in the context of the free verse controversy, in order to understand the impact of Loy's poems on those readers who kept them around for months and dug them out of corners to read to each other.

I

Mina Loy's chief source of information about the New York avant-garde prior to her arrival was Mabel Dodge, her close friend from the Anglo-American expatriate community in Florence. While Loy remained in Florence until 1916, Dodge had returned to New York in 1912, having, as she said, "done" the Renaissance and wishing to catch the tempo of modern life. Soon Dodge's name was linked with modernism in the arts and radicalism in social and political thought. By 1913, her elegant salon in Greenwich Village brought together "Socialists, Trade-Unionists, Anarchists, Suffragists, Poets, Relations, Lawyers, Murderers, 'Old Friends,' Psychoanalysts, I.W.W.'s, Single Taxers, Birth Controlists, Newspapermen, Artists, Modern-Artists, Clubwomen, Woman's-place-is-in-the-home Women, Clergymen, and just plain men." Dodge wanted to see what would happen when "all sorts of people could meet under one roof and talk together freely on all subjects." At this point, Dodge considered herself one of the "pioneers for the renewed expression of life in art," for whom radicalism in all domains sprang from the same impulse.

Dodge wrote to Loy of her many activities on behalf of the new spirit. She organized publicity for the controversial Armory Show, published a provocative appreciation of Gertrude Stein's prose, and distributed Stein's "Portrait of Mabel Dodge at the Villa Curonia" as if it were a sort of press release. She also worked in support of the new socialist magazine *The Masses* and the reenactment of the Paterson strike, where she began an affair with journalist John Reed. Reed was, however, less certain than Dodge that changes in the means of expression would go hand in hand with changes in forms of social organization. When she waxed enthusiastic over his coverage of the Mexican revolution, he bantered, "Mabel has already decided that the rebels are part of the great world-movement. . . . I think she expects to find General Villa a sort of male Gertrude Stein, or at least a Mexican Steiglitz." But at this point, she was still convinced that the radicals, herself included, were "out in the untried—feeling our way towards the truth of tomorrow."

Still digesting the philosophy of Henri Bergson, which she had read in Florence with Mina Loy, Dodge decided that a sort of cosmic "élan vital" was at work, and that she and her friends were playing their parts in its unfolding. Did not Bergson's visit to New York at the time of the Armory Show confirm her intuitions? She was equally enthusiastic about Loy's quasi-Bergsonian prose poem, "Aphorisms on Futurism," and recommended it to Steiglitz for *Camera Work.* Loy's first published writing, **"Aphorisms,"** reads like a set of prescriptions for psychic liberation.

> TODAY is the crisis in consciousness.
>
> CONSCIOUSNESS cannot spontaneously accept or reject new forms, as offered by creative genius; it is the new form, for however great a period of time it may remain a mere irritant—that moulds consciousness to the necessary amplitude for holding it.
>
> CONSCIOUSNESS has no climax.
>
> LET the Universe flow into your consciousness, there is no limit to its capacity, nothing that it shall not re-create.

Although they would later grow apart, at this point, Dodge included Loy in her world movement for psychic and social emancipation.

Another new woman whom she met in radical circles soon showed Dodge the way to her vocation as a priestess of "It," or a mystical eroticism. Although Margaret Sanger was still involved in the political struggles of the International Workers of the World (IWW) in 1913, she was, in Dodge's view, more important as a prophet of sexual liberation. "It was as if she had been more or less arbitrarily chosen by the powers that be to voice a new gospel of not only sex knowledge in regard to conception, but sex knowledge about copulation and its intrinsic importance." At the same time that she was forming her commitment to birth control, Sanger was also "an ardent propagandist for the joys of the flesh. . . . It was her belief that the attitude towards sex in the past of the race was infantile, archaic, and ignorant." Dodge learned that the body was full of wondrous possibilities for "sex expression," a sacred yet scientific mode of communion. She received Sanger's teaching as if it were the new gospel and Sanger herself a female precursor of D. H. Lawrence.

Although Mabel Dodge showed little interest in birth control, Mina Loy was curious about Sanger's activities. She asked Dodge for the details of Sanger's legal battles and may have been familiar with Sanger's magazine, *The Woman Rebel.* When Sanger began to publish information on contraception and sexual hygiene, another friend in New York commented on the scandal to Loy, "There are those of us over here who won't believe that 'That's' all Love is." Loy in turn observed to Dodge that their friend was having "virginal hysterics. . . . Of course *'Thats'* all nothing and yet *'Thats'* all it is—the *more* is spiritual effervescence." Loy was sympathetic to efforts for greater sexual honesty, which she saw as a prerequisite for psychic and social liberation. Even though Sanger's activities might put "That" in proper perspective, however, activism was not Loy's way: "what I feel now are feminine politics—but in a cosmic way that may not fit in anywhere."

In an effort to define her version of "feminine politics," Loy wrote her own "Feminist Manifesto" and sent a copy to Mabel Dodge. She added, "Do tell me what you are making of Feminism. . . . Have you any idea in what direction the sex must be shoved—psychological I mean." Apparently uninterested in what she called the "bread and butter" issues, the vote and other political solutions to the woman question on the basis of equality, Loy emphasized instead the differences between the sexes. Her manifesto calls for women to "leave off looking to men to find out what you are *not*—seek within yourselves to find out what you are." Convinced that "no scratching on the surface of the rubbish heap of tradition will bring about Reform," she concluded, "the only method is Absolute Demolition." Loy agreed with Sanger, however, that women's ignorance of sexual realities stood in the way of their self-fulfillment: "Nature has endowed the complete woman," Loy wrote, "with a faculty for expressing herself through all her functions—there are no restrictions." Furthermore, like Sanger, she believed that "every woman has a right to maternity," whether married or not. Children should no longer be defined according to the marital status of their parents, who, in turn, should remain free to follow their own paths of personal development. Such freedom would restore the "spontaneous creative quality" long repressed by "the Anglo-Saxon covered up-ness," she wrote to another friend, adding, "all this modern movement—is keeping entirely on the surface—and gets no further psychologically." Loy's manifesto prescribed psychic liberation as the necessary prelude to both artistic and social regeneration. Her conclusion would have been appropriate in the pages of *The Woman Rebel*: "There is nothing impure in sex—except in the mental attitude to it."

Such views were not shared by the American postal authorities, however. Sanger was soon indicted for publishing "a pamphlet of obscene, lewd and lascivious character, containing articles of such vile, obscene, filthy and indecent nature that a description of them would defile the records of the United States District Court." Sanger gathered numerous supporters in New York and abroad, while the newspapers gave her case increasingly abundant publicity. By the time of her trial early in 1916 (when the indictment was dropped), birth control had become the central social issue of the period, dividing pro-family progressives from radicals, who saw the issue in the larger context of the class struggle.

Although Sanger later disavowed her friendship with Emma Goldman, she first learned of birth control methods in Goldman's anarchist circles. The first issue of *The Woman Rebel* carried an article in which Goldman declared that the modern woman "desires fewer and better children, begotten and reared in love and through free choice, not by compulsion, as marriage imposes." Like Mina Loy, Goldman believed that most exponents of women's rights held too narrow a conception of female emancipation. In her view, "independence from external tyrannies" was not enough, for the "internal tyrants . . . —ethical and social conventions" still ruled the hearts and heads of most feminists. Since women's access to information about their sexuality was a prerequisite for dealing with these tyrants, Goldman took up the cause of birth control again soon after Sanger's indictment and served a brief sentence in a New York jail in the winter of 1916. Throughout this period, Greenwich Village feminists (including Henrietta Rodman, Ida Rauh, Floyd Dell, Crystal and Max Eastman, and John Reed) lectured, wrote editorials, and organized protest meetings in support of the cause. This publicity was so effective that by the summer of 1916, large groups of people were voicing their opposition to the classification of birth control literature as obscene, and the police no longer arrested those who distributed it. By the time of Mina Loy's arrival in the autumn of 1916, many were ready to agree that "a woman's body belongs to herself alone."

In this context, it is not surprising that Loy's poems on sexual love and its consequences were read as if they were the statements of the woman rebel. She had dared to write of the "lascivious revelation" of childbirth in **"Parturition"** (1914) and of free love in her infamous *Love Songs* (1915). Like Dodge, Loy called for freedom of "sex expression"; like Sanger, she wrote of female sexuality as the woman's own prerogative; and like Goldman, she questioned the sway of the inner tyrants that caused even emancipated women to accept the conventions of romantic love and patriarchal marriage. Her writing confirmed the popular view that free verse probably led to free love. Before turning to a reading of her poetry in this context, I would like to illustrate the important literary issue of 1915–16—the vers libre controversy—by discussing critical responses to *Others* in relation to the question of the new woman.

## II

Depending upon one's point of view during the prewar years, new developments in the arts were seen either as "conditions of vital growth" or as immoral and decadent. Progressives and conservatives agreed that "much of the expression of those explosive days was the same, whether in art, literature, labor expansion, or sexual experience." The *New York Times*'s art critic considered the modernists "cousins to the anarchists in politics," and as if in confir-

mation of his view, Emma Goldman called *The Little Review* "a note of rebellion in creative endeavor" [in *A Heritage of Her Own*, 1979]. At Mabel Dodge's salon, friends discussed the connections among what their hostess called "the possibles: the possible revolution, the possible New Art, the possible new relation between men and women." The general sense that political, artistic, and sexual experimentation spring from the same impulse lay behind the vers libre controversy. Free verse was denounced by the press and taken up by the public as yet another symptom of the impulse of the day.

William Carlos Williams remembered that the summer of 1915 saw "a strange quickening of artistic life" with the publication of Alfred Kreymborg's *Others*. Kreymborg and Walter Conrad Arensberg, his financial backer, intended to publish more experimental verse than could be found in *Poetry*, which, they felt, "admitted too many compromises" [*Egoist*, 1916]. The first issue featured Orrick Johns's "Olives" and Mina Loy's **Love Songs**, both of which caused something of an uproar in the press. One could be amused by Johns's "Now I know / I have been eating apple-pie for breakfast/ In the New England/ Of your sexuality," but few readers knew what to make of Loy's peculiar love songs:

      Spawn   of   Fantasies
      Silting  the  appraisable
      Pig Cupid   his rosy snout
      Rooting erotic garbage
      "Once upon a time"
      Pulls a weed      white and star-topped
      Among wild oats      sewn in mucous-membrane

      I would an  eye  in a bengal light
      Eternity in a sky-rocket
      Constellations in an ocean
      Whose rivers run no fresher
      Than a trickle of saliva

Although Kreymborg noted approvingly at the time, "Women are finding their most intimate expression through free verse," he recalled later that many readers "shuddered at Mina Loy's subject matter and derided her elimination of punctuation marks and the audacious spacing of her lines" [*The Troubadour, An Autobiography,* 1925]. Perhaps these readers sensed that Loy's antisentimental stance and formal experimentation subverted both literary decorum and received cultural norms.

For supporters of *Others,* however, "it seemed that the weight of centuries was about to be lifted. . . . America had at last found a democratic means of expression." Not the least of their excitement was caused by the realization that the magazine had created "wild enthusiasm among free-verse writers, slightly less enthusiasm among Sunday Magazine Section reporters, and really quite a stir in the country at large." Detractors soon objected that the unrestrained expression of individualistic emotions produced only crank insurgency, "a perfumed and purposeless revolt." A letter in the *New York Sun* denounced poetry like Loy's as "erotic and erratic." Soon the newspapers, eager to promote a controversy, were ridiculing the new poetry: it was skinny, impoverished, preoccupied with sex and empty of thought, save the thought of its own emancipation. Parodies of the poems in the first issues of *Others* appeared throughout the autumn and winter of 1915.

Don Marquis devoted a number of columns in the *New York Evening Sun* to gentle mockery of the new fashion. "A Key to the New Verse" declares:

> Not only do we understand the New Verse, but we are the only person who does understand all of it. When Alfred Kreymborg writes one of his mushroom poems, no one but Mina Loy knows exactly what it means, and she never tells anyone but Sadakichi Hartmann. Sadakichi Hartmann is sometimes comprehended by Ezra Pound, but never by himself.

After linking free verse to the activities of Gertrude Stein and Alfred Steiglitz, Don Marquis shared his key with the reader: such poems need only to be rearranged into traditional meters to be understood, for "in every *vers libre* poem of the wilder sort, a poem of the academic, old fashioned conventional type . . . is hidden" [*New York Evening Sun,* July 24, 1915]. Those who were bewildered by the new poetry could, at last, breathe a sigh of relief.

But it would have been impossible to find reassuringly old-fashioned poems hidden in Loy's **Love Songs**. Readers accustomed to the conventions of romantic poetry were totally unprepared for her frank exploration of sexual love from a woman's perspective. Even the ostensibly modern Amy Lowell was so shocked by Loy's poems that she threatened to withdraw her support from *Others*. In the meantime, readers alarmed by the image of Eros as **"Pig Cupid"** denounced Loy's verse as "swill poetry" or, more succinctly, "Hoggerel." What Kreymborg described as her "utter nonchalance in revealing the secrets of sex," others saw as lewd and lascivious writing, in the same class as the pamphlets of Margaret Sanger or the lectures of Emma Goldman. Worse still, Loy did not imitate their straightforward prose but wrote "in a madly elliptical style scornful of the regulation grammar, syntax and punctuation." Kreymborg concluded [in his *Our Singing Strength: An Outline of American Poetry, 1620-1930,* 1929], "To reduce eroticism to the sty was an outrage, and to do so without verbs, sentence structure, punctuation, even more offensive. . . . Had a man written these poems, the town might have viewed them with comparative comfort." His point is well taken: Loy's frankness and experimentalism were all the more unacceptable because she was a woman.

When Loy decided to write about the predicament of the modern woman as avant-garde artist, she chose as her model an acquaintance from the expatriate colony in Florence, Isadora Duncan. Possibly she recalled her fellow radicals' high esteem for the dancer's art: when Duncan appeared in New York in 1915, she seemed to represent "woman's emancipation, sexual liberation, artistic freedom and political protest" all in one. Floyd Dell asserted in *The Masses,* "It is not enough to throw God from his pedestal, to dream of superman and the cooperative com-

monwealth: one must have seen Isadora Duncan to die happily." Mabel Dodge thought Duncan "the most truly living being I had ever seen," the embodiment of the élan vital. Her unfettered movement, which seemed to the modernists to express creativity in its pure state, soon suggested a metaphor for the "free feet" of free verse. The image of bare feet, emancipated from the stiff shoes and outworn choreographies of classical ballet, recurred whenever reporters began to write of the revolution in poetry.

When, for example, the *New York Tribune* sent a reporter to the artists' colony in New Jersey where Kreymborg printed *Others,* the story appeared under the provocative headline, "Free Footed Verse is Danced in Ridgefield, N.J." Although the reporter concentrated on the more bohemian aspects of life in Ridgefield, she discussed free verse as a new cultural phenomenon. After comparing the poems in *Others* to the paintings in the Armory Show, she explained that *vers libre* demands an intellectual effort of the reader: "in the new poetry there is a riddle, something to be solved. It is like . . . a Gertrude Stein rhapsody or a Shoenberg [*sic*] symphony." To illustrate the point she quoted not Loy's infamous lines about Pig Cupid, but the puzzling conclusion of her first love song:

> I must live in my lantern
> Trimming subliminal flicker
> Virginal   to the bellows
> Of experience
>               Coloured glass

After a glance at Loy's significant blank spaces, the rest of the article [published on July 25, 1915] details the poets' attempts to live in a style appropriate to their verse. The reporter did, however, observe that a "notable feature of the movement is the early prominence taken in it by women." The connection was implicit: like Isadora Duncan, the emancipated female poet would naturally express herself in "free-footed verse."

Of course there were those who doubted the wisdom of allowing either poets or women to dance as they desired, and parodists continued to mock the Isadora-like abandon affected by free verse writers. The author of "Lines to the Free Feet of Free Verse" (the *New York Tribune*) noted that once poetry was emancipated, it lost its grace and hobbled clumsily. He concluded with an argument familiar from other controversies: the feet that once pattered prettily were being deprived of their natural rhythm by the new freedom; everyone knew that they were happiest when dancing to the familiar choreographies. Soon Don Marquis was explaining that modernism in verse was merely a return to a language freed of Victorian excrescences. Under the guidance of Harriet Monroe, "a rather conservatively inclined chaperone of the radical brood," vers librists would return to their senses [*The Business of Poetry,* 1915]. Although a few *Others* poets did return to meter and to romantic love poetry, Loy had irrevocably abandoned the chaperonage of the late Victorian sensibility. Her unsentimental depiction of sexuality—"No love or the other thing / Only the impact of lighted bodies / Knocking sparks off each other / In chaos"—suggested a modernist disillusionment with both the myth and metrics of romance. Her poetry appeared, furthermore, to corroborate a contemporary's observation: "When the world began to change, the restlessness of women was the main cause."

### III

As an English woman familiar with contemporary artistic movements on the Continent, Mina Loy brought an original perspective to the American scene. Although she too was in revolt against Victorian social and aesthetic standards, unlike the American modernists she did not have to do combat with a genteel poetic tradition. In fact, Loy had the peculiar advantage of knowing very little of literary convention. She began to write poetry around 1912 in a kind of historical vacuum, as if there were no models of poetic speech for or by women. In the 1910s, Emily Dickinson was known by very few readers, and she was, in any case, too idiosyncratic to serve as a model. Although Elizabeth Barrett Browning wrote suggestively of "woman's claim," she was at once too learned and too much of her own generation (that of Loy's grandparents). Similarly, although Loy read Christina Rossetti's poetry with great interest, its eroticized piety and self-deprivation provided her with a negative model only. Loy was, however, reading Gertrude Stein's experimental rhythmic prose as early as 1911, when they met in Florence. In contrast to nineteenth-century poetry, Stein's writing revealed a strikingly contemporary concern with psychological analysis and the effects of consciousness upon perception. For Loy, Stein's battle with grammatical, rhetorical, and narrative convention actually "stretches the muscles of the intellect." Loy's writing was undoubtedly stimulated by Stein's innovations, which may have pointed the way toward her own development of a highly visual form of free verse. In any case, she praised Stein as a type of female genius:

> Curie
> of the laboratory
> of vocabulary
>     she crushed
> the tonnage of consciousness
> congealed to phrases
>     to extract
> a radium of the word

In a similar spirit, the new poetry might also liberate language from the weight of tradition.

Both Stein and Loy could approach writing in this typically modernist spirit, in part because of their familiarity with contemporary art movements, especially cubism. Loy actually studied painting in London, Munich, and Paris during the 1890s and 1900s and achieved recognition for her work at the Salon d'Automne before moving to Florence in 1907. Like her contemporary Guillaume Apollinaire, whose *Soirées de Paris* column on modern art she probably read, Loy was a "poète fondé en peinture." But even if she knew Apollinaire's *Alcools* and *Zone,* she was already composing her own visually oriented, "simultanist" poetry when Apollinaire began to publish his spatially ordered *calligrammes.* (Indeed, Loy's 1913 **"Costa San Giorgio"** may have been one of the first English poems to employ simultaneity and juxtaposition as formal principles.) Furthermore, by 1913, Loy was involved with the Italian Futurists. Marinetti and his followers claimed in their provocative manifestos that they intended to break down the barriers between art and life, as well as the barriers separating one art from another. To Loy, their reorientation of artistic attention to the urban flow and bustle seemed to throw open the windows of both poetry and art to modern life. In spite of her later criticisms of Futurist misogyny, Loy wrote that Marinetti nevertheless deserved credit for waking her up: his theories of dynamism suggested a way out of the passivity of *fin de siècle* aestheticism. Although her own poetry was never as extreme in its syntactic and grammatical emancipation as Marinetti's *parole in libertà,* like Stein he acted as a catalyst in her own personal and artistic awakening.

It is not surprising that American modernists welcomed a poet with this impressive background in European avant-gardisms. They saw Loy as a sophisticated expatriate at home with the latest developments of modern art, as well as an ally in their battle with the genteel tradition. What they did not see was that Loy, like themselves, had her own "subconscious archives," the layers of interwoven images and memories that had to be exhumed and analyzed while she was finding her voice as a modern woman. As an art student in London during the nineties, Loy attempted to distance herself from her middle-class family and the waning ideals of Victorian womanhood by adopting the aestheticism and antibourgeois stance of the Decadents. Later, when she began to write poetry from a woman's perspective, the imagery of the nineties rose to the surface of her consciousness: women were either sensitive Ophelias or dangerous Salomés, or these two extremes might seem to be combined in such complex female presences as the imaginary Mona Lisa or the real Sarah Bernhardt. Although few women spent their lives in languorous poses outside the art studio, such images retained their hold on her imagination. Several groups of poems from the early 1910s constitute a kind of aesthetic and personal self-analysis, in which images of gender and sexuality are dredged up from the subconscious, carefully examined, and, finally, demystified.

In **"Three Moments in Paris,"** a sequence of three related poems, Loy paints portraits of women whose dependence upon a traditional view of the sexes shapes their self-awareness. This *fin de siècle* Paris is, of course, as much a state of mind or an artistic vision (suggesting Toulouse-Lautrec or the early Picasso) as it is an actual city, and Loy's perceptive female speakers all acknowledge the limitations of its aesthetic ambience. In the first poem, **"One O'Clock at Night,"** the speaker is bemused by her response to a male companion's virile posturings. While this man tries to argue his interlocutor into accepting his theories of "Plastic Velocity," the woman falls asleep at his side:

> Indifferent to cerebral gymnastics
> Or regarding them as the self-indulgent play of

children
Or the thunder of alien gods

When she wakes to catch the thread of the argument, however, and assumes "a personal mental attitude," she ceases to be "a mere woman / The animal woman / Understanding nothing of man." Asleep, she had been "indifferent," or unaware of the structure of sexual difference, but now she awakens to an understanding of its effects. She could criticize their "pugilis(m) of the intellect" if she chose to abandon the security of living "indifferent." The ironic conclusion—"Let us go home she is tired and wants to go to bed."—appears to give the last word to the men while permitting their arguments to be undercut by the physical presence of the "mere woman."

The second poem evokes an imaginary **"Café du Néant,"** whose airless atmosphere and melancholy poses suggest a Symbolist painting. In this world of artifice, seeing is not necessarily believing, when "eyes that are full of love" become "eyes that are full of kohl." Pairs of lovers are grouped in a composition that focuses on the central figure, again a woman defined by her male companion's power over her. Acquiescing in her role as dependent, however, the women "As usual / Is smiling as bravely / As it is given to her to be brave." Although her languid acceptance of self-abasement marks her as a Symbolist ideal, the speaker's heavy irony makes it clear that there are, nevertheless, alternatives to this morbid romantic script. The final line—"Yet there are cabs outside the door."—implies that this woman (and women in general) must distance herself from the aestheticism of the Café du Néant before she can see what it has made of her. Perception and consciousness are intimately related. One whose eyes are blurred with love may lack the ability to perceive her own complicity in the process of being reduced to an image.

In **"Magasins du Louvre,"** the final poem of the sequence, another watchful speaker studies the images of femininity available for purchase at the Paris department store. Boxes of dolls are on display: their vacant glass eyes see nothing, like the "virgin eyes" they represent, "Beckoning / Smiling / In a profound silence." The speaker also studies the other women in the shop, who, like the dolls, are available objects of the female sex. Both the salesgirl harassed by the shop-walker and the two *cocottes* in provocative costumes are defined by their subordination to masculine powers. When the *cocottes* catch sight of the dolls, their knowing eyes are held by the vacant gazes of these icons of innocence: "their eyes relax / And now averted / Seek each other's surreptitiously." The speaker, meanwhile, watches this double exchange of glances, then lowers her own eyes in shame, "Having surprised a gesture that is ultimately intimate." She regrets the loss of innocence that her lucidity entails. The complex relationship between the "eye" and the "I," between perception and (self) consciousness, sets her apart from these women even in her attempt to understand their situation. The sequence of poems as a whole rethinks masculinity and femininity as perceptual and conceptual categories, or as habits of the eye and the mind.

Loy's *Love Songs*, published in the same year as **"Three Moments in Paris"** but more innovative both thematically and formally, constitute a passionately clinical analysis of a failed love affair from a woman's perspective. The first person speaker's focus has moved in them from the exterior world to an inner space or psychological reality. There, the conventions of romantic love may be reenacted rhythmically and imagistically to evoke both their power and their status as illusory fictions. The entire sequence of thirty-four poems deserves attention in the context of modernist experimentation by her contemporaries T. S. Eliot, Williams, Pound, and Marianne Moore. A kind of verse collage, Loy's fragmented form itself participates in the thematic examination of the gaps between art and life, but her shards of "colored glass" (the final image of the first poem) constitute a kaleidoscope of psychic and sensual impressions rather than a stable mosaic. The experience they embody is the disintegration of an ideal, or, more positively, the process of "deconstruction" that Gertrude Stein described to Loy as the aim and technique of modernist art. In the deeply ironic last line of the sequence, "Love———the preeminent litterateur," romantic love is "deconstructed" and dismissed as a self-enclosed system of creative illusions.

What shocked her contemporaries, however, was Loy's treatment of gender and sexuality in these so-called love songs. She alluded to the "suspect places" of sexual intercourse with such frankness that no one could miss her meaning. As if references to female sexuality in a series of water images (e.g., "an ocean / Whose rivers run no fresher / Than a trickle of saliva") were not sufficiently scandalous, poem II evokes both the male sexual principle and the apparently insurmountable differences between the sexes.

> The skin-sack
> In which a wanton duality
> Packed
> All the completions of my infructuous impulses
> Something the shape of a man
> To the casual vulgarity of the merely observant
> More of a clock-work mechanism
> Running down against time
> To which I am not paced
>     My finger-tips are numb from fretting your hair
> A God's door-mat
>         On the threshold of your mind

Her sexual timing is incompatible with the lover's "clock-work mechanism," yet their intercourse could fulfill both her physical desires and her spiritual aspirations, were they similarly "paced." Given the biological and emotional scripts for heterosexual romance, communion between the sexes seems doomed to frustration.

Loy's *Love Songs* may be compared with similarly antiromantic poetry by her better-known contemporaries. Despite Harriet Monroe's misgivings, *Poetry* published T. S. Eliot's "The Love Song of J. Alfred Prufrock" in 1915, and his "Portrait of a Lady" appeared in *Others* soon after the publication of Loy's *Love Songs*. Although both poets share an ironic approach to the demise of romantic love and traditional love poetry, Eliot's tepid tales are emotionally evasive and self-protective, while Loy's verses spring from passionate self-revelation. Where Eliot writes of what did not happen, of "carefully caught regrets," Loy plunges the reader into the suspect places of sexuality and generates surrealistic images of spiritual transgression. Unlike Eliot, the generally shy William Carlos Williams nevertheless "frankly and fearlessly undressed himself down to the ground" in his poetry during this period, when he was close to Mina Loy. Her daring subject matter and technique probably stimulated him to attempt more contemporary subjects and greater stylistic innovation. His "Romance Moderne" (published in *Others* in 1919) evokes "the unseen power of words" in the shaping of desire and juxtaposes romantic declarations of love with violently antisentimental references to its physical apparatus: "God how I love you!—or, as I say, / a plunge into the ditch. The end. I sit / examining my red handful. . . ." Loy's love poems exhibit a lingering fondness for "something the shape of a man," compared with Williams's deliberately crude demystification of the phallic principle. Although hardly a feminist, Williams was intensely interested in the woman's perspective, especially when he wanted to appropriate it for his own uses. Like Loy, he learned to make sexual difference a poetic subject, and he undoubtedly agreed with her that women's experience differed radically from men's.

If sexual intercourse simultaneously heightened and frustrated the female subject's sense of herself, the experience of childbirth provided another, perhaps even more extreme occasion for the definition of female difference. Fifty years before such a subject became acceptable, Loy traced what she called the "spatial contours" of childbirth in **"Parturition"** (1914). Her originality and daring should not be underestimated. Few women discussed childbirth in public, except in the pages of *The Woman Rebel,* and none wrote poems about it. Whitman's ecstatic celebration of physical being may have provided Loy with a distant precedent, but she had to revise his song of the (male) self to suit a female subject. While his Biblically cadenced free verse sang the body electric by casting aside poetic conventions as if they were tight-fitting garments, Loy, by contrast, worked out a compact, compressed free verse line that could simulate the rhythmic contractions and expansions of labor. At the same time, she approached the blank page as if it were a canvas: a visual medium in which to recreate the inner spaces of the female body.

> I am the centre
> Of a circle of pain
> Exceeding its boundaries in every direction
>
> The business of the bland sun
> Has no affair with me
> In my congested cosmos of agony
> From which there is no escape
> On infinitely prolonged nerve-vibrations
> Or in contraction
> To the pin-point nucleus of being

> Locate an irritation      without
> It is      within
>            within
> It is without

The white space around the words joins in the play of speech and silence. Gradually the spaces between words and phrases become the inner space from which the birth/ poem is issuing, and the area around the poem becomes a version of the larger cosmos in which the birth is taking place. By abandoning punctuation, Loy creates a kinesthetic sensation of opening from within: childbirth becomes the process of "knowing / All about / Unfolding," an "elusion of the circumscribed." The female subject is released from dependence upon the male into an unbounded knowledge of female libido, a "lascivious revelation." In giving birth to the child, she also gives birth to the poem and to herself in an almost mystical acknowledgment of female creative potential. **"Parturition"** answered the prescription for psychic liberation in Loy's **"Feminist Manifesto"**: "leave off looking to men to find out what you are *not*—seek within yourselves to find out what you are."

But even in the radical literary and political circles of pre–World War I Greenwich Village, few readers were prepared for poetry like Loy's. Probably it demanded too much of them, intellectually, aesthetically, and emotionally, because, as Kreymborg pointed out, it was spoken in a woman's voice. Even sympathetic literary men generally saw women poets first "as humans," then "as lovers," and finally "as artists," as in the appropriate chapter title from Kreymborg's *Our Singing Strength,* a history of American Poetry. (In it, Kreymborg observes that women are better craftsmen because they set themselves "a narrower range.") John Reed, for example, lent his support to feminist causes but responded with ambivalence to the new woman's writing. His mixed feelings are apparent in the mock drama that he composed for Mabel Dodge, which included a part for Mina Loy: the play is of interest because it concerns God's efforts to create the ideal woman from a pattern book containing all the familiar stereotypes. Only the formula for a femme fatale has been slightly modernized: "Figure that will stand a Greenwich Village uniform; thorough comprehension of Matisse; more than a touch of languor; a dash of economic independence; dark hair, dark eyes, dark past." Reed might have been describing Mina Loy or someone like her, except that this femme fatale would have painted her own canvases or written her own poems. Even the most committed radicals were often intimidated by the modern woman's conjunction of independence, intellect, and what Loy called her "personal mental attitude."

Always on the alert for what was "new," however, Ezra Pound was not so much intimidated as surprised by the presence of intellect in poetry by women. After championing H. D. as the exemplary "imagiste," he asserted in 1918 that Mina Loy and Marianne Moore both wrote "logopoeia," a kind of poetry which he described as "a dance of the intelligence among words and ideas." While welcoming them to the club of intellectual poets (including Pope, Laforgue, and T. S. Eliot), he warned that their poetry would disconcert readers unaccustomed to using their wits. Moreover, he found in their poetry "the utterance of clever people in despair." Although Pound went out of his way to avoid speaking of Moore and Loy as women, his criticism of their poetry is typically astigmatic, however, because it ignores both the striking differences between them and the fact that being a woman mattered to each of them as much as being intelligent. Pound concluded that both poets were "interesting and readable," but that their poems "would drive numerous not wholly unintelligent readers into a fury of rage-out-of-puzzlement."

Although Moore's relation to feminism is ambiguous, her poetry is well known today, while Loy's still puzzles numerous not unintelligen readers. In a gloss on Pound's comments, Kenneth Rexroth offered a provocative explanation for Loy's neglect that made a clear connection between the politics of the new woman and the poetics of the new poetry:

> Erotic poetry is usually lyric. Hers is elegiac and satirical. . . . If it is bitter and dissatisfied, it is at least passionate. She commonly transforms the characteristic envy of little girls into the superciliousness of an unhappy suffragette. People don't like poetry like that.

Arguing for Loy's importance in the history of American modernism, he observed, "her material is self evidently more important than Miss Moore's. . . . She writes of . . . the presence or absence of sexual satisfaction; and of the results: recreation, marriage, procreation; sterility, disorder, disaster, death." It was no wonder that adventurous readers kept Loy's poems around for months and more conservative readers were shocked. Perhaps as the reporter suspected in their 1917 interview, women like Mina Loy were indeed a "cause of modernism, whatever that is."

**Lisa Ress** (essay date 1993)

SOURCE: "From Futurism to Feminism: The Poetry of Mina Loy," in *Gender, Culture, and the Arts: Women, the Arts, and Society,* edited by Ronald Dotterer and Susan Bowers, Associated University Presses, 1993, pp. 115-27.

[*In the following essay, Ress determines the primary influences on Loy's poetry and discusses how she appropriated collage and other Futurist literary techniques to give her own work "violence and energy."* ]

In a 1921 letter Ezra Pound, that entrepreneur of modernism, asked Marianne Moore, "P.S. Entre nooz, is there anyone in America besides you, Bill [W. C. Williams], and Mina Loy who can write anything of interest in verse?" [*The Last Lunar Baedeker,* edited by Roger L. Conover, 1982]. Both he and Eliot considered Loy "the most radical of the radical set whose work began appearing" in avant-garde literary magazines of the period. In 1926 Yvor Winters, writing in *The Dial,* asked, "Who will poets of

my generation look back to as the ablest master of the Experimental Generation?" His answer: William Carlos Williams and Mina Loy. Winters repeated this assessment in a 1930 article, and again in 1967. Writing to Loy in 1931, Kay Boyle characterized her work as "glorious, sharp, miraculous," and went on to "wonder if you know how terribly much your writing matters to us." In 1944 Kenneth Rexroth, comparing Loy's work with that of Marianne Moore, found "her material . . . self-evidently more important . . . and treated with great earnestness . . ." and the poetry "tough, forthright, very witty, atypical, antirhetorical, devoid of chi-chi." As Denise Levertov noted in 1958, Loy's poems contain "something of great value that had been needed and mislaid. . . . The value is—indivisibly—technical and moral."

That Loy's poems have been "mislaid," there can be no doubt. Despite the esteem of illustrious colleagues and Winters's conviction that she was one of "the two living poets who have the most . . . to offer the younger generation of American writers," her book, *Lunar Baedeker* (published by Contact Press in 1923), was not reprinted until 1958, her individual poems were rarely anthologized, and Loy's place in the development of modernism and feminism nearly forgotten. Thus that influence on future generations Winters predicted for her work was severely curtailed. Loy has indeed been so thoroughly mislaid, that nothing of hers was included in the recent massive and otherwise excellent *Norton Anthology of Literature by Women.* Nevertheless, a poet whose work was so radical in form deserves consideration in the history of modernism. And a poet whose work was, and in my opinion remains, so radical in content deserves a place in the history of feminist thought.

If Loy—and how many others?—could disappear so completely from the history of this century's creative endeavor, then the history we know remains subtly falsified, not yet true, not yet our own. Loy's career, and the circumstances of her life as she struggled to live both as an artist and as a woman, can teach us much about our own circumstances as writers, painters, scholars, and women. "Those who do not remember their history," as Santayana remarked, and as has been intoned so often since, "are doomed to repeat it." I would like, therefore, to contribute to the project of making his/story also her/story, our story, a glimpse of some of the influences that shaped Loy as a person and as an artist, and how these contributed both to the nature of her work and to its having been mislaid.

Born Mina Gertrude Lowy in 1882 to a fairly prosperous London family, Loy's mother was English, her father the son of immigrant Hungarian Jews. Her unpublished autobiographical writings show her to have been a thoughtful, willful, and highly imaginative child, a rebel from the outset, embroiled early in a war against her parents' restrictive and Victorian attitudes. The ideas she expressed as a child elicited consternation; "the insane logic of my infant mind," she recalled, ". . . made chaos of their cosmos." Gifted both as a writer and a painter, young Mina spent much of her time reading, drawing, and writing, pursuits her very conventional parents found alarming in a girl. At the birth of a sister, Loy's mother, "already convinced [Mina's] unladylike urge toward occupation constituted a social menace . . . would lock the nursery door against [her] 'coming near her' . . . ," shutting Mina out to peer at the door "from the limitless hell of a mis-handled childhood. . . ." Home was unbearable, outside contact severely restricted. She and her sisters were for-bidden "to . . . set foot outside the house," and Loy recalls her father pacing before his daughters, "dropping in his heat, watch words from his restricted ideation to be our safeguard through the dangerous day." Girls who went about freely "became 'bad women.'" With characteristic brio, Loy answered back, thoroughly scandalizing her fa-ther. On the contrary, she said, it was "Our present outra-geous social system [that made] the poor wretched pros-titute inevitable." Loy fought not only these restrictions, but also those imposed on her intellectual and artistic development, waging an intense campaign to convince her parents to send her and her sisters to a more progressive school. As she noted,

> As sometimes neglected illness will put an end to itself, at intervals the sheer desperation of my being alive abated, clearing the way for spells of apparently rootless courage; when they occurred I became indiscriminately militant on behalf of myself or my sisters who seemed quite contented as they were.

At home, Loy's reading was censored, bookcases locked against her, and her room frequently searched by her mother, who destroyed the drawings and writings she found there. It is not surprising that Mina Lowy began early on to plan her escape from her family, from Lon-don, and from the way of life she knew there.

But how was she to achieve her freedom? Two ways pre-sented themselves: the first traditional (marriage), and the second radically unconventional (art). After protracted struggle, Mina Lowy persuaded her parents to allow her to study art, and in 1900 she left London for Munich and then Paris, putting England and the nineteenth century firmly behind her. In 1903 she changed her name from Lowy to Loy, "forging her own passport to Bohemia," and by 1906 had achieved recognition and critical acclaim as an avant-garde painter, exhibiting work in the Salon d'Automn show at which Fauvism was born. Her friend-ships with Leo and Gertrude Stein date from this period, and it was through them that she met Apollinaire, Picasso, and Rousseau. Having chosen art as an escape route, Loy clinched her independence from her family by marriage to British painter Stephan Haweis in 1903.

In 1906 she and Haweis left Paris for Florence, where she spent the next ten years. There she became involved with a number of painters and writers, among them Futurists F. T. Marinetti and Giovanni Papini. Although she disavowed the movement less than a year after aligning herself with it, Futurism was to have a profound influence on her work. While she continued her activities as a painter and a de-signer, from 1914 to 1925 Loy produced a quantity of important poems, and it was her contact with Futurism and Futurists that encouraged this new creative focus.

Marinetti "is one of the most satisfying personalities I ever came in contact with," she wrote to her friend Mabel Luhan in 1914, and, later in the year, "I am indebted to [him] for twenty years added to my life from mere contact with his exuberant vitality."

The Futurist call, first articulated by Marinetti in his 1909 "Futurist Manifesto," "was for revolution—for a complete break with the past." "Obsess[ed] with the machine, with speed, dynamism and energy" it was the first movement "to have grasped . . . that our age, the age of big industry, of the large proletarian city and of intense and tumultuous life, . . . was in need of new forms of art, philosophy, behaviour and language." Marinetti exhorted poets "to sing the love of danger, the habit of energy and fearlessness." "Essential elements of . . . poetry" were to be "courage, audacity, and revolt." Literature of the past, he declared, had exalted "a pensive immobility, ecstasy and sleep. We intend to exalt aggressive action, a feverish insomnia, the racer's stride, the mortal leap, the punch and the slap," and he proposed a new aesthetic: "the beauty of speed." "A roaring car that seems to ride on grapeshot is more beautiful than the Victory of Samothrace."

"Love of danger," "energy and fearlessness," "courage, audacity and revolt," "aggressive action": these attributes had been Loy's from birth. Small wonder that she was attracted to Futurism. However, like so many women who have bitten eagerly into the alluring apple of revolution, Loy was immediately to discover the worm inside. The ninth tenet of Marinetti's 1909 Manifesto reads: "We will glorify war—the world's only hygiene—militarism, patriotism, the destructive gesture of freedom-bringers, beautiful ideas worth dying for, and scorn of woman." It was not, however, Futurism's sexism but its militarism, culminating in its support of Fascism, with which Loy initially took issue. "I am in the throes of conversion to Futurism," she wrote Mabel Luhan in February, 1914: ". . . But I shall never convince myself—there is no hope in any system that 'combats le mal avec le mal'—(can't help it) and that is really Marinetti's philosophy." Sex-ism was, however, an equally alienating factor. As did many women in revolutionary movements before and after her, Loy discovered that the new freedoms advocated either were not applied at all or would be applied differ-ently to women. Marinetti's formulation makes it clear that "woman" is other; that the category signified by woman is not included in the category designated "Fu-turist." As a woman, therefore, Loy must remain outside the circle. "I am so interested," she wrote Luhan in October, 1914, "to find I am a sort of pseudo Futurist."

Although rejected by and herself rejecting much of the Futurist social program, Loy nevertheless made selective use of Futurist literary techniques. Aware that the use of new, and newly rapid, means of communication and trans-portation in the early part of the century was altering the experience of space and time, giving those experiencing the change "the sense of being everywhere at once," Fu-turism promoted techniques of simultaneity, "spatial and temporal distortions" that "collapse[d] present and past," to reflect contemporary experience truthfully. "The simultaneousness of states of mind in the work of art," said Boccioni in his 1912 manifesto, "that is the intoxicating aim of our art." "In this context," notes Marjorie Perloff, "it is not surprising that simultaneity became a central theme as well as a formal and structured principle." Collage, which, by juxtaposing disparate elements, collapsed conventional contexts of meaning, was first suggested by Apollinaire and first executed by Futurist painter Severini in 1912. "The single most revolutionary formal innovation in artistic representation to occur in our century;" in collage, "each cited element breaks the continuity or linearity of the discourse and leads necessarily to a double reading; that of the fragment in relation to its text of origin; that of the same fragment as incorporated into a new whole."

---

**A buccaneer of diction, Loy appropriated for herself and for all women the vocabulary until then used only by classically educated men.**

*—Lisa Ress*

---

Futurism called for other radical changes in written language as well. "How," Marinetti asked, "can traditional discourse with its complete sentences . . . convey this new language of telephones, phonographs, airplanes, the cinema, the great newspaper . . . ? The 'old syntax' must be abolished," likewise, the adverb, which in Marinetti's words, "preserves the tedious unity of tone within a phrase," and "the foolish pauses made by commas and periods" which "suppress the continuity of a living style." Loy's syntax and punctuation were clearly affected by Marinetti's ideas. Her poems use typically Futurist orthographic elements, a mix of upper and lower case words and phrases, for example, and minimal punctuation, as well as concise, often brutally vivid images, disjunction, and variable line length and placement. Both Loy's style and subject matter demonstrate her concurrence with Marinetti's declaration that "Poetry demands violence and energy . . . a kind of 'fever' in which the life of the modern city merges with the exotic Other . . . the off-beat, the erotic, the populist." To be truly in accord with modern life, poetry, he said, must include the free and open expression of sexual energy and appetite.

In **"Love Songs to Joannes"** (written between 1915 and 1917, preceding Eliot's *The Waste Land* by at least four years) Loy was among the first, along with Apollinaire and Cendrars, to adapt collage to literature. Characteristically undetered by her status as "pseudo Futurist," and heedless of what the phrase, "scorn of woman," implied—namely that Futurist ideas were for men, not for women, to use—Loy took seriously this call for free and open expression of sexual energy and appetite. Her marriage's disintegration during these years and her emotional and sexual involvement with Futurists—two months with Marinetti, two years with Giovanni Papini—powerfully

influenced her poetry's subject matter, and as powerfully provided the impetus for its expression. **"Love Songs to Joannes,"** Loy's exploration of her relationship with Papini, is radical not only in form but in its attack on romantic love and in its depiction of sexuality. She was made to suffer, however, for her Futurist-female frankness.

In 1915, when poems 1 through 4 were published in New York's avant-garde *Others,* as Alfred Kreymbourg, its editor, recalled:

> Detractors shuddered at . . . Loy's subject matter and derided her elimination of punctuation marks and the audacious spacing of her lines. . . . such sophistry, clinical frankness, sardonic conclusions, wedded to a madly elliptical style scornful of the regulation grammar, syntax and punctuation horrified our gentry and drove our critics into furious despair. The nudity of emotion and thought . . . roused the worst disturbance, and the utter nonchalance in revealing the secrets of sex was denounced as nothing less than lewd. . . . Had a man written these poems, the town might have viewed them with comparative comfort.

Her husband, from whom she had separated, warned her she was "losing [her] good name writing as [she] did," as she told Carl Van Vechten, and threatened her custody of their children. Even Van Vechten, a longtime friend acting as her literary agent, drew back, asking that she write "something without a sexual undercurrent." Loy replied, "I know nothing but life—and that is generally reducible to sex!" "What I feel now are feminist politics." [According to Virginia M. Kouidis, in *Mina Loy: American Modernist Poet,* 1980]. The writing that resulted, however, was both Futurist and feminist, "distinctively feminine in its exploration of female oppression," as well as "Futurist inspired in its aggressive assertion of selfhood and in its structural experiment."

Never one to submit meekly to limitation or rejection, and stimulated by her quarrel with the Futurists, in 1914 Loy wrote her own **"Feminist Manifesto,"** although, unlike Marinetti's, it remained unpublished until 1982. "The Feminist Movement as instituted at present," she declared, "is INADEQUATE. . . . The lies of centuries have got to be discarded. . . .":

> There is no half-measure, no scratching on the surface of the rubbish heap of tradition. Nothing short of Absolute Demolition will bring about reform. Cease to place your confidence in economic legislation, vice-crusades and uniform education. . . . Professional and commercial careers are opening up for you. *Is that all you want?*

"Leave off looking to men to find out what you are *not,*" she exhorted. "Seek within yourselves to find out what you are. As conditions are at present constituted you have the choice between Parasitism, Prostitution, or Negation." "As protection against the manmade bogey of virtue," Loy advocated "*unconditional* surgical *destruction of virginity*" finally, and what a familiar ring this has in this boom-time of books on co-dependency: "Woman must destroy in herself the desire to be loved. . . . Honor, grief, sentimentality, pride, and consequent jealousy must be detached from sex."

Long concerned with women's issues, between 1914 and 1923 Loy wrote a number of poems analyzing and often satirizing the situation of women in and outside marriage. **"Virgins Plus Curtains Minus Dots"** gives voice to young women confined inside houses who can only "'Bore curtains with eyes'" (1:4):

> Somebody who was never a virgin
> Has bolted the door
> Put curtains at our windows
> See the men pass
> They          are going somewhere
>
> (1:43–47)

These "virgins," however, are not going anywhere, for they have no dowries.

> We have been taught
> Love is a god
> White          with soft wings
>               Nobody shouts
> VIRGINS FOR SALE
> Yet where are our coins
> for buying a purchaser
>
> (1:29–35)

In **"The Effectual Marriage"** Loy tackled the inequalities between men and women. The poem relates "the insipid narrative" of Gina and Miovanni, a couple who "In the evening [look] out of their two windows":

> Miovanni out of his library window
> Gina from the kitchen window
> From among his pots and pans
> Where he so kindly kept her
> Where she so wisely busied herself
>
> (1:11–16)

The assignment of rooms, the choice of pronouns and adverbs, tell the story behind the story. As a wife, Gina is all that a man might require:

> Miovanni     Gina called
> Would it be fitting for you to tell
> The time for supper
> Pooh     said Miovanni     I am
> Outside time and space
> Patience     said Gina     is an attribute
> And she learned at any hour to offer
> The dish     appropriately delectable
>
> (1:42–49)

From her place in the kitchen Gina "suppose[s] that peeping" into the library "While Miovanni thought alone in the dark,"

>               she might see
> A round light     shining     where his mind was
> She never opened the door

> Fearing that this might blind her
> Or even
> That she should see     Nothing at all
>
> (1:69–75)

While **"Virgins Plus Curtains"** allowed Loy to examine and satirize social restrictions placed on young women without dowries, and **"The Effectual Marriage"** allowed her a cool ironic look at marriage, a number of other poems provided her with a vehicle in which to present her case against the Futurists. In **"Giovanni Franchi,"** for example, she creates a devastating portrait of Giovanni Papini, Marinetti's chief propagandist, and her "friendly enemy," as she called him. "His adolescence was all there was of him / Whatever was left was rather awkward" (11:11–12). In a scene that trenchantly foresees Fascist rallies to come, we see Franchi (Papini) "scuttl[ing] winsomely" to distribute pro-war leaflets.

> His acolytian sincerity
> The sensitive down among the freckles
> Fell in with the patriotic souls of     flags
> Red white and green flags fillipping piazzas
> When the "National Idea" arrived on the Milan
>     Express
>
> (1:48–52)

Futurist misogyny is also targeted. Franchi, the acolyte devoted to Bapini (Marinetti), listens

> at the elder's lips
> That taught him of earthquakes and
> of women— . . . And what he told
> Giovanni Franchi
> About these pernicious persons
> was so extremely good for him
> It entirely spoilt his first love-affair
> To such an extent     it never came off
>
> (1:100–13)

Loy's **"Parturition,"** written in 1914, to my knowledge the first poem to depict the process of childbirth from the laboring woman's point of view, "is significant," too, as Virginia Kouidis notes, "because it details an area of femaleness rarely thought suitable for literature." Although Roger Conover, editor of *The Last Lunar Baedeker,* the recent, and indispensable collection of Loy's work, placed the poem among Loy's satires, the poem's satiric component is minor. Remarkable in its powerful enactment of labor, the poem combines the physical process with the consciousness of the woman giving birth, uniting her physical circumstances and sensations with her "spiritual and intellectual life." "In giving birth to the child, she gives birth to herself."

> I am the centre
> Of a circle of pain
> Exceeding its boundaries in every direction
> The business of the bland sun
> Has no affair with me
> In my congested cosmos of agony
> From which there is no escape

On infinitely prolonged nerve-vibrations
Or in contraction
To the pin-point nucleus of being

(1:1–10)

Although the narrator is gripped by biological forces, she is far from being eclipsed by them; her language—crisp, spare, latinate—signals a mind that stands beyond the activities of her body, a self both highly conscious and strong.

Pain is no stronger than the resisting force
Pain calls up in me
The struggle is equal

(1:24–26)

Momentarily, the narrator becomes aware of "a fashionable portrait-painter / running up-stairs to a woman's apartment" (Loy's husband was himself a painter), but the implied betrayal is secondary to the powerful process of which she is a part.

At the back of the thoughts to which I permit
    crystallization
The conception Brute
Why?
    The irresponsibility of the male
Leaves woman her superior Inferiority
He is running up-stairs
I am climbing a distorted mountain of agony

(1:35–41)

"Incidentally with the exhaustion of control," she reaches "the summit and gradually subside[s] into anticipation of / Repose / Which never comes / For another mountain is growing up / Which goaded by the unavoidable / I must traverse / Traversing myself" (1:42–50) While her body struggles, her sense of self remains detached, intact, even enhanced.

. . . the gurgling of a crucified wild beast
Is no part of myself
There is a climax in sensibility
When plain surpassing itself
Becomes exotic
And the ego succeeds in unifying the positive and
                                    negative
    poles of sensation
Uniting the opposing and resisting forces
in lascivious revelation

(1:55–63)

Between contractions, the narrator reflects on her situation in the light of biological theory: "I should have been emptied of life / Giving life / For consciousness in crises races / Through the subliminal deposits of evolutionary processes" (1:69–72). But the "stir of incipient life" does not reduce but expand the narrator's sense of self, "Precipitating into [her], / The contents of the universe" (1:96–98). "I am absorbed / Into / The was-is-ever-shall-be / Of cosmic reproductivity" (1:104–07). Through conscious participation in giving birth, she has learned much, even, as the line break suggests, become "knowing" itself:

Death
Life
I am knowing
All about
    Unfolding

(1:120–24)

And Loy ends the poem with a tribute to all women who participate in bringing human life into the world: "Each woman-of-the-people / Tiptoeing the red pile of the carpet / Doing hushed service / Each woman-of-the-people / Wearing a halo / A ludicrous little halo / Of which she is sublimely unaware" (1:125–31).

"Leave off looking to men to find out what you are *not*. Seek within yourself to find out what you *are*," Loy had declared in her **Feminist Manifesto**. She took her own exhortation seriously: refusing to accept others' definitions, she created a body of work that defined herself and her situation as woman and artist on her own terms. Acutely aware of the connection between her own situation and that of all women, of the connection between the personal and the political, Loy chose daily life, viewed from her independent and feminist perspective, as her subject. In doing so, she pioneered in the exploration of the female self. "Intensely cerebral," as Yvor Winters noted,

her work ordinarily presents [a] broken, unemotional, and witty observation of undeniable facts. . . . she has written seven or eight of the most brilliant and unshakably solid satirical poems of our time, and at least two non-satirical pieces that possess for me a beauty that is unspeakably moving and profound.

"The essence of her style is its directness in which she is exceeded by no one," as William Carlos Williams remarked. It was to describe her poetry that Pound coined the word *logopoeia,* "poetry . . akin to nothing but language, . . . a dance of the intelligence among words and ideas and modifications of ideas and characters." Loy deploys language brilliant and subtle, graphic and cerebral, which by its cerebrality and wit, by its linguistic play, refutes strictures patriarchal culture forces on women, to be voiceless vessels, obedient domestics, adoring groupies marginal to male activities. A buccaneer of diction, Loy appropriated for herself and for all women the vocabulary until then used only by classically educated men.

"The major reasons for her obscurity today," as Roger Conover observes in his introduction to Loy's collected works, "are self-imposed, the result of her own intransigence and intrepidness." Yet it is precisely these qualities that give her work its value. In her writings, she spoke as no woman in history had hitherto dared to speak, and of things long considered taboo. "Significantly," Virginia Kouidis remarks, "the gradual recovery of [Loy's] poetry began with the emergence of the post-modern poets of the 1950's and '60's." And, citing Jerome Rothenberg, she notes that

like Rexroth he praises her vigorous defense and practice of artistic freedom and deplores her submergence by the reactionary modernism of mid-century. He situates her among the first, "circa 1914," to awaken to the "revolution in consciousness" and subsequently to explore "the relationship between consciousness, language and poetic structure: what is seen, said and made." Rothenberg joins the few . . . who have discovered in Mina Loy's oeuvre . . . a body of poetry important to an understanding of the modernist vortex. Her poetry aligns itself with that of Stevens-Pound-Williams to form a "counter-poetics" that by generating postmodern poetry is emerging as the most vital force in 20th-century American poetry [*Boundary* 27, No. 3, 1980].

---

## FURTHER READING

### Criticism

Arnold, Elizabeth. "Mina Loy and the Futurists." *Sagetrieb* 8, Nos. 1 & 2 (Spring-Fall 1989): 83-117.
　Determines the extent to which Loy both utilizes and rejects Futurist approaches to language.

Burke, Carolyn. "Mina Loy's 'Love Songs' and the Limits of Imagism." *San Jose Studies* XIII, No. 3 (Fall 1987): 37-46.
　Compares Loy's Futurist-inspired *Love Songs* with the Imagist and Vorticist techniques of Ezra Pound.

DuPlessis, Rachel Blau. "'Seismic Orgasm': Sexual Intercourse, Gender Narratives, and Lyric Ideology in Mina Loy." In *Studies in Historical Change*, edited by Ralph Cohen, pp. 264-91. Charlottesville: University Press of Virginia, 1992.
　Analyzes aspects of Loy's *Love Songs*, contending that she "produced a work whose depiction of sexuality, if not unique, is a provocation to the study of the social codes of the lyric and some historical meanings of the representation of sex."

Kenner, Hugh. "To Be the Brancusi of Poetry." *The New York Times Book Review* (16 May 1982): 7, 30.
　Favorable review of *The Last Lunar Baedeker*.

Kouidis, Virginia. *Mina Loy: American Modernist Poet.* Baton Rouge: Louisiana State University Press, 1980, 148 p.
　Provides a comprehensive overview of Loy's career, in its feminist, modernist, and poetic contexts.

Morse, Samuel French. "The Rediscovery of Mina Loy and the Avant Garde." *Wisconsin Studies in Contemporary Literature* 2, No. 2 (Spring-Summer 1961): 12-19.
　Traces the anthologization of Loy's work in light of her vacillating critical reputation.

Schaum, Melita. "'Moon-flowers out of Muck': Mina Loy and the Female Autobiographical Epic." *Massachusetts Studies in English* 10, No. 4 (Fall 1986): 254-76.
　Maintains that Loy's *Anglo-Mongrels and the Rose* "stands less as a work 'ahead of its time' than as a poetic response very much *in* its time, as a conscious revolution against tendencies and directions beginning to dominate the literary-cultural milieu of the 1920s."

Tuma, Keith. "Anglo-Mongrels and the Rose." *Sagetrieb* II, Nos. 1 & 2 (Spring-Fall 1992): 207-25.
　Examines the satiric, didactic, and lyrical qualities of Loy's autobiographical poem.

# Mary Wortley Montagu
## 1689–1762

(Full name Lady Mary Pierrepont Wortley Montagu; also Montague) English epistler, poet, essayist, and playwright.

## INTRODUCTION

Known simply as Lady Mary to her contemporaries, Montagu is appreciated primarily for her witty, candid letters, which span the years 1708 to 1762 and address diverse correspondents and themes. A controversial figure of her time, she perhaps enhanced her reputation with the publication of satirical attacks of Alexander Pope and Jonathan Swift. Although much of her verse was written extempore, Montagu used a full range of poetic forms, including Ovidian and Horatian epistles, mock eclogues, ballads, and songs. Isobel Grundy remarked that "[Montagu's] poems demonstrate the continuing vitality of the Augustan tradition within which she wrote," but they are "none the less distinctively her own."

### Biographical Information

Montagu was the daughter of Evelyn Pierrepont, the fifth earl and first duke of Kingston. As a child she devised a rigorous academic program for herself, which included writing poetry and learning to speak Latin. In 1712 she eloped with Edward Wortley Montagu. By 1715 they were circulating among prominent social and literary circles in London, where she befriended poets John Gay and Alexander Pope. She accompanied her husband when he was named ambassador to Constantinople in 1716; her subsequent correspondence with London friends became the basis for her famous "Turkish Embassy Letters." Montagu returned to London in 1718 and for the next two decades presided over high society, which celebrated her sparkling wit and flamboyant behavior. In 1722 she anonymously published an essay arguing for the practice of smallpox inoculation in England, after observing the procedure performed successfully abroad. Around 1722 she also engaged Pope in a bitter, public quarrel that began for unknown reasons and culminated in her *Verses Address'd to the Imitator of the First Satire of the Second Book of Horace* (1733), which further incensed Pope. In 1736 she met and fell in love with Francesco Algarotti, a young Italian count. She wrote an anonymous feminist periodical, *The Nonsense of Common Sense* (1937-1938), before she left her husband and England in 1739. For over twenty years Montagu lived abroad mainly in Italy, and wrote many more letters, mostly to her daughter, Lady Bute. Shortly after Montagu returned to England in 1762, she died of cancer.

### Major Works

As a female aristocrat, Montagu abhorred the notion of writing for print and circulated her poems primarily in manuscript. A few were published during her lifetime, usually without her knowledge. For instance, Montagu, in collaboration with Gay and Pope wrote a series of eclogues which satirizes the manners and immorality of the court of George I; three of them were stolen and published anonymously in 1716 by the notorious Edmund Curll as *Court Poems*. The original grouping was later issued as *Six Town Eclogues. With Some Other Poems* (1747). Yet, Montagu may have intended to print her verse attacks on Pope and Swift. Enraged over Pope's repeated lampoons of her in his poems, Montagu wrote *Verses Address'd to the Imitator of the First Satire of the Second Book of Horace*, assisted by another of Pope's foes, Lord Hervey. The *Verses* is considered the best satire of Pope written at that time, mockingly equating Pope's offensive satire to his hunchbacked body. *The Dean's Provocation for Writing the Lady's Dressing-Room* (1734) expresses Montagu's disapproval of the "excremental vision" in Swift's poem, "The Lady's Dressing Room" (1732); her poem accuses Swift of being impotent and stingy. Among surviving manuscript poems, several treat the wretched conditions of women enduring miserable marriages, divorces, and attempted rapes, but some are contemplative musings about love, politics, and personal opinions. A hastily edited collection of some of her poems appeared in 1748 to her chagrin, and *The Poetical Works of the Right Honourable Lady M—y W—y M—e* was printed posthumously in 1768.

## Critical Reception

Montagu's literary reputation rests chiefly on her erudite but entertaining correspondence, particularly the "Turkish Embassy Letters," although her contemporaries also "took her verse very seriously," according to Grundy. Such arbiters of literary taste as Pope, Lord Hervey, Horace Walpole, and Voltaire numbered themselves among admirers of her poetry. In the nineteenth century critics generally received Montagu's letters better than her other writings, especially her poetry, which most rejected as unpoetic. Twentieth-century scholarship has scrutinized her canon for feminist impulses and orientalist elements, yet again with slight attention given her verse. Montagu is considered a minor poet, but several critics have described her poetry as competent if not brilliant. Grundy suggested that "today Lady Mary's poems need no apology," adding that the range of her poetic forms is "remarkable." As Carol Barash recently noted, "Montagu remains the one eighteenth-century woman poet of whom there is both a standard edition and a critical biography."

## PRINCIPAL WORKS

### Poetry

*Court Poems*  1716
*An Elegy to a Young Lady, In the manner of Ovid . . . With an answer. By a Lady, author of the Verses to the Imitator of Horace* [with James Hammond]  1733
*Verses Address'd to the Imitator of the First Satire of the Second Book of Horace* [with John, Lord Hervey]  1733
*The Dean's Provocation for Writing the Lady's Dressing-Room*  1734
*\*Six Town Eclogues. With Some Other Poems*  1747
*The Poetical Works of the Right Honourable Lady My—W—y M—e*  1768

†*Essays and Poems* and *Simplicity, A Comedy*  1977

### Other Major Works

"A Plain Account of the Inoculating of the Small Pox by a Turkey Merchant" (essay)  1722; published in newspaper *The Flying-Post; or, Post-Master*
*Letters of the Right Honourable Lady M—y W—y M—e: Written, during her Travels in Europe, Asia and Africa, to Persons of Distinction, Men of Letters, &c. in*

*different Parts of Europe.*  3 vols. (letters)  1763
††*The Nonsense of Common-Sense*  (essays)  1947
†††*The Complete Letters of Lady Mary Wortley Montagu.* 3 vols. (letters)  1965-67

\*This work includes the earlier *Court Poems.*

††This work contains the play *Simplicity*, an adaptation in English of Pierre Carlet de Chamblain de Marivaux's *Le jeu de l'amour et du hasard* (1730).

‡This work was published as a periodical in nine numbers from 16 December 1737 to 14 March 1738.

††† This work is also known as "Turkish Embassy Letters."

---

## CRITICISM

### Isobel Grundy  (essay date 1975)

SOURCE: An introduction in *Essays and Poems and Simplicity, A Comedy,* edited by Robert Halsband and Isobel Grundy, Oxford at the Clarendon Press, 1977, pp. 171-75.

[*The following excerpt appears as the introduction to a collection of Montagu's work titled* Essays and Poems and Simplicity, A Comedy. *Grundy, one of the editors of the collection, discusses the construction of Montagu's poetry canon and specifically the selections that she made for this volume.*]

Throughout her life Lady Mary liked to refer to herself as a poet, often with a touch of irony or self-deprecation. At fifteen or so she confessed to the folly of having 'trespass'd wickedly in Rhime', her confession taking the form of an eight-line poem. At sixty-nine she described herself as 'haunted . . . by the Dæmon of Poesie'.

Her contemporaries took her verse seriously. John Sheffield, Duke of Buckingham, referred to her fame in a 'sessions of the poets' piece. Many of the voices raised to honour her are suspect—seekers for her patronage or protesters against Pope's satire. Admirers who carry more weight included the young Pope himself, who longed to read her 'Sonnets'; Lord Hervey, who got her verses by heart; Horace Walpole, who found them as first 'too womanish' but later 'excessively good'; the distinguished foreigners Antonio Conti, who translated them into Italian, and Voltaire and Algarotti, who quoted them; and perhaps most surprising of all, Lord Auchinleck, father of James Boswell. Late in this chorus of praise, resisting the new definitions of poetry to which he had himself contributed, came Byron, demanding of the fourth stanza of **'The Lover'**, 'Is not her "Champaigne and Chicken" worth a forest or two? Is it not poetry?' [*Letters and Journals,* 1898-1901]. The nineteenth century in general (Wordsworth, Leigh Hunt, Walter Bagehot) thought it was not. George Saintsbury ruled out poetry, the true diamond, when he wrote that her 'verse flashes with the very best paste in Dodsley' [*The Peace of the Augustans,* 1916].

Yet today Lady Mary's poems need no apology. She herself would not have claimed diamond quality for them, though she did claim to have inscribed eleven lines on a window pane with a diamond. This rather unlikely verve and facility, this small scale, was what she aimed at in poetry. She had the habit of dashing off verse extempore. Her poems demonstrate the continuing vitality of the Augustan tradition within which she wrote, its power to shape the voice and even the thinking of a minor talent. The tradition supplied her not only with forms but with satirical or moral stances based on inheritance from or reaction against the past. She had the gift of successfully embodying her idiosyncratic opinions and attitudes in a verse style heavily influenced by her contemporaries and immediate predecessors, especially Dryden and the Pope of the 1717 *Works*.

Packed with allusion, echoes, parody, her verse is none the less distinctively her own. Its range is remarkable: Ovidian and Horatian epistles, mock-eclogue, mock-epic, songs and ballads, description, meditation, and translation. Despite her reference to the daemon of poesie, most of her poems owe their existence to the provocation of some outside stimulus, some love-affair, political issue, or debating point to be made.

As a woman and an aristocrat, Lady Mary frequently expressed horror at the idea of writing for print. Yet she may well have connived at or even arranged for the publication of her verse attacks on Pope and Swift. Perhaps for reasons of prudence, she copied neither of these printed poems into the album, now Harrowby MS. 256, which bore her claim, 'all the verses and Prose in this Book were wrote by me, without the assistance of one Line from any other. Mary Wortley Montagu.' This volume contains most of her more successful poems, but with some notable omissions. Others she kept in rough draft, in separate copies, or not at all. Individual poems strayed into print in her lifetime, beginning with the three eclogues stolen and printed anonymously by Curll in 1716 [the critic identifies these in a footnote: *"Court Poems*: **'Monday', 'Thursday',** and **'Friday'**]. The first collection was published by Horace Walpole in 1747, with her initials on the title-page. He and Joseph Spence had both read her poems, probably in what is now H MS. 256, in Italy; Spence had many of them copied into a volume which he corrected himself. The number of pieces in print as hers was enlarged by the *London Magazine* and by Dodsley's *Collection*, 1748. Dodsley's second edition, published later that year, transferred Lady Mary's poems from volume three to volume one; later editions added a few more poems. Issac Reed gathered most of what was available from these sources in a volume of **Poetical Works,** 1768; James Dallaway enlarged the canon in the last volume of his edition of Lady Mary's *Works*, 1803. Despite her family's permission to use her papers he reproduced existing inaccurate printed texts, and when printing from MS. adapted freely. Later editors of her works added only a few poems and corrected none. Nor did they explain the grounds on which they accepted or rejected attributions to her.

[*Essays and Poems and* Simplicity, *A Comedy*] is as far as possible and within certain definable limits complete. She wrote other poems of which no copies survive, as comments by her contemporaries indicate. She also adapted other people's work. [This collection includes] such poems as **'A Satyr',** modelled on Boileau but substantially an original piece, while omitting some in which Lady Mary made only the most minimal alterations to her source. These include poems previously printed among her works, like **'The Bride in the Country'** (which she adapted from another satirical ballad to apply to the marriage of her niece), **'A Character'** (adapted from verse by Robert Wolseley and William Wharton), and **'To the Same'** ('Thô old in ill, the Traitor sure shall find', which she condensed from Creech's translation of Juvenal). An imitation of Dorset's famous ballad, beginning 'To all you ladies now at Bath' and entitled 'Farewell to Bath', appeared in the *Gentleman's Magazine* in 1731 as by 'Lady M. Montagu', and has been anthologized as Lady Mary's. I have omitted it since even if the ascription is accurate, Lady Mary's name was extremely unlikely to be formulated this way except on the Continent. The designation fits at least two other ladies, daughters of Charles Montagu, Earl of Halifax, and the 2nd Duke of Montagu.

I have omitted the poems from Lady Mary's two juvenile albums, composed at the age of fourteen or a little older. These are interesting as late re-workings of various seventeenth-century conventions, but have too little intrinsic merit and too great length to justify inclusion. I have omitted fragments and insignificant separate couplets, except those already printed. Passages of verse available among her *Complete Letters* (mainly epistles to Hervey and fragments to Algarotti) are likewise not included here. I have, however, reprinted her poetic rendering **'Turkish Verses',** and her epitaph on the lovers struck by lightning, which readers may expect to find among her poems.

The problem of attribution is a tricky one. I have printed, with brief comment, poems in which other writers besides Lady Mary shared, like the **'Friday'** eclogue, *Dunciad* imitations, and the *Verses to the Imitator of Horace*. There can be little doubt about the poems from H MS. 256, and these are all included here. A few poems in another album (H MS. 255) are marked with her monogram MWM; yet two of these come under the category of adaptations made by the substitution of only a word here and there. Of these one seemed worth inclusion, the other not. The same volume yields a few unmarked poems which seem to be by Lady Mary.

She transcribed many poems without giving any author's name, and she also saved copies made by other people. Some of these poems may be by her, but without further evidence I have supposed that they are not. Sometimes heavy correction in her hand supplies evidence of authorship. I have accepted some but not all of the attributions of those with fairly close knowledge of her: Horace Walpole, Sir James Caldwell, and Lady Oxford and her daughter the Duchess of Portland. This volume therefore contains only poems which are almost certainly by Lady Mary, without the many which *may* be by her, or which have been wrongly attributed to her.

## Isobel Grundy  (essay date 1977)

SOURCE: *"Verses Address'd to the Imitator of Horace:
A Skirmish between Pope and Some Persons of Rank and
Fortune,"* in *Studies in Bibliography,* Vol. 30, 1977, pp.
96-119.

[*In the following excerpt, Grundy discusses the events
surrounding the publication of* Verses, *compares various
claims to authorship of the poem, and concludes that it
was probably a cooperative effort for Montagu and her
close friend Lord Hervey.*]

Pope's imitations of Horace take as grist to their mill the
attacks of those writers rash enough to oppose him. Mr. J.
V. Guerinot, cataloguing their attempts, considers only
one 'a worthy adversary' to Pope, which caught something of his 'own satiric brilliance'. That one, the *Verses
Address'd to the Imitator of the First Satire of the Second Book of Horace,* 1733, has been briefly discussed
not only by Guerinot but also by Professor Robert Halsband in his lives of its confederate authors, Lord Hervey
and Lady Mary Wortley Montagu. Much, however, remains to be told. . . . This article will give a short account
of Lady Mary's previous attacks on Pope, of her denial of
any connection with the *Verses* and Hervey's silence about
them; it will then . . . analyse the evidence we have about
authorship from contemporary and later opinion and from
examination of the *Verses* themselves, and show the part
which they later played in shaping some of Pope's own
most brilliant attacking lines.

Pope published his *First Satire of the Second Book of
Horace, Imitated,* on 15 Feb. 1733. He devoted some
attention (lines 81-84) to his former friend Lady Mary,
who had already crossed pens with him:

> Slander or Poyson, dread from *Delia*'s Rage,
> Hard Words or Hanging, if your Judge be *Page.*
> From furious *Sappho* scarce a milder Fate,
> P-x'd by her Love, or libell'd by her Hate.

Lord Hervey, who was politically opposed to Pope's
friends, but had offered no show of hostility in print, received only a glance of disparagement (lines 5-6):

> The Lines are weak, another's pleas'd to say,
> Lord *Fanny* spins a thousand such a Day.

There was, however, a common element in the two attacks, in that each aimed at the victim's activities as a
writer. Lady Mary tried non-literary means to ensure
Pope's future silence, first through Lord Peterborough
and then through Sir Robert Walpole. Her first attempt
met with humiliating failure; while the second was still
under discussion she must have turned back to the idea
of verse retaliation.

Despite its rashness and its liability to the charge from
Pope of 'fulfilling the veracity of my prophecy', this idea
was not new to Lady Mary. After Pope's thrust in the
*Dunciad,* 1728 (ii. 127-128):

> (Whence hapless Monsieur much complains at Paris
> Of wrongs from Duchesses and Lady Mary's),

she had begun work on a mock-epic counterblast. Its action takes place before Queen Anne's death: Dullness,
aided by Prophanation, Obscænity and in an early version
Cloacina, has settled (anachronistically) in a certain grotto
beneath a muddy road: she plots to reverse the national
educative process being carried out by Addison; each
goddess supports her own candidate for leadership of their
forces, and the young Pope is chosen as commander in
preference to Swift, Gay, and Arbuthnot [as found in *Essays
and Poems and Simplicity, a Comedy,* edited by R. Halsband and I. Grundy, 1977, revised ed. 1993]. Lady Mary
had re-worked the material of Pope's masterpiece and
copied his tone with some skill. She had also enlisted her
cousin Henry Fielding, at that time a very young writer
looking for patronage, as ally. He too, loyally rather than
personally indignant, had attacked the *Dunciad* in *Dunciad*-like fragments, related to hers, the draft of which he
left with her. The subject-matter of this epic story makes
it hard to see how either Fielding's or Lady Mary's part
could ever have been finished, let alone printed. Any satisfaction which she derived from this counter-attack must
have remained private.

After Pope's new offensive of 1733, Fielding composed
his sympathetic 'Epistle to Mr Lyttleton, occasioned by
two Lines in Mr Pope's Paraphrase on the first Satire of
the 2d Book of Horace', either at Lady Mary's prompting
or on his own initiative. Again he left the manuscript with
her; again it remained unpublished. Meanwhile, however,
as contemporary opinions about the *Verses to the Imitator* suggest, Lady Mary struck up the same sort of alliance
with Lord Hervey that she had previously had with Fielding. No record of this remains among her letters: the following account comes from other sources than herself.
She denied any part in the *Verses,* saying two years later
that they had been written '(without my knowledge) by a
Gentleman of great merit, whom I very much esteem, who
[Pope] will never guess, and who, if he did know, he durst
not attack'. This denial, sent to Arbuthnot the day after
the publication of Pope's *Epistle* to him, can be ignored
as a desperate defensive stroke in her mortal combat with
Pope. If it is incredible, so are Pope's denials to Peterborough and to Hervey: that he 'never applied that name
[Sappho] to her in any verse of mine, public or private;
and, I firmly believe, not in any letter or conversation.'
Neither of the two enemies could be trusted to speak truth
of the other.

Lady Mary cannot be *proved* a liar. As her biographer
writes, 'no documentary evidence survives to prove [her]
authorship of the *Verses'.* No copy in her hand is now
known, either in the Harrowby Manuscripts Trust with the
bulk of her papers, or elsewhere. Her great-grandson and
editor, Lord Wharncliffe, claimed that the poem was 'contained in the collection of poems verified by Lady Mary's
own hand as written by her'; and this was repeated by a
later editor and a biographer. Yet the surviving album
verified by Lady Mary in this way, Harrowby MS 256,
shows no sign of anything having been removed from it.

Either a copy of the *Verses* was once lodged, though not bound, in the album, and has since vanished; or a whole volume of Lady Mary's manuscripts, also verified by her hand, has similarly disappeared; or Lord Wharncliffe was entirely mistaken.

Hervey also says nothing of the poem in his surviving letters (which do not, however, include those he wrote to Lady Mary); but he is linked with it by documentary evidence, which will be discussed in detail later. He made two sets of corrections, differing slightly from each other: to a scribal copy now in the British Museum and to a printed copy now at Ickworth, Suffolk. He also wrote a manuscript preface *'To the Reader',* assuming rather than claiming authorship, now bound inside the Ickworth copy which he called 'corrected by the Author'; it is the closest we have to an assertion of literary ownership. He refrained from asserting the same thing elsewhere. He mentioned *The First Satire of the Second Book* without annoyance two days after its publication. Early in 1734, *à propos* his *Epistle From a Nobleman to a Doctor of Divinity,* he told Arbuthnot he was sorry 'to enter into a Paper-War' with Pope, apparently not expecting Arbuthnot to reply that he had entered already. In letters he gloried in his severity on Pope, but only the severity of *An Epistle,* which he disclaimed in the press and discussed at length with his correspondents. Where Lady Mary protests too much, Hervey protests less than might be expected. . . .

[The] next possible source for evidence of authorship is contemporary and later critical opinion. The *Verses* seem to have been identified as Lady Mary's from the first, and Hervey's contribution recognized only later. Two of the four early transcripts ascribed them to her [so did contemporary hands in copies of Dodd's first, 5th, and 6th editions (Texas)]. On 8 March, the day of publication, Pope wrote to Fortescue of 'that Lady's having taken her own Satisfaction in an avowed Libell'; this sounds more sincere than his later suggestion that he considered the Dodd title-page ascription, 'By a Lady', to be her deliberate confession of authorship. Two days later Theobald told Warburton that Pope had been 'most handsomely depicted in a severe Poem by Lady Mary W. Mountague'. On [18] March Pope again wrote of the 'Libel' as hers alone; he did not link Hervey's name with hers until 2[0] April. Irish opinion also believed the *Verses* were 'certainly hers'. Voltaire (who never mentioned the *Verses* in his letters to Hervey) seems to have asked for them as Lady Mary's in early May 1733 [Voltaire, *Corr.*, edited by Theodore Besterman, ii, 1969, 333].

Her authorship was again assumed three weeks after publication by whoever was responsible for printing the *Answer* to Hammond's *Elegy* as 'By a LADY, Author of the Verses to the Imitator of HORACE.' (Dodsley's *Collection,* however, reprinting the *Answer* as Hervey's, thereby implied his authorship of the *Verses* too.) Hervey himself kept a copy of the *Elegy* and *Answer* (now bound with his copy of the *Verses* at Ickworth), but he made no mark in it as he did in the other pamphlets collected in this volume as his.

Hostile squadrons gathering against the *Verses* had no doubt whom to attack. *A Proper Reply to a Lady,* 'By a Gentleman' (3 April), began with the question of authorship:

> What Lust of Malice, what salacious Spite
> 'Gainst her *Alcaeus Sappho* moves to write?
> It must be *Sappho,*—Who can chuse but guess
> Whence springs this clam'rous Womanish Address?

This 'Gentleman' not only detected feminine ignorance of razors in lines 25-26, but amply hinted at Lady Mary's identity, mentioning her poetry and the scandal over her deranged sister. Another combatant, the 'Gentlewoman' who printed at her own expense her *Advice to Sappho* (received by Lord Oxford on 12 April [Badminton MSS Fm T/B1/4.4; Bod. M. 3. 19. Art.]), made it clear that her quarry was Lady Mary. An unympathetic commentator in MS agreed. On the other side, the anonymous author of 'In Defence of Lady Mary Wortley' described how 'Ingenious *Wortley* draws her conq'ring Pen.'

By 2[0] April Pope had heard more of the complicated story of 'Lady M—'s or Lord H—'s performance. . . . it was labour'd, corrected, præcommended and postdisapprov'd, so far as to be dis-own'd by themselves, after each had highly cry'd it up for the others'. On the first of May Swift wrote of the authors as 'they', not knowing whether 'the production you mention came from the Lady or the Lord'. In any case he was not impressed:

> I did not imagine that they were at least so bad versifyers, Therefore, facit indignation versum [*sic:* he must have seen a copy of the second Dodd edition], is only to be applyed when the indignation is against general vilany, and never operates when a vilian writes to defend himself. I love to hear them reproach you for dulness; Onely I would be satisfied, since you are so dull, why are they so angry?

Thereafter, opinions continued uncertain or ambiguous— none more so than Pope's own in his *Letter to a Noble Lord,* 30 Nov. 1733. Here he began with a clear statement of Lady Mary's responsibility: 'I wonder yet more, how a lady, of great wit, beauty, and fame for her poetry . . . could be prevailed upon to take a part in that proceeding.' Further on he implied that her denial of authorship, brought to him by Lord Peterborough, had caused him to change his mind about her part in the *Verses*; but this he almost immediately contradicted, in a passage famous for suggestiveness rather than for precision:

> Your Lordship indeed said you had it from a lady, and the lady said it was your Lordship's; some thought the beautiful bye-blow had two fathers, or (if one of them will hardly be allowed a man) two mothers; indeed I think both sexes had a share in it, but which was uppermost, I know not. I pretend not to determine the exact method of this witty fornication.

Pope never again admitted to believing Lady Mary's disclaimer. He continued to couple her with Hervey as authors of unworthy libels against him, either as *'some Per-*

*sons of Rank and Fortune'* or by name. By this time Hervey had struck again in his *Epistle From a Nobleman to a Doctor of Divinity*; Pope did not make it clear whether he was blaming Hervey for that alone, or for a share with Lady Mary in the *Verses.*

More than a year after the *Verses* were published, a third name was added to those of the suspected authors. Lord Oxford wrote on his copy of the first Dodd edition, 'The Authors of this poem are Lady Mary Wortley, Lord Harvey and Mr Windham under Tutor to the Duke of Cumberland and married to my Lady Deloraine'. Since William Windham married Lady Delorain only in April 1734, Oxford's identification was written more than a year after the *Verses* were published—very likely at the same time that he annotated his copy of the 'Fifth Edition', January 1735. Despite this time-lag Windham is a plausible third collaborator. His courtship of Lady Delorain (the 'Delia' Pope linked with 'Sappho') provided ample grounds for reprisals by him. He might be the esteemed gentleman whom Lady Mary considered Pope would not guess or dare to attack—a description by that time entirely unfitted to Hervey, who had just been trounced as Sporus. *A Letter to a Noble Lord* mentions 'your friend *W—m*'. Professor Maynard Mack has argued that Windham's marriage and his part in the *Verses* are glanced at in the *Epistle to Arbuthnot:*

> To please a *Mistress,* One aspers'd his life;
> He lash'd him not, but let her be his *Wife.*

Lord Oxford may have been simply following this same reasoning, or he may have had positive information. His wife was a close friend of Lady Mary, and their daughter the Duchess of Portland (whose transcript of the *Verses,* ascribed to Lady Mary, has already been mentioned) an equally close friend of Lady Mary's daughter. The paragraph in the *Verses* beginning

> Not even Youth and Beauty can controul
> The universal Rancour of thy Soul

was taken by W. J. Courthope to be a tribute to Lady Mary, but is more appropriate to Lady Delorain, who was eleven years younger. These lines, if no others in the *Verses,* may well be Windham's contribution. If he took a larger part, it seems odd that it attracted such slight and tardy notice.

Later attributions of the *Verses* followed one or other contemporary view. In 1768 Isaac Reed, editing Lady Mary's *Poetical Works,* reprinted them from the *Monthly Review,* 1767, without suggesting that she was not sole author. Lady Mary's son quoted the *Verses* as hers. James Dallaway, first editor to be allowed by her family to use her papers, mentioned that the poem was 'said to have been the joint performance' of her and Hervey [in Jonathan Curling, *Edward Wortley Montagu* (1954), 208]. J. W. Croker, who edited Hervey's *Memoirs,* decided on the basis of the manuscript evidence that Hervey wrote it—but decided against his own critical judgement, for he found it

smoother, keener, and in every way better than any of Lord Hervey's single-handed productions—except (if that be one) the *'Answer'* to Hammond. . . . a marked superiority over Lord Hervey's other works, both in vigour and polish—

and especially over *An Epistle From a Nobleman.* W. J. Courthope found in the poem various characteristics of Hervey (triplets, enjambement, lack of cæsura), but also 'greater vigour than is usually found in Lord Hervey's style, which, when he uses metre, is, as a rule, mean and dull.' A modern critic finds *An Epistle* 'inferior to the *Verses,* lacking the crack and sparkle which frequently distinguish' them. Halkett and Laing's *Dictionary of Anonymous and Pseudonymous Literature* ascribes the *Verses* to Lady Mary (rev. ed., 1926-43). Hervey's most recent editor gives as 'the accepted view' that she wrote them, possibly with Hervey's help. His biographer, wittily elaborating Pope's paradoxes, finds in the poem 'a crude vitality and masculine robustness more characteristic of Lady Mary . . . than it is of Hervey, most of whose verse is monotonously fluent and nerveless', and concludes it to be hers.

It still remains to analyse the poem more closely and to compare it in some detail with others by each writer. This analysis will confirm the view of Lady Mary's dominance, but with some qualifications. The opening of the *Verses* is strongly Herveyesque: antitheses as thick as bees o'er vernal blossoms, and six lines of subordinate clauses (in most of Lady Mary's poems the first main verb occurs in the first or second line). On the other hand the extended climactic image occupying the last paragraph has many parallels among her verse, while Hervey usually prefers to end with a detached, pointed couplet. If genuine collaboration went into the *Verses,* then the influence of each contributor enabled the other to surpass his or her usual level. They have none of the prolixity which was Hervey's besetting sin, and little of the careless syntax and construction which was Lady Mary's. She seldom uses 'thou' and 'thee' with so few lapses into 'you'. The balance of lines and couplets (especially in the series of antitheses at lines 93-100) is more exactly judged than is usual in any but short passages of her writing. Hervey was certainly no fonder of triplets than she was; but while his generally enclose their sense within the three lines in the approved manner, she treated this device in more cavalier fashion, often making the third line introduce a new idea or lead hurriedly on towards the following couplet, as it does in all the triplets of the *Verses* except the first.

In content the poem reflects sometimes one author, sometimes the other. The sneer at Pope's classicism in the first paragraph expresses an attitude which Hervey (like Fielding) consistently took towards him: that of one who has enjoyed the classical education proper to a gentleman. In his revisions to the *Verses* and also in later attacks, Hervey accuses Pope of inability to appreciate the ancients; in *An Epistle From a Nobleman* he laments the increasing rustiness of his own classical learning, with a polite air of deprecating a grace which in fact his correspondent knows him to possess. This poem, like the *Verses* (line 4), compares Pope to his disadvantage with the 'ancient Sense' which Hervey felt himself better equipped to savour.

The *Verses*'s admission (line 96) that many people had formerly prized Pope's work possibly reflects the fact that Lady Mary, who never liked his satires, had once deeply admired his pre-*Dunciad* poems. By 1728 she had lost her admiration sufficiently to call them 'smooth unmeaning Rhime'; perhaps a contrast with that smoothness is implied in the *Verses,* line 19: 'none thy crabbed Numbers can endure'. Hervey made no distinctions as to chronology when attacking Pope's work.

The reference (*Verses,* line 61) to physical weakness as 'The Female Scold's Protection in Offence' would read oddly coming from Lady Mary. So would the gibe at Pope as one who may legitimately be beaten since he 'cannot fight' (line 62), which may imply a contrast with Hervey's surprisingly bold conduct in his duel with Pulteney in 1731. The threat of inflicting punishment is in itself harder to assign; there are innumerable parallels in other people's pamphlet attacks on Pope, and some elsewhere in Hervey's and Lady Mary's writings. Hervey had mentioned late in December 1731, and again in January 1733, the likelihood of physical chastisement for Pope: on the first occasion he seems to have been quoting a phrase of Lady Mary's, as reported by Horace Walpole; on the second he used, like the *Verses,* line 65, the word 'cudgel'. This passage goes on to depict Pope escaping actual punishment ('Limbs unbroken, Skin without a Stain, / Unwhipt, unblanketed, unkick'd, unslain'), as does the concluding line of Lady Mary's **'P[ope] to Bolingbroke'**, written after *An Essay on Man*: 'You scape the Block, and I the Whipping-Post'. The effect in both poems is that of a barely-suppressed rather than a direct threat.

The *Verses* contain no unique accusations, only those repeated elsewhere by Hervey, Lady Mary, Fielding, and others. Yet some distinctions may be drawn. Pope wrote of the *Verses*:

> 'Tis a pleasure & a comfort at once to find, that with so much mind, as so much Malice must have to accuse or blacken my character, it can fix upon no one ill or immoral thing in my Life; & must content itself to say my Poetry is dull, & my Person ugly.

Insofar as this is accurate, it suggests a contrast with Lady Mary's other verse attacks on him, which fix on a large number of specific if unjust moral charges: superstition, obscenity, profaning religion, unfairness to Addison, Tickell, Lintot, Walpole, and Mme Dacier; toad-eating, cheating subscribers, causing bad blood between husband and wife, boasting of fictious amatory exploits, and having the clap. From the beginning, and increasingly with time, she points at Pope's personality rather than his writing, abusing his 'Father, Mother, Body, Soul' as well as 'Muse' with more inclusiveness and particularity than Hervey. Oddly, in view of the latter's career, her attacks outside the *Verses* are more politically angled than his; they present Pope linked with Bolingbroke and others, a poison working in the body of the state, while Hervey presents him as an obscure private lampooner.

Hervey also moves away from the literary towards the personal in his attacks, but never becomes so specific in his personalities as Lady Mary. His *Epistle From a Nobleman,* devoting only part of its space to attacking Pope, singles out poor translation and plagiarism. His prose *Letter to Mr. C-b-r,* 1742, reproves Cibber for attacking 'nothing but his Morals, which no body defends', and goes on to criticise his poetry. *The Difference between Verbal and Practical Virtue,* published a few days later, says that Pope should be castigated for 'that worse Deformity, his Mind', mentioning specifically literary faults as well as vindictiveness, lying, and ingratitude. Of the major ideas of the *Verses,* that of Pope as inhuman is more characteristic of Lady Mary; that of his verse as unintentionally innocuous is more like Hervey.

In their plan the *Verses* differ from Lady Mary's other poetic attacks. Those are all cast in dramatic form, involving more than one character (Dullness, her 'subservient Pow'rs', and the Scriblerians; Swift and a prostitute; Pope and Bolingbroke), whereas Hervey always chooses to argue directly in his own person, like an orator speaking for the prosecution. The *Verses* come closer to his method, though the fact that they are addressed to Pope, like an epistle, gives them greater immediacy of attack than an address to a third party, and they are not without dramatic characterization.

Hervey undoubtedly made use of the *Verses'* second paragraph,

> Thine is just such an Image of *his* Pen,
> As thou thy self art of the Sons of Men:
> Where our own Species in Burlesque we trace,
> A Sign-Post Likeness of the noble Race;
> That is at once Resemblance and Disgrace,

nine years later in *The Difference Between Verbal and Practical Virtue:*

> But whilst such Features in his Works we trace,
> And Gifts like these his happy Genius grace. . . .
> It seems the Counterpart by Heav'n design'd
> A Symbol and a Warning to Mankind:
> As at some Door we find hung out a Sign,
> Type of the Monster to be found within.

But the image of Pope's body as sign and type of his mind weakens the fearsome image of his body as a signpainter's travesty of a man. Later and inferior re-workings are not evidence either for or against authorship; but it is of some interest that Hervey's *The Difference* re-works many ideas from the *Verses* and weakens almost all of them. For instance, it reduces to a run-of-the-mill accusation of impotence the force of 'the gross *Lust* of Hate' (*Verses,* line 30) and 'No more for loving made, then to be lov'd (*Verses,* line 49), and in making a statement of the suitability of Pope's mind to his body misses half the point of *Verses,* lines 50-51:

It was the Equity of righteous Heav'n,
That such a Soul to such a Form was giv'n.

These details add up to a real and important difference between the pictures which the two poems present. *The Difference* takes the form of a general essay on the failure of poets to practise what they preach: Pope, though likened to a monster, to Domitian, to 'some yelping Mungril', remains recognisably an actual writer, who has faults which Horace, Seneca and others had, only worse. Despite the shrill tone which is *de riguer* among Pope's antagonists, it remains a rational argument, as does that part of *An Epistle From a Nobleman* which deals with Pope. (Hervey points out in *An Epistle* that Pope has mangled 'what *Homer* thought', which is a derogatory opinion; Lady Mary in **'P[ope] to Bolingbroke'** makes him refer casually to himself as 'The Homer, and the Horace of the Age', which is a dramatization.) Though the *Verses* do not, like other works by Lady Mary, present Pope as a developed fictional character, they go further than Hervey's in transforming the raw material which he represents.

The first paragraph of the *Verses,* perhaps Hervey's, is entirely logical if one accepts its premises. Thereafter, non-rational suggestion takes over. The images of the poem cluster round several central ideas: that of Pope as non-human, which the sign-post image introduces; that of his works as instruments of hurt, a whole catalogue of which succeed each other between lines 21 and 37, and 73 and 88; that of unavailing effort in 'Weeds, as they are, they seem produc'd by Toil', 'doubly bent to force a Dart', the lines on beauty, 'rancorous Will', 'stings and dies' and 'try at least t'assassinate' (all of which assert the opposite of Pope's own claim to Horatian ease); and that of oneman warfare against the rest of mankind. This idea dominates the poem, steadily growing in importance and incidentally producing some fine lines ('The Object of thy Spleen is Human Kind', line 33; 'To Thee 'tis Provocation to exist', line 35). As an enemy to mankind (and first of all to women), Pope is linked with Milton's Satan in his later, ignoble stages, Whether snake, porcupine or wasp, he is something the surrounding human beings look at with wonder and contempt. At last he becomes the outcast homicide Cain. One can see how indispensable to the design is the most offensive aspect of the poem, the use it makes (from the second paragraph to the last couplet) of Pope's deformity.

Whether or not it is true, as J. V. Guerinot thinks, that 'the experience of years of friendship, possibly of love . . . made it possible for Lady Mary to wound deepest of all', it is true that the *Verses* inflict some wounds which are almost caressing. There is insulting pity in 'thy poor Corps' (line 91), in 'wretched little Carcass' and 'angry little Monster' (lines 70 and 76), and in lines 81-82 (surely Lady Mary's, since Hervey struck them out in both his copies):

One over-match'd by ev'ry Blast of Wind,
Insulting and provoking all Mankind.

This glimpse of embattled mock-pathos is vivid enough to oppose to self-portraits of the heroic satirist; yet despite hints of pathos or even amusement, the Pope created in the *Verses* is a creature whom in the end it is appropriate to banish with Old-Testament rigour.

The *Verses* make comparatively little effort to take up points from the *First Satire of the Second Book*. One might expect Hervey to look for debating points, or Lady Mary to be provoked by its celebration of Pope's friends, 'Chiefs out of war, and statesmen out of place', since they were her habitual targets in polemical verse. But all is subordinated to the substitution of the imaginary pest for the real man or for the modest crusader depicted in the *Satire*. Where the *Verses* do allude to specific lines it is always on this point of self-portraiture. Their 'if thou drawst thy Pen to aid the Law' (line 64) refers to the *Satire's* passage, lines 105ff.:

What? arm'd for *Virtue* when I point the Pen,
Brand the bold Front of shameless, guilty Men. . . .

The second of these two lines also suggested the image of Pope's deformity as the brand 'Mark'd on thy Back, like *Cain,* by God's own Hand'. Line 84, *'To make those tremble who escape the Law',* paraphrases Pope's claim in his line 118. Immediately afterwards, lines 85-86,

Is this *Ridicule* to live so long,
The deathless Satire, and *immortal Song?*

refer to Pope's seeing the victim of his satire in his lines 79-80:

Sacred to Ridicule! his whole Life long,
And the sad Burthen of some merry Song.

This distorts Pope's claim by over-stating it and ignoring its irony and humour.

Pope surpassed his attackers in turning their weapons back upon themselves. Five years later he took 'But *Horace,* Sir, was delicate, was nice' from the *Verses,* line 16: '*Horace* can laugh, is delicate, is clear'. He may also have recalled 'none thy crabbed Numbers can endure' (line 19) when he wrote in the *Epistle to Arbuthnot* that '*Congreve* lov'd, and *Swift* endur'd my Lays' (line 138). But of all his re-workings of the lines of others against him, laying them low with words from their own mouths, the most striking is the Sporus portrait (*Arbuthnol,* lines 305-333), which can be seen as virtually a composite portrait of the two collaborators.

In the Sporus passage the *Verses* seem to live a ghastly resurrected life. One of their accusations is re-animated in 'florid Impotence', one of their techniques alluded to in 'vile Antithesis'. Pope used their comparison of himself (line 55) with *'the Snake of Eve'* for 'at the Ear of *Eve,* familiar Toad'. 'This painted Child of Dirt that stinks and stings' has its source in 'as we're told of Wasps, it stings and dies' (*Verses,* line 88). He was already fond of insect-imagery, but his identification of Sporus-Hervey with butterfly and bug acquires an extra force from the *Verses'* use of this very image. Indeed, for readers—let alone the writers—of the *Verses,* an additional layer of meaning informs this passage. No wonder if on the publication of Pope's epistle someone 'supposed that some copies would be called for'. The poem had acquired notoriety as an assault on Pope of which 'Your Lordship indeed said you had it from a lady, and the lady said it was your Lordship's'. Although 'both sexes had a share in it', the lady, more sorely provoked and more poetically inventive, probably had the greater. Yet the lord was taking public acknowledgement and blame. The Sporus portrait, already rich with complex allusions to Hervey's sexual reputation, his influence on Queen Caroline, the behind-the-scenes nature of his court and pamphlet politics, acquires a new level of significance through the unacknowledged place in it of Lady Mary. Like Walpole she speaks through Hervey's mouth, like the Queen she is corrupted by him:

> as the Prompter breathes, the Puppet squeaks;
> Or at the Ear of *Eve,* familiar Toad,
> Half Froth, half Venom, spits himself abroad. . . .
> His Wit all see-saw between *that* and *this,*
> Now high, now low, now Master up, now Miss,
> And he himself one vile Antithesis.
> Amphibious Thing! that acting either Part . . .
> Now trips a Lady, and now struts a Lord.
> *Eve*'s Tempter thus the Rabbins have exprest,
> A Cherub's face, a Reptile all the rest.

The sexual innuendoes of *A Letter to a Noble Lord* can be seen as a preliminary draft for this portrait, clumsy in comparison with the finished product.

The authors of the *Verses* had put up a fierce fight, but the champion was not to be worsted. He gave Hervey what is probably the most memorable of all his satirical lashings; he allowed Lady Mary (like her own later imagined version of himself) to escape the public whipping-post. In private she was not exempt. Pope deflected the weighty blow of the *Verses'* closing lines by skilful paraphrase:

> Sapho enrag'd crys out your Back is round,
> Adonis screams—Ah! Foe to all Mankind!

It appears that he was not blind to the element of insulting pity in the poem, for he took up that weapon and with that too proved himself the victor:

> Thanks, dirty Pair! you teach me what to say,
> When you attack my Morals, Sense, or Truth,
> I answer thus—poor Sapho you grow grey,
> And sweet Adonis—you have lost a Tooth.

The annals of poetic warfare can hardly show a finer example of wounding, as the *Verses* have it (line 26), 'with a Touch, that's scarcely felt or seen.'

## Robert Halsband (essay date 1978)

SOURCE: "Condemned to Petticoats: Lady Mary Wortley Montagu as Feminist and Writer," in *The Dress of Words:* *Essays on Restoration and Eighteenth Century Literature in Honor of Richmond P. Bond,* edited by Robert B. White, Jr., University of Kansas Libraries, 1978, pp. 35-52.

[*In the following excerpt Halsband investigates Montagu's feminism as it is displayed in her writings.*]

Lady Mary Wortley Montagu is sufficiently well known so that mention of her name need not be followed by the rhetorical question with which *Time* magazine headed its review of her *Complete Letters*—"Lady *Who?*" I have elsewhere touched on her stature as a lady of letters and on the general predicament of women writers in her time; ["Ladies of Letters in the Eighteenth Century," *Stuart and Georgian Moments,* 1972] her ideas and writings on feminism and her career as a miscellaneous writer deserve re-examination now because they are clarified and amplified in the recently published edition of her wide-ranging prose and verse [*Essays and Poems* and *Simplicity, A Comedy,* 1977]. It may seem anachronistic to call an eighteenth-century woman a feminist, a word applied to that movement a century later, yet Lady Mary, because of her life-long preoccupation with women as women, their privileges and disabilities, rights and wrongs, deserves an honorable place in that movement.

Lady Mary was an aristocratic, stubborn, and self-educated woman. Her dates, 1689 to 1762, span the lifetimes of the two most conspicuous feminist women of the century—Mary Astell (whom she knew) and Mary Wollstonecraft. She is thus one of a trinity of Marys. Unlike the other two she did not enunciate feminist principles in boldly signed pamphlets and books advocating that cause with revolutionary fervor. Yet she states or clearly implies this doctrine in her private correspondence with friends and family, and in her essays and poems, whether published or not. As a feminist she earns her credentials also by her vigorous activity in the profession of writing, which in her time was dominated by men. What better proof of women's equality with the other sex than competing on this intellectual battlefield!

Lady Mary's feminist ideas were not static, but became emancipated as she grew older. Whether or not women are inferior to men was a frequently debated question, and often decided on a theological basis. When Lady Mary, at the age of twenty-one, translated the *Enchiridion* of Epictetus (from a Latin version) and sent it to Bishop Burnet for correction she says this of women: "I am not now arguing for an Equality for the 2 Sexes; I do not doubt God and Nature has thrown us into an Inferior Rank. We are a lower part of the Creation; we owe Obedience and Submission to the Superior Sex; and any Woman who suffers her Vanity and folly to deny this, Rebells against the Law of the Creator and indisputable Order of Nature." No doubt her conventional posture was stiffened by her awareness that the good Bishop was not guilty of holding advanced notions of creatures whose genealogy begins with Adam's rib. (It was he who probably dissuaded the future Queen Anne from endowing the college for women as envisioned by Mary Astell.) Like any sensitive letter-writer Lady Mary tailored her ideas to her correspondents' interests and expectations.

Forty years later, as an expatriate in Italy—when she boasted of being "old without peevishness, superstition, or slander"—she writes that in her opinion "Nature has not plac'd us in an inferior Rank to Men, no more than the Females of other Animals, where we see no distinction of capacity, thô I am persuaded if there was a Common-wealth of rational Horses (as Doctor Swift has suppos'd) it would be an establish'd maxim amongst them that a mare could not be taught to pace." Whether or not women were intrinsically inferior to men was a moot question since they were undoubtedly treated as though they were, especially in their education. . . .

[T]here can be no doubt that as a writer [Montagu] was engaged by feminist topics—that, in other words, she combines both roles of my title, feminist and writer. Her very first publication, in fact, was an essay in the *Spectator* that satirically treated marriage from a wife's point of view. (She was the only woman, incidentally, who contributed to that periodical.) In June 1714 the *Spectator* had printed a letter written by Addison in the role of "a tall, broad-shoulderd, impudent, black Fellow . . . every way qualified for a rich Widow." He complains that he has been unable to capture a rich widow in marriage because his courtships have been obstructed by the Widow-Club, made up of "nine experienced Dames" who meet to pool their information about widow-hunters, and are thus able to resist suitors like himself. "Their Conversation," he continues, "often turns upon their former Husbands, and it is very diverting to hear them relate their several Arts and Stratagems, with which they amused the Jealous, pacified the Cholerick, or wheedled the Good-natured Man, 'till at last, to use the Club-phrase, *They sent him out of the House with his Heels foremost.*" In its gentle raillery and condescension Addison's fictitious letter is typical of his attitude toward women in most of his essays.

A month later, *Spectator* No. 573 printed a reply from Mrs. President, head of the Widow-Club, and it was Lady Mary who had held her pen. "You are pleased to be very Merry, as you imagine, with us Widows," she begins; and then in her counter-attack as well as defence of the club she relates the history of her own extensive marital career: having disposed of six husbands, she intends to take a seventh. (She thus outranks Chaucer's Wife of Bath, who could boast of only five husbands.) Her constant suitor, the seventh husband-to-be, is called the Hon. Edward Waitfort, evidently Lady Mary's private little joke about her husband Edward Wortley's long and querulous courtship. At the end of her account she sums up her marriages: "I do not believe all the unreasonable Malice of Mankind can give a Pretence why I should have been constant to the Memory of any of the deceased, or have spent much time in grieving for an insolent, insignificant, negligent, extravagant, splenatick, or covetous Husband; my first insulted me, my second was nothing to me, my third disgusted me, the fourth would have ruined me, the fifth tormented me, and the sixth would have starved me. If the other Ladies you name would thus give in their Husbands Pictures, at length, you would see, they have had as little Reason as my self to lose their Hours in

weeping and wailing." At the head of the essay Lady Mary put a Latin motto from Juvenal that sums up her reply: "Being reproved they bite back." This needs to be kept in mind, for the portrait of the widow is far from idealized; she displays some characteristics that are less than admirable. Mrs. President shows herself to be both frivolous and mercenary, but her various husbands easily surpass her in their faults. Lady Mary as a feminist regarded women as human creatures of mixed qualities and not as idealized saints.

She had more opportunity to "bite back" in a periodical that she herself conducted in 1737-38. The chief mission of her paper, which she called *The Nonsense of Common-Sense,* was political, as its title implied, for it supported Robert Walpole's administration against the Opposition paper *Common Sense.* . . .

In Number VI of *The Nonsense of Common-Sense,* Lady Mary devotes the entire paper to an impassioned and enlightened defence of womankind. . . .

In the entire canon of Lady Mary's letters, essays, and poems this is her most extended, articulate, and reasoned defence of women. . . .

Besides essays in a weekly journal, an earnest propagandist could utilize pamphlets, especially if the argument could be spun out in elegant verse couplets. (The recently issued bibliography by David Foxon lists the enormous number of verse pamphlets that were published between 1700 and 1750.) Lady Mary used this means at least twice for feminist propaganda: once to defend women in general against a satirist's scorn, and once to set forth her thoughts on courtship and marriage.

Jonathan Swift's *The Lady's Dressing Room,* published in 1732, vividly depicts how a naif Strephon explores his Celia's dressing room, with its evidence of slatternly filth (including an unemptied chamber-pot), and steals away disgusted,

> Repeating in his amorous Fits,
> Oh! *Celia, Celia, Celia* shits!

Among the various responses to the poem—it caused Mrs. Pilkington's mother to vomit—four writers issued anonymous pamphlets; one of them has only recently been identified as being by Lady Mary. Swift's poem, like others of his "excremental vision," is sometimes cited as proof of misogyny; one may wonder how a woman writer would treat it. She might scold him for his lack of charity, reprove him for his obscenity, accuse him of undue bias in choosing such a nymph as heroine. Lady Mary does none of these; the title of her poem indicates her strategy: ***The Dean's Provocation for Writing the Lady's Dressing Room.*** She spins out a fiction of how he had gone to a prostitute, who demanded payment before her services; how when he proved impotent and demanded the return of his payment, the prostitute refused; whereupon he vowed that in revenge he would ruin her trade by describing her dressing room.

In her *jeu d'esprit* Lady Mary very cleverly parodies Swift's own verse style—his octosyllabic couplets, his blunt, unpoetic diction, his digression, animal parallels, sententiae, and even his use of scatological words—as in her concluding lines. The prostitute, refusing to return the money, says:

> Perhaps you have no better Luck in
> The Knack of Rhyming than of———.

When the Dean replies with the threat that he will describe her dressing-room:

> She answer'd short, I'm glad you'll write,
> You'll furnish Paper when I Sh—e.

In this poem Lady Mary is not at all lady-like, but why should she be? Although "condemned to petticoats" (as she phrased it) she neither demanded nor expected consideration for being a woman. Is that not the frame of mind fitted for sexual equality, the "equal opportunity" that feminists strive for today?

Her other feminist poem, published as a pamphlet (in 1733), is about courtship and marriage. It is *The Answer* to a love elegy (printed along with it) by James Hammond, an impecunious young man who had fallen in love with a young woman at court. In her reply to the man's love-poem Lady Mary, answering for the woman, realistically points out that a marriage without financial safeguards would cause bitter regret for both: the woman would be "a poor *Virtuous* Wretch for Life"; and as for both: "*Love* soon would cease to smile, when *Fortune* frown'd." And so at the conclusion the woman makes a firm resolve not to encourage him:

> Whilst other Maids a shameless Path pursue,
> Neither to Honour, nor to Int'rest true;
> And proud to swell the Triumphs of their Eyes,
> Exult in Love from Lovers they despise;
> Their Maxims all revers'd, I mean to prove,
> And tho' I like the Lover quit the Love.

In her view of marriage Lady Mary recognizes the stringencies of her social class, where in a successful match financial settlements had to accompany love as a protection for the wife (as well as the husband). At the same time she sharply condemns a purely mercenary marriage, a "Nuptial Sale," and characterizes women who marry for that reason "legal Prostitutes." The phrase had already been used, in slightly different form, by Steele in the *Tatler* and by Defoe; it was made famous by Mary Wollstonecraft in *A Vindication of the Rights of Woman*. With or without Lady Mary's consent, her printer revealed her authorship by putting on the pamphlet's title page "By a Lady, Author of the Verses to the Imitator of Horace." The printer no doubt hoped to profit by the notoriety of her feud with Alexander Pope.

Lady Mary had already devoted a long poem to women's disabilities after marriage, to the cruel punishment suffered by wives because of the double moral standard imposed by society. In the **"Epistle from Mrs. Y[onge] to her Husband,"** purportedly written by a cast-off wife, Lady Mary criticizes the moral code that permits a husband to commit adultery with impunity yet punishes his wife for the same crime:

> Too, too severely Laws of Honour bind
> The Weak Submissive Sex of Woman-kind.

She then asks:

> From whence is this unjust Distinction grown?
> Are we not form'd with Passions like your own?
> Nature with equal Fire our Souls endu'd,
> Our Minds as Haughty, and as warm our blood,
> O're the wide World your pleasures you persue,
> The Change is justify'd by something new;
> But we must sigh in Silence—and be true.

The eloquence of this poem seems to reflect Lady Mary's urgent convictions; and whether or not she intended it to be printed, it remained unpublished among her manuscripts.

Adultery and divorce were so common among those she knew that she once suggested (in a letter to her sister) "a genneral Act of Divorceing all the people of England. You know, those that pleas'd might marry over again, and it would save the Reputations of several Ladys that are now in peril of being expos'd every day." Often in verse as well as in prose she scornfully attacked men's "gallantry," whether in or out of marriage, and particularly condemned the injustice of punishing or ostracizing women when their seducers were really the guilty ones. . . .

How do her ideas on marriage contribute to her advocacy of feminism? The faults of conventional marriage of the time are to the woman's disadvantage—the mercenary principle that treats her as a financial commodity, and the double standard of morality that permits a husband's infidelity but harshly punishes a wife's. Woman's lot would be improved, Lady Mary implies, if the institution of marriage were accepted honestly and seriously as a union between equals.

All of her writings that I have so far discussed illustrate both parts of my title simultaneously: her ideas on feminism and her activity as a writer concerned with those ideas. But in most of her writings she did not confine herself to that subject; she stands out as a woman whose literary energy and passion drove her to compete in an activity ruled by men. She is thus a feminist in practice.

### Ann Messenger (essay date 1986)

SOURCE: "Town Eclogues: Lady Mary Wortley Montagu and John Gay," in *His and Hers: Essays in Restoration and Eighteenth-Century Literature*, University Press of Kentucky, 1986, pp. 84-107.

*[In the following excerpt, Messenger compares John Gay's version of the eclogue "The Toilette" with Montagu's*

*version which appreared in* Six Town Eclogues, *and also provides a synopsis of the remaining five poems.*]

Before she went to Constantinople and wrote the letters for which perhaps she is best known today, Lady Mary Wortley Montagu spent a year and a half in London. While her husband worked at his government job, eventually winning the post of Ambassador to the court of Turkey, Lady Mary shone in court society, continued her old friendship with Congreve and other literary men, and made the acquaintance of still others, including John Gay. She also continued writing. She had read voraciously and had written both prose and verse from the age of twelve. Some of her early writing is pastoral: in her first manuscript album she called herself "Strephon"; she wrote poems praising the country, and she imitated Virgil's tenth eclogue. In London, the pastoral was to reappear in her poetry in a different form.

John Gay, today best known as the author of *The Beggar's Opera* and the *Fables,* is credited with having written the first English "town eclogue," "Araminta" (1713). The genre is a curious one, part pastoral, part burlesque, sometimes imitating a classical model, sometimes not. It is clearly enough defined to be recognizable, yet loose enough to allow a variety of attitudes and forms. Adina Forsgren, in her two-volume study of Gay, describes the genre and its mixed nature in detail. Gay published five such poems, following "Araminta" with "The Toilette" and three more in his collected poems of 1720. Lady Mary wrote six, published for the first time as a group in 1747, but composed during her stay in London in 1715-1716 when she first met Gay. One of her eclogues is also called **"The Toilette"**; it is the **"Friday"** poem in the group of six that is arranged in a "week" like Gay's *Shepherd's Week* (1714). Clearly there are connections, although, with one exception, the relationships among the poems by the two poets are general rather than particular.

The exception is **"The Toilette,"** in which the relationship is direct, even intimate—bewilderingly so. **"The Toilette"** was first published in 1716 by the unspeakable Edmund Curll, in (of course) an unauthorized edition. He suggested that Lady Mary might have written the poem, or Pope, or Gay. A much revised text, authorized, appeared in Gay's *Poems on Several Occasions* in 1720. But a manuscript album of Lady Mary's includes not only Curll's version of the poem but also a statement that she wrote every line of it herself. Pope thought it was "almost wholly Gay's"; Walpole republished it in 1747 as Lady Mary's, whose eclogues he preferred to Gay's. Robert Halsband surveys and analyzes the whole problem and concludes that Lady Mary could not seriously claim it as hers, but Isobel Grundy, in the Halsband/Grundy edition of Lady Mary's work, not only includes the poem in the earliest version but also says that Gay's version of 1720 "really amounts to a different poem." It could be the product of some sort of collaboration, with Gay and Lady Mary working together on the first version and Gay adapting and lengthening it for his 1720 version. We can never really know. And even if one could call up their ghosts and ask just who wrote what, they might not be able to

answer. When two minds, working closely together, produce a poem or a novel or other literary work, ideas and words and phrases are somehow generated by the partnership in a manner that mysteriously defies individual attribution. Perhaps that is the explanation.

But no matter who wrote what, Gay clearly laid claim to the 1720 version, consisting of 106 lines, while Lady Mary laid claim to the 1716/1747 version, consisting of 78 lines. If she did not write all of it, she at least preferred it enough to call it her own. These claims represent an inextricable tangle of creative and critical activities: the generating of words and phrases and the revisions, omissions, and additions of words and phrases. The result of all this, as Grundy says, is indeed two quite different poems, which I shall call for convenience Lady Mary's poem and Gay's poem. What matters, at least for my purposes here, is not the technical question of attribution, but which poet laid claim to which version—that is, which poet took responsibility for which ideas and point of view. For this comparison I shall use Lady Mary's text as printed in Grundy and Halsband, and Gay's text as printed in Dearing and Beckwith, without considering the minutiae of variations from one edition to another of either poem. Nor shall I look at every verbal variant between the two basic texts; many are so slight as to be insignificant, and besides, it would be foolish to search for significance on a microscopic level when the whole question of authorship is so tangled. But major differences in content and organization, in omissions and inclusions, and even, occasionally, in single words, are worth examining in order to show how two different sensibilities, a woman's and a man's, perceived and felt about the same female character and the same urban scene.

Lady Mary's poem opens with ten lines describing Lydia, now thirty-five years old, deserted by the many lovers who had once crowded the street before her door; now she has nothing to do but look out her window or into her mirror. The body of the poem (ll. 11-68) is Lydia's lament for her lost youth, speculation about how she shall pass the time today, and fury at Damon, her faithless lover, who has deserted her for his own young wife, Cloe. Lydia heaps abuse on Cloe and on the institution of marriage until her maid appears, carrying her bandbox, and compliments Lydia fulsomely on her appearance. Lydia then smiles and prepares to go to the playhouse (ll. 69-78).

Gay's poem opens with twenty-two lines describing the deserted Lydia, with much more detail about her dressing room, populated by "Shocks, monkeys and mockaws" (l. 9) who behave in a comically human fashion, and with observations about her hair and make-up. The fuller detail does not include a window as Lady Mary's poem does, however; Gay does not give us a Lydia who feels trapped. Again, the body of the poem is Lydia's lament (ll. 23-98), also more detailed but covering the same ground of regret for lost youth, distress about how to spend the time today, and jealousy of fifteen-year-old Chloe. This Chloe, however, is not Damon's wife but a rival mistress. Lydia speculates unhappily about the possible marriage and Chloe's probable behavior as a wife. She breaks down in passionate sobbing until the maid appears with band-box and flattery. The upshot is the same—a smile and preparation for the playhouse (ll. 99-106). . . .

Gay's Lydia is foolish and pitiable, and Gay's sympathy for her takes away the bite of his satire; as Spacks says, "The satirist's energy disappears in . . . compassion." Lady Mary's Lydia is also foolish and pitiable, but she is something more—she is, . . . in some senses admirable as well. This quality complicates and strengthens the satire immeasurably. The world that dictates the values and behavior of such a potentially strong character is the more strongly condemned, and we regret the loss of her potentialities. We smile when Gay's Lydia stops raving and smiles. When Lady Mary's Lydia smiles, we do not. . . .

The greater vigor of the central character and unambiguous though multipronged satire of [Montagu's] version of **"The Toilette"** are characteristic of her eclogues and of her attitudes in general, in both verse and prose.

To see Lady Mary's strength in prose, one can open her collected letters almost at random and find strong expression, no matter how complex the feeling she is discussing and no matter how often she changes her mind. She is particularly vigorous in her opinions of her own sex, opinions often far more purely condemnatory than those of Gay the gentle man. For instance, she praises her friend Philippa Mundy at the expense of most other women: "I wish Mr. M. may be sensible how happy he is in that uncommon thing (so rare that like the Phoenix its very existence is disputed), a Woman of Youth and Beauty without Coquetry. In this vile Town, the Universal follys of the fair, the ugly, in short, the whole sex that way ought to make all Husbands revere those Wives that have sense enough not to be led by the Croud, and Virtuous Courrage enough to stand the Laugh that will infailibly insult them with the name of Prudes." She addresses Philippa again: "I confesse, contrary to the Generallity of my Sex, I am of Opinion that both good and ill Husbands are of their Wives' making, for as Folly is the root of all matrimonial Quarrells, that distemper commonly runs highest of the Woman's side." Women, beware women! And foolish women are her target in all but one of her town eclogues.

Gay's town eclogues are discrete poems; Lady Mary's form a "week" from Monday through Saturday, like Gay's *Shepherd's Week* (1714). Written between February 1715 and July 1716, the order in which she finally arranged them is not that of composition, so it must have some rationale. It can be seen as an order of increasing complexity of satiric tone and increasing intensity of theme—the theme of loss, observed caustically in others at the beginning and drawing closer and closer to home toward the end. Neither the theme nor the organization is absolutely strict or all-pervasive; it would take a very convoluted argument indeed to force every detail, indeed every poem, into the pattern. And, of course, the theme of lost love is the standard stock-in-trade of the pastoral, urban or otherwise; Gay uses it often. Nevertheless, one can see a special treatment of that theme and a degree of coherence in Lady Mary's group of poems.

**"Monday: Roxana; or The Drawing-room"** is the most politically dangerous of the poems and the most personal argument *ad feminam*. Returning from court, oppressed by sorrows even more than her chairmen are by their "cruel load" (l. 5)—the lady is fat—Roxana laments the loss of an appointment in the Princess's household which she had expected to obtain. The satiric attack is at least two-pronged. Roxana the prude has engaged in immodest behavior, attending "filthy Plays" (l. 16) and the like, to win the favor of the Princess; the poem suggests that her prudery was hypocrisy in the first place and that her ambition, given her age (she has three grown daughters) and general unattractiveness, is foolish. The second and more dangerous prong is levelled at the Princess: if frivolous, even lewd, behavior is believed necessary to win her favor, her own standards are called into question, although Roxana hypocritically (or diplomatically) says that the Princess is miraculously virtuous in the midst of a corrupt court (l. 54). Court life in general, as well as Roxana and the Princess in particular, is satirized. Lady Mary has no sympathy for any of her objects in this poem. A personal tone gives it added bite: the young, slender, Whig Lady Mary obviously enjoyed getting her knife into the middle-aged, fat, Tory "Roxana," the Duchess of Roxburghe. Roxana's lost appointment stirred up no compassion. The verse pattern may occasionally echo Gay's "Araminta," but the tone certainly does not.

**"Tuesday: St. James's Coffee-house: Silliander and Patch"** is the odd poem out in the Week. It is a wonderfully funny bragging match between two gentlemen, Silliander (silly plus man [Greek: *anēr, andros*]) and Patch ("a paltry fellow": Johnson). They compare notes on the favors they have won from various unnamed but noble ladies—rings, shoe buckles, snuff boxes, and opportunities to view specific areas of flesh. Patch wins. Like Gay's "The *Tea-table*" and "Monday" in his *Week,* it is a parody of the pastoral singing contests in which shepherds praise the charms of their mistresses, and as such it expresses, as do all the town eclogues, a sense of the loss of rural innocence. The gentleman to whom it was addressed and the two gentlemen disguised as Silliander and Patch may have felt some loss of dignity. But the poem has no important link to the theme of loss in the rest of the group. It stands with Lady Mary's **"Monday,"** however, as an example of satire that is relatively simple because it is entirely unsympathetic.

The tone begins to change with **"Wednesday: The Tête à Tête,"** the one poem other than **"Friday: The Toilette"** in which Lady Mary uses Gay's trick of an ironic twist at the end to create satire. For eighty-two lines, the poem could be a truly rural pastoral. Dancinda laments the loss of her heart to Strephon, describing his courtship and complaining in classic style that she dare not yield to him because he would then despise her. The loving woman's eternal dilemma is expressed in conventional terms and yet with strength and passion. Real questions and real issues are raised: dare a woman confess that she loves? how can she conceal it? is love anything more than lust? how can she prove her love without losing the man who asks her to prove it? But then "She paus'd; and fix'd her

Eyes upon her Fan" (l. 83), the first hint, apart from the context of the whole group of poems, that we are not in a pasture. Strephon confirms the town setting by taking a pinch of snuff in the next line, and all the lady's passionate argument is called into question. Her image of her own virtue is unequivocally destroyed when the maid knocks at the door and warns her of her husband's approach; Strephon "cursing slips down the back Stairs" (l. 92). The poem has other endings as well. Pope wanted Lady Mary to conclude, after the maid's knock, with Dancinda blaming Strephon for wasting time: "You have but listen'd when you should have kist!" Another ending, by Lady Mary, gives Strephon a speech in which he differentiates between lust and love, apparently successfully, because the lady allows him to "put out the Light, / And all that follow'd was Eternal Night." Lady Mary's first ending has the advantage of brevity, which makes the shock sharper. But all three serve the same purpose, the undercutting of the lady's lament. Yet one cannot forget that the lament raises real issues, real not only for an innocent shepherdess but also for any woman who loves in a social context that limits her sexual freedom.

This poem has a doubleness, but it is unlike Gay's doubleness, which Spacks calls "ambiguity." Gay's town eclogues arouse mixed feelings toward his characters—scorn blended with pity, contempt blended with tolerant amusement. Lady Mary's **"Wednesday"** creates two separate reactions: concern for the issues raised and then contempt for the lady raising them. The two levels are sharply distinguished. The issues are obviously important ones, and, being aware of the writer's sex, the reader takes them all the more seriously: here is the voice of authority and perhaps of experience. The ironic twist shows, in a flash, that the speaker is a hypocrite and either an adulteress or fast on the way to becoming one. The condemnation is unambiguous. Although she has been speaking of serious issues, she has not emerged as an individualized character, so she is easy to condemn. But the issues remain.

Concern and condemnation are not kept tidily apart in **"Thursday: The Bassette Table: Smilinda, Cardelia."** The satiric tone is growing more complex. The theme of loss is central: Cardelia has lost at cards and Smilinda has lost at love. The two ladies debate which loss is the greater, in pastoral singing-contest form. The terms of the two topics mix and cross: the faithless lover is a "sharper" and basset is a "passion." Both love and cards are games, as in *The Rape of the Lock,* and both are passions. The emphasis, however, falls upon the game, for Smilinda too plays cards and indeed lost her lover to her rival at the gaming table. Both the ladies are being satirized: one has trivialized love and the other inflated the importance of cards. They even seem to be boasting about their suffering, as each tries to top the other in detailing her pain. Both passions are uncontrollable: "I know the Bite, yet to my ruin run, / And see the Folly which I cannot shun," Cardelia laments (ll. 74-75). Cardelia loses her reason when she looks on the charms of basset (ll. 86-87), while Smilinda loses her prudence in the arms of her sharper (ll. 98-99). The lady who is to judge this contest is Betty Loveit. If this were Restoration comedy, one would expect the

name to indicate simply sexual eagerness, as it does in Etherege's *Man of Mode.* But this Loveit "all the pains of Love and Play does know" (l. 23), having often tried both. And at the end of the poem, impatient for her tea, she awards prizes to both the contenders. The judge in Gay's "Monday" similarly declares a draw and expresses his boredom with the songs. That conclusion is purely comic, but there are satiric complexities in Loveit's judgment in Lady Mary's poem. It implies that love and cards are equally significant, or equally trivial; that both are games; that in the world of the town eclogue, all passions are the same, though perhaps the passion for tea is strongest. If we had expected love to be more important, as Loveit's name leads us to do and as our own priorities should, we find the poem's satire leveled at us because we do not understand the town.

The same strategy is part of the complexity of **"Friday: The Toilette: Lydia,"** complicated . . . by the admiration we are made to feel for the emotional honesty and self-assertion of Lydia, until we find that she "raves."

**"Saturday: The Small Pox: Flavia"** brings the complexities to a climax. While Smilinda, the forsaken lover in **"Thursday,"** might be modeled on Lady Mary herself, Flavia, lamenting the loss of her beauty to the ravages of smallpox, definitely is. Lady Mary, who was disfigured by the disease in 1715, said she expressed her own feelings in this poem. The value of beauty is the satiric center of the poem. In the marriage market, and in fashionable society in general, beauty was a precious commodity. Money could buy a husband when beauty was lacking, but with beauty, one had a wider field to choose from and needed rather less money. But beauty is ephemeral, especially in an age of primitive medicine and dentistry, and, like other things of the flesh, has no value for the orthodox moralist. That beauty confers power, indeed wealth, on a woman is thus evidence of the corruption of the world. Also, beauty has aesthetic value, which has nothing to do with morality and on which one cannot set a price. All this, along with the fact that the author was expressing her own feelings, creates a poem of great complexity and power.

Like **"The Toilette,"** **"The Small Pox"** consists almost entirely of the protagonist's speech lamenting her loss. Flavia lies on her couch. "A Glass revers'd in her right hand she bore" (l. 3); the detail is emblematic, ceremonial, like the reversed arms of the escort in a military funeral. Flavia is now *hors de combat.* It is a small detail, but it sets the mock heroic tone of the poem, a tone that comes and goes throughout both Lady Mary's and Gay's town ecologues and that dominates this poem more than any other. Perhaps Lady Mary chose the mock heroic tone because the subject is beauty and its power, as in *The Rape of the Lock.* Certainly that tone works: its elevation and importance fit her own real feelings and the value that beauty had in her world, while its ironic gap shows the littleness of the topic from the moral point of view—the insignificance of ephemeral beauty and the wrongness of those who value it. The mock heroic poet can have it both ways.

Flavia laments, "How am I chang'd!" (l. 5), regretting the loss of her complexion "That promis'd Happyness for Years to come" (l. 8). She is already an object of satire, if she believes that beauty could last. She is morally wrong to think that it could confer happiness on its possessor. And yet, in some respects and to some extent, in this world, could it not? Flavia goes on to reveal how enchanted she used to be with her own image, as Belinda worshiped hers in *The Rape of the Lock*. She dwells sadly on former evidences of her power: gifts of opera tickets, cherries, china, and much attention:

> For me, the Patriot has the House forsook,
> And left debates to catch a passing look,
> For me, the Soldier has soft verses writ,
> For me, the Beau has aim'd to be a Wit,
> For me, the Wit to Nonsense was betraid,
> The Gamester has for me his Dun delaid. . . .
> [ll. 28-33]

Perhaps one should add this passage to the list of Pope's sources for the following lines in *An Essay on Man:*

> Ask for what end the heav'nly bodies shine,
> Earth for whose use? Pride answers, "'Tis for mine:
> For me kind Nature wakes her genial pow'r,
> Suckles each herb, and spreads out ev'ry flow'r;
> Annual for me, the grape, the rose renew
> The juice nectareous, and the balmy dew;
> For me, the mine a thousand treasures brings;
> For me, health gushes from a thousand springs;
> Seas roll to waft me, suns to light me rise;
> My foot-stool earth, my canopy the skies."
> [I, 131-40]

Both poets are attacking pride. Pope's proud man lays claim to cosmic importance, while Flavia claims power equally vast, given the scope of her world, power to make various kinds of men contradict their own essential natures. Flavia, who is Lady Mary herself, the men, and their world are all objects of satire in these lines, and yet the grief, like some degree of the power, is real.

Next, Flavia glances around the room and exclaims over her portrait, now out of date, and her toilette, now useless. "Meaner Beauties" (l. 55) may now shine but only because they have no competition from her. The pride, the former self-worship, the boasting are all obvious. And yet, so is the sadness of her loss. Doctors had promised she would be well and beautiful again, but their oaths were false. In the last two verse paragraphs, Flavia counsels herself to "bid the World Adieu" (l. 84), since "Monarchs, and Beauties" (l. 85) are unpitied, even mocked, when they are deposed. The comparison shows her awareness that, in losing her beauty, she has lost her power. She will retire to an "obscure recess" (l. 89) from the parks, operas, and parties of the world, and hide her face "in shades" (l. 94). Real pastoral landscape is to be a retreat from the urban pastoral world, a morally superior retreat in which no false friend will pretend compassion (l. 91) and "Where Gentle streams will weep at [her] distress" (l. 90). And yet, this world, pathetic fallacy and all, is of course a fiction, a literary fiction. There is no place to hide.

Each of Lady Mary's town eclogues can stand alone as a skillfully wrought, interesting poem, sometimes complex and sometimes simple in satire, sometimes topical, sometimes autobiographical. Gay's town eclogues, with their different kind of appeal, are intended as single poems, but Lady Mary has put hers together in a series in which the whole is greater than the sum of its parts. One's admiration for her artistic skill and control and for her penetrating vision of her social world grows as the series unfolds. That admiration reaches its peak when, at the end, she shows us herself, disfigured and in tears, making, as many poets have, good art out of grief.

## FURTHER READING

### Biography

Halsband, Robert. *The Life of Lady Mary Wortley Montagu.* Oxford: Clarendon Press, 1956, 313 p.
    Definitive biography.

### Criticism

Bataille, Robert R. "The Dating of *The Lady's Curiosity* and Lady Montagu's 'The Fifth Ode of Horace Imitated.'" *American Notes and Queries* XVIII, No. 6 (February 1980): 87-8.
    Searches bibliographic evidence to ascertain when Montagu wrote her "Ode."

Grundy, Isobel. "'The Entire Works of Clarinda': Unpublished Juvenile Verse by Lady Mary Wortley Montagu." *Yearbook of English Studies* 7 (1977): 91-107.
    Thorough overview of Montagu's juvenile verse.

——. "A 'Spurious' Poem by Lady Mary Wortley Montagu?" *Notes and Queries* 27, No. 5 (October 1980): 407-10.
    Investigates claims attributing the poem "To Clio, occasioned by her verses on friendship" to Montagu.

——. "'New' Verse by Lady Mary Wortley Montagu." *The Bodleian Library Record* X, No. 4 (February 1981): 237-49.
    Detects strains of erotic attraction and friendly debate in recently discovered manuscript poems.

——. "The Politics of Female Authorship." *The Book Collector* 31, No. 1 (Spring 1982): 19-37.
    Discusses Montagu's reaction to the printing of her poems.

Halsband, Robert. "Ladies of Letters in the Eighteenth Century." In *Stuart and Georgian Moments,* edited by Earl Miner, pp. 271-91. Berkeley: University of California Press, 1972.

Comprehensive overview of Montagu's writings, contrasting her literary career with those of other eighteenth-century woman authors.

Lerner, Laurence. "Subverting the Canon." *The British Journal of Aesthetics* 32, No. 4 (October 1992): 347-58.

Reexamines Montagu's poems in the context of an analysis of the male-dominated canon of great poetry. Although he finds "some good poems, and a fresh perspective on love poems" in Montagu's work, Lerner maintains that there is little reason for "establishing alternative criteria of poetic merit."

Looser, Devoney. "Scolding Lady Mary Wortley Montagu? The Problematics of Sisterhood in Feminist Criticism." In *Feminist Nightmares: Women at Odds; Feminism and the Problem of Sisterhood,* edited by Susan Ostrov Weisser and Jennifer Fleischner, pp. 44-61. New York: New York University Press, 1994.

Questions Montagu's status as a "feminist authorial model" in an overview of her changing feminist reputations.

Spacks, Patricia Meyer. "Imaginations Warm and Tender: Pope and Lady Mary." *South Atlantic Quarterly* 83, No. 2 (Spring 1984): 207-15.

Examines the letters written between Montagu and Pope before their quarrel, discerning a subtext of struggle.

Van Ostade, Ingrid Tieken-Boon. "*Do*—Support in the Writings of Lady Mary Wortley Montagu: A Change in Progress." *Folia Linguistica Historica* VI, No. 1 (1985): 127-51.

Analyzes Montagu's use and non-use of the word "do," "as it can be detected in the language of one single educated upper-class author."

**Additional coverage of Montagu's life and career is contained in the following sources published by Gale Research:** *Literature Criticism 1400-1800,* **Vol. 9; and** *Dictionary of Literary Biography,* **Vols. 95, 101.**

# Poetry Criticism
# INDEXES

*Literary Criticism Series*
*Cumulative Author Index*

*Cumulative Nationality Index*

*Cumulative Title Index*

# How to Use This Index

# Literary Criticism Series
# Cumulative Author Index

**A. E.** . . . . . . . . . . . . . . . . . . . . . . . **TCLC 3, 10**
See also Russell, George William

**Abasiyanik, Sait Faik** 1906-1954
See Sait Faik
See also CA 123

**Abbey, Edward** 1927-1989 . . . . . . **CLC 36, 59**
See also CA 45-48; 128; CANR 2, 41

**Abbott, Lee K(ittredge)** 1947- . . . . . . **CLC 48**
See also CA 124; CANR 51; DLB 130

**Abe, Kobo**
1924-1993 . . . . . . . . . **CLC 8, 22, 53, 81;**
**DAM NOV**
See also CA 65-68; 140; CANR 24; MTCW

**Abelard, Peter** c. 1079-c. 1142 . . . **CMLC 11**
See also DLB 115

**Abell, Kjeld** 1901-1961 . . . . . . . . . . . **CLC 15**
See also CA 111

**Abish, Walter** 1931- . . . . . . . . . . . . . **CLC 22**
See also CA 101; CANR 37; DLB 130

**Abrahams, Peter (Henry)** 1919- . . . . . **CLC 4**
See also BW 1; CA 57-60; CANR 26;
DLB 117; MTCW

**Abrams, M(eyer) H(oward)** 1912- . . . **CLC 24**
See also CA 57-60; CANR 13, 33; DLB 67

**Abse, Dannie**
1923- . . . **CLC 7, 29; DAB; DAM POET**
See also CA 53-56; CAAS 1; CANR 4, 46;
DLB 27

**Achebe, (Albert) Chinua(lumogu)**
1930- . . . . . **CLC 1, 3, 5, 7, 11, 26, 51, 75;**
**BLC; DA; DAB; DAC; DAM MST,**
**MULT, NOV; WLC**
See also AAYA 15; BW 2; CA 1-4R;
CANR 6, 26, 47; CLR 20; DLB 117;
MAICYA; MTCW; SATA 40;
SATA-Brief 38

**Acker, Kathy** 1948- . . . . . . . . . . . . . . **CLC 45**
See also CA 117; 122

**Ackroyd, Peter** 1949- . . . . . . . . . **CLC 34, 52**
See also CA 123; 127; CANR 51; DLB 155;
INT 127

**Acorn, Milton** 1923- . . . . . . . . **CLC 15; DAC**
See also CA 103; DLB 53; INT 103

**Adamov, Arthur**
1908-1970 . . . . **CLC 4, 25; DAM DRAM**
See also CA 17-18; 25-28R; CAP 2; MTCW

**Adams, Alice (Boyd)** 1926- . . . **CLC 6, 13, 46**
See also CA 81-84; CANR 26, 53;
DLBY 86; INT CANR-26; MTCW

**Adams, Andy** 1859-1935 . . . . . . . . . **TCLC 56**
See also YABC 1

**Adams, Douglas (Noel)**
1952- . . . . . . . . . **CLC 27, 60; DAM POP**
See also AAYA 4; BEST 89:3; CA 106;
CANR 34; DLBY 83; JRDA

**Adams, Francis** 1862-1893 . . . . . . **NCLC 33**

**Adams, Henry (Brooks)**
1838-1918 . . . . . . **TCLC 4, 52; DA; DAB;**
**DAC; DAM MST**
See also CA 104; 133; DLB 12, 47

**Adams, Richard (George)**
1920- . . . . . . . **CLC 4, 5, 18; DAM NOV**
See also AAYA 16; AITN 1, 2; CA 49-52;
CANR 3, 35; CLR 20; JRDA; MAICYA;
MTCW; SATA 7, 69

**Adamson, Joy(-Friederike Victoria)**
1910-1980 . . . . . . . . . . . . . . . . . . . **CLC 17**
See also CA 69-72; 93-96; CANR 22;
MTCW; SATA 11; SATA-Obit 22

**Adcock, Fleur** 1934- . . . . . . . . . . . . . **CLC 41**
See also CA 25-28R; CAAS 23; CANR 11,
34; DLB 40

**Addams, Charles (Samuel)**
1912-1988 . . . . . . . . . . . . . . . . . . . **CLC 30**
See also CA 61-64; 126; CANR 12

**Addison, Joseph** 1672-1719 . . . . . . . . **LC 18**
See also CDBLB 1660-1789; DLB 101

**Adler, Alfred (F.)** 1870-1937 . . . . . **TCLC 61**
See also CA 119

**Adler, C(arole) S(chwerdtfeger)**
1932- . . . . . . . . . . . . . . . . . . . . . . . **CLC 35**
See also AAYA 4; CA 89-92; CANR 19,
40; JRDA; MAICYA; SAAS 15;
SATA 26, 63

**Adler, Renata** 1938- . . . . . . . . . . . **CLC 8, 31**
See also CA 49-52; CANR 5, 22, 52;
MTCW

**Ady, Endre** 1877-1919 . . . . . . . . . . **TCLC 11**
See also CA 107

**Aeschylus**
525B.C.-456B.C. . . . . . . . **CMLC 11; DA;**
**DAB; DAC; DAM DRAM, MST**

**Afton, Effie**
See Harper, Frances Ellen Watkins

**Agapida, Fray Antonio**
See Irving, Washington

**Agee, James (Rufus)**
1909-1955 . . . . **TCLC 1, 19; DAM NOV**
See also AITN 1; CA 108; 148;
CDALB 1941-1968; DLB 2, 26, 152

**Aghill, Gordon**
See Silverberg, Robert

**Agnon, S(hmuel) Y(osef Halevi)**
1888-1970 . . . . . . . . . . . . . . **CLC 4, 8, 14**
See also CA 17-18; 25-28R; CAP 2; MTCW

**Agrippa von Nettesheim, Henry Cornelius**
1486-1535 . . . . . . . . . . . . . . . . . . . . **LC 27**

**Aherne, Owen**
See Cassill, R(onald) V(erlin)

**Ai** 1947- . . . . . . . . . . . . . . . . . . **CLC 4, 14, 69**
See also CA 85-88; CAAS 13; DLB 120

**Aickman, Robert (Fordyce)**
1914-1981 . . . . . . . . . . . . . . . . . . . **CLC 57**
See also CA 5-8R; CANR 3

**Aiken, Conrad (Potter)**
1889-1973 . . . . . . . . . **CLC 1, 3, 5, 10, 52;**
**DAM NOV, POET; SSC 9**
See also CA 5-8R; 45-48; CANR 4;
CDALB 1929-1941; DLB 9, 45, 102;
MTCW; SATA 3, 30

**Aiken, Joan (Delano)** 1924- . . . . . . . . **CLC 35**
See also AAYA 1; CA 9-12R; CANR 4, 23,
34; CLR 1, 19; DLB 161; JRDA;
MAICYA; MTCW; SAAS 1; SATA 2,
30, 73

**Ainsworth, William Harrison**
1805-1882 . . . . . . . . . . . . . . . . **NCLC 13**
See also DLB 21; SATA 24

**Aitmatov, Chingiz (Torekulovich)**
1928- . . . . . . . . . . . . . . . . . . . . . . . **CLC 71**
See also CA 103; CANR 38; MTCW;
SATA 56

**Akers, Floyd**
See Baum, L(yman) Frank

**Akhmadulina, Bella Akhatovna**
1937- . . . . . . . . . . . **CLC 53; DAM POET**
See also CA 65-68

**Akhmatova, Anna**
1888-1966 . . . . . . . . . . . **CLC 11, 25, 64;**
**DAM POET; PC 2**
See also CA 19-20; 25-28R; CANR 35;
CAP 1; MTCW

**Aksakov, Sergei Timofeyvich**
1791-1859 . . . . . . . . . . . . . . . . . **NCLC 2**

**Aksenov, Vassily**
See Aksyonov, Vassily (Pavlovich)

**Aksyonov, Vassily (Pavlovich)**
1932- . . . . . . . . . . . . . . . . . . . . **CLC 22, 37**
See also CA 53-56; CANR 12, 48

**Akutagawa Ryunosuke**
1892-1927 . . . . . . . . . . . . . . . . . **TCLC 16**
See also CA 117

**Alain** 1868-1951 . . . . . . . . . . . . . . . **TCLC 41**

**Alain-Fournier** . . . . . . . . . . . . . . . . . **TCLC 6**
See also Fournier, Henri Alban
See also DLB 65

**Alarcon, Pedro Antonio de**
1833-1891 . . . . . . . . . . . . . . . . . **NCLC 1**

**Alas (y Urena), Leopoldo (Enrique Garcia)**
1852-1901 . . . . . . . . . . . . . . . . **TCLC 29**
See also CA 113; 131; HW

**Albee, Edward (Franklin III)**
1928- . . . . . . **CLC 1, 2, 3, 5, 9, 11, 13, 25,**
**53, 86; DA; DAB; DAC; DAM DRAM,**
**MST; WLC**
See also AITN 1; CA 5-8R; CABS 3;
CANR 8; CDALB 1941-1968; DLB 7;
INT CANR-8; MTCW

**Alberti, Rafael** 1902- . . . . . . . . . . . . . **CLC 7**
See also CA 85-88; DLB 108

**Albert the Great** 1200(?)-1280 . . . . **CMLC 16**
See also DLB 115

**Andouard**
See Giraudoux, (Hippolyte) Jean

**Andrade, Carlos Drummond de** . . . . . . **CLC 18**
See also Drummond de Andrade, Carlos

**Andrade, Mario de**   1893-1945 . . . . . **TCLC 43**

**Andreae, Johann V(alentin)**
1586-1654 . . . . . . . . . . . . . . . . . . . . **LC 32**
See also DLB 164

**Andreas-Salome, Lou**   1861-1937 . . . **TCLC 56**
See also DLB 66

**Andrewes, Lancelot**   1555-1626 . . . . . . . **LC 5**
See also DLB 151

**Andrews, Cicily Fairfield**
See West, Rebecca

**Andrews, Elton V.**
See Pohl, Frederik

**Andreyev, Leonid (Nikolaevich)**
1871-1919 . . . . . . . . . . . . . . . . . . . **TCLC 3**
See also CA 104

**Andric, Ivo**   1892-1975 . . . . . . . . . . . . . **CLC 8**
See also CA 81-84; 57-60; CANR 43;
DLB 147; MTCW

**Angelique, Pierre**
See Bataille, Georges

**Angell, Roger**   1920- . . . . . . . . . . . . . . **CLC 26**
See also CA 57-60; CANR 13, 44

**Angelou, Maya**
1928- . . . . **CLC 12, 35, 64, 77; BLC; DA;
DAB; DAC; DAM MST, MULT, POET,
POP**
See also AAYA 7; BW 2; CA 65-68;
CANR 19, 42; DLB 38; MTCW;
SATA 49

**Annensky, Innokenty Fyodorovich**
1856-1909 . . . . . . . . . . . . . . . . . . **TCLC 14**
See also CA 110

**Anon, Charles Robert**
See Pessoa, Fernando (Antonio Nogueira)

**Anouilh, Jean (Marie Lucien Pierre)**
1910-1987 . . . . . . **CLC 1, 3, 8, 13, 40, 50;
DAM DRAM**
See also CA 17-20R; 123; CANR 32;
MTCW

**Anthony, Florence**
See Ai

**Anthony, John**
See Ciardi, John (Anthony)

**Anthony, Peter**
See Shaffer, Anthony (Joshua); Shaffer,
Peter (Levin)

**Anthony, Piers**   1934- . . **CLC 35; DAM POP**
See also AAYA 11; CA 21-24R; CANR 28;
DLB 8; MTCW; SAAS 22; SATA 84

**Antoine, Marc**
See Proust, (Valentin-Louis-George-Eugene-)
Marcel

**Antoninus, Brother**
See Everson, William (Oliver)

**Antonioni, Michelangelo**   1912- . . . . . **CLC 20**
See also CA 73-76; CANR 45

**Antschel, Paul**   1920-1970
See Celan, Paul
See also CA 85-88; CANR 33; MTCW

**Anwar, Chairil**   1922-1949 . . . . . . . . **TCLC 22**
See also CA 121

**Apollinaire, Guillaume**
1880-1918 . . . . . . . . . . . . . **TCLC 3, 8, 51;
DAM POET; PC 7**
See also Kostrowitzki, Wilhelm Apollinaris
de
See also CA 152

**Appelfeld, Aharon**   1932- . . . . . . . **CLC 23, 47**
See also CA 112; 133

**Apple, Max (Isaac)**   1941- . . . . . . . . **CLC 9, 33**
See also CA 81-84; CANR 19; DLB 130

**Appleman, Philip (Dean)**   1926- . . . . . **CLC 51**
See also CA 13-16R; CAAS 18; CANR 6,
29

**Appleton, Lawrence**
See Lovecraft, H(oward) P(hillips)

**Apteryx**
See Eliot, T(homas) S(tearns)

**Apuleius, (Lucius Madaurensis)**
125(?)-175(?) . . . . . . . . . . . . . . . **CMLC 1**

**Aquin, Hubert**   1929-1977 . . . . . . . . . **CLC 15**
See also CA 105; DLB 53

**Aragon, Louis**
1897-1982 . . . . . **CLC 3, 22; DAM NOV,
POET**
See also CA 69-72; 108; CANR 28;
DLB 72; MTCW

**Arany, Janos**   1817-1882 . . . . . . . . **NCLC 34**

**Arbuthnot, John**   1667-1735 . . . . . . . . . . **LC 1**
See also DLB 101

**Archer, Herbert Winslow**
See Mencken, H(enry) L(ouis)

**Archer, Jeffrey (Howard)**
1940- . . . . . . . . . . . . **CLC 28; DAM POP**
See also AAYA 16; BEST 89:3; CA 77-80;
CANR 22, 52; INT CANR-22

**Archer, Jules**   1915- . . . . . . . . . . . . . . **CLC 12**
See also CA 9-12R; CANR 6; SAAS 5;
SATA 4, 85

**Archer, Lee**
See Ellison, Harlan (Jay)

**Arden, John**
1930- . . . . . **CLC 6, 13, 15; DAM DRAM**
See also CA 13-16R; CAAS 4; CANR 31;
DLB 13; MTCW

**Arenas, Reinaldo**
1943-1990 . . . . . . **CLC 41; DAM MULT;
HLC**
See also CA 124; 128; 133; DLB 145; HW

**Arendt, Hannah**   1906-1975 . . . . . . . . **CLC 66**
See also CA 17-20R; 61-64; CANR 26;
MTCW

**Aretino, Pietro**   1492-1556 . . . . . . . . . . **LC 12**

**Arghezi, Tudor** . . . . . . . . . . . . . . . . . . . . **CLC 80**
See also Theodorescu, Ion N.

**Arguedas, Jose Maria**
1911-1969 . . . . . . . . . . . . . . . . **CLC 10, 18**
See also CA 89-92; DLB 113; HW

**Argueta, Manlio**   1936- . . . . . . . . . . . . **CLC 31**
See also CA 131; DLB 145; HW

**Ariosto, Ludovico**   1474-1533 . . . . . . . . **LC 6**

**Aristides**
See Epstein, Joseph

**Aristophanes**
450B.C.-385B.C. . . . . . . . . **CMLC 4; DA;
DAB; DAC; DAM DRAM, MST; DC 2**

**Arlt, Roberto (Godofredo Christophersen)**
1900-1942 . . . . . **TCLC 29; DAM MULT;
HLC**
See also CA 123; 131; HW

**Armah, Ayi Kwei**
1939- . . . . . . . . . . . . . . **CLC 5, 33; BLC;
DAM MULT, POET**
See also BW 1; CA 61-64; CANR 21;
DLB 117; MTCW

**Armatrading, Joan**   1950- . . . . . . . . . . **CLC 17**
See also CA 114

**Arnette, Robert**
See Silverberg, Robert

**Arnim, Achim von (Ludwig Joachim von
Arnim)**   1781-1831 . . . . . . . . . . **NCLC 5**
See also DLB 90

**Arnim, Bettina von**   1785-1859 . . . . **NCLC 38**
See also DLB 90

**Arnold, Matthew**
1822-1888 . . . . . **NCLC 6, 29; DA; DAB;
DAC; DAM MST, POET; PC 5; WLC**
See also CDBLB 1832-1890; DLB 32, 57

**Arnold, Thomas**   1795-1842 . . . . . . **NCLC 18**
See also DLB 55

**Arnow, Harriette (Louisa) Simpson**
1908-1986 . . . . . . . . . . . . . . . **CLC 2, 7, 18**
See also CA 9-12R; 118; CANR 14; DLB 6;
MTCW; SATA 42; SATA-Obit 47

**Arp, Hans**
See Arp, Jean

**Arp, Jean**   1887-1966 . . . . . . . . . . . . . . **CLC 5**
See also CA 81-84; 25-28R; CANR 42

**Arrabal**
See Arrabal, Fernando

**Arrabal, Fernando**   1932- . . . **CLC 2, 9, 18, 58**
See also CA 9-12R; CANR 15

**Arrick, Fran** . . . . . . . . . . . . . . . . . . . . . . **CLC 30**
See also Gaberman, Judie Angell

**Artaud, Antonin (Marie Joseph)**
1896-1948 . . . **TCLC 3, 36; DAM DRAM**
See also CA 104; 149

**Arthur, Ruth M(abel)**   1905-1979 . . . . **CLC 12**
See also CA 9-12R; 85-88; CANR 4;
SATA 7, 26

**Artsybashev, Mikhail (Petrovich)**
1878-1927 . . . . . . . . . . . . . . . . . . **TCLC 31**

**Arundel, Honor (Morfydd)**
1919-1973 . . . . . . . . . . . . . . . . . . . **CLC 17**
See also CA 21-22; 41-44R; CAP 2;
CLR 35; SATA 4; SATA-Obit 24

**Asch, Sholem**   1880-1957 . . . . . . . . . . **TCLC 3**
See also CA 105

**Ash, Shalom**
See Asch, Sholem

**Ashbery, John (Lawrence)**
1927- . . . . . . **CLC 2, 3, 4, 6, 9, 13, 15, 25,
41, 77; DAM POET**
See also CA 5-8R; CANR 9, 37; DLB 5,
165; DLBY 81; INT CANR-9; MTCW

**Ashdown, Clifford**
See Freeman, R(ichard) Austin

**Bakshi, Ralph** 1938(?)-............ **CLC 26**
See also CA 112; 138

**Bakunin, Mikhail (Alexandrovich)**
1814-1876 ................ **NCLC 25**

**Baldwin, James (Arthur)**
1924-1987 ...... **CLC 1, 2, 3, 4, 5, 8, 13,
15, 17, 42, 50, 67, 90; BLC; DA; DAB;
DAC; DAM MST, MULT, NOV, POP;
DC 1; SSC 10; WLC**
See also AAYA 4; BW 1; CA 1-4R; 124;
CABS 1; CANR 3, 24;
CDALB 1941-1968; DLB 2, 7, 33;
DLBY 87; MTCW; SATA 9;
SATA-Obit 54

**Ballard, J(ames) G(raham)**
1930- .... **CLC 3, 6, 14, 36; DAM NOV,
POP; SSC 1**
See also AAYA 3; CA 5-8R; CANR 15, 39;
DLB 14; MTCW

**Balmont, Konstantin (Dmitriyevich)**
1867-1943 ................. **TCLC 11**
See also CA 109

**Balzac, Honore de**
1799-1850 ........ **NCLC 5, 35, 53; DA;
DAB; DAC; DAM MST, NOV; SSC 5;
WLC**
See also DLB 119

**Bambara, Toni Cade**
1939-1995 ...... **CLC 19, 88; BLC; DA;
DAC; DAM MST, MULT**
See also AAYA 5; BW 2; CA 29-32R; 150;
CANR 24, 49; DLB 38; MTCW

**Bamdad, A.**
See Shamlu, Ahmad

**Banat, D. R.**
See Bradbury, Ray (Douglas)

**Bancroft, Laura**
See Baum, L(yman) Frank

**Banim, John** 1798-1842 ........ **NCLC 13**
See also DLB 116, 158, 159

**Banim, Michael** 1796-1874 ...... **NCLC 13**
See also DLB 158, 159

**Banks, Iain**
See Banks, Iain M(enzies)

**Banks, Iain M(enzies)** 1954- ....... **CLC 34**
See also CA 123; 128; INT 128

**Banks, Lynne Reid** ................ **CLC 23**
See also Reid Banks, Lynne
See also AAYA 6

**Banks, Russell** 1940- ........ **CLC 37, 72**
See also CA 65-68; CAAS 15; CANR 19,
52; DLB 130

**Banville, John** 1945-............. **CLC 46**
See also CA 117; 128; DLB 14; INT 128

**Banville, Theodore (Faullain) de**
1832-1891 ................. **NCLC 9**

**Baraka, Amiri**
1934- ........ **CLC 1, 2, 3, 5, 10, 14, 33;
BLC; DA; DAC; DAM MST, MULT,
POET, POP; DC 6; PC 4**
See also Jones, LeRoi
See also BW 2; CA 21-24R; CABS 3;
CANR 27, 38; CDALB 1941-1968;
DLB 5, 7, 16, 38; DLBD 8; MTCW

**Barbauld, Anna Laetitia**
1743-1825 ................. **NCLC 50**
See also DLB 107, 109, 142, 158

**Barbellion, W. N. P.** .............. **TCLC 24**
See also Cummings, Bruce F(rederick)

**Barbera, Jack (Vincent)** 1945-...... **CLC 44**
See also CA 110; CANR 45

**Barbey d'Aurevilly, Jules Amedee**
1808-1889 ........... **NCLC 1; SSC 17**
See also DLB 119

**Barbusse, Henri** 1873-1935 ........ **TCLC 5**
See also CA 105; DLB 65

**Barclay, Bill**
See Moorcock, Michael (John)

**Barclay, William Ewert**
See Moorcock, Michael (John)

**Barea, Arturo** 1897-1957 ........ **TCLC 14**
See also CA 111

**Barfoot, Joan** 1946- .............. **CLC 18**
See also CA 105

**Baring, Maurice** 1874-1945 ....... **TCLC 8**
See also CA 105; DLB 34

**Barker, Clive** 1952- ... **CLC 52; DAM POP**
See also AAYA 10; BEST 90:3; CA 121;
129; INT 129; MTCW

**Barker, George Granville**
1913-1991 ...... **CLC 8, 48; DAM POET**
See also CA 9-12R; 135; CANR 7, 38;
DLB 20; MTCW

**Barker, Harley Granville**
See Granville-Barker, Harley
See also DLB 10

**Barker, Howard** 1946-............ **CLC 37**
See also CA 102; DLB 13

**Barker, Pat(ricia)** 1943-........ **CLC 32, 94**
See also CA 117; 122; CANR 50; INT 122

**Barlow, Joel** 1754-1812 ......... **NCLC 23**
See also DLB 37

**Barnard, Mary (Ethel)** 1909-....... **CLC 48**
See also CA 21-22; CAP 2

**Barnes, Djuna**
1892-1982 ... **CLC 3, 4, 8, 11, 29; SSC 3**
See also CA 9-12R; 107; CANR 16; DLB 4,
9, 45; MTCW

**Barnes, Julian** 1946-........ **CLC 42; DAB**
See also CA 102; CANR 19; DLBY 93

**Barnes, Peter** 1931- ............ **CLC 5, 56**
See also CA 65-68; CAAS 12; CANR 33,
34; DLB 13; MTCW

**Baroja (y Nessi), Pio**
1872-1956 ............ **TCLC 8; HLC**
See also CA 104

**Baron, David**
See Pinter, Harold

**Baron Corvo**
See Rolfe, Frederick (William Serafino
Austin Lewis Mary)

**Barondess, Sue K(aufman)**
1926-1977 ................... **CLC 8**
See also Kaufman, Sue
See also CA 1-4R; 69-72; CANR 1

**Baron de Teive**
See Pessoa, Fernando (Antonio Nogueira)

**Barres, Maurice** 1862-1923 ....... **TCLC 47**
See also DLB 123

**Barreto, Afonso Henrique de Lima**
See Lima Barreto, Afonso Henrique de

**Barrett, (Roger) Syd** 1946- ........ **CLC 35**

**Barrett, William (Christopher)**
1913-1992 ................. **CLC 27**
See also CA 13-16R; 139; CANR 11;
INT CANR-11

**Barrie, J(ames) M(atthew)**
1860-1937 ............. **TCLC 2; DAB;
DAM DRAM**
See also CA 104; 136; CDBLB 1890-1914;
CLR 16; DLB 10, 141, 156; MAICYA;
YABC 1

**Barrington, Michael**
See Moorcock, Michael (John)

**Barrol, Grady**
See Bograd, Larry

**Barry, Mike**
See Malzberg, Barry N(athaniel)

**Barry, Philip** 1896-1949.......... **TCLC 11**
See also CA 109; DLB 7

**Bart, Andre Schwarz**
See Schwarz-Bart, Andre

**Barth, John (Simmons)**
1930- ...... **CLC 1, 2, 3, 5, 7, 9, 10, 14,
27, 51, 89; DAM NOV; SSC 10**
See also AITN 1, 2; CA 1-4R; CABS 1;
CANR 5, 23, 49; DLB 2; MTCW

**Barthelme, Donald**
1931-1989 ...... **CLC 1, 2, 3, 5, 6, 8, 13,
23, 46, 59; DAM NOV; SSC 2**
See also CA 21-24R; 129; CANR 20;
DLB 2; DLBY 80, 89; MTCW; SATA 7;
SATA-Obit 62

**Barthelme, Frederick** 1943-........ **CLC 36**
See also CA 114; 122; DLBY 85; INT 122

**Barthes, Roland (Gerard)**
1915-1980 ................ **CLC 24, 83**
See also CA 130; 97-100; MTCW

**Barzun, Jacques (Martin)** 1907- .... **CLC 51**
See also CA 61-64; CANR 22

**Bashevis, Isaac**
See Singer, Isaac Bashevis

**Bashkirtseff, Marie** 1859-1884 ... **NCLC 27**

**Basho**
See Matsuo Basho

**Bass, Kingsley B., Jr.**
See Bullins, Ed

**Bass, Rick** 1958-................. **CLC 79**
See also CA 126; CANR 53

**Bassani, Giorgio** 1916-............. **CLC 9**
See also CA 65-68; CANR 33; DLB 128;
MTCW

**Bastos, Augusto (Antonio) Roa**
See Roa Bastos, Augusto (Antonio)

**Bataille, Georges** 1897-1962 ....... **CLC 29**
See also CA 101; 89-92

**Bates, H(erbert) E(rnest)**
1905-1974 ............ **CLC 46; DAB;
DAM POP; SSC 10**
See also CA 93-96; 45-48; CANR 34;
DLB 162; MTCW

**Bauchart**
　See Camus, Albert

**Baudelaire, Charles**
　　　1821-1867 . . . . . . . . NCLC 6, 29, 55; DA;
　　　DAB; DAC; DAM MST, POET; PC 1;
　　　　　　　　　　　　　　SSC 18; WLC

**Baudrillard, Jean**　1929- . . . . . . . . . . CLC 60

**Baum, L(yman) Frank**　1856-1919 . . . TCLC 7
　See also CA 108; 133; CLR 15; DLB 22;
　JRDA; MAICYA; MTCW; SATA 18

**Baum, Louis F.**
　See Baum, L(yman) Frank

**Baumbach, Jonathan**　1933- . . . . . . CLC 6, 23
　See also CA 13-16R; CAAS 5; CANR 12;
　DLBY 80; INT CANR-12; MTCW

**Bausch, Richard (Carl)**　1945- . . . . . . CLC 51
　See also CA 101; CAAS 14; CANR 43;
　DLB 130

**Baxter, Charles**
　　　1947- . . . . . . . . CLC 45, 78; DAM POP
　See also CA 57-60; CANR 40; DLB 130

**Baxter, George Owen**
　See Faust, Frederick (Schiller)

**Baxter, James K(eir)**　1926-1972 . . . . CLC 14
　See also CA 77-80

**Baxter, John**
　See Hunt, E(verette) Howard, (Jr.)

**Bayer, Sylvia**
　See Glassco, John

**Baynton, Barbara**　1857-1929 . . . . . . TCLC 57

**Beagle, Peter S(oyer)**　1939- . . . . . . . . CLC 7
　See also CA 9-12R; CANR 4, 51;
　DLBY 80; INT CANR-4; SATA 60

**Bean, Normal**
　See Burroughs, Edgar Rice

**Beard, Charles A(ustin)**
　　　1874-1948 . . . . . . . . . . . . . . . . TCLC 15
　See also CA 115; DLB 17; SATA 18

**Beardsley, Aubrey**　1872-1898 . . . . . NCLC 6

**Beattie, Ann**
　　　1947- . . . . . . . . . . CLC 8, 13, 18, 40, 63;
　　　　　　　　　　DAM NOV, POP; SSC 11
　See also BEST 90:2; CA 81-84; CANR 53;
　DLBY 82; MTCW

**Beattie, James**　1735-1803 . . . . . . . NCLC 25
　See also DLB 109

**Beauchamp, Kathleen Mansfield**　1888-1923
　See Mansfield, Katherine
　See also CA 104; 134; DA; DAC;
　DAM MST

**Beaumarchais, Pierre-Augustin Caron de**
　　　1732-1799 . . . . . . . . . . . . . . . . . . . DC 4
　See also DAM DRAM

**Beaumont, Francis**
　　　1584(?)-1616 . . . . . . . . . . . . LC 33; DC 6
　See also CDBLB Before 1660; DLB 58, 121

**Beauvoir, Simone (Lucie Ernestine Marie
　Bertrand) de**
　　　1908-1986 . . . . CLC 1, 2, 4, 8, 14, 31, 44,
　　　　　50, 71; DA; DAB; DAC; DAM MST,
　　　　　　　　　　　　　　　　　　NOV; WLC
　See also CA 9-12R; 118; CANR 28;
　DLB 72; DLBY 86; MTCW

**Becker, Carl**　1873-1945 . . . . . . . . TCLC 63:
　See also DLB 17

**Becker, Jurek**　1937- . . . . . . . . . . . CLC 7, 19
　See also CA 85-88; DLB 75

**Becker, Walter**　1950- . . . . . . . . . . . . CLC 26

**Beckett, Samuel (Barclay)**
　　　1906-1989 . . . . . CLC 1, 2, 3, 4, 6, 9, 10,
　　　11, 14, 18, 29, 57, 59, 83; DA; DAB;
　　　DAC; DAM DRAM, MST, NOV;
　　　　　　　　　　　　　　SSC 16; WLC
　See also CA 5-8R; 130; CANR 33;
　CDBLB 1945-1960; DLB 13, 15;
　DLBY 90; MTCW

**Beckford, William**　1760-1844 . . . . NCLC 16
　See also DLB 39

**Beckman, Gunnel**　1910- . . . . . . . . . . CLC 26
　See also CA 33-36R; CANR 15; CLR 25;
　MAICYA; SAAS 9; SATA 6

**Becque, Henri**　1837-1899 . . . . . . . . NCLC 3

**Beddoes, Thomas Lovell**
　　　1803-1849 . . . . . . . . . . . . . . . . NCLC 3
　See also DLB 96

**Bedford, Donald F.**
　See Fearing, Kenneth (Flexner)

**Beecher, Catharine Esther**
　　　1800-1878 . . . . . . . . . . . . . . . NCLC 30
　See also DLB 1

**Beecher, John**　1904-1980 . . . . . . . . . . CLC 6
　See also AITN 1; CA 5-8R; 105; CANR 8

**Beer, Johann**　1655-1700 . . . . . . . . . . . . LC 5
　See also DLB 168

**Beer, Patricia**　1924- . . . . . . . . . . . . . CLC 58
　See also CA 61-64; CANR 13, 46; DLB 40

**Beerbohm, Henry Maximilian**
　　　1872-1956 . . . . . . . . . . . . . . . TCLC 1, 24
　See also CA 104; DLB 34, 100

**Beerbohm, Max**
　See Beerbohm, Henry Maximilian

**Beer-Hofmann, Richard**
　　　1866-1945 . . . . . . . . . . . . . . . . TCLC 60
　See also DLB 81

**Begiebing, Robert J(ohn)**　1946- . . . . . CLC 70
　See also CA 122; CANR 40

**Behan, Brendan**
　　　1923-1964 . . . . . . . . CLC 1, 8, 11, 15, 79;
　　　　　　　　　　　　　　　　DAM DRAM
　See also CA 73-76; CANR 33;
　CDBLB 1945-1960; DLB 13; MTCW

**Behn, Aphra**
　　　1640(?)-1689 . . . . . . LC 1, 30; DA; DAB;
　　　DAC; DAM DRAM, MST, NOV,
　　　　　　　　　　POET; DC 4; PC 13; WLC
　See also DLB 39, 80, 131

**Behrman, S(amuel) N(athaniel)**
　　　1893-1973 . . . . . . . . . . . . . . . . CLC 40
　See also CA 13-16; 45-48; CAP 1; DLB 7,
　44

**Belasco, David**　1853-1931 . . . . . . . . TCLC 3
　See also CA 104; DLB 7

**Belcheva, Elisaveta**　1893- . . . . . . . . . CLC 10
　See also Bagryana, Elisaveta

**Beldone, Phil "Cheech"**
　See Ellison, Harlan (Jay)

**Beleno**
　See Azuela, Mariano

**Belinski, Vissarion Grigoryevich**
　　　1811-1848 . . . . . . . . . . . . . . . . NCLC 5

**Belitt, Ben**　1911- . . . . . . . . . . . . . . CLC 22
　See also CA 13-16R; CAAS 4; CANR 7;
　DLB 5

**Bell, James Madison**
　　　1826-1902 . . . . . . . . . . . TCLC 43; BLC;
　　　　　　　　　　　　　　　　DAM MULT
　See also BW 1; CA 122; 124; DLB 50

**Bell, Madison (Smartt)**　1957- . . . . . . CLC 41
　See also CA 111; CANR 28

**Bell, Marvin (Hartley)**
　　　1937- . . . . . . . . . CLC 8, 31; DAM POET
　See also CA 21-24R; CAAS 14; DLB 5;
　MTCW

**Bell, W. L. D.**
　See Mencken, H(enry) L(ouis)

**Bellamy, Atwood C.**
　See Mencken, H(enry) L(ouis)

**Bellamy, Edward**　1850-1898 . . . . . . NCLC 4
　See also DLB 12

**Bellin, Edward J.**
　See Kuttner, Henry

**Belloc, (Joseph) Hilaire (Pierre)**
　　　1870-1953 . . . TCLC 7, 18; DAM POET
　See also CA 106; 152; DLB 19, 100, 141;
　YABC 1

**Belloc, Joseph Peter Rene Hilaire**
　See Belloc, (Joseph) Hilaire (Pierre)

**Belloc, Joseph Pierre Hilaire**
　See Belloc, (Joseph) Hilaire (Pierre)

**Belloc, M. A.**
　See Lowndes, Marie Adelaide (Belloc)

**Bellow, Saul**
　　　1915- . . . . . . CLC 1, 2, 3, 6, 8, 10, 13, 15,
　　　25, 33, 34, 63, 79; DA; DAB; DAC;
　　　DAM MST, NOV, POP; SSC 14; WLC
　See also AITN 2; BEST 89:3; CA 5-8R;
　CABS 1; CANR 29, 53;
　CDALB 1941-1968; DLB 2, 28; DLBD 3;
　DLBY 82; MTCW

**Belser, Reimond Karel Maria de**　1929-
　See Ruyslinck, Ward
　See also CA 152

**Bely, Andrey** . . . . . . . . . . . . . TCLC 7; PC 11
　See also Bugayev, Boris Nikolayevich

**Benary, Margot**
　See Benary-Isbert, Margot

**Benary-Isbert, Margot**　1889-1979 . . . CLC 12
　See also CA 5-8R; 89-92; CANR 4;
　CLR 12; MAICYA; SATA 2;
　SATA-Obit 21

**Benavente (y Martinez), Jacinto**
　　　1866-1954 . . . . . TCLC 3; DAM DRAM,
　　　　　　　　　　　　　　　　　　　MULT
　See also CA 106; 131; HW; MTCW

**Benchley, Peter (Bradford)**
　　　1940- . . . . . CLC 4, 8; DAM NOV, POP
　See also AAYA 14; AITN 2; CA 17-20R;
　CANR 12, 35; MTCW; SATA 3, 89

**Benchley, Robert (Charles)**
　　　1889-1945 . . . . . . . . . . . . . . TCLC 1, 55
　See also CA 105; DLB 11

**Benda, Julien**　1867-1956 . . . . . . . . TCLC 60
　See also CA 120

**Benedict, Ruth**　1887-1948 . . . . . . . TCLC 60

**Benedikt, Michael**　1935-　........　**CLC 4, 14**
See also CA 13-16R; CANR 7; DLB 5

**Benet, Juan**　1927-................　**CLC 28**
See also CA 143

**Benet, Stephen Vincent**
1898-1943　......　**TCLC 7; DAM POET;**
**SSC 10**
See also CA 104; 152; DLB 4, 48, 102;
YABC 1

**Benet, William Rose**
1886-1950　......　**TCLC 28; DAM POET**
See also CA 118; 152; DLB 45

**Benford, Gregory (Albert)**　1941-....　**CLC 52**
See also CA 69-72; CANR 12, 24, 49;
DLBY 82

**Bengtsson, Frans (Gunnar)**
1894-1954　.................　**TCLC 48**

**Benjamin, David**
See Slavitt, David R(ytman)

**Benjamin, Lois**
See Gould, Lois

**Benjamin, Walter**　1892-1940.....　**TCLC 39**

**Benn, Gottfried**　1886-1956........　**TCLC 3**
See also CA 106; DLB 56

**Bennett, Alan**
1934-　...　**CLC 45, 77; DAB; DAM MST**
See also CA 103; CANR 35; MTCW

**Bennett, (Enoch) Arnold**
1867-1931　...............　**TCLC 5, 20**
See also CA 106; CDBLB 1890-1914;
DLB 10, 34, 98, 135

**Bennett, Elizabeth**
See Mitchell, Margaret (Munnerlyn)

**Bennett, George Harold**　1930-
See Bennett, Hal
See also BW 1; CA 97-100

**Bennett, Hal**　.....................　**CLC 5**
See also Bennett, George Harold
See also DLB 33

**Bennett, Jay**　1912-................　**CLC 35**
See also AAYA 10; CA 69-72; CANR 11,
42; JRDA; SAAS 4; SATA 41, 87;
SATA-Brief 27

**Bennett, Louise (Simone)**
1919-　.....　**CLC 28; BLC; DAM MULT**
See also BW 2; CA 151; DLB 117

**Benson, E(dward) F(rederic)**
1867-1940　.................　**TCLC 27**
See also CA 114; DLB 135, 153

**Benson, Jackson J.**　1930-..........　**CLC 34**
See also CA 25-28R; DLB 111

**Benson, Sally**　1900-1972　..........　**CLC 17**
See also CA 19-20; 37-40R; CAP 1;
SATA 1, 35; SATA-Obit 27

**Benson, Stella**　1892-1933........　**TCLC 17**
See also CA 117; DLB 36, 162

**Bentham, Jeremy**　1748-1832　.....　**NCLC 38**
See also DLB 107, 158

**Bentley, E(dmund) C(lerihew)**
1875-1956　.................　**TCLC 12**
See also CA 108; DLB 70

**Bentley, Eric (Russell)**　1916-.......　**CLC 24**
See also CA 5-8R; CANR 6; INT CANR-6

**Beranger, Pierre Jean de**
1780-1857　.................　**NCLC 34**

**Berendt, John (Lawrence)**　1939-....　**CLC 86**
See also CA 146

**Berger, Colonel**
See Malraux, (Georges-)Andre

**Berger, John (Peter)**　1926-　......　**CLC 2, 19**
See also CA 81-84; CANR 51; DLB 14

**Berger, Melvin H.**　1927-..........　**CLC 12**
See also CA 5-8R; CANR 4; CLR 32;
SAAS 2; SATA 5, 88

**Berger, Thomas (Louis)**
1924-　..........　**CLC 3, 5, 8, 11, 18, 38;**
**DAM NOV**
See also CA 1-4R; CANR 5, 28, 51; DLB 2;
DLBY 80; INT CANR-28; MTCW

**Bergman, (Ernst) Ingmar**
1918-　....................　**CLC 16, 72**
See also CA 81-84; CANR 33

**Bergson, Henri**　1859-1941.......　**TCLC 32**

**Bergstein, Eleanor**　1938-..........　**CLC 4**
See also CA 53-56; CANR 5

**Berkoff, Steven**　1937-.............　**CLC 56**
See also CA 104

**Bermant, Chaim (Icyk)**　1929-　......　**CLC 40**
See also CA 57-60; CANR 6, 31

**Bern, Victoria**
See Fisher, M(ary) F(rances) K(ennedy)

**Bernanos, (Paul Louis) Georges**
1888-1948　...................　**TCLC 3**
See also CA 104; 130; DLB 72

**Bernard, April**　1956-　.............　**CLC 59**
See also CA 131

**Berne, Victoria**
See Fisher, M(ary) F(rances) K(ennedy)

**Bernhard, Thomas**
1931-1989　.............　**CLC 3, 32, 61**
See also CA 85-88; 127; CANR 32;
DLB 85, 124; MTCW

**Berriault, Gina**　1926-.............　**CLC 54**
See also CA 116; 129; DLB 130

**Berrigan, Daniel**　1921-.............　**CLC 4**
See also CA 33-36R; CAAS 1; CANR 11,
43; DLB 5

**Berrigan, Edmund Joseph Michael, Jr.**
1934-1983
See Berrigan, Ted
See also CA 61-64; 110; CANR 14

**Berrigan, Ted**.....................　**CLC 37**
See also Berrigan, Edmund Joseph Michael,
Jr.
See also DLB 5

**Berry, Charles Edward Anderson**　1931-
See Berry, Chuck
See also CA 115

**Berry, Chuck**.....................　**CLC 17**
See also Berry, Charles Edward Anderson

**Berry, Jonas**
See Ashbery, John (Lawrence)

**Berry, Wendell (Erdman)**
1934-　.............　**CLC 4, 6, 8, 27, 46;**
**DAM POET**
See also AITN 1; CA 73-76; CANR 50;
DLB 5, 6

**Berryman, John**
1914-1972　......　**CLC 1, 2, 3, 4, 6, 8, 10,**
**13, 25, 62; DAM POET**
See also CA 13-16; 33-36R; CABS 2;
CANR 35; CAP 1; CDALB 1941-1968;
DLB 48; MTCW

**Bertolucci, Bernardo**　1940-........　**CLC 16**
See also CA 106

**Bertrand, Aloysius**　1807-1841....　**NCLC 31**

**Bertran de Born**　c. 1140-1215.....　**CMLC 5**

**Besant, Annie (Wood)**　1847-1933　...　**TCLC 9**
See also CA 105

**Bessie, Alvah**　1904-1985..........　**CLC 23**
See also CA 5-8R; 116; CANR 2; DLB 26

**Bethlen, T. D.**
See Silverberg, Robert

**Beti, Mongo**....　**CLC 27; BLC; DAM MULT**
See also Biyidi, Alexandre

**Betjeman, John**
1906-1984　.......　**CLC 2, 6, 10, 34, 43;**
**DAB; DAM MST, POET**
See also CA 9-12R; 112; CANR 33;
CDBLB 1945-1960; DLB 20; DLBY 84;
MTCW

**Bettelheim, Bruno**　1903-1990　......　**CLC 79**
See also CA 81-84; 131; CANR 23; MTCW

**Betti, Ugo**　1892-1953.............　**TCLC 5**
See also CA 104

**Betts, Doris (Waugh)**　1932-....　**CLC 3, 6, 28**
See also CA 13-16R; CANR 9; DLBY 82;
INT CANR-9

**Bevan, Alistair**
See Roberts, Keith (John Kingston)

**Bialik, Chaim Nachman**
1873-1934　.................　**TCLC 25**

**Bickerstaff, Isaac**
See Swift, Jonathan

**Bidart, Frank**　1939-..............　**CLC 33**
See also CA 140

**Bienek, Horst**　1930-..........　**CLC 7, 11**
See also CA 73-76; DLB 75

**Bierce, Ambrose (Gwinett)**
1842-1914(?)　.......　**TCLC 1, 7, 44; DA;**
**DAC; DAM MST; SSC 9; WLC**
See also CA 104; 139; CDALB 1865-1917;
DLB 11, 12, 23, 71, 74

**Biggers, Earl Derr**　1884-1933　.....　**TCLC 65**
See also CA 108

**Billings, Josh**
See Shaw, Henry Wheeler

**Billington, (Lady) Rachel (Mary)**
1942-　.....................　**CLC 43**
See also AITN 2; CA 33-36R; CANR 44

**Binyon, T(imothy) J(ohn)**　1936-　....　**CLC 34**
See also CA 111; CANR 28

**Bioy Casares, Adolfo**
1914-　..............　**CLC 4, 8, 13, 88;**
**DAM MULT; HLC; SSC 17**
See also CA 29-32R; CANR 19, 43;
DLB 113; HW; MTCW

**Bird, Cordwainer**
See Ellison, Harlan (Jay)

**Bird, Robert Montgomery**
1806-1854　.................　**NCLC 1**

**Birney, (Alfred) Earle**
    1904- . . . . . . . . . . CLC 1, 4, 6, 11; DAC;
                            DAM MST, POET
    See also CA 1-4R; CANR 5, 20; DLB 88;
    MTCW

**Bishop, Elizabeth**
    1911-1979 . . . . . . CLC 1, 4, 9, 13, 15, 32;
                    DA; DAC; DAM MST, POET; PC 3
    See also CA 5-8R; 89-92; CABS 2;
    CANR 26; CDALB 1968-1988; DLB 5;
    MTCW; SATA-Obit 24

**Bishop, John**   1935- . . . . . . . . . . . . . . CLC 10
    See also CA 105

**Bissett, Bill**   1939- . . . . . . . . . CLC 18; PC 14
    See also CA 69-72; CAAS 19; CANR 15;
    DLB 53; MTCW

**Bitov, Andrei (Georgievich)**   1937- . . . CLC 57
    See also CA 142

**Biyidi, Alexandre**   1932-
    See Beti, Mongo
    See also BW 1; CA 114; 124; MTCW

**Bjarme, Brynjolf**
    See Ibsen, Henrik (Johan)

**Bjornson, Bjornstjerne (Martinius)**
    1832-1910 . . . . . . . . . . . . . . TCLC 7, 37
    See also CA 104

**Black, Robert**
    See Holdstock, Robert P.

**Blackburn, Paul**   1926-1971 . . . . . . CLC 9, 43
    See also CA 81-84; 33-36R; CANR 34;
    DLB 16; DLBY 81

**Black Elk**
    1863-1950 . . . . . TCLC 33; DAM MULT
    See also CA 144; NNAL

**Black Hobart**
    See Sanders, (James) Ed(ward)

**Blacklin, Malcolm**
    See Chambers, Aidan

**Blackmore, R(ichard) D(oddridge)**
    1825-1900 . . . . . . . . . . . . . . . . TCLC 27
    See also CA 120; DLB 18

**Blackmur, R(ichard) P(almer)**
    1904-1965 . . . . . . . . . . . . . . . CLC 2, 24
    See also CA 11-12; 25-28R; CAP 1; DLB 63

**Black Tarantula, The**
    See Acker, Kathy

**Blackwood, Algernon (Henry)**
    1869-1951 . . . . . . . . . . . . . . . . . TCLC 5
    See also CA 105; 150; DLB 153, 156

**Blackwood, Caroline**   1931-1996 . . . CLC 6, 9
    See also CA 85-88; 151; CANR 32;
    DLB 14; MTCW

**Blade, Alexander**
    See Hamilton, Edmond; Silverberg, Robert

**Blaga, Lucian**   1895-1961 . . . . . . . . . CLC 75

**Blair, Eric (Arthur)**   1903-1950
    See Orwell, George
    See also CA 104; 132; DA; DAB; DAC;
    DAM MST, NOV; MTCW; SATA 29

**Blais, Marie-Claire**
    1939- . . . . . . . CLC 2, 4, 6, 13, 22; DAC;
                                    DAM MST
    See also CA 21-24R; CAAS 4; CANR 38;
    DLB 53; MTCW

**Blaise, Clark**   1940- . . . . . . . . . . . . . . CLC 29
    See also AITN 2; CA 53-56; CAAS 3;
    CANR 5; DLB 53

**Blake, Nicholas**
    See Day Lewis, C(ecil)
    See also DLB 77

**Blake, William**
    1757-1827 . . . . . . . NCLC 13, 37, 57; DA;
                    DAB; DAC; DAM MST, POET; PC 12;
                                            WLC
    See also CDBLB 1789-1832; DLB 93, 163;
    MAICYA; SATA 30

**Blake, William J(ames)**   1894-1969 . . . PC 12
    See also CA 5-8R; 25-28R

**Blasco Ibanez, Vicente**
    1867-1928 . . . . . . . TCLC 12; DAM NOV
    See also CA 110; 131; HW; MTCW

**Blatty, William Peter**
    1928- . . . . . . . . . . . . . CLC 2; DAM POP
    See also CA 5-8R; CANR 9

**Bleeck, Oliver**
    See Thomas, Ross (Elmore)

**Blessing, Lee**   1949- . . . . . . . . . . . . . . CLC 54

**Blish, James (Benjamin)**
    1921-1975 . . . . . . . . . . . . . . . . . CLC 14
    See also CA 1-4R; 57-60; CANR 3; DLB 8;
    MTCW; SATA 66

**Bliss, Reginald**
    See Wells, H(erbert) G(eorge)

**Blixen, Karen (Christentze Dinesen)**
    1885-1962
    See Dinesen, Isak
    See also CA 25-28; CANR 22, 50; CAP 2;
    MTCW; SATA 44

**Bloch, Robert (Albert)**   1917-1994 . . . CLC 33
    See also CA 5-8R; 146; CAAS 20; CANR 5;
    DLB 44; INT CANR-5; SATA 12;
    SATA-Obit 82

**Blok, Alexander (Alexandrovich)**
    1880-1921 . . . . . . . . . . . . . . . . . TCLC 5
    See also CA 104

**Blom, Jan**
    See Breytenbach, Breyten

**Bloom, Harold**   1930- . . . . . . . . . . . . . CLC 24
    See also CA 13-16R; CANR 39; DLB 67

**Bloomfield, Aurelius**
    See Bourne, Randolph S(illiman)

**Blount, Roy (Alton), Jr.**   1941- . . . . . CLC 38
    See also CA 53-56; CANR 10, 28;
    INT CANR-28; MTCW

**Bloy, Leon**   1846-1917. . . . . . . . . . . . TCLC 22
    See also CA 121; DLB 123

**Blume, Judy (Sussman)**
    1938- . . . CLC 12, 30; DAM NOV, POP
    See also AAYA 3; CA 29-32R; CANR 13,
    37; CLR 2, 15; DLB 52; JRDA;
    MAICYA; MTCW; SATA 2, 31, 79

**Blunden, Edmund (Charles)**
    1896-1974 . . . . . . . . . . . . . . . CLC 2, 56
    See also CA 17-18; 45-48; CAP 2; DLB 20,
    100, 155; MTCW

**Bly, Robert (Elwood)**
    1926- . . . . . . . . . CLC 1, 2, 5, 10, 15, 38;
                                    DAM POET
    See also CA 5-8R; CANR 41; DLB 5;
    MTCW

**Boas, Franz**   1858-1942. . . . . . . . . . TCLC 56
    See also CA 115

**Bobette**
    See Simenon, Georges (Jacques Christian)

**Boccaccio, Giovanni**
    1313-1375 . . . . . . . . . CMLC 13; SSC 10

**Bochco, Steven**   1943- . . . . . . . . . . . . CLC 35
    See also AAYA 11; CA 124; 138

**Bodenheim, Maxwell**   1892-1954 . . . TCLC 44
    See also CA 110; DLB 9, 45

**Bodker, Cecil**   1927- . . . . . . . . . . . . . . CLC 21
    See also CA 73-76; CANR 13, 44; CLR 23;
    MAICYA; SATA 14

**Boell, Heinrich (Theodor)**
    1917-1985 . . . . CLC 2, 3, 6, 9, 11, 15, 27,
                    32, 72; DA; DAB; DAC; DAM MST,
                    NOV; SSC 23; WLC
    See also CA 21-24R; 116; CANR 24;
    DLB 69; DLBY 85; MTCW

**Boerne, Alfred**
    See Doeblin, Alfred

**Boethius**   480(?)-524(?) . . . . . . . . . CMLC 15
    See also DLB 115

**Bogan, Louise**
    1897-1970 . . . . . . . . . CLC 4, 39, 46, 93;
                                    DAM POET; PC 12
    See also CA 73-76; 25-28R; CANR 33;
    DLB 45; MTCW

**Bogarde, Dirk** . . . . . . . . . . . . . . . . . CLC 19
    See also Van Den Bogarde, Derek Jules
    Gaspard Ulric Niven
    See also DLB 14

**Bogosian, Eric**   1953- . . . . . . . . . . . . CLC 45
    See also CA 138

**Bograd, Larry**   1953- . . . . . . . . . . . . . CLC 35
    See also CA 93-96; SAAS 21; SATA 33, 89

**Boiardo, Matteo Maria**   1441-1494 . . . . LC 6

**Boileau-Despreaux, Nicolas**
    1636-1711 . . . . . . . . . . . . . . . . . . LC 3

**Bojer, Johan**   1872-1959. . . . . . . . . TCLC 64

**Boland, Eavan (Aisling)**
    1944- . . . . . . . CLC 40, 67; DAM POET
    See also CA 143; DLB 40

**Bolt, Lee**
    See Faust, Frederick (Schiller)

**Bolt, Robert (Oxton)**
    1924-1995 . . . . . . CLC 14; DAM DRAM
    See also CA 17-20R; 147; CANR 35;
    DLB 13; MTCW

**Bombet, Louis-Alexandre-Cesar**
    See Stendhal

**Bomkauf**
    See Kaufman, Bob (Garnell)

**Bonaventura**. . . . . . . . . . . . . . . . . . NCLC 35
    See also DLB 90

**Bond, Edward**
    1934- . . . CLC 4, 6, 13, 23; DAM DRAM
    See also CA 25-28R; CANR 38; DLB 13;
    MTCW

**Bonham, Frank**   1914-1989. . . . . . . . CLC 12
    See also AAYA 1; CA 9-12R; CANR 4, 36;
    JRDA; MAICYA; SAAS 3; SATA 1, 49;
    SATA-Obit 62

**Bonnefoy, Yves**
1923- ...... **CLC 9, 15, 58; DAM MST, POET**
See also CA 85-88; CANR 33; MTCW

**Bontemps, Arna(ud Wendell)**
1902-1973 ........... **CLC 1, 18; BLC; DAM MULT, NOV, POET**
See also BW 1; CA 1-4R; 41-44R; CANR 4, 35; CLR 6; DLB 48, 51; JRDA; MAICYA; MTCW; SATA 2, 44; SATA-Obit 24

**Booth, Martin** 1944- .............. **CLC 13**
See also CA 93-96; CAAS 2

**Booth, Philip** 1925- .............. **CLC 23**
See also CA 5-8R; CANR 5; DLBY 82

**Booth, Wayne C(layson)** 1921- ..... **CLC 24**
See also CA 1-4R; CAAS 5; CANR 3, 43; DLB 67

**Borchert, Wolfgang** 1921-1947 ..... **TCLC 5**
See also CA 104; DLB 69, 124

**Borel, Petrus** 1809-1859 ........ **NCLC 41**

**Borges, Jorge Luis**
1899-1986 ... **CLC 1, 2, 3, 4, 6, 8, 9, 10, 13, 19, 44, 48, 83; DA; DAB; DAC; DAM MST, MULT; HLC; SSC 4; WLC**
See also CA 21-24R; CANR 19, 33; DLB 113; DLBY 86; HW; MTCW

**Borowski, Tadeusz** 1922-1951 ...... **TCLC 9**
See also CA 106

**Borrow, George (Henry)**
1803-1881 .................. **NCLC 9**
See also DLB 21, 55, 166

**Bosman, Herman Charles**
1905-1951 .................. **TCLC 49**

**Bosschere, Jean de** 1878(?)-1953 ... **TCLC 19**
See also CA 115

**Boswell, James**
1740-1795 ...... **LC 4; DA; DAB; DAC; DAM MST; WLC**
See also CDBLB 1660-1789; DLB 104, 142

**Bottoms, David** 1949- ............ **CLC 53**
See also CA 105; CANR 22; DLB 120; DLBY 83

**Boucicault, Dion** 1820-1890 ...... **NCLC 41**

**Boucolon, Maryse** 1937(?)-
See Conde, Maryse
See also CA 110; CANR 30, 53

**Bourget, Paul (Charles Joseph)**
1852-1935 .................. **TCLC 12**
See also CA 107; DLB 123

**Bourjaily, Vance (Nye)** 1922- .... **CLC 8, 62**
See also CA 1-4R; CAAS 1; CANR 2; DLB 2, 143

**Bourne, Randolph S(illiman)**
1886-1918 .................. **TCLC 16**
See also CA 117; DLB 63

**Bova, Ben(jamin William)** 1932- .... **CLC 45**
See also AAYA 16; CA 5-8R; CAAS 18; CANR 11; CLR 3; DLBY 81; INT CANR-11; MAICYA; MTCW; SATA 6, 68

**Bowen, Elizabeth (Dorothea Cole)**
1899-1973 ...... **CLC 1, 3, 6, 11, 15, 22; DAM NOV; SSC 3**
See also CA 17-18; 41-44R; CANR 35; CAP 2; CDBLB 1945-1960; DLB 15, 162; MTCW

**Bowering, George** 1935- ........ **CLC 15, 47**
See also CA 21-24R; CAAS 16; CANR 10; DLB 53

**Bowering, Marilyn R(uthe)** 1949- ... **CLC 32**
See also CA 101; CANR 49

**Bowers, Edgar** 1924- .............. **CLC 9**
See also CA 5-8R; CANR 24; DLB 5

**Bowie, David** ..................... **CLC 17**
See also Jones, David Robert

**Bowles, Jane (Sydney)**
1917-1973 ................. **CLC 3, 68**
See also CA 19-20; 41-44R; CAP 2

**Bowles, Paul (Frederick)**
1910- ........ **CLC 1, 2, 19, 53; SSC 3**
See also CA 1-4R; CAAS 1; CANR 1, 19, 50; DLB 5, 6; MTCW

**Box, Edgar**
See Vidal, Gore

**Boyd, Nancy**
See Millay, Edna St. Vincent

**Boyd, William** 1952- ........ **CLC 28, 53, 70**
See also CA 114; 120; CANR 51

**Boyle, Kay**
1902-1992 ..... **CLC 1, 5, 19, 58; SSC 5**
See also CA 13-16R; 140; CAAS 1; CANR 29; DLB 4, 9, 48, 86; DLBY 93; MTCW

**Boyle, Mark**
See Kienzle, William X(avier)

**Boyle, Patrick** 1905-1982 ......... **CLC 19**
See also CA 127

**Boyle, T. C.** 1948-
See Boyle, T(homas) Coraghessan

**Boyle, T(homas) Coraghessan**
1948- ..... **CLC 36, 55, 90; DAM POP; SSC 16**
See also BEST 90:4; CA 120; CANR 44; DLBY 86

**Boz**
See Dickens, Charles (John Huffam)

**Brackenridge, Hugh Henry**
1748-1816 .................. **NCLC 7**
See also DLB 11, 37

**Bradbury, Edward P.**
See Moorcock, Michael (John)

**Bradbury, Malcolm (Stanley)**
1932- ......... **CLC 32, 61; DAM NOV**
See also CA 1-4R; CANR 1, 33; DLB 14; MTCW

**Bradbury, Ray (Douglas)**
1920- ........ **CLC 1, 3, 10, 15, 42; DA; DAB; DAC; DAM MST, NOV, POP; WLC**
See also AAYA 15; AITN 1, 2; CA 1-4R; CANR 2, 30; CDALB 1968-1988; DLB 2, 8; INT CANR-30; MTCW; SATA 11, 64

**Bradford, Gamaliel** 1863-1932 ..... **TCLC 36**
See also DLB 17

**Bradley, David (Henry, Jr.)**
1950- ..... **CLC 23; BLC; DAM MULT**
See also BW 1; CA 104; CANR 26; DLB 33

**Bradley, John Ed(mund, Jr.)**
1958- ...................... **CLC 55**
See also CA 139

**Bradley, Marion Zimmer**
1930- ............ **CLC 30; DAM POP**
See also AAYA 9; CA 57-60; CAAS 10; CANR 7, 31, 51; DLB 8; MTCW

**Bradstreet, Anne**
1612(?)-1672 ...... **LC 4, 30; DA; DAC; DAM MST, POET; PC 10**
See also CDALB 1640-1865; DLB 24

**Brady, Joan** 1939- .............. **CLC 86**
See also CA 141

**Bragg, Melvyn** 1939- ............. **CLC 10**
See also BEST 89:3; CA 57-60; CANR 10, 48; DLB 14

**Braine, John (Gerard)**
1922-1986 ............... **CLC 1, 3, 41**
See also CA 1-4R; 120; CANR 1, 33; CDBLB 1945-1960; DLB 15; DLBY 86; MTCW

**Brammer, William** 1930(?)-1978 .... **CLC 31**
See also CA 77-80

**Brancati, Vitaliano** 1907-1954 ..... **TCLC 12**
See also CA 109

**Brancato, Robin F(idler)** 1936- ..... **CLC 35**
See also AAYA 9; CA 69-72; CANR 11, 45; CLR 32; JRDA; SAAS 9; SATA 23

**Brand, Max**
See Faust, Frederick (Schiller)

**Brand, Millen** 1906-1980 .......... **CLC 7**
See also CA 21-24R; 97-100

**Branden, Barbara** ................. **CLC 44**
See also CA 148

**Brandes, Georg (Morris Cohen)**
1842-1927 .................. **TCLC 10**
See also CA 105

**Brandys, Kazimierz** 1916- ......... **CLC 62**

**Branley, Franklyn M(ansfield)**
1915- ...................... **CLC 21**
See also CA 33-36R; CANR 14, 39; CLR 13; MAICYA; SAAS 16; SATA 4, 68

**Brathwaite, Edward Kamau**
1930- ........... **CLC 11; DAM POET**
See also BW 2; CA 25-28R; CANR 11, 26, 47; DLB 125

**Brautigan, Richard (Gary)**
1935-1984 .... **CLC 1, 3, 5, 9, 12, 34, 42; DAM NOV**
See also CA 53-56; 113; CANR 34; DLB 2, 5; DLBY 80, 84; MTCW; SATA 56

**Brave Bird, Mary** 1953-
See Crow Dog, Mary
See also NNAL

**Braverman, Kate** 1950- ........... **CLC 67**
See also CA 89-92

**Brecht, Bertolt**
1898-1956 ...... **TCLC 1, 6, 13, 35; DA; DAB; DAC; DAM DRAM, MST; DC 3; WLC**
See also CA 104; 133; DLB 56, 124; MTCW

Brecht, Eugen Berthold Friedrich
See Brecht, Bertolt

Bremer, Fredrika 1801-1865 ..... NCLC 11

Brennan, Christopher John
1870-1932 ................. TCLC 17
See also CA 117

Brennan, Maeve 1917-............. CLC 5
See also CA 81-84

Brentano, Clemens (Maria)
1778-1842 ................. NCLC 1
See also DLB 90

Brent of Bin Bin
See Franklin, (Stella Maraia Sarah) Miles

Brenton, Howard 1942-........... CLC 31
See also CA 69-72; CANR 33; DLB 13;
MTCW

Breslin, James 1930-
See Breslin, Jimmy
See also CA 73-76; CANR 31; DAM NOV;
MTCW

Breslin, Jimmy ................. CLC 4, 43
See also Breslin, James
See also AITN 1

Bresson, Robert 1901-............. CLC 16
See also CA 110; CANR 49

Breton, Andre
1896-1966 ..... CLC 2, 9, 15, 54; PC 15
See also CA 19-20; 25-28R; CANR 40;
CAP 2; DLB 65; MTCW

Breytenbach, Breyten
1939(?)-...... CLC 23, 37; DAM POET
See also CA 113; 129

Bridgers, Sue Ellen 1942-......... CLC 26
See also AAYA 8; CA 65-68; CANR 11,
36; CLR 18; DLB 52; JRDA; MAICYA;
SAAS 1; SATA 22

Bridges, Robert (Seymour)
1844-1930 .......TCLC 1; DAM POET
See also CA 104; 152; CDBLB 1890-1914;
DLB 19, 98

Bridie, James.................... TCLC 3
See also Mavor, Osborne Henry
See also DLB 10

Brin, David 1950-............... CLC 34
See also CA 102; CANR 24;
INT CANR-24; SATA 65

Brink, Andre (Philippus)
1935- .................... CLC 18, 36
See also CA 104; CANR 39; INT 103;
MTCW

Brinsmead, H(esba) F(ay) 1922-.... CLC 21
See also CA 21-24R; CANR 10; MAICYA;
SAAS 5; SATA 18, 78

Brittain, Vera (Mary)
1893(?)-1970 ................. CLC 23
See also CA 13-16; 25-28R; CAP 1; MTCW

Broch, Hermann 1886-1951....... TCLC 20
See also CA 117; DLB 85, 124

Brock, Rose
See Hansen, Joseph

Brodkey, Harold (Roy) 1930-1996 .. CLC 56
See also CA 111; 151; DLB 130

Brodsky, Iosif Alexandrovich 1940-1996
See Brodsky, Joseph
See also AITN 1; CA 41-44R; 151;
CANR 37; DAM POET; MTCW

Brodsky, Joseph .. CLC 4, 6, 13, 36, 50; PC 9
See also Brodsky, Iosif Alexandrovich

Brodsky, Michael Mark 1948- ..... CLC 19
See also CA 102; CANR 18, 41

Bromell, Henry 1947-............. CLC 5
See also CA 53-56; CANR 9

Bromfield, Louis (Brucker)
1896-1956 ................. TCLC 11
See also CA 107; DLB 4, 9, 86

Broner, E(sther) M(asserman)
1930- ...................... CLC 19
See also CA 17-20R; CANR 8, 25; DLB 28

Bronk, William 1918-............. CLC 10
See also CA 89-92; CANR 23; DLB 165

Bronstein, Lev Davidovich
See Trotsky, Leon

Bronte, Anne 1820-1849......... NCLC 4
See also DLB 21

Bronte, Charlotte
1816-1855 ........ NCLC 3, 8, 33; DA;
DAB; DAC; DAM MST, NOV; WLC
See also AAYA 17; CDBLB 1832-1890;
DLB 21, 159

Bronte, Emily (Jane)
1818-1848 .... NCLC 16, 35; DA; DAB;
DAC; DAM MST, NOV, POET; PC 8;
WLC
See also AAYA 17; CDBLB 1832-1890;
DLB 21, 32

Brooke, Frances 1724-1789 ......... LC 6
See also DLB 39, 99

Brooke, Henry 1703(?)-1783 ........ LC 1
See also DLB 39

Brooke, Rupert (Chawner)
1887-1915 ....... TCLC 2, 7; DA; DAB;
DAC; DAM MST, POET; WLC
See also CA 104; 132; CDBLB 1914-1945;
DLB 19; MTCW

Brooke-Haven, P.
See Wodehouse, P(elham) G(renville)

Brooke-Rose, Christine 1926-...... CLC 40
See also CA 13-16R; DLB 14

Brookner, Anita
1928- ........... CLC 32, 34, 51; DAB;
DAM POP
See also CA 114; 120; CANR 37; DLBY 87;
MTCW

Brooks, Cleanth 1906-1994 ..... CLC 24, 86
See also CA 17-20R; 145; CANR 33, 35;
DLB 63; DLBY 94; INT CANR-35;
MTCW

Brooks, George
See Baum, L(yman) Frank

Brooks, Gwendolyn
1917- ...... CLC 1, 2, 4, 5, 15, 49; BLC;
DA; DAC; DAM MST, MULT, POET;
PC 7; WLC
See also AITN 1; BW 2; CA 1-4R;
CANR 1, 27, 52; CDALB 1941-1968;
CLR 27; DLB 5, 76, 165; MTCW;
SATA 6

Brooks, Mel..................... CLC 12
See also Kaminsky, Melvin
See also AAYA 13; DLB 26

Brooks, Peter 1938-............. CLC 34
See also CA 45-48; CANR 1

Brooks, Van Wyck 1886-1963...... CLC 29
See also CA 1-4R; CANR 6; DLB 45, 63,
103

Brophy, Brigid (Antonia)
1929-1995 ............ CLC 6, 11, 29
See also CA 5-8R; 149; CAAS 4; CANR 25,
53; DLB 14; MTCW

Brosman, Catharine Savage 1934-.... CLC 9
See also CA 61-64; CANR 21, 46

Brother Antoninus
See Everson, William (Oliver)

Broughton, T(homas) Alan 1936- ... CLC 19
See also CA 45-48; CANR 2, 23, 48

Broumas, Olga 1949-.......... CLC 10, 73
See also CA 85-88; CANR 20

Brown, Charles Brockden
1771-1810 ................. NCLC 22
See also CDALB 1640-1865; DLB 37, 59,
73

Brown, Christy 1932-1981......... CLC 63
See also CA 105; 104; DLB 14

Brown, Claude
1937- ..... CLC 30; BLC; DAM MULT
See also AAYA 7; BW 1; CA 73-76

Brown, Dee (Alexander)
1908- ......... CLC 18, 47; DAM POP
See also CA 13-16R; CAAS 6; CANR 11,
45; DLBY 80; MTCW; SATA 5

Brown, George
See Wertmueller, Lina

Brown, George Douglas
1869-1902 ................. TCLC 28

Brown, George Mackay
1921-1996 ................. CLC 5, 48
See also CA 21-24R; 151; CAAS 6;
CANR 12, 37; DLB 14, 27, 139; MTCW;
SATA 35

Brown, (William) Larry 1951-...... CLC 73
See also CA 130; 134; INT 133

Brown, Moses
See Barrett, William (Christopher)

Brown, Rita Mae
1944- ..... CLC 18, 43, 79; DAM NOV,
POP
See also CA 45-48; CANR 2, 11, 35;
INT CANR-11; MTCW

Brown, Roderick (Langmere) Haig-
See Haig-Brown, Roderick (Langmere)

Brown, Rosellen 1939-............ CLC 32
See also CA 77-80; CAAS 10; CANR 14, 44

Brown, Sterling Allen
1901-1989 ........ CLC 1, 23, 59; BLC;
DAM MULT, POET
See also BW 1; CA 85-88; 127; CANR 26;
DLB 48, 51, 63; MTCW

Brown, Will
See Ainsworth, William Harrison

Carey, Ernestine Gilbreth   1908- .... **CLC 17**
See also CA 5-8R; SATA 2

Carey, Peter   1943- ........ **CLC 40, 55, 96**
See also CA 123; 127; CANR 53; INT 127;
MTCW

Carleton, William   1794-1869 ...... **NCLC 3**
See also DLB 159

Carlisle, Henry (Coffin)   1926- ..... **CLC 33**
See also CA 13-16R; CANR 15

Carlsen, Chris
See Holdstock, Robert P.

Carlson, Ron(ald F.)   1947- ........ **CLC 54**
See also CA 105; CANR 27

Carlyle, Thomas
1795-1881 ....... **NCLC 22; DA; DAB;
DAC; DAM MST**
See also CDBLB 1789-1832; DLB 55; 144

Carman, (William) Bliss
1861-1929 ............. **TCLC 7; DAC**
See also CA 104; 152; DLB 92

Carnegie, Dale   1888-1955 ....... **TCLC 53**

Carossa, Hans   1878-1956 ........ **TCLC 48**
See also DLB 66

Carpenter, Don(ald Richard)
1931-1995 .................... **CLC 41**
See also CA 45-48; 149; CANR 1

Carpentier (y Valmont), Alejo
1904-1980 ............. **CLC 8, 11, 38;
DAM MULT; HLC**
See also CA 65-68; 97-100; CANR 11;
DLB 113; HW

Carr, Caleb   1955(?)- .............. **CLC 86**
See also CA 147

Carr, Emily   1871-1945 ........... **TCLC 32**
See also DLB 68

Carr, John Dickson   1906-1977 ...... **CLC 3**
See also CA 49-52; 69-72; CANR 3, 33;
MTCW

Carr, Philippa
See Hibbert, Eleanor Alice Burford

Carr, Virginia Spencer   1929- ...... **CLC 34**
See also CA 61-64; DLB 111

Carrere, Emmanuel   1957- ......... **CLC 89**

Carrier, Roch
1937- ... **CLC 13, 78; DAC; DAM MST**
See also CA 130; DLB 53

Carroll, James P.   1943(?)- ........ **CLC 38**
See also CA 81-84

Carroll, Jim   1951- ................ **CLC 35**
See also AAYA 17; CA 45-48; CANR 42

Carroll, Lewis ........... **NCLC 2, 53; WLC**
See also Dodgson, Charles Lutwidge
See also CDBLB 1832-1890; CLR 2, 18;
DLB 18, 163; JRDA

Carroll, Paul Vincent   1900-1968 .... **CLC 10**
See also CA 9-12R; 25-28R; DLB 10

Carruth, Hayden
1921- ...... **CLC 4, 7, 10, 18, 84; PC 10**
See also CA 9-12R; CANR 4, 38; DLB 5,
165; INT CANR-4; MTCW; SATA 47

Carson, Rachel Louise
1907-1964 ....... **CLC 71; DAM POP**
See also CA 77-80; CANR 35; MTCW;
SATA 23

Carter, Angela (Olive)
1940-1992 ...... **CLC 5, 41, 76; SSC 13**
See also CA 53-56; 136; CANR 12, 36;
DLB 14; MTCW; SATA 66;
SATA-Obit 70

Carter, Nick
See Smith, Martin Cruz

Carver, Raymond
1938-1988 ........ **CLC 22, 36, 53, 55;
DAM NOV; SSC 8**
See also CA 33-36R; 126; CANR 17, 34;
DLB 130; DLBY 84, 88; MTCW

Cary, Elizabeth, Lady Falkland
1585-1639 .................... **LC 30**

Cary, (Arthur) Joyce (Lunel)
1888-1957 ................ **TCLC 1, 29**
See also CA 104; CDBLB 1914-1945;
DLB 15, 100

Casanova de Seingalt, Giovanni Jacopo
1725-1798 .................... **LC 13**

Casares, Adolfo Bioy
See Bioy Casares, Adolfo

Casely-Hayford, J(oseph) E(phraim)
1866-1930 ............ **TCLC 24; BLC;
DAM MULT**
See also BW 2; CA 123; 152

Casey, John (Dudley)   1939- ........ **CLC 59**
See also BEST 90:2; CA 69-72; CANR 23

Casey, Michael   1947- .............. **CLC 2**
See also CA 65-68; DLB 5

Casey, Patrick
See Thurman, Wallace (Henry)

Casey, Warren (Peter)   1935-1988 ... **CLC 12**
See also CA 101; 127; INT 101

Casona, Alejandro ................. **CLC 49**
See also Alvarez, Alejandro Rodriguez

Cassavetes, John   1929-1989 ........ **CLC 20**
See also CA 85-88; 127

Cassill, R(onald) V(erlin)   1919- ... **CLC 4, 23**
See also CA 9-12R; CAAS 1; CANR 7, 45;
DLB 6

Cassirer, Ernst   1874-1945 ....... **TCLC 61**

Cassity, (Allen) Turner   1929- .... **CLC 6, 42**
See also CA 17-20R; CAAS 8; CANR 11;
DLB 105

Castaneda, Carlos   1931(?)- ......... **CLC 12**
See also CA 25-28R; CANR 32; HW;
MTCW

Castedo, Elena   1937- ............. **CLC 65**
See also CA 132

Castedo-Ellerman, Elena
See Castedo, Elena

Castellanos, Rosario
1925-1974 ...... **CLC 66; DAM MULT;
HLC**
See also CA 131; 53-56; DLB 113; HW

Castelvetro, Lodovico   1505-1571 ..... **LC 12**

Castiglione, Baldassare   1478-1529 ... **LC 12**

Castle, Robert
See Hamilton, Edmond

Castro, Guillen de   1569-1631 ........ **LC 19**

Castro, Rosalia de
1837-1885 ...... **NCLC 3; DAM MULT**

Cather, Willa
See Cather, Willa Sibert

Cather, Willa Sibert
1873-1947 ....... **TCLC 1, 11, 31; DA;
DAB; DAC; DAM MST, NOV; SSC 2;
WLC**
See also CA 104; 128; CDALB 1865-1917;
DLB 9, 54, 78; DLBD 1; MTCW;
SATA 30

Catton, (Charles) Bruce
1899-1978 .................... **CLC 35**
See also AITN 1; CA 5-8R; 81-84;
CANR 7; DLB 17; SATA 2;
SATA-Obit 24

Catullus   c. 84B.C.-c. 54B.C. ..... **CMLC 18**

Cauldwell, Frank
See King, Francis (Henry)

Caunitz, William J.   1933-1996 ..... **CLC 34**
See also BEST 89:3; CA 125; 130; 152;
INT 130

Causley, Charles (Stanley)   1917- ..... **CLC 7**
See also CA 9-12R; CANR 5, 35; CLR 30;
DLB 27; MTCW; SATA 3, 66

Caute, David   1936- .... **CLC 29; DAM NOV**
See also CA 1-4R; CAAS 4; CANR 1, 33;
DLB 14

Cavafy, C(onstantine) P(eter)
1863-1933 .... **TCLC 2, 7; DAM POET**
See also Kavafis, Konstantinos Petrou
See also CA 148

Cavallo, Evelyn
See Spark, Muriel (Sarah)

Cavanna, Betty .................. **CLC 12**
See also Harrison, Elizabeth Cavanna
See also JRDA; MAICYA; SAAS 4;
SATA 1, 30

Cavendish, Margaret Lucas
1623-1673 .................... **LC 30**
See also DLB 131

Caxton, William   1421(?)-1491(?) ..... **LC 17**

Cayrol, Jean   1911- ................ **CLC 11**
See also CA 89-92; DLB 83

Cela, Camilo Jose
1916- ..... **CLC 4, 13, 59; DAM MULT;
HLC**
See also BEST 90:2; CA 21-24R; CAAS 10;
CANR 21, 32; DLBY 89; HW; MTCW

Celan, Paul ...... **CLC 10, 19, 53, 82; PC 10**
See also Antschel, Paul
See also DLB 69

Celine, Louis-Ferdinand
............. **CLC 1, 3, 4, 7, 9, 15, 47**
See also Destouches, Louis-Ferdinand
See also DLB 72

Cellini, Benvenuto   1500-1571 ........ **LC 7**

Cendrars, Blaise ................. **CLC 18**
See also Sauser-Hall, Frederic

Cernuda (y Bidon), Luis
1902-1963 ....... **CLC 54; DAM POET**
See also CA 131; 89-92; DLB 134; HW

Cervantes (Saavedra), Miguel de
1547-1616 ........ **LC 6, 23; DA; DAB;
DAC; DAM MST, NOV; SSC 12; WLC**

**Cesaire, Aime (Fernand)**
1913- . . . . . . . . . . . . **CLC 19, 32; BLC;**
**DAM MULT, POET**
See also BW 2; CA 65-68; CANR 24, 43;
MTCW

**Chabon, Michael** 1965(?)- . . . . . . . . **CLC 55**
See also CA 139

**Chabrol, Claude** 1930- . . . . . . . . . . . **CLC 16**
See also CA 110

**Challans, Mary** 1905-1983
See Renault, Mary
See also CA 81-84; 111; SATA 23;
SATA-Obit 36

**Challis, George**
See Faust, Frederick (Schiller)

**Chambers, Aidan** 1934- . . . . . . . . . . **CLC 35**
See also CA 25-28R; CANR 12, 31; JRDA;
MAICYA; SAAS 12; SATA 1, 69

**Chambers, James** 1948-
See Cliff, Jimmy
See also CA 124

**Chambers, Jessie**
See Lawrence, D(avid) H(erbert Richards)

**Chambers, Robert W.** 1865-1933. . . TCLC 41

**Chandler, Raymond (Thornton)**
1888-1959 . . . . . . . . TCLC 1, 7; SSC 23
See also CA 104; 129; CDALB 1929-1941;
DLBD 6; MTCW

**Chang, Jung** 1952- . . . . . . . . . . . . . **CLC 71**
See also CA 142

**Channing, William Ellery**
1780-1842 . . . . . . . . . . . . . . . **NCLC 17**
See also DLB 1, 59

**Chaplin, Charles Spencer**
1889-1977 . . . . . . . . . . . . . . . . **CLC 16**
See also Chaplin, Charlie
See also CA 81-84; 73-76

**Chaplin, Charlie**
See Chaplin, Charles Spencer
See also DLB 44

**Chapman, George**
1559(?)-1634 . . . . . **LC 22; DAM DRAM**
See also DLB 62, 121

**Chapman, Graham** 1941-1989 . . . . . . **CLC 21**
See also Monty Python
See also CA 116; 129; CANR 35

**Chapman, John Jay** 1862-1933 . . . . . **TCLC 7**
See also CA 104

**Chapman, Lee**
See Bradley, Marion Zimmer

**Chapman, Walker**
See Silverberg, Robert

**Chappell, Fred (Davis)** 1936- . . . . **CLC 40, 78**
See also CA 5-8R; CAAS 4; CANR 8, 33;
DLB 6, 105

**Char, Rene(-Emile)**
1907-1988 . . . . . . . . . **CLC 9, 11, 14, 55;**
**DAM POET**
See also CA 13-16R; 124; CANR 32;
MTCW

**Charby, Jay**
See Ellison, Harlan (Jay)

**Chardin, Pierre Teilhard de**
See Teilhard de Chardin, (Marie Joseph)
Pierre

**Charles I** 1600-1649 . . . . . . . . . . . . . . **LC 13**

**Charyn, Jerome** 1937- . . . . . . . . **CLC 5, 8, 18**
See also CA 5-8R; CAAS 1; CANR 7;
DLBY 83; MTCW

**Chase, Mary (Coyle)** 1907-1981 . . . . . . **DC 1**
See also CA 77-80; 105; SATA 17;
SATA-Obit 29

**Chase, Mary Ellen** 1887-1973 . . . . . . . **CLC 2**
See also CA 13-16; 41-44R; CAP 1;
SATA 10

**Chase, Nicholas**
See Hyde, Anthony

**Chateaubriand, Francois Rene de**
1768-1848 . . . . . . . . . . . . . . . . **NCLC 3**
See also DLB 119

**Chatterje, Sarat Chandra** 1876-1936(?)
See Chatterji, Saratchandra
See also CA 109

**Chatterji, Bankim Chandra**
1838-1894 . . . . . . . . . . . . . . . **NCLC 19**

**Chatterji, Saratchandra** . . . . . . . . . . **TCLC 13**
See also Chatterje, Sarat Chandra

**Chatterton, Thomas**
1752-1770 . . . . . . . . **LC 3; DAM POET**
See also DLB 109

**Chatwin, (Charles) Bruce**
1940-1989 . . **CLC 28, 57, 59; DAM POP**
See also AAYA 4; BEST 90:1; CA 85-88;
127

**Chaucer, Daniel**
See Ford, Ford Madox

**Chaucer, Geoffrey**
1340(?)-1400 . . . . . . . . **LC 17; DA; DAB;**
**DAC; DAM MST, POET**
See also CDBLB Before 1660; DLB 146

**Chaviaras, Strates** 1935-
See Haviaras, Stratis
See also CA 105

**Chayefsky, Paddy** . . . . . . . . . . . . . . . **CLC 23**
See also Chayefsky, Sidney
See also DLB 7, 44; DLBY 81

**Chayefsky, Sidney** 1923-1981
See Chayefsky, Paddy
See also CA 9-12R; 104; CANR 18;
DAM DRAM

**Chedid, Andree** 1920- . . . . . . . . . . . . . **CLC 47**
See also CA 145

**Cheever, John**
1912-1982 . . . . . . **CLC 3, 7, 8, 11, 15, 25,**
**64; DA; DAB; DAC; DAM MST, NOV,**
**POP; SSC 1; WLC**
See also CA 5-8R; 106; CABS 1; CANR 5,
27; CDALB 1941-1968; DLB 2, 102;
DLBY 80, 82; INT CANR-5; MTCW

**Cheever, Susan** 1943- . . . . . . . . . . **CLC 18, 48**
See also CA 103; CANR 27, 51; DLBY 82;
INT CANR-27

**Chekhonte, Antosha**
See Chekhov, Anton (Pavlovich)

**Chekhov, Anton (Pavlovich)**
1860-1904 . . . . . **TCLC 3, 10, 31, 55; DA;**
**DAB; DAC; DAM DRAM, MST; SSC 2;**
**WLC**
See also CA 104; 124

**Chernyshevsky, Nikolay Gavrilovich**
1828-1889 . . . . . . . . . . . . . . . . . **NCLC 1**

**Cherry, Carolyn Janice** 1942-
See Cherryh, C. J.
See also CA 65-68; CANR 10

**Cherryh, C. J.** . . . . . . . . . . . . . . . . . . . **CLC 35**
See also Cherry, Carolyn Janice
See also DLBY 80

**Chesnutt, Charles W(addell)**
1858-1932 . . . . . . . . . **TCLC 5, 39; BLC;**
**DAM MULT; SSC 7**
See also BW 1; CA 106; 125; DLB 12, 50,
78; MTCW

**Chester, Alfred** 1929(?)-1971 . . . . . . . **CLC 49**
See also CA 33-36R; DLB 130

**Chesterton, G(ilbert) K(eith)**
1874-1936 . . . . . . . . . . . . **TCLC 1, 6, 64;**
**DAM NOV, POET; SSC 1**
See also CA 104; 132; CDBLB 1914-1945;
DLB 10, 19, 34, 70, 98, 149; MTCW;
SATA 27

**Chiang Pin-chin** 1904-1986
See Ding Ling
See also CA 118

**Ch'ien Chung-shu** 1910- . . . . . . . . . . . **CLC 22**
See also CA 130; MTCW

**Child, L. Maria**
See Child, Lydia Maria

**Child, Lydia Maria** 1802-1880 . . . . **NCLC 6**
See also DLB 1, 74; SATA 67

**Child, Mrs.**
See Child, Lydia Maria

**Child, Philip** 1898-1978 . . . . . . . . **CLC 19, 68**
See also CA 13-14; CAP 1; SATA 47

**Childers, (Robert) Erskine**
1870-1922 . . . . . . . . . . . . . . . . . **TCLC 65**
See also CA 113; DLB 70

**Childress, Alice**
1920-1994 . . . . **CLC 12, 15, 86, 96; BLC;**
**DAM DRAM, MULT, NOV; DC 4**
See also AAYA 8; BW 2; CA 45-48; 146;
CANR 3, 27, 50; CLR 14; DLB 7, 38;
JRDA; MAICYA; MTCW; SATA 7, 48,
81

**Chislett, (Margaret) Anne** 1943- . . . . **CLC 34**
See also CA 151

**Chitty, Thomas Willes** 1926- . . . . . . . **CLC 11**
See also Hinde, Thomas
See also CA 5-8R

**Chivers, Thomas Holley**
1809-1858 . . . . . . . . . . . . . . . . . **NCLC 49**
See also DLB 3

**Chomette, Rene Lucien** 1898-1981
See Clair, Rene
See also CA 103

**Chopin, Kate**
. . . . . . . . **TCLC 5, 14; DA; DAB; SSC 8**
See also Chopin, Katherine
See also CDALB 1865-1917; DLB 12, 78

**Chopin, Katherine** 1851-1904
See Chopin, Kate
See also CA 104; 122; DAC; DAM MST,
NOV

**Chretien de Troyes**
c. 12th cent. - . . . . . . . . . . . . . **CMLC 10**

**Christie**
See Ichikawa, Kon

**Christie, Agatha (Mary Clarissa)**
1890-1976 ...... **CLC 1, 6, 8, 12, 39, 48;**
**DAB; DAC; DAM NOV**
See also AAYA 9; AITN 1, 2; CA 17-20R;
61-64; CANR 10, 37; CDBLB 1914-1945;
DLB 13, 77; MTCW; SATA 36

**Christie, (Ann) Philippa**
See Pearce, Philippa
See also CA 5-8R; CANR 4

**Christine de Pizan** 1365(?)-1431(?) .... **LC 9**

**Chubb, Elmer**
See Masters, Edgar Lee

**Chulkov, Mikhail Dmitrievich**
1743-1792 ...................... **LC 2**
See also DLB 150

**Churchill, Caryl** 1938-... **CLC 31, 55; DC 5**
See also CA 102; CANR 22, 46; DLB 13;
MTCW

**Churchill, Charles** 1731-1764........ **LC 3**
See also DLB 109

**Chute, Carolyn** 1947-.............. **CLC 39**
See also CA 123

**Ciardi, John (Anthony)**
1916-1986 ........... **CLC 10, 40, 44;**
**DAM POET**
See also CA 5-8R; 118; CAAS 2; CANR 5,
33; CLR 19; DLB 5; DLBY 86;
INT CANR-5; MAICYA; MTCW;
SATA 1, 65; SATA-Obit 46

**Cicero, Marcus Tullius**
106B.C.-43B.C............... **CMLC 3**

**Cimino, Michael** 1943-........... **CLC 16**
See also CA 105

**Cioran, E(mil) M.** 1911-1995....... **CLC 64**
See also CA 25-28R; 149

**Cisneros, Sandra**
1954- ..... **CLC 69; DAM MULT; HLC**
See also AAYA 9; CA 131; DLB 122, 152;
HW

**Cixous, Helene** 1937-............. **CLC 92**
See also CA 126; DLB 83; MTCW

**Clair, Rene**...................... **CLC 20**
See also Chomette, Rene Lucien

**Clampitt, Amy** 1920-1994 ......... **CLC 32**
See also CA 110; 146; CANR 29; DLB 105

**Clancy, Thomas L., Jr.** 1947-
See Clancy, Tom
See also CA 125; 131; INT 131; MTCW

**Clancy, Tom**..... **CLC 45; DAM NOV, POP**
See also Clancy, Thomas L., Jr.
See also AAYA 9; BEST 89:1, 90:1

**Clare, John**
1793-1864 ........... **NCLC 9; DAB;**
**DAM POET**
See also DLB 55, 96

**Clarin**
See Alas (y Urena), Leopoldo (Enrique
Garcia)

**Clark, Al C.**
See Goines, Donald

**Clark, (Robert) Brian** 1932-........ **CLC 29**
See also CA 41-44R

**Clark, Curt**
See Westlake, Donald E(dwin)

**Clark, Eleanor** 1913-1996 ....... **CLC 5, 19**
See also CA 9-12R; 151; CANR 41; DLB 6

**Clark, J. P.**
See Clark, John Pepper
See also DLB 117

**Clark, John Pepper**
1935- .... **CLC 38; BLC; DAM DRAM,**
**MULT; DC 5**
See also Clark, J. P.
See also BW 1; CA 65-68; CANR 16

**Clark, M. R.**
See Clark, Mavis Thorpe

**Clark, Mavis Thorpe** 1909-........ **CLC 12**
See also CA 57-60; CANR 8, 37; CLR 30;
MAICYA; SAAS 5; SATA 8, 74

**Clark, Walter Van Tilburg**
1909-1971 .................. **CLC 28**
See also CA 9-12R; 33-36R; DLB 9;
SATA 8

**Clarke, Arthur C(harles)**
1917- ........... **CLC 1, 4, 13, 18, 35;**
**DAM POP; SSC 3**
See also AAYA 4; CA 1-4R; CANR 2, 28;
JRDA; MAICYA; MTCW; SATA 13, 70

**Clarke, Austin**
1896-1974 ...... **CLC 6, 9; DAM POET**
See also CA 29-32; 49-52; CAP 2; DLB 10,
20

**Clarke, Austin C(hesterfield)**
1934- .......... **CLC 8, 53; BLC; DAC;**
**DAM MULT**
See also BW 1; CA 25-28R; CAAS 16;
CANR 14, 32; DLB 53, 125

**Clarke, Gillian** 1937-............. **CLC 61**
See also CA 106; DLB 40

**Clarke, Marcus (Andrew Hislop)**
1846-1881 ................ **NCLC 19**

**Clarke, Shirley** 1925-............. **CLC 16**

**Clash, The**
See Headon, (Nicky) Topper; Jones, Mick;
Simonon, Paul; Strummer, Joe

**Claudel, Paul (Louis Charles Marie)**
1868-1955 ............... **TCLC 2, 10**
See also CA 104

**Clavell, James (duMaresq)**
1925-1994 ............. **CLC 6, 25, 87;**
**DAM NOV, POP**
See also CA 25-28R; 146; CANR 26, 48;
MTCW

**Cleaver, (Leroy) Eldridge**
1935- ..... **CLC 30; BLC; DAM MULT**
See also BW 1; CA 21-24R; CANR 16

**Cleese, John (Marwood)** 1939-..... **CLC 21**
See also Monty Python
See also CA 112; 116; CANR 35; MTCW

**Cleishbotham, Jebediah**
See Scott, Walter

**Cleland, John** 1710-1789 ............ **LC 2**
See also DLB 39

**Clemens, Samuel Langhorne** 1835-1910
See Twain, Mark
See also CA 104; 135; CDALB 1865-1917;
DA; DAB; DAC; DAM MST, NOV;
DLB 11, 12, 23, 64, 74; JRDA;
MAICYA; YABC 2

**Cleophil**
See Congreve, William

**Clerihew, E.**
See Bentley, E(dmund) C(lerihew)

**Clerk, N. W.**
See Lewis, C(live) S(taples)

**Cliff, Jimmy**...................... **CLC 21**
See also Chambers, James

**Clifton, (Thelma) Lucille**
1936- .............. **CLC 19, 66; BLC;**
**DAM MULT, POET**
See also BW 2; CA 49-52; CANR 2, 24, 42;
CLR 5; DLB 5, 41; MAICYA; MTCW;
SATA 20, 69

**Clinton, Dirk**
See Silverberg, Robert

**Clough, Arthur Hugh** 1819-1861.. **NCLC 27**
See also DLB 32

**Clutha, Janet Paterson Frame** 1924-
See Frame, Janet
See also CA 1-4R; CANR 2, 36; MTCW

**Clyne, Terence**
See Blatty, William Peter

**Cobalt, Martin**
See Mayne, William (James Carter)

**Cobbett, William** 1763-1835 ..... **NCLC 49**
See also DLB 43, 107, 158

**Coburn, D(onald) L(ee)** 1938-...... **CLC 10**
See also CA 89-92

**Cocteau, Jean (Maurice Eugene Clement)**
1889-1963 .... **CLC 1, 8, 15, 16, 43; DA;**
**DAB; DAC; DAM DRAM, MST, NOV;**
**WLC**
See also CA 25-28; CANR 40; CAP 2;
DLB 65; MTCW

**Codrescu, Andrei**
1946- ........... **CLC 46; DAM POET**
See also CA 33-36R; CAAS 19; CANR 13,
34, 53

**Coe, Max**
See Bourne, Randolph S(illiman)

**Coe, Tucker**
See Westlake, Donald E(dwin)

**Coetzee, J(ohn) M(ichael)**
1940- ...... **CLC 23, 33, 66; DAM NOV**
See also CA 77-80; CANR 41; MTCW

**Coffey, Brian**
See Koontz, Dean R(ay)

**Cohan, George M.** 1878-1942 ..... **TCLC 60**

**Cohen, Arthur A(llen)**
1928-1986 ................. **CLC 7, 31**
See also CA 1-4R; 120; CANR 1, 17, 42;
DLB 28

**Cohen, Leonard (Norman)**
1934- .... **CLC 3, 38; DAC; DAM MST**
See also CA 21-24R; CANR 14; DLB 53;
MTCW

**Cormier, Robert (Edmund)**
1925- .... **CLC 12, 30; DA; DAB; DAC; DAM MST, NOV**
See also AAYA 3; CA 1-4R; CANR 5, 23; CDALB 1968-1988; CLR 12; DLB 52; INT CANR-23; JRDA; MAICYA; MTCW; SATA 10, 45, 83

**Corn, Alfred (DeWitt III)** 1943- .... **CLC 33**
See also CA 104; CANR 44; DLB 120; DLBY 80

**Corneille, Pierre**
1606-1684 .... **LC 28; DAB; DAM MST**

**Cornwell, David (John Moore)**
1931- .......... **CLC 9, 15; DAM POP**
See also le Carre, John
See also CA 5-8R; CANR 13, 33; MTCW

**Corso, (Nunzio) Gregory** 1930-... **CLC 1, 11**
See also CA 5-8R; CANR 41; DLB 5, 16; MTCW

**Cortazar, Julio**
1914-1984 ...... **CLC 2, 3, 5, 10, 13, 15, 33, 34, 92; DAM MULT, NOV; HLC; SSC 7**
See also CA 21-24R; CANR 12, 32; DLB 113; HW; MTCW

**CORTES, HERNAN** 1484-1547..... **LC 31**

**Corwin, Cecil**
See Kornbluth, C(yril) M.

**Cosic, Dobrica** 1921- ............. **CLC 14**
See also CA 122; 138

**Costain, Thomas B(ertram)**
1885-1965 ................... **CLC 30**
See also CA 5-8R; 25-28R; DLB 9

**Costantini, Humberto**
1924(?)-1987 ................ **CLC 49**
See also CA 131; 122; HW

**Costello, Elvis** 1955-............. **CLC 21**

**Cotter, Joseph Seamon Sr.**
1861-1949 ............ **TCLC 28; BLC; DAM MULT**
See also BW 1; CA 124; DLB 50

**Couch, Arthur Thomas Quiller**
See Quiller-Couch, Arthur Thomas

**Coulton, James**
See Hansen, Joseph

**Couperus, Louis (Marie Anne)**
1863-1923 ................. **TCLC 15**
See also CA 115

**Coupland, Douglas**
1961- ....... **CLC 85; DAC; DAM POP**
See also CA 142

**Court, Wesli**
See Turco, Lewis (Putnam)

**Courtenay, Bryce** 1933-........... **CLC 59**
See also CA 138

**Courtney, Robert**
See Ellison, Harlan (Jay)

**Cousteau, Jacques-Yves** 1910-...... **CLC 30**
See also CA 65-68; CANR 15; MTCW; SATA 38

**Coward, Noel (Peirce)**
1899-1973 .......... **CLC 1, 9, 29, 51; DAM DRAM**
See also AITN 1; CA 17-18; 41-44R; CANR 35; CAP 2; CDBLB 1914-1945; DLB 10; MTCW

**Cowley, Malcolm** 1898-1989 ....... **CLC 39**
See also CA 5-8R; 128; CANR 3; DLB 4, 48; DLBY 81, 89; MTCW

**Cowper, William**
1731-1800 ..... **NCLC 8; DAM POET**
See also DLB 104, 109

**Cox, William Trevor**
1928- ....... **CLC 9, 14, 71; DAM NOV**
See also Trevor, William
See also CA 9-12R; CANR 4, 37; DLB 14; INT CANR-37; MTCW

**Coyne, P. J.**
See Masters, Hilary

**Cozzens, James Gould**
1903-1978 ............ **CLC 1, 4, 11, 92**
See also CA 9-12R; 81-84; CANR 19; CDALB 1941-1968; DLB 9; DLBD 2; DLBY 84; MTCW

**Crabbe, George** 1754-1832....... **NCLC 26**
See also DLB 93

**Craddock, Charles Egbert**
See Murfree, Mary Noailles

**Craig, A. A.**
See Anderson, Poul (William)

**Craik, Dinah Maria (Mulock)**
1826-1887 ................ **NCLC 38**
See also DLB 35, 163; MAICYA; SATA 34

**Cram, Ralph Adams** 1863-1942.... **TCLC 45**

**Crane, (Harold) Hart**
1899-1932 ....... **TCLC 2, 5; DA; DAB; DAC; DAM MST, POET; PC 3; WLC**
See also CA 104; 127; CDALB 1917-1929; DLB 4, 48; MTCW

**Crane, R(onald) S(almon)**
1886-1967 ................... **CLC 27**
See also CA 85-88; DLB 63

**Crane, Stephen (Townley)**
1871-1900 ....... **TCLC 11, 17, 32; DA; DAB; DAC; DAM MST, NOV, POET; SSC 7; WLC**
See also CA 109; 140; CDALB 1865-1917; DLB 12, 54, 78; YABC 2

**Crase, Douglas** 1944- ............. **CLC 58**
See also CA 106

**Crashaw, Richard** 1612(?)-1649...... **LC 24**
See also DLB 126

**Craven, Margaret**
1901-1980 ............. **CLC 17; DAC**
See also CA 103

**Crawford, F(rancis) Marion**
1854-1909 ................. **TCLC 10**
See also CA 107; DLB 71

**Crawford, Isabella Valancy**
1850-1887 ................ **NCLC 12**
See also DLB 92

**Crayon, Geoffrey**
See Irving, Washington

**Creasey, John** 1908-1973 ......... **CLC 11**
See also CA 5-8R; 41-44R; CANR 8; DLB 77; MTCW

**Crebillon, Claude Prosper Jolyot de (fils)**
1707-1777 .................... **LC 28**

**Credo**
See Creasey, John

**Creeley, Robert (White)**
1926- ..... **CLC 1, 2, 4, 8, 11, 15, 36, 78; DAM POET**
See also CA 1-4R; CAAS 10; CANR 23, 43; DLB 5, 16; MTCW

**Crews, Harry (Eugene)**
1935- ................. **CLC 6, 23, 49**
See also AITN 1; CA 25-28R; CANR 20; DLB 6, 143; MTCW

**Crichton, (John) Michael**
1942- .... **CLC 2, 6, 54, 90; DAM NOV, POP**
See also AAYA 10; AITN 2; CA 25-28R; CANR 13, 40; DLBY 81; INT CANR-13; JRDA; MTCW; SATA 9, 88

**Crispin, Edmund** ................. **CLC 22**
See also Montgomery, (Robert) Bruce
See also DLB 87

**Cristofer, Michael**
1945(?)- ........ **CLC 28; DAM DRAM**
See also CA 110; 152; DLB 7

**Croce, Benedetto** 1866-1952 ...... **TCLC 37**
See also CA 120

**Crockett, David** 1786-1836 ....... **NCLC 8**
See also DLB 3, 11

**Crockett, Davy**
See Crockett, David

**Crofts, Freeman Wills**
1879-1957 ................. **TCLC 55**
See also CA 115; DLB 77

**Croker, John Wilson** 1780-1857 .. **NCLC 10**
See also DLB 110

**Crommelynck, Fernand** 1885-1970 .. **CLC 75**
See also CA 89-92

**Cronin, A(rchibald) J(oseph)**
1896-1981 ................... **CLC 32**
See also CA 1-4R; 102; CANR 5; SATA 47; SATA-Obit 25

**Cross, Amanda**
See Heilbrun, Carolyn G(old)

**Crothers, Rachel** 1878(?)-1958..... **TCLC 19**
See also CA 113; DLB 7

**Croves, Hal**
See Traven, B.

**Crow Dog, Mary**.................. **CLC 93**
See also Brave Bird, Mary

**Crowfield, Christopher**
See Stowe, Harriet (Elizabeth) Beecher

**Crowley, Aleister**.................. **TCLC 7**
See also Crowley, Edward Alexander

**Crowley, Edward Alexander** 1875-1947
See Crowley, Aleister
See also CA 104

**Crowley, John** 1942-.............. **CLC 57**
See also CA 61-64; CANR 43; DLBY 82; SATA 65

**Crud**
See Crumb, R(obert)

**Crumarums**
See Crumb, R(obert)

**Davis, Richard Harding**
1864-1916 ............... **TCLC 24**
See also CA 114; DLB 12, 23, 78, 79;
DLBD 13

**Davison, Frank Dalby** 1893-1970 ... **CLC 15**
See also CA 116

**Davison, Lawrence H.**
See Lawrence, D(avid) H(erbert Richards)

**Davison, Peter (Hubert)** 1928- ..... **CLC 28**
See also CA 9-12R; CAAS 4; CANR 3, 43;
DLB 5

**Davys, Mary** 1674-1732 ............ **LC 1**
See also DLB 39

**Dawson, Fielding** 1930- ........... **CLC 6**
See also CA 85-88; DLB 130

**Dawson, Peter**
See Faust, Frederick (Schiller)

**Day, Clarence (Shepard, Jr.)**
1874-1935 ................. **TCLC 25**
See also CA 108; DLB 11

**Day, Thomas** 1748-1789 ............ **LC 1**
See also DLB 39; YABC 1

**Day Lewis, C(ecil)**
1904-1972 .............. **CLC 1, 6, 10;**
**DAM POET; PC 11**
See also Blake, Nicholas
See also CA 13-16; 33-36R; CANR 34;
CAP 1; DLB 15, 20; MTCW

**Dazai, Osamu** ................... **TCLC 11**
See also Tsushima, Shuji

**de Andrade, Carlos Drummond**
See Drummond de Andrade, Carlos

**Deane, Norman**
See Creasey, John

**de Beauvoir, Simone (Lucie Ernestine Marie**
**Bertrand)**
See Beauvoir, Simone (Lucie Ernestine
Marie Bertrand) de

**de Brissac, Malcolm**
See Dickinson, Peter (Malcolm)

**de Chardin, Pierre Teilhard**
See Teilhard de Chardin, (Marie Joseph)
Pierre

**Dee, John** 1527-1608 ............. **LC 20**

**Deer, Sandra** 1940- ............... **CLC 45**

**De Ferrari, Gabriella** 1941- ........ **CLC 65**
See also CA 146

**Defoe, Daniel**
1660(?)-1731 .... **LC 1; DA; DAB; DAC;**
**DAM MST, NOV; WLC**
See also CDBLB 1660-1789; DLB 39, 95,
101; JRDA; MAICYA; SATA 22

**de Gourmont, Remy(-Marie-Charles)**
See Gourmont, Remy (-Marie-Charles) de

**de Hartog, Jan** 1914- ............. **CLC 19**
See also CA 1-4R; CANR 1

**de Hostos, E. M.**
See Hostos (y Bonilla), Eugenio Maria de

**de Hostos, Eugenio M.**
See Hostos (y Bonilla), Eugenio Maria de

**Deighton, Len** ............ **CLC 4, 7, 22, 46**
See also Deighton, Leonard Cyril
See also AAYA 6; BEST 89:2;
CDBLB 1960 to Present; DLB 87

**Deighton, Leonard Cyril** 1929-
See Deighton, Len
See also CA 9-12R; CANR 19, 33;
DAM NOV, POP; MTCW

**Dekker, Thomas**
1572(?)-1632 ..... **LC 22; DAM DRAM**
See also CDBLB Before 1660; DLB 62

**Delafield, E. M.** 1890-1943 ....... **TCLC 61**
See also Dashwood, Edmee Elizabeth
Monica de la Pasture
See also DLB 34

**de la Mare, Walter (John)**
1873-1956 .... **TCLC 4, 53; DAB; DAC;**
**DAM MST, POET; SSC 14; WLC**
See also CDBLB 1914-1945; CLR 23;
DLB 162; SATA 16

**Delaney, Franey**
See O'Hara, John (Henry)

**Delaney, Shelagh**
1939- ......... **CLC 29; DAM DRAM**
See also CA 17-20R; CANR 30;
CDBLB 1960 to Present; DLB 13;
MTCW

**Delany, Mary (Granville Pendarves)**
1700-1788 ................... **LC 12**

**Delany, Samuel R(ay, Jr.)**
1942- ........... **CLC 8, 14, 38; BLC;**
**DAM MULT**
See also BW 2; CA 81-84; CANR 27, 43;
DLB 8, 33; MTCW

**De La Ramee, (Marie) Louise** 1839-1908
See Ouida
See also SATA 20

**de la Roche, Mazo** 1879-1961 ...... **CLC 14**
See also CA 85-88; CANR 30; DLB 68;
SATA 64

**Delbanco, Nicholas (Franklin)**
1942- .................... **CLC 6, 13**
See also CA 17-20R; CAAS 2; CANR 29;
DLB 6

**del Castillo, Michel** 1933- ........ **CLC 38**
See also CA 109

**Deledda, Grazia (Cosima)**
1875(?)-1936 ............... **TCLC 23**
See also CA 123

**Delibes, Miguel** ................. **CLC 8, 18**
See also Delibes Setien, Miguel

**Delibes Setien, Miguel** 1920-
See Delibes, Miguel
See also CA 45-48; CANR 1, 32; HW;
MTCW

**DeLillo, Don**
1936- ..... **CLC 8, 10, 13, 27, 39, 54, 76;**
**DAM NOV, POP**
See also BEST 89:1; CA 81-84; CANR 21;
DLB 6; MTCW

**de Lisser, H. G.**
See De Lisser, Herbert George
See also DLB 117

**De Lisser, Herbert George**
1878-1944 ................. **TCLC 12**
See also de Lisser, H. G.
See also BW 2; CA 109; 152

**Deloria, Vine (Victor), Jr.**
1933- ......... **CLC 21; DAM MULT**
See also CA 53-56; CANR 5, 20, 48;
MTCW; NNAL; SATA 21

**Del Vecchio, John M(ichael)**
1947- ..................... **CLC 29**
See also CA 110; DLBD 9

**de Man, Paul (Adolph Michel)**
1919-1983 ................... **CLC 55**
See also CA 128; 111; DLB 67; MTCW

**De Marinis, Rick** 1934- ........... **CLC 54**
See also CA 57-60; CAAS 24; CANR 9, 25,
50

**Dembry, R. Emmet**
See Murfree, Mary Noailles

**Demby, William**
1922- ..... **CLC 53; BLC; DAM MULT**
See also BW 1; CA 81-84; DLB 33

**Demijohn, Thom**
See Disch, Thomas M(ichael)

**de Montherlant, Henry (Milon)**
See Montherlant, Henry (Milon) de

**Demosthenes** 384B.C.-322B.C. ... **CMLC 13**

**de Natale, Francine**
See Malzberg, Barry N(athaniel)

**Denby, Edwin (Orr)** 1903-1983 ..... **CLC 48**
See also CA 138; 110

**Denis, Julio**
See Cortazar, Julio

**Denmark, Harrison**
See Zelazny, Roger (Joseph)

**Dennis, John** 1658-1734 ........... **LC 11**
See also DLB 101

**Dennis, Nigel (Forbes)** 1912-1989 .... **CLC 8**
See also CA 25-28R; 129; DLB 13, 15;
MTCW

**De Palma, Brian (Russell)** 1940- .... **CLC 20**
See also CA 109

**De Quincey, Thomas** 1785-1859 ... **NCLC 4**
See also CDBLB 1789-1832; DLB 110; 144

**Deren, Eleanora** 1908(?)-1961
See Deren, Maya
See also CA 111

**Deren, Maya** ..................... **CLC 16**
See also Deren, Eleanora

**Derleth, August (William)**
1909-1971 ................... **CLC 31**
See also CA 1-4R; 29-32R; CANR 4;
DLB 9; SATA 5

**Der Nister** 1884-1950 ........... **TCLC 56**

**de Routisie, Albert**
See Aragon, Louis

**Derrida, Jacques** 1930- ......... **CLC 24, 87**
See also CA 124; 127

**Derry Down Derry**
See Lear, Edward

**Dersonnes, Jacques**
See Simenon, Georges (Jacques Christian)

**Desai, Anita**
1937- ... **CLC 19, 37; DAB; DAM NOV**
See also CA 81-84; CANR 33, 53; MTCW;
SATA 63

**de Saint-Luc, Jean**
See Glassco, John

**de Saint Roman, Arnaud**
See Aragon, Louis

**Descartes, Rene** 1596-1650 ...... LC 20, 35

**De Sica, Vittorio** 1901(?)-1974 ..... CLC 20
See also CA 117

**Desnos, Robert** 1900-1945 ........ TCLC 22
See also CA 121; 151

**Destouches, Louis-Ferdinand**
1894-1961 ................. CLC 9, 15
See also Celine, Louis-Ferdinand
See also CA 85-88; CANR 28; MTCW

**Deutsch, Babette** 1895-1982 ....... CLC 18
See also CA 1-4R; 108; CANR 4; DLB 45;
SATA 1; SATA-Obit 33

**Devenant, William** 1606-1649 ....... LC 13

**Devkota, Laxmiprasad**
1909-1959 .................. TCLC 23
See also CA 123

**De Voto, Bernard (Augustine)**
1897-1955 ................. TCLC 29
See also CA 113; DLB 9

**De Vries, Peter**
1910-1993 .... CLC 1, 2, 3, 7, 10, 28, 46;
DAM NOV
See also CA 17-20R; 142; CANR 41;
DLB 6; DLBY 82; MTCW

**Dexter, John**
See Bradley, Marion Zimmer

**Dexter, Martin**
See Faust, Frederick (Schiller)

**Dexter, Pete**
1943- ........ CLC 34, 55; DAM POP
See also BEST 89:2; CA 127; 131; INT 131;
MTCW

**Diamano, Silmang**
See Senghor, Leopold Sedar

**Diamond, Neil** 1941- ............. CLC 30
See also CA 108

**Diaz del Castillo, Bernal** 1496-1584 .. LC 31

**di Bassetto, Corno**
See Shaw, George Bernard

**Dick, Philip K(indred)**
1928-1982 ........... CLC 10, 30, 72;
DAM NOV, POP
See also CA 49-52; 106; CANR 2, 16;
DLB 8; MTCW

**Dickens, Charles (John Huffam)**
1812-1870 ...... NCLC 3, 8, 18, 26, 37,
50; DA; DAB; DAC; DAM MST, NOV;
SSC 17; WLC
See also CDBLB 1832-1890; DLB 21, 55,
70, 159, 166; JRDA; MAICYA; SATA 15

**Dickey, James (Lafayette)**
1923- ........ CLC 1, 2, 4, 7, 10, 15, 47;
DAM NOV, POET, POP
See also AITN 1, 2; CA 9-12R; CABS 2;
CANR 10, 48; CDALB 1968-1988;
DLB 5; DLBD 7; DLBY 82, 93;
INT CANR-10; MTCW

**Dickey, William** 1928-1994 ...... CLC 3, 28
See also CA 9-12R; 145; CANR 24; DLB 5

**Dickinson, Charles** 1951- .......... CLC 49
See also CA 128

**Dickinson, Emily (Elizabeth)**
1830-1886 ...... NCLC 21; DA; DAB;
DAC; DAM MST, POET; PC 1; WLC
See also CDALB 1865-1917; DLB 1;
SATA 29

**Dickinson, Peter (Malcolm)**
1927- ..................... CLC 12, 35
See also AAYA 9; CA 41-44R; CANR 31;
CLR 29; DLB 87, 161; JRDA; MAICYA;
SATA 5, 62

**Dickson, Carr**
See Carr, John Dickson

**Dickson, Carter**
See Carr, John Dickson

**Diderot, Denis** 1713-1784 .......... LC 26

**Didion, Joan**
1934- .. CLC 1, 3, 8, 14, 32; DAM NOV
See also AITN 1; CA 5-8R; CANR 14, 52;
CDALB 1968-1988; DLB 2; DLBY 81,
86; MTCW

**Dietrich, Robert**
See Hunt, E(verette) Howard, (Jr.)

**Dillard, Annie**
1945- .......... CLC 9, 60; DAM NOV
See also AAYA 6; CA 49-52; CANR 3, 43;
DLBY 80; MTCW; SATA 10

**Dillard, R(ichard) H(enry) W(ilde)**
1937- ....................... CLC 5
See also CA 21-24R; CAAS 7; CANR 10;
DLB 5

**Dillon, Eilis** 1920-1994 ........... CLC 17
See also CA 9-12R; 147; CAAS 3; CANR 4,
38; CLR 26; MAICYA; SATA 2, 74;
SATA-Obit 83

**Dimont, Penelope**
See Mortimer, Penelope (Ruth)

**Dinesen, Isak** ....... CLC 10, 29, 95; SSC 7
See also Blixen, Karen (Christentze
Dinesen)

**Ding Ling** ....................... CLC 68
See also Chiang Pin-chin

**Disch, Thomas M(ichael)** 1940- ... CLC 7, 36
See also AAYA 17; CA 21-24R; CAAS 4;
CANR 17, 36; CLR 18; DLB 8;
MAICYA; MTCW; SAAS 15; SATA 54

**Disch, Tom**
See Disch, Thomas M(ichael)

**d'Isly, Georges**
See Simenon, Georges (Jacques Christian)

**Disraeli, Benjamin** 1804-1881 .. NCLC 2, 39
See also DLB 21, 55

**Ditcum, Steve**
See Crumb, R(obert)

**Dixon, Paige**
See Corcoran, Barbara

**Dixon, Stephen** 1936- ..... CLC 52; SSC 16
See also CA 89-92; CANR 17, 40; DLB 130

**Dobell, Sydney Thompson**
1824-1874 ................. NCLC 43
See also DLB 32

**Doblin, Alfred** ................. TCLC 13
See also Doeblin, Alfred

**Dobrolyubov, Nikolai Alexandrovich**
1836-1861 ................. NCLC 5

**Dobyns, Stephen** 1941- ............ CLC 37
See also CA 45-48; CANR 2, 18

**Doctorow, E(dgar) L(aurence)**
1931- ..... CLC 6, 11, 15, 18, 37, 44, 65;
DAM NOV, POP
See also AITN 2; BEST 89:3; CA 45-48;
CANR 2, 33, 51; CDALB 1968-1988;
DLB 2, 28; DLBY 80; MTCW

**Dodgson, Charles Lutwidge** 1832-1898
See Carroll, Lewis
See also CLR 2; DA; DAB; DAC;
DAM MST, NOV, POET; MAICYA;
YABC 2

**Dodson, Owen (Vincent)**
1914-1983 ............. CLC 79; BLC;
DAM MULT
See also BW 1; CA 65-68; 110; CANR 24;
DLB 76

**Doeblin, Alfred** 1878-1957 ........ TCLC 13
See also Doblin, Alfred
See also CA 110; 141; DLB 66

**Doerr, Harriet** 1910- ............. CLC 34
See also CA 117; 122; CANR 47; INT 122

**Domecq, H(onorio) Bustos**
See Bioy Casares, Adolfo; Borges, Jorge
Luis

**Domini, Rey**
See Lorde, Audre (Geraldine)

**Dominique**
See Proust, (Valentin-Louis-George-Eugene-)
Marcel

**Don, A**
See Stephen, Leslie

**Donaldson, Stephen R.**
1947- ............ CLC 46; DAM POP
See also CA 89-92; CANR 13;
INT CANR-13

**Donleavy, J(ames) P(atrick)**
1926- ............. CLC 1, 4, 6, 10, 45
See also AITN 2; CA 9-12R; CANR 24, 49;
DLB 6; INT CANR-24; MTCW

**Donne, John**
1572-1631 ....... LC 10, 24; DA; DAB;
DAC; DAM MST, POET; PC 1
See also CDBLB Before 1660; DLB 121,
151

**Donnell, David** 1939(?)- ........... CLC 34

**Donoghue, P. S.**
See Hunt, E(verette) Howard, (Jr.)

**Donoso (Yanez), Jose**
1924- ............... CLC 4, 8, 11, 32;
DAM MULT; HLC
See also CA 81-84; CANR 32; DLB 113;
HW; MTCW

**Donovan, John** 1928-1992 ........ CLC 35
See also CA 97-100; 137; CLR 3;
MAICYA; SATA 72; SATA-Brief 29

**Don Roberto**
See Cunninghame Graham, R(obert)
B(ontine)

**Doolittle, Hilda**
1886-1961 ..... CLC 3, 8, 14, 31, 34, 73;
DA; DAC; DAM MST, POET; PC 5;
WLC
See also H. D.
See also CA 97-100; CANR 35; DLB 4, 45;
MTCW

**Dorfman, Ariel**
1942- ....... CLC 48, 77; DAM MULT;
HLC
See also CA 124; 130; HW; INT 130

**Dorn, Edward (Merton)** 1929- ... CLC 10, 18
See also CA 93-96; CANR 42; DLB 5;
INT 93-96

**Dorsan, Luc**
See Simenon, Georges (Jacques Christian)

**Dorsange, Jean**
See Simenon, Georges (Jacques Christian)

**Dos Passos, John (Roderigo)**
1896-1970 ...... CLC 1, 4, 8, 11, 15, 25,
34, 82; DA; DAB; DAC; DAM MST,
NOV; WLC
See also CA 1-4R; 29-32R; CANR 3;
CDALB 1929-1941; DLB 4, 9; DLBD 1;
MTCW

**Dossage, Jean**
See Simenon, Georges (Jacques Christian)

**Dostoevsky, Fedor Mikhailovich**
1821-1881 ...... NCLC 2, 7, 21, 33, 43;
DA; DAB; DAC; DAM MST, NOV;
SSC 2; WLC

**Doughty, Charles M(ontagu)**
1843-1926 .................... TCLC 27
See also CA 115; DLB 19, 57

**Douglas, Ellen** .................... CLC 73
See also Haxton, Josephine Ayres;
Williamson, Ellen Douglas

**Douglas, Gavin** 1475(?)-1522 ....... LC 20

**Douglas, Keith** 1920-1944 ....... TCLC 40
See also DLB 27

**Douglas, Leonard**
See Bradbury, Ray (Douglas)

**Douglas, Michael**
See Crichton, (John) Michael

**Douglass, Frederick**
1817(?)-1895 .... NCLC 7, 55; BLC; DA;
DAC; DAM MST, MULT; WLC
See also CDALB 1640-1865; DLB 1, 43, 50,
79; SATA 29

**Dourado, (Waldomiro Freitas) Autran**
1926- .................... CLC 23, 60
See also CA 25-28R; CANR 34

**Dourado, Waldomiro Autran**
See Dourado, (Waldomiro Freitas) Autran

**Dove, Rita (Frances)**
1952- ....... CLC 50, 81; DAM MULT,
POET; PC 6
See also BW 2; CA 109; CAAS 19;
CANR 27, 42; DLB 120

**Dowell, Coleman** 1925-1985 ....... CLC 60
See also CA 25-28R; 117; CANR 10;
DLB 130

**Dowson, Ernest (Christopher)**
1867-1900 .................... TCLC 4
See also CA 105; 150; DLB 19, 135

**Doyle, A. Conan**
See Doyle, Arthur Conan

**Doyle, Arthur Conan**
1859-1930 ......... TCLC 7; DA; DAB;
DAC; DAM MST, NOV; SSC 12; WLC
See also AAYA 14; CA 104; 122;
CDBLB 1890-1914; DLB 18, 70, 156;
MTCW; SATA 24

**Doyle, Conan**
See Doyle, Arthur Conan

**Doyle, John**
See Graves, Robert (von Ranke)

**Doyle, Roddy** 1958(?)- ............ CLC 81
See also AAYA 14; CA 143

**Doyle, Sir A. Conan**
See Doyle, Arthur Conan

**Doyle, Sir Arthur Conan**
See Doyle, Arthur Conan

**Dr. A**
See Asimov, Isaac; Silverstein, Alvin

**Drabble, Margaret**
1939- ........ CLC 2, 3, 5, 8, 10, 22, 53;
DAB; DAC; DAM MST, NOV, POP
See also CA 13-16R; CANR 18, 35;
CDBLB 1960 to Present; DLB 14, 155;
MTCW; SATA 48

**Drapier, M. B.**
See Swift, Jonathan

**Drayham, James**
See Mencken, H(enry) L(ouis)

**Drayton, Michael** 1563-1631 ........ LC 8

**Dreadstone, Carl**
See Campbell, (John) Ramsey

**Dreiser, Theodore (Herman Albert)**
1871-1945 ....... TCLC 10, 18, 35; DA;
DAC; DAM MST, NOV; WLC
See also CA 106; 132; CDALB 1865-1917;
DLB 9, 12, 102, 137; DLBD 1; MTCW

**Drexler, Rosalyn** 1926- .......... CLC 2, 6
See also CA 81-84

**Dreyer, Carl Theodor** 1889-1968.... CLC 16
See also CA 116

**Drieu la Rochelle, Pierre(-Eugene)**
1893-1945 .................. TCLC 21
See also CA 117; DLB 72

**Drinkwater, John** 1882-1937 ...... TCLC 57
See also CA 109; 149; DLB 10, 19, 149

**Drop Shot**
See Cable, George Washington

**Droste-Hulshoff, Annette Freiin von**
1797-1848 .................. NCLC 3
See also DLB 133

**Drummond, Walter**
See Silverberg, Robert

**Drummond, William Henry**
1854-1907 .................. TCLC 25
See also DLB 92

**Drummond de Andrade, Carlos**
1902-1987 .................... CLC 18
See also Andrade, Carlos Drummond de
See also CA 132; 123

**Drury, Allen (Stuart)** 1918- ........ CLC 37
See also CA 57-60; CANR 18, 52;
INT CANR-18

**Dryden, John**
1631-1700 ........ LC 3, 21; DA; DAB;
DAC; DAM DRAM, MST, POET;
DC 3; WLC
See also CDBLB 1660-1789; DLB 80, 101,
131

**Duberman, Martin** 1930- .......... CLC 8
See also CA 1-4R; CANR 2

**Dubie, Norman (Evans)** 1945- ...... CLC 36
See also CA 69-72; CANR 12; DLB 120

**Du Bois, W(illiam) E(dward) B(urghardt)**
1868-1963 ........ CLC 1, 2, 13, 64, 96;
BLC; DA; DAC; DAM MST, MULT,
NOV; WLC
See also BW 1; CA 85-88; CANR 34;
CDALB 1865-1917; DLB 47, 50, 91;
MTCW; SATA 42

**Dubus, Andre** 1936- ... CLC 13, 36; SSC 15
See also CA 21-24R; CANR 17; DLB 130;
INT CANR-17

**Duca Minimo**
See D'Annunzio, Gabriele

**Ducharme, Rejean** 1941- .......... CLC 74
See also DLB 60

**Duclos, Charles Pinot** 1704-1772 ..... LC 1

**Dudek, Louis** 1918- ........... CLC 11, 19
See also CA 45-48; CAAS 14; CANR 1;
DLB 88

**Duerrenmatt, Friedrich**
1921-1990 ...... CLC 1, 4, 8, 11, 15, 43;
DAM DRAM
See also CA 17-20R; CANR 33; DLB 69,
124; MTCW

**Duffy, Bruce** (?)- ................. CLC 50

**Duffy, Maureen** 1933- ............ CLC 37
See also CA 25-28R; CANR 33; DLB 14;
MTCW

**Dugan, Alan** 1923- ............... CLC 2, 6
See also CA 81-84; DLB 5

**du Gard, Roger Martin**
See Martin du Gard, Roger

**Duhamel, Georges** 1884-1966 ....... CLC 8
See also CA 81-84; 25-28R; CANR 35;
DLB 65; MTCW

**Dujardin, Edouard (Emile Louis)**
1861-1949 .................. TCLC 13
See also CA 109; DLB 123

**Dumas, Alexandre (Davy de la Pailleterie)**
1802-1870 ....... NCLC 11; DA; DAB;
DAC; DAM MST, NOV; WLC
See also DLB 119; SATA 18

**Dumas, Alexandre**
1824-1895 ............. NCLC 9; DC 1

**Dumas, Claudine**
See Malzberg, Barry N(athaniel)

**Dumas, Henry L.** 1934-1968 ..... CLC 6, 62
See also BW 1; CA 85-88; DLB 41

**du Maurier, Daphne**
1907-1989 ........ CLC 6, 11, 59; DAB;
DAC; DAM MST, POP; SSC 18
See also CA 5-8R; 128; CANR 6; MTCW;
SATA 27; SATA-Obit 60

**Dunbar, Paul Laurence**
1872-1906 . . . . . TCLC 2, 12; BLC; DA;
DAC; DAM MST, MULT, POET; PC 5;
SSC 8; WLC
See also BW 1; CA 104; 124;
CDALB 1865-1917; DLB 50, 54, 78;
SATA 34

**Dunbar, William** 1460(?)-1530(?) . . . . LC 20
See also DLB 132, 146

**Duncan, Lois** 1934- . . . . . . . . . . . . . CLC 26
See also AAYA 4; CA 1-4R; CANR 2, 23,
36; CLR 29; JRDA; MAICYA; SAAS 2;
SATA 1, 36, 75

**Duncan, Robert (Edward)**
1919-1988 . . . . CLC 1, 2, 4, 7, 15, 41, 55;
DAM POET; PC 2
See also CA 9-12R; 124; CANR 28; DLB 5,
16; MTCW

**Duncan, Sara Jeannette**
1861-1922 . . . . . . . . . . . . . . . . TCLC 60
See also DLB 92

**Dunlap, William** 1766-1839 . . . . . . . NCLC 2
See also DLB 30, 37, 59

**Dunn, Douglas (Eaglesham)**
1942- . . . . . . . . . . . . . . . . . . . CLC 6, 40
See also CA 45-48; CANR 2, 33; DLB 40;
MTCW

**Dunn, Katherine (Karen)** 1945- . . . . . CLC 71
See also CA 33-36R

**Dunn, Stephen** 1939- . . . . . . . . . . . . . CLC 36
See also CA 33-36R; CANR 12, 48, 53;
DLB 105

**Dunne, Finley Peter** 1867-1936 . . . . TCLC 28
See also CA 108; DLB 11, 23

**Dunne, John Gregory** 1932- . . . . . . . . CLC 28
See also CA 25-28R; CANR 14, 50;
DLBY 80

**Dunsany, Edward John Moreton Drax
Plunkett** 1878-1957
See Dunsany, Lord
See also CA 104; 148; DLB 10

**Dunsany, Lord** . . . . . . . . . . . . . . . TCLC 2, 59
See also Dunsany, Edward John Moreton
Drax Plunkett
See also DLB 77, 153, 156

**du Perry, Jean**
See Simenon, Georges (Jacques Christian)

**Durang, Christopher (Ferdinand)**
1949- . . . . . . . . . . . . . . . . . . . CLC 27, 38
See also CA 105; CANR 50

**Duras, Marguerite**
1914-1996 . . CLC 3, 6, 11, 20, 34, 40, 68
See also CA 25-28R; 151; CANR 50;
DLB 83; MTCW

**Durban, (Rosa) Pam** 1947- . . . . . . . . CLC 39
See also CA 123

**Durcan, Paul**
1944- . . . . . . . . CLC 43, 70; DAM POET
See also CA 134

**Durkheim, Emile** 1858-1917 . . . . . . TCLC 55

**Durrell, Lawrence (George)**
1912-1990 . . . . CLC 1, 4, 6, 8, 13, 27, 41;
DAM NOV
See also CA 9-12R; 132; CANR 40;
CDBLB 1945-1960; DLB 15, 27;
DLBY 90; MTCW

**Durrenmatt, Friedrich**
See Duerrenmatt, Friedrich

**Dutt, Toru** 1856-1877 . . . . . . . . . . NCLC 29

**Dwight, Timothy** 1752-1817 . . . . . . NCLC 13
See also DLB 37

**Dworkin, Andrea** 1946- . . . . . . . . . . CLC 43
See also CA 77-80; CAAS 21; CANR 16,
39; INT CANR-16; MTCW

**Dwyer, Deanna**
See Koontz, Dean R(ay)

**Dwyer, K. R.**
See Koontz, Dean R(ay)

**Dylan, Bob** 1941- . . . . . . CLC 3, 4, 6, 12, 77
See also CA 41-44R; DLB 16

**Eagleton, Terence (Francis)** 1943-
See Eagleton, Terry
See also CA 57-60; CANR 7, 23; MTCW

**Eagleton, Terry** . . . . . . . . . . . . . . . . CLC 63
See also Eagleton, Terence (Francis)

**Early, Jack**
See Scoppettone, Sandra

**East, Michael**
See West, Morris L(anglo)

**Eastaway, Edward**
See Thomas, (Philip) Edward

**Eastlake, William (Derry)** 1917- . . . . . CLC 8
See also CA 5-8R; CAAS 1; CANR 5;
DLB 6; INT CANR-5

**Eastman, Charles A(lexander)**
1858-1939 . . . . . TCLC 55; DAM MULT
See also NNAL; YABC 1

**Eberhart, Richard (Ghormley)**
1904- . . CLC 3, 11, 19, 56; DAM POET
See also CA 1-4R; CANR 2;
CDALB 1941-1968; DLB 48; MTCW

**Eberstadt, Fernanda** 1960- . . . . . . . . CLC 39
See also CA 136

**Echegaray (y Eizaguirre), Jose (Maria Waldo)**
1832-1916 . . . . . . . . . . . . . . . . . TCLC 4
See also CA 104; CANR 32; HW; MTCW

**Echeverria, (Jose) Esteban (Antonino)**
1805-1851 . . . . . . . . . . . . . . . . NCLC 18

**Echo**
See Proust, (Valentin-Louis-George-Eugene-)
Marcel

**Eckert, Allan W.** 1931- . . . . . . . . . . . CLC 17
See also AAYA 18; CA 13-16R; CANR 14,
45; INT CANR-14; SAAS 21; SATA 29;
SATA-Brief 27

**Eckhart, Meister** 1260(?)-1328(?) . . CMLC 9
See also DLB 115

**Eckmar, F. R.**
See de Hartog, Jan

**Eco, Umberto**
1932- . . . CLC 28, 60; DAM NOV, POP
See also BEST 90:1; CA 77-80; CANR 12,
33; MTCW

**Eddison, E(ric) R(ucker)**
1882-1945 . . . . . . . . . . . . . . . . TCLC 15
See also CA 109

**Edel, (Joseph) Leon** 1907- . . . . . . CLC 29, 34
See also CA 1-4R; CANR 1, 22; DLB 103;
INT CANR-22

**Eden, Emily** 1797-1869 . . . . . . . . NCLC 10

**Edgar, David**
1948- . . . . . . . . . CLC 42; DAM DRAM
See also CA 57-60; CANR 12; DLB 13;
MTCW

**Edgerton, Clyde (Carlyle)** 1944- . . . . CLC 39
See also AAYA 17; CA 118; 134; INT 134

**Edgeworth, Maria** 1768-1849 . . . NCLC 1, 51
See also DLB 116, 159, 163; SATA 21

**Edmonds, Paul**
See Kuttner, Henry

**Edmonds, Walter D(umaux)** 1903- . . CLC 35
See also CA 5-8R; CANR 2; DLB 9;
MAICYA; SAAS 4; SATA 1, 27

**Edmondson, Wallace**
See Ellison, Harlan (Jay)

**Edson, Russell** . . . . . . . . . . . . . . . . . CLC 13
See also CA 33-36R

**Edwards, Bronwen Elizabeth**
See Rose, Wendy

**Edwards, G(erald) B(asil)**
1899-1976 . . . . . . . . . . . . . . . . . CLC 25
See also CA 110

**Edwards, Gus** 1939- . . . . . . . . . . . . . CLC 43
See also CA 108; INT 108

**Edwards, Jonathan**
1703-1758 . . . . . . . . . . . LC 7; DA; DAC;
DAM MST
See also DLB 24

**Efron, Marina Ivanovna Tsvetaeva**
See Tsvetaeva (Efron), Marina (Ivanovna)

**Ehle, John (Marsden, Jr.)** 1925- . . . . CLC 27
See also CA 9-12R

**Ehrenbourg, Ilya (Grigoryevich)**
See Ehrenburg, Ilya (Grigoryevich)

**Ehrenburg, Ilya (Grigoryevich)**
1891-1967 . . . . . . . . . . CLC 18, 34, 62
See also CA 102; 25-28R

**Ehrenburg, Ilyo (Grigoryevich)**
See Ehrenburg, Ilya (Grigoryevich)

**Eich, Guenter** 1907-1972 . . . . . . . . . . CLC 15
See also CA 111; 93-96; DLB 69, 124

**Eichendorff, Joseph Freiherr von**
1788-1857 . . . . . . . . . . . . . . . . . NCLC 8
See also DLB 90

**Eigner, Larry** . . . . . . . . . . . . . . . . . . . CLC 9
See also Eigner, Laurence (Joel)
See also CAAS 23; DLB 5

**Eigner, Laurence (Joel)** 1927-1996
See Eigner, Larry
See also CA 9-12R; 151; CANR 6

**Einstein, Albert** 1879-1955 . . . . . . . TCLC 65
See also CA 121; 133; MTCW

**Eiseley, Loren Corey** 1907-1977 . . . . . CLC 7
See also AAYA 5; CA 1-4R; 73-76;
CANR 6

**Eisenstadt, Jill** 1963- . . . . . . . . . . . . . CLC 50
See also CA 140

**Eisenstein, Sergei (Mikhailovich)**
1898-1948 . . . . . . . . . . . . . . . . TCLC 57
See also CA 114; 149

**Eisner, Simon**
See Kornbluth, C(yril) M.

**Ekeloef, (Bengt) Gunnar**
1907-1968 ....... **CLC 27; DAM POET**
See also CA 123; 25-28R

**Ekelof, (Bengt) Gunnar**
See Ekeloef, (Bengt) Gunnar

**Ekwensi, C. O. D.**
See Ekwensi, Cyprian (Odiatu Duaka)

**Ekwensi, Cyprian (Odiatu Duaka)**
1921- ...... **CLC 4; BLC; DAM MULT**
See also BW 2; CA 29-32R; CANR 18, 42;
DLB 117; MTCW; SATA 66

**Elaine** ......................... **TCLC 18**
See also Leverson, Ada

**El Crummo**
See Crumb, R(obert)

**Elia**
See Lamb, Charles

**Eliade, Mircea** 1907-1986 ......... **CLC 19**
See also CA 65-68; 119; CANR 30; MTCW

**Eliot, A. D.**
See Jewett, (Theodora) Sarah Orne

**Eliot, Alice**
See Jewett, (Theodora) Sarah Orne

**Eliot, Dan**
See Silverberg, Robert

**Eliot, George**
1819-1880 ..... **NCLC 4, 13, 23, 41, 49;**
**DA; DAB; DAC; DAM MST, NOV;**
**WLC**
See also CDBLB 1832-1890; DLB 21, 35, 55

**Eliot, John** 1604-1690 .............. **LC 5**
See also DLB 24

**Eliot, T(homas) S(tearns)**
1888-1965 ..... **CLC 1, 2, 3, 6, 9, 10, 13,**
**15, 24, 34, 41, 55, 57; DA; DAB; DAC;**
**DAM DRAM, MST, POET; PC 5;**
**WLC 2**
See also CA 5-8R; 25-28R; CANR 41;
CDALB 1929-1941; DLB 7, 10, 45, 63;
DLBY 88; MTCW

**Elizabeth** 1866-1941 ............. **TCLC 41**

**Elkin, Stanley L(awrence)**
1930-1995 ...... **CLC 4, 6, 9, 14, 27, 51,**
**91; DAM NOV, POP; SSC 12**
See also CA 9-12R; 148; CANR 8, 46;
DLB 2, 28; DLBY 80; INT CANR-8;
MTCW

**Elledge, Scott** ................... **CLC 34**

**Elliott, Don**
See Silverberg, Robert

**Elliott, George P(aul)** 1918-1980 ..... **CLC 2**
See also CA 1-4R; 97-100; CANR 2

**Elliott, Janice** 1931- .............. **CLC 47**
See also CA 13-16R; CANR 8, 29; DLB 14

**Elliott, Sumner Locke** 1917-1991 ... **CLC 38**
See also CA 5-8R; 134; CANR 2, 21

**Elliott, William**
See Bradbury, Ray (Douglas)

**Ellis, A. E.** .................... **CLC 7**

**Ellis, Alice Thomas** ............... **CLC 40**
See also Haycraft, Anna

**Ellis, Bret Easton**
1964- ......... **CLC 39, 71; DAM POP**
See also AAYA 2; CA 118; 123; CANR 51;
INT 123

**Ellis, (Henry) Havelock**
1859-1939 .................. **TCLC 14**
See also CA 109

**Ellis, Landon**
See Ellison, Harlan (Jay)

**Ellis, Trey** 1962- ................. **CLC 55**
See also CA 146

**Ellison, Harlan (Jay)**
1934- ...... **CLC 1, 13, 42; DAM POP;**
**SSC 14**
See also CA 5-8R; CANR 5, 46; DLB 8;
INT CANR-5; MTCW

**Ellison, Ralph (Waldo)**
1914-1994 ........ **CLC 1, 3, 11, 54, 86;**
**BLC; DA; DAB; DAC; DAM MST,**
**MULT, NOV; WLC**
See also BW 1; CA 9-12R; 145; CANR 24,
53; CDALB 1941-1968; DLB 2, 76;
DLBY 94; MTCW

**Ellmann, Lucy (Elizabeth)** 1956- .... **CLC 61**
See also CA 128

**Ellmann, Richard (David)**
1918-1987 ................... **CLC 50**
See also BEST 89:2; CA 1-4R; 122;
CANR 2, 28; DLB 103; DLBY 87;
MTCW

**Elman, Richard** 1934- ............. **CLC 19**
See also CA 17-20R; CAAS 3; CANR 47

**Elron**
See Hubbard, L(afayette) Ron(ald)

**Eluard, Paul** ................... **TCLC 7, 41**
See also Grindel, Eugene

**Elyot, Sir Thomas** 1490(?)-1546 ..... **LC 11**

**Elytis, Odysseus**
1911-1996 .... **CLC 15, 49; DAM POET**
See also CA 102; 151; MTCW

**Emecheta, (Florence Onye) Buchi**
1944- .. **CLC 14, 48; BLC; DAM MULT**
See also BW 2; CA 81-84; CANR 27;
DLB 117; MTCW; SATA 66

**Emerson, Ralph Waldo**
1803-1882 ..... **NCLC 1, 38; DA; DAB;**
**DAC; DAM MST, POET; WLC**
See also CDALB 1640-1865; DLB 1, 59, 73

**Eminescu, Mihail** 1850-1889 ..... **NCLC 33**

**Empson, William**
1906-1984 ....... **CLC 3, 8, 19, 33, 34**
See also CA 17-20R; 112; CANR 31;
DLB 20; MTCW

**Enchi Fumiko (Ueda)** 1905-1986 .... **CLC 31**
See also CA 129; 121

**Ende, Michael (Andreas Helmuth)**
1929-1995 ................... **CLC 31**
See also CA 118; 124; 149; CANR 36;
CLR 14; DLB 75; MAICYA; SATA 61;
SATA-Brief 42; SATA-Obit 86

**Endo, Shusaku**
1923- ... **CLC 7, 14, 19, 54; DAM NOV**
See also CA 29-32R; CANR 21; MTCW

**Engel, Marian** 1933-1985 ......... **CLC 36**
See also CA 25-28R; CANR 12; DLB 53;
INT CANR-12

**Engelhardt, Frederick**
See Hubbard, L(afayette) Ron(ald)

**Enright, D(ennis) J(oseph)**
1920- ................... **CLC 4, 8, 31**
See also CA 1-4R; CANR 1, 42; DLB 27;
SATA 25

**Enzensberger, Hans Magnus**
1929- ...................... **CLC 43**
See also CA 116; 119

**Ephron, Nora** 1941- ........... **CLC 17, 31**
See also AITN 2; CA 65-68; CANR 12, 39

**Epsilon**
See Betjeman, John

**Epstein, Daniel Mark** 1948- ........ **CLC 7**
See also CA 49-52; CANR 2, 53

**Epstein, Jacob** 1956- ............. **CLC 19**
See also CA 114

**Epstein, Joseph** 1937- ............. **CLC 39**
See also CA 112; 119; CANR 50

**Epstein, Leslie** 1938- ............. **CLC 27**
See also CA 73-76; CAAS 12; CANR 23

**Equiano, Olaudah**
1745(?)-1797 ............. **LC 16; BLC;**
**DAM MULT**
See also DLB 37, 50

**Erasmus, Desiderius** 1469(?)-1536.... **LC 16**

**Erdman, Paul E(mil)** 1932- ........ **CLC 25**
See also AITN 1; CA 61-64; CANR 13, 43

**Erdrich, Louise**
1954- ....... **CLC 39, 54; DAM MULT,**
**NOV, POP**
See also AAYA 10; BEST 89:1; CA 114;
CANR 41; DLB 152; MTCW; NNAL

**Erenburg, Ilya (Grigoryevich)**
See Ehrenburg, Ilya (Grigoryevich)

**Erickson, Stephen Michael** 1950-
See Erickson, Steve
See also CA 129

**Erickson, Steve** ................... **CLC 64**
See also Erickson, Stephen Michael

**Ericson, Walter**
See Fast, Howard (Melvin)

**Eriksson, Buntel**
See Bergman, (Ernst) Ingmar

**Ernaux, Annie** 1940- ............. **CLC 88**
See also CA 147

**Eschenbach, Wolfram von**
See Wolfram von Eschenbach

**Eseki, Bruno**
See Mphahlele, Ezekiel

**Esenin, Sergei (Alexandrovich)**
1895-1925 .................. **TCLC 4**
See also CA 104

**Eshleman, Clayton** 1935- ........... **CLC 7**
See also CA 33-36R; CAAS 6; DLB 5

**Espriella, Don Manuel Alvarez**
See Southey, Robert

**Espriu, Salvador** 1913-1985 ......... **CLC 9**
See also CA 115; DLB 134

**Espronceda, Jose de** 1808-1842... **NCLC 39**

**Esse, James**
See Stephens, James

**Esterbrook, Tom**
See Hubbard, L(afayette) Ron(ald)

**Estleman, Loren D.**
1952- . . . . . . **CLC 48; DAM NOV, POP**
See also CA 85-88; CANR 27;
INT CANR-27; MTCW

**Eugenides, Jeffrey** 1960(?)- . . . . . . . . **CLC 81**
See also CA 144

**Euripides** c. 485B.C.-406B.C. . . . . . . . . **DC 4**
See also DA; DAB; DAC; DAM DRAM,
MST

**Evan, Evin**
See Faust, Frederick (Schiller)

**Evans, Evan**
See Faust, Frederick (Schiller)

**Evans, Marian**
See Eliot, George

**Evans, Mary Ann**
See Eliot, George

**Evarts, Esther**
See Benson, Sally

**Everett, Percival L.** 1956- . . . . . . . . **CLC 57**
See also BW 2; CA 129

**Everson, R(onald) G(ilmour)**
1903- . . . . . . . . . . . . . . . . . . . . . . **CLC 27**
See also CA 17-20R; DLB 88

**Everson, William (Oliver)**
1912-1994 . . . . . . . . . . . . . . **CLC 1, 5, 14**
See also CA 9-12R; 145; CANR 20; DLB 5,
16; MTCW

**Evtushenko, Evgenii Aleksandrovich**
See Yevtushenko, Yevgeny (Alexandrovich)

**Ewart, Gavin (Buchanan)**
1916-1995 . . . . . . . . . . . . . . . **CLC 13, 46**
See also CA 89-92; 150; CANR 17, 46;
DLB 40; MTCW

**Ewers, Hanns Heinz** 1871-1943 . . . **TCLC 12**
See also CA 109; 149

**Ewing, Frederick R.**
See Sturgeon, Theodore (Hamilton)

**Exley, Frederick (Earl)**
1929-1992 . . . . . . . . . . . . . . . . **CLC 6, 11**
See also AITN 2; CA 81-84; 138; DLB 143;
DLBY 81

**Eynhardt, Guillermo**
See Quiroga, Horacio (Sylvestre)

**Ezekiel, Nissim** 1924- . . . . . . . . . . . . **CLC 61**
See also CA 61-64

**Ezekiel, Tish O'Dowd** 1943- . . . . . . . **CLC 34**
See also CA 129

**Fadeyev, A.**
See Bulgya, Alexander Alexandrovich

**Fadeyev, Alexander** . . . . . . . . . . . . . . **TCLC 53**
See also Bulgya, Alexander Alexandrovich

**Fagen, Donald** 1948- . . . . . . . . . . . . . **CLC 26**

**Fainzilberg, Ilya Arnoldovich** 1897-1937
See Ilf, Ilya
See also CA 120

**Fair, Ronald L.** 1932- . . . . . . . . . . . . . **CLC 18**
See also BW 1; CA 69-72; CANR 25;
DLB 33

**Fairbairns, Zoe (Ann)** 1948- . . . . . . . **CLC 32**
See also CA 103; CANR 21

**Falco, Gian**
See Papini, Giovanni

**Falconer, James**
See Kirkup, James

**Falconer, Kenneth**
See Kornbluth, C(yril) M.

**Falkland, Samuel**
See Heijermans, Herman

**Fallaci, Oriana** 1930- . . . . . . . . . . . . . **CLC 11**
See also CA 77-80; CANR 15; MTCW

**Faludy, George** 1913- . . . . . . . . . . . . . **CLC 42**
See also CA 21-24R

**Faludy, Gyoergy**
See Faludy, George

**Fanon, Frantz**
1925-1961 . . . . . . . . . . . . . **CLC 74; BLC;**
**DAM MULT**
See also BW 1; CA 116; 89-92

**Fanshawe, Ann** 1625-1680 . . . . . . . . . . **LC 11**

**Fante, John (Thomas)** 1911-1983 . . . **CLC 60**
See also CA 69-72; 109; CANR 23;
DLB 130; DLBY 83

**Farah, Nuruddin**
1945- . . . . . **CLC 53; BLC; DAM MULT**
See also BW 2; CA 106; DLB 125

**Fargue, Leon-Paul** 1876(?)-1947 . . . **TCLC 11**
See also CA 109

**Farigoule, Louis**
See Romains, Jules

**Farina, Richard** 1936(?)-1966 . . . . . . . **CLC 9**
See also CA 81-84; 25-28R

**Farley, Walter (Lorimer)**
1915-1989 . . . . . . . . . . . . . . . . . . **CLC 17**
See also CA 17-20R; CANR 8, 29; DLB 22;
JRDA; MAICYA; SATA 2, 43

**Farmer, Philip Jose** 1918- . . . . . . . **CLC 1, 19**
See also CA 1-4R; CANR 4, 35; DLB 8;
MTCW

**Farquhar, George**
1677-1707 . . . . . . . **LC 21; DAM DRAM**
See also DLB 84

**Farrell, J(ames) G(ordon)**
1935-1979 . . . . . . . . . . . . . . . . . . . **CLC 6**
See also CA 73-76; 89-92; CANR 36;
DLB 14; MTCW

**Farrell, James T(homas)**
1904-1979 . . . . . . . . **CLC 1, 4, 8, 11, 66**
See also CA 5-8R; 89-92; CANR 9; DLB 4,
9, 86; DLBD 2; MTCW

**Farren, Richard J.**
See Betjeman, John

**Farren, Richard M.**
See Betjeman, John

**Fassbinder, Rainer Werner**
1946-1982 . . . . . . . . . . . . . . . . . . **CLC 20**
See also CA 93-96; 106; CANR 31

**Fast, Howard (Melvin)**
1914- . . . . . . . . . . . **CLC 23; DAM NOV**
See also AAYA 16; CA 1-4R; CAAS 18;
CANR 1, 33; DLB 9; INT CANR-33;
SATA 7

**Faulcon, Robert**
See Holdstock, Robert P.

**Faulkner, William (Cuthbert)**
1897-1962 . . . . . **CLC 1, 3, 6, 8, 9, 11, 14,**
**18, 28, 52, 68; DA; DAB; DAC;**
**DAM MST, NOV; SSC 1; WLC**
See also AAYA 7; CA 81-84; CANR 33;
CDALB 1929-1941; DLB 9, 11, 44, 102;
DLBD 2; DLBY 86; MTCW

**Fauset, Jessie Redmon**
1884(?)-1961 . . . . . . . . **CLC 19, 54; BLC;**
**DAM MULT**
See also BW 1; CA 109; DLB 51

**Faust, Frederick (Schiller)**
1892-1944(?) . . . . . **TCLC 49; DAM POP**
See also CA 108; 152

**Faust, Irvin** 1924- . . . . . . . . . . . . . . . . . **CLC 8**
See also CA 33-36R; CANR 28; DLB 2, 28;
DLBY 80

**Fawkes, Guy**
See Benchley, Robert (Charles)

**Fearing, Kenneth (Flexner)**
1902-1961 . . . . . . . . . . . . . . . . . . **CLC 51**
See also CA 93-96; DLB 9

**Fecamps, Elise**
See Creasey, John

**Federman, Raymond** 1928- . . . . . . **CLC 6, 47**
See also CA 17-20R; CAAS 8; CANR 10,
43; DLBY 80

**Federspiel, J(uerg) F.** 1931- . . . . . . . . **CLC 42**
See also CA 146

**Feiffer, Jules (Ralph)**
1929- . . . . . . **CLC 2, 8, 64; DAM DRAM**
See also AAYA 3; CA 17-20R; CANR 30;
DLB 7, 44; INT CANR-30; MTCW;
SATA 8, 61

**Feige, Hermann Albert Otto Maximilian**
See Traven, B.

**Feinberg, David B.** 1956-1994 . . . . . . **CLC 59**
See also CA 135; 147

**Feinstein, Elaine** 1930- . . . . . . . . . . . . **CLC 36**
See also CA 69-72; CAAS 1; CANR 31;
DLB 14, 40; MTCW

**Feldman, Irving (Mordecai)** 1928- . . . . **CLC 7**
See also CA 1-4R; CANR 1

**Fellini, Federico** 1920-1993 . . . . . **CLC 16, 85**
See also CA 65-68; 143; CANR 33

**Felsen, Henry Gregor** 1916- . . . . . . . **CLC 17**
See also CA 1-4R; CANR 1; SAAS 2;
SATA 1

**Fenton, James Martin** 1949- . . . . . . . **CLC 32**
See also CA 102; DLB 40

**Ferber, Edna** 1887-1968 . . . . . . . . **CLC 18, 93**
See also AITN 1; CA 5-8R; 25-28R; DLB 9,
28, 86; MTCW; SATA 7

**Ferguson, Helen**
See Kavan, Anna

**Ferguson, Samuel** 1810-1886 . . . . . **NCLC 33**
See also DLB 32

**Fergusson, Robert** 1750-1774 . . . . . . . **LC 29**
See also DLB 109

**Ferling, Lawrence**
See Ferlinghetti, Lawrence (Monsanto)

**Fornes, Maria Irene** 1930-..... **CLC 39, 61**
See also CA 25-28R; CANR 28; DLB 7;
HW; INT CANR-28; MTCW

**Forrest, Leon** 1937- .............. **CLC 4**
See also BW 2; CA 89-92; CAAS 7;
CANR 25, 52; DLB 33

**Forster, E(dward) M(organ)**
1879-1970 ..... **CLC 1, 2, 3, 4, 9, 10, 13,
15, 22, 45, 77; DA; DAB; DAC;
DAM MST, NOV; WLC**
See also AAYA 2; CA 13-14; 25-28R;
CANR 45; CAP 1; CDBLB 1914-1945;
DLB 34, 98, 162; DLBD 10; MTCW;
SATA 57

**Forster, John** 1812-1876 ........ **NCLC 11**
See also DLB 144

**Forsyth, Frederick**
1938- .. **CLC 2, 5, 36; DAM NOV, POP**
See also BEST 89:4; CA 85-88; CANR 38;
DLB 87; MTCW

**Forten, Charlotte L.** ......... **TCLC 16; BLC**
See also Grimke, Charlotte L(ottie) Forten
See also DLB 50

**Foscolo, Ugo** 1778-1827.......... **NCLC 8**

**Fosse, Bob** ...................... **CLC 20**
See also Fosse, Robert Louis

**Fosse, Robert Louis** 1927-1987
See Fosse, Bob
See also CA 110; 123

**Foster, Stephen Collins**
1826-1864 ................. **NCLC 26**

**Foucault, Michel**
1926-1984 ............. **CLC 31, 34, 69**
See also CA 105; 113; CANR 34; MTCW

**Fouque, Friedrich (Heinrich Karl) de la Motte**
1777-1843 ................... **NCLC 2**
See also DLB 90

**Fourier, Charles** 1772-1837 ...... **NCLC 51**

**Fournier, Henri Alban** 1886-1914
See Alain-Fournier
See also CA 104

**Fournier, Pierre** 1916-............. **CLC 11**
See also Gascar, Pierre
See also CA 89-92; CANR 16, 40

**Fowles, John**
1926-...... **CLC 1, 2, 3, 4, 6, 9, 10, 15,
33, 87; DAB; DAC; DAM MST**
See also CA 5-8R; CANR 25; CDBLB 1960
to Present; DLB 14, 139; MTCW;
SATA 22

**Fox, Paula** 1923-................ **CLC 2, 8**
See also AAYA 3; CA 73-76; CANR 20,
36; CLR 1; DLB 52; JRDA; MAICYA;
MTCW; SATA 17, 60

**Fox, William Price (Jr.)** 1926- ..... **CLC 22**
See also CA 17-20R; CAAS 19; CANR 11;
DLB 2; DLBY 81

**Foxe, John** 1516(?)-1587 ........... **LC 14**

**Frame, Janet**
1924-........ **CLC 2, 3, 6, 22, 66, 96**
See also Clutha, Janet Paterson Frame

**France, Anatole** ................ **TCLC 9**
See also Thibault, Jacques Anatole Francois
See also DLB 123

**Francis, Claude** 19(?)- ............ **CLC 50**

**Francis, Dick**
1920- ....... **CLC 2, 22, 42; DAM POP**
See also AAYA 5; BEST 89:3; CA 5-8R;
CANR 9, 42; CDBLB 1960 to Present;
DLB 87; INT CANR-9; MTCW

**Francis, Robert (Churchill)**
1901-1987 ................... **CLC 15**
See also CA 1-4R; 123; CANR 1

**Frank, Anne(lies Marie)**
1929-1945 ........ **TCLC 17; DA; DAB;
DAC; DAM MST; WLC**
See also AAYA 12; CA 113; 133; MTCW;
SATA 87; SATA-Brief 42

**Frank, Elizabeth** 1945-............ **CLC 39**
See also CA 121; 126; INT 126

**Frankl, Viktor E(mil)** 1905-........ **CLC 93**
See also CA 65-68

**Franklin, Benjamin**
See Hasek, Jaroslav (Matej Frantisek)

**Franklin, Benjamin**
1706-1790 ..... **LC 25; DA; DAB; DAC;
DAM MST**
See also CDALB 1640-1865; DLB 24, 43,
73

**Franklin, (Stella Maraia Sarah) Miles**
1879-1954 ................... **TCLC 7**
See also CA 104

**Fraser, (Lady) Antonia (Pakenham)**
1932-...................... **CLC 32**
See also CA 85-88; CANR 44; MTCW;
SATA-Brief 32

**Fraser, George MacDonald** 1925-.... **CLC 7**
See also CA 45-48; CANR 2, 48

**Fraser, Sylvia** 1935-.............. **CLC 64**
See also CA 45-48; CANR 1, 16

**Frayn, Michael**
1933-............... **CLC 3, 7, 31, 47;
DAM DRAM, NOV**
See also CA 5-8R; CANR 30; DLB 13, 14;
MTCW

**Fraze, Candida (Merrill)** 1945- ..... **CLC 50**
See also CA 126

**Frazer, J(ames) G(eorge)**
1854-1941 ................. **TCLC 32**
See also CA 118

**Frazer, Robert Caine**
See Creasey, John

**Frazer, Sir James George**
See Frazer, J(ames) G(eorge)

**Frazier, Ian** 1951-................ **CLC 46**
See also CA 130

**Frederic, Harold** 1856-1898...... **NCLC 10**
See also DLB 12, 23; DLBD 13

**Frederick, John**
See Faust, Frederick (Schiller)

**Frederick the Great** 1712-1786 ...... **LC 14**

**Fredro, Aleksander** 1793-1876..... **NCLC 8**

**Freeling, Nicolas** 1927- ........... **CLC 38**
See also CA 49-52; CAAS 12; CANR 1, 17,
50; DLB 87

**Freeman, Douglas Southall**
1886-1953 ................. **TCLC 11**
See also CA 109; DLB 17

**Freeman, Judith** 1946-............ **CLC 55**
See also CA 148

**Freeman, Mary Eleanor Wilkins**
1852-1930 ........... **TCLC 9; SSC 1**
See also CA 106; DLB 12, 78

**Freeman, R(ichard) Austin**
1862-1943 ................. **TCLC 21**
See also CA 113; DLB 70

**French, Albert** 1943- ............. **CLC 86**

**French, Marilyn**
1929-............... **CLC 10, 18, 60;
DAM DRAM, NOV, POP**
See also CA 69-72; CANR 3, 31;
INT CANR-31; MTCW

**French, Paul**
See Asimov, Isaac

**Freneau, Philip Morin** 1752-1832.. **NCLC 1**
See also DLB 37, 43

**Freud, Sigmund** 1856-1939 ....... **TCLC 52**
See also CA 115; 133; MTCW

**Friedan, Betty (Naomi)** 1921-...... **CLC 74**
See also CA 65-68; CANR 18, 45; MTCW

**Friedlander, Saul** 1932-........... **CLC 90**
See also CA 117; 130

**Friedman, B(ernard) H(arper)**
1926-........................ **CLC 7**
See also CA 1-4R; CANR 3, 48

**Friedman, Bruce Jay** 1930-.... **CLC 3, 5, 56**
See also CA 9-12R; CANR 25, 52; DLB 2,
28; INT CANR-25

**Friel, Brian** 1929-........... **CLC 5, 42, 59**
See also CA 21-24R; CANR 33; DLB 13;
MTCW

**Friis-Baastad, Babbis Ellinor**
1921-1970 ................... **CLC 12**
See also CA 17-20R; 134; SATA 7

**Frisch, Max (Rudolf)**
1911-1991 ..... **CLC 3, 9, 14, 18, 32, 44;
DAM DRAM, NOV**
See also CA 85-88; 134; CANR 32;
DLB 69, 124; MTCW

**Fromentin, Eugene (Samuel Auguste)**
1820-1876 ................. **NCLC 10**
See also DLB 123

**Frost, Frederick**
See Faust, Frederick (Schiller)

**Frost, Robert (Lee)**
1874-1963 .... **CLC 1, 3, 4, 9, 10, 13, 15,
26, 34, 44; DA; DAB; DAC; DAM MST,
POET; PC 1; WLC**
See also CA 89-92; CANR 33;
CDALB 1917-1929; DLB 54; DLBD 7;
MTCW; SATA 14

**Froude, James Anthony**
1818-1894 ................. **NCLC 43**
See also DLB 18, 57, 144

**Froy, Herald**
See Waterhouse, Keith (Spencer)

**Fry, Christopher**
1907- ..... **CLC 2, 10, 14; DAM DRAM**
See also CA 17-20R; CAAS 23; CANR 9,
30; DLB 13; MTCW; SATA 66

**Frye, (Herman) Northrop**
1912-1991 ................ **CLC 24, 70**
See also CA 5-8R; 133; CANR 8, 37;
DLB 67, 68; MTCW**

**Fuchs, Daniel** 1909-1993 . . . . . . . **CLC 8, 22**
See also CA 81-84; 142; CAAS 5;
CANR 40; DLB 9, 26, 28; DLBY 93

**Fuchs, Daniel** 1934- . . . . . . . . . . . . . . **CLC 34**
See also CA 37-40R; CANR 14, 48

**Fuentes, Carlos**
1928- . . . . . . **CLC 3, 8, 10, 13, 22, 41, 60;**
**DA; DAB; DAC; DAM MST, MULT,**
**NOV; HLC; WLC**
See also AAYA 4; AITN 2; CA 69-72;
CANR 10, 32; DLB 113; HW; MTCW

**Fuentes, Gregorio Lopez y**
See Lopez y Fuentes, Gregorio

**Fugard, (Harold) Athol**
1932- . . . . . . . . . **CLC 5, 9, 14, 25, 40, 80;**
**DAM DRAM; DC 3**
See also AAYA 17; CA 85-88; CANR 32;
MTCW

**Fugard, Sheila** 1932- . . . . . . . . . . . . . **CLC 48**
See also CA 125

**Fuller, Charles (H., Jr.)**
1939- . . . . **CLC 25; BLC; DAM DRAM,**
**MULT; DC 1**
See also BW 2; CA 108; 112; DLB 38;
INT 112; MTCW

**Fuller, John (Leopold)** 1937- . . . . . . . **CLC 62**
See also CA 21-24R; CANR 9, 44; DLB 40

**Fuller, Margaret** . . . . . . . . . . . . . . **NCLC 5, 50**
See also Ossoli, Sarah Margaret (Fuller
marchesa d')

**Fuller, Roy (Broadbent)**
1912-1991 . . . . . . . . . . . . . . . . **CLC 4, 28**
See also CA 5-8R; 135; CAAS 10;
CANR 53; DLB 15, 20; SATA 87

**Fulton, Alice** 1952- . . . . . . . . . . . . . . **CLC 52**
See also CA 116

**Furphy, Joseph** 1843-1912 . . . . . . . **TCLC 25**

**Fussell, Paul** 1924- . . . . . . . . . . . . . . **CLC 74**
See also BEST 90:1; CA 17-20R; CANR 8,
21, 35; INT CANR-21; MTCW

**Futabatei, Shimei** 1864-1909 . . . . . **TCLC 44**

**Futrelle, Jacques** 1875-1912 . . . . . **TCLC 19**
See also CA 113

**Gaboriau, Emile** 1835-1873 . . . . . . **NCLC 14**

**Gadda, Carlo Emilio** 1893-1973 . . . . **CLC 11**
See also CA 89-92

**Gaddis, William**
1922- . . . **CLC 1, 3, 6, 8, 10, 19, 43, 86**
See also CA 17-20R; CANR 21, 48; DLB 2;
MTCW

**Gaines, Ernest J(ames)**
1933- . . . . . . . . . **CLC 3, 11, 18, 86; BLC;**
**DAM MULT**
See also AAYA 18; AITN 1; BW 2;
CA 9-12R; CANR 6, 24, 42;
CDALB 1968-1988; DLB 2, 33, 152;
DLBY 80; MTCW; SATA 86

**Gaitskill, Mary** 1954- . . . . . . . . . . . . . **CLC 69**
See also CA 128

**Galdos, Benito Perez**
See Perez Galdos, Benito

**Gale, Zona**
1874-1938 . . . . . . **TCLC 7; DAM DRAM**
See also CA 105; DLB 9, 78

**Galeano, Eduardo (Hughes)** 1940- . . . **CLC 72**
See also CA 29-32R; CANR 13, 32; HW

**Galiano, Juan Valera y Alcala**
See Valera y Alcala-Galiano, Juan

**Gallagher, Tess**
1943- . . **CLC 18, 63; DAM POET; PC 9**
See also CA 106; DLB 120

**Gallant, Mavis**
1922- . . . . . . . . . . . **CLC 7, 18, 38; DAC;**
**DAM MST; SSC 5**
See also CA 69-72; CANR 29; DLB 53;
MTCW

**Gallant, Roy A(rthur)** 1924- . . . . . . . **CLC 17**
See also CA 5-8R; CANR 4, 29; CLR 30;
MAICYA; SATA 4, 68

**Gallico, Paul (William)** 1897-1976 . . . **CLC 2**
See also AITN 1; CA 5-8R; 69-72;
CANR 23; DLB 9; MAICYA; SATA 13

**Gallo, Max Louis** 1932- . . . . . . . . . . . **CLC 95**
See also CA 85-88

**Gallois, Lucien**
See Desnos, Robert

**Gallup, Ralph**
See Whitemore, Hugh (John)

**Galsworthy, John**
1867-1933 . . . . . . **TCLC 1, 45; DA; DAB;**
**DAC; DAM DRAM, MST, NOV;**
**SSC 22; WLC 2**
See also CA 104; 141; CDBLB 1890-1914;
DLB 10, 34, 98, 162

**Galt, John** 1779-1839 . . . . . . . . . . . **NCLC 1**
See also DLB 99, 116, 159

**Galvin, James** 1951- . . . . . . . . . . . . . . **CLC 38**
See also CA 108; CANR 26

**Gamboa, Federico** 1864-1939 . . . . . **TCLC 36**

**Gandhi, M. K.**
See Gandhi, Mohandas Karamchand

**Gandhi, Mahatma**
See Gandhi, Mohandas Karamchand

**Gandhi, Mohandas Karamchand**
1869-1948 . . . . . **TCLC 59; DAM MULT**
See also CA 121; 132; MTCW

**Gann, Ernest Kellogg** 1910-1991 . . . . **CLC 23**
See also AITN 1; CA 1-4R; 136; CANR 1

**Garcia, Cristina** 1958- . . . . . . . . . . . . **CLC 76**
See also CA 141

**Garcia Lorca, Federico**
1898-1936 . . . **TCLC 1, 7, 49; DA; DAB;**
**DAC; DAM DRAM, MST, MULT,**
**POET; DC 2; HLC; PC 3; WLC**
See also CA 104; 131; DLB 108; HW;
MTCW

**Garcia Marquez, Gabriel (Jose)**
1928- . . . . **CLC 2, 3, 8, 10, 15, 27, 47, 55,**
**68; DA; DAB; DAC; DAM MST,**
**MULT, NOV, POP; HLC; SSC 8; WLC**
See also AAYA 3; BEST 89:1, 90:4;
CA 33-36R; CANR 10, 28, 50; DLB 113;
HW; MTCW

**Gard, Janice**
See Latham, Jean Lee

**Gard, Roger Martin du**
See Martin du Gard, Roger

**Gardam, Jane** 1928- . . . . . . . . . . . . . . **CLC 43**
See also CA 49-52; CANR 2, 18, 33;
CLR 12; DLB 14, 161; MAICYA;
MTCW; SAAS 9; SATA 39, 76;
SATA-Brief 28

**Gardner, Herb(ert)** 1934- . . . . . . . . . **CLC 44**
See also CA 149

**Gardner, John (Champlin), Jr.**
1933-1982 . . . . . **CLC 2, 3, 5, 7, 8, 10, 18,**
**28, 34; DAM NOV, POP; SSC 7**
See also AITN 1; CA 65-68; 107;
CANR 33; DLB 2; DLBY 82; MTCW;
SATA 40; SATA-Obit 31

**Gardner, John (Edmund)**
1926- . . . . . . . . . . . . **CLC 30; DAM POP**
See also CA 103; CANR 15; MTCW

**Gardner, Miriam**
See Bradley, Marion Zimmer

**Gardner, Noel**
See Kuttner, Henry

**Gardons, S. S.**
See Snodgrass, W(illiam) D(e Witt)

**Garfield, Leon** 1921-1996 . . . . . . . . . . **CLC 12**
See also AAYA 8; CA 17-20R; 152;
CANR 38, 41; CLR 21; DLB 161; JRDA;
MAICYA; SATA 1, 32, 76

**Garland, (Hannibal) Hamlin**
1860-1940 . . . . . . . . . . . **TCLC 3; SSC 18**
See also CA 104; DLB 12, 71, 78

**Garneau, (Hector de) Saint-Denys**
1912-1943 . . . . . . . . . . . . . . . . . **TCLC 13**
See also CA 111; DLB 88

**Garner, Alan**
1934- . . . . . . . **CLC 17; DAB; DAM POP**
See also AAYA 18; CA 73-76; CANR 15;
CLR 20; DLB 161; MAICYA; MTCW;
SATA 18, 69

**Garner, Hugh** 1913-1979 . . . . . . . . . . **CLC 13**
See also CA 69-72; CANR 31; DLB 68

**Garnett, David** 1892-1981 . . . . . . . . . . **CLC 3**
See also CA 5-8R; 103; CANR 17; DLB 34

**Garos, Stephanie**
See Katz, Steve

**Garrett, George (Palmer)**
1929- . . . . . . . . . . . . . . . . . **CLC 3, 11, 51**
See also CA 1-4R; CAAS 5; CANR 1, 42;
DLB 2, 5, 130, 152; DLBY 83

**Garrick, David**
1717-1779 . . . . . . . **LC 15; DAM DRAM**
See also DLB 84

**Garrigue, Jean** 1914-1972 . . . . . . . . **CLC 2, 8**
See also CA 5-8R; 37-40R; CANR 20

**Garrison, Frederick**
See Sinclair, Upton (Beall)

**Garth, Will**
See Hamilton, Edmond; Kuttner, Henry

**Garvey, Marcus (Moziah, Jr.)**
1887-1940 . . . . . . . . . . . **TCLC 41; BLC;**
**DAM MULT**
See also BW 1; CA 120; 124

**Gary, Romain** . . . . . . . . . . . . . . . . . . . **CLC 25**
See also Kacew, Romain
See also DLB 83

**Gascar, Pierre** . . . . . . . . . . . . . . . . . . . **CLC 11**
See also Fournier, Pierre

**Gascoyne, David (Emery)** 1916- .... **CLC 45**
See also CA 65-68; CANR 10, 28; DLB 20;
MTCW

**Gaskell, Elizabeth Cleghorn**
1810-1865 .. **NCLC 5; DAB; DAM MST**
See also CDBLB 1832-1890; DLB 21, 144,
159

**Gass, William H(oward)**
1924- ... **CLC 1, 2, 8, 11, 15, 39; SSC 12**
See also CA 17-20R; CANR 30; DLB 2;
MTCW

**Gasset, Jose Ortega y**
See Ortega y Gasset, Jose

**Gates, Henry Louis, Jr.**
1950- ......... **CLC 65; DAM MULT**
See also BW 2; CA 109; CANR 25, 53;
DLB 67

**Gautier, Theophile**
1811-1872 ...... **NCLC 1; DAM POET;**
**SSC 20**
See also DLB 119

**Gawsworth, John**
See Bates, H(erbert) E(rnest)

**Gay, Oliver**
See Gogarty, Oliver St. John

**Gaye, Marvin (Penze)** 1939-1984 ... **CLC 26**
See also CA 112

**Gebler, Carlo (Ernest)** 1954- ....... **CLC 39**
See also CA 119; 133

**Gee, Maggie (Mary)** 1948-......... **CLC 57**
See also CA 130

**Gee, Maurice (Gough)** 1931- ....... **CLC 29**
See also CA 97-100; SATA 46

**Gelbart, Larry (Simon)** 1923- ... **CLC 21, 61**
See also CA 73-76; CANR 45

**Gelber, Jack** 1932-........ **CLC 1, 6, 14, 79**
See also CA 1-4R; CANR 2; DLB 7

**Gellhorn, Martha (Ellis)** 1908- .. **CLC 14, 60**
See also CA 77-80; CANR 44; DLBY 82

**Genet, Jean**
1910-1986 ...... **CLC 1, 2, 5, 10, 14, 44,**
**46; DAM DRAM**
See also CA 13-16R; CANR 18; DLB 72;
DLBY 86; MTCW

**Gent, Peter** 1942-................ **CLC 29**
See also AITN 1; CA 89-92; DLBY 82

**Gentlewoman in New England, A**
See Bradstreet, Anne

**Gentlewoman in Those Parts, A**
See Bradstreet, Anne

**George, Jean Craighead** 1919-...... **CLC 35**
See also AAYA 8; CA 5-8R; CANR 25;
CLR 1; DLB 52; JRDA; MAICYA;
SATA 2, 68

**George, Stefan (Anton)**
1868-1933 ............... **TCLC 2, 14**
See also CA 104

**Georges, Georges Martin**
See Simenon, Georges (Jacques Christian)

**Gerhardi, William Alexander**
See Gerhardie, William Alexander

**Gerhardie, William Alexander**
1895-1977 .................... **CLC 5**
See also CA 25-28R; 73-76; CANR 18;
DLB 36

**Gerstler, Amy** 1956-............. **CLC 70**
See also CA 146

**Gertler, T.** ...................... **CLC 34**
See also CA 116; 121; INT 121

**gfgg**....................... **CLC XvXzc**

**Ghalib**........................ **NCLC 39**
See also Ghalib, Hsadullah Khan

**Ghalib, Hsadullah Khan** 1797-1869
See Ghalib
See also DAM POET

**Ghelderode, Michel de**
1898-1962 .... **CLC 6, 11; DAM DRAM**
See also CA 85-88; CANR 40

**Ghiselin, Brewster** 1903-......... **CLC 23**
See also CA 13-16R; CAAS 10; CANR 13

**Ghose, Zulfikar** 1935-............ **CLC 42**
See also CA 65-68

**Ghosh, Amitav** 1956-............. **CLC 44**
See also CA 147

**Giacosa, Giuseppe** 1847-1906 ...... **TCLC 7**
See also CA 104

**Gibb, Lee**
See Waterhouse, Keith (Spencer)

**Gibbon, Lewis Grassic** ............. **TCLC 4**
See also Mitchell, James Leslie

**Gibbons, Kaye**
1960- ........ **CLC 50, 88; DAM POP**
See also CA 151

**Gibran, Kahlil**
1883-1931 .... **TCLC 1, 9; DAM POET,**
**POP; PC 9**
See also CA 104; 150

**Gibran, Khalil**
See Gibran, Kahlil

**Gibson, William**
1914- ........ **CLC 23; DA; DAB; DAC;**
**DAM DRAM, MST**
See also CA 9-12R; CANR 9, 42; DLB 7;
SATA 66

**Gibson, William (Ford)**
1948- ........ **CLC 39, 63; DAM POP**
See also AAYA 12; CA 126; 133; CANR 52

**Gide, Andre (Paul Guillaume)**
1869-1951 ...... **TCLC 5, 12, 36; DA;**
**DAB; DAC; DAM MST, NOV; SSC 13;**
**WLC**
See also CA 104; 124; DLB 65; MTCW

**Gifford, Barry (Colby)** 1946-...... **CLC 34**
See also CA 65-68; CANR 9, 30, 40

**Gilbert, W(illiam) S(chwenck)**
1836-1911 ..... **TCLC 3; DAM DRAM,**
**POET**
See also CA 104; SATA 36

**Gilbreth, Frank B., Jr.** 1911-....... **CLC 17**
See also CA 9-12R; SATA 2

**Gilchrist, Ellen**
1935- ........ **CLC 34, 48; DAM POP;**
**SSC 14**
See also CA 113; 116; CANR 41; DLB 130;
MTCW

**Giles, Molly** 1942-............... **CLC 39**
See also CA 126

**Gill, Patrick**
See Creasey, John

**Gilliam, Terry (Vance)** 1940-...... **CLC 21**
See also Monty Python
See also CA 108; 113; CANR 35; INT 113

**Gillian, Jerry**
See Gilliam, Terry (Vance)

**Gilliatt, Penelope (Ann Douglass)**
1932-1993 .......... **CLC 2, 10, 13, 53**
See also AITN 2; CA 13-16R; 141;
CANR 49; DLB 14

**Gilman, Charlotte (Anna) Perkins (Stetson)**
1860-1935 ........ **TCLC 9, 37; SSC 13**
See also CA 106; 150

**Gilmour, David** 1949-............. **CLC 35**
See also CA 138, 147

**Gilpin, William** 1724-1804...... **NCLC 30**

**Gilray, J. D.**
See Mencken, H(enry) L(ouis)

**Gilroy, Frank D(aniel)** 1925-........ **CLC 2**
See also CA 81-84; CANR 32; DLB 7

**Ginsberg, Allen**
1926- ...... **CLC 1, 2, 3, 4, 6, 13, 36, 69;**
**DA; DAB; DAC; DAM MST, POET;**
**PC 4; WLC 3**
See also AITN 1; CA 1-4R; CANR 2, 41;
CDALB 1941-1968; DLB 5, 16; MTCW

**Ginzburg, Natalia**
1916-1991 ........... **CLC 5, 11, 54, 70**
See also CA 85-88; 135; CANR 33; MTCW

**Giono, Jean** 1895-1970......... **CLC 4, 11**
See also CA 45-48; 29-32R; CANR 2, 35;
DLB 72; MTCW

**Giovanni, Nikki**
1943- ...... **CLC 2, 4, 19, 64; BLC; DA;**
**DAB; DAC; DAM MST, MULT, POET**
See also AITN 1; BW 2; CA 29-32R;
CAAS 6; CANR 18, 41; CLR 6; DLB 5,
41; INT CANR-18; MAICYA; MTCW;
SATA 24

**Giovene, Andrea** 1904-............. **CLC 7**
See also CA 85-88

**Gippius, Zinaida (Nikolayevna)** 1869-1945
See Hippius, Zinaida
See also CA 106

**Giraudoux, (Hippolyte) Jean**
1882-1944 .... **TCLC 2, 7; DAM DRAM**
See also CA 104; DLB 65

**Gironella, Jose Maria** 1917- ....... **CLC 11**
See also CA 101

**Gissing, George (Robert)**
1857-1903 ............ **TCLC 3, 24, 47**
See also CA 105; DLB 18, 135

**Giurlani, Aldo**
See Palazzeschi, Aldo

**Gladkov, Fyodor (Vasilyevich)**
1883-1958 ................. **TCLC 27**

**Glanville, Brian (Lester)** 1931- ...... **CLC 6**
See also CA 5-8R; CAAS 9; CANR 3;
DLB 15, 139; SATA 42

**Glasgow, Ellen (Anderson Gholson)**
1873(?)-1945 .............. **TCLC 2, 7**
See also CA 104; DLB 9, 12

**Glaspell, Susan (Keating)**
1882(?)-1948 ............... **TCLC 55**
See also CA 110; DLB 7, 9, 78; YABC 2

**Glassco, John** 1909-1981 .......... **CLC 9**
See also CA 13-16R; 102; CANR 15;
DLB 68

**Glasscock, Amnesia**
See Steinbeck, John (Ernst)

**Glasser, Ronald J.** 1940(?)- ........ **CLC 37**

**Glassman, Joyce**
See Johnson, Joyce

**Glendinning, Victoria** 1937-........ **CLC 50**
See also CA 120; 127; DLB 155

**Glissant, Edouard**
1928- ....... **CLC 10, 68; DAM MULT**

**Gloag, Julian** 1930- .............. **CLC 40**
See also AITN 1; CA 65-68; CANR 10

**Glowacki, Aleksander**
See Prus, Boleslaw

**Gluck, Louise (Elisabeth)**
1943- .............. **CLC 7, 22, 44, 81;**
**DAM POET; PC 16**
See also CA 33-36R; CANR 40; DLB 5

**Gobineau, Joseph Arthur (Comte) de**
1816-1882 ................. **NCLC 17**
See also DLB 123

**Godard, Jean-Luc** 1930-.......... **CLC 20**
See also CA 93-96

**Godden, (Margaret) Rumer** 1907-... **CLC 53**
See also AAYA 6; CA 5-8R; CANR 4, 27,
36; CLR 20; DLB 161; MAICYA;
SAAS 12; SATA 3, 36

**Godoy Alcayaga, Lucila** 1889-1957
See Mistral, Gabriela
See also BW 2; CA 104; 131; DAM MULT;
HW; MTCW

**Godwin, Gail (Kathleen)**
1937- ........... **CLC 5, 8, 22, 31, 69;**
**DAM POP**
See also CA 29-32R; CANR 15, 43; DLB 6;
INT CANR-15; MTCW

**Godwin, William** 1756-1836...... **NCLC 14**
See also CDBLB 1789-1832; DLB 39, 104,
142, 158, 163

**Goethe, Johann Wolfgang von**
1749-1832 ........ **NCLC 4, 22, 34; DA;**
**DAB; DAC; DAM DRAM, MST,**
**POET; PC 5; WLC 3**
See also DLB 94

**Gogarty, Oliver St. John**
1878-1957 ................. **TCLC 15**
See also CA 109; 150; DLB 15, 19

**Gogol, Nikolai (Vasilyevich)**
1809-1852 ......NCLC 5, 15, 31; DA;
**DAB; DAC; DAM DRAM, MST; DC 1;**
**SSC 4; WLC**

**Goines, Donald**
1937(?)-1974 .......... **CLC 80; BLC;**
**DAM MULT, POP**
See also AITN 1; BW 1; CA 124; 114;
DLB 33

**Gold, Herbert** 1924-....... **CLC 4, 7, 14, 42**
See also CA 9-12R; CANR 17, 45; DLB 2;
DLBY 81

**Goldbarth, Albert** 1948-......... **CLC 5, 38**
See also CA 53-56; CANR 6, 40; DLB 120

**Goldberg, Anatol** 1910-1982 ....... **CLC 34**
See also CA 131; 117

**Goldemberg, Isaac** 1945-.......... **CLC 52**
See also CA 69-72; CAAS 12; CANR 11,
32; HW

**Golding, William (Gerald)**
1911-1993 .... **CLC 1, 2, 3, 8, 10, 17, 27,**
**58, 81; DA; DAB; DAC; DAM MST,**
**NOV; WLC**
See also AAYA 5; CA 5-8R; 141;
CANR 13, 33; CDBLB 1945-1960;
DLB 15, 100; MTCW

**Goldman, Emma** 1869-1940...... **TCLC 13**
See also CA 110; 150

**Goldman, Francisco** 1955-......... **CLC 76**

**Goldman, William (W.)** 1931-.... **CLC 1, 48**
See also CA 9-12R; CANR 29; DLB 44

**Goldmann, Lucien** 1913-1970 ...... **CLC 24**
See also CA 25-28; CAP 2

**Goldoni, Carlo**
1707-1793 ....... **LC 4; DAM DRAM**

**Goldsberry, Steven** 1949-.......... **CLC 34**
See also CA 131

**Goldsmith, Oliver**
1728-1774 ...... **LC 2; DA; DAB; DAC;**
**DAM DRAM, MST, NOV, POET;**
**WLC**
See also CDBLB 1660-1789; DLB 39, 89,
104, 109, 142; SATA 26

**Goldsmith, Peter**
See Priestley, J(ohn) B(oynton)

**Gombrowicz, Witold**
1904-1969 .......... **CLC 4, 7, 11, 49;**
**DAM DRAM**
See also CA 19-20; 25-28R; CAP 2

**Gomez de la Serna, Ramon**
1888-1963 .................... **CLC 9**
See also CA 116; HW

**Goncharov, Ivan Alexandrovich**
1812-1891 .................. **NCLC 1**

**Goncourt, Edmond (Louis Antoine Huot) de**
1822-1896 .................. **NCLC 7**
See also DLB 123

**Goncourt, Jules (Alfred Huot) de**
1830-1870 .................. **NCLC 7**
See also DLB 123

**Gontier, Fernande** 19(?)- .......... **CLC 50**

**Goodman, Paul** 1911-1972.... **CLC 1, 2, 4, 7**
See also CA 19-20; 37-40R; CANR 34;
CAP 2; DLB 130; MTCW

**Gordimer, Nadine**
1923- .... **CLC 3, 5, 7, 10, 18, 33, 51, 70;**
**DA; DAB; DAC; DAM MST, NOV;**
**SSC 17**
See also CA 5-8R; CANR 3, 28;
INT CANR-28; MTCW

**Gordon, Adam Lindsay**
1833-1870 ................. **NCLC 21**

**Gordon, Caroline**
1895-1981 ... **CLC 6, 13, 29, 83; SSC 15**
See also CA 11-12; 103; CANR 36; CAP 1;
DLB 4, 9, 102; DLBY 81; MTCW

**Gordon, Charles William** 1860-1937
See Connor, Ralph
See also CA 109

**Gordon, Mary (Catherine)**
1949- ..................... **CLC 13, 22**
See also CA 102; CANR 44; DLB 6;
DLBY 81; INT 102; MTCW

**Gordon, Sol** 1923-................. **CLC 26**
See also CA 53-56; CANR 4; SATA 11

**Gordone, Charles**
1925-1995 ..... **CLC 1, 4; DAM DRAM**
See also BW 1; CA 93-96; 150; DLB 7;
INT 93-96; MTCW

**Gorenko, Anna Andreevna**
See Akhmatova, Anna

**Gorky, Maxim.........** **TCLC 8; DAB; WLC**
See also Peshkov, Alexei Maximovich

**Goryan, Sirak**
See Saroyan, William

**Gosse, Edmund (William)**
1849-1928 .................. **TCLC 28**
See also CA 117; DLB 57, 144

**Gotlieb, Phyllis Fay (Bloom)**
1926- ....................... **CLC 18**
See also CA 13-16R; CANR 7; DLB 88

**Gottesman, S. D.**
See Kornbluth, C(yril) M.; Pohl, Frederik

**Gottfried von Strassburg**
fl. c. 1210-................. **CMLC 10**
See also DLB 138

**Gould, Lois** ..................... **CLC 4, 10**
See also CA 77-80; CANR 29; MTCW

**Gourmont, Remy (-Marie-Charles) de**
1858-1915 ................... **TCLC 17**
See also CA 109; 150

**Govier, Katherine** 1948-........... **CLC 51**
See also CA 101; CANR 18, 40

**Goyen, (Charles) William**
1915-1983 ...........CLC 5, 8, 14, 40
See also AITN 2; CA 5-8R; 110; CANR 6;
DLB 2; DLBY 83; INT CANR-6

**Goytisolo, Juan**
1931- ..... **CLC 5, 10, 23; DAM MULT;**
**HLC**
See also CA 85-88; CANR 32; HW; MTCW

**Gozzano, Guido** 1883-1916 ......... **PC 10**
See also DLB 114

**Gozzi, (Conte) Carlo** 1720-1806 .. **NCLC 23**

**Grabbe, Christian Dietrich**
1801-1836 .................. **NCLC 2**
See also DLB 133

**Grace, Patricia** 1937-............. **CLC 56**

**Gracian y Morales, Baltasar**
1601-1658 .................. **LC 15**

**Gracq, Julien** ................. **CLC 11, 48**
See also Poirier, Louis
See also DLB 83

**Grade, Chaim** 1910-1982 .......... **CLC 10**
See also CA 93-96; 107

**Graduate of Oxford, A**
See Ruskin, John

**Graham, John**
See Phillips, David Graham

**Graham, Jorie** 1951-.............. **CLC 48**
See also CA 111; DLB 120

**Graham, R(obert) B(ontine) Cunninghame**
See Cunninghame Graham, R(obert)
B(ontine)
See also DLB 98, 135

**Graham, Robert**
See Haldeman, Joe (William)

**Graham, Tom**
See Lewis, (Harry) Sinclair

**Graham, W(illiam) S(ydney)**
1918-1986 . . . . . . . . . . . . . . . . . CLC 29
See also CA 73-76; 118; DLB 20

**Graham, Winston (Mawdsley)**
1910- . . . . . . . . . . . . . . . . . . . . . CLC 23
See also CA 49-52; CANR 2, 22, 45;
DLB 77

**Grahame, Kenneth**
1859-1932 . . . . . . . . . . . . TCLC 64; DAB
See also CA 108; 136; CLR 5; DLB 34, 141;
MAICYA; YABC 1

**Grant, Skeeter**
See Spiegelman, Art

**Granville-Barker, Harley**
1877-1946 . . . . . . TCLC 2; DAM DRAM
See also Barker, Harley Granville
See also CA 104

**Grass, Guenter (Wilhelm)**
1927- . . . . . CLC 1, 2, 4, 6, 11, 15, 22, 32,
49, 88; DA; DAB; DAC; DAM MST,
NOV; WLC
See also CA 13-16R; CANR 20; DLB 75,
124; MTCW

**Gratton, Thomas**
See Hulme, T(homas) E(rnest)

**Grau, Shirley Ann**
1929- . . . . . . . . . . . . . . CLC 4, 9; SSC 15
See also CA 89-92; CANR 22; DLB 2;
INT CANR-22; MTCW

**Gravel, Fern**
See Hall, James Norman

**Graver, Elizabeth** 1964- . . . . . . . . . . CLC 70
See also CA 135

**Graves, Richard Perceval** 1945- . . . . CLC 44
See also CA 65-68; CANR 9, 26, 51

**Graves, Robert (von Ranke)**
1895-1985 . . . . . . CLC 1, 2, 6, 11, 39, 44,
45; DAB; DAC; DAM MST, POET;
PC 6
See also CA 5-8R; 117; CANR 5, 36;
CDBLB 1914-1945; DLB 20, 100;
DLBY 85; MTCW; SATA 45

**Graves, Valerie**
See Bradley, Marion Zimmer

**Gray, Alasdair (James)** 1934- . . . . . . CLC 41
See also CA 126; CANR 47; INT 126;
MTCW

**Gray, Amlin** 1946- . . . . . . . . . . . . . . CLC 29
See also CA 138

**Gray, Francine du Plessix**
1930- . . . . . . . . . . . CLC 22; DAM NOV
See also BEST 90:3; CA 61-64; CAAS 2;
CANR 11, 33; INT CANR-11; MTCW

**Gray, John (Henry)** 1866-1934 . . . . TCLC 19
See also CA 119

**Gray, Simon (James Holliday)**
1936- . . . . . . . . . . . . . . . . . CLC 9, 14, 36
See also AITN 1; CA 21-24R; CAAS 3;
CANR 32; DLB 13; MTCW

**Gray, Spalding** 1941- . . CLC 49; DAM POP
See also CA 128

**Gray, Thomas**
1716-1771 . . . . . . LC 4; DA; DAB; DAC;
DAM MST; PC 2; WLC
See also CDBLB 1660-1789; DLB 109

**Grayson, David**
See Baker, Ray Stannard

**Grayson, Richard (A.)** 1951- . . . . . . . CLC 38
See also CA 85-88; CANR 14, 31

**Greeley, Andrew M(oran)**
1928- . . . . . . . . . . . CLC 28; DAM POP
See also CA 5-8R; CAAS 7; CANR 7, 43;
MTCW

**Green, Anna Katharine**
1846-1935 . . . . . . . . . . . . . . . . . TCLC 63
See also CA 112

**Green, Brian**
See Card, Orson Scott

**Green, Hannah**
See Greenberg, Joanne (Goldenberg)

**Green, Hannah** . . . . . . . . . . . . . . . . . CLC 3
See also CA 73-76

**Green, Henry** . . . . . . . . . . . . . . . . CLC 2, 13
See also Yorke, Henry Vincent
See also DLB 15

**Green, Julian (Hartridge)** 1900-
See Green, Julien
See also CA 21-24R; CANR 33; DLB 4, 72;
MTCW

**Green, Julien** . . . . . . . . . . . . . . CLC 3, 11, 77
See also Green, Julian (Hartridge)

**Green, Paul (Eliot)**
1894-1981 . . . . . . CLC 25; DAM DRAM
See also AITN 1; CA 5-8R; 103; CANR 3;
DLB 7, 9; DLBY 81

**Greenberg, Ivan** 1908-1973
See Rahv, Philip
See also CA 85-88

**Greenberg, Joanne (Goldenberg)**
1932- . . . . . . . . . . . . . . . . . . CLC 7, 30
See also AAYA 12; CA 5-8R; CANR 14,
32; SATA 25

**Greenberg, Richard** 1959(?)- . . . . . . . CLC 57
See also CA 138

**Greene, Bette** 1934- . . . . . . . . . . . . . . CLC 30
See also AAYA 7; CA 53-56; CANR 4;
CLR 2; JRDA; MAICYA; SAAS 16;
SATA 8

**Greene, Gael** . . . . . . . . . . . . . . . . . . . CLC 8
See also CA 13-16R; CANR 10

**Greene, Graham**
1904-1991 . . . . CLC 1, 3, 6, 9, 14, 18, 27,
37, 70, 72; DA; DAB; DAC; DAM MST,
NOV; WLC
See also AITN 2; CA 13-16R; 133;
CANR 35; CDBLB 1945-1960; DLB 13,
15, 77, 100, 162; DLBY 91; MTCW;
SATA 20

**Greer, Richard**
See Silverberg, Robert

**Gregor, Arthur** 1923- . . . . . . . . . . . . . CLC 9
See also CA 25-28R; CAAS 10; CANR 11;
SATA 36

**Gregor, Lee**
See Pohl, Frederik

**Gregory, Isabella Augusta (Persse)**
1852-1932 . . . . . . . . . . . . . . . . . . TCLC 1
See also CA 104; DLB 10

**Gregory, J. Dennis**
See Williams, John A(lfred)

**Grendon, Stephen**
See Derleth, August (William)

**Grenville, Kate** 1950- . . . . . . . . . . . . . CLC 61
See also CA 118; CANR 53

**Grenville, Pelham**
See Wodehouse, P(elham) G(renville)

**Greve, Felix Paul (Berthold Friedrich)**
1879-1948
See Grove, Frederick Philip
See also CA 104; 141; DAC; DAM MST

**Grey, Zane**
1872-1939 . . . . . . . . TCLC 6; DAM POP
See also CA 104; 132; DLB 9; MTCW

**Grieg, (Johan) Nordahl (Brun)**
1902-1943 . . . . . . . . . . . . . . . . . TCLC 10
See also CA 107

**Grieve, C(hristopher) M(urray)**
1892-1978 . . . . CLC 11, 19; DAM POET
See also MacDiarmid, Hugh; Pteleon
See also CA 5-8R; 85-88; CANR 33;
MTCW

**Griffin, Gerald** 1803-1840 . . . . . . . . NCLC 7
See also DLB 159

**Griffin, John Howard** 1920-1980 . . . . CLC 68
See also AITN 1; CA 1-4R; 101; CANR 2

**Griffin, Peter** 1942- . . . . . . . . . . . . . . CLC 39
See also CA 136

**Griffiths, Trevor** 1935- . . . . . . . . . CLC 13, 52
See also CA 97-100; CANR 45; DLB 13

**Grigson, Geoffrey (Edward Harvey)**
1905-1985 . . . . . . . . . . . . . . . . CLC 7, 39
See also CA 25-28R; 118; CANR 20, 33;
DLB 27; MTCW

**Grillparzer, Franz** 1791-1872 . . . . . . NCLC 1
See also DLB 133

**Grimble, Reverend Charles James**
See Eliot, T(homas) S(tearns)

**Grimke, Charlotte L(ottie) Forten**
1837(?)-1914
See Forten, Charlotte L.
See also BW 1; CA 117; 124; DAM MULT,
POET

**Grimm, Jacob Ludwig Karl**
1785-1863 . . . . . . . . . . . . . . . . . NCLC 3
See also DLB 90; MAICYA; SATA 22

**Grimm, Wilhelm Karl** 1786-1859 . . NCLC 3
See also DLB 90; MAICYA; SATA 22

**Grimmelshausen, Johann Jakob Christoffel**
von 1621-1676 . . . . . . . . . . . . . . . . LC 6
See also DLB 168

**Grindel, Eugene** 1895-1952
See Eluard, Paul
See also CA 104

**Grisham, John** 1955- . . CLC 84; DAM POP
See also AAYA 14; CA 138; CANR 47

Grossman, David 1954- .......... CLC 67
See also CA 138

Grossman, Vasily (Semenovich)
1905-1964 ................. CLC 41
See also CA 124; 130; MTCW

Grove, Frederick Philip ........... TCLC 4
See also Greve, Felix Paul (Berthold
Friedrich)
See also DLB 92

Grubb
See Crumb, R(obert)

Grumbach, Doris (Isaac)
1918- ................ CLC 13, 22, 64
See also CA 5-8R; CAAS 2; CANR 9, 42;
INT CANR-9

Grundtvig, Nicolai Frederik Severin
1783-1872 ................. NCLC 1

Grunge
See Crumb, R(obert)

Grunwald, Lisa 1959- ............. CLC 44
See also CA 120

Guare, John
1938- ............. CLC 8, 14, 29, 67;
DAM DRAM
See also CA 73-76; CANR 21; DLB 7;
MTCW

Gudjonsson, Halldor Kiljan 1902-
See Laxness, Halldor
See also CA 103

Guenter, Erich
See Eich, Guenter

Guest, Barbara 1920- ............. CLC 34
See also CA 25-28R; CANR 11, 44; DLB 5

Guest, Judith (Ann)
1936- .... CLC 8, 30; DAM NOV, POP
See also AAYA 7; CA 77-80; CANR 15;
INT CANR-15; MTCW

Guevara, Che .............. CLC 87; HLC
See also Guevara (Serna), Ernesto

Guevara (Serna), Ernesto 1928-1967
See Guevara, Che
See also CA 127; 111; DAM MULT; HW

Guild, Nicholas M. 1944- ......... CLC 33
See also CA 93-96

Guillemin, Jacques
See Sartre, Jean-Paul

Guillen, Jorge
1893-1984 ...... CLC 11; DAM MULT,
POET
See also CA 89-92; 112; DLB 108; HW

Guillen, Nicolas (Cristobal)
1902-1989 ......... CLC 48, 79; BLC;
DAM MST, MULT, POET; HLC
See also BW 2; CA 116; 125; 129; HW

Guillevic, (Eugene) 1907- ......... CLC 33
See also CA 93-96

Guillois
See Desnos, Robert

Guillois, Valentin
See Desnos, Robert

Guiney, Louise Imogen
1861-1920 ................. TCLC 41
See also DLB 54

Guiraldes, Ricardo (Guillermo)
1886-1927 ................. TCLC 39
See also CA 131; HW; MTCW

Gumilev, Nikolai Stephanovich
1886-1921 ................. TCLC 60

Gunesekcra, Romesh .............. CLC 91

Gunn, Bill ....................... CLC 5
See also Gunn, William Harrison
See also DLB 38

Gunn, Thom(son William)
1929- ........... CLC 3, 6, 18, 32, 81;
DAM POET
See also CA 17-20R; CANR 9, 33;
CDBLB 1960 to Present; DLB 27;
INT CANR-33; MTCW

Gunn, William Harrison 1934(?)-1989
See Gunn, Bill
See also AITN 1; BW 1; CA 13-16R; 128;
CANR 12, 25

Gunnars, Kristjana 1948- ......... CLC 69
See also CA 113; DLB 60

Gurganus, Allan
1947- ............ CLC 70; DAM POP
See also BEST 90:1; CA 135

Gurney, A(lbert) R(amsdell), Jr.
1930- .... CLC 32, 50, 54; DAM DRAM
See also CA 77-80; CANR 32

Gurney, Ivor (Bertie) 1890-1937 ... TCLC 33

Gurney, Peter
See Gurney, A(lbert) R(amsdell), Jr.

Guro, Elena 1877-1913 .......... TCLC 56

Gustafson, Ralph (Barker) 1909- .... CLC 36
See also CA 21-24R; CANR 8, 45; DLB 88

Gut, Gom
See Simenon, Georges (Jacques Christian)

Guterson, David 1956- ............ CLC 91
See also CA 132

Guthrie, A(lfred) B(ertram), Jr.
1901-1991 ................. CLC 23
See also CA 57-60; 134; CANR 24; DLB 6;
SATA 62; SATA-Obit 67

Guthrie, Isobel
See Grieve, C(hristopher) M(urray)

Guthrie, Woodrow Wilson 1912-1967
See Guthrie, Woody
See also CA 113; 93-96

Guthrie, Woody .................. CLC 35
See also Guthrie, Woodrow Wilson

Guy, Rosa (Cuthbert) 1928- ........ CLC 26
See also AAYA 4; BW 2; CA 17-20R;
CANR 14, 34; CLR 13; DLB 33; JRDA;
MAICYA; SATA 14, 62

Gwendolyn
See Bennett, (Enoch) Arnold

H. D. ........ CLC 3, 8, 14, 31, 34, 73; PC 5
See also Doolittle, Hilda

H. de V.
See Buchan, John

Haavikko, Paavo Juhani
1931- .................... CLC 18, 34
See also CA 106

Habbema, Koos
See Heijermans, Herman

Hacker, Marilyn
1942- ........... CLC 5, 9, 23, 72, 91;
DAM POET
See also CA 77-80; DLB 120

Haggard, H(enry) Rider
1856-1925 ................. TCLC 11
See also CA 108; 148; DLB 70, 156;
SATA 16

Hagiosy, L.
See Larbaud, Valery (Nicolas)

Hagiwara Sakutaro 1886-1942 .... TCLC 60

Haig, Fenil
See Ford, Ford Madox

Haig-Brown, Roderick (Langmere)
1908-1976 ................. CLC 21
See also CA 5-8R; 69-72; CANR 4, 38;
CLR 31; DLB 88; MAICYA; SATA 12

Hailey, Arthur
1920- ....... CLC 5; DAM NOV, POP
See also AITN 2; BEST 90:3; CA 1-4R;
CANR 2, 36; DLB 88; DLBY 82; MTCW

Hailey, Elizabeth Forsythe 1938- ... CLC 40
See also CA 93-96; CAAS 1; CANR 15, 48;
INT CANR-15

Haines, John (Meade) 1924- ....... CLC 58
See also CA 17-20R; CANR 13, 34; DLB 5

Hakluyt, Richard 1552-1616 ....... LC 31

Haldeman, Joe (William) 1943- ..... CLC 61
See also CA 53-56; CANR 6; DLB 8;
INT CANR-6

Haley, Alex(ander Murray Palmer)
1921-1992 .... CLC 8, 12, 76; BLC; DA;
DAB; DAC; DAM MST, MULT, POP
See also BW 2; CA 77-80; 136; DLB 38;
MTCW

Haliburton, Thomas Chandler
1796-1865 ................. NCLC 15
See also DLB 11, 99

Hall, Donald (Andrew, Jr.)
1928- .. CLC 1, 13, 37, 59; DAM POET
See also CA 5-8R; CAAS 7; CANR 2, 44;
DLB 5; SATA 23

Hall, Frederic Sauser
See Sauser-Hall, Frederic

Hall, James
See Kuttner, Henry

Hall, James Norman 1887-1951 ... TCLC 23
See also CA 123; SATA 21

Hall, (Marguerite) Radclyffe
1886-1943 ................. TCLC 12
See also CA 110; 150

Hall, Rodney 1935- .............. CLC 51
See also CA 109

Halleck, Fitz-Greene 1790-1867 .. NCLC 47
See also DLB 3

Halliday, Michael
See Creasey, John

Halpern, Daniel 1945- ............ CLC 14
See also CA 33-36R

Hamburger, Michael (Peter Leopold)
1924- .................... CLC 5, 14
See also CA 5-8R; CAAS 4; CANR 2, 47;
DLB 27

Hamill, Pete 1935- .............. CLC 10
See also CA 25-28R; CANR 18

**Hatteras, Amelia**
See Mencken, H(enry) L(ouis)

**Hatteras, Owen** . . . . . . . . . . . . . . . . . **TCLC 18**
See also Mencken, H(enry) L(ouis); Nathan, George Jean

**Hauptmann, Gerhart (Johann Robert)**
1862-1946 . . . . . . **TCLC 4; DAM DRAM**
See also CA 104; DLB 66, 118

**Havel, Vaclav**
1936- . . . . . . . . . . . . . . **CLC 25, 58, 65;**
**DAM DRAM; DC 6**
See also CA 104; CANR 36; MTCW

**Haviaras, Stratis** . . . . . . . . . . . . . . . . . **CLC 33**
See also Chaviaras, Strates

**Hawes, Stephen** 1475(?)-1523(?) . . . . . **LC 17**

**Hawkes, John (Clendennin Burne, Jr.)**
1925- . . . . . . **CLC 1, 2, 3, 4, 7, 9, 14, 15,**
**27, 49**
See also CA 1-4R; CANR 2, 47; DLB 2, 7; DLBY 80; MTCW

**Hawking, S. W.**
See Hawking, Stephen W(illiam)

**Hawking, Stephen W(illiam)**
1942- . . . . . . . . . . . . . . . . . . . . . . **CLC 63**
See also AAYA 13; BEST 89:1; CA 126; 129; CANR 48

**Hawthorne, Julian** 1846-1934 . . . . . **TCLC 25**

**Hawthorne, Nathaniel**
1804-1864 . . . . . . . **NCLC 39; DA; DAB;**
**DAC; DAM MST, NOV; SSC 3; WLC**
See also AAYA 18; CDALB 1640-1865; DLB 1, 74; YABC 2

**Haxton, Josephine Ayres** 1921-
See Douglas, Ellen
See also CA 115; CANR 41

**Hayaseca y Eizaguirre, Jorge**
See Echegaray (y Eizaguirre), Jose (Maria Waldo)

**Hayashi Fumiko** 1904-1951 . . . . . . **TCLC 27**

**Haycraft, Anna**
See Ellis, Alice Thomas
See also CA 122

**Hayden, Robert E(arl)**
1913-1980 . . . . . . **CLC 5, 9, 14, 37; BLC;**
**DA; DAC; DAM MST, MULT, POET;**
**PC 6**
See also BW 1; CA 69-72; 97-100; CABS 2; CANR 24; CDALB 1941-1968; DLB 5, 76; MTCW; SATA 19; SATA-Obit 26

**Hayford, J(oseph) E(phraim) Casely**
See Casely-Hayford, J(oseph) E(phraim)

**Hayman, Ronald** 1932- . . . . . . . . . . . **CLC 44**
See also CA 25-28R; CANR 18, 50; DLB 155

**Haywood, Eliza (Fowler)**
1693(?)-1756 . . . . . . . . . . . . . . . . . . **LC 1**

**Hazlitt, William** 1778-1830 . . . . . . **NCLC 29**
See also DLB 110, 158

**Hazzard, Shirley** 1931- . . . . . . . . . . . **CLC 18**
See also CA 9-12R; CANR 4; DLBY 82; MTCW

**Head, Bessie**
1937-1986 . . . . . . . . . **CLC 25, 67; BLC;**
**DAM MULT**
See also BW 2; CA 29-32R; 119; CANR 25; DLB 117; MTCW

**Headon, (Nicky) Topper** 1956(?)- . . . **CLC 30**

**Heaney, Seamus (Justin)**
1939- . . . . . . **CLC 5, 7, 14, 25, 37, 74, 91;**
**DAB; DAM POET**
See also CA 85-88; CANR 25, 48; CDBLB 1960 to Present; DLB 40; DLBY 95; MTCW

**Hearn, (Patricio) Lafcadio (Tessima Carlos)**
1850-1904 . . . . . . . . . . . . . . . . . . **TCLC 9**
See also CA 105; DLB 12, 78

**Hearne, Vicki** 1946- . . . . . . . . . . . . . **CLC 56**
See also CA 139

**Hearon, Shelby** 1931- . . . . . . . . . . . . **CLC 63**
See also AITN 2; CA 25-28R; CANR 18, 48

**Heat-Moon, William Least** . . . . . . . . . **CLC 29**
See also Trogdon, William (Lewis)
See also AAYA 9

**Hebbel, Friedrich**
1813-1863 . . . . **NCLC 43; DAM DRAM**
See also DLB 129

**Hebert, Anne**
1916- . . . . . . . . . . . **CLC 4, 13, 29; DAC;**
**DAM MST, POET**
See also CA 85-88; DLB 68; MTCW

**Hecht, Anthony (Evan)**
1923- . . . . . . **CLC 8, 13, 19; DAM POET**
See also CA 9-12R; CANR 6; DLB 5

**Hecht, Ben** 1894-1964 . . . . . . . . . . . . . **CLC 8**
See also CA 85-88; DLB 7, 9, 25, 26, 28, 86

**Hedayat, Sadeq** 1903-1951 . . . . . . . **TCLC 21**
See also CA 120

**Hegel, Georg Wilhelm Friedrich**
1770-1831 . . . . . . . . . . . . . . . . **NCLC 46**
See also DLB 90

**Heidegger, Martin** 1889-1976 . . . . . . **CLC 24**
See also CA 81-84; 65-68; CANR 34; MTCW

**Heidenstam, (Carl Gustaf) Verner von**
1859-1940 . . . . . . . . . . . . . . . . . **TCLC 5**
See also CA 104

**Heifner, Jack** 1946- . . . . . . . . . . . . . . **CLC 11**
See also CA 105; CANR 47

**Heijermans, Herman** 1864-1924 . . . **TCLC 24**
See also CA 123

**Heilbrun, Carolyn G(old)** 1926- . . . . . **CLC 25**
See also CA 45-48; CANR 1, 28

**Heine, Heinrich** 1797-1856 . . . . **NCLC 4, 54**
See also DLB 90

**Heinemann, Larry (Curtiss)** 1944- . . **CLC 50**
See also CA 110; CAAS 21; CANR 31; DLBD 9; INT CANR-31

**Heiney, Donald (William)** 1921-1993
See Harris, MacDonald
See also CA 1-4R; 142; CANR 3

**Heinlein, Robert A(nson)**
1907-1988 . . . . . . **CLC 1, 3, 8, 14, 26, 55;**
**DAM POP**
See also AAYA 17; CA 1-4R; 125; CANR 1, 20, 53; DLB 8; JRDA; MAICYA; MTCW; SATA 9, 69; SATA-Obit 56

**Helforth, John**
See Doolittle, Hilda

**Hellenhofferu, Vojtech Kapristian z**
See Hasek, Jaroslav (Matej Frantisek)

**Heller, Joseph**
1923- . . . . **CLC 1, 3, 5, 8, 11, 36, 63; DA;**
**DAB; DAC; DAM MST, NOV, POP;**
**WLC**
See also AITN 1; CA 5-8R; CABS 1; CANR 8, 42; DLB 2, 28; DLBY 80; INT CANR-8; MTCW

**Hellman, Lillian (Florence)**
1906-1984 . . . . . . **CLC 2, 4, 8, 14, 18, 34,**
**44, 52; DAM DRAM; DC 1**
See also AITN 1, 2; CA 13-16R; 112; CANR 33; DLB 7; DLBY 84; MTCW

**Helprin, Mark**
1947- . . . . . . . . . . . . . . **CLC 7, 10, 22, 32;**
**DAM NOV, POP**
See also CA 81-84; CANR 47; DLBY 85; MTCW

**Helvetius, Claude-Adrien**
1715-1771 . . . . . . . . . . . . . . . . . . **LC 26**

**Helyar, Jane Penelope Josephine** 1933-
See Poole, Josephine
See also CA 21-24R; CANR 10, 26; SATA 82

**Hemans, Felicia** 1793-1835 . . . . . . **NCLC 29**
See also DLB 96

**Hemingway, Ernest (Miller)**
1899-1961 . . . . **CLC 1, 3, 6, 8, 10, 13, 19,**
**30, 34, 39, 41, 44, 50, 61, 80; DA; DAB;**
**DAC; DAM MST, NOV; SSC 1; WLC**
See also CA 77-80; CANR 34; CDALB 1917-1929; DLB 4, 9, 102; DLBD 1; DLBY 81, 87; MTCW

**Hempel, Amy** 1951- . . . . . . . . . . . . . . **CLC 39**
See also CA 118; 137

**Henderson, F. C.**
See Mencken, H(enry) L(ouis)

**Henderson, Sylvia**
See Ashton-Warner, Sylvia (Constance)

**Henley, Beth** . . . . . . . . . . . . . . **CLC 23; DC 6**
See also Henley, Elizabeth Becker
See also CABS 3; DLBY 86

**Henley, Elizabeth Becker** 1952-
See Henley, Beth
See also CA 107; CANR 32; DAM DRAM, MST; MTCW

**Henley, William Ernest**
1849-1903 . . . . . . . . . . . . . . . . . **TCLC 8**
See also CA 105; DLB 19

**Hennissart, Martha**
See Lathen, Emma
See also CA 85-88

**Henry, O.** . . . . . . . . **TCLC 1, 19; SSC 5; WLC**
See also Porter, William Sydney

**Henry, Patrick** 1736-1799 . . . . . . . . . **LC 25**

**Henryson, Robert** 1430(?)-1506(?).... **LC 20**
See also DLB 146

**Henry VIII** 1491-1547............. **LC 10**

**Henschke, Alfred**
See Klabund

**Hentoff, Nat(han Irving)** 1925-..... **CLC 26**
See also AAYA 4; CA 1-4R; CAAS 6;
CANR 5, 25; CLR 1; INT CANR-25;
JRDA; MAICYA; SATA 42, 69;
SATA-Brief 27

**Heppenstall, (John) Rayner**
1911-1981 ................... **CLC 10**
See also CA 1-4R; 103; CANR 29

**Herbert, Frank (Patrick)**
1920-1986 ...... **CLC 12, 23, 35, 44, 85;**
**DAM POP**
See also CA 53-56; 118; CANR 5, 43;
DLB 8; INT CANR-5; MTCW; SATA 9,
37; SATA-Obit 47

**Herbert, George**
1593-1633 ............. **LC 24; DAB;**
**DAM POET; PC 4**
See also CDBLB Before 1660; DLB 126

**Herbert, Zbigniew**
1924- ........ **CLC 9, 43; DAM POET**
See also CA 89-92; CANR 36; MTCW

**Herbst, Josephine (Frey)**
1897-1969 .................. **CLC 34**
See also CA 5-8R; 25-28R; DLB 9

**Hergesheimer, Joseph**
1880-1954 .................. **TCLC 11**
See also CA 109; DLB 102, 9

**Herlihy, James Leo** 1927-1993 ...... **CLC 6**
See also CA 1-4R; 143; CANR 2

**Hermogenes** fl. c. 175-........... **CMLC 6**

**Hernandez, Jose** 1834-1886...... **NCLC 17**

**Herodotus** c. 484B.C.-429B.C..... **CMLC 17**

**Herrick, Robert**
1591-1674 ..... **LC 13; DA; DAB; DAC;**
**DAM MST, POP; PC 9**
See also DLB 126

**Herring, Guilles**
See Somerville, Edith

**Herriot, James**
1916-1995 ........ **CLC 12; DAM POP**
See also Wight, James Alfred
See also AAYA 1; CA 148; CANR 40;
SATA 86

**Herrmann, Dorothy** 1941-......... **CLC 44**
See also CA 107

**Herrmann, Taffy**
See Herrmann, Dorothy

**Hersey, John (Richard)**
1914-1993 ....... **CLC 1, 2, 7, 9, 40, 81;**
**DAM POP**
See also CA 17-20R; 140; CANR 33;
DLB 6; MTCW; SATA 25;
SATA-Obit 76

**Herzen, Aleksandr Ivanovich**
1812-1870 ................. **NCLC 10**

**Herzl, Theodor** 1860-1904........ **TCLC 36**

**Herzog, Werner** 1942-............. **CLC 16**
See also CA 89-92

**Hesiod** c. 8th cent. B.C.-......... **CMLC 5**

**Hesse, Hermann**
1877-1962 .... **CLC 1, 2, 3, 6, 11, 17, 25,**
**69; DA; DAB; DAC; DAM MST, NOV;**
**SSC 9; WLC**
See also CA 17-18; CAP 2; DLB 66;
MTCW; SATA 50

**Hewes, Cady**
See De Voto, Bernard (Augustine)

**Heyen, William** 1940- ........ **CLC 13, 18**
See also CA 33-36R; CAAS 9; DLB 5

**Heyerdahl, Thor** 1914-............ **CLC 26**
See also CA 5-8R; CANR 5, 22; MTCW;
SATA 2, 52

**Heym, Georg (Theodor Franz Arthur)**
1887-1912 ................. **TCLC 9**
See also CA 106

**Heym, Stefan** 1913-.............. **CLC 41**
See also CA 9-12R; CANR 4; DLB 69

**Heyse, Paul (Johann Ludwig von)**
1830-1914 .................. **TCLC 8**
See also CA 104; DLB 129

**Heyward, (Edwin) DuBose**
1885-1940 .................. **TCLC 59**
See also CA 108; DLB 7, 9, 45; SATA 21

**Hibbert, Eleanor Alice Burford**
1906-1993 ........ **CLC 7; DAM POP**
See also BEST 90:4; CA 17-20R; 140;
CANR 9, 28; SATA 2; SATA-Obit 74

**Hichens, Robert S.** 1864-1950..... **TCLC 64**
See also DLB 153

**Higgins, George V(incent)**
1939- ................ **CLC 4, 7, 10, 18**
See also CA 77-80; CAAS 5; CANR 17, 51;
DLB 2; DLBY 81; INT CANR-17;
MTCW

**Higginson, Thomas Wentworth**
1823-1911 .................. **TCLC 36**
See also DLB 1, 64

**Highet, Helen**
See MacInnes, Helen (Clark)

**Highsmith, (Mary) Patricia**
1921-1995 ........... **CLC 2, 4, 14, 42;**
**DAM NOV, POP**
See also CA 1-4R; 147; CANR 1, 20, 48;
MTCW

**Highwater, Jamake (Mamake)**
1942(?)- ..................... **CLC 12**
See also AAYA 7; CA 65-68; CAAS 7;
CANR 10, 34; CLR 17; DLB 52;
DLBY 85; JRDA; MAICYA; SATA 32,
69; SATA-Brief 30

**Highway, Tomson**
1951- ..... **CLC 92; DAC; DAM MULT**
See also CA 151; NNAL

**Higuchi, Ichiyo** 1872-1896....... **NCLC 49**

**Hijuelos, Oscar**
1951- .... **CLC 65; DAM MULT, POP;**
**HLC**
See also BEST 90:1; CA 123; CANR 50;
DLB 145; HW

**Hikmet, Nazim** 1902(?)-1963....... **CLC 40**
See also CA 141; 93-96

**Hildesheimer, Wolfgang**
1916-1991 ................... **CLC 49**
See also CA 101; 135; DLB 69, 124

**Hill, Geoffrey (William)**
1932- ... **CLC 5, 8, 18, 45; DAM POET**
See also CA 81-84; CANR 21;
CDBLB 1960 to Present; DLB 40;
MTCW

**Hill, George Roy** 1921-.......... **CLC 26**
See also CA 110; 122

**Hill, John**
See Koontz, Dean R(ay)

**Hill, Susan (Elizabeth)**
1942-.. **CLC 4; DAB; DAM MST, NOV**
See also CA 33-36R; CANR 29; DLB 14,
139; MTCW

**Hillerman, Tony**
1925-............. **CLC 62; DAM POP**
See also AAYA 6; BEST 89:1; CA 29-32R;
CANR 21, 42; SATA 6

**Hillesum, Etty** 1914-1943 ........ **TCLC 49**
See also CA 137

**Hilliard, Noel (Harvey)** 1929-...... **CLC 15**
See also CA 9-12R; CANR 7

**Hillis, Rick** 1956-................ **CLC 66**
See also CA 134

**Hilton, James** 1900-1954........ **TCLC 21**
See also CA 108; DLB 34, 77; SATA 34

**Himes, Chester (Bomar)**
1909-1984 .... **CLC 2, 4, 7, 18, 58; BLC;**
**DAM MULT**
See also BW 2; CA 25-28R; 114; CANR 22;
DLB 2, 76, 143; MTCW

**Hinde, Thomas** ................. **CLC 6, 11**
See also Chitty, Thomas Willes

**Hindin, Nathan**
See Bloch, Robert (Albert)

**Hine, (William) Daryl** 1936-....... **CLC 15**
See also CA 1-4R; CAAS 15; CANR 1, 20;
DLB 60

**Hinkson, Katharine Tynan**
See Tynan, Katharine

**Hinton, S(usan) E(loise)**
1950- ........ **CLC 30; DA; DAB; DAC;**
**DAM MST, NOV**
See also AAYA 2; CA 81-84; CANR 32;
CLR 3, 23; JRDA; MAICYA; MTCW;
SATA 19, 58

**Hippius, Zinaida** ................. **TCLC 9**
See also Gippius, Zinaida (Nikolayevna)

**Hiraoka, Kimitake** 1925-1970
See Mishima, Yukio
See also CA 97-100; 29-32R; DAM DRAM;
MTCW

**Hirsch, E(ric) D(onald), Jr.** 1928-... **CLC 79**
See also CA 25-28R; CANR 27, 51;
DLB 67; INT CANR-27; MTCW

**Hirsch, Edward** 1950- ......... **CLC 31, 50**
See also CA 104; CANR 20, 42; DLB 120

**Hitchcock, Alfred (Joseph)**
1899-1980 .................. **CLC 16**
See also CA 97-100; SATA 27;
SATA-Obit 24

**Hitler, Adolf** 1889-1945......... **TCLC 53**
See also CA 117; 147

**Hoagland, Edward** 1932-.......... **CLC 28**
See also CA 1-4R; CANR 2, 31; DLB 6;
SATA 51

**Hoban, Russell (Conwell)**
    1925- ......... **CLC 7, 25; DAM NOV**
    See also CA 5-8R; CANR 23, 37; CLR 3;
    DLB 52; MAICYA; MTCW; SATA 1,
    40, 78

**Hobbs, Perry**
    See Blackmur, R(ichard) P(almer)

**Hobson, Laura Z(ametkin)**
    1900-1986 ................. **CLC 7, 25**
    See also CA 17-20R; 118; DLB 28;
    SATA 52

**Hochhuth, Rolf**
    1931- ..... **CLC 4, 11, 18; DAM DRAM**
    See also CA 5-8R; CANR 33; DLB 124;
    MTCW

**Hochman, Sandra** 1936- ......... **CLC 3, 8**
    See also CA 5-8R; DLB 5

**Hochwaelder, Fritz**
    1911-1986 ...... **CLC 36; DAM DRAM**
    See also CA 29-32R; 120; CANR 42;
    MTCW

**Hochwalder, Fritz**
    See Hochwaelder, Fritz

**Hocking, Mary (Eunice)** 1921- ..... **CLC 13**
    See also CA 101; CANR 18, 40

**Hodgins, Jack** 1938- ............. **CLC 23**
    See also CA 93-96; DLB 60

**Hodgson, William Hope**
    1877(?)-1918 ............... **TCLC 13**
    See also CA 111; DLB 70, 153, 156

**Hoeg, Peter** 1957- ............... **CLC 95**
    See also CA 151

**Hoffman, Alice**
    1952- ............ **CLC 51; DAM NOV**
    See also CA 77-80; CANR 34; MTCW

**Hoffman, Daniel (Gerard)**
    1923- ................. **CLC 6, 13, 23**
    See also CA 1-4R; CANR 4; DLB 5

**Hoffman, Stanley** 1944- ............. **CLC 5**
    See also CA 77-80

**Hoffman, William M(oses)** 1939- ... **CLC 40**
    See also CA 57-60; CANR 11

**Hoffmann, E(rnst) T(heodor) A(madeus)**
    1776-1822 ...... **NCLC 2; SSC 13**
    See also DLB 90; SATA 27

**Hofmann, Gert** 1931- ............. **CLC 54**
    See also CA 128

**Hofmannsthal, Hugo von**
    1874-1929 .... **TCLC 11; DAM DRAM;
                                        DC 4**
    See also CA 106; DLB 81, 118

**Hogan, Linda**
    1947- ......... **CLC 73; DAM MULT**
    See also CA 120; CANR 45; NNAL

**Hogarth, Charles**
    See Creasey, John

**Hogarth, Emmett**
    See Polonsky, Abraham (Lincoln)

**Hogg, James** 1770-1835 ......... **NCLC 4**
    See also DLB 93, 116, 159

**Holbach, Paul Henri Thiry Baron**
    1723-1789 ................... **LC 14**

**Holberg, Ludvig** 1684-1754 ......... **LC 6**

**Holden, Ursula** 1921- ............ **CLC 18**
    See also CA 101; CAAS 8; CANR 22

**Holderlin, (Johann Christian) Friedrich**
    1770-1843 ........... **NCLC 16; PC 4**

**Holdstock, Robert**
    See Holdstock, Robert P.

**Holdstock, Robert P.** 1948- ........ **CLC 39**
    See also CA 131

**Holland, Isabelle** 1920- ........... **CLC 21**
    See also AAYA 11; CA 21-24R; CANR 10,
    25, 47; JRDA; MAICYA; SATA 8, 70

**Holland, Marcus**
    See Caldwell, (Janet Miriam) Taylor
    (Holland)

**Hollander, John** 1929- ...... **CLC 2, 5, 8, 14**
    See also CA 1-4R; CANR 1, 52; DLB 5;
    SATA 13

**Hollander, Paul**
    See Silverberg, Robert

**Holleran, Andrew** 1943(?)- ......... **CLC 38**
    See also CA 144

**Hollinghurst, Alan** 1954- ....... **CLC 55, 91**
    See also CA 114

**Hollis, Jim**
    See Summers, Hollis (Spurgeon, Jr.)

**Holly, Buddy** 1936-1959 ........ **TCLC 65**

**Holmes, John**
    See Souster, (Holmes) Raymond

**Holmes, John Clellon** 1926-1988.... **CLC 56**
    See also CA 9-12R; 125; CANR 4; DLB 16

**Holmes, Oliver Wendell**
    1809-1894 ................. **NCLC 14**
    See also CDALB 1640-1865; DLB 1;
    SATA 34

**Holmes, Raymond**
    See Souster, (Holmes) Raymond

**Holt, Victoria**
    See Hibbert, Eleanor Alice Burford

**Holub, Miroslav** 1923- ............. **CLC 4**
    See also CA 21-24R; CANR 10

**Homer**
    c. 8th cent. B.C.- ..... **CMLC 1, 16; DA;
                                        DAB; DAC; DAM MST, POET**

**Honig, Edwin** 1919- ............... **CLC 33**
    See also CA 5-8R; CAAS 8; CANR 4, 45;
    DLB 5

**Hood, Hugh (John Blagdon)**
    1928- ..................... **CLC 15, 28**
    See also CA 49-52; CAAS 17; CANR 1, 33;
    DLB 53

**Hood, Thomas** 1799-1845........ **NCLC 16**
    See also DLB 96

**Hooker, (Peter) Jeremy** 1941- ...... **CLC 43**
    See also CA 77-80; CANR 22; DLB 40

**hooks, bell** ...................... **CLC 94**
    See also Watkins, Gloria

**Hope, A(lec) D(erwent)** 1907- .... **CLC 3, 51**
    See also CA 21-24R; CANR 33; MTCW

**Hope, Brian**
    See Creasey, John

**Hope, Christopher (David Tully)**
    1944- ..................... **CLC 52**
    See also CA 106; CANR 47; SATA 62

**Hopkins, Gerard Manley**
    1844-1889 ....... **NCLC 17; DA; DAB;
                DAC; DAM MST, POET; PC 15; WLC**
    See also CDBLB 1890-1914; DLB 35, 57

**Hopkins, John (Richard)** 1931- ...... **CLC 4**
    See also CA 85-88

**Hopkins, Pauline Elizabeth**
    1859-1930 ............ **TCLC 28; BLC;
                                        DAM MULT**
    See also BW 2; CA 141; DLB 50

**Hopkinson, Francis** 1737-1791 ...... **LC 25**
    See also DLB 31

**Hopley-Woolrich, Cornell George** 1903-1968
    See Woolrich, Cornell
    See also CA 13-14; CAP 1

**Horatio**
    See Proust, (Valentin-Louis-George-Eugene-)
    Marcel

**Horgan, Paul (George Vincent O'Shaughnessy)**
    1903-1995 ...... **CLC 9, 53; DAM NOV**
    See also CA 13-16R; 147; CANR 9, 35;
    DLB 102; DLBY 85; INT CANR-9;
    MTCW; SATA 13; SATA-Obit 84

**Horn, Peter**
    See Kuttner, Henry

**Hornem, Horace Esq.**
    See Byron, George Gordon (Noel)

**Hornung, E(rnest) W(illiam)**
    1866-1921 ................. **TCLC 59**
    See also CA 108; DLB 70

**Horovitz, Israel (Arthur)**
    1939- .......... **CLC 56; DAM DRAM**
    See also CA 33-36R; CANR 46; DLB 7

**Horvath, Odon von**
    See Horvath, Oedoen von
    See also DLB 85, 124

**Horvath, Oedoen von** 1901-1938... **TCLC 45**
    See also Horvath, Odon von
    See also CA 118

**Horwitz, Julius** 1920-1986......... **CLC 14**
    See also CA 9-12R; 119; CANR 12

**Hospital, Janette Turner** 1942-..... **CLC 42**
    See also CA 108; CANR 48

**Hostos, E. M. de**
    See Hostos (y Bonilla), Eugenio Maria de

**Hostos, Eugenio M. de**
    See Hostos (y Bonilla), Eugenio Maria de

**Hostos, Eugenio Maria**
    See Hostos (y Bonilla), Eugenio Maria de

**Hostos (y Bonilla), Eugenio Maria de**
    1839-1903 ................. **TCLC 24**
    See also CA 123; 131; HW

**Houdini**
    See Lovecraft, H(oward) P(hillips)

**Hougan, Carolyn** 1943- .......... **CLC 34**
    See also CA 139

**Household, Geoffrey (Edward West)**
    1900-1988 .................. **CLC 11**
    See also CA 77-80; 126; DLB 87; SATA 14;
    SATA-Obit 59

**Housman, A(lfred) E(dward)**
    1859-1936 ...... **TCLC 1, 10; DA; DAB;
                DAC; DAM MST, POET; PC 2**
    See also CA 104; 125; DLB 19; MTCW

Housman, Laurence 1865-1959 . . . . . TCLC 7
See also CA 106; DLB 10; SATA 25

Howard, Elizabeth Jane 1923- . . . CLC 7, 29
See also CA 5-8R; CANR 8

Howard, Maureen 1930- . . . . . CLC 5, 14, 46
See also CA 53-56; CANR 31; DLBY 83;
INT CANR-31; MTCW

Howard, Richard 1929- . . . . . . CLC 7, 10, 47
See also AITN 1; CA 85-88; CANR 25;
DLB 5; INT CANR-25

Howard, Robert Ervin 1906-1936 . . . TCLC 8
See also CA 105

Howard, Warren F.
See Pohl, Frederik

Howe, Fanny 1940- . . . . . . . . . . . . . . CLC 47
See also CA 117; SATA-Brief 52

Howe, Irving 1920-1993 . . . . . . . . . . . CLC 85
See also CA 9-12R; 141; CANR 21, 50;
DLB 67; MTCW

Howe, Julia Ward 1819-1910 . . . . . TCLC 21
See also CA 117; DLB 1

Howe, Susan 1937- . . . . . . . . . . . . . . . CLC 72
See also DLB 120

Howe, Tina 1937- . . . . . . . . . . . . . . . . CLC 48
See also CA 109

Howell, James 1594(?)-1666 . . . . . . . . LC 13
See also DLB 151

Howells, W. D.
See Howells, William Dean

Howells, William D.
See Howells, William Dean

Howells, William Dean
1837-1920 . . . . . . . . . . . . TCLC 7, 17, 41
See also CA 104; 134; CDALB 1865-1917;
DLB 12, 64, 74, 79

Howes, Barbara 1914-1996 . . . . . . . . CLC 15
See also CA 9-12R; 151; CAAS 3;
CANR 53; SATA 5

Hrabal, Bohumil 1914- . . . . . . . . CLC 13, 67
See also CA 106; CAAS 12

Hsun, Lu
See Lu Hsun

Hubbard, L(afayette) Ron(ald)
1911-1986 . . . . . . . . CLC 43; DAM POP
See also CA 77-80; 118; CANR 52

Huch, Ricarda (Octavia)
1864-1947 . . . . . . . . . . . . . . . . . TCLC 13
See also CA 111; DLB 66

Huddle, David 1942- . . . . . . . . . . . . . CLC 49
See also CA 57-60; CAAS 20; DLB 130

Hudson, Jeffrey
See Crichton, (John) Michael

Hudson, W(illiam) H(enry)
1841-1922 . . . . . . . . . . . . . . . . . TCLC 29
See also CA 115; DLB 98, 153; SATA 35

Hueffer, Ford Madox
See Ford, Ford Madox

Hughart, Barry 1934- . . . . . . . . . . . . . CLC 39
See also CA 137

Hughes, Colin
See Creasey, John

Hughes, David (John) 1930- . . . . . . . CLC 48
See also CA 116; 129; DLB 14

Hughes, Edward James
See Hughes, Ted
See also DAM MST, POET

Hughes, (James) Langston
1902-1967 . . . . . CLC 1, 5, 10, 15, 35, 44;
BLC; DA; DAB; DAC; DAM DRAM,
MST, MULT, POET; DC 3; PC 1;
SSC 6; WLC
See also AAYA 12; BW 1; CA 1-4R;
25-28R; CANR 1, 34; CDALB 1929-1941;
CLR 17; DLB 4, 7, 48, 51, 86; JRDA;
MAICYA; MTCW; SATA 4, 33

Hughes, Richard (Arthur Warren)
1900-1976 . . . . . . CLC 1, 11; DAM NOV
See also CA 5-8R; 65-68; CANR 4;
DLB 15, 161; MTCW; SATA 8;
SATA-Obit 25

Hughes, Ted
1930- . . . . . . . CLC 2, 4, 9, 14, 37; DAB;
DAC; PC 7
See also Hughes, Edward James
See also CA 1-4R; CANR 1, 33; CLR 3;
DLB 40, 161; MAICYA; MTCW;
SATA 49; SATA-Brief 27

Hugo, Richard F(ranklin)
1923-1982 . . . . . . . . . . . . . CLC 6, 18, 32;
DAM POET
See also CA 49-52; 108; CANR 3; DLB 5

Hugo, Victor (Marie)
1802-1885 . . . . . . . . NCLC 3, 10, 21; DA;
DAB; DAC; DAM DRAM, MST, NOV,
POET; WLC
See also DLB 119; SATA 47

Huidobro, Vicente
See Huidobro Fernandez, Vicente Garcia

Huidobro Fernandez, Vicente Garcia
1893-1948 . . . . . . . . . . . . . . . . . TCLC 31
See also CA 131; HW

Hulme, Keri 1947- . . . . . . . . . . . . . . . CLC 39
See also CA 125; INT 125

Hulme, T(homas) E(rnest)
1883-1917 . . . . . . . . . . . . . . . . . TCLC 21
See also CA 117; DLB 19

Hume, David 1711-1776 . . . . . . . . . . . . . LC 7
See also DLB 104

Humphrey, William 1924- . . . . . . . . . CLC 45
See also CA 77-80; DLB 6

Humphreys, Emyr Owen 1919- . . . . . CLC 47
See also CA 5-8R; CANR 3, 24; DLB 15

Humphreys, Josephine 1945- . . . . CLC 34, 57
See also CA 121; 127; INT 127

Huneker, James Gibbons
1857-1921 . . . . . . . . . . . . . . . . . TCLC 65
See also DLB 71

Hungerford, Pixie
See Brinsmead, H(esba) F(ay)

Hunt, E(verette) Howard, (Jr.)
1918- . . . . . . . . . . . . . . . . . . . . . . CLC 3
See also AITN 1; CA 45-48; CANR 2, 47

Hunt, Kyle
See Creasey, John

Hunt, (James Henry) Leigh
1784-1859 . . . . . . NCLC 1; DAM POET

Hunt, Marsha 1946- . . . . . . . . . . . . . . CLC 70
See also BW 2; CA 143

Hunt, Violet 1866-1942 . . . . . . . . . TCLC 53
See also DLB 162

Hunter, E. Waldo
See Sturgeon, Theodore (Hamilton)

Hunter, Evan
1926- . . . . . . . . . CLC 11, 31; DAM POP
See also CA 5-8R; CANR 5, 38; DLBY 82;
INT CANR-5; MTCW; SATA 25

Hunter, Kristin (Eggleston) 1931- . . . CLC 35
See also AITN 1; BW 1; CA 13-16R;
CANR 13; CLR 3; DLB 33;
INT CANR-13; MAICYA; SAAS 10;
SATA 12

Hunter, Mollie 1922- . . . . . . . . . . . . . CLC 21
See also McIlwraith, Maureen Mollie
Hunter
See also AAYA 13; CANR 37; CLR 25;
DLB 161; JRDA; MAICYA; SAAS 7;
SATA 54

Hunter, Robert (?)-1734 . . . . . . . . . . . . LC 7

Hurston, Zora Neale
1903-1960 . . . . CLC 7, 30, 61; BLC; DA;
DAC; DAM MST, MULT, NOV; SSC 4
See also AAYA 15; BW 1; CA 85-88;
DLB 51, 86; MTCW

Huston, John (Marcellus)
1906-1987 . . . . . . . . . . . . . . . . . . CLC 20
See also CA 73-76; 123; CANR 34; DLB 26

Hustvedt, Siri 1955- . . . . . . . . . . . . . . CLC 76
See also CA 137

Hutten, Ulrich von 1488-1523 . . . . . . . LC 16

Huxley, Aldous (Leonard)
1894-1963 . . . . . CLC 1, 3, 4, 5, 8, 11, 18,
35, 79; DA; DAB; DAC; DAM MST,
NOV; WLC
See also AAYA 11; CA 85-88; CANR 44;
CDBLB 1914-1945; DLB 36, 100, 162;
MTCW; SATA 63

Huysmans, Charles Marie Georges
1848-1907
See Huysmans, Joris-Karl
See also CA 104

Huysmans, Joris-Karl . . . . . . . . . . . . . TCLC 7
See also Huysmans, Charles Marie Georges
See also DLB 123

Hwang, David Henry
1957- . . . . CLC 55; DAM DRAM; DC 4
See also CA 127; 132; INT 132

Hyde, Anthony 1946- . . . . . . . . . . . . . CLC 42
See also CA 136

Hyde, Margaret O(ldroyd) 1917- . . . CLC 21
See also CA 1-4R; CANR 1, 36; CLR 23;
JRDA; MAICYA; SAAS 8; SATA 1, 42,
76

Hynes, James 1956(?)- . . . . . . . . . . . . CLC 65

Ian, Janis 1951- . . . . . . . . . . . . . . . . . CLC 21
See also CA 105

Ibanez, Vicente Blasco
See Blasco Ibanez, Vicente

Ibarguengoitia, Jorge 1928-1983 . . . . CLC 37
See also CA 124; 113; HW

Ibsen, Henrik (Johan)
1828-1906 . . . . . . . TCLC 2, 8, 16, 37, 52;
DA; DAB; DAC; DAM DRAM, MST;
DC 2; WLC
See also CA 104; 141

**Ibuse Masuji** 1898-1993 . . . . . . . . . . **CLC 22**
See also CA 127; 141

**Ichikawa, Kon** 1915- . . . . . . . . . . . . . **CLC 20**
See also CA 121

**Idle, Eric** 1943- . . . . . . . . . . . . . . . . . **CLC 21**
See also Monty Python
See also CA 116; CANR 35

**Ignatow, David** 1914- . . . . . . **CLC 4, 7, 14, 40**
See also CA 9-12R; CAAS 3; CANR 31;
DLB 5

**Ihimaera, Witi** 1944- . . . . . . . . . . . . **CLC 46**
See also CA 77-80

**Ilf, Ilya** . . . . . . . . . . . . . . . . . . . . . . . **TCLC 21**
See also Fainzilberg, Ilya Arnoldovich

**Illyes, Gyula** 1902-1983 . . . . . . . . . . . **PC 16**
See also CA 114; 109

**Immermann, Karl (Lebrecht)**
1796-1840 . . . . . . . . . . . . . . **NCLC 4, 49**
See also DLB 133

**Inclan, Ramon (Maria) del Valle**
See Valle-Inclan, Ramon (Maria) del

**Infante, G(uillermo) Cabrera**
See Cabrera Infante, G(uillermo)

**Ingalls, Rachel (Holmes)** 1940- . . . . . **CLC 42**
See also CA 123; 127

**Ingamells, Rex** 1913-1955 . . . . . . . . **TCLC 35**

**Inge, William Motter**
1913-1973 . . **CLC 1, 8, 19; DAM DRAM**
See also CA 9-12R; CDALB 1941-1968;
DLB 7; MTCW

**Ingelow, Jean** 1820-1897 . . . . . . . . **NCLC 39**
See also DLB 35, 163; SATA 33

**Ingram, Willis J.**
See Harris, Mark

**Innaurato, Albert (F.)** 1948(?)- . . **CLC 21, 60**
See also CA 115; 122; INT 122

**Innes, Michael**
See Stewart, J(ohn) I(nnes) M(ackintosh)

**Ionesco, Eugene**
1909-1994 . . . . **CLC 1, 4, 6, 9, 11, 15, 41,
86; DA; DAB; DAC; DAM DRAM,
MST; WLC**
See also CA 9-12R; 144; MTCW; SATA 7;
SATA-Obit 79

**Iqbal, Muhammad** 1873-1938 . . . . . **TCLC 28**

**Ireland, Patrick**
See O'Doherty, Brian

**Iron, Ralph**
See Schreiner, Olive (Emilie Albertina)

**Irving, John (Winslow)**
1942- . . . . . **CLC 13, 23, 38; DAM NOV,
POP**
See also AAYA 8; BEST 89:3; CA 25-28R;
CANR 28; DLB 6; DLBY 82; MTCW

**Irving, Washington**
1783-1859 . . . . . **NCLC 2, 19; DA; DAB;
DAM MST; SSC 2; WLC**
See also CDALB 1640-1865; DLB 3, 11, 30,
59, 73, 74; YABC 2

**Irwin, P. K.**
See Page, P(atricia) K(athleen)

**Isaacs, Susan** 1943- . . . **CLC 32; DAM POP**
See also BEST 89:1; CA 89-92; CANR 20,
41; INT CANR-20; MTCW

**Isherwood, Christopher (William Bradshaw)**
1904-1986 . . . . . . . **CLC 1, 9, 11, 14, 44;
DAM DRAM, NOV**
See also CA 13-16R; 117; CANR 35;
DLB 15; DLBY 86; MTCW

**Ishiguro, Kazuo**
1954- . . . . . . **CLC 27, 56, 59; DAM NOV**
See also BEST 90:2; CA 120; CANR 49;
MTCW

**Ishikawa, Takuboku**
1886(?)-1912 . . . . . . . . . . . . . . **TCLC 15;
DAM POET; PC 10**
See also CA 113

**Iskander, Fazil** 1929- . . . . . . . . . . . . . **CLC 47**
See also CA 102

**Isler, Alan** . . . . . . . . . . . . . . . . . . . . . **CLC 91**

**Ivan IV** 1530-1584 . . . . . . . . . . . . . . . **LC 17**

**Ivanov, Vyacheslav Ivanovich**
1866-1949 . . . . . . . . . . . . . . . . **TCLC 33**
See also CA 122

**Ivask, Ivar Vidrik** 1927-1992 . . . . . . **CLC 14**
See also CA 37-40R; 139; CANR 24

**Ives, Morgan**
See Bradley, Marion Zimmer

**J. R. S.**
See Gogarty, Oliver St. John

**Jabran, Kahlil**
See Gibran, Kahlil

**Jabran, Khalil**
See Gibran, Kahlil

**Jackson, Daniel**
See Wingrove, David (John)

**Jackson, Jesse** 1908-1983 . . . . . . . . . **CLC 12**
See also BW 1; CA 25-28R; 109; CANR 27;
CLR 28; MAICYA; SATA 2, 29;
SATA-Obit 48

**Jackson, Laura (Riding)** 1901-1991
See Riding, Laura
See also CA 65-68; 135; CANR 28; DLB 48

**Jackson, Sam**
See Trumbo, Dalton

**Jackson, Sara**
See Wingrove, David (John)

**Jackson, Shirley**
1919-1965 . . . . . . . . **CLC 11, 60, 87; DA;
DAC; DAM MST; SSC 9; WLC**
See also AAYA 9; CA 1-4R; 25-28R;
CANR 4, 52; CDALB 1941-1968; DLB 6;
SATA 2

**Jacob, (Cyprien-)Max** 1876-1944 . . . **TCLC 6**
See also CA 104

**Jacobs, Jim** 1942- . . . . . . . . . . . . . . . . **CLC 12**
See also CA 97-100; INT 97-100

**Jacobs, W(illiam) W(ymark)**
1863-1943 . . . . . . . . . . . . . . . . . . **TCLC 22**
See also CA 121; DLB 135

**Jacobsen, Jens Peter** 1847-1885 . . **NCLC 34**

**Jacobsen, Josephine** 1908- . . . . . . . . . **CLC 48**
See also CA 33-36R; CAAS 18; CANR 23,
48

**Jacobson, Dan** 1929- . . . . . . . . . . . **CLC 4, 14**
See also CA 1-4R; CANR 2, 25; DLB 14;
MTCW

**Jacqueline**
See Carpentier (y Valmont), Alejo

**Jagger, Mick** 1944- . . . . . . . . . . . . . . . **CLC 17**

**Jakes, John (William)**
1932- . . . . . . **CLC 29; DAM NOV, POP**
See also BEST 89:4; CA 57-60; CANR 10,
43; DLBY 83; INT CANR-10; MTCW;
SATA 62

**James, Andrew**
See Kirkup, James

**James, C(yril) L(ionel) R(obert)**
1901-1989 . . . . . . . . . . . . . . . . . . **CLC 33**
See also BW 2; CA 117; 125; 128; DLB 125;
MTCW

**James, Daniel (Lewis)** 1911-1988
See Santiago, Danny
See also CA 125

**James, Dynely**
See Mayne, William (James Carter)

**James, Henry Sr.** 1811-1882 . . . . . **NCLC 53**

**James, Henry**
1843-1916 . . . . . . **TCLC 2, 11, 24, 40, 47,
64; DA; DAB; DAC; DAM MST, NOV;
SSC 8; WLC**
See also CA 104; 132; CDALB 1865-1917;
DLB 12, 71, 74; DLBD 13; MTCW

**James, M. R.**
See James, Montague (Rhodes)
See also DLB 156

**James, Montague (Rhodes)**
1862-1936 . . . . . . . . . . . **TCLC 6; SSC 16**
See also CA 104

**James, P. D.** . . . . . . . . . . . . . . . . . **CLC 18, 46**
See also White, Phyllis Dorothy James
See also BEST 90:2; CDBLB 1960 to
Present; DLB 87

**James, Philip**
See Moorcock, Michael (John)

**James, William** 1842-1910 . . . . . **TCLC 15, 32**
See also CA 109

**James I** 1394-1437 . . . . . . . . . . . . . . . **LC 20**

**Jameson, Anna** 1794-1860 . . . . . . . **NCLC 43**
See also DLB 99, 166

**Jami, Nur al-Din 'Abd al-Rahman**
1414-1492 . . . . . . . . . . . . . . . . . . . **LC 9**

**Jandl, Ernst** 1925- . . . . . . . . . . . . . . . **CLC 34**

**Janowitz, Tama**
1957- . . . . . . . . . . . . **CLC 43; DAM POP**
See also CA 106; CANR 52

**Japrisot, Sebastien** 1931- . . . . . . . . . . **CLC 90**

**Jarrell, Randall**
1914-1965 . . . . . . . **CLC 1, 2, 6, 9, 13, 49;
DAM POET**
See also CA 5-8R; 25-28R; CABS 2;
CANR 6, 34; CDALB 1941-1968; CLR 6;
DLB 48, 52; MAICYA; MTCW; SATA 7

**Jarry, Alfred**
1873-1907 . . . . . . . . . . . . . . . **TCLC 2, 14;
DAM DRAM; SSC 20**
See also CA 104

**Jarvis, E. K.**
See Bloch, Robert (Albert); Ellison, Harlan
(Jay); Silverberg, Robert

**Jeake, Samuel, Jr.**
See Aiken, Conrad (Potter)

**Jean Paul** 1763-1825 . . . . . . . . . . . NCLC 7

**Jefferies, (John) Richard**
1848-1887 . . . . . . . . . . . . . . . NCLC 47
See also DLB 98, 141; SATA 16

**Jeffers, (John) Robinson**
1887-1962 . . . . CLC 2, 3, 11, 15, 54; DA;
DAC; DAM MST, POET; WLC
See also CA 85-88; CANR 35;
CDALB 1917-1929; DLB 45; MTCW

**Jefferson, Janet**
See Mencken, H(enry) L(ouis)

**Jefferson, Thomas** 1743-1826 . . . . NCLC 11
See also CDALB 1640-1865; DLB 31

**Jeffrey, Francis** 1773-1850. . . . . . . NCLC 33
See also DLB 107

**Jelakowitch, Ivan**
See Heijermans, Herman

**Jellicoe, (Patricia) Ann** 1927- . . . . . . CLC 27
See also CA 85-88; DLB 13

**Jen, Gish** . . . . . . . . . . . . . . . . . . . . . . CLC 70
See also Jen, Lillian

**Jen, Lillian** 1956(?)-
See Jen, Gish
See also CA 135

**Jenkins, (John) Robin** 1912- . . . . . . . CLC 52
See also CA 1-4R; CANR 1; DLB 14

**Jennings, Elizabeth (Joan)**
1926- . . . . . . . . . . . . . . . . . . . . CLC 5, 14
See also CA 61-64; CAAS 5; CANR 8, 39;
DLB 27; MTCW; SATA 66

**Jennings, Waylon** 1937- . . . . . . . . . . CLC 21

**Jensen, Johannes V.** 1873-1950. . . . TCLC 41

**Jensen, Laura (Linnea)** 1948- . . . . . . CLC 37
See also CA 103

**Jerome, Jerome K(lapka)**
1859-1927 . . . . . . . . . . . . . . . . . TCLC 23
See also CA 119; DLB 10, 34, 135

**Jerrold, Douglas William**
1803-1857 . . . . . . . . . . . . . . . . . NCLC 2
See also DLB 158, 159

**Jewett, (Theodora) Sarah Orne**
1849-1909 . . . . . . . . TCLC 1, 22; SSC 6
See also CA 108; 127; DLB 12, 74;
SATA 15

**Jewsbury, Geraldine (Endsor)**
1812-1880 . . . . . . . . . . . . . . . . . NCLC 22
See also DLB 21

**Jhabvala, Ruth Prawer**
1927- . . . . . . . . . CLC 4, 8, 29, 94; DAB;
DAM NOV
See also CA 1-4R; CANR 2, 29, 51;
DLB 139; INT CANR-29; MTCW

**Jibran, Kahlil**
See Gibran, Kahlil

**Jibran, Khalil**
See Gibran, Kahlil

**Jiles, Paulette** 1943- . . . . . . . . . . CLC 13, 58
See also CA 101

**Jimenez (Mantecon), Juan Ramon**
1881-1958 . . . . . TCLC 4; DAM MULT,
POET; HLC; PC 7
See also CA 104; 131; DLB 134; HW;
MTCW

**Jimenez, Ramon**
See Jimenez (Mantecon), Juan Ramon

**Jimenez Mantecon, Juan**
See Jimenez (Mantecon), Juan Ramon

**Joel, Billy** . . . . . . . . . . . . . . . . . . . . . CLC 26
See also Joel, William Martin

**Joel, William Martin** 1949-
See Joel, Billy
See also CA 108

**John of the Cross, St.** 1542-1591 . . . . LC 18

**Johnson, B(ryan) S(tanley William)**
1933-1973 . . . . . . . . . . . . . . . . CLC 6, 9
See also CA 9-12R; 53-56; CANR 9;
DLB 14, 40

**Johnson, Benj. F. of Boo**
See Riley, James Whitcomb

**Johnson, Benjamin F. of Boo**
See Riley, James Whitcomb

**Johnson, Charles (Richard)**
1948- . . . . . . . . . . . CLC 7, 51, 65; BLC;
DAM MULT
See also BW 2; CA 116; CAAS 18;
CANR 42; DLB 33

**Johnson, Denis** 1949- . . . . . . . . . . . . CLC 52
See also CA 117; 121; DLB 120

**Johnson, Diane** 1934- . . . . . . . CLC 5, 13, 48
See also CA 41-44R; CANR 17, 40;
DLBY 80; INT CANR-17; MTCW

**Johnson, Eyvind (Olof Verner)**
1900-1976 . . . . . . . . . . . . . . . . . CLC 14
See also CA 73-76; 69-72; CANR 34

**Johnson, J. R.**
See James, C(yril) L(ionel) R(obert)

**Johnson, James Weldon**
1871-1938 . . . . . . . . . TCLC 3, 19; BLC;
DAM MULT, POET
See also BW 1; CA 104; 125;
CDALB 1917-1929; CLR 32; DLB 51;
MTCW; SATA 31

**Johnson, Joyce** 1935- . . . . . . . . . . . . CLC 58
See also CA 125; 129

**Johnson, Lionel (Pigot)**
1867-1902 . . . . . . . . . . . . . . . . . TCLC 19
See also CA 117; DLB 19

**Johnson, Mel**
See Malzberg, Barry N(athaniel)

**Johnson, Pamela Hansford**
1912-1981 . . . . . . . . . . . . . CLC 1, 7, 27
See also CA 1-4R; 104; CANR 2, 28;
DLB 15; MTCW

**Johnson, Samuel**
1709-1784 . . . . . LC 15; DA; DAB; DAC;
DAM MST; WLC
See also CDBLB 1660-1789; DLB 39, 95,
104, 142

**Johnson, Uwe**
1934-1984 . . . . . . . . . . . CLC 5, 10, 15, 40
See also CA 1-4R; 112; CANR 1, 39;
DLB 75; MTCW

**Johnston, George (Benson)** 1913- . . . CLC 51
See also CA 1-4R; CANR 5, 20; DLB 88

**Johnston, Jennifer** 1930- . . . . . . . . . . CLC 7
See also CA 85-88; DLB 14

**Jolley, (Monica) Elizabeth**
1923- . . . . . . . . . . . . . . CLC 46; SSC 19
See also CA 127; CAAS 13

**Jones, Arthur Llewellyn** 1863-1947
See Machen, Arthur
See also CA 104

**Jones, D(ouglas) G(ordon)** 1929-. . . . CLC 10
See also CA 29-32R; CANR 13; DLB 53

**Jones, David (Michael)**
1895-1974 . . . . . . . . CLC 2, 4, 7, 13, 42
See also CA 9-12R; 53-56; CANR 28;
CDBLB 1945-1960; DLB 20, 100; MTCW

**Jones, David Robert** 1947-
See Bowie, David
See also CA 103

**Jones, Diana Wynne** 1934- . . . . . . . . CLC 26
See also AAYA 12; CA 49-52; CANR 4,
26; CLR 23; DLB 161; JRDA; MAICYA;
SAAS 7; SATA 9, 70

**Jones, Edward P.** 1950- . . . . . . . . . . . CLC 76
See also BW 2; CA 142

**Jones, Gayl**
1949- . . . . CLC 6, 9; BLC; DAM MULT
See also BW 2; CA 77-80; CANR 27;
DLB 33; MTCW

**Jones, James** 1921-1977. . . . CLC 1, 3, 10, 39
See also AITN 1, 2; CA 1-4R; 69-72;
CANR 6; DLB 2, 143; MTCW

**Jones, John J.**
See Lovecraft, H(oward) P(hillips)

**Jones, LeRoi** . . . . . . CLC 1, 2, 3, 5, 10, 14
See also Baraka, Amiri

**Jones, Louis B.** . . . . . . . . . . . . . . . . . CLC 65
See also CA 141

**Jones, Madison (Percy, Jr.)** 1925- . . . CLC 4
See also CA 13-16R; CAAS 11; CANR 7;
DLB 152

**Jones, Mervyn** 1922- . . . . . . . . . . CLC 10, 52
See also CA 45-48; CAAS 5; CANR 1;
MTCW

**Jones, Mick** 1956(?)- . . . . . . . . . . . . . CLC 30

**Jones, Nettie (Pearl)** 1941- . . . . . . . . CLC 34
See also BW 2; CA 137; CAAS 20

**Jones, Preston** 1936-1979 . . . . . . . . . CLC 10
See also CA 73-76; 89-92; DLB 7

**Jones, Robert F(rancis)** 1934- . . . . . . CLC 7
See also CA 49-52; CANR 2

**Jones, Rod** 1953- . . . . . . . . . . . . . . . . CLC 50
See also CA 128

**Jones, Terence Graham Parry**
1942- . . . . . . . . . . . . . . . . . . . . . . CLC 21
See also Jones, Terry; Monty Python
See also CA 112; 116; CANR 35; INT 116

**Jones, Terry**
See Jones, Terence Graham Parry
See also SATA 67; SATA-Brief 51

**Jones, Thom** 1945(?)- . . . . . . . . . . . . . CLC 81

**Jong, Erica**
1942- . . . . . . . . . . . . . CLC 4, 6, 8, 18, 83;
DAM NOV, POP
See also AITN 1; BEST 90:2; CA 73-76;
CANR 26, 52; DLB 2, 5, 28, 152;
INT CANR-26; MTCW

**Jonson, Ben(jamin)**
1572(?)-1637 ...... **LC 6, 33; DA; DAB;
DAC; DAM DRAM, MST, POET;
DC 4; WLC**
See also CDBLB Before 1660; DLB 62, 121

**Jordan, June**
1936- ..... **CLC 5, 11, 23; DAM MULT,
POET**
See also AAYA 2; BW 2; CA 33-36R;
CANR 25; CLR 10; DLB 38; MAICYA;
MTCW; SATA 4

**Jordan, Pat(rick M.)** 1941- ........ **CLC 37**
See also CA 33-36R

**Jorgensen, Ivar**
See Ellison, Harlan (Jay)

**Jorgenson, Ivar**
See Silverberg, Robert

**Josephus, Flavius** c. 37-100 ...... **CMLC 13**

**Josipovici, Gabriel** 1940- ........ **CLC 6, 43**
See also CA 37-40R; CAAS 8; CANR 47;
DLB 14

**Joubert, Joseph** 1754-1824 ....... **NCLC 9**

**Jouve, Pierre Jean** 1887-1976 ...... **CLC 47**
See also CA 65-68

**Joyce, James (Augustine Aloysius)**
1882-1941 ....... **TCLC 3, 8, 16, 35, 52;
DA; DAB; DAC; DAM MST, NOV,
POET; SSC 3; WLC**
See also CA 104; 126; CDBLB 1914-1945;
DLB 10, 19, 36, 162; MTCW

**Jozsef, Attila** 1905-1937 ......... **TCLC 22**
See also CA 116

**Juana Ines de la Cruz** 1651(?)-1695 ... **LC 5**

**Judd, Cyril**
See Kornbluth, C(yril) M.; Pohl, Frederik

**Julian of Norwich** 1342(?)-1416(?) .... **LC 6**
See also DLB 146

**Juniper, Alex**
See Hospital, Janette Turner

**Junius**
See Luxemburg, Rosa

**Just, Ward (Swift)** 1935- ........ **CLC 4, 27**
See also CA 25-28R; CANR 32;
INT CANR-32

**Justice, Donald (Rodney)**
1925- ........ **CLC 6, 19; DAM POET**
See also CA 5-8R; CANR 26; DLBY 83;
INT CANR-26

**Juvenal** c. 55-c. 127 ............. **CMLC 8**

**Juvenis**
See Bourne, Randolph S(illiman)

**Kacew, Romain** 1914-1980
See Gary, Romain
See also CA 108; 102

**Kadare, Ismail** 1936- ............. **CLC 52**

**Kadohata, Cynthia** ............... **CLC 59**
See also CA 140

**Kafka, Franz**
1883-1924 .... **TCLC 2, 6, 13, 29, 47, 53;
DA; DAB; DAC; DAM MST, NOV;
SSC 5; WLC**
See also CA 105; 126; DLB 81; MTCW

**Kahanovitsch, Pinkhes**
See Der Nister

**Kahn, Roger** 1927- ............... **CLC 30**
See also CA 25-28R; CANR 44; SATA 37

**Kain, Saul**
See Sassoon, Siegfried (Lorraine)

**Kaiser, Georg** 1878-1945 ......... **TCLC 9**
See also CA 106; DLB 124

**Kaletski, Alexander** 1946- ........ **CLC 39**
See also CA 118; 143

**Kalidasa** fl. c. 400- .............. **CMLC 9**

**Kallman, Chester (Simon)**
1921-1975 ................... **CLC 2**
See also CA 45-48; 53-56; CANR 3

**Kaminsky, Melvin** 1926-
See Brooks, Mel
See also CA 65-68; CANR 16

**Kaminsky, Stuart M(elvin)** 1934- ... **CLC 59**
See also CA 73-76; CANR 29, 53

**Kane, Paul**
See Simon, Paul

**Kane, Wilson**
See Bloch, Robert (Albert)

**Kanin, Garson** 1912- .............. **CLC 22**
See also AITN 1; CA 5-8R; CANR 7;
DLB 7

**Kaniuk, Yoram** 1930- ............. **CLC 19**
See also CA 134

**Kant, Immanuel** 1724-1804 ...... **NCLC 27**
See also DLB 94

**Kantor, MacKinlay** 1904-1977 ...... **CLC 7**
See also CA 61-64; 73-76; DLB 9, 102

**Kaplan, David Michael** 1946- ...... **CLC 50**

**Kaplan, James** 1951- ............. **CLC 59**
See also CA 135

**Karageorge, Michael**
See Anderson, Poul (William)

**Karamzin, Nikolai Mikhailovich**
1766-1826 .................. **NCLC 3**
See also DLB 150

**Karapanou, Margarita** 1946- ....... **CLC 13**
See also CA 101

**Karinthy, Frigyes** 1887-1938 ...... **TCLC 47**

**Karl, Frederick R(obert)** 1927- ..... **CLC 34**
See also CA 5-8R; CANR 3, 44

**Kastel, Warren**
See Silverberg, Robert

**Kataev, Evgeny Petrovich** 1903-1942
See Petrov, Evgeny
See also CA 120

**Kataphusin**
See Ruskin, John

**Katz, Steve** 1935- ................. **CLC 47**
See also CA 25-28R; CAAS 14; CANR 12;
DLBY 83

**Kauffman, Janet** 1945- ............ **CLC 42**
See also CA 117; CANR 43; DLBY 86

**Kaufman, Bob (Garnell)**
1925-1986 ................... **CLC 49**
See also BW 1; CA 41-44R; 118; CANR 22;
DLB 16, 41

**Kaufman, George S.**
1889-1961 ...... **CLC 38; DAM DRAM**
See also CA 108; 93-96; DLB 7; INT 108

**Kaufman, Sue** ................... **CLC 3, 8**
See also Barondess, Sue K(aufman)

**Kavafis, Konstantinos Petrou** 1863-1933
See Cavafy, C(onstantine) P(eter)
See also CA 104

**Kavan, Anna** 1901-1968 ...... **CLC 5, 13, 82**
See also CA 5-8R; CANR 6; MTCW

**Kavanagh, Dan**
See Barnes, Julian

**Kavanagh, Patrick (Joseph)**
1904-1967 ................... **CLC 22**
See also CA 123; 25-28R; DLB 15, 20;
MTCW

**Kawabata, Yasunari**
1899-1972 ............ **CLC 2, 5, 9, 18;
DAM MULT; SSC 17**
See also CA 93-96; 33-36R

**Kaye, M(ary) M(argaret)** 1909- ..... **CLC 28**
See also CA 89-92; CANR 24; MTCW;
SATA 62

**Kaye, Mollie**
See Kaye, M(ary) M(argaret)

**Kaye-Smith, Sheila** 1887-1956 ..... **TCLC 20**
See also CA 118; DLB 36

**Kaymor, Patrice Maguilene**
See Senghor, Leopold Sedar

**Kazan, Elia** 1909- ........... **CLC 6, 16, 63**
See also CA 21-24R; CANR 32

**Kazantzakis, Nikos**
1883(?)-1957 ........... **TCLC 2, 5, 33**
See also CA 105; 132; MTCW

**Kazin, Alfred** 1915- ........... **CLC 34, 38**
See also CA 1-4R; CAAS 7; CANR 1, 45;
DLB 67

**Keane, Mary Nesta (Skrine)** 1904-1996
See Keane, Molly
See also CA 108; 114; 151

**Keane, Molly** .................... **CLC 31**
See also Keane, Mary Nesta (Skrine)
See also INT 114

**Keates, Jonathan** 19(?)- ........... **CLC 34**

**Keaton, Buster** 1895-1966 ......... **CLC 20**

**Keats, John**
1795-1821 ........ **NCLC 8; DA; DAB;
DAC; DAM MST, POET; PC 1; WLC**
See also CDBLB 1789-1832; DLB 96, 110

**Keene, Donald** 1922- .............. **CLC 34**
See also CA 1-4R; CANR 5

**Keillor, Garrison** ................. **CLC 40**
See also Keillor, Gary (Edward)
See also AAYA 2; BEST 89:3; DLBY 87;
SATA 58

**Keillor, Gary (Edward)** 1942-
See Keillor, Garrison
See also CA 111; 117; CANR 36;
DAM POP; MTCW

**Keith, Michael**
See Hubbard, L(afayette) Ron(ald)

**Keller, Gottfried** 1819-1890 ....... **NCLC 2**
See also DLB 129

**Kellerman, Jonathan**
1949- ........... **CLC 44; DAM POP**
See also BEST 90:1; CA 106; CANR 29, 51;
INT CANR-29

**Kipling, (Joseph) Rudyard**
1865-1936 ...... **TCLC 8, 17; DA; DAB; DAC; DAM MST, POET; PC 3; SSC 5; WLC**
See also CA 105; 120; CANR 33; CDBLB 1890-1914; CLR 39; DLB 19, 34, 141, 156; MAICYA; MTCW; YABC 2

**Kirkup, James** 1918- .............. **CLC 1**
See also CA 1-4R; CAAS 4; CANR 2; DLB 27; SATA 12

**Kirkwood, James** 1930(?)-1989 ...... **CLC 9**
See also AITN 2; CA 1-4R; 128; CANR 6, 40

**Kirshner, Sidney**
See Kingsley, Sidney

**Kis, Danilo** 1935-1989 ............ **CLC 57**
See also CA 109; 118; 129; MTCW

**Kivi, Aleksis** 1834-1872 ........ **NCLC 30**

**Kizer, Carolyn (Ashley)**
1925- ..... **CLC 15, 39, 80; DAM POET**
See also CA 65-68; CAAS 5; CANR 24; DLB 5

**Klabund** 1890-1928.............. **TCLC 44**
See also DLB 66

**Klappert, Peter** 1942-............. **CLC 57**
See also CA 33-36R; DLB 5

**Klein, A(braham) M(oses)**
1909-1972 ........ **CLC 19; DAB; DAC; DAM MST**
See also CA 101; 37-40R; DLB 68

**Klein, Norma** 1938-1989 .......... **CLC 30**
See also AAYA 2; CA 41-44R; 128; CANR 15, 37; CLR 2, 19; INT CANR-15; JRDA; MAICYA; SAAS 1; SATA 7, 57

**Klein, T(heodore) E(ibon) D(onald)**
1947- ....................... **CLC 34**
See also CA 119; CANR 44

**Kleist, Heinrich von**
1777-1811 .............. **NCLC 2, 37; DAM DRAM; SSC 22**
See also DLB 90

**Klima, Ivan** 1931-..... **CLC 56; DAM NOV**
See also CA 25-28R; CANR 17, 50

**Klimentov, Andrei Platonovich** 1899-1951
See Platonov, Andrei
See also CA 108

**Klinger, Friedrich Maximilian von**
1752-1831 ................. **NCLC 1**
See also DLB 94

**Klopstock, Friedrich Gottlieb**
1724-1803 ................. **NCLC 11**
See also DLB 97

**Knebel, Fletcher** 1911-1993 ....... **CLC 14**
See also AITN 1; CA 1-4R; 140; CAAS 3; CANR 1, 36; SATA 36; SATA-Obit 75

**Knickerbocker, Diedrich**
See Irving, Washington

**Knight, Etheridge**
1931-1991 ............. **CLC 40; BLC; DAM POET; PC 14**
See also BW 1; CA 21-24R; 133; CANR 23; DLB 41

**Knight, Sarah Kemble** 1666-1727 ..... **LC 7**
See also DLB 24

**Knister, Raymond** 1899-1932...... **TCLC 56**
See also DLB 68

**Knowles, John**
1926- ...... **CLC 1, 4, 10, 26; DA; DAC; DAM MST, NOV**
See also AAYA 10; CA 17-20R; CANR 40; CDALB 1968-1988; DLB 6; MTCW; SATA 8, 89

**Knox, Calvin M.**
See Silverberg, Robert

**Knye, Cassandra**
See Disch, Thomas M(ichael)

**Koch, C(hristopher) J(ohn)** 1932- ... **CLC 42**
See also CA 127

**Koch, Christopher**
See Koch, C(hristopher) J(ohn)

**Koch, Kenneth**
1925- ....... **CLC 5, 8, 44; DAM POET**
See also CA 1-4R; CANR 6, 36; DLB 5; INT CANR-36; SATA 65

**Kochanowski, Jan** 1530-1584........ **LC 10**

**Kock, Charles Paul de**
1794-1871 ................. **NCLC 16**

**Koda Shigeyuki** 1867-1947
See Rohan, Koda
See also CA 121

**Koestler, Arthur**
1905-1983 ....... **CLC 1, 3, 6, 8, 15, 33**
See also CA 1-4R; 109; CANR 1, 33; CDBLB 1945-1960; DLBY 83; MTCW

**Kogawa, Joy Nozomi**
1935- ...... **CLC 78; DAC; DAM MST, MULT**
See also CA 101; CANR 19

**Kohout, Pavel** 1928-.............. **CLC 13**
See also CA 45-48; CANR 3

**Koizumi, Yakumo**
See Hearn, (Patricio) Lafcadio (Tessima Carlos)

**Kolmar, Gertrud** 1894-1943 ...... **TCLC 40**

**Komunyakaa, Yusef** 1947-...... **CLC 86, 94**
See also CA 147; DLB 120

**Konrad, George**
See Konrad, Gyoergy

**Konrad, Gyoergy** 1933-...... **CLC 4, 10, 73**
See also CA 85-88

**Konwicki, Tadeusz** 1926-..... **CLC 8, 28, 54**
See also CA 101; CAAS 9; CANR 39; MTCW

**Koontz, Dean R(ay)**
1945- ...... **CLC 78; DAM NOV, POP**
See also AAYA 9; BEST 89:3, 90:2; CA 108; CANR 19, 36, 52; MTCW

**Kopit, Arthur (Lee)**
1937- ..... **CLC 1, 18, 33; DAM DRAM**
See also AITN 1; CA 81-84; CABS 3; DLB 7; MTCW

**Kops, Bernard** 1926-.............. **CLC 4**
See also CA 5-8R; DLB 13

**Kornbluth, C(yril) M.** 1923-1958.... **TCLC 8**
See also CA 105; DLB 8

**Korolenko, V. G.**
See Korolenko, Vladimir Galaktionovich

**Korolenko, Vladimir**
See Korolenko, Vladimir Galaktionovich

**Korolenko, Vladimir G.**
See Korolenko, Vladimir Galaktionovich

**Korolenko, Vladimir Galaktionovich**
1853-1921 ................. **TCLC 22**
See also CA 121

**Korzybski, Alfred (Habdank Skarbek)**
1879-1950 ................. **TCLC 61**
See also CA 123

**Kosinski, Jerzy (Nikodem)**
1933-1991 .... **CLC 1, 2, 3, 6, 10, 15, 53, 70; DAM NOV**
See also CA 17-20R; 134; CANR 9, 46; DLB 2; DLBY 82; MTCW

**Kostelanetz, Richard (Cory)** 1940- .. **CLC 28**
See also CA 13-16R; CAAS 8; CANR 38

**Kostrowitzki, Wilhelm Apollinaris de**
1880-1918
See Apollinaire, Guillaume
See also CA 104

**Kotlowitz, Robert** 1924-............ **CLC 4**
See also CA 33-36R; CANR 36

**Kotzebue, August (Friedrich Ferdinand) von**
1761-1819 ................. **NCLC 25**
See also DLB 94

**Kotzwinkle, William** 1938- ... **CLC 5, 14, 35**
See also CA 45-48; CANR 3, 44; CLR 6; MAICYA; SATA 24, 70

**Kozol, Jonathan** 1936-............ **CLC 17**
See also CA 61-64; CANR 16, 45

**Kozoll, Michael** 1940(?)- .......... **CLC 35**

**Kramer, Kathryn** 19(?)- ........... **CLC 34**

**Kramer, Larry** 1935- .. **CLC 42; DAM POP**
See also CA 124; 126

**Krasicki, Ignacy** 1735-1801 ....... **NCLC 8**

**Krasinski, Zygmunt** 1812-1859 .... **NCLC 4**

**Kraus, Karl** 1874-1936........... **TCLC 5**
See also CA 104; DLB 118

**Kreve (Mickevicius), Vincas**
1882-1954 ................. **TCLC 27**

**Kristeva, Julia** 1941- ............. **CLC 77**

**Kristofferson, Kris** 1936-.......... **CLC 26**
See also CA 104

**Krizanc, John** 1956-.............. **CLC 57**

**Krleza, Miroslav** 1893-1981........ **CLC 8**
See also CA 97-100; 105; CANR 50; DLB 147

**Kroetsch, Robert**
1927- ............ **CLC 5, 23, 57; DAC; DAM POET**
See also CA 17-20R; CANR 8, 38; DLB 53; MTCW

**Kroetz, Franz**
See Kroetz, Franz Xaver

**Kroetz, Franz Xaver** 1946- ........ **CLC 41**
See also CA 130

**Kroker, Arthur** 1945-............. **CLC 77**

**Kropotkin, Peter (Alekseievich)**
1842-1921 ................. **TCLC 36**
See also CA 119

**Krotkov, Yuri** 1917-.............. **CLC 19**
See also CA 102

**Krumb**
See Crumb, R(obert)

**Krumgold, Joseph (Quincy)**
1908-1980 ................. CLC 12
See also CA 9-12R; 101; CANR 7;
MAICYA; SATA 1, 48; SATA-Obit 23

**Krumwitz**
See Crumb, R(obert)

**Krutch, Joseph Wood** 1893-1970.... CLC 24
See also CA 1-4R; 25-28R; CANR 4;
DLB 63

**Krutzch, Gus**
See Eliot, T(homas) S(tearns)

**Krylov, Ivan Andreevich**
1768(?)-1844 ................ NCLC 1
See also DLB 150

**Kubin, Alfred (Leopold Isidor)**
1877-1959 ................. TCLC 23
See also CA 112; 149; DLB 81

**Kubrick, Stanley** 1928-............ CLC 16
See also CA 81-84; CANR 33; DLB 26

**Kumin, Maxine (Winokur)**
1925- ..... CLC 5, 13, 28; DAM POET;
PC 15
See also AITN 2; CA 1-4R; CAAS 8;
CANR 1, 21; DLB 5; MTCW; SATA 12

**Kundera, Milan**
1929- ............ CLC 4, 9, 19, 32, 68;
DAM NOV
See also AAYA 2; CA 85-88; CANR 19,
52; MTCW

**Kunene, Mazisi (Raymond)** 1930-... CLC 85
See also BW 1; CA 125; DLB 117

**Kunitz, Stanley (Jasspon)**
1905- ................. CLC 6, 11, 14
See also CA 41-44R; CANR 26; DLB 48;
INT CANR-26; MTCW

**Kunze, Reiner** 1933-.............. CLC 10
See also CA 93-96; DLB 75

**Kuprin, Aleksandr Ivanovich**
1870-1938 ................. TCLC 5
See also CA 104

**Kureishi, Hanif** 1954(?)-........... CLC 64
See also CA 139

**Kurosawa, Akira**
1910- ......... CLC 16; DAM MULT
See also AAYA 11; CA 101; CANR 46

**Kushner, Tony**
1957(?)-........ CLC 81; DAM DRAM
See also CA 144

**Kuttner, Henry** 1915-1958....... TCLC 10
See also CA 107; DLB 8

**Kuzma, Greg** 1944-............... CLC 7
See also CA 33-36R

**Kuzmin, Mikhail** 1872(?)-1936 .... TCLC 40

**Kyd, Thomas**
1558-1594 ...... LC 22; DAM DRAM;
DC 3
See also DLB 62

**Kyprianos, Iossif**
See Samarakis, Antonis

**La Bruyere, Jean de** 1645-1696...... LC 17

**Lacan, Jacques (Marie Emile)**
1901-1981 ................. CLC 75
See also CA 121; 104

**Laclos, Pierre Ambroise Francois Choderlos
de** 1741-1803 .............. NCLC 4

**Lacolere, Francois**
See Aragon, Louis

**La Colere, Francois**
See Aragon, Louis

**La Deshabilleuse**
See Simenon, Georges (Jacques Christian)

**Lady Gregory**
See Gregory, Isabella Augusta (Persse)

**Lady of Quality, A**
See Bagnold, Enid

**La Fayette, Marie (Madelaine Pioche de la
Vergne Comtes** 1634-1693...... LC 2

**Lafayette, Rene**
See Hubbard, L(afayette) Ron(ald)

**Laforgue, Jules**
1860-1887 ....... NCLC 5, 53; PC 14;
SSC 20

**Lagerkvist, Paer (Fabian)**
1891-1974 ......... CLC 7, 10, 13, 54;
DAM DRAM, NOV
See also Lagerkvist, Par
See also CA 85-88; 49-52; MTCW

**Lagerkvist, Par** ................... SSC 12
See also Lagerkvist, Paer (Fabian)

**Lagerloef, Selma (Ottiliana Lovisa)**
1858-1940 ............... TCLC 4, 36
See also Lagerlof, Selma (Ottiliana Lovisa)
See also CA 108; SATA 15

**Lagerlof, Selma (Ottiliana Lovisa)**
See Lagerloef, Selma (Ottiliana Lovisa)
See also CLR 7; SATA 15

**La Guma, (Justin) Alex(ander)**
1925-1985 ....... CLC 19; DAM NOV
See also BW 1; CA 49-52; 118; CANR 25;
DLB 117; MTCW

**Laidlaw, A. K.**
See Grieve, C(hristopher) M(urray)

**Lainez, Manuel Mujica**
See Mujica Lainez, Manuel
See also HW

**Laing, R(onald) D(avid)**
1927-1989 ................. CLC 95
See also CA 107; 129; CANR 34; MTCW

**Lamartine, Alphonse (Marie Louis Prat) de**
1790-1869 ..... NCLC 11; DAM POET;
PC 16

**Lamb, Charles**
1775-1834 ....... NCLC 10; DA; DAB;
DAC; DAM MST; WLC
See also CDBLB 1789-1832; DLB 93, 107,
163; SATA 17

**Lamb, Lady Caroline** 1785-1828.. NCLC 38
See also DLB 116

**Lamming, George (William)**
1927- ............ CLC 2, 4, 66; BLC;
DAM MULT
See also BW 2; CA 85-88; CANR 26;
DLB 125; MTCW

**L'Amour, Louis (Dearborn)**
1908-1988 .... CLC 25, 55; DAM NOV,
POP
See also AAYA 16; AITN 2; BEST 89:2;
CA 1-4R; 125; CANR 3, 25, 40;
DLBY 80; MTCW

**Lampedusa, Giuseppe (Tomasi) di ... TCLC 13**
See also Tomasi di Lampedusa, Giuseppe

**Lampman, Archibald** 1861-1899 .. NCLC 25
See also DLB 92

**Lancaster, Bruce** 1896-1963........ CLC 36
See also CA 9-10; CAP 1; SATA 9

**Landau, Mark Alexandrovich**
See Aldanov, Mark (Alexandrovich)

**Landau-Aldanov, Mark Alexandrovich**
See Aldanov, Mark (Alexandrovich)

**Landis, John** 1950-................ CLC 26
See also CA 112; 122

**Landolfi, Tommaso** 1908-1979... CLC 11, 49
See also CA 127; 117

**Landon, Letitia Elizabeth**
1802-1838 ................. NCLC 15
See also DLB 96

**Landor, Walter Savage**
1775-1864 ................. NCLC 14
See also DLB 93, 107

**Landwirth, Heinz** 1927-
See Lind, Jakov
See also CA 9-12R; CANR 7

**Lane, Patrick**
1939- ........... CLC 25; DAM POET
See also CA 97-100; DLB 53; INT 97-100

**Lang, Andrew** 1844-1912........ TCLC 16
See also CA 114; 137; DLB 98, 141;
MAICYA; SATA 16

**Lang, Fritz** 1890-1976 ............ CLC 20
See also CA 77-80; 69-72; CANR 30

**Lange, John**
See Crichton, (John) Michael

**Langer, Elinor** 1939- .............. CLC 34
See also CA 121

**Langland, William**
1330(?)-1400(?) ...... LC 19; DA; DAB;
DAC; DAM MST, POET
See also DLB 146

**Langstaff, Launcelot**
See Irving, Washington

**Lanier, Sidney**
1842-1881 ...... NCLC 6; DAM POET
See also DLB 64; DLBD 13; MAICYA;
SATA 18

**Lanyer, Aemilia** 1569-1645 ...... LC 10, 30
See also DLB 121

**Lao Tzu** ....................... CMLC 7

**Lapine, James (Elliot)** 1949-....... CLC 39
See also CA 123; 130; INT 130

**Larbaud, Valery (Nicolas)**
1881-1957 ................. TCLC 9
See also CA 106; 152

**Lardner, Ring**
See Lardner, Ring(gold) W(ilmer)

**Lardner, Ring W., Jr.**
See Lardner, Ring(gold) W(ilmer)

**Lardner, Ring(gold) W(ilmer)**
1885-1933 . . . . . . . . . . . . . . **TCLC 2, 14**
See also CA 104; 131; CDALB 1917-1929;
DLB 11, 25, 86; MTCW

**Laredo, Betty**
See Codrescu, Andrei

**Larkin, Maia**
See Wojciechowska, Maia (Teresa)

**Larkin, Philip (Arthur)**
1922-1985 . . . . **CLC 3, 5, 8, 9, 13, 18, 33,
39, 64; DAB; DAM MST, POET**
See also CA 5-8R; 117; CANR 24;
CDBLB 1960 to Present; DLB 27;
MTCW

**Larra (y Sanchez de Castro), Mariano Jose de**
1809-1837 . . . . . . . . . . . . . . . **NCLC 17**

**Larsen, Eric** 1941- . . . . . . . . . . . . . . **CLC 55**
See also CA 132

**Larsen, Nella**
1891-1964 . . . . . . . . . . . . . **CLC 37; BLC;
DAM MULT**
See also BW 1; CA 125; DLB 51

**Larson, Charles R(aymond)** 1938- . . . **CLC 31**
See also CA 53-56; CANR 4

**Las Casas, Bartolome de** 1474-1566 . . **LC 31**

**Lasker-Schueler, Else** 1869-1945 . . **TCLC 57**
See also DLB 66, 124

**Latham, Jean Lee** 1902- . . . . . . . . . . **CLC 12**
See also AITN 1; CA 5-8R; CANR 7;
MAICYA; SATA 2, 68

**Latham, Mavis**
See Clark, Mavis Thorpe

**Lathen, Emma** . . . . . . . . . . . . . . . . . . . . **CLC 2**
See also Hennissart, Martha; Latsis, Mary
J(ane)

**Lathrop, Francis**
See Leiber, Fritz (Reuter, Jr.)

**Latsis, Mary J(ane)**
See Lathen, Emma
See also CA 85-88

**Lattimore, Richmond (Alexander)**
1906-1984 . . . . . . . . . . . . . . . . . . **CLC 3**
See also CA 1-4R; 112; CANR 1

**Laughlin, James** 1914- . . . . . . . . . . . . **CLC 49**
See also CA 21-24R; CAAS 22; CANR 9,
47; DLB 48

**Laurence, (Jean) Margaret (Wemyss)**
1926-1987 . . . . . . . **CLC 3, 6, 13, 50, 62;
DAC; DAM MST; SSC 7**
See also CA 5-8R; 121; CANR 33; DLB 53;
MTCW; SATA-Obit 50

**Laurent, Antoine** 1952- . . . . . . . . . . **CLC 50**

**Lauscher, Hermann**
See Hesse, Hermann

**Lautreamont, Comte de**
1846-1870 . . . . . . . . . **NCLC 12; SSC 14**

**Laverty, Donald**
See Blish, James (Benjamin)

**Lavin, Mary** 1912-1996 . . **CLC 4, 18; SSC 4**
See also CA 9-12R; 151; CANR 33;
DLB 15; MTCW

**Lavond, Paul Dennis**
See Kornbluth, C(yril) M.; Pohl, Frederik

**Lawler, Raymond Evenor** 1922- . . . . **CLC 58**
See also CA 103

**Lawrence, D(avid) H(erbert Richards)**
1885-1930 . . . . **TCLC 2, 9, 16, 33, 48, 61;
DA; DAB; DAC; DAM MST, NOV,
POET; SSC 4, 19; WLC**
See also CA 104; 121; CDBLB 1914-1945;
DLB 10, 19, 36, 98, 162; MTCW

**Lawrence, T(homas) E(dward)**
1888-1935 . . . . . . . . . . . . . . . . **TCLC 18**
See also Dale, Colin
See also CA 115

**Lawrence of Arabia**
See Lawrence, T(homas) E(dward)

**Lawson, Henry (Archibald Hertzberg)**
1867-1922 . . . . . . . . . **TCLC 27; SSC 18**
See also CA 120

**Lawton, Dennis**
See Faust, Frederick (Schiller)

**Laxness, Halldor** . . . . . . . . . . . . . . . . **CLC 25**
See also Gudjonsson, Halldor Kiljan

**Layamon** fl. c. 1200- . . . . . . . . . . . **CMLC 10**
See also DLB 146

**Laye, Camara**
1928-1980 . . . . . . . . . . **CLC 4, 38; BLC;
DAM MULT**
See also BW 1; CA 85-88; 97-100;
CANR 25; MTCW

**Layton, Irving (Peter)**
1912- . . . . **CLC 2, 15; DAC; DAM MST,
POET**
See also CA 1-4R; CANR 2, 33, 43;
DLB 88; MTCW

**Lazarus, Emma** 1849-1887 . . . . . . . . **NCLC 8**

**Lazarus, Felix**
See Cable, George Washington

**Lazarus, Henry**
See Slavitt, David R(ytman)

**Lea, Joan**
See Neufeld, John (Arthur)

**Leacock, Stephen (Butler)**
1869-1944 . . **TCLC 2; DAC; DAM MST**
See also CA 104; 141; DLB 92

**Lear, Edward** 1812-1888 . . . . . . . . . **NCLC 3**
See also CLR 1; DLB 32, 163, 166;
MAICYA; SATA 18

**Lear, Norman (Milton)** 1922- . . . . . . **CLC 12**
See also CA 73-76

**Leavis, F(rank) R(aymond)**
1895-1978 . . . . . . . . . . . . . . . . . . **CLC 24**
See also CA 21-24R; 77-80; CANR 44;
MTCW

**Leavitt, David** 1961- . . . **CLC 34; DAM POP**
See also CA 116; 122; CANR 50; DLB 130;
INT 122

**Leblanc, Maurice (Marie Emile)**
1864-1941 . . . . . . . . . . . . . . . . **TCLC 49**
See also CA 110

**Lebowitz, Fran(ces Ann)**
1951(?)- . . . . . . . . . . . . . . . . . **CLC 11, 36**
See also CA 81-84; CANR 14;
INT CANR-14; MTCW

**Lebrecht, Peter**
See Tieck, (Johann) Ludwig

**le Carre, John** . . . . . . . . . . **CLC 3, 5, 9, 15, 28**
See also Cornwell, David (John Moore)
See also BEST 89:4; CDBLB 1960 to
Present; DLB 87

**Le Clezio, J(ean) M(arie) G(ustave)**
1940- . . . . . . . . . . . . . . . . . . . . . **CLC 31**
See also CA 116; 128; DLB 83

**Leconte de Lisle, Charles-Marie-Rene**
1818-1894 . . . . . . . . . . . . . . . . . **NCLC 29**

**Le Coq, Monsieur**
See Simenon, Georges (Jacques Christian)

**Leduc, Violette** 1907-1972 . . . . . . . . . **CLC 22**
See also CA 13-14; 33-36R; CAP 1

**Ledwidge, Francis** 1887(?)-1917 . . . **TCLC 23**
See also CA 123; DLB 20

**Lee, Andrea**
1953- . . . . . **CLC 36; BLC; DAM MULT**
See also BW 1; CA 125

**Lee, Andrew**
See Auchincloss, Louis (Stanton)

**Lee, Chang-rae** 1965- . . . . . . . . . . . . . **CLC 91**
See also CA 148

**Lee, Don L.** . . . . . . . . . . . . . . . . . . . . . **CLC 2**
See also Madhubuti, Haki R.

**Lee, George W(ashington)**
1894-1976 . . . . . . . . . . . . **CLC 52; BLC;
DAM MULT**
See also BW 1; CA 125; DLB 51

**Lee, (Nelle) Harper**
1926- . . . . **CLC 12, 60; DA; DAB; DAC;
DAM MST, NOV; WLC**
See also AAYA 13; CA 13-16R; CANR 51;
CDALB 1941-1968; DLB 6; MTCW;
SATA 11

**Lee, Helen Elaine** 1959(?)- . . . . . . . . **CLC 86**
See also CA 148

**Lee, Julian**
See Latham, Jean Lee

**Lee, Larry**
See Lee, Lawrence

**Lee, Laurie**
1914- . . . . . . . **CLC 90; DAB; DAM POP**
See also CA 77-80; CANR 33; DLB 27;
MTCW

**Lee, Lawrence** 1941-1990 . . . . . . . . . **CLC 34**
See also CA 131; CANR 43

**Lee, Manfred B(ennington)**
1905-1971 . . . . . . . . . . . . . . . . . . **CLC 11**
See also Queen, Ellery
See also CA 1-4R; 29-32R; CANR 2;
DLB 137

**Lee, Stan** 1922- . . . . . . . . . . . . . . . . . . **CLC 17**
See also AAYA 5; CA 108; 111; INT 111

**Lee, Tanith** 1947- . . . . . . . . . . . . . . . **CLC 46**
See also AAYA 15; CA 37-40R; CANR 53;
SATA 8, 88

**Lee, Vernon** . . . . . . . . . . . . . . . . . . . . **TCLC 5**
See also Paget, Violet
See also DLB 57, 153, 156

**Lee, William**
See Burroughs, William S(eward)

**Lee, Willy**
See Burroughs, William S(eward)

**Lee-Hamilton, Eugene (Jacob)**
1845-1907 . . . . . . . . . . . . . . . . . TCLC 22
See also CA 117

**Leet, Judith** 1935- . . . . . . . . . . . . . . CLC 11

**Le Fanu, Joseph Sheridan**
1814-1873 . . . . . . . NCLC 9; DAM POP;
SSC 14
See also DLB 21, 70, 159

**Leffland, Ella** 1931- . . . . . . . . . . . . . CLC 19
See also CA 29-32R; CANR 35; DLBY 84;
INT CANR-35; SATA 65

**Leger, Alexis**
See Leger, (Marie-Rene Auguste) Alexis
Saint-Leger

**Leger, (Marie-Rene Auguste) Alexis**
**Saint-Leger**
1887-1975 . . . . . . . CLC 11; DAM POET
See also Perse, St.-John
See also CA 13-16R; 61-64; CANR 43;
MTCW

**Leger, Saintleger**
See Leger, (Marie-Rene Auguste) Alexis
Saint-Leger

**Le Guin, Ursula K(roeber)**
1929- . . . . . . CLC 8, 13, 22, 45, 71; DAB;
DAC; DAM MST, POP; SSC 12
See also AAYA 9; AITN 1; CA 21-24R;
CANR 9, 32, 52; CDALB 1968-1988;
CLR 3, 28; DLB 8, 52; INT CANR-32;
JRDA; MAICYA; MTCW; SATA 4, 52

**Lehmann, Rosamond (Nina)**
1901-1990 . . . . . . . . . . . . . . . . . CLC 5
See also CA 77-80; 131; CANR 8; DLB 15

**Leiber, Fritz (Reuter, Jr.)**
1910-1992 . . . . . . . . . . . . . . . . . CLC 25
See also CA 45-48; 139; CANR 2, 40;
DLB 8; MTCW; SATA 45;
SATA-Obit 73

**Leibniz, Gottfried Wilhelm von**
1646-1716 . . . . . . . . . . . . . . . . . LC 35
See also DLB 168

**Leimbach, Martha** 1963-
See Leimbach, Marti
See also CA 130

**Leimbach, Marti** . . . . . . . . . . . . . . . CLC 65
See also Leimbach, Martha

**Leino, Eino** . . . . . . . . . . . . . . . . . TCLC 24
See also Loennbohm, Armas Eino Leopold

**Leiris, Michel (Julien)** 1901-1990 . . . CLC 61
See also CA 119; 128; 132

**Leithauser, Brad** 1953- . . . . . . . . . . . CLC 27
See also CA 107; CANR 27; DLB 120

**Lelchuk, Alan** 1938- . . . . . . . . . . . . . CLC 5
See also CA 45-48; CAAS 20; CANR 1

**Lem, Stanislaw** 1921- . . . . . . . . CLC 8, 15, 40
See also CA 105; CAAS 1; CANR 32;
MTCW

**Lemann, Nancy** 1956- . . . . . . . . . . . . CLC 39
See also CA 118; 136

**Lemonnier, (Antoine Louis) Camille**
1844-1913 . . . . . . . . . . . . . . . . TCLC 22
See also CA 121

**Lenau, Nikolaus** 1802-1850 . . . . . . NCLC 16

**L'Engle, Madeleine (Camp Franklin)**
1918- . . . . . . . . . . . CLC 12; DAM POP
See also AAYA 1; AITN 2; CA 1-4R;
CANR 3, 21, 39; CLR 1, 14; DLB 52;
JRDA; MAICYA; MTCW; SAAS 15;
SATA 1, 27, 75

**Lengyel, Jozsef** 1896-1975 . . . . . . . . . CLC 7
See also CA 85-88; 57-60

**Lennon, John (Ono)**
1940-1980 . . . . . . . . . . . . . . . CLC 12, 35
See also CA 102

**Lennox, Charlotte Ramsay**
1729(?)-1804 . . . . . . . . . . . . . . NCLC 23
See also DLB 39

**Lentricchia, Frank (Jr.)** 1940- . . . . . . CLC 34
See also CA 25-28R; CANR 19

**Lenz, Siegfried** 1926- . . . . . . . . . . . . CLC 27
See also CA 89-92; DLB 75

**Leonard, Elmore (John, Jr.)**
1925- . . . . . . CLC 28, 34, 71; DAM POP
See also AITN 1; BEST 89:1, 90:4;
CA 81-84; CANR 12, 28, 53;
INT CANR-28; MTCW

**Leonard, Hugh** . . . . . . . . . . . . . . . . CLC 19
See also Byrne, John Keyes
See also DLB 13

**Leonov, Leonid (Maximovich)**
1899-1994 . . . . . . . . CLC 92; DAM NOV
See also CA 129; MTCW

**Leopardi, (Conte) Giacomo**
1798-1837 . . . . . . . . . . . . . . . . NCLC 22

**Le Reveler**
See Artaud, Antonin (Marie Joseph)

**Lerman, Eleanor** 1952- . . . . . . . . . . . CLC 9
See also CA 85-88

**Lerman, Rhoda** 1936- . . . . . . . . . . . . CLC 56
See also CA 49-52

**Lermontov, Mikhail Yuryevich**
1814-1841 . . . . . . . . . . . . . . . . NCLC 47

**Leroux, Gaston** 1868-1927 . . . . . . . . TCLC 25
See also CA 108; 136; SATA 65

**Lesage, Alain-Rene** 1668-1747 . . . . . . LC 28

**Leskov, Nikolai (Semyonovich)**
1831-1895 . . . . . . . . . . . . . . . . NCLC 25

**Lessing, Doris (May)**
1919- . . . . . CLC 1, 2, 3, 6, 10, 15, 22, 40,
94; DA; DAB; DAC; DAM MST, NOV;
SSC 6
See also CA 9-12R; CAAS 14; CANR 33;
CDBLB 1960 to Present; DLB 15, 139;
DLBY 85; MTCW

**Lessing, Gotthold Ephraim**
1729-1781 . . . . . . . . . . . . . . . . . LC 8
See also DLB 97

**Lester, Richard** 1932- . . . . . . . . . . . . CLC 20

**Lever, Charles (James)**
1806-1872 . . . . . . . . . . . . . . . . NCLC 23
See also DLB 21

**Leverson, Ada** 1865(?)-1936(?) . . . . TCLC 18
See also Elaine
See also CA 117; DLB 153

**Levertov, Denise**
1923- . . . . . . CLC 1, 2, 3, 5, 8, 15, 28, 66;
DAM POET; PC 11
See also CA 1-4R; CAAS 19; CANR 3, 29,
50; DLB 5, 165; INT CANR-29; MTCW

**Levi, Jonathan** . . . . . . . . . . . . . . . . CLC 76

**Levi, Peter (Chad Tigar)** 1931- . . . . . CLC 41
See also CA 5-8R; CANR 34; DLB 40

**Levi, Primo**
1919-1987 . . . . . . . . CLC 37, 50; SSC 12
See also CA 13-16R; 122; CANR 12, 33;
MTCW

**Levin, Ira** 1929- . . . . . CLC 3, 6; DAM POP
See also CA 21-24R; CANR 17, 44;
MTCW; SATA 66

**Levin, Meyer**
1905-1981 . . . . . . . . . CLC 7; DAM POP
See also AITN 1; CA 9-12R; 104;
CANR 15; DLB 9, 28; DLBY 81;
SATA 21; SATA-Obit 27

**Levine, Norman** 1924- . . . . . . . . . . . CLC 54
See also CA 73-76; CAAS 23; CANR 14;
DLB 88

**Levine, Philip**
1928- . . . . . . . . . . CLC 2, 4, 5, 9, 14, 33;
DAM POET
See also CA 9-12R; CANR 9, 37, 52;
DLB 5

**Levinson, Deirdre** 1931- . . . . . . . . . . CLC 49
See also CA 73-76

**Levi-Strauss, Claude** 1908- . . . . . . . . CLC 38
See also CA 1-4R; CANR 6, 32; MTCW

**Levitin, Sonia (Wolff)** 1934- . . . . . . . CLC 17
See also AAYA 13; CA 29-32R; CANR 14,
32; JRDA; MAICYA; SAAS 2; SATA 4,
68

**Levon, O. U.**
See Kesey, Ken (Elton)

**Lewes, George Henry**
1817-1878 . . . . . . . . . . . . . . . . NCLC 25
See also DLB 55, 144

**Lewis, Alun** 1915-1944 . . . . . . . . . . . TCLC 3
See also CA 104; DLB 20, 162

**Lewis, C. Day**
See Day Lewis, C(ecil)

**Lewis, C(live) S(taples)**
1898-1963 . . . . . CLC 1, 3, 6, 14, 27; DA;
DAB; DAC; DAM MST, NOV, POP;
WLC
See also AAYA 3; CA 81-84; CANR 33;
CDBLB 1945-1960; CLR 3, 27; DLB 15,
100, 160; JRDA; MAICYA; MTCW;
SATA 13

**Lewis, Janet** 1899- . . . . . . . . . . . . . . CLC 41
See also Winters, Janet Lewis
See also CA 9-12R; CANR 29; CAP 1;
DLBY 87

**Lewis, Matthew Gregory**
1775-1818 . . . . . . . . . . . . . . . . NCLC 11
See also DLB 39, 158

**Lewis, (Harry) Sinclair**
1885-1951 . . . . . TCLC 4, 13, 23, 39; DA;
DAB; DAC; DAM MST, NOV; WLC
See also CA 104; 133; CDALB 1917-1929;
DLB 9, 102; DLBD 1; MTCW

**Lewis, (Percy) Wyndham**
1884(?)-1957 . . . . . . . . . . . . . . TCLC **2, 9**
See also CA 104; DLB 15

**Lewisohn, Ludwig** 1883-1955 . . . . . . TCLC **19**
See also CA 107; DLB 4, 9, 28, 102

**Leyner, Mark** 1956- . . . . . . . . . . . . . . CLC **92**
See also CA 110; CANR 28, 53

**Lezama Lima, Jose**
1910-1976 . . . . CLC **4, 10; DAM MULT**
See also CA 77-80; DLB 113; HW

**L'Heureux, John (Clarke)** 1934- . . . . CLC **52**
See also CA 13-16R; CANR 23, 45

**Liddell, C. H.**
See Kuttner, Henry

**Lie, Jonas (Lauritz Idemil)**
1833-1908(?) . . . . . . . . . . . . . . . . TCLC **5**
See also CA 115

**Lieber, Joel** 1937-1971 . . . . . . . . . . . . CLC **6**
See also CA 73-76; 29-32R

**Lieber, Stanley Martin**
See Lee, Stan

**Lieberman, Laurence (James)**
1935- . . . . . . . . . . . . . . . . . . . . . CLC **4, 36**
See also CA 17-20R; CANR 8, 36

**Lieksman, Anders**
See Haavikko, Paavo Juhani

**Li Fei-kan** 1904-
See Pa Chin
See also CA 105

**Lifton, Robert Jay** 1926- . . . . . . . . . . CLC **67**
See also CA 17-20R; CANR 27;
INT CANR-27; SATA 66

**Lightfoot, Gordon** 1938- . . . . . . . . . . CLC **26**
See also CA 109

**Lightman, Alan P.** 1948- . . . . . . . . . . CLC **81**
See also CA 141

**Ligotti, Thomas (Robert)**
1953- . . . . . . . . . . . . . . . . CLC **44; SSC 16**
See also CA 123; CANR 49

**Li Ho** 791-817 . . . . . . . . . . . . . . . . . . . PC **13**

**Liliencron, (Friedrich Adolf Axel) Detlev von**
1844-1909 . . . . . . . . . . . . . . . . . . TCLC **18**
See also CA 117

**Lilly, William** 1602-1681 . . . . . . . . . . . LC **27**

**Lima, Jose Lezama**
See Lezama Lima, Jose

**Lima Barreto, Afonso Henrique de**
1881-1922 . . . . . . . . . . . . . . . . . . TCLC **23**
See also CA 117

**Limonov, Edward** 1944- . . . . . . . . . . . CLC **67**
See also CA 137

**Lin, Frank**
See Atherton, Gertrude (Franklin Horn)

**Lincoln, Abraham** 1809-1865 . . . . . NCLC **18**

**Lind, Jakov** . . . . . . . . . . . . CLC **1, 2, 4, 27, 82**
See also Landwirth, Heinz
See also CAAS 4

**Lindbergh, Anne (Spencer) Morrow**
1906- . . . . . . . . . . CLC **82; DAM NOV**
See also CA 17-20R; CANR 16; MTCW;
SATA 33

**Lindsay, David** 1878-1945 . . . . . . . . TCLC **15**
See also CA 113

**Lindsay, (Nicholas) Vachel**
1879-1931 . . . . . . . TCLC **17; DA; DAC;**
**DAM MST, POET; WLC**
See also CA 114; 135; CDALB 1865-1917;
DLB 54; SATA 40

**Linke-Poot**
See Doeblin, Alfred

**Linney, Romulus** 1930- . . . . . . . . . . . CLC **51**
See also CA 1-4R; CANR 40, 44

**Linton, Eliza Lynn** 1822-1898 . . . . NCLC **41**
See also DLB 18

**Li Po** 701-763 . . . . . . . . . . . . . . . . . . CMLC **2**

**Lipsius, Justus** 1547-1606 . . . . . . . . . LC **16**

**Lipsyte, Robert (Michael)**
1938- . . . . . . . . . . . . . CLC **21; DA; DAC;**
**DAM MST, NOV**
See also AAYA 7; CA 17-20R; CANR 8;
CLR 23; JRDA; MAICYA; SATA 5, 68

**Lish, Gordon (Jay)** 1934- . . CLC **45; SSC 18**
See also CA 113; 117; DLB 130; INT 117

**Lispector, Clarice** 1925-1977 . . . . . . CLC **43**
See also CA 139; 116; DLB 113

**Littell, Robert** 1935(?)- . . . . . . . . . . . CLC **42**
See also CA 109; 112

**Little, Malcolm** 1925-1965
See Malcolm X
See also BW 1; CA 125; 111; DA; DAB;
DAC; DAM MST, MULT; MTCW

**Littlewit, Humphrey Gent.**
See Lovecraft, H(oward) P(hillips)

**Litwos**
See Sienkiewicz, Henryk (Adam Alexander
Pius)

**Liu E** 1857-1909 . . . . . . . . . . . . . . . . TCLC **15**
See also CA 115

**Lively, Penelope (Margaret)**
1933- . . . . . . . . . CLC **32, 50; DAM NOV**
See also CA 41-44R; CANR 29; CLR 7;
DLB 14, 161; JRDA; MAICYA; MTCW;
SATA 7, 60

**Livesay, Dorothy (Kathleen)**
1909- . . . . . . . . . . . CLC **4, 15, 79; DAC;**
**DAM MST, POET**
See also AITN 2; CA 25-28R; CAAS 8;
CANR 36; DLB 68; MTCW

**Livy** c. 59B.C.-c. 17 . . . . . . . . . . . . CMLC **11**

**Lizardi, Jose Joaquin Fernandez de**
1776-1827 . . . . . . . . . . . . . . . . . NCLC **30**

**Llewellyn, Richard**
See Llewellyn Lloyd, Richard Dafydd
Vivian
See also DLB 15

**Llewellyn Lloyd, Richard Dafydd Vivian**
1906-1983 . . . . . . . . . . . . . . . . CLC **7, 80**
See also Llewellyn, Richard
See also CA 53-56; 111; CANR 7;
SATA 11; SATA-Obit 37

**Llosa, (Jorge) Mario (Pedro) Vargas**
See Vargas Llosa, (Jorge) Mario (Pedro)

**Lloyd Webber, Andrew** 1948-
See Webber, Andrew Lloyd
See also AAYA 1; CA 116; 149;
DAM DRAM; SATA 56

**Llull, Ramon** c. 1235-c. 1316 . . . . . CMLC **12**

**Locke, Alain (Le Roy)**
1886-1954 . . . . . . . . . . . . . . . . . . TCLC **43**
See also BW 1; CA 106; 124; DLB 51

**Locke, John** 1632-1704 . . . . . . . . . . LC **7, 35**
See also DLB 101

**Locke-Elliott, Sumner**
See Elliott, Sumner Locke

**Lockhart, John Gibson**
1794-1854 . . . . . . . . . . . . . . . . . . NCLC **6**
See also DLB 110, 116, 144

**Lodge, David (John)**
1935- . . . . . . . . . . . . CLC **36; DAM POP**
See also BEST 90:1; CA 17-20R; CANR 19,
53; DLB 14; INT CANR-19; MTCW

**Loennbohm, Armas Eino Leopold** 1878-1926
See Leino, Eino
See also CA 123

**Loewinsohn, Ron(ald William)**
1937- . . . . . . . . . . . . . . . . . . . . . . . CLC **52**
See also CA 25-28R

**Logan, Jake**
See Smith, Martin Cruz

**Logan, John (Burton)** 1923-1987 . . . . . CLC **5**
See also CA 77-80; 124; CANR 45; DLB 5

**Lo Kuan-chung** 1330(?)-1400(?) . . . . . . LC **12**

**Lombard, Nap**
See Johnson, Pamela Hansford

**London, Jack** . . TCLC **9, 15, 39; SSC 4; WLC**
See also London, John Griffith
See also AAYA 13; AITN 2;
CDALB 1865-1917; DLB 8, 12, 78;
SATA 18

**London, John Griffith** 1876-1916
See London, Jack
See also CA 110; 119; DA; DAB; DAC;
DAM MST, NOV; JRDA; MAICYA;
MTCW

**Long, Emmett**
See Leonard, Elmore (John, Jr.)

**Longbaugh, Harry**
See Goldman, William (W.)

**Longfellow, Henry Wadsworth**
1807-1882 . . . . . NCLC **2, 45; DA; DAB;**
**DAC; DAM MST, POET**
See also CDALB 1640-1865; DLB 1, 59;
SATA 19

**Longley, Michael** 1939- . . . . . . . . . . . CLC **29**
See also CA 102; DLB 40

**Longus** fl. c. 2nd cent. - . . . . . . . . . . CMLC **7**

**Longway, A. Hugh**
See Lang, Andrew

**Lonnrot, Elias** 1802-1884 . . . . . . . . NCLC **53**

**Lopate, Phillip** 1943- . . . . . . . . . . . . . CLC **29**
See also CA 97-100; DLBY 80; INT 97-100

**Lopez Portillo (y Pacheco), Jose**
1920- . . . . . . . . . . . . . . . . . . . . . . CLC **46**
See also CA 129; HW

**Lopez y Fuentes, Gregorio**
1897(?)-1966 . . . . . . . . . . . . . . . . . CLC **32**
See also CA 131; HW

**Lorca, Federico Garcia**
See Garcia Lorca, Federico

**Machiavelli, Niccolo**
1469-1527 . . . . . . LC 8; DA; DAB; DAC;
DAM MST

**MacInnes, Colin** 1914-1976 . . . . . CLC 4, 23
See also CA 69-72; 65-68; CANR 21;
DLB 14; MTCW

**MacInnes, Helen (Clark)**
1907-1985 . . . . . CLC 27, 39; DAM POP
See also CA 1-4R; 117; CANR 1, 28;
DLB 87; MTCW; SATA 22;
SATA-Obit 44

**Mackay, Mary** 1855-1924
See Corelli, Marie
See also CA 118

**Mackenzie, Compton (Edward Montague)**
1883-1972 . . . . . . . . . . . . . . . . . . CLC 18
See also CA 21-22; 37-40R; CAP 2;
DLB 34, 100

**Mackenzie, Henry** 1745-1831 . . . . NCLC 41
See also DLB 39

**Mackintosh, Elizabeth** 1896(?)-1952
See Tey, Josephine
See also CA 110

**MacLaren, James**
See Grieve, C(hristopher) M(urray)

**Mac Laverty, Bernard** 1942- . . . . . . CLC 31
See also CA 116; 118; CANR 43; INT 118

**MacLean, Alistair (Stuart)**
1922-1987 . . . . . . . . . CLC 3, 13, 50, 63;
DAM POP
See also CA 57-60; 121; CANR 28; MTCW;
SATA 23; SATA-Obit 50

**Maclean, Norman (Fitzroy)**
1902-1990 . . . . . . . . CLC 78; DAM POP;
SSC 13
See also CA 102; 132; CANR 49

**MacLeish, Archibald**
1892-1982 . . . . . . . . . . . CLC 3, 8, 14, 68;
DAM POET
See also CA 9-12R; 106; CANR 33; DLB 4,
7, 45; DLBY 82; MTCW

**MacLennan, (John) Hugh**
1907-1990 . . . . . . . . CLC 2, 14, 92; DAC;
DAM MST
See also CA 5-8R; 142; CANR 33; DLB 68;
MTCW

**MacLeod, Alistair**
1936- . . . . . . CLC 56; DAC; DAM MST
See also CA 123; DLB 60

**MacNeice, (Frederick) Louis**
1907-1963 . . . . . . CLC 1, 4, 10, 53; DAB;
DAM POET
See also CA 85-88; DLB 10, 20; MTCW

**MacNeill, Dand**
See Fraser, George MacDonald

**Macpherson, James** 1736-1796 . . . . . . LC 29
See also DLB 109

**Macpherson, (Jean) Jay** 1931- . . . . . . CLC 14
See also CA 5-8R; DLB 53

**MacShane, Frank** 1927- . . . . . . . . . . . CLC 39
See also CA 9-12R; CANR 3, 33; DLB 111

**Macumber, Mari**
See Sandoz, Mari(e Susette)

**Madach, Imre** 1823-1864 . . . . . . . NCLC 19

**Madden, (Jerry) David** 1933- . . . . CLC 5, 15
See also CA 1-4R; CAAS 3; CANR 4, 45;
DLB 6; MTCW

**Maddern, Al(an)**
See Ellison, Harlan (Jay)

**Madhubuti, Haki R.**
1942- . . . . . . . . . . . . . . . CLC 6, 73; BLC;
DAM MULT, POET; PC 5
See also Lee, Don L.
See also BW 2; CA 73-76; CANR 24, 51;
DLB 5, 41; DLBD 8

**Maepenn, Hugh**
See Kuttner, Henry

**Maepenn, K. H.**
See Kuttner, Henry

**Maeterlinck, Maurice**
1862-1949 . . . . . . TCLC 3; DAM DRAM
See also CA 104; 136; SATA 66

**Maginn, William** 1794-1842 . . . . . . NCLC 8
See also DLB 110, 159

**Mahapatra, Jayanta**
1928- . . . . . . . . . . . CLC 33; DAM MULT
See also CA 73-76; CAAS 9; CANR 15, 33

**Mahfouz, Naguib (Abdel Aziz Al-Sabilgi)**
1911(?)-
See Mahfuz, Najib
See also BEST 89:2; CA 128; DAM NOV;
MTCW

**Mahfuz, Najib** . . . . . . . . . . . . . . . CLC 52, 55
See also Mahfouz, Naguib (Abdel Aziz
Al-Sabilgi)
See also DLBY 88

**Mahon, Derek** 1941- . . . . . . . . . . . . . CLC 27
See also CA 113; 128; DLB 40

**Mailer, Norman**
1923- . . . . . . CLC 1, 2, 3, 4, 5, 8, 11, 14,
28, 39, 74; DA; DAB; DAC; DAM MST,
NOV, POP
See also AITN 2; CA 9-12R; CABS 1;
CANR 28; CDALB 1968-1988; DLB 2,
16, 28; DLBD 3; DLBY 80, 83; MTCW

**Maillet, Antonine** 1929- . . . . . . CLC 54; DAC
See also CA 115; 120; CANR 46; DLB 60;
INT 120

**Mais, Roger** 1905-1955 . . . . . . . . . . TCLC 8
See also BW 1; CA 105; 124; DLB 125;
MTCW

**Maistre, Joseph de** 1753-1821 . . . . NCLC 37

**Maitland, Frederic** 1850-1906 . . . . . TCLC 65

**Maitland, Sara (Louise)** 1950- . . . . . . CLC 49
See also CA 69-72; CANR 13

**Major, Clarence**
1936- . . . . . . . . . . . CLC 3, 19, 48; BLC;
DAM MULT
See also BW 2; CA 21-24R; CAAS 6;
CANR 13, 25, 53; DLB 33

**Major, Kevin (Gerald)**
1949- . . . . . . . . . . . . . . . . . . CLC 26; DAC
See also AAYA 16; CA 97-100; CANR 21,
38; CLR 11; DLB 60; INT CANR-21;
JRDA; MAICYA; SATA 32, 82

**Maki, James**
See Ozu, Yasujiro

**Malabaila, Damiano**
See Levi, Primo

**Malamud, Bernard**
1914-1986 . . . . . . CLC 1, 2, 3, 5, 8, 9, 11,
18, 27, 44, 78, 85; DA; DAB; DAC;
DAM MST, NOV, POP; SSC 15; WLC
See also AAYA 16; CA 5-8R; 118; CABS 1;
CANR 28; CDALB 1941-1968; DLB 2,
28, 152; DLBY 80, 86; MTCW

**Malaparte, Curzio** 1898-1957 . . . . . TCLC 52

**Malcolm, Dan**
See Silverberg, Robert

**Malcolm X** . . . . . . . . . . . . . . . CLC 82; BLC
See also Little, Malcolm

**Malherbe, Francois de** 1555-1628 . . . . . LC 5

**Mallarme, Stephane**
1842-1898 . . . . . . . . . . . . . . NCLC 4, 41;
DAM POET; PC 4

**Mallet-Joris, Francoise** 1930- . . . . . . CLC 11
See also CA 65-68; CANR 17; DLB 83

**Malley, Ern**
See McAuley, James Phillip

**Mallowan, Agatha Christie**
See Christie, Agatha (Mary Clarissa)

**Maloff, Saul** 1922- . . . . . . . . . . . . . . . CLC 5
See also CA 33-36R

**Malone, Louis**
See MacNeice, (Frederick) Louis

**Malone, Michael (Christopher)**
1942- . . . . . . . . . . . . . . . . . . . . . . CLC 43
See also CA 77-80; CANR 14, 32

**Malory, (Sir) Thomas**
1410(?)-1471(?) . . . . . . LC 11; DA; DAB;
DAC; DAM MST
See also CDBLB Before 1660; DLB 146;
SATA 59; SATA-Brief 33

**Malouf, (George Joseph) David**
1934- . . . . . . . . . . . . . . . . . . CLC 28, 86
See also CA 124; CANR 50

**Malraux, (Georges-)Andre**
1901-1976 . . . . . . CLC 1, 4, 9, 13, 15, 57;
DAM NOV
See also CA 21-22; 69-72; CANR 34;
CAP 2; DLB 72; MTCW

**Malzberg, Barry N(athaniel)** 1939- . . . CLC 7
See also CA 61-64; CAAS 4; CANR 16;
DLB 8

**Mamet, David (Alan)**
1947- . . . . . . . . . . . CLC 9, 15, 34, 46, 91;
DAM DRAM; DC 4
See also AAYA 3; CA 81-84; CABS 3;
CANR 15, 41; DLB 7; MTCW

**Mamoulian, Rouben (Zachary)**
1897-1987 . . . . . . . . . . . . . . . . . . CLC 16
See also CA 25-28R; 124

**Mandelstam, Osip (Emilievich)**
1891(?)-1938(?) . . . . . . TCLC 2, 6; PC 14
See also CA 104; 150

**Mander, (Mary) Jane** 1877-1949 . . . TCLC 31

**Mandiargues, Andre Pieyre de** . . . . . . CLC 41
See also Pieyre de Mandiargues, Andre
See also DLB 83

**Mandrake, Ethel Belle**
See Thurman, Wallace (Henry)

**Mangan, James Clarence**
1803-1849 . . . . . . . . . . . . . . . NCLC 27

**Maniere, J.-E.**
See Giraudoux, (Hippolyte) Jean

**Manley, (Mary) Delariviere**
1672(?)-1724 . . . . . . . . . . . . . . . . . **LC 1**
See also DLB 39, 80

**Mann, Abel**
See Creasey, John

**Mann, (Luiz) Heinrich** 1871-1950 . . . **TCLC 9**
See also CA 106; DLB 66

**Mann, (Paul) Thomas**
1875-1955 . . . . **TCLC 2, 8, 14, 21, 35, 44,**
**60; DA; DAB; DAC; DAM MST, NOV;**
**SSC 5; WLC**
See also CA 104; 128; DLB 66; MTCW

**Mannheim, Karl** 1893-1947 . . . . . . **TCLC 65**

**Manning, David**
See Faust, Frederick (Schiller)

**Manning, Frederic** 1887(?)-1935 . . . **TCLC 25**
See also CA 124

**Manning, Olivia** 1915-1980 . . . . . . **CLC 5, 19**
See also CA 5-8R; 101; CANR 29; MTCW

**Mano, D. Keith** 1942- . . . . . . . . . **CLC 2, 10**
See also CA 25-28R; CAAS 6; CANR 26;
DLB 6

**Mansfield, Katherine**
. . **TCLC 2, 8, 39; DAB; SSC 9, 23; WLC**
See also Beauchamp, Kathleen Mansfield
See also DLB 162

**Manso, Peter** 1940- . . . . . . . . . . . . . **CLC 39**
See also CA 29-32R; CANR 44

**Mantecon, Juan Jimenez**
See Jimenez (Mantecon), Juan Ramon

**Manton, Peter**
See Creasey, John

**Man Without a Spleen, A**
See Chekhov, Anton (Pavlovich)

**Manzoni, Alessandro** 1785-1873 . . **NCLC 29**

**Mapu, Abraham (ben Jekutiel)**
1808-1867 . . . . . . . . . . . . . . . . . **NCLC 18**

**Mara, Sally**
See Queneau, Raymond

**Marat, Jean Paul** 1743-1793 . . . . . . . **LC 10**

**Marcel, Gabriel Honore**
1889-1973 . . . . . . . . . . . . . . . . . . **CLC 15**
See also CA 102; 45-48; MTCW

**Marchbanks, Samuel**
See Davies, (William) Robertson

**Marchi, Giacomo**
See Bassani, Giorgio

**Margulies, Donald** . . . . . . . . . . . . . . **CLC 76**

**Marie de France** c. 12th cent. - . . . . **CMLC 8**

**Marie de l'Incarnation** 1599-1672 . . . . **LC 10**

**Mariner, Scott**
See Pohl, Frederik

**Marinetti, Filippo Tommaso**
1876-1944 . . . . . . . . . . . . . . . . **TCLC 10**
See also CA 107; DLB 114

**Marivaux, Pierre Carlet de Chamblain de**
1688-1763 . . . . . . . . . . . . . . . . . . . **LC 4**

**Markandaya, Kamala** . . . . . . . . . . . **CLC 8, 38**
See also Taylor, Kamala (Purnaiya)

**Markfield, Wallace** 1926- . . . . . . . . . . **CLC 8**
See also CA 69-72; CAAS 3; DLB 2, 28

**Markham, Edwin** 1852-1940 . . . . . . **TCLC 47**
See also DLB 54

**Markham, Robert**
See Amis, Kingsley (William)

**Marks, J**
See Highwater, Jamake (Mamake)

**Marks-Highwater, J**
See Highwater, Jamake (Mamake)

**Markson, David M(errill)** 1927- . . . . **CLC 67**
See also CA 49-52; CANR 1

**Marley, Bob** . . . . . . . . . . . . . . . . . . . **CLC 17**
See also Marley, Robert Nesta

**Marley, Robert Nesta** 1945-1981
See Marley, Bob
See also CA 107; 103

**Marlowe, Christopher**
1564-1593 . . . . . **LC 22; DA; DAB; DAC;**
**DAM DRAM, MST; DC 1; WLC**
See also CDBLB Before 1660; DLB 62

**Marmontel, Jean-Francois**
1723-1799 . . . . . . . . . . . . . . . . . . . **LC 2**

**Marquand, John P(hillips)**
1893-1960 . . . . . . . . . . . . . . . **CLC 2, 10**
See also CA 85-88; DLB 9, 102

**Marques, Rene**
1919-1979 . . . . . . **CLC 96; DAM MULT;**
**HLC**
See also CA 97-100; 85-88; DLB 113; HW

**Marquez, Gabriel (Jose) Garcia**
See Garcia Marquez, Gabriel (Jose)

**Marquis, Don(ald Robert Perry)**
1878-1937 . . . . . . . . . . . . . . . . . . **TCLC 7**
See also CA 104; DLB 11, 25

**Marric, J. J.**
See Creasey, John

**Marrow, Bernard**
See Moore, Brian

**Marryat, Frederick** 1792-1848 . . . . **NCLC 3**
See also DLB 21, 163

**Marsden, James**
See Creasey, John

**Marsh, (Edith) Ngaio**
1899-1982 . . . . . . **CLC 7, 53; DAM POP**
See also CA 9-12R; CANR 6; DLB 77;
MTCW

**Marshall, Garry** 1934- . . . . . . . . . . . . **CLC 17**
See also AAYA 3; CA 111; SATA 60

**Marshall, Paule**
1929- . . . . . . . . . . . . . . **CLC 27, 72; BLC;**
**DAM MULT; SSC 3**
See also BW 2; CA 77-80; CANR 25;
DLB 157; MTCW

**Marsten, Richard**
See Hunter, Evan

**Marston, John**
1576-1634 . . . . . . . **LC 33; DAM DRAM**
See also DLB 58

**Martha, Henry**
See Harris, Mark

**Martial** c. 40-c. 104 . . . . . . . . . . . . . **PC 10**

**Martin, Ken**
See Hubbard, L(afayette) Ron(ald)

**Martin, Richard**
See Creasey, John

**Martin, Steve** 1945- . . . . . . . . . . . . . **CLC 30**
See also CA 97-100; CANR 30; MTCW

**Martin, Valerie** 1948- . . . . . . . . . . . . **CLC 89**
See also BEST 90:2; CA 85-88; CANR 49

**Martin, Violet Florence**
1862-1915 . . . . . . . . . . . . . . . . . **TCLC 51**

**Martin, Webber**
See Silverberg, Robert

**Martindale, Patrick Victor**
See White, Patrick (Victor Martindale)

**Martin du Gard, Roger**
1881-1958 . . . . . . . . . . . . . . . . . **TCLC 24**
See also CA 118; DLB 65

**Martineau, Harriet** 1802-1876 . . . . **NCLC 26**
See also DLB 21, 55, 159, 163, 166;
YABC 2

**Martines, Julia**
See O'Faolain, Julia

**Martinez, Jacinto Benavente y**
See Benavente (y Martinez), Jacinto

**Martinez Ruiz, Jose** 1873-1967
See Azorin; Ruiz, Jose Martinez
See also CA 93-96; HW

**Martinez Sierra, Gregorio**
1881-1947 . . . . . . . . . . . . . . . . . . **TCLC 6**
See also CA 115

**Martinez Sierra, Maria (de la O'LeJarraga)**
1874-1974 . . . . . . . . . . . . . . . . . . **TCLC 6**
See also CA 115

**Martinsen, Martin**
See Follett, Ken(neth Martin)

**Martinson, Harry (Edmund)**
1904-1978 . . . . . . . . . . . . . . . . . . **CLC 14**
See also CA 77-80; CANR 34

**Marut, Ret**
See Traven, B.

**Marut, Robert**
See Traven, B.

**Marvell, Andrew**
1621-1678 . . . . . . **LC 4; DA; DAB; DAC;**
**DAM MST, POET; PC 10; WLC**
See also CDBLB 1660-1789; DLB 131

**Marx, Karl (Heinrich)**
1818-1883 . . . . . . . . . . . . . . . . . **NCLC 17**
See also DLB 129

**Masaoka Shiki** . . . . . . . . . . . . . . . . . **TCLC 18**
See also Masaoka Tsunenori

**Masaoka Tsunenori** 1867-1902
See Masaoka Shiki
See also CA 117

**Masefield, John (Edward)**
1878-1967 . . . . **CLC 11, 47; DAM POET**
See also CA 19-20; 25-28R; CANR 33;
CAP 2; CDBLB 1890-1914; DLB 10, 19,
153, 160; MTCW; SATA 19

**Maso, Carole** 19(?)- . . . . . . . . . . . . . **CLC 44**

**Mason, Bobbie Ann**
1940- . . . . . . . . . **CLC 28, 43, 82; SSC 4**
See also AAYA 5; CA 53-56; CANR 11,
31; DLBY 87; INT CANR-31; MTCW

**Mason, Ernst**
See Pohl, Frederik

**Mason, Lee W.**
See Malzberg, Barry N(athaniel)

**Mason, Nick** 1945- ............... **CLC 35**

**Mason, Tally**
See Derleth, August (William)

**Mass, William**
See Gibson, William

**Masters, Edgar Lee**
1868-1950 ...... **TCLC 2, 25; DA; DAC; DAM MST, POET; PC 1**
See also CA 104; 133; CDALB 1865-1917; DLB 54; MTCW

**Masters, Hilary** 1928- ............ **CLC 48**
See also CA 25-28R; CANR 13, 47

**Mastrosimone, William** 19(?)- ...... **CLC 36**

**Mathe, Albert**
See Camus, Albert

**Matheson, Richard Burton** 1926- ... **CLC 37**
See also CA 97-100; DLB 8, 44; INT 97-100

**Mathews, Harry** 1930- ......... **CLC 6, 52**
See also CA 21-24R; CAAS 6; CANR 18, 40

**Mathews, John Joseph**
1894-1979 ...... **CLC 84; DAM MULT**
See also CA 19-20; 142; CANR 45; CAP 2; NNAL

**Mathias, Roland (Glyn)** 1915- ...... **CLC 45**
See also CA 97-100; CANR 19, 41; DLB 27

**Matsuo Basho** 1644-1694 ........... **PC 3**
See also DAM POET

**Mattheson, Rodney**
See Creasey, John

**Matthews, Greg** 1949- ............ **CLC 45**
See also CA 135

**Matthews, William** 1942- ......... **CLC 40**
See also CA 29-32R; CAAS 18; CANR 12; DLB 5

**Matthias, John (Edward)** 1941- ...... **CLC 9**
See also CA 33-36R

**Matthiessen, Peter**
1927- ............ **CLC 5, 7, 11, 32, 64; DAM NOV**
See also AAYA 6; BEST 90:4; CA 9-12R; CANR 21, 50; DLB 6; MTCW; SATA 27

**Maturin, Charles Robert**
1780(?)-1824 ............... **NCLC 6**

**Matute (Ausejo), Ana Maria**
1925- ..................... **CLC 11**
See also CA 89-92; MTCW

**Maugham, W. S.**
See Maugham, W(illiam) Somerset

**Maugham, W(illiam) Somerset**
1874-1965 ....... **CLC 1, 11, 15, 67, 93; DA; DAB; DAC; DAM DRAM, MST, NOV; SSC 8; WLC**
See also CA 5-8R; 25-28R; CANR 40; CDBLB 1914-1945; DLB 10, 36, 77, 100, 162; MTCW; SATA 54

**Maugham, William Somerset**
See Maugham, W(illiam) Somerset

**Maupassant, (Henri Rene Albert) Guy de**
1850-1893 ..... **NCLC 1, 42; DA; DAB; DAC; DAM MST; SSC 1; WLC**
See also DLB 123

**Maupin, Armistead**
1944- ........... **CLC 95; DAM POP**
See also CA 125; 130; INT 130

**Maurhut, Richard**
See Traven, B.

**Mauriac, Claude** 1914-1996 ........ **CLC 9**
See also CA 89-92; 152; DLB 83

**Mauriac, Francois (Charles)**
1885-1970 ............... **CLC 4, 9, 56**
See also CA 25-28; CAP 2; DLB 65; MTCW

**Mavor, Osborne Henry** 1888-1951
See Bridie, James
See also CA 104

**Maxwell, William (Keepers, Jr.)**
1908- ..................... **CLC 19**
See also CA 93-96; DLBY 80; INT 93-96

**May, Elaine** 1932- ............... **CLC 16**
See also CA 124; 142; DLB 44

**Mayakovski, Vladimir (Vladimirovich)**
1893-1930 ............... **TCLC 4, 18**
See also CA 104

**Mayhew, Henry** 1812-1887 ...... **NCLC 31**
See also DLB 18, 55

**Mayle, Peter** 1939(?)- ............ **CLC 89**
See also CA 139

**Maynard, Joyce** 1953- ............ **CLC 23**
See also CA 111; 129

**Mayne, William (James Carter)**
1928- ..................... **CLC 12**
See also CA 9-12R; CANR 37; CLR 25; JRDA; MAICYA; SAAS 11; SATA 6, 68

**Mayo, Jim**
See L'Amour, Louis (Dearborn)

**Maysles, Albert** 1926- ............ **CLC 16**
See also CA 29-32R

**Maysles, David** 1932- ............ **CLC 16**

**Mazer, Norma Fox** 1931- ......... **CLC 26**
See also AAYA 5; CA 69-72; CANR 12, 32; CLR 23; JRDA; MAICYA; SAAS 1; SATA 24, 67

**Mazzini, Guiseppe** 1805-1872 .... **NCLC 34**

**McAuley, James Phillip**
1917-1976 .................. **CLC 45**
See also CA 97-100

**McBain, Ed**
See Hunter, Evan

**McBrien, William Augustine**
1930- ..................... **CLC 44**
See also CA 107

**McCaffrey, Anne (Inez)**
1926- ...... **CLC 17; DAM NOV, POP**
See also AAYA 6; AITN 2; BEST 89:2; CA 25-28R; CANR 15, 35; DLB 8; JRDA; MAICYA; MTCW; SAAS 11; SATA 8, 70

**McCall, Nathan** 1955(?)- .......... **CLC 86**
See also CA 146

**McCann, Arthur**
See Campbell, John W(ood, Jr.)

**McCann, Edson**
See Pohl, Frederik

**McCarthy, Charles, Jr.** 1933-
See McCarthy, Cormac
See also CANR 42; DAM POP

**McCarthy, Cormac** 1933- ..... **CLC 4, 57, 59**
See also McCarthy, Charles, Jr.
See also DLB 6, 143

**McCarthy, Mary (Therese)**
1912-1989 ... **CLC 1, 3, 5, 14, 24, 39, 59**
See also CA 5-8R; 129; CANR 16, 50; DLB 2; DLBY 81; INT CANR-16; MTCW

**McCartney, (James) Paul**
1942- .................... **CLC 12, 35**
See also CA 146

**McCauley, Stephen (D.)** 1955- ..... **CLC 50**
See also CA 141

**McClure, Michael (Thomas)**
1932- .................... **CLC 6, 10**
See also CA 21-24R; CANR 17, 46; DLB 16

**McCorkle, Jill (Collins)** 1958- ...... **CLC 51**
See also CA 121; DLBY 87

**McCourt, James** 1941- ............ **CLC 5**
See also CA 57-60

**McCoy, Horace (Stanley)**
1897-1955 ................. **TCLC 28**
See also CA 108; DLB 9

**McCrae, John** 1872-1918 ........ **TCLC 12**
See also CA 109; DLB 92

**McCreigh, James**
See Pohl, Frederik

**McCullers, (Lula) Carson (Smith)**
1917-1967 .... **CLC 1, 4, 10, 12, 48; DA; DAB; DAC; DAM MST, NOV; SSC 9; WLC**
See also CA 5-8R; 25-28R; CABS 1, 3; CANR 18; CDALB 1941-1968; DLB 2, 7; MTCW; SATA 27

**McCulloch, John Tyler**
See Burroughs, Edgar Rice

**McCullough, Colleen**
1938(?)- .... **CLC 27; DAM NOV, POP**
See also CA 81-84; CANR 17, 46; MTCW

**McDermott, Alice** 1953- .......... **CLC 90**
See also CA 109; CANR 40

**McElroy, Joseph** 1930- ........ **CLC 5, 47**
See also CA 17-20R

**McEwan, Ian (Russell)**
1948- ........ **CLC 13, 66; DAM NOV**
See also BEST 90:4; CA 61-64; CANR 14, 41; DLB 14; MTCW

**McFadden, David** 1940- .......... **CLC 48**
See also CA 104; DLB 60; INT 104

**McFarland, Dennis** 1950- ........ **CLC 65**

**McGahern, John**
1934- ........... **CLC 5, 9, 48; SSC 17**
See also CA 17-20R; CANR 29; DLB 14; MTCW

**McGinley, Patrick (Anthony)**
1937- ..................... **CLC 41**
See also CA 120; 127; INT 127

**McGinley, Phyllis** 1905-1978 ...... **CLC 14**
See also CA 9-12R; 77-80; CANR 19; DLB 11, 48; SATA 2, 44; SATA-Obit 24

**McGinniss, Joe** 1942- ............ **CLC 32**
See also AITN 2; BEST 89:2; CA 25-28R; CANR 26; INT CANR-26

McGivern, Maureen Daly
See Daly, Maureen

McGrath, Patrick 1950-.......... **CLC 55**
See also CA 136

McGrath, Thomas (Matthew)
1916-1990 .... **CLC 28, 59; DAM POET**
See also CA 9-12R; 132; CANR 6, 33;
MTCW; SATA 41; SATA-Obit 66

McGuane, Thomas (Francis III)
1939-................**CLC 3, 7, 18, 45**
See also AITN 2; CA 49-52; CANR 5, 24,
49; DLB 2; DLBY 80; INT CANR-24;
MTCW

McGuckian, Medbh
1950-.......... **CLC 48; DAM POET**
See also CA 143; DLB 40

McHale, Tom 1942(?)-1982....... **CLC 3, 5**
See also AITN 1; CA 77-80; 106

McIlvanney, William 1936-........ **CLC 42**
See also CA 25-28R; DLB 14

McIlwraith, Maureen Mollie Hunter
See Hunter, Mollie
See also SATA 2

McInerney, Jay
1955-............ **CLC 34; DAM POP**
See also AAYA 18; CA 116; 123;
CANR 45; INT 123

McIntyre, Vonda N(eel) 1948- ..... **CLC 18**
See also CA 81-84; CANR 17, 34; MTCW

McKay, Claude
........**TCLC 7, 41; BLC; DAB; PC 2**
See also McKay, Festus Claudius
See also DLB 4, 45, 51, 117

McKay, Festus Claudius 1889-1948
See McKay, Claude
See also BW 1; CA 104; 124; DA; DAC;
DAM MST, MULT, NOV, POET;
MTCW; WLC

McKuen, Rod 1933-............. **CLC 1, 3**
See also AITN 1; CA 41-44R; CANR 40

McLoughlin, R. B.
See Mencken, H(enry) L(ouis)

McLuhan, (Herbert) Marshall
1911-1980 ............... **CLC 37, 83**
See also CA 9-12R; 102; CANR 12, 34;
DLB 88; INT CANR-12; MTCW

McMillan, Terry (L.)
1951- ....... **CLC 50, 61; DAM MULT,**
**NOV, POP**
See also BW 2; CA 140

McMurtry, Larry (Jeff)
1936- .......... **CLC 2, 3, 7, 11, 27, 44;**
**DAM NOV, POP**
See also AAYA 15; AITN 2; BEST 89:2;
CA 5-8R; CANR 19, 43;
CDALB 1968-1988; DLB 2, 143;
DLBY 80, 87; MTCW

McNally, T. M. 1961- ............ **CLC 82**

McNally, Terrence
1939-... **CLC 4, 7, 41, 91; DAM DRAM**
See also CA 45-48; CANR 2; DLB 7

McNamer, Deirdre 1950-.......... **CLC 70**

McNeile, Herman Cyril 1888-1937
See Sapper
See also DLB 77

McNickle, (William) D'Arcy
1904-1977 ...... **CLC 89; DAM MULT**
See also CA 9-12R; 85-88; CANR 5, 45;
NNAL; SATA-Obit 22

McPhee, John (Angus) 1931- ...... **CLC 36**
See also BEST 90:1; CA 65-68; CANR 20,
46; MTCW

McPherson, James Alan
1943-.....................**CLC 19, 77**
See also BW 1; CA 25-28R; CAAS 17;
CANR 24; DLB 38; MTCW

McPherson, William (Alexander)
1933-.....................**CLC 34**
See also CA 69-72; CANR 28;
INT CANR-28

Mead, Margaret 1901-1978........ **CLC 37**
See also AITN 1; CA 1-4R; 81-84;
CANR 4; MTCW; SATA-Obit 20

Meaker, Marijane (Agnes) 1927-
See Kerr, M. E.
See also CA 107; CANR 37; INT 107;
JRDA; MAICYA; MTCW; SATA 20, 61

Medoff, Mark (Howard)
1940- ........ **CLC 6, 23; DAM DRAM**
See also AITN 1; CA 53-56; CANR 5;
DLB 7; INT CANR-5

Medvedev, P. N.
See Bakhtin, Mikhail Mikhailovich

Meged, Aharon
See Megged, Aharon

Meged, Aron
See Megged, Aharon

Megged, Aharon 1920-............. **CLC 9**
See also CA 49-52; CAAS 13; CANR 1

Mehta, Ved (Parkash) 1934-....... **CLC 37**
See also CA 1-4R; CANR 2, 23; MTCW

Melanter
See Blackmore, R(ichard) D(oddridge)

Melikow, Loris
See Hofmannsthal, Hugo von

Melmoth, Sebastian
See Wilde, Oscar (Fingal O'Flahertie Wills)

Meltzer, Milton 1915-............ **CLC 26**
See also AAYA 8; CA 13-16R; CANR 38;
CLR 13; DLB 61; JRDA; MAICYA;
SAAS 1; SATA 1, 50, 80

Melville, Herman
1819-1891 ..... **NCLC 3, 12, 29, 45, 49;**
**DA; DAB; DAC; DAM MST, NOV;**
**SSC 1, 17; WLC**
See also CDALB 1640-1865; DLB 3, 74;
SATA 59

Menander
c. 342B.C.-c. 292B.C........ **CMLC 9;**
**DAM DRAM; DC 3**

Mencken, H(enry) L(ouis)
1880-1956 .................. **TCLC 13**
See also CA 105; 125; CDALB 1917-1929;
DLB 11, 29, 63, 137; MTCW

Mercer, David
1928-1980 ....... **CLC 5; DAM DRAM**
See also CA 9-12R; 102; CANR 23;
DLB 13; MTCW

Merchant, Paul
See Ellison, Harlan (Jay)

Meredith, George
1828-1909 .. **TCLC 17, 43; DAM POET**
See also CA 117; CDBLB 1832-1890;
DLB 18, 35, 57, 159

Meredith, William (Morris)
1919- .. **CLC 4, 13, 22, 55; DAM POET**
See also CA 9-12R; CAAS 14; CANR 6, 40;
DLB 5

Merezhkovsky, Dmitry Sergeyevich
1865-1941 .................. **TCLC 29**

Merimee, Prosper
1803-1870 ............ **NCLC 6; SSC 7**
See also DLB 119

Merkin, Daphne 1954-............ **CLC 44**
See also CA 123

Merlin, Arthur
See Blish, James (Benjamin)

Merrill, James (Ingram)
1926-1995 .... **CLC 2, 3, 6, 8, 13, 18, 34,**
**91; DAM POET**
See also CA 13-16R; 147; CANR 10, 49;
DLB 5, 165; DLBY 85; INT CANR-10;
MTCW

Merriman, Alex
See Silverberg, Robert

Merritt, E. B.
See Waddington, Miriam

Merton, Thomas
1915-1968 .. **CLC 1, 3, 11, 34, 83; PC 10**
See also CA 5-8R; 25-28R; CANR 22, 53;
DLB 48; DLBY 81; MTCW

Merwin, W(illiam) S(tanley)
1927- ...... **CLC 1, 2, 3, 5, 8, 13, 18, 45,**
**88; DAM POET**
See also CA 13-16R; CANR 15, 51; DLB 5;
INT CANR-15; MTCW

Metcalf, John 1938-.............. **CLC 37**
See also CA 113; DLB 60

Metcalf, Suzanne
See Baum, L(yman) Frank

Mew, Charlotte (Mary)
1870-1928 .................. **TCLC 8**
See also CA 105; DLB 19, 135

Mewshaw, Michael 1943-.......... **CLC 9**
See also CA 53-56; CANR 7, 47; DLBY 80

Meyer, June
See Jordan, June

Meyer, Lynn
See Slavitt, David R(ytman)

Meyer-Meyrink, Gustav 1868-1932
See Meyrink, Gustav
See also CA 117

Meyers, Jeffrey 1939- ............ **CLC 39**
See also CA 73-76; DLB 111

Meynell, Alice (Christina Gertrude Thompson)
1847-1922 .................. **TCLC 6**
See also CA 104; DLB 19, 98

Meyrink, Gustav ................ **TCLC 21**
See also Meyer-Meyrink, Gustav
See also DLB 81

Michaels, Leonard
1933- ............. **CLC 6, 25; SSC 16**
See also CA 61-64; CANR 21; DLB 130;
MTCW

Michaux, Henri  1899-1984 . . . . . **CLC 8, 19**
See also CA 85-88; 114

Michelangelo  1475-1564. . . . . . . . . . . **LC 12**

Michelet, Jules  1798-1874. . . . . . **NCLC 31**

Michener, James A(lbert)
1907(?)- . . . . . . . . . . **CLC 1, 5, 11, 29, 60;**
**DAM NOV, POP**
See also AITN 1; BEST 90:1; CA 5-8R;
CANR 21, 45; DLB 6; MTCW

Mickiewicz, Adam  1798-1855 . . . . . **NCLC 3**

Middleton, Christopher  1926- . . . . . . **CLC 13**
See also CA 13-16R; CANR 29; DLB 40

Middleton, Richard (Barham)
1882-1911 . . . . . . . . . . . . . . . . . **TCLC 56**
See also DLB 156

Middleton, Stanley  1919- . . . . . . . . **CLC 7, 38**
See also CA 25-28R; CAAS 23; CANR 21,
46; DLB 14

Middleton, Thomas
1580-1627 . . . . . . . **LC 33; DAM DRAM,**
**MST; DC 5**
See also DLB 58

Migueis, Jose Rodrigues  1901- . . . . . **CLC 10**

Mikszath, Kalman  1847-1910 . . . . . **TCLC 31**

Miles, Josephine
1911-1985 . . . . . . . . **CLC 1, 2, 14, 34, 39;**
**DAM POET**
See also CA 1-4R; 116; CANR 2; DLB 48

Militant
See Sandburg, Carl (August)

Mill, John Stuart  1806-1873 . . . . . **NCLC 11**
See also CDBLB 1832-1890; DLB 55

Millar, Kenneth
1915-1983 . . . . . . . . **CLC 14; DAM POP**
See also Macdonald, Ross
See also CA 9-12R; 110; CANR 16; DLB 2;
DLBD 6; DLBY 83; MTCW

Millay, E. Vincent
See Millay, Edna St. Vincent

Millay, Edna St. Vincent
1892-1950 . . . . . . **TCLC 4, 49; DA; DAB;**
**DAC; DAM MST, POET; PC 6**
See also CA 104; 130; CDALB 1917-1929;
DLB 45; MTCW

Miller, Arthur
1915- . . . . **CLC 1, 2, 6, 10, 15, 26, 47, 78;**
**DA; DAB; DAC; DAM DRAM, MST;**
**DC 1; WLC**
See also AAYA 15; AITN 1; CA 1-4R;
CABS 3; CANR 2, 30;
CDALB 1941-1968; DLB 7; MTCW

Miller, Henry (Valentine)
1891-1980 . . . . **CLC 1, 2, 4, 9, 14, 43, 84;**
**DA; DAB; DAC; DAM MST, NOV;**
**WLC**
See also CA 9-12R; 97-100; CANR 33;
CDALB 1929-1941; DLB 4, 9; DLBY 80;
MTCW

Miller, Jason  1939(?)- . . . . . . . . . . . . **CLC 2**
See also AITN 1; CA 73-76; DLB 7

Miller, Sue  1943- . . . . . **CLC 44; DAM POP**
See also BEST 90:3; CA 139; DLB 143

Miller, Walter M(ichael, Jr.)
1923- . . . . . . . . . . . . . . . . . . . **CLC 4, 30**
See also CA 85-88; DLB 8

Millett, Kate  1934- . . . . . . . . . . . . . . **CLC 67**
See also AITN 1; CA 73-76; CANR 32, 53;
MTCW

Millhauser, Steven  1943- . . . . . . . **CLC 21, 54**
See also CA 110; 111; DLB 2; INT 111

Millin, Sarah Gertrude  1889-1968 . . **CLC 49**
See also CA 102; 93-96

Milne, A(lan) A(lexander)
1882-1956 . . . . . . . **TCLC 6; DAB; DAC;**
**DAM MST**
See also CA 104; 133; CLR 1, 26; DLB 10,
77, 100, 160; MAICYA; MTCW;
YABC 1

Milner, Ron(ald)
1938- . . . . . . . . **CLC 56; BLC; DAM MULT**
See also AITN 1; BW 1; CA 73-76;
CANR 24; DLB 38; MTCW

Milosz, Czeslaw
1911- . . . . . . . . **CLC 5, 11, 22, 31, 56, 82;**
**DAM MST, POET; PC 8**
See also CA 81-84; CANR 23, 51; MTCW

Milton, John
1608-1674 . . . . . . **LC 9; DA; DAB; DAC;**
**DAM MST, POET; WLC**
See also CDBLB 1660-1789; DLB 131, 151

Min, Anchee  1957- . . . . . . . . . . . . . . **CLC 86**
See also CA 146

Minehaha, Cornelius
See Wedekind, (Benjamin) Frank(lin)

Miner, Valerie  1947- . . . . . . . . . . . . . **CLC 40**
See also CA 97-100

Minimo, Duca
See D'Annunzio, Gabriele

Minot, Susan  1956- . . . . . . . . . . . . . . **CLC 44**
See also CA 134

Minus, Ed  1938- . . . . . . . . . . . . . . . . **CLC 39**

Miranda, Javier
See Bioy Casares, Adolfo

Mirbeau, Octave  1848-1917. . . . . . . **TCLC 55**
See also DLB 123

Miro (Ferrer), Gabriel (Francisco Victor)
1879-1930 . . . . . . . . . . . . . . . . . . **TCLC 5**
See also CA 104

Mishima, Yukio
. . . . . . . **CLC 2, 4, 6, 9, 27; DC 1; SSC 4**
See also Hiraoka, Kimitake

Mistral, Frederic  1830-1914 . . . . . . **TCLC 51**
See also CA 122

Mistral, Gabriela. . . . . . . . . . . **TCLC 2; HLC**
See also Godoy Alcayaga, Lucila

Mistry, Rohinton  1952- . . . . . . **CLC 71; DAC**
See also CA 141

Mitchell, Clyde
See Ellison, Harlan (Jay); Silverberg, Robert

Mitchell, James Leslie  1901-1935
See Gibbon, Lewis Grassic
See also CA 104; DLB 15

Mitchell, Joni  1943- . . . . . . . . . . . . . . **CLC 12**
See also CA 112

Mitchell, Margaret (Munnerlyn)
1900-1949 . . . . . . **TCLC 11; DAM NOV,**
**POP**
See also CA 109; 125; DLB 9; MTCW

Mitchell, Peggy
See Mitchell, Margaret (Munnerlyn)

Mitchell, S(ilas) Weir  1829-1914 . . **TCLC 36**

Mitchell, W(illiam) O(rmond)
1914- . . . . . . **CLC 25; DAC; DAM MST**
See also CA 77-80; CANR 15, 43; DLB 88

Mitford, Mary Russell  1787-1855. . **NCLC 4**
See also DLB 110, 116

Mitford, Nancy  1904-1973. . . . . . . . **CLC 44**
See also CA 9-12R

Miyamoto, Yuriko  1899-1951 . . . . . **TCLC 37**

Mo, Timothy (Peter)  1950(?)- . . . . . . **CLC 46**
See also CA 117; MTCW

Modarressi, Taghi (M.)  1931- . . . . . . **CLC 44**
See also CA 121; 134; INT 134

Modiano, Patrick (Jean)  1945- . . . . . **CLC 18**
See also CA 85-88; CANR 17, 40; DLB 83

Moerck, Paal
See Roelvaag, O(le) E(dvart)

Mofolo, Thomas (Mokopu)
1875(?)-1948 . . . . . . . . . . **TCLC 22; BLC;**
**DAM MULT**
See also CA 121

Mohr, Nicholasa
1935- . . . . . **CLC 12; DAM MULT; HLC**
See also AAYA 8; CA 49-52; CANR 1, 32;
CLR 22; DLB 145; HW; JRDA; SAAS 8;
SATA 8

Mojtabai, A(nn) G(race)
1938- . . . . . . . . . . . . . . **CLC 5, 9, 15, 29**
See also CA 85-88

Moliere
1622-1673 . . . . . **LC 28; DA; DAB; DAC;**
**DAM DRAM, MST; WLC**

Molin, Charles
See Mayne, William (James Carter)

Molnar, Ferenc
1878-1952 . . . . . **TCLC 20; DAM DRAM**
See also CA 109

Momaday, N(avarre) Scott
1934- . . . . . **CLC 2, 19, 85, 95; DA; DAB;**
**DAC; DAM MST, MULT, NOV, POP**
See also AAYA 11; CA 25-28R; CANR 14,
34; DLB 143; INT CANR-14; MTCW;
NNAL; SATA 48; SATA-Brief 30

Monette, Paul  1945-1995. . . . . . . . . . **CLC 82**
See also CA 139; 147

Monroe, Harriet  1860-1936. . . . . . . **TCLC 12**
See also CA 109; DLB 54, 91

Monroe, Lyle
See Heinlein, Robert A(nson)

Montagu, Elizabeth  1917- . . . . . . . . **NCLC 7**
See also CA 9-12R

Montagu, Mary (Pierrepont) Wortley
1689-1762 . . . . . . . . . . . . . . **LC 9; PC 16**
See also DLB 95, 101

Montagu, W. H.
See Coleridge, Samuel Taylor

Montague, John (Patrick)
1929- . . . . . . . . . . . . . . . . . . . **CLC 13, 46**
See also CA 9-12R; CANR 9; DLB 40;
MTCW

                                                    

**Montaigne, Michel (Eyquem) de**
1533-1592 ..... **LC 8; DA; DAB; DAC;
DAM MST; WLC**

**Montale, Eugenio**
1896-1981 ....... **CLC 7, 9, 18; PC 13**
See also CA 17-20R; 104; CANR 30;
DLB 114; MTCW

**Montesquieu, Charles-Louis de Secondat**
1689-1755 ................... **LC 7**

**Montgomery, (Robert) Bruce**   1921-1978
See Crispin, Edmund
See also CA 104

**Montgomery, L(ucy) M(aud)**
1874-1942 ............ **TCLC 51; DAC;
DAM MST**
See also AAYA 12; CA 108; 137; CLR 8;
DLB 92; DLBD 14; JRDA; MAICYA;
YABC 1

**Montgomery, Marion H., Jr.**   1925-.. **CLC 7**
See also AITN 1; CA 1-4R; CANR 3, 48;
DLB 6

**Montgomery, Max**
See Davenport, Guy (Mattison, Jr.)

**Montherlant, Henry (Milon) de**
1896-1972 .... **CLC 8, 19; DAM DRAM**
See also CA 85-88; 37-40R; DLB 72;
MTCW

**Monty Python**
See Chapman, Graham; Cleese, John
(Marwood); Gilliam, Terry (Vance); Idle,
Eric; Jones, Terence Graham Parry; Palin,
Michael (Edward)
See also AAYA 7

**Moodie, Susanna (Strickland)**
1803-1885 ................. **NCLC 14**
See also DLB 99

**Mooney, Edward**   1951-
See Mooney, Ted
See also CA 130

**Mooney, Ted** ...................... **CLC 25**
See also Mooney, Edward

**Moorcock, Michael (John)**
1939- .................. **CLC 5, 27, 58**
See also CA 45-48; CAAS 5; CANR 2, 17,
38; DLB 14; MTCW

**Moore, Brian**
1921- ...... **CLC 1, 3, 5, 7, 8, 19, 32, 90;
DAB; DAC; DAM MST**
See also CA 1-4R; CANR 1, 25, 42; MTCW

**Moore, Edward**
See Muir, Edwin

**Moore, George Augustus**
1852-1933 .......... **TCLC 7; SSC 19**
See also CA 104; DLB 10, 18, 57, 135

**Moore, Lorrie** .............. **CLC 39, 45, 68**
See also Moore, Marie Lorena

**Moore, Marianne (Craig)**
1887-1972 .... **CLC 1, 2, 4, 8, 10, 13, 19,
47; DA; DAB; DAC; DAM MST, POET;
PC 4**
See also CA 1-4R; 33-36R; CANR 3;
CDALB 1929-1941; DLB 45; DLBD 7;
MTCW; SATA 20

**Moore, Marie Lorena**   1957-
See Moore, Lorrie
See also CA 116; CANR 39

**Moore, Thomas**   1779-1852........ **NCLC 6**
See also DLB 96, 144

**Morand, Paul**   1888-1976 .. **CLC 41; SSC 22**
See also CA 69-72; DLB 65

**Morante, Elsa**   1918-1985........ **CLC 8, 47**
See also CA 85-88; 117; CANR 35; MTCW

**Moravia, Alberto**....... **CLC 2, 7, 11, 27, 46**
See also Pincherle, Alberto

**More, Hannah**   1745-1833 ....... **NCLC 27**
See also DLB 107, 109, 116, 158

**More, Henry**   1614-1687............ **LC 9**
See also DLB 126

**More, Sir Thomas**   1478-1535 .... **LC 10, 32**

**Moreas, Jean**.................... **TCLC 18**
See also Papadiamantopoulos, Johannes

**Morgan, Berry**   1919- .............. **CLC 6**
See also CA 49-52; DLB 6

**Morgan, Claire**
See Highsmith, (Mary) Patricia

**Morgan, Edwin (George)**   1920-..... **CLC 31**
See also CA 5-8R; CANR 3, 43; DLB 27

**Morgan, (George) Frederick**
1922- ...................... **CLC 23**
See also CA 17-20R; CANR 21

**Morgan, Harriet**
See Mencken, H(enry) L(ouis)

**Morgan, Jane**
See Cooper, James Fenimore

**Morgan, Janet**   1945- ............. **CLC 39**
See also CA 65-68

**Morgan, Lady**   1776(?)-1859...... **NCLC 29**
See also DLB 116, 158

**Morgan, Robin**   1941-.............. **CLC 2**
See also CA 69-72; CANR 29; MTCW;
SATA 80

**Morgan, Scott**
See Kuttner, Henry

**Morgan, Seth**   1949(?)-1990 ........ **CLC 65**
See also CA 132

**Morgenstern, Christian**
1871-1914 ................. **TCLC 8**
See also CA 105

**Morgenstern, S.**
See Goldman, William (W.)

**Moricz, Zsigmond**   1879-1942 ..... **TCLC 33**

**Morike, Eduard (Friedrich)**
1804-1875 ................. **NCLC 10**
See also DLB 133

**Mori Ogai** ...................... **TCLC 14**
See also Mori Rintaro

**Mori Rintaro**   1862-1922
See Mori Ogai
See also CA 110

**Moritz, Karl Philipp**   1756-1793 ...... **LC 2**
See also DLB 94

**Morland, Peter Henry**
See Faust, Frederick (Schiller)

**Morren, Theophil**
See Hofmannsthal, Hugo von

**Morris, Bill**   1952-............... **CLC 76**

**Morris, Julian**
See West, Morris L(anglo)

**Morris, Steveland Judkins**   1950(?)-
See Wonder, Stevie
See also CA 111

**Morris, William**   1834-1896 ....... **NCLC 4**
See also CDBLB 1832-1890; DLB 18, 35,
57, 156

**Morris, Wright**   1910-... **CLC 1, 3, 7, 18, 37**
See also CA 9-12R; CANR 21; DLB 2;
DLBY 81; MTCW

**Morrison, Chloe Anthony Wofford**
See Morrison, Toni

**Morrison, James Douglas**   1943-1971
See Morrison, Jim
See also CA 73-76; CANR 40

**Morrison, Jim** ..................... **CLC 17**
See also Morrison, James Douglas

**Morrison, Toni**
1931- ........ **CLC 4, 10, 22, 55, 81, 87;
BLC; DA; DAB; DAC; DAM MST,
MULT, NOV, POP**
See also AAYA 1; BW 2; CA 29-32R;
CANR 27, 42; CDALB 1968-1988;
DLB 6, 33, 143; DLBY 81; MTCW;
SATA 57

**Morrison, Van**   1945- ............. **CLC 21**
See also CA 116

**Mortimer, John (Clifford)**
1923- ...... **CLC 28, 43; DAM DRAM,
POP**
See also CA 13-16R; CANR 21;
CDBLB 1960 to Present; DLB 13;
INT CANR-21; MTCW

**Mortimer, Penelope (Ruth)**   1918-.... **CLC 5**
See also CA 57-60; CANR 45

**Morton, Anthony**
See Creasey, John

**Mosher, Howard Frank**   1943-...... **CLC 62**
See also CA 139

**Mosley, Nicholas**   1923-........ **CLC 43, 70**
See also CA 69-72; CANR 41; DLB 14

**Moss, Howard**
1922-1987 .......... **CLC 7, 14, 45, 50;
DAM POET**
See also CA 1-4R; 123; CANR 1, 44;
DLB 5

**Mossgiel, Rab**
See Burns, Robert

**Motion, Andrew (Peter)**   1952-...... **CLC 47**
See also CA 146; DLB 40

**Motley, Willard (Francis)**
1909-1965 .................. **CLC 18**
See also BW 1; CA 117; 106; DLB 76, 143

**Motoori, Norinaga**   1730-1801 .... **NCLC 45**

**Mott, Michael (Charles Alston)**
1930- .................... **CLC 15, 34**
See also CA 5-8R; CAAS 7; CANR 7, 29

**Mountain Wolf Woman**
1884-1960 .................. **CLC 92**
See also CA 144; NNAL

**Moure, Erin**   1955- .............. **CLC 88**
See also CA 113; DLB 60

**Nervo, (Jose) Amado (Ruiz de)**
1870-1919 . . . . . . . . . . . . . . . . . **TCLC 11**
See also CA 109; 131; HW

**Nessi, Pio Baroja y**
See Baroja (y Nessi), Pio

**Nestroy, Johann** 1801-1862 . . . . . . **NCLC 42**
See also DLB 133

**Neufeld, John (Arthur)** 1938- . . . . . . **CLC 17**
See also AAYA 11; CA 25-28R; CANR 11,
37; MAICYA; SAAS 3; SATA 6, 81

**Neville, Emily Cheney** 1919- . . . . . . . **CLC 12**
See also CA 5-8R; CANR 3, 37; JRDA;
MAICYA; SAAS 2; SATA 1

**Newbound, Bernard Slade** 1930-
See Slade, Bernard
See also CA 81-84; CANR 49;
DAM DRAM

**Newby, P(ercy) H(oward)**
1918- . . . . . . . . . . **CLC 2, 13; DAM NOV**
See also CA 5-8R; CANR 32; DLB 15;
MTCW

**Newlove, Donald** 1928- . . . . . . . . . . . **CLC 6**
See also CA 29-32R; CANR 25

**Newlove, John (Herbert)** 1938- . . . . . **CLC 14**
See also CA 21-24R; CANR 9, 25

**Newman, Charles** 1938- . . . . . . . . . . **CLC 2, 8**
See also CA 21-24R

**Newman, Edwin (Harold)** 1919- . . . . **CLC 14**
See also AITN 1; CA 69-72; CANR 5

**Newman, John Henry**
1801-1890 . . . . . . . . . . . . . . . . . **NCLC 38**
See also DLB 18, 32, 55

**Newton, Suzanne** 1936- . . . . . . . . . . . **CLC 35**
See also CA 41-44R; CANR 14; JRDA;
SATA 5, 77

**Nexo, Martin Andersen**
1869-1954 . . . . . . . . . . . . . . . . . **TCLC 43**

**Nezval, Vitezslav** 1900-1958 . . . . . . **TCLC 44**
See also CA 123

**Ng, Fae Myenne** 1957(?)- . . . . . . . . . **CLC 81**
See also CA 146

**Ngema, Mbongeni** 1955- . . . . . . . . . . **CLC 57**
See also BW 2; CA 143

**Ngugi, James T(hiong'o)** . . . . . . . . **CLC 3, 7, 13**
See also Ngugi wa Thiong'o

**Ngugi wa Thiong'o**
1938- . . . . . **CLC 36; BLC; DAM MULT,
NOV**
See also Ngugi, James T(hiong'o)
See also BW 2; CA 81-84; CANR 27;
DLB 125; MTCW

**Nichol, B(arrie) P(hillip)**
1944-1988 . . . . . . . . . . . . . . . . . . **CLC 18**
See also CA 53-56; DLB 53; SATA 66

**Nichols, John (Treadwell)** 1940- . . . . **CLC 38**
See also CA 9-12R; CAAS 2; CANR 6;
DLBY 82

**Nichols, Leigh**
See Koontz, Dean R(ay)

**Nichols, Peter (Richard)**
1927- . . . . . . . . . . . . . . . . . **CLC 5, 36, 65**
See also CA 104; CANR 33; DLB 13;
MTCW

**Nicolas, F. R. E.**
See Freeling, Nicolas

**Niedecker, Lorine**
1903-1970 . . . . **CLC 10, 42; DAM POET**
See also CA 25-28; CAP 2; DLB 48

**Nietzsche, Friedrich (Wilhelm)**
1844-1900 . . . . . . . . . . **TCLC 10, 18, 55**
See also CA 107; 121; DLB 129

**Nievo, Ippolito** 1831-1861 . . . . . . . **NCLC 22**

**Nightingale, Anne Redmon** 1943-
See Redmon, Anne
See also CA 103

**Nik. T. O.**
See Annensky, Innokenty Fyodorovich

**Nin, Anais**
1903-1977 . . . . . . **CLC 1, 4, 8, 11, 14, 60;
DAM NOV, POP; SSC 10**
See also AITN 2; CA 13-16R; 69-72;
CANR 22, 53; DLB 2, 4, 152; MTCW

**Nishiwaki, Junzaburo** 1894-1982 . . . . **PC 15**
See also CA 107

**Nissenson, Hugh** 1933- . . . . . . . . . . **CLC 4, 9**
See also CA 17-20R; CANR 27; DLB 28

**Niven, Larry** . . . . . . . . . . . . . . . . . . . **CLC 8**
See also Niven, Laurence Van Cott
See also DLB 8

**Niven, Laurence Van Cott** 1938-
See Niven, Larry
See also CA 21-24R; CAAS 12; CANR 14,
44; DAM POP; MTCW

**Nixon, Agnes Eckhardt** 1927- . . . . . . **CLC 21**
See also CA 110

**Nizan, Paul** 1905-1940 . . . . . . . . . . **TCLC 40**
See also DLB 72

**Nkosi, Lewis**
1936- . . . . . **CLC 45; BLC; DAM MULT**
See also BW 1; CA 65-68; CANR 27;
DLB 157

**Nodier, (Jean) Charles (Emmanuel)**
1780-1844 . . . . . . . . . . . . . . . . . **NCLC 19**
See also DLB 119

**Nolan, Christopher** 1965- . . . . . . . . . **CLC 58**
See also CA 111

**Noon, Jeff** 1957- . . . . . . . . . . . . . . . . **CLC 91**
See also CA 148

**Norden, Charles**
See Durrell, Lawrence (George)

**Nordhoff, Charles (Bernard)**
1887-1947 . . . . . . . . . . . . . . . . . **TCLC 23**
See also CA 108; DLB 9; SATA 23

**Norfolk, Lawrence** 1963- . . . . . . . . . **CLC 76**
See also CA 144

**Norman, Marsha**
1947- . . . . . . . . . **CLC 28; DAM DRAM**
See also CA 105; CABS 3; CANR 41;
DLBY 84

**Norris, Benjamin Franklin, Jr.**
1870-1902 . . . . . . . . . . . . . . . . . **TCLC 24**
See also Norris, Frank
See also CA 110

**Norris, Frank**
See Norris, Benjamin Franklin, Jr.
See also CDALB 1865-1917; DLB 12, 71

**Norris, Leslie** 1921- . . . . . . . . . . . . . **CLC 14**
See also CA 11-12; CANR 14; CAP 1;
DLB 27

**North, Andrew**
See Norton, Andre

**North, Anthony**
See Koontz, Dean R(ay)

**North, Captain George**
See Stevenson, Robert Louis (Balfour)

**North, Milou**
See Erdrich, Louise

**Northrup, B. A.**
See Hubbard, L(afayette) Ron(ald)

**North Staffs**
See Hulme, T(homas) E(rnest)

**Norton, Alice Mary**
See Norton, Andre
See also MAICYA; SATA 1, 43

**Norton, Andre** 1912- . . . . . . . . . . . . . **CLC 12**
See also Norton, Alice Mary
See also AAYA 14; CA 1-4R; CANR 2, 31;
DLB 8, 52; JRDA; MTCW

**Norton, Caroline** 1808-1877 . . . . . . **NCLC 47**
See also DLB 21, 159

**Norway, Nevil Shute** 1899-1960
See Shute, Nevil
See also CA 102; 93-96

**Norwid, Cyprian Kamil**
1821-1883 . . . . . . . . . . . . . . . . . **NCLC 17**

**Nosille, Nabrah**
See Ellison, Harlan (Jay)

**Nossack, Hans Erich** 1901-1978 . . . . . **CLC 6**
See also CA 93-96; 85-88; DLB 69

**Nostradamus** 1503-1566 . . . . . . . . . . . **LC 27**

**Nosu, Chuji**
See Ozu, Yasujiro

**Notenburg, Eleanora (Genrikhovna) von**
See Guro, Elena

**Nova, Craig** 1945- . . . . . . . . . . . . . . **CLC 7, 31**
See also CA 45-48; CANR 2, 53

**Novak, Joseph**
See Kosinski, Jerzy (Nikodem)

**Novalis** 1772-1801 . . . . . . . . . . . . . **NCLC 13**
See also DLB 90

**Nowlan, Alden (Albert)**
1933-1983 . . **CLC 15; DAC; DAM MST**
See also CA 9-12R; CANR 5; DLB 53

**Noyes, Alfred** 1880-1958 . . . . . . . . . . **TCLC 7**
See also CA 104; DLB 20

**Nunn, Kem** 19(?)- . . . . . . . . . . . . . . . **CLC 34**

**Nye, Robert**
1939- . . . . . . . . **CLC 13, 42; DAM NOV**
See also CA 33-36R; CANR 29; DLB 14;
MTCW; SATA 6

**Nyro, Laura** 1947- . . . . . . . . . . . . . . **CLC 17**

**Oates, Joyce Carol**
1938- . . . . . . **CLC 1, 2, 3, 6, 9, 11, 15, 19,
33, 52; DA; DAB; DAC; DAM MST,
NOV, POP; SSC 6; WLC**
See also AAYA 15; AITN 1; BEST 89:2;
CA 5-8R; CANR 25, 45;
CDALB 1968-1988; DLB 2, 5, 130;
DLBY 81; INT CANR-25; MTCW

**O'Brien, Darcy** 1939- . . . . . . . . . . . . . **CLC 11**
See also CA 21-24R; CANR 8

**O'Brien, E. G.**
See Clarke, Arthur C(harles)

**O'Brien, Edna**
1936-......... CLC 3, 5, 8, 13, 36, 65;
DAM NOV; SSC 10
See also CA 1-4R; CANR 6, 41;
CDBLB 1960 to Present; DLB 14;
MTCW

**O'Brien, Fitz-James** 1828-1862... NCLC 21
See also DLB 74

**O'Brien, Flann**....... CLC 1, 4, 5, 7, 10, 47
See also O Nuallain, Brian

**O'Brien, Richard** 1942-........... CLC 17
See also CA 124

**O'Brien, Tim**
1946-....... CLC 7, 19, 40; DAM POP
See also AAYA 16; CA 85-88; CANR 40;
DLB 152; DLBD 9; DLBY 80

**Obstfelder, Sigbjoern** 1866-1900... TCLC 23
See also CA 123

**O'Casey, Sean**
1880-1964...... CLC 1, 5, 9, 11, 15, 88;
DAB; DAC; DAM DRAM, MST
See also CA 89-92; CDBLB 1914-1945;
DLB 10; MTCW

**O'Cathasaigh, Sean**
See O'Casey, Sean

**Ochs, Phil** 1940-1976............. CLC 17
See also CA 65-68

**O'Connor, Edwin (Greene)**
1918-1968 .................. CLC 14
See also CA 93-96; 25-28R

**O'Connor, (Mary) Flannery**
1925-1964 .... CLC 1, 2, 3, 6, 10, 13, 15,
21, 66; DA; DAB; DAC; DAM MST,
NOV; SSC 1, 23; WLC
See also AAYA 7; CA 1-4R; CANR 3, 41;
CDALB 1941-1968; DLB 2, 152;
DLBD 12; DLBY 80; MTCW

**O'Connor, Frank**.......... CLC 23; SSC 5
See also O'Donovan, Michael John
See also DLB 162

**O'Dell, Scott** 1898-1989........... CLC 30
See also AAYA 3; CA 61-64; 129;
CANR 12, 30; CLR 1, 16; DLB 52;
JRDA; MAICYA; SATA 12, 60

**Odets, Clifford**
1906-1963 ... CLC 2, 28; DAM DRAM;
DC 6
See also CA 85-88; DLB 7, 26; MTCW

**O'Doherty, Brian** 1934-........... CLC 76
See also CA 105

**O'Donnell, K. M.**
See Malzberg, Barry N(athaniel)

**O'Donnell, Lawrence**
See Kuttner, Henry

**O'Donovan, Michael John**
1903-1966 ............... CLC 14
See also O'Connor, Frank
See also CA 93-96

**Oe, Kenzaburo**
1935-..... CLC 10, 36, 86; DAM NOV;
SSC 20
See also CA 97-100; CANR 36, 50;
DLBY 94; MTCW

**O'Faolain, Julia** 1932-....... CLC 6, 19, 47
See also CA 81-84; CAAS 2; CANR 12;
DLB 14; MTCW

**O'Faolain, Sean**
1900-1991 ....... CLC 1, 7, 14, 32, 70;
SSC 13
See also CA 61-64; 134; CANR 12;
DLB 15, 162; MTCW

**O'Flaherty, Liam**
1896-1984 .......... CLC 5, 34; SSC 6
See also CA 101; 113; CANR 35; DLB 36,
162; DLBY 84; MTCW

**Ogilvy, Gavin**
See Barrie, J(ames) M(atthew)

**O'Grady, Standish James**
1846-1928 .................. TCLC 5
See also CA 104

**O'Grady, Timothy** 1951-.......... CLC 59
See also CA 138

**O'Hara, Frank**
1926-1966 .......... CLC 2, 5, 13, 78;
DAM POET
See also CA 9-12R; 25-28R; CANR 33;
DLB 5, 16; MTCW

**O'Hara, John (Henry)**
1905-1970 ....... CLC 1, 2, 3, 6, 11, 42;
DAM NOV; SSC 15
See also CA 5-8R; 25-28R; CANR 31;
CDALB 1929-1941; DLB 9, 86; DLBD 2;
MTCW

**O Hehir, Diana** 1922- ............. CLC 41
See also CA 93-96

**Okigbo, Christopher (Ifenayichukwu)**
1932-1967 ......... CLC 25, 84; BLC;
DAM MULT, POET; PC 7
See also BW 1; CA 77-80; DLB 125;
MTCW

**Okri, Ben** 1959- .................. CLC 87
See also BW 2; CA 130; 138; DLB 157;
INT 138

**Olds, Sharon**
1942- ..... CLC 32, 39, 85; DAM POET
See also CA 101; CANR 18, 41; DLB 120

**Oldstyle, Jonathan**
See Irving, Washington

**Olesha, Yuri (Karlovich)**
1899-1960 ................... CLC 8
See also CA 85-88

**Oliphant, Laurence**
1829(?)-1888 ............... NCLC 47
See also DLB 18, 166

**Oliphant, Margaret (Oliphant Wilson)**
1828-1897 ................. NCLC 11
See also DLB 18, 159

**Oliver, Mary** 1935-............ CLC 19, 34
See also CA 21-24R; CANR 9, 43; DLB 5

**Olivier, Laurence (Kerr)**
1907-1989 .................. CLC 20
See also CA 111; 150; 129

**Olsen, Tillie**
1913- ..... CLC 4, 13; DA; DAB; DAC;
DAM MST; SSC 11
See also CA 1-4R; CANR 1, 43; DLB 28;
DLBY 80; MTCW

**Olson, Charles (John)**
1910-1970 ..... CLC 1, 2, 5, 6, 9, 11, 29;
DAM POET
See also CA 13-16; 25-28R; CABS 2;
CANR 35; CAP 1; DLB 5, 16; MTCW

**Olson, Toby** 1937- .............. CLC 28
See also CA 65-68; CANR 9, 31

**Olyesha, Yuri**
See Olesha, Yuri (Karlovich)

**Ondaatje, (Philip) Michael**
1943- ........ CLC 14, 29, 51, 76; DAB;
DAC; DAM MST
See also CA 77-80; CANR 42; DLB 60

**Oneal, Elizabeth** 1934-
See Oneal, Zibby
See also CA 106; CANR 28; MAICYA;
SATA 30, 82

**Oneal, Zibby** ..................... CLC 30
See also Oneal, Elizabeth
See also AAYA 5; CLR 13; JRDA

**O'Neill, Eugene (Gladstone)**
1888-1953 ...... TCLC 1, 6, 27, 49; DA;
DAB; DAC; DAM DRAM, MST; WLC
See also AITN 1; CA 110; 132;
CDALB 1929-1941; DLB 7; MTCW

**Onetti, Juan Carlos**
1909-1994 .... CLC 7, 10; DAM MULT,
NOV; SSC 23
See also CA 85-88; 145; CANR 32;
DLB 113; HW; MTCW

**O Nuallain, Brian** 1911-1966
See O'Brien, Flann
See also CA 21-22; 25-28R; CAP 2

**Oppen, George** 1908-1984 .... CLC 7, 13, 34
See also CA 13-16R; 113; CANR 8; DLB 5,
165

**Oppenheim, E(dward) Phillips**
1866-1946 .................. TCLC 45
See also CA 111; DLB 70

**Orlovitz, Gil** 1918-1973 ........... CLC 22
See also CA 77-80; 45-48; DLB 2, 5

**Orris**
See Ingelow, Jean

**Ortega y Gasset, Jose**
1883-1955 ..... TCLC 9; DAM MULT;
HLC
See also CA 106; 130; HW; MTCW

**Ortese, Anna Maria** 1914-........ CLC 89

**Ortiz, Simon J(oseph)**
1941- .... CLC 45; DAM MULT, POET
See also CA 134; DLB 120; NNAL

**Orton, Joe** ........... CLC 4, 13, 43; DC 3
See also Orton, John Kingsley
See also CDBLB 1960 to Present; DLB 13

**Orton, John Kingsley** 1933-1967
See Orton, Joe
See also CA 85-88; CANR 35;
DAM DRAM; MTCW

**Orwell, George**
.... TCLC 2, 6, 15, 31, 51; DAB; WLC
See also Blair, Eric (Arthur)
See also CDBLB 1945-1960; DLB 15, 98

**Osborne, David**
See Silverberg, Robert

**Osborne, George**
See Silverberg, Robert

**Osborne, John (James)**
1929-1994 ..... CLC 1, 2, 5, 11, 45; DA;
DAB; DAC; DAM DRAM, MST; WLC
See also CA 13-16R; 147; CANR 21;
CDBLB 1945-1960; DLB 13; MTCW

Osborne, Lawrence 1958- ......... **CLC 50**

Oshima, Nagisa 1932- ............ **CLC 20**
See also CA 116; 121

Oskison, John Milton
1874-1947 ..... **TCLC 35; DAM MULT**
See also CA 144; NNAL

Ossoli, Sarah Margaret (Fuller marchesa d')
1810-1850
See Fuller, Margaret
See also SATA 25

Ostrovsky, Alexander
1823-1886 .............. **NCLC 30, 57**

Otero, Blas de 1916-1979......... **CLC 11**
See also CA 89-92; DLB 134

Otto, Whitney 1955-.............. **CLC 70**
See also CA 140

Ouida......................... **TCLC 43**
See also De La Ramee, (Marie) Louise
See also DLB 18, 156

Ousmane, Sembene 1923- .... **CLC 66; BLC**
See also BW 1; CA 117; 125; MTCW

Ovid
43B.C.-18(?) ... **CMLC 7; DAM POET;
PC 2**

Owen, Hugh
See Faust, Frederick (Schiller)

Owen, Wilfred (Edward Salter)
1893-1918 ...... **TCLC 5, 27; DA; DAB;
DAC; DAM MST, POET; WLC**
See also CA 104; 141; CDBLB 1914-1945;
DLB 20

Owens, Rochelle 1936-............. **CLC 8**
See also CA 17-20R; CAAS 2; CANR 39

Oz, Amos
1939- ......... **CLC 5, 8, 11, 27, 33, 54;
DAM NOV**
See also CA 53-56; CANR 27, 47; MTCW

Ozick, Cynthia
1928- .... **CLC 3, 7, 28, 62; DAM NOV,
POP; SSC 15**
See also BEST 90:1; CA 17-20R; CANR 23;
DLB 28, 152; DLBY 82; INT CANR-23;
MTCW

Ozu, Yasujiro 1903-1963.......... **CLC 16**
See also CA 112

Pacheco, C.
See Pessoa, Fernando (Antonio Nogueira)

Pa Chin......................... **CLC 18**
See also Li Fei-kan

Pack, Robert 1929-............... **CLC 13**
See also CA 1-4R; CANR 3, 44; DLB 5

Padgett, Lewis
See Kuttner, Henry

Padilla (Lorenzo), Heberto 1932-... **CLC 38**
See also AITN 1; CA 123; 131; HW

Page, Jimmy 1944-............... **CLC 12**

Page, Louise 1955-............... **CLC 40**
See also CA 140

Page, P(atricia) K(athleen)
1916- .... **CLC 7, 18; DAC; DAM MST;
PC 12**
See also CA 53-56; CANR 4, 22; DLB 68;
MTCW

Page, Thomas Nelson 1853-1922.... **SSC 23**
See also CA 118; DLB 12, 78; DLBD 13

Paget, Violet 1856-1935
See Lee, Vernon
See also CA 104

Paget-Lowe, Henry
See Lovecraft, H(oward) P(hillips)

Paglia, Camille (Anna) 1947-....... **CLC 68**
See also CA 140

Paige, Richard
See Koontz, Dean R(ay)

Pakenham, Antonia
See Fraser, (Lady) Antonia (Pakenham)

Palamas, Kostes 1859-1943 ....... **TCLC 5**
See also CA 105

Palazzeschi, Aldo 1885-1974....... **CLC 11**
See also CA 89-92; 53-56; DLB 114

Paley, Grace
1922- ....... **CLC 4, 6, 37; DAM POP;
SSC 8**
See also CA 25-28R; CANR 13, 46;
DLB 28; INT CANR-13; MTCW

Palin, Michael (Edward) 1943-..... **CLC 21**
See also Monty Python
See also CA 107; CANR 35; SATA 67

Palliser, Charles 1947-........... **CLC 65**
See also CA 136

Palma, Ricardo 1833-1919........ **TCLC 29**

Pancake, Breece Dexter 1952-1979
See Pancake, Breece D'J
See also CA 123; 109

Pancake, Breece D'J.............. **CLC 29**
See also Pancake, Breece Dexter
See also DLB 130

Panko, Rudy
See Gogol, Nikolai (Vasilyevich)

Papadiamantis, Alexandros
1851-1911 .................. **TCLC 29**

Papadiamantopoulos, Johannes 1856-1910
See Moreas, Jean
See also CA 117

Papini, Giovanni 1881-1956....... **TCLC 22**
See also CA 121

Paracelsus 1493-1541.............. **LC 14**

Parasol, Peter
See Stevens, Wallace

Parfenie, Maria
See Codrescu, Andrei

Parini, Jay (Lee) 1948- ........... **CLC 54**
See also CA 97-100; CAAS 16; CANR 32

Park, Jordan
See Kornbluth, C(yril) M.; Pohl, Frederik

Parker, Bert
See Ellison, Harlan (Jay)

Parker, Dorothy (Rothschild)
1893-1967 .............. **CLC 15, 68;
DAM POET; SSC 2**
See also CA 19-20; 25-28R; CAP 2;
DLB 11, 45, 86; MTCW

Parker, Robert B(rown)
1932- ...... **CLC 27; DAM NOV, POP**
See also BEST 89:4; CA 49-52; CANR 1,
26, 52; INT CANR-26; MTCW

Parkin, Frank 1940-.............. **CLC 43**
See also CA 147

Parkman, Francis, Jr.
1823-1893 ................ **NCLC 12**
See also DLB 1, 30

Parks, Gordon (Alexander Buchanan)
1912- ... **CLC 1, 16; BLC; DAM MULT**
See also AITN 2; BW 2; CA 41-44R;
CANR 26; DLB 33; SATA 8

Parnell, Thomas 1679-1718......... **LC 3**
See also DLB 94

Parra, Nicanor
1914- ...... **CLC 2; DAM MULT; HLC**
See also CA 85-88; CANR 32; HW; MTCW

Parrish, Mary Frances
See Fisher, M(ary) F(rances) K(ennedy)

Parson
See Coleridge, Samuel Taylor

Parson Lot
See Kingsley, Charles

Partridge, Anthony
See Oppenheim, E(dward) Phillips

Pascal, Blaise 1623-1662........... **LC 35**

Pascoli, Giovanni 1855-1912...... **TCLC 45**

Pasolini, Pier Paolo
1922-1975 ............... **CLC 20, 37**
See also CA 93-96; 61-64; DLB 128;
MTCW

Pasquini
See Silone, Ignazio

Pastan, Linda (Olenik)
1932- ........... **CLC 27; DAM POET**
See also CA 61-64; CANR 18, 40; DLB 5

Pasternak, Boris (Leonidovich)
1890-1960 ...... **CLC 7, 10, 18, 63; DA;
DAB; DAC; DAM MST, NOV, POET;
PC 6; WLC**
See also CA 127; 116; MTCW

Patchen, Kenneth
1911-1972 ... **CLC 1, 2, 18; DAM POET**
See also CA 1-4R; 33-36R; CANR 3, 35;
DLB 16, 48; MTCW

Pater, Walter (Horatio)
1839-1894 .................. **NCLC 7**
See also CDBLB 1832-1890; DLB 57, 156

Paterson, A(ndrew) B(arton)
1864-1941 .................. **TCLC 32**

Paterson, Katherine (Womeldorf)
1932- .................... **CLC 12, 30**
See also AAYA 1; CA 21-24R; CANR 28;
CLR 7; DLB 52; JRDA; MAICYA;
MTCW; SATA 13, 53

Patmore, Coventry Kersey Dighton
1823-1896 .................. **NCLC 9**
See also DLB 35, 98

Paton, Alan (Stewart)
1903-1988 ...... **CLC 4, 10, 25, 55; DA;
DAB; DAC; DAM MST, NOV; WLC**
See also CA 13-16; 125; CANR 22; CAP 1;
MTCW; SATA 11; SATA-Obit 56

Paton Walsh, Gillian 1937-
See Walsh, Jill Paton
See also CANR 38; JRDA; MAICYA;
SAAS 3; SATA 4, 72

**Paulding, James Kirke**  1778-1860.. **NCLC 2**
See also DLB 3, 59, 74

**Paulin, Thomas Neilson**  1949-
See Paulin, Tom
See also CA 123; 128

**Paulin, Tom**.................... **CLC 37**
See also Paulin, Thomas Neilson
See also DLB 40

**Paustovsky, Konstantin (Georgievich)**
1892-1968 .................. **CLC 40**
See also CA 93-96; 25-28R

**Pavese, Cesare**
1908-1950 ..... **TCLC 3; PC 13; SSC 19**
See also CA 104; DLB 128

**Pavic, Milorad**  1929-............. **CLC 60**
See also CA 136

**Payne, Alan**
See Jakes, John (William)

**Paz, Gil**
See Lugones, Leopoldo

**Paz, Octavio**
1914- ....... **CLC 3, 4, 6, 10, 19, 51, 65;**
**DA; DAB; DAC; DAM MST, MULT,**
**POET; HLC; PC 1; WLC**
See also CA 73-76; CANR 32; DLBY 90;
HW; MTCW

**p'Bitek, Okot**
1931-1982 ............. **CLC 96; BLC;**
**DAM MULT**
See also BW 2; CA 124; 107; DLB 125;
MTCW

**Peacock, Molly**  1947-............. **CLC 60**
See also CA 103; CAAS 21; CANR 52;
DLB 120

**Peacock, Thomas Love**
1785-1866 ................ **NCLC 22**
See also DLB 96, 116

**Peake, Mervyn**  1911-1968....... **CLC 7, 54**
See also CA 5-8R; 25-28R; CANR 3;
DLB 15, 160; MTCW; SATA 23

**Pearce, Philippa** .................. **CLC 21**
See also Christie, (Ann) Philippa
See also CLR 9; DLB 161; MAICYA;
SATA 1, 67

**Pearl, Eric**
See Elman, Richard

**Pearson, T(homas) R(eid)**  1956- .... **CLC 39**
See also CA 120; 130; INT 130

**Peck, Dale**  1967- ................ **CLC 81**
See also CA 146

**Peck, John**  1941- ................. **CLC 3**
See also CA 49-52; CANR 3

**Peck, Richard (Wayne)**  1934- ...... **CLC 21**
See also AAYA 1; CA 85-88; CANR 19,
38; CLR 15; INT CANR-19; JRDA;
MAICYA; SAAS 2; SATA 18, 55

**Peck, Robert Newton**
1928- .. **CLC 17; DA; DAC; DAM MST**
See also AAYA 3; CA 81-84; CANR 31;
JRDA; MAICYA; SAAS 1; SATA 21, 62

**Peckinpah, (David) Sam(uel)**
1925-1984 .................. **CLC 20**
See also CA 109; 114

**Pedersen, Knut**  1859-1952
See Hamsun, Knut
See also CA 104; 119; MTCW

**Peeslake, Gaffer**
See Durrell, Lawrence (George)

**Peguy, Charles Pierre**
1873-1914 ................. **TCLC 10**
See also CA 107

**Pena, Ramon del Valle y**
See Valle-Inclan, Ramon (Maria) del

**Pendennis, Arthur Esquir**
See Thackeray, William Makepeace

**Penn, William**  1644-1718.......... **LC 25**
See also DLB 24

**Pepys, Samuel**
1633-1703 ..... **LC 11; DA; DAB; DAC;**
**DAM MST; WLC**
See also CDBLB 1660-1789; DLB 101

**Percy, Walker**
1916-1990 .... **CLC 2, 3, 6, 8, 14, 18, 47,**
**65; DAM NOV, POP**
See also CA 1-4R; 131; CANR 1, 23;
DLB 2; DLBY 80, 90; MTCW

**Perec, Georges**  1936-1982 ........ **CLC 56**
See also CA 141; DLB 83

**Pereda (y Sanchez de Porrua), Jose Maria de**
1833-1906 .................. **TCLC 16**
See also CA 117

**Pereda y Porrua, Jose Maria de**
See Pereda (y Sanchez de Porrua), Jose
Maria de

**Peregoy, George Weems**
See Mencken, H(enry) L(ouis)

**Perelman, S(idney) J(oseph)**
1904-1979 ...... **CLC 3, 5, 9, 15, 23, 44,**
**49; DAM DRAM**
See also AITN 1, 2; CA 73-76; 89-92;
CANR 18; DLB 11, 44; MTCW

**Peret, Benjamin**  1899-1959 ....... **TCLC 20**
See also CA 117

**Peretz, Isaac Loeb**  1851(?)-1915... **TCLC 16**
See also CA 109

**Peretz, Yitzkhok Leibush**
See Peretz, Isaac Loeb

**Perez Galdos, Benito**  1843-1920 ... **TCLC 27**
See also CA 125; HW

**Perrault, Charles**  1628-1703 ......... **LC 2**
See also MAICYA; SATA 25

**Perry, Brighton**
See Sherwood, Robert E(mmet)

**Perse, St.-John** .............. **CLC 4, 11, 46**
See also Leger, (Marie-Rene Auguste) Alexis
Saint-Leger

**Perutz, Leo**  1882-1957.......... **TCLC 60**
See also DLB 81

**Peseenz, Tulio F.**
See Lopez y Fuentes, Gregorio

**Pesetsky, Bette**  1932-............. **CLC 28**
See also CA 133; DLB 130

**Peshkov, Alexei Maximovich**  1868-1936
See Gorky, Maxim
See also CA 105; 141; DA; DAC;
DAM DRAM, MST, NOV

**Pessoa, Fernando (Antonio Nogueira)**
1888-1935 ............ **TCLC 27; HLC**
See also CA 125

**Peterkin, Julia Mood**  1880-1961.... **CLC 31**
See also CA 102; DLB 9

**Peters, Joan K.**  1945-............. **CLC 39**

**Peters, Robert L(ouis)**  1924-...... **CLC 7**
See also CA 13-16R; CAAS 8; DLB 105

**Petofi, Sandor**  1823-1849........ **NCLC 21**

**Petrakis, Harry Mark**  1923-........ **CLC 3**
See also CA 9-12R; CANR 4, 30

**Petrarch**  1304-1374.................. **PC 8**
See also DAM POET

**Petrov, Evgeny** ................... **TCLC 21**
See also Kataev, Evgeny Petrovich

**Petry, Ann (Lane)**  1908- ...... **CLC 1, 7, 18**
See also BW 1; CA 5-8R; CAAS 6;
CANR 4, 46; CLR 12; DLB 76; JRDA;
MAICYA; MTCW; SATA 5

**Petursson, Halligrimur**  1614-1674 .... **LC 8**

**Philips, Katherine**  1632-1664....... **LC 30**
See also DLB 131

**Philipson, Morris H.**  1926- ........ **CLC 53**
See also CA 1-4R; CANR 4

**Phillips, Caryl**
1958- .......... **CLC 96; DAM MULT**
See also BW 2; CA 141; DLB 157

**Phillips, David Graham**
1867-1911 .................. **TCLC 44**
See also CA 108; DLB 9, 12

**Phillips, Jack**
See Sandburg, Carl (August)

**Phillips, Jayne Anne**
1952- ............. **CLC 15, 33; SSC 16**
See also CA 101; CANR 24, 50; DLBY 80;
INT CANR-24; MTCW

**Phillips, Richard**
See Dick, Philip K(indred)

**Phillips, Robert (Schaeffer)**  1938-... **CLC 28**
See also CA 17-20R; CAAS 13; CANR 8;
DLB 105

**Phillips, Ward**
See Lovecraft, H(oward) P(hillips)

**Piccolo, Lucio**  1901-1969.......... **CLC 13**
See also CA 97-100; DLB 114

**Pickthall, Marjorie L(owry) C(hristie)**
1883-1922 .................. **TCLC 21**
See also CA 107; DLB 92

**Pico della Mirandola, Giovanni**
1463-1494 ................... **LC 15**

**Piercy, Marge**
1936- ......... **CLC 3, 6, 14, 18, 27, 62**
See also CA 21-24R; CAAS 1; CANR 13,
43; DLB 120; MTCW

**Piers, Robert**
See Anthony, Piers

**Pieyre de Mandiargues, Andre**  1909-1991
See Mandiargues, Andre Pieyre de
See also CA 103; 136; CANR 22

**Pilnyak, Boris** ................... **TCLC 23**
See also Vogau, Boris Andreyevich

Pincherle, Alberto
1907-1990 ..... CLC 11, 18; DAM NOV
See also Moravia, Alberto
See also CA 25-28R; 132; CANR 33;
MTCW

Pinckney, Darryl 1953- .......... CLC 76
See also BW 2; CA 143

Pindar 518B.C.-446B.C. ......... CMLC 12

Pineda, Cecile 1942-............. CLC 39
See also CA 118

Pinero, Arthur Wing
1855-1934 ..... TCLC 32; DAM DRAM
See also CA 110; DLB 10

Pinero, Miguel (Antonio Gomez)
1946-1988 ................. CLC 4, 55
See also CA 61-64; 125; CANR 29; HW

Pinget, Robert 1919- ........ CLC 7, 13, 37
See also CA 85-88; DLB 83

Pink Floyd
See Barrett, (Roger) Syd; Gilmour, David;
Mason, Nick; Waters, Roger; Wright,
Rick

Pinkney, Edward 1802-1828 ..... NCLC 31

Pinkwater, Daniel Manus 1941-.... CLC 35
See also Pinkwater, Manus
See also AAYA 1; CA 29-32R; CANR 12,
38; CLR 4; JRDA; MAICYA; SAAS 3;
SATA 46, 76

Pinkwater, Manus
See Pinkwater, Daniel Manus
See also SATA 8

Pinsky, Robert
1940-.. CLC 9, 19, 38, 94; DAM POET
See also CA 29-32R; CAAS 4; DLBY 82

Pinta, Harold
See Pinter, Harold

Pinter, Harold
1930-..... CLC 1, 3, 6, 9, 11, 15, 27, 58,
73; DA; DAB; DAC; DAM DRAM,
MST; WLC
See also CA 5-8R; CANR 33; CDBLB 1960
to Present; DLB 13; MTCW

Piozzi, Hester Lynch (Thrale)
1741-1821 ................. NCLC 57
See also DLB 104, 142

Pirandello, Luigi
1867-1936 ...... TCLC 4, 29; DA; DAB;
DAC; DAM DRAM, MST; DC 5;
SSC 22; WLC
See also CA 104

Pirsig, Robert M(aynard)
1928- ........ CLC 4, 6, 73; DAM POP
See also CA 53-56; CANR 42; MTCW;
SATA 39

Pisarev, Dmitry Ivanovich
1840-1868 ................. NCLC 25

Pix, Mary (Griffith) 1666-1709 ....... LC 8
See also DLB 80

Pixerecourt, Guilbert de
1773-1844 ................. NCLC 39

Plaidy, Jean
See Hibbert, Eleanor Alice Burford

Planche, James Robinson
1796-1880 ................. NCLC 42

Plant, Robert 1948- .............. CLC 12

Plante, David (Robert)
1940- ....... CLC 7, 23, 38; DAM NOV
See also CA 37-40R; CANR 12, 36;
DLBY 83; INT CANR-12; MTCW

Plath, Sylvia
1932-1963 ..... CLC 1, 2, 3, 5, 9, 11, 14,
17, 50, 51, 62; DA; DAB; DAC;
DAM MST, POET; PC 1; WLC
See also AAYA 13; CA 19-20; CANR 34;
CAP 2; CDALB 1941-1968; DLB 5, 6,
152; MTCW

Plato
428(?)B.C.-348(?)B.C..... CMLC 8; DA;
DAB; DAC; DAM MST

Platonov, Andrei ................. TCLC 14
See also Klimentov, Andrei Platonovich

Platt, Kin 1911- ................. CLC 26
See also AAYA 11; CA 17-20R; CANR 11;
JRDA; SAAS 17; SATA 21, 86

Plautus c. 251B.C.-184B.C. .......... DC 6

Plick et Plock
See Simenon, Georges (Jacques Christian)

Plimpton, George (Ames) 1927-..... CLC 36
See also AITN 1; CA 21-24R; CANR 32;
MTCW; SATA 10

Plomer, William Charles Franklin
1903-1973 ................. CLC 4, 8
See also CA 21-22; CANR 34; CAP 2;
DLB 20, 162; MTCW; SATA 24

Plowman, Piers
See Kavanagh, Patrick (Joseph)

Plum, J.
See Wodehouse, P(elham) G(renville)

Plumly, Stanley (Ross) 1939- ...... CLC 33
See also CA 108; 110; DLB 5; INT 110

Plumpe, Friedrich Wilhelm
1888-1931 ................. TCLC 53
See also CA 112

Poe, Edgar Allan
1809-1849 ........ NCLC 1, 16, 55; DA;
DAB; DAC; DAM MST, POET; PC 1;
SSC 1, 22; WLC
See also AAYA 14; CDALB 1640-1865;
DLB 3, 59, 73, 74; SATA 23

Poet of Titchfield Street, The
See Pound, Ezra (Weston Loomis)

Pohl, Frederik 1919- ............. CLC 18
See also CA 61-64; CAAS 1; CANR 11, 37;
DLB 8; INT CANR-11; MTCW;
SATA 24

Poirier, Louis 1910-
See Gracq, Julien
See also CA 122; 126

Poitier, Sidney 1927-............. CLC 26
See also BW 1; CA 117

Polanski, Roman 1933- ........... CLC 16
See also CA 77-80

Poliakoff, Stephen 1952- .......... CLC 38
See also CA 106; DLB 13

Police, The
See Copeland, Stewart (Armstrong);
Summers, Andrew James; Sumner,
Gordon Matthew

Polidori, John William
1795-1821 ................. NCLC 51
See also DLB 116

Pollitt, Katha 1949-.............. CLC 28
See also CA 120; 122; MTCW

Pollock, (Mary) Sharon
1936- .... CLC 50; DAC; DAM DRAM,
MST
See also CA 141; DLB 60

Polo, Marco 1254-1324 ......... CMLC 15

Polonsky, Abraham (Lincoln)
1910- ...................... CLC 92
See also CA 104; DLB 26; INT 104

Polybius c. 200B.C.-c. 118B.C. .... CMLC 17

Pomerance, Bernard
1940- .......... CLC 13; DAM DRAM
See also CA 101; CANR 49

Ponge, Francis (Jean Gaston Alfred)
1899-1988 ..... CLC 6, 18; DAM POET
See also CA 85-88; 126; CANR 40

Pontoppidan, Henrik 1857-1943 ... TCLC 29

Poole, Josephine ................. CLC 17
See also Helyar, Jane Penelope Josephine
See also SAAS 2; SATA 5

Popa, Vasko 1922-1991 ........... CLC 19
See also CA 112; 148

Pope, Alexander
1688-1744 ...... LC 3; DA; DAB; DAC;
DAM MST, POET; WLC
See also CDBLB 1660-1789; DLB 95, 101

Porter, Connie (Rose) 1959(?)- ..... CLC 70
See also BW 2; CA 142; SATA 81

Porter, Gene(va Grace) Stratton
1863(?)-1924 ................. TCLC 21
See also CA 112

Porter, Katherine Anne
1890-1980 ...... CLC 1, 3, 7, 10, 13, 15,
27; DA; DAB; DAC; DAM MST, NOV;
SSC 4
See also AITN 2; CA 1-4R; 101; CANR 1;
DLB 4, 9, 102; DLBD 12; DLBY 80;
MTCW; SATA 39; SATA-Obit 23

Porter, Peter (Neville Frederick)
1929- ................. CLC 5, 13, 33
See also CA 85-88; DLB 40

Porter, William Sydney 1862-1910
See Henry, O.
See also CA 104; 131; CDALB 1865-1917;
DA; DAB; DAC; DAM MST; DLB 12,
78, 79; MTCW; YABC 2

Portillo (y Pacheco), Jose Lopez
See Lopez Portillo (y Pacheco), Jose

Post, Melville Davisson
1869-1930 ................. TCLC 39
See also CA 110

Potok, Chaim
1929- .... CLC 2, 7, 14, 26; DAM NOV
See also AAYA 15; AITN 1, 2; CA 17-20R;
CANR 19, 35; DLB 28, 152;
INT CANR-19; MTCW; SATA 33

Potter, Beatrice
See Webb, (Martha) Beatrice (Potter)
See also MAICYA

Author Index

Potter, Dennis (Christopher George)
1935-1994 ................ CLC 58, 86
See also CA 107; 145; CANR 33; MTCW

Pound, Ezra (Weston Loomis)
1885-1972 ...... CLC 1, 2, 3, 4, 5, 7, 10,
13, 18, 34, 48, 50; DA; DAB; DAC;
DAM MST, POET; PC 4; WLC
See also CA 5-8R; 37-40R; CANR 40;
CDALB 1917-1929; DLB 4, 45, 63;
MTCW

Povod, Reinaldo 1959-1994 ....... CLC 44
See also CA 136; 146

Powell, Adam Clayton, Jr.
1908-1972 ............. CLC 89; BLC;
DAM MULT
See also BW 1; CA 102; 33-36R

Powell, Anthony (Dymoke)
1905- .......... CLC 1, 3, 7, 9, 10, 31
See also CA 1-4R; CANR 1, 32;
CDBLB 1945-1960; DLB 15; MTCW

Powell, Dawn 1897-1965 ......... CLC 66
See also CA 5-8R

Powell, Padgett 1952-............. CLC 34
See also CA 126

Power, Susan..................... CLC 91

Powers, J(ames) F(arl)
1917- ......... CLC 1, 4, 8, 57; SSC 4
See also CA 1-4R; CANR 2; DLB 130;
MTCW

Powers, John J(ames) 1945-
See Powers, John R.
See also CA 69-72

Powers, John R. .................. CLC 66
See also Powers, John J(ames)

Powers, Richard (S.) 1957- ........ CLC 93
See also CA 148

Pownall, David 1938-............. CLC 10
See also CA 89-92; CAAS 18; CANR 49;
DLB 14

Powys, John Cowper
1872-1963 ........... CLC 7, 9, 15, 46
See also CA 85-88; DLB 15; MTCW

Powys, T(heodore) F(rancis)
1875-1953 .................... TCLC 9
See also CA 106; DLB 36, 162

Prager, Emily 1952-............. CLC 56

Pratt, E(dwin) J(ohn)
1883(?)-1964 .......... CLC 19; DAC;
DAM POET
See also CA 141; 93-96; DLB 92

Premchand..................... TCLC 21
See also Srivastava, Dhanpat Rai

Preussler, Otfried 1923-.......... CLC 17
See also CA 77-80; SATA 24

Prevert, Jacques (Henri Marie)
1900-1977 ............... CLC 15
See also CA 77-80; 69-72; CANR 29;
MTCW; SATA-Obit 30

Prevost, Abbe (Antoine Francois)
1697-1763 .................... LC 1

Price, (Edward) Reynolds
1933- ......... CLC 3, 6, 13, 43, 50, 63;
DAM NOV; SSC 22
See also CA 1-4R; CANR 1, 37; DLB 2;
INT CANR-37

Price, Richard 1949- .......... CLC 6, 12
See also CA 49-52; CANR 3; DLBY 81

Prichard, Katharine Susannah
1883-1969 .................... CLC 46
See also CA 11-12; CANR 33; CAP 1;
MTCW; SATA 66

Priestley, J(ohn) B(oynton)
1894-1984 .......... CLC 2, 5, 9, 34;
DAM DRAM, NOV
See also CA 9-12R; 113; CANR 33;
CDBLB 1914-1945; DLB 10, 34, 77, 100,
139; DLBY 84; MTCW

Prince 1958(?)- .................. CLC 35

Prince, F(rank) T(empleton) 1912- .. CLC 22
See also CA 101; CANR 43; DLB 20

Prince Kropotkin
See Kropotkin, Peter (Aleksieevich)

Prior, Matthew 1664-1721.......... LC 4
See also DLB 95

Pritchard, William H(arrison)
1932-....................... CLC 34
See also CA 65-68; CANR 23; DLB 111

Pritchett, V(ictor) S(awdon)
1900- ............. CLC 5, 13, 15, 41;
DAM NOV; SSC 14
See also CA 61-64; CANR 31; DLB 15,
139; MTCW

Private 19022
See Manning, Frederic

Probst, Mark 1925- ............. CLC 59
See also CA 130

Prokosch, Frederic 1908-1989.... CLC 4, 48
See also CA 73-76; 128; DLB 48

Prophet, The
See Dreiser, Theodore (Herman Albert)

Prose, Francine 1947-............ CLC 45
See also CA 109; 112; CANR 46

Proudhon
See Cunha, Euclides (Rodrigues Pimenta) da

Proulx, E. Annie 1935- ........... CLC 81

Proust, (Valentin-Louis-George-Eugene-)
Marcel
1871-1922 ....... TCLC 7, 13, 33; DA;
DAB; DAC; DAM MST, NOV; WLC
See also CA 104; 120; DLB 65; MTCW

Prowler, Harley
See Masters, Edgar Lee

Prus, Boleslaw 1845-1912 ....... TCLC 48

Pryor, Richard (Franklin Lenox Thomas)
1940-....................... CLC 26
See also CA 122

Przybyszewski, Stanislaw
1868-1927 .................... TCLC 36
See also DLB 66

Pteleon
See Grieve, C(hristopher) M(urray)
See also DAM POET

Puckett, Lute
See Masters, Edgar Lee

Puig, Manuel
1932-1990 ....... CLC 3, 5, 10, 28, 65;
DAM MULT; HLC
See also CA 45-48; CANR 2, 32; DLB 113;
HW; MTCW

Purdy, Al(fred Wellington)
1918- ......... CLC 3, 6, 14, 50; DAC;
DAM MST, POET
See also CA 81-84; CAAS 17; CANR 42;
DLB 88

Purdy, James (Amos)
1923- ............ CLC 2, 4, 10, 28, 52
See also CA 33-36R; CAAS 1; CANR 19,
51; DLB 2; INT CANR-19; MTCW

Pure, Simon
See Swinnerton, Frank Arthur

Pushkin, Alexander (Sergeyevich)
1799-1837 ..... NCLC 3, 27; DA; DAB;
DAC; DAM DRAM, MST, POET;
PC 10; WLC
See also SATA 61

P'u Sung-ling 1640-1715 ............ LC 3

Putnam, Arthur Lee
See Alger, Horatio, Jr.

Puzo, Mario
1920- ..... CLC 1, 2, 6, 36; DAM NOV,
POP
See also CA 65-68; CANR 4, 42; DLB 6;
MTCW

Pym, Barbara (Mary Crampton)
1913-1980 ............. CLC 13, 19, 37
See also CA 13-14; 97-100; CANR 13, 34;
CAP 1; DLB 14; DLBY 87; MTCW

Pynchon, Thomas (Ruggles, Jr.)
1937- ..... CLC 2, 3, 6, 9, 11, 18, 33, 62,
72; DA; DAB; DAC; DAM MST, NOV;
POP; SSC 14; WLC
See also BEST 90:2; CA 17-20R; CANR 22,
46; DLB 2; MTCW

Qian Zhongshu
See Ch'ien Chung-shu

Qroll
See Dagerman, Stig (Halvard)

Quarrington, Paul (Lewis) 1953-.... CLC 65
See also CA 129

Quasimodo, Salvatore 1901-1968 ... CLC 10
See also CA 13-16; 25-28R; CAP 1;
DLB 114; MTCW

Quay, Stephen 1947- ............. CLC 95

Quay, The Brothers
See Quay, Stephen; Quay, Timothy

Quay, Timothy 1947- ............. CLC 95

Queen, Ellery.................... CLC 3, 11
See also Dannay, Frederic; Davidson,
Avram; Lee, Manfred B(ennington);
Sturgeon, Theodore (Hamilton); Vance,
John Holbrook

Queen, Ellery, Jr.
See Dannay, Frederic; Lee, Manfred
B(ennington)

Queneau, Raymond
1903-1976 ............ CLC 2, 5, 10, 42
See also CA 77-80; 69-72; CANR 32;
DLB 72; MTCW

Quevedo, Francisco de 1580-1645 .... LC 23

Quiller-Couch, Arthur Thomas
1863-1944 ................. TCLC 53
See also CA 118; DLB 135, 153

Quin, Ann (Marie) 1936-1973 ....... CLC 6
See also CA 9-12R; 45-48; DLB 14

**Quinn, Martin**
See Smith, Martin Cruz

**Quinn, Peter** 1947-............... **CLC 91**

**Quinn, Simon**
See Smith, Martin Cruz

**Quiroga, Horacio (Sylvestre)**
1878-1937 ..... **TCLC 20; DAM MULT;**
**HLC**
See also CA 117; 131; HW; MTCW

**Quoirez, Francoise** 1935-........... **CLC 9**
See also Sagan, Francoise
See also CA 49-52; CANR 6, 39; MTCW

**Raabe, Wilhelm** 1831-1910 ....... **TCLC 45**
See also DLB 129

**Rabe, David (William)**
1940- ...... **CLC 4, 8, 33; DAM DRAM**
See also CA 85-88; CABS 3; DLB 7

**Rabelais, Francois**
1483-1553 ...... **LC 5; DA; DAB; DAC;**
**DAM MST; WLC**

**Rabinovitch, Sholem** 1859-1916
See Aleichem, Sholom
See also CA 104

**Racine, Jean**
1639-1699 .... **LC 28; DAB; DAM MST**

**Radcliffe, Ann (Ward)**
1764-1823 ............... **NCLC 6, 55**
See also DLB 39

**Radiguet, Raymond** 1903-1923 .... **TCLC 29**
See also DLB 65

**Radnoti, Miklos** 1909-1944 ....... **TCLC 16**
See also CA 118

**Rado, James** 1939-............... **CLC 17**
See also CA 105

**Radvanyi, Netty** 1900-1983
See Seghers, Anna
See also CA 85-88; 110

**Rae, Ben**
See Griffiths, Trevor

**Raeburn, John (Hay)** 1941-........ **CLC 34**
See also CA 57-60

**Ragni, Gerome** 1942-1991 ......... **CLC 17**
See also CA 105; 134

**Rahv, Philip** 1908-1973 ........... **CLC 24**
See also Greenberg, Ivan
See also DLB 137

**Raine, Craig** 1944-............... **CLC 32**
See also CA 108; CANR 29, 51; DLB 40

**Raine, Kathleen (Jessie)** 1908- ... **CLC 7, 45**
See also CA 85-88; CANR 46; DLB 20;
MTCW

**Rainis, Janis** 1865-1929.......... **TCLC 29**

**Rakosi, Carl**.................... **CLC 47**
See also Rawley, Callman
See also CAAS 5

**Raleigh, Richard**
See Lovecraft, H(oward) P(hillips)

**Raleigh, Sir Walter** 1554(?)-1618 .... **LC 31**
See also CDBLB Before 1660

**Rallentando, H. P.**
See Sayers, Dorothy L(eigh)

**Ramal, Walter**
See de la Mare, Walter (John)

**Ramon, Juan**
See Jimenez (Mantecon), Juan Ramon

**Ramos, Graciliano** 1892-1953 ..... **TCLC 32**

**Rampersad, Arnold** 1941-.......... **CLC 44**
See also BW 2; CA 127; 133; DLB 111;
INT 133

**Rampling, Anne**
See Rice, Anne

**Ramsay, Allan** 1684(?)-1758 ....... **LC 29**
See also DLB 95

**Ramuz, Charles-Ferdinand**
1878-1947 ................. **TCLC 33**

**Rand, Ayn**
1905-1982 ...... **CLC 3, 30, 44, 79; DA;**
**DAC; DAM MST, NOV, POP; WLC**
See also AAYA 10; CA 13-16R; 105;
CANR 27; MTCW

**Randall, Dudley (Felker)**
1914- ...... **CLC 1; BLC; DAM MULT**
See also BW 1; CA 25-28R; CANR 23;
DLB 41

**Randall, Robert**
See Silverberg, Robert

**Ranger, Ken**
See Creasey, John

**Ransom, John Crowe**
1888-1974 ......... **CLC 2, 4, 5, 11, 24;**
**DAM POET**
See also CA 5-8R; 49-52; CANR 6, 34;
DLB 45, 63; MTCW

**Rao, Raja** 1909- ... **CLC 25, 56; DAM NOV**
See also CA 73-76; CANR 51; MTCW

**Raphael, Frederic (Michael)**
1931- .................... **CLC 2, 14**
See also CA 1-4R; CANR 1; DLB 14

**Ratcliffe, James P.**
See Mencken, H(enry) L(ouis)

**Rathbone, Julian** 1935- ........... **CLC 41**
See also CA 101; CANR 34

**Rattigan, Terence (Mervyn)**
1911-1977 ....... **CLC 7; DAM DRAM**
See also CA 85-88; 73-76;
CDBLB 1945-1960; DLB 13; MTCW

**Ratushinskaya, Irina** 1954-........ **CLC 54**
See also CA 129

**Raven, Simon (Arthur Noel)**
1927- .................... **CLC 14**
See also CA 81-84

**Rawley, Callman** 1903-
See Rakosi, Carl
See also CA 21-24R; CANR 12, 32

**Rawlings, Marjorie Kinnan**
1896-1953 ................... **TCLC 4**
See also CA 104; 137; DLB 9, 22, 102;
JRDA; MAICYA; YABC 1

**Ray, Satyajit**
1921-1992 ... **CLC 16, 76; DAM MULT**
See also CA 114; 137

**Read, Herbert Edward** 1893-1968.... **CLC 4**
See also CA 85-88; 25-28R; DLB 20, 149

**Read, Piers Paul** 1941- ...... **CLC 4, 10, 25**
See also CA 21-24R; CANR 38; DLB 14;
SATA 21

**Reade, Charles** 1814-1884 ........ **NCLC 2**
See also DLB 21

**Reade, Hamish**
See Gray, Simon (James Holliday)

**Reading, Peter** 1946-............. **CLC 47**
See also CA 103; CANR 46; DLB 40

**Reaney, James**
1926- ...... **CLC 13; DAC; DAM MST**
See also CA 41-44R; CAAS 15; CANR 42;
DLB 68; SATA 43

**Rebreanu, Liviu** 1885-1944 ....... **TCLC 28**

**Rechy, John (Francisco)**
1934-............... **CLC 1, 7, 14, 18;**
**DAM MULT; HLC**
See also CA 5-8R; CAAS 4; CANR 6, 32;
DLB 122; DLBY 82; HW; INT CANR-6

**Redcam, Tom** 1870-1933 ......... **TCLC 25**

**Reddin, Keith**.................... **CLC 67**

**Redgrove, Peter (William)**
1932-.................... **CLC 6, 41**
See also CA 1-4R; CANR 3, 39; DLB 40

**Redmon, Anne**.................... **CLC 22**
See also Nightingale, Anne Redmon
See also DLBY 86

**Reed, Eliot**
See Ambler, Eric

**Reed, Ishmael**
1938-........ **CLC 2, 3, 5, 6, 13, 32, 60;**
**BLC; DAM MULT**
See also BW 2; CA 21-24R; CANR 25, 48;
DLB 2, 5, 33; DLBD 8; MTCW

**Reed, John (Silas)** 1887-1920 ...... **TCLC 9**
See also CA 106

**Reed, Lou**........................ **CLC 21**
See also Firbank, Louis

**Reeve, Clara** 1729-1807......... **NCLC 19**
See also DLB 39

**Reich, Wilhelm** 1897-1957........ **TCLC 57**

**Reid, Christopher (John)** 1949-..... **CLC 33**
See also CA 140; DLB 40

**Reid, Desmond**
See Moorcock, Michael (John)

**Reid Banks, Lynne** 1929-
See Banks, Lynne Reid
See also CA 1-4R; CANR 6, 22, 38;
CLR 24; JRDA; MAICYA; SATA 22, 75

**Reilly, William K.**
See Creasey, John

**Reiner, Max**
See Caldwell, (Janet Miriam) Taylor
(Holland)

**Reis, Ricardo**
See Pessoa, Fernando (Antonio Nogueira)

**Remarque, Erich Maria**
1898-1970 .... **CLC 21; DA; DAB; DAC;**
**DAM MST, NOV**
See also CA 77-80; 29-32R; DLB 56;
MTCW

**Remizov, A.**
See Remizov, Aleksei (Mikhailovich)

**Remizov, A. M.**
See Remizov, Aleksei (Mikhailovich)

**Remizov, Aleksei (Mikhailovich)**
1877-1957 ................. **TCLC 27**
See also CA 125; 133

**Renan, Joseph Ernest**
        1823-1892 ................ NCLC 26

**Renard, Jules**  1864-1910 ........ TCLC 17
        See also CA 117

**Renault, Mary** .............. CLC 3, 11, 17
        See also Challans, Mary
        See also DLBY 83

**Rendell, Ruth (Barbara)**
        1930- ......... CLC 28, 48; DAM POP
        See also Vine, Barbara
        See also CA 109; CANR 32, 52; DLB 87;
        INT CANR-32; MTCW

**Renoir, Jean**  1894-1979 .......... CLC 20
        See also CA 129; 85-88

**Resnais, Alain**  1922- .............. CLC 16

**Reverdy, Pierre**  1889-1960 ........ CLC 53
        See also CA 97-100; 89-92

**Rexroth, Kenneth**
        1905-1982 ...... CLC 1, 2, 6, 11, 22, 49;
                                        DAM POET
        See also CA 5-8R; 107; CANR 14, 34;
        CDALB 1941-1968; DLB 16, 48, 165;
        DLBY 82; INT CANR-14; MTCW

**Reyes, Alfonso**  1889-1959 ....... TCLC 33
        See also CA 131; HW

**Reyes y Basoalto, Ricardo Eliecer Neftali**
        See Neruda, Pablo

**Reymont, Wladyslaw (Stanislaw)**
        1868(?)-1925 ................ TCLC 5
        See also CA 104

**Reynolds, Jonathan**  1942- ....... CLC 6, 38
        See also CA 65-68; CANR 28

**Reynolds, Joshua**  1723-1792 ........ LC 15
        See also DLB 104

**Reynolds, Michael Shane**  1937- .... CLC 44
        See also CA 65-68; CANR 9

**Reznikoff, Charles**  1894-1976 ....... CLC 9
        See also CA 33-36; 61-64; CAP 2; DLB 28,
        45

**Rezzori (d'Arezzo), Gregor von**
        1914- ....................... CLC 25
        See also CA 122; 136

**Rhine, Richard**
        See Silverstein, Alvin

**Rhodes, Eugene Manlove**
        1869-1934 ................ TCLC 53

**R'hoone**
        See Balzac, Honore de

**Rhys, Jean**
        1890(?)-1979 .... CLC 2, 4, 6, 14, 19, 51;
                                        DAM NOV; SSC 21
        See also CA 25-28R; 85-88; CANR 35;
        CDBLB 1945-1960; DLB 36, 117, 162;
        MTCW

**Ribeiro, Darcy**  1922- ............. CLC 34
        See also CA 33-36R

**Ribeiro, Joao Ubaldo (Osorio Pimentel)**
        1941- ................... CLC 10, 67
        See also CA 81-84

**Ribman, Ronald (Burt)**  1932- ....... CLC 7
        See also CA 21-24R; CANR 46

**Ricci, Nino**  1959- ................ CLC 70
        See also CA 137

**Rice, Anne**  1941- ..... CLC 41; DAM POP
        See also AAYA 9; BEST 89:2; CA 65-68;
        CANR 12, 36, 53

**Rice, Elmer (Leopold)**
        1892-1967 .... CLC 7, 49; DAM DRAM
        See also CA 21-22; 25-28R; CAP 2; DLB 4,
        7; MTCW

**Rice, Tim(othy Miles Bindon)**
        1944- ....................... CLC 21
        See also CA 103; CANR 46

**Rich, Adrienne (Cecile)**
        1929- .... CLC 3, 6, 7, 11, 18, 36, 73, 76;
                                        DAM POET; PC 5
        See also CA 9-12R; CANR 20, 53; DLB 5,
        67; MTCW

**Rich, Barbara**
        See Graves, Robert (von Ranke)

**Rich, Robert**
        See Trumbo, Dalton

**Richard, Keith** .................... CLC 17
        See also Richards, Keith

**Richards, David Adams**
        1950- .................. CLC 59; DAC
        See also CA 93-96; DLB 53

**Richards, I(vor) A(rmstrong)**
        1893-1979 ............... CLC 14, 24
        See also CA 41-44R; 89-92; CANR 34;
        DLB 27

**Richards, Keith**  1943-
        See Richard, Keith
        See also CA 107

**Richardson, Anne**
        See Roiphe, Anne (Richardson)

**Richardson, Dorothy Miller**
        1873-1957 .................. TCLC 3
        See also CA 104; DLB 36

**Richardson, Ethel Florence (Lindesay)**
        1870-1946
        See Richardson, Henry Handel
        See also CA 105

**Richardson, Henry Handel** ......... TCLC 4
        See also Richardson, Ethel Florence
        (Lindesay)

**Richardson, John**
        1796-1852 ............ NCLC 55; DAC
        See also DLB 99

**Richardson, Samuel**
        1689-1761 ...... LC 1; DA; DAB; DAC;
                                        DAM MST, NOV; WLC
        See also CDBLB 1660-1789; DLB 39

**Richler, Mordecai**
        1931- ....... CLC 3, 5, 9, 13, 18, 46, 70;
                                        DAC; DAM MST, NOV
        See also AITN 1; CA 65-68; CANR 31;
        CLR 17; DLB 53; MAICYA; MTCW;
        SATA 44; SATA-Brief 27

**Richter, Conrad (Michael)**
        1890-1968 ................... CLC 30
        See also CA 5-8R; 25-28R; CANR 23;
        DLB 9; MTCW; SATA 3

**Ricostranza, Tom**
        See Ellis, Trey

**Riddell, J. H.**  1832-1906 ........ TCLC 40

**Riding, Laura** .................... CLC 3, 7
        See also Jackson, Laura (Riding)

**Riefenstahl, Berta Helene Amalia**  1902-
        See Riefenstahl, Leni
        See also CA 108

**Riefenstahl, Leni** ................. CLC 16
        See also Riefenstahl, Berta Helene Amalia

**Riffe, Ernest**
        See Bergman, (Ernst) Ingmar

**Riggs, (Rolla) Lynn**
        1899-1954 ..... TCLC 56; DAM MULT
        See also CA 144; NNAL

**Riley, James Whitcomb**
        1849-1916 ...... TCLC 51; DAM POET
        See also CA 118; 137; MAICYA; SATA 17

**Riley, Tex**
        See Creasey, John

**Rilke, Rainer Maria**
        1875-1926 ............. TCLC 1, 6, 19;
                                        DAM POET; PC 2
        See also CA 104; 132; DLB 81; MTCW

**Rimbaud, (Jean Nicolas) Arthur**
        1854-1891 ..... NCLC 4, 35; DA; DAB;
                                        DAC; DAM MST, POET; PC 3; WLC

**Rinehart, Mary Roberts**
        1876-1958 ................ TCLC 52
        See also CA 108

**Ringmaster, The**
        See Mencken, H(enry) L(ouis)

**Ringwood, Gwen(dolyn Margaret) Pharis**
        1910-1984 ................... CLC 48
        See also CA 148; 112; DLB 88

**Rio, Michel**  19(?)- ................ CLC 43

**Ritsos, Giannes**
        See Ritsos, Yannis

**Ritsos, Yannis**  1909-1990 ..... CLC 6, 13, 31
        See also CA 77-80; 133; CANR 39; MTCW

**Ritter, Erika**  1948(?)- ............. CLC 52

**Rivera, Jose Eustasio**  1889-1928... TCLC 35
        See also HW

**Rivers, Conrad Kent**  1933-1968...... CLC 1
        See also BW 1; CA 85-88; DLB 41

**Rivers, Elfrida**
        See Bradley, Marion Zimmer

**Riverside, John**
        See Heinlein, Robert A(nson)

**Rizal, Jose**  1861-1896 ........... NCLC 27

**Roa Bastos, Augusto (Antonio)**
        1917- ..... CLC 45; DAM MULT; HLC
        See also CA 131; DLB 113; HW

**Robbe-Grillet, Alain**
        1922- ...... CLC 1, 2, 4, 6, 8, 10, 14, 43
        See also CA 9-12R; CANR 33; DLB 83;
        MTCW

**Robbins, Harold**
        1916- ............. CLC 5; DAM NOV
        See also CA 73-76; CANR 26; MTCW

**Robbins, Thomas Eugene**  1936-
        See Robbins, Tom
        See also CA 81-84; CANR 29; DAM NOV,
        POP; MTCW

**Robbins, Tom** ............... CLC 9, 32, 64
        See also Robbins, Thomas Eugene
        See also BEST 90:3; DLBY 80

**Robbins, Trina**  1938- ............. CLC 21
        See also CA 128

Roberts, Charles G(eorge) D(ouglas)
1860-1943 .................. **TCLC 8**
See also CA 105; CLR 33; DLB 92;
SATA 88; SATA-Brief 29

Roberts, Kate 1891-1985 ......... **CLC 15**
See also CA 107; 116

Roberts, Keith (John Kingston)
1935- ...................... **CLC 14**
See also CA 25-28R; CANR 46

Roberts, Kenneth (Lewis)
1885-1957 ................. **TCLC 23**
See also CA 109; DLB 9

Roberts, Michele (B.) 1949-........ **CLC 48**
See also CA 115

Robertson, Ellis
See Ellison, Harlan (Jay); Silverberg, Robert

Robertson, Thomas William
1829-1871 .... **NCLC 35; DAM DRAM**

Robinson, Edwin Arlington
1869-1935 ........ **TCLC 5; DA; DAC;**
**DAM MST, POET; PC 1**
See also CA 104; 133; CDALB 1865-1917;
DLB 54; MTCW

Robinson, Henry Crabb
1775-1867 ................ **NCLC 15**
See also DLB 107

Robinson, Jill 1936-.............. **CLC 10**
See also CA 102; INT 102

Robinson, Kim Stanley 1952- ...... **CLC 34**
See also CA 126

Robinson, Lloyd
See Silverberg, Robert

Robinson, Marilynne 1944-........ **CLC 25**
See also CA 116

Robinson, Smokey................. **CLC 21**
See also Robinson, William, Jr.

Robinson, William, Jr. 1940-
See Robinson, Smokey
See also CA 116

Robison, Mary 1949-............. **CLC 42**
See also CA 113; 116; DLB 130; INT 116

Rod, Edouard 1857-1910 ........ **TCLC 52**

Roddenberry, Eugene Wesley 1921-1991
See Roddenberry, Gene
See also CA 110; 135; CANR 37; SATA 45;
SATA-Obit 69

Roddenberry, Gene .............. **CLC 17**
See also Roddenberry, Eugene Wesley
See also AAYA 5; SATA-Obit 69

Rodgers, Mary 1931-............. **CLC 12**
See also CA 49-52; CANR 8; CLR 20;
INT CANR-8; JRDA; MAICYA;
SATA 8

Rodgers, W(illiam) R(obert)
1909-1969 ..................... **CLC 7**
See also CA 85-88; DLB 20

Rodman, Eric
See Silverberg, Robert

Rodman, Howard 1920(?)-1985..... **CLC 65**
See also CA 118

Rodman, Maia
See Wojciechowska, Maia (Teresa)

Rodriguez, Claudio 1934-.......... **CLC 10**
See also DLB 134

Roelvaag, O(le) E(dvart)
1876-1931 ................. **TCLC 17**
See also CA 117; DLB 9

Roethke, Theodore (Huebner)
1908-1963 ...... **CLC 1, 3, 8, 11, 19, 46;**
**DAM POET; PC 15**
See also CA 81-84; CABS 2;
CDALB 1941-1968; DLB 5; MTCW

Rogers, Thomas Hunton 1927- ..... **CLC 57**
See also CA 89-92; INT 89-92

Rogers, Will(iam Penn Adair)
1879-1935 ...... **TCLC 8; DAM MULT**
See also CA 105; 144; DLB 11; NNAL

Rogin, Gilbert 1929-.............. **CLC 18**
See also CA 65-68; CANR 15

Rohan, Koda .................... **TCLC 22**
See also Koda Shigeyuki

Rohmer, Eric.................... **CLC 16**
See also Scherer, Jean-Marie Maurice

Rohmer, Sax .................... **TCLC 28**
See also Ward, Arthur Henry Sarsfield
See also DLB 70

Roiphe, Anne (Richardson)
1935- ...................... **CLC 3, 9**
See also CA 89-92; CANR 45; DLBY 80;
INT 89-92

Rojas, Fernando de 1465-1541 ...... **LC 23**

Rolfe, Frederick (William Serafino Austin
Lewis Mary) 1860-1913...... **TCLC 12**
See also CA 107; DLB 34, 156

Rolland, Romain 1866-1944...... **TCLC 23**
See also CA 118; DLB 65

Rolvaag, O(le) E(dvart)
See Roelvaag, O(le) E(dvart)

Romain Arnaud, Saint
See Aragon, Louis

Romains, Jules 1885-1972.......... **CLC 7**
See also CA 85-88; CANR 34; DLB 65;
MTCW

Romero, Jose Ruben 1890-1952 ... **TCLC 14**
See also CA 114; 131; HW

Ronsard, Pierre de
1524-1585 ............... **LC 6; PC 11**

Rooke, Leon
1934- ......... **CLC 25, 34; DAM POP**
See also CA 25-28R; CANR 23, 53

Roper, William 1498-1578 .......... **LC 10**

Roquelaure, A. N.
See Rice, Anne

Rosa, Joao Guimaraes 1908-1967 ... **CLC 23**
See also CA 89-92; DLB 113

Rose, Wendy
1948- .... **CLC 85; DAM MULT; PC 13**
See also CA 53-56; CANR 5, 51; NNAL;
SATA 12

Rosen, Richard (Dean) 1949-....... **CLC 39**
See also CA 77-80; INT CANR-30

Rosenberg, Isaac 1890-1918....... **TCLC 12**
See also CA 107; DLB 20

Rosenblatt, Joe .................. **CLC 15**
See also Rosenblatt, Joseph

Rosenblatt, Joseph 1933-
See Rosenblatt, Joe
See also CA 89-92; INT 89-92

Rosenfeld, Samuel 1896-1963
See Tzara, Tristan
See also CA 89-92

Rosenthal, M(acha) L(ouis)
1917-1996 .................. **CLC 28**
See also CA 1-4R; 152; CAAS 6; CANR 4,
51; DLB 5; SATA 59

Ross, Barnaby
See Dannay, Frederic

Ross, Bernard L.
See Follett, Ken(neth Martin)

Ross, J. H.
See Lawrence, T(homas) E(dward)

Ross, Martin
See Martin, Violet Florence
See also DLB 135

Ross, (James) Sinclair
1908- ...... **CLC 13; DAC; DAM MST**
See also CA 73-76; DLB 88

Rossetti, Christina (Georgina)
1830-1894 ..... **NCLC 2, 50; DA; DAB;**
**DAC; DAM MST, POET; PC 7; WLC**
See also DLB 35, 163; MAICYA; SATA 20

Rossetti, Dante Gabriel
1828-1882 ........ **NCLC 4; DA; DAB;**
**DAC; DAM MST, POET; WLC**
See also CDBLB 1832-1890; DLB 35

Rossner, Judith (Perelman)
1935- .................... **CLC 6, 9, 29**
See also AITN 2; BEST 90:3; CA 17-20R;
CANR 18, 51; DLB 6; INT CANR-18;
MTCW

Rostand, Edmond (Eugene Alexis)
1868-1918 ...... **TCLC 6, 37; DA; DAB;**
**DAC; DAM DRAM, MST**
See also CA 104; 126; MTCW

Roth, Henry 1906-1995 ....... **CLC 2, 6, 11**
See also CA 11-12; 149; CANR 38; CAP 1;
DLB 28; MTCW

Roth, Joseph 1894-1939.......... **TCLC 33**
See also DLB 85

Roth, Philip (Milton)
1933- ...... **CLC 1, 2, 3, 4, 6, 9, 15, 22,**
**31, 47, 66, 86; DA; DAB; DAC;**
**DAM MST, NOV, POP; WLC**
See also BEST 90:3; CA 1-4R; CANR 1, 22,
36; CDALB 1968-1988; DLB 2, 28;
DLBY 82; MTCW

Rothenberg, Jerome 1931-....... **CLC 6, 57**
See also CA 45-48; CANR 1; DLB 5

Roumain, Jacques (Jean Baptiste)
1907-1944 ........... **TCLC 19; BLC;**
**DAM MULT**
See also BW 1; CA 117; 125

Rourke, Constance (Mayfield)
1885-1941 ................ **TCLC 12**
See also CA 107; YABC 1

Rousseau, Jean-Baptiste 1671-1741 ... **LC 9**

Rousseau, Jean-Jacques
1712-1778 ..... **LC 14; DA; DAB; DAC;**
**DAM MST; WLC**

Roussel, Raymond 1877-1933 ..... **TCLC 20**
See also CA 117

Rovit, Earl (Herbert) 1927-......... **CLC 7**
See also CA 5-8R; CANR 12

Sanchez, Sonia
1934- ...... CLC 5; BLC; DAM MULT;
PC 9
See also BW 2; CA 33-36R; CANR 24, 49;
CLR 18; DLB 41; DLBD 8; MAICYA;
MTCW; SATA 22

Sand, George
1804-1876 ....... NCLC 2, 42, 57; DA;
DAB; DAC; DAM MST, NOV; WLC
See also DLB 119

Sandburg, Carl (August)
1878-1967 .... CLC 1, 4, 10, 15, 35; DA;
DAB; DAC; DAM MST, POET; PC 2;
WLC
See also CA 5-8R; 25-28R; CANR 35;
CDALB 1865-1917; DLB 17, 54;
MAICYA; MTCW; SATA 8

Sandburg, Charles
See Sandburg, Carl (August)

Sandburg, Charles A.
See Sandburg, Carl (August)

Sanders, (James) Ed(ward) 1939- ... CLC 53
See also CA 13-16R; CAAS 21; CANR 13,
44; DLB 16

Sanders, Lawrence
1920- ........... CLC 41; DAM POP
See also BEST 89:4; CA 81-84; CANR 33;
MTCW

Sanders, Noah
See Blount, Roy (Alton), Jr.

Sanders, Winston P.
See Anderson, Poul (William)

Sandoz, Mari(e Susette)
1896-1966 .................. CLC 28
See also CA 1-4R; 25-28R; CANR 17;
DLB 9; MTCW; SATA 5

Saner, Reg(inald Anthony) 1931- .... CLC 9
See also CA 65-68

Sannazaro, Jacopo 1456(?)-1530 ...... LC 8

Sansom, William
1912-1976 ...... CLC 2, 6; DAM NOV;
SSC 21
See also CA 5-8R; 65-68; CANR 42;
DLB 139; MTCW

Santayana, George 1863-1952 ..... TCLC 40
See also CA 115; DLB 54, 71; DLBD 13

Santiago, Danny .................. CLC 33
See also James, Daniel (Lewis)
See also DLB 122

Santmyer, Helen Hoover
1895-1986 .................. CLC 33
See also CA 1-4R; 118; CANR 15, 33;
DLBY 84; MTCW

Santos, Bienvenido N(uqui)
1911-1996 ...... CLC 22; DAM MULT
See also CA 101; 151; CANR 19, 46

Sapper ......................... TCLC 44
See also McNeile, Herman Cyril

Sappho
fl. 6th cent. B.C.- ........... CMLC 3;
DAM POET; PC 5

Sarduy, Severo 1937-1993 ....... CLC 6, 96
See also CA 89-92; 142; DLB 113; HW

Sargeson, Frank 1903-1982 ........ CLC 31
See also CA 25-28R; 106; CANR 38

Sarmiento, Felix Ruben Garcia
See Dario, Ruben

Saroyan, William
1908-1981 ..... CLC 1, 8, 10, 29, 34, 56;
DA; DAB; DAC; DAM DRAM, MST,
NOV; SSC 21; WLC
See also CA 5-8R; 103; CANR 30; DLB 7,
9, 86; DLBY 81; MTCW; SATA 23;
SATA-Obit 24

Sarraute, Nathalie
1900- ........ CLC 1, 2, 4, 8, 10, 31, 80
See also CA 9-12R; CANR 23; DLB 83;
MTCW

Sarton, (Eleanor) May
1912-1995 ......... CLC 4, 14, 49, 91;
DAM POET
See also CA 1-4R; 149; CANR 1, 34;
DLB 48; DLBY 81; INT CANR-34;
MTCW; SATA 36; SATA-Obit 86

Sartre, Jean-Paul
1905-1980 .... CLC 1, 4, 7, 9, 13, 18, 24,
44, 50, 52; DA; DAB; DAC;
DAM DRAM, MST, NOV; DC 3; WLC
See also CA 9-12R; 97-100; CANR 21;
DLB 72; MTCW

Sassoon, Siegfried (Lorraine)
1886-1967 ............. CLC 36; DAB;
DAM MST, NOV, POET; PC 12
See also CA 104; 25-28R; CANR 36;
DLB 20; MTCW

Satterfield, Charles
See Pohl, Frederik

Saul, John (W. III)
1942- ...... CLC 46; DAM NOV, POP
See also AAYA 10; BEST 90:4; CA 81-84;
CANR 16, 40

Saunders, Caleb
See Heinlein, Robert A(nson)

Saura (Atares), Carlos 1932- ....... CLC 20
See also CA 114; 131; HW

Sauser-Hall, Frederic 1887-1961.... CLC 18
See also Cendrars, Blaise
See also CA 102; 93-96; CANR 36; MTCW

Saussure, Ferdinand de
1857-1913 .................. TCLC 49

Savage, Catharine
See Brosman, Catharine Savage

Savage, Thomas 1915- ............ CLC 40
See also CA 126; 132; CAAS 15; INT 132

Savan, Glenn 19(?)- .............. CLC 50

Sayers, Dorothy L(eigh)
1893-1957 ..... TCLC 2, 15; DAM POP
See also CA 104; 119; CDBLB 1914-1945;
DLB 10, 36, 77, 100; MTCW

Sayers, Valerie 1952- ............. CLC 50
See also CA 134

Sayles, John (Thomas)
1950- ................. CLC 7, 10, 14
See also CA 57-60; CANR 41; DLB 44

Scammell, Michael ................ CLC 34

Scannell, Vernon 1922- ........... CLC 49
See also CA 5-8R; CANR 8, 24; DLB 27;
SATA 59

Scarlett, Susan
See Streatfeild, (Mary) Noel

Schaeffer, Susan Fromberg
1941- .................. CLC 6, 11, 22
See also CA 49-52; CANR 18; DLB 28;
MTCW; SATA 22

Schary, Jill
See Robinson, Jill

Schell, Jonathan 1943-............ CLC 35
See also CA 73-76; CANR 12

Schelling, Friedrich Wilhelm Joseph von
1775-1854 ................. NCLC 30
See also DLB 90

Schendel, Arthur van 1874-1946... TCLC 56

Scherer, Jean-Marie Maurice 1920-
See Rohmer, Eric
See also CA 110

Schevill, James (Erwin) 1920-....... CLC 7
See also CA 5-8R; CAAS 12

Schiller, Friedrich
1759-1805 .... NCLC 39; DAM DRAM
See also DLB 94

Schisgal, Murray (Joseph) 1926-..... CLC 6
See also CA 21-24R; CANR 48

Schlee, Ann 1934-................. CLC 35
See also CA 101; CANR 29; SATA 44;
SATA-Brief 36

Schlegel, August Wilhelm von
1767-1845 ................. NCLC 15
See also DLB 94

Schlegel, Friedrich 1772-1829 .... NCLC 45
See also DLB 90

Schlegel, Johann Elias (von)
1719(?)-1749 .................. LC 5

Schlesinger, Arthur M(eier), Jr.
1917- ...................... CLC 84
See also AITN 1; CA 1-4R; CANR 1, 28;
DLB 17; INT CANR-28; MTCW;
SATA 61

Schmidt, Arno (Otto) 1914-1979.... CLC 56
See also CA 128; 109; DLB 69

Schmitz, Aron Hector 1861-1928
See Svevo, Italo
See also CA 104; 122; MTCW

Schnackenberg, Gjertrud 1953-..... CLC 40
See also CA 116; DLB 120

Schneider, Leonard Alfred 1925-1966
See Bruce, Lenny
See also CA 89-92

Schnitzler, Arthur
1862-1931 .......... TCLC 4; SSC 15
See also CA 104; DLB 81, 118

Schopenhauer, Arthur
1788-1860 ................. NCLC 51
See also DLB 90

Schor, Sandra (M.) 1932(?)-1990 ... CLC 65
See also CA 132

Schorer, Mark 1908-1977 .......... CLC 9
See also CA 5-8R; 73-76; CANR 7;
DLB 103

Schrader, Paul (Joseph) 1946-...... CLC 26
See also CA 37-40R; CANR 41; DLB 44

Schreiner, Olive (Emilie Albertina)
1855-1920 .................... TCLC 9
See also CA 105; DLB 18, 156

**Schulberg, Budd (Wilson)**
 1914- . . . . . . . . . . . . . . . . . . . **CLC 7, 48**
 See also CA 25-28R; CANR 19; DLB 6, 26, 28; DLBY 81

**Schulz, Bruno**
 1892-1942 . . . . . . . **TCLC 5, 51; SSC 13**
 See also CA 115; 123

**Schulz, Charles M(onroe)** 1922- . . . . **CLC 12**
 See also CA 9-12R; CANR 6; INT CANR-6; SATA 10

**Schumacher, E(rnst) F(riedrich)**
 1911-1977 . . . . . . . . . . . . . . . . . **CLC 80**
 See also CA 81-84; 73-76; CANR 34

**Schuyler, James Marcus**
 1923-1991 . . . . . **CLC 5, 23; DAM POET**
 See also CA 101; 134; DLB 5; INT 101

**Schwartz, Delmore (David)**
 1913-1966 . . . **CLC 2, 4, 10, 45, 87; PC 8**
 See also CA 17-18; 25-28R; CANR 35; CAP 2; DLB 28, 48; MTCW

**Schwartz, Ernst**
 See Ozu, Yasujiro

**Schwartz, John Burnham** 1965- . . . . **CLC 59**
 See also CA 132

**Schwartz, Lynne Sharon** 1939- . . . . . **CLC 31**
 See also CA 103; CANR 44

**Schwartz, Muriel A.**
 See Eliot, T(homas) S(tearns)

**Schwarz-Bart, Andre** 1928- . . . . . . . **CLC 2, 4**
 See also CA 89-92

**Schwarz-Bart, Simone** 1938- . . . . . . . . **CLC 7**
 See also BW 2; CA 97-100

**Schwob, (Mayer Andre) Marcel**
 1867-1905 . . . . . . . . . . . . . . . . . **TCLC 20**
 See also CA 117; DLB 123

**Sciascia, Leonardo**
 1921-1989 . . . . . . . . . . . . . **CLC 8, 9, 41**
 See also CA 85-88; 130; CANR 35; MTCW

**Scoppettone, Sandra** 1936- . . . . . . . . **CLC 26**
 See also AAYA 11; CA 5-8R; CANR 41; SATA 9

**Scorsese, Martin** 1942- . . . . . . . . **CLC 20, 89**
 See also CA 110; 114; CANR 46

**Scotland, Jay**
 See Jakes, John (William)

**Scott, Duncan Campbell**
 1862-1947 . . . . . . . . . . . . **TCLC 6; DAC**
 See also CA 104; DLB 92

**Scott, Evelyn** 1893-1963 . . . . . . . . . . **CLC 43**
 See also CA 104; 112; DLB 9, 48

**Scott, F(rancis) R(eginald)**
 1899-1985 . . . . . . . . . . . . . . . . . **CLC 22**
 See also CA 101; 114; DLB 88; INT 101

**Scott, Frank**
 See Scott, F(rancis) R(eginald)

**Scott, Joanna** 1960- . . . . . . . . . . . . . **CLC 50**
 See also CA 126; CANR 53

**Scott, Paul (Mark)** 1920-1978 . . . . **CLC 9, 60**
 See also CA 81-84; 77-80; CANR 33; DLB 14; MTCW

**Scott, Walter**
 1771-1832 . . . . . . . **NCLC 15; DA; DAB; DAC; DAM MST, NOV, POET; PC 13; WLC**
 See also CDBLB 1789-1832; DLB 93, 107, 116, 144, 159; YABC 2

**Scribe, (Augustin) Eugene**
 1791-1861 . . . . **NCLC 16; DAM DRAM; DC 5**

**Scrum, R.**
 See Crumb, R(obert)

**Scudery, Madeleine de** 1607-1701 . . . . . **LC 2**

**Scum**
 See Crumb, R(obert)

**Scumbag, Little Bobby**
 See Crumb, R(obert)

**Seabrook, John**
 See Hubbard, L(afayette) Ron(ald)

**Sealy, I. Allan** 1951- . . . . . . . . . . . . . **CLC 55**

**Search, Alexander**
 See Pessoa, Fernando (Antonio Nogueira)

**Sebastian, Lee**
 See Silverberg, Robert

**Sebastian Owl**
 See Thompson, Hunter S(tockton)

**Sebestyen, Ouida** 1924- . . . . . . . . . . **CLC 30**
 See also AAYA 8; CA 107; CANR 40; CLR 17; JRDA; MAICYA; SAAS 10; SATA 39

**Secundus, H. Scriblerus**
 See Fielding, Henry

**Sedges, John**
 See Buck, Pearl S(ydenstricker)

**Sedgwick, Catharine Maria**
 1789-1867 . . . . . . . . . . . . . . . . **NCLC 19**
 See also DLB 1, 74

**Seelye, John** 1931- . . . . . . . . . . . . . . . **CLC 7**

**Seferiades, Giorgos Stylianou** 1900-1971
 See Seferis, George
 See also CA 5-8R; 33-36R; CANR 5, 36; MTCW

**Seferis, George** . . . . . . . . . . . . . . . **CLC 5, 11**
 See also Seferiades, Giorgos Stylianou

**Segal, Erich (Wolf)**
 1937- . . . . . . . . . . **CLC 3, 10; DAM POP**
 See also BEST 89:1; CA 25-28R; CANR 20, 36; DLBY 86; INT CANR-20; MTCW

**Seger, Bob** 1945- . . . . . . . . . . . . . . . . **CLC 35**

**Seghers, Anna** . . . . . . . . . . . . . . . . . . . **CLC 7**
 See also Radvanyi, Netty
 See also DLB 69

**Seidel, Frederick (Lewis)** 1936- . . . . . **CLC 18**
 See also CA 13-16R; CANR 8; DLBY 84

**Seifert, Jaroslav**
 1901-1986 . . . . . . . . . . . **CLC 34, 44, 93**
 See also CA 127; MTCW

**Sei Shonagon** c. 966-1017(?) . . . . . . **CMLC 6**

**Selby, Hubert, Jr.**
 1928- . . . . . . . . . **CLC 1, 2, 4, 8; SSC 20**
 See also CA 13-16R; CANR 33; DLB 2

**Selzer, Richard** 1928- . . . . . . . . . . . . **CLC 74**
 See also CA 65-68; CANR 14

**Sembene, Ousmane**
 See Ousmane, Sembene

**Senancour, Etienne Pivert de**
 1770-1846 . . . . . . . . . . . . . . . . **NCLC 16**
 See also DLB 119

**Sender, Ramon (Jose)**
 1902-1982 . . **CLC 8; DAM MULT; HLC**
 See also CA 5-8R; 105; CANR 8; HW; MTCW

**Seneca, Lucius Annaeus**
 4B.C.-65 . . . . . . **CMLC 6; DAM DRAM; DC 5**

**Senghor, Leopold Sedar**
 1906- . . . . . **CLC 54; BLC; DAM MULT, POET**
 See also BW 2; CA 116; 125; CANR 47; MTCW

**Serling, (Edward) Rod(man)**
 1924-1975 . . . . . . . . . . . . . . . . . **CLC 30**
 See also AAYA 14; AITN 1; CA 65-68; 57-60; DLB 26

**Serna, Ramon Gomez de la**
 See Gomez de la Serna, Ramon

**Serpieres**
 See Guillevic, (Eugene)

**Service, Robert**
 See Service, Robert W(illiam)
 See also DAB; DLB 92

**Service, Robert W(illiam)**
 1874(?)-1958 . . . . . . **TCLC 15; DA; DAC; DAM MST, POET; WLC**
 See also Service, Robert
 See also CA 115; 140; SATA 20

**Seth, Vikram**
 1952- . . . . . . . **CLC 43, 90; DAM MULT**
 See also CA 121; 127; CANR 50; DLB 120; INT 127

**Seton, Cynthia Propper**
 1926-1982 . . . . . . . . . . . . . . . . . **CLC 27**
 See also CA 5-8R; 108; CANR 7

**Seton, Ernest (Evan) Thompson**
 1860-1946 . . . . . . . . . . . . . . . . . **TCLC 31**
 See also CA 109; DLB 92; DLBD 13; JRDA; SATA 18

**Seton-Thompson, Ernest**
 See Seton, Ernest (Evan) Thompson

**Settle, Mary Lee** 1918- . . . . . . . . **CLC 19, 61**
 See also CA 89-92; CAAS 1; CANR 44; DLB 6; INT 89-92

**Seuphor, Michel**
 See Arp, Jean

**Sevigne, Marie (de Rabutin-Chantal) Marquise de** 1626-1696 . . . . . . . . . . . . . . . **LC 11**

**Sexton, Anne (Harvey)**
 1928-1974 . . . . **CLC 2, 4, 6, 8, 10, 15, 53; DA; DAB; DAC; DAM MST, POET; PC 2; WLC**
 See also CA 1-4R; 53-56; CABS 2; CANR 3, 36; CDALB 1941-1968; DLB 5; MTCW; SATA 10

**Shaara, Michael (Joseph, Jr.)**
 1929-1988 . . . . . . . . **CLC 15; DAM POP**
 See also AITN 1; CA 102; 125; CANR 52; DLBY 83

**Shackleton, C. C.**
 See Aldiss, Brian W(ilson)

**Shacochis, Bob** . . . . . . . . . . . . . . . . . **CLC 39**
 See also Shacochis, Robert G.

**Shacochis, Robert G.** 1951-
See Shacochis, Bob
See also CA 119; 124; INT 124

**Shaffer, Anthony (Joshua)**
1926- ......... **CLC 19; DAM DRAM**
See also CA 110; 116; DLB 13

**Shaffer, Peter (Levin)**
1926- ...... **CLC 5, 14, 18, 37, 60; DAB;**
**DAM DRAM, MST**
See also CA 25-28R; CANR 25, 47;
CDBLB 1960 to Present; DLB 13;
MTCW

**Shakey, Bernard**
See Young, Neil

**Shalamov, Varlam (Tikhonovich)**
1907(?)-1982 ................. **CLC 18**
See also CA 129; 105

**Shamlu, Ahmad** 1925- ............ **CLC 10**

**Shammas, Anton** 1951-............ **CLC 55**

**Shange, Ntozake**
1948- ........ **CLC 8, 25, 38, 74; BLC;**
**DAM DRAM, MULT; DC 3**
See also AAYA 9; BW 2; CA 85-88;
CABS 3; CANR 27, 48; DLB 38; MTCW

**Shanley, John Patrick** 1950- ....... **CLC 75**
See also CA 128; 133

**Shapcott, Thomas W(illiam)** 1935- .. **CLC 38**
See also CA 69-72; CANR 49

**Shapiro, Jane**..................... **CLC 76**

**Shapiro, Karl (Jay)** 1913- .. **CLC 4, 8, 15, 53**
See also CA 1-4R; CAAS 6; CANR 1, 36;
DLB 48; MTCW

**Sharp, William** 1855-1905 ........ **TCLC 39**
See also DLB 156

**Sharpe, Thomas Ridley** 1928-
See Sharpe, Tom
See also CA 114; 122; INT 122

**Sharpe, Tom**..................... **CLC 36**
See also Sharpe, Thomas Ridley
See also DLB 14

**Shaw, Bernard**................... **TCLC 45**
See also Shaw, George Bernard
See also BW 1

**Shaw, G. Bernard**
See Shaw, George Bernard

**Shaw, George Bernard**
1856-1950 ... **TCLC 3, 9, 21; DA; DAB;**
**DAC; DAM DRAM, MST; WLC**
See also Shaw, Bernard
See also CA 104; 128; CDBLB 1914-1945;
DLB 10, 57; MTCW

**Shaw, Henry Wheeler**
1818-1885 ................. **NCLC 15**
See also DLB 11

**Shaw, Irwin**
1913-1984 ............. **CLC 7, 23, 34;**
**DAM DRAM, POP**
See also AITN 1; CA 13-16R; 112;
CANR 21; CDALB 1941-1968; DLB 6,
102; DLBY 84; MTCW

**Shaw, Robert** 1927-1978 .......... **CLC 5**
See also AITN 1; CA 1-4R; 81-84;
CANR 4; DLB 13, 14

**Shaw, T. E.**
See Lawrence, T(homas) E(dward)

**Shawn, Wallace** 1943- ........... **CLC 41**
See also CA 112

**Shea, Lisa** 1953-................. **CLC 86**
See also CA 147

**Sheed, Wilfrid (John Joseph)**
1930- ............... **CLC 2, 4, 10, 53**
See also CA 65-68; CANR 30; DLB 6;
MTCW

**Sheldon, Alice Hastings Bradley**
1915(?)-1987
See Tiptree, James, Jr.
See also CA 108; 122; CANR 34; INT 108;
MTCW

**Sheldon, John**
See Bloch, Robert (Albert)

**Shelley, Mary Wollstonecraft (Godwin)**
1797-1851 ....... **NCLC 14; DA; DAB;**
**DAC; DAM MST, NOV; WLC**
See also CDBLB 1789-1832; DLB 110, 116,
159; SATA 29

**Shelley, Percy Bysshe**
1792-1822 ....... **NCLC 18; DA; DAB;**
**DAC; DAM MST, POET; PC 14; WLC**
See also CDBLB 1789-1832; DLB 96, 110,
158

**Shepard, Jim** 1956-............... **CLC 36**
See also CA 137

**Shepard, Lucius** 1947- ............ **CLC 34**
See also CA 128; 141

**Shepard, Sam**
1943- ........ **CLC 4, 6, 17, 34, 41, 44;**
**DAM DRAM; DC 5**
See also AAYA 1; CA 69-72; CABS 3;
CANR 22; DLB 7; MTCW

**Shepherd, Michael**
See Ludlum, Robert

**Sherburne, Zoa (Morin)** 1912-...... **CLC 30**
See also AAYA 13; CA 1-4R; CANR 3, 37;
MAICYA; SAAS 18; SATA 3

**Sheridan, Frances** 1724-1766........ **LC 7**
See also DLB 39, 84

**Sheridan, Richard Brinsley**
1751-1816 ....... **NCLC 5; DA; DAB;**
**DAC; DAM DRAM, MST; DC 1; WLC**
See also CDBLB 1660-1789; DLB 89

**Sherman, Jonathan Marc**........... **CLC 55**

**Sherman, Martin** 1941(?)- ......... **CLC 19**
See also CA 116; 123

**Sherwin, Judith Johnson** 1936-... **CLC 7, 15**
See also CA 25-28R; CANR 34

**Sherwood, Frances** 1940-.......... **CLC 81**
See also CA 146

**Sherwood, Robert E(mmet)**
1896-1955 ...... **TCLC 3; DAM DRAM**
See also CA 104; DLB 7, 26

**Shestov, Lev** 1866-1938 ......... **TCLC 56**

**Shevchenko, Taras** 1814-1861 .... **NCLC 54**

**Shiel, M(atthew) P(hipps)**
1865-1947 ................... **TCLC 8**
See also CA 106; DLB 153

**Shields, Carol** 1935-......... **CLC 91; DAC**
See also CA 81-84; CANR 51

**Shiga, Naoya** 1883-1971... **CLC 33; SSC 23**
See also CA 101; 33-36R

**Shilts, Randy** 1951-1994 ......... **CLC 85**
See also CA 115; 127; 144; CANR 45;
INT 127

**Shimazaki, Haruki** 1872-1943
See Shimazaki Toson
See also CA 105; 134

**Shimazaki Toson**................. **TCLC 5**
See also Shimazaki, Haruki

**Sholokhov, Mikhail (Aleksandrovich)**
1905-1984 ................ **CLC 7, 15**
See also CA 101; 112; MTCW;
SATA-Obit 36

**Shone, Patric**
See Hanley, James

**Shreve, Susan Richards** 1939-...... **CLC 23**
See also CA 49-52; CAAS 5; CANR 5, 38;
MAICYA; SATA 46; SATA-Brief 41

**Shue, Larry**
1946-1985 ...... **CLC 52; DAM DRAM**
See also CA 145; 117

**Shu-Jen, Chou** 1881-1936
See Lu Hsun
See also CA 104

**Shulman, Alix Kates** 1932-...... **CLC 2, 10**
See also CA 29-32R; CANR 43; SATA 7

**Shuster, Joe** 1914- ............... **CLC 21**

**Shute, Nevil**..................... **CLC 30**
See also Norway, Nevil Shute

**Shuttle, Penelope (Diane)** 1947- ..... **CLC 7**
See also CA 93-96; CANR 39; DLB 14, 40

**Sidney, Mary** 1561-1621 ........... **LC 19**

**Sidney, Sir Philip**
1554-1586 ..... **LC 19; DA; DAB; DAC;**
**DAM MST, POET**
See also CDBLB Before 1660; DLB 167

**Siegel, Jerome** 1914-1996 ......... **CLC 21**
See also CA 116; 151

**Siegel, Jerry**
See Siegel, Jerome

**Sienkiewicz, Henryk (Adam Alexander Pius)**
1846-1916 ................... **TCLC 3**
See also CA 104; 134

**Sierra, Gregorio Martinez**
See Martinez Sierra, Gregorio

**Sierra, Maria (de la O'LeJarraga) Martinez**
See Martinez Sierra, Maria (de la
O'LeJarraga)

**Sigal, Clancy** 1926-............... **CLC 7**
See also CA 1-4R

**Sigourney, Lydia Howard (Huntley)**
1791-1865 ................. **NCLC 21**
See also DLB 1, 42, 73

**Siguenza y Gongora, Carlos de**
1645-1700 .................... **LC 8**

**Sigurjonsson, Johann** 1880-1919... **TCLC 27**

**Sikelianos, Angelos** 1884-1951 .... **TCLC 39**

**Silkin, Jon** 1930- ............ **CLC 2, 6, 43**
See also CA 5-8R; CAAS 5; DLB 27

**Silko, Leslie (Marmon)**
1948- .......... **CLC 23, 74; DA; DAC;**
**DAM MST, MULT, POP**
See also AAYA 14; CA 115; 122;
CANR 45; DLB 143; NNAL

**Sillanpaa, Frans Eemil** 1888-1964... **CLC 19**
See also CA 129; 93-96; MTCW

**Sillitoe, Alan**
1928- ......... **CLC 1, 3, 6, 10, 19, 57**
See also AITN 1; CA 9-12R; CAAS 2;
CANR 8, 26; CDBLB 1960 to Present;
DLB 14, 139; MTCW; SATA 61

**Silone, Ignazio** 1900-1978 .......... **CLC 4**
See also CA 25-28; 81-84; CANR 34;
CAP 2; MTCW

**Silver, Joan Micklin** 1935- ........ **CLC 20**
See also CA 114; 121; INT 121

**Silver, Nicholas**
See Faust, Frederick (Schiller)

**Silverberg, Robert**
1935- ................. **CLC 7; DAM POP**
See also CA 1-4R; CAAS 3; CANR 1, 20,
36; DLB 8; INT CANR-20; MAICYA;
MTCW; SATA 13

**Silverstein, Alvin** 1933- .......... **CLC 17**
See also CA 49-52; CANR 2; CLR 25;
JRDA; MAICYA; SATA 8, 69

**Silverstein, Virginia B(arbara Opshelor)**
1937- ...................... **CLC 17**
See also CA 49-52; CANR 2; CLR 25;
JRDA; MAICYA; SATA 8, 69

**Sim, Georges**
See Simenon, Georges (Jacques Christian)

**Simak, Clifford D(onald)**
1904-1988 ................. **CLC 1, 55**
See also CA 1-4R; 125; CANR 1, 35;
DLB 8; MTCW; SATA-Obit 56

**Simenon, Georges (Jacques Christian)**
1903-1989 ....... **CLC 1, 2, 3, 8, 18, 47;**
**DAM POP**
See also CA 85-88; 129; CANR 35;
DLB 72; DLBY 89; MTCW

**Simic, Charles**
1938- ........... **CLC 6, 9, 22, 49, 68;**
**DAM POET**
See also CA 29-32R; CAAS 4; CANR 12,
33, 52; DLB 105

**Simmel, Georg** 1858-1918 ....... **TCLC 64**

**Simmons, Charles (Paul)** 1924- ..... **CLC 57**
See also CA 89-92; INT 89-92

**Simmons, Dan** 1948- ... **CLC 44; DAM POP**
See also AAYA 16; CA 138; CANR 53

**Simmons, James (Stewart Alexander)**
1933- ...................... **CLC 43**
See also CA 105; CAAS 21; DLB 40

**Simms, William Gilmore**
1806-1870 ................. **NCLC 3**
See also DLB 3, 30, 59, 73

**Simon, Carly** 1945- .............. **CLC 26**
See also CA 105

**Simon, Claude**
1913- .... **CLC 4, 9, 15, 39; DAM NOV**
See also CA 89-92; CANR 33; DLB 83;
MTCW

**Simon, (Marvin) Neil**
1927- .......... **CLC 6, 11, 31, 39, 70;**
**DAM DRAM**
See also AITN 1; CA 21-24R; CANR 26;
DLB 7; MTCW

**Simon, Paul** 1942(?)- ............ **CLC 17**
See also CA 116

**Simonon, Paul** 1956(?)- ........... **CLC 30**

**Simpson, Harriette**
See Arnow, Harriette (Louisa) Simpson

**Simpson, Louis (Aston Marantz)**
1923- .... **CLC 4, 7, 9, 32; DAM POET**
See also CA 1-4R; CAAS 4; CANR 1;
DLB 5; MTCW

**Simpson, Mona (Elizabeth)** 1957- ... **CLC 44**
See also CA 122; 135

**Simpson, N(orman) F(rederick)**
1919- ...................... **CLC 29**
See also CA 13-16R; DLB 13

**Sinclair, Andrew (Annandale)**
1935- ..................... **CLC 2, 14**
See also CA 9-12R; CAAS 5; CANR 14, 38;
DLB 14; MTCW

**Sinclair, Emil**
See Hesse, Hermann

**Sinclair, Iain** 1943- .............. **CLC 76**
See also CA 132

**Sinclair, Iain MacGregor**
See Sinclair, Iain

**Sinclair, Mary Amelia St. Clair** 1865(?)-1946
See Sinclair, May
See also CA 104

**Sinclair, May** ................. **TCLC 3, 11**
See also Sinclair, Mary Amelia St. Clair
See also DLB 36, 135

**Sinclair, Upton (Beall)**
1878-1968 ...... **CLC 1, 11, 15, 63; DA;**
**DAB; DAC; DAM MST, NOV; WLC**
See also CA 5-8R; 25-28R; CANR 7;
CDALB 1929-1941; DLB 9;
INT CANR-7; MTCW; SATA 9

**Singer, Isaac**
See Singer, Isaac Bashevis

**Singer, Isaac Bashevis**
1904-1991 .... **CLC 1, 3, 6, 9, 11, 15, 23,**
**38, 69; DA; DAB; DAC; DAM MST,**
**NOV; SSC 3; WLC**
See also AITN 1, 2; CA 1-4R; 134;
CANR 1, 39; CDALB 1941-1968; CLR 1;
DLB 6, 28, 52; DLBY 91; JRDA;
MAICYA; MTCW; SATA 3, 27;
SATA-Obit 68

**Singer, Israel Joshua** 1893-1944 ... **TCLC 33**

**Singh, Khushwant** 1915- .......... **CLC 11**
See also CA 9-12R; CAAS 9; CANR 6

**Sinjohn, John**
See Galsworthy, John

**Sinyavsky, Andrei (Donatevich)**
1925- ...................... **CLC 8**
See also CA 85-88

**Sirin, V.**
See Nabokov, Vladimir (Vladimirovich)

**Sissman, L(ouis) E(dward)**
1928-1976 ................. **CLC 9, 18**
See also CA 21-24R; 65-68; CANR 13;
DLB 5

**Sisson, C(harles) H(ubert)** 1914- .... **CLC 8**
See also CA 1-4R; CAAS 3; CANR 3, 48;
DLB 27

**Sitwell, Dame Edith**
1887-1964 .............. **CLC 2, 9, 67;**
**DAM POET; PC 3**
See also CA 9-12R; CANR 35;
CDBLB 1945-1960; DLB 20; MTCW

**Sjoewall, Maj** 1935- ............... **CLC 7**
See also CA 65-68

**Sjowall, Maj**
See Sjoewall, Maj

**Skelton, Robin** 1925- ............. **CLC 13**
See also AITN 2; CA 5-8R; CAAS 5;
CANR 28; DLB 27, 53

**Skolimowski, Jerzy** 1938- ......... **CLC 20**
See also CA 128

**Skram, Amalie (Bertha)**
1847-1905 ................. **TCLC 25**

**Skvorecky, Josef (Vaclav)**
1924- .......... **CLC 15, 39, 69; DAC;**
**DAM NOV**
See also CA 61-64; CAAS 1; CANR 10, 34;
MTCW

**Slade, Bernard** ................. **CLC 11, 46**
See also Newbound, Bernard Slade
See also CAAS 9; DLB 53

**Slaughter, Carolyn** 1946- .......... **CLC 56**
See also CA 85-88

**Slaughter, Frank G(ill)** 1908- ...... **CLC 29**
See also AITN 2; CA 5-8R; CANR 5;
INT CANR-5

**Slavitt, David R(ytman)** 1935- .... **CLC 5, 14**
See also CA 21-24R; CAAS 3; CANR 41;
DLB 5, 6

**Slesinger, Tess** 1905-1945 ........ **TCLC 10**
See also CA 107; DLB 102

**Slessor, Kenneth** 1901-1971 ....... **CLC 14**
See also CA 102; 89-92

**Slowacki, Juliusz** 1809-1849 ..... **NCLC 15**

**Smart, Christopher**
1722-1771 ... **LC 3; DAM POET; PC 13**
See also DLB 109

**Smart, Elizabeth** 1913-1986 ........ **CLC 54**
See also CA 81-84; 118; DLB 88

**Smiley, Jane (Graves)**
1949- ......... **CLC 53, 76; DAM POP**
See also CA 104; CANR 30, 50;
INT CANR-30

**Smith, A(rthur) J(ames) M(arshall)**
1902-1980 ............. **CLC 15; DAC**
See also CA 1-4R; 102; CANR 4; DLB 88

**Smith, Anna Deavere** 1950- ........ **CLC 86**
See also CA 133

**Smith, Betty (Wehner)** 1896-1972... **CLC 19**
See also CA 5-8R; 33-36R; DLBY 82;
SATA 6

**Smith, Charlotte (Turner)**
1749-1806 ................. **NCLC 23**
See also DLB 39, 109

**Smith, Clark Ashton** 1893-1961 .... **CLC 43**
See also CA 143

**Smith, Dave** ................... **CLC 22, 42**
See also Smith, David (Jeddie)
See also CAAS 7; DLB 5

**Smith, David (Jeddie)** 1942-
See Smith, Dave
See also CA 49-52; CANR 1; DAM POET

Smith, Florence Margaret    1902-1971
    See Smith, Stevie
    See also CA 17-18; 29-32R; CANR 35;
    CAP 2; DAM POET; MTCW

Smith, Iain Crichton    1928- ........ CLC 64
    See also CA 21-24R; DLB 40, 139

Smith, John    1580(?)-1631 ........... LC 9

Smith, Johnston
    See Crane, Stephen (Townley)

Smith, Joseph, Jr.    1805-1844 .... NCLC 53

Smith, Lee    1944-.............. CLC 25, 73
    See also CA 114; 119; CANR 46; DLB 143;
    DLBY 83; INT 119

Smith, Martin
    See Smith, Martin Cruz

Smith, Martin Cruz
    1942- ..... CLC 25; DAM MULT, POP
    See also BEST 89:4; CA 85-88; CANR 6,
    23, 43; INT CANR-23; NNAL

Smith, Mary-Ann Tirone    1944-..... CLC 39
    See also CA 118; 136

Smith, Patti    1946- .............. CLC 12
    See also CA 93-96

Smith, Pauline (Urmson)
    1882-1959 ................. TCLC 25

Smith, Rosamond
    See Oates, Joyce Carol

Smith, Sheila Kaye
    See Kaye-Smith, Sheila

Smith, Stevie ....... CLC 3, 8, 25, 44; PC 12
    See also Smith, Florence Margaret
    See also DLB 20

Smith, Wilbur (Addison)    1933-..... CLC 33
    See also CA 13-16R; CANR 7, 46; MTCW

Smith, William Jay    1918- .......... CLC 6
    See also CA 5-8R; CANR 44; DLB 5;
    MAICYA; SAAS 22; SATA 2, 68

Smith, Woodrow Wilson
    See Kuttner, Henry

Smolenskin, Peretz    1842-1885.... NCLC 30

Smollett, Tobias (George)    1721-1771 .. LC 2
    See also CDBLB 1660-1789; DLB 39, 104

Snodgrass, W(illiam) D(e Witt)
    1926- ........... CLC 2, 6, 10, 18, 68;
                                    DAM POET
    See also CA 1-4R; CANR 6, 36; DLB 5;
    MTCW

Snow, C(harles) P(ercy)
    1905-1980 ....... CLC 1, 4, 6, 9, 13, 19;
                                    DAM NOV
    See also CA 5-8R; 101; CANR 28;
    CDBLB 1945-1960; DLB 15, 77; MTCW

Snow, Frances Compton
    See Adams, Henry (Brooks)

Snyder, Gary (Sherman)
    1930- .. CLC 1, 2, 5, 9, 32; DAM POET
    See also CA 17-20R; CANR 30; DLB 5, 16,
    165

Snyder, Zilpha Keatley    1927- ...... CLC 17
    See also AAYA 15; CA 9-12R; CANR 38;
    CLR 31; JRDA; MAICYA; SAAS 2;
    SATA 1, 28, 75

Soares, Bernardo
    See Pessoa, Fernando (Antonio Nogueira)

Sobh, A.
    See Shamlu, Ahmad

Sobol, Joshua................... CLC 60

Soderberg, Hjalmar    1869-1941 .... TCLC 39

Sodergran, Edith (Irene)
    See Soedergran, Edith (Irene)

Soedergran, Edith (Irene)
    1892-1923 ................. TCLC 31

Softly, Edgar
    See Lovecraft, H(oward) P(hillips)

Softly, Edward
    See Lovecraft, H(oward) P(hillips)

Sokolov, Raymond    1941-........... CLC 7
    See also CA 85-88

Solo, Jay
    See Ellison, Harlan (Jay)

Sologub, Fyodor .................. TCLC 9
    See also Teternikov, Fyodor Kuzmich

Solomons, Ikey Esquir
    See Thackeray, William Makepeace

Solomos, Dionysios    1798-1857 ... NCLC 15

Solwoska, Mara
    See French, Marilyn

Solzhenitsyn, Aleksandr I(sayevich)
    1918- ...... CLC 1, 2, 4, 7, 9, 10, 18, 26,
        34, 78; DA; DAB; DAC; DAM MST,
                                    NOV; WLC
    See also AITN 1; CA 69-72; CANR 40;
    MTCW

Somers, Jane
    See Lessing, Doris (May)

Somerville, Edith    1858-1949 ...... TCLC 51
    See also DLB 135

Somerville & Ross
    See Martin, Violet Florence; Somerville,
    Edith

Sommer, Scott    1951- ............. CLC 25
    See also CA 106

Sondheim, Stephen (Joshua)
    1930- ....... CLC 30, 39; DAM DRAM
    See also AAYA 11; CA 103; CANR 47

Sontag, Susan
    1933- ............ CLC 1, 2, 10, 13, 31;
                                    DAM POP
    See also CA 17-20R; CANR 25, 51; DLB 2,
    67; MTCW

Sophocles
    496(?)B.C.-406(?)B.C..... CMLC 2; DA;
        DAB; DAC; DAM DRAM, MST; DC 1

Sordello    1189-1269............. CMLC 15

Sorel, Julia
    See Drexler, Rosalyn

Sorrentino, Gilbert
    1929- ........... CLC 3, 7, 14, 22, 40
    See also CA 77-80; CANR 14, 33; DLB 5;
    DLBY 80; INT CANR-14

Soto, Gary
    1952- ....... CLC 32, 80; DAM MULT;
                                    HLC
    See also AAYA 10; CA 119; 125;
    CANR 50; CLR 38; DLB 82; HW;
    INT 125; JRDA; SATA 80

Soupault, Philippe    1897-1990 ...... CLC 68
    See also CA 116; 147; 131

Souster, (Holmes) Raymond
    1921- ... CLC 5, 14; DAC; DAM POET
    See also CA 13-16R; CAAS 14; CANR 13,
    29, 53; DLB 88; SATA 63

Southern, Terry    1924(?)-1995 ...... CLC 7
    See also CA 1-4R; 150; CANR 1; DLB 2

Southey, Robert    1774-1843 ....... NCLC 8
    See also DLB 93, 107, 142; SATA 54

Southworth, Emma Dorothy Eliza Nevitte
    1819-1899 ................. NCLC 26

Souza, Ernest
    See Scott, Evelyn

Soyinka, Wole
    1934- ....... CLC 3, 5, 14, 36, 44; BLC;
        DA; DAB; DAC; DAM DRAM, MST,
                                MULT; DC 2; WLC
    See also BW 2; CA 13-16R; CANR 27, 39;
    DLB 125; MTCW

Spackman, W(illiam) M(ode)
    1905-1990 ................. CLC 46
    See also CA 81-84; 132

Spacks, Barry    1931-.............. CLC 14
    See also CA 29-32R; CANR 33; DLB 105

Spanidou, Irini    1946- ............. CLC 44

Spark, Muriel (Sarah)
    1918- ..... CLC 2, 3, 5, 8, 13, 18, 40, 94;
        DAB; DAC; DAM MST, NOV; SSC 10
    See also CA 5-8R; CANR 12, 36;
    CDBLB 1945-1960; DLB 15, 139;
    INT CANR-12; MTCW

Spaulding, Douglas
    See Bradbury, Ray (Douglas)

Spaulding, Leonard
    See Bradbury, Ray (Douglas)

Spence, J. A. D.
    See Eliot, T(homas) S(tearns)

Spencer, Elizabeth    1921-.......... CLC 22
    See also CA 13-16R; CANR 32; DLB 6;
    MTCW; SATA 14

Spencer, Leonard G.
    See Silverberg, Robert

Spencer, Scott    1945-.............. CLC 30
    See also CA 113; CANR 51; DLBY 86

Spender, Stephen (Harold)
    1909-1995 ...... CLC 1, 2, 5, 10, 41, 91;
                                    DAM POET
    See also CA 9-12R; 149; CANR 31;
    CDBLB 1945-1960; DLB 20; MTCW

Spengler, Oswald (Arnold Gottfried)
    1880-1936 ................. TCLC 25
    See also CA 118

Spenser, Edmund
    1552(?)-1599 .... LC 5; DA; DAB; DAC;
        DAM MST, POET; PC 8; WLC
    See also CDBLB Before 1660; DLB 167

Spicer, Jack
    1925-1965 ............. CLC 8, 18, 72;
                                    DAM POET
    See also CA 85-88; DLB 5, 16

Spiegelman, Art    1948-............. CLC 76
    See also AAYA 10; CA 125; CANR 41

Spielberg, Peter    1929-............. CLC 6
    See also CA 5-8R; CANR 4, 48; DLBY 81

Spielberg, Steven  1947- . . . . . . . . . .  **CLC 20**
See also AAYA 8; CA 77-80; CANR 32;
SATA 32

Spillane, Frank Morrison  1918-
See Spillane, Mickey
See also CA 25-28R; CANR 28; MTCW;
SATA 66

Spillane, Mickey . . . . . . . . . . . . . . .  **CLC 3, 13**
See also Spillane, Frank Morrison

Spinoza, Benedictus de  1632-1677 . . . .  **LC 9**

Spinrad, Norman (Richard)  1940-. . .  **CLC 46**
See also CA 37-40R; CAAS 19; CANR 20;
DLB 8; INT CANR-20

Spitteler, Carl (Friedrich Georg)
1845-1924 . . . . . . . . . . . . . . . . .  **TCLC 12**
See also CA 109; DLB 129

Spivack, Kathleen (Romola Drucker)
1938- . . . . . . . . . . . . . . . . . . . . . .  **CLC 6**
See also CA 49-52

Spoto, Donald  1941-. . . . . . . . . . . . .  **CLC 39**
See also CA 65-68; CANR 11

Springsteen, Bruce (F.)  1949- . . . . . .  **CLC 17**
See also CA 111

Spurling, Hilary  1940- . . . . . . . . . . . .  **CLC 34**
See also CA 104; CANR 25, 52

Spyker, John Howland
See Elman, Richard

Squires, (James) Radcliffe
1917-1993 . . . . . . . . . . . . . . . . . . .  **CLC 51**
See also CA 1-4R; 140; CANR 6, 21

Srivastava, Dhanpat Rai  1880(?)-1936
See Premchand
See also CA 118

Stacy, Donald
See Pohl, Frederik

Stael, Germaine de
See Stael-Holstein, Anne Louise Germaine
Necker Baronn
See also DLB 119

Stael-Holstein, Anne Louise Germaine Necker
Baronn  1766-1817 . . . . . . . . . .  **NCLC 3**
See also Stael, Germaine de

Stafford, Jean  1915-1979. . .  **CLC 4, 7, 19, 68**
See also CA 1-4R; 85-88; CANR 3; DLB 2;
MTCW; SATA-Obit 22

Stafford, William (Edgar)
1914-1993 . . .  **CLC 4, 7, 29; DAM POET**
See also CA 5-8R; 142; CAAS 3; CANR 5,
22; DLB 5; INT CANR-22

Staines, Trevor
See Brunner, John (Kilian Houston)

Stairs, Gordon
See Austin, Mary (Hunter)

Stannard, Martin  1947- . . . . . . . . . . .  **CLC 44**
See also CA 142; DLB 155

Stanton, Maura  1946- . . . . . . . . . . . . .  **CLC 9**
See also CA 89-92; CANR 15; DLB 120

Stanton, Schuyler
See Baum, L(yman) Frank

Stapledon, (William) Olaf
1886-1950 . . . . . . . . . . . . . . . . .  **TCLC 22**
See also CA 111; DLB 15

Starbuck, George (Edwin)
1931- . . . . . . . . . . .  **CLC 53; DAM POET**
See also CA 21-24R; CANR 23

Stark, Richard
See Westlake, Donald E(dwin)

Staunton, Schuyler
See Baum, L(yman) Frank

Stead, Christina (Ellen)
1902-1983 . . . . . . . .  **CLC 2, 5, 8, 32, 80**
See also CA 13-16R; 109; CANR 33, 40;
MTCW

Stead, William Thomas
1849-1912 . . . . . . . . . . . . . . . . .  **TCLC 48**

Steele, Richard  1672-1729 . . . . . . . . . .  **LC 18**
See also CDBLB 1660-1789; DLB 84, 101

Steele, Timothy (Reid)  1948-. . . . . . .  **CLC 45**
See also CA 93-96; CANR 16, 50; DLB 120

Steffens, (Joseph) Lincoln
1866-1936 . . . . . . . . . . . . . . . . .  **TCLC 20**
See also CA 117

Stegner, Wallace (Earle)
1909-1993 . . .  **CLC 9, 49, 81; DAM NOV**
See also AITN 1; BEST 90:3; CA 1-4R;
141; CAAS 9; CANR 1, 21, 46; DLB 9;
DLBY 93; MTCW

Stein, Gertrude
1874-1946 . . . . . .  **TCLC 1, 6, 28, 48; DA;**
**DAB; DAC; DAM MST, NOV, POET;**
**WLC**
See also CA 104; 132; CDALB 1917-1929;
DLB 4, 54, 86; MTCW

Steinbeck, John (Ernst)
1902-1968 . . . . . .  **CLC 1, 5, 9, 13, 21, 34,**
**45, 75; DA; DAB; DAC; DAM DRAM,**
**MST, NOV; SSC 11; WLC**
See also AAYA 12; CA 1-4R; 25-28R;
CANR 1, 35; CDALB 1929-1941; DLB 7,
9; DLBD 2; MTCW; SATA 9

Steinem, Gloria  1934-. . . . . . . . . . . .  **CLC 63**
See also CA 53-56; CANR 28, 51; MTCW

Steiner, George
1929- . . . . . . . . . . . .  **CLC 24; DAM NOV**
See also CA 73-76; CANR 31; DLB 67;
MTCW; SATA 62

Steiner, K. Leslie
See Delany, Samuel R(ay, Jr.)

Steiner, Rudolf  1861-1925. . . . . . . .  **TCLC 13**
See also CA 107

Stendhal
1783-1842 . . . .  **NCLC 23, 46; DA; DAB;**
**DAC; DAM MST, NOV; WLC**
See also DLB 119

Stephen, Leslie  1832-1904 . . . . . . . .  **TCLC 23**
See also CA 123; DLB 57, 144

Stephen, Sir Leslie
See Stephen, Leslie

Stephen, Virginia
See Woolf, (Adeline) Virginia

Stephens, James  1882(?)-1950 . . . . . .  **TCLC 4**
See also CA 104; DLB 19, 153, 162

Stephens, Reed
See Donaldson, Stephen R.

Steptoe, Lydia
See Barnes, Djuna

Sterchi, Beat  1949-. . . . . . . . . . . . . .  **CLC 65**

Sterling, Brett
See Bradbury, Ray (Douglas); Hamilton,
Edmond

Sterling, Bruce  1954-. . . . . . . . . . . . .  **CLC 72**
See also CA 119; CANR 44

Sterling, George  1869-1926 . . . . . . .  **TCLC 20**
See also CA 117; DLB 54

Stern, Gerald  1925- . . . . . . . . . . . . . .  **CLC 40**
See also CA 81-84; CANR 28; DLB 105

Stern, Richard (Gustave)  1928-. . .  **CLC 4, 39**
See also CA 1-4R; CANR 1, 25, 52;
DLBY 87; INT CANR-25

Sternberg, Josef von  1894-1969. . . . .  **CLC 20**
See also CA 81-84

Sterne, Laurence
1713-1768 . . . . . .  **LC 2; DA; DAB; DAC;**
**DAM MST, NOV; WLC**
See also CDBLB 1660-1789; DLB 39

Sternheim, (William Adolf) Carl
1878-1942 . . . . . . . . . . . . . . . . . .  **TCLC 8**
See also CA 105; DLB 56, 118

Stevens, Mark  1951-. . . . . . . . . . . . . .  **CLC 34**
See also CA 122

Stevens, Wallace
1879-1955 . . . . . . . .  **TCLC 3, 12, 45; DA;**
**DAB; DAC; DAM MST, POET; PC 6;**
**WLC**
See also CA 104; 124; CDALB 1929-1941;
DLB 54; MTCW

Stevenson, Anne (Katharine)
1933-. . . . . . . . . . . . . . . . . . . .  **CLC 7, 33**
See also CA 17-20R; CAAS 9; CANR 9, 33;
DLB 40; MTCW

Stevenson, Robert Louis (Balfour)
1850-1894 . . . . . .  **NCLC 5, 14; DA; DAB;**
**DAC; DAM MST, NOV; SSC 11; WLC**
See also CDBLB 1890-1914; CLR 10, 11;
DLB 18, 57, 141, 156; DLBD 13; JRDA;
MAICYA; YABC 2

Stewart, J(ohn) I(nnes) M(ackintosh)
1906-1994 . . . . . . . . . . . . . .  **CLC 7, 14, 32**
See also CA 85-88; 147; CAAS 3;
CANR 47; MTCW

Stewart, Mary (Florence Elinor)
1916- . . . . . . . . . . . . . . .  **CLC 7, 35; DAB**
See also CA 1-4R; CANR 1; SATA 12

Stewart, Mary Rainbow
See Stewart, Mary (Florence Elinor)

Stifle, June
See Campbell, Maria

Stifter, Adalbert  1805-1868 . . . . . .  **NCLC 41**
See also DLB 133

Still, James  1906-. . . . . . . . . . . . . . . .  **CLC 49**
See also CA 65-68; CAAS 17; CANR 10,
26; DLB 9; SATA 29

Sting
See Sumner, Gordon Matthew

Stirling, Arthur
See Sinclair, Upton (Beall)

Stitt, Milan  1941-. . . . . . . . . . . . . . . .  **CLC 29**
See also CA 69-72

Stockton, Francis Richard  1834-1902
See Stockton, Frank R.
See also CA 108; 137; MAICYA; SATA 44

**Swenson, May**
1919-1989 .... **CLC 4, 14, 61; DA; DAB;**
**DAC; DAM MST, POET; PC 14**
See also CA 5-8R; 130; CANR 36; DLB 5;
MTCW; SATA 15

**Swift, Augustus**
See Lovecraft, H(oward) P(hillips)

**Swift, Graham (Colin)** 1949- .... **CLC 41, 88**
See also CA 117; 122; CANR 46

**Swift, Jonathan**
1667-1745 ...... **LC 1; DA; DAB; DAC;**
**DAM MST, NOV, POET; PC 9; WLC**
See also CDBLB 1660-1789; DLB 39, 95,
101; SATA 19

**Swinburne, Algernon Charles**
1837-1909 ...... **TCLC 8, 36; DA; DAB;**
**DAC; DAM MST, POET; WLC**
See also CA 105; 140; CDBLB 1832-1890;
DLB 35, 57

**Swinfen, Ann** ..................... **CLC 34**

**Swinnerton, Frank Arthur**
1884-1982 ................... **CLC 31**
See also CA 108; DLB 34

**Swithen, John**
See King, Stephen (Edwin)

**Sylvia**
See Ashton-Warner, Sylvia (Constance)

**Symmes, Robert Edward**
See Duncan, Robert (Edward)

**Symonds, John Addington**
1840-1893 ................ **NCLC 34**
See also DLB 57, 144

**Symons, Arthur** 1865-1945 ....... **TCLC 11**
See also CA 107; DLB 19, 57, 149

**Symons, Julian (Gustave)**
1912-1994 .............. **CLC 2, 14, 32**
See also CA 49-52; 147; CAAS 3; CANR 3,
33; DLB 87, 155; DLBY 92; MTCW

**Synge, (Edmund) J(ohn) M(illington)**
1871-1909 .............. **TCLC 6, 37;**
**DAM DRAM; DC 2**
See also CA 104; 141; CDBLB 1890-1914;
DLB 10, 19

**Syruc, J.**
See Milosz, Czeslaw

**Szirtes, George** 1948- ............. **CLC 46**
See also CA 109; CANR 27

**Tabori, George** 1914- ............. **CLC 19**
See also CA 49-52; CANR 4

**Tagore, Rabindranath**
1861-1941 .............. **TCLC 3, 53;**
**DAM DRAM, POET; PC 8**
See also CA 104; 120; MTCW

**Taine, Hippolyte Adolphe**
1828-1893 ................ **NCLC 15**

**Talese, Gay** 1932- ................. **CLC 37**
See also AITN 1; CA 1-4R; CANR 9;
INT CANR-9; MTCW

**Tallent, Elizabeth (Ann)** 1954- ..... **CLC 45**
See also CA 117; DLB 130

**Tally, Ted** 1952- ................. **CLC 42**
See also CA 120; 124; INT 124

**Tamayo y Baus, Manuel**
1829-1898 ................. **NCLC 1**

**Tammsaare, A(nton) H(ansen)**
1878-1940 ................. **TCLC 27**

**Tan, Amy**
1952- .... **CLC 59; DAM MULT, NOV,**
**POP**
See also AAYA 9; BEST 89:3; CA 136;
SATA 75

**Tandem, Felix**
See Spitteler, Carl (Friedrich Georg)

**Tanizaki, Jun'ichiro**
1886-1965 ...... **CLC 8, 14, 28; SSC 21**
See also CA 93-96; 25-28R

**Tanner, William**
See Amis, Kingsley (William)

**Tao Lao**
See Storni, Alfonsina

**Tarassoff, Lev**
See Troyat, Henri

**Tarbell, Ida M(inerva)**
1857-1944 ................. **TCLC 40**
See also CA 122; DLB 47

**Tarkington, (Newton) Booth**
1869-1946 ................. **TCLC 9**
See also CA 110; 143; DLB 9, 102;
SATA 17

**Tarkovsky, Andrei (Arsenyevich)**
1932-1986 ................. **CLC 75**
See also CA 127

**Tartt, Donna** 1964(?)- ............. **CLC 76**
See also CA 142

**Tasso, Torquato** 1544-1595 ......... **LC 5**

**Tate, (John Orley) Allen**
1899-1979 .... **CLC 2, 4, 6, 9, 11, 14, 24**
See also CA 5-8R; 85-88; CANR 32;
DLB 4, 45, 63; MTCW

**Tate, Ellalice**
See Hibbert, Eleanor Alice Burford

**Tate, James (Vincent)** 1943- ... **CLC 2, 6, 25**
See also CA 21-24R; CANR 29; DLB 5

**Tavel, Ronald** 1940- ............... **CLC 6**
See also CA 21-24R; CANR 33

**Taylor, C(ecil) P(hilip)** 1929-1981... **CLC 27**
See also CA 25-28R; 105; CANR 47

**Taylor, Edward**
1642(?)-1729 ........ **LC 11; DA; DAB;**
**DAC; DAM MST, POET**
See also DLB 24

**Taylor, Eleanor Ross** 1920- ........ **CLC 5**
See also CA 81-84

**Taylor, Elizabeth** 1912-1975 ... **CLC 2, 4, 29**
See also CA 13-16R; CANR 9; DLB 139;
MTCW; SATA 13

**Taylor, Henry (Splawn)** 1942- ...... **CLC 44**
See also CA 33-36R; CAAS 7; CANR 31;
DLB 5

**Taylor, Kamala (Purnaiya)** 1924-
See Markandaya, Kamala
See also CA 77-80

**Taylor, Mildred D.** ................ **CLC 21**
See also AAYA 10; BW 1; CA 85-88;
CANR 25; CLR 9; DLB 52; JRDA;
MAICYA; SAAS 5; SATA 15, 70

**Taylor, Peter (Hillsman)**
1917-1994 ..... **CLC 1, 4, 18, 37, 44, 50,**
**71; SSC 10**
See also CA 13-16R; 147; CANR 9, 50;
DLBY 81, 94; INT CANR-9; MTCW

**Taylor, Robert Lewis** 1912- ........ **CLC 14**
See also CA 1-4R; CANR 3; SATA 10

**Tchekhov, Anton**
See Chekhov, Anton (Pavlovich)

**Teasdale, Sara** 1884-1933 .......... **TCLC 4**
See also CA 104; DLB 45; SATA 32

**Tegner, Esaias** 1782-1846 ......... **NCLC 2**

**Teilhard de Chardin, (Marie Joseph) Pierre**
1881-1955 ................. **TCLC 9**
See also CA 105

**Temple, Ann**
See Mortimer, Penelope (Ruth)

**Tennant, Emma (Christina)**
1937- ................... **CLC 13, 52**
See also CA 65-68; CAAS 9; CANR 10, 38;
DLB 14

**Tenneshaw, S. M.**
See Silverberg, Robert

**Tennyson, Alfred**
1809-1892 ....... **NCLC 30; DA; DAB;**
**DAC; DAM MST, POET; PC 6; WLC**
See also CDBLB 1832-1890; DLB 32

**Teran, Lisa St. Aubin de** ........... **CLC 36**
See also St. Aubin de Teran, Lisa

**Terence** 195(?)B.C.-159B.C. ...... **CMLC 14**

**Teresa de Jesus, St.** 1515-1582 ...... **LC 18**

**Terkel, Louis** 1912-
See Terkel, Studs
See also CA 57-60; CANR 18, 45; MTCW

**Terkel, Studs** ..................... **CLC 38**
See also Terkel, Louis
See also AITN 1

**Terry, C. V.**
See Slaughter, Frank G(ill)

**Terry, Megan** 1932- .............. **CLC 19**
See also CA 77-80; CABS 3; CANR 43;
DLB 7

**Tertz, Abram**
See Sinyavsky, Andrei (Donatevich)

**Tesich, Steve** 1943(?)-1996 ...... **CLC 40, 69**
See also CA 105; 152; DLBY 83

**Teternikov, Fyodor Kuzmich** 1863-1927
See Sologub, Fyodor
See also CA 104

**Tevis, Walter** 1928-1984 .......... **CLC 42**
See also CA 113

**Tey, Josephine** .................... **TCLC 14**
See also Mackintosh, Elizabeth
See also DLB 77

**Thackeray, William Makepeace**
1811-1863 .... **NCLC 5, 14, 22, 43; DA;**
**DAB; DAC; DAM MST, NOV; WLC**
See also CDBLB 1832-1890; DLB 21, 55,
159, 163; SATA 23

**Thakura, Ravindranatha**
See Tagore, Rabindranath

**Tharoor, Shashi** 1956- ............ **CLC 70**
See also CA 141

**Thelwell, Michael Miles**  1939- . . . . . **CLC 22**
See also BW 2; CA 101

**Theobald, Lewis, Jr.**
See Lovecraft, H(oward) P(hillips)

**Theodorescu, Ion N.**  1880-1967
See Arghezi, Tudor
See also CA 116

**Theriault, Yves**
1915-1983 . . **CLC 79; DAC; DAM MST**
See also CA 102; DLB 88

**Theroux, Alexander (Louis)**
1939- . . . . . . . . . . . . . . . . . . . . **CLC 2, 25**
See also CA 85-88; CANR 20

**Theroux, Paul (Edward)**
1941- . . . . . . . . **CLC 5, 8, 11, 15, 28, 46;**
**DAM POP**
See also BEST 89:4; CA 33-36R; CANR 20,
45; DLB 2; MTCW; SATA 44

**Thesen, Sharon**  1946- . . . . . . . . . . . **CLC 56**

**Thevenin, Denis**
See Duhamel, Georges

**Thibault, Jacques Anatole Francois**
1844-1924
See France, Anatole
See also CA 106; 127; DAM NOV; MTCW

**Thiele, Colin (Milton)**  1920- . . . . . . . **CLC 17**
See also CA 29-32R; CANR 12, 28, 53;
CLR 27; MAICYA; SAAS 2; SATA 14,
72

**Thomas, Audrey (Callahan)**
1935- . . . . . . . . . **CLC 7, 13, 37; SSC 20**
See also AITN 2; CA 21-24R; CAAS 19;
CANR 36; DLB 60; MTCW

**Thomas, D(onald) M(ichael)**
1935- . . . . . . . . . . . . . . . . **CLC 13, 22, 31**
See also CA 61-64; CAAS 11; CANR 17,
45; CDBLB 1960 to Present; DLB 40;
INT CANR-17; MTCW

**Thomas, Dylan (Marlais)**
1914-1953 . . . **TCLC 1, 8, 45; DA; DAB;**
**DAC; DAM DRAM, MST, POET;**
**PC 2; SSC 3; WLC**
See also CA 104; 120; CDBLB 1945-1960;
DLB 13, 20, 139; MTCW; SATA 60

**Thomas, (Philip) Edward**
1878-1917 . . . . . . **TCLC 10; DAM POET**
See also CA 106; DLB 19

**Thomas, Joyce Carol**  1938- . . . . . . . . **CLC 35**
See also AAYA 12; BW 2; CA 113; 116;
CANR 48; CLR 19; DLB 33; INT 116;
JRDA; MAICYA; SAAS 7;
SATA 40, 78

**Thomas, Lewis**  1913-1993 . . . . . . . . **CLC 35**
See also CA 85-88; 143; CANR 38; MTCW

**Thomas, Paul**
See Mann, (Paul) Thomas

**Thomas, Piri**  1928- . . . . . . . . . . . . . . **CLC 17**
See also CA 73-76; HW

**Thomas, R(onald) S(tuart)**
1913- . . . . . . . . . . . **CLC 6, 13, 48; DAB;**
**DAM POET**
See also CA 89-92; CAAS 4; CANR 30;
CDBLB 1960 to Present; DLB 27;
MTCW

**Thomas, Ross (Elmore)**  1926-1995 . . **CLC 39**
See also CA 33-36R; 150; CANR 22

**Thompson, Francis Clegg**
See Mencken, H(enry) L(ouis)

**Thompson, Francis Joseph**
1859-1907 . . . . . . . . . . . . . . . . . . **TCLC 4**
See also CA 104; CDBLB 1890-1914;
DLB 19

**Thompson, Hunter S(tockton)**
1939- . . . . . . . **CLC 9, 17, 40; DAM POP**
See also BEST 89:1; CA 17-20R; CANR 23,
46; MTCW

**Thompson, James Myers**
See Thompson, Jim (Myers)

**Thompson, Jim (Myers)**
1906-1977(?) . . . . . . . . . . . . . . . . **CLC 69**
See also CA 140

**Thompson, Judith** . . . . . . . . . . . . . . . **CLC 39**

**Thomson, James**
1700-1748 . . . . . **LC 16, 29; DAM POET**
See also DLB 95

**Thomson, James**
1834-1882 . . . . . **NCLC 18; DAM POET**
See also DLB 35

**Thoreau, Henry David**
1817-1862 . . . . . **NCLC 7, 21; DA; DAB;**
**DAC; DAM MST; WLC**
See also CDALB 1640-1865; DLB 1

**Thornton, Hall**
See Silverberg, Robert

**Thucydides**  c. 455B.C.-399B.C. . . . . **CMLC 17**

**Thurber, James (Grover)**
1894-1961 . . . . **CLC 5, 11, 25; DA; DAB;**
**DAC; DAM DRAM, MST, NOV; SSC 1**
See also CA 73-76; CANR 17, 39;
CDALB 1929-1941; DLB 4, 11, 22, 102;
MAICYA; MTCW; SATA 13

**Thurman, Wallace (Henry)**
1902-1934 . . . . . . . . . . . . . **TCLC 6; BLC;**
**DAM MULT**
See also BW 1; CA 104; 124; DLB 51

**Ticheburn, Cheviot**
See Ainsworth, William Harrison

**Tieck, (Johann) Ludwig**
1773-1853 . . . . . . . . . . . . . . **NCLC 5, 46**
See also DLB 90

**Tiger, Derry**
See Ellison, Harlan (Jay)

**Tilghman, Christopher**  1948(?)- . . . . . **CLC 65**

**Tillinghast, Richard (Williford)**
1940- . . . . . . . . . . . . . . . . . . . . . . **CLC 29**
See also CA 29-32R; CAAS 23; CANR 26,
51

**Timrod, Henry**  1828-1867 . . . . . . . **NCLC 25**
See also DLB 3

**Tindall, Gillian**  1938- . . . . . . . . . . . . . **CLC 7**
See also CA 21-24R; CANR 11

**Tiptree, James, Jr.** . . . . . . . . . . . **CLC 48, 50**
See also Sheldon, Alice Hastings Bradley
See also DLB 8

**Titmarsh, Michael Angelo**
See Thackeray, William Makepeace

**Tocqueville, Alexis (Charles Henri Maurice**
**Clerel Comte)**  1805-1859 . . . . . **NCLC 7**

**Tolkien, J(ohn) R(onald) R(euel)**
1892-1973 . . . . . . . **CLC 1, 2, 3, 8, 12, 38;**
**DA; DAB; DAC; DAM MST, NOV,**
**POP; WLC**
See also AAYA 10; AITN 1; CA 17-18;
45-48; CANR 36; CAP 2;
CDBLB 1914-1945; DLB 15, 160; JRDA;
MAICYA; MTCW; SATA 2, 32;
SATA-Obit 24

**Toller, Ernst**  1893-1939 . . . . . . . . . **TCLC 10**
See also CA 107; DLB 124

**Tolson, M. B.**
See Tolson, Melvin B(eaunorus)

**Tolson, Melvin B(eaunorus)**
1898(?)-1966 . . . . . . . . . . . **CLC 36; BLC;**
**DAM MULT, POET**
See also BW 1; CA 124; 89-92; DLB 48, 76

**Tolstoi, Aleksei Nikolaevich**
See Tolstoy, Alexey Nikolaevich

**Tolstoy, Alexey Nikolaevich**
1882-1945 . . . . . . . . . . . . . . . . . **TCLC 18**
See also CA 107

**Tolstoy, Count Leo**
See Tolstoy, Leo (Nikolaevich)

**Tolstoy, Leo (Nikolaevich)**
1828-1910 . . . . . . **TCLC 4, 11, 17, 28, 44;**
**DA; DAB; DAC; DAM MST, NOV;**
**SSC 9; WLC**
See also CA 104; 123; SATA 26

**Tomasi di Lampedusa, Giuseppe**  1896-1957
See Lampedusa, Giuseppe (Tomasi) di
See also CA 111

**Tomlin, Lily** . . . . . . . . . . . . . . . . . . . . **CLC 17**
See also Tomlin, Mary Jean

**Tomlin, Mary Jean**  1939(?)-
See Tomlin, Lily
See also CA 117

**Tomlinson, (Alfred) Charles**
1927- . . . . . . . . . . . . . . **CLC 2, 4, 6, 13, 45;**
**DAM POET**
See also CA 5-8R; CANR 33; DLB 40

**Tonson, Jacob**
See Bennett, (Enoch) Arnold

**Toole, John Kennedy**
1937-1969 . . . . . . . . . . . . . . . **CLC 19, 64**
See also CA 104; DLBY 81

**Toomer, Jean**
1894-1967 . . . . . . **CLC 1, 4, 13, 22; BLC;**
**DAM MULT; PC 7; SSC 1**
See also BW 1; CA 85-88;
CDALB 1917-1929; DLB 45, 51; MTCW

**Torley, Luke**
See Blish, James (Benjamin)

**Tornimparte, Alessandra**
See Ginzburg, Natalia

**Torre, Raoul della**
See Mencken, H(enry) L(ouis)

**Torrey, E(dwin) Fuller**  1937- . . . . . . . **CLC 34**
See also CA 119

**Torsvan, Ben Traven**
See Traven, B.

**Torsvan, Benno Traven**
See Traven, B.

**Torsvan, Berick Traven**
See Traven, B.

**Torsvan, Berwick Traven**
See Traven, B.

**Torsvan, Bruno Traven**
See Traven, B.

**Torsvan, Traven**
See Traven, B.

**Tournier, Michel (Edouard)**
1924- . . . . . . . . . . . . . . CLC 6, 23, 36, 95
See also CA 49-52; CANR 3, 36; DLB 83;
MTCW; SATA 23

**Tournimparte, Alessandra**
See Ginzburg, Natalia

**Towers, Ivar**
See Kornbluth, C(yril) M.

**Towne, Robert (Burton)** 1936(?)- . . . . CLC 87
See also CA 108; DLB 44

**Townsend, Sue** 1946- . . CLC 61; DAB; DAC
See also CA 119; 127; INT 127; MTCW;
SATA 55; SATA-Brief 48

**Townshend, Peter (Dennis Blandford)**
1945- . . . . . . . . . . . . . . . . . . . CLC 17, 42
See also CA 107

**Tozzi, Federigo** 1883-1920 . . . . . . . TCLC 31

**Traill, Catharine Parr**
1802-1899 . . . . . . . . . . . . . . . . NCLC 31
See also DLB 99

**Trakl, Georg** 1887-1914 . . . . . . . . . . TCLC 5
See also CA 104

**Transtroemer, Tomas (Goesta)**
1931- . . . . . . . . CLC 52, 65; DAM POET
See also CA 117; 129; CAAS 17

**Transtromer, Tomas Gosta**
See Transtroemer, Tomas (Goesta)

**Traven, B.** (?)-1969 . . . . . . . . . . . . CLC 8, 11
See also CA 19-20; 25-28R; CAP 2; DLB 9,
56; MTCW

**Treitel, Jonathan** 1959- . . . . . . . . . . . CLC 70

**Tremain, Rose** 1943- . . . . . . . . . . . . . CLC 42
See also CA 97-100; CANR 44; DLB 14

**Tremblay, Michel**
1942- . . . . . . CLC 29; DAC; DAM MST
See also CA 116; 128; DLB 60; MTCW

**Trevanian** . . . . . . . . . . . . . . . . . . . . . CLC 29
See also Whitaker, Rod(ney)

**Trevor, Glen**
See Hilton, James

**Trevor, William**
1928- . . . . . CLC 7, 9, 14, 25, 71; SSC 21
See also Cox, William Trevor
See also DLB 14, 139

**Trifonov, Yuri (Valentinovich)**
1925-1981 . . . . . . . . . . . . . . . . . CLC 45
See also CA 126; 103; MTCW

**Trilling, Lionel** 1905-1975 . . . . CLC 9, 11, 24
See also CA 9-12R; 61-64; CANR 10;
DLB 28, 63; INT CANR-10; MTCW

**Trimball, W. H.**
See Mencken, H(enry) L(ouis)

**Tristan**
See Gomez de la Serna, Ramon

**Tristram**
See Housman, A(lfred) E(dward)

**Trogdon, William (Lewis)** 1939-
See Heat-Moon, William Least
See also CA 115; 119; CANR 47; INT 119

**Trollope, Anthony**
1815-1882 . . . . . NCLC 6, 33; DA; DAB;
DAC; DAM MST, NOV; WLC
See also CDBLB 1832-1890; DLB 21, 57,
159; SATA 22

**Trollope, Frances** 1779-1863 . . . . . NCLC 30
See also DLB 21, 166

**Trotsky, Leon** 1879-1940 . . . . . . . . TCLC 22
See also CA 118

**Trotter (Cockburn), Catharine**
1679-1749 . . . . . . . . . . . . . . . . . . LC 8
See also DLB 84

**Trout, Kilgore**
See Farmer, Philip Jose

**Trow, George W. S.** 1943- . . . . . . . . CLC 52
See also CA 126

**Troyat, Henri** 1911- . . . . . . . . . . . . . CLC 23
See also CA 45-48; CANR 2, 33; MTCW

**Trudeau, G(arretson) B(eekman)** 1948-
See Trudeau, Garry B.
See also CA 81-84; CANR 31; SATA 35

**Trudeau, Garry B.** . . . . . . . . . . . . . . . CLC 12
See also Trudeau, G(arretson) B(eekman)
See also AAYA 10; AITN 2

**Truffaut, Francois** 1932-1984 . . . . . . CLC 20
See also CA 81-84; 113; CANR 34

**Trumbo, Dalton** 1905-1976 . . . . . . . . CLC 19
See also CA 21-24R; 69-72; CANR 10;
DLB 26

**Trumbull, John** 1750-1831 . . . . . . NCLC 30
See also DLB 31

**Trundlett, Helen B.**
See Eliot, T(homas) S(tearns)

**Tryon, Thomas**
1926-1991 . . . . . . CLC 3, 11; DAM POP
See also AITN 1; CA 29-32R; 135;
CANR 32; MTCW

**Tryon, Tom**
See Tryon, Thomas

**Ts'ao Hsueh-ch'in** 1715(?)-1763 . . . . . . . LC 1

**Tsushima, Shuji** 1909-1948
See Dazai, Osamu
See also CA 107

**Tsvetaeva (Efron), Marina (Ivanovna)**
1892-1941 . . . . . . . . TCLC 7, 35; PC 14
See also CA 104; 128; MTCW

**Tuck, Lily** 1938- . . . . . . . . . . . . . . . . CLC 70
See also CA 139

**Tu Fu** 712-770 . . . . . . . . . . . . . . . . . . PC 9
See also DAM MULT

**Tunis, John R(oberts)** 1889-1975 . . . CLC 12
See also CA 61-64; DLB 22; JRDA;
MAICYA; SATA 37; SATA-Brief 30

**Tuohy, Frank** . . . . . . . . . . . . . . . . . . CLC 37
See also Tuohy, John Francis
See also DLB 14, 139

**Tuohy, John Francis** 1925-
See Tuohy, Frank
See also CA 5-8R; CANR 3, 47

**Turco, Lewis (Putnam)** 1934- . . . CLC 11, 63
See also CA 13-16R; CAAS 22; CANR 24,
51; DLBY 84

**Turgenev, Ivan**
1818-1883 . . . . . . . NCLC 21; DA; DAB;
DAC; DAM MST, NOV; SSC 7; WLC

**Turgot, Anne-Robert-Jacques**
1727-1781 . . . . . . . . . . . . . . . . . . LC 26

**Turner, Frederick** 1943- . . . . . . . . . . CLC 48
See also CA 73-76; CAAS 10; CANR 12,
30; DLB 40

**Tutu, Desmond M(pilo)**
1931- . . . . . CLC 80; BLC; DAM MULT
See also BW 1; CA 125

**Tutuola, Amos**
1920- . . . . . . . . . . . . CLC 5, 14, 29; BLC;
DAM MULT
See also BW 2; CA 9-12R; CANR 27;
DLB 125; MTCW

**Twain, Mark**
. . . . . TCLC 6, 12, 19, 36, 48, 59; SSC 6;
WLC
See also Clemens, Samuel Langhorne
See also DLB 11, 12, 23, 64, 74

**Tyler, Anne**
1941- . . . . . . . . CLC 7, 11, 18, 28, 44, 59;
DAM NOV, POP
See also AAYA 18; BEST 89:1; CA 9-12R;
CANR 11, 33, 53; DLB 6, 143; DLBY 82;
MTCW; SATA 7

**Tyler, Royall** 1757-1826 . . . . . . . . . . NCLC 3
See also DLB 37

**Tynan, Katharine** 1861-1931 . . . . . . TCLC 3
See also CA 104; DLB 153

**Tyutchev, Fyodor** 1803-1873 . . . . . NCLC 34

**Tzara, Tristan** . . . . . . . . CLC 47; DAM POET
See also Rosenfeld, Samuel

**Uhry, Alfred**
1936- . . . . . CLC 55; DAM DRAM, POP
See also CA 127; 133; INT 133

**Ulf, Haerved**
See Strindberg, (Johan) August

**Ulf, Harved**
See Strindberg, (Johan) August

**Ulibarri, Sabine R(eyes)**
1919- . . . . . . . . . . CLC 83; DAM MULT
See also CA 131; DLB 82; HW

**Unamuno (y Jugo), Miguel de**
1864-1936 . . . TCLC 2, 9; DAM MULT,
NOV; HLC; SSC 11
See also CA 104; 131; DLB 108; HW;
MTCW

**Undercliffe, Errol**
See Campbell, (John) Ramsey

**Underwood, Miles**
See Glassco, John

**Undset, Sigrid**
1882-1949 . . . . . . . . TCLC 3; DA; DAB;
DAC; DAM MST, NOV; WLC
See also CA 104; 129; MTCW

**Ungaretti, Giuseppe**
1888-1970 . . . . . . . . . . . . . CLC 7, 11, 15
See also CA 19-20; 25-28R; CAP 2;
DLB 114

**Unger, Douglas** 1952-............ **CLC 34**
See also CA 130

**Unsworth, Barry (Forster)** 1930-.... **CLC 76**
See also CA 25-28R; CANR 30

**Updike, John (Hoyer)**
1932-...... **CLC 1, 2, 3, 5, 7, 9, 13, 15,**
**23, 34, 43, 70; DA; DAB; DAC;**
**DAM MST, NOV, POET, POP;**
**SSC 13; WLC**
See also CA 1-4R; CABS 1; CANR 4, 33,
51; CDALB 1968-1988; DLB 2, 5, 143;
DLBD 3; DLBY 80, 82; MTCW

**Upshaw, Margaret Mitchell**
See Mitchell, Margaret (Munnerlyn)

**Upton, Mark**
See Sanders, Lawrence

**Urdang, Constance (Henriette)**
1922-...................... **CLC 47**
See also CA 21-24R; CANR 9, 24

**Uriel, Henry**
See Faust, Frederick (Schiller)

**Uris, Leon (Marcus)**
1924-.... **CLC 7, 32; DAM NOV, POP**
See also AITN 1, 2; BEST 89:2; CA 1-4R;
CANR 1, 40; MTCW; SATA 49

**Urmuz**
See Codrescu, Andrei

**Urquhart, Jane** 1949-........ **CLC 90; DAC**
See also CA 113; CANR 32

**Ustinov, Peter (Alexander)** 1921-.... **CLC 1**
See also AITN 1; CA 13-16R; CANR 25,
51; DLB 13

**Vaculik, Ludvik** 1926-............. **CLC 7**
See also CA 53-56

**Valdez, Luis (Miguel)**
1940-..... **CLC 84; DAM MULT; HLC**
See also CA 101; CANR 32; DLB 122; HW

**Valenzuela, Luisa**
1938-... **CLC 31; DAM MULT; SSC 14**
See also CA 101; CANR 32; DLB 113; HW

**Valera y Alcala-Galiano, Juan**
1824-1905 .................. **TCLC 10**
See also CA 106

**Valery, (Ambroise) Paul (Toussaint Jules)**
1871-1945 ............... **TCLC 4, 15;**
**DAM POET; PC 9**
See also CA 104; 122; MTCW

**Valle-Inclan, Ramon (Maria) del**
1866-1936 ..... **TCLC 5; DAM MULT;**
**HLC**
See also CA 106; DLB 134

**Vallejo, Antonio Buero**
See Buero Vallejo, Antonio

**Vallejo, Cesar (Abraham)**
1892-1938 .............. **TCLC 3, 56;**
**DAM MULT; HLC**
See also CA 105; HW

**Valle Y Pena, Ramon del**
See Valle-Inclan, Ramon (Maria) del

**Van Ash, Cay** 1918-............. **CLC 34**

**Vanbrugh, Sir John**
1664-1726 ...... **LC 21; DAM DRAM**
See also DLB 80

**Van Campen, Karl**
See Campbell, John W(ood, Jr.)

**Vance, Gerald**
See Silverberg, Robert

**Vance, Jack** ...................... **CLC 35**
See also Vance, John Holbrook
See also DLB 8

**Vance, John Holbrook** 1916-
See Queen, Ellery; Vance, Jack
See also CA 29-32R; CANR 17; MTCW

**Van Den Bogarde, Derek Jules Gaspard Ulric
Niven** 1921-
See Bogarde, Dirk
See also CA 77-80

**Vandenburgh, Jane** ................ **CLC 59**

**Vanderhaeghe, Guy** 1951- ......... **CLC 41**
See also CA 113

**van der Post, Laurens (Jan)** 1906- ... **CLC 5**
See also CA 5-8R; CANR 35

**van de Wetering, Janwillem** 1931- .. **CLC 47**
See also CA 49-52; CANR 4

**Van Dine, S. S.** ................... **TCLC 23**
See also Wright, Willard Huntington

**Van Doren, Carl (Clinton)**
1885-1950 .................. **TCLC 18**
See also CA 111

**Van Doren, Mark** 1894-1972..... **CLC 6, 10**
See also CA 1-4R; 37-40R; CANR 3;
DLB 45; MTCW

**Van Druten, John (William)**
1901-1957 ................... **TCLC 2**
See also CA 104; DLB 10

**Van Duyn, Mona (Jane)**
1921- ....... **CLC 3, 7, 63; DAM POET**
See also CA 9-12R; CANR 7, 38; DLB 5

**Van Dyne, Edith**
See Baum, L(yman) Frank

**van Itallie, Jean-Claude** 1936-....... **CLC 3**
See also CA 45-48; CAAS 2; CANR 1, 48;
DLB 7

**van Ostaijen, Paul** 1896-1928 ..... **TCLC 33**

**Van Peebles, Melvin**
1932- ........ **CLC 2, 20; DAM MULT**
See also BW 2; CA 85-88; CANR 27

**Vansittart, Peter** 1920-............ **CLC 42**
See also CA 1-4R; CANR 3, 49

**Van Vechten, Carl** 1880-1964 ...... **CLC 33**
See also CA 89-92; DLB 4, 9, 51

**Van Vogt, A(lfred) E(lton)** 1912-..... **CLC 1**
See also CA 21-24R; CANR 28; DLB 8;
SATA 14

**Varda, Agnes** 1928- .............. **CLC 16**
See also CA 116; 122

**Vargas Llosa, (Jorge) Mario (Pedro)**
1936- .... **CLC 3, 6, 9, 10, 15, 31, 42, 85;**
**DA; DAB; DAC; DAM MST, MULT,**
**NOV; HLC**
See also CA 73-76; CANR 18, 32, 42;
DLB 145; HW; MTCW

**Vasiliu, Gheorghe** 1881-1957
See Bacovia, George
See also CA 123

**Vassa, Gustavus**
See Equiano, Olaudah

**Vassilikos, Vassilis** 1933-........ **CLC 4, 8**
See also CA 81-84

**Vaughan, Henry** 1621-1695 ........ **LC 27**
See also DLB 131

**Vaughn, Stephanie** ................. **CLC 62**

**Vazov, Ivan (Minchov)**
1850-1921 .................. **TCLC 25**
See also CA 121; DLB 147

**Veblen, Thorstein (Bunde)**
1857-1929 .................. **TCLC 31**
See also CA 115

**Vega, Lope de** 1562-1635 .......... **LC 23**

**Venison, Alfred**
See Pound, Ezra (Weston Loomis)

**Verdi, Marie de**
See Mencken, H(enry) L(ouis)

**Verdu, Matilde**
See Cela, Camilo Jose

**Verga, Giovanni (Carmelo)**
1840-1922 .......... **TCLC 3; SSC 21**
See also CA 104; 123

**Vergil**
70B.C.-19B.C..... **CMLC 9; DA; DAB;**
**DAC; DAM MST, POET; PC 12**

**Verhaeren, Emile (Adolphe Gustave)**
1855-1916 .................. **TCLC 12**
See also CA 109

**Verlaine, Paul (Marie)**
1844-1896 .............. **NCLC 2, 51;**
**DAM POET; PC 2**

**Verne, Jules (Gabriel)**
1828-1905 ................ **TCLC 6, 52**
See also AAYA 16; CA 110; 131; DLB 123;
JRDA; MAICYA; SATA 21

**Very, Jones** 1813-1880 .......... **NCLC 9**
See also DLB 1

**Vesaas, Tarjei** 1897-1970 ......... **CLC 48**
See also CA 29-32R

**Vialis, Gaston**
See Simenon, Georges (Jacques Christian)

**Vian, Boris** 1920-1959 ............ **TCLC 9**
See also CA 106; DLB 72

**Viaud, (Louis Marie) Julien** 1850-1923
See Loti, Pierre
See also CA 107

**Vicar, Henry**
See Felsen, Henry Gregor

**Vicker, Angus**
See Felsen, Henry Gregor

**Vidal, Gore**
1925- ..... **CLC 2, 4, 6, 8, 10, 22, 33, 72;**
**DAM NOV, POP**
See also AITN 1; BEST 90:2; CA 5-8R;
CANR 13, 45; DLB 6, 152;
INT CANR-13; MTCW

**Viereck, Peter (Robert Edwin)**
1916-...................... **CLC 4**
See also CA 1-4R; CANR 1, 47; DLB 5

**Vigny, Alfred (Victor) de**
1797-1863 ...... **NCLC 7; DAM POET**
See also DLB 119

**Vilakazi, Benedict Wallet**
1906-1947 ................. **TCLC 37**

**Villiers de l'Isle Adam, Jean Marie Mathias Philippe Auguste Comte**
1838-1889 . . . . . . . . . . **NCLC 3; SSC 14**
See also DLB 123

**Villon, Francois** 1431-1463(?) . . . . . . . **PC 13**

**Vinci, Leonardo da** 1452-1519 . . . . . . **LC 12**

**Vine, Barbara** . . . . . . . . . . . . . . . . . . . **CLC 50**
See also Rendell, Ruth (Barbara)
See also BEST 90:4

**Vinge, Joan D(ennison)** 1948- . . . . . . **CLC 30**
See also CA 93-96; SATA 36

**Violis, G.**
See Simenon, Georges (Jacques Christian)

**Visconti, Luchino** 1906-1976 . . . . . . . **CLC 16**
See also CA 81-84; 65-68; CANR 39

**Vittorini, Elio** 1908-1966 . . . . . . **CLC 6, 9, 14**
See also CA 133; 25-28R

**Vizinczey, Stephen** 1933- . . . . . . . . . . **CLC 40**
See also CA 128; INT 128

**Vliet, R(ussell) G(ordon)**
1929-1984 . . . . . . . . . . . . . . . . . **CLC 22**
See also CA 37-40R; 112; CANR 18

**Vogau, Boris Andreyevich** 1894-1937(?)
See Pilnyak, Boris
See also CA 123

**Vogel, Paula A(nne)** 1951- . . . . . . . . . **CLC 76**
See also CA 108

**Voight, Ellen Bryant** 1943- . . . . . . . . **CLC 54**
See also CA 69-72; CANR 11, 29; DLB 120

**Voigt, Cynthia** 1942- . . . . . . . . . . . . . **CLC 30**
See also AAYA 3; CA 106; CANR 18, 37,
40; CLR 13; INT CANR-18; JRDA;
MAICYA; SATA 48, 79; SATA-Brief 33

**Voinovich, Vladimir (Nikolaevich)**
1932- . . . . . . . . . . . . . . . . . . . **CLC 10, 49**
See also CA 81-84; CAAS 12; CANR 33;
MTCW

**Vollmann, William T.**
1959- . . . . . . **CLC 89; DAM NOV, POP**
See also CA 134

**Voloshinov, V. N.**
See Bakhtin, Mikhail Mikhailovich

**Voltaire**
1694-1778 . . . . . **LC 14; DA; DAB; DAC;
DAM DRAM, MST; SSC 12; WLC**

**von Daeniken, Erich** 1935- . . . . . . . . **CLC 30**
See also AITN 1; CA 37-40R; CANR 17,
44

**von Daniken, Erich**
See von Daeniken, Erich

**von Heidenstam, (Carl Gustaf) Verner**
See Heidenstam, (Carl Gustaf) Verner von

**von Heyse, Paul (Johann Ludwig)**
See Heyse, Paul (Johann Ludwig von)

**von Hofmannsthal, Hugo**
See Hofmannsthal, Hugo von

**von Horvath, Odon**
See Horvath, Oedoen von

**von Horvath, Oedoen**
See Horvath, Oedoen von

**von Liliencron, (Friedrich Adolf Axel) Detlev**
See Liliencron, (Friedrich Adolf Axel)
Detlev von

**Vonnegut, Kurt, Jr.**
1922- . . . . . . **CLC 1, 2, 3, 4, 5, 8, 12, 22,
40, 60; DA; DAB; DAC; DAM MST,
NOV, POP; SSC 8; WLC**
See also AAYA 6; AITN 1; BEST 90:4;
CA 1-4R; CANR 1, 25, 49;
CDALB 1968-1988; DLB 2, 8, 152;
DLBD 3; DLBY 80; MTCW

**Von Rachen, Kurt**
See Hubbard, L(afayette) Ron(ald)

**von Rezzori (d'Arezzo), Gregor**
See Rezzori (d'Arezzo), Gregor von

**von Sternberg, Josef**
See Sternberg, Josef von

**Vorster, Gordon** 1924- . . . . . . . . . . . **CLC 34**
See also CA 133

**Vosce, Trudie**
See Ozick, Cynthia

**Voznesensky, Andrei (Andreievich)**
1933- . . . . . . **CLC 1, 15, 57; DAM POET**
See also CA 89-92; CANR 37; MTCW

**Waddington, Miriam** 1917- . . . . . . . . **CLC 28**
See also CA 21-24R; CANR 12, 30;
DLB 68

**Wagman, Fredrica** 1937- . . . . . . . . . . **CLC 7**
See also CA 97-100; INT 97-100

**Wagner, Richard** 1813-1883 . . . . . . . **NCLC 9**
See also DLB 129

**Wagner-Martin, Linda** 1936- . . . . . . **CLC 50**

**Wagoner, David (Russell)**
1926- . . . . . . . . . . . . . . . . . . **CLC 3, 5, 15**
See also CA 1-4R; CAAS 3; CANR 2;
DLB 5; SATA 14

**Wah, Fred(erick James)** 1939- . . . . . . **CLC 44**
See also CA 107; 141; DLB 60

**Wahloo, Per** 1926-1975 . . . . . . . . . . . . **CLC 7**
See also CA 61-64

**Wahloo, Peter**
See Wahloo, Per

**Wain, John (Barrington)**
1925-1994 . . . . . . . . . . . **CLC 2, 11, 15, 46**
See also CA 5-8R; 145; CAAS 4; CANR 23;
CDBLB 1960 to Present; DLB 15, 27,
139, 155; MTCW

**Wajda, Andrzej** 1926- . . . . . . . . . . . . . **CLC 16**
See also CA 102

**Wakefield, Dan** 1932- . . . . . . . . . . . . . **CLC 7**
See also CA 21-24R; CAAS 7

**Wakoski, Diane**
1937- . . . . . . . . . . **CLC 2, 4, 7, 9, 11, 40;
DAM POET; PC 15**
See also CA 13-16R; CAAS 1; CANR 9;
DLB 5; INT CANR-9

**Wakoski-Sherbell, Diane**
See Wakoski, Diane

**Walcott, Derek (Alton)**
1930- . . . . **CLC 2, 4, 9, 14, 25, 42, 67, 76;
BLC; DAB; DAC; DAM MST, MULT,
POET**
See also BW 2; CA 89-92; CANR 26, 47;
DLB 117; DLBY 81; MTCW

**Waldman, Anne** 1945- . . . . . . . . . . . . **CLC 7**
See also CA 37-40R; CAAS 17; CANR 34;
DLB 16

**Waldo, E. Hunter**
See Sturgeon, Theodore (Hamilton)

**Waldo, Edward Hamilton**
See Sturgeon, Theodore (Hamilton)

**Walker, Alice (Malsenior)**
1944- . . . . . . . **CLC 5, 6, 9, 19, 27, 46, 58;
BLC; DA; DAB; DAC; DAM MST,
MULT, NOV, POET, POP; SSC 5**
See also AAYA 3; BEST 89:4; BW 2;
CA 37-40R; CANR 9, 27, 49;
CDALB 1968-1988; DLB 6, 33, 143;
INT CANR-27; MTCW; SATA 31

**Walker, David Harry** 1911-1992 . . . . **CLC 14**
See also CA 1-4R; 137; CANR 1; SATA 8;
SATA-Obit 71

**Walker, Edward Joseph** 1934-
See Walker, Ted
See also CA 21-24R; CANR 12, 28, 53

**Walker, George F.**
1947- . . . . . . . . **CLC 44, 61; DAB; DAC;
DAM MST**
See also CA 103; CANR 21, 43; DLB 60

**Walker, Joseph A.**
1935- . . . . **CLC 19; DAM DRAM, MST**
See also BW 1; CA 89-92; CANR 26;
DLB 38

**Walker, Margaret (Abigail)**
1915- . . . . **CLC 1, 6; BLC; DAM MULT**
See also BW 2; CA 73-76; CANR 26;
DLB 76, 152; MTCW

**Walker, Ted** . . . . . . . . . . . . . . . . . . . . **CLC 13**
See also Walker, Edward Joseph
See also DLB 40

**Wallace, David Foster** 1962- . . . . . . . **CLC 50**
See also CA 132

**Wallace, Dexter**
See Masters, Edgar Lee

**Wallace, (Richard Horatio) Edgar**
1875-1932 . . . . . . . . . . . . . . . . . **TCLC 57**
See also CA 115; DLB 70

**Wallace, Irving**
1916-1990 . . . . . **CLC 7, 13; DAM NOV,
POP**
See also AITN 1; CA 1-4R; 132; CAAS 1;
CANR 1, 27; INT CANR-27; MTCW

**Wallant, Edward Lewis**
1926-1962 . . . . . . . . . . . . . . . . **CLC 5, 10**
See also CA 1-4R; CANR 22; DLB 2, 28,
143; MTCW

**Walley, Byron**
See Card, Orson Scott

**Walpole, Horace** 1717-1797 . . . . . . . . . . **LC 2**
See also DLB 39, 104

**Walpole, Hugh (Seymour)**
1884-1941 . . . . . . . . . . . . . . . . . . . **TCLC 5**
See also CA 104; DLB 34

**Walser, Martin** 1927- . . . . . . . . . . . . . **CLC 27**
See also CA 57-60; CANR 8, 46; DLB 75,
124

**Walser, Robert**
1878-1956 . . . . . . . . . . **TCLC 18; SSC 20**
See also CA 118; DLB 66

**Walsh, Jill Paton** . . . . . . . . . . . . . . . . . **CLC 35**
See also Paton Walsh, Gillian
See also AAYA 11; CLR 2; DLB 161;
SAAS 3

**Walter, Villiam Christian**
See Andersen, Hans Christian

**Wambaugh, Joseph (Aloysius, Jr.)**
1937- .... **CLC 3, 18; DAM NOV, POP**
See also AITN 1; BEST 89:3; CA 33-36R;
CANR 42; DLB 6; DLBY 83; MTCW

**Ward, Arthur Henry Sarsfield** 1883-1959
See Rohmer, Sax
See also CA 108

**Ward, Douglas Turner** 1930- ....... **CLC 19**
See also BW 1; CA 81-84; CANR 27;
DLB 7, 38

**Ward, Mary Augusta**
See Ward, Mrs. Humphry

**Ward, Mrs. Humphry**
1851-1920 ................. **TCLC 55**
See also DLB 18

**Ward, Peter**
See Faust, Frederick (Schiller)

**Warhol, Andy** 1928(?)-1987 ....... **CLC 20**
See also AAYA 12; BEST 89:4; CA 89-92;
121; CANR 34

**Warner, Francis (Robert le Plastrier)**
1937- ...................... **CLC 14**
See also CA 53-56; CANR 11

**Warner, Marina** 1946- ........... **CLC 59**
See also CA 65-68; CANR 21

**Warner, Rex (Ernest)** 1905-1986.... **CLC 45**
See also CA 89-92; 119; DLB 15

**Warner, Susan (Bogert)**
1819-1885 ................. **NCLC 31**
See also DLB 3, 42

**Warner, Sylvia (Constance) Ashton**
See Ashton-Warner, Sylvia (Constance)

**Warner, Sylvia Townsend**
1893-1978 ......... **CLC 7, 19; SSC 23**
See also CA 61-64; 77-80; CANR 16;
DLB 34, 139; MTCW

**Warren, Mercy Otis** 1728-1814... **NCLC 13**
See also DLB 31

**Warren, Robert Penn**
1905-1989 .... **CLC 1, 4, 6, 8, 10, 13, 18,**
**39, 53, 59; DA; DAB; DAC; DAM MST,**
**NOV, POET; SSC 4; WLC**
See also AITN 1; CA 13-16R; 129;
CANR 10, 47; CDALB 1968-1988;
DLB 2, 48, 152; DLBY 80, 89;
INT CANR-10; MTCW; SATA 46;
SATA-Obit 63

**Warshofsky, Isaac**
See Singer, Isaac Bashevis

**Warton, Thomas**
1728-1790 ....... **LC 15; DAM POET**
See also DLB 104, 109

**Waruk, Kona**
See Harris, (Theodore) Wilson

**Warung, Price** 1855-1911........ **TCLC 45**

**Warwick, Jarvis**
See Garner, Hugh

**Washington, Alex**
See Harris, Mark

**Washington, Booker T(aliaferro)**
1856-1915 ........... **TCLC 10; BLC;**
**DAM MULT**
See also BW 1; CA 114; 125; SATA 28

**Washington, George** 1732-1799 ..... **LC 25**
See also DLB 31

**Wassermann, (Karl) Jakob**
1873-1934 ................... **TCLC 6**
See also CA 104; DLB 66

**Wasserstein, Wendy**
1950- ............... **CLC 32, 59, 90;**
**DAM DRAM; DC 4**
See also CA 121; 129; CABS 3; CANR 53;
INT 129

**Waterhouse, Keith (Spencer)**
1929- ...................... **CLC 47**
See also CA 5-8R; CANR 38; DLB 13, 15;
MTCW

**Waters, Frank (Joseph)**
1902-1995 ................... **CLC 88**
See also CA 5-8R; 149; CAAS 13; CANR 3,
18; DLBY 86

**Waters, Roger** 1944- ............. **CLC 35**

**Watkins, Frances Ellen**
See Harper, Frances Ellen Watkins

**Watkins, Gerrold**
See Malzberg, Barry N(athaniel)

**Watkins, Gloria** 1955(?)-
See hooks, bell
See also BW 2; CA 143

**Watkins, Paul** 1964- ............. **CLC 55**
See also CA 132

**Watkins, Vernon Phillips**
1906-1967 ................... **CLC 43**
See also CA 9-10; 25-28R; CAP 1; DLB 20

**Watson, Irving S.**
See Mencken, H(enry) L(ouis)

**Watson, John H.**
See Farmer, Philip Jose

**Watson, Richard F.**
See Silverberg, Robert

**Waugh, Auberon (Alexander)** 1939- .. **CLC 7**
See also CA 45-48; CANR 6, 22; DLB 14

**Waugh, Evelyn (Arthur St. John)**
1903-1966 ...... **CLC 1, 3, 8, 13, 19, 27,**
**44; DA; DAB; DAC; DAM MST, NOV,**
**POP; WLC**
See also CA 85-88; 25-28R; CANR 22;
CDBLB 1914-1945; DLB 15, 162; MTCW

**Waugh, Harriet** 1944- ............. **CLC 6**
See also CA 85-88; CANR 22

**Ways, C. R.**
See Blount, Roy (Alton), Jr.

**Waystaff, Simon**
See Swift, Jonathan

**Webb, (Martha) Beatrice (Potter)**
1858-1943 ................. **TCLC 22**
See also Potter, Beatrice
See also CA 117

**Webb, Charles (Richard)** 1939- ...... **CLC 7**
See also CA 25-28R

**Webb, James H(enry), Jr.** 1946- .... **CLC 22**
See also CA 81-84

**Webb, Mary (Gladys Meredith)**
1881-1927 ................. **TCLC 24**
See also CA 123; DLB 34

**Webb, Mrs. Sidney**
See Webb, (Martha) Beatrice (Potter)

**Webb, Phyllis** 1927- .............. **CLC 18**
See also CA 104; CANR 23; DLB 53

**Webb, Sidney (James)**
1859-1947 ................. **TCLC 22**
See also CA 117

**Webber, Andrew Lloyd.............. CLC 21**
See also Lloyd Webber, Andrew

**Weber, Lenora Mattingly**
1895-1971 ................... **CLC 12**
See also CA 19-20; 29-32R; CAP 1;
SATA 2; SATA-Obit 26

**Webster, John**
1579(?)-1634(?) ...... **LC 33; DA; DAB;**
**DAC; DAM DRAM, MST; DC 2; WLC**
See also CDBLB Before 1660; DLB 58

**Webster, Noah** 1758-1843 ....... **NCLC 30**

**Wedekind, (Benjamin) Frank(lin)**
1864-1918 ...... **TCLC 7; DAM DRAM**
See also CA 104; DLB 118

**Weidman, Jerome** 1913- ............ **CLC 7**
See also AITN 2; CA 1-4R; CANR 1;
DLB 28

**Weil, Simone (Adolphine)**
1909-1943 ................. **TCLC 23**
See also CA 117

**Weinstein, Nathan**
See West, Nathanael

**Weinstein, Nathan von Wallenstein**
See West, Nathanael

**Weir, Peter (Lindsay)** 1944- ....... **CLC 20**
See also CA 113; 123

**Weiss, Peter (Ulrich)**
1916-1982 ............. **CLC 3, 15, 51;**
**DAM DRAM**
See also CA 45-48; 106; CANR 3; DLB 69,
124

**Weiss, Theodore (Russell)**
1916- .................... **CLC 3, 8, 14**
See also CA 9-12R; CAAS 2; CANR 46;
DLB 5

**Welch, (Maurice) Denton**
1915-1948 ................. **TCLC 22**
See also CA 121; 148

**Welch, James**
1940- ..... **CLC 6, 14, 52; DAM MULT,**
**POP**
See also CA 85-88; CANR 42; NNAL

**Weldon, Fay**
1933- ......... **CLC 6, 9, 11, 19, 36, 59;**
**DAM POP**
See also CA 21-24R; CANR 16, 46;
CDBLB 1960 to Present; DLB 14;
INT CANR-16; MTCW

**Wellek, Rene** 1903-1995.......... **CLC 28**
See also CA 5-8R; 150; CAAS 7; CANR 8;
DLB 63; INT CANR-8

**Weller, Michael** 1942- ......... **CLC 10, 53**
See also CA 85-88

**Weller, Paul** 1958- .............. **CLC 26**

**Wellershoff, Dieter** 1925- ......... **CLC 46**
See also CA 89-92; CANR 16, 37

**Welles, (George) Orson**
1915-1985 ................ **CLC 20, 80**
See also CA 93-96; 117

**Wellman, Mac** 1945- ............. **CLC 65**

Wellman, Manly Wade   1903-1986 .. **CLC 49**
See also CA 1-4R; 118; CANR 6, 16, 44;
SATA 6; SATA-Obit 47

Wells, Carolyn   1869(?)-1942 ...... **TCLC 35**
See also CA 113; DLB 11

Wells, H(erbert) G(eorge)
1866-1946 ........ **TCLC 6, 12, 19; DA;**
**DAB; DAC; DAM MST, NOV; SSC 6;**
**WLC**
See also AAYA 18; CA 110; 121;
CDBLB 1914-1945; DLB 34, 70, 156;
MTCW; SATA 20

Wells, Rosemary   1943-............ **CLC 12**
See also AAYA 13; CA 85-88; CANR 48;
CLR 16; MAICYA; SAAS 1; SATA 18,
69

Welty, Eudora
1909- ...... **CLC 1, 2, 5, 14, 22, 33; DA;**
**DAB; DAC; DAM MST, NOV; SSC 1;**
**WLC**
See also CA 9-12R; CABS 1; CANR 32;
CDALB 1941-1968; DLB 2, 102, 143;
DLBD 12; DLBY 87; MTCW

Wen I-to   1899-1946 ............. **TCLC 28**

Wentworth, Robert
See Hamilton, Edmond

Werfel, Franz (V.)   1890-1945 ...... **TCLC 8**
See also CA 104; DLB 81, 124

Wergeland, Henrik Arnold
1808-1845 ................. **NCLC 5**

Wersba, Barbara   1932-............ **CLC 30**
See also AAYA 2; CA 29-32R; CANR 16,
38; CLR 3; DLB 52; JRDA; MAICYA;
SAAS 2; SATA 1, 58

Wertmueller, Lina   1928- .......... **CLC 16**
See also CA 97-100; CANR 39

Wescott, Glenway   1901-1987....... **CLC 13**
See also CA 13-16R; 121; CANR 23;
DLB 4, 9, 102

Wesker, Arnold
1932- ............. **CLC 3, 5, 42; DAB;**
**DAM DRAM**
See also CA 1-4R; CAAS 7; CANR 1, 33;
CDBLB 1960 to Present; DLB 13;
MTCW

Wesley, Richard (Errol)   1945-....... **CLC 7**
See also BW 1; CA 57-60; CANR 27;
DLB 38

Wessel, Johan Herman   1742-1785 .... **LC 7**

West, Anthony (Panther)
1914-1987 ................. **CLC 50**
See also CA 45-48; 124; CANR 3, 19;
DLB 15

West, C. P.
See Wodehouse, P(elham) G(renville)

West, (Mary) Jessamyn
1902-1984 ................. **CLC 7, 17**
See also CA 9-12R; 112; CANR 27; DLB 6;
DLBY 84; MTCW; SATA-Obit 37

West, Morris L(anglo)   1916-..... **CLC 6, 33**
See also CA 5-8R; CANR 24, 49; MTCW

West, Nathanael
1903-1940 ..... **TCLC 1, 14, 44; SSC 16**
See also CA 104; 125; CDALB 1929-1941;
DLB 4, 9, 28; MTCW

West, Owen
See Koontz, Dean R(ay)

West, Paul   1930- ........... **CLC 7, 14, 96**
See also CA 13-16R; CAAS 7; CANR 22,
53; DLB 14; INT CANR-22

West, Rebecca   1892-1983 .. **CLC 7, 9, 31, 50**
See also CA 5-8R; 109; CANR 19; DLB 36;
DLBY 83; MTCW

Westall, Robert (Atkinson)
1929-1993 ................... **CLC 17**
See also AAYA 12; CA 69-72; 141;
CANR 18; CLR 13; JRDA; MAICYA;
SAAS 2; SATA 23, 69; SATA-Obit 75

Westlake, Donald E(dwin)
1933- ......... **CLC 7, 33; DAM POP**
See also CA 17-20R; CAAS 13; CANR 16,
44; INT CANR-16

Westmacott, Mary
See Christie, Agatha (Mary Clarissa)

Weston, Allen
See Norton, Andre

Wetcheek, J. L.
See Feuchtwanger, Lion

Wetering, Janwillem van de
See van de Wetering, Janwillem

Wetherell, Elizabeth
See Warner, Susan (Bogert)

Whale, James   1889-1957 ........ **TCLC 63**

Whalen, Philip   1923- ........... **CLC 6, 29**
See also CA 9-12R; CANR 5, 39; DLB 16

Wharton, Edith (Newbold Jones)
1862-1937 ...... **TCLC 3, 9, 27, 53; DA;**
**DAB; DAC; DAM MST, NOV; SSC 6;**
**WLC**
See also CA 104; 132; CDALB 1865-1917;
DLB 4, 9, 12, 78; DLBD 13; MTCW

Wharton, James
See Mencken, H(enry) L(ouis)

Wharton, William (a pseudonym)
.................... **CLC 18, 37**
See also CA 93-96; DLBY 80; INT 93-96

Wheatley (Peters), Phillis
1754(?)-1784 .... **LC 3; BLC; DA; DAC;**
**DAM MST, MULT, POET; PC 3; WLC**
See also CDALB 1640-1865; DLB 31, 50

Wheelock, John Hall   1886-1978.... **CLC 14**
See also CA 13-16R; 77-80; CANR 14;
DLB 45

White, E(lwyn) B(rooks)
1899-1985 .. **CLC 10, 34, 39; DAM POP**
See also AITN 2; CA 13-16R; 116;
CANR 16, 37; CLR 1, 21; DLB 11, 22;
MAICYA; MTCW; SATA 2, 29;
SATA-Obit 44

White, Edmund (Valentine III)
1940- ........... **CLC 27; DAM POP**
See also AAYA 7; CA 45-48; CANR 3, 19,
36; MTCW

White, Patrick (Victor Martindale)
1912-1990 .. **CLC 3, 4, 5, 7, 9, 18, 65, 69**
See also CA 81-84; 132; CANR 43; MTCW

White, Phyllis Dorothy James   1920-
See James, P. D.
See also CA 21-24R; CANR 17, 43;
DAM POP; MTCW

White, T(erence) H(anbury)
1906-1964 ................. **CLC 30**
See also CA 73-76; CANR 37; DLB 160;
JRDA; MAICYA; SATA 12

White, Terence de Vere
1912-1994 ................. **CLC 49**
See also CA 49-52; 145; CANR 3

White, Walter F(rancis)
1893-1955 ................. **TCLC 15**
See White, Walter
See also BW 1; CA 115; 124; DLB 51

White, William Hale   1831-1913
See Rutherford, Mark
See also CA 121

Whitehead, E(dward) A(nthony)
1933- ...................... **CLC 5**
See also CA 65-68

Whitemore, Hugh (John)   1936-..... **CLC 37**
See also CA 132; INT 132

Whitman, Sarah Helen (Power)
1803-1878 ................. **NCLC 19**
See also DLB 1

Whitman, Walt(er)
1819-1892 ..... **NCLC 4, 31; DA; DAB;**
**DAC; DAM MST, POET; PC 3; WLC**
See also CDALB 1640-1865; DLB 3, 64;
SATA 20

Whitney, Phyllis A(yame)
1903- ............. **CLC 42; DAM POP**
See also AITN 2; BEST 90:3; CA 1-4R;
CANR 3, 25, 38; JRDA; MAICYA;
SATA 1, 30

Whittemore, (Edward) Reed (Jr.)
1919- ...................... **CLC 4**
See also CA 9-12R; CAAS 8; CANR 4;
DLB 5

Whittier, John Greenleaf
1807-1892 ................. **NCLC 8**
See also DLB 1

Whittlebot, Hernia
See Coward, Noel (Peirce)

Wicker, Thomas Grey   1926-
See Wicker, Tom
See also CA 65-68; CANR 21, 46

Wicker, Tom ...................... **CLC 7**
See also Wicker, Thomas Grey

Wideman, John Edgar
1941- ........ **CLC 5, 34, 36, 67; BLC;**
**DAM MULT**
See also BW 2; CA 85-88; CANR 14, 42;
DLB 33, 143

Wiebe, Rudy (Henry)
1934- ............ **CLC 6, 11, 14; DAC;**
**DAM MST**
See also CA 37-40R; CANR 42; DLB 60

Wieland, Christoph Martin
1733-1813 ................. **NCLC 17**
See also DLB 97

Wiene, Robert   1881-1938........ **TCLC 56**

Wieners, John   1934-............... **CLC 7**
See also CA 13-16R; DLB 16

**Wister, Owen** 1860-1938 . . . . . . . . **TCLC 21**
See also CA 108; DLB 9, 78; SATA 62

**Witkacy**
See Witkiewicz, Stanislaw Ignacy

**Witkiewicz, Stanislaw Ignacy**
1885-1939 . . . . . . . . . . . . . . . . . **TCLC 8**
See also CA 105

**Wittgenstein, Ludwig (Josef Johann)**
1889-1951 . . . . . . . . . . . . . . . . **TCLC 59**
See also CA 113

**Wittig, Monique** 1935(?)- . . . . . . . . . **CLC 22**
See also CA 116; 135; DLB 83

**Wittlin, Jozef** 1896-1976 . . . . . . . . . **CLC 25**
See also CA 49-52; 65-68; CANR 3

**Wodehouse, P(elham) G(renville)**
1881-1975 . . . **CLC 1, 2, 5, 10, 22; DAB;
DAC; DAM NOV; SSC 2**
See also AITN 2; CA 45-48; 57-60;
CANR 3, 33; CDBLB 1914-1945;
DLB 34, 162; MTCW; SATA 22

**Woiwode, L.**
See Woiwode, Larry (Alfred)

**Woiwode, Larry (Alfred)** 1941- . . . **CLC 6, 10**
See also CA 73-76; CANR 16; DLB 6;
INT CANR-16

**Wojciechowska, Maia (Teresa)**
1927- . . . . . . . . . . . . . . . . . . . . . . **CLC 26**
See also AAYA 8; CA 9-12R; CANR 4, 41;
CLR 1; JRDA; MAICYA; SAAS 1;
SATA 1, 28, 83

**Wolf, Christa** 1929- . . . . . . . . **CLC 14, 29, 58**
See also CA 85-88; CANR 45; DLB 75;
MTCW

**Wolfe, Gene (Rodman)**
1931- . . . . . . . . . . . . **CLC 25; DAM POP**
See also CA 57-60; CAAS 9; CANR 6, 32;
DLB 8

**Wolfe, George C.** 1954- . . . . . . . . . . **CLC 49**
See also CA 149

**Wolfe, Thomas (Clayton)**
1900-1938 . . . . . **TCLC 4, 13, 29, 61; DA;
DAB; DAC; DAM MST, NOV; WLC**
See also CA 104; 132; CDALB 1929-1941;
DLB 9, 102; DLBD 2; DLBY 85; MTCW

**Wolfe, Thomas Kennerly, Jr.** 1931-
See Wolfe, Tom
See also CA 13-16R; CANR 9, 33;
DAM POP; INT CANR-9; MTCW

**Wolfe, Tom** . . . . . . . . **CLC 1, 2, 9, 15, 35, 51**
See also Wolfe, Thomas Kennerly, Jr.
See also AAYA 8; AITN 2; BEST 89:1;
DLB 152

**Wolff, Geoffrey (Ansell)** 1937- . . . . . **CLC 41**
See also CA 29-32R; CANR 29, 43

**Wolff, Sonia**
See Levitin, Sonia (Wolff)

**Wolff, Tobias (Jonathan Ansell)**
1945- . . . . . . . . . . . . . . . . . . . **CLC 39, 64**
See also AAYA 16; BEST 90:2; CA 114;
117; CAAS 22; DLB 130; INT 117

**Wolfram von Eschenbach**
c. 1170-c. 1220 . . . . . . . . . . . . . **CMLC 5**
See also DLB 138

**Wolitzer, Hilma** 1930- . . . . . . . . . . . **CLC 17**
See also CA 65-68; CANR 18, 40;
INT CANR-18; SATA 31

**Wollstonecraft, Mary** 1759-1797 . . . . . . **LC 5**
See also CDBLB 1789-1832; DLB 39, 104,
158

**Wonder, Stevie** . . . . . . . . . . . . . . . . **CLC 12**
See also Morris, Steveland Judkins

**Wong, Jade Snow** 1922- . . . . . . . . . . **CLC 17**
See also CA 109

**Woodcott, Keith**
See Brunner, John (Kilian Houston)

**Woodruff, Robert W.**
See Mencken, H(enry) L(ouis)

**Woolf, (Adeline) Virginia**
1882-1941 . . . . . . **TCLC 1, 5, 20, 43, 56;
DA; DAB; DAC; DAM MST, NOV;
SSC 7; WLC**
See also CA 104; 130; CDBLB 1914-1945;
DLB 36, 100, 162; DLBD 10; MTCW

**Woollcott, Alexander (Humphreys)**
1887-1943 . . . . . . . . . . . . . . . . . **TCLC 5**
See also CA 105; DLB 29

**Woolrich, Cornell** 1903-1968 . . . . . . **CLC 77**
See also Hopley-Woolrich, Cornell George

**Wordsworth, Dorothy**
1771-1855 . . . . . . . . . . . . . . . . **NCLC 25**
See also DLB 107

**Wordsworth, William**
1770-1850 . . . . **NCLC 12, 38; DA; DAB;
DAC; DAM MST, POET; PC 4; WLC**
See also CDBLB 1789-1832; DLB 93, 107

**Wouk, Herman**
1915- . . . **CLC 1, 9, 38; DAM NOV, POP**
See also CA 5-8R; CANR 6, 33; DLBY 82;
INT CANR-6; MTCW

**Wright, Charles (Penzel, Jr.)**
1935- . . . . . . . . . . . . . . . . **CLC 6, 13, 28**
See also CA 29-32R; CAAS 7; CANR 23,
36; DLB 165; DLBY 82; MTCW

**Wright, Charles Stevenson**
1932- . . . . . . . . . . . . . . . **CLC 49; BLC 3;
DAM MULT, POET**
See also BW 1; CA 9-12R; CANR 26;
DLB 33

**Wright, Jack R.**
See Harris, Mark

**Wright, James (Arlington)**
1927-1980 . . . . . . . . . . **CLC 3, 5, 10, 28;
DAM POET**
See also AITN 2; CA 49-52; 97-100;
CANR 4, 34; DLB 5; MTCW

**Wright, Judith (Arundell)**
1915- . . . . . . . . . . . . . **CLC 11, 53; PC 14**
See also CA 13-16R; CANR 31; MTCW;
SATA 14

**Wright, L(aurali) R.** 1939- . . . . . . . . **CLC 44**
See also CA 138

**Wright, Richard (Nathaniel)**
1908-1960 . . . . **CLC 1, 3, 4, 9, 14, 21, 48,
74; BLC; DA; DAB; DAC; DAM MST,
MULT, NOV; SSC 2; WLC**
See also AAYA 5; BW 1; CA 108;
CDALB 1929-1941; DLB 76, 102;
DLBD 2; MTCW

**Wright, Richard B(ruce)** 1937- . . . . . . **CLC 6**
See also CA 85-88; DLB 53

**Wright, Rick** 1945- . . . . . . . . . . . . . . **CLC 35**

**Wright, Rowland**
See Wells, Carolyn

**Wright, Stephen Caldwell** 1946- . . . . **CLC 33**
See also BW 2

**Wright, Willard Huntington** 1888-1939
See Van Dine, S. S.
See also CA 115

**Wright, William** 1930- . . . . . . . . . . . **CLC 44**
See also CA 53-56; CANR 7, 23

**Wroth, LadyMary** 1587-1653(?) . . . . . **LC 30**
See also DLB 121

**Wu Ch'eng-en** 1500(?)-1582(?) . . . . . . . **LC 7**

**Wu Ching-tzu** 1701-1754 . . . . . . . . . . . **LC 2**

**Wurlitzer, Rudolph** 1938(?)- . . . **CLC 2, 4, 15**
See also CA 85-88

**Wycherley, William**
1641-1715 . . . . . **LC 8, 21; DAM DRAM**
See also CDBLB 1660-1789; DLB 80

**Wylie, Elinor (Morton Hoyt)**
1885-1928 . . . . . . . . . . . . . . . . . **TCLC 8**
See also CA 105; DLB 9, 45

**Wylie, Philip (Gordon)** 1902-1971 . . . **CLC 43**
See also CA 21-22; 33-36R; CAP 2; DLB 9

**Wyndham, John** . . . . . . . . . . . . . . . . **CLC 19**
See also Harris, John (Wyndham Parkes
Lucas) Beynon

**Wyss, Johann David Von**
1743-1818 . . . . . . . . . . . . . . . . **NCLC 10**
See also JRDA; MAICYA; SATA 29;
SATA-Brief 27

**Xenophon**
c. 430B.C.-c. 354B.C. . . . . . . . . **CMLC 17**

**Yakumo Koizumi**
See Hearn, (Patricio) Lafcadio (Tessima
Carlos)

**Yanez, Jose Donoso**
See Donoso (Yanez), Jose

**Yanovsky, Basile S.**
See Yanovsky, V(assily) S(emenovich)

**Yanovsky, V(assily) S(emenovich)**
1906-1989 . . . . . . . . . . . . . . . . **CLC 2, 18**
See also CA 97-100; 129

**Yates, Richard** 1926-1992 . . . . . **CLC 7, 8, 23**
See also CA 5-8R; 139; CANR 10, 43;
DLB 2; DLBY 81, 92; INT CANR-10

**Yeats, W. B.**
See Yeats, William Butler

**Yeats, William Butler**
1865-1939 . . . . . **TCLC 1, 11, 18, 31; DA;
DAB; DAC; DAM DRAM, MST,
POET; WLC**
See also CA 104; 127; CANR 45;
CDBLB 1890-1914; DLB 10, 19, 98, 156;
MTCW

**Yehoshua, A(braham) B.**
1936- . . . . . . . . . . . . . . . . . . . **CLC 13, 31**
See also CA 33-36R; CANR 43

**Yep, Laurence Michael** 1948- . . . . . . **CLC 35**
See also AAYA 5; CA 49-52; CANR 1, 46;
CLR 3, 17; DLB 52; JRDA; MAICYA;
SATA 7, 69

# *PC* Cumulative Nationality Index

## AMERICAN

Ammons, A(rchie) R(andolph)  **16**
Auden, W(ystan) H(ugh)  **1**
Baraka, Amiri  **4**
Bishop, Elizabeth  **3**
Blake, William J(ames)  **12**
Bogan, Louise  **12**
Bradstreet, Anne  **10**
Brodsky, Joseph  **9**
Brooks, Gwendolyn  **7**
Carruth, Hayden  **10**
Crane, (Harold) Hart  **3**
Cummings, E(dward) E(stlin)  **5**
Dickinson, Emily (Elizabeth)  **1**
Doolittle, Hilda  **5**
Dove, Rita (Frances)  **6**
Dunbar, Paul Laurence  **5**
Duncan, Robert (Edward)  **2**
Eliot, T(homas) S(tearns)  **5**
Ferlinghetti, Lawrence (Monsanto)  **1**
Forche, Carolyn (Louise)  **10**
Frost, Robert (Lee)  **1**
Gallagher, Tess  **9**
Ginsberg, Allen  **4**
Gluck, Louise (Elisabeth)  **16**
Hammon, Jupiter  **16**
Hass, Robert  **16**
Hayden, Robert E(arl)  **6**
H. D.  **5**
Hughes, (James) Langston  **1**
Knight, Etheridge  **14**
Kumin, Maxine (Winokur)  **15**
Levertov, Denise  **11**
Lorde, Audre (Geraldine)  **12**
Lowell, Amy  **13**
Lowell, Robert (Traill Spence Jr.)  **3**
Loy, Mina  **16**
Madhubuti, Haki R.  **5**
Masters, Edgar Lee  **1**

McKay, Claude  **2**
Merton, Thomas  **10**
Millay, Edna St. Vincent  **6**
Moore, Marianne (Craig)  **4**
Plath, Sylvia  **1**
Poe, Edgar Allan  **1**
Pound, Ezra (Weston Loomis)  **4**
Rich, Adrienne (Cecile)  **5**
Robinson, Edwin Arlington  **1**
Roethke, Theodore (Huebner)  **15**
Rose, Wendy  **13**
Rukeyser, Muriel  **12**
Sanchez, Sonia  **9**
Sandburg, Carl (August)  **2**
Schwartz, Delmore (David)  **8**
Sexton, Anne (Harvey)  **2**
Stevens, Wallace  **6**
Swenson, May  **14**
Toomer, Jean  **7**
Wakoski, Diane  **15**
Wheatley (Peters), Phillis  **3**
Whitman, Walt(er)  **3**
Williams, William Carlos  **7**
Zukofsky, Louis  **11**

## AUSTRALIAN

Wright, Judith (Arandell)  **14**

## CANADIAN

Atwood, Margaret (Eleanor)  **8**
Bissett, Bill  **14**
Page, P(atricia) K(athleen)  **12**

## CHILEAN

Neruda, Pablo  **4**

## CHINESE

Li Ho  **13**
Tu Fu  **9**

## ENGLISH

Arnold, Matthew  **5**
Auden, W(ystan) H(ugh)  **1**
Behn, Aphra  **13**
Blake, William  **12**
Bradstreet, Anne  **10**
Bronte, Emily (Jane)  **8**
Browning, Elizabeth Barrett  **6**
Browning, Robert  **2**
Byron, George Gordon (Noel)  **16**
Coleridge, Samuel Taylor  **11**
Day Lewis, C(ecil)  **11**
Donne, John  **1**
Eliot, T(homas) S(tearns)  **5**
Graves, Robert (von Ranke)  **6**
Gray, Thomas  **2**
Hardy, Thomas  **8**
Herbert, George  **4**
Herrick, Robert  **9**
Hopkins, Gerard Manley  **15**
Housman, A(lfred) E(dward)  **2**
Hughes, Ted  **7**
Keats, John  **1**
Kipling, (Joseph) Rudyard  **3**
Levertov, Denise  **11**
Loy, Mina  **16**
Marvell, Andrew  **10**
Montagu, Mary (Pierrepont) Wortley  **16**
Page, P(atricia) K(athleen)  **12**
Rossetti, Christina (Georgina)  **7**
Sassoon, Siegfried (Lorraine)  **12**
Shelley, Percy Bysshe  **14**
Sitwell, Dame Edith  **3**
Smart, Christopher  **13**
Smith, Stevie  **12**
Spenser, Edmund  **8**
Swift, Jonathan  **9**
Tennyson, Alfred  **6**
Wordsworth, William  **4**

## FRENCH
Apollinaire, Guillaume  7
Baudelaire, Charles  1
Breton, Andre  15
Laforgue, Jules  14
Lamartine, Alphonse (Marie Louis Prat) de
    16
Mallarme, Stephane  4
Merton, Thomas  10
Nerval, Gerard de  13
Rimbaud, (Jean Nicolas) Arthur  3
Ronsard, Pierre de  11
Valery, (Ambroise) Paul (Toussaint Jules)
    9
Verlaine, Paul (Marie)  2
Villon, Francois  13

## GERMAN
Goethe, Johann Wolfgang von  5
Holderlin, (Johann Christian) Friedrich  4
Rilke, Rainer Maria  2

## GREEK
Sappho  5

## HUNGARIAN
Illyes, Gyula  16

## INDIAN
Tagore, Rabindranath  8

## IRISH
Day Lewis, C(ecil)  11
Swift, Jonathan  9

## ITALIAN
Gozzano, Guido  10
Martial  10
Montale, Eugenio  13
Pavese, Cesare  13
Petrarch  8

## JAMAICAN
McKay, Claude  2

## JAPANESE
Ishikawa, Takuboku  10
Matsuo Basho  3
Nishiwaki, Junzaburo  15
Yosano Akiko  11

## LEBANESE
Gibran, Kahlil  9

## MEXICAN
Paz, Octavio  1

## NICARAGUAN
Dario, Ruben  15

## NIGERIAN
Okigbo, Christopher (Ifenayichukwu)  7

## PERSIAN
Khayyam, Omar  8

## POLISH
Milosz, Czeslaw  8

## ROMAN
Ovid  2
Vergil  12

## ROMANIAN
Celan, Paul  10

## RUSSIAN
Akhmatova, Anna  2
Bely, Andrey  11
Brodsky, Joseph  9
Mandelstam, Osip (Emilievich)  14
Pasternak, Boris (Leonidovich)  6
Pushkin, Alexander (Sergeyevich)  10
Tsvetaeva (Efron), Marina (Ivanovna)  14

## SCOTTISH
Burns, Robert  6
MacDiarmid, Hugh  9
Scott, Walter  13

## SPANISH
Aleixandre, Vicente  15
Garcia Lorca, Federico  3
Jimenez (Mantecon), Juan Ramon  7

## SYRIAN
Gibran, Kahlil  9

## WELSH
Thomas, Dylan (Marlais)  2

# *PC* Cumulative Title Index

Title Index

"Little Fugue" (Plath) **1**:390
"The Little Ghost" (Millay) **6**:206
"Little Gidding" (Eliot) **5**:165-67, 169-70, 181-83, 185, 193, 204-05, 208, 210-11
"The Little Girl Found" (Blake) **12**:7, 33-4, 61
"A Little Girl Lost" (Blake) **12**:7, 33-4, 61
"Little Girl, My String Bean, My Lovely Woman" (Sexton) **2**:363
"Little Girls" (Page) **12**:176-77
"Little Green Tree" (Hughes) **1**:243
"The Little Hill" (Millay) **6**:214, 233
*The Little House of Kolomna* (Pushkin)
    See *Domik v Kolomne*
"Little Jim" (McKay) **2**:216, 222
"The Little June Book" (Stevens) **6**:332-33
"Little Lion Face" (Swenson) **14**:280
"Little Lobeila's Song" (Bogan) **12**:100-01, 111
"Little Lyric" (Hughes) **1**:240
"Little Mattie" (Browning) **6**:24
"Little Old Letter" (Hughes) **1**:243
"The Little Old Women" (Baudelaire)
    See "Les petites vielles"
"The Little Peasant" (Sexton) **2**:364, 368
*Little Poems in Prose* (Baudelaire)
    See *Petits poèmes en prose: Le spleen de Paris*
"The Little Rapids" (Swenson) **14**:262
"Little T. C." (Marvell)
    See "The Picture of Little T. C. in a Prospect of Flowers"
"A Little Testament" (Montale)
    See "Piccolo testamento"
"Little Tree" (Cummings) **5**:93
"A Little Uncomplicated Hymn" (Sexton) **2**:363
"The Little Vagabond" (Blake) **12**:7
"The Little White Rose" (MacDiarmid) **9**:154, 176, 186
"Littleblood" (Hughes) **7**:153, 168-69
*Liturgies intimes* (Verlaine) **2**:417-18
"Liubliu moroznoe dykhan'e" ("I love frosty breath . . . and reality is reality") (Mandelstam) **14**:154
"Live" (Sexton) **2**:351, 364
"Live Niggers--Stop Bullshitting" (Baraka) **4**:18
*Live or Die* (Sexton) **2**:349, 351, 356, 362-65
"Lives" (Rukeyser) **12**:207, 217, 228
"Living" (Levertov) **11**:186
"Living Earth" (Toomer) **7**:336-37
"Living in Sin" (Rich) **5**:351, 369
"LIVING WITH TH VISHYUN" (Bissett) **14**:34
*living with th vishyun* (Bissett) **14**:16-17
*Llanto por Ignacio Sánchez Mejías* (*Lament for Ignacio Sánchez Mejías*; *Lament for the Death of a Bullfighter*) (Garcia Lorca) **3**:121-22, 124, 126, 128
"Llewellyn and the Tree" (Robinson) **1**:462, 468
"Lo! A Child Is Born" (MacDiarmid) **9**:178-79
"Lo fatal" ("Doom") (Dario) **15**:96
"The Load of Sugar-Cane" (Stevens) **6**:293
"The Lockless Door" (Frost) **1**:218
"Locksley Hall" (Tennyson) **6**:354, 357, 359-60, 363
"Locus" (Hayden) **6**:189, 194, 196
"The Locust Tree in Flower" (Williams) **7**:363
"Locutions des Pierrots, I" (Laforgue) **14**:81

"Locutions des Pierrots XIV" (Laforgue) **14**:89
"Logos" (Hughes) **7**:120, 159
"Loin Cloth" (Sandburg) **2**:329
"Loin des oiseaux" (Rimbaud) **3**:274
"Loin du pigeonnier" ("The Depths") (Apollinaire) **7**:18, 21, 23
"Loitering with a Vacant Eye" (Housman) **2**:193
"Lollocks" (Graves) **6**:137, 142, 144
"London" (Blake) **12**:7, 25, 34
"London Bridge" (Robinson) **1**:466, 468
*Loneliness* (Paz)
    See *Soledad*
"The Lonely Street" (Williams) **7**:362
"Lonesome" (Dunbar) **5**:119
*Long Ago and Not So Long Ago* (Verlaine)
    See *Jadis et naguère*
"The Long Alley" (Roethke) **15**:248, 254
*The Long Approach* (Kumin) **15**:214, 221
*Long Division: A Tribal History* (Rose) **13**:232
"Long John Brown & Little Mary Bell" (Blake) **12**:35
"Long Past Moncada" (Rukeyser) **12**:231-32
"Long Screams" (Hughes) **7**:150
"The Long Shadow of Lincoln: A Litany" (Sandburg) **2**:334
"A Long Story" (Gray) **2**:143, 152-53
"Long To'ds Night" (Dunbar) **5**:147
"The Long Tunnel Ceiling" (Hughes) **7**:148
"The Long Waters" (Roethke) **15**:310, 316-17
"Longing" (Arnold) **5**:42-3
"The Longing" (Roethke) **15**:272, 274, 310, 312-15
*Longing* (Ishikawa)
    See *Akogare*
"Longing for Heaven" (Bradstreet) **10**:27, 30, 42
*A Longing for the Light: Selected Poems of Vicente Aleixandre* (Aleixandre) **15**:24
"Longing Is Like the Seed" (Dickinson) **1**:111
"the lonliness of literacy" (Bissett) **14**:34
"Look!" (Smith) **12**:342
"Look for You Yesterday, Here You Come Today" (Baraka) **4**:14-15
"Look on This Picture and on This" (Rossetti) **7**:277
"Look, Stranger, on This Island Now" (*On This Island*) (Auden) **1**:7-8, 12, 22, 30
"Looking at a Picture on an Anniversary" (Hardy) **8**:137-38
*Looking for Luck* (Kumin) **15**:213, 216, 221, 223-24
"Looking for Luck in Bangkok" (Kumin) **15**:214
"Looking for th Lammas" (Bissett) **14**:7
"Looking Forward" (Rossetti) **7**:277
"Looking in a Mirror" (Atwood) **8**:32, 38
"The Loom" (Masters) **1**:333
"The Loop" (Masters) **1**:329
"Loot" (Kipling) **3**:160, 163, 174, 187
"Lord of Elbë, on Elbë Hill" (Bronte) **8**:73
*The Lord of the Isles* (Scott) **13**:277, 281, 288, 294, 296, 304, 311-12, 318, 321
*Lord Weary's Castle* (Lowell) **3**:200, 202-03, 206-07, 211-12, 216-18, 224, 230-33
"Lorelei" (Plath) **1**:388-89
"L'lorloge de demain" ("The Clock of Tomorrow") (Apollinaire) **7**:32
"Losing Track" (Levertov) **11**:160, 169
"Loss" (H. D.) **5**:303

"The Loss of the Eurydice" (Hopkins) **15**:147, 162
"The Loss of The Nabara" (Day Lewis)
    See "The Nabara"
"Lost" (Sandburg) **2**:303
*lost angel mining company* (Bissett) **14**:6-7, 9, 17, 19
"The Lost Bower" (Browning) **6**:7
"Lost Child" (Wright) **14**:349, 352
*Lost Copper* (Rose) **13**:235, 237-38, 240
"The Lost Dancer" (Toomer) **7**:336
"The Lost Ingredient" (Sexton) **2**:350, 359
"Lost Love" (Graves) **6**:129
"The Lost Man" (Wright) **14**:339, 346
"The Lost Mistress" (Browning) **2**:38
"The Lost Son" (Roethke) **15**:248, 250, 255, 262-63, 267-68, 270, 272, 275-76, 278, 284, 298-99, 301-02
*The Lost Son, and Other Poems* (Roethke) **15**:246-50, 260, 282-83, 290-91, 296-97, 304, 308-09
"The Lost Wine" (Valery)
    See "Le vin perdu"
"The Lotos-Eaters" (Tennyson) **6**:352, 358-60, 409-12
"Louenge a la court" (Villon) **13**:394-95
"Love" (Herbert) ::100, 114
"Love III" (Herbert) **4**:121
"Love among the Ruins" (Browning) **2**:88
"Love and Friendship" (Bronte) **8**:51
"Love and Harmony Combine" (Blake) **12**:32
"Love Arm'd" ("Love in Fantastic Triumph Sat"; "Song") (Behn) **13**:4, 7, 15, 23-5
"Love Despoiled" (Dunbar) **5**:125
*Love Elegies* (Donne)
    See *Elegies*
"Love from the North" (Rossetti) **7**:260, 278, 280, 289
"Love in Barrenness" (Graves) **6**:172
"Love in Fantastic Triumph Sat" (Behn)
    See "Love Arm'd"
"Love in Moonlight" (Gluck) **16**:169
"Love in the Museum" (Rich) **5**:393
"Love Is" (Swenson) **14**:283
"Love is More Thicker than Forget" (Cummings) **5**:108
"Love is the Only God" (Cummings) **5**:107
"Love Joy" (Herbert) **4**:122-23, 125
"A Love Letter" (Dunbar) **5**:147
"Love Letter Postmarked Van Beethoven" (Wakoski) **15**:326, 331
"Love Me!" (Smith) **12**:346
"The Love Nut" (Ferlinghetti) **1**:187
"The Love of Christ which Passeth Knowledge" (Rossetti) **7**:268, 290
"LOVE OF LIFE, the 49th parallel" (Bissett) **14**:7, 10, 18
"Love Passes Beyond the Incredible Hawk of Innocence" (Wakoski) **15**:351
"Love Poem" (Gluck) **16**:150
"Love Poem" (Lorde) **12**:158
"Love Poem" (Page) **12**:177
*Love Poems* (Sanchez) **9**:207, 212, 216, 218-21, 227, 229, 234, 237, 242
*Love Poems* (Sexton) **2**:349, 351-53, 355, 364-65
*The Love Poems of May Swenson* (Swenson) **14**:274-75, 280, 283-84
*Love Respelt* (Graves) **6**:154, 156
"Love Sex and Romance" (Wakoski) **15**:357
"Love Song" (Levertov) **11**:159, 171
"Love Song" (Sexton) **2**:363

"Materia humana" (Aleixandre)  **15**:34

"Maternità" (Pavese)  **13**:213

"Mathilde in Normady" (Rich)  **5**:352, 359

"Matinée d'ivresse" (Rimbaud)  **3**:261, 263, 271-73, 281-82

"Matins" (Gluck)  **16**:170-71

"Matins" (Levertov)  **11**:166

"Matros v Moskve" ("Sailor in Moscow") (Pasternak)  **6**:283

"Mattens" (Herbert)  **4**:119

"Mattens, or Morning Prayer" (Herrick)  **9**:118

*Matthias at the Door* (Robinson)  **1**:473-74, 479

"Mattino" (Pavese)  **13**:230

"Maturity" (Ginsberg)  **4**:87

*Maud, and Other Poems* (Tennyson)  **6**:354, 356-57, 360, 363, 366, 373, 379-80, 383, 385, 387, 407

"Maude Clare" (Rossetti)  **7**:260, 280, 291

"Mausfallen-Sprüchlein" (Morike)  **1**:114

"Le mauvais moine" ("The Indolent Monk") (Baudelaire)  **1**:59

"Le mauvais vitrier" ("The Bad Glazier") (Baudelaire)  **1**:67

"Mawu" (Lorde)  **12**:143

"May" (Rossetti)  **7**:265

"May 24, 1980" (Brodsky)  **9**:24

"May 1943" (H. D.)  **5**:307

"may all thes blessings" (Bissett)  **14**:30

"May Festival" (Goethe)
See "Maifest"

"May It Be" (Pasternak)  **6**:261

"The May Magnificat" (Hopkins)  **15**:124-25, 165

*The May Queen* (Tennyson)  **6**:359

"Mayavada" ("Theory of Maya") (Tagore)  **8**:408

"Maybe this is a sign of madness" (Mandelstam)  **14**:155

"Maybe this is the beginning of madness" (Mandelstam)
See "Mozhet byt' eto tochka bezumiia"

"The Mayor of Gary" (Sandburg)  **2**:304, 308

"The Maypole Is Up" (Herrick)  **9**:102, 145

"May's Love" (Browning)  **6**:24

*Mazeppa* (Byron)  **16**:83

"M.B." (Brodsky)  **9**:10

"McAndrew's Hymn" (Kipling)  **3**:161, 167, 170, 186, 192

*Me Again: Uncollected Writings of Stevie Smith* (Smith)  **12**:314, 333-34, 340, 343-44, 346-47

"Me from Myself to Banish" (Dickinson)  **1**:94

"Me Whoppin' Big-Tree Boy" (McKay)  **2**:226

"Meadow Milk" (Bogan)  **12**:110

*Meadowlands* (Gluck)  **16**:171-73

"Meadowlands 3" (Gluck)  **16**:171

"Meaning" (Milosz)  **8**:215

"Meat without Mirth" (Herrick)  **9**:98

"Mechanism" (Ammons)  **16**:40

"Le médaillon toujours ferme" (Apollinaire)  **7**:22

*Medea the Sorceress* (Wakoski)  **15**:372-73

*Le médecin malgré lui* (Williams)  **7**:349

*Medicamina Faciei* (Ovid)  **2**:238-39, 243, 251, 253, 258

"MEDICINE" (Bissett)  **14**:20

*MEDICINE my mouths on fire* (Bissett)  **14**:16, 19, 27

*Medieval Scenes* (Duncan)  **2**:109

"Médiocriteé" (Laforgue)  **14**:88

"Meditation" (Baudelaire)
See "Recueillement"

"Meditation at Lagunitas" (Hass)  **16**:200, 209, 211, 219

"Meditation at Oyster River" (Roethke)  **15**:265, 276, 310, 313, 316

"A Meditation for His Mistresse" (Herrick)  **9**:101

"A Meditation in Tuscany" (Browning)  **6**:16

*Les meditations* (Lamartine)  **16**:256-62, 265, 268-69

"Meditations of an Old Woman" (Roethke)  **15**:262, 264-65, 273

*Méditations poétiques* (*The Poetical Meditations of M. Alphonse de La Martine*) (Lamartine)  **16**:270, 272-82, 284-85, 287, 289-93, 302

"Mediterraneo" (Montale)  **13**:115

*Medny Vsadnik* (*The Bronze Horseman*) (Pushkin)  **10**:367-68, 373-74, 385, 390-400, 414

"Medusa" (Bogan)  **12**:85, 104-06, 111-12, 115, 117

"Medusa" (Dove)  **6**:123

"Meeting" (Arnold)  **5**:42

"Meeting" (Montale)
See "Incontro"

"A Meeting" (Pasternak)
See "Vstrecha"

"The Meeting" (Rukeyser)  **12**:231

"A Meeting of Minds" (Lorde)  **12**:135

"Meeting-House Hill" (Lowell)  **13**:67

"Mein Karren knarrt nicht mehr" (Celan)  **10**:124

"A Mei-p'i Lake Song" (Tu Fu)  **9**:330-31, 333

"Melancholia en Orizba" ("Melancholy in Orizaba") (Neruda)  **4**:281

"Melancholy" (Bely)  **11**:6

"Melancholy in Orizaba" (Neruda)
See "Melancholia en Orizba"

"A Melancholy Moon" (Baudelaire)
See "Les tristesses de la lune"

*Melancolía* (Jimenez)  **7**:211

"Melancthon" (Moore)  **4**:254

"Mélange adultère de tout" (Eliot)  **5**:185

"Memo from the Cave" (Gluck)  **16**:147-48

"Mémoire" (Rimbaud)  **3**:262, 268

"Memorabilia" (Masters)  **1**:343

"Memorandum Confided by a Yucca to a Passion-Vine" (Lowell)  **13**:61, 64

"Memorial" (Sanchez)  **9**:224

"Memorial II" (Lorde)  **12**:140, 157

"Memorial for the City" (Auden)  **1**:23

"Memorial Tablet" (Sassoon)  **12**:269

"Memories..." (Jimenez)
See "Recuerdos..."

"Memories of the Forest" (Ishikawa)
See "Mori no omoide"

"Memories of West Street and Lepke" (Lowell)  **3**:206, 208, 220, 223, 237

"Memory" (Bogan)  **12**:101, 120, 122

"A Memory" (Pavese)  **13**:203

"Memory" (Roethke)  **15**:275

"Memory" (Sassoon)  **12**:269

"Memory" (Wright)  **14**:376

"Memory I" (Rossetti)  **7**:277

"The Memory of Elena" ("In Memory of Elena") (Forche)  **10**:136, 139, 152-53, 166, 169

"Memory of V. I. Ulianov" (Zukofsky)  **11**:396

"A Memory Picture" (Arnold)  **5**:49

"Men" (Toomer)  **7**:336

*Men and Women* (Browning)  **2**:66, 77, 94

"Men Loved Wholly beyond Wisdom" (Bogan)  **12**:104, 126

*Men, Women, and Ghosts* (Lowell)  **13**:63, 71, 73, 76, 79, 85, 93

"Mending Wall" (Frost)  **1**:225, 227, 229

"Menons Klagen um Diotima" ("Menon's Lament for Diotime") (Holderlin)  **4**:141-42

"Menon's Lament for Diotime" (Holderlin)
See "Menons Klagen um Diotima"

"Mensaje" ("Message") (Aleixandre)  **15**:6, 10

"Menschenbeitfall" ("Human Applause") (Holderlin)  **4**:165

"Menses" (Millay)  **6**:233

"Menstruation at Forty" (Sexton)  **2**:363 .

"The Mental Traveller" (Blake)  **12**:36, 46, 48

"The Merchantmen" (Kipling)  **3**:161

"Merely Statement" (Lowell)  **13**:86

"Meriggiare pallido e assorto" ("Pale, Intent Noontide") (Montale)  **13**:105

*Merlin: A Poem* (Robinson)  **1**:462-63, 465, 468-71, 482-83, 488-89, 491

"Merlin and the Gleam" (Tennyson)  **6**:389, 407

"The Mermaid's Children" (Lowell)  **3**:241

"The Mermen" (Crane)  **3**:90

*Merope* (Arnold)  **5**:8, 12, 35, 37, 45, 47, 58-60, 62-3

"The Merry Guide" (Housman)  **2**:180, 192

"The Merry Muses" (Burns)  **6**:96

"Merveilles de la guerre" (Apollinaire)  **7**:3, 22

"Mes bouguins refemés" (Mallarme)  **4**:199

"Mes petites amoureuses" ("My Little Lovers") (Rimbaud)  **3**:262, 284

"Mescaline" (Ginsberg)  **4**:74, 81

"Un mese fra i bambini" ("A Month among Children") (Montale)  **13**:134

*Les meslanges* (Ronsard)  **11**:247, 266

"Message" (Aleixandre)
See "Mensaje"

"Message" (Forche)  **10**:139, 144, 154-55

"The Message" (Levertov)  **11**:171

"The Message" (Sassoon)  **12**:248

"A Message All Blackpeople Can Dig (& A Few Negroes Too)" ("And a Few Negroes Too") (Madhubuti)  **5**:329, 341

"Message for the Sinecurist" (Gallagher)  **9**:62

"Message from the NAACP" (Baraka)  **4**:11

"Message to a Black Soldier" (Madhubuti)  **5**:339

"The Messenger" (Atwood)  **8**:18

"The Messenger" (Merton)  **10**:339

"The Messenger" (Sassoon)  **12**:259

"A Messenger from the Horizon" (Merton)  **10**:334

"Messengers" (Gluck)  **16**:127, 133, 142

"Messianic Eclogue" (Vergil)
See "Eclogue 4"

"The Metal and the Flower" (Page)  **12**:168, 178

*The Metal and the Flower* (Page)  **12**:167, 171, 193

*Die Metamorphose der Pflanzen* (Goethe)  **5**:239-40

*Metamorphoses* (*Metamorphosis; The Transformation/Transformations*) (Ovid)  **2**:233, 238-241, 244-45, 260

"R. A. F." (H. D.)  **5**:307
"The Rabbi" (Hayden)  **6**:195, 198
"Rabbi Ben Ezra" (Browning)  **2**:51, 75, 95
"The Rabbi's Song" (Kipling)  **3**:183
"The Rabbit" (Millay)  **6**:238
"Race" (Dario)
  See "Raza"
"The Racer's Widow" (Gluck)  **16**:139
"Rack" (Ammons)  **16**:39
"Raft" (Ammons)  **16**:20, 27
"The Rag Man" (Hayden)  **6**:195
"Rages de césars" (Rimbaud)  **3**:283
"The Ragged Schools of London" (Browning)
  See "A Song for the Ragged Schools of
  London"
"Railroad Avenue" (Hughes)  **1**:237
"The Rain" (Levertov)  **11**:176
"Rain" (Williams)  **7**:349
"Rain Charm for the Duchy, a Blessed,
  Devout Drench for the Christening of a
  Prince Harry" (Hughes)  **7**:171
"Rain Festival" (Tagore)
  See "Varsha-mangal"
"The Rain, It Streams on Stone and Hillock"
  (Housman)  **2**:162
"Rain on a Grave" (Hardy)  **8**:134
"Rain or Hail" (Cummings)  **5**:88
"rainbow music" (Bissett)  **14**:24
"Rainforest" (Wright)  **14**:375, 377
"Rain-Song" (Dunbar)  **5**:125
"Raise the Shade" (Cummings)  **5**:89
"Raleigh Was Right" (Williams)  **7**:360
"La rameur" (Valery)  **9**:367, 395-96
"Rano Raraku" (Breton)  **15**:53-4
"Rap of a Fan..." (Apollinaire)
  See "Coup d'evential..."
"Rape" (Rich)  **5**:361
"The Raper from Passenack" (Williams)
  **7**:353, 368, 399
"Rapids" (Ammons)  **16**:63
"Rapunzel" (Sexton)  **2**:368
"Rapunzel, Rapunzel" (Smith)  **12**:341
"Rasshchelina" ("The Crevasse") (Tsvetaeva)
  **14**:306-08
"The Ratcatcher" (Tsvetaeva)
  See "Krysolov"
"Rational Man" (Rukeyser)  **12**:220, 230
"rattle poem" (Bissett)  **14**:21
"The Raven" (Poe)  **1**:419-20, 424, 427, 429-
  34, 436, 439-40, 443-44, 447, 452-53
"The Raven: A Christmas Tale" (Coleridge)
  **11**:109-17
*The Raven, and Other Poems* (Poe)  **1**:437,
  449
"The Ravine" (Carruth)  **10**:85, 90
"Raza" ("Race") (Dario)  **15**:115
"Razgovor s geniem" ("Conversation with my
  Inspiration") (Tsvetaeva)  **14**:325
*Rbaiyyat* (Khayyam)
  See *Rubáiyát*
"Reaching Out with the Hands of the Sun"
  (Wakoski)  **15**:363
"Re-Act for Action" (Madhubuti)  **5**:338
"The Reader over My Shoulder" (Graves)
  **6**:143, 151
"Reading Aloud" (Gallagher)  **9**:60
"Reading Apollinaire by the Rouge River"
  (Ferlinghetti)  **1**:181, 187
"Reading Holderlin on the Patio with the Aid
  of a Dictionary" (Dove)  **6**:109
"Reading Myself" (Lowell)  **3**:229

"Reading the Japanese Poet Issa" (Milosz)
  **8**:189
"Reading the Will" (Kipling)  **3**:190
"Reading Time: 1 Minute 26 Seconds"
  (Rukeyser)  **12**:206
"Readings of History" (Rich)  **5**:355
"The Real Estate Agents Tale" (Lowell)
  **13**:84
"Real Life" (Baraka)  **4**:30
*La realidad invisible* (*Invisible Reality*)
  (Jimenez)  **7**:207
*Reality Sandwiches* (Ginsberg)  **4**:67, 81
"Reapers" (Toomer)  **7**:319, 333-34
"Reaping" (Lowell)  **13**:60
"The Rear-Guard" (Sassoon)  **12**:266
"Reason and Imagination" (Smart)  **13**:341,
  347
"Reawakening" (Pavese)
  See "Risveglio"
"Le rebelle" (Baudelaire)  **1**:55
"Rebellion" (Lowell)  **3**:318
"The Rebels" (Ferlinghetti)  **1**:184
"Rebirth" (Pushkin)  **10**:408
"A Rebus by I. B." (Wheatley)  **3**:338
"Recalling War" (Graves)  **6**:137, 142, 144,
  165
"The Recantation: An Ode. By S. T.
  Coleridge" (Coleridge)  **11**:94, 99
"Recessional" (Masters)  **1**:333
"Recipe for Happiness in Khaboronsky"
  (Ferlinghetti)  **1**:183
"Recitative" (Crane)  **3**:81, 83
*Recklings* (Hughes)  **7**:120, 122-23
"The Recluse" (Smith)  **12**:299, 331, 333
*The Recluse; or Views on Man, Nature, and on
  Human Life* (Wordsworth)  **4**:406-07, 409
"Recollection" (Wheatley)
  See "On Recollection"
"Recollections of the Arabian Nights"
  (Tennyson)  **6**:347, 359, 389, 406, 408-09
*Recollections of Tsarskoe-Selo* (Pushkin)
  See "Vospominanie v Tsarskom Sele"
"Reconciliation" (Day Lewis)  **11**:147
"Reconciliation" (Milosz)  **8**:213
"Reconciliation" (Sassoon)  **12**:289
"Reconciliation" (Whitman)  **3**:378
*Records of a Weather Exposed Skeleton*
  (Matsuo Basho)
  See *Nozarashi kiko*
"Recovering" (Rukeyser)  **12**:225
"Recovery" (Ammons)  **16**:6
"The Recovery" (Pushkin)  **10**:408
*Recovery* (Tagore)
  See *Árogya*
*Recovery* (Tagore)
  See *Árogya*
"Recreaciones arqueológicas" (Dario)  **15**:96
"The Recruit" (Housman)  **2**:196
"A Recruit on the Corpy" (McKay)  **2**:226
"Recueillement" ("Meditation") (Baudelaire)
  **1**:65
*Les recueillements poétiques* (*Poetic
  Contemplations*) (Lamartine)  **16**:263, 268,
  284-85
"Recuerdo" (Millay)  **6**:215
"Recuerdos..." ("Memories...") (Jimenez)
  **7**:199
"The Red Knight" (Lowell)  **13**:84
"The Red Lacquer Music Stand" (Lowell)
  **13**:78
"Red Poppy" (Gallagher)  **9**:64
"A Red, Red Rose" (Burns)

  See "My Luve Is Like a Red, Red Rose"
"Red Riding Hood" (Sexton)  **2**:354, 364
*Red Roses for Bronze* (H. D.)  **5**:270-71, 304
"Red Silk Stockings" (Hughes)  **1**:269
"Red Slippers" (Lowell)  **13**:79
"The Red Steer" (Tsvetaeva)
  See "Krasnyi bychok"
"The Red Wheelbarrow" (Williams)  **7**:378,
  401-02, 409-10
"The Redbreast and the Butterfly"
  (Wordsworth)  **4**:376
"Red-Cotton Nightcap Country" (Browning)
  **2**:96
"The Redeemer" (Sassoon)  **12**:242, 249-51,
  261-62, 276, 278, 287
"Redemption" (Herbert)  **4**:119, 130
"Redwing" (Gallagher)  **9**:62
"The Reefy Coast" (Ishikawa)
  See "Ariso"
"The Reflection: A Song" (Behn)  **13**:18, 20-1
"Reflection in a Forest" (Auden)  **1**:17
"Reflection in an Ironworks" (MacDiarmid)
  **9**:155
"Reflections at Lake Louise" (Ginsberg)  **4**:84
"Reflections on a Scottish Slum"
  (MacDiarmid)  **9**:181
"Reflections on Having Left a Place of
  Retirement" (Coleridge)  **11**:81
"Reflective" (Ammons)  **16**:6
"Reflexion" (Lamartine)  **16**:266, 285
"Refrain" (Dove)  **6**:117
"A Refusal to Mourn the Death, by Fire, of a
  Child in London" (Thomas)  **2**:382-83, 386,
  388, 390, 398, 400
"Regrets of the Belle Heaumiere" (Villon)
  See "Lament of the Belle Heaulmiere"
"Rehabilitation & Treatment in the Prisons of
  America" (Knight)  **14**:53
"The Rehearsal" (Smith)  **12**:330
"El reino interior" ("The Inner Kingdom")
  (Dario)  **15**:79-80, 92, 96, 114
"Rejoice in the Lamb" (Smart)
  See "Jubilate Agno"
*Rekviem: Tsikl stikhotvorenii* (*Requiem: A
  Cycle of Poems*) (Akhmatova)  **2**:4, 7, 9, 15-
  16, 19-20
"Relearning the Alphabet" (Levertov)
  **11**:195-98
*Relearning the Alphabet* (Levertov)  **11**:176-78,
  180, 193-94
"Religion" (Dunbar)  **5**:125
"Religious Isolation" (Arnold)  **5**:42
"A Religious Man" (Smith)  **12**:352
"Religious Musings" (Coleridge)  **11**:49-51,
  53, 80-2, 93-6
"Religious Propaganda" (Tagore)
  See "Dharma prachar"
"The Relique" (Donne)  **1**:126, 130
*Remains of Elmet* (Hughes)  **7**:146, 149, 162
"Rembrandt to Rembrandt" (Robinson)
  **1**:487
"Remember" (Rossetti)  **7**:269, 280
"Rememberance" (Holderlin)
  See "Andenken"
"Remembering Pearl Harbor at the
  Tutankhamen Exhibit" (Kumin)  **15**:196,
  206, 208
"Remembrance" ("Cold in the Earth")
  (Bronte)  **8**:52, 56, 60, 65, 68, 74-5
"Remembrance Has a Rear and Front"
  (Dickinson)  **1**:94
"Remembrance in Tsarskoe Selo" (Pushkin)

"The Unfaithful Married Woman" (Garcia Lorca)
See "La casada infiel"
"The Unfaithful Wife" (Garcia Lorca)
See "La casada infiel"
"Unfold! Unfold!" (Roethke)   **15**:248, 254, 276, 300-03
"The Unfortunate Lover" (Marvell)   **10**:265-66, 271, 300, 302
"Ungratefulnesse" (Herbert)   **4**:119, 133-34
"Unidentified Flying Object" (Hayden)   **6**:196
"L'Union libre" (Breton)   **15**:51, 62
"The Unions at the Front" (Neruda)
See "Los Grernios en el frente"
"A Unison" (Williams)   **7**:360
"La United Fruit Company" ("The United Fruit Company") (Neruda)   **4**:296
"The United Fruit Company" (Neruda)
See "La United Fruit Company"
"U.S. 1946 King's X" (Frost)   **1**:200
*U.S. One* (Rukeyser)   **12**:203-04, 211
"The Universal Andalusia" (Jimenez)
See "El andaluz universal"
"Universal Sorrow" (Tagore)
See "Vishvashoka"
"The Universe" (Swenson)   **14**:258, 268, 281
"The Unknown" (Williams)   **7**:369
"Unknown Girl in the Maternity Ward" (Sexton)   **2**:349, 355
"Unknown Water" (Wright)   **14**:341, 353
"Unresolved" (Levertov)   **11**:198
"Les uns et les autres" (Verlaine)   **2**:416
"An Unsaid Word" (Rich)   **5**:359, 393
"Unsleeping City (Brooklyn Bridge Nocturne)" (Garcia Lorca)
See "Ciudad sin sueño"
"Unsounded" (Rich)   **5**:359
"The Unsung Heroes" (Dunbar)   **5**:131
"Unsuspecting" (Toomer)   **7**:336
"Untitled" (Swenson)   **14**:274, 285
"Unto the Whole—How Add?" (Dickinson)   **1**:103
"The Untrustworthy Speaker" (Gluck)   **16**:157
"Gli uomini che si voltano" (Montale)   **13**:133
"Up and Down" (Smith)   **12**:316
"Up at a Villa-Down in the City, as Distinguished by an Italian Person of Quality" (Browning)   **2**:38
*Up Country: Poems of New England* (Kumin)   **15**:181-83, 187, 189, 194, 208
"Up Hill" (Rossetti)   **7**:261, 298
"The Up Rising" (Duncan)   **2**:104
"Upahar" ("Gift") (Tagore)   **8**:407
"The Upas Tree" (Pushkin)
See "Anchar"
"An Upbraiding" (Hardy)   **8**:93
"Uplands" (Ammons)   **16**:31
*Uplands* (Ammons)   **16**:22, 28, 46, 61
"Upon a Beautiful Young Nymph Going to Bed" (Swift)
See "A Beautiful Young Nymph Going to Bed. Written for the Honour of the Fair Sex"
"Upon a Child. An Epitaph" (Herrick)   **9**:129-31
"Upon a Child That Died" ("Here she lies, a pretty bud") (Herrick)   **9**:130-31
"Upon a Comely and Curious Maide" (Herrick)   **9**:129
"Upon a fit of Sickness, Anno 1632" (Bradstreet)   **10**:20, 26, 34, 59

"Upon Appleton House" ("Appleton House") (Marvell)   **10**:260, 265-67, 269, 271-73, 289-91, 294, 298, 303-04, 314-15, 318
"Upon Ben Jonson" (Herrick)   **9**:86
"Upon Her Blush" (Herrick)   **9**:143
"Upon Himself" (Herrick)   **9**:89, 109
"Upon Himselfe Being Buried" (Herrick)   **9**:128, 131
"Upon His Kinswoman Mistris Elizabeth Herrick" (Herrick)   **9**:131
"Upon His Last Request to Julia" (Herrick)   **9**:108
"Upon Julia's Clothes" ("On Julia's Clothes") (Herrick)   **9**:135-36
"Upon Julia's Recovery" (Herrick)   **9**:102
"Upon Julia's Washing Her Self in the River" (Herrick)   **9**:143
"Upon Meeting Don L. Lee, in a Dream" (Dove)   **6**:104-05, 108
"Upon My Daughter Hannah Wiggin Her Recovery from a Dangerous Fever" (Bradstreet)   **10**:34
"Upon My Dear and Loving Husband His Goeing into England" (Bradstreet)
See "To My Dear and Loving Husband His Goeing into England"
"Upon My Son Samuel His Going to England, November 6, 1959" (Bradstreet)   **10**:26, 34, 36, 63
"Upon the Annunciation and Passion" (Donne)   **1**:139
"Upon the Death of the Lord Protector" (Marvell)
See "Poem upon the Death of O. C."
"Upon the Hill and Grove at Billborow" ("The Hill and Grove at Bill-Borrow"; "On the Hill and Grove at Billborow") (Marvell)   **10**:269
"Upon the Much Lamented, Master J. Warr" (Herrick)   **9**:129
"Upon the Nipples of Julia's Breast" (Herrick)   **9**:143
"Upon the Roses in Julias Bosome" (Herrick)   **9**:143
"Upon Your Held-Out Hand" (Thomas)   **2**:406
"Uptown" (Ginsberg)   **4**:47
"The Urals" (Pasternak)   **6**:268
"Urania" ("Excuse") (Arnold)   **5**:43
*Urbasi* (Tagore)   **8**:403
*The Urn* (Bely)
See *Urna*
*Urna* (*The Urn*) (Bely)   **11**:3-4, 6-7, 24, 32-3
"Urvashi" (Tagore)   **8**:409
"Us" (Sexton)   **2**:352
"The Use of 'Tu" (Montale)   **13**:145
"Used Up" (Sandburg)   **2**:303
"Useless" (Atwood)   **8**:27
"Ustica" (Paz)   **1**:355, 360-61
"Utopie" (Lamartine)   **16**:263, 284
"Utsarga" ("Offering") (Tagore)   **8**:409
"V bol'nitse" ("In Hospital") (Pasternak)   **6**:266, 269, 286-87
"V den' Blagoveshchen'ia" ("On Annunciation Day") (Tsvetaeva)   **14**:322
"V. L. Davydovu" ("To V. L. Davydovu") (Pushkin)   **10**:412
"V lesu" ("In the Forest") (Pasternak)   **6**:280
"V ony dni, ty mne byla kak mat" ("In those days you were like a moter to me") (Tsvetaeva)   **14**:321
"vaalee daancers" (Bissett)   **14**:33

"The Vacant Lot" (Brooks)   **7**:69
"Vagabonds" (Rimbaud)   **3**:261
"Vain and Careless" (Graves)   **6**:141, 150
"Les vaines danseuses" (Valery)   **9**:392
"Vaishnava kavita" ("Vaishnava Poetry") (Tagore)   **8**:408
"Vaishnava Poetry" (Tagore)
See "Vaishnava kavita"
"Vaivén" (Paz)   **1**:359
*Vala* (Blake)
See *The Four Zoas: The Torments of Love and Jealousy in the Death and Judgement of Albion the Ancient Man*
*Vala* (Blake)
See *The Four Zoas: The Torments of Love and Jealousy in the Death and Judgement of Albion the Ancient Man*
*Vale Ave* (H. D.)   **5**:282
"The Vale of Esthwaite" (Wordsworth)   **4**:417
"A Valediction: forbidding mourning" ("As virtuous men pass mildly away") (Donne)   **1**:124, 126, 130, 135
"A Valediction Forbidding Mourning" (Rich)   **5**:371, 395
"A Valediction: of my name, in the window" (Donne)   **1**:152
"A Valediction: of the booke" ("I'll tell thee now (dear love) what thou shalt doe") (Donne)   **1**:128, 130
"A Valediction: of weeping" (Donne)   **1**:124, 130, 153
"A Valentine" (Poe)   **1**:445
"Valentine" (Zukofsky)   **11**:349
"Valentine Delivered by a Raven" (Gallagher)   **9**:63
"Valentine I" (Bishop)   **3**:36
"Valley Candle" (Stevens)   **6**:338
"The Valley of the Shadow" (Robinson)   **1**:490
"The Valley of Unrest" (Poe)   **1**:438
"Le vallon" ("The Dale") (Lamartine)   **16**:268, 276, 283, 290, 298-301
"Valuable" (Smith)   **12**:296
"Values in Use" (Moore)   **4**:261
"Valvins" (Valery)   **9**:392
"The Vampire" (Baudelaire)
See "Les métamorphoses du vampire"
"Le Vampire" (Baudelaire)
See "Les métamorphoses du vampire"
"The Vampire" (Kipling)   **3**:166
"Van Winkle" (Crane)   **3**:100, 109
"Vanaspati" ("Vegetation") (Tagore)   **8**:415
"Vandracour" (Wordsworth)   **4**:399
"Vanishing Point: Urban Indian" (Rose)   **13**:232
"Vanitie" (Herbert)   **4**:120
"Vanitie I" (Herbert)   **4**:132
"The Vanity of All Worldly Things" ("Of the Vanity of All Worldly Creatures") (Bradstreet)   **10**:2, 6, 21
"Vanna's Twins" (Rossetti)   **7**:291
"Variation and Reflection on a Poem by Rilke" (Levertov)   **11**:206
"Variation and Reflection on a Theme by Rilke (The Book of Hours Book I Poem 7)" (Levertov)   **11**:203
"Variation on a Theme by Rilke" (Levertov)   **11**:202
"Variations on a Theme by Rilke (The Book of Hours Book I Poem 4)" (Levertov)   **11**:203
"Variations on Two Dicta of William Blake" (Duncan)   **2**:103

ISBN 0-7876-0475-5

90000